fourth edition/cuarta edición 2002

© HarperCollins Publishers 1995, 1999, 2002
© William Collins Sons & Co. Ltd. 1990

HarperCollins Publishers
Westerhill Road, Bishopbriggs, Glasgow G64 2QT,
Great Britain

www.collins.co.uk

Collins® and Bank of English® are registered trademarks
of HarperCollins Publishers Limited

Collins is an imprint of HarperCollins Publishers

ISBN 0-00-712291-8

HarperCollins Publishers, Inc.
10 East 53rd Street, New York, NY 10022

ISBN 0-06-008451-0

Library of Congress Cataloging-in-Publication Data
has been applied for

www.harpercollins.com

Typeset by Morton Word Processing Ltd, Scarborough

Printed and bound in Italy by Amadeus S.p.A.

Collins

Pocket
Spanish
Dictionary

Spanish » English English » Spanish

Collins

An Imprint of HarperCollins*Publishers*

editors/redactores
Mike Gonzalez • Alicia de Benito de Harland
Soledad Pérez-López • José Ramón Parrondo

contributors/colaboradores
Bob Grossmith • Teresa Álvarez García
Sharon Hunter • Claire Evans

editorial staff/redacción
Joyce Littlejohn • Val McNulty

series editor/colección dirigida por
Lorna Sinclair Knight

INTRODUCTION

We are delighted that you have decided to buy the Collins Pocket Spanish Dictionary, and hope you will enjoy and benefit from using it at home, at school, on holiday or at work.

The innovative use of colour guides you quickly and efficiently to the word you want, and the comprehensive wordlist provides a wealth of modern and idiomatic phrases not normally found in a dictionary this size.

In addition, the supplement provides you with guidance on using the dictionary, along with entertaining ways of improving your dictionary skills.

We hope that you will enjoy using it and that it will significantly enhance your language studies.

ABREVIATURAS

ABBREVIATIONS

adjetivo, locución adjetiva	adj	adjective, adjectival phrase
abreviatura	ab(b)r	abbreviation
adverbio, locución adverbial	adv	adverb, adverbial phrase
administración, lengua administrativa	ADMIN	administration
agricultura	AGR	agriculture
América Latina	AM	Latin America
anatomía	ANAT	anatomy
arquitectura	ARQ, ARCH	architecture
artículo	art	article
el automóvil	AUT(O)	the motor car and motoring
aviación, viajes aéreos	AVIAT	flying, air travel
biología	BIO(L)	biology
botánica, flores	BOT	botany
inglés británico	BRIT	British English
química	CHEM	chemistry
comercio, finanzas, banca	COM(M)	commerce, finance, banking
comparativo	compar	comparative
informática	COMPUT	computers
conjunción	conj	conjunction
construcción	CONSTR	building
compuesto	cpd	compound element
cocina	CULIN	cookery
definido	def	definite
demostrativo	demos	demonstrative
economía	ECON	economics
electricidad, electrónica	ELEC	electricity, electronics
enseñanza, sistema escolar y universitario	ESCOL	schooling, schools and universities
España	ESP	Spain
especialmente	esp	especially
exclamación, interjección	excl	exclamation, interjection
femenino	f	feminine
lengua familiar (! vulgar)	fam(!)	informal usage (! particularly offensive)
ferrocarril	FERRO	railways
uso figurado	fig	figurative use
fotografía	FOTO	photography
(verbo inglés) del cual la partícula es inseparable	fus	(phrasal verb) where the particle is inseparable
generalmente	gen	generally
geografía, geología	GEO	geography, geology
geometría	GEOM	geometry
indefinido	indef	indefinite
lengua familiar (! vulgar)	inf(!)	informal usage
infinitivo	infin	infinitive
informática	INFORM	computers
interrogativo	interr	interrogative
invariable	inv	invariable
irregular	irreg	irregular
lo jurídico	JUR	law

ABREVIATURAS

ABBREVIATIONS

América Latina	**LAM**	Latin America
gramática, lingüística	**LING**	grammar, linguistics
masculino	**m**	masculine
matemáticas	**MAT(H)**	mathematics
medicina	**MED**	medical term, medicine
masculino/femenino	**m/f**	masculine/feminine
lo militar, ejército	**MIL**	military matters
música	**MUS**	music
sustantivo, nombre	**n**	noun
navegación, náutica	**NAUT**	sailing, navigation
sustantivo numérico	**num**	numeral noun
complemento	**obj**	(grammatical) object
	o.s.	oneself
peyorativo	**pey, pej**	derogatory, pejorative
fotografía	**PHOT**	photography
fisiología	**PHYSIOL**	physiology
plural	**pl**	plural
política	**POL**	politics
participio de pasado	**pp**	past participle
preposición	**prep**	preposition
pronombre	**pron**	pronoun
psicología, psiquiatría	**PSICO, PSYCH**	psychology, psychiatry
tiempo pasado	**pt**	past tense
química	**QUIM**	chemistry
ferrocarril	**RAIL**	railways
religión, lo eclesiástico	**REL**	religion, church service
	sb	somebody
enseñanza, sistema escolar y universitario	**SCH**	schooling, schools and universities
singular	**sg**	singular
España	**SP**	Spain
	sth	something
sujeto	**su(b)j**	(grammatical) subject
subjuntivo	**subjun**	subjunctive
superlativo	**superl**	superlative
tauromaquia	**TAUR**	bullfighting
también	**tb**	also
técnica, tecnología	**TEC(H)**	technical term, technology
telecomunicaciones	**TELEC, TEL**	telecommunications
televisión	**TV**	television
imprenta, tipografía	**TIP, TYP**	typography, printing
inglés norteamericano	**US**	American English
verbo	**vb**	verb
verbo intransitivo	**vi**	intransitive verb
verbo pronominal	**vr**	reflexive verb
verbo transitivo	**vt**	transitive verb
zoología, animales	**ZOOL**	zoology
marca registrada	®	registered trademark
indica un equivalente cultural	≈	introduces a cultural equivalent

SPANISH PRONUNCIATION

Consonants

b	[b, ß]	**b**oda **b**om**b**a la**b**or	see notes on **v** below
c	[k]	**c**aja	**c** before **a, o** or **u** is pronounced as in **c**at
ce, ci	[θe, θi]	**c**ero **c**ielo	**c** before **e** or **i** is pronounced as in **thir**
ch	[tʃ]	**ch**iste	**ch** is pronounced as **ch** in **ch**air
d	[d, ð]	**d**anés ciu**dad**	at the beginning of a phrase or after or **n, d** is pronounced as in English. In any other position it is pronounced like **th** in **the**
g	[g, ɣ]	**g**afas pa**g**a	**g** before **a, o** or **u** is pronounced as in **g**ap, if at the beginning of a phrase or after **n**. In other positions the sound is softened
ge, gi	[xe, xi]	**g**ente **g**irar	**g** before **e** or **i** is pronounced similar to **ch** in Scottish lo**ch**
h		**h**aber	**h** is always silent in Spanish
j	[x]	**j**ugar	**j** is pronounced similar to **ch** in Scottish lo**ch**
ll	[ʎ]	ta**ll**e	**ll** is pronounced like the **lli** in mi**lli**on
ñ	[ɲ]	ni**ñ**o	**ñ** is pronounced like the **ni** in o**ni**on
q	[k]	**q**ue	**q** is pronounced as **k** in **k**ing
r, rr	[r, rr]	quita**r** ga**rr**a	**r** is always pronounced in Spanish, unlike the silent **r** in dance**r**. **rr** is trilled, like a Scottish **r**
s	[s]	quizá**s** i**s**la	**s** is usually pronounced as in pa**ss**, but before **b, d, g, l, m** or **n** it is pronounced as in ro**s**e
v	[b, ß]	**v**ía di**v**idir	**v** is pronounced something like **b**. At the beginning of a phrase or after **m** or **n** it is pronounced as **b** in **b**oy. In any other position the sound is softened
z	[θ]	tena**z**	**z** is pronounced as **th** in **th**in

f, k, l, m, n, p, t and **x** are pronounced as in English.

Vowels

	[a]	p**a**ta	not as long as **a** in f**a**r. When followed by a consonant in the same syllable (i.e. in a closed syllable), as in am**a**nte, the **a** is short, as in b**a**t
	[e]	m**e**	like **e** in th**e**y. In a closed syllable, as in g**e**nte, the **e** is short as in p**e**t
	[i]	p**i**no	as in m**ea**n or mach**i**ne
	[o]	l**o**	as in l**o**cal. In a closed syllable, as in c**o**ntrol, the **o** is short as in c**o**t
	[u]	l**u**nes	as in r**u**le. It is silent after **q**, and in **gue, gui**, unless marked **güe, güi** e.g. anti**gü**edad, when it is pronounced like **w** in **w**olf

Semivowels

| y | [j] | b**i**en
h**i**elo
yunta | pronounced like **y** in **y**es |
| | [w] | h**u**evo
f**u**ento
anti**gü**edad | unstressed **u** between consonant and vowel is pronounced like **w** in **w**ell. See also notes on **u** above |

Diphthongs

i, ay	[ai]	b**ai**le	as **i** in r**i**de
u	[au]	**au**to	as **ou** in sh**ou**t
, ey	[ei]	bu**ey**	as **ey** in gr**ey**
u	[eu]	d**eu**da	both elements pronounced independently [e] + [u]
, oy	[oi]	h**oy**	as **oy** in t**oy**

Stress

The rules of stress in Spanish are as follows:

(a) when a word ends in a vowel or in **n** or **s**, the second last syllable is stressed: pa**ta**ta, pa**ta**tas, **co**me, **co**men

(b) when a word ends in a consonant other than **n** or **s**, the stress falls on the last syllable: pa**red**, ha**blar**

(c) when the rules set out in (a) and (b) are not applied, an acute accent appears over the stressed vowel: co**mún**, geogra**fía**, in**glés**

In the phonetic transcription, the symbol ['] precedes the syllable on which the stress falls.

ix

PRONUNCIACIÓN INGLESA

Vocales y diptongos

	Ejemplo inglés	*Ejemplo español/explicación*
ɑː	f**a**ther	Entre **a** de p**a**dre y **o** de n**o**che
ʌ	b**u**t, c**o**me	**a** muy breve
æ	m**a**n, c**a**t	Con los labios en la posición de **e** en p**e**na se pronuncia el sonido **a** parecido a la **a** de c**a**rro
ə	fath**er**, **a**go	Vocal neutra parecida a una **e** u **o** casi mudas
əː	b**i**rd, h**ea**rd	Entre **e** abierta, y **o** cerrada, sonido alargado
ɛ	g**e**t, b**e**d	Como en p**e**rro
ɪ	**i**t, b**i**g	Más breve que en s**i**
iː	t**ea**, s**ee**	Como en f**i**no
ɔ	h**o**t, w**a**sh	Como en t**o**rre
ɔː	s**aw**, **a**ll	Como en p**o**r
u	p**u**t, b**oo**k	Sonido breve, más cerrado que b**u**rro
uː	t**oo**, y**ou**	Sonido largo, como en **u**no
aɪ	fl**y**, h**igh**	Como en fr**ai**le
au	h**ow**, h**ou**se	Como en p**au**sa
ɛə	th**ere**, b**ear**	Casi como en v**ea**, pero el segundo elemento es la vocal neutra [ə]
eɪ	d**ay**, ob**ey**	**e** cerrada seguida por una **i** débil
ɪə	h**ere**, h**ear**	Como en man**ía**, mezclándose el sonido **a** con la vocal neutra [ə]
əu	g**o**, n**o**te	[ə] seguido por una breve **u**
ɔɪ	b**oy**, **oi**l	Como en v**oy**
uə	p**oor**, s**ure**	**u** bastante larga más la vocal neutra [ə]

	Ejemplo inglés	*Ejemplo español/explicación*
	big, lo**bb**y	Como en tum**b**a
	men**ded**	Como en con**d**e, an**d**ar
	go, **g**et, bi**g**	Como en **g**rande, **g**ol
3	**g**in, ju**dge**	Como en la **ll** andaluza y en **G**eneralitat (catalán)
	si**ng**	Como en ví**n**culo
	house, **h**e	Como la jota hispanoamericana
	young, **y**es	Como en **y**a
	come, mo**ck**	Como en **c**aña, Es**c**ocia
	red, t**r**ead	Se pronuncia con la punta de la lengua hacia atrás y sin hacerla vibrar
	sand, ye**s**	Como en ca**s**a, **s**esión
	ro**s**e, **z**ebra	Como en de**s**de, mi**s**mo
	she, ma**ch**ine	Como en **ch**ambre (francés), ro**x**o (portugués)
	chin, ri**ch**	Como en **ch**ocolate
	valley	Como en f, pero se retiran los dientes superiores vibrándolos contra el labio inferior
	water, **wh**ich	Como en la **u** de h**u**evo, p**u**ede
	vi**s**ion	Como en **j**ournal (francés)
	think, my**th**	Como en re**c**eta, **z**apato
	this, **th**e	Como en la **d** de habla**d**o, verda**d**

f, m, n, l, t iguales que en español

El signo * indica que la r final escrita apenas se pronuncia en inglés británico cuando la palabra siguiente empieza con vocal. El signo ['] indica la sílaba acentuada.

SPANISH VERB TABLES

1 Gerund *2* Imperative *3* Present *4* Preterite *5* Future *6* Present subjunctive *7* Imperfect subjunctive *8* Past participle *9* Imperfect. *Etc* indicates that the irregular root is used for all persons of the tense, e.g. **oír**: *6* oiga *etc* = oigas, oigamos, oigáis, oigan. Forms which consist of the unmodified verb root + verb ending are not shown, e.g. acertamos, acertáis.

acertar *2* acierta *3* acierto, aciertas, acierta, aciertan *6* acierte, aciertes, acierte, acierten

acordar *2* acuerda *3* acuerdo, acuerdas, acuerda, acuerdan *6* acuerde, acuerdes, acuerde, acuerden

advertir *1* advirtiendo *2* advierte *3* advierto, adviertes, advierte, advierten *4* advirtió, advirtieron *6* advierta, adviertas, advierta, advirtamos, advirtáis, adviertan *7* advirtiera *etc*

agradecer *3* agradezco *6* agradezca *etc*

aparecer *3* aparezco *6* aparezca *etc*

aprobar *2* aprueba *3* apruebo, apruebas, aprueba, aprueban *6* apruebe, apruebes, apruebe, aprueben

atravesar *2* atraviesa *3* atravieso, atraviesas, atraviesa, atraviesan *6* atraviese, atravieses, atraviese, atraviesen

caber *3* quepo *4* cupe, cupiste, cupo, cupimos, cupisteis, cupieron *5* cabré *etc* *6* quepa *etc* *7* cupiera *etc*

caer *1* cayendo *3* caigo *4* cayó, cayeron *6* caiga *etc* *7* cayera *etc*

calentar *2* calienta *3* caliento, calientas, calienta, calientan *6* caliente, calientes, caliente, calienten

cerrar *2* cierra *3* cierro, cierras, cierra, cierran *6* cierre, cierres, cierre, cierren

COMER *1* comiendo *2* come, comed *3* como, comes, come, comemos, coméis, comen *4* comí, comiste, comió, comimos, comisteis, comieron *5* comeré, comerás, comerá, comeremos, comeréis, comerán *6* coma, comas, coma, comamos, comáis, coman *7* comiera, comieras, comiera, comiéramos, comierais, comieran *8* comido *9* comía, comías, comía, comíamos, comíais, comían

conocer *3* conozco *6* conozca *etc*

contar *2* cuenta *3* cuento, cuentas, cuenta, cuentan *6* cuente, cuentes, cuente, cuenten

costar *3* cuesta *3* cuesto, cuestas, cuesta, cuestan *6* cueste, cuestes, cueste, cuesten

dar *3* doy *4* di, diste, dio, dimos, disteis, dieron *7* diera *etc*

decir *2* di *3* digo *4* dije, dijiste, dijo, dijimos, dijisteis, dijeron *5* diré *etc* *6* diga *etc* *7* dijera *etc* *8* dicho

despertar *2* despierta *3* despierto, despiertas, despierta, despiertan *6* despierte, despiertes, despierte, despierten

divertir *1* divirtiendo *2* divierte *3* divierto, diviertes, divierte, divierten *4* divirtió, divirtieron *6* divierta, diviertas, divierta, divirtamos, divirtáis, diviertan *7* divirtiera *etc*

dormir *1* durmiendo *2* duerme *3* duermo, duermes, duerme, duermen *4* durmió, durmieron *6* duerma, duermas, duerma, durmamos, durmáis, duerman *7* durmiera *etc*

empezar *2* empieza *3* empiezo, empiezas, empieza, empiezan *4* empecé *6* empiece, empieces, empiece, empecemos, empecéis, empiecen

entender *2* entiende *3* entiendo, entiendes, entiende, entienden *6* entienda, entiendas, entienda, entiendan

ESTAR *2* está *3* estoy, estás, está, están *4* estuve, estuviste, estuvo, estuvimos, estuvisteis, estuvieron *6* esté, estés, esté, estén *7* estuviera *etc*

HABER *3* he, has, ha, hemos, han *4* hube, hubiste, hubo, hubimos, hubisteis, hubieron *5* habré *etc* *6* haya *etc* *7* hubiera *etc*

HABLAR *1* hablando *2* habla, hablad *3* hablo, hablas, habla, hablamos, habláis, hablan *4* hablé, hablaste, habló, hablamos, hablasteis, hablaron *5* hablaré, hablarás, hablará, hablaremos, hablaréis, hablarán *6* hable, hables, hable, hablemos, habléis, hablen *7* hablara, hablaras, hablara, habláramos, hablarais, hablaran *8* hablado *9* hablaba, hablabas, hablaba, hablábamos, hablabais, hablaban

hacer *2* haz *3* hago *4* hice, hiciste, hizo, hicimos, hicisteis, hicieron *5* haré *etc* *6* haga *etc* *7* hiciera *etc* *8* hecho

instruir *1* instruyendo *2* instruye *3* instruyo, instruyes, instruye, instruyen *4* instruyó, instruyeron *6* instruya *etc* *7* instruyera *etc*

ir *1* yendo *2* ve *3* voy, vas, va, vamos, vais, van *4* fui, fuiste, fue, fuimos, fuisteis, fueron *6* vaya, vayas, vaya, vayamos, vayáis, vayan

7 fuera *etc* 9 iba, ibas, iba, íbamos, ibais, iban

jugar 2 juega 3 juego, juegas, juega, juegan 4 jugué 6 juegue *etc*

leer 1 leyendo 4 leyó, leyeron 7 leyera *etc*

morir 1 muriendo 2 muere 3 muero, mueres, muere, mueren 4 murió, murieron 6 muera, mueras, muera, muramos, muráis, mueran 7 muriera *etc* 8 muerto

mostrar 2 muestra 3 muestro, muestras, muestra, muestran 6 muestre, muestres, muestre, muestren

mover 2 mueve 3 muevo, mueves, mueve, mueven 6 mueva, muevas, mueva, muevan

negar 2 niega 3 niego, niegas, niega, niegan 4 negué 6 niegue, niegues, niegue, neguemos, neguéis, nieguen

ofrecer 3 ofrezco 6 ofrezca *etc*

oír 1 oyendo 2 oye 3 oigo, oyes, oye, oyen 4 oyó, oyeron 6 oiga *etc* 7 oyera *etc*

oler 2 huele 3 huelo, hueles, huele, huelen 6 huela, huelas, huela, huelan

parecer 3 parezco 6 parezca *etc*

pedir 1 pidiendo 2 pide 3 pido, pides, pide, piden 4 pidió, pidieron 6 pida *etc* 7 pidiera *etc*

pensar 2 piensa 3 pienso, piensas, piensa, piensan 6 piense, pienses, piense, piensen

perder 2 pierde 3 pierdo, pierdes, pierde, pierden 6 pierda, pierdas, pierda, pierdan

poder 1 pudiendo 2 puede 3 puedo, puedes, puede, pueden 4 pude, pudiste, pudo, pudimos, pudisteis, pudieron 5 podré *etc* 6 pueda, puedas, pueda, puedan 7 pudiera *etc*

poner 2 pon 3 pongo 4 puse, pusiste, puso, pusimos, pusisteis, pusieron 5 pondré *etc* 6 ponga *etc* 7 pusiera *etc* 8 puesto

preferir 1 prefiriendo 2 prefiere 3 prefiero, prefieres, prefiere, prefieren 4 prefirió, prefirieron 6 prefiera, prefieras, prefiera, prefiramos, prefiráis, prefieran 7 prefiriera *etc*

querer 2 quiere 3 quiero, quieres, quiere, quieren 4 quise, quisiste, quiso, quisimos, quisisteis, quisieron 5 querré 6 quiera, quieras, quiera, quieran 7 quisiera *etc*

reír 2 ríe 3 río, ríes, ríe, ríen 4 rio, rieron 6 ría, rías, ría, riamos, riáis, rían 7 riera *etc*

repetir 1 repitiendo 2 repite 3 repito, repites, repite, repiten 4 repitió, repitieron 6 repita *etc* 7 repitiera *etc*

rogar 2 ruega 3 ruego, ruegas, ruega, ruegan 4 rogué 6 ruegue, ruegues, ruegue, roguemos, roguéis, rueguen

saber 3 sé 4 supe, supiste, supo, supimos, supisteis, supieron 5 sabré *etc* 6 sepa *etc* 7 supiera *etc*

salir 2 sal 3 salgo 5 saldré *etc* 6 salga *etc*

seguir 1 siguiendo 2 sigue 3 sigo, sigues, sigue, siguen 4 siguió, siguieron 6 siga *etc* 7 siguiera *etc*

sentar 2 sienta 3 siento, sientas, sienta, sientan 6 siente, sientes, siente, sienten

sentir 1 sintiendo 2 siente 3 siento, sientes, siente, sienten 4 sintió, sintieron 6 sienta, sientas, sienta, sintamos, sintáis, sientan 7 sintiera *etc*

SER 2 sé 3 soy, eres, es, somos, sois, son 4 fui, fuiste, fue, fuimos, fuisteis, fueron 6 sea *etc* fuera *etc* 9 era, eras, era, éramos, erais, eran

servir 1 sirviendo 2 sirve 3 sirvo, sirves, sirve, sirven 4 sirvió, sirvieron 6 sirva *etc* 7 sirviera *etc*

soñar 2 sueña 3 sueño, sueñas, sueña, sueñan 6 sueñe, sueñes, sueñe, sueñen

tener 2 ten 3 tengo, tienes, tiene, tienen 4 tuve, tuviste, tuvo, tuvimos, tuvisteis, tuvieron 5 tendré *etc* 6 tenga *etc* 7 tuviera *etc*

traer 1 trayendo 3 traigo 4 traje, trajiste, trajo, trajimos, trajisteis, trajeron 6 traiga *etc* 7 trajera *etc*

valer 2 val 3 valgo 5 valdré *etc* 6 valga *etc*

venir 2 ven 3 vengo, vienes, viene, vienen 4 vine, viniste, vino, vinimos, vinisteis, vinieron 5 vendré *etc* 6 venga *etc* 7 viniera *etc*

ver 3 veo 6 vea *etc* 8 visto 9 veía *etc*

vestir 1 vistiendo 2 viste 3 visto, vistes, viste, visten 4 vistió, vistieron 6 vista *etc* 7 vistiera *etc*

VIVIR 1 viviendo 2 vive, vivid 3 vivo, vives, vive, vivimos, vivís, viven 4 viví, viviste, vivió, vivimos, vivisteis, vivieron 5 viviré, vivirás, vivirá, viviremos, viviréis, vivirán 6 viva, vivas, viva, vivamos, viváis, vivan 7 viviera, vivieras, viviera, viviéramos, vivierais, vivieran 8 vivido 9 vivía, vivías, vivía, vivíamos, vivíais, vivían

volver 2 vuelve 3 vuelvo, vuelves, vuelve, vuelven 6 vuelva, vuelvas, vuelva, vuelvan 8 vuelto

VERBOS IRREGULARES EN INGLÉS

present	pt	pp	present	pt	pp
arise	arose	arisen	feed	fed	fed
awake	awoke	awoken	feel	felt	felt
be (am, is, are; being)	was, were	been	fight	fought	fought
			find	found	found
bear	bore	born(e)	flee	fled	fled
beat	beat	beaten	fling	flung	flung
become	became	become	fly (flies)	flew	flown
begin	began	begun	forbid	forbade	forbidden
behold	beheld	beheld	forecast	forecast	forecast
bend	bent	bent	forego	forewent	foregone
beseech	besought	besought	foresee	foresaw	foreseen
beset	beset	beset	foretell	foretold	foretold
bet	bet, betted	bet, betted	forget	forgot	forgotten
bid	bid, bade	bid, bidden	forgive	forgave	forgiven
bind	bound	bound	forsake	forsook	forsaken
bite	bit	bitten	freeze	froze	frozen
bleed	bled	bled	get	got	got, (US) gotten
blow	blew	blown			
break	broke	broken	give	gave	given
breed	bred	bred	go (goes)	went	gone
bring	brought	brought	grind	ground	ground
build	built	built	grow	grew	grown
burn	burnt, burned	burnt, burned	hang	hung, hanged	hung, hanged
burst	burst	burst	have (has; having)	had	had
buy	bought	bought			
can	could	(been able)	hear	heard	heard
cast	cast	cast	hide	hid	hidden
catch	caught	caught	hit	hit	hit
choose	chose	chosen	hold	held	held
cling	clung	clung	hurt	hurt	hurt
come	came	come	keep	kept	kept
cost	cost	cost	kneel	knelt, kneeled	knelt, kneeled
creep	crept	crept			
cut	cut	cut	know	knew	known
deal	dealt	dealt	lay	laid	laid
dig	dug	dug	lead	led	led
do (3rd person: he/she/it does)	did	done	lean	leant, leaned	leant, leaned
			leap	leapt, leaped	leapt, leaped
draw	drew	drawn			
dream	dreamed, dreamt	dreamed, dreamt	learn	learnt, learned	learnt, learned
drink	drank	drunk	leave	left	left
drive	drove	driven	lend	lent	lent
dwell	dwelt	dwelt	let	let	let
eat	ate	eaten	lie (lying)	lay	lain
fall	fell	fallen	light	lit, lighted	lit, lighted

present	pt	pp	present	pt	pp
lose	lost	lost	spell	spelt, spelled	spelt, spelled
make	made	made			
may	might	—	spend	spent	spent
mean	meant	meant	spill	spilt, spilled	spilt, spilled
meet	met	met			
mistake	mistook	mistaken	spin	spun	spun
mow	mowed	mown, mowed	spit	spat	spat
must	(had to)	(had to)	split	split	split
pay	paid	paid	spoil	spoiled, spoilt	spoiled, spoilt
put	put	put			
quit	quit, quitted	quit, quitted	spread	spread	spread
			spring	sprang	sprung
read	read	read	stand	stood	stood
rid	rid	rid	steal	stole	stolen
ride	rode	ridden	stick	stuck	stuck
ring	rang	rung	sting	stung	stung
rise	rose	risen	stink	stank	stunk
run	ran	run	stride	strode	stridden
saw	sawed	sawn	strike	struck	struck, stricken
say	said	said			
see	saw	seen	strive	strove	striven
seek	sought	sought	swear	swore	sworn
sell	sold	sold	sweep	swept	swept
send	sent	sent	swell	swelled	swollen, swelled
set	set	set			
shake	shook	shaken	swim	swam	swum
shall	should	—	swing	swung	swung
shear	sheared	shorn, sheared	take	took	taken
shed	shed	shed	teach	taught	taught
shine	shone	shone	tear	tore	torn
shoot	shot	shot	tell	told	told
show	showed	shown	think	thought	thought
shrink	shrank	shrunk	throw	threw	thrown
shut	shut	shut	thrust	thrust	thrust
sing	sang	sung	tread	trod	trodden
sink	sank	sunk	wake	woke	woken
sit	sat	sat	waylay	waylaid	waylaid
slay	slew	slain	wear	wore	worn
sleep	slept	slept	weave	wove, weaved	woven, weaved
slide	slid	slid			
sling	slung	slung	wed	wedded, wed	wedded, wed
slit	slit	slit			
smell	smelt, smelled	smelt, smelled	weep	wept	wept
			win	won	won
sow	sowed	sown, sowed	wind	wound	wound
speak	spoke	spoken	wring	wrung	wrung
speed	sped, speeded	sped, speeded	write	wrote	written

LOS NÚMEROS

NUMBERS

un, uno(a)	1	one
dos	2	two
tres	3	three
cuatro	4	four
cinco	5	five
seis	6	six
siete	7	seven
ocho	8	eight
nueve	9	nine
diez	10	ten
once	11	eleven
doce	12	twelve
trece	13	thirteen
catorce	14	fourteen
quince	15	fifteen
dieciséis	16	sixteen
diecisiete	17	seventeen
dieciocho	18	eighteen
diecinueve	19	nineteen
veinte	20	twenty
veintiuno	21	twenty-one
veintidós	22	twenty-two
treinta	30	thirty
treinta y uno(a)	31	thirty-one
treinta y dos	32	thirty-two
cuarenta	40	forty
cuarenta y uno(a)	41	forty-one
cincuenta	50	fifty
sesenta	60	sixty
setenta	70	seventy
ochenta	80	eighty
noventa	90	ninety
cien, ciento	100	a hundred, one hundred
ciento uno(a)	101	a hundred and one
doscientos(as)	200	two hundred
doscientos(as) uno(a)	201	two hundred and one
trescientos(as)	300	three hundred
trescientos(as) uno(a)	301	three hundred and one
cuatrocientos(as)	400	four hundred
quinientos(as)	500	five hundred
seiscientos(as)	600	six hundred
setecientos(as)	700	seven hundred
ochocientos(as)	800	eight hundred
novecientos(as)	900	nine hundred
mil	1000	a thousand
mil dos	1002	a thousand and two
cinco mil	5000	five thousand
un millón	1000000	a million

OS NÚMEROS

NUMBERS

…imer, primero(a), 1º, 1ᵉʳ (1ª, 1ᵉʳᵃ)	first, 1st
…gundo(a), 2º (2ª)	second, 2nd
…rcer, tercero(a), 3º (3ª)	third, 3rd
…uarto(a), 4º (4ª)	fourth, 4th
…uinto(a), 5º (5ª)	fifth, 5th
…xto(a), 6º (6ª)	sixth, 6th
…ptimo(a)	seventh
…tavo(a)	eighth
…veno(a)	ninth
…cimo(a)	tenth
…décimo(a)	eleventh
…odécimo(a)	twelfth
…cimotercio(a)	thirteenth
…cimocuarto(a)	fourteenth
…cimoquinto(a)	fifteenth
…cimosexto(a)	sixteenth
…cimoséptimo(a)	seventeenth
…cimoctavo(a)	eighteenth
…cimonoveno(a)	nineteenth
…gésimo(a)	twentieth
…gésimo(a) primero(a)	twenty-first
…gésimo(a) segundo(a)	twenty-second
…igésimo(a)	thirtieth
…ntésimo(a)	hundredth
…ntésimo(a) primero(a)	hundred-and-first
…ilésimo(a)	thousandth

Números Quebrados etc

Fractions etc

…n medio	a half
…n tercio	a third
…s tercios	two thirds
…n cuarto	a quarter
…n quinto	a fifth
…ro coma cinco, 0,5	(nought) point five, 0.5
…es coma cuatro, 3,4	three point four, 3.4
…ez por cien(to)	ten per cent
…en por cien	a hundred per cent

Ejemplos

Examples

…a a llegar el 7 (de mayo)	he's arriving on the 7th (of May)
…ve en el número 7	he lives at number 7
…capítulo/la página 7	chapter/page 7
…egó séptimo	he came in 7th

…B. In Spanish the ordinal numbers from 1 to 10 are commonly used; from 11 to … rather less; above 21 they are rarely written and almost never heard in speech. …he custom is to replace the forms for 21 and above by the cardinal number.

LA HORA

¿qué hora es?

es/son

medianoche, las doce (de la noche)
la una (de la madrugada)
la una y cinco
la una y diez
la una y cuarto *or* quince
la una y veinticinco
la una y media *or* treinta
las dos menos veinticinco, la una
  treinta y cinco
las dos menos veinte, la una cuarenta
las dos menos cuarto, la una cuarenta
  y cinco
las dos menos diez, la una cincuenta
mediodía, las doce (de la tarde)
la una (de la tarde)

las siete (de la tarde)

¿a qué hora?

a medianoche
a las siete

en veinte minutos
hace quince minutos

THE TIME

what time is it?

it's o it is

midnight, twelve p.m.
one o'clock (in the morning), one (a.m
five past one
ten past one
a quarter past one, one fifteen
twenty-five past one, one twenty-five
half-past one, one thirty
twenty-five to two, one thirty-five

twenty to two, one forty
a quarter to two, one forty-five

ten to two, one fifty
twelve o'clock, midday, noon
one o'clock (in the afternoon), one
  (p.m.)
seven o'clock (in the evening), seven
  (p.m.)

(at) what time?

at midnight
at seven o'clock

in twenty minutes
fifteen minutes ago

ESPAÑOL – INGLÉS
SPANISH – ENGLISH

A, a

a [a] (*a+el = al*) *prep* **1** (*dirección*) to; **fueron ~ Madrid/Grecia** they went to Madrid/Greece; **me voy ~ casa** I'm going home

2 (*distancia*): **está ~ 15 km de aquí** it's 15 kms from here

3 (*posición*): **estar ~ la mesa** to be at table; **al lado de** next to, beside; *ver tb* **puerta**

4 (*tiempo*): **~ las 10/~ medianoche** at 10/midnight; **~ la mañana siguiente** the following morning; **~ los pocos días** after a few days; **estamos ~ 9 de julio** it's the ninth of July; **~ los 24 años** at the age of 24; **al año/~ la semana** (*AM*) a year/week later

5 (*manera*): **~ la francesa** the French way; **~ caballo** on horseback; **~ oscuras** in the dark

6 (*medio, instrumento*): **~ lápiz** in pencil; **~ mano** by hand; **cocina ~ gas** gas stove

7 (*razón*): **~ 30 ptas el kilo** at 30 pesetas el kilo; **~ más de 50 km/h** at more than 50 kms per hour

8 (*dativo*): **se lo di ~ él** I gave it to him; **vi al policía** I saw the policeman; **se lo compré ~ él** I bought it from him

9 (*tras ciertos verbos*): **voy ~ verle** I'm going to see him; **empezó ~ trabajar** he started working *o* to work

10 (*+infin*): **al verle, le reconocí inmediatamente** when I saw him I recognized him at once; **el camino ~ recorrer** the distance we (*etc*) have to travel; **¡~ callar!** keep quiet!; **¡~ comer!** let's eat!

abad, esa [a'ßað, 'ðesa] *nm/f* abbot/

abbess; **~ía** *nf* abbey

abajo [a'ßaxo] *adv* (*situación*) (down) below, underneath; (*en edificio*) downstairs; (*dirección*) down, downwards; **el piso de ~** the downstairs flat; **la parte de ~** the lower part; **¡~ el gobierno!** down with the government!; **cuesta/río ~** downhill/downstream; **de arriba ~** from top to bottom; **el ~ firmante** the undersigned; **más ~** lower *o* further down

abalanzarse [aßalan'θarse] *vr*: **~ sobre** *o* **contra** to throw o.s. at

abandonado, a [aßando'nað̞o, a] *adj* derelict; (*desatendido*) abandoned; (*desierto*) deserted; (*descuidado*) neglected

abandonar [aßando'nar] *vt* to leave; (*persona*) to abandon, desert; (*cosa*) to abandon, leave behind; (*descuidar*) to neglect; (*renunciar a*) to give up; (*INFORM*) to quit; **~se** *vr*: **~se a** to abandon o.s. to; **abandono** *nm* (*acto*) desertion, abandonment; (*estado*) abandon, neglect; (*renuncia*) withdrawal, retirement; **ganar por abandono** to win by default

abanicar [aßani'kar] *vt* to fan; **abanico** *nm* fan; (*NAUT*) derrick

abaratar [aßara'tar] *vt* to lower the price of; **~se** *vr* to go *o* come down in price

abarcar [aßar'kar] *vt* to include, embrace; (*AM*) to monopolize

abarrotado, a [aßarro'tað̞o, a] *adj* packed

abarrotar [aßarro'tar] *vt* (*local, estadio, teatro*) to fill, pack

abarrotero, a [aßarro'tero, a] (*AM*) *nm/f* grocer; **abarrotes** *nmpl* (*AM*) groceries, provisions

abastecer [aßaste'θer] *vt*: **~ (de)** to supply (with); **abastecimiento** *nm* supply

abasto [a'ßasto] *nm* supply; **no dar ~ a** to be unable to cope with

abatido, a [aβa'tiðo, a] *adj* dejected, downcast

abatimiento [aβati'mjento] *nm* (*depresión*) dejection, depression

abatir [aβa'tir] *vt* (*muro*) to demolish; (*pájaro*) to shoot *o* bring down; (*fig*) to depress; **~se** *vr* to get depressed; **~se sobre** to swoop *o* pounce on

abdicación [aβðika'θjon] *nf* abdication

abdicar [aβði'kar] *vi* to abdicate

abdomen [aβ'ðomen] *nm* abdomen; **abdominales** *nmpl* (*tb: ejercicios abdominales*) sit-ups

abecedario [aβeθe'ðarjo] *nm* alphabet

abedul [aβe'ðul] *nm* birch

abeja [a'βexa] *nf* bee

abejorro [aβe'xorro] *nm* bumblebee

abertura [aβer'tura] *nf* = **apertura**

abeto [a'βeto] *nm* fir

abierto, a [a'βjerto, a] *pp de* **abrir** ♦ *adj* open; (*AM*) generous

abigarrado, a [aβiɣa'rraðo, a] *adj* multi-coloured

abismal [aβis'mal] *adj* (*fig*) vast, enormous

abismar [aβis'mar] *vt* to humble, cast down; **~se** *vr* to sink; **~se en** (*fig*) to be plunged into

abismo [a'βismo] *nm* abyss

abjurar [aβxu'rar] *vi*: **~ de** to abjure, forswear

ablandar [aβlan'dar] *vt* to soften; **~se** *vr* to get softer

abnegación [aβneɣa'θjon] *nf* self-denial

abnegado, a [aβne'ɣaðo, a] *adj* self-sacrificing

abocado, a [aβo'kaðo, a] *adj*: **verse ~ al desastre** to be heading for disaster

abochornar [aβotʃor'nar] *vt* to embarrass

abofetear [aβofete'ar] *vt* to slap (in the face)

abogado, a [aβo'ɣaðo, a] *nm/f* lawyer; (*notario*) solicitor; (*en tribunal*) barrister (*BRIT*), attorney (*US*); **~ defensor** defence lawyer *o* attorney (*US*)

abogar [aβo'ɣar] *vi*: **~ por** to plead for; (*fig*) to advocate

abolengo [aβo'leŋgo] *nm* ancestry, lineage

abolición [aβoli'θjon] *nf* abolition

abolir [aβo'lir] *vt* to abolish; (*cancelar*) to cancel

abolladura [aβoʎa'ðura] *nf* dent

abollar [aβo'ʎar] *vt* to dent

abominable [aβomi'naβle] *adj* abominable

abonado, a [aβo'naðo, a] *adj* (*deuda*) paid(-up) ♦ *nm/f* subscriber

abonar [aβo'nar] *vt* (*deuda*) to settle; (*terreno*) to fertilize; (*idea*) to endorse; **~se** *vr* to subscribe; **abono** *nm* payment; fertilizer; subscription

abordar [aβor'ðar] *vt* (*barco*) to board; (*asunto*) to broach

aborigen [aβo'rixen] *nm/f* aborigine

aborrecer [aβorre'θer] *vt* to hate, loathe

abortar [aβor'tar] *vi* (*malparir*) to have a miscarriage; (*deliberadamente*) to have an abortion; **aborto** *nm* miscarriage; abortion

abotonar [aβoto'nar] *vt* to button (up), do up

abovedado, a [aβoβe'ðaðo, a] *adj* vaulted, domed

abrasar [aβra'sar] *vt* to burn (up); (*AGR*) to dry up, parch

abrazar [aβra'θar] *vt* to embrace, hug

abrazo [a'βraθo] *nm* embrace, hug; **un ~** (*en carta*) with best wishes

abrebotellas [aβreβo'teʎas] *nm inv* bottle opener

abrecartas [aβre'kartas] *nm inv* letter opener

abrelatas [aβre'latas] *nm inv* tin (*BRIT*) *o* can opener

abreviar [aβre'βjar] *vt* to abbreviate; (*texto*) to abridge; (*plazo*) to reduce; **abreviatura** *nf* abbreviation

abridor [aβri'ðor] *nm* bottle opener; (*de latas*) tin (*BRIT*) *o* can opener

abrigar [aβri'ɣar] *vt* (*proteger*) to shelter; (*suj: ropa*) to keep warm; (*fig*) to cherish

abrigo [a'βriɣo] *nm* (*prenda*) coat, overcoat; (*lugar protegido*) shelter

abril [a'βril] *nm* April

brillantar [aßriλan'tar] vt to polish

brir [a'ßrir] vt to open (up) ♦ vi to open; **~se** vr to open (up); (extenderse) to open out; (cielo) to clear; **~se paso** to find o force a way through

brochar [aßro'tʃar] vt (con botones) to button (up); (zapato, con broche) to do up

brumar [aßru'mar] vt to overwhelm; (sobrecargar) to weigh down

brupto, a [a'ßrupto, a] adj abrupt; (empinado) steep

bsceso [aßs'θeso] nm abscess

bsentismo [aßsen'tismo] nm absenteeism

bsolución [aßsolu'θjon] nf (REL) absolution; (JUR) acquittal

bsoluto, a [aßso'luto, a] adj absolute; **en ~** adv not at all

bsolver [aßsol'ßer] vt to absolve; (JUR) to pardon; (: acusado) to acquit

bsorbente [aßsor'ßente] adj absorbent; (interesante) absorbing

bsorber [aßsor'ßer] vt to absorb; (embeber) to soak up

bsorción [aßsor'θjon] nf absorption; (COM) takeover

bsorto, a [aß'sorto, a] pp de **absorber** ♦ adj absorbed, engrossed

bstemio, a [aßs'temjo, a] adj teetotal

bstención [aßsten'θjon] nf abstention

bstenerse [aßste'nerse] vr: **~ (de)** to abstain o refrain (from)

bstinencia [aßsti'nenθja] nf abstinence; (ayuno) fasting

bstracción [aßstrak'θjon] nf abstraction

bstracto, a [aß'strakto, a] adj abstract

bstraer [aßstra'er] vt to abstract; **~se** vr to be o become absorbed

bstraído, a [aßstra'iðo, a] adj absent-minded

bsuelto [aß'swelto] pp de **absolver**

bsurdo, a [aß'surðo, a] adj absurd

buchear [aßutʃe'ar] vt to boo

buelo, a [a'ßwelo, a] nm/f grandfather/ nother; **~s** nmpl grandparents

bulia [a'ßulja] nf apathy

abultado, a [aßul'taðo, a] adj bulky

abultar [aßul'tar] vi to be bulky

abundancia [aßun'danθja] nf: **una ~ de** plenty of; **abundante** adj abundant, plentiful

abundar [aßun'dar] vi to abound, be plentiful

aburguesarse [aßurγe'sarse] vr to become middle-class

aburrido, a [aßu'rriðo, a] adj (hastiado) bored; (que aburre) boring; **aburrimiento** nm boredom, tedium

aburrir [aßu'rrir] vt to bore; **~se** vr to be bored, get bored

abusar [aßu'sar] vi to go too far; **~ de** to abuse

abusivo, a [aßu'sißo, a] adj (precio) exorbitant

abuso [a'ßuso] nm abuse

abyecto, a [aß'jekto, a] adj wretched, abject

acá [a'ka] adv (lugar) here; **¿de cuándo ~?** since when?

acabado, a [aka'ßaðo, a] adj finished, complete; (perfecto) perfect; (agotado) worn out; (fig) masterly ♦ nm finish

acabar [aka'ßar] vt (llevar a su fin) to finish, complete; (consumir) to use up; (rematar) to finish off ♦ vi to finish, end; **~se** vr to finish, stop; (terminarse) to be over; (agotarse) to run out; **~ con** to put an end to; **~ de llegar** to have just arrived; **~ por hacer** to end (up) by doing; **¡se acabó!** it's all over!; (¡basta!) that's enough!

acabóse [aka'ßose] nm: **esto es el ~** this is the last straw

academia [aka'ðemja] nf academy; **académico, a** adj academic

acaecer [akae'θer] vi to happen, occur

acallar [aka'λar] vt (persona) to silence; (protestas, rumores) to suppress

acalorado, a [akalo'raðo, a] adj (discusión) heated

acalorarse [akalo'rarse] vr (fig) to get heated

acampar [akam'par] vi to camp

acantilado [akanti'laðo] nm cliff
acaparar [akapa'rar] vt to monopolize; (*acumular*) to hoard
acariciar [akari'θjar] vt to caress; (*esperanza*) to cherish
acarrear [akarre'ar] vt to transport; (*fig*) to cause, result in
acaso [a'kaso] adv perhaps, maybe; **(por) si ~** (just) in case
acatamiento [akata'mjento] nm respect; (*ley*) observance
acatar [aka'tar] vt to respect; (*ley*) obey
acatarrarse [akata'rrarse] vr to catch a cold
acaudalado, a [akauða'laðo, a] adj well-off
acaudillar [akauði'ʎar] vt to lead, command
acceder [akθe'ðer] vi: **~ a** (*petición etc*) to agree to; (*tener acceso a*) to have access to; (*INFORM*) to access
accesible [akθe'siβle] adj accessible
acceso [ak'θeso] nm access, entry; (*camino*) access, approach; (*MED*) attack, fit
accesorio, a [akθe'sorjo, a] adj, nm accessory
accidentado, a [akθiðen'taðo, a] adj uneven; (*montañoso*) hilly; (*azaroso*) eventful ♦ nm/f accident victim
accidental [akθiðen'tal] adj accidental; **accidentarse** vr to have an accident
accidente [akθi'ðente] nm accident; **~s** nmpl (*de terreno*) unevenness sg
acción [ak'θjon] nf action; (*acto*) action, act; (*COM*) share; (*JUR*) action, lawsuit; **accionar** vt to work, operate; (*INFORM*) to drive
accionista [akθjo'nista] nm/f shareholder, stockholder
acebo [a'θeβo] nm holly; (*árbol*) holly tree
acechar [aθe'tʃar] vt to spy on; (*aguardar*) to lie in wait for; **acecho** nm: **estar al acecho (de)** to lie in wait (for)
aceitar [aθei'tar] vt to oil, lubricate
aceite [a'θeite] nm oil; (*de oliva*) olive oil; **~ra** nf oilcan; **aceitoso, a** adj oily

aceituna [aθei'tuna] nf olive
acelerador [aθelera'ðor] nm accelerator
acelerar [aθele'rar] vt to accelerate
acelga [a'θelɣa] nf chard, beet
acento [a'θento] nm accent; (*acentuación*) stress
acentuar [aθen'twar] vt to accent; to stress; (*fig*) to accentuate
acepción [aθep'θjon] nf meaning
aceptable [aθep'taβle] adj acceptable
aceptación [aθepta'θjon] nf acceptance; (*aprobación*) approval
aceptar [aθep'tar] vt to accept; (*aprobar*) to approve
acequia [a'θekja] nf irrigation ditch
acera [a'θera] nf pavement (*BRIT*), sidewalk (*US*)
acerca [a'θerka]: **~ de** prep about, concerning
acercar [aθer'kar] vt to bring o move nearer; **~se** vr to approach, come near
acerico [aθe'riko] nm pincushion
acero [a'θero] nm steel
acérrimo, a [a'θerrimo, a] adj (*partidario*) staunch; (*enemigo*) bitter
acertado, a [aθer'taðo, a] adj correct; (*apropiado*) apt; (*sensato*) sensible
acertar [aθer'tar] vt (*blanco*) to hit; (*solución*) to get right; (*adivinar*) to guess ♦ vi to get it right, be right; **~ a** to manage to; **~ con** to happen o hit on
acertijo [aθer'tixo] nm riddle, puzzle
achacar [atʃa'kar] vt to attribute
achacoso, a [atʃa'koso, a] adj sickly
achantar [atʃan'tar] (*fam*) vt to scare, frighten; **~se** vr to back down
achaque etc [a'tʃake] vb ver **achacar** ♦ nm ailment
achicar [atʃi'kar] vt to reduce; (*NAUT*) to bale out
achicharrar [atʃitʃa'rrar] vt to scorch, burn
achicoria [atʃi'korja] nf chicory
aciago, a [a'θjaɣo, a] adj ill-fated, fateful
acicalar [aθika'lar] vt to polish; (*persona*) to dress up; **~se** vr to get dressed up
acicate [aθi'kate] nm spur

acidez [aθi'ðeθ] *nf* acidity

ácido, a ['aθiðo, a] *adj* sour, acid ♦ *nm* acid

acierto *etc* [a'θjerto] *vb ver* **acertar** ♦ *nm* success; (*buen paso*) wise move; (*solución*) solution; (*habilidad*) skill, ability

aclamación [aklama'θjon] *nf* acclamation; (*aplausos*) applause

aclamar [akla'mar] *vt* to acclaim; (*aplaudir*) to applaud

aclaración [aklara'θjon] *nf* clarification, explanation

aclarar [akla'rar] *vt* to clarify, explain; (*ropa*) to rinse ♦ *vi* to clear up; **~se** *vr* (*explicarse*) to understand; **~se la garganta** to clear one's throat

aclaratorio, a [aklara'torjo, a] *adj* explanatory

aclimatación [aklimata'θjon] *nf* acclimatization

aclimatar [aklima'tar] *vt* to acclimatize; **~se** *vr* to become acclimatized

acné [ak'ne] *nm* acne

acobardar [akoβar'ðar] *vt* to intimidate

acodarse [ako'ðarse] *vr*: **~ en** to lean on

acogedor, a [akoxe'ðor, a] *adj* welcoming; (*hospitalario*) hospitable

acoger [ako'xer] *vt* to welcome; (*abrigar*) to shelter; **~se** *vr* to take refuge

acogida [ako'xiða] *nf* reception; refuge

acometer [akome'ter] *vt* to attack; (*emprender*) to undertake; **acometida** *nf* attack, assault

acomodado, a [akomo'ðaðo, a] *adj* (*persona*) well-to-do

acomodador, a [akomoða'ðor, a] *nm/f* usher(ette)

acomodar [akomo'ðar] *vt* to adjust; (*alojar*) to accommodate; **~se** *vr* to conform; (*instalarse*) to install o.s.; (*adaptarse*): **~se (a)** to adapt (to)

acompañar [akompa'ɲar] *vt* to accompany; (*documentos*) to enclose

acondicionar [akondiθjo'nar] *vt* to arrange, prepare; (*pelo*) to condition

acongojar [akongo'xar] *vt* to distress, grieve

aconsejar [akonse'xar] *vt* to advise, counsel; **~se** *vr*: **~se con** to consult

acontecer [akonte'θer] *vi* to happen, occur; **acontecimiento** *nm* event

acopio [a'kopjo] *nm* store, stock

acoplamiento [akopla'mjento] *nm* coupling, joint; **acoplar** *vt* to fit; (*ELEC*) to connect; (*vagones*) to couple

acorazado, a [akora'θaðo, a] *adj* armour-plated, armoured ♦ *nm* battleship

acordar [akor'ðar] *vt* (*resolver*) to agree, resolve; (*recordar*) to remind; **~se** *vr* to agree; **~se (de algo)** to remember (sth); **acorde** *adj* (*MUS*) harmonious ♦ *nm* chord; **acorde con** (*medidas etc*) in keeping with

acordeón [akorðe'on] *nm* accordion

acordonado, a [akorðo'naðo, a] *adj* (*calle*) cordoned-off

acorralar [akorra'lar] *vt* to round up, corral

acortar [akor'tar] *vt* to shorten; (*duración*) to cut short; (*cantidad*) to reduce; **~se** *vr* to become shorter

acosar [ako'sar] *vt* to pursue relentlessly; (*fig*) to hound, pester; **acoso** *nm* harassment; **acoso sexual** sexual harassment

acostar [akos'tar] *vt* (*en cama*) to put to bed; (*en suelo*) to lay down; **~se** *vr* to go to bed; to lie down; **~se con uno** to sleep with sb

acostumbrado, a [akostum'braðo, a] *adj* usual; **~ a** used to

acostumbrar [akostum'brar] *vt*: **~ a uno a algo** to get sb used to sth ♦ *vi*: **~ (a) hacer** to be in the habit of doing; **~se** *vr*: **~se a** to get used to

acotación [akota'θjon] *nf* marginal note; (*GEO*) elevation mark; (*de límite*) boundary mark; (*TEATRO*) stage direction

ácrata ['akrata] *adj, nm/f* anarchist

acre ['akre] *adj* (*olor*) acrid; (*fig*) biting ♦ *nm* acre

acrecentar [akreθen'tar] *vt* to increase, augment

acreditar [akreði'tar] *vt* (*garantizar*) to

vouch for, guarantee; (*autorizar*) to
authorize; (*dar prueba de*) to prove; (COM:
abonar) to credit; (*embajador*) to accredit;
~se *vr* to become famous

acreedor, a [akree'ðor, a] *adj*: **~ de**
worthy of ♦ *nm/f* creditor

acribillar [akriβi'ʎar] *vt*: **~ a balazos** to
riddle with bullets

acróbata [a'kroβata] *nm/f* acrobat

acta ['akta] *nf* certificate; (*de comisión*)
minutes *pl*, record; **~ de nacimiento/de
matrimonio** birth/marriage certificate; **~
notarial** affidavit

actitud [akti'tuð] *nf* attitude; (*postura*)
posture

activar [akti'βar] *vt* to activate; (*acelerar*)
to speed up

actividad [aktiβi'ðað] *nf* activity

activo, a [ak'tiβo, a] *adj* active; (*vivo*)
lively ♦ *nm* (COM) assets *pl*

acto ['akto] *nm* act, action; (*ceremonia*)
ceremony; (TEATRO) act; **en el ~**
immediately

actor [ak'tor] *nm* actor; (JUR) plaintiff
♦ *adj*: **parte ~a** prosecution

actriz [ak'triθ] *nf* actress

actuación [aktwa'θjon] *nf* action;
(*comportamiento*) conduct, behaviour;
(JUR) proceedings *pl*; (*desempeño*)
performance

actual [ak'twal] *adj* present(-day), current;
~idad *nf* present; **~idades** *nfpl* (*noticias*)
news *sg*; **en la ~idad** at present; (*hoy día*)
nowadays

actualizar [aktwali'θar] *vt* to update,
modernize

actualmente [aktwal'mente] *adv* at
present; (*hoy día*) nowadays

actuar [ak'twar] *vi* (*obrar*) to work,
operate; (*actor*) to act, perform ♦ *vt* to
work, operate; **~ de** to act as

acuarela [akwa'rela] *nf* watercolour

acuario [a'kwarjo] *nm* aquarium;
(ASTROLOGÍA): **A~** Aquarius

acuartelar [akwarte'lar] *vt* (MIL) to confine
to barracks

acuático, a [a'kwatiko, a] *adj* aquatic

acuchillar [akutʃi'ʎar] *vt* (TEC) to plane
(down), smooth

acuciante [aku'θjante] *adj* urgent

acuciar [aku'θjar] *vt* to urge on

acudir [aku'ðir] *vi* (*asistir*) to attend; (*ir*) to
go; **~ a** (*fig*) to turn to; **~ en ayuda de** to
go to the aid of

acuerdo *etc* [a'kwerðo] *vb ver* **acordar**
♦ *nm* agreement; **¡de ~!** agreed!; **de ~
con** (*persona*) in agreement with; (*acción,
documento*) in accordance with; **estar de
~** to be agreed, agree

acumular [akumu'lar] *vt* to accumulate,
collect

acuñar [aku'ɲar] *vt* (*moneda*) to mint;
(*frase*) to coin

acupuntura [akupun'tura] *nf* acupuncture

acurrucarse [akurru'karse] *vr* to crouch;
(*ovillarse*) to curl up

acusación [akusa'θjon] *nf* accusation

acusar [aku'sar] *vt* to accuse; (*revelar*) to
reveal; (*denunciar*) to denounce

acuse [a'kuse] *nm*: **~ de recibo**
acknowledgement of receipt

acústica [a'kustika] *nf* acoustics *pl*

acústico, a [a'kustiko, a] *adj* acoustic

adaptación [aðapta'θjon] *nf* adaptation

adaptador [aðapta'ðor] *nm* (ELEC) adapter

adaptar [aðap'tar] *vt* to adapt; (*acomodar*)
to fit

adecuado, a [aðe'kwaðo, a] *adj* (*apto*)
suitable; (*oportuno*) appropriate

adecuar [aðe'kwar] *vt* to adapt; to make
suitable

a. de J.C. *abr* (= *antes de Jesucristo*) B.C.

adelantado, a [aðelan'taðo, a] *adj*
advanced; (*reloj*) fast; **pagar por ~** to pay
in advance

adelantamiento [aðelanta'mjento] *nm*
(AUTO) overtaking

adelantar [aðelan'tar] *vt* to move forward;
(*avanzar*) to advance; (*acelerar*) to speed
up; (AUTO) to overtake ♦ *vi* to go
forward, advance; **~se** *vr* to go forward,
advance

adelante [aðe'lante] *adv* forward(s), ahead
♦ *excl* come in!; **de hoy en ~** from now

on; **más ~** later on; (*más allá*) further on
adelanto [aðe'lanto] *nm* advance; (*mejora*)
improvement; (*progreso*) progress
adelgazar [aðelɣa'θar] *vt* to thin (down)
♦ *vi* to get thin; (*con régimen*) to slim
down, lose weight
ademán [aðe'man] *nm* gesture;
ademanes *nmpl* manners; **en ~ de** as if
to
además [aðe'mas] *adv* besides; (*por otra
parte*) moreover; (*también*) also; **~ de**
besides, in addition to
adentrarse [aðen'trarse] *vr*: **~ en** to go
into, get inside; (*penetrar*) to penetrate
(into)
adentro [a'ðentro] *adv* inside, in; **mar ~**
out at sea; **tierra ~** inland
adepto, a [a'ðepto, a] *nm/f* supporter
aderezar [aðere'θar] *vt* (*ensalada*) to dress;
(*comida*) to season; **aderezo** *nm*
dressing; seasoning
adeudar [aðeu'ðar] *vt* to owe; **~se** *vr* to
run into debt
adherirse [aðe'rirse] *vr*: **~ a** to adhere to;
(*partido*) to join
adhesión [aðe'sjon] *nf* adhesion; (*fig*)
adherence
adicción [aðik'θjon] *nf* addiction
adición [aði'θjon] *nf* addition
adicto, a [a'ðikto, a] *adj*: **~ a** addicted to;
(*dedicado*) devoted to ♦ *nm/f* supporter,
follower; (*toxicómano etc*) addict
adiestrar [aðjes'trar] *vt* to train, teach;
(*conducir*) to guide, lead; **~se** *vr* to
practise; (*enseñarse*) to train o.s.
adinerado, a [aðine'raðo, a] *adj* wealthy
adiós [a'ðjos] *excl* (*para despedirse*)
goodbye!, cheerio!; (*al pasar*) hello!
aditivo [aði'tiβo] *nm* additive
adivinanza [aðiβi'nanθa] *nf* riddle
adivinar [aðiβi'nar] *vt* to prophesy;
(*conjeturar*) to guess; **adivino, a** *nm/f*
fortune-teller
adj *abr* (= **adjunto**) encl.
adjetivo [aðxe'tiβo] *nm* adjective
adjudicación [aðxuðika'θjon] *nf* award;
adjudication

adjudicar [aðxuði'kar] *vt* to award; **~se**
vr: **~se algo** to appropriate sth
adjuntar [aðxun'tar] *vt* to attach, enclose;
adjunto, a *adj* attached, enclosed
♦ *nm/f* assistant
administración [aðministra'θjon] *nf*
administration; (*dirección*) management;
administrador, a *nm/f* administrator;
manager(ess)
administrar [aðminis'trar] *vt* to
administer; **administrativo, a** *adj*
administrative
admirable [aðmi'raβle] *adj* admirable
admiración [aðmira'θjon] *nf* admiration;
(*asombro*) wonder; (*LING*) exclamation
mark
admirar [aðmi'rar] *vt* to admire; (*extrañar*)
to surprise; **~se** *vr* to be surprised
admisible [aðmi'siβle] *adj* admissible
admisión [aðmi'sjon] *nf* admission;
(*reconocimiento*) acceptance
admitir [aðmi'tir] *vt* to admit; (*aceptar*) to
accept
admonición [aðmoni'θjon] *nf* warning
adobar [aðo'βar] *vt* (*CULIN*) to season
adobe [a'ðoβe] *nm* adobe, sun-dried brick
adoctrinar [aðoktri'nar] *vt*: **~ en** to
indoctrinate with
adolecer [aðole'θer] *vi*: **~ de** to suffer
from
adolescente [aðoles'θente] *nm/f*
adolescent, teenager
adonde [a'ðonde] *conj* (to) where
adónde [a'ðonde] *adv* = **dónde**
adopción [aðop'θjon] *nf* adoption
adoptar [aðop'tar] *vt* to adopt
adoptivo, a [aðop'tiβo, a] *adj* (*padres*)
adoptive; (*hijo*) adopted
adoquín [aðo'kin] *nm* paving stone
adorar [aðo'rar] *vt* to adore
adormecer [aðorme'θer] *vt* to put to
sleep; **~se** *vr* to become sleepy; (*dormirse*)
to fall asleep
adornar [aðor'nar] *vt* to adorn
adorno [a'ðorno] *nm* ornament;
(*decoración*) decoration
adosado, a [aðo'saðo, a] *adj*: **casa**

adosada semi-detached house
adquiero *etc vb ver* **adquirir**
adquirir [aðki'rir] *vt* to acquire, obtain
adquisición [aðkisi'θjon] *nf* acquisition
adrede [a'ðreðe] *adv* on purpose
adscribir [aðskri'ßir] *vt* to appoint
adscrito *pp de* **adscribir**
aduana [a'ðwana] *nf* customs *pl*
aduanero, a [aðwa'nero, a] *adj* customs *cpd* ♦ *nm/f* customs officer
aducir [aðu'θir] *vt* to adduce; (*dar como prueba*) to offer as proof
adueñarse [aðwe'narse] *vr*: ~ **de** to take possession of
adulación [aðula'θjon] *nf* flattery
adular [aðu'lar] *vt* to flatter
adulterar [aðulte'rar] *vt* to adulterate
adulterio [aðul'terjo] *nm* adultery
adúltero, a [a'ðultero, a] *adj* adulterous ♦ *nm/f* adulterer/adulteress
adulto, a [a'ðulto, a] *adj, nm/f* adult
adusto, a [a'ðusto, a] *adj* stern; (*austero*) austere
advenedizo, a [aðßene'ðiθo, a] *nm/f* upstart
advenimiento [aðßeni'mjento] *nm* arrival; (*al trono*) accession
adverbio [að'ßerßjo] *nm* adverb
adversario, a [aðßer'sarjo, a] *nm/f* adversary
adversidad [aðßersi'ðað] *nf* adversity; (*contratiempo*) setback
adverso, a [að'ßerso, a] *adj* adverse
advertencia [aðßer'tenθja] *nf* warning; (*prefacio*) preface, foreword
advertir [aðßer'tir] *vt* to notice; (*avisar*): ~ **a uno de** to warn sb about *o* of
Adviento [að'ßjento] *nm* Advent
advierto *etc vb ver* **advertir**
adyacente [aðja'θente] *adj* adjacent
aéreo, a [a'ereo, a] *adj* aerial
aerobic [ae'roßik] *nm* aerobics *sg*
aerodeslizador [aeroðesliθa'ðor] *nm* hovercraft
aeromozo, a [aero'moθo, a] *(AM) nm/f* air steward(ess)
aeronáutica [aero'nautika] *nf* aeronautics

sg
aeronave [aero'naße] *nm* spaceship
aeroplano [aero'plano] *nm* aeroplane
aeropuerto [aero'pwerto] *nm* airport
aerosol [aero'sol] *nm* aerosol
afabilidad [afaßili'ðað] *nf* friendliness; **afable** *adj* affable
afamado, a [afa'maðo, a] *adj* famous
afán [a'fan] *nm* hard work; (*deseo*) desire
afanar [afa'nar] *vt* to harass; (*fam*) to pinch; ~**se** *vr*: ~**se por hacer** to strive to do
afear [afe'ar] *vt* to disfigure
afección [afek'θjon] *nf* (*MED*) disease
afectación [afekta'θjon] *nf* affectation; **afectado, a** *adj* affected
afectar [afek'tar] *vt* to affect
afectísimo, a [afek'tisimo, a] *adj* affectionate; **suyo** ~ yours truly
afectivo, a [afek'tißo, a] *adj* (*problema etc*) emotional
afecto [a'fekto] *nm* affection; **tenerle** ~ **a uno** to be fond of sb
afectuoso, a [afek'twoso, a] *adj* affectionate
afeitar [afei'tar] *vt* to shave; ~**se** *vr* to shave
afeminado, a [afemi'naðo, a] *adj* effeminate
Afganistán [afɣanis'tan] *nm* Afghanistan
afianzamiento [afjanθa'mjento] *nm* strengthening; security
afianzar [afjan'θar] *vt* to strengthen; to secure; ~**se** *vr* to become established
afiche [a'fitʃe] *(AM) nm* poster
afición [afi'θjon] *nf* fondness, liking; **la** ~ the fans *pl*; **pinto por** ~ I paint as a hobby; **aficionado, a** *adj* keen, enthusiastic; (*no profesional*) amateur ♦ *nm/f* enthusiast, fan; amateur; **ser aficionado a algo** to be very keen on *o* fond of sth
aficionar [afiθjo'nar] *vt*: ~ **a uno a algo** to make sb like sth; ~**se** *vr*: ~**se a algo** to grow fond of sth
afilado, a [afi'laðo, a] *adj* sharp
afilar [afi'lar] *vt* to sharpen

afiliarse [afi'ljarse] *vr* to affiliate

afín [a'fin] *adj* (*parecido*) similar; (*conexo*) related

afinar [afi'nar] *vt* (*TEC*) to refine; (*MUS*) to tune ♦ *vi* (*tocar*) to play in tune; (*cantar*) to sing in tune

afincarse [afin'karse] *vr* to settle

afinidad [afini'ðað] *nf* affinity; (*parentesco*) relationship; **por ~** by marriage

afirmación [afirma'θjon] *nf* affirmation

afirmar [afir'mar] *vt* to affirm, state; **afirmativo, a** *adj* affirmative

aflicción [aflik'θjon] *nf* affliction; (*dolor*) grief

afligir [afli'xir] *vt* to afflict; (*apenar*) to distress; **~se** *vr* to grieve

aflojar [aflo'xar] *vt* to slacken; (*desatar*) to loosen, undo; (*relajar*) to relax ♦ *vi* to drop; (*bajar*) to go down; **~se** *vr* to relax

aflorar [aflo'rar] *vi* to come to the surface, emerge

afluente [aflu'ente] *adj* flowing ♦ *nm* tributary

afluir [aflu'ir] *vi* to flow

afmo, a *abr* (= *afectísimo(a) suyo(a)*) Yours

afónico, a [a'foniko, a] *adj*: **estar ~** to have a sore throat; to have lost one's voice

aforo [a'foro] *nm* (*de teatro etc*) capacity

afortunado, a [afortu'naðo, a] *adj* fortunate, lucky

afrancesado, a [afranθe'saðo, a] *adj* francophile; (*pey*) Frenchified

afrenta [a'frenta] *nf* affront, insult; (*deshonra*) dishonour, shame

África ['afrika] *nf* Africa; **africano, a** *adj*, *nm/f* African

afrontar [afron'tar] *vt* to confront; (*poner cara a cara*) to bring face to face

afuera [a'fwera] *adv* out, outside; **~s** *nfpl* outskirts

agachar [aɣa'tʃar] *vt* to bend, bow; **~se** *vr* to stoop, bend

agalla [a'ɣaʎa] *nf* (*ZOOL*) gill; **tener ~s** (*fam*) to have guts

agarradera [aɣarra'ðera] *nf* (*esp AM*) handle

agarrado, a [aɣa'rraðo, a] *adj* mean, stingy

agarrar [aɣa'rrar] *vt* to grasp, grab; (*AM*) to take, catch; (*recoger*) to pick up ♦ *vi* (*planta*) to take root; **~se** *vr* to hold on (tightly)

agarrotar [aɣarro'tar] *vt* (*persona*) to squeeze tightly; (*reo*) to garrotte; **~se** *vr* (*motor*) to seize up; (*MED*) to stiffen

agasajar [aɣasa'xar] *vt* to treat well, fête

agazaparse [aɣaθa'parse] *vr* to crouch down

agencia [a'xenθja] *nf* agency; **~ inmobiliaria** estate (*BRIT*) *o* real estate (*US*) agent's (office); **~ de viajes** travel agency

agenciarse [axen'θjarse] *vr* to obtain, procure

agenda [a'xenda] *nf* diary

agente [a'xente] *nm/f* agent; (*de policía*) policeman/policewoman; **~ inmobiliario** estate agent (*BRIT*), realtor (*US*); **~ de seguros** insurance agent

ágil ['axil] *adj* agile, nimble; **agilidad** *nf* agility, nimbleness

agilizar [axili'θar] *vt* (*trámites*) to speed up

agitación [axita'θjon] *nf* (*de mano etc*) shaking, waving; (*de líquido etc*) stirring; (*fig*) agitation

agitado, a [axi'aðo, a] *adj* hectic; (*viaje*) bumpy

agitar [axi'tar] *vt* to wave, shake; (*líquido*) to stir; (*fig*) to stir up, excite; **~se** *vr* to get excited; (*inquietarse*) to get worried *o* upset

aglomeración [aɣlomera'θjon] *nf*: **~ de tráfico/gente** traffic jam/mass of people

aglomerar [aɣlome'rar] *vt* to crowd together; **~se** *vr* to crowd together

agnóstico, a [aɣ'nostiko, a] *adj*, *nm/f* agnostic

agobiar [aɣo'βjar] *vt* to weigh down; (*oprimir*) to oppress; (*cargar*) to burden

agolparse [aɣol'parse] *vr* to crowd together

agonía [aɣo'nia] *nf* death throes *pl*; (*fig*)

agony, anguish
agonizante [aɣoni'θante] *adj* dying
agonizar [aɣoni'θar] *vi* to be dying
agosto [a'ɣosto] *nm* August
agotado, a [aɣo'taðo, a] *adj* (*persona*) exhausted; (*libros*) out of print; (*acabado*) finished; (COM) sold out
agotador, a [aɣota'ðor, a] *adj* exhausting
agotamiento [aɣota'mjento] *nm* exhaustion
agotar [aɣo'tar] *vt* to exhaust; (*consumir*) to drain; (*recursos*) to use up, deplete; **~se** *vr* to be exhausted; (*acabarse*) to run out; (*libro*) to go out of print
agraciado, a [aɣra'θjaðo, a] *adj* (*atractivo*) attractive; (*en sorteo etc*) lucky
agradable [aɣra'ðaßle] *adj* pleasant, nice
agradar [aɣra'ðar] *vt*: **él me agrada** I like him
agradecer [aɣraðe'θer] *vt* to thank; (*favor etc*) to be grateful for; **agradecido, a** *adj* grateful; **¡muy agradecido!** thanks a lot!; **agradecimiento** *nm* thanks *pl*; gratitude
agradezco *etc vb ver* **agradecer**
agrado [a'ɣraðo] *nm*: **ser de tu** *etc* **~** to be to your *etc* liking
agrandar [aɣran'dar] *vt* to enlarge; (*fig*) to exaggerate; **~se** *vr* to get bigger
agrario, a [a'ɣrarjo, a] *adj* agrarian, land *cpd*; (*política*) agricultural, farming
agravante [aɣra'ßante] *adj* aggravating
♦ *nm*: **con el ~ de que ...** with the further difficulty that ...
agravar [aɣra'ßar] *vt* (*pesar sobre*) to make heavier; (*irritar*) to aggravate; **~se** *vr* to worsen, get worse
agraviar [aɣra'ßjar] *vt* to offend; (*ser injusto con*) to wrong; **~se** *vr* to take offence; **agravio** *nm* offence; wrong; (JUR) grievance
agredir [aɣre'ðir] *vt* to attack
agregado, a [aɣre'xaðo, a] *nm/f*: **A~** ≈ teacher (*who is not head of department*)
♦ *nm* aggregate; (*persona*) attaché
agregar [aɣre'ɣar] *vt* to gather; (*añadir*) to add; (*persona*) to appoint

agresión [aɣre'sjon] *nf* aggression
agresivo, a [aɣre'sißo, a] *adj* aggressive
agriar [a'ɣrjar] *vt* to (turn) sour; **~se** *vr* to turn sour
agrícola [a'ɣrikola] *adj* farming *cpd*, agricultural
agricultor, a [aɣrikul'tor, a] *nm/f* farmer
agricultura [aɣrikul'tura] *nf* agriculture, farming
agridulce [aɣri'ðulθe] *adj* bittersweet; (CULIN) sweet and sour
agrietarse [aɣrje'tarse] *vr* to crack; (*piel*) to chap
agrimensor, a [aɣrimen'sor, a] *nm/f* surveyor
agrio, a ['aɣrjo, a] *adj* bitter
agrupación [aɣrupa'θjon] *nf* group; (*acto*) grouping
agrupar [aɣru'par] *vt* to group
agua ['aɣwa] *nf* water; (NAUT) wake; (ARQ) slope of a roof; **~s** *nfpl* (*de piedra*) water *sg*, sparkle *sg*; (MED) water *sg*, urine *sg*; (NAUT) waters; **~s abajo/arriba** downstream/upstream; **~ bendita/destilada/potable** holy/distilled/drinking water; **~ caliente** hot water; **~ corriente** running water; **~ de colonia** eau de cologne; **~ mineral (con/sin gas)** (carbonated/uncarbonated) mineral water; **~ oxigenada** hydrogen peroxide; **~s jurisdiccionales** territorial waters
aguacate [aɣwa'kate] *nm* avocado (pear)
aguacero [aɣwa'θero] *nm* (heavy) shower, downpour
aguado, a [a'ɣwaðo, a] *adj* watery, watered down
aguafiestas [aɣwa'fjestas] *nm/f inv* spoilsport, killjoy
aguanieve [aɣwa'njeße] *nf* sleet
aguantar [aɣwan'tar] *vt* to bear, put up with; (*sostener*) to hold up ♦ *vi* to last; **~se** *vr* to restrain o.s.; **aguante** *nm* (*paciencia*) patience; (*resistencia*) endurance
aguar [a'ɣwar] *vt* to water down
aguardar [aɣwar'ðar] *vt* to wait for
aguardiente [aɣwar'ðjente] *nm* brandy,

liquor

aguarrás [aɣwa'rras] *nm* turpentine

agudeza [aɣu'ðeθa] *nf* sharpness; (*ingenio*) wit

agudizar [aɣuði'θar] *vt* (*crisis*) to make worse; **~se** *vr* to get worse

agudo, a [a'ɣuðo, a] *adj* sharp; (*voz*) high-pitched, piercing; (*dolor, enfermedad*) acute

agüero [a'ɣwero] *nm*: **buen/mal ~** good/ bad omen

aguijón [aɣi'xon] *nm* sting; (*fig*) spur

águila ['aɣila] *nf* eagle; (*fig*) genius

aguileño, a [aɣi'leɲo, a] *adj* (*nariz*) aquiline; (*rostro*) sharp-featured

aguinaldo [aɣi'naldo] *nm* Christmas box

aguja [a'ɣuxa] *nf* needle; (*de reloj*) hand; (*ARQ*) spire; (*TEC*) firing-pin; **~s** *nfpl* (*ZOOL*) ribs; (*FERRO*) points

agujerear [aɣuxere'ar] *vt* to make holes in

agujero [aɣu'xero] *nm* hole

agujetas [aɣu'xetas] *nfpl* stitch *sg*; (*rigidez*) stiffness *sg*

aguzar [aɣu'θar] *vt* to sharpen; (*fig*) to incite

ahí [a'i] *adv* there; **de ~ que** so that, with the result that; **~ llega** here he comes; **por ~** that way; (*allá*) over there; **200 o por ~** 200 or so

ahijado, a [ai'xaðo, a] *nm/f* godson/ daughter

ahínco [a'inko] *nm* earnestness

ahogar [ao'ɣar] *vt* to drown; (*asfixiar*) to suffocate, smother; (*fuego*) to put out; **~se** *vr* (*en el agua*) to drown; (*por asfixia*) to suffocate

ahogo [a'oɣo] *nm* breathlessness; (*fig*) financial difficulty

ahondar [aon'dar] *vt* to deepen, make deeper; (*fig*) to study thoroughly ♦ *vi*: **~ en** to study thoroughly

ahora [a'ora] *adv* now; (*hace poco*) a moment ago, just now; (*dentro de poco*) in a moment; **~ voy** I'm coming; **~ mismo** right now; **~ bien** now then; **por ~** for the present

ahorcar [aor'kar] *vt* to hang

ahorita [ao'rita] (*fam: esp AM*) *adv* right now

ahorrar [ao'rrar] *vt* (*dinero*) to save; (*esfuerzos*) to save, avoid; **ahorro** *nm* (*acto*) saving; **ahorros** *nmpl* (*dinero*) savings

ahuecar [awe'kar] *vt* to hollow (out); (*voz*) to deepen; **~se** *vr* to give o.s. airs

ahumar [au'mar] *vt* to smoke, cure; (*llenar de humo*) to fill with smoke ♦ *vi* to smoke; **~se** *vr* to fill with smoke

ahuyentar [aujen'tar] *vt* to drive off, frighten off; (*fig*) to dispel

airado, a [ai'raðo, a] *adj* angry

airar [ai'rar] *vt* to anger; **~se** *vr* to get angry

aire ['aire] *nm* air; (*viento*) wind; (*corriente*) draught; (*MUS*) tune; **~s** *nmpl*: **darse ~s** to give o.s. airs; **al ~ libre** in the open air; **~ acondicionado** air conditioning; **airearse** *vr* (*persona*) to go out for a breath of fresh air; **airoso, a** *adj* windy; draughty; (*fig*) graceful

aislado, a [ais'laðo, a] *adj* isolated; (*incomunicado*) cut-off; (*ELEC*) insulated

aislar [ais'lar] *vt* to isolate; (*ELEC*) to insulate

ajardinado, a [axarði'naðo, a] *adj* landscaped

ajedrez [axe'ðreθ] *nm* chess

ajeno, a [a'xeno, a] *adj* (*que pertenece a otro*) somebody else's; **~ a** foreign to

ajetreado, a [axetre'aðo, a] *adj* busy

ajetreo [axe'treo] *nm* bustle

ají [a'xi] (*AM*) *nm* chil(l)i, red pepper; (*salsa*) chil(l)i sauce

ajillo [a'xiʎo] *nm*: **gambas al ~** garlic prawns

ajo ['axo] *nm* garlic

ajuar [a'xwar] *nm* household furnishings *pl*; (*de novia*) trousseau; (*de niño*) layette

ajustado, a [axus'taðo, a] *adj* (*tornillo*) tight; (*cálculo*) right; (*ropa*) tight(-fitting); (*resultado*) close

ajustar [axus'tar] *vt* (*adaptar*) to adjust; (*encajar*) to fit; (*TEC*) to engage; (*IMPRENTA*) to make up; (*apretar*) to tighten; (*concertar*) to agree (on); (*reconciliar*) to reconcile; (*cuentas, deudas*) to settle ♦ *vi* to fit; **~se** *vr*: **~se** (*precio etc*) to be in keeping with, fit in with; **~ las cuentas a uno** to get even with sb

ajuste [a'xuste] *nm* adjustment; (COSTURA) fitting; (*acuerdo*) compromise; (*de cuenta*) settlement

al [al] (= **a +el**) *ver* **a**

ala ['ala] *nf* wing; (*de sombrero*) brim; (*futbolista*) winger; **~ delta** *nf* hang-glider

alabanza [ala'ßanθa] *nf* praise

alabar [ala'ßar] *vt* to praise

alacena [ala'θena] *nf* kitchen cupboard (BRIT), kitchen closet (US)

alacrán [ala'kran] *nm* scorpion

alambique [alam'bike] *nm* still

alambrada [alam'braða] *nf* wire fence; (*red*) wire netting

alambrado [alam'braðo] *nm* = **alambrada**

alambre [a'lambre] *nm* wire; **~ de púas** barbed wire

alameda [ala'meða] *nf* (*plantío*) poplar grove; (*lugar de paseo*) avenue, boulevard

álamo ['alamo] *nm* poplar; **~ temblón** aspen

alarde [a'larðe] *nm* show, display; **hacer ~ de** to boast of

alargador [alarɣa'ðor] *nm* (ELEC) extension lead

alargar [alar'ɣar] *vt* to lengthen, extend; (*paso*) to hasten; (*brazo*) to stretch out; (*cuerda*) to pay out; (*conversación*) to spin out; **~se** *vr* to get longer

alarido [ala'riðo] *nm* shriek

alarma [a'larma] *nf* alarm

alarmar [alar'mar] *vt* to alarm; **~se** *vr* to get alarmed; **alarmante** [alar'mante] *adj* alarming

alba ['alßa] *nf* dawn

albacea [alßa'θea] *nm/f* executor/executrix

albahaca [al'ßaka] *nf* basil

Albania [al'ßanja] *nf* Albania

albañil [alßa'ɲil] *nm* bricklayer; (*cantero*) mason

albarán [alßa'ran] *nm* (COM) delivery note,

invoice

albaricoque [alßari'koke] *nm* apricot

albedrío [alße'ðrio] *nm*: **libre ~** free will

alberca [al'ßerka] *nf* reservoir; (AM) swimming pool

albergar [alßer'var] *vt* to shelter

albergue *etc* [al'ßerve] *vb ver* **albergar** ♦ *nm* shelter, refuge; **~ juvenil** youth hostel

albóndiga [al'ßondiva] *nf* meatball

albornoz [alßor'noθ] *nm* (*de los árabes*) burnous; (*para el baño*) bathrobe

alborotar [alßoro'tar] *vi* to make a row ♦ *vt* to agitate, stir up; **~se** *vr* to get excited; (*mar*) to get rough; **alboroto** *nm* row, uproar

alborozar [alßoro'θar] *vt* to gladden; **~se** *vr* to rejoice

alborozo [alßo'roθo] *nm* joy

álbum ['alßum] (*pl* **~s, ~es**) *nm* album; **~ de recortes** scrapbook

alcachofa [alka'tʃofa] *nf* artichoke

alcalde, esa [al'kalde, esa] *nm/f* mayor(ess)

alcaldía [alkal'dia] *nf* mayoralty; (*lugar*) mayor's office

alcance *etc* [al'kanθe] *vb ver* **alcanzar** ♦ *nm* reach; (COM) adverse balance

alcantarilla [alkanta'riʎa] *nf* (*de aguas cloacales*) sewer; (*en la calle*) gutter

alcanzar [alkan'θar] *vt* (*algo: con la mano, el pie*) to reach; (*alguien: en el camino etc*) to catch up (with); (*autobús*) to catch; (*suj: bala*) to hit, strike ♦ *vi* (*ser suficiente*) to be enough; **~ a hacer** to manage to do

alcaparra [alka'parra] *nf* caper

alcayata [alka'jata] *nf* hook

alcázar [al'kaθar] *nm* fortress; (NAUT) quarter-deck

alcoba [al'koßa] *nf* bedroom

alcohol [al'kol] *nm* alcohol; **~ metílico** methylated spirits *pl* (BRIT), wood alcohol (US); **alcohólico, a** *adj, nm/f* alcoholic

alcoholímetro [alko'limetro] *nm* Breathalyser ® (BRIT), drunkometer (US)

alcoholismo [alko'lismo] *nm* alcoholism

alcornoque [alkor'noke] *nm* cork tree; *(fam)* idiot

alcurnia [al'kurnja] *nf* lineage

aldaba [al'daßa] *nf* (door) knocker

aldea [al'dea] *nf* village; **~no, a** *adj* village *cpd* ♦ *nm/f* villager

aleación [alea'θjon] *nf* alloy

aleatorio, a [alea'torjo, a] *adj* random

aleccionar [alekθjo'nar] *vt* to instruct; *(adiestrar)* to train

alegación [aleγa'θjon] *nf* allegation

alegar [ale'γar] *vt* to claim; *(JUR)* to plead ♦ *vi (AM)* to argue

alegato [ale'γato] *nm (JUR)* allegation; *(AM)* argument

alegoría [aleγo'ria] *nf* allegory

alegrar [ale'γrar] *vt (causar alegría)* to cheer up; *(fuego)* to poke; *(fiesta)* to liven up; **~se** *vr (fam)* to get merry *o* tight; **~se de** to be glad about

alegre [a'leγre] *adj* happy, cheerful; *(fam)* merry, tight; *(chiste)* risqué, blue; **alegría** *nf* happiness; merriment

alejamiento [alexa'mjento] *nm* removal; *(distancia)* remoteness

alejar [ale'xar] *vt* to remove; *(fig)* to estrange; **~se** *vr* to move away

alemán, ana [ale'man, ana] *adj, nm/f* German ♦ *nm (LING)* German

Alemania [ale'manja] *nf*: **~ Occidental/ Oriental** West/East Germany

alentador, a [alenta'ðor, a] *adj* encouraging

alentar [alen'tar] *vt* to encourage

alergia [a'lerxja] *nf* allergy

alero [a'lero] *nm (de tejado)* eaves *pl*; *(de carruaje)* mudguard

alerta [a'lerta] *adj, nm* alert

aleta [a'leta] *nf (de pez)* fin; *(de ave)* wing; *(de foca, DEPORTE)* flipper; *(AUTO)* mudguard

aletargar [aletar'γar] *vt* to make drowsy; *(entumecer)* to make numb; **~se** *vr* to grow drowsy; to become numb

aletear [alete'ar] *vi* to flutter

alevín [ale'ßin] *nm* fry, young fish

alevosía [aleßo'sia] *nf* treachery

alfabeto [alfa'ßeto] *nm* alphabet

alfalfa [al'falfa] *nf* alfalfa, lucerne

alfarería [alfare'ria] *nf* pottery; *(tienda)* pottery shop; **alfarero, a** *nm/f* potter

alféizar [al'feiθar] *nm* window-sill

alférez [al'fereθ] *nm (MIL)* second lieutenant; *(NAUT)* ensign

alfil [al'fil] *nm (AJEDREZ)* bishop

alfiler [alfi'ler] *nm* pin; *(broche)* clip

alfiletero [alfile'tero] *nm* needlecase

alfombra [al'fombra] *nf* carpet; *(más pequeña)* rug; **alfombrar** *vt* to carpet; **alfombrilla** *nf* rug, mat; *(INFORM)* mouse mat *o* pad

alforja [al'forxa] *nf* saddlebag

algarabía [alγara'ßia] *(fam) nf* gibberish; *(griterío)* hullabaloo

algas [alγas] *nfpl* seaweed

álgebra ['alxeßra] *nf* algebra

álgido, a ['alxiðo, a] *adj (momento etc)* crucial, decisive

algo ['alγo] *pron* something; anything ♦ *adv* somewhat, rather; **¿~ más?** anything else?; *(en tienda)* is that all?; **por ~ será** there must be some reason for it

algodón [alγo'ðon] *nm* cotton; *(planta)* cotton plant; **~ de azúcar** candy floss *(BRIT)*, cotton candy *(US)*; **~ hidrófilo** cotton wool *(BRIT)*, absorbent cotton *(US)*

algodonero, a [alγoðo'nero, a] *adj* cotton *cpd* ♦ *nm/f* cotton grower ♦ *nm* cotton plant

alguacil [alγwa'θil] *nm* bailiff; *(TAUR)* mounted official

alguien ['alγjen] *pron* someone, somebody; *(en frases interrogativas)* anyone, anybody

alguno, a [al'γuno, a] *adj (delante de nm:* **algún**) some; *(después de n)*: **no tiene talento ~** he has no talent, he doesn't have any talent ♦ *pron (alguien)* someone, somebody; **algún que otro libro** some book or other; **algún día iré** I'll go one *o* some day; **sin interés ~** without the slightest interest; **~ que otro** an occasional one; **~s piensan** some (people) think

alhaja [a'laxa] *nf* jewel; *(tesoro)* precious

object, treasure
alhelí [ale'li] *nm* wallflower, stock
aliado, a [a'ljaðo, a] *adj* allied
alianza [a'ljanθa] *nf* alliance; (*anillo*) wedding ring
aliar [a'ljar] *vt* to ally; **~se** *vr* to form an alliance
alias ['aljas] *adv* alias
alicates [ali'kates] *nmpl* pliers; **~ de uñas** nail clippers
aliciente [ali'θjente] *nm* incentive; (*atracción*) attraction
alienación [aljena'θjon] *nf* alienation
aliento [a'ljento] *nm* breath; (*respiración*) breathing; **sin ~** breathless
aligerar [alixe'rar] *vt* to lighten; (*reducir*) to shorten; (*aliviar*) to alleviate; (*mitigar*) to ease; (*paso*) to quicken
alijo [a'lixo] *nm* consignment
alimaña [ali'maɲa] *nf* pest
alimentación [alimenta'θjon] *nf* (*comida*) food; (*acción*) feeding; (*tienda*) grocer's (shop); **alimentador** *nm*: **alimentador de papel** sheet-feeder
alimentar [alimen'tar] *vt* to feed; (*nutrir*) to nourish; **~se** *vr* to feed
alimenticio, a [alimen'tiθjo, a] *adj* food *cpd*; (*nutritivo*) nourishing, nutritious
alimento [ali'mento] *nm* food; (*nutrición*) nourishment
alineación [alinea'θjon] *nf* alignment; (*DEPORTE*) line-up
alinear [aline'ar] *vt* to align; **~se** *vr* (*DEPORTE*) to line up; **~se en** to fall in with
aliñar [ali'ɲar] *vt* (*CULIN*) to season; **aliño** *nm* (*CULIN*) dressing
alioli [ali'oli] *nm* garlic mayonnaise
alisar [ali'sar] *vt* to smooth
aliso [a'liso] *nm* alder
alistarse [alis'tarse] *vr* to enlist; (*inscribirse*) to enrol
aliviar [ali'βjar] *vt* (*carga*) to lighten; (*persona*) to relieve; (*dolor*) to relieve, alleviate
alivio [a'liβjo] *nm* alleviation, relief
aljibe [al'xiβe] *nm* cistern

allá [a'ʎa] *adv* (*lugar*) there; (*por ahí*) over there; (*tiempo*) then; **~ abajo** down there; **más ~** further on; **más ~ de** beyond; **¡~ tú!** that's your problem!
allanamiento [aʎana'mjento] *nm*: **~ de morada** burglary
allanar [aʎa'nar] *vt* to flatten, level (out); (*igualar*) to smooth (out); (*fig*) to subdue; (*JUR*) to burgle, break into
allegado, a [aʎe'xaðo, a] *adj* near, close ♦ *nm/f* relation
allí [a'ʎi] *adv* there; **~ mismo** right there; **por ~** over there; (*por ese camino*) that way
alma ['alma] *nf* soul; (*persona*) person
almacén [alma'θen] *nm* (*depósito*) warehouse, store; (*MIL*) magazine; (*AM*) shop; **(grandes) almacenes** *nmpl* department store *sg*; **almacenaje** *nm* storage
almacenar [almaθe'nar] *vt* to store, put in storage; (*proveerse*) to stock up with; **almacenero** *nm* (*AM*) shopkeeper
almanaque [alma'nake] *nm* almanac
almeja [al'mexa] *nf* clam
almendra [al'mendra] *nf* almond; **almendro** *nm* almond tree
almíbar [al'miβar] *nm* syrup
almidón [almi'ðon] *nm* starch; **almidonar** *vt* to starch
almirante [almi'rante] *nm* admiral
almirez [almi'reθ] *nm* mortar
almizcle [al'miθkle] *nm* musk
almohada [almo'aða] *nf* pillow; (*funda*) pillowcase; **almohadilla** *nf* cushion; (*TEC*) pad; (*AM*) pincushion
almohadón [almoa'ðon] *nm* large pillow; bolster
almorranas [almo'rranas] *nfpl* piles, haemorrhoids
almorzar [almor'θar] *vt*: **~ una tortilla** to have an omelette for lunch ♦ *vi* to (have) lunch
almuerzo *etc* [al'mwerθo] *vb ver* **almorzar** ♦ *nm* lunch
alocado, a [alo'kaðo, a] *adj* crazy
alojamiento [aloxa'mjento] *nm* lodging(s)

(*pl*); (*viviendas*) housing

alojar [alo'xar] *vt* to lodge; **~se** *vr* to lodge, stay

alondra [a'londra] *nf* lark, skylark

alpargata [alpar'vata] *nf* rope-soled sandal, espadrille

Alpes ['alpes] *nmpl*: **los ~** the Alps

alpinismo [alpi'nismo] *nm* mountaineering, climbing; **alpinista** *nm/f* mountaineer, climber

alpiste [al'piste] *nm* birdseed

alquilar [alki'lar] *vt* (*suj: propietario: inmuebles*) to let, rent (out); (: *coche*) to hire out; (: *TV*) to rent (out); (*suj: alquilador: inmuebles, TV*) to rent; (: *coche*) to hire; **"se alquila casa"** "house to let (*BRIT*) o for rent (*US*)"

alquiler [alki'ler] *nm* renting; letting; hiring; (*arriendo*) rent; hire charge; **~ de automóviles** car hire; **de ~** for hire

alquimia [al'kimja] *nf* alchemy

alquitrán [alki'tran] *nm* tar

alrededor [alreðe'ðor] *adv* around, about; **~ de** around, about; **mirar a su ~** to look (round) about one; **~es** *nmpl* surroundings

alta ['alta] *nf* (certificate of) discharge; **dar de ~** to discharge

altanería [altane'ria] *nf* haughtiness, arrogance; **altanero, a** *adj* arrogant, haughty

altar [al'tar] *nm* altar

altavoz [alta'ßoθ] *nm* loudspeaker; (*amplificador*) amplifier

alteración [altera'θjon] *nf* alteration; (*alboroto*) disturbance

alterar [alte'rar] *vt* to alter; to disturb; **~se** *vr* (*persona*) to get upset

altercado [alter'kaðo] *nm* argument

alternar [alter'nar] *vt* to alternate ♦ *vi* to alternate; (*turnar*) to take turns; **~se** *vr* to alternate; to take turns; **~ con** to mix with; **alternativa** *nf* alternative; (*elección*) choice; **alternativo, a** *adj* alternative; (*alterno*) alternating; **alterno, a** *adj* alternate; (*ELEC*) alternating

alteza [al'teθa] *nf* (*tratamiento*) Highness

altibajos [alti'ßaxos] *nmpl* ups and downs

altiplanicie [altipla'niθje] *nf* high plateau

altiplano [alti'plano] *nm* = **altiplanicie**

altisonante [altiso'nante] *adj* high-flown, high-sounding

altitud [alti'tuð] *nf* height; (*AVIAT, GEO*) altitude

altivez [alti'ßeθ] *nf* haughtiness, arrogance; **altivo, a** *adj* haughty, arrogant

alto, a ['alto, a] *adj* high; (*persona*) tall; (*sonido*) high, sharp; (*noble*) high, lofty ♦ *nm* halt; (*MUS*) alto; (*GEO*) hill; (*AM*) pile ♦ *adv* (*de sitio*) high; (*de sonido*) loud, loudly ♦ *excl* halt!; **la pared tiene 2 metros de ~** the wall is 2 metres high; **en alta mar** on the high seas; **en voz alta** in a loud voice; **las altas horas de la noche** the small *o* wee hours; **en lo ~ de** at the top of; **pasar por ~** to overlook

altoparlante [altopar'lante] (*AM*) *nm* loudspeaker

altruismo [altru'ismo] *nm* altruism

altura [al'tura] *nf* height; (*NAUT*) depth; (*GEO*) latitude; **la pared tiene 1.80 de ~** the wall is 1 metre 80cm high; **a estas ~s** at this stage; **a estas ~s del año** at this time of the year

alubia [a'lußja] *nf* bean

alucinación [aluθina'θjon] *nf* hallucination

alucinar [aluθi'nar] *vi* to hallucinate ♦ *vt* to deceive; (*fascinar*) to fascinate

alud [a'luð] *nm* avalanche; (*fig*) flood

aludir [alu'ðir] *vi*: **~ a** to allude to; **darse por aludido** to take the hint

alumbrado [alum'braðo] *nm* lighting; **alumbramiento** *nm* lighting; (*MED*) childbirth, delivery

alumbrar [alum'brar] *vt* to light (up) ♦ *vi* (*MED*) to give birth

aluminio [alu'minjo] *nm* aluminium (*BRIT*), aluminum (*US*)

alumno, a [a'lumno, a] *nm/f* pupil, student

alunizar [aluni'θar] *vi* to land on the moon

alusión [alu'sjon] nf allusion

alusivo, a [alu'siβo, a] adj allusive

aluvión [alu'βjon] nm alluvium; (fig) flood

alverja [al'βerxa] (AM) nf pea

alza ['alθa] nf rise; (MIL) sight

alzada [al'θaða] nf (de caballos) height; (JUR) appeal

alzamiento [alθa'mjento] nm (rebelión) rising

alzar [al'θar] vt to lift (up); (precio, muro) to raise; (cuello de abrigo) to turn up; (AGR) to gather in; (IMPRENTA) to gather; **~se** vr to get up, rise; (rebelarse) to revolt; (COM) to go fraudulently bankrupt; (JUR) to appeal

ama ['ama] nf lady of the house; (dueña) owner; (institutriz) governess; (madre adoptiva) foster mother; **~ de casa** housewife; **~ de llaves** housekeeper

amabilidad [amaβili'ðað] nf kindness; (simpatía) niceness; **amable** adj kind; nice; **es usted muy amable** that's very kind of you

amaestrado, a [amaes'traðo, a] adj (animal: en circo etc) performing

amaestrar [amaes'trar] vt to train

amago [a'maγo] nm threat; (gesto) threatening gesture; (MED) symptom

amainar [amai'nar] vi (viento) to die down

amalgama [amal'γama] nf amalgam; **amalgamar** vt to amalgamate; (combinar) to combine, mix

amamantar [amaman'tar] vt to suckle, nurse

amanecer [amane'θer] vi to dawn ♦ nm dawn; **~ afiebrado** to wake up with a fever

amanerado, a [amane'raðo, a] adj affected

amansar [aman'sar] vt to tame; (persona) to subdue; **~se** vr (persona) to calm down

amante [a'mante] adj: **~ de** fond of ♦ nm/f lover

amapola [ama'pola] nf poppy

amar [a'mar] vt to love

amargado, a [amar'γaðo, a] adj bitter

amargar [amar'γar] vt to make bitter; (fig) to embitter; **~se** vr to become embittered

amargo, a [a'marγo, a] adj bitter; **amargura** nf bitterness

amarillento, a [amari'ʎento, a] adj yellowish; (tez) sallow; **amarillo, a** adj, nm yellow

amarrar [ama'rrar] vt to moor; (sujetar) to tie up

amarras [a'marras] nfpl: **soltar ~** to set sail

amasar [ama'sar] vt (masa) to knead; (mezclar) to mix, prepare; (confeccionar) to concoct; **amasijo** nm kneading; mixing; (fig) hotchpotch

amateur ['amatur] nm/f amateur

amazona [ama'θona] nf horsewoman; **A~s** nm: **el A~s** the Amazon

ambages [am'baxes] nmpl: **sin ~** in plain language

ámbar ['ambar] nm amber

ambición [ambi'θjon] nf ambition; **ambicionar** vt to aspire to; **ambicioso, a** adj ambitious

ambidextro, a [ambi'ðekstro, a] adj ambidextrous

ambientación [ambjenta'θjon] nf (CINE, TEATRO etc) setting; (RADIO) sound effects

ambiente [am'bjente] nm (tb fig) atmosphere; (medio) environment

ambigüedad [ambiγwe'ðað] nf ambiguity; **ambiguo, a** adj ambiguous

ámbito ['ambito] nm (campo) field; (fig) scope

ambos, as ['ambos, as] adj pl, pron pl both

ambulancia [ambu'lanθja] nf ambulance

ambulante [ambu'lante] adj travelling cpd, itinerant

ambulatorio [ambula'torio] nm state health-service clinic

amedrentar [ameðren'tar] vt to scare

amén [a'men] excl amen; **~ de** besides

amenaza [ame'naθa] nf threat

amenazar [amena'θar] vt to threaten ♦ vi: **~ con hacer** to threaten to do

amenidad [ameni'ðað] nf pleasantness

ameno, a [a'meno, a] *adj* pleasant
América [a'merika] *nf* America; **~ del Norte/del Sur** North/South America; **~ Central/Latina** Central/Latin America; **americana** *nf* coat, jacket; *ver tb* **americano**; **americano, a** *adj, nm/f* American
amerizar [ameri'θar] *vi* (*avión*) to land (on the sea)
ametralladora [ametraʎa'ðora] *nf* machine gun
amianto [a'mjanto] *nm* asbestos
amigable [ami'yaßle] *adj* friendly
amígdala [a'mixðala] *nf* tonsil; **amigdalitis** *nf* tonsillitis
amigo, a [a'mixo, a] *adj* friendly ♦ *nm/f* friend; (*amante*) lover; **ser ~ de algo** to be fond of sth; **ser muy ~s** to be close friends
amilanar [amila'nar] *vt* to scare; **~se** *vr* to get scared
aminorar [amino'rar] *vt* to diminish; (*reducir*) to reduce; **~ la marcha** to slow down
amistad [amis'tað] *nf* friendship; **~es** *nfpl* (*amigos*) friends; **amistoso, a** *adj* friendly
amnesia [am'nesja] *nf* amnesia
amnistía [amnis'tia] *nf* amnesty
amo [a'mo] *nm* owner; (*jefe*) boss
amodorrarse [amoðo'rrarse] *vr* to get sleepy
amoldar [amol'dar] *vt* to mould; (*adaptar*) to adapt
amonestación [amonesta'θjon] *nf* warning; **amonestaciones** *nfpl* (*REL*) marriage banns
amonestar [amones'tar] *vt* to warn; (*REL*) to publish the banns of
amontonar [amonto'nar] *vt* to collect, pile up; **~se** *vr* to crowd together; (*acumularse*) to pile up
amor [a'mor] *nm* love; (*amante*) lover; **hacer el ~** to make love; **~ propio** self-respect
amoratado, a [amora'taðo, a] *adj* purple
amordazar [amorða'θar] *vt* to muzzle;

(*fig*) to gag
amorfo, a [a'morfo, a] *adj* amorphous, shapeless
amoroso, a [amo'roso, a] *adj* affectionate, loving
amortajar [amorta'xar] *vt* to shroud
amortiguador [amortigwa'ðor] *nm* shock absorber; (*parachoques*) bumper; **~es** *nmpl* (*AUTO*) suspension *sg*
amortiguar [amorti'ɣwar] *vt* to deaden; (*ruido*) to muffle; (*color*) to soften
amortización [amortiθa'θjon] *nf* (*de deuda*) repayment; (*de bono*) redemption
amotinar [amoti'nar] *vt* to stir up, incite (to riot); **~se** *vr* to mutiny
amparar [ampa'rar] *vt* to protect; **~se** *vr* to seek protection; (*de la lluvia etc*) to shelter; **amparo** *nm* help, protection; **al amparo de** under the protection of
amperio [am'perjo] *nm* ampère, amp
ampliación [amplja'θjon] *nf* enlargement; (*extensión*) extension
ampliar [am'pljar] *vt* to enlarge; to extend
amplificación [amplifika'θjon] *nf* enlargement; **amplificador** *nm* amplifier
amplificar [amplifi'kar] *vt* to amplify
amplio, a ['ampljo, a] *adj* spacious; (*de falda etc*) full; (*extenso*) extensive; (*ancho*) wide; **amplitud** *nf* spaciousness; extent; (*fig*) amplitude
ampolla [am'poʎa] *nf* blister; (*MED*) ampoule
ampuloso, a [ampu'loso, a] *adj* bombastic, pompous
amputar [ampu'tar] *vt* to cut off, amputate
amueblar [amwe'ßlar] *vt* to furnish
amurallar [amura'ʎar] *vt* to wall up o in
anacronismo [anakro'nismo] *nm* anachronism
anales [a'nales] *nmpl* annals
analfabetismo [analfaße'tismo] *nm* illiteracy; **analfabeto, a** *adj, nm/f* illiterate
analgésico [anal'xesiko] *nm* painkiller, analgesic

análisis [a'nalisis] *nm inv* analysis

analista [ana'lista] *nm/f* (*gen*) analyst

analizar [anali'θar] *vt* to analyse

analogía [analo'xia] *nf* analogy

analógico, a [ana'loxiko, a] *adj* (*INFORM*) analog; (*reloj*) analogue (*BRIT*), analog (*US*)

análogo, a [a'naloɣo, a] *adj* analogous, similar

ananá(s) [ana'na(s)] (*AM*) *nm* pineapple

anaquel [ana'kel] *nm* shelf

anarquía [anar'kia] *nf* anarchy; **anarquismo** *nm* anarchism; **anarquista** *nm/f* anarchist

anatomía [anato'mia] *nf* anatomy

anca ['anka] *nf* rump, haunch; **~s** *nfpl* (*fam*) behind *sg*

ancho, a ['antʃo, a] *adj* wide; (*falda*) full; (*fig*) liberal ♦ *nm* width; (*FERRO*) gauge; **ponerse ~** to get conceited; **estar a sus anchas** to be at one's ease

anchoa [an'tʃoa] *nf* anchovy

anchura [an'tʃura] *nf* width; (*extensión*) wideness

anciano, a [an'θjano, a] *adj* old, aged ♦ *nm/f* old man/woman; elder

ancla ['ankla] *nf* anchor; **~dero** *nm* anchorage; **anclar** *vi* to (drop) anchor

andadura [anda'ðura] *nf* gait; (*de caballo*) pace

Andalucía [andalu'θia] *nf* Andalusia; **andaluz, a** *adj*, *nm/f* Andalusian

andamiaje [anda'mjaxe] *nm* = **andamio**

andamio [an'damjo] *nm* scaffold(ing)

andar [an'dar] *vt* to go, cover, travel ♦ *vi* to go, walk, travel; (*funcionar*) to go, work; (*estar*) to be ♦ *nm* walk, gait, pace; **~se** *vr* to go away; **~ a pie/a caballo/en bicicleta** to go on foot/on horseback/by bicycle; **~ haciendo algo** to be doing sth; **¡anda!** (*sorpresa*) come on!; **anda por o en los 40** he's about 40

andén [an'den] *nm* (*FERRO*) platform; (*NAUT*) quayside; (*AM: de la calle*) pavement (*BRIT*), sidewalk (*US*)

Andes ['andes] *nmpl*: **los ~** the Andes

Andorra [an'dorra] *nf* Andorra

andrajo [an'draxo] *nm* rag; **~so, a** *adj* ragged

anduve *etc* [an'duβe] *vb ver* **andar**

anécdota [a'nekðota] *nf* anecdote, story

anegar [ane'ɣar] *vt* to flood; (*ahogar*) to drown; **~se** *vr* to drown; (*hundirse*) to sink

anejo, a [a'nexo, a] *adj*, *nm* = **anexo**

anemia [a'nemja] *nf* anaemia

anestesia [anes'tesja] *nf* (*sustancia*) anaesthetic; (*proceso*) anaesthesia

anexar [anek'sar] *vt* to annex; (*documento*) to attach; **anexión** *nf* annexation; **anexionamiento** *nm* annexation; **anexo, a** *adj* attached ♦ *nm* annexe

anfibio, a [an'fiβjo, a] *adj* amphibious ♦ *nm* amphibian

anfiteatro [anfite'atro] *nm* amphitheatre; (*TEATRO*) dress circle

anfitrión, ona [anfi'trjon, ona] *nm/f* host(ess)

ángel ['anxel] *nm* angel; **~ de la guarda** guardian angel; **tener ~** to be charming; **angelical** *adj*, **angélico, a** *adj* angelic(al)

angina [an'xina] *nf* (*MED*) inflammation of the throat; **~ de pecho** angina; **tener ~s** to have tonsillitis

anglicano, a [angli'kano, a] *adj*, *nm/f* Anglican

anglosajón, ona [anglosa'xon, ona] *adj* Anglo-Saxon

angosto, a [an'gosto, a] *adj* narrow

anguila [an'gila] *nf* eel

angula [an'gula] *nf* elver, baby eel

ángulo ['angulo] *nm* angle; (*esquina*) corner; (*curva*) bend

angustia [an'gustja] *nf* anguish; **angustiar** *vt* to distress, grieve

anhelar [ane'lar] *vt* to be eager for; (*desear*) to long for, desire ♦ *vi* to pant, gasp; **anhelo** *nm* eagerness; desire

anidar [ani'ðar] *vi* to nest

anillo [a'niλo] *nm* ring; **~ de boda** wedding ring

animación [anima'θjon] *nf* liveliness; (*vitalidad*) life; (*actividad*) activity; bustle

animado, a [ani'maðo, a] *adj* lively;

(*vivaz*) animated; **animador, a** *nm/f*
(*TV*) host(ess), compère; (*DEPORTE*)
cheerleader

animadversión [animaðßer'sjon] *nf* ill-
will, antagonism

animal [ani'mal] *adj* animal; (*fig*) stupid
♦ *nm* animal; (*fig*) fool; (*bestia*) brute

animar [ani'mar] *vt* (*BIO*) to animate, give
life to; (*fig*) to liven up, brighten up,
cheer up; (*estimular*) to stimulate; **~se** *vr*
to cheer up; to feel encouraged;
(*decidirse*) to make up one's mind

ánimo ['animo] *nm* (*alma*) soul; (*mente*)
mind; (*valentía*) courage ♦ *excl* cheer up!

animoso, a [ani'moso, a] *adj* brave; (*vivo*)
lively

aniquilar [aniki'lar] *vt* to annihilate,
destroy

anís [a'nis] *nm* aniseed; (*licor*) anisette

aniversario [anißer'sarjo] *nm* anniversary

anoche [a'notʃe] *adv* last night; **antes de**
~ the night before last

anochecer [anotʃe'θer] *vi* to get dark
♦ *nm* nightfall, dark; **al ~** at nightfall

anodino, a [ano'ðino, a] *adj* dull,
anodyne

anomalía [anoma'lia] *nf* anomaly

anonadado, a [anona'ðaðo, a] *adj*:
estar/quedar/sentirse ~ to be
overwhelmed *o* amazed

anonimato [anoni'mato] *nm* anonymity

anónimo, a [a'nonimo, a] *adj*
anonymous; (*COM*) limited ♦ *nm* (*carta*)
anonymous letter; (: *maliciosa*) poison-
pen letter

anormal [anor'mal] *adj* abnormal

anotación [anota'θjon] *nf* note;
annotation

anotar [ano'tar] *vt* to note down;
(*comentar*) to annotate

anquilosamiento [ankilosa'mjento] *nm*
(*fig*) paralysis; stagnation

anquilosarse [ankilo'sarse] *vr* (*fig*:
persona) to get out of touch; (*método,*
costumbres) to go out of date

ansia ['ansja] *nf* anxiety; (*añoranza*)
yearning; **ansiar** *vt* to long for

ansiedad [ansje'ðað] *nf* anxiety

ansioso, a [an'sjoso, a] *adj* anxious;
(*anhelante*) eager; **~ de** *o* **por algo**
greedy for sth

antagónico, a [anta'xoniko, a] *adj*
antagonistic; (*opuesto*) contrasting;
antagonista *nm/f* antagonist

antaño [an'taɲo] *adv* long ago, formerly

Antártico [an'tartiko] *nm*: **el ~** the
Antarctic

ante ['ante] *prep* before, in the presence
of; (*problema etc*) faced with ♦ *nm* (*piel*)
suede; **~ todo** above all

anteanoche [antea'notʃe] *adv* the night
before last

anteayer [antea'jer] *adv* the day before
yesterday

antebrazo [ante'ßraθo] *nm* forearm

antecedente [anteθe'ðente] *adj* previous
♦ *nm* antecedent; **~s** *nmpl* (*JUR*): **~s**
penales criminal record; (*procedencia*)
background

anteceder [anteθe'ðer] *vt* to precede, go
before

antecesor, a [anteθe'sor, a] *nm/f*
predecessor

antedicho, a [ante'ðitʃo, a] *adj*
aforementioned

antelación [antela'θjon] *nf*: **con ~** in
advance

antemano [ante'mano]: **de ~** *adv*
beforehand, in advance

antena [an'tena] *nf* antenna; (*de televisión*
etc) aerial; **~ parabólica** satellite dish

anteojo [ante'oxo] *nm* eyeglass; **~s** *nmpl*
(*AM*) glasses, spectacles

antepasados [antepa'saðos] *nmpl*
ancestors

anteponer [antepo'ner] *vt* to place in
front; (*fig*) to prefer

anteproyecto [antepro'jekto] *nm*
preliminary sketch; (*fig*) blueprint

anterior [ante'rjor] *adj* preceding,
previous; **~idad** *nf*: **con ~idad a** prior to,
before

antes ['antes] *adv* (*con prioridad*) before
♦ *prep*: **~ de** before ♦ *conj*: **~ de ir/de**

que te vayas before going/before you go; **~ bien** (but) rather; **dos días ~** two days before *o* previously; **no quiso venir ~** she didn't want to come any earlier; **tomo el avión ~ que el barco** I take the plane rather than the boat; **~ que yo** before me; **lo ~ posible** as soon as possible; **cuanto ~ mejor** the sooner the better

antiaéreo, a [antia'ereo, a] *adj* anti-aircraft

antibalas [anti'βalas] *adj inv*: **chaleco ~** bullet-proof jacket

antibiótico [anti'βjotiko] *nm* antibiotic

anticipación [antiθipa'θjon] *nf* anticipation; **con 10 minutos de ~** 10 minutes early

anticipado, a [antiθi'paðo, a] *adj* (*pago*) advance; **por ~** in advance

anticipar [antiθi'par] *vt* to anticipate; (*adelantar*) to bring forward; (*COM*) to advance; **~se** *vr*: **~se a su época** to be ahead of one's time

anticipo [anti'θipo] *nm* (*COM*) advance

anticonceptivo, a [antikonθep'tiβo, a] *adj, nm* contraceptive

anticongelante [antikonxe'lante] *nm* antifreeze

anticuado, a [anti'kwaðo, a] *adj* out-of-date, old-fashioned; (*desusado*) obsolete

anticuario [anti'kwarjo] *nm* antique dealer

anticuerpo [anti'kwerpo] *nm* (*MED*) antibody

antidepresivo [antiðepre'siβo] *nm* antidepressant

antídoto [an'tiðoto] *nm* antidote

antiestético, a [anties'tetiko, a] *adj* unsightly

antifaz [anti'faθ] *nm* mask; (*velo*) veil

antigualla [anti'ɣwaʎa] *nf* antique; (*reliquia*) relic

antiguamente [antiɣwa'mente] *adv* formerly; (*hace mucho tiempo*) long ago

antigüedad [antiɣwe'ðað] *nf* antiquity; (*artículo*) antique; (*rango*) seniority

antiguo, a [an'tiɣwo, a] *adj* old, ancient; (*que fue*) former

Antillas [an'tiʎas] *nfpl*: **las ~** the West Indies

antílope [an'tilope] *nm* antelope

antinatural [antinatu'ral] *adj* unnatural

antipatía [antipa'tia] *nf* antipathy, dislike; **antipático, a** *adj* disagreeable, unpleasant

antirrobo [anti'rroβo] *adj inv* (*alarma etc*) anti-theft

antisemita [antise'mita] *adj* anti-Semitic ♦ *nm/f* anti-Semite

antiséptico, a [anti'septiko, a] *adj* antiseptic ♦ *nm* antiseptic

antítesis [an'titesis] *nf inv* antithesis

antojadizo, a [antoxa'ðiθo, a] *adj* capricious

antojarse [anto'xarse] *vr* (*desear*): **se me antoja comprarlo** I have a mind to buy it; (*pensar*): **se me antoja que** I have a feeling that

antojo [an'toxo] *nm* caprice, whim; (*rosa*) birthmark; (*lunar*) mole

antología [antolo'xia] *nf* anthology

antorcha [an'tortʃa] *nf* torch

antro ['antro] *nm* cavern

antropófago, a [antro'pofaɣo, a] *adj, nm/f* cannibal

antropología [antropolo'xia] *nf* anthropology

anual [a'nwal] *adj* annual

anuario [a'nwarjo] *nm* yearbook

anudar [anu'ðar] *vt* to knot, tie; (*unir*) to join; **~se** *vr* to get tied up

anulación [anula'θjon] *nf* annulment; (*cancelación*) cancellation

anular [anu'lar] *vt* (*contrato*) to annul, cancel; (*ley*) to revoke, repeal; (*suscripción*) to cancel ♦ *nm* ring finger

Anunciación [anunθja'θjon] *nf* (*REL*) Annunciation

anunciante [anun'θjante] *nm/f* (*COM*) advertiser

anunciar [anun'θjar] *vt* to announce; (*proclamar*) to proclaim; (*COM*) to advertise

anuncio [a'nunθjo] *nm* announcement; (*señal*) sign; (*COM*) advertisement; (*cartel*) poster

anzuelo [an'θwelo] *nm* hook; (*para pescar*) fish hook

añadidura [aɲaði'ðura] *nf* addition, extra; **por ~** besides, in addition

añadir [aɲa'ðir] *vt* to add

añejo, a [a'ɲexo, a] *adj* old; (*vino*) mellow

añicos [a'ɲikos] *nmpl*: **hacer ~** to smash, shatter

añil [a'ɲil] *nm* (*BOT, color*) indigo

año ['aɲo] *nm* year; **¡Feliz A~ Nuevo!** Happy New Year!; **tener 15 ~s** to be 15 (years old); **los ~s 90** the nineties; **~ bisiesto/escolar** leap/school year; **el ~ que viene** next year

añoranza [aɲo'ranθa] *nf* nostalgia; (*anhelo*) longing

apabullar [apaβu'ʎar] *vt* (*tb fig*) to crush, squash

apacentar [apaθen'tar] *vt* to pasture, graze

apacible [apa'θiβle] *adj* gentle, mild

apaciguar [apaθi'ɣwar] *vt* to pacify, calm (down)

apadrinar [apaðri'nar] *vt* to sponsor, support; (*REL*) to be godfather to

apagado, a [apa'ɣaðo, a] *adj* (*volcán*) extinct; (*color*) dull; (*voz*) quiet; (*sonido*) muted, muffled; (*persona: apático*) listless; **estar ~** (*fuego, luz*) to be out; (*RADIO, TV etc*) to be off

apagar [apa'ɣar] *vt* to put out; (*ELEC, RADIO, TV*) to turn off; (*sonido*) to silence, muffle; (*sed*) to quench

apagón [apa'ɣon] *nm* blackout; power cut

apalabrar [apala'βrar] *vt* to agree to; (*contratar*) to engage

apalear [apale'ar] *vt* to beat, thrash

apañar [apa'ɲar] *vt* to pick up; (*asir*) to take hold of, grasp; (*reparar*) to mend, patch up; **~se** *vr* to manage, get along

aparador [apara'ðor] *nm* sideboard; (*AM: escaparate*) shop window

aparato [apa'rato] *nm* apparatus; (*máquina*) machine; (*doméstico*) appliance; (*boato*) ostentation; **~ de facsímil** facsimile (machine), fax; **~ digestivo** (*ANAT*) digestive system; **~so,**

a *adj* showy, ostentatious

aparcamiento [aparka'mjento] *nm* car park (*BRIT*), parking lot (*US*)

aparcar [apar'kar] *vt, vi* to park

aparear [apare'ar] *vt* (*objetos*) to pair, match; (*animales*) to mate; **~se** *vr* to make a pair; to mate

aparecer [apare'θer] *vi* to appear; **~se** *vr* to appear

aparejado, a [apare'xaðo, a] *adj* fit, suitable; **llevar** *o* **traer ~** to involve;

aparejador, a *nm/f* (*ARQ*) master builder

aparejo [apa'rexo] *nm* harness; rigging; (*de poleas*) block and tackle

aparentar [aparen'tar] *vt* (*edad*) to look; (*fingir*): **~ tristeza** to pretend to be sad

aparente [apa'rente] *adj* apparent; (*adecuado*) suitable

aparezco *etc vb ver* **aparecer**

aparición [apari'θjon] *nf* appearance; (*de libro*) publication; (*espectro*) apparition

apariencia [apa'rjenθja] *nf* (*outward*) appearance; **en ~** outwardly, seemingly

apartado, a [apar'taðo, a] *adj* separate; (*lejano*) remote ♦ *nm* (*tipográfico*) paragraph; **~ (de correos)** post office box

apartamento [aparta'mento] *nm* apartment, flat (*BRIT*)

apartamiento [aparta'mjento] *nm* separation; (*aislamiento*) remoteness, isolation; (*AM*) apartment, flat (*BRIT*)

apartar [apar'tar] *vt* to separate; (*quitar*) to remove; **~se** *vr* to separate, part; (*irse*) to move away; to keep away

aparte [a'parte] *adv* (*separadamente*) separately; (*además*) besides ♦ *nm* aside; (*tipográfico*) new paragraph

aparthotel [aparto'tel] *nm* serviced apartments

apasionado, a [apasjo'naðo, a] *adj* passionate

apasionar [apasjo'nar] *vt* to excite; **le apasiona el fútbol** she's crazy about football; **~se** *vr* to get excited

apatía [apa'tia] *nf* apathy

apático, a [a'patiko, a] *adj* apathetic

Apdo *abr* (= *Apartado (de Correos)*) PO Box

apeadero [apea'ðero] *nm* halt, stop, stopping place

apearse [ape'arse] *vr* (*jinete*) to dismount; (*bajarse*) to get down *o* out; (*AUTO, FERRO*) to get off *o* out

apechugar [apetʃu'ɣar] *vr*: **~ con algo** to face up to sth

apedrear [apeðre'ar] *vt* to stone

apegarse [ape'ɣarse] *vr*: **~ a** to become attached to; **apego** *nm* attachment, devotion

apelación [apela'θjon] *nf* appeal

apelar [ape'lar] *vi* to appeal; **~ a** (*fig*) to resort to

apellidar [apeʎi'ðar] *vt* to call, name; **~se** *vr*: **se apellida Pérez** her (sur)name's Pérez

apellido [ape'ʎiðo] *nm* surname

apelmazarse [apelma'θarse] *vr* (*masa, arroz*) to go hard; (*prenda de lana*) to shrink

apenar [ape'nar] *vt* to grieve, trouble; (*AM: avergonzar*) to embarrass; **~se** *vr* to grieve; (*AM*) to be embarrassed

apenas [a'penas] *adv* scarcely, hardly ♦ *conj* as soon as, no sooner

apéndice [a'pendiθe] *nm* appendix; **apendicitis** *nf* appendicitis

aperitivo [aperi'tiβo] *nm* (*bebida*) aperitif; (*comida*) appetizer

apero [a'pero] *nm* (*AGR*) implement; **~s** *nmpl* farm equipment *sg*

apertura [aper'tura] *nf* opening; (*POL*) liberalization

apesadumbrar [apesaðum'brar] *vt* to grieve, sadden; **~se** *vr* to distress o.s.

apestar [apes'tar] *vt* to infect ♦ *vi*: **~ (a)** to stink (of)

apetecer [apete'θer] *vt*: **¿te apetece un café?** do you fancy a (cup of) coffee?; **apetecible** *adj* desirable; (*comida*) appetizing

apetito [ape'tito] *nm* appetite; **~so, a** *adj* appetizing; (*fig*) tempting

apiadarse [apja'ðarse] *vr*: **~ de** to take pity on

ápice ['apiθe] *nm* whit, iota

apilar [api'lar] *vt* to pile *o* heap up; **~se** *vr* to pile up

apiñarse [api'ɲarse] *vr* to crowd *o* press together

apio ['apjo] *nm* celery

apisonadora [apisona'ðora] *nf* steamroller

aplacar [apla'kar] *vt* to placate; **~se** *vr* to calm down

aplanar [apla'nar] *vt* to smooth, level; (*allanar*) to roll flat, flatten

aplastante [aplas'tante] *adj* overwhelming; (*lógica*) compelling

aplastar [aplas'tar] *vt* to squash (flat); (*fig*) to crush

aplatanarse [aplata'narse] *vr* to get lethargic

aplaudir [aplau'ðir] *vt* to applaud

aplauso [a'plauso] *nm* applause; (*fig*) approval, acclaim

aplazamiento [aplaθa'mjento] *nm* postponement

aplazar [apla'θar] *vt* to postpone, defer

aplicación [aplika'θjon] *nf* application; (*esfuerzo*) effort

aplicado, a [apli'kaðo, a] *adj* diligent, hard-working

aplicar [apli'kar] *vt* (*ejecutar*) to apply; **~se** *vr* to apply o.s.

aplique *etc* [a'plike] *vb ver* **aplicar** ♦ *nm* wall light

aplomo [a'plomo] *nm* aplomb, self-assurance

apocado, a [apo'kaðo, a] *adj* timid

apodar [apo'ðar] *vt* to nickname

apoderado [apoðe'raðo] *nm* agent, representative

apoderarse [apoðe'rarse] *vr*: **~ de** to take possession of

apodo [a'poðo] *nm* nickname

apogeo [apo'xeo] *nm* peak, summit

apolillarse [apoli'ʎarse] *vr* to get moth-eaten

apología [apolo'xia] *nf* eulogy; (*defensa*) defence

apoltronarse [apoltro'narse] *vr* to get

lazy

apoplejía [apople'xia] *nf* apoplexy, stroke

apoquinar [apoki'nar] *(fam) vt* to fork out, cough up

aporrear [aporre'ar] *vt* to beat (up)

aportar [apor'tar] *vt* to contribute ♦ *vi* to reach port; **~se** *vr* (AM: *llegar*) to arrive, come

aposento [apo'sento] *nm* lodging; (*habitación*) room

aposta [a'posta] *adv* deliberately, on purpose

apostar [apos'tar] *vt* to bet, stake; (*tropas etc*) to station, post ♦ *vi* to bet

apóstol [a'postol] *nm* apostle

apóstrofo [a'postrofo] *nm* apostrophe

apoyar [apo'jar] *vt* to lean, rest; (*fig*) to support, back; **~se** *vr*: **~se en** to lean on; **apoyo** *nm* (*gen*) support; backing, help

apreciable [apre'θjaßle] *adj* considerable; (*fig*) esteemed

apreciar [apre'θjar] *vt* to evaluate, assess; (COM) to appreciate, value; (*persona*) to respect; (*tamaño*) to gauge, assess; (*detalles*) to notice

aprecio [a'preθjo] *nm* valuation, estimate; (*fig*) appreciation

aprehender [apreen'der] *vt* to apprehend, detain

apremiante [apre'mjante] *adj* urgent, pressing

apremiar [apre'mjar] *vt* to compel, force ♦ *vi* to be urgent, press; **apremio** *nm* urgency

aprender [apren'der] *vt, vi* to learn

aprendiz, a [apren'diθ, a] *nm/f* apprentice; (*principiante*) learner; **~ de conductor** learner driver; **~aje** *nm* apprenticeship

aprensión [apren'sjon] *nm* apprehension, fear; **aprensivo, a** *adj* apprehensive

apresar [apre'sar] *vt* to seize; (*capturar*) to capture

aprestar [apres'tar] *vt* to prepare, get ready; (TEC) to prime, size; **~se** *vr* to get ready

apresurado, a [apresu'raðo, a] *adj* hurried, hasty; **apresuramiento** *nm* hurry, haste

apresurar [apresu'rar] *vt* to hurry, accelerate; **~se** *vr* to hurry, make haste

apretado, a [apre'taðo, a] *adj* tight; (*escritura*) cramped

apretar [apre'tar] *vt* to squeeze; (TEC) to tighten; (*presionar*) to press together, pack ♦ *vi* to be too tight

apretón [apre'ton] *nm* squeeze; **~ de manos** handshake

aprieto [a'prjeto] *nm* squeeze; (*dificultad*) difficulty; **estar en un ~** to be in a fix

aprisa [a'prisa] *adv* quickly, hurriedly

aprisionar [aprisjo'nar] *vt* to imprison

aprobación [aproßa'θjon] *nf* approval

aprobar [apro'ßar] *vt* to approve (of); (*examen, materia*) to pass ♦ *vi* to pass

apropiación [apropja'θjon] *nf* appropriation

apropiado, a [apro'pjaðo, a] *adj* suitable

apropiarse [apro'pjarse] *vr*: **~ de** to appropriate

aprovechado, a [aproße'tʃaðo, a] *adj* industrious, hard-working; (*económico*) thrifty; (*pey*) unscrupulous; **aprovechamiento** *nm* use; exploitation

aprovechar [aproße'tʃar] *vt* to use; (*explotar*) to exploit; (*experiencia*) to profit from; (*oferta, oportunidad*) to take advantage of ♦ *vi* to progress, improve; **~se** *vr*: **~se de** to make use of; to take advantage of; **¡que aproveche!** enjoy your meal!

aproximación [aproksima'θjon] *nf* approximation; (*de lotería*) consolation prize; **aproximado, a** *adj* approximate

aproximar [aproksi'mar] *vt* to bring nearer; **~se** *vr* to come near, approach

apruebo etc *vb ver* **aprobar**

aptitud [apti'tuð] *nf* aptitude

apto, a ['apto, a] *adj* suitable

apuesta [a'pwesta] *nf* bet, wager

apuesto, a [a'pwesto, a] *adj* neat, elegant

apuntador [apunta'ðor] *nm* prompter

apuntalar [apunta'lar] *vt* to prop up

apuntar [apun'tar] vt (con arma) to aim at; (con dedo) to point at o to; (anotar) to note (down); (TEATRO) to prompt; **~se** vr (DEPORTE: tanto, victoria) to score; (ESCOL) to enrol

apunte [a'punte] nm note

apuñalar [apuɲa'lar] vt to stab

apurado, a [apu'raðo, a] adj needy; (difícil) difficult; (peligroso) dangerous; (AM) hurried, rushed

apurar [apu'rar] vt (agotar) to drain; (recursos) to use up; (molestar) to annoy; **~se** vr (preocuparse) to worry; (darse prisa) to hurry

apuro [a'puro] nm (aprieto) fix, jam; (escasez) want, hardship; (vergüenza) embarrassment; (AM) haste, urgency

aquejado, a [ake'xaðo, a] adj: ~ **de** (MED) afflicted by

aquél, aquélla [a'kel, a'keʎa] (pl **aquéllos, as**) pron that (one); (pl) those (ones)

aquel, aquella [a'kel, a'keʎa] (pl **aquellos, as**) adj that; (pl) those

aquello [a'keʎo] pron that, that business

aquí [a'ki] adv (lugar) here; (tiempo) now; **~ arriba** up here; **~ mismo** right here; **~ yace** here lies; **de ~ a siete días** a week from now

aquietar [akje'tar] vt to quieten (down), calm (down)

ara ['ara] nf: **en ~s de** for the sake of

árabe ['araβe] adj, nm/f Arab ♦ nm (LING) Arabic

Arabia [a'raβja] nf: ~ **Saudí** o **Saudita** Saudi Arabia

arado [a'raðo] nm plough

Aragón [ara'ɣon] nm Aragon; **aragonés, esa** adj, nm/f Aragonese

arancel [aran'θel] nm tariff, duty; ~ **de aduanas** customs (duty)

arandela [aran'dela] nf (TEC) washer

araña [a'raɲa] nf (ZOOL) spider; (lámpara) chandelier

arañar [ara'ɲar] vt to scratch

arañazo [ara'ɲaθo] nm scratch

arar [a'rar] vt to plough, till

arbitraje [arβi'traxe] nm arbitration

arbitrar [arβi'trar] vt to arbitrate in; (DEPORTE) to referee ♦ vi to arbitrate

arbitrariedad [arβitrarje'ðað] nf arbitrariness; (acto) arbitrary act; **arbitrario, a** adj arbitrary

arbitrio [ar'βitrjo] nm free will; (JUR) adjudication, decision

árbitro ['arβitro] nm arbitrator; (DEPORTE) referee; (TENIS) umpire

árbol ['arβol] nm (BOT) tree; (NAUT) mast; (TEC) axle, shaft; **arbolado, a** adj wooded; (camino etc) tree-lined ♦ nm woodland

arboleda [arβo'leða] nf grove, plantation

arbusto [ar'βusto] nm bush, shrub

arca ['arka] nf chest, box

arcada [ar'kaða] nf arcade; (de puente) arch, span; **~s** nfpl (náuseas) retching sg

arcaico, a [ar'kaiko, a] adj archaic

arce ['arθe] nm maple tree

arcén [ar'θen] nm (de autopista) hard shoulder; (de carretera) verge

archipiélago [artʃi'pjelaɣo] nm archipelago

archivador [artʃiβa'ðor] nm filing cabinet

archivar [artʃi'βar] vt to file (away); **archivo** nm file, archive(s) (pl)

arcilla [ar'θiʎa] nf clay

arco ['arko] nm arch; (MAT) arc; (MIL, MUS) bow; **~ iris** rainbow

arder [ar'ðer] vi to burn; **estar que arde** (persona) to fume

ardid [ar'ðið] nm ploy, trick

ardiente [ar'ðjente] adj burning, ardent

ardilla [ar'ðiʎa] nf squirrel

ardor [ar'ðor] nm (calor) heat; (fig) ardour; **~ de estómago** heartburn

arduo, a ['arðwo, a] adj arduous

área ['area] nf area; (DEPORTE) penalty area

arena [a'rena] nf sand; (de una lucha) arena; **~s movedizas** quicksand sg

arenal [are'nal] nm (arena movediza) quicksand

arengar [aren'ɡar] vt to harangue

arenisca [are'niska] nf sandstone; (cascajo) grit

arenoso, a [are'noso, a] adj sandy
arenque [a'renke] nm herring
argamasa [arva'masa] nf mortar, plaster
Argel [ar'xel] n Algiers; **Argelia** nf
Algeria; **argelino, a** adj, nm/f Algerian
Argentina [arxen'tina] nf: **(la) ~** Argentina
argentino, a [arxen'tino, a] adj
Argentinian; (de plata) silvery ♦ nm/f
Argentinian
argolla [ar'voʎa] nf (large) ring
argot [ar'vo] (pl **~s**) nm slang
argucia [ar'vuθja] nf subtlety, sophistry
argüir [ar'xwir] vt to deduce; (discutir) to
argue; (indicar) to indicate, imply;
(censurar) to reproach ♦ vi to argue
argumentación [arvumenta'θjon] nf (line
of) argument
argumentar [arvumen'tar] vt, vi to argue
argumento [arvu'mento] nm argument;
(razonamiento) reasoning; (de novela etc)
plot; (CINE, TV) storyline
aria ['arja] nf aria
aridez [ari'ðeθ] nf aridity, dryness
árido, a ['ariðo, a] adj arid, dry; **~s** nmpl
(COM) dry goods
Aries ['arjes] nm Aries
ario, a ['arjo, a] adj Aryan
arisco, a [a'risko, a] adj surly; (insociable)
unsociable
aristócrata [aris'tokrata] nm/f aristocrat
aritmética [arit'metika] nf arithmetic
arma ['arma] nf arm; **~s** nfpl arms; **~
blanca** blade, knife; (espada) sword; **~ de
fuego** firearm; **~s cortas** small arms
armada [ar'maða] nf armada; (flota) fleet
armadillo [arma'ðiʎo] nm armadillo
armado, a [ar'maðo, a] adj armed; (TEC)
reinforced
armador [arma'ðor] nm (NAUT) shipowner
armadura [arma'ðura] nf (MIL) armour;
(TEC) framework; (ZOOL) skeleton; (FÍSICA)
armature
armamento [arma'mento] nm armament;
(NAUT) fitting-out
armar [ar'mar] vt (soldado) to arm;
(máquina) to assemble; (navío) to fit out;
~la, ~ un lío to start a row, kick up a fuss

armario [ar'marjo] nm wardrobe; (de
cocina, baño) cupboard
armatoste [arma'toste] nm (mueble)
monstrosity; (máquina) contraption
armazón [arma'θon] nf o m body, chassis;
(de mueble etc) frame; (ARQ) skeleton
armería [arme'ria] nf gunsmith's
armiño [ar'miɲo] nm stoat; (piel) ermine
armisticio [armis'tiθjo] nm armistice
armonía [armo'nia] nf harmony
armónica [ar'monika] nf harmonica
armonioso, a [armo'njoso, a] adj
harmonious
armonizar [armoni'θar] vt to harmonize;
(diferencias) to reconcile ♦ vi: **~ con** (fig)
to be in keeping with; (colores) to tone in
with, blend
arnés [ar'nes] nm armour; **arneses** nmpl
(de caballo etc) harness sg
aro ['aro] nm ring; (tejo) quoit; (AM:
pendiente) earring
aroma [a'roma] nm aroma, scent
aromático, a [aro'matiko, a] adj aromatic
arpa ['arpa] nf harp
arpía [ar'pia] nf shrew
arpillera [arpi'ʎera] nf sacking, sackcloth
arpón [ar'pon] nm harpoon
arquear [arke'ar] vt to arch, bend; **~se** vr
to arch, bend
arqueología [arkeolo'xia] nf archaeology;
arqueólogo, a nm/f archaeologist
arquero [ar'kero] nm archer, bowman
arquetipo [arke'tipo] nm archetype
arquitecto [arki'tekto] nm architect;
arquitectura nf architecture
arrabal [arra'ßal] nm suburb; (AM) slum;
~es nmpl (afueras) outskirts
arraigado, a [arrai'xaðo, a] adj deep-
rooted; (fig) established
arraigar [arrai'var] vt to establish ♦ vi to
take root; **~se** vr to take root; (persona)
to settle
arrancar [arran'kar] vt (sacar) to extract,
pull out; (arrebatar) to snatch (away);
(INFORM) to boot; (fig) to extract ♦ vi
(AUTO, máquina) to start; (ponerse en
marcha) to get going; **~ de** to stem from

arranque *etc* [a'rranke] *vb ver* **arrancar**
♦ *nm* sudden start; (*AUTO*) start; (*fig*) fit, outburst

arrasar [arra'sar] *vt* (*aplanar*) to level, flatten; (*destruir*) to demolish

arrastrado, a [arras'traðo, a] *adj* poor, wretched; (*AM*) servile

arrastrar [arras'trar] *vt* to drag (along); (*fig*) to drag down, degrade; (*suj: agua, viento*) to carry away ♦ *vi* to drag, trail on the ground; **~se** *vr* to crawl; (*fig*) to grovel; **llevar algo arrastrado** to drag sth along

arrastre [a'rrastre] *nm* drag, dragging

arre ['arre] *excl* gee up!

arrear [arre'ar] *vt* to drive on, urge on ♦ *vi* to hurry along

arrebatado, a [arreßa'taðo, a] *adj* rash, impetuous; (*repentino*) sudden, hasty

arrebatar [arreßa'tar] *vt* to snatch (away), seize; (*fig*) to captivate; **~se** *vr* to get carried away, get excited

arrebato [arre'ßato] *nm* fit of rage, fury; (*éxtasis*) rapture

arrecife [arre'θife] *nm* (*tb:* **~ de coral**) reef

arredrarse [arre'ðrarse] *vr*: **~ (ante algo)** to be intimidated (by sth)

arreglado, a [arre'ɣlaðo, a] *adj* (*ordenado*) neat, orderly; (*moderado*) moderate, reasonable

arreglar [arre'ɣlar] *vt* (*poner orden*) to tidy up; (*algo roto*) to fix, repair; (*problema*) to solve; **~se** *vr* to reach an understanding; **arreglárselas** (*fam*) to get by, manage

arreglo [a'rreɣlo] *nm* settlement; (*orden*) order; (*acuerdo*) agreement; (*MUS*) arrangement, setting

arrellanarse [arreʎa'narse] *vr*: **~ en** to sit back in/on

arremangar [arreman'gar] *vt* to roll up, turn up; **~se** *vr* to roll up one's sleeves

arremeter [arreme'ter] *vi*: **~ contra** to attack, rush at

arrendamiento [arrenda'mjento] *nm* letting; (*alquilar*) hiring; (*contrato*) lease; (*alquiler*) rent; **arrendar** *vt* to let, lease; to rent; **arrendatario, a** *nm/f* tenant

arreos [a'rreos] *nmpl* (*de caballo*) harness *sg*, trappings

arrepentimiento [arrepenti'mjento] *nm* regret, repentance

arrepentirse [arrepen'tirse] *vr* to repent; **~ de** to regret

arrestar [arres'tar] *vt* to arrest; (*encarcelar*) to imprison; **arresto** *nm* arrest; (*MIL*) detention; (*audacia*) boldness, daring; **arresto domiciliario** house arrest

arriar [a'rrjar] *vt* (*velas*) to haul down; (*bandera*) to lower, strike; (*cable*) to pay out

---

PALABRA CLAVE

arriba [a'rrißa] *adv* **1** (*posición*) above; **desde ~** from above; **~ de todo** at the very top, right on top; **Juan está ~** Juan is upstairs; **lo ~ mencionado** the aforementioned

2 (*dirección*): **calle ~** up the street

3: **de ~ abajo** from top to bottom; **mirar a uno de ~ abajo** to look sb up and down

4: **para ~: de 5000 pesetas para ~** from 5000 pesetas up(wards)

♦ *adj*: **de ~: el piso de ~** the upstairs flat (*BRIT*) *o* apartment; **la parte de ~** the top *o* upper part

♦ *prep*: **~ de** (*AM*) above; **~ de 200 dólares** more than 200 dollars

♦ *excl*: **¡~!** up!; **¡manos ~!** hands up!; **¡~ España!** long live Spain!

---

arribar [arri'ßar] *vi* to put into port; (*llegar*) to arrive

arribista [arri'ßista] *nm/f* parvenu(e), upstart

arriendo *etc* [a'rrjendo] *vb ver* **arrendar**
♦ *nm* = **arrendamiento**

arriero [a'rrjero] *nm* muleteer

arriesgado, a [arrjes'ɣaðo, a] *adj* (*peligroso*) risky; (*audaz*) bold, daring

arriesgar [arrjes'ɣar] *vt* to risk; (*poner en peligro*) to endanger; **~se** *vr* to take a risk

arrimar [arri'mar] *vt* (*acercar*) to bring close; (*poner de lado*) to set aside; **~se** *vr* to come close *o* closer; **~se a** to lean on

arrinconar [arrinko'nar] *vt* (*colocar*) to put in a corner; (*enemigo*) to corner; (*fig*) to put on one side; (*abandonar*) to push aside

arrodillarse [arroði'ʎarse] *vr* to kneel (down)

arrogancia [arro'vanθja] *nf* arrogance; **arrogante** *adj* arrogant

arrojar [arro'xar] *vt* to throw, hurl; (*humo*) to emit, give out; (*COM*) to yield, produce; **~se** *vr* to throw *o* hurl o.s.

arrojo [a'rroxo] *nm* daring

arrollador, a [arroʎa'ðor, a] *adj* overwhelming

arrollar [arro'ʎar] *vt* (*AUTO etc*) to run over, knock down; (*DEPORTE*) to crush

arropar [arro'par] *vt* to cover, wrap up; **~se** *vr* to wrap o.s. up

arroyo [a'rrojo] *nm* stream; (*de la calle*) gutter

arroz [a'rroθ] *nm* rice; **~ con leche** rice pudding

arruga [a'rruxa] *nf* (*de cara*) wrinkle; (*de vestido*) crease

arrugar [arru'xar] *vt* to wrinkle; to crease; **~se** *vr* to get creased

arruinar [arrwi'nar] *vt* to ruin, wreck; **~se** *vr* to be ruined, go bankrupt

arrullar [arru'ʎar] *vi* to coo ♦ *vt* to lull to sleep

arsenal [arse'nal] *nm* naval dockyard; (*MIL*) arsenal

arsénico [ar'seniko] *nm* arsenic

arte ['arte] (*gen m en sg y siempre f en pl*) *nm* art; (*maña*) skill, guile; **~s** *nfpl* (*bellas ~s*) arts

artefacto [arte'fakto] *nm* appliance

arteria [ar'terja] *nf* artery

artesanía [artesa'nia] *nf* craftsmanship; (*artículos*) handicrafts *pl*; **artesano, a** *nm/f* artisan, craftsman/woman

ártico, a ['artiko, a] *adj* Arctic ♦ *nm*: **el Á~** the Arctic

articulación [artikula'θjon] *nf* articulation; (*MED, TEC*) joint; **articulado, a** *adj* articulated; jointed

articular [artiku'lar] *vt* to articulate; to join together

artículo [ar'tikulo] *nm* article; (*cosa*) thing, article; **~s** *nmpl* (*COM*) goods

artífice [ar'tifiθe] *nm/f* (*fig*) architect

artificial [artifi'θjal] *adj* artificial

artificio [arti'fiθjo] *nm* art, skill; (*astucia*) cunning

artillería [artiʎe'ria] *nf* artillery

artillero [arti'ʎero] *nm* artilleryman, gunner

artilugio [arti'luxjo] *nm* gadget

artimaña [arti'maɲa] *nf* trap, snare; (*astucia*) cunning

artista [ar'tista] *nm/f* (*pintor*) artist, painter; (*TEATRO*) artist, artiste; **~ de cine** film actor/actress; **artístico, a** *adj* artistic

artritis [ar'tritis] *nf* arthritis

arveja [ar'ßexa] (*AM*) *nf* pea

arzobispo [arθo'ßispo] *nm* archbishop

as [as] *nm* ace

asa ['asa] *nf* handle; (*fig*) lever

asado [a'saðo] *nm* roast (meat); (*AM: barbacoa*) barbecue

asador [asa'ðor] *nm* spit

asadura [asa'ðura] *nf* entrails *pl*, offal

asalariado, a [asala'rjaðo, a] *adj* paid, salaried ♦ *nm/f* wage earner

asaltante [asal'tante] *nm/f* attacker

asaltar [asal'tar] *vt* to attack, assault; (*fig*) to assail; **asalto** *nm* attack, assault; (*DEPORTE*) round

asamblea [asam'blea] *nf* assembly; (*reunión*) meeting

asar [a'sar] *vt* to roast

asbesto [as'ßesto] *nm* asbestos

ascendencia [asθen'denθja] *nf* ancestry; (*AM*) ascendancy; **de ~ francesa** of French origin

ascender [asθen'der] *vi* (*subir*) to ascend, rise; (*ser promovido*) to gain promotion ♦ *vt* to promote; **~ a** to amount to; **ascendiente** *nm* influence ♦ *nm/f* ancestor

ascensión [asθen'sjon] *nf* ascent; (*REL*): **la A~** the Ascension

ascenso [as'θenso] *nm* ascent; (*promoción*) promotion

ascensor [asθen'sor] *nm* lift (*BRIT*), elevator (*US*)

ascético, a [as'θetiko, a] *adj* ascetic

asco ['asko] *nm*: **¡qué ~!** how revolting *o* disgusting; **el ajo me da ~** I hate *o* loathe garlic; **estar hecho un ~** to be filthy

ascua ['askwa] *nf* ember; **estar en ~s** to be on tenterhooks

aseado, a [ase'aðo, a] *adj* clean; (*arreglado*) tidy; (*pulcro*) smart

asear [ase'ar] *vt* to clean, wash; to tidy (up)

asediar [ase'ðjar] *vt* (*MIL*) to besiege, lay siege to; (*fig*) to chase, pester; **asedio** *nm* siege; (*COM*) run

asegurado, a [aseɣu'raðo, a] *adj* insured

asegurador, a [aseɣu'rar] *nm/f* insurer

asegurar [aseɣu'rar] *vt* (*consolidar*) to secure, fasten; (*dar garantía de*) to guarantee; (*preservar*) to safeguard; (*afirmar, dar por cierto*) to assure, affirm; (*tranquilizar*) to reassure; (*tomar un seguro*) to insure; **~se** *vr* to assure o.s., make sure

asemejarse [aseme'xarse] *vr* to be alike; **~ a** to be like, resemble

asentado, a [asen'taðo, a] *adj* established, settled

asentar [asen'tar] *vt* (*sentar*) to seat, sit down; (*poner*) to place, establish; (*alisar*) to level, smooth down *o* out; (*anotar*) to note down ♦ *vi* to be suitable, suit

asentir [asen'tir] *vi* to assent, agree; **~ con la cabeza** to nod (one's head)

aseo [a'seo] *nm* cleanliness; **~s** *nmpl* (*servicios*) toilet *sg* (*BRIT*), cloakroom *sg* (*BRIT*), restroom *sg* (*US*)

aséptico, a [a'septiko, a] *adj* germ-free, free from infection

asequible [ase'kiβle] *adj* (*precio*) reasonable; (*meta*) attainable; (*persona*) approachable

aserradero [aserra'ðero] *nm* sawmill; **aserrar** *vt* to saw

asesinar [asesi'nar] *vt* to murder; (*POL*) to assassinate; **asesinato** *nm* murder; assassination

asesino, a [ase'sino, a] *nm/f* murderer, killer; (*POL*) assassin

asesor, a [ase'sor, a] *nm/f* adviser, consultant

asesorar [aseso'rar] *vt* (*JUR*) to advise, give legal advice to; (*COM*) to act as consultant to; **~se** *vr*: **~se con** *o* **de** to take advice from, consult; **asesoría** *nf* (*cargo*) consultancy; (*oficina*) consultant's office

asestar [ases'tar] *vt* (*golpe*) to deal, strike

asfalto [as'falto] *nm* asphalt

asfixia [as'fiksja] *nf* asphyxia, suffocation

asfixiar [asfik'sjar] *vt* to asphyxiate, suffocate; (*suffocate*) ~**se** *vr* to be asphyxiated, suffocate

asgo *etc vb ver* **asir**

así [a'si] *adv* (*de esta manera*) in this way, like this, thus; (*aunque*) although; (*tan pronto como*) as soon as; **~ que** so; **~ como** as well as; **~ y todo** even so; **¿no es ~?** isn't it?, didn't you? *etc*; **~ de grande** this big

Asia ['asja] *nf* Asia; **asiático, a** *adj, nm/f* Asian, Asiatic

asidero [asi'ðero] *nm* handle

asiduidad [asiðwi'ðað] *nf* assiduousness; **asiduo, a** *adj* assiduous; (*frecuente*) frequent ♦ *nm/f* regular (customer)

asiento [a'sjento] *nm* (*mueble*) seat, chair; (*de coche, en tribunal etc*) seat; (*localidad*) seat, place; (*fundamento*) site; **~ delantero/trasero** front/back seat

asignación [asiɣna'θjon] *nf* (*atribución*) assignment; (*reparto*) allocation; (*sueldo*) salary; **~ (semanal)** pocket money

asignar [asiɣ'nar] *vt* to assign, allocate

asignatura [asiɣna'tura] *nf* subject; course

asilado, a [asi'laðo, a] *nm/f* inmate; (*POL*) refugee

asilo [a'silo] *nm* (*refugio*) asylum, refuge; (*establecimiento*) home, institution; **~ político** political asylum

asimilación [asimila'θjon] *nf* assimilation

asimilar [asimi'lar] *vt* to assimilate

asimismo [asi'mismo] *adv* in the same

way, likewise

sir [a'sir] *vt* to seize, grasp

sistencia [asis'tenθja] *nf* audience; (*MED*) attendance; (*ayuda*) assistance;
asistente *nm/f* assistant; **los asistentes** those present; **asistente social** social worker

sistido, a [asis'tiðo, a] *adj*: ~ **por ordenador** computer-assisted

sistir [asis'tir] *vt* to assist, help ♦ *vi*: ~ **a** to attend, be present at

sma ['asma] *nf* asthma

sno ['asno] *nm* donkey; (*fig*) ass

sociación [asoθja'θjon] *nf* association; (*COM*) partnership; **asociado, a** *adj* associate ♦ *nm/f* associate; (*COM*) partner

sociar [aso'θjar] *vt* to associate

solar [aso'lar] *vt* to destroy

somar [aso'mar] *vt* to show, stick out ♦ *vi* to appear; **~se** *vr* to appear, show up; ~ **la cabeza por la ventana** to put one's head out of the window

sombrar [asom'brar] *vt* to amaze, astonish; **~se** *vr* (*sorprenderse*) to be amazed; (*asustarse*) to get a fright; **asombro** *nm* amazement, astonishment; (*susto*) fright; **asombroso, a** *adj* astonishing, amazing

somo [a'somo] *nm* hint, sign

spa ['aspa] *nf* (*cruz*) cross; (*de molino*) sail; **en** ~ X-shaped

spaviento [aspa'βjento] *nm* exaggerated display of feeling; (*fam*) fuss

specto [as'pekto] *nm* (*apariencia*) look, appearance; (*fig*) aspect

spereza [aspe'reθa] *nf* roughness; (*agrura*) sourness; (*de carácter*) surliness; **áspero, a** *adj* rough; bitter, sour; harsh

spersión [asper'sjon] *nf* sprinkling

spiración [aspira'θjon] *nf* breath, inhalation; (*MUS*) short pause; **aspiraciones** *nfpl* (*ambiciones*) aspirations

spirador [aspira'ðor] *nm* = **aspiradora**

spiradora [aspira'ðora] *nf* vacuum cleaner, Hoover ®

spirante [aspi'rante] *nm/f* (*candidato*) candidate; (*DEPORTE*) contender

aspirar [aspi'rar] *vt* to breathe in ♦ *vi*: ~ **a** to aspire to

aspirina [aspi'rina] *nf* aspirin

asquear [aske'ar] *vt* to sicken ♦ *vi* to be sickening; **~se** *vr* to feel disgusted; **asqueroso, a** *adj* disgusting, sickening

asta ['asta] *nf* lance; (*arpón*) spear; (*mango*) shaft, handle; (*ZOOL*) horn; **a media** ~ at half mast

asterisco [aste'risko] *nm* asterisk

astilla [as'tiʎa] *nf* splinter; (*pedacito*) chip; **~s** *nfpl* (*leña*) firewood *sg*

astillero [asti'ʎero] *nm* shipyard

astringente [astrin'xente] *adj, nm* astringent

astro ['astro] *nm* star

astrología [astrolo'xia] *nf* astrology; **astrólogo, a** *nm/f* astrologer

astronauta [astro'nauta] *nm/f* astronaut

astronave [astro'naβe] *nm* spaceship

astronomía [astrono'mia] *nf* astronomy; **astrónomo, a** *nm/f* astronomer

astucia [as'tuθja] *nf* astuteness; (*ardid*) clever trick

asturiano, a [astu'rjano, a] *adj, nm/f* Asturian

astuto, a [as'tuto, a] *adj* astute; (*taimado*) cunning

asumir [asu'mir] *vt* to assume

asunción [asun'θjon] *nf* assumption; (*REL*): **A~** Assumption

asunto [a'sunto] *nm* (*tema*) matter, subject; (*negocio*) business

asustar [asus'tar] *vt* to frighten; **~se** *vr* to be (o become) frightened

atacar [ata'kar] *vt* to attack

atadura [ata'ðura] *nf* bond, tie

atajar [ata'xar] *vt* (*enfermedad, mal*) to stop ♦ *vi* (*persona*) to take a short cut

atajo [a'taxo] *nm* short cut

atañer [ata'ɲer] *vi*: ~ **a** to concern

ataque *etc* [a'take] *vb ver* **atacar** ♦ *nm* attack; ~ **cardíaco** heart attack

atar [a'tar] *vt* to tie, tie up

atardecer [atarðe'θer] *vi* to get dark ♦ *nm* evening; (*crepúsculo*) dusk

atareado, a [atare'aðo, a] *adj* busy

atascar [atas'kar] *vt* to clog up; *(obstruir)* to jam; *(fig)* to hinder; **~se** *vr* to stall; *(cañería)* to get blocked up; **atasco** *nm* obstruction; *(AUTO)* traffic jam

ataúd [ata'uð] *nm* coffin

ataviar [ata'ßjar] *vt* to deck, array; **~se** *vr* to dress up

atavío [ata'ßio] *nm* attire, dress; **~s** *nmpl* finery *sg*

atemorizar [atemori'θar] *vt* to frighten, scare; **~se** *vr* to get scared

Atenas [a'tenas] *n* Athens

atención [aten'θjon] *nf* attention; *(bondad)* kindness ♦ *excl* (be) careful!, look out!

atender [aten'der] *vt* to attend to, look after ♦ *vi* to pay attention

atenerse [ate'nerse] *vr*: **~ a** to abide by, adhere to

atentado [aten'taðo] *nm* crime, illegal act; *(asalto)* assault; **~ contra la vida de uno** attempt on sb's life

atentamente [atenta'mente] *adv*: **Le saluda ~** Yours faithfully

atentar [aten'tar] *vi*: **~ a** *o* **contra** to commit an outrage against

atento, a [a'tento, a] *adj* attentive, observant; *(cortés)* polite, thoughtful

atenuante [ate'nwante] *adj* extenuating

atenuar [ate'nwar] *vt (disminuir)* to lessen, minimize

ateo, a [a'teo, a] *adj* atheistic ♦ *nm/f* atheist

aterciopelado, a [aterθjope'laðo, a] *adj* velvety

aterido, a [ate'riðo, a] *adj*: **~ de frío** frozen stiff

aterrador, a [aterra'ðor, a] *adj* frightening

aterrar [ate'rrar] *vt* to frighten; to terrify

aterrizaje [aterri'θaxe] *nm* landing

aterrizar [aterri'θar] *vi* to land

aterrorizar [aterrori'θar] *vt* to terrify

atesorar [ateso'rar] *vt* to hoard

atestado, a [ates'taðo, a] *adj* packed ♦ *nm (JUR)* affidavit

atestar [ates'tar] *vt* to pack, stuff; *(JUR)* to attest, testify to

atestiguar [atesti'ɣwar] *vt* to testify to, bear witness to

atiborrar [atiβo'rrar] *vt* to fill, stuff; **~se** *vr* to stuff o.s.

ático ['atiko] *nm* attic; **~ de lujo** penthouse (flat *(BRIT)* o apartment)

atinado, a [ati'naðo, a] *adj (sensato)* wise; *(correcto)* right, correct

atinar [ati'nar] *vi (al disparar)*: **~ al blanco** to hit the target; *(fig)* to be right

atisbar [atis'ßar] *vt* to spy on; *(echar una ojeada)* to peep at

atizar [ati'θar] *vt* to poke; *(horno etc)* to stoke; *(fig)* to stir up, rouse

atlántico, a [at'lantiko, a] *adj* Atlantic ♦ *nm*: **el (océano) A~** the Atlantic (Ocean)

atlas ['atlas] *nm inv* atlas

atleta [at'leta] *nm* athlete; **atlético, a** *adj* athletic; **atletismo** *nm* athletics *sg*

atmósfera [at'mosfera] *nf* atmosphere

atolladero [atoʎa'ðero] *nm (fig)* jam, fix

atolondramiento [atolondra'mjento] *nm* bewilderment; *(insensatez)* silliness

atómico, a [a'tomiko, a] *adj* atomic

atomizador [atomiθa'ðor] *nm* atomizer; *(de perfume)* spray

átomo ['atomo] *nm* atom

atónito, a [a'tonito, a] *adj* astonished, amazed

atontado, a [aton'taðo, a] *adj* stunned; *(bobo)* silly, daft

atontar [aton'tar] *vt* to stun; **~se** *vr* to become confused

atormentar [atormen'tar] *vt* to torture; *(molestar)* to torment; *(acosar)* to plague, harass

atornillar [atorni'ʎar] *vt* to screw on *o* down

atosigar [atosi'ɣar] *vt* to harass, pester

atracador, a [atraka'ðor, a] *nm/f* robber

atracar [atra'kar] *vt (NAUT)* to moor; *(robar)* to hold up, rob ♦ *vi* to moor; **~se** *vr*: **~se (de)** to stuff o.s. (with)

atracción [atrak'θjon] *nf* attraction

atraco [a'trako] *nm* holdup, robbery

atracón [atra'kon] *nm*: **darse** *o* **pegarse**

un ~ (de) (fam) to stuff o.s. (with)
atractivo, a [atrak'tiβo, a] adj attractive
♦ nm appeal
atraer [atra'er] vt to attract
atragantarse [atraɣan'tarse] vr: ~ (con) to choke (on); **se me ha atragantado el chico** I can't stand the boy
atrancar [atraŋ'kar] vt (puerta) to bar, bolt
atrapar [atra'par] vt to trap; (resfriado etc) to catch
atrás [a'tras] adv (movimiento) back (-wards); (lugar) behind; (tiempo) previously; **ir hacia ~** to go back(wards); to go to the rear; **estar ~** to be behind o at the back
atrasado, a [atra'saðo, a] adj slow; (pago) overdue, late; (país) backward
atrasar [atra'sar] vi to be slow; **~se** vr to remain behind; (tren) to be o run late; **atraso** nm slowness; lateness, delay; (de país) backwardness; **atrasos** nmpl (COM) arrears
atravesar [atraβe'sar] vt (cruzar) to cross (over); (traspasar) to pierce; to go through; (poner al través) to lay o put across; **~se** vr to come in between; (intervenir) to interfere
atravieso etc vb ver **atravesar**
atrayente [atra'jente] adj attractive
atreverse [atre'βerse] vr to dare; (insolentarse) to be insolent; **atrevido, a** adj daring; insolent; **atrevimiento** nm daring; insolence
atribución [atriβu'θjon] nf: **atribuciones** (POL) powers; (ADMIN) responsibilities
atribuir [atriβu'ir] vt to attribute; (funciones) to confer
atribular [atriβu'lar] vt to afflict, distress
atributo [atri'βuto] nm attribute
atril [a'tril] nm (para libro) lectern; (MUS) music stand
atrocidad [atroθi'ðað] nf atrocity, outrage
atropellar [atrope'ʎar] vt (derribar) to knock over o down; (empujar) to push (aside); (AUTO) to run over, run down; (agraviar) to insult; **~se** vr to act hastily; **atropello** nm (AUTO) accident; (empujón)

push; (agravio) wrong; (atrocidad) outrage
atroz [a'troθ] adj atrocious, awful
ATS nm/f abr (= Ayudante Técnico Sanitario) nurse
atto, a abr = **atento**
atuendo [a'twendo] nm attire
atún [a'tun] nm tuna
aturdir [atur'ðir] vt to stun; (de ruido) to deafen; (fig) to dumbfound, bewilder
atusar [atu'sar] vt to smooth (down)
audacia [au'ðaθja] nf boldness, audacity; **audaz** adj bold, audacious
audible [au'ðiβle] adj audible
audición [auði'θjon] nf hearing; (TEATRO) audition
audiencia [au'ðjenθja] nf audience; **A~** (JUR) High Court
audífono [au'ðifono] nm (para sordos) hearing aid
auditor [auði'tor] nm (JUR) judge advocate; (COM) auditor
auditorio [auði'torjo] nm audience; (sala) auditorium
auge ['auxe] nm boom; (clímax) climax
augurar [auɣu'rar] vt to predict; (presagiar) to portend
augurio [au'ɣurjo] nm omen
aula ['aula] nf classroom; (en universidad etc) lecture room
aullar [au'ʎar] vi to howl, yell
aullido [au'ʎiðo] nm howl, yell
aumentar [aumen'tar] vt to increase; (precios) to put up; (producción) to step up; (con microscopio, anteojos) to magnify ♦ vi to increase, be on the increase; **~se** vr to increase, be on the increase; **aumento** nm increase; rise
aun [a'un] adv even; **~ así** even so; **~ más** even o yet more
aún [a'un] adv: **~ está aquí** he's still here; **~ no lo sabemos** we don't know yet; **¿no ha venido ~?** hasn't she come yet?
aunque [a'unke] conj though, although, even though
aúpa [a'upa] excl come on!
aureola [aure'ola] nf halo
auricular [auriku'lar] nm (TEL) earpiece,

receiver; **~es** *nmpl* (*para escuchar música etc*) headphones

aurora [auˈrora] *nf* dawn

auscultar [auskulˈtar] *vt* (*MED: pecho*) to listen to, sound

ausencia [auˈsenθja] *nf* absence

ausentarse [ausenˈtarse] *vr* to go away; (*por poco tiempo*) to go out

ausente [auˈsente] *adj* absent

auspicios [ausˈpiθjos] *nmpl* auspices

austero, a [ausˈtero, a] *adj* austere

austral [ausˈtral] *adj* southern ♦ *nm* monetary unit of Argentina

Australia [ausˈtralja] *nf* Australia; **australiano, a** *adj, nm/f* Australian

Austria [ˈaustrja] *nf* Austria; **austríaco, a** *adj, nm/f* Austrian

auténtico, a [auˈtentiko, a] *adj* authentic

auto [ˈauto] *nm* (*JUR*) edict, decree; (: *orden*) writ; (*AUTO*) car; **~s** *nmpl* (*JUR*) proceedings; (: *acta*) court record *sg*

autoadhesivo [autoaðeˈsiβo] *adj* self-adhesive; (*sobre*) self-sealing

autobiografía [autoβjoɣraˈfia] *nf* autobiography

autobronceador [autoβronθeaˈðor] *adj* self-tanning

autobús [autoˈβus] *nm* bus

autocar [autoˈkar] *nm* coach (*BRIT*), (passenger) bus (*US*)

autóctono, a [auˈtoktono, a] *adj* native

autodefensa [autoðeˈfensa] *nf* self-defence

autodeterminación [autoðeterminaˈθjon] *nf* self-determination

autodidacta [autoðiˈðakta] *adj* self-taught

autoescuela [autoesˈkwela] *nf* driving school

autógrafo [auˈtoɣrafo] *nm* autograph

autómata [auˈtomata] *nm* automaton

automático, a [autoˈmatiko, a] *adj* automatic ♦ *nm* press stud

automotor, triz [automoˈtor, ˈtriθ] *adj* self-propelled ♦ *nm* diesel train

automóvil [autoˈmoβil] *nm* (motor) car (*BRIT*), automobile (*US*); **automovilismo** *nm* (*actividad*) motoring; (*DEPORTE*) motor

racing; **automovilista** *nm/f* motorist, driver; **automovilístico, a** *adj* (*industria*) motor *cpd*

autonomía [autonoˈmia] *nf* autonomy; **autónomo, a** (*ESP*), **autonómico, a** (*ESP*) *adj* (*POL*) autonomous

autopista [autoˈpista] *nf* motorway (*BRIT*), freeway (*US*); **~ de peaje** toll road (*BRIT*), turnpike road (*US*)

autopsia [auˈtopsja] *nf* autopsy, postmortem

autor, a [auˈtor, a] *nm/f* author

autoridad [autoriˈðað] *nf* authority; **autoritario, a** *adj* authoritarian

autorización [autoriθaˈθjon] *nf* authorization; **autorizado, a** *adj* authorized; (*aprobado*) approved

autorizar [autoriˈθar] *vt* to authorize; (*aprobar*) to approve

autorretrato [autorreˈtrato] *nm* self-portrait

autoservicio [autoserˈβiθjo] *nm* (*tienda*) self-service shop (*BRIT*) *o* store (*US*); (*restaurante*) self-service restaurant

autostop [autoˈstop] *nm* hitch-hiking; **hacer ~** to hitch-hike; **~ista** *nm/f* hitch-hiker

autosuficiencia [autosufiˈθjenθja] *nf* self-sufficiency

autovía [autoˈβia] *nf* ≈ A-road (*BRIT*), dual carriageway (*BRIT*), ≈ state highway (*US*)

auxiliar [auksiˈljar] *vt* to help ♦ *nm/f* assistant; **auxilio** *nm* assistance, help; **primeros auxilios** first aid *sg*

Av *abr* (= *Avenida*) Av(e).

aval [aˈβal] *nm* guarantee; (*persona*) guarantor

avalancha [aβaˈlantʃa] *nf* avalanche

avance [aˈβanθe] *nm* advance; (*pago*) advance payment; (*CINE*) trailer

avanzar [aβanˈθar] *vt, vi* to advance

avaricia [aβaˈriθja] *nf* avarice, greed; **avaricioso, a** *adj* avaricious, greedy

avaro, a [aˈβaro, a] *adj* miserly, mean ♦ *nm/f* miser

avasallar [aβasaˈʎar] *vt* to subdue, subjugate

Avda *abr* (= *Avenida*) Av(e).
AVE ['aße] *nm abr* (= *Alta Velocidad Española*) ≈ bullet train
ave ['aße] *nf* bird; ~ **de rapiña** bird of prey
avecinarse [aße θi'narse] *vr* (*tormenta, fig*) to be on the way
avellana [aße'ʎana] *nf* hazelnut; **avellano** *nm* hazel tree
avemaría [aßema'ria] *nm* Hail Mary, Ave Maria
avena [a'ßena] *nf* oats *pl*
avenida [aße'niða] *nf* (*calle*) avenue
avenir [aße'nir] *vt* to reconcile; ~**se** *vr* to come to an agreement, reach a compromise
aventajado, a [aßenta'xaðo, a] *adj* outstanding
aventajar [aßenta'xar] *vt* (*sobrepasar*) to surpass, outstrip
aventura [aßen'tura] *nf* adventure; **aventurado, a** *adj* risky; **aventurero, a** *adj* adventurous
avergonzar [aßerɣon'θar] *vt* to shame; (*desconcertar*) to embarrass; ~**se** *vr* to be ashamed; to be embarrassed
avería [aße'ria] *nf* (*TEC*) breakdown, fault
averiado, a [aße'rjaðo, a] *adj* broken down; "~" "out of order"
averiguación [aßeriɣwa'θjon] *nf* investigation; (*descubrimiento*) ascertainment
averiguar [aßeri'ɣwar] *vt* to investigate; (*descubrir*) to find out, ascertain
aversión [aßer'sjon] *nf* aversion, dislike
avestruz [aßes'truθ] *nm* ostrich
aviación [aßja'θjon] *nf* aviation; (*fuerzas aéreas*) air force
aviador, a [aßja'ðor, a] *nm/f* aviator, airman/woman
avicultura [aßikul'tura] *nf* poultry farming
avidez [aßi'ðeθ] *nf* avidity, eagerness; **ávido, a** *adj* avid, eager
avinagrado, a [aßina'ɣraðo, a] *adj* sour, acid
avión [a'ßjon] *nm* aeroplane; (*ave*) martin; ~ **de reacción** jet (plane)
avioneta [aßjo'neta] *nf* light aircraft

avisar [aßi'sar] *vt* (*advertir*) to warn, notify; (*informar*) to tell; (*aconsejar*) to advise, counsel; **aviso** *nm* warning; (*noticia*) notice
avispa [a'ßispa] *nf* wasp
avispado, a [aßis'paðo, a] *adj* sharp, clever
avispero [aßis'pero] *nm* wasp's nest
avispón [aßis'pon] *nm* hornet
avistar [aßis'tar] *vt* to sight, spot
avituallar [aßitwa'ʎar] *vt* to supply with food
avivar [aßi'ßar] *vt* to strengthen, intensify; ~**se** *vr* to revive, acquire new life
axila [ak'sila] *nf* armpit
axioma [ak'sjoma] *nm* axiom
ay [ai] *excl* (*dolor*) ow!, ouch!; (*aflicción*) oh!, oh dear!; **¡~ de mí!** poor me!
aya ['aja] *nf* governess; (*niñera*) nanny
ayer [a'jer] *adv, nm* yesterday; **antes de ~** the day before yesterday
ayote [a'jote] (*AM*) *nm* pumpkin
ayuda [a'juða] *nf* help, assistance ♦ *nm* page; **ayudante, a** *nm/f* assistant, helper; (*ESCOL*) assistant; (*MIL*) adjutant
ayudar [aju'ðar] *vt* to help, assist
ayunar [aju'nar] *vi* to fast; **ayunas** *nfpl*: **estar en ayunas** to be fasting; **ayuno** *nm* fast; fasting
ayuntamiento [ajunta'mjento] *nm* (*consejo*) town (o city) council; (*edificio*) town (o city) hall
azabache [aθa'ßatʃe] *nm* jet
azada [a'θaða] *nf* hoe
azafata [aθa'fata] *nf* air stewardess
azafrán [aθa'fran] *nm* saffron
azahar [aθa'ar] *nm* orange/lemon blossom
azar [a'θar] *nm* (*casualidad*) chance, fate; (*desgracia*) misfortune, accident; **por ~** by chance; **al ~** at random
azoramiento [aθora'mjento] *nm* alarm; (*confusión*) confusion
azorar [aθo'rar] *vt* to alarm; ~**se** *vr* to get alarmed
Azores [a'θores] *nfpl*: **las ~** the Azores
azotar [aθo'tar] *vt* to whip, beat; (*pegar*) to spank; **azote** *nm* (*látigo*) whip;

(*latigazo*) lash, stroke; (*en las nalgas*) spank; (*calamidad*) calamity

azotea [aθo'tea] *nf* (flat) roof

azteca [aθ'teka] *adj, nm/f* Aztec

azúcar [a'θukar] *nm* sugar; **azucarado, a** *adj* sugary, sweet

azucarero, a [aθuka'rero, a] *adj* sugar *cpd* ♦ *nm* sugar bowl

azucena [aθu'θena] *nf* white lily

azufre [a'θufre] *nm* sulphur

azul [a'θul] *adj, nm* blue; ~ **marino** navy blue

azulejo [aθu'lexo] *nm* tile

azuzar [aθu'θar] *vt* to incite, egg on

B, b

B.A. *abr* (= *Buenos Aires*) B.A.

baba ['baβa] *nf* spittle, saliva; **babear** *vi* to drool, slaver

babero [ba'βero] *nm* bib

babor [ba'βor] *nm* port (side)

baboso, a [ba'βoso, a] (*AM: fam*) *adj* silly

baca ['baka] *nf* (*AUTO*) luggage *o* roof rack

bacalao [baka'lao] *nm* cod(fish)

bache ['batʃe] *nm* pothole, rut; (*fig*) bad patch

bachillerato [batʃiʎe'rato] *nm* higher secondary school course

bacteria [bak'terja] *nf* bacterium, germ

báculo ['bakulo] *nm* stick, staff

bagaje [ba'vaxe] *nm* baggage, luggage

Bahama [ba'ama]: **las (Islas) ~** *nfpl* the Bahamas

bahía [ba'ia] *nf* bay

bailar [bai'lar] *vt, vi* to dance; ~**ín, ina** *nm/f* (*ballet*) dancer; **baile** *nm* dance; (*formal*) ball

baja ['baxa] *nf* drop, fall; (*MIL*) casualty; **dar de ~** (*soldado*) to discharge; (*empleado*) to dismiss

bajada [ba'xaða] *nf* descent; (*camino*) slope; (*de aguas*) ebb

bajar [ba'xar] *vi* to go down, come down; (*temperatura, precios*) to drop, fall ♦ *vt* (*cabeza*) to bow; (*escalera*) to go down, come down; (*precio, voz*) to lower; (*llevar abajo*) to take down; ~**se** *vr* (*de coche*) to get out; (*de autobús, tren*) to get off; ~ **de** (*coche*) to get out of; (*autobús, tren*) to get off

bajeza [ba'xeθa] *nf* baseness *no pl*; (*una ~*) vile deed

bajío [ba'xio] *nm* (*AM*) lowlands *pl*

bajo, a ['baxo, a] *adj* (*mueble, número, precio*) low; (*piso*) ground; (*de estatura*) small, short; (*color*) pale; (*sonido*) faint, soft, low; (*voz: en tono*) deep; (*metal*) base; (*humilde*) low, humble ♦ *adv* (*hablar*) softly, quietly; (*volar*) low ♦ *prep* under, below, underneath ♦ *nm* (*MUS*) bass; ~ **la lluvia** in the rain

bajón [ba'xon] *nm* fall, drop

bakalao [baka'lao] (*fam*) *nm* rave (music)

bala ['bala] *nf* bullet

balance [ba'lanθe] *nm* (*COM*) balance; (*: libro*) balance sheet; (*: cuenta general*) stocktaking

balancear [balanθe'ar] *vt* to balance ♦ *vi* to swing (to and fro); (*vacilar*) to hesitate; ~**se** *vr* to swing (to and fro); to hesitate; **balanceo** *nm* swinging

balanza [ba'lanθa] *nf* scales *pl*, balance; (*ASTROLOGÍA*): **B~** Libra; ~ **comercial** balance of trade; ~ **de pagos** balance of payments

balar [ba'lar] *vi* to bleat

balaustrada [balaus'traða] *nf* balustrade; (*pasamanos*) banisters *pl*

balazo [ba'laθo] *nm* (*golpe*) shot; (*herida*) bullet wound

balbucear [balβuθe'ar] *vi, vt* to stammer, stutter; **balbuceo** *nm* stammering, stuttering

balbucir [balβu'θir] *vi, vt* to stammer, stutter

balcón [bal'kon] *nm* balcony

balde ['balde] *nm* bucket, pail; **de ~** (for) free, for nothing; **en ~** in vain

baldío, a [bal'dio, a] *adj* uncultivated; (*terreno*) waste ♦ *nm* waste land

baldosa [bal'dosa] *nf* (*azulejo*) floor tile; (*grande*) flagstone; **baldosín** *nm* (small) tile

Baleares [bale'ares] *nfpl*: **las (Islas) ~** the Balearic Islands

balido [ba'liðo] *nm* bleat, bleating

baliza [ba'liθa] *nf* (AVIAT) beacon; (NAUT) buoy

ballena [ba'ʎena] *nf* whale

ballesta [ba'ʎesta] *nf* crossbow; (AUTO) spring

ballet [ba'le] (*pl* ~**s**) *nm* ballet

balneario, a [balne'arjo, a] *adj*: **estación balnearia** (AM) (bathing) resort ♦ *nm* spa, health resort

balón [ba'lon] *nm* ball

baloncesto [balon'θesto] *nm* basketball

balonmano [balon'mano] *nm* handball

balonvolea [balombo'lea] *nm* volleyball

balsa ['balsa] *nf* raft; (BOT) balsa wood

bálsamo ['balsamo] *nm* balsam, balm

baluarte [ba'lwarte] *nm* bastion, bulwark

bambolear [bambole'ar] *vi* to swing, sway; (*silla*) to wobble; **~se** *vr* to swing, sway; to wobble; **bamboleo** *nm* swinging, swaying; wobbling

bambú [bam'bu] *nm* bamboo

banana [ba'nana] (AM) *nf* banana; **banano** (AM) banana tree

banca ['banka] *nf* (COM) banking

bancario, a [ban'karjo, a] *adj* banking *cpd*, bank *cpd*

bancarrota [banka'rrota] *nf* bankruptcy; **hacer ~** to go bankrupt

banco ['banko] *nm* bench; (ESCOL) desk; (COM) bank; (GEO) stratum; **~ de crédito/de ahorros** credit/savings bank; **~ de arena** sandbank; **~ de datos** databank

banda ['banda] *nf* band; (*pandilla*) gang; (NAUT) side, edge; **la B~ Oriental** Uruguay; **~ sonora** soundtrack

bandada [ban'daða] *nf* (*de pájaros*) flock; (*de peces*) shoal

bandazo [ban'daθo] *nm*: **dar ~s** to sway from side to side

bandeja [ban'dexa] *nf* tray

bandera [ban'dera] *nf* flag

banderilla [bande'riʎa] *nf* banderilla

banderín [bande'rin] *nm* pennant, small flag

bandido [ban'diðo] *nm* bandit

bando ['bando] *nm* (*edicto*) edict, proclamation; (*facción*) faction; **los ~s** (REL) the banns

bandolera [bando'lera] *nf*: **llevar en ~** to wear across one's chest

bandolero [bando'lero] *nm* bandit, brigand

banquero [ban'kero] *nm* banker

banqueta [ban'keta] *nf* stool; (AM: *en la calle*) pavement (BRIT), sidewalk (US)

banquete [ban'kete] *nm* banquet; (*para convidados*) formal dinner

banquillo [ban'kiʎo] *nm* (JUR) dock, prisoner's bench; (*banco*) bench; (*para los pies*) footstool

bañador [baɲa'ðor] *nm* swimming costume (BRIT), bathing suit (US)

bañar [ba'ɲar] *vt* to bath, bathe; (*objeto*) to dip; (*de barniz*) to coat; **~se** *vr* (*en el mar*) to bathe, swim; (*en la bañera*) to have a bath

bañera [ba'ɲera] *nf* bath(tub)

bañero, a [ba'ɲero, a] (AM) *nm/f* lifeguard

bañista [ba'ɲista] *nm/f* bather

baño ['baɲo] *nm* (*en bañera*) bath; (*en río*) dip, swim; (*cuarto*) bathroom; (*bañera*) bath(tub); (*capa*) coating

baqueta [ba'keta] *nf* (MUS) drumstick

bar [bar] *nm* bar

barahúnda [bara'unda] *nf* uproar, hubbub

baraja [ba'raxa] *nf* pack (of cards); **barajar** *vt* (*naipes*) to shuffle; (*fig*) to jumble up

baranda [ba'randa] *nf* = **barandilla**

barandilla [baran'diʎa] *nf* rail, railing

baratija [bara'tixa] *nf* trinket

baratillo [bara'tiʎo] *nm* (*tienda*) junkshop; (*subasta*) bargain sale; (*conjunto de cosas*) secondhand goods *pl*

barato, a [ba'rato, a] *adj* cheap ♦ *adv* cheap, cheaply

baraúnda [bara'unda] *nf* = **barahúnda**

barba ['barβa] *nf* (*mentón*) chin; (*pelo*) beard

barbacoa [barˈβaˈkoa] *nf* (*parrilla*) barbecue; (*carne*) barbecued meat

barbaridad [barβariˈðað] *nf* barbarity; (*acto*) barbarism; (*atrocidad*) outrage; **una ~** (*fam*) loads; **¡qué ~!** (*fam*) how awful!

barbarie [barˈβarje] *nf* barbarism, savagery; (*crueldad*) barbarity

barbarismo [barβaˈrismo] *nm* = **barbarie**

bárbaro, a [ˈbarβaro, a] *adj* barbarous, cruel; (*grosero*) rough, uncouth ♦ *nm/f* barbarian ♦ *adv*: **lo pasamos ~** (*fam*) we had a great time; **¡qué ~!** (*fam*) how marvellous!; **un éxito ~** (*fam*) a terrific success; **es un tipo ~** (*fam*) he's a great bloke

barbecho [barˈβetʃo] *nm* fallow land

barbero [barˈβero] *nm* barber, hairdresser

barbilla [barˈβiʎa] *nf* chin, tip of the chin

barbo [ˈbarβo] *nm* barbel; **~ de mar** red mullet

barbotear [barβoteˈar] *vt, vi* to mutter, mumble

barbudo, a [barˈβuðo, a] *adj* bearded

barca [ˈbarka] *nf* (small) boat; **~ pesquera** fishing boat; **~ de pasaje** ferry; **~za** *nf* barge; **~za de desembarco** landing craft

Barcelona [barθeˈlona] *n* Barcelona

barcelonés, esa [barθeloˈnes, esa] *adj* of *o* from Barcelona

barco [ˈbarko] *nm* boat; (*grande*) ship; **~ de carga** cargo boat; **~ de vela** sailing ship

baremo [baˈremo] *nm* (*MAT, fig*) scale

barítono [baˈritono] *nm* baritone

barman [ˈbarman] *nm* barman

Barna *n* = **Barcelona**

barniz [barˈniθ] *nm* varnish; (*en la loza*) glaze; (*fig*) veneer; **~ar** *vt* to varnish; (*loza*) to glaze

barómetro [baˈrometro] *nm* barometer

barquero [barˈkero] *nm* boatman

barquillo [barˈkiʎo] *nm* cone, cornet

barra [ˈbarra] *nf* bar, rod; (*de un bar, café*) bar; (*de pan*) French stick; (*palanca*) lever; **~ de carmín** *o* **de labios** lipstick; **~ libre** free bar

barraca [baˈrraka] *nf* hut, cabin

barranco [baˈrranko] *nm* ravine; (*fig*) difficulty

barrena [baˈrrena] *nf* drill; **barrenar** *vt* to drill (through), bore; **barreno** *nm* large drill

barrer [baˈrrer] *vt* to sweep; (*quitar*) to sweep away

barrera [baˈrrera] *nf* barrier

barriada [baˈrrjaða] *nf* quarter, district

barricada [barriˈkaða] *nf* barricade

barrida [baˈrriða] *nf* sweep, sweeping

barrido [baˈrriðo] *nm* = **barrida**

barriga [baˈrriɣa] *nf* belly; (*panza*) paunch; **barrigón, ona** *adj* potbellied; **barrigudo, a** *adj* potbellied

barril [baˈrril] *nm* barrel, cask

barrio [ˈbarrjo] *nm* (*vecindad*) area, neighborhood (*US*); (*en las afueras*) suburb; **~ chino** red-light district

barro [ˈbarro] *nm* (*lodo*) mud; (*objetos*) earthenware; (*MED*) pimple

barroco, a [baˈrroko, a] *adj, nm* baroque

barrote [baˈrrote] *nm* (*de ventana*) bar

barruntar [barrunˈtar] *vt* (*conjeturar*) to guess; (*presentir*) to suspect; **barrunto** *nm* guess; suspicion

bartola [barˈtola]: **a la ~** *adv*: **tirarse a la ~** to take it easy, be lazy

bártulos [ˈbartulos] *nmpl* things, belongings

barullo [baˈruʎo] *nm* row, uproar

basar [baˈsar] *vt* to base; **~se** *vr*: **~se en** to be based on

báscula [ˈbaskula] *nf* (*platform*) scales

base [ˈbase] *nf* base; **a ~ de** on the basis of; (*mediante*) by means of; **~ de datos** (*INFORM*) database

básico, a [ˈbasiko, a] *adj* basic

basílica [baˈsilika] *nf* basilica

PALABRA CLAVE

bastante [basˈtante] *adj* **1** (*suficiente*) enough; **~ dinero** enough *o* sufficient money; **~s libros** enough books
2 (*valor intensivo*): **~ gente** quite a lot of people; **tener ~ calor** to be rather hot
♦ *adv*: **~ bueno/malo** quite good/rather

bad; **~ rico** pretty rich; **(lo) ~ inteligente (como) para hacer algo** clever enough *o* sufficiently clever to do sth

bastar [bas'tar] *vi* to be enough *o* sufficient; **~se** *vr* to be self-sufficient; **~ para** to be enough to; **¡basta!** (that's) enough!

bastardilla [bastar'ðiʎa] *nf* italics

bastardo, a [bas'tarðo, a] *adj, nm/f* bastard

bastidor [basti'ðor] *nm* frame; *(de coche)* chassis; *(TEATRO)* wing; **entre ~es** *(fig)* behind the scenes

basto, a ['basto, a] *adj* coarse, rough; **~s** *nmpl (NAIPES)* ≈ clubs

bastón [bas'ton] *nm* stick, staff; *(para pasear)* walking stick

bastoncillo [baston'θiʎo] *nm* cotton bud

basura [ba'sura] *nf* rubbish *(BRIT)*, garbage *(US)*

basurero [basu'rero] *nm (hombre)* dustman *(BRIT)*, garbage man *(US)*; *(lugar)* dump; *(cubo)* (rubbish) bin *(BRIT)*, trash can *(US)*

bata ['bata] *nf (gen)* dressing gown; *(cubretodo)* smock, overall; *(MED, TEC etc)* lab(oratory) coat

batalla [ba'taʎa] *nf* battle; **de ~** *(fig)* for everyday use

batallar [bata'ʎar] *vi* to fight

batallón [bata'ʎon] *nm* battalion

batata [ba'tata] *nf* sweet potato

batería [bate'ria] *nf* battery; *(MUS)* drums; **~ de cocina** kitchen utensils

batido, a [ba'tiðo, a] *adj (camino)* beaten, well-trodden ♦ *nm (CULIN)*: **~ (de leche)** milk shake

batidora [bati'ðora] *nf* beater, mixer; **~ eléctrica** food mixer, blender

batir [ba'tir] *vt* to beat, strike; *(vencer)* to beat, defeat; *(revolver)* to beat, mix; **~se** *vr* to fight; **~ palmas** to clap, applaud

batuta [ba'tuta] *nf* baton; **llevar la ~** *(fig)* to be the boss, be in charge

baúl [ba'ul] *nm* trunk; *(AUTO)* boot *(BRIT)*, trunk *(US)*

bautismo [bau'tismo] *nm* baptism, christening

bautizar [bauti'θar] *vt* to baptize, christen; *(fam: diluir)* to water down; **bautizo** *nm* baptism, christening

baya ['baja] *nf* berry

bayeta [ba'jeta] *nf* floorcloth

baza ['baθa] *nf* trick; **meter ~** to butt in

bazar [ba'θar] *nm* bazaar

bazofia [ba'θofja] *nf* trash

BCE *nm abr (= Banco Central Europeo)* ECB

beato, a [be'ato, a] *adj* blessed; *(piadoso)* pious

bebé [be'ße] *(pl ~s)* *nm* baby

bebedor, a [beße'ðor, a] *adj* hard-drinking

beber [be'ßer] *vt, vi* to drink

bebida [be'ßiða] *nf* drink; **bebido, a** *adj* drunk

beca ['beka] *nf* grant, scholarship

becario, a [be'karjo, a] *nm/f* scholarship holder, grant holder

bedel [be'ðel] *nm (ESCOL)* janitor; *(UNIV)* porter

béisbol ['beisßol] *nm (DEPORTE)* baseball

belén [be'len] *nm (de navidad)* nativity scene, crib; **B~** Bethlehem

belga ['belxa] *adj, nm/f* Belgian

Bélgica ['belxika] *nf* Belgium

bélico, a ['beliko, a] *adj (actitud)* warlike; **belicoso, a** *adj (guerrero)* warlike; *(agresivo)* aggressive, bellicose

beligerante [belixe'rante] *adj* belligerent

belleza [be'ʎeθa] *nf* beauty

bello, a ['beʎo, a] *adj* beautiful, lovely; **Bellas Artes** Fine Art

bellota [be'ʎota] *nf* acorn

bemol [be'mol] *nm (MUS)* flat; **esto tiene ~es** *(fam)* this is a tough one

bencina [ben'θina] *nf (AM)* petrol *(BRIT)*, gasoline *(US)*

bendecir [bende'θir] *vt* to bless

bendición [bendi'θjon] *nf* blessing

bendito, a [ben'dito, a] *pp de* **bendecir** ♦ *adj* holy; *(afortunado)* lucky; *(feliz)* happy; *(sencillo)* simple ♦ *nm/f* simple soul

beneficencia [benefi'θenθja] *nf* charity
beneficiar [benefi'θjar] *vt* to benefit, be
of benefit to; **~se** *vr* to benefit, profit;
~io, a *nm/f* beneficiary
beneficio [bene'fiθjo] *nm* (*bien*) benefit,
advantage; (*ganancia*) profit, gain; **~so,
a** *adj* beneficial
benéfico, a [be'nefiko, a] *adj*
charitable
beneplácito [bene'plaθito] *nm* approval,
consent
benevolencia [beneβo'lenθja] *nf*
benevolence, kindness; **benévolo, a** *adj*
benevolent, kind
benigno, a [be'niɣno, a] *adj* kind; (*suave*)
mild; (*MED: tumor*) benign, non-malignant
berberecho [berβe'retʃo] *nm* (*ZOOL,
CULIN*) cockle
berenjena [beren'xena] *nf* aubergine
(*BRIT*), eggplant (*US*)
Berlín [ber'lin] *n* Berlin; **berlinés, esa**
adj of o from Berlin ♦ *nm/f* Berliner
bermudas [ber'muðas] *nfpl* Bermuda
shorts
berrear [berre'ar] *vi* to bellow, low
berrido [be'rriðo] *nm* bellow(ing)
berrinche [be'rrintʃe] (*fam*) *nm* temper,
tantrum
berro ['berro] *nm* watercress
berza ['berθa] *nf* cabbage
besamel [besa'mel] *nf* (*CULIN*) white
sauce, bechamel sauce
besar [be'sar] *vt* to kiss; (*fig: tocar*) to
graze; **~se** *vr* to kiss (one another); **beso**
nm kiss
bestia ['bestja] *nf* beast, animal; (*fig*) idiot;
~ de carga beast of burden
bestial [bes'tjal] *adj* bestial; (*fam*) terrific;
~idad *nf* bestiality; (*fam*) stupidity
besugo [be'suɣo] *nm* sea bream; (*fam*)
idiot
besuquear [besuke'ar] *vt* to cover with
kisses; **~se** *vr* to kiss and cuddle
betún [be'tun] *nm* shoe polish; (*QUÍM*)
bitumen
biberón [biβe'ron] *nm* feeding bottle
Biblia ['biβlja] *nf* Bible

bibliografía [biβljoɣra'fia] *nf* bibliography
biblioteca [biβljo'teka] *nf* library; (*mueble*)
bookshelves; **~ de consulta** reference
library; **~rio, a** *nm/f* librarian
bicarbonato [bikarβo'nato] *nm*
bicarbonate
bicho ['bitʃo] *nm* (*animal*) small animal;
(*sabandija*) bug, insect; (*TAUR*) bull
bici ['biθi] (*fam*) *nf* bike
bicicleta [biθi'kleta] *nf* bicycle, cycle; **ir en
~** to cycle
bidé [bi'ðe] (*pl* **~s**) *nm* bidet
bidón [bi'ðon] *nm* (*de aceite*) drum; (*de
gasolina*) can

PALABRA CLAVE
---

bien [bjen] *nm* 1 (*bienestar*) good; **te lo
digo por tu ~** I'm telling you for your
own good; **el ~ y el mal** good and evil
2 (*posesión*): **~es** goods; **~es de
consumo** consumer goods; **~es
inmuebles** *o* **raíces/~es muebles** real
estate *sg*/personal property *sg*
♦ *adv* 1 (*de manera satisfactoria, correcta
etc*) well; **trabaja/come ~** she works/eats
well; **contestó ~** he answered correctly;
me siento ~ I feel fine; **no me siento ~** I
don't feel very well; **se está ~ aquí** it's
nice here
2 (*frases*): **hiciste ~ en llamarme** you
were right to call me
3 (*valor intensivo*) very; **un cuarto ~
caliente** a nice warm room; **~ se ve que
...** it's quite clear that ...
4: **estar ~: estoy muy ~ aquí** I feel very
happy here; **está ~ que vengan** it's all
right for them to come; **¡está ~! lo haré**
oh all right, I'll do it
5 (*de buena gana*): **yo ~ que iría pero ...**
I'd gladly go but ...
♦ *excl*: **¡~!** (*aprobación*) O.K.!; **¡muy ~!**
well done!
♦ *adj inv* (*matiz despectivo*): **niño ~** rich
kid; **gente ~** posh people
♦ *conj* 1: **~ ... ~: ~ en coche ~ en tren**
either by car or by train
2: **no ~** (*esp AM*): **no ~ llegue te llamaré**

as soon as I arrive I'll call you
3: **si** ~ even though; *ver tb* **más**

ienal [bje'nal] *adj* biennial

enaventurado, a [bjenaßentu'raðo, a] *adj (feliz)* happy, fortunate

ienestar [bjenes'tar] *nm* well-being, welfare

enhechor, a [bjene'tʃor, a] *adj* beneficent ♦ *nm/f* benefactor/benefactress

envenida [bjembe'niða] *nf* welcome; **dar la ~ a uno** to welcome sb

ienvenido [bjembe'niðo] *excl* welcome!

ife ['bife] (AM) *nm* steak

ifurcación [bifurka'θjon] *nf* fork

ifurcarse [bifur'karse] *vr (camino, carretera, río)* to fork

igamia [bi'vamja] *nf* bigamy; **bígamo, a** *adj* bigamous ♦ *nm/f* bigamist

igote [bi'vote] *nm* moustache; **bigotudo, a** *adj* with a big moustache

ikini [bi'kini] *nm* bikini; (CULIN) toasted ham and cheese sandwich

ilbaíno, a [bilßa'ino, a] *adj* from *o* of Bilbao

ilingüe [bi'lingwe] *adj* bilingual

illar [bi'ʎar] *nm* billiards *sg*; *(lugar)* billiard hall; *(mini-casino)* amusement arcade; **~ americano** pool

illete [bi'ʎete] *nm* ticket; *(de banco)* (bank)note (BRIT), bill (US); *(carta)* note; **~ sencillo, ~ de ida solamente** single (BRIT) *o* one-way (US) ticket; **~ de ida y vuelta** return (BRIT) *o* round-trip (US) ticket; **~ de 20 libras** £20 note

illetera [biʎe'tera] *nf* wallet

illetero [biʎe'tero] *nm* = **billetera**

illón [bi'ʎon] *nm* billion

imensual [bimen'swal] *adj* twice monthly

imotor [bimo'tor] *adj* twin-engined ♦ *nm* twin-engined plane

iodegradable [bioðevra'ðaßle] *adj* biodegradable

iografía [bjovra'fia] *nf* biography; **biógrafo, a** *nm/f* biographer

biología [bjolo'xia] *nf* biology; **biológico, a** *adj* biological; *(cultivo, producto)* organic; **biólogo, a** *nm/f* biologist

biombo ['bjombo] *nm* (folding) screen

biopsia [bi'opsja] *nf* biopsy

biquini [bi'kini] *nm* bikini

birlar [bir'lar] *(fam) vt* to pinch

Birmania [bir'manja] *nf* Burma

birria ['birrja] *nf*: **ser una ~** *(película, libro)* to be rubbish

bis [bis] *excl* encore! ♦ *adv*: **viven en el 27 ~** they live at 27a

bisabuelo, a [bisa'ßwelo, a] *nm/f* great-grandfather/mother

bisagra [bi'saɣra] *nf* hinge

bisiesto [bi'sjesto] *adj*: **año ~** leap year

bisnieto, a [bis'njeto, a] *nm/f* great-grandson/daughter

bisonte [bi'sonte] *nm* bison

bisté [bis'te] *nm* = **bistec**

bistec [bis'tek] *nm* steak

bisturí [bistu'ri] *nm* scalpel

bisutería [bisute'ria] *nf* imitation *o* costume jewellery

bit [bit] *nm* (INFORM) bit

bizco, a ['biθko, a] *adj* cross-eyed

bizcocho [biθ'kotʃo] *nm* (CULIN) sponge cake

bizquear [biθke'ar] *vi* to squint

blanca ['blanka] *nf* (MUS) minim; **estar sin ~** to be broke; *ver tb* **blanco**

blanco, a ['blanko, a] *adj* white ♦ *nm/f* white man/woman, white ♦ *nm (color)* white; *(en texto)* blank; *(MIL, fig)* target; **en ~** blank; **noche en ~** sleepless night

blancura [blan'kura] *nf* whiteness

blandir [blan'dir] *vt* to brandish

blando, a ['blando, a] *adj* soft; *(tierno)* tender, gentle; *(carácter)* mild; *(fam)* cowardly; **blandura** *nf* softness; tenderness; mildness

blanquear [blanke'ar] *vt* to whiten; *(fachada)* to whitewash; *(paño)* to bleach ♦ *vi* to turn white; **blanquecino, a** *adj* whitish

blasfemar [blasfe'mar] *vi* to blaspheme, curse; **blasfemia** *nf* blasphemy

blasón [bla'son] *nm* coat of arms

bledo ['bleðo] *nm*: **me importa un ~** I couldn't care less

blindado, a [blin'daðo, a] *adj* (*MIL*) armour-plated; (*antibala*) bullet-proof; **coche** (*ESP*) *o* **carro** (*AM*) ~ armoured car

blindaje [blin'daxe] *nm* armour, armour-plating

bloc [blok] (*pl* ~**s**) *nm* writing pad

bloque ['bloke] *nm* block; (*POL*) bloc; ~ **de cilindros** cylinder block

bloquear [bloke'ar] *vt* to blockade; **bloqueo** *nm* blockade; (*COM*) freezing, blocking

blusa ['blusa] *nf* blouse

boato [bo'ato] *nm* show, ostentation

bobada [bo'βaða] *nf* foolish action; foolish statement; **decir ~s** to talk nonsense

bobería [boβe'ria] *nf* = **bobada**

bobina [bo'βina] *nf* (*TEC*) bobbin; (*FOTO*) spool; (*ELEC*) coil

bobo, a ['boβo, a] *adj* (*tonto*) daft, silly; (*cándido*) naïve ♦ *nm/f* fool, idiot ♦ *nm* (*TEATRO*) clown, funny man

boca ['boka] *nf* mouth; (*de crustáceo*) pincer; (*de cañón*) muzzle; (*entrada*) mouth, entrance; ~**s** *nfpl* (*de río*) mouth *sg*; ~ **abajo/arriba** face down/up; **se me hace agua la ~** my mouth is watering

bocacalle [boka'kaʎe] *nf* (*entrance to a*) street; **la primera ~** the first turning *o* street

bocadillo [boka'ðiʎo] *nm* sandwich

bocado [bo'kaðo] *nm* mouthful, bite; (*de caballo*) bridle; ~ **de Adán** Adam's apple

bocajarro [boka'xarro]: **a ~** *adv* (*disparar, preguntar*) point-blank

bocanada [boka'naða] *nf* (*de vino*) mouthful, swallow; (*de aire*) gust, puff

bocata [bo'kata] (*fam*) *nm* sandwich

bocazas [bo'kaθas] (*fam*) *nm inv* bigmouth

boceto [bo'θeto] *nm* sketch, outline

bochorno [bo'tʃorno] *nm* (*vergüenza*) embarrassment; (*color*): **hace ~** it's very muggy; ~**so, a** *adj* muggy; embarrassing

bocina [bo'θina] *nf* (*MUS*) trumpet; (*AUTO*) horn; (*para hablar*) megaphone

boda ['boða] *nf* (*tb*: ~**s**) wedding, marriage; (*fiesta*) wedding reception; ~**s de plata/de oro** silver/golden wedding

bodega [bo'ðeɣa] *nf* (*de vino*) (wine) cellar; (*depósito*) storeroom; (*de barco*) hold

bodegón [boðe'ɣon] *nm* (*ARTE*) still life

bofe ['bofe] *nm* (*tb*: ~**s**: **de res**) lights

bofetada [bofe'taða] *nf* slap (in the face)

bofetón [bofe'ton] *nm* = **bofetada**

boga ['boɣa] *nf*: **en ~** (*fig*) in vogue

bogar [bo'ɣar] *vi* (*remar*) to row; (*navegar*) to sail

bogavante [boɣa'βante] *nm* lobster

Bogotá [boɣo'ta] *n* Bogotá

bohemio, a [bo'emjo, a] *adj*, *nm/f* Bohemian

boicot [boi'kot] (*pl* ~**s**) *nm* boycott; ~**ear** *vt* to boycott; ~**eo** *nm* boycott

boina ['boina] *nf* beret

bola ['bola] *nf* ball; (*canica*) marble; (*NAIPES*) (grand) slam; (*betún*) shoe polish; (*mentira*) tale, story; ~**s** (*AM*) *nfpl* bolas *sg*; ~ **de billar** billiard ball; ~ **de nieve** snowball

bolchevique [boltʃe'βike] *adj*, *nm/f* Bolshevik

boleadoras [bolea'ðoras] (*AM*) *nfpl* bolas *sg*

bolera [bo'lera] *nf* skittle *o* bowling alley

boleta [bo'leta] (*AM*) *nf* (*billete*) ticket; (*permiso*) pass, permit

boletería [bolete'ria] (*AM*) *nf* ticket office

boletín [bole'tin] *nm* bulletin; (*periódico*) journal, review; ~ **de noticias** news bulletin

boleto [bo'leto] *nm* ticket

boli ['boli] (*fam*) *nm* Biro ®, pen

bolígrafo [bo'liɣrafo] *nm* ball-point pen, Biro ®

bolívar [bo'liβar] *nm* monetary unit of Venezuela

Bolivia [bo'liβja] *nf* Bolivia; **boliviano, a** *adj*, *nm/f* Bolivian

bollería [boʎe'ria] *nf* cakes *pl* and pastries *pl*

bollo ['boʎo] nm (pan) roll; (bulto) bump, lump; (abolladura) dent

bolo ['bolo] nm skittle; (píldora) (large) pill; **(juego de) ~s** nmpl skittles sg

bolsa ['bolsa] nf bag; (AM) pocket; (ANAT) cavity, sac; (COM) stock exchange; (MINERÍA) pocket; **de ~** pocket cpd; **~ de agua caliente** hot water bottle; **~ de aire** air pocket; **~ de papel** paper bag; **~ de plástico** plastic bag

bolsillo [bol'siʎo] nm pocket; (cartera) purse; **de ~** pocket(-size)

bolsista [bol'sista] nm/f stockbroker

bolso ['bolso] nm (bolsa) bag; (de mujer) handbag

bomba ['bomba] nf (MIL) bomb; (TEC) pump ♦ (fam) adj: **noticia ~** bombshell ♦ (fam) adv: **pasarlo ~** to have a great time; **~ atómica/de humo/de efecto retardado** atomic/smoke/time bomb

bombardear [bombarðe'ar] vt to bombard; (MIL) to bomb; **bombardeo** nm bombardment; bombing

bombardero [bombar'ðero] nm bomber

bombear [bombe'ar] vt (agua) to pump (out o up); **~se** vr to warp

bombero [bom'bero] nm fireman

bombilla [bom'biʎa] (ESP) nf (light) bulb

bombín [bom'bin] nm bowler hat

bombo ['bombo] nm (MUS) bass drum; (TEC) drum

bombón [bom'bon] nm chocolate

bombona [bom'bona] nf (de butano, oxígeno) cylinder

bonachón, ona [bona'tʃon, ona] adj good-natured, easy-going

bonanza [bo'nanθa] nf (NAUT) fair weather; (fig) bonanza; (MINERÍA) rich pocket o vein

bondad [bon'dað] nf goodness, kindness; **tenga la ~ de** (please) be good enough to; **~oso, a** adj good, kind

bonificación [bonifika'θjon] nf bonus

bonito, a [bo'nito, a] adj pretty; (agradable) nice ♦ nm (atún) tuna (fish)

bono ['bono] nm voucher; (FIN) bond

bonobús [bono'βus] (ESP) nm bus pass

bonoloto [bono'loto] nf state-run weekly lottery

boquerón [boke'ron] nm (pez) (kind of) anchovy; (agujero) large hole

boquete [bo'kete] nm gap, hole

boquiabierto, a [bokia'βjerto, a] adj: **quedar ~** to be amazed o flabbergasted

boquilla [bo'kiʎa] nf (para riego) nozzle; (para cigarro) cigarette holder; (MUS) mouthpiece

borbotón [borβo'ton] nm: **salir a borbotones** to gush out

borda ['borða] nf (NAUT) (ship's) rail; **tirar algo/caerse por la ~** to throw sth/fall overboard

bordado [bor'ðaðo] nm embroidery

bordar [bor'ðar] vt to embroider

borde ['borðe] nm edge, border; (de camino etc) side; (en la costura) hem; **al ~ de** (fig) on the verge o brink of; **ser ~** (ESP: fam) to be rude; **~ar** vt to border

bordillo [bor'ðiʎo] nm kerb (BRIT), curb (US)

bordo ['borðo] nm (NAUT) side; **a ~** on board

borinqueño, a [borin'kenjo, a] adj, nm/f Puerto Rican

borla ['borla] nf (adorno) tassel

borrachera [borra'tʃera] nf (ebriedad) drunkenness; (orgía) spree, binge

borracho, a [bo'rratʃo, a] adj drunk ♦ nm/f (habitual) drunkard, drunk; (temporal) drunk, drunk man/woman

borrador [borra'ðor] nm (escritura) first draft, rough sketch; (goma) rubber (BRIT), eraser

borrar [bo'rrar] vt to erase, rub out

borrasca [bo'rraska] nf storm

borrico, a [bo'rriko, a] nm/f donkey/she-donkey; (fig) stupid man/woman

borrón [bo'rron] nm (mancha) stain

borroso, a [bo'rroso, a] adj vague, unclear; (escritura) illegible

bosque ['boske] nm wood; (grande) forest

bosquejar [boske'xar] vt to sketch; **bosquejo** nm sketch

bostezar [boste'θar] vi to yawn; **bostezo**

nm yawn

bota ['bota] *nf* (*calzado*) boot; (*para vino*) leather wine bottle; **~s de agua, ~s de goma** Wellingtons

botánica [bo'tanika] *nf* (*ciencia*) botany; *ver tb* **botánico**

botánico, a [bo'taniko, a] *adj* botanical ♦ *nm/f* botanist

botar [bo'tar] *vt* to throw, hurl; (*NAUT*) to launch; (*AM*) to throw out ♦ *vi* to bounce

bote ['bote] *nm* (*salto*) bounce; (*golpe*) thrust; (*vasija*) tin, can; (*embarcación*) boat; **de ~ en ~** packed, jammed full; **~ de la basura** (*AM*) dustbin (*BRIT*), trashcan (*US*); **~ salvavidas** lifeboat

botella [bo'teʎa] *nf* bottle; **botellín** *nm* small bottle

botica [bo'tika] *nf* chemist's (shop) (*BRIT*), pharmacy; **~rio, a** *nm/f* chemist (*BRIT*), pharmacist

botijo [bo'tixo] *nm* (earthenware) jug

botín [bo'tin] *nm* (*calzado*) half boot; (*polaina*) spat; (*MIL*) booty

botiquín [boti'kin] *nm* (*armario*) medicine cabinet; (*portátil*) first-aid kit

botón [bo'ton] *nm* button; (*BOT*) bud; **~ de oro** buttercup

botones [bo'tones] *nm inv* bellboy (*BRIT*), bellhop (*US*)

bóveda ['boβeða] *nf* (*ARQ*) vault

boxeador [boksea'ðor] *nm* boxer

boxear [bokse'ar] *vi* to box

boxeo [bok'seo] *nm* boxing

boya ['boja] *nf* (*NAUT*) buoy; (*de caña*) float

boyante [bo'jante] *adj* prosperous

bozal [bo'θal] *nm* (*de caballo*) halter; (*de perro*) muzzle

bracear [braθe'ar] *vi* (*agitar los brazos*) to wave one's arms

bracero [bra'θero] *nm* labourer; (*en el campo*) farmhand

bragas ['braɣas] *nfpl* (*de mujer*) panties, knickers (*BRIT*)

bragueta [bra'ɣeta] *nf* fly, flies *pl*

braille [breil] *nm* braille

bramar [bra'mar] *vi* to bellow, roar;

bramido *nm* bellow, roar

brasa ['brasa] *nf* live *o* hot coal

brasero [bra'sero] *nm* brazier

Brasil [bra'sil] *nm*: **(el) ~** Brazil; **brasileño, a** *adj, nm/f* Brazilian

bravata [bra'βata] *nf* boast

braveza [bra'βeθa] *nf* (*valor*) bravery; (*ferocidad*) ferocity

bravío, a [bra'βio, a] *adj* wild; (*feroz*) fierce

bravo, a ['braβo, a] *adj* (*valiente*) brave; (*feroz*) ferocious; (*salvaje*) wild; (*mar etc*) rough, stormy ♦ *excl* bravo!; **bravura** *nf* bravery; ferocity

braza ['braθa] *nf* fathom; **nadar a la ~** to swim (the) breast-stroke

brazada [bra'θaða] *nf* stroke

brazado [bra'θaðo] *nm* armful

brazalete [braθa'lete] *nm* (*pulsera*) bracelet; (*banda*) armband

brazo ['braθo] *nm* arm; (*ZOOL*) foreleg; (*BOT*) limb, branch; **luchar a ~ partido** to fight hand-to-hand; **ir cogidos del ~** to walk arm in arm

brea ['brea] *nf* pitch, tar

brebaje [bre'βaxe] *nm* potion

brecha ['bretʃa] *nf* (*hoyo, vacío*) gap, opening; (*MIL, fig*) breach

brega ['breɣa] *nf* (*lucha*) struggle; (*trabajo*) hard work

breva ['breβa] *nf* early fig

breve ['breβe] *adj* short, brief ♦ *nf* (*MUS*) breve; **~dad** *nf* brevity, shortness

brezo ['breθo] *nm* heather

bribón, ona [bri'βon, ona] *adj* idle, lazy ♦ *nm/f* (*pícaro*) rascal, rogue

bricolaje [briko'laxe] *nm* do-it-yourself, DIY

brida ['briða] *nf* bridle, rein; (*TEC*) clamp; **a toda ~** at top speed

bridge [britʃ] *nm* bridge

brigada [bri'ɣaða] *nf* (*unidad*) brigade; (*trabajadores*) squad, gang ♦ *nm* ≈ staff-sergeant, sergeant-major

brillante [bri'ʎante] *adj* brilliant ♦ *nm* diamond

brillar [bri'ʎar] *vi* (*tb fig*) to shine; (*joyas*)

~ to sparkle

illo ['briʎo] nm shine; (brillantez) brilliance; (fig) splendour; **sacar ~ a** to polish

incar [brin'kar] vi to skip about, hop about, jump about; **está que brinca** he's hopping mad

inco ['brinko] nm jump, leap

indar [brin'dar] vi: **~ o por** to drink (a toast) to ♦ vt to offer, present

indis ['brindis] nm inv toast

ío ['brio] nm spirit, dash; **brioso, a** adj spirited, dashing

isa ['brisa] nf breeze

itánico, a [bri'taniko, a] adj British ♦ nm/f Briton, British person

izna ['briθna] nf (de hierba, paja) blade; (de tabaco) leaf

oca ['broka] nf (TEC) drill, bit

ocal [bro'kal] nm rim

ocha ['brotʃa] nf (large) paintbrush; **~ de afeitar** shaving brush

oche ['brotʃe] nm brooch

oma ['broma] nf joke; **en ~** in fun, as a joke; **~ pesada** practical joke; **bromear** vi to joke

omista [bro'mista] adj fond of joking ♦ nm/f joker, wag

onca ['bronka] nf row; **echar una ~ a uno** to tick sb off

once ['bronθe] nm bronze; **~ado, a** adj bronze; (por el sol) tanned ♦ nm (sun)tan; (TEC) bronzing

onceador [bronθea'ðor] nm suntan lotion

oncearse [bronθe'arse] vr to get a suntan

onco, a ['bronko, a] adj (manera) rude, surly; (voz) harsh

onquio ['bronkjo] nm (ANAT) bronchial tube

onquitis [bron'kitis] nf inv bronchitis

otar [bro'tar] vi (BOT) to sprout; (aguas) to gush (forth); (MED) to break out

ote ['brote] nm (BOT) shoot; (MED, fig) outbreak

ruces ['bruθes]: **de ~** adv: **caer o dar de**

~ to fall headlong, fall flat

bruja ['bruxa] nf witch; **brujería** nf witchcraft

brujo ['bruxo] nm wizard, magician

brújula ['bruxula] nf compass

bruma ['bruma] nf mist; **brumoso, a** adj misty

bruñir [bru'ɲir] vt to polish

brusco, a ['brusko, a] adj (súbito) sudden; (áspero) brusque

Bruselas [bru'selas] n Brussels

brutal [bru'tal] adj brutal

brutalidad [brutali'ðað] nf brutality

bruto, a ['bruto, a] adj (idiota) stupid; (bestial) brutish; (peso) gross; **en ~** raw, unworked

Bs.As. abr (= Buenos Aires) B.A.

bucal [bu'kal] adj oral; **por vía ~** orally

bucear [buθe'ar] vi to dive ♦ vt to explore; **buceo** nm diving

bucle ['bukle] nm curl

budismo [bu'ðismo] nm Buddhism

buen [bwen] adj V **bueno**

buenamente [bwena'mente] adv (fácilmente) easily; (voluntariamente) willingly

buenaventura [bwenaβen'tura] nf (suerte) good luck; (adivinación) fortune

---

PALABRA CLAVE

---

bueno, a ['bweno, a] adj (antes de nmsg: **buen**) 1 (excelente etc) good; **es un libro ~, es un buen libro** it's a good book; **hace ~, hace buen tiempo** the weather is fine, it is fine; **el ~ de Paco** good old Paco; **fue muy ~ conmigo** he was very nice o kind to me

2 (apropiado): **ser ~ para** to be good for; **creo que vamos por buen camino** I think we're on the right track

3 (irónico): **le di un buen rapapolvo** I gave him a good o real ticking off; **¡buen conductor estás hecho!** some o a fine driver you are!; **¡estaría ~ que ...!** a fine thing it would be if ...!

4 (atractivo, sabroso): **está ~ este bizcocho** this sponge is delicious;

Carmen está muy buena Carmen is gorgeous
5 (*saludos*): **¡buen día!, ¡~s días!** (good) morning!; **¡buenas (tardes)!** (good) afternoon!; (*más tarde*): **(good) evening!; ¡buenas noches!** good night!
6 (*otras locuciones*): **estar de buenas** to be in a good mood; **por las buenas o por las malas** by hook or by crook; **de buenas a primeras** all of a sudden ♦ *excl*: **¡~!** all right!; **~, ¿y qué?** well, so what?

Buenos Aires *nm* Buenos Aires
buey [bwei] *nm* ox
búfalo ['bufalo] *nm* buffalo
bufanda [bu'fanda] *nf* scarf
bufar [bu'far] *vi* to snort
bufete [bu'fete] *nm* (*despacho de abogado*) lawyer's office
buffer ['bufer] *nm* (*INFORM*) buffer
bufón [bu'fon] *nm* clown
buhardilla [buar'ðiʎa] *nf* attic
búho ['buo] *nm* owl; (*fig*) hermit, recluse
buhonero [buo'nero] *nm* pedlar
buitre ['bwitre] *nm* vulture
bujía [bu'xia] *nf* (*vela*) candle; (*ELEC*) candle (power); (*AUTO*) spark plug
bula ['bula] *nf* (*papal*) bull
bulbo ['bulßo] *nm* bulb
bulevar [bule'ßar] *nm* boulevard
Bulgaria [bul'xarja] *nf* Bulgaria; **búlgaro, a** *adj*, *nm/f* Bulgarian
bulla ['buʎa] *nf* (*ruido*) uproar; (*de gente*) crowd
bullicio [bu'ʎiθjo] *nm* (*ruido*) uproar; (*movimiento*) bustle
bullir [bu'ʎir] *vi* (*hervir*) to boil; (*burbujear*) to bubble
bulto ['bulto] *nm* (*paquete*) package; (*fardo*) bundle; (*tamaño*) size, bulkiness; (*MED*) swelling, lump; (*silueta*) vague shape
buñuelo [bu'ɲwelo] *nm* ≈ doughnut (*BRIT*), ≈ donut (*US*); (*fruta de sartén*) fritter
BUP [bup] *nm abr* (*ESP*: = *Bachillerato*

Unificado Polivalente) *secondary education and leaving certificate for 14–17 age group*
buque ['buke] *nm* ship, vessel
burbuja [bur'ßuxa] *nf* bubble; **burbujear** *vi* to bubble
burdel [bur'ðel] *nm* brothel
burdo, a ['burðo, a] *adj* coarse, rough
burgués, esa [bur'ɣes, esa] *adj* middle-class, bourgeois; **burguesía** *nf* middle class, bourgeoisie
burla ['burla] *nf* (*mofa*) gibe; (*broma*) joke; (*engaño*) trick
burladero [burla'ðero] *nm* (bullfighter's) refuge
burlar [bur'lar] *vt* (*engañar*) to deceive ♦ *vi* to joke; **~se** *vr* to joke; **~se de** to make fun of
burlesco, a [bur'lesko, a] *adj* burlesque
burlón, ona [bur'lon, ona] *adj* mocking
burocracia [buro'kraθja] *nf* civil service
burócrata [bu'rokrata] *nm/f* civil servant
burrada [bu'rraða] *nf*: **decir/soltar ~s** to talk nonsense; **hacer ~s** to act stupid; **una ~** (*mucho*) a (hell of a) lot
burro, a ['burro, a] *nm/f* donkey/she-donkey; (*fig*) ass, idiot
bursátil [bur'satil] *adj* stock-exchange *cpd*
bus [bus] *nm* bus
busca ['buska] *nf* search, hunt ♦ *nm* (*TEL*) bleeper; **en ~ de** in search of
buscar [bus'kar] *vt* to look for, search for, seek ♦ *vi* to look, search, seek; **se busca secretaria** secretary wanted
busque *etc vb ver* **buscar**
búsqueda ['buskeða] *nf* = **busca** *nf*
busto ['busto] *nm* (*ANAT*, *ARTE*) bust
butaca [bu'taka] *nf* armchair; (*de cine*, *teatro*) stall, seat
butano [bu'tano] *nm* butane (gas)
buzo ['buθo] *nm* diver
buzón [bu'θon] *nm* (*en puerta*) letter box; (*en la calle*) pillar box

C, c

abr (= *centígrado*) C; (= *compañía*) Co.

abr (= *capítulo*) ch.

abr (= *calle*) St

abr (= *corriente alterna*) AC

al [ka'βal] *adj* (*exacto*) exact; (*correcto*) ght, proper; (*acabado*) finished, omplete; **~es** *nmpl*: **estar en sus ~es** o be in one's right mind

alas ['kaβalas] *nfpl*: **hacer ~** to guess

algar [kaβal'γar] *vt, vi* to ride

algata [kaβal'vata] *nf* procession

alla [ka'βaʎa] *nf* mackerel

alleresco, a [kaβaʎe'resko, a] *adj* oble, chivalrous

allería [kaβaʎe'ria] *nf* mount; (*MIL*) avalry

alleriza [kaβaʎe'riθa] *nf* stable; **abalerizo** *nm* groom, stableman

allero [kaβa'ʎero] *nm* gentleman; (*de orden de caballería*) knight; (*trato irecto*) sir

allerosidad [kaβaʎerosi'ðað] *nf* nivalry

allete [kaβa'ʎete] *nm* (*ARTE*) easel; rEC) trestle

allito [kaβa'ʎito] *nm* (*caballo pequeño*) mall horse, pony; **~s** *nmpl* (*en verbena*) oundabout, merry-go-round

allo [ka'βaʎo] *nm* horse; (*AJEDREZ*) night; (*NAIPES*) queen; **ir en ~** to ride; **~ e vapor** *o* **de fuerza** horsepower; **~ de arreras** racehorse

aña [ka'βaɲa] *nf* (*casita*) hut, cabin

aré [kaβa're] (*pl* **~s**) *nm* cabaret

aret [kaβa're] (*pl* **~s**) *nm* cabaret

ecear [kaβeθe'ar] *vt, vi* to nod

ecera [kaβe'θera] *nf* head; (*IMPRENTA*) eadline

ecilla [kaβe'θiʎa] *nm* ringleader

ellera [kaβe'ʎera] *nf* (head of) hair; (*de ometa*) tail

ello [ka'βeʎo] *nm* (*tb*: **~s**) hair

er [ka'βer] *vi* (*entrar*) to fit, go; **caben**

3 más there's room for 3 more

cabestrillo [kaβes'triʎo] *nm* sling

cabestro [ka'βestro] *nm* halter

cabeza [ka'βeθa] *nf* head; (*POL*) chief, leader; **~ rapada** skinhead; **~ da** *nf* (*golpe*) butt; **dar ~das** to nod off; **cabezón, ona** *adj* (*vino*) heady; (*fam: persona*) pig-headed

cabida [ka'βiða] *nf* space

cabildo [ka'βildo] *nm* (*de iglesia*) chapter; (*POL*) town council

cabina [ka'βina] *nf* cabin; (*de camión*) cab; **~ telefónica** telephone box (*BRIT*) *o* booth

cabizbajo, a [kaβiθ'βaxo, a] *adj* crestfallen, dejected

cable ['kaβle] *nm* cable

cabo ['kaβo] *nm* (*de objeto*) end, extremity; (*MIL*) corporal; (*NAUT*) rope, cable; (*GEO*) cape; **al ~ de 3 días** after 3 days

cabra ['kaβra] *nf* goat

cabré *etc vb ver* **caber**

cabrear [kaβre'ar] (*fam*) *vt* to bug; **~se** *vr* (*enfadarse*) to fly off the handle

cabrío, a [ka'βrio, a] *adj* goatish; **macho ~** (he-)goat, billy goat

cabriola [ka'βrjola] *nf* caper

cabritilla [kaβri'tiʎa] *nf* kid, kidskin

cabrito [ka'βrito] *nm* kid

cabrón [ka'βron] *nm* cuckold; (*fam!*) bastard (*!*)

caca ['kaka] (*fam*) *nf* pooh

cacahuete [kaka'wete] (*ESP*) *nm* peanut

cacao [ka'kao] *nm* cocoa; (*BOT*) cacao

cacarear [kakare'ar] *vi* (*persona*) to boast; (*gallina*) to crow

cacería [kaθe'ria] *nf* hunt

cacerola [kaθe'rola] *nf* pan, saucepan

cachalote [katʃa'lote] *nm* (*ZOOL*) sperm whale

cacharro [ka'tʃarro] *nm* earthenware pot; **~s** *nmpl* pots and pans

cachear [katʃe'ar] *vt* to search, frisk

cachemir [katʃe'mir] *nm* cashmere

cacheo [ka'tʃeo] *nm* searching, frisking

cachete [ka'tʃete] *nm* (*ANAT*) cheek; (*bofetada*) slap (in the face)

cachiporra [katʃi'porra] nf truncheon

cachivache [katʃi'ßatʃe] nm (trasto) piece of junk; **~s** nmpl junk sg

cacho ['katʃo] nm (small) bit; (AM: cuerno) horn

cachondeo [katʃon'deo] (fam) nm farce, joke

cachondo, a [ka'tʃondo, a] adj (ZOOL) on heat; (fam: sexualmente) randy; (: gracioso) funny

cachorro, a [ka'tʃorro, a] nm/f (perro) pup, puppy; (león) cub

cacique [ka'ðike] nm chief, local ruler; (POL) local party boss; **caciquismo** nm system of control by the local boss

caco ['kako] nm pickpocket

cacto ['kakto] nm cactus

cactus ['kaktus] nm inv cactus

cada ['kaða] adj inv each; (antes de número) every; **~ día** each day, every day; **~ dos días** every other day; **~ uno/a** each one, every one; **~ vez más/menos** more and more/less and less; **uno de ~ diez** one out of every ten

cadalso [ka'ðalso] nm scaffold

cadáver [ka'ðaßer] nm (dead) body, corpse

cadena [ka'ðena] nf chain; (TV) channel; **trabajo en ~** assembly line work; **~ perpetua** (JUR) life imprisonment

cadencia [ka'ðenθja] nf rhythm

cadera [ka'ðera] nf hip

cadete [ka'ðete] nm cadet

caducar [kaðu'kar] vi to expire; **caduco, a** adj expired; (persona) very old

caer [ka'er] vi to fall (down); **~se** vr to fall (down); **me cae bien/mal** I get on well with him/I can't stand him; **~ en la cuenta** to realize; **su cumpleaños cae en viernes** her birthday falls on a Friday

café [ka'fe] (pl **~s**) nm (bebida, planta) coffee; (lugar) café ♦ adj (color) brown; **~ con leche** white coffee; **~ solo** black coffee

cafetera [kafe'tera] nf coffee pot

cafetería [kafete'ria] nf (gen) café

cafetero, a [kafe'tero, a] adj coffee cpd;

ser muy ~ to be a coffee addict

cagar [ka'var] (fam!) vt to bungle, mess u ♦ vi to have a shit (!)

caída [ka'iða] nf fall; (declive) slope; (disminución) fall, drop

caído, a [ka'iðo, a] adj drooping

caiga etc vb ver **caer**

caimán [kai'man] nm alligator

caja ['kaxa] nf box; (para reloj) case; (de ascensor) shaft; (COM) cashbox; (donde se hacen los pagos) cashdesk; (: en supermercado) checkout, till; **~ de ahorros** savings bank; **~ de cambios** gearbox; **~ fuerte, ~ de caudales** safe, strongbox

cajero, a [ka'xero, a] nm/f cashier; **~ automático** cash dispenser

cajetilla [kaxe'tiʎa] nf (de cigarrillos) packet

cajón [ka'xon] nm big box; (de mueble) drawer

cal [kal] nf lime

cala ['kala] nf (GEO) cove, inlet; (de barco) hold

calabacín [kalaßa'θin] nm (BOT) baby marrow; (: más pequeño) courgette (BRIT), zucchini (US)

calabaza [kala'ßaθa] nf (BOT) pumpkin

calabozo [kala'ßoθo] nm (cárcel) prison; (celda) cell

calada [ka'laða] nf (de cigarrillo) puff

calado, a [ka'laðo, a] adj (prenda) lace cpd ♦ nm (NAUT) draught

calamar [kala'mar] nm squid no pl

calambre [ka'lambre] nm (tb: **~s**) cramp

calamidad [kalami'ðað] nf calamity, disaster

calar [ka'lar] vt to soak, drench; (penetrar) to pierce, penetrate; (comprender) to see through; (vela) to lower; **~se** vr (AUTO) to stall; **~se las gafas** to stick one's glasses on

calavera [kala'ßera] nf skull

calcar [kal'kar] vt (reproducir) to trace; (imitar) to copy

calcetín [kalθe'tin] nm sock

calcinar [kalθi'nar] vt to burn, blacken

cio ['kalθjo] nm calcium

comanía [kalkoma'nia] nf transfer

culador, a [kalkula'ðor, a] adj *persona*) calculating

culadora [kalkula'ðora] nf calculator

cular [kalku'lar] vt (MAT) to calculate, ompute; ~ **que ...** to reckon that ...;

álculo nm

dear [kalde'ar] vt to warm (up), heat up)

dera [kal'dera] nf boiler

derilla [kalde'riʎa] nf (*moneda*) small hange

dero [kal'dero] nm small boiler

do ['kaldo] nm stock; (*consomé*) onsommé

efacción [kalefak'θjon] nf heating; ~ **entral** central heating

endario [kalen'darjo] nm calendar

entador [kalenta'ðor] nm heater

entamiento [kalenta'mjento] nm *DEPORTE*) warm-up

entar [kalen'tar] vt to heat (up); **~se** vr o heat up, warm up; (*fig: discusión etc*) o get heated

entura [kalen'tura] nf (MED) fever, high) temperature

ibrar [kali'βrar] vt to gauge, measure; **alibre** nm (*de cañón*) calibre, bore; *diámetro*) diameter; (*fig*) calibre

idad [kali'ðað] nf quality; **de ~** quality *pd*; **en ~ de** in the capacity of, as

ido, a ['kaliðo, a] adj hot; (*fig*) warm

iente [ka'ljente] vb ver **calentar** adj hot; (*fig*) fiery; (*disputa*) heated; *am: cachondo*) randy

ificación [kalifika'θjon] nf qualification; *de alumno*) grade, mark

ificar [kalifi'kar] vt to qualify; (*alumno*) o grade, mark; ~ **de** to describe as

ima [ka'lima] nf (*cerca del mar*) mist

iz ['kaliθ] nm chalice

iza [ka'liθa] nf limestone

izo, a [ka'liθo, a] adj lime *cpd*

llado, a [ka'ʎaðo, a] adj quiet

llar [ka'ʎar] vt (*asunto delicado*) to keep quiet about, say nothing about; (*persona*,

opinión) to silence ♦ vi to keep quiet, be silent; **~se** vr to keep quiet, be silent; **¡cállate!** be quiet!, shut up!

calle ['kaʎe] nf street; (DEPORTE) lane; ~ **arriba/abajo** up/down the street; ~ **de un solo sentido** one-way street

calleja [ka'ʎexa] nf alley, narrow street; **callejear** vi to wander (about) the streets; **callejero, a** adj street *cpd* ♦ nm street map; **callejón** nm alley, passage; **callejón sin salida** cul-de-sac; **callejuela** nf side-street, alley

callista [ka'ʎista] nm/f chiropodist

callo ['kaʎo] nm callus; (*en el pie*) corn; **~s** nmpl (CULIN) tripe *sg*

calma ['kalma] nf calm

calmante [kal'mante] nm sedative, tranquillizer

calmar [kal'mar] vt to calm, calm down ♦ vi (*tempestad*) to abate; (*mente etc*) to become calm

calmoso, a [kal'moso, a] adj calm, quiet

calor [ka'lor] nm heat; (*agradable*) warmth; **hace ~** it's hot; **tener ~** to be hot

caloría [kalo'ria] nf calorie

calumnia [ka'lumnja] nf calumny, slander; **calumnioso, a** adj slanderous

caluroso, a [kalu'roso, a] adj hot; (*sin exceso*) warm; (*fig*) enthusiastic

calva ['kalβa] nf bald patch; (*en bosque*) clearing

calvario [kal'βarjo] nm stations pl of the cross

calvicie [kal'βiθje] nf baldness

calvo, a ['kalβo, a] adj bald; (*terreno*) bare, barren; (*tejido*) threadbare

calza ['kalθa] nf wedge, chock

calzada [kal'θaða] nf roadway, highway

calzado, a [kal'θaðo, a] adj shod ♦ nm footwear

calzador [kalθa'ðor] nm shoehorn

calzar [kal'θar] vt (*zapatos etc*) to wear; (*un mueble*) to put a wedge under; **~se** vr: **~se los zapatos** to put on one's shoes; **¿qué (número) calza?** what size do you take?

calzón [kal'θon] nm (tb: **calzones** nmpl)

shorts; (*AM: de hombre*) (under)pants;
(: *de mujer*) panties
calzoncillos [kalθon'θiλos] *nmpl*
underpants
cama ['kama] *nf* bed; ~ **individual/de
matrimonio** single/double bed
camafeo [kama'feo] *nm* cameo
camaleón [kamale'on] *nm* chameleon
cámara ['kamara] *nf* chamber; (*habitación*)
room; (*sala*) hall; (*CINE*) cine camera;
(*fotográfica*) camera; ~ **de aire** inner tube;
~ **de comercio** chamber of commerce; ~
frigorífica cold-storage room
camarada [kama'raða] *nm* comrade,
companion
camarera [kama'rera] *nf* (*en restaurante*)
waitress; (*en casa, hotel*) maid
camarero [kama'rero] *nm* waiter
camarilla [kama'riλa] *nf* clique
camarón [kama'ron] *nm* shrimp
camarote [kama'rote] *nm* cabin
cambiable [kam'bjaßle] *adj* (*variable*)
changeable, variable; (*intercambiable*)
interchangeable
cambiante [kam'bjante] *adj* variable
cambiar [kam'bjar] *vt* to change; (*dinero*)
to exchange ♦ *vi* to change; ~**se** *vr*
(*mudarse*) to move; (*de ropa*) to change;
~ **de idea** to change one's mind; ~ **de
ropa** to change (one's clothes)
cambio ['kambjo] *nm* change; (*trueque*)
exchange; (*COM*) rate of exchange;
(*oficina*) bureau de change; (*dinero
menudo*) small change; **en** ~ on the other
hand; (*en lugar de*) instead; ~ **de divisas**
foreign exchange; ~ **de velocidades** gear
lever
camelar [kame'lar] *vt* to sweet-talk
camello [ka'meλo] *nm* camel; (*fam:
traficante*) pusher
camerino [kame'rino] *nm* dressing room
camilla [ka'miλa] *nf* (*MED*) stretcher
caminante [kami'nante] *nm/f* traveller
caminar [kami'nar] *vi* (*marchar*) to walk,
go ♦ *vt* (*recorrer*) to cover, travel
caminata [kami'nata] *nf* long walk; (*por el
campo*) hike

camino [ka'mino] *nm* way, road; (*sendero*)
track; **a medio** ~ halfway (there); **en el** ~
on the way, en route; ~ **de** on the way
to; ~ **particular** private road

Camino de Santiago

> *The **Camino de Santiago** is a
> medieval pilgrim route stretching from
> the Pyrenees to Santiago de Compostela in
> north-west Spain, where tradition has it
> the body of the Apostle James is buried.
> Nowadays it is a popular tourist route as
> well as a religious one.*

---

camión [ka'mjon] *nm* lorry (*BRIT*), truck
(*US*); ~ **cisterna** tanker; **camionero, a**
nm/f lorry *o* truck driver
camioneta [kamjo'neta] *nf* van, light
truck
camisa [ka'misa] *nf* shirt; (*BOT*) skin; ~ **de
fuerza** straitjacket; **camisería** *nf*
outfitter's (shop)
camiseta [kami'seta] *nf* (*prenda*) tee-shirt;
(: *ropa interior*) vest; (*de deportista*) top
camisón [kami'son] *nm* nightdress,
nightgown
camorra [ka'morra] *nf*: **buscar** ~ to look
for trouble
campamento [kampa'mento] *nm* camp
campana [kam'pana] *nf* bell; ~ **de cristal**
bell jar; ~**da** *nf* peal; ~**rio** *nm* belfry
campanilla [kampa'niλa] *nf* small bell
campaña [kam'paɲa] *nf* (*MIL, POL*)
campaign
campechano, a [kampe'tʃano, a] *adj*
(*franco*) open
campeón, ona [kampe'on, ona] *nm/f*
champion; **campeonato** *nm*
championship
campesino, a [kampe'sino, a] *adj*
country *cpd*, rural; (*gente*) peasant *cpd*
♦ *nm/f* countryman/woman; (*agricultor*)
farmer
campestre [kam'pestre] *adj* country *cpd*,
rural
camping ['kampin] (*pl* ~**s**) *nm* camping;
(*lugar*) campsite; **ir de** *o* **hacer** ~ to go

camping

campo ['kampo] nm (fuera de la ciudad) country, countryside; (AGR, ELEC) field; (de fútbol) pitch; (de golf) course; (MIL) camp; **~ de batalla** battlefield; **~ de deportes** sports ground, playing field

camposanto [kampo'santo] nm cemetery

camuflaje [kamu'flaxe] nm camouflage

cana ['kana] nf white o grey hair; **tener ~s** to be going grey

Canadá [kana'ða] nm Canada; **canadiense** adj, nm/f Canadian ♦ nf fur-lined jacket

canal [ka'nal] nm canal; (GEO) channel, strait; (de televisión) channel; (de tejado) gutter; **~ de Panamá** Panama Canal; **~izar** vt to channel

canalla [ka'naʎa] nf rabble, mob ♦ nm swine

canalón [kana'lon] nm (conducto vertical) drainpipe; (del tejado) gutter

canapé [kana'pe] (pl **~s**) nm sofa, settee; (CULIN) canapé

Canarias [ka'narjas] nfpl: **(las Islas) ~** the Canary Islands, the Canaries

canario, a [ka'narjo, a] adj, nm/f (native) of the Canary Isles ♦ nm (ZOOL) canary

canasta [ka'nasta] nf (round) basket; **canastilla** nf small basket; (de niño) layette

canasto [ka'nasto] nm large basket

cancela [kan'θela] nf gate

cancelación [kanθela'θjon] nf cancellation

cancelar [kanθe'lar] vt to cancel; (una deuda) to write off

cáncer ['kanθer] nm (MED) cancer; (ASTROLOGÍA): **C~** Cancer

cancha ['kantʃa] nf (de baloncesto, tenis etc) court; (de fútbol) pitch

canciller [kanθi'ʎer] nm chancellor

canción [kan'θjon] nf song; **~ de cuna** lullaby; **cancionero** nm song book

candado [kan'daðo] nm padlock

candente [kan'dente] adj red-hot; (fig: tema) burning

candidato, a [kandi'ðato, a] nm/f candidate

candidez [kandi'ðeθ] nf (sencillez) simplicity; (simpleza) naiveté; **cándido, a** adj simple; naive

candil [kan'dil] nm oil lamp; **~ejas** nfpl (TEATRO) footlights

candor [kan'dor] nm (sinceridad) frankness; (inocencia) innocence

canela [ka'nela] nf cinnamon

canelones [kane'lones] nmpl cannelloni

cangrejo [kan'grexo] nm crab

canguro [kan'guro] nm kangaroo; **hacer de ~** to babysit

caníbal [ka'nißal] adj, nm/f cannibal

canica [ka'nika] nf marble

canijo, a [ka'nixo, a] adj frail, sickly

canino, a [ka'nino, a] adj canine ♦ nm canine (tooth)

canjear [kanxe'ar] vt to exchange

cano, a ['kano, a] adj grey-haired, white-haired

canoa [ka'noa] nf canoe

canon ['kanon] nm canon; (pensión) rent; (COM) tax

canónigo [ka'noniɣo] nm canon

canonizar [kanoni'θar] vt to canonize

canoso, a [ka'noso, a] adj grey-haired

cansado, a [kan'saðo, a] adj tired, weary; (tedioso) tedious, boring

cansancio [kan'sanθjo] nm tiredness, fatigue

cansar [kan'sar] vt (fatigar) to tire, tire out; (aburrir) to bore; (fastidiar) to bother; **~se** vr to tire, get tired; (aburrirse) to get bored

cantábrico, a [kan'taßriko, a] adj Cantabrian; **mar C~** Bay of Biscay

cantante [kan'tante] adj singing ♦ nm/f singer

cantar [kan'tar] vt to sing ♦ vi to sing; (insecto) to chirp ♦ nm (acción) singing; (canción) song; (poema) poem

cántara ['kantara] nf large pitcher

cántaro ['kantaro] nm pitcher, jug; **llover a ~s** to rain cats and dogs

cante ['kante] nm: **~ jondo** flamenco singing

cantera [kan'tera] *nf* quarry

cantidad [kanti'ðað] *nf* quantity, amount

cantimplora [kantim'plora] *nf* (*frasco*) water bottle, canteen

cantina [kan'tina] *nf* canteen; (*de estación*) buffet

canto ['kanto] *nm* singing; (*canción*) song; (*borde*) edge, rim; (*de un cuchillo*) back; ~ **rodado** boulder

cantor, a [kan'tor, a] *nm/f* singer

canturrear [kanturre'ar] *vi* to sing softly

canuto [ka'nuto] *nm* (*tubo*) small tube; (*fam: droga*) joint

caña ['kaɲa] *nf* (*BOT: tallo*) stem, stalk; (*carrizo*) reed; (*vaso*) tumbler; (*de cerveza*) glass of beer; (*ANAT*) shinbone; ~ **de azúcar** sugar cane; ~ **de pescar** fishing rod

cañada [ka'ɲaða] *nf* (*entre dos montañas*) gully, ravine; (*camino*) cattle track

cáñamo ['kaɲamo] *nm* hemp

cañería [kaɲe'ria] *nf* (*tubo*) pipe

caño ['kaɲo] *nm* (*tubo*) tube, pipe; (*de albañal*) sewer; (*MUS*) pipe; (*de fuente*) jet

cañón [ka'ɲon] *nm* (*MIL*) cannon; (*de fusil*) barrel; (*GEO*) canyon, gorge

caoba [ka'oβa] *nf* mahogany

caos ['kaos] *nm* chaos

cap. *abr* (= *capítulo*) ch.

capa ['kapa] *nf* cloak, cape; (*GEO*) layer, stratum; **so** ~ **de** under the pretext of; ~ **de ozono** ozone layer

capacidad [kapaθi'ðað] *nf* (*medida*) capacity; (*aptitud*) capacity, ability

capacitar [kapaθi'tar] *vt*: ~ **a algn para (hacer)** to enable sb to (do)

capar [ka'par] *vt* to castrate, geld

caparazón [kapara'θon] *nm* shell

capataz [kapa'taθ] *nm* foreman

capaz [ka'paθ] *adj* able, capable; (*amplio*) capacious, roomy

capcioso, a [kap'θjoso, a] *adj* wily, deceitful

capellán [kape'ʎan] *nm* chaplain; (*sacerdote*) priest

caperuza [kape'ruθa] *nf* hood

capicúa [kapi'kua] *adj inv* (*número, fecha*)

reversible

capilla [ka'piʎa] *nf* chapel

capital [kapi'tal] *adj* capital ♦ *nm* (*COM*) capital ♦ *nf* (*ciudad*) capital; ~ **social** share *o* authorized capital

capitalismo [kapita'lismo] *nm* capitalism; **capitalista** *adj, nm/f* capitalist

capitán [kapi'tan] *nm* captain

capitanear [kapitane'ar] *vt* to captain

capitulación [kapitula'θjon] *nf* (*rendición*) capitulation, surrender; (*acuerdo*) agreement, pact; **capitulaciones (matrimoniales)** *nfpl* marriage contract *sg*

capitular [kapitu'lar] *vi* to make an agreement

capítulo [ka'pitulo] *nm* chapter

capó [ka'po] *nm* (*AUTO*) bonnet

capón [ka'pon] *nm* (*gallo*) capon

capota [ka'pota] *nf* (*de mujer*) bonnet; (*AUTO*) hood (*BRIT*), top (*US*)

capote [ka'pote] *nm* (*abrigo: de militar*) greatcoat; (: *de torero*) cloak

capricho [ka'pritʃo] *nm* whim, caprice; ~**so, a** *adj* capricious

Capricornio [kapri'kornjo] *nm* Capricorn

cápsula ['kapsula] *nf* capsule

captar [kap'tar] *vt* (*comprender*) to understand; (*RADIO*) to pick up; (*atención, apoyo*) to attract

captura [kap'tura] *nf* capture; (*JUR*) arrest; **capturar** *vt* to capture; to arrest

capucha [ka'putʃa] *nf* hood, cowl

capullo [ka'puʎo] *nm* (*BOT*) bud; (*ZOOL*) cocoon; (*fam*) idiot

caqui ['kaki] *nm* khaki

cara ['kara] *nf* (*ANAT, de moneda*) face; (*de disco*) side; (*descaro*) boldness; ~ **a** facing; **de** ~ opposite, facing; **dar la** ~ to face the consequences; **¿~ o cruz?** heads or tails?; **¡qué ~ (más dura)!** what a nerve!

carabina [kara'βina] *nf* carbine, rifle; (*persona*) chaperone

Caracas [ka'rakas] *n* Caracas

caracol [kara'kol] *nm* (*ZOOL*) snail; (*concha*) (sea) shell

carácter [ka'rakter] (*pl* **caracteres**) *nm*

character; **tener buen/mal ~** to be good natured/bad tempered

aracterística [karakte'ristika] nf characteristic

aracterístico, a [karakte'ristiko, a] adj characteristic

aracterizar [karakteri'θar] vt to characterize, typify

aradura [kara'ðura] nm/f: **es un ~** he's got a nerve

arajillo [kara'xiλo] nm coffee with a dash of brandy

arajo [ka'raxo] (fam!) nm: **¡~!** shit! (!)

aramba [ka'ramba] excl good gracious!

arámbano [ka'rambano] nm icicle

aramelo [kara'melo] nm (dulce) sweet; (azúcar fundida) caramel

aravana [kara'ßana] nf caravan; (fig) group; (AUTO) tailback

arbón [kar'ßon] nm coal; **papel ~** carbon paper; **carboncillo** nm (ARTE) charcoal; **carbonero, a** nm/f coal merchant; **carbonilla** [-'niλa] nf coal dust

arbonizar [karßoni'θar] vt to carbonize; (quemar) to char

arbono [kar'ßono] nm carbon

arburador [karßura'ðor] nm carburettor

arburante [karßu'rante] nm (para motor) fuel

arcajada [karka'xaða] nf (loud) laugh, guffaw

árcel [kar'θel] nf prison, jail; (TEC) clamp; **carcelero, a** adj prison cpd ♦ nm/f warder

arcoma [kar'koma] nf woodworm

arcomer [karko'mer] vt to bore into, eat into; (fig) to undermine; **~se** vr to become worm-eaten; (fig) to decay

ardar [kar'ðar] vt (pelo) to backcomb

ardenal [karðe'nal] nm (REL) cardinal; (MED) bruise

ardíaco, a [kar'ðiako, a] adj cardiac, heart cpd

ardinal [karði'nal] adj cardinal

ardo ['karðo] nm thistle

arearse [kare'arse] vr to come face to face

carecer [kare'θer] vi: **~ de** to lack, be in need of

carencia [ka'renθja] nf lack; (escasez) shortage; (MED) deficiency

carente [ka'rente] adj: **~ de** lacking in, devoid of

carestía [kares'tia] nf (escasez) scarcity, shortage; (COM) high cost

careta [ka'reta] nf mask

carga ['karßa] nf (peso, ELEC) load; (de barco) cargo, freight; (MIL) charge; (responsabilidad) duty, obligation

cargado, a [kar'ßaðo, a] adj loaded; (ELEC) live; (café, té) strong; (cielo) overcast

cargamento [karßa'mento] nm (acción) loading; (mercancías) load, cargo

cargar [kar'ßar] vt (barco, arma) to load; (ELEC) to charge; (COM: algo en cuenta) to charge; (INFORM) to load ♦ vi (MIL) to charge; (AUTO) to load (up); **~ con** to pick up, carry away; (peso, fig) to shoulder, bear; **~se** (fam) vr (estropear) to break; (matar) to bump off

cargo ['karßo] nm (puesto) post, office; (responsabilidad) duty, obligation; (JUR) charge; **hacerse ~ de** to take charge of o responsibility for

carguero [kar'ßero] nm freighter, cargo boat; (avión) freight plane

Caribe [ka'riße] nm: **el ~** the Caribbean; **del ~** Caribbean

caribeño, a [kari'ßeɲo, a] adj Caribbean

caricatura [karika'tura] nf caricature

caricia [ka'riθja] nf caress

caridad [kari'ðað] nf charity

caries ['karjes] nf inv tooth decay

cariño [ka'riɲo] nm affection, love; (caricia) caress; (en carta) love ...; **tener ~ a** to be fond of; **~so, a** adj affectionate

carisma [ka'risma] nm charisma

caritativo, a [karita'tißo, a] adj charitable

cariz [ka'riθ] nm: **tener o tomar buen/ mal ~** to look good/bad

carmesí [karme'si] adj, nm crimson

carmín [kar'min] nm lipstick

carnal [kar'nal] adj carnal; **primo ~** first cousin

carnaval [karna'ßal] *nm* carnival

---
carnaval

ℹ **Carnaval** *is the traditional period of fun, feasting and partying which takes place in the three days before the start of Lent ("Cuaresma"). Although in decline during the Franco years the carnival has grown in popularity recently in Spain. Cádiz and Tenerife are particularly well-known for their flamboyant celebrations with fancy-dress parties, parades and firework displays being the order of the day.*

carne ['karne] *nf* flesh; (CULIN) meat; **~ de cerdo/cordero/ternera/vaca** pork/lamb/veal/beef; **~ de gallina** (*fig*): **se me pone la ~ de gallina sólo verlo** I get the creeps just seeing it

carné [kar'ne] (*pl* **~s**) *nm*: **~ de conducir** driving licence (BRIT), driver's license (US); **~ de identidad** identity card

carnero [kar'nero] *nm* sheep, ram; (*carne*) mutton

carnet [kar'ne] (*pl* **~s**) *nm* = **carné**

carnicería [karniθe'ria] *nf* butcher's (shop); (*fig*: *matanza*) carnage, slaughter

carnicero, a [karni'θero, a] *adj* carnivorous ♦ *nm/f* (*tb fig*) butcher; (*carnívoro*) carnivore

carnívoro, a [kar'nißoro, a] *adj* carnivorous

carnoso, a [kar'noso, a] *adj* beefy, fat

caro, a ['karo, a] *adj* dear; (COM) dear, expensive ♦ *adv* dear, dearly

carpa ['karpa] *nf* (*pez*) carp; (*de circo*) big top; (AM: *de camping*) tent

carpeta [kar'peta] *nf* folder, file

carpintería [karpinte'ria] *nf* carpentry, joinery; **carpintero** *nm* carpenter

carraspear [karraspe'ar] *vi* to clear one's throat

carraspera [karras'pera] *nf* hoarseness

carrera [ka'rrera] *nf* (*acción*) run(ning); (*espacio recorrido*) run; (*competición*) race; (*trayecto*) course; (*profesión*) career;

carreta [ka'rreta] *nf* wagon, cart

carrete [ka'rrete] *nm* reel, spool; (TEC) coil

carretera [karre'tera] *nf* (main) road, highway; **~ de circunvalación** ring road; **~ nacional** ≈ A road (BRIT), ≈ state highway (US)

carretilla [karre'tiʎa] *nf* trolley; (AGR) (wheel)barrow

carril [ka'rril] *nm* furrow; (*de autopista*) lane; (FERRO) rail

carrillo [ka'rriʎo] *nm* (ANAT) cheek; (TEC) pulley

carrito [ka'rrito] *nm* trolley

carro ['karro] *nm* cart, wagon; (MIL) tank; (AM: *coche*) car

carrocería [karroθe'ria] *nf* bodywork, coachwork

carroña [ka'rroɲa] *nf* carrion *no pl*

carroza [ka'rroθa] *nf* (*carruaje*) coach

carrusel [karru'sel] *nm* merry-go-round, roundabout

carta ['karta] *nf* letter; (CULIN) menu; (*naipe*) card; (*mapa*) map; (JUR) document; **~ de ajuste** (TV) test card; **~ de crédito** credit card; **~ certificada** registered letter; **~ marítima** chart; **~ verde** (AUTO) green card

cartabón [karta'ßon] *nm* set square

cartel [kar'tel] *nm* (*anuncio*) poster, placard; (ESCOL) wall chart; (COM) cartel; **~era** *nf* hoarding, billboard; (*en periódico etc*) entertainments guide; **"en ~era"** "showing"

cartera [kar'tera] *nf* (*de bolsillo*) wallet; (*de colegial, cobrador*) satchel; (*de señora*) handbag; (*para documentos*) briefcase; (COM) portfolio; **ocupa la ~ de Agricultura** she is Minister of Agriculture

carterista [karte'rista] *nm/f* pickpocket

cartero [kar'tero] *nm* postman

cartilla [kar'tiʎa] *nf* primer, first reading book; **~ de ahorros** savings book

cartón [kar'ton] *nm* cardboard; **~ piedra** papier-mâché

cartucho [kar'tutʃo] *nm* (MIL) cartridge

cartulina [kartu'lina] *nf* card

asa ['kasa] nf house; (*hogar*) home; (*COM*) firm, company; **en ~** at home; **~ consistorial** town hall; **~ de huéspedes** boarding house; **~ de socorro** first aid post

asado, a [ka'saðo, a] adj married ♦ nm/f married man/woman

asamiento [kasa'mjento] nm marriage, wedding

asar [ka'sar] vt to marry; (*JUR*) to quash, annul; **~se** vr to marry, get married

ascabel [kaska'ßel] nm (small) bell

ascada [kas'kaða] nf waterfall

ascanueces [kaska'nweθes] nm inv nutcrackers pl

ascar [kas'kar] vt to crack, split, break (open); **~se** vr to crack, split, break (open)

ascara ['kaskara] nf (*de huevo, fruta seca*) shell; (*de fruta*) skin; (*de limón*) peel

asco ['kasko] nm (*de bombero, soldado*) helmet; (*NAUT: de barco*) hull; (*ZOOL: de caballo*) hoof; (*botella*) empty bottle; (*de ciudad*): **el ~ antiguo** the old part; **el ~ urbano** the town centre; **los ~s azules** the UN peace-keeping force, the blue berets

ascote [kas'kote] nm rubble

aserío [kase'rio] nm hamlet; (*casa*) country house

asero, a [ka'sero, a] adj (*pan etc*) home-made ♦ nm/f (*propietario*) landlord/lady; **er muy ~** to be home-loving; **"comida asera"** "home cooking"

aseta [ka'seta] nf hut; (*para bañista*) cubicle; (*de feria*) stall

asete [ka'sete] nm o f cassette

asi ['kasi] adv almost, nearly; **~ nada** hardly anything; **~ nunca** hardly ever, most never; **~ te caes** you almost fell

asilla [ka'siʎa] nf (*casita*) hut, cabin; (*AJEDREZ*) square; (*para cartas*) pigeonhole; **asillero** nm (*para cartas*) pigeonholes

asino [ka'sino] nm club; (*de juego*) casino

aso ['kaso] nm case; **en ~ de ...** in case ...; **en ~ de que ...** in case ...; **el ~ es**

que the fact is that; **en ese ~** in that case; **hacer ~ a** to pay attention to; **hacer o venir al ~** to be relevant

caspa ['kaspa] nf dandruff

cassette [ka'sete] nm o f = **casete**

casta ['kasta] nf caste; (*raza*) breed; (*linaje*) lineage

castaña [kas'taɲa] nf chestnut

castañetear [kastaɲete'ar] vi (*dientes*) to chatter

castaño, a [kas'taɲo, a] adj chestnut (-coloured), brown ♦ nm chestnut tree

castañuelas [kasta'ɲwelas] nfpl castanets

castellano, a [kaste'ʎano, a] adj, nm/f Castilian ♦ nm (*LING*) Castilian, Spanish

castidad [kasti'ðað] nf chastity, purity

castigar [kasti'var] vt to punish; (*DEPORTE*) to penalize; **castigo** nm punishment; (*DEPORTE*) penalty

Castilla [kas'tiʎa] nf Castille

castillo [kas'tiʎo] nm castle

castizo, a [kas'tiθo, a] adj (*LING*) pure

casto, a ['kasto, a] adj chaste, pure

castor [kas'tor] nm beaver

castrar [kas'trar] vt to castrate

castrense [kas'trense] adj (*disciplina, vida*) military

casual [ka'swal] adj chance, accidental; **~idad** nf chance, accident; (*combinación de circunstancias*) coincidence; **¡qué ~idad!** what a coincidence!

cataclismo [kata'klismo] nm cataclysm

catador, a [kata'ðor, a] nm/f wine taster

catalán, ana [kata'lan, ana] adj, nm/f Catalan ♦ nm (*LING*) Catalan

catalizador [kataliθa'ðor] nm catalyst; (*AUT*) catalytic convertor

catalogar [katalo'var] vt to catalogue; **~ a algn (de)** (*fig*) to categorize sb (as)

catálogo [ka'talovo] nm catalogue

Cataluña [kata'luɲa] nf Catalonia

catar [ka'tar] vt to taste, sample

catarata [kata'rata] nf (*GEO*) waterfall; (*MED*) cataract

catarro [ka'tarro] nm catarrh; (*constipado*) cold

catástrofe [ka'tastrofe] nf catastrophe

catear [kate'ar] (*fam*) *vt* (*examen, alumno*) to fail
cátedra ['kateðra] *nf* (*UNIV*) chair, professorship
catedral [kate'ðral] *nf* cathedral
catedrático, a [kate'ðratiko, a] *nm/f* professor
categoría [kateɣo'ria] *nf* category; (*rango*) rank, standing; (*calidad*) quality; **de ~** (*hotel*) top-class
categórico, a [kate'ɣoriko, a] *adj* categorical
cateto, a ['kateto, a] (*pey*) *nm/f* peasant
catolicismo [katoli'θismo] *nm* Catholicism
católico, a [ka'toliko, a] *adj, nm/f* Catholic
catorce [ka'torθe] *num* fourteen
cauce ['kauθe] *nm* (*de río*) riverbed; (*fig*) channel
caucho ['kautʃo] *nm* rubber; (*AM: llanta*) tyre
caución [kau'θjon] *nf* bail; **caucionar** *vt* (*JUR*) to bail, go bail for
caudal [kau'ðal] *nm* (*de río*) volume, flow; (*fortuna*) wealth; (*abundancia*) abundance; **~oso, a** *adj* (*río*) large
caudillo [kau'ðiʎo] *nm* leader, chief
causa ['kausa] *nf* cause; (*razón*) reason; (*JUR*) lawsuit, case; **a ~ de** because of
causar [kau'sar] *vt* to cause
cautela [kau'tela] *nf* caution, cautiousness; **cauteloso, a** *adj* cautious, wary
cautivar [kauti'ßar] *vt* to capture; (*atraer*) to captivate
cautiverio [kauti'ßerjo] *nm* captivity
cautividad [kautißi'ðað] *nf* = **cautiverio**
cautivo, a [kau'tißo, a] *adj, nm/f* captive
cauto, a ['kauto, a] *adj* cautious, careful
cava ['kaßa] *nm* champagne-type wine
cavar [ka'ßar] *vt* to dig
caverna [ka'ßerna] *nf* cave, cavern
cavidad [kaßi'ðað] *nf* cavity
cavilar [kaßi'lar] *vt* to ponder
cayado [ka'jaðo] *nm* (*de pastor*) crook; (*de obispo*) crozier
cayendo *etc vb ver* **caer**
caza ['kaθa] *nf* (*acción: gen*) hunting;

(*: con fusil*) shooting; (*una ~*) hunt, chase, (*animales*) game ♦ *nm* (*AVIAT*) fighter
cazador, a [kaθa'ðor, a] *nm/f* hunter; **cazadora** *nf* jacket
cazar [ka'θar] *vt* to hunt; (*perseguir*) to chase; (*prender*) to catch
cazo ['kaθo] *nm* saucepan
cazuela [ka'θwela] *nf* (*vasija*) pan; (*guisado*) casserole
CD *abbr* (= *compact disc*) CD
CD-ROM *abbr* CD-ROM
CE *nf abr* (= *Comunidad Europea*) EC
cebada [θe'ßaða] *nf* barley
cebar [θe'ßar] *vt* (*animal*) to fatten (up); (*anzuelo*) to bait; (*MIL, TEC*) to prime
cebo ['θeßo] *nm* (*para animales*) feed, food; (*para peces, fig*) bait; (*de arma*) charge
cebolla [θe'ßoʎa] *nf* onion; **cebolleta** *nf* spring onion; **cebollín** *nm* spring onion
cebra ['θeßra] *nf* zebra
cecear [θeθe'ar] *vi* to lisp; **ceceo** *nm* lisp
ceder [θe'ðer] *vt* to hand over, give up, part with ♦ *vi* (*renunciar*) to give in, yield; (*disminuir*) to diminish, decline; (*romperse*) to give way
cedro ['θeðro] *nm* cedar
cédula ['θeðula] *nf* certificate, document
cegar [θe'ɣar] *vt* to blind; (*tubería etc*) to block up, stop up ♦ *vi* to go blind; **~se** *vr*: **~se (de)** to be blinded (by)
ceguera [θe'ɣera] *nf* blindness
CEI *abbr* (= *Confederación de Estados Independientes*) CIS
ceja ['θexa] *nf* eyebrow
cejar [θe'xar] *vi* (*fig*) to back down
celador, a [θela'ðor, a] *nm/f* (*de edificio*) watchman; (*de museo etc*) attendant
celda ['θelda] *nf* cell
celebración [θeleßra'θjon] *nf* celebration
celebrar [θele'ßrar] *vt* to celebrate; (*alabar*) to praise ♦ *vi* to be glad; **~se** *vr* to occur, take place
célebre ['θelebre] *adj* famous
celebridad [θeleßri'ðað] *nf* fame; (*persona*) celebrity
celeste [θe'leste] *adj* (*azul*) sky-blue

celestial [θeles'tjal] adj celestial, heavenly
celibato [θeli'ßato] nm celibacy
célibe ['θeliße] adj, nm/f celibate
celo¹ ['θelo] nm zeal; (REL) fervour; (ZOOL):
en ~ on heat; ~s nmpl jealousy sg; tener
~s to be jealous
celo² ® ['θelo] nm Sellotape ®
celofán [θelo'fan] nm cellophane
celoso, a [θe'loso, a] adj jealous;
(trabajador) zealous
celta ['θelta] adj Celtic ♦ nm/f Celt
célula ['θelula] nf cell; ~ solar solar cell
celulitis [θelu'litis] nf cellulite
cementerio [θemen'terjo] nm cemetery,
graveyard
cemento [θe'mento] nm cement;
(hormigón) concrete; (AM: cola) glue
cena ['θena] nf evening meal, dinner
cenagal [θena'yal] nm bog, quagmire
cenar [θe'nar] vt to have for dinner ♦ vi to
have dinner
cenicero [θeni'θero] nm ashtray
cenit [θe'nit] nm zenith
ceniza [θe'niθa] nf ash, ashes pl
censo ['θenso] nm census; ~ electoral
electoral roll
censura [θen'sura] nf (POL) censorship
censurar [θensu'rar] vt (idea) to censure;
(cortar: película) to censor
centella [θen'teʎa] nf spark
centellear [θenteʎe'ar] vi (metal) to
gleam; (estrella) to twinkle; (fig) to sparkle
centenar [θente'nar] nm hundred
centenario, a [θente'narjo, a] adj
centenary; hundred-year-old ♦ nm
centenary
centeno [θen'teno] nm (BOT) rye
centésimo, a [θen'tesimo, a] adj
hundredth
centígrado [θen'tiɣraðo] adj centigrade
centímetro [θen'timetro] nm centimetre
(BRIT), centimeter (US)
céntimo [θentimo] nm cent
centinela [θenti'nela] nm sentry, guard
centollo [θen'toʎo] nm spider crab
central [θen'tral] adj central ♦ nf head
office; (TEC) plant; (TEL) exchange; ~

eléctrica power station; ~ nuclear
nuclear power station; ~ telefónica
telephone exchange
centralita [θentra'lita] nf switchboard
centralizar [θentrali'θar] vt to centralize
centrar [θen'trar] vt to centre
céntrico, a ['θentriko, a] adj central
centrifugar [θentrifu'var] vt to spin-dry
centrista [θen'trista] adj centre cpd
centro ['θentro] nm centre; ~ comercial
shopping centre; ~ juvenil youth club; ~
de atención al cliente call centre
centroamericano, a [θentroameri'kano,
a] adj, nm/f Central American
ceñido, a [θe'niðo, a] adj (chaqueta,
pantalón) tight(-fitting)
ceñir [θe'nir] vt (rodear) to encircle,
surround; (ajustar) to fit (tightly)
ceño ['θeno] nm frown, scowl; fruncir el ~
to frown, knit one's brow
CEOE nf abr (ESP: = Confederación
Española de Organizaciones Empresariales)
≈ CBI (BRIT), employers' organization
cepillar [θepi'ʎar] vt to brush; (madera) to
plane (down)
cepillo [θe'piʎo] nm brush; (para madera)
plane; ~ de dientes toothbrush
cera ['θera] nf wax
cerámica [θe'ramika] nf pottery; (arte)
ceramics
cerca ['θerka] nf fence ♦ adv near, nearby,
close; ~ de near, close to
cercanías [θerka'nias] nfpl (afueras)
outskirts, suburbs
cercano, a [θer'kano, a] adj close, near
cercar [θer'kar] vt to fence in; (rodear) to
surround
cerciorar [θerθjo'rar] vt (asegurar) to
assure; ~se vr (asegurarse) to make sure
cerco ['θerko] nm (AGR) enclosure; (AM)
fence; (MIL) siege
cerdo, a ['θerðo, a] nm/f pig/sow
cereal [θere'al] nm cereal; ~es nmpl
cereals, grain sg
cerebro [θe'reßro] nm brain; (fig) brains pl
ceremonia [θere'monja] nf ceremony;
ceremonial adj, nm ceremonial;

ceremonioso, a *adj* ceremonious

cereza [θe'reθa] *nf* cherry

cerilla [θe'riʎa] *nf* (*fósforo*) match

cernerse [θer'nerse] *vr* to hover

cero ['θero] *nm* nothing, zero

cerrado, a [θe'rraðo, a] *adj* closed, shut; (*con llave*) locked; (*tiempo*) cloudy, overcast; (*curva*) sharp; (*acento*) thick, broad

cerradura [θerra'ðura] *nf* (*acción*) closing; (*mecanismo*) lock

cerrajero [θerra'xero] *nm* locksmith

cerrar [θe'rrar] *vt* to close, shut; (*paso, carretera*) to close; (*grifo*) to turn off; (*cuenta, negocio*) to close ♦ *vi* to close, shut; (*la noche*) to come down; ~se *vr* to close, shut; ~ con llave to lock; ~ un trato to strike a bargain

cerro ['θerro] *nm* hill

cerrojo [θe'rroxo] *nm* (*herramienta*) bolt; (*de puerta*) latch

certamen [θer'tamen] *nm* competition, contest

certero, a [θer'tero, a] *adj* (*gen*) accurate

certeza [θer'teθa] *nf* certainty

certidumbre [θerti'ðumßre] *nf* = certeza

certificado [θertifi'kaðo] *nm* certificate

certificar [θertifi'kar] *vt* to certify, atestar) to certify

cervatillo [θerßa'tiʎo] *nm* fawn

cervecería [θerßeθe'ria] *nf* (*fábrica*) brewery; (*bar*) public house, pub

cerveza [θer'ßeθa] *nf* beer

cesante [θe'sante] *adj* redundant

cesar [θe'sar] *vi* to cease, stop ♦ *vt* (*funcionario*) to remove from office

cesárea [θe'sarea] *nf* (*MED*) Caesarean operation o section

cese ['θese] *nm* (*de trabajo*) dismissal; (*de pago*) suspension

césped ['θespeð] *nm* grass, lawn

cesta ['θesta] *nf* basket

cesto ['θesto] *nm* (large) basket, hamper

cetro ['θetro] *nm* sceptre

cfr *abr* = confróntese) cf.

chabacano, a [tʃaßa'kano, a] *adj* vulgar, coarse

chabola [tʃa'ßola] *nf* shack; barrio de ~s shanty town *sg*

chacal [tʃa'kal] *nm* jackal

chacha ['tʃatʃa] (*fam*) *nf* maid

cháchara ['tʃatʃara] *nf* chatter; estar de ~ to chatter away

chacra ['tʃakra] (*AM*) *nf* smallholding

chafar [tʃa'far] *vt* (*aplastar*) to crush; (*plan etc*) to ruin

chal [tʃal] *nm* shawl

chalado, a [tʃa'lado, a] (*fam*) *adj* crazy

chalé [tʃa'le] (*pl* ~s) *nm* villa; ≈ detached house

chaleco [tʃa'leko] *nm* waistcoat, vest (*US*); ~ salvavidas life jacket

chalet [tʃa'le] (*pl* ~s) *nm* = chalé

champán [tʃam'pan] *nm* champagne

champaña [tʃam'paɲa] *nm* = champán

champiñón [tʃampi'ɲon] *nm* mushroom

champú [tʃam'pu] (*pl* champúes, champús) *nm* shampoo

chamuscar [tʃamus'kar] *vt* to scorch, sear, singe

chance ['tʃanθe] (*AM*) *nm* chance

chancho, a ['tʃantʃo, a] (*AM*) *nm/f* pig

chanchullo [tʃan'tʃuʎo] (*fam*) *nm* fiddle

chandal [tʃan'dal] *nm* tracksuit

chantaje [tʃan'taxe] *nm* blackmail

chapa ['tʃapa] *nf* (*de metal*) plate, sheet; (*de madera*) board, panel; (*AM: AUTO*) number (*BRIT*) o license (*US*) plate; ~do, a *adj*: ~do en oro gold-plated

chaparrón [tʃapa'rron] *nm* downpour, cloudburst

chapotear [tʃapote'ar] *vi* to splash about

chapurrear [tʃapurre'ar] *vt* (*idioma*) to speak badly

chapuza [tʃa'puθa] *nf* botched job

chapuzón [tʃapu'θon] *nm*: darse un ~ to go for a dip

chaqueta [tʃa'keta] *nf* jacket

chaquetón [tʃake'ton] *nm* long jacket

charca ['tʃarka] *nf* pond, pool

charco ['tʃarko] *nm* pool, puddle

charcutería [tʃarkute'ria] *nf* (*tienda*) shop selling chiefly pork meat products; (*productos*) cooked pork meats *pl*

charla ['tʃarla] *nf* talk, chat; (*conferencia*) lecture

charlar [tʃar'lar] *vi* to talk, chat

charlatán, ana [tʃarla'tan, ana] *nm/f* (*hablador*) chatterbox; (*estafador*) trickster

charol [tʃa'rol] *nm* varnish; (*cuero*) patent leather

chascarrillo [tʃaska'rriʎo] (*fam*) *nm* funny story

chasco ['tʃasko] *nm* (*desengaño*) disappointment

chasis ['tʃasis] *nm inv* chassis

chasquear [tʃaske'ar] *vt* (*látigo*) to crack; (*lengua*) to click; **chasquido** *nm* crack; click

chatarra [tʃa'tarra] *nf* scrap (metal)

chato, a ['tʃato, a] *adj* flat; (*nariz*) snub

chaval, a [tʃa'ßal, a] *nm/f* kid, lad/lass

checo, a ['tʃeko, a] *adj*, *nm/f* Czech ♦ *nm* (*LING*) Czech

checo(e)slovaco, a [tʃeko(e)slo'ßako, a] *adj*, *nm/f* Czech, Czechoslovak

checo(e)slovaquia [tʃeko(e)slo'ßakja] *nf* Czechoslovakia

cheque ['tʃeke] *nm* cheque (*BRIT*), check (*US*); **~ de viajero** traveller's cheque (*BRIT*), traveler's check (*US*)

chequeo [tʃe'keo] *nm* (*MED*) check-up; (*AUTO*) service

chequera [tʃe'kera] (*AM*) *nf* chequebook (*BRIT*), checkbook (*US*)

chicano, a [tʃi'kano, a] *adj*, *nm/f* chicano

chícharo ['tʃitʃaro] (*AM*) *nm* pea

chichón [tʃi'tʃon] *nm* bump, lump

chicle ['tʃikle] *nm* chewing gum

chico, a ['tʃiko, a] *adj* small, little ♦ *nm/f* (*niño*) child; (*muchacho*) boy/girl

chiflado, a [tʃi'flaðo, a] *adj* crazy

chiflar [tʃi'flar] *vt* to hiss, boo

Chile ['tʃile] *nm* Chile; **chileno, a** *adj*, *nm/f* Chilean

chile ['tʃile] *nm* chilli pepper

chillar [tʃi'ʎar] *vi* (*persona*) to yell, scream; (*animal salvaje*) to howl; (*cerdo*) to squeal

chillido [tʃi'ʎiðo] *nm* (*de persona*) yell, scream; (*de animal*) howl

chillón, ona [tʃi'ʎon, ona] *adj* (*niño*) noisy; (*color*) loud, gaudy

chimenea [tʃime'nea] *nf* chimney; (*hogar*) fireplace

China ['tʃina] *nf*: **(la) ~** China

chinche ['tʃintʃe] *nf* (*insecto*) (bed)bug; (*TEC*) drawing pin (*BRIT*), thumbtack (*US*) ♦ *nm/f* nuisance, pest

chincheta [tʃin'tʃeta] *nf* drawing pin (*BRIT*), thumbtack (*US*)

chino, a ['tʃino, a] *adj*, *nm/f* Chinese ♦ *nm* (*LING*) Chinese

chipirón [tʃipi'ron] *nm* (*ZOOL*, *CULIN*) squid

Chipre ['tʃipre] *nf* Cyprus; **chipriota** *adj*, *nm/f* Cypriot

chiquillo, a [tʃi'kiʎo, a] *nm/f* (*fam*) kid

chirimoya [tʃiri'moja] *nf* custard apple

chiringuito [tʃirin'vito] *nm* small open-air bar

chiripa [tʃi'ripa] *nf* fluke

chirriar [tʃi'rrjar] *vi* to creak, squeak

chirrido [tʃi'rriðo] *nm* creak(ing), squeak(ing)

chis [tʃis] *excl* sh!

chisme ['tʃisme] *nm* (*habladurías*) piece of gossip; (*fam: objeto*) thingummyjig

chismoso, a [tʃis'moso, a] *adj* gossiping ♦ *nm/f* gossip

chispa ['tʃispa] *nf* spark; (*fig*) sparkle; (*ingenio*) wit; (*fam*) drunkenness

chispear [tʃispe'ar] *vi* (*lloviznar*) to drizzle

chisporrotear [tʃisporrote'ar] *vi* (*fuego*) to throw out sparks; (*leña*) to crackle; (*aceite*) to hiss, splutter

chiste ['tʃiste] *nm* joke, funny story

chistoso, a [tʃis'toso, a] *adj* funny, amusing

chivo, a ['tʃißo, a] *nm/f* (billy-/nanny-) goat; **~ expiatorio** scapegoat

chocante [tʃo'kante] *adj* startling; (*extraño*) odd; (*ofensivo*) shocking

chocar [tʃo'kar] *vi* (*coches etc*) to collide, crash ♦ *vt* to shock; (*sorprender*) to startle; **~ con** to collide with; (*fig*) to run into, run up against; **¡chócala!** (*fam*) put it there!

chochear [tʃotʃe'ar] *vi* to dodder, be senile

chocho, a ['tʃotʃo, a] *adj* doddering, senile; *(fig)* soft, doting

chocolate [tʃoko'late] *adj, nm* chocolate; **chocolatina** *nf* chocolate

chofer [tʃo'fer] *nm* = **chófer**

chófer ['tʃofer] *nm* driver

chollo ['tʃoʎo] *(fam) nm* bargain, snip

choque *etc* ['tʃoke] *vb ver* **chocar ♦** *nm* *(impacto)* impact; *(golpe)* jolt; *(AUTO)* crash; *(fig)* conflict; ~ **frontal** head-on collision

chorizo [tʃo'riθo] *nm* hard pork sausage

chorrada [tʃo'rraða] *(fam) nf*: **¡es una ~!** that's crap! *(!)*; **decir ~s** to talk crap *(!)*

chorrear [tʃorre'ar] *vi* to gush (out), spout (out); *(gotear)* to drip, trickle

chorro ['tʃorro] *nm* jet; *(fig)* stream

choza ['tʃoθa] *nf* hut, shack

chubasco [tʃu'ßasko] *nm* squall

chubasquero [tʃußas'kero] *nm* lightweight raincoat

chuchería [tʃutʃe'ria] *nf* trinket

chuleta [tʃu'leta] *nf* chop, cutlet

chulo ['tʃulo] *nm (de prostituta)* pimp

chupar [tʃu'par] *vt* to suck; *(absorber)* to absorb; **~se** *vr* to grow thin

chupete [tʃu'pete] *nm* dummy *(BRIT)*, pacifier *(US)*

chupito [tʃu'pito] *(fam) nm* shot

churro ['tʃurro] *nm* (type of) fritter

chusma ['tʃusma] *nf* rabble, mob

chutar [tʃu'tar] *vi* to shoot (at goal)

Cía *abr* (= *compañía*) Co.

cianuro [θja'nuro] *nm* cyanide

cibercafé [θißerka'fe] *nm* cybercafé

cicatriz [θika'triθ] *nf* scar; **~arse** *vr* to heal (up), form a scar

ciclismo [θi'klismo] *nm* cycling

ciclista [θi'klista] *adj* cycle *cpd* ♦ *nm/f* cyclist

ciclo ['θiklo] *nm* cycle

ciclón [θi'klon] *nm* cyclone

cicloturismo [θiklotu'rismo] *nm*: **hacer ~** to go on a cycling holiday

ciego, a ['θjeɣo, a] *adj* blind ♦ *nm/f* blind man/woman

cielo ['θjelo] *nm* sky; *(REL)* heaven; **¡~s!** good heavens!

ciempiés [θjem'pjes] *nm inv* centipede

cien [θjen] *num ver* **ciento**

ciénaga ['θjenaɣa] *nf* marsh, swamp

ciencia ['θjenθja] *nf* science; **~s** *nfpl* *(ESCOL)* science *sg*; **~-ficción** *nf* science fiction

cieno ['θjeno] *nm* mud, mire

científico, a [θjen'tifiko, a] *adj* scientific ♦ *nm/f* scientist

ciento ['θjento] *(tb: cien) num* hundred; **pagar al 10 por ~** to pay at 10 per cent

cierre *etc* ['θjerre] *vb ver* **cerrar** ♦ *nm* closing, shutting; *(con llave)* locking; ~ **de cremallera** zip (fastener)

cierro *etc vb ver* **cerrar**

cierto, a ['θjerto, a] *adj* sure, certain; *(un tal)* a certain; *(correcto)* right, correct; ~ **hombre** a certain man; **ciertas personas** certain *o* some people; **sí, es ~** yes, that's correct

ciervo ['θjerßo] *nm* deer; *(macho)* stag

cierzo ['θjerθo] *nm* north wind

cifra ['θifra] *nf* number; *(secreta)* code

cifrar [θi'frar] *vt* to code, write in code

cigala [θi'ɣala] *nf* Norway lobster

cigarra [θi'ɣarra] *nf* cicada

cigarrillo [θiɣa'rriʎo] *nm* cigarette

cigarro [θi'ɣarro] *nm* cigarette; *(puro)* cigar

cigüeña [θi'ɣweɲa] *nf* stork

cilíndrico, a [θi'lindriko, a] *adj* cylindrical

cilindro [θi'lindro] *nm* cylinder

cima ['θima] *nf (de montaña)* top, peak; *(de árbol)* top; *(fig)* height

cimbrearse [θimbre'arse] *vr* to sway

cimentar [θimen'tar] *vt* to lay the foundations of; *(fig: fundar)* to found

cimiento [θi'mjento] *nm* foundation

cinc [θink] *nm* zinc

cincel [θin'θel] *nm* chisel; **~ar** *vt* to chisel

cinco ['θinko] *num* five

cincuenta [θin'kwenta] *num* fifty

cine ['θine] *nm* cinema

cineasta [θine'asta] *nm/f* film director

cinematográfico, a [θinemato'ɣrafiko, a] *adj* cine-, film *cpd*

ínico, a ['θiniko, a] *adj* cynical ♦ *nm/f* cynic

inismo [θi'nismo] *nm* cynicism

inta ['θinta] *nf* band, strip; (*de tela*) ribbon; (*película*) reel; (*de máquina de escribir*) ribbon; ~ **adhesiva** sticky tape; ~ **de vídeo** videotape; ~ **magnetofónica** tape; ~ **métrica** tape measure

intura [θin'tura] *nf* waist

inturón [θintu'ron] *nm* belt; ~ **de seguridad** safety belt

iprés [θi'pres] *nm* cypress (tree)

rco ['θirko] *nm* circus

ircuito [θir'kwito] *nm* circuit

rculación [θirkula'θjon] *nf* circulation; (*AUTO*) traffic

rcular [θirku'lar] *adj, nf* circular ♦ *vi, vt* to circulate ♦ *vi* (*AUTO*) to drive; **"circule por la derecha"** "keep to (the) right"

rculo ['θirkulo] *nm* circle; ~ **vicioso** vicious circle

rcuncidar [θirkunθi'dar] *vt* to circumcise

rcundar [θirkun'dar] *vt* to surround

rcunferencia [θirkunfe'renθja] *nf* circumference

rcunscribir [θirkunskri'βir] *vt* to circumscribe; ~**se** *vr* to be limited

rcunscripción [θirkunskrip'θjon] *nf* (*POL*) constituency

rcunspecto, a [θirkuns'pekto, a] *adj* circumspect, cautious

rcunstancia [θirkuns'tanθja] *nf* circumstance

io ['θirjo] *nm* (wax) candle

uela [θi'rwela] *nf* plum; ~ **pasa** prune

ugía [θiru'xia] *nf* surgery; ~ **estética** o **lástica** plastic surgery

ujano [θiru'xano] *nm* surgeon

ne ['θisne] *nm* swan

terna [θis'terna] *nf* cistern, tank

a ['θita] *nf* appointment, meeting; (*de ovios*) date; (*referencia*) quotation

ación [θita'θjon] *nf* (*JUR*) summons *sg*

ar [θi'tar] *vt* (*gen*) to make an ppointment with; (*JUR*) to summons; (*un utor, texto*) to quote; ~**se** *vr*: **se citaron n el cine** they arranged to meet at the cinema

cítricos ['θitrikos] *nmpl* citrus fruit(s)

ciudad [θju'ðað] *nf* town; (*más grande*) city; ~**anía** *nf* citizenship; ~**ano, a** *nm/f* citizen

cívico, a ['θiβiko, a] *adj* civic

civil [θi'βil] *adj* civil ♦ *nm* (*guardia*) policeman

civilización [θiβiliθa'θjon] *nf* civilization

civilizar [θiβili'θar] *vt* to civilize

civismo [θi'βismo] *nm* public spirit

cizaña [θi'θaɲa] *nf* (*fig*) discord

cl. *abr* (= *centilitro*) cl.

clamar [kla'mar] *vt* to clamour for, cry out for ♦ *vi* to cry out, clamour

clamor [kla'mor] *nm* clamour, protest

clandestino, a [klandes'tino, a] *adj* clandestine; (*POL*) underground

clara ['klara] *nf* (*de huevo*) egg white

claraboya [klara'βoja] *nf* skylight

clarear [klare'ar] *vi* (*el día*) to dawn; (*el cielo*) to clear up, brighten up; ~**se** *vr* to be transparent

clarete [kla'rete] *nm* rosé (wine)

claridad [klari'ðað] *nf* (*del día*) brightness; (*de estilo*) clarity

clarificar [klarifi'kar] *vt* to clarify

clarinete [klari'nete] *nm* clarinet

clarividencia [klariβi'ðenθja] *nf* clairvoyance; (*fig*) far-sightedness

claro, a ['klaro, a] *adj* clear; (*luminoso*) bright; (*color*) light; (*evidente*) clear, evident; (*poco espeso*) thin ♦ *nm* (*en bosque*) clearing ♦ *adv* clearly ♦ *excl* (*tb*: ~ **que sí**) of course!

clase ['klase] *nf* class; ~ **alta/media/ obrera** upper/middle/working class; ~**s particulares** private lessons, private tuition *sg*

clásico, a ['klasiko, a] *adj* classical

clasificación [klasifika'θjon] *nf* classification; (*DEPORTE*) league (table)

clasificar [klasifi'kar] *vt* to classify

claudicar [klauði'kar] *vi* to give in

claustro ['klaustro] *nm* cloister

cláusula ['klausula] *nf* clause

clausura [klau'sura] *nf* closing, closure;

clausurar vt (congreso etc) to bring to a close

clavar [kla'βar] vt (clavo) to hammer in; (cuchillo) to stick, thrust

clave ['klaβe] nf key; (MUS) clef

clavel [kla'βel] nm carnation

clavícula [kla'βikula] nf collar bone

clavija [kla'βixa] nf peg, dowel, pin; (ELEC) plug

clavo ['klaβo] nm (de metal) nail; (BOT) clove

claxon ['klakson] (pl ~s) nm horn

clemencia [kle'menθja] nf mercy, clemency

cleptómano, a [klep'tomano, a] nm/f kleptomaniac

clérigo ['kleriɣo] nm priest

clero ['klero] nm clergy

cliché [kli'tʃe] nm cliché; (FOTO) negative

cliente, a ['kljente, a] nm/f client, customer

clientela [kljen'tela] nf clientele, customers pl

clima ['klima] nm climate

climatizado, a [klimati'θaðo, a] adj air-conditioned

clímax ['klimaks] nm inv climax

clínica ['klinika] nf clinic; (particular) private hospital

clip [klip] (pl ~s) nm paper clip

clítoris ['klitoris] nm inv (ANAT) clitoris

cloaca [klo'aka] nf sewer

cloro ['kloro] nm chlorine

club [klub] (pl ~s o ~es) nm club; ~ de jóvenes youth club

cm abr (= centímetro, centímetros) cm

C.N.T. (ESP) abr = Confederación Nacional de Trabajo

coacción [koak'θjon] nf coercion, compulsion; **coaccionar** vt to coerce

coagular [koaɣu'lar] vt (leche, sangre) to clot; **~se** vr to clot; **coágulo** nm clot

coalición [koali'θjon] nf coalition

coartada [koar'taða] nf alibi

coartar [koar'tar] vt to limit, restrict

coba ['koβa] nf: **dar ~ a uno** to soft-soap sb

cobarde [ko'βarðe] adj cowardly ♦ nm coward; **cobardía** nf cowardice

cobaya [ko'βaja] nf guinea pig

cobertizo [koβer'tiθo] nm shelter

cobertura [koβer'tura] nf cover

cobija [ko'βixa] (AM) nf blanket

cobijar [koβi'xar] vt (cubrir) to cover; (proteger) to shelter; **cobijo** nm shelter

cobra ['koβra] nf cobra

cobrador, a [koβra'ðor, a] nm/f (de autobús) conductor/conductress; (de impuestos, gas) collector

cobrar [ko'βrar] vt (cheque) to cash; (sueldo) to collect, draw; (objeto) to recover; (precio) to charge; (deuda) to collect ♦ vi to be paid; **cóbrese al entregar** cash on delivery

cobre ['koβre] nm copper; **~s** nmpl (MUS) brass instruments

cobro ['koβro] nm (de cheque) cashing; **presentar al ~** to cash

cocaína [koka'ina] nf cocaine

cocción [kok'θjon] nf (CULIN) cooking; (en agua) boiling

cocear [koθe'ar] vi to kick

cocer [ko'θer] vt, vi to cook; (en agua) to boil; (en horno) to bake

coche ['kotʃe] nm (AUTO) car (BRIT), automobile (US); (de tren, de caballos) coach, carriage; (para niños) pram (BRIT), baby carriage (US); **ir en ~** to drive; **~ celular** Black Maria, prison van; **~ de bomberos** fire engine; **~ fúnebre** hearse; **coche-cama** (pl **coches-cama**) nm (FERRO) sleeping car, sleeper

cochera [ko'tʃera] nf garage; (de autobuses, trenes) depot

coche restaurante (pl **coches restaurante**) nm (FERRO) dining car, diner

cochinillo [kotʃi'niʎo] nm (CULIN) suckling pig, sucking pig

cochino, a [ko'tʃino, a] adj filthy, dirty ♦ nm/f pig

cocido [ko'θiðo] nm stew

cocina [ko'θina] nf kitchen; (aparato) cooker, stove; (acto) cookery; **~ eléctrica/de gas** electric/gas cooker; **~**

ncesa French cuisine; **cocinar** vt, vi cook

inero, a [koθi'nero, a] nm/f cook

o ['koko] nm coconut

odrilo [koko'ðrilo] nm crocodile

otero [koko'tero] nm coconut palm

tel ['koktel] nm cocktail

azo [ko'ðaθo] nm: **dar un ~ a uno** to dge sb

icia [ko'ðiθja] nf greed; **codiciar** vt covet; **codicioso, a** adj covetous

igo ['koðiɣo] nm code; **~ de barras** r code; **~ civil** common law; **~ de (la) rculación** highway code; **~ postal** stcode

illo [ko'ðiλo] nm (ZOOL) knee; (TEC) ow (joint)

o ['koðo] nm (ANAT, de tubo) elbow; OOL) knee

orniz [koðor'niθ] nf quail

rción [koer'θjon] nf coercion

táneo, a [koe'taneo, a] adj, nm/f ntemporary

xistir [koe(k)sis'tir] vi to coexist

adía [kofra'ðia] nf brotherhood, ternity

e ['kofre] nm (de joyas) case; (de ero) chest

er [ko'xer] (ESP) vt to take (hold of); *bjeto caído*) to pick up; (frutas) to pick, rvest; (resfriado, ladrón, pelota) to catch vi: **~ por el buen camino** to take the ght road; **~se** vr (el dedo) to catch; **~se algo** to get hold of sth

ollo [ko'ɣoλo] nm (de lechuga) heart

ote [ko'ɣote] nm back o nape of the ck

abitar [koaβi'tar] vi to live together, habit

echo [ko'etʃo] nm (acción) bribery; (*borno*) bribe

erente [koe'rente] adj coherent

esión [koe'sjon] nm cohesion

ete [ko'ete] nm rocket

ibido, a [koi'βiðo, a] adj (PSICO) ibited; (tímido) shy

ibir [koi'βir] vt to restrain, restrict

coincidencia [koinθi'ðenθja] nf coincidence

coincidir [koinθi'ðir] vi (en idea) to coincide, agree; (en lugar) to coincide

coito ['koito] nm intercourse, coitus

coja etc vb ver **coger**

cojear [koxe'ar] vi (persona) to limp, hobble; (mueble) to wobble, rock

cojera [ko'xera] nf limp

cojín [ko'xin] nm cushion; **cojinete** nm (TEC) ball bearing

cojo, a etc ['koxo, a] vb ver **coger** ♦ adj (que no puede andar) lame, crippled; (mueble) wobbly ♦ nm/f lame person, cripple

cojón [ko'xon] (fam) nm: **¡cojones!** shit! (!); **cojonudo, a** (fam) adj great, fantastic

col [kol] nf cabbage; **~es de Bruselas** Brussels sprouts

cola ['kola] nf tail; (de gente) queue; (lugar) end, last place; (para pegar) glue, gum; **hacer ~** to queue (up)

colaborador, a [kolaβora'ðor, a] nm/f collaborator

colaborar [kolaβo'rar] vi to collaborate

colada [ko'laða] nf: **hacer la ~** to do the washing

colador [kola'ðor] nm (de líquidos) strainer; (para verduras etc) colander

colapso [ko'lapso] nm collapse; **~ nervioso** nervous breakdown

colar [ko'lar] vt (líquido) to strain off; (metal) to cast ♦ vi to ooze, seep (through); **~se** vr to jump the queue; **~se en** to get into without paying; (fiesta) to gatecrash

colcha ['koltʃa] nf bedspread

colchón [kol'tʃon] nm mattress; **~ inflable** o **neumático** air bed, air mattress

colchoneta [koltʃo'neta] nf (en gimnasio) mat; (de playa) air bed

colección [kolek'θjon] nf collection; **coleccionar** vt to collect; **coleccionista** nm/f collector

colecta [ko'lekta] nf collection

colectivo, a [kolek'tiβo, a] adj collective,

joint ♦ nm (AM) (small) bus

colega [ko'leɣa] nm/f colleague

colegial, a [kole'xjal, a] nm/f schoolboy/
girl

colegio [ko'lexjo] nm college; (escuela)
school; (de abogados etc) association; ~
electoral polling station; ~ **mayor** hall of
residence

---
colegio

> ⓘ A **colegio** is normally a private
> primary or secondary school. In the
> state system it means a primary school
> although these are also called **escuelas**.
> State secondary schools are called
> **institutos**.

---

colegir [kole'xir] vt to infer, conclude

cólera ['kolera] nf (ira) anger ♦ nm (MED)
cholera; **colérico, a** [ko'leriko, a] adj
irascible, bad-tempered

colesterol [koleste'rol] nm cholesterol

coleta [ko'leta] nf pigtail

colgante [kol'ɣante] adj hanging ♦ nm
(joya) pendant

colgar [kol'ɣar] vt to hang (up); (ropa) to
hang out ♦ vi to hang; (TELEC) to hang
up

cólico ['koliko] nm colic

coliflor [koli'flor] nf cauliflower

colilla [ko'liʎa] nf cigarette end, butt

colina [ko'lina] nf hill

colisión [koli'sjon] nf collision; ~ **de**
frente head-on crash

collar [ko'ʎar] nm necklace; (de perro)
collar

colmar [kol'mar] vt to fill to the brim; (fig)
to fulfil, realize

colmena [kol'mena] nf beehive

colmillo [kol'miʎo] nm (diente) eye tooth;
(de elefante) tusk; (de perro) fang

colmo ['kolmo] nm: **¡es el ~!** it's the limit!

colocación [koloka'θjon] nf (acto)
placing; (empleo) position

colocar [kolo'kar] vt to place, put,
position; (dinero) to invest; (poner en
empleo) to find a job for; **~se** vr to get a

job

Colombia [ko'lombja] nf Colombia;
colombiano, a adj, nm/f Colombian

colonia [ko'lonja] nf colony; (de casas)
housing estate; (agua de ~) cologne

colonización [koloniθa'θjon] nf
colonization; **colonizador, a**
[koloniθa'ðor, a] adj colonizing ♦ nm/f
colonist, settler

colonizar [koloni'θar] vt to colonize

coloquio [ko'lokjo] nm conversation;
(congreso) conference

color [ko'lor] nm colour

colorado, a [kolo'raðo, a] adj (rojo) red;
(LAM: chiste) rude

colorante [kolo'rante] nm colouring

colorear [kolore'ar] vt to colour

colorete [kolo'rete] nm blusher

colorido [kolo'riðo] nm colouring

columna [ko'lumna] nf column; (pilar)
pillar; (apoyo) support

columpiar [kolum'pjar] vt to swing; **~se**
vr to swing; **columpio** nm swing

coma ['koma] nf comma ♦ nm (MED)
coma

comadre [ko'maðre] nf (madrina)
godmother; (chismosa) gossip;
comadrona nf midwife

comandancia [koman'danθja] nf
command

comandante [koman'dante] nm
commandant

comarca [ko'marka] nf region

comba ['komba] nf (curva) curve; (cuerda)
skipping rope; **saltar a la ~** to skip

combar [kom'bar] vt to bend, curve

combate [kom'bate] nm fight;
combatiente nm combatant

combatir [komba'tir] vt to fight, combat

combinación [kombina'θjon] nf
combination; (QUÍM) compound; (prenda)
slip

combinar [kombi'nar] vt to combine

combustible [kombus'tiβle] nm fuel

combustión [kombus'tjon] nf combustio

comedia [ko'meðja] nf comedy; (TEATRO)
play, drama

mediante [kome'ðjante] *nm/f* (comic) ctor/actress

medido, a [kome'ðiðo, a] *adj* moderate

medor, a [kome'ðor, a] *nm* (*habitación*) ning room; (*cantina*) canteen

mensal [komen'sal] *nm/f* fellow guest diner)

mentar [komen'tar] *vt* to comment on

mentario [komen'tarjo] *nm* comment, emark; (*literario*) commentary; **~s** *nmpl* *hismes*) gossip *sg*

mentarista [komenta'rista] *nm/f* ommentator

menzar [komen'θar] *vt*, *vi* to begin, tart; **~ a hacer algo** to begin *o* start oing sth

mer [ko'mer] *vt* to eat; (*DAMAS, AJEDREZ*) o take, capture ♦ *vi* to eat; (*almorzar*) to ave lunch; **~se** *vr* to eat up

mercial [komer'θjal] *adj* commercial; *relativo al negocio*) business *cpd*;

omercializar *vt* (*producto*) to market; *pey*) to commercialize

merciante [komer'θjante] *nm/f* trader, nerchant

merciar [komer'θjar] *vi* to trade, do usiness

mercio [ko'merθjo] *nm* commerce, rade; (*negocio*) business; (*fig*) dealings *pl*; **electrónico** e-commerce

mestible [komes'tißle] *adj* eatable, dible; **~s** *nmpl* food *sg*, foodstuffs

meta [ko'meta] *nm* comet ♦ *nf* kite

meter [kome'ter] *vt* to commit

metido [kome'tiðo] *nm* task, ssignment

mezón [kome'θon] *nf* itch, itching

mic [ko'mik] *nm* comic

micios [ko'miθjos] *nmpl* elections

mico, a ['komiko, a] *adj* comic(al) *nm/f* comedian

mida [ko'miða] *nf* (*alimento*) food; *cena*) meal; (*de mediodía*) lunch

midilla [komi'ðiʎa] *nf*: **ser la ~ de la iudad** to be the talk of the town

mienzo *etc* [ko'mjenθo] *vb ver*

omenzar ♦ *nm* beginning, start

comillas [ko'miʎas] *nfpl* quotation marks

comilona [komi'lona] (*fam*) *nf* blow-out

comino [ko'mino] *nm*: **(no) me importa un ~** I don't give a damn

comisaría [komisa'ria] *nf* (*de policía*) police station; (*MIL*) commissariat

comisario [komi'sarjo] *nm* (*MIL etc*) commissary; (*POL*) commissar

comisión [komi'sjon] *nf* commission

comité [komi'te] (*pl* **~s**) *nm* committee

comitiva [komi'tißa] *nf* retinue

como ['komo] *adv* as; (*tal ~*) like; (*aproximadamente*) about, approximately ♦ *conj* (*ya que, puesto que*) as, since; **¡~ no!** of course!; **~ no lo haga hoy** unless he does it today; **~ si** as if; **es tan alto ~ ancho** it is as high as it is wide

cómo ['komo] *adv* how?, why? ♦ *excl* what?, I beg your pardon? ♦ *nm*: **el ~ y el porqué** the whys and wherefores

cómoda ['komoða] *nf* chest of drawers

comodidad [komoði'ðað] *nf* comfort; **venga a su ~** come at your convenience

comodín [komo'ðin] *nm* joker

cómodo, a ['komoðo, a] *adj* comfortable; (*práctico, de fácil uso*) convenient

compact disc *nm* compact disk player

compacto, a [kom'pakto, a] *adj* compact

compadecer [kompaðe'θer] *vt* to pity, be sorry for; **~se** *vr*: **~se de** to pity, be *o* feel sorry for

compadre [kom'paðre] *nm* (*padrino*) godfather; (*amigo*) friend, pal

compañero, a [kompa'ɲero, a] *nm/f* companion; (*novio*) boy/girlfriend; **~ de clase** classmate

compañía [kompa'ɲia] *nf* company

comparación [kompara'θjon] *nf* comparison; **en ~ con** in comparison with

comparar [kompa'rar] *vt* to compare

comparecer [kompare'θer] *vi* to appear (in court)

comparsa [kom'parsa] *nm/f* (*TEATRO*) extra

compartimiento [komparti'mjento] *nm* (*FERRO*) compartment

compartir [kompar'tir] *vt* to share; (*dinero,*

comida etc) to divide (up), share (out)
compás [kom'pas] nm (MUS) beat,
rhythm; (MAT) compasses pl; (NAUT etc)
compass
compasión [kompa'sjon] nf compassion,
pity
compasivo, a [kompa'sißo, a] adj
compassionate
compatibilidad [kompatißili'ðað] nf
compatibility
compatible [kompa'tißle] adj compatible
compatriota [kompa'trjota] nm/f
compatriot, fellow countryman/woman
compendiar [kompen'djar] vt to
summarize; **compendio** nm summary
compenetrarse [kompene'trarse] vr to
be in tune
compensación [kompensa'θjon] nf
compensation
compensar [kompen'sar] vt to
compensate
competencia [kompe'tenθja] nf
(incumbencia) domain, field; (JUR,
habilidad) competence; (rivalidad)
competition
competente [kompe'tente] adj competent
competición [kompeti'θjon] nf
competition
competir [kompe'tir] vi to compete
compilar [kompi'lar] vt to compile
complacencia [kompla'θenθja] nf (placer)
pleasure; (tolerancia excesiva)
complacency
complacer [kompla'θer] vt to please; ~se
vr to be pleased
complaciente [kompla'θjente] adj kind,
obliging, helpful
complejo, a [kom'plexo, a] adj, nm
complex
complementario, a [komplemen'tarjo, a]
adj complementary
completar [komple'tar] vt to complete
completo, a [kom'pleto, a] adj complete;
(perfecto) perfect; (lleno) full ♦ nm full
complement
complicado, a [kompli'kaðo, a] adj
complicated; **estar ~ en** to be mixed up

in
cómplice ['kompliθe] nm/f accomplice
complot [kom'plo(t)] (pl ~s) nm plot
componer [kompo'ner] vt (MUS,
LITERATURA, IMPRENTA) to compose; (algo
roto) to mend, repair; (arreglar) to
arrange; ~se vr: ~se de to consist of;
componérselas para hacer algo to
manage to do sth
comportamiento [komporta'mjento] n
behaviour, conduct
comportarse [kompor'tarse] vr to beha
composición [komposi'θjon] nf
composition
compositor, a [komposi'tor, a] nm/f
composer
compostura [kompos'tura] nf (actitud)
composure
compra ['kompra] nf purchase; **ir de ~s**
go shopping; **comprador, a** nm/f
buyer, purchaser
comprar [kom'prar] vt to buy, purchase
comprender [kompren'der] vt to
understand; (incluir) to comprise, includ
comprensión [kompren'sjon] nf
understanding; **comprensivo, a** adj
(actitud) understanding
compresa [kom'presa] nf: ~ **higiénica**
sanitary towel (BRIT) o napkin (US)
comprimido, a [kompri'miðo, a] adj
compressed ♦ nm (MED) pill, tablet
comprimir [kompri'mir] vt to compress
comprobante [kompro'ßante] nm proof
(COM) voucher; ~ **de recibo** receipt
comprobar [kompro'ßar] vt to check;
(probar) to prove; (TEC) to check, test
comprometer [komprome'ter] vt to
compromise; (poner en peligro) to
endanger; ~se vr (involucrarse) to get
involved
compromiso [kompro'miso] nm
(obligación) obligation; (cometido)
commitment; (convenio) agreement;
(apuro) awkward situation
compuesto, a [kom'pwesto, a] adj: ~ de
composed of, made up of ♦ nm
compound

computador [komputa'ðor] *nm* computer; ~ **central** mainframe computer; ~ **personal** personal computer

computadora [komputa'ðora] *nf* = **computador**

cómputo ['komputo] *nm* calculation

comulgar [komul'var] *vi* to receive communion

común [ko'mun] *adj* common ♦ *nm*: **el ~** the community

comunicación [komunika'θjon] *nf* communication; (*informe*) report

comunicado [komuni'kaðo] *nm* announcement; ~ **de prensa** press release

comunicar [komuni'kar] *vt*, *vi* to communicate; ~**se** *vr* to communicate; **está comunicando** (*TEL*) the line's engaged (*BRIT*) o busy (*US*);

comunicativo, a *adj* communicative

comunidad [komuni'ðað] *nf* community; ~ **autónoma** (*POL*) autonomous region; **C~ Económica Europea** European Economic Community

comunión [komu'njon] *nf* communion

comunismo [komu'nismo] *nm* communism; **comunista** *adj*, *nm/f* communist

---

con [kon] *prep* **1** (*medio, compañía*) with; **comer ~ cuchara** to eat with a spoon; **pasear ~ uno** to go for a walk with sb

2 (*a pesar de*): ~ **todo, merece nuestros respetos** all the same, he deserves our respect

3 (*para ~*): **es muy bueno para ~ los niños** he's very good with (the) children

4 (*+infin*): ~ **llegar tan tarde se quedó sin comer** by arriving so late he missed out on eating

♦ *conj*: ~ **que: será suficiente ~ que le escribas** it will be sufficient if you write to her

---

conato [ko'nato] *nm* attempt; ~ **de robo** ttempted robbery

concebir [konθe'ßir] *vt*, *vi* to conceive

conceder [konθe'ðer] *vt* to concede

concejal, a [konθe'xal, a] *nm/f* town councillor

concentración [konθentra'θjon] *nf* concentration

concentrar [konθen'trar] *vt* to concentrate; ~**se** *vr* to concentrate

concepción [konθep'θjon] *nf* conception

concepto [kon'θepto] *nm* concept

concernir [konθer'nir] *vi* to concern; **en lo que concierne a ...** as far as ... is concerned; **en lo que a mí concierne** as far as I'm concerned

concertar [konθer'tar] *vt* (*MUS*) to harmonize; (*acordar: precio*) to agree; (: *tratado*) to conclude; (*trato*) to arrange, fix up; (*combinar: esfuerzos*) to coordinate ♦ *vi* to harmonize, be in tune

concesión [konθe'sjon] *nf* concession

concesionario [konθesjo'narjo] *nm* (licensed) dealer, agent

concha ['kontʃa] *nf* shell

conciencia [kon'θjenθja] *nf* conscience; **tener/tomar ~ de** to be/become aware of; **tener la ~ limpia/tranquila** to have a clear conscience

concienciar [konθjen'θjar] *vt* to make aware; ~**se** *vr* to become aware

concienzudo, a [konθjen'θuðo, a] *adj* conscientious

concierto *etc* [kon'θjerto] *vb ver* **concertar** ♦ *nm* concert; (*obra*) concerto

conciliar [konθi'ljar] *vt* to reconcile

concilio [kon'θiljo] *nm* council

conciso, a [kon'θiso, a] *adj* concise

concluir [konklu'ir] *vt*, *vi* to conclude; ~**se** *vr* to conclude

conclusión [konklu'sjon] *nf* conclusion

concluyente [konklu'jente] *adj* (*prueba, información*) conclusive

concordar [konkor'ðar] *vt* to reconcile ♦ *vi* to agree, tally

concordia [kon'korðja] *nf* harmony

concretar [konkre'tar] *vt* to make concrete, make more specific; ~**se** *vr* to become more definite

concreto, a [kon'kreto, a] *adj*, *nm* (*AM*)

concrete; **en ~** (*en resumen*) to sum up; (*específicamente*) specifically; **no hay nada en ~** there's nothing definite

concurrencia [konkuˈrrenθja] *nf* turnout

concurrido, a [konkuˈrriðo, a] *adj* (*calle*) busy; (*local, reunión*) crowded

concurrir [konkuˈrrir] *vi* (*juntarse: ríos*) to meet, come together; (: *personas*) to gather, meet

concursante [konkurˈsante] *nm/f* competitor

concurso [konˈkurso] *nm* (*de público*) crowd; (*ESCOL, DEPORTE, competencia*) competition; (*ayuda*) help, cooperation

condal [konˈdal] *adj*: **la Ciudad C~** Barcelona

conde [ˈkonde] *nm* count

condecoración [kondekoraˈθjon] *nf* (*MIL*) medal

condecorar [kondekoˈrar] *vt* (*MIL*) to decorate

condena [konˈdena] *nf* sentence

condenación [kondenaˈθjon] *nf* condemnation; (*REL*) damnation

condenar [kondeˈnar] *vt* to condemn; (*JUR*) to convict; **~se** *vr* (*REL*) to be damned

condensar [kondenˈsar] *vt* to condense

condesa [konˈdesa] *nf* countess

condición [kondiˈθjon] *nf* condition; **condicional** *adj* conditional

condicionar [kondiθjoˈnar] *vt* (*acondicionar*) to condition; **~ algo a** to make sth conditional on

condimento [kondiˈmento] *nm* seasoning

condolerse [kondoˈlerse] *vr* to sympathize

condón [konˈdon] *nm* condom

conducir [konduˈθir] *vt* to take, convey; (*AUTO*) to drive ♦ *vi* to drive; (*fig*) to lead; **~se** *vr* to behave

conducta [konˈdukta] *nf* conduct, behaviour

conducto [konˈdukto] *nm* pipe, tube; (*fig*) channel

conductor, a [kondukˈtor, a] *adj* leading, guiding ♦ *nm* (*FÍSICA*) conductor; (*de vehículo*) driver

conduje *etc vb ver* **conducir**

conduzco *etc vb ver* **conducir**

conectado, a [konekˈtaðo, a] *adj* (*INFORM*) on-line

conectar [konekˈtar] *vt* to connect (up); (*enchufar*) plug in

conejillo [koneˈxiʎo] *nm*: **~ de Indias** (*ZOOL*) guinea pig

conejo [koˈnexo] *nm* rabbit

conexión [konekˈsjon] *nf* connection

confección [konfe(k)ˈθjon] *nf* preparation; (*industria*) clothing industry

confeccionar [konfekθjoˈnar] *vt* to make (up)

confederación [konfeðeraˈθjon] *nf* confederation

conferencia [konfeˈrenθja] *nf* conference; (*lección*) lecture; (*TEL*) call

conferir [konfeˈrir] *vt* to award

confesar [konfeˈsar] *vt* to confess, admit

confesión [konfeˈsjon] *nf* confession

confesionario [konfesjoˈnarjo] *nm* confessional

confeti [konˈfeti] *nm* confetti

confiado, a [konˈfjaðo, a] *adj* (*crédulo*) trusting; (*seguro*) confident

confianza [konˈfjanθa] *nf* trust; (*seguridad*) confidence; (*familiaridad*) intimacy, familiarity

confiar [konˈfjar] *vt* to entrust ♦ *vi* to trust

confidencia [konfiˈðenθja] *nf* confidence

confidencial [konfiðenˈθjal] *adj* confidential

confidente [konfiˈðente] *nm/f* confidant/ e; (*policial*) informer

configurar [konfixuˈrar] *vt* to shape, form

confín [konˈfin] *nm* limit; **confines** *nmpl* confines, limits

confinar [konfiˈnar] *vi* to confine; (*desterrar*) to banish

confirmar [konfirˈmar] *vt* to confirm

confiscar [konfisˈkar] *vt* to confiscate

confite [konˈfite] *nm* sweet (*BRIT*), candy (*US*)

confitería [konfiteˈria] *nf* (*tienda*) confectioner's (shop)

confitura [konfi'tura] *nf* jam

conflictivo, a [konflik'tiβo, a] *adj* (*asunto, propuesta*) controversial; (*país, situación*) troubled

conflicto [kon'flikto] *nm* conflict; (*fig*) clash

confluir [kon'flwir] *vi* (*ríos*) to meet; (*gente*) to gather

conformar [konfor'mar] *vt* to shape, fashion ♦ *vi* to agree; **~se** *vr* to conform; (*resignarse*) to resign o.s.

conforme [kon'forme] *adj* (*correspondiente*): **~ con** in line with; (*de acuerdo*): **estar ~s (con algo)** to be in agreement (with sth) ♦ *adv* as ♦ *excl* agreed! ♦ *prep*: **~ a** in accordance with; **quedarse ~ (con algo)** to be satisfied (with sth)

conformidad [konformi'ðað] *nf* (*semejanza*) similarity; (*acuerdo*) agreement; **conformista** *adj, nm/f* conformist

confortable [konfor'taβle] *adj* comfortable

confortar [konfor'tar] *vt* to comfort

confrontar [konfron'tar] *vt* to confront; (*dos personas*) to bring face to face; (*cotejar*) to compare

confundir [konfun'dir] *vt* (*equivocar*) to mistake, confuse; (*turbar*) to confuse; **~se** *vr* (*turbarse*) to get confused; (*equivocarse*) to make a mistake; (*mezclarse*) to mix

confusión [konfu'sjon] *nf* confusion

confuso, a [kon'fuso, a] *adj* confused

congelado, a [konxe'laðo, a] *adj* frozen; **~s** *nmpl* frozen food(s); **congelador** *nm* (*aparato*) freezer, deep freeze

congelar [konxe'lar] *vt* to freeze; **~se** *vr* (*sangre, grasa*) to congeal

congeniar [konxe'njar] *vi* to get on (*BRIT*), to along (*US*) well

congestión [konxes'tjon] *nf* congestion

congestionar [konxestjo'nar] *vt* to congest

congoja [kon'goxa] *nf* distress, grief

congraciarse [kongra'θjarse] *vr* to ingratiate o.s.

congratular [kongratu'lar] *vt* to congratulate

congregación [kongreγa'θjon] *nf* congregation

congregar [kongre'γar] *vt* to gather together; **~se** *vr* to gather together

congresista [kongre'sista] *nm/f* delegate, congressman/woman

congreso [kon'greso] *nm* congress

congrio ['kongrjo] *nm* conger eel

conjetura [konxe'tura] *nf* guess; **conjeturar** *vt* to guess

conjugar [konxu'γar] *vt* to combine, fit together; (*LING*) to conjugate

conjunción [konxun'θjon] *nf* conjunction

conjunto, a [kon'xunto, a] *adj* joint, united ♦ *nm* whole; (*MUS*) band; **en ~** as a whole

conjurar [konxu'rar] *vt* (*REL*) to exorcise; (*fig*) to ward off ♦ *vi* to plot

conmemoración [konmemora'θjon] *nf* commemoration

conmemorar [konmemo'rar] *vt* to commemorate

conmigo [kon'miγo] *pron* with me

conmoción [konmo'θjon] *nf* shock; (*fig*) upheaval; **~ cerebral** (*MED*) concussion

conmovedor, a [konmoβe'ðor, a] *adj* touching, moving; (*emocionante*) exciting

conmover [konmo'βer] *vt* to shake, disturb; (*fig*) to move

conmutador [konmuta'ðor] *nm* switch; (*AM: TEL: centralita*) switchboard; (: *central*) telephone exchange

cono ['kono] *nm* cone

conocedor, a [konoθe'ðor, a] *adj* expert, knowledgeable ♦ *nm/f* expert

conocer [kono'θer] *vt* to know; (*por primera vez*) to meet, get to know; (*entender*) to know about; (*reconocer*) to recognize; **~se** *vr* (*una persona*) to know o.s.; (*dos personas*) to (get to) know each other

conocido, a [kono'θiðo, a] *adj* (well-)known ♦ *nm/f* acquaintance

conocimiento [konoθi'mjento] *nm*

knowledge; (MED) consciousness; **~s** nmpl (saber) knowledge sg

conozco etc vb ver **conocer**

conque ['konke] conj and so, so then

conquista [kon'kista] nf conquest; **conquistador, a** adj conquering ♦ nm conqueror

conquistar [konkis'tar] vt to conquer

consagrar [konsa'xrar] vt (REL) to consecrate; (fig) to devote

consciente [kons'θjente] adj conscious

consecución [konseku'θjon] nf acquisition; (de fin) attainment

consecuencia [konse'kwenθja] nf consequence, outcome; (coherencia) consistency

consecuente [konse'kwente] adj consistent

consecutivo, a [konseku'tiβo, a] adj consecutive

conseguir [konse'xir] vt to get, obtain; (objetivo) to attain

consejero, a [konse'xero, a] nm/f adviser, consultant; (POL) councillor

consejo [kon'sexo] nm advice; (POL) council; **~ de administración** (COM) board of directors; **~ de guerra** court martial; **~ de ministros** cabinet meeting

consenso [kon'senso] nm consensus

consentimiento [konsenti'mjento] nm consent

consentir [konsen'tir] vt (permitir, tolerar) to consent to; (mimar) to pamper, spoil; (aguantar) to put up with ♦ vi to agree, consent; **~ que uno haga algo** to allow sb to do sth

conserje [kon'serxe] nm caretaker; (portero) porter

conservación [konserβa'θjon] nf conservation; (de alimentos, vida) preservation

conservador, a [konserβa'ðor, a] adj (POL) conservative ♦ nm/f conservative

conservante [konser'βante] nm preservative

conservar [konser'βar] vt to conserve, keep; (alimentos, vida) to preserve; **~se** vr

to survive

conservas [kon'serβas] nfpl canned food(s) (pl)

conservatorio [konserβa'torjo] nm (MUS) conservatoire, conservatory

considerable [konsiðe'raβle] adj considerable

consideración [konsiðera'θjon] nf consideration; (estimación) respect

considerado, a [konsiðe'raðo, a] adj (atento) considerate; (respetado) respected

considerar [konsiðe'rar] vt to consider

consigna [kon'sixna] nf (orden) order, instruction; (para equipajes) left-luggage office

consigo etc [kon'sixo] vb ver **conseguir** ♦ pron (m) with him; (f) with her; (Vd) with you; (reflexivo) with o.s.

consiguiendo etc vb ver **conseguir**

consiguiente [konsi'xjente] adj consequent; **por ~** and so, therefore, consequently

consistente [konsis'tente] adj consistent; (sólido) solid, firm; (válido) sound

consistir [konsis'tir] vi: **~ en** (componerse de) to consist of

consola [kon'sola] nf (mueble) console table; (de videojuegos) console

consolación [konsola'θjon] nf consolation

consolar [konso'lar] vt to console

consolidar [konsoli'ðar] vt to consolidate

consomé [konso'me] (pl ~s) nm consommé, clear soup

consonante [konso'nante] adj consonant, harmonious ♦ nf consonant

consorcio [kon'sorθjo] nm consortium

conspiración [konspira'θjon] nf conspiracy

conspirador, a [konspira'ðor, a] nm/f conspirator

conspirar [konspi'rar] vi to conspire

constancia [kon'stanθja] nf constancy; **dejar ~ de** to put on record

constante [kons'tante] adj, nf constant

constar [kons'tar] vi (evidenciarse) to be clear o evident; **~ de** to consist of

constatar [konsta'tar] vt to verify

consternación [konsterna'θjon] *nf* consternation

constipado, a [konsti'paðo, a] *adj*: **estar ~** to have a cold ♦ *nm* cold

constitución [konstitu'θjon] *nf* constitution; **constitucional** *adj* constitutional

constituir [konstitu'ir] *vt* (*formar, componer*) to constitute, make up; (*fundar, erigir, ordenar*) to constitute, establish

constituyente [konstitu'jente] *adj* constituent

constreñir [konstre'nir] *vt* (*restringir*) to restrict

construcción [konstruk'θjon] *nf* construction, building

constructor, a [konstruk'tor, a] *nm/f* builder

construir [konstru'ir] *vt* to build, construct

construyendo *etc vb ver* **construir**

consuelo [kon'swelo] *nm* consolation, solace

cónsul ['konsul] *nm* consul; **consulado** *nm* consulate

consulta [kon'sulta] *nf* consultation; (*MED*): **horas de ~** surgery hours

consultar [konsul'tar] *vt* to consult

consultorio [konsul'torjo] *nm* (*MED*) surgery

consumar [konsu'mar] *vt* to complete, carry out; (*crimen*) to commit; (*sentencia*) to carry out

consumición [konsumi'θjon] *nf* consumption; (*bebida*) drink; (*comida*) food; **~ mínima** cover charge

consumidor, a [konsumi'ðor, a] *nm/f* consumer

consumir [konsu'mir] *vt* to consume; **~se** *vr* to be consumed; (*persona*) to waste away

consumismo [konsu'mismo] *nm* consumerism

consumo [kon'sumo] *nm* consumption

contabilidad [kontaβili'ðað] *nf* accounting, book-keeping; (*profesión*) accountancy; **contable** *nm/f* accountant

contacto [kon'takto] *nm* contact; (*AUTO*) ignition

contado, a [kon'taðo, a] *adj*: **~s** (*escasos*) numbered, scarce, few ♦ *nm*: **pagar al ~** to pay (in) cash

contador [konta'ðor] *nm* (*aparato*) meter; (*AM*: *contante*) accountant

contagiar [konta'xjar] *vt* (*enfermedad*) to pass on, transmit; (*persona*) to infect; **~se** *vr* to become infected

contagio [kon'taxjo] *nm* infection; **contagioso, a** *adj* infectious; (*fig*) catching

contaminación [kontamina'θjon] *nf* contamination; (*polución*) pollution

contaminar [kontami'nar] *vt* to contaminate; (*aire, agua*) to pollute

contante [kon'tante] *adj*: **dinero ~ (y sonante)** cash

contar [kon'tar] *vt* (*páginas, dinero*) to count; (*anécdota, chiste etc*) to tell ♦ *vi* to count; **~ con** to rely on, count on

contemplación [kontempla'θjon] *nf* contemplation

contemplar [kontem'plar] *vt* to contemplate; (*mirar*) to look at

contemporáneo, a [kontempo'raneo, a] *adj, nm/f* contemporary

contendiente [konten'djente] *nm/f* contestant

contenedor [kontene'ðor] *nm* container

contener [konte'ner] *vt* to contain, hold; (*retener*) to hold back, contain; **~se** *vr* to control *o* restrain o.s.

contenido, a [konte'niðo, a] *adj* (*moderado*) restrained; (*risa etc*) suppressed ♦ *nm* contents *pl*, content

contentar [konten'tar] *vt* (*satisfacer*) to satisfy; (*complacer*) to please; **~se** *vr* to be satisfied

contento, a [kon'tento, a] *adj* (*alegre*) pleased; (*feliz*) happy

contestación [kontesta'θjon] *nf* answer, reply

contestador [kontesta'ðor] *nm*: **~ automático** answering machine

contestar [kontes'tar] *vt* to answer, reply;

(*JUR*) to corroborate, confirm

contexto [kon'te(k)sto] *nm* context

contienda [kon'tjenda] *nf* contest

contigo [kon'tiɣo] *pron* with you

contiguo, a [kon'tiɣwo, a] *adj* adjacent, adjoining

continente [konti'nente] *adj, nm* continent

contingencia [kontin'xenθja] *nf* contingency; (*riesgo*) risk; **contingente** *adj, nm* contingent

continuación [kontinwa'θjon] *nf* continuation; **a ~** then, next

continuar [konti'nwar] *vt* to continue, go on with ♦ *vi* to continue, go on; **~ hablando** to continue talking *o* to talk

continuidad [kontinwi'ðað] *nf* continuity

continuo, a [kon'tinwo, a] *adj* (*sin interrupción*) continuous; (*acción perseverante*) continual

contorno [kon'torno] *nm* outline; (*GEO*) contour; **~s** *nmpl* neighbourhood *sg*, surrounding area *sg*

contorsión [kontor'sjon] *nf* contortion

contra ['kontra] *prep, adv* against ♦ *nm inv* con ♦ *nf*: **la C~** (*de Nicaragua*) the Contras *pl*

contraataque [kontraa'take] *nm* counter-attack

contrabajo [kontra'ßaxo] *nm* double bass

contrabandista [kontraßan'dista] *nm/f* smuggler

contrabando [kontra'ßando] *nm* (*acción*) smuggling; (*mercancías*) contraband

contracción [kontrak'θjon] *nf* contraction

contracorriente [kontrako'rrjente]: **(a) ~** *adv* against the current

contradecir [kontraðe'θir] *vt* to contradict

contradicción [kontraðik'θjon] *nf* contradiction

contradictorio, a [kontraðik'torjo, a] *adj* contradictory

contraer [kontra'er] *vt* to contract; (*limitar*) to restrict; **~se** *vr* to contract; (*limitarse*) to limit o.s.

contraluz [kontra'luθ] *nf*: **a ~** against the light

contrapartida [kontrapar'tiða] *nf*: **como ~ (de)** in return (for)

contrapelo [kontra'pelo]: **a ~** *adv* the wrong way

contrapesar [kontrape'sar] *vt* to counterbalance; (*fig*) to offset; **contrapeso** *nm* counterweight

contraportada [kontrapor'taða] *nf* (*de revista*) back cover

contraproducente [kontraproðu'θente] *adj* counterproductive

contrariar [kontra'rjar] *vt* (*oponerse*) to oppose; (*poner obstáculo*) to impede; (*enfadar*) to vex

contrariedad [kontrarje'ðað] *nf* (*obstáculo*) obstacle, setback; (*disgusto*) vexation, annoyance

contrario, a [kon'trarjo, a] *adj* contrary; (*persona*) opposed; (*sentido, lado*) opposite ♦ *nm/f* enemy, adversary; (*DEPORTE*) opponent; **al/por el ~** on the contrary; **de lo ~** otherwise

contrarreloj [kontrarre'lo] *nf* (*tb*: **prueba ~**) time trial

contrarrestar [kontrarres'tar] *vt* to counteract

contrasentido [kontrasen'tiðo] *nm*: **es un ~ que él ...** it doesn't make sense for him to ...

contraseña [kontra'seɲa] *nf* (*INFORM*) password

contrastar [kontras'tar] *vt, vi* to contrast

contraste [kon'traste] *nm* contrast

contratar [kontra'tar] *vt* (*firmar un acuerdo para*) to contract for; (*empleados, obreros*) to hire, engage; **~se** *vr* to sign on

contratiempo [kontra'tjempo] *nm* setback

contratista [kontra'tista] *nm/f* contractor

contrato [kon'trato] *nm* contract

contravenir [kontraße'nir] *vi*: **~ a** to contravene, violate

contraventana [kontraßen'tana] *nf* shutter

contribución [kontrißu'θjon] *nf* (*municipal etc*) tax; (*ayuda*) contribution

contribuir [kontrißu'ir] *vt, vi* to

contribute; (COM) to pay (in taxes)

contribuyente [kontriβu'jente] *nm/f* (COM) taxpayer; (que ayuda) contributor

contrincante [kontrin'kante] *nm* opponent

control [kon'trol] *nm* control; (inspección) inspection, check; **~ador, a** *nm/f* controller; **~ador aéreo** air-traffic controller

controlar [kontro'lar] *vt* to control; (inspeccionar) to inspect, check

controversia [kontro'βersja] *nf* controversy

contundente [kontun'dente] *adj* (instrumento) blunt; (argumento, derrota) overwhelming

contusión [kontu'sjon] *nf* bruise

convalecencia [kombale'θenθja] *nf* convalescence

convalecer [kombale'θer] *vi* to convalesce, get better

convaleciente [kombale'θjente] *adj, nm/f* convalescent

convalidar [kombali'ðar] *vt* (título) to recognize

convencer [komben'θer] *vt* to convince

convencimiento [kombenθi'mjento] *nm* (certidumbre) conviction

convención [komben'θjon] *nf* convention

conveniencia [kombe'njenθja] *nf* suitability; (conformidad) agreement; (utilidad, provecho) usefulness; **~s** *nfpl* (convenciones) conventions; (COM) property *sg*

conveniente [kombe'njente] *adj* suitable; (útil) useful

convenio [kom'benjo] *nm* agreement, treaty

convenir [kombe'nir] *vi* (estar de acuerdo) to agree; (venir bien) to suit, be suitable

convento [kom'bento] *nm* convent

convenza *etc vb ver* **convencer**

converger [komber'xer] *vi* to converge

convergir [komber'xir] *vi* = **converger**

conversación [kombersa'θjon] *nf* conversation

conversar [komber'sar] *vi* to talk, converse

conversión [komber'sjon] *nf* conversion

convertir [komber'tir] *vt* to convert

convicción [kombik'θjon] *nf* conviction

convicto, a [kom'bikto, a] *adj* convicted

convidado, a [kombi'ðaðo, a] *nm/f* guest

convidar [kombi'ðar] *vt* to invite

convincente [kombin'θente] *adj* convincing

convite [kom'bite] *nm* invitation; (banquete) banquet

convivencia [kombi'βenθja] *nf* coexistence, living together

convivir [kombi'βir] *vi* to live together

convocar [kombo'kar] *vt* to summon, call (together)

convocatoria [komboka'torja] *nf* (de oposiciones, elecciones) notice; (de huelga) call

convulsión [kombul'sjon] *nf* convulsion

conyugal [konju'γal] *adj* conjugal; **cónyuge** ['konjuxe] *nm/f* spouse

coñac [ko'ɲa(k)] (*pl* **~s**) *nm* cognac, brandy

coño ['koɲo] (fam!) *excl* (enfado) shit! (!); (sorpresa) bloody hell! (!)

cooperación [koopera'θjon] *nf* cooperation

cooperar [koope'rar] *vi* to cooperate

cooperativa [koopera'tiβa] *nf* cooperative

coordinadora [koorðina'ðora] *nf* (comité) coordinating committee

coordinar [koorði'nar] *vt* to coordinate

copa ['kopa] *nf* cup; (vaso) glass; (bebida): **(tomar una) ~** (to have a) drink; (de árbol) top; (de sombrero) crown; **~s** *nfpl* (NAIPES) ≈ hearts

copia ['kopja] *nf* copy; **~ de respaldo** *o* **seguridad** (INFORM) back-up copy; **copiar** *vt* to copy

copioso, a [ko'pjoso, a] *adj* copious, plentiful

copla ['kopla] *nf* verse; (canción) (popular) song

copo ['kopo] *nm*: **~ de nieve** snowflake; **~s de maíz** cornflakes

coqueta [ko'keta] *adj* flirtatious,

coquettish; **coquetear** *vi* to flirt

coraje [ko'raxe] *nm* courage; *(ánimo)* spirit; *(ira)* anger

coral [ko'ral] *adj* choral ♦ *nf* (*MUS*) choir ♦ *nm* (*ZOOL*) coral

coraza [ko'raθa] *nf* (*armadura*) armour; *(blindaje)* armour-plating

corazón [kora'θon] *nm* heart

corazonada [koraθo'naða] *nf* impulse; *(presentimiento)* hunch

corbata [kor'ßata] *nf* tie

corchete [kor'tʃete] *nm* catch, clasp

corcho ['kortʃo] *nm* cork; *(PESCA)* float

cordel [kor'ðel] *nm* cord, line

cordero [kor'ðero] *nm* lamb

cordial [kor'ðjal] *adj* cordial; **~idad** *nf* warmth, cordiality

cordillera [korði'ʎera] *nf* range (of mountains)

Córdoba ['korðoßa] *n* Cordova

cordón [kor'ðon] *nm* (*cuerda*) cord, string; *(de zapatos)* lace; (*MIL etc*) cordon

cordura [kor'ðura] *nf*: **con ~** *(obrar, hablar)* sensibly

corneta [kor'neta] *nf* bugle

cornisa [kor'nisa] *nf* (*ARQ*) cornice

coro ['koro] *nm* chorus; *(conjunto de cantores)* choir

corona [ko'rona] *nf* crown; *(de flores)* garland; **coronación** *nf* coronation; **coronar** *vt* to crown

coronel [koro'nel] *nm* colonel

coronilla [koro'niʎa] *nf* (*ANAT*) crown (of the head)

corporación [korpora'θjon] *nf* corporation

corporal [korpo'ral] *adj* corporal, bodily

corpulento, a [korpu'lento a] *adj* *(persona)* heavily-built

corral [ko'rral] *nm* farmyard

correa [ko'rrea] *nf* strap; *(cinturón)* belt; *(de perro)* lead, leash

corrección [korrek'θjon] *nf* correction; *(reprensión)* rebuke; **correccional** *nm* reformatory

correcto, a [ko'rrekto a] *adj* correct; *(persona)* well-mannered

corredizo, a [korre'ðiθo, a] *adj* (*puerta etc*) sliding

corredor, a [korre'ðor, a] *nm* (*pasillo*) corridor; *(balcón corrido)* gallery; (*COM*) agent, broker ♦ *nm/f* (*DEPORTE*) runner

corregir [korre'xir] *vt* (*error*) to correct; **~se** *vr* to reform

correo [ko'rreo] *nm* post, mail; *(persona)* courier; **C~s** *nmpl* Post Office *sg*; **~ aéreo** airmail; **~ electrónico** electronic mail, e-mail

correr [ko'rrer] *vt* to run; *(cortinas)* to draw; *(cerrojo)* to shoot ♦ *vi* to run; *(líquido)* to run, flow; **~se** *vr* to slide, move; *(colores)* to run

correspondencia [korrespon'denθja] *nf* correspondence; *(FERRO)* connection

corresponder [korrespon'der] *vi* to correspond; *(convenir)* to be suitable; *(pertenecer)* to belong; *(concernir)* to concern; **~se** *vr* (*por escrito*) to correspond; *(amarse)* to love one another

correspondiente [korrespon'djente] *adj* corresponding

corresponsal [korrespon'sal] *nm/f* correspondent

corrida [ko'rriða] *nf* (*de toros*) bullfight

corrido, a [ko'rriðo, a] *adj* (*avergonzado*) abashed; **3 noches corridas** 3 nights running; **un kilo ~** a good kilo

corriente [ko'rrjente] *adj* (*agua*) running; *(dinero etc)* current; *(común)* ordinary, normal ♦ *nf* current ♦ *nm* current month; **~ eléctrica** electric current

corrija *etc vb ver* **corregir**

corrillo [ko'rriʎo] *nm* ring, circle (of people); *(fig)* clique

corro ['korro] *nm* ring, circle (of people)

corroborar [korroßo'rar] *vt* to corroborate

corroer [korro'er] *vt* to corrode; *(GEO)* to erode

corromper [korrom'per] *vt* (*madera*) to rot; *(fig)* to corrupt

corrosivo, a [korro'sißo, a] *adj* corrosive

corrupción [korrup'θjon] *nf* rot, decay; *(fig)* corruption

corsé [kor'se] *nm* corset

cortacésped [korta'θespeð] *nm* lawn mower

cortado, a [kor'taðo, a] *adj* (*gen*) cut; (*leche*) sour; (*tímido*) shy; (*avergonzado*) embarrassed ♦ *nm* coffee (with a little milk)

cortar [kor'tar] *vt* to cut; (*suministro*) to cut off; (*un pasaje*) to cut out ♦ *vi* to cut; **~se** *vr* (*avergonzarse*) to become embarrassed; (*leche*) to turn, curdle; **~se el pelo** to have one's hair cut

cortaúñas [korta'uɲas] *nm inv* nail clippers *pl*

corte ['korte] *nm* cut, cutting; (*de tela*) piece, length ♦ *nf*: **las C~s** the Spanish Parliament; **~ y confección** dressmaking; **~ de luz** power cut

cortejar [korte'xar] *vt* to court

cortejo [kor'texo] *nm* entourage; **~ fúnebre** funeral procession

cortés [kor'tes] *adj* courteous, polite

cortesía [korte'sia] *nf* courtesy

corteza [kor'teθa] *nf* (*de árbol*) bark; (*de pan*) crust

cortijo [kor'tixo] *nm* farm, farmhouse

cortina [kor'tina] *nf* curtain

corto, a ['korto, a] *adj* (*breve*) short; (*tímido*) bashful; **~ de luces** not very bright; **~ de vista** short-sighted; **estar ~ de fondos** to be short of funds; **~circuito** *nm* short circuit; **~metraje** *nm* (*CINE*) short

cosa ['kosa] *nf* thing; **~ de** about; **eso es ~ mía** that's my business

coscorrón [kosko'rron] *nm* bump on the head

cosecha [ko'setʃa] *nf* (*AGR*) harvest; (*de vino*) vintage

cosechar [kose'tʃar] *vt* to harvest, gather (in)

coser [ko'ser] *vt* to sew

cosmético, a [kos'metiko, a] *adj, nm* cosmetic

cosquillas [kos'kiʎas] *nfpl*: **hacer ~** to tickle; **tener ~** to be ticklish

costa ['kosta] *nf* (*GEO*) coast; **C~ Brava** Costa Brava; **C~ Cantábrica** Cantabrian Coast; **C~ del Sol** Costa del Sol; **a toda ~** at all costs

costado [kos'taðo] *nm* side

costar [kos'tar] *vt* (*valer*) to cost; **me cuesta hablarle** I find it hard to talk to him

Costa Rica *nf* Costa Rica; **costarricense** *adj, nm/f* Costa Rican; **costarriqueño, a** *adj, nm/f* Costa Rican

coste ['koste] *nm* = **costo**

costear [koste'ar] *vt* to pay for

costero, a [kos'tero, a] *adj* (*pueblecito, camino*) coastal

costilla [kos'tiʎa] *nf* rib; (*CULIN*) cutlet

costo ['kosto] *nm* cost, price; **~ de la vida** cost of living; **~so, a** *adj* costly, expensive

costra ['kostra] *nf* (*corteza*) crust; (*MED*) scab

costumbre [kos'tumbre] *nf* custom, habit

costura [kos'tura] *nf* sewing, needlework; (*zurcido*) seam

costurera [kostu'rera] *nf* dressmaker

costurero [kostu'rero] *nm* sewing box *o* case

cotejar [kote'xar] *vt* to compare

cotidiano, a [koti'ðjano, a] *adj* daily, day to day

cotilla [ko'tiʎa] *nm/f* (*fam*) gossip; **cotillear** *vi* to gossip; **cotilleo** *nm* gossip(ing)

cotización [kotiθa'θjon] *nf* (*COM*) quotation, price; (*de club*) dues *pl*

cotizar [koti'θar] *vt* (*COM*) to quote, price; **~se** *vr*: **~se a** to sell at, fetch; (*BOLSA*) to stand at, be quoted at

coto ['koto] *nm* (*terreno cercado*) enclosure; (*de caza*) reserve

cotorra [ko'torra] *nf* parrot

COU [kou] (*ESP*) *nm abr* (= *Curso de Orientación Universitaria*) 1 year course leading to final school-leaving certificate and university entrance examinations

coyote [ko'jote] *nm* coyote, prairie wolf

coyuntura [kojun'tura] *nf* juncture, occasion

coz [koθ] nf kick

crack [krak] nm (droga) crack

cráneo ['kraneo] nm skull, cranium

cráter ['krater] nm crater

creación [krea'θjon] nf creation

creador, a [krea'ðor, a] adj creative
♦ nm/f creator

crear [kre'ar] vt to create, make

crecer [kre'θer] vi to grow; (precio) to rise

creces ['kreθes]: **con ~** adv amply, fully

crecido, a [kre'θiðo, a] adj (persona, planta) full-grown; (cantidad) large

creciente [kre'θjente] adj growing; (cantidad) increasing; (luna) crescent
♦ nm crescent

crecimiento [kreθi'mjento] nm growth; (aumento) increase

credenciales [kreðen'θjales] nfpl credentials

crédito ['kreðito] nm credit

credo ['kreðo] nm creed

crédulo, a ['kreðulo, a] adj credulous

creencia [kre'enθja] nf belief

creer [kre'er] vt, vi to think, believe; **~se** vr to believe o.s. (to be); **~ en** to believe in; **¡ya lo creo!** I should think so!

creíble [kre'iβle] adj credible, believable

creído, a [kre'iðo, a] adj (engreído) conceited

crema ['krema] nf cream; **~ pastelera** (confectioner's) custard

cremallera [krema'ʎera] nf zip (fastener)

crematorio [krema'torjo] nm (tb: **horno ~**) crematorium

crepitar [krepi'tar] vi to crackle

crepúsculo [kre'puskulo] nm twilight, dusk

cresta ['kresta] nf (GEO, ZOOL) crest

creyendo vb ver **creer**

creyente [kre'jente] nm/f believer

creyó etc vb ver **creer**

crezco etc vb ver **crecer**

cría etc ['kria] vb ver **criar** ♦ nf (de animales) rearing, breeding; (animal) young; ver tb **crío**

criadero [kria'ðero] nm (ZOOL) breeding place

criado, a [kria'ðo, a] nm servant ♦ nf servant, maid

criador [kria'ðor] nm breeder

crianza [kri'anθa] nf rearing, breeding; (fig) breeding

criar [kri'ar] vt (educar) to bring up; (producir) to grow, produce; (animales) to breed

criatura [kria'tura] nf creature; (niño) baby, (small) child

criba ['kriβa] nf sieve; **cribar** vt to sieve

crimen ['krimen] nm crime

criminal [krimi'nal] adj, nm/f criminal

crin [krin] nf (tb: **-es** nfpl) mane

crío, a ['krio, a] (fam) nm/f (niño) kid

crisis ['krisis] nf inv crisis; **~ nerviosa** nervous breakdown

crispar [kris'par] vt (nervios) to set on edge

cristal [kris'tal] nm crystal; (de ventana) glass, pane; (lente) lens; **~ino, a** adj crystalline; (fig) clear ♦ nm lens (of the eye); **~izar** vt, vi to crystallize

cristiandad [kristjan'daθ] nf Christendom

cristianismo [kristja'nismo] nm Christianity

cristiano, a [kris'tjano, a] adj, nm/f Christian

Cristo ['kristo] nm Christ; (crucifijo) crucifix

criterio [kri'terjo] nm criterion; (juicio) judgement

crítica ['kritika] nf criticism; ver tb **crítico**

criticar [kriti'kar] vt to criticize

crítico, a ['kritiko, a] adj critical ♦ nm/f critic

Croacia [kro'aθja] nf Croatia

croar [kro'ar] vi to croak

cromo ['kromo] nm chrome

crónica ['kronika] nf chronicle, account

crónico, a ['kroniko, a] adj chronic

cronómetro [kro'nometro] nm stopwatch

croqueta [kro'keta] nf croquette

cruce etc ['kruθe] vb ver **cruzar** ♦ nm crossing; (de carreteras) crossroads

crucificar [kruθifi'kar] vt to crucify

crucifijo [kruθi'fixo] nm crucifix

crucigrama [kruθi'ɣrama] nm crossword

(puzzle)

crudo, a ['kruðo, a] *adj* raw; *(no maduro)* unripe; *(petróleo)* crude; *(rudo, cruel)* cruel ♦ *nm* crude (oil)

cruel [krwel] *adj* cruel; **~dad** *nf* cruelty

crujido [kru'xiðo] *nm (de madera etc)* creak

crujiente [kru'xjente] *adj (galleta etc)* crunchy

crujir [kru'xir] *vi (madera etc)* to creak; *(dedos)* to crack; *(dientes)* to grind; *(nieve, arena)* to crunch

cruz [kruθ] *nf* cross; *(de moneda)* tails *sg*; **~ gamada** swastika

cruzada [kru'θaða] *nf* crusade

cruzado, a [kru'θaðo, a] *adj* crossed ♦ *nm* crusader

cruzar [kru'θar] *vt* to cross; **~se** *vr (líneas etc)* to cross; *(personas)* to pass each other

Cruz Roja *nf* Red Cross

cuaderno [kwa'ðerno] *nm* notebook; *(de escuela)* exercise book; *(NAUT)* logbook

cuadra ['kwaðra] *nf (caballeriza)* stable; *(AM)* block

cuadrado, a [kwa'ðraðo, a] *adj* square ♦ *nm (MAT)* square

cuadrar [kwa'ðrar] *vt* to square ♦ *vi:* **~ con** to square with, tally with; **~se** *vr (soldado)* to stand to attention

cuadrilátero [kwaðri'latero] *nm (DEPORTE)* boxing ring; *(GEOM)* quadrilateral

cuadrilla [kwa'ðriʎa] *nf* party, group

cuadro ['kwaðro] *nm* square; *(ARTE)* painting; *(TEATRO)* scene; *(diagrama)* chart; *(DEPORTE, MED)* team; **tela a ~s** checked *(BRIT)* o chequered *(US)* material

cuádruple ['kwaðruple] *adj* quadruple

cuajar [kwa'xar] *vt (leche)* to curdle; *(sangre)* to congeal; *(CULIN)* to set; **~se** *vr* to curdle; to congeal; to set; *(llenarse)* to fill up

cuajo ['kwaxo] *nm:* **de ~** *(arrancar)* by the roots; *(cortar)* completely

cual [kwal] *adv* like, as ♦ *pron:* **el ~** *etc* which; *(persona: sujeto)* who; *(: objeto)* whom ♦ *adj* such as; **cada ~** each one;

déjalo tal ~ leave it just as it is

cuál [kwal] *pron interr* which (one)

cualesquier(a) [kwales'kjer(a)] *pl de* **cualquier(a)**

cualidad [kwali'ðað] *nf* quality

cualquier [kwal'kjer] *adj ver* **cualquiera**

cualquiera [kwal'kjera] *(pl* **cualesquiera)** *adj (delante de nm y f:* **cualquier)** any ♦ *pron* anybody; **un coche ~ servirá** any car will do; **no es un hombre ~** he isn't just anybody; **cualquier día/libro** any day/book; **eso ~ lo sabe hacer** anybody can do that; **es un ~** he's a nobody

cuando ['kwando] *adv* when; *(aún si)* if, even if ♦ *conj (puesto que)* since ♦ *prep:* **yo, ~ niño ...** when I was a child ...; **~ no sea así** even if it is not so; **~ más** at (the) most; **~ menos** at least; **~ no** if not, otherwise; **de ~ en ~** from time to time

cuándo ['kwando] *adv* when; **¿desde ~?, ¿de ~ acá?** since when?

cuantía [kwan'tia] *nf (importe: de pérdidas, deuda, daños)* extent

cuantioso, a [kwan'tjoso, a] *adj* substantial

PALABRA CLAVE

cuanto, a ['kwanto, a] *adj* **1** *(todo):* **tiene todo ~ desea** he's got everything he wants; **le daremos ~s ejemplares necesite** we'll give him as many copies as *o* all the copies he needs; **~s hombres la ven** all the men who see her

2: **unos ~s:** **había unos ~s periodistas** there were a few journalists

3 *(+más):* **~ más vino bebes peor te sentirás** the more wine you drink the worse you'll feel

♦ *pron:* **tiene ~ desea** he has everything he wants; **tome ~/~s quiera** take as much/many as you want

♦ *adv:* **en ~:** **en ~ profesor** as a teacher; **en ~ a mí** as for me; **ver tb antes**

♦ *conj* **1:** **~ más gana menos gasta** the more he earns the less he spends; **~ más joven más confiado** the younger you are the more trusting you are

2: en ~: en ~ llegue/llegué as soon as I
arrive/arrived

cuánto, a ['kwanto, a] *adj (exclamación)*
what a lot of; *(interr: sg)* how much?;
(: pl) how many?; ♦ *pron, adv* how;
(interr: sg) how much?; *(: pl)* how many?;
¡cuánta gente! what a lot of people!; **¿~
cuesta?** how much does it cost?; **¿a ~s
estamos?** what's the date?; **Señor no sé
~s** Mr. So-and-So

cuarenta [kwa'renta] *num* forty

cuarentena [kwaren'tena] *nf* quarantine

cuaresma [kwa'resma] *nf* Lent

cuarta ['kwarta] *nf (MAT)* quarter, fourth;
(palmo) span

cuartel [kwar'tel] *nm (MIL)* barracks *pl*; **~
general** headquarters *pl*

cuarteto [kwar'teto] *nm* quartet

cuarto, a ['kwarto, a] *adj* fourth ♦ *nm
(MAT)* quarter, fourth; *(habitación)* room;
~ de baño bathroom; **~ de estar** living
room; **~ de hora** quarter (of an) hour; **~
de kilo** quarter kilo

cuatro ['kwatro] *num* four

Cuba ['kuβa] *nf* Cuba; **cubano, a** *adj,
nm/f* Cuban

cuba ['kuβa] *nf* cask, barrel

cubata [ku'βata] *nm (fam)* large drink *(of
rum and coke etc)*

cúbico, a ['kuβiko, a] *adj* cubic

cubierta [ku'βjerta] *nf* cover, covering;
(neumático) tyre; *(NAUT)* deck

cubierto, a [ku'βjerto, a] *pp de* **cubrir**
♦ *adj* covered ♦ *nm* cover; *(lugar en la
mesa)* place; **~s** *nmpl* cutlery *sg*; **a ~**
under cover

cubil [ku'βil] *nm* den; **~ete** *nm (en
juegos)* cup

cubito [ku'βito] *nm*: **~ de hielo** ice-cube

cubo ['kuβo] *nm (MATH)* cube; *(balde)*
bucket, tub; *(TEC)* drum

cubrecama [kuβre'kama] *nm* bedspread

cubrir [ku'βrir] *vt* to cover; **~se** *vr (cielo)*
to become overcast

cucaracha [kuka'ratʃa] *nf* cockroach

cuchara [ku'tʃara] *nf* spoon; *(TEC)* scoop;

~da *nf* spoonful; **~dita** *nf* teaspoonful

cucharilla [kutʃa'riʎa] *nf* teaspoon

cucharón [kutʃa'ron] *nm* ladle

cuchichear [kutʃitʃe'ar] *vi* to whisper

cuchilla [ku'tʃiʎa] *nf (large)* knife; *(de
arma blanca)* blade; **~ de afeitar** razor
blade

cuchillo [ku'tʃiʎo] *nm* knife

cuchitril [kutʃi'tril] *nm* hovel

cuclillas [ku'kliʎas] *nfpl*: **en ~** squatting

cuco, a ['kuko, a] *adj* pretty; *(astuto)*
sharp ♦ *nm* cuckoo

cucurucho [kuku'rutʃo] *nm* cornet

cuello ['kweʎo] *nm (ANAT)* neck; *(de
vestido, camisa)* collar

cuenca ['kwenka] *nf (ANAT)* eye socket;
(GEO) bowl, deep valley

cuenco ['kwenko] *nm* bowl

cuenta *etc* ['kwenta] *vb ver* **contar** ♦ *nf
(cálculo)* count, counting; *(en café,
restaurante)* bill *(BRIT)*, check *(US)*; *(COM)*
account; *(de collar)* bead; **a fin de ~s** in
the end; **caer en la ~** to catch on; **darse
~ de** to realize; **tener en ~** to bear in
mind; **echar ~s** to take stock; **~
corriente/de ahorros** current/savings
account; **~ atrás** countdown;
~kilómetros *nm inv* ≈ milometer; *(de
velocidad)* speedometer

cuento *etc* ['kwento] *vb ver* **contar** ♦ *nm*
story

cuerda ['kwerða] *nf* rope; *(fina)* string; *(de
reloj)* spring; **dar ~ a un reloj** to wind up
a clock; **~ floja** tightrope

cuerdo, a ['kwerðo, a] *adj* sane; *(prudente)*
wise, sensible

cuerno ['kwerno] *nm* horn

cuero ['kwero] *nm* leather; **en ~s** stark
naked; **~ cabelludo** scalp

cuerpo ['kwerpo] *nm* body

cuervo ['kwerβo] *nm* crow

cuesta *etc* ['kwesta] *vb ver* **costar** ♦ *nf*
slope; *(en camino etc)* hill; **~ arriba/abajo**
uphill/downhill; **a ~s** on one's back

cueste *etc* *vb ver* **costar**

cuestión [kwes'tjon] *nf* matter, question,
issue

cueva ['kweβa] nf cave
cuidado [kwi'ðaðo] nm care, carefulness; (preocupación) care, worry ♦ excl careful!, look out!
cuidadoso, a [kwiða'ðoso, a] adj careful; (preocupado) anxious
cuidar [kwi'ðar] vt (MED) to care for; (ocuparse de) to take care of, look after ♦ vi: ~ de to take care of, look after; ~se vr to look after o.s.; ~se de hacer algo to take care to do sth
culata [ku'lata] nf (de fusil) butt
culebra [ku'leβra] nf snake
culebrón [kule'βron] (fam) nm (TV) soap(-opera)
culinario, a [kuli'narjo, a] adj culinary, cooking cpd
culminación [kulmina'θjon] nf culmination
culo ['kulo] nm bottom, backside; (de vaso, botella) bottom
culpa ['kulpa] nf fault; (JUR) guilt; por ~ de because of; tener la ~ (de) to be to blame (for); ~bilidad nf guilt; ~ble adj guilty ♦ nm/f culprit
culpar [kul'par] vt to blame; (acusar) to accuse
cultivar [kulti'βar] vt to cultivate
cultivo [kul'tiβo] nm (acto) cultivation; (plantas) crop
culto, a ['kulto, a] adj (que tiene cultura) cultured, educated ♦ nm (homenaje) worship; (religión) cult
cultura [kul'tura] nf culture
culturismo [kultu'rismo] nm body-building
cumbre ['kumbre] nf summit, top
cumpleaños [kumple'aɲos] nm inv birthday
cumplido, a [kum'pliðo, a] adj (abundante) plentiful; (cortés) courteous ♦ nm compliment; visita de ~ courtesy call
cumplidor, a [kumpli'ðor, a] adj reliable
cumplimentar [kumplimen'tar] vt to congratulate
cumplimiento [kumpli'mjento] nm (de un

deber) fulfilment; (acabamiento) completion
cumplir [kum'plir] vt (orden) to carry out, obey; (promesa) to carry out, fulfil; (condena) to serve ♦ vi: ~ con (deberes) to carry out, fulfil; ~se vr (plazo) to expire; hoy cumple dieciocho años he is eighteen today
cúmulo ['kumulo] nm heap
cuna ['kuna] nf cradle, cot
cundir [kun'dir] vi (noticia, rumor, pánico) to spread; (rendir) to go a long way
cuneta [ku'neta] nf ditch
cuña ['kuɲa] nf wedge
cuñado, a [ku'ɲaðo, a] nm/f brother-/sister-in-law
cuota ['kwota] nf (parte proporcional) share; (cotización) fee, dues pl
cupe etc vb ver caber
cupiera etc vb ver caber
cupo ['kupo] vb ver caber ♦ nm quota
cupón [ku'pon] nm coupon
cúpula ['kupula] nf dome
cura ['kura] nf (curación) cure; (método curativo) treatment ♦ nm priest
curación [kura'θjon] nf cure; (acción) curing
curandero, a [kuran'dero, a] nm/f quack
curar [ku'rar] vt (MED: herida) to treat, dress; (: enfermo) to cure; (CULIN) to cure, salt; (cuero) to tan; ~se vr to get well, recover
curiosear [kurjose'ar] vt to glance at, look over ♦ vi to look round, wander round; (explorar) to poke about
curiosidad [kurjosi'ðað] nf curiosity
curioso, a [ku'rjoso, a] adj curious ♦ nm/f bystander, onlooker
currante [ku'rrante] (fam) nm/f worker
currar [ku'rrar] (fam) vi to work
currículo [ku'rrikulo] = curriculum
curriculum [ku'rrikulum] nm curriculum vitae
cursi ['kursi] (fam) adj affected
cursillo [kur'siλo] nm short course
cursiva [kur'siβa] nf italics pl
curso ['kurso] nm course; en ~ (año)

current; (*proceso*) going on, under way

cursor [kur'sor] *nm* (*INFORM*) cursor

curtido, a [kur'tiðo, a] *adj* (*cara etc*) weather-beaten; (*fig: persona*) experienced

curtir [kur'tir] *vt* (*cuero etc*) to tan

curva ['kurßa] *nf* curve, bend

cúspide ['kuspiðe] *nf* (*GEO*) peak; (*fig*) top

custodia [kus'toðja] *nf* safekeeping; custody; **custodiar** *vt* (*conservar*) to take care of; (*vigilar*) to guard

cutis ['kutis] *nm inv* skin, complexion

cutre ['kutre] (*fam*) *adj* (*lugar*) grotty

cuyo, a ['kujo, a] *pron* (*de quien*) whose; (*de que*) whose, of which; **en ~ caso** in which case

C.V. *abr* (= *caballos de vapor*) H.P.

D, d

D. *abr* (= *Don*) Esq.

Da. *abr* = **Doña**

dádiva ['daðißa] *nf* (*donación*) donation; (*regalo*) gift; **dadivoso, a** *adj* generous

dado, a ['daðo, a] *pp de* **dar** ♦ *nm* die; **~s** *nmpl* dice; **~ que** given that

daltónico, a [dal'toniko, a] *adj* colour-blind

dama ['dama] *nf* (*gen*) lady; (*AJEDREZ*) queen; **~s** *nfpl* (*juego*) draughts *sg*

damnificar [damnifi'kar] *vt* to harm; (*persona*) to injure

danés, esa [da'nes, esa] *adj* Danish ♦ *nm/f* Dane

danzar [dan'θar] *vt, vi* to dance

dañar [da'ɲar] *vt* (*objeto*) to damage; (*persona*) to hurt; **~se** *vr* (*objeto*) to get damaged

dañino, a [da'ɲino, a] *adj* harmful

daño ['daɲo] *nm* (*a un objeto*) damage; (*a una persona*) harm, injury; **~s y perjuicios** (*JUR*) damages; **hacer ~ a** to damage; (*persona*) to hurt, injure; **hacerse ~** to hurt o.s.

PALABRA CLAVE

dar [dar] *vt* **1** (*gen*) to give; (*obra de teatro*) to put on; (*film*) to show; (*fiesta*) to hold; **~ algo a uno** to give sb sth *o* sth to sb; **~ de beber a uno** to give sb a drink

2 (*producir: intereses*) to yield; (*fruta*) to produce

3 (*locuciones +n*): **da gusto escucharle** it's a pleasure to listen to him; *ver tb* **paseo** *y otros sustantivos*

4 (*+n: = perífrasis de verbo*): **me da asco** it sickens me

5 (*considerar*): **~ algo por descontado/ entendido** to take sth for granted/as read; **~ algo por concluido** to consider sth finished

6 (*hora*): **el reloj dio las 6** the clock struck 6 (o'clock)

7: **me da lo mismo** it's all the same to me; *ver tb* **igual, más**

♦ *vi* **1**: **~ con**: **dimos con él dos horas más tarde** we came across him two hours later; **al final di con la solución** I eventually came up with the answer

2: **~ en** (*blanco, suelo*) to hit; **el sol me da en la cara** the sun is shining (right) on my face

3: **~ de sí** (*zapatos etc*) to stretch, give

♦ **~se** *vr* **1**: **~se por vencido** to give up

2 (*ocurrir*): **se han dado muchos casos** there have been a lot of cases

3: **~se a**: **se ha dado a la bebida** he's taken to drinking

4: **se me dan bien/mal las ciencias** I'm good/bad at science

5: **dárselas de**: **se las da de experto** he fancies himself *o* poses as an expert

---

dardo ['darðo] *nm* dart

datar [da'tar] *vi*: **~ de** to date from

dátil ['datil] *nm* date

dato ['dato] *nm* fact, piece of information; **~s personales** personal details

DC *abbr m* (= *disco compacto*) CD

dcha. *abr* (= *derecha*) r.h.

. de J.C. abr (= después de Jesucristo)
A.D.

PALABRA CLAVE

e [de] prep (de+el = del) 1 (posesión) of;
la casa ~ Isabel/mis padres Isabel's/my
parents' house; **es ~ ellos** it's theirs
2 (origen, distancia, con números) from;
soy ~ Gijón I'm from Gijón; **~ 8 a 20**
from 8 to 20; **salir del cine** to go out of
o leave the cinema; **~ 2 en 2** 2 by 2, 2 at
a time
3 (valor descriptivo): **una copa ~ vino** a
glass of wine; **la mesa ~ la cocina** the
kitchen table; **un billete ~ 1000 pesetas**
a 1000 peseta note; **un niño ~ tres años**
a three-year-old (child); **una máquina ~
coser** a sewing machine; **ir vestido ~
gris** to be dressed in grey; **la niña del
vestido azul** the girl in the blue dress;
trabaja ~ profesora she works as a
teacher; **~ lado** sideways; **~ atrás/
delante** rear/front
4 (hora, tiempo): **a las 8 ~ la mañana** at
8 o'clock in the morning; **~ día/noche**
by day/night; **~ hoy en ocho días** a week
from now; **~ niño era gordo** as a child
he was fat
5 (comparaciones): **más/menos ~ cien
personas** more/less than a hundred
people; **el más caro ~ la tienda** the
most expensive in the shop; **menos/más
~ lo pensado** less/more than expected
6 (causa): **del calor** from the heat; **~
puro tonto** out of sheer stupidity
7 (tema) about; **clases ~ inglés** English
classes; **¿sabes algo ~ él?** do you know
anything about him?; **un libro ~ física** a
physics book
8 (adj +de +infin): **fácil ~ entender** easy
to understand
9 (oraciones pasivas): **fue respetado ~
todos** he was loved by all
10 (condicional +infin) if; **~ ser posible** if
possible; **~ no terminarlo hoy** if I etc
don't finish it today

---

dé vb ver **dar**
deambular [deambu'lar] vi to wander
debajo [de'βaxo] adv underneath; **~ de**
below, under; **por ~ de** beneath
debate [de'βate] nm debate; **debatir** vt
to debate
deber [de'βer] nm duty ♦ vt to owe ♦ vi:
debe (de) it must, it should; **~es** nmpl
(ESCOL) homework; **debo hacerlo** I must
do it; **debe de ir** he should go; **~se** vr:
~se a to be owing o due to
debido, a [de'βiðo, a] adj proper, just; **~ a**
due to, because of
débil ['deβil] adj (persona, carácter) weak;
(luz) dim; **debilidad** nf weakness;
dimness
debilitar [deβili'tar] vt to weaken; **~se** vr
to grow weak
debutar [deβu'tar] vi to make one's debut
década ['dekaða] nf decade
decadencia [deka'ðenθja] nf (estado)
decadence; (proceso) decline, decay
decaer [deka'er] vi (declinar) to decline;
(debilitarse) to weaken
decaído, a [deka'iðo, a] adj: **estar ~**
(abatido) to be down
decaimiento [dekai'mjento] nm
(declinación) decline; (desaliento)
discouragement; (MED: estado débil)
weakness
decano, a [de'kano, a] nm/f (de
universidad etc) dean
decapitar [dekapi'tar] vt to behead
decena [de'θena] nf: **una ~** ten (or so)
decencia [de'θenθja] nf decency
decente [de'θente] adj decent
decepción [deθep'θjon] nf
disappointment
decepcionar [deθepθjo'nar] vt to
disappoint
decidir [deθi'ðir] vt, vi to decide; **~se** vr:
~se a to make up one's mind to
décimo, a ['deθimo, a] adj tenth ♦ nm
tenth
decir [de'θir] vt to say; (contar) to tell;
(hablar) to speak ♦ nm saying; **~se** vr: **se
dice que** it is said that; **~ para** o **entre sí**

to say to o.s.; **querer ~** to mean;
¡dígame! (*TEL*) hello!; (*en tienda*) can I
help you?

decisión [deθi'sjon] *nf* (*resolución*)
decision; (*firmeza*) decisiveness

decisivo, a [deθi'siβo, a] *adj* decisive

declaración [deklara'θjon] *nf*
(*manifestación*) statement; (*de amor*)
declaration; **~ de ingresos** *o* **de la renta**
o **fiscal** income-tax return

declarar [dekla'rar] *vt* to declare ♦ *vi* to
declare; (*JUR*) to testify; **~se** *vr* to propose

declinar [dekli'nar] *vt* (*gen*) to decline;
(*JUR*) to reject ♦ *vi* (*el día*) to draw to a
close

declive [de'kliβe] *nm* (*cuesta*) slope; (*fig*)
decline

decodificador [dekoðifika'ðor] *nm*
decoder

decolorarse [dekolo'rarse] *vr* to become
discoloured

decoración [dekora'θjon] *nf* decoration

decorado [deko'raðo] *nm* (*CINE, TEATRO*)
scenery, set

decorar [deko'rar] *vt* to decorate;
decorativo, a *adj* ornamental,
decorative

decoro [de'koro] *nm* (*respeto*) respect;
(*dignidad*) decency; (*recato*) propriety;
~so, a *adj* (*decente*) decent; (*modesto*)
modest; (*digno*) proper

decrecer [dekre'θer] *vi* to decrease,
diminish

decrépito, a [de'krepito, a] *adj* decrepit

decretar [dekre'tar] *vt* to decree; **decreto**
nm decree

dedal [de'ðal] *nm* thimble

dedicación [deðika'θjon] *nf* dedication

dedicar [deði'kar] *vt* (*libro*) to dedicate;
(*tiempo, dinero*) to devote; (*palabras:
decir, consagrar*) to dedicate, devote;
dedicatoria *nf* (*de libro*) dedication

dedo ['deðo] *nm* finger; **~ (del pie)** toe; **~
pulgar** thumb; **~ índice** index finger; **~
corazón** middle finger; **~ anular** ring
finger; **~ meñique** little finger; **hacer ~**
(*fam*) to hitch (a lift)

deducción [deðuk'θjon] *nf* deduction

deducir [deðu'θir] *vt* (*concluir*) to deduce,
infer; (*COM*) to deduct

defecto [de'fekto] *nm* defect, flaw;
defectuoso, a *adj* defective, faulty

defender [defen'der] *vt* to defend

defensa [de'fensa] *nf* defence ♦ *nm*
(*DEPORTE*) defender, back; **defensivo, a**
adj defensive; **a la defensiva** on the
defensive

defensor, a [defen'sor, a] *adj* defending
♦ *nm/f* (*abogado ~*) defending counsel;
(*protector*) protector

deficiencia [defi'θjenθja] *nf* deficiency

deficiente [defi'θjente] *adj* (*defectuoso*)
defective; (*carente*): **~ en** lacking *o* deficient in; **ser
un ~ mental** to be mentally handicapped

déficit ['defiθit] (*pl* **~s**) *nm* deficit

definición [defini'θjon] *nf* definition

definir [defi'nir] *vt* (*determinar*) to
determine, establish; (*decidir*) to define;
(*aclarar*) to clarify; **definitivo, a** *adj*
definitive; **en definitiva** definitively; (*en
resumen*) in short

deformación [deforma'θjon] *nf*
(*alteración*) deformation; (*RADIO etc*)
distortion

deformar [defor'mar] *vt* (*gen*) to deform;
~se *vr* to become deformed; **deforme**
adj (*informe*) deformed; (*feo*) ugly;
(*malhecho*) misshapen

defraudar [defrau'ðar] *vt* (*decepcionar*) to
disappoint; (*estafar*) to defraud

defunción [defun'θjon] *nf* death, demise

degeneración [dexenera'θjon] *nf* (*de las
células*) degeneration; (*moral*) degeneracy

degenerar [dexene'rar] *vi* to degenerate

degollar [deɣo'ʎar] *vt* to behead; (*fig*) to
slaughter

degradar [deɣra'ðar] *vt* to debase,
degrade; **~se** *vr* to demean o.s.

degustación [deɣusta'θjon] *nf* sampling,
tasting

deificar [deifi'kar] *vt* to deify

dejadez [dexa'ðeθ] *nf* (*negligencia*)
neglect; (*descuido*) untidiness, carelessness

dejar [de'xar] *vt* to leave; (*permitir*) to

allow, let; (*abandonar*) to abandon, forsake; (*beneficios*) to produce, yield ♦ *vi*: ~ **de** (*parar*) to stop; (*no hacer*) to fail to; **no dejes de comprar un billete** make sure you buy a ticket; ~ **a un lado** to leave *o* set aside

dejo ['dexo] *nm* (*LING*) accent

del [del] (= **de+el**) *ver* **de**

delantal [delan'tal] *nm* apron

delante [de'lante] *adv* in front, (*enfrente*) opposite; (*adelante*) ahead; ~ **de** in front of, before

delantera [delan'tera] *nf* (*de vestido, casa etc*) front part; (*DEPORTE*) forward line; **llevar la ~ (a uno)** to be ahead (of sb)

delantero, a [delan'tero, a] *adj* front ♦ *nm* (*DEPORTE*) forward, striker

delatar [dela'tar] *vt* to inform on *o* against, betray; **delator, a** *nm/f* informer

delegación [deleɣa'θjon] *nf* (*acción, delegados*) delegation; (*COM: oficina*) office, branch; ~ **de policía** police station

delegado, a [dele'ɣaðo, a] *nm/f* delegate; (*COM*) agent

delegar [dele'ɣar] *vt* to delegate

deletrear [deletre'ar] *vt* to spell (out)

deleznable [deleθ'naßle] *adj* brittle; (*excusa, idea*) feeble

delfín [del'fin] *nm* dolphin

delgadez [delɣa'ðeθ] *nf* thinness, slimness

delgado, a [del'ɣaðo, a] *adj* thin; (*persona*) slim, thin; (*tela etc*) light, delicate

deliberación [delißera'θjon] *nf* deliberation

deliberar [deliße'rar] *vt* to debate, discuss

delicadeza [delika'ðeθa] *nf* (*gen*) delicacy; (*refinamiento, sutileza*) refinement

delicado, a [deli'kaðo, a] *adj* (*gen*) delicate; (*sensible*) sensitive; (*quisquilloso*) touchy

delicia [de'liθja] *nf* delight

delicioso, a [deli'θjoso, a] *adj* (*gracioso*) delightful; (*exquisito*) delicious

delimitar [delimi'tar] *vt* (*funciones, responsabilidades*) to define

delincuencia [delin'kwenθja] *nf* delinquency; **delincuente** *nm/f* delinquent; (*criminal*) criminal

delineante [deline'ante] *nm/f* draughtsman/woman

delinear [deline'ar] *vt* (*dibujo*) to draw; (*fig, contornos*) to outline

delinquir [delin'kir] *vi* to commit an offence

delirante [deli'rante] *adj* delirious

delirar [deli'rar] *vi* to be delirious, rave

delirio [de'lirjo] *nm* (*MED*) delirium; (*palabras insensatas*) ravings *pl*

delito [de'lito] *nm* (*gen*) crime; (*infracción*) offence

delta ['delta] *nm* delta

demacrado, a [dema'kraðo, a] *adj*: **estar ~** to look pale and drawn, be wasted away

demagogo, a [dema'ɣoɣo, a] *nm/f* demagogue

demanda [de'manda] *nf* (*pedido, COM*) demand; (*petición*) request; (*JUR*) action, lawsuit

demandante [deman'dante] *nm/f* claimant

demandar [deman'dar] *vt* (*gen*) to demand; (*JUR*) to sue, file a lawsuit against

demarcación [demarka'θjon] *nf* (*de terreno*) demarcation

demás [de'mas] *adj*: **los ~ niños** the other children, the remaining children ♦ *pron*: **los/las ~** the others, the rest (of them); **lo ~** the rest (of it)

demasía [dema'sia] *nf* (*exceso*) excess, surplus; **comer en ~** to eat to excess

demasiado, a [dema'sjaðo, a] *adj*: ~ **vino** too much wine ♦ *adv* (*antes de adj, adv*) too; ~**s libros** too many books; ¡**esto es ~!** that's the limit!; **hace ~ calor** it's too hot; ~ **despacio** too slowly; ~**s** too many

demencia [de'menθja] *nf* (*locura*) madness; **demente** *nm/f* lunatic ♦ *adj* mad, insane

democracia [demo'kraθja] *nf* democracy

demócrata [de'mokrata] *nm/f* democrat;

democrático, a *adj* democratic

demoler [demo'ler] *vt* to demolish; demolición *nf* demolition

demonio [de'monjo] *nm* devil, demon; ¡~s! hell!, damn!; ¿cómo ~s? how the hell?

demora [de'mora] *nf* delay; demorar *vt* (*retardar*) to delay, hold back; (*detener*) to hold up ♦ *vi* to linger, stay on; ~se *vr* to be delayed

demos *vb ver* dar

demostración [demostra'θjon] *nf* (MAT) proof; (*de afecto*) show, display

demostrar [demos'trar] *vt* (*probar*) to prove; (*mostrar*) to show; (*manifestar*) to demonstrate

demudado, a [demu'ðaðo, a] *adj* (*rostro*) pale

den *vb ver* dar

denegar [dene'var] *vt* (*rechazar*) to refuse; (JUR) to reject

denigrar [deni'vrar] *vt* (*desacreditar, infamar*) to denigrate; (*injuriar*) to insult

---

Denominación de Origen

ⓘ The **Denominación de Origen**, abbreviated to **D.O.**, is a prestigious classification awarded to food products such as wines, cheeses, sausages and hams which meet the stringent quality and production standards of the designated region. **D.O.** labels serve as a guarantee of quality.

---

denotar [deno'tar] *vt* to denote

densidad [densi'ðað] *nf* density; (*fig*) thickness

denso, a ['denso, a] *adj* dense; (*espeso, pastoso*) thick; (*fig*) heavy

dentadura [denta'ðura] *nf* (set of) teeth *pl*; ~ postiza false teeth *pl*

dentera [den'tera] *nf* (*sensación desagradable*) the shivers *pl*

dentífrico, a [den'tifriko, a] *adj* dental ♦ *nm* toothpaste

dentista [den'tista] *nm/f* dentist

dentro ['dentro] *adv* inside ♦ *prep*: ~ de in, inside, within; **por** ~ (on the) inside; **mirar por** ~ to look inside; ~ **de tres meses** within three months

denuncia [de'nunθja] *nf* (*delación*) denunciation; (*acusación*) accusation; (*de accidente*) report; denunciar *vt* to report; (*delatar*) to inform on *o* against

departamento [departa'mento] *nm* (*sección administrativa*) department, section; (AM: *apartamento*) flat (BRIT), apartment

dependencia [depen'denθja] *nf* dependence; (POL) dependency; (COM) office, section

depender [depen'der] *vi*: ~ **de** to depend on

dependienta [depen'djenta] *nf* saleswoman, shop assistant

dependiente [depen'djente] *adj* dependent ♦ *nm* salesman, shop assistant

depilar [depi'lar] *vt* (*con cera*) to wax; (*cejas*) to pluck; depilatorio *nm* hair remover

deplorable [deplo'raßle] *adj* deplorable

deplorar [deplo'rar] *vt* to deplore

deponer [depo'ner] *vt* to lay down ♦ *vi* (JUR) to give evidence; (*declarar*) to make a statement

deportar [depor'tar] *vt* to deport

deporte [de'porte] *nm* sport; hacer ~ to play sports; deportista *adj* sports *cpd* ♦ *nm/f* sportsman/woman; deportivo, a *adj* (*club, periódico*) sports *cpd* ♦ *nm* sports car

depositar [deposi'tar] *vt* (*dinero*) to deposit; (*mercancías*) to put away, store; ~se *vr* to settle; ~io, a *nm/f* trustee

depósito [de'posito] *nm* (*gen*) deposit; (*almacén*) warehouse, store; (*de agua, gasolina etc*) tank; ~ **de cadáveres** mortuary

depreciar [depre'θjar] *vt* to depreciate, reduce the value of; ~se *vr* to depreciate, lose value

depredador, a [depreða'ðor, a] *adj* predatory ♦ *nm* predator

depresión [depre'sjon] *nf* depression

deprimido, a [depri'miðo, a] *adj*
depressed

deprimir [depri'mir] *vt* to depress; **~se** *vr*
(*persona*) to become depressed

deprisa [de'prisa] *adv* quickly, hurriedly

depuración [depura'θjon] *nf* purification;
(*POL*) purge

depurar [depu'rar] *vt* to purify; (*purgar*) to
purge

derecha [de'retʃa] *nf* right(-hand) side;
(*POL*) right; **a la ~** (*estar*) on the right;
(*torcer etc*) (to the) right

derecho, a [de'retʃo, a] *adj* right, right-
hand ♦ *nm* (*privilegio*) right; (*lado*)
right(-hand) side; (*leyes*) law ♦ *adv*
straight, directly; **~s** *nmpl* (*de aduana*)
duty *sg*; (*de autor*) royalties; **tener ~ a** to
have a right to

deriva [de'riβa] *nf*: **ir** *o* **estar a la ~** to
drift, be adrift

derivado [deri'βaðo] *nm* (*COM*) by-
product

derivar [deri'βar] *vt* to derive; (*desviar*) to
direct ♦ *vi* to derive, be derived; (*NAUT*)
to drift; **~se** *vr* to derive, be derived; to
drift

derramamiento [derrama'mjento] *nm*
(*dispersión*) spilling; **~ de sangre**
bloodshed

derramar [derra'mar] *vt* to spill; (*verter*) to
pour out; (*esparcir*) to scatter; **~se** *vr* to
pour out; **~ lágrimas** to weep

derrame [de'rrame] *nm* (*de líquido*)
spilling; (*de sangre*) shedding; (*de tubo
etc*) overflow; (*pérdida*) leakage; (*MED*)
discharge

derredor [derre'ðor] *adv*: **al** *o* **en ~ de**
around, about

derretido, a [derre'tiðo, a] *adj* melted;
(*metal*) molten

derretir [derre'tir] *vt* (*gen*) to melt; (*nieve*)
to thaw; **~se** *vr* to melt

derribar [derri'βar] *vt* to knock down;
(*construcción*) to demolish; (*persona,
gobierno, político*) to bring down

derrocar [derro'kar] *vt* (*gobierno*) to bring
down, overthrow

derrochar [derro'tʃar] *vt* to squander;
derroche *nm* (*despilfarro*) waste,
squandering

derrota [de'rrota] *nf* (*NAUT*) course; (*MIL,
DEPORTE etc*) defeat, rout; **derrotar** *vt*
(*gen*) to defeat; **derrotero** *nm* (*rumbo*)
course

derruir [derru'ir] *vt* (*edificio*) to demolish

derrumbar [derrum'bar] *vt* (*edificio*) to
knock down; **~se** *vr* to collapse

derruyendo *etc vb ver* **derruir**

des *vb ver* **dar**

desabotonar [desaβoto'nar] *vt* to
unbutton, undo; **~se** *vr* to come undone

desabrido, a [desa'βriðo, a] *adj* (*comida*)
insipid, tasteless; (*persona*) rude, surly;
(*respuesta*) sharp; (*tiempo*) unpleasant

desabrochar [desaβro'tʃar] *vt* (*botones,
broches*) to undo, unfasten; **~se** *vr* (*ropa
etc*) to come undone

desacato [desa'kato] *nm* (*falta de respeto*)
disrespect; (*JUR*) contempt

desacertado, a [desaθer'taðo, a] *adj*
(*equivocado*) mistaken; (*inoportuno*)
unwise

desacierto [desa'θjerto] *nm* mistake, error

desaconsejado, a [desakonse'xaðo, a]
adj ill-advised

desaconsejar [desakonse'xar] *vt* to advise
against

desacreditar [desakreði'tar] *vt*
(*desprestigiar*) to discredit, bring into
disrepute; (*denigrar*) to run down

desacuerdo [desa'kwerðo] *nm*
disagreement, discord

desafiar [desa'fjar] *vt* (*retar*) to challenge;
(*enfrentarse a*) to defy

desafilado, a [desafi'laðo, a] *adj* blunt

desafinado, a [desafi'naðo, a] *adj*: **estar
~** to be out of tune

desafinar [desafi'nar] *vi* (*al cantar*) to be
o go out of tune

desafío *etc* [desa'fio] *vb ver* **desafiar**
♦ *nm* (*reto*) challenge; (*combate*) duel;
(*resistencia*) defiance

desaforado, a [desafo'raðo, a] *adj* (*grito*)
ear-splitting; (*comportamiento*) outrageous

desafortunadamente
[desafortunaða'mente] *adv* unfortunately
desafortunado, a [desafortu'naðo, a] *adj*
(*desgraciado*) unfortunate, unlucky
desagradable [desaɣra'ðaßle] *adj*
(*fastidioso, enojoso*) unpleasant; (*irritante*)
disagreeable
desagradar [desaɣra'ðar] *vi* (*disgustar*) to
displease; (*molestar*) to bother
desagradecido, a [desaɣraðe'θiðo, a] *adj*
ungrateful
desagrado [desa'ɣraðo] *nm* (*disgusto*)
displeasure; (*contrariedad*) dissatisfaction
desagraviar [desaɣra'ßjar] *vt* to make
amends to
desagüe [des'aɣwe] *nm* (*de un líquido*)
drainage; (*cañería*) drainpipe; (*salida*)
outlet, drain
desaguisado [desaɣi'saðo] *nm* outrage
desahogado, a [desao'ɣaðo, a] *adj*
(*holgado*) comfortable; (*espacioso*) roomy,
large
desahogar [desao'ɣar] *vt* (*aliviar*) to ease,
relieve; (*ira*) to vent; **~se** *vr* (*relajarse*) to
relax; (*desfogarse*) to let off steam
desahogo [desa'oɣo] *nm* (*alivio*) relief;
(*comodidad*) comfort, ease
desahuciar [desau'θjar] *vt* (*enfermo*) to
give up hope for; (*inquilino*) to evict;
desahucio *nm* eviction
desairar [desai'rar] *vt* (*menospreciar*) to
slight, snub
desaire [des'aire] *nm* (*menosprecio*) slight;
(*falta de garbo*) unattractiveness
desajustar [desaxus'tar] *vt* (*desarreglar*) to
disarrange; (*desconcertar*) to throw off
balance; **~se** *vr* to get out of order;
(*aflojarse*) to loosen
desajuste [desa'xuste] *nm* (*de máquina*)
disorder; (*situación*) imbalance
desalentador, a [desalenta'ðor, a] *adj*
discouraging
desalentar [desalen'tar] *vt* (*desanimar*) to
discourage
desaliento *etc* [desa'ljento] *vb ver*
desalentar ♦ *nm* discouragement
desaliño [desa'liŋo] *nm* slovenliness

desalmado, a [desal'maðo, a] *adj* (*cruel*)
cruel, heartless
desalojar [desalo'xar] *vt* (*expulsar, echar*)
to eject; (*abandonar*) to move out of ♦ *vi*
to move out
desamor [desa'mor] *nm* (*frialdad*)
indifference; (*odio*) dislike
desamparado, a [desampa'raðo, a] *adj*
(*persona*) helpless; (*lugar: expuesto*)
exposed; (*desierto*) deserted
desamparar [desampa'rar] *vt* (*abandonar*)
to desert, abandon; (*JUR*) to leave
defenceless; (*barco*) to abandon
desandar [desan'dar] *vt*: **~ lo andado** o **el
camino** to retrace one's steps
desangrar [desan'grar] *vt* to bleed; (*fig:
persona*) to bleed dry; **~se** *vr* to lose a lot
of blood
desanimado, a [desani'maðo, a] *adj*
(*persona*) downhearted; (*espectáculo,
fiesta*) dull
desanimar [desani'mar] *vt* (*desalentar*) to
discourage; (*deprimir*) to depress; **~se** *vr*
to lose heart
desapacible [desapa'θißle] *adj* (*gen*)
unpleasant
desaparecer [desapare'θer] *vi* (*gen*) to
disappear; (*el sol, la luz*) to vanish;
desaparecido, a *adj* missing;
desaparición *nf* disappearance
desapasionado, a [desapasjo'naðo, a]
adj dispassionate, impartial
desapego [desa'peɣo] *nm* (*frialdad*)
coolness; (*distancia*) detachment
desapercibido, a [desaperθi'ßiðo, a] *adj*
(*desprevenido*) unprepared; **pasar ~** to go
unnoticed
desaprensivo, a [desapren'sißo, a] *adj*
unscrupulous
desaprobar [desapro'ßar] *vt* (*reprobar*) to
disapprove of; (*condenar*) to condemn;
(*no consentir*) to reject
desaprovechado, a [desaproße'tʃaðo, a]
adj (*oportunidad, tiempo*) wasted;
(*estudiante*) slack
desaprovechar [desaproße'tʃar] *vt* to
waste

desarmar [desar'mar] vt (MIL, fig) to disarm; (TEC) to take apart, dismantle; **desarme** nm disarmament

desarraigar [desarrai'var] vt to uproot; **desarraigo** nm uprooting

desarreglar [desarre'vlar] vt (desordenar) to disarrange; (trastocar) to upset, disturb

desarreglo [desa'rrevlo] nm (de casa, persona) untidiness; (desorden) disorder

desarrollar [desarro'ʎar] vt (gen) to develop; **~se** vr to develop; (ocurrir) to take place; (FOTO) to develop; **desarrollo** nm development

desarticular [desartiku'lar] vt (hueso) to dislocate; (objeto) to take apart; (fig) to break up

desasir [desa'sir] vt to loosen

desasosegar [desasose'var] vt (inquietar) to disturb, make uneasy; **~se** vr to become uneasy

desasosiego etc [desaso'sjevo] vb ver **desasosegar** ♦ nm (intranquilidad) uneasiness, restlessness; (ansiedad) anxiety

desastrado, a [desas'traðo, a] adj (desaliñado) shabby; (sucio) dirty

desastre [de'sastre] nm disaster; **desastroso, a** adj disastrous

desatado, a [desa'taðo, a] adj (desligado) untied; (violento) violent, wild

desatar [desa'tar] vt (nudo) to untie; (paquete) to undo; (separar) to detach; **~se** vr (zapatos) to come untied; (tormenta) to break

desatascar [desatas'kar] vt (cañería) to unblock, clear

desatender [desaten'der] vt (no prestar atención a) to disregard; (abandonar) to neglect

desatento, a [desa'tento, a] adj (distraído) inattentive; (descortés) discourteous

desatinado, a [desati'naðo, a] adj foolish, silly; **desatino** nm (idiotez) foolishness, folly; (error) blunder

desatornillar [desatorni'ʎar] vt to unscrew

desatrancar [desatran'kar] vt (puerta) to unbolt; (cañería) to clear, unblock

desautorizado, a [desautori'θaðo, a] adj unauthorized

desautorizar [desautori'θar] vt (oficial) to deprive of authority; (informe) to deny

desavenencia [desaβe'nenθja] nf (desacuerdo) disagreement; (discrepancia) quarrel

desayunar [desaju'nar] vi to have breakfast ♦ vt to have for breakfast; **desayuno** nm breakfast

desazón [desa'θon] nf anxiety

desazonarse [desaθo'narse] vr to worry, be anxious

desbandarse [desβan'darse] vr (MIL) to disband; (fig) to flee in disorder

desbarajuste [desβara'xuste] nm confusion, disorder

desbaratar [desβara'tar] vt (deshacer, destruir) to ruin

desbloquear [desβloke'ar] vt (negociaciones, tráfico) to get going again; (COM: cuenta) to unfreeze

desbocado, a [desβo'kaðo, a] adj (caballo) runaway

desbordar [desβor'ðar] vt (sobrepasar) to go beyond; (exceder) to exceed; **~se** vr (río) to overflow; (entusiasmo) to erupt

descabalgar [deskaβal'var] vi to dismount

descabellado, a [deskaβe'ʎaðo, a] adj (disparatado) wild, crazy

descafeinado, a [deskafei'naðo, a] adj decaffeinated ♦ nm decaffeinated coffee

descalabro [deska'laβro] nm blow; (desgracia) misfortune

descalificar [deskalifi'kar] vt to disqualify; (desacreditar) to discredit

descalzar [deskal'θar] vt (zapato) to take off; **descalzo, a** adj barefoot(ed)

descambiar [deskam'bjar] vt to exchange

descaminado, a [deskami'naðo, a] adj (equivocado) on the wrong road; (fig) misguided

descampado [deskam'paðo] nm open space

descansado, a [deskan'saðo, a] adj (gen) rested; (que tranquiliza) restful

descansar [deskan'sar] *vt* (*gen*) to rest
♦ *vi* to rest, have a rest; (*echarse*) to lie down

descansillo [deskan'siʎo] *nm* (*de escalera*) landing

descanso [des'kanso] *nm* (*reposo*) rest; (*alivio*) relief; (*pausa*) break; (*DEPORTE*) interval, half time

descapotable [deskapo'taβle] *nm* (*tb:* **coche ~**) convertible

descarado, a [deska'raðo, a] *adj* shameless; (*insolente*) cheeky

descarga [des'karɣa] *nf* (*ARQ, ELEC, MIL*) discharge; (*NAUT*) unloading

descargar [deskar'ɣar] *vt* to unload; (*golpe*) to let fly; **~se** *vr* to unburden o.s.; **descargo** *nm* (*COM*) receipt; (*JUR*) evidence

descaro [des'karo] *nm* nerve

descarriar [deska'rrjar] *vt* (*descaminar*) to misdirect; (*fig*) to lead astray; **~se** *vr* (*perderse*) to lose one's way; (*separarse*) to stray; (*pervertirse*) to err, go astray

descarrilamiento [deskarrila'mjento] *nm* (*de tren*) derailment

descarrilar [deskarri'lar] *vi* to be derailed

descartar [deskar'tar] *vt* (*rechazar*) to reject; (*eliminar*) to rule out; **~se** *vr* (*NAIPES*) to discard; **~se de** to shirk

descascarillado, a [deskaskari'ʎaðo, a] *adj* (*paredes*) peeling

descendencia [desθen'denθja] *nf* (*origen*) origin, descent; (*hijos*) offspring

descender [desθen'der] *vt* (*bajar: escalera*) to go down ♦ *vi* to descend; (*temperatura, nivel*) to fall, drop; **~ de** to be descended from

descendiente [desθen'djente] *nm/f* descendant

descenso [des'θenso] *nm* descent; (*de temperatura*) drop

descifrar [desθi'frar] *vt* to decipher; (*mensaje*) to decode

descolgar [deskol'ɣar] *vt* (*bajar*) to take down; (*teléfono*) to pick up; **~se** *vr* to let o.s. down

descolorido, a [deskolo'riðo, a] *adj*

faded; (*pálido*) pale

descompasado, a [deskompa'saðo, a] *adj* (*sin proporción*) out of all proportion; (*excesivo*) excessive

descomponer [deskompo'ner] *vt* (*desordenar*) to disarrange, disturb; (*TEC*) to put out of order; (*dividir*) to break down (into parts); (*fig*) to provoke; **~se** *vr* (*corromperse*) to rot, decompose; (*TEC*) to break down

descomposición [deskomposi'θjon] *nf* (*de un objeto*) breakdown; (*de fruta etc*) decomposition; **~ de vientre** stomach upset, diarrhoea

descompuesto, a [deskom'pwesto, a] *adj* (*corrompido*) decomposed; (*roto*) broken

descomunal [deskomu'nal] *adj* (*enorme*) huge

desconcertado, a [deskonθer'taðo, a] *adj* disconcerted, bewildered

desconcertar [deskonθer'tar] *vt* (*confundir*) to baffle; (*incomodar*) to upset, put out; **~se** *vr* (*turbarse*) to be upset

deschochado, a [deskon'tʃaðo, a] *adj* (*pintura*) peeling

desconcierto *etc* [deskon'θjerto] *vb ver* **desconcertar** ♦ *nm* (*gen*) disorder; (*desorientación*) uncertainty; (*inquietud*) uneasiness

desconectar [deskonek'tar] *vt* to disconnect

desconfianza [deskon'fjanθa] *nf* distrust

desconfiar [deskon'fjar] *vi* to be distrustful; **~ de** to distrust, suspect

descongelar [deskonxe'lar] *vt* to defrost; (*COM, POL*) to unfreeze

descongestionar [deskonxestjo'nar] *vt* (*cabeza, tráfico*) to clear

desconocer [deskono'θer] *vt* (*ignorar*) not to know, be ignorant of

desconocido, a [deskono'θiðo, a] *adj* unknown ♦ *nm/f* stranger

desconocimiento [deskonoθi'mjento] *nm* (*falta de conocimientos*) ignorance

desconsiderado, a [deskonsiðe'raðo, a] *adj* inconsiderate; (*insensible*) thoughtless desconsolar [deskonso'lar] vt to distress; ~se vr to despair

desconsuelo etc [deskon'swelo] vb ver desconsolar ♦ nm (tristeza) distress; (desesperación) despair

descontado, a [deskon'taðo, a] adj: dar por ~ (que) to take (it) for granted (that)

descontar [deskon'tar] vt (deducir) to take away, deduct; (rebajar) to discount

descontento, a [deskon'tento, a] adj dissatisfied ♦ nm dissatisfaction, discontent

descorazonar [deskoraθo'nar] vt to discourage, dishearten

descorchar [deskor'tʃar] vt to uncork

descorrer [desko'rrer] vt (cortinas, cerrojo) to draw back

descortés [deskor'tes] adj (mal educado) discourteous; (grosero) rude

descoser [desko'ser] vt to unstitch; ~se vr to come apart (at the seams)

descosido, a [desko'siðo, a] adj (COSTURA) unstitched

descrédito [des'kreðito] nm discredit

descreído, a [deskre'iðo, a] adj (incrédulo) incredulous; (falto de fe) unbelieving

descremado, a [deskre'maðo, a] adj skimmed

describir [deskri'ßir] vt to describe; descripción [deskrip'θjon] nf description

descrito [des'krito] pp de describir

descuartizar [deskwarti'θar] vt (animal) to cut up

descubierto, a [desku'ßjerto, a] pp de descubrir ♦ adj uncovered, bare; (persona) bareheaded ♦ nm (bancario) overdraft; al ~ in the open

descubrimiento [deskußri'mjento] nm (hallazgo) discovery; (revelación) revelation

descubrir [desku'ßrir] vt to discover, find; (inaugurar) to unveil; (vislumbrar) to detect; (revelar) to reveal, show; (destapar) to uncover; ~se vr to reveal o.s.; (quitarse sombrero) to take off one's hat; (confesar) to confess

descuento etc [des'kwento] vb ver

descontar ♦ nm discount

descuidado, a [deskwi'ðaðo, a] adj (sin cuidado) careless; (desordenado) untidy; (olvidadizo) forgetful; (dejado) neglected; (desprevenido) unprepared

descuidar [deskwi'ðar] vt (dejar) to neglect; (olvidar) to overlook; ~se vr (distraerse) to be careless; (abandonarse) to let o.s. go; (desprevenirse) to drop one's guard; ¡descuida! don't worry!; descuido nm (dejadez) carelessness; (olvido) negligence

PALABRA CLAVE

desde ['desðe] prep 1 (lugar) from; ~ Burgos hasta mi casa hay 30 km it's 30 kms from Burgos to my house
2 (posición): hablaba ~ el balcón she was speaking from the balcony
3 (tiempo: +adv, n): ~ ahora from now on; ~ la boda since the wedding; ~ niño since I etc was a child; ~ 3 años atrás since 3 years ago
4 (tiempo: +vb, fecha) since; for; nos conocemos ~ 1992/ ~ hace 20 años we've known each other since 1992/for 20 years; no le veo ~ 1997/~ hace 5 años I haven't seen him since 1997/for 5 years
5 (gama): ~ los más lujosos hasta los más económicos from the most luxurious to the most reasonably priced
6: ~ luego (que no) of course (not)
♦ conj: ~ que: ~ que recuerdo for as long as I can remember; ~ que llegó no ha salido he hasn't been out since he arrived

desdecirse [desðe'θirse] vr to retract; ~ de to go back on

desdén [des'ðen] nm scorn

desdeñar [desðe'ɲar] vt (despreciar) to scorn

desdicha [des'ðitʃa] nf (desgracia) misfortune; (infelicidad) unhappiness; desdichado, a adj (sin suerte) unlucky; (infeliz) unhappy desdoblar [desðo'βlar] vt (extender) to spread out; (desplegar) to unfold

desear [dese'ar] vt to want, desire, wish for

desecar [dese'kar] vt to dry up; ~se vr to dry up

desechar [dese'tʃar] vt (basura) to throw out o away; (ideas) to reject, discard; desechos nmpl rubbish sg, waste sg

desembalar [desemba'lar] vt to unpack

desembarazar [desembara'θar] vt (desocupar) to clear; (desenredar) to free; ~se vr: ~se de to free o.s. of, get rid of

desembarcar [desembar'kar] vt (mercancías etc) to unload ♦ vi to disembark; ~se vr to disembark

desembocadura [desemboka'ðura] nf (de río) mouth; (de calle) opening

desembocar [desembo'kar] vi (río) to flow into; (fig) to result in

desembolso [desem'bolso] nm payment

desembragar [desembra'ɣar] vi to declutch

desembrollar [desembro'ʎar] vt (madeja) to unravel; (asunto, malentendido) to sort out

desemejanza [deseme'xanθa] nf dissimilarity

desempaquetar [desempake'tar] vt (regalo) to unwrap; (mercancía) to unpack

desempatar [desempa'tar] vt to replay, hold a play-off; desempate nm (FÚTBOL) replay, play-off; (TENIS) tie-break(er)

desempeñar [desempe'ɲar] vt (cargo) to hold; (papel) to perform; (lo empeñado) to redeem; ~ un papel (fig) to play (a role)

desempeño [desem'peɲo] nm redeeming; (de cargo) occupation

desempleado, a [desemple'aðo, a] nm/f unemployed person; desempleo nm unemployment

desempolvar [desempol'βar] vt (muebles etc) to dust; (lo olvidado) to revive

desencadenar [desenkaðe'nar] vt to unchain; (ira) to unleash; ~se vr to break loose; (tormenta) to burst; (guerra) to break out

desencajar [desenka'xar] vt (hueso) to dislocate; (mecanismo, pieza) to disconnect, disengage

desencanto [desen'kanto] nm disillusionment

desenchufar [desentʃu'far] vt to unplug

desenfadado, a [desenfa'ðaðo, a] adj (desenvuelto) uninhibited; (descarado) forward; desenfado nm (libertad) freedom; (comportamiento) free and easy manner; (descaro) forwardness

desenfocado, a [desenfo'kaðo, a] adj (FOTO) out of focus

desenfrenado, a [desenfre'naðo, a] adj (descontrolado) uncontrolled; (inmoderado) unbridled; desenfreno nm wildness; (de las pasiones) lack of self-control

desenganchar [desengan'tʃar] vt (gen) to unhook; (FERRO) to uncouple

desengañar [desenga'ɲar] vt to disillusion; ~se vr to become disillusioned; desengaño nm disillusionment; (decepción) disappointment

desenlace [desen'laθe] nm outcome

desenmarañar [desenmara'ɲar] vt (fig) to unravel

desenmascarar [desenmaska'rar] vt to unmask

desenredar [desenre'ðar] vt (pelo) to untangle; (problema) to sort out

desenroscar [desenros'kar] vt to unscrew

desentenderse [desenten'derse] vr: ~ de to pretend not to know about; (apartarse) to have nothing to do with

desenterrar [desente'rrar] vt to exhume; (tesoro, fig) to unearth, dig up

desentonar [desento'nar] vi (MUS) to sing (o play) out of tune; (color) to clash

desentrañar [desentra'ɲar] vt (misterio) to unravel

desentumecer [desentume'θer] vt (pierna etc) to stretch

desenvoltura [desenβol'tura] nf ease

desenvolver [desenβol'βer] vt (paquete) to unwrap; (fig) to develop; ~se vr (desarrollarse) to unfold, develop;

(arreglárselas) to cope

deseo [de'seo] nm desire, wish; ~**so, a** adj: **estar** ~**so de** to be anxious to

desequilibrado, a [desekili'ßraðo, a] adj unbalanced

desertar [deser'tar] vi to desert

desértico, a [de'sertiko, a] adj desert cpd

desesperación [desespera'θjon] nf (impaciencia) desperation, despair; (irritación) fury

desesperar [desespe'rar] vt to drive to despair; (exasperar) to drive to distraction ♦ vi: ~ **de** to despair of; ~**se** vr to despair, lose hope

desestabilizar [desestaßili'θar] vt to destabilize

desestimar [desesti'mar] vt (menospreciar) to have a low opinion of; (rechazar) to reject

desfachatez [desfatʃa'teθ] nf (insolencia) impudence; (descaro) rudeness

desfalco [des'falko] nm embezzlement

desfallecer [desfaʎe'θer] vi (perder las fuerzas) to become weak; (desvanecerse) to faint

desfasado, a [desfa'saðo, a] adj (anticuado) old-fashioned; **desfase** nm (diferencia) gap

desfavorable [desfaßo'raßle] adj unfavourable

desfigurar [desfixu'rar] vt (cara) to disfigure; (cuerpo) to deform

desfiladero [desfila'ðero] nm gorge

desfilar [desfi'lar] vi to parade; **desfile** nm procession

desfogarse [desfo'varse] vr (fig) to let off steam

desgajar [desva'xar] vt (arrancar) to tear off; (romper) to break off; ~**se** vr to come off

desgana [des'vana] nf (falta de apetito) loss of appetite; (apatía) unwillingness; ~**do, a** adj: **estar** ~**do** (sin apetito) to have no appetite; (sin entusiasmo) to have lost interest

desgarrador, a [desvarra'ðor, a] adj (fig) heartrending

desgarrar [desva'rrar] vt to tear (up); (fig) to shatter; **desgarro** nm (en tela) tear; (aflicción) grief

desgastar [desvas'tar] vt (deteriorar) to wear away o down; (estropear) to spoil; ~**se** vr to get worn out; **desgaste** nm wear (and tear)

desglosar [desvlo'sar] vt (factura) to break down

desgracia [des'vraθja] nf misfortune; (accidente) accident; (vergüenza) disgrace; (contratiempo) setback; **por** ~ unfortunately

desgraciado, a [desvra'θjaðo, a] adj (sin suerte) unlucky, unfortunate; (miserable) wretched; (infeliz) miserable

desgravación [desvraßa'θjon] nf (COM): ~ **fiscal** tax relief

desgravar [desvra'ßar] vt (impuestos) to reduce the tax o duty on

deshabitado, a [desaßi'taðo, a] adj uninhabited

deshacer [desa'θer] vt (casa) to break up; (TEC) to take apart; (enemigo) to defeat; (diluir) to melt; (contrato) to break; (intriga) to solve; ~**se** vr (disolverse) to melt; (despedazarse) to come apart o undone; ~**se de** to get rid of; ~**se en lágrimas** to burst into tears

desharrapado, a [desarra'paðo, a] adj (persona) shabby

deshecho, a [des'etʃo, a] adj undone; (roto) smashed; (persona): **estar** ~ to be shattered

desheredar [desere'ðar] vt to disinherit

deshidratar [desiðra'tar] vt to dehydrate

deshielo [des'jelo] nm thaw

deshonesto, a [deso'nesto, a] adj indecent

deshonra [des'onra] nf (deshonor) dishonour; (vergüenza) shame

deshora [des'ora]: **a** ~ adv at the wrong time

deshuesar [deswe'sar] vt (carne) to bone; (fruta) to stone

desierto, a [de'sjerto, a] adj (casa, calle, negocio) deserted ♦ nm desert

designar [desiɣ'nar] *vt* (*nombrar*) to designate; (*indicar*) to fix

designio [de'siɣnjo] *nm* plan

desigual [desi'ɣwal] *adj* (*terreno*) uneven; (*lucha etc*) unequal

desilusión [desilu'sjon] *nf* disillusionment; (*decepción*) disappointment; **desilusionar** *vt* to disillusion; to disappoint; **desilusionarse** *vr* to become disillusioned

desinfectar [desinfek'tar] *vt* to disinfect

desinflar [desin'flar] *vt* to deflate

desintegración [desinteɣra'θjon] *nf* disintegration

desinterés [desinte'res] *nm* (*desgana*) lack of interest; (*altruismo*) unselfishness

desintoxicarse [desintoksi'karse] *vr* (*drogadicto*) to undergo detoxification

desistir [desis'tir] *vi* (*renunciar*) to stop, desist

desleal [desle'al] *adj* (*infiel*) disloyal; (COM: *competencia*) unfair; ~**tad** *nf* disloyalty

desleír [desle'ir] *vt* (*líquido*) to dilute; (*sólido*) to dissolve

deslenguado, a [deslen'gwaðo, a] *adj* (*grosero*) foul-mouthed

desligar [desli'ɣar] *vt* (*desatar*) to untie, undo; (*separar*) to separate; ~**se** *vr* (*de un compromiso*) to extricate o.s.

desliz [des'liθ] *nm* (*fig*) lapse; ~**ar** *vt* to slip, slide

deslucido, a [deslu'θiðo, a] *adj* dull; (*torpe*) awkward, graceless; (*deslustrado*) tarnished

deslumbrar [deslum'brar] *vt* to dazzle

desmadrarse [desma'ðrarse] (*fam*) *vr* (*descontrolarse*) to run wild; (*divertirse*) to let one's hair down; **desmadre** (*fam*) *nm* (*desorganización*) chaos; (*jaleo*) commotion

desmán [des'man] *nm* (*exceso*) outrage; (*abuso de poder*) abuse

desmandarse [desman'darse] *vr* (*portarse mal*) to behave badly; (*excederse*) to get out of hand; (*caballo*) to bolt

desmantelar [desmante'lar] *vt* (*deshacer*) to dismantle; (*casa*) to strip

desmaquillador [desmaki'ʎa'ðor] *nm* make-up remover

desmayar [desma'jar] *vi* to lose heart; ~**se** *vr* (MED) to faint; **desmayo** *nm* (MED: *acto*) faint; (: *estado*) unconsciousness

desmedido, a [desme'ðiðo, a] *adj* excessive

desmejorar [desmexo'rar] *vt* (*dañar*) to impair, spoil; (MED) to weaken

desmembrar [desmem'brar] *vt* (MED) to dismember; (*fig*) to separate

desmemoriado, a [desmemo'rjado, a] *adj* forgetful

desmentir [desmen'tir] *vt* (*contradecir*) to contradict; (*refutar*) to deny

desmenuzar [desmenu'θar] *vt* (*deshacer*) to crumble; (*carne*) to chop; (*examinar*) to examine closely

desmerecer [desmere'θer] *vt* to be unworthy of ♦ *vi* (*deteriorarse*) to deteriorate

desmesurado, a [desmesu'rado, a] *adj* disproportionate

desmontable [desmon'taßle] *adj* (*que se quita*: *pieza*) detachable; (*que se puede plegar etc*) collapsible, folding

desmontar [desmon'tar] *vt* (*deshacer*) to dismantle; (*tierra*) to level ♦ *vi* to dismount

desmoralizar [desmorali'θar] *vt* to demoralize

desmoronar [desmoro'nar] *vt* to wear away, erode; ~**se** *vr* (*edificio, dique*) to collapse; (*economía*) to decline

desnatado, a [desna'taðo, a] *adj* skimmed

desnivel [desni'ßel] *nm* (*de terreno*) unevenness

desnudar [desnu'ðar] *vt* (*desvestir*) to undress; (*despojar*) to strip; ~**se** *vr* (*desvestirse*) to get undressed; **desnudo, a** *adj* naked ♦ *nm/f* nude; **desnudo de** devoid o bereft of

desnutrición [desnutri'θjon] *nf* malnutrition; **desnutrido, a** *adj* undernourished

desobedecer [desoβeðe'θer] *vt, vi* to disobey; **desobediencia** *nf* disobedience

desocupado, a [desoku'paðo, a] *adj* at leisure; (*desempleado*) unemployed; (*deshabitado*) empty, vacant

desocupar [desoku'par] *vt* to vacate

desodorante [desoðo'rante] *nm* deodorant

desolación [desola'θjon] *nf* (*de lugar*) desolation; (*fig*) grief

desolar [deso'lar] *vt* to ruin, lay waste

desorbitado, a [desorβi'taðo, a] *adj* (*excesivo: ambición*) boundless; (*deseos*) excessive; (: *precio*) exorbitant

desorden [des'orðen] *nm* confusion; (*político*) disorder, unrest

desorganizar [desorvani'θar] *vt* (*desordenar*) to disorganize; **desorganización** *nf* (*de persona*) disorganization; (*en empresa, oficina*) disorder, chaos

desorientar [desorjen'tar] *vt* (*extraviar*) to mislead; (*confundir, desconcertar*) to confuse; ~**se** *vr* (*perderse*) to lose one's way

despabilado, a [despaβi'laðo, a] *adj* (*despierto*) wide-awake; (*fig*) alert, sharp

despabilar [despaβi'lar] *vt* (*el ingenio*) to sharpen ♦ *vi* to wake up; (*fig*) to get a move on; ~**se** *vr* to wake up; to get a move on

despachar [despa'tʃar] *vt* (*negocio*) to do, complete; (*enviar*) to send, dispatch; (*vender*) to sell, deal in; (*billete*) to issue; (*mandar ir*) to send away

despacho [des'patʃo] *nm* (*oficina*) office; (*de paquetes*) dispatch; (*venta*) sale; (*comunicación*) message

despacio [des'paθjo] *adv* slowly

desparpajo [despar'paxo] *nm* self-confidence; (*pey*) nerve

desparramar [desparra'mar] *vt* (*esparcir*) to scatter; (*líquido*) to spill

despavorido, a [despaβo'riðo, a] *adj* terrified

despecho [des'petʃo] *nm* spite; **a ~ de** in

spite of

despectivo, a [despek'tiβo, a] *adj* (*despreciativo*) derogatory; (*LING*) pejorative

despedazar [despeða'θar] *vt* to tear to pieces

despedida [despe'ðiða] *nf* (*adiós*) farewell; (*de obrero*) sacking

despedir [despe'ðir] *vt* (*visita*) to see off, show out; (*empleado*) to dismiss; (*inquilino*) to evict; (*objeto*) to hurl; (*olor etc*) to give out *o* off; ~**se** *vr*: ~**se de** to say goodbye to

despegar [despe'var] *vt* to unstick ♦ *vi* (*avión*) to take off; ~**se** *vr* to come loose, come unstuck; **despego** *nm* detachment

despegue *etc* [des'peve] *vb ver* **despegar** ♦ *nm* takeoff

despeinado, a [despei'naðo, a] *adj* dishevelled, unkempt

despejado, a [despe'xaðo, a] *adj* (*lugar*) clear, free; (*cielo*) clear; (*persona*) wide-awake, bright

despejar [despe'xar] *vt* (*gen*) to clear; (*misterio*) to clear up ♦ *vi* (*el tiempo*) to clear; ~**se** *vr* (*tiempo, cielo*) to clear (up); (*misterio*) to become clearer; (*cabeza*) to clear

despellejar [despeλe'xar] *vt* (*animal*) to skin

despensa [des'pensa] *nf* larder

despeñadero [despeɲa'ðero] *nm* (*GEO*) cliff, precipice

despeñarse [despe'ɲarse] *vr* to hurl o.s. down; (*coche*) to tumble over

desperdicio [desper'ðiθjo] *nm* (*despilfarro*) squandering; ~**s** *nmpl* (*basura*) rubbish *sg* (*BRIT*), garbage *sg* (*US*); (*residuos*) waste *sg*

desperdigarse [desperði'varse] *vr* (*rebaño, familia*) to scatter, spread out; (*granos de arroz, semillas*) to scatter

desperezarse [despere'θarse] *vr* to stretch

desperfecto [desper'fekto] *nm* (*deterioro*) slight damage; (*defecto*) flaw, imperfection

despertador [desperta'ðor] *nm* alarm clock

despertar [desper'tar] *nm* awakening ♦ *vt* (*persona*) to wake up; (*recuerdos*) to revive; (*sentimiento*) to arouse ♦ *vi* to awaken, wake up; **~se** *vr* to awaken, wake up

despiadado, a [despja'ðaðo, a] *adj* (*ataque*) merciless; (*persona*) heartless

despido *etc* [des'piðo] *vb ver* **despedir** ♦ *nm* dismissal, sacking

despierto, a *etc* [des'pjerto, a] *vb ver* **despertar** ♦ *adj* awake; (*fig*) sharp, alert

despilfarro [despil'farro] *nm* (*derroche*) squandering; (*lujo desmedido*) extravagance

despistar [despis'tar] *vt* to throw off the track *o* scent; (*confundir*) to mislead, confuse; **~se** *vr* to take the wrong road; (*confundirse*) to become confused

despiste [des'piste] *nm* absent-mindedness; **un ~** a mistake, slip

desplazamiento [desplaθa'mjento] *nm* displacement

desplazar [despla'θar] *vt* to move; (*NAUT*) to displace; (*INFORM*) to scroll; (*fig*) to oust; **~se** *vr* (*persona*) to travel

desplegar [desple'ɣar] *vt* (*tela, papel*) to unfold, open out; (*bandera*) to unfurl; **despliegue** *etc* [des'pleɣe] *vb ver* **desplegar** ♦ *nm* display

desplomarse [desplo'marse] *vr* (*edificio, gobierno, persona*) to collapse

desplumar [desplu'mar] *vt* (*ave*) to pluck; (*fam: estafar*) to fleece

despoblado, a [despo'ßlaðo, a] *adj* (*sin habitantes*) uninhabited

despojar [despo'xar] *vt* (*alguien: de sus bienes*) to divest of, deprive of; (*casa*) to strip, leave bare; (*alguien: de su cargo*) to strip of

despojo [des'poxo] *nm* (*acto*) plundering; (*objetos*) plunder, loot; **~s** *nmpl* (*de ave, res*) offal *sg*

desposado, a [despo'saðo, a] *adj, nm/f* newly-wed

desposar [despo'sar] *vt* to marry; **~se** *vr* to get married

desposeer [despose'er] *vt*: **~ a uno de** (*puesto, autoridad*) to strip sb of

déspota ['despota] *nm/f* despot

despreciar [despre'θjar] *vt* (*desdeñar*) to despise, scorn; (*afrentar*) to slight; **desprecio** *nm* scorn, contempt; slight

desprender [despren'der] *vt* (*broche*) to unfasten; (*olor*) to give off; **~se** *vr* (*botón: caerse*) to fall off; (*broche*) to come unfastened; (*olor, perfume*) to be given off; **~se de algo que ...** to draw from sth that ...

desprendimiento [desprendi'mjento] *nm* (*gen*) loosening; (*generosidad*) disinterestedness; (*de tierra, rocas*) landslide

despreocupado, a [despreoku'paðo, a] *adj* (*sin preocupación*) unworried, nonchalant; (*negligente*) careless

despreocuparse [despreoku'parse] *vr* not to worry; **~ de** to have no interest in

desprestigiar [despresti'xjar] *vt* (*criticar*) to run down; (*desacreditar*) to discredit

desprevenido, a [despreße'niðo, a] *adj* (*no preparado*) unprepared, unready

desproporcionado, a [desproporθjo'naðo, a] *adj* disproportionate, out of proportion

desprovisto, a [despro'ßisto, a] *adj*: **~ de** devoid of

después [des'pwes] *adv* afterwards, later; (*próximo paso*) next; **~ de comer** after lunch; **un año ~** a year later; **~ se debatió el tema** next the matter was discussed; **~ de corregido el texto** after the text had been corrected; **~ de todo** after all

desquiciado, a [deski'θjaðo, a] *adj* deranged

desquite [des'kite] *nm* (*satisfacción*) satisfaction; (*venganza*) revenge

destacar [desta'kar] *vt* to emphasize, point up; (*MIL*) to detach, detail ♦ *vi* (*resaltarse*) to stand out; (*persona*) to be outstanding *o* exceptional; **~se** *vr* to

stand out; to be outstanding o
exceptional

destajo [des'taxo] *nm*: **trabajar a ~** to do
piecework

destapar [desta'par] *vt* (*botella*) to open;
(*cacerola*) to take the lid off; (*descubrir*) to
uncover; **~se** *vr* (*revelarse*) to reveal one's
true character

destartalado, a [destarta'laðo, a] *adj*
(*desordenado*) untidy; (*ruinoso*)
tumbledown

destello [des'teʎo] *nm* (*de estrella*) twinkle;
(*de faro*) signal light

destemplado, a [destem'plaðo, a] *adj*
(*MUS*) out of tune; (*voz*) harsh; (*MED*) out
of sorts; (*tiempo*) unpleasant, nasty

desteñir [deste'ɲir] *vt* to fade ♦ *vi* to fade;
~se *vr* to fade; **esta tela no destiñe** this
fabric will not run

desternillarse [desterni'ʎarse] *vr*: **~ de
risa** to split one's sides laughing

desterrar [deste'rrar] *vt* (*exilar*) to exile;
(*fig*) to banish, dismiss

destiempo [des'tjempo]: **a ~** *adv* out of
turn

destierro *etc* [des'tjerro] *vb ver* **desterrar**
♦ *nm* exile

destilar [desti'lar] *vt* to distil; **destilería**
nf distillery

destinar [desti'nar] *vt* (*funcionario*) to
appoint, assign; (*fondos*): **~ (a)** to set
aside (for)

destinatario, a [destina'tarjo, a] *nm/f*
addressee

destino [des'tino] *nm* (*suerte*) destiny; (*de
avión, viajero*) destination

destituir [destitu'ir] *vt* to dismiss

destornillador [destorniʎa'ðor] *nm*
screwdriver

destornillar [destorni'ʎar] *vt* (*tornillo*) to
unscrew; **~se** *vr* to unscrew

destreza [des'treθa] *nf* (*habilidad*) skill;
(*maña*) dexterity

destrozar [destro'θar] *vt* (*romper*) to
smash, break (up); (*estropear*) to ruin;
(*nervios*) to shatter

destrozo [des'troθo] *nm* (*acción*)

destruction; (*desastre*) smashing; **~s** *nmpl*
(*pedazos*) pieces; (*daños*) havoc *sg*

destrucción [destruk'θjon] *nf* destruction

destruir [destru'ir] *vt* to destroy

desuso [des'uso] *nm* disuse; **caer en ~** to
become obsolete

desvalido, a [desβa'liðo, a] *adj*
(*desprotegido*) destitute; (*sin fuerzas*)
helpless

desvalijar [desβali'xar] *vt* (*persona*) to rob;
(*casa, tienda*) to burgle; (*coche*) to break
into

desván [des'βan] *nm* attic

desvanecer [desβane'θer] *vt* (*disipar*) to
dispel; (*borrar*) to blur; **~se** *vr* (*humo etc*)
to vanish, disappear; (*color*) to fade;
(*recuerdo, sonido*) to fade away; (*MED*) to
pass out; (*duda*) to be dispelled

desvanecimiento [desβaneθi'mjento] *nm*
(*desaparición*) disappearance; (*de colores*)
fading; (*evaporación*) evaporation; (*MED*)
fainting fit

desvariar [desβa'rjar] *vi* (*enfermo*) to be
delirious; **desvarío** *nm* delirium

desvelar [desβe'lar] *vt* to keep awake; **~se**
vr (*no poder dormir*) to stay awake;
(*preocuparse*) to be vigilant o watchful

desvelos [des'βelos] *nmpl* worrying *sg*

desvencijado, a [desβenθi'xaðo, a] *adj*
(*silla*) rickety; (*máquina*) broken-down

desventaja [desβen'taxa] *nf* disadvantage

desventura [desβen'tura] *nf* misfortune

desvergonzado, a [desβerɣon'θaðo, a]
adj shameless

desvergüenza [desβer'ɣwenθa] *nf*
(*descaro*) shamelessness; (*insolencia*)
impudence; (*mala conducta*) effrontery

desvestir [desβes'tir] *vt* to undress; **~se** *vr*
to undress

desviación [desβja'θjon] *nf* deviation;
(*AUTO*) diversion, detour

desviar [desβ'jar] *vt* to turn aside; (*río*) to
alter the course of; (*navío*) to divert, re-
route; (*conversación*) to sidetrack; **~se** *vr*
(*apartarse del camino*) to turn aside;
(*: barco*) to go off course

desvío *etc* [des'βio] *vb ver* **desviar** ♦ *nm*

(*desviación*) detour, diversion; (*fig*) indifference

desvirtuar [desβir'twar] *vt* to distort

desvivirse [desβi'βirse] *vr*: ~ **por** (*anhelar*) to long for, crave for; (*hacer lo posible por*) to do one's utmost for

detallar [deta'ʎar] *vt* to detail

detalle [de'taʎe] *nm* detail; (*gesto*) gesture, token; **al ~** in detail; (COM) retail

detallista [deta'ʎista] *nm/f* (COM) retailer

detective [detek'tiβe] *nm/f* detective

detener [dete'ner] *vt* (*gen*) to stop; (JUR) to arrest; (*objeto*) to keep; ~**se** *vr* to stop; (*demorarse*): ~**se en** to delay over, linger over

detenidamente [deteniða'mente] *adv* (*minuciosamente*) carefully; (*extensamente*) at great length

detenido, a [dete'niðo, a] *adj* (*arrestado*) under arrest ♦ *nm/f* person under arrest, prisoner

detenimiento [deteni'mjento] *nm*: **con ~** thoroughly; (*observar, considerar*) carefully

detergente [deter'xente] *nm* detergent

deteriorar [deterjo'rar] *vt* to spoil, damage; ~**se** *vr* to deteriorate; **deterioro** *nm* deterioration

determinación [determina'θjon] *nf* (*empeño*) determination; (*decisión*) decision; **determinado, a** *adj* specific

determinar [determi'nar] *vt* (*plazo*) to fix; (*precio*) to settle; ~**se** *vr* to decide

detestar [detes'tar] *vt* to detest

detractor, a [detrak'tor, a] *nm/f* slanderer, libeller

detrás [de'tras] *adv* behind; (*atrás*) at the back; ~ **de** behind

detrimento [detri'mento] *nm*: **en ~ de** to the detriment of

deuda ['deuða] *nf* debt

devaluación [deβalwa'θjon] *nf* devaluation

devastar [deβas'tar] *vt* (*destruir*) to devastate

devoción [deβo'θjon] *nf* devotion

devolución [deβolu'θjon] *nf* (*reenvío*) return, sending back; (*reembolso*)

repayment; (JUR) devolution

devolver [deβol'βer] *vt* to return; (*lo extraviado, lo prestado*) to give back; (*carta al correo*) to send back; (COM) to repay, refund ♦ *vi* (*vomitar*) to be sick

devorar [deβo'rar] *vt* to devour

devoto, a [de'βoto, a] *adj* devout ♦ *nm/f* admirer

devuelto *pp de* **devolver**

devuelva *etc vb ver* **devolver**

di *vb ver* **dar; decir**

día ['dia] *nm* day; **¿qué ~ es?** what's the date?; **estar/poner al ~** to be/keep up to date; **el ~ de hoy/de mañana** today/tomorrow; **al ~ siguiente** (on) the following day; **vivir al ~** to live from hand to mouth; **de ~** by day, in daylight; **en pleno ~** in full daylight; **D~ de Reyes** Epiphany; **~ festivo** (ESP) *o* **feriado** (AM) holiday; **~ libre** day off

diabetes [dja'βetes] *nf* diabetes

diablo ['djaβlo] *nm* devil; **diablura** *nf* prank

diadema [dja'ðema] *nf* tiara

diafragma [dja'frayma] *nm* diaphragm

diagnosis [djay'nosis] *nf inv* diagnosis

diagnóstico [djay'nostiko] *nm =* **diagnosis**

diagonal [djayo'nal] *adj* diagonal

diagrama [dja'yrama] *nm* diagram; **~ de flujo** flowchart

dial [djal] *nm* dial

dialecto [dja'lekto] *nm* dialect

dialogar [djalo'var] *vi*: ~ **con** (POL) to hold talks with

diálogo ['djaloyo] *nm* dialogue

diamante [dja'mante] *nm* diamond

diana ['djana] *nf* (MIL) reveille; (*de blanco*) centre, bull's-eye

diapositiva [djaposi'tiβa] *nf* (FOTO) slide, transparency

diario, a [djarjo, a] *adj* daily ♦ *nm* newspaper; **a ~** daily; **de ~** everyday

diarrea [dja'rrea] *nf* diarrhoea

dibujar [diβu'xar] *vt* to draw, sketch; **dibujo** *nm* drawing; **dibujos animados** cartoons

diccionario [dikθjo'narjo] *nm* dictionary

dice *etc vb ver* **decir**

dicho, a ['ditʃo, a] *pp de* **decir** ♦ *adj*: **en ~s países** in the aforementioned countries ♦ *nm* saying

dichoso, a [di'tʃoso, a] *adj* happy

diciembre [di'θjembre] *nm* December

dictado [dik'taðo] *nm* dictation

dictador [dikta'ðor] *nm* dictator; **dictadura** *nf* dictatorship

dictamen [dik'tamen] *nm* (*opinión*) opinion; (*juicio*) judgment; (*informe*) report

dictar [dik'tar] *vt* (*carta*) to dictate; (*JUR: sentencia*) to pronounce; (*decreto*) to issue; (*AM: clase*) to give

didáctico, a [di'ðaktiko, a] *adj* educational

diecinueve [djeθi'nweße] *num* nineteen

dieciocho [djeθi'otʃo] *num* eighteen

dieciséis [djeθi'seis] *num* sixteen

diecisiete [djeθi'sjete] *num* seventeen

diente ['djente] *nm* (*ANAT, TEC*) tooth; (*ZOOL*) fang; (: *de elefante*) tusk; (*de ajo*) clove; **hablar entre ~s** to mutter, mumble

diera *etc vb ver* **dar**

diesel ['disel] *adj*: **motor ~** diesel engine

diestro, a ['djestro, a] *adj* (*derecho*) right; (*hábil*) skilful

dieta ['djeta] *nf* diet; **dietética** *nf*: **tienda de dietética** health food shop; **dietético, a** *adj* diet (*atr*), dietary

diez [djeθ] *num* ten

diezmar [djeθ'mar] *vt* (*población*) to decimate

difamar [difa'mar] *vt* (*JUR: hablando*) to slander; (: *por escrito*) to libel

diferencia [dife'renθja] *nf* difference; **diferenciar** *vt* to differentiate between ♦ *vi* to differ; **diferenciarse** *vr* to differ, be different; (*distinguirse*) to distinguish o.s.

diferente [dife'rente] *adj* different

diferido [dife'riðo] *nm*: **en ~** (*TV etc*) recorded

difícil [di'fiθil] *adj* difficult

dificultad [difikul'taθ] *nf* difficulty; (*problema*) trouble

dificultar [difikul'tar] *vt* (*complicar*) to complicate, make difficult; (*estorbar*) to obstruct

difteria [dif'terja] *nf* diphtheria

difundir [difun'dir] *vt* (*calor, luz*) to diffuse; (*RADIO, TV*) to broadcast; **~ una noticia** to spread a piece of news; **~se** *vr* to spread (out)

difunto, a [di'funto, a] *adj* dead, deceased ♦ *nm/f* deceased (person)

difusión [difu'sjon] *nf* (*RADIO, TV*) broadcasting

diga *etc vb ver* **decir**

digerir [dixe'rir] *vt* to digest; (*fig*) to absorb; **digestión** *nf* digestion; **digestivo, a** *adj* digestive

digital [dixi'tal] *adj* digital

dignarse [dix'narse] *vr* to deign to

dignatario, a [dixna'tarjo, a] *nm/f* dignitary

dignidad [divni'ðaθ] *nf* dignity

digno, a ['divno, a] *adj* worthy

digo *etc vb ver* **decir**

dije *etc vb ver* **decir**

dilapidar [dilapi'ðar] *vt* (*dinero, herencia*) to squander, waste

dilatar [dila'tar] *vt* (*cuerpo*) to dilate; (*prolongar*) to prolong

dilema [di'lema] *nm* dilemma

diligencia [dili'xenθja] *nf* diligence; (*ocupación*) errand, job; **~s** *nfpl* (*JUR*) formalities; **diligente** *adj* diligent

diluir [dilu'ir] *vt* to dilute

diluvio [di'lußjo] *nm* deluge, flood

dimensión [dimen'sjon] *nf* dimension

diminuto, a [dimi'nuto, a] *adj* tiny, diminutive

dimitir [dimi'tir] *vi* to resign

dimos *vb ver* **dar**

Dinamarca [dina'marka] *nf* Denmark

dinámico, a [di'namiko, a] *adj* dynamic

dinamita [dina'mita] *nf* dynamite

dínamo ['dinamo] *nf* dynamo

dineral [dine'ral] *nm* large sum of money, fortune

dinero [di'nero] *nm* money; **~ contante, ~ efectivo** (ready) cash; **~ suelto** (loose) change

dio *vb ver* **dar**

dios [djos] *nm* god; **¡D~ mío!** (oh,) my God!

diosa ['djosa] *nf* goddess

diploma [di'ploma] *nm* diploma

diplomacia [diplo'maθja] *nf* diplomacy; (*fig*) tact

diplomado, a [diplo'maðo, a] *adj* qualified

diplomático, a [diplo'matiko, a] *adj* diplomatic ♦ *nm/f* diplomat

diputación [diputa'θjon] *nf* (*tb:* **~ provincial**) ≈ county council

diputado, a [dipu'taðo, a] *nm/f* delegate; (*POL*) ≈ member of parliament (*BRIT*), ≈ representative (*US*)

dique ['dike] *nm* dyke

diré *etc vb ver* **decir**

dirección [direk'θjon] *nf* direction; (*señas*) address; (*AUTO*) steering; (*gerencia*) management; (*POL*) leadership; **~ única/ prohibida** one-way street/no entry

directa [di'rekta] *nf* (*AUT*) top gear

directiva [direk'tißa] *nf* (*DEP, tb:* **junta ~**) board of directors

directo, a [di'rekto, a] *adj* direct; (*RADIO, TV*) live; **transmitir en ~** to broadcast live

director, a [direk'tor, a] *adj* leading ♦ *nm/f* director; (*ESCOL*) head(teacher) (*BRIT*), principal (*US*); (*gerente*) manager(ess); (*PRENSA*) editor; **~ de cine** film director; **~ general** managing director

dirigente [diri'xente] *nm/f* (*POL*) leader

dirigir [diri'xir] *vt* to direct; (*carta*) to address; (*obra de teatro, film*) to direct; (*MUS*) to conduct; (*negocio*) to manage; **~se** *vr*: **~se a** to go towards, make one's way towards; (*hablar con*) to speak to

dirija *etc vb ver* **dirigir**

discernir [disθer'nir] *vt* to discern

disciplina [disθi'plina] *nf* discipline

discípulo, a [dis'θipulo, a] *nm/f* disciple

disco ['disko] *nm* disc; (*DEPORTE*) discus;

(*TEL*) dial; (*AUTO: semáforo*) light; (*MUS*) record; (*INFORM*): **~ flexible/rígido** floppy/hard disk; **~ compacto/de larga duración** compact disc/long-playing record; **~ de freno** brake disc

disconforme [diskon'forme] *adj* differing; **estar ~ (con)** to be in disagreement (with)

discordia [dis'korðja] *nf* discord

discoteca [disko'teka] *nf* disco(theque)

discreción [diskre'θjon] *nf* discretion; (*reserva*) prudence; **comer a ~** to eat as much as one wishes; **discrecional** *adj* (*facultativo*) discretionary

discrepancia [diskre'panθja] *nf* (*diferencia*) discrepancy; (*desacuerdo*) disagreement

discreto, a [dis'kreto, a] *adj* discreet

discriminación [diskrimina'θjon] *nf* discrimination

disculpa [dis'kulpa] *nf* excuse; (*pedir perdón*) apology; **pedir ~s a/por** to apologize to/for; **disculpar** *vt* to excuse, pardon; **disculparse** *vr* to excuse o.s.; to apologize

discurrir [disku'rrir] *vi* (*pensar, reflexionar*) to think, meditate; (*el tiempo*) to pass, go by

discurso [dis'kurso] *nm* speech

discusión [disku'sjon] *nf* (*diálogo*) discussion; (*riña*) argument

discutir [disku'tir] *vt* (*debatir*) to discuss; (*pelear*) to argue about; (*contradecir*) to argue against ♦ *vi* (*debatir*) to discuss; (*pelearse*) to argue

disecar [dise'kar] *vt* (*conservar: animal*) to stuff; (*: planta*) to dry

diseminar [disemi'nar] *vt* to disseminate, spread

diseñar [dise'nar] *vt, vi* to design

diseño [di'seno] *nm* design

disfraz [dis'fraθ] *nm* (*máscara*) disguise; (*excusa*) pretext; **~ar** *vt* to disguise; **~arse** *vr*: **~arse de** to disguise o.s. as

disfrutar [disfru'tar] *vt* to enjoy ♦ *vi* to enjoy o.s.; **~ de** to enjoy, possess

disgregarse [disɣre'varse] *vr*

disgustar [disɣus'tar] vt (no gustar) to displease; (contrariar, enojar) to annoy, upset; **~se** vr (enfadarse) to get upset; (dos personas) to fall out

disgusto [dis'ɣusto] nm (contrariedad) annoyance; (tristeza) grief; (riña) quarrel

disidente [disi'ðente] nm dissident

disimular [disimu'lar] vt (ocultar) to hide, conceal ♦ vi to dissemble

disipar [disi'par] vt to dispel; (fortuna) to squander; **~se** vr (nubes) to vanish; (indisciplinarse) to dissipate

dislocarse [dislo'karse] vr (articulación) to sprain, dislocate

disminución [disminu'θjon] nf decrease, reduction

disminuido, a [disminui'ðo, a] nm/f: ~ **mental/físico** mentally/physically handicapped person

disminuir [disminu'ir] vt to decrease, diminish

disociarse [diso'θjarse] vr: ~ **(de)** to dissociate o.s. (from)

disolver [disol'ßer] vt (gen) to dissolve; **~se** vr to dissolve; (COM) to go into liquidation

dispar [dis'par] adj different

disparar [dispa'rar] vt, vi to shoot, fire

disparate [dispa'rate] nm (tontería) foolish remark; (error) blunder; **decir ~s** to talk nonsense

disparo [dis'paro] nm shot

dispensar [dispen'sar] vt to dispense; (disculpar) to excuse

dispersar [disper'sar] vt to disperse; **~se** vr to scatter

disponer [dispo'ner] vt (arreglar) to arrange; (ordenar) to put in order; (preparar) to prepare, get ready ♦ vi: ~ **de** to have, own; **~se** vr: **~se a** o **para hacer** to prepare to do

disponible [dispo'nißle] adj available

disposición [disposi'θjon] nf arrangement, disposition; (INFORM) layout; **a la ~** at the disposal of; **~ de ánimo** state of mind

dispositivo [disposi'tiβo] nm device, mechanism

dispuesto, a [dis'pwesto, a] pp de **disponer** ♦ adj (arreglado) arranged; (preparado) disposed

disputar [dispu'tar] vt (carrera) to compete in

disquete [dis'kete] nm floppy disk, diskette

distancia [dis'tanθja] nf distance

distanciar [distan'θjar] vt to space out; **~se** vr to become estranged

distante [dis'tante] adj distant

distar [dis'tar] vi: **dista 5km de aquí** it is 5km from here

diste vb ver **dar**

disteis ['disteis] vb ver **dar**

distension [disten'sjon] nf (en las relaciones) relaxation; (POL) détente; (muscular) strain

distinción [distin'θjon] nf distinction; (elegancia) elegance; (honor) honour

distinguido, a [distin'giðo, a] adj distinguished

distinguir [distin'gir] vt to distinguish; (escoger) to single out; **~se** vr to be distinguished

distintivo [distin'tiβo] nm badge; (fig) characteristic

distinto, a [dis'tinto, a] adj different; (claro) clear

distracción [distrak'θjon] nf distraction; (pasatiempo) hobby, pastime; (olvido) absent-mindedness, distraction

distraer [distra'er] vt (atención) to distract; (divertir) to amuse; (fondos) to embezzle; **~se** vr (entretenerse) to amuse o.s.; (perder la concentración) to allow one's attention to wander

distraído, a [distra'iðo, a] adj (gen) absent-minded; (entretenido) amusing

distribuidor, a [distrißui'ðor, a] nm/f distributor; **distribuidora** nf (COM) dealer, agent; (CINE) distributor

distribuir [distrißu'ir] vt to distribute

distrito [dis'trito] nm (sector, territorio) region; (barrio) district

disturbio [dis'turβjo] *nm* disturbance; (*desorden*) riot

disuadir [diswa'ðir] *vt* to dissuade

disuelto [di'swelto] *pp de* **disolver**

disyuntiva [disjun'tiβa] *nf* dilemma

DIU *nm abr* (= *dispositivo intrauterino*) IUD

diurno, a ['djurno, a] *adj* day *cpd*

divagar [diβa'γar] *vi* (*desviarse*) to digress

diván [di'βan] *nm* divan

divergencia [diβer'xenθja] *nf* divergence

diversidad [diβersi'ðað] *nf* diversity, variety

diversificar [diβersifi'kar] *vt* to diversify

diversión [diβer'sjon] *nf* (*gen*) entertainment; (*actividad*) hobby, pastime

diverso, a [di'βerso, a] *adj* diverse; **~s libros** several books; **~s** *nmpl* sundries

divertido, a [diβer'tiðo, a] *adj* (*chiste*) amusing; (*fiesta etc*) enjoyable

divertir [diβer'tir] *vt* (*entretener, recrear*) to amuse; **~se** *vr* (*pasarlo bien*) to have a good time; (*distraerse*) to amuse o.s.

dividendos [diβi'ðendos] *nmpl* (*COM*) dividends

dividir [diβi'ðir] *vt* (*gen*) to divide; (*distribuir*) to distribute, share out

divierta *etc vb ver* **divertir**

divino, a [di'βino, a] *adj* divine

divirtiendo *etc vb ver* **divertir**

divisa [di'βisa] *nf* (*emblema*) emblem, badge; **~s** *nfpl* foreign exchange *sg*

divisar [diβi'sar] *vt* to make out, distinguish

división [diβi'sjon] *nf* (*gen*) division; (*de partido*) split; (*de país*) partition

divorciar [diβor'θjar] *vt* to divorce; **~se** *vr* to get divorced; **divorcio** *nm* divorce

divulgar [diβul'γar] *vt* (*ideas*) to spread; (*secreto*) to divulge

DNI (*ESP*) *nm abr* (= *Documento Nacional de Identidad*) national identity card

DNI

i The **Documento Nacional de Identidad** *is a Spanish ID card which must be carried at all times and produced on request for the police. It contains the*

holder's photo, fingerprints and personal details. It is also known as the DNI or "carnet de identidad".

Dña. *abr* (= *doña*) Mrs

do [do] *nm* (*MUS*) do, C

dobladillo [doβla'ðiʎo] *nm* (*de vestido*) hem; (*de pantalón: vuelta*) turn-up (*BRIT*), cuff (*US*)

doblar [do'βlar] *vt* to double; (*papel*) to fold; (*caño*) to bend; (*la esquina*) to turn, go round; (*film*) to dub ♦ *vi* to turn; (*campana*) to toll; **~se** *vr* (*plegarse*) to fold (up), crease; (*encorvarse*) to bend

doble ['doβle] *adj* double; (*de dos aspectos*) dual; (*fig*) two-faced ♦ *nm* double ♦ *nm/f* (*TEATRO*) double, stand-in; **~s** *nmpl* (*DEPORTE*) doubles *sg*; **con sentido ~** with a double meaning

doblegar [doβle'γar] *vt* to fold, crease; **~se** *vr* to yield

doblez [do'βleθ] *nm* fold, hem ♦ *nf* insincerity, duplicity

doce ['doθe] *num* twelve; **~na** *nf* dozen

docente [do'θente] *adj*: **centro/personal ~** teaching establishment/staff

dócil [do'θil] *adj* (*pasivo*) docile; (*obediente*) obedient

docto, a ['dokto, a] *adj*: **~ en** instructed in

doctor, a [dok'tor, a] *nm/f* doctor

doctorado [dokto'raðo] *nm* doctorate

doctrina [dok'trina] *nf* doctrine, teaching

documentación [dokumenta'θjon] *nf* documentation, papers *pl*

documental [dokumen'tal] *adj, nm* documentary

documento [doku'mento] *nm* (*certificado*) document; **~ nacional de identidad** identity card

dólar ['dolar] *nm* dollar

doler [do'ler] *vt, vi* to hurt; (*fig*) to grieve; **~se** *vr* (*de su situación*) to grieve, feel sorry; (*de las desgracias ajenas*) to sympathize; **me duele el brazo** my arm hurts

dolor [do'lor] *nm* pain; (*fig*) grief, sorrow; **~ de cabeza** headache; **~ de estómago**

stomachache

domar [do'mar] *vt* to tame

domesticar [domesti'kar] *vt* = **domar**

doméstico, a [do'mestiko, a] *adj* (*vida, servicio*) home; (*tareas*) household; (*animal*) tame, pet

domiciliación [domiθilia'θjon] *nf*: ~ **de pagos** (COM) standing order

domicilio [domi'θiljo] *nm* home; ~ **particular** private residence; ~ **social** (COM) head office; **sin ~ fijo** of no fixed abode

dominante [domi'nante] *adj* dominant; (*persona*) domineering

dominar [domi'nar] *vt* (*gen*) to dominate; (*idiomas*) to be fluent in ♦ *vi* to dominate, prevail; **~se** *vr* to control o.s.

domingo [do'mingo] *nm* Sunday

dominio [do'minjo] *nm* (*tierras*) domain; (*autoridad*) power, authority; (*de las pasiones*) grip, hold; (*de idiomas*) command

don [don] *nm* (*talento*) gift; ~ **Juan Gómez** Mr Juan Gómez, Juan Gómez Esq (BRIT)

Don/Doña

i *The term* **don/doña** *often abbreviated to* **D./Dña** *is placed before the first name as a mark of respect to an older or more senior person - eg Don Diego, Doña Inés. Although becoming rarer in Spain it is still used with names and surnames on official documents and formal correspondence - eg "Sr. D. Pedro Rodríguez Hernández", "Sra. Dña. Inés Rodríguez Hernández".*

---

donaire [do'naire] *nm* charm

donar [do'nar] *vt* to donate

donativo [dona'tiβo] *nm* donation

doncella [don'θeʎa] *nf* (*criada*) maid

donde ['donde] *adv* where ♦ *prep*: **el coche está allí ~ el farol** the car is over there by the lamppost *o* where the lamppost is; **en ~** where, in which

dónde ['donde] *adv interrogativo* where?; **¿a ~ vas?** where are you going (to)?;

¿de ~ vienes? where have you been?; **¿por ~?** where?, whereabouts?

dondequiera [donde'kjera] *adv* anywhere; **por ~** everywhere, all over the place ♦ *conj*: ~ **que** wherever

doña ['doɲa] *nf*: ~ **Alicia** Alicia; ~ **Victoria Benito** Mrs Victoria Benito

dorado, a [do'raðo, a] *adj* (*color*) golden; (TEC) gilt

dormir [dor'mir] *vt*: ~ **la siesta** to have an afternoon nap ♦ *vi* to sleep; **~se** *vr* to fall asleep

dormitar [dormi'tar] *vi* to doze

dormitorio [dormi'torjo] *nm* bedroom; ~ **común** dormitory

dorsal [dor'sal] *nm* (DEPORTE) number

dorso ['dorso] *nm* (*de mano*) back; (*de hoja*) other side

dos [dos] *num* two

dosis ['dosis] *nf inv* dose, dosage

dotado, a [do'taðo, a] *adj* gifted; ~ **de** endowed with

dotar [do'tar] *vt* to endow; **dote** *nf* dowry; **dotes** *nfpl* (*talentos*) gifts

doy *vb ver* **dar**

dragar [dra'var] *vt* (*río*) to dredge; (*minas*) to sweep

drama ['drama] *nm* drama

dramaturgo [drama'turvo] *nm* dramatist, playwright

drástico, a ['drastiko, a] *adj* drastic

drenaje [dre'naxe] *nm* drainage

droga ['drova] *nf* drug

drogadicto, a [drova'ðikto, a] *nm/f* drug addict

droguería [drove'ria] *nf* hardware shop (BRIT) *o* store (US)

ducha ['dutʃa] *nf* (*baño*) shower; (MED) douche; **ducharse** *vr* to take a shower

duda ['duða] *nf* doubt; **dudar** *vt, vi* to doubt; **dudoso, a** [du'ðoso, a] *adj* (*incierto*) hesitant; (*sospechoso*) doubtful

duela *etc vb ver* **doler**

duelo ['dwelo] *vb ver* **doler** ♦ *nm* (*combate*) duel; (*luto*) mourning

duende ['dwende] *nm* imp, goblin

dueño, a ['dweɲo, a] *nm/f* (*propietario*)

owner; (*de pensión, taberna*) landlord/
lady; (*empresario*) employer
duermo *etc vb ver* **dormir**
dulce ['dulθe] *adj* sweet ♦ *adv* gently,
softly ♦ *nm* sweet
dulzura [dul'θura] *nf* sweetness; (*ternura*)
gentleness
duna ['duna] *nf* (GEO) dune
dúo ['duo] *nm* duet
duplicar [dupli'kar] *vt* (*hacer el doble de*)
to duplicate; ~**se** *vr* to double
duque ['duke] *nm* duke; ~**sa** *nf* duchess
duración [dura'θjon] *nf* (*de película, disco
etc*) length; (*de pila etc*) life; (*curso: de
acontecimientos etc*) duration
duradero, a [dura'ðero, a] *adj* (*tela etc*)
hard-wearing; (*fe, paz*) lasting
durante [du'rante] *prep* during
durar [du'rar] *vi* to last; (*recuerdo*) to remain
durazno [du'raθno] (AM) *nm* (*fruta*) peach;
(*árbol*) peach tree
durex ['dureks] (AM) *nm* (*tira adhesiva*)
Sellotape ® (BRIT), Scotch tape ® (US)
dureza [du'reθa] *nf* (*calidad*) hardness
duro, a ['duro, a] *adj* hard; (*carácter*)
tough ♦ *adv* hard ♦ *nm* (*moneda*) five
peseta coin o piece
DVD *nm abr* (= *disco de vídeo digital*)
DVD

E, e

E *abr* (= *este*) E
e [e] *conj* and
ebanista [eßa'nista] *nm/f* cabinetmaker
ébano ['eßano] *nm* ebony
ebrio, a ['eßrjo, a] *adj* drunk
ebullición [eßuʎi'θjon] *nf* boiling
eccema [ek'θema] *nf* (MED) eczema
echar [e'tʃar] *vt* to throw; (*agua, vino*) to
pour (out); (*empleado: despedir*) to fire,
sack; (*hojas*) to sprout; (*cartas*) to post;
(*humo*) to emit, give out ♦ *vi*: ~ **a**
correr/llorar to run off/burst into tears;
~**se** *vr* to lie down; ~ **llave a** to lock (up);
~ **abajo** (*gobierno*) to overthrow; (*edificio*)

to demolish; ~ **mano a** to lay hands on;
~ **una mano a uno** (*ayudar*) to give sb a
hand; ~ **de menos** to miss
eclesiástico, a [ekle'sjastiko, a] *adj*
ecclesiastical
eco ['eko] *nm* echo; **tener** ~ to catch on
ecología [ekolo'xia] *nf* ecology;
ecológico, a *adj* (*producto, método*)
environmentally-friendly; (*agricultura*)
organic; **ecologista** *adj* ecological,
environmental ♦ *nm/f* environmentalist
economato [ekono'mato] *nm* cooperative
store
economía [ekono'mia] *nf* (*sistema*)
economy; (*carrera*) economics
económico, a [eko'nomiko, a] *adj*
(*barato*) cheap, economical; (*ahorrativo*)
thrifty; (COM: *año etc*) financial;
(: *situación*) economic
economista [ekono'mista] *nm/f*
economist
ECU [eku] *nm* ECU
ecuador [ekwa'ðor] *nm* equator; **(el) E~**
Ecuador
ecuánime [e'kwanime] *adj* (*carácter*)
level-headed; (*estado*) calm
ecuatoriano, a [ekwato'rjano, a] *adj*,
nm/f Ecuadorian
ecuestre [e'kwestre] *adj* equestrian
eczema [ek'θema] *nm* = **eccema**
edad [e'ðað] *nf* age; **¿qué ~ tienes?** how
old are you?; **tiene ocho años de ~** he is
eight (years old); **de ~ mediana/**
avanzada middle-aged/advanced in
years; **la E~ Media** the Middle Ages
edición [eði'θjon] *nf* (*acto*) publication;
(*ejemplar*) edition
edificar [eðifi'kar] *vt, vi* to build
edificio [eði'fiθjo] *nm* building; (*fig*)
edifice, structure
Edimburgo [eðim'burvo] *nm* Edinburgh
editar [eði'tar] *vt* (*publicar*) to publish;
(*preparar textos*) to edit
editor, a [eði'tor, a] *nm/f* (*que publica*)
publisher; (*redactor*) editor ♦ *adj*: **casa ~a**
publishing house, publisher; ~**ial** *adj*
editorial ♦ *nm* leading article, editorial;

casa ~ial publishing house, publisher

edredon [eðreˈðon] nm duvet

educación [eðukaˈθjon] nf education; (crianza) upbringing; (modales) (good) manners pl

educado, a [eðuˈkaðo, a] adj: **bien/mal ~** well/badly behaved

educar [eðuˈkar] vt to educate; (criar) to bring up; (voz) to train

E. UU. nmpl abr (= Estados Unidos) US(A)

efectista [efekˈtista] adj sensationalist

efectivamente [efektiβaˈmente] adv (como respuesta) exactly, precisely; (verdaderamente) really; (de hecho) in fact

efectivo, a [efekˈtiβo, a] adj effective; (real) actual, real ♦ nm: **pagar en ~** to pay (in) cash; **hacer ~ un cheque** to cash a cheque

efecto [eˈfekto] nm effect, result; **~s** nmpl (~s personales) effects; (bienes) goods; (COM) assets; **en ~** in fact; (respuesta) exactly, indeed; **~ 2000** millennium bug; **~ invernadero** greenhouse effect

efectuar [efekˈtwar] vt to carry out; (viaje) to make

eficacia [efiˈkaθja] nf (de persona) efficiency; (de medicamento etc) effectiveness

eficaz [efiˈkaθ] adj (persona) efficient; (acción) effective

eficiente [efiˈθjente] adj efficient

efusivo, a [efuˈsiβo, a] adj effusive; **mis más efusivas gracias** my warmest thanks

EGB (ESP) nf abr (ESCOL) = Educación General Básica

egipcio, a [eˈxipθjo, a] adj, nm/f Egyptian

Egipto [eˈxipto] nm Egypt

egoísmo [eɣoˈismo] nm egoism

egoísta [eɣoˈista] adj egoistical, selfish ♦ nm/f egoist

egregio, a [eˈɣrexjo, a] adj eminent, distinguished

Eire [ˈeire] nm Eire

ej. abr (= ejemplo) eg

eje [ˈexe] nm (GEO, MAT) axis; (de rueda)

axle; (de máquina) shaft, spindle

ejecución [exekuˈθjon] nf execution; (cumplimiento) fulfilment; (MUS) performance; (JUR: embargo de deudor) attachment

ejecutar [exekuˈtar] vt to execute, carry out; (matar) to execute; (cumplir) to fulfil; (MUS) to perform; (JUR: embargar) to attach, distrain (on)

ejecutivo, a [exekuˈtiβo, a] adj executive; **el (poder) ~** the executive (power)

ejemplar [exemˈplar] adj exemplary ♦ nm example; (ZOOL) specimen; (de libro) copy; (de periódico) number, issue

ejemplo [eˈxemplo] nm example; **por ~** for example

ejercer [exerˈθer] vt to exercise; (influencia) to exert; (un oficio) to practise ♦ vi (practicar): **~ (de)** to practise (as)

ejercicio [exerˈθiθjo] nm exercise; (período) tenure; **~ comercial** financial year

ejército [eˈxerθito] nm army; **entrar en el ~** to join the army, join up

ejote [eˈxote] (AM) nm green bean

PALABRA CLAVE

---

el [el] (f **la**, pl **los, las,** neutro **lo**) art def **1** the; **el libro/la mesa/los estudiantes** the book/table/students
2 (con n abstracto: no se traduce): **el amor/la juventud** love/youth
3 (posesión: se traduce a menudo por adj posesivo): **romperse el brazo** to break one's arm; **levantó la mano** he put his hand up; **se puso el sombrero** she put her hat on
4 (valor descriptivo): **tener la boca grande/los ojos azules** to have a big mouth/blue eyes
5 (con días) on; **me iré el viernes** I'll leave on Friday; **los domingos suelo ir a nadar** on Sundays I generally go swimming
6 (lo +adj): **lo difícil/caro** what is difficult/expensive; (= cuán): **no se da cuenta de lo pesado que es** he doesn't

realise how boring he is

♦ *pron demos* **1**: **mi libro y el de usted** my book and yours; **las de Pepe son mejores** Pepe's are better; **no la(s) blanca(s) sino la(s) gris(es)** not the white one(s) but the grey one(s) **2**: **lo de**: **lo de ayer** what happened yesterday; **lo de las facturas** that business about the invoices

♦ *pron relativo*: **el que** *etc* **1** (*indef*): **el (los) que quiera(n) que se vaya(n)** anyone who wants to can leave; **llévese el que más le guste** take the one you like best

2 (*def*): **el que compré ayer** the one I bought yesterday; **los que se van** those who leave

3: **lo que**: **lo que pienso yo/más me gusta** what I think/like most

♦ *conj*: **el que**: **el que lo diga** the fact that he says so; **el que sea tan vago me molesta** his being so lazy bothers me

♦ *excl*: **¡el susto que me diste!** what a fright you gave me!

♦ *pron personal* **1** (*persona: m*) him; (*: f*) her; (*: pl*) them; **lo/las veo** I can see him/them

2 (*animal, cosa: sg*) it; (*: pl*) them; **lo** (*o* **la**) **veo** I can see it; **los** (*o* **las**) **veo** I can see them

3: **lo** (*como sustituto de frase*): **no lo sabía** I didn't know; **ya lo entiendo** I understand now

él [el] *pron* (*persona*) he; (*cosa*) it; (*después de prep: persona*) him; (*: cosa*) it; **de ~** his
elaborar [elaβo'rar] *vt* (*producto*) to make, manufacture; (*preparar*) to prepare; (*madera, metal etc*) to work; (*proyecto etc*) to work on *o* out
elasticidad [elastiθi'ðað] *nf* elasticity
elástico, a [e'lastiko, a] *adj* elastic; (*flexible*) flexible ♦ *nm* elastic; (*un ~*) elastic band
elección [elek'θjon] *nf* election; (*selección*) choice, selection
electorado [elekto'raðo] *nm* electorate,

voters *pl*
electricidad [elektriθi'ðað] *nf* electricity
electricista [elektri'θista] *nm/f* electrician
eléctrico, a [e'lektriko, a] *adj* electric
electro... [elektro] *prefijo* electro...;
~**cardiograma** *nm* electrocardiogram;
~**cutar** *vt* to electrocute; ~**do** *nm* electrode; ~**domésticos** *nmpl* (electrical) household appliances;
~**magnético, a** *adj* electromagnetic
electrónica [elek'tronika] *nf* electronics *sg*
electrónico, a [elek'troniko, a] *adj* electronic
elefante [ele'fante] *nm* elephant
elegancia [ele'γanθja] *nf* elegance, grace; (*estilo*) stylishness
elegante [ele'γante] *adj* elegant, graceful; (*estiloso*) stylish, fashionable
elegir [ele'xir] *vt* (*escoger*) to choose, select; (*optar*) to opt for; (*presidente*) to elect
elemental [elemen'tal] *adj* (*claro, obvio*) elementary; (*fundamental*) elemental, fundamental
elemento [ele'mento] *nm* element; (*fig*) ingredient; ~**s** *nmpl* elements, rudiments
elepé [ele'pe] (*pl* ~**s**) *nm* L.P.
elevación [eleβa'θjon] *nf* elevation; (*acto*) raising, lifting; (*de precios*) rise; (*GEO etc*) height, altitude
elevar [ele'βar] *vt* to raise, lift (up); (*precio*) to put up; ~**se** *vr* (*edificio*) to rise; (*precios*) to go up
eligiendo *etc vb ver* **elegir**
elija *etc vb ver* **elegir**
eliminar [elimi'nar] *vt* to eliminate, remove
eliminatoria [elimina'torja] *nf* heat, preliminary (round)
elite [e'lite] *nf* elite
ella ['eʎa] *pron* (*persona*) she; (*cosa*) it; (*después de prep: persona*) her; (*: cosa*) it; **de ~** hers
ellas ['eʎas] *pron* (*personas y cosas*) they; (*después de prep*) them; **de ~** theirs
ello ['eʎo] *pron* it
ellos ['eʎos] *pron* they; (*después de prep*)

them; **de ~** theirs

elocuencia [elo'kwenθja] nf eloquence

elogiar [elo'xjar] vt to praise; **elogio** nm praise

elote [e'lote] (AM) nm corn on the cob

eludir [elu'ðir] vt to avoid

emanar [ema'nar] vi: **~ de** to emanate from, come from; (derivar de) to originate in

emancipar [emanθi'par] vt to emancipate; **~se** vr to become emancipated, free o.s.

embadurnar [embaður'nar] vt to smear

embajada [emba'xaða] nf embassy

embajador, a [embaxa'ðor, a] nm/f ambassador/ambassadress

embalaje [emba'laxe] nm packing

embalar [emba'lar] vt to parcel, wrap (up); **~se** vr to go fast

embalsamar [embalsa'mar] vt to embalm

embalse [em'balse] nm (presa) dam; (lago) reservoir

embarazada [embara'θaða] adj pregnant ♦ nf pregnant woman

embarazo [emba'raθo] nm (de mujer) pregnancy; (impedimento) obstacle, obstruction; (timidez) embarrassment; **embarazoso, a** adj awkward, embarrassing

embarcación [embarka'θjon] nf (barco) boat, craft; (acto) embarkation, boarding

embarcadero [embarka'ðero] nm pier, landing stage

embarcar [embar'kar] vt (cargamento) to ship, stow; (persona) to embark, put on board; **~se** vr to embark, go on board

embargar [embar'var] vt (JUR) to seize, impound

embargo [em'barvo] nm (JUR) seizure; (COM, POL) embargo

embargue [em'barve] etc vb ver **embargar**

embarque etc [em'barke] vb ver **embarcar** ♦ nm shipment, loading

embaucar [embau'kar] vt to trick, fool

embeber [embe'ßer] vt (absorber) to absorb, soak up; (empapar) to saturate ♦ vi to shrink; **~se** vr: **~se en un libro** to be engrossed o absorbed in a book

embellecer [embeʎe'θer] vt to embellish, beautify

embestida [embes'tiða] nf attack, onslaught; (carga) charge

embestir [embes'tir] vt to attack, assault; to charge, attack ♦ vi to attack

emblema [em'blema] nm emblem

embobado, a [embo'ßaðo, a] adj (atontado) stunned, bewildered

embolia [em'bolja] nf (MED) clot

émbolo ['embolo] nm (AUTO) piston

embolsar [embol'sar] vt to pocket, put in one's pocket

emborrachar [emborra'tʃar] vt to make drunk, intoxicate; **~se** vr to get drunk

emboscada [embos'kaða] nf ambush

embotar [embo'tar] vt to blunt, dull; **~se** vr (adormecerse) to go numb

embotellamiento [emboteʎa'mjento] nm (AUTO) traffic jam

embotellar [embote'ʎar] vt to bottle

embrague [em'braɣe] nm (tb: **pedal de ~**) clutch

embriagar [embrja'var] vt (emborrachar) to make drunk; **~se** vr (emborracharse) to get drunk

embrión [em'brjon] nm embryo

embrollar [embro'ʎar] vt (el asunto) to confuse, complicate; (implicar) to involve, embroil; **~se** vr (confundirse) to get into a muddle o mess

embrollo [em'broʎo] nm (enredo) muddle, confusion; (aprieto) fix, jam

embrujado, a [embru'xado, a] adj bewitched; **casa embrujada** haunted house

embrutecer [embrute'θer] vt (atontar) to stupefy; **~se** vr to be stupefied

embudo [em'buðo] nm funnel

embuste [em'buste] nm (mentira) lie; **~ro, a** adj lying, deceitful ♦ nm/f (mentiroso) liar

embutido [embu'tiðo] nm (CULIN) sausage; (TEC) inlay

emergencia [emer'xenθja] nf emergency;

(surgimiento) emergence

emerger [emer'ver] *vi* to emerge, appear

emigración [emiɣra'θjon] *nf* emigration; *(de pájaros)* migration

emigrar [emi'ɣrar] *vi (personas)* to emigrate; *(pájaros)* to migrate

eminencia [emi'nenθja] *nf* eminence; **eminente** *adj* eminent, distinguished; *(elevado)* high

emisario [emi'sarjo] *nm* emissary

emisión [emi'sjon] *nf (acto)* emission; *(COM etc)* issue; *(RADIO, TV: acto)* broadcasting; *(: programa)* broadcast, programme *(BRIT)*, program *(US)*

emisora [emi'sora] *nf* radio o broadcasting station

emitir [emi'tir] *vt (olor etc)* to emit, give off; *(moneda etc)* to issue; *(opinión)* to express; *(RADIO)* to broadcast

emoción [emo'θjon] *nf* emotion; *(excitación)* excitement; *(sentimiento)* feeling

emocionante [emoθjo'nante] *adj (excitante)* exciting, thrilling

emocionar [emoθjo'nar] *vt (excitar)* to excite, thrill; *(conmover)* to move, touch; *(impresionar)* to impress

emotivo, a [emo'tißo, a] *adj* emotional

empacar [empa'kar] *vt (gen)* to pack; *(en caja etc)* to bale, crate

empacho [em'patʃo] *nm (MED)* indigestion; *(fig)* embarrassment

empadronarse [empaðro'narse] *vr (POL: como elector)* to register

empalagoso, a [empala'ɣoso, a] *adj* cloying; *(fig)* tiresome

empalmar [empal'mar] *vt* to join, connect ♦ *vi (dos caminos)* to meet, join; **empalme** *nm* joint, connection; junction; *(de trenes)* connection

empanada [empa'naða] *nf* pie, pasty

empantanarse [empanta'narse] *vr* to get swamped; *(fig)* to get bogged down

empañarse [empa'narse] *vr (cristales etc)* to steam up

empapar [empa'par] *vt (mojar)* to soak, saturate; *(absorber)* to soak up, absorb;

~se *vr*: **~se de** to soak up

empapelar [empape'lar] *vt (paredes)* to paper

empaquetar [empake'tar] *vt* to pack, parcel up

empastar [empas'tar] *vt (embadurnar)* to paste; *(diente)* to fill

empaste [em'paste] *nm (de diente)* filling

empatar [empa'tar] *vi* to draw, tie; **empate** *nm* draw, tie

empecé *etc vb ver* **empezar**

empedernido, a [empeðer'niðo, a] *adj* hard, heartless; *(fumador)* inveterate

empedrado, a [empe'ðraðo, a] *adj* paved ♦ *nm* paving

empeine [em'peine] *nm (de pie, zapato)* instep

empellón [empe'ʎon] *nm* push, shove

empeñado, a [empe'naðo, a] *adj (persona)* determined; *(objeto)* pawned

empeñar [empe'nar] *vt (objeto)* to pawn, pledge; *(persona)* to compel; **~se** *vr (endeudarse)* to get into debt; **~se en** to be set on, be determined to

empeño [em'peno] *nm (determinación, insistencia)* determination, insistence; **casa de ~s** pawnshop

empeorar [empeo'rar] *vt* to make worse, worsen ♦ *vi* to get worse, deteriorate

empequeñecer [empekene'θer] *vt* to dwarf; *(minusvalorar)* to belittle

emperador [empera'ðor] *nm* emperor; **emperatriz** *nf* empress

empezar [empe'θar] *vt, vi* to begin, start

empiece *etc vb ver* **empezar**

empiezo *etc vb ver* **empezar**

empinar [empi'nar] *vt* to raise; **~se** *vr (persona)* to stand on tiptoe; *(animal)* to rear up; *(camino)* to climb steeply

empírico, a [em'piriko, a] *adj* empirical

emplasto [em'plasto] *nm (MED)* plaster

emplazamiento [emplaθa'mjento] *nm* site, location; *(JUR)* summons *sg*

emplazar [empla'θar] *vt (ubicar)* to site, place, locate; *(JUR)* to summons; *(convocar)* to summon

empleado, a [emple'aðo, a] *nm/f (gen)*

mployee; (*de banco etc*) clerk

mplear [emple'ar] *vt* (*usar*) to use,
mploy; (*dar trabajo a*) to employ; **~se** *vr*
(*conseguir trabajo*) to be employed;
(*ocuparse*) to occupy o.s.

mpleo [em'pleo] *nm* (*puesto*) job;
(*puestos: colectivamente*) employment;
(*uso*) use, employment

mpobrecer [empoβre'θer] *vt* to
mpoverish; **~se** *vr* to become poor *o*
mpoverished

mpollar [empo'ʎar] (*fam*) *vt*, *vi* to swot
up; **empollón, ona** (*fam*) *nm/f* swot

mporio [em'porjo] *nm* (*AM: gran
almacén*) department store

mpotrado, a [empo'traðo, a] *adj*
(*armario etc*) built-in

mprender [empren'der] *vt* (*empezar*) to
begin, embark on; (*acometer*) to tackle,
take on

mpresa [em'presa] *nf* (*de espíritu etc*)
enterprise; (*COM*) company, firm; **~rio, a**
nm/f (*COM*) businessman/woman

mpréstito [em'prestito] *nm* (public) loan

mpujar [empu'xar] *vt* to push, shove

mpujón [empu'xon] *nm* push, shove

mpuñar [empu'ɲar] *vt* (*asir*) to grasp,
take (firm) hold of

mular [emu'lar] *vt* to emulate; (*rivalizar*)
to rival

PALABRA CLAVE

n [en] *prep* 1 (*posición*) in; (*: sobre*) on;
está ~ el cajón it's in the drawer; **~
Argentina/La Paz** in Argentina/La Paz; **~
la oficina/el colegio** at the office/school;
está ~ el suelo/quinto piso it's on the
floor/the fifth floor

2 (*dirección*) into; **entró ~ el aula** she
went into the classroom; **meter algo ~ el
bolso** to put sth into one's bag

3 (*tiempo*) in; on; **~ 1605/3 semanas/
invierno** in 1605/3 weeks/winter; **~ (el
mes de) enero** in (the month of)
January; **~ aquella ocasión/época** on
that occasion/at that time

4 (*precio*) for; **lo vendió ~ 20 dólares** he

sold it for 20 dollars

5 (*diferencia*) by; **reducir/aumentar ~
una tercera parte/un 20 por ciento** to
reduce/increase by a third/20 per cent

6 (*manera*): **~ avión/autobús** by plane/
bus; **escrito ~ inglés** written in English

7 (*después de vb que indica gastar etc*) on;
han cobrado demasiado ~ dietas
they've charged too much to expenses;
se le va la mitad del sueldo ~ comida
he spends half his salary on food

8 (*tema, ocupación*): **experto ~ la
materia** expert on the subject; **trabaja ~
la construcción** he works in the building
industry

9 (*adj* + **~** + *infin*): **lento ~ reaccionar**
slow to react

enaguas [e'naɣwas] *nfpl* petticoat *sg*,
underskirt *sg*

enajenación [enaxena'θjon] *nf*: **~ mental**
mental derangement

enajenar [enaxe'nar] *vt* (*volver loco*) to
drive mad

enamorado, a [enamo'raðo, a] *adj* in
love ♦ *nm/f* lover

enamorar [enamo'rar] *vt* to win the love
of; **~se** *vr*: **~se de alguien** to fall in love
with sb

enano, a [e'nano, a] *adj* tiny ♦ *nm/f*
dwarf

enardecer [enarðe'θer] *vt* (*pasiones*) to
fire, inflame; (*persona*) to fill with
enthusiasm; **~se** *vr*: **~se por** to get
excited about; (*entusiasmarse*) to get
enthusiastic about

encabezamiento [enkaβeθa'mjento] *nm*
(*de carta*) heading; (*de periódico*) headline

encabezar [enkaβe'θar] *vt* (*movimiento,
revolución*) to lead, head; (*lista*) to head,
be at the top of; (*carta*) to put a heading
to

encadenar [enkaðe'nar] *vt* to chain
(together); (*poner grilletes a*) to shackle

encajar [enka'xar] *vt* (*ajustar*): **~ (en)** to fit
(into); (*fam: golpe*) to take ♦ *vi* to fit
(well); (*fig: corresponder a*) to match; **~se**

vr: **~se en un sillón** to squeeze into a chair

encaje [enˈkaxe] *nm* (*labor*) lace

encalar [enkaˈlar] *vt* (*pared*) to whitewash

encallar [enkaˈʎar] *vi* (NAUT) to run aground

encaminar [enkamiˈnar] *vt* to direct, send; **~se** *vr*: **~se a** to set out for

encantado, a [enkanˈtaðo, a] *adj* (*hechizado*) bewitched; (*muy contento*) delighted; **¡~!** how do you do, pleased to meet you

encantador, a [enkantaˈðor, a] *adj* charming, lovely ♦ *nm/f* magician, enchanter/enchantress

encantar [enkanˈtar] *vt* (*agradar*) to charm, delight; (*hechizar*) to bewitch, cast a spell on; **me encanta eso** I love that; **encanto** *nm* (*hechizo*) spell, charm; (*fig*) charm, delight

encarcelar [enkarθeˈlar] *vt* to imprison, jail

encarecer [enkareˈθer] *vt* to put up the price of; **~se** *vr* to get dearer

encarecimiento [enkareθiˈmjento] *nm* price increase

encargado, a [enkarˈɣaðo, a] *adj* in charge ♦ *nm/f* agent, representative; (*responsable*) person in charge

encargar [enkarˈɣar] *vt* to entrust; (*recomendar*) to urge, recommend; **~se** *vr*: **~se de** to look after, take charge of

encargo [enˈkarɣo] *nm* (*tarea*) assignment, job; (*responsabilidad*) responsibility; (COM) order

encariñarse [enkariˈɲarse] *vr*: **~ con** to grow fond of, get attached to

encarnación [enkarnaˈθjon] *nf* incarnation, embodiment

encarnizado, a [enkarniˈθaðo, a] *adj* (*lucha*) bloody, fierce

encarrilar [enkarriˈlar] *vt* (*tren*) to put back on the rails; (*fig*) to correct, put on the right track

encasillar [enkasiˈʎar] *vt* (*tb fig*) to pigeonhole; (*actor*) to typecast

encauzar [enkauˈθar] *vt* to channel

encendedor [enθendeˈðor] *nm* lighter

encender [enθenˈder] *vt* (*con fuego*) to light; (*luz, radio*) to put on, switch on; (*avivar: pasiones*) to inflame; **~se** *vr* to catch fire; (*excitarse*) to get excited; (*de cólera*) to flare up; (*el rostro*) to blush

encendido [enθenˈdiðo] *nm* (AUTO) ignition

encerado [enθeˈraðo] *nm* (ESCOL) blackboard

encerar [enθeˈrar] *vt* (*suelo*) to wax, polish

encerrar [enθeˈrrar] *vt* (*confinar*) to shut in, shut up; (*comprender, incluir*) to include, contain

encharcado, a [entʃarˈkaðo, a] *adj* (*terreno*) flooded

encharcarse [entʃarˈkarse] *vr* to get flooded

enchufado, a [entʃuˈfaðo, a] (*fam*) *nm/f* well-connected person

enchufar [entʃuˈfar] *vt* (ELEC) to plug in; (TEC) to connect, fit together; **enchufe** *nm* (ELEC: *clavija*) plug; (: *toma*) socket; (*de dos tubos*) joint, connection; (*fam: influencia*) contact, connection; (: *puesto*) cushy job

encía [enˈθia] *nf* gum

encienda *etc vb ver* **encender**

encierro *etc* [enˈθjerro] *vb ver* **encerrar** ♦ *nm* shutting in, shutting up; (*calabozo*) prison

encima [enˈθima] *adv* (*sobre*) above, over; (*además*) besides; **~ de** (*en*) on, on top of; (*sobre*) above; (*además de*) besides, on top of; **por ~ de** over; **¿llevas dinero ~?** have you (got) any money on you?; **se me vino ~** it took me by surprise

encina [enˈθina] *nf* holm oak

encinta [enˈθinta] *adj* pregnant

enclenque [enˈklenke] *adj* weak, sickly

encoger [enkoˈxer] *vt* to shrink, contract; **~se** *vr* to shrink, contract; (*fig*) to cringe; **~se de hombros** to shrug one's shoulders

encolar [enkoˈlar] *vt* (*engomar*) to glue, paste; (*pegar*) to stick down

encolerizar [enkoleri'θar] *vt* to anger, provoke; **~se** *vr* to get angry

encomendar [enkomen'dar] *vt* to entrust, commend; **~se** *vr*: **~se a** to put one's trust in

encomiar [enko'mjar] *vt* to praise, pay tribute to

encomienda *etc* [enko'mjenda] *vb ver* **encomendar** ♦ *nf* (*encargo*) charge, commission; (*elogio*) tribute; **~ postal** (*AM*) parcel post

encontrado, a [enkon'traðo, a] *adj* (*contrario*) contrary, conflicting

encontrar [enkon'trar] *vt* (*hallar*) to find; (*inesperadamente*) to meet, run into; **~se** *vr* to meet (each other); (*situarse*) to be (situated); **~se con** to meet; **~se bien (de salud)** to feel well

encrespar [enkres'par] *vt* (*cabellos*) to curl; (*fig*) to anger, irritate; **~se** *vr* (*el mar*) to get rough; (*fig*) to get cross, get irritated

encrucijada [enkruθi'xaða] *nf* crossroads *sg*

encuadernación [enkwaðerna'θjon] *nf* binding

encuadernador, a [enkwaðerna'ðor, a] *nm/f* bookbinder

encuadrar [enkwa'ðrar] *vt* (*retrato*) to frame; (*ajustar*) to fit, insert; (*contener*) to contain

encubrir [enku'ßrir] *vt* (*ocultar*) to hide, conceal; (*criminal*) to harbour, shelter

encuentro *etc* [en'kwentro] *vb ver* **encontrar** ♦ *nm* (*de personas*) meeting; (*AUTO etc*) collision, crash; (*DEPORTE*) match, game; (*MIL*) encounter

encuesta [en'kwesta] *nf* inquiry, investigation; (*sondeo*) (public) opinion poll; **~ judicial** post mortem

encumbrar [enkum'brar] *vt* (*persona*) to exalt

endeble [en'deßle] *adj* (*argumento, excusa, persona*) weak

endémico, a [en'demiko, a] *adj* (*MED*) endemic; (*fig*) rife, chronic

endemoniado, a [endemo'njaðo, a] *adj* possessed (of the devil); (*travieso*) devilish

enderezar [endere'θar] *vt* (*poner derecho*) to straighten (out); (: *verticalmente*) to set upright; (*situación*) to straighten *o* sort out; (*dirigir*) to direct; **~se** *vr* (*persona sentada*) to straighten up

endeudarse [endeu'ðarse] *vr* to get into debt

endiablado, a [endja'ßlaðo, a] *adj* devilish, diabolical; (*travieso*) mischievous

endilgar [endil'var] (*fam*) *vt*: **~le algo a uno** to lumber sb with sth; **~le un sermón a uno** to lecture sb

endiñar [endi'nar] (*fam*) *vt* (*bofetón*) to land, belt

endosar [endo'sar] *vt* (*cheque etc*) to endorse

endulzar [endul'θar] *vt* to sweeten; (*suavizar*) to soften

endurecer [endure'θer] *vt* to harden; **~se** *vr* to harden, grow hard

enema [e'nema] *nm* (*MED*) enema

enemigo, a [ene'mixo, a] *adj* enemy, hostile ♦ *nm/f* enemy

enemistad [enemis'tað] *nf* enmity

enemistar [enemis'tar] *vt* to make enemies of, cause a rift between; **~se** *vr* to become enemies; (*amigos*) to fall out

energía [ener'xia] *nf* (*vigor*) energy, drive; (*empuje*) push; (*TEC, ELEC*) energy, power; **~ eolica** wind power; **~ solar** solar energy/power

enérgico, a [e'nerxiko, a] *adj* (*gen*) energetic; (*voz, modales*) forceful

energúmeno, a [ener'vumeno, a] (*fam*) *nm/f* (*fig*) madman/woman

enero [e'nero] *nm* January

enfadado, a [enfa'ðaðo, a] *adj* angry, annoyed

enfadar [enfa'ðar] *vt* to anger, annoy; **~se** *vr* to get angry *o* annoyed

enfado [en'faðo] *nm* (*enojo*) anger, annoyance; (*disgusto*) trouble, bother

énfasis ['enfasis] *nm* emphasis, stress

enfático, a [en'fatiko, a] *adj* emphatic

enfermar [enfer'mar] *vt* to make ill ♦ *vi* to fall ill, be taken ill

enfermedad [enferme'ðað] *nf* illness; **~ venérea** venereal disease

enfermera [enfer'mera] *nf* nurse

enfermería [enferme'ria] *nf* infirmary; *(de colegio etc)* sick bay

enfermero [enfer'mero] *nm* (male) nurse

enfermizo, a [enfer'miθo, a] *adj (persona)* sickly, unhealthy; *(fig)* unhealthy

enfermo, a [en'fermo, a] *adj* ill, sick ♦ *nm/f* invalid, sick person; *(en hospital)* patient

enflaquecer [enflake'θer] *vt (adelgazar)* to make thin; *(debilitar)* to weaken

enfocar [enfo'kar] *vt (foto etc)* to focus; *(problema etc)* to approach

enfoque [en'foke] *vb ver* **enfocar** ♦ *nm* focus.

enfrascarse [enfras'karse] *vr:* **~ en algo** to bury o.s. in sth

enfrentar [enfren'tar] *vt (peligro)* to face (up to), confront; *(oponer)* to bring face to face; **~se** *vr (dos personas)* to face o confront each other; *(DEPORTE: dos equipos)* to meet; **~se a** o **con** to face up to, confront

enfrente [en'frente] *adv* opposite; **la casa de ~** the house opposite, the house across the street; **~ de** opposite, facing

enfriamiento [enfria'mjento] *nm* chilling, refrigeration; *(MED)* cold, chill

enfriar [enfri'ar] *vt (alimentos)* to cool, chill; *(algo caliente)* to cool down; **~se** *vr* to cool down; *(MED)* to catch a chill; *(amistad)* to cool

enfurecer [enfure'θer] *vt* to enrage, madden; **~se** *vr* to become furious, fly into a rage; *(mar)* to get rough

engalanar [engala'nar] *vt (adornar)* to adorn; *(ciudad)* to decorate; **~se** *vr* to get dressed up

enganchar [engan'tʃar] *vt* to hook; *(dos vagones)* to hitch up; *(TEC)* to couple, connect; *(MIL)* to recruit; **~se** *vr (MIL)* to enlist, join up

enganche [en'gantʃe] *nm* hook; *(TEC)* coupling, connection; *(acto)* hooking (up); *(MIL)* recruitment, enlistment; *(AM:*

depósito) deposit

engañar [enga'nar] *vt* to deceive; *(estafar)* to cheat, swindle; **~se** *vr (equivocarse)* to be wrong; *(disimular la verdad)* to deceive o.s.

engaño [en'gaɲo] *nm* deceit; *(estafa)* trick, swindle; *(error)* mistake, misunderstanding; *(ilusión)* delusion; **~so, a** *adj (tramposo)* crooked; *(mentiroso)* dishonest, deceitful; *(aspecto)* deceptive; *(consejo)* misleading

engarzar [engar'θar] *vt (joya)* to set, mount; *(fig)* to link, connect

engatusar [engatu'sar] *(fam) vt* to coax

engendrar [enxen'drar] *vt* to breed; *(procrear)* to beget; *(causar)* to cause, produce; **engendro** *nm (BIO)* foetus; *(fig)* monstrosity

englobar [englo'ßar] *vt* to include, comprise

engordar [engor'ðar] *vt* to fatten ♦ *vi* to get fat, put on weight

engorroso, a [engo'rroso, a] *adj* bothersome, trying

engranaje [engra'naxe] *nm (AUTO)* gear

engrandecer [engrande'θer] *vt* to enlarge, magnify; *(alabar)* to praise, speak highly of; *(exagerar)* to exaggerate

engrasar [engra'sar] *vt (TEC: poner grasa)* to grease; *(: lubricar)* to lubricate, oil; *(manchar)* to make greasy

engreído, a [engre'iðo, a] *adj* vain, conceited

engrosar [engro'sar] *vt (ensanchar)* to enlarge; *(aumentar)* to increase; *(hinchar)* to swell

enhebrar [ene'ßrar] *vt* to thread

enhorabuena [enora'ßwena] *excl:* **¡~!** congratulations! ♦ *nf:* **dar la ~ a** to congratulate

enigma [e'nivma] *nm* enigma; *(problema)* puzzle; *(misterio)* mystery

enjabonar [enxaßo'nar] *vt* to soap; *(fam: adular)* to soft-soap

enjambre [en'xambre] *nm* swarm

enjaular [enxau'lar] *vt* to (put in a) cage; *(fam)* to jail, lock up

uagar [enxwa'ɣar] vt (ropa) to rinse
ut)

uague etc [en'xwaɣe] vb ver **enjuagar**

nm (MED) mouthwash; (de ropa) rinse,
sing

ugar [enxu'ɣar] vt to wipe (off);
ágrimas) to dry; (déficit) to wipe out

uiciar [enxwi'θjar] vt (JUR: procesar) to
rosecute, try; (fig) to judge

uto, a [en'xuto, a] adj (flaco) lean,
inny

ace [en'laθe] nm link, connection;
elación) relationship; (tb: ~ **matrimonial**)
arriage; (de carretera, trenes)
nnection; ~ **sindical** shop steward

atado, a [enla'taðo, a] adj (comida,
roductos) tinned, canned

azar [enla'θar] vt (unir con lazos) to
nd together; (atar) to tie; (conectar) to
k, connect; (AM) to lasso

odar [enlo'ðar] vt to cover in mud; (fig:
anchar) to stain; (: rebajar) to debase

oquecer [enloke'θer] vt to drive mad
vi to go mad; ~**se** vr to go mad

utado, a [enlu'taðo, a] adj (persona) in
ourning

marañar [enmara'ɲar] vt (enredar) to
ngle (up), entangle; (complicar) to
mplicate; (confundir) to confuse; ~**se** vr
nredarse) to become entangled;
onfundirse) to get confused

marcar [enmar'kar] vt (cuadro) to frame

mascarar [enmaska'rar] vt to mask;
se vr to put on a mask

mendar [enmen'dar] vt to emend,
orrect; (constitución etc) to amend;
omportamiento) to reform; ~**se** vr to
form, mend one's ways; **enmienda** nf
rrection; amendment; reform

mohecerse [enmoe'θerse] vr (metal) to
st, go rusty; (muro, plantas) to get
ouldy

mudecer [enmuðe'θer] vi (perder el
bla) to fall silent; (guardar silencio) to
main silent

egrecer [enneɣre'θer] vt (poner negro)
blacken; (oscurecer) to darken; ~**se** vr

to turn black; (oscurecerse) to get dark,
darken

ennoblecer [ennoβle'θer] vt to ennoble

enojar [eno'xar] vt (encolerizar) to anger;
(disgustar) to annoy, upset; ~**se** vr to get
angry; to get annoyed

enojo [e'noxo] nm (cólera) anger;
(irritación) annoyance; ~**so, a** adj
annoying

enorgullecerse [enorɣuʎe'θerse] vr to be
proud; ~ **de** to pride o.s. on, be proud of

enorme [e'norme] adj enormous, huge;
(fig) monstrous; **enormidad** nf
hugeness, immensity

enrarecido, a [enrare'θiðo, a] adj
(atmósfera, aire) rarefied

enredadera [enreða'ðera] nf (BOT)
creeper, climbing plant

enredar [enre'ðar] vt (cables, hilos etc) to
tangle (up), entangle; (situación) to
complicate, confuse; (meter cizaña) to
sow discord among o between; (implicar)
to embroil, implicate; ~**se** vr to get
entangled, get tangled (up); (situación) to
get complicated; (persona) to get
embroiled; (AM: fam) to meddle

enredo [en'reðo] nm (maraña) tangle;
(confusión) mix-up, confusion; (intriga)
intrigue

enrejado [enre'xaðo] nm fence, railings pl

enrevesado, a [enreβe'saðo, a] adj
(asunto) complicated, involved

enriquecer [enrike'θer] vt to make rich,
enrich; ~**se** vr to get rich

enrojecer [enroxe'θer] vt to redden ♦ vi
(persona) to blush; ~**se** vr to blush

enrolar [enro'lar] vt (MIL) to enlist;
(reclutar) to recruit; ~**se** vr (MIL) to join
up; (afiliarse) to enrol

enrollar [enro'ʎar] vt to roll (up), wind
(up)

enroscar [enros'kar] vt (torcer, doblar) to
coil (round), wind; (tornillo, rosca) to
screw in; ~**se** vr to coil, wind

ensalada [ensa'laða] nf salad;
ensaladilla (rusa) nf Russian salad

ensalzar [ensal'θar] vt (alabar) to praise,

extol; (*exaltar*) to exalt

ensamblaje [ensam'blaxe] *nm* assembly; (*TEC*) joint

ensanchar [ensan'tʃar] *vt* (*hacer más ancho*) to widen; (*agrandar*) to enlarge, expand; (*COSTURA*) to let out; **~se** *vr* to get wider, expand; **ensanche** *nm* (*de calle*) widening

ensangrentar [ensangren'tar] *vt* to stain with blood

ensañar [ensa'ɲar] *vt* to enrage; **~se** *vr*: **~se con** to treat brutally

ensartar [ensar'tar] *vt* (*cuentas, perlas etc*) to string (together)

ensayar [ensa'jar] *vt* to test, try (out); (*TEATRO*) to rehearse

ensayo [en'sajo] *nm* test, trial; (*QUÍM*) experiment; (*TEATRO*) rehearsal; (*DEPORTE*) try; (*ESCOL, LITERATURA*) essay

enseguida [ense'βiða] *adv* at once, right away

ensenada [ense'naða] *nf* inlet, cove

enseñanza [ense'naɲθa] *nf* (*educación*) education; (*acción*) teaching; (*doctrina*) teaching, doctrine

enseñar [ense'ɲar] *vt* (*educar*) to teach; (*mostrar, señalar*) to show

enseres [en'seres] *nmpl* belongings

ensillar [ensi'ʎar] *vt* to saddle (up)

ensimismarse [ensimis'marse] *vr* (*abstraerse*) to become lost in thought; (*AM*) to become conceited

ensombrecer [ensombre'θer] *vt* to darken, cast a shadow over; (*fig*) to overshadow, put in the shade

ensordecer [ensorðe'θer] *vt* to deafen ♦ *vi* to go deaf

ensortijado, a [ensorti'xaðo, a] *adj* (*pelo*) curly

ensuciar [ensu'θjar] *vt* (*manchar*) to dirty, soil; (*fig*) to defile; **~se** *vr* to get dirty; (*niño*) to wet o.s.

ensueño [en'sweɲo] *nm* (*sueño*) dream, fantasy; (*ilusión*) illusion; (*soñando despierto*) daydream

entablar [enta'βlar] *vt* (*recubrir*) to board (up); (*AJEDREZ, DAMAS*) to set up;

(*conversación*) to strike up; (*JUR*) to file ♦ *vi* to draw

entablillar [entaβli'ʎar] *vt* (*MED*) to (put in a) splint

entallar [enta'ʎar] *vt* (*traje*) to tailor ♦ *vi*: **el traje entalla bien** the suit fits well

ente ['ente] *nm* (*organización*) body, organization; (*fam: persona*) odd character

entender [enten'der] *vt* (*comprender*) to understand; (*darse cuenta*) to realize ♦ *vi* to understand; (*creer*) to think, believe; **~se** *vr* (*comprenderse*) to be understood; (*2 personas*) to get on together; (*ponerse de acuerdo*) to agree, reach an agreement; **~ de** to know all about; **~ algo de** to know a little about; **~ en** to deal with, have to do with; **~se mal** (*2 personas*) to get on badly

entendido, a [enten'diðo, a] *adj* (*comprendido*) understood; (*hábil*) skilled; (*inteligente*) knowledgeable ♦ *nm/f* (*experto*) expert ♦ *excl* agreed!; **entendimiento** *nm* (*comprensión*) understanding; (*inteligencia*) mind, intellect; (*juicio*) judgement

enterado, a [ente'raðo, a] *adj* well-informed; **estar ~ de** to know about, be aware of

enteramente [entera'mente] *adv* entirely, completely

enterar [ente'rar] *vt* (*informar*) to inform, tell; **~se** *vr* to find out, get to know

entereza [ente'reθa] *nf* (*totalidad*) entirety (*fig: carácter*) strength of mind; (*: honradez*) integrity

enternecer [enterne'θer] *vt* (*ablandar*) to soften; (*apiadar*) to touch, move; **~se** *vr* to be touched, be moved

entero, a [en'tero, a] *adj* (*total*) whole, entire; (*fig: honesto*) honest; (*: firme*) firm, resolute ♦ *nm* (*COM: punto*) point; (*AM: pago*) payment

enterrador [enterra'ðor] *nm* gravedigger

enterrar [ente'rrar] *vt* to bury

entibiar [enti'βjar] *vt* (*enfriar*) to cool; (*calentar*) to warm; **~se** *vr* (*fig*) to cool

entidad [enti'ðað] *nf* (*empresa*) firm, company; (*organismo*) body; (*sociedad*) society; (FILOSOFÍA) entity

entiendo *etc vb ver* **entender**

entierro [en'tjerro] *nm* (*acción*) burial; (*funeral*) funeral

entonación [entona'θjon] *nf* (LING) intonation

entonar [ento'nar] *vt* (*canción*) to intone; (*colores*) to tone; (MED) to tone up ♦ *vi* to be in tune

entonces [en'tonθes] *adv* then, at that time; **desde ~** since then; **en aquel ~** at that time; **(pues) ~** and so

entornar [entor'nar] *vt* (*puerta, ventana*) to half close, leave ajar; (*los ojos*) to screw up

entorpecer [entorpe'θer] *vt* (*entendimiento*) to dull; (*impedir*) to obstruct, hinder; (: *tránsito*) to slow down, delay

entrada [en'traða] *nf* (*acción*) entry, access; (*sitio*) entrance, way in; (INFORM) input; (COM) receipts *pl*, takings *pl*; (CULIN) starter; (DEPORTE) innings *sg*; (TEATRO) house, audience; (*billete*) ticket; (COM): **~s y salidas** income and expenditure; (TEC): **~ de aire** air intake *o* inlet; **de ~** from the outset

entrado, a [en'traðo, a] *adj*: **~ en años** elderly; **una vez ~ el verano** in the summer(time), when summer comes

entramparse [entram'parse] *vr* to get into debt

entrante [en'trante] *adj* next, coming; **mes/año ~** next month/year; **~s** *nmpl* starters

entraña [en'traɲa] *nf* (*fig: centro*) heart, core; (*raíz*) root; **~s** *nfpl* (ANAT) entrails; (*fig*) heart *sg*; **sin ~s** (*fig*) heartless; **entrañable** *adj* close, intimate; **entrañar** *vt* to entail

entrar [en'trar] *vt* (*introducir*) to bring in; (INFORM) to input ♦ *vi* (*meterse*) to go in, come in, enter; (*comenzar*): **~ diciendo** to begin by saying; **hacer ~** to show in; **no me entra** I can't get the hang of it

entre ['entre] *prep* (*dos*) between; (*más de dos*) among(st)

entreabrir [entrea'ßrir] *vt* to half-open, open halfway

entrecejo [entre'θexo] *nm*: **fruncir el ~** to frown

entrecortado, a [entrekor'taðo, a] *adj* (*respiración*) difficult; (*habla*) faltering

entredicho [entre'ðitʃo] *nm* (JUR) injunction; **poner en ~** to cast doubt on; **estar en ~** to be in doubt

entrega [en'treya] *nf* (*de mercancías*) delivery; (*de novela etc*) instalment

entregar [entre'yar] *vt* (*dar*) to hand (over), deliver; **~se** *vr* (*rendirse*) to surrender, give in, submit; (*dedicarse*) to devote o.s.

entrelazar [entrela'θar] *vt* to entwine

entremeses [entre'meses] *nmpl* hors d'œuvres

entremeter [entreme'ter] *vt* to insert, put in; **~se** *vr* to meddle, interfere; **entremetido, a** *adj* meddling, interfering

entremezclar [entremeθ'klar] *vt* to intermingle; **~se** *vr* to intermingle

entrenador, a [entrena'ðor, a] *nm/f* trainer, coach

entrenarse [entre'narse] *vr* to train

entrepierna [entre'pjerna] *nf* crotch

entresacar [entresa'kar] *vt* to pick out, select

entresuelo [entre'swelo] *nm* mezzanine

entretanto [entre'tanto] *adv* meanwhile, meantime

entretejer [entrete'xer] *vt* to interweave

entretener [entrete'ner] *vt* (*divertir*) to entertain, amuse; (*detener*) to hold up, delay; **~se** *vr* (*divertirse*) to amuse o.s.; (*retrasarse*) to delay, linger; **entretenido, a** *adj* entertaining, amusing; **entretenimiento** *nm* entertainment, amusement

entrever [entre'ßer] *vt* to glimpse, catch a glimpse of

entrevista [entre'ßista] *nf* interview; **entrevistar** *vt* to interview;

entrevistarse *vr* to have an interview
entristecer [entriste'θer] *vt* to sadden, grieve; **~se** *vr* to grow sad
entrometerse [entrome'terse] *vr*: ~ **(en)** to interfere (in *o* with)
entroncar [entron'kar] *vi* to be connected *o* related
entumecer [entume'θer] *vt* to numb, benumb; **~se** *vr* (*por el frío*) to go *o* become numb; **entumecido, a** *adj* numb, stiff
enturbiar [entur'βjar] *vt* (*el agua*) to make cloudy; (*fig*) to confuse; **~se** *vr* (*oscurecerse*) to become cloudy; (*fig*) to get confused, become obscure
entusiasmar [entusjas'mar] *vt* to excite, fill with enthusiasm; (*gustar mucho*) to delight; **~se con** *o* **por** to get enthusiastic *o* excited about
entusiasmo [entu'sjasmo] *nm* enthusiasm; (*excitación*) excitement
entusiasta [entu'sjasta] *adj* enthusiastic ♦ *nm/f* enthusiast
enumerar [enume'rar] *vt* to enumerate
enunciación [enunθja'θjon] *nf* enunciation
enunciado [enun'θjaðo] *nm* enunciation
envainar [embai'nar] *vt* to sheathe
envalentonar [embalento'nar] *vt* to give courage to; **~se** *vr* (*pey: jactarse*) to boast, brag
envanecer [embane'θer] *vt* to make conceited; **~se** *vr* to grow conceited
envasar [emba'sar] *vt* (*empaquetar*) to pack, wrap; (*enfrascar*) to bottle; (*enlatar*) to can; (*embolsar*) to pocket
envase [em'base] *nm* (*en paquete*) packing, wrapping; (*en botella*) bottling; (*en lata*) canning; (*recipiente*) container; (*paquete*) package; (*botella*) bottle; (*lata*) tin (*BRIT*), can
envejecer [embexe'θer] *vt* to make old, age ♦ *vi* (*volverse viejo*) to grow old; (*parecer viejo*) to age; **~se** *vr* to grow old; to age
envenenar [embene'nar] *vt* to poison; (*fig*) to embitter

envergadura [emberɣa'ðura] *nf* (*fig*) scope, compass
envés [em'bes] *nm* (*de tela*) back, wrong side
enviar [em'bjar] *vt* to send
enviciarse [embi'θjarse] *vr*: ~ **(con)** to get addicted (to)
envidia [em'biðja] *nf* envy; **tener ~ a** to envy, be jealous of; **envidiar** *vt* to envy
envío [em'bio] *nm* (*acción*) sending; (*de mercancías*) consignment; (*de dinero*) remittance
enviudar [embju'ðar] *vi* to be widowed
envoltura [embol'tura] *nf* (*cobertura*) cover; (*embalaje*) wrapper, wrapping; **envoltorio** *nm* package
envolver [embol'βer] *vt* to wrap (up); (*cubrir*) to cover; (*enemigo*) to surround; (*implicar*) to involve, implicate
envuelto [em'bwelto] *pp de* **envolver**
enyesar [enje'sar] *vt* (*pared*) to plaster; (*MED*) to put in plaster
enzarzarse [enθar'θarse] *vr*: ~ **en** (*pelea*) to get mixed up in; (*disputa*) to get involved in
épica ['epika] *nf* epic
épico, a ['epiko, a] *adj* epic
epidemia [epi'ðemja] *nf* epidemic
epilepsia [epi'lepsja] *nf* epilepsy
epílogo [e'piloɣo] *nm* epilogue
episodio [epi'soðjo] *nm* episode
epístola [e'pistola] *nf* epistle
época ['epoka] *nf* period, time; (*HISTORIA*) age, epoch; **hacer ~** to be epoch-making
equilibrar [ekili'βrar] *vt* to balance; **equilibrio** *nm* balance, equilibrium; **equilibrista** *nm/f* (*funámbulo*) tightrope walker; (*acróbata*) acrobat
equipaje [eki'paxe] *nm* luggage; (*avíos*): ~ **de mano** hand luggage
equipar [eki'par] *vt* (*proveer*) to equip
equipararse [ekipa'rarse] *vr*: ~ **con** to be on a level with
equipo [e'kipo] *nm* (*conjunto de cosas*) equipment; (*DEPORTE*) team; (*de obreros*) shift
equis ['ekis] *nf inv* (the letter) X

equitación [ekita'θjon] *nf* horse riding

equitativo, a [ekita'tiβo, a] *adj* equitable, fair

equivalente [ekiβa'lente] *adj, nm* equivalent

equivaler [ekiβa'ler] *vi* to be equivalent o equal

equivocación [ekiβoka'θjon] *nf* mistake, error

equivocado, a [ekiβo'kaðo, a] *adj* wrong, mistaken

equivocarse [ekiβo'karse] *vr* to be wrong, make a mistake; **~ de camino** to take the wrong road

equívoco, a [e'kiβoko, a] *adj* (*dudoso*) suspect; (*ambiguo*) ambiguous ♦ *nm* ambiguity; (*malentendido*) misunderstanding

era ['era] *vb ver* **ser** ♦ *nf* era, age

erais *vb ver* **ser**

eramos *vb ver* **ser**

eran *vb ver* **ser**

erario [e'rarjo] *nm* exchequer (*BRIT*), treasury

eras *vb ver* **ser**

erección [erek'θjon] *nf* erection

eres *vb ver* **ser**

erguir [er'vir] *vt* to raise, lift; (*poner derecho*) to straighten; **~se** *vr* to straighten up

erigir [eri'xir] *vt* to erect, build; **~se** *vr*: **~se en** to set o.s. up as

erizarse [eri'θarse] *vr* (*pelo: de perro*) to bristle; (*: de persona*) to stand on end

erizo [e'riθo] *nm* (*ZOOL*) hedgehog; **~ de mar** sea-urchin

ermita [er'mita] *nf* hermitage

ermitaño, a [ermi'taɲo, a] *nm/f* hermit

erosión [ero'sjon] *nf* erosion

erosionar [erosjo'nar] *vt* to erode

erótico, a [e'rotiko, a] *adj* erotic; **erotismo** *nm* eroticism

erradicar [erraði'kar] *vt* to eradicate

errante [e'rrante] *adj* wandering, errant

errar [e'rrar] *vi* (*vagar*) to wander, roam; (*equivocarse*) to be mistaken ♦ *vt*: **~ el camino** to take the wrong road; **~ el tiro** to miss

erróneo, a [e'rroneo, a] *adj* (*equivocado*) wrong, mistaken

error [e'rror] *nm* error, mistake; (*INFORM*) bug; **~ de imprenta** misprint

eructar [eruk'tar] *vt* to belch, burp

erudito, a [eru'ðito, a] *adj* erudite, learned

erupción [erup'θjon] *nf* eruption; (*MED*) rash

es *vb ver* **ser**

esa ['esa] (*pl* **esas**) *adj demos ver* **ese**

ésa ['esa] (*pl* **ésas**) *pron ver* **ése**

esbelto, a [es'βelto, a] *adj* slim, slender

esbozo [es'βoθo] *nm* sketch, outline

escabeche [eska'βetʃe] *nm* brine; (*de aceitunas etc*) pickle; **en ~** pickled

escabroso, a [eska'βroso, a] *adj* (*accidentado*) rough, uneven; (*fig*) tough, difficult; (*: atrevido*) risqué

escabullirse [eskaβuʎ'irse] *vr* to slip away, to clear out

escafandra [eska'fandra] *nf* (*buzo*) diving suit; (**~ espacial**) space suit

escala [es'kala] *nf* (*proporción, MUS*) scale; (*de mano*) ladder; (*AVIAT*) stopover; **hacer ~ en** to stop o call in at

escalafón [eskala'fon] *nm* (*escala de salarios*) salary scale, wage scale

escalar [eska'lar] *vt* to climb, scale

escalera [eska'lera] *nf* stairs *pl*, staircase; (*escala*) ladder; (*NAIPES*) run; **~ mecánica** escalator; **~ de caracol** spiral staircase

escalfar [eskal'far] *vt* (*huevos*) to poach

escalinata [eskali'nata] *nf* staircase

escalofriante [eskalo'frjante] *adj* chilling

escalofrío [eskalo'frio] *nm* (*MED*) chill; **~s** *nmpl* (*fig*) shivers

escalón [eska'lon] *nm* step, stair; (*de escalera*) rung

escalope [eska'lope] *nm* (*CULIN*) escalope

escama [es'kama] *nf* (*de pez, serpiente*) scale; (*de jabón*) flake; (*fig*) resentment

escamar [eska'mar] *vt* (*fig*) to make wary o suspicious

escamotear [eskamote'ar] *vt* (*robar*) to lift, swipe; (*hacer desaparecer*) to make disappear

escampar [eskam'par] *vb impers* to stop raining

escandalizar [eskandali'θar] *vt* to scandalize, shock; **~se** *vr* to be shocked; (*ofenderse*) to be offended

escándalo [es'kandalo] *nm* scandal; (*alboroto, tumulto*) row, uproar; **escandaloso, a** *adj* scandalous, shocking

escandinavo, a [eskandi'naβo, a] *adj, nm/f* Scandinavian

escaño [es'kaɲo] *nm* bench; (*POL*) seat

escapar [eska'par] *vi* (*gen*) to escape, run away; (*DEPORTE*) to break away; **~se** *vr* to escape, get away; (*agua, gas*) to leak (out)

escaparate [eskapa'rate] *nm* shop window

escape [es'kape] *nm* (*de agua, gas*) leak; (*de motor*) exhaust

escarabajo [eskara'βaxo] *nm* beetle

escaramuza [eskara'muθa] *nf* skirmish

escarbar [eskar'βar] *vt* (*tierra*) to scratch

escarceos [eskar'θeos] *nmpl* (*fig*): **en mis ~ con la política ...** in my dealings with politics ...; **~ amorosos** love affairs

escarcha [es'kartʃa] *nf* frost

escarchado, a [eskar'tʃaðo, a] *adj* (*CULIN: fruta*) crystallized

escarlata [eskar'lata] *adj inv* scarlet; **escarlatina** *nf* scarlet fever

escarmentar [eskarmen'tar] *vt* to punish severely ♦ *vi* to learn one's lesson

escarmiento *etc* [eskar'mjento] *vb ver* **escarmentar** ♦ *nm* (*ejemplo*) lesson; (*castigo*) punishment

escarnio [es'karnjo] *nm* mockery; (*injuria*) insult

escarola [eska'rola] *nf* endive

escarpado, a [eskar'paðo, a] *adj* (*pendiente*) sheer, steep; (*rocas*) craggy

escasear [eskase'ar] *vi* to be scarce

escasez [eska'seθ] *nf* (*falta*) shortage, scarcity; (*pobreza*) poverty

escaso, a [es'kaso, a] *adj* (*poco*) scarce; (*raro*) rare; (*ralo*) thin, sparse; (*limitado*) limited

escatimar [eskati'mar] *vt* to skimp (on), be sparing with

escayola [eska'jola] *nf* plaster

escena [es'θena] *nf* scene

escenario [esθe'narjo] *nm* (*TEATRO*) stage; (*CINE*) set; (*fig*) scene; **escenografía** *nf* set design

escepticismo [esθepti'θismo] *nm* scepticism; **escéptico, a** *adj* sceptical ♦ *nm/f* sceptic

escisión [esθi'sjon] *nf* (*de partido, secta*) split

esclarecer [esklare'θer] *vt* (*misterio, problema*) to shed light on

esclavitud [esklaβi'tuð] *nf* slavery

esclavizar [esklaβi'θar] *vt* to enslave

esclavo, a [es'klaβo, a] *nm/f* slave

esclusa [es'klusa] *nf* (*de canal*) lock; (*compuerta*) floodgate

escoba [es'koβa] *nf* broom; **escobilla** *nf* brush

escocer [esko'θer] *vi* to burn, sting; **~se** *vr* to chafe, get chafed

escocés, esa [esko'θes, esa] *adj* Scottish ♦ *nm/f* Scotsman/woman, Scot

Escocia [es'koθja] *nf* Scotland

escoger [esko'xer] *vt* to choose, pick, select; **escogido, a** *adj* chosen, selected

escolar [esko'lar] *adj* school *cpd* ♦ *nm/f* schoolboy/girl, pupil

escollo [es'koʎo] *nm* (*obstáculo*) pitfall

escolta [es'kolta] *nf* escort; **escoltar** *vt* to escort

escombros [es'kombros] *nmpl* (*basura*) rubbish *sg*; (*restos*) debris *sg*

esconder [eskon'der] *vt* to hide, conceal; **~se** *vr* to hide; **escondidas** (*AM*) *nfpl*: **a escondidas** secretly; **escondite** *nm* hiding place; (*juego*) hide-and-seek; **escondrijo** *nm* hiding place, hideout

escopeta [esko'peta] *nf* shotgun

escoria [es'korja] *nf* (*de alto horno*) slag; (*fig*) scum, dregs *pl*

Escorpio [es'korpjo] *nm* Scorpio

escorpión [eskor'pjon] *nm* scorpion

escotado, a [esko'taðo, a] *adj* low-cut

escote [es'kote] *nm* (*de vestido*) low neck;

-agar a ~ to share the expenses
-cotilla [esko'tiʎa] nf (NAUT) hatch(way)
-cozor [esko'θor] nm (dolor) sting(ing)
-cribir [eskri'ßir] vt, vi to write; **~ a**
-áquina to type; **¿cómo se escribe?**
ow do you spell it?
-crito, a [es'krito, a] pp de **escribir** ♦ nm
(documento) document; (manuscrito) text,
manuscript; **por ~** in writing
-critor, a [eskri'tor, a] nm/f writer
-critorio [eskri'torjo] nm desk
-critura [eskri'tura] nf (acción) writing;
(caligrafía) (hand)writing; (JUR: documento)
eed
-crúpulo [es'krupulo] nm scruple;
(minuciosidad) scrupulousness;
-scrupuloso, a adj scrupulous
-crutar [eskru'tar] vt to scrutinize,
examine; (votos) to count
-crutinio [eskru'tinjo] nm (examen
atento) scrutiny; (POL: recuento de votos)
count(ing)
-cuadra [es'kwaðra] nf (MIL etc) squad;
(NAUT) squadron; (de coches etc) fleet;
-scuadrilla nf (de aviones) squadron;
(AM: de obreros) gang
-cuadrón [eskwa'ðron] nm squadron
-cuálido, a [es'kwaliðo, a] adj skinny,
scraggy; (sucio) squalid
-cuchar [esku'tʃar] vt to listen to ♦ vi to
listen
-cudilla [esku'ðiʎa] nf bowl, basin
-cudo [es'kuðo] nm shield
-cudriñar [eskuðri'ɲar] vt (examinar) to
investigate, scrutinize; (mirar de lejos) to
scan
-cuela [es'kwela] nf school; **~ de artes y
-ficios** (ESP) ≈ technical college; **~
-ormal** teacher training college
-cueto, a [es'kweto, a] adj plain; (estilo)
simple
-cuincle [es'kwinkle] (AM: fam) nm/f kid
-culpir [eskul'pir] vt to sculpt; (grabar) to
engrave; (tallar) to carve; **escultor, a**
nm/f sculptor/tress; **escultura** nf
sculpture
-upidera [eskupi'ðera] nf spittoon

escupir [esku'pir] vt, vi to spit (out)
escurreplatos [eskurre'platos] nm inv
plate rack
escurridizo, a [eskurri'ðiθo, a] adj
slippery
escurridor [eskurri'ðor] nm colander
escurrir [esku'rrir] vt (ropa) to wring out;
(verduras, platos) to drain ♦ vi (líquidos)
to drip; **~se** vr (secarse) to drain;
(resbalarse) to slip, slide; (escaparse) to
slip away
ese ['ese] (f **esa**, pl **esos, esas**) adj demos
(sg) that; (pl) those
ése ['ese] (f **ésa**, pl **ésos, ésas**) pron (sg)
that (one); (pl) those (ones); **~ ... éste ...**
the former ... the latter ...; **no me vengas
con ésas** don't give me any more of that
nonsense
esencia [e'senθja] nf essence; **esencial**
adj essential
esfera [es'fera] nf sphere; (de reloj) face;
esférico, a adj spherical
esforzarse [esfor'θarse] vr to exert o.s.,
make an effort
esfuerzo etc [es'fwerθo] vb ver **esforzar**
♦ nm effort
esfumarse [esfu'marse] vr (apoyo,
esperanzas) to fade away
esgrima [es'ɣrima] nf fencing
esgrimir [esɣri'mir] vt (arma) to brandish;
(argumento) to use
esguince [es'ɣinθe] nm (MED) sprain
eslabón [esla'ßon] nm link
eslip [es'lip] nm pants pl (BRIT), briefs pl
eslovaco, a [eslo'ßako, a] adj, nm/f
Slovak, Slovakian ♦ nm (LING) Slovak,
Slovakian
Eslovaquia [eslo'ßakja] nf Slovakia
esmaltar [esmal'tar] vt to enamel;
esmalte nm enamel; **esmalte de uñas**
nail varnish o polish
esmerado, a [esme'raðo, a] adj careful,
neat
esmeralda [esme'ralda] nf emerald
esmerarse [esme'rarse] vr (aplicarse) to
take great pains, exercise great care;
(afanarse) to work hard

esmero [es'mero] *nm* (great) care
esnob [es'nob] (*pl* ~s) *adj* (*persona*)
snobbish ♦ *nm/f* snob; ~**ismo** *nm*
snobbery
eso ['eso] *pron* that, that thing *o* matter; ~
de su coche that business about his car;
~ **de ir al cine** all that about going to the
cinema; **a ~ de las cinco** at about five
o'clock; **en ~** thereupon, at that point; ~
es that's it; **¡~ sí que es vida!** now that
is really living!; **por ~ te lo dije** that's why
I told you; **y ~ que llovía** in spite of the
fact it was raining
esos ['esos] *adj demos ver* **ese**
ésos ['esos] *pron ver* **ése**
espabilar *etc* [espaßi'lar] = **despabilar** *etc*
espacial [espa'θjal] *adj* (*del espacio*) space
cpd
espaciar [espa'θjar] *vt* to space (out)
espacio [es'paθjo] *nm* space; (*MUS*)
interval; (*RADIO, TV*) programme (*BRIT*),
program (*US*); **el ~** space; ~**so, a** *adj*
spacious, roomy
espada [es'paða] *nf* sword; ~**s** *nfpl*
(*NAIPES*) spades
espaguetis [espa'ɣetis] *nmpl* spaghetti *sg*
espalda [es'palda] *nf* (*gen*) back; ~**s** *nfpl*
(*hombros*) shoulders; **a ~s de uno** behind
sb's back; **tenderse de ~s** to lie (down)
on one's back; **volver la ~ a alguien** to
cold-shoulder sb
espantajo [espan'taxo] *nm* = **espantapájaros**
espantapájaros [espanta'paxaros] *nm inv*
scarecrow
espantar [espan'tar] *vt* (*asustar*) to
frighten, scare; (*ahuyentar*) to frighten off;
(*asombrar*) to horrify, appal; ~**se** *vr* to get
frightened *o* scared; to be appalled
espanto [es'panto] *nm* (*susto*) fright;
(*terror*) terror; (*asombro*) astonishment;
~**so, a** *adj* frightening; terrifying;
astonishing
España [es'paɲa] *nf* Spain; **español, a**
adj Spanish ♦ *nm/f* Spaniard ♦ *nm* (*LING*)
Spanish
esparadrapo [espara'ðrapo] *nm* (sticking)

plaster (*BRIT*), adhesive tape (*US*)
esparcimiento [esparθi'mjento] *nm*
(*dispersión*) spreading; (*diseminación*)
scattering; (*fig*) cheerfulness
esparcir [espar'θir] *vt* to spread;
(*diseminar*) to scatter; ~**se** *vr* to spread
(out); to scatter; (*divertirse*) to enjoy o.s.
espárrago [es'parrayo] *nm* asparagus
esparto [es'parto] *nm* esparto (grass)
espasmo [es'pasmo] *nm* spasm
espátula [es'patula] *nf* spatula
especia [es'peθja] *nf* spice
especial [espe'θjal] *adj* special; ~**idad** *nf*
speciality (*BRIT*), specialty (*US*)
especie [es'peθje] *nf* (*BIO*) species; (*clase*)
kind, sort; **en ~** in kind
especificar [espeθifi'kar] *vt* to specify;
específico, a *adj* specific
espécimen [es'peθimen] (*pl*
especímenes) *nm* specimen
espectáculo [espek'takulo] *nm* (*gen*)
spectacle; (*TEATRO etc*) show
espectador, a [espekta'ðor, a] *nm/f*
spectator
espectro [es'pektro] *nm* ghost; (*fig*)
spectre
especular [espeku'lar] *vt, vi* to speculate
espejismo [espe'xismo] *nm* mirage
espejo [es'pexo] *nm* mirror; ~ **retrovisor**
rear-view mirror
espeluznante [espeluθ'nante] *adj*
horrifying, hair-raising
espera [es'pera] *nf* (*pausa, intervalo*) wait;
(*JUR: plazo*) respite; **en ~ de** waiting for;
(*con expectativa*) expecting
esperanza [espe'ranθa] *nf* (*confianza*)
hope; (*expectativa*) expectation; **hay
pocas ~s de que venga** there is little
prospect of his coming
esperar [espe'rar] *vt* (*aguardar*) to wait
for; (*tener expectativa de*) to expect;
(*desear*) to hope for ♦ *vi* to wait; to
expect; to hope
esperma [es'perma] *nf* sperm
espesar [espe'sar] *vt* to thicken; ~**se** *vr* to
thicken, get thicker
espeso, a [es'peso, a] *adj* thick; **espesor**

nm thickness

spía [es'pia] *nm/f* spy; **espiar** *vt* (*observar*) to spy on

spiga [es'piɣa] *nf* (*BOT: de trigo etc*) ear

spigón [espi'ɣon] *nm* (*BOT*) ear; (*NAUT*) breakwater

spina [es'pina] *nf* thorn; (*de pez*) bone; ~ **dorsal** (*ANAT*) spine

spinaca [espi'naka] *nf* spinach

spinazo [espi'naθo] *nm* spine, backbone

spinilla [espi'niʎa] *nf* (*ANAT: tibia*) shin(bone); (*grano*) blackhead

spinoso, a [espi'noso, a] *adj* (*planta*) thorny, prickly; (*asunto*) difficult

spionaje [espjo'naxe] *nm* spying, espionage

spiral [espi'ral] *adj, nf* spiral

spirar [espi'rar] *vt* to breathe out, exhale

spiritista [espiri'tista] *adj, nm/f* spiritualist

spíritu [es'piritu] *nm* spirit; **espiritual** *adj* spiritual

spita [es'pita] *nf* tap

spléndido, a [es'plendiðo, a] *adj* (*magnífico*) magnificent, splendid; (*generoso*) generous

splendor [esplen'dor] *nm* splendour

spolear [espole'ar] *vt* to spur on

spoleta [espo'leta] *nf* (*de bomba*) fuse

spolón [espo'lon] *nm* sea wall

spolvorear [espolßore'ar] *vt* to dust, sprinkle

sponja [es'ponxa] *nf* sponge; (*fig*) sponger; **esponjoso, a** *adj* spongy

spontaneidad [espontanei'ðað] *nf* spontaneity; **espontáneo, a** *adj* spontaneous

sposa [es'posa] *nf* wife; ~**s** *nfpl* handcuffs; **esposar** *vt* to handcuff

sposo [es'poso] *nm* husband

spray [es'prai] *nm* spray

spuela [es'pwela] *nf* spur

spuma [es'puma] *nf* foam; (*de cerveza*) froth, head; (*de jabón*) lather; **espumadera** *nf* (*utensilio*) skimmer; **espumoso, a** *adj* frothy, foamy; (*vino*) sparkling

esqueleto [eske'leto] *nm* skeleton

esquema [es'kema] *nm* (*diagrama*) diagram; (*dibujo*) plan; (*FILOSOFÍA*) schema

esquí [es'ki] (*pl* ~**s**) *nm* (*objeto*) ski; (*DEPORTE*) skiing; ~ **acúatico** water-skiing; **esquiar** *vi* to ski

esquilar [eski'lar] *vt* to shear

esquimal [eski'mal] *adj, nm/f* Eskimo

esquina [es'kina] *nf* corner

esquinazo [eski'naθo] *nm*: **dar ~ a algn** to give sb the slip

esquirol [eski'rol] *nm* blackleg

esquivar [eski'ßar] *vt* to avoid

esquivo, a [es'kißo, a] *adj* evasive; (*tímido*) reserved; (*huraño*) unsociable

esta [esta] *adj demos ver* **este²**

está *vb ver* **estar**

ésta ['esta] *pron ver* **éste**

estabilidad [estaßili'ðað] *nf* stability; **estable** *adj* stable

establecer [estaßle'θer] *vt* to establish; ~**se** *vr* to establish o.s.; (*echar raíces*) to settle (down); **establecimiento** *nm* establishment

establo [es'taßlo] *nm* (*AGR*) stable

estaca [es'taka] *nf* stake, post; (*de tienda de campaña*) peg

estacada [esta'kaða] *nf* (*cerca*) fence, fencing; (*palenque*) stockade

estación [esta'θjon] *nf* station; (*del año*) season; ~ **de autobuses** bus station; ~ **balnearia** seaside resort; ~ **de servicio** service station

estacionamiento [estaθjona'mjento] *nm* (*AUTO*) parking; (*MIL*) stationing

estacionar [estaθjo'nar] *vt* (*AUTO*) to park; (*MIL*) to station; ~**io, a** *adj* stationary; (*COM: mercado*) slack

estadio [es'taðjo] *nm* (*fase*) stage, phase; (*DEPORTE*) stadium

estadista [esta'ðista] *nm* (*POL*) statesman; (*ESTADÍSTICA*) statistician

estadística [esta'ðistika] *nf* figure, statistic; (*ciencia*) statistics *sg*

estado [es'taðo] *nm* (*POL: condición*) state; ~ **de ánimo** state of mind; ~ **de cuenta** bank statement; ~ **de sitio** state of siege;

~ **civil** marital status; ~ **mayor** staff; **estar en** ~ to be pregnant; **(los) E~s Unidos** *nmpl* the United States (of America) *sg*

estadounidense [estaðouniˈðense] *adj* United States *cpd*, American ♦ *nm/f* American

estafa [esˈtafa] *nf* swindle, trick; **estafar** *vt* to swindle, defraud

estafeta [estaˈfeta] *nf* (*oficina de correos*) post office; ~ **diplomática** diplomatic bag

estáis *vb ver* **estar**

estallar [estaˈʎar] *vi* to burst; (*bomba*) to explode, go off; (*epidemia, guerra, rebelión*) to break out; ~ **en llanto** to burst into tears; **estallido** *nm* explosion; (*fig*) outbreak

estampa [esˈtampa] *nf* print, engraving

estampado, a [estamˈpaðo, a] *adj* printed ♦ *nm* (*impresión: acción*) printing; (: *efecto*) print; (*marca*) stamping

estampar [estamˈpar] *vt* (*imprimir*) to print; (*marcar*) to stamp; (*metal*) to engrave; (*poner sello en*) to stamp; (*fig*) to stamp, imprint

estampida [estamˈpiða] *nf* stampede

estampido [estamˈpiðo] *nm* bang, report

están *vb ver* **estar**

estancado, a [estanˈkaðo, a] *adj* stagnant

estancar [estanˈkar] *vt* (*aguas*) to hold up, hold back; (*COM*) to monopolize; (*fig*) to block, hold up; **~se** *vr* to stagnate

estancia [esˈtanθja] *nf* (*permanencia*) stay; (*sala*) room; (*AM*) farm, ranch; **estanciero** (*AM*) *nm* farmer, rancher

estanco, a [esˈtanko, a] *adj* watertight ♦ *nm* tobacconist's (shop), cigar store (*US*)

Estanco

ⓘ Cigarettes, tobacco, postage stamps and official forms are all sold under state monopoly in shops called an **estanco**. Although tobacco products can also be bought in bars and **quioscos** they are generally more expensive.

---

estándar [esˈtandar] *adj, nm* standard;

estandarizar *vt* to standardize

estandarte [estanˈdarte] *nm* banner, standard

estanque [esˈtanke] *nm* (*lago*) pool, pond; (*AGR*) reservoir

estanquero, a [estanˈkero, a] *nm/f* tobacconist

estante [esˈtante] *nm* (*armario*) rack, stand; (*biblioteca*) bookcase; (*anaquel*) shelf; (*AM*) prop; **estantería** *nf* shelving, shelves *pl*

estaño [esˈtaɲo] *nm* tin

PALABRA CLAVE
---

estar [esˈtar] *vi* 1 (*posición*) to be; **está en la plaza** it's in the square; **¿está Juan?** is Juan in?; **estamos a 30 km de Junín** we're 30 kms from Junín

2 (+*adj: estado*) to be; ~ **enfermo** to be ill; **está muy elegante** he's looking very smart; **¿cómo estás?** how are you keeping?

3 (+*gerundio*) to be; **estoy leyendo** I'm reading

4 (*uso pasivo*): **está condenado a muerte** he's been condemned to death; **está envasado en ...** it's packed in ...

5 (*con fechas*): **¿a cuántos estamos?** what's the date today?; **estamos a 5 de mayo** it's the 5th of May

6 (*locuciones*): **¿estamos?** (*¿de acuerdo?*) okay?; (*¿listo?*) ready?; **¡ya está bien!** that's enough!

7: ~ **de**: ~ **de vacaciones/viaje** to be on holiday/away *o* on a trip; **está de camarero** he's working as a waiter

8: ~ **para**: **está para salir** he's about to leave; **no estoy para bromas** I'm not in the mood for jokes

9: ~ **por** (*propuesta etc*) to be in favour of; (*persona etc*) to support, side with; **está por limpiar** it still has to be cleaned

10: ~ **sin**: ~ **sin dinero** to have no money; **está sin terminar** it isn't finished yet

♦ **~se** *vr*: **se estuvo en la cama toda la tarde** he stayed in bed all afternoon

estas ['estas] adj demos ver **este²**

éstas ['estas] pron ver **éste**

estatal [esta'tal] adj state cpd

estático, a [es'tatiko, a] adj static

estatua [es'tatwa] nf statue

estatura [esta'tura] nf stature, height

estatuto [esta'tuto] nm (JUR) statute; (de ciudad) bye-law; (de comité) rule

este¹ ['este] nm east

este² ['este] (f **esta**, pl **estos, estas**) adj demos (sg) this; (pl) these

esté etc vb ver **estar**

éste ['este] (f **ésta**, pl **éstos, éstas**) pron (sg) this (one); (pl) these (ones); **ése ... ~** ... the former ... the latter ....

estelar [este'lar] adj (ASTRO) stellar; (actuación, reparto) star (atr)

estén etc vb ver **estar**

estepa [es'tepa] nf (GEO) steppe

estera [es'tera] nf mat(ting)

estéreo [es'tereo] adj inv, nm stereo; **estereotipo** nm stereotype

estéril [es'teril] adj sterile, barren; (fig) vain, futile; **esterilizar** vt to sterilize

esterlina [ester'lina] adj: **libra ~** pound sterling

estés etc vb ver **estar**

estética [es'tetika] nf aesthetics sg

estético, a [es'tetiko, a] adj aesthetic

estibador [estiβa'ðor] nm stevedore, docker

estiércol [es'tjerkol] nm dung, manure

estigma [es'tiɣma] nm stigma

estilarse [esti'larse] vr to be in fashion

estilo [es'tilo] nm style; (TEC) stylus; (NATACIÓN) stroke; **algo por el ~** something along those lines

estima [es'tima] nf esteem, respect

estimación [estima'θjon] nf (evaluación) estimation; (aprecio, afecto) esteem, regard

estimar [esti'mar] vt (evaluar) to estimate; (valorar) to value; (apreciar) to esteem, respect; (pensar, considerar) to think, reckon

estimulante [estimu'lante] adj stimulating ♦ nm stimulant

estimular [estimu'lar] vt to stimulate; (excitar) to excite

estímulo [es'timulo] nm stimulus; (ánimo) encouragement

estipulación [estipula'θjon] nf stipulation, condition

estipular [estipu'lar] vt to stipulate

estirado, a [esti'raðo, a] adj (tenso) (stretched o drawn) tight; (fig: persona) stiff, pompous

estirar [esti'rar] vt to stretch; (dinero, suma etc) to stretch out; **~se** vr to stretch

estirón [esti'ron] nm pull, tug; (crecimiento) spurt, sudden growth; **dar un ~** (niño) to shoot up

estirpe [es'tirpe] nf stock, lineage

estival [esti'βal] adj summer cpd

esto ['esto] pron this, this thing o matter; **~ de la boda** this business about the wedding

Estocolmo [esto'kolmo] nm Stockholm

estofado [esto'faðo] nm stew

estofar [esto'far] vt to stew

estómago [es'tomaɣo] nm stomach; **tener ~** to be thick-skinned

estorbar [estor'βar] vt to hinder, obstruct; (molestar) to bother, disturb ♦ vi to be in the way; **estorbo** nm (molestia) bother, nuisance; (obstáculo) hindrance, obstacle

estornudar [estornu'ðar] vi to sneeze

estos ['estos] adj demos ver **este²**

éstos ['estos] pron ver **éste**

estoy vb ver **estar**

estrado [es'traðo] nm platform

estrafalario, a [estrafa'larjo, a] adj odd, eccentric

estrago [es'traɣo] nm ruin, destruction; **hacer ~s en** to wreak havoc among

estragón [estra'ɣon] nm tarragon

estrambótico, a [estram'botiko, a] adj (persona) eccentric; (peinado, ropa) outlandish

estrangulador, a [estrangula'ðor, a] nm/f strangler ♦ nm (TEC) throttle; (AUTO) choke

estrangular [estrangu'lar] vt (persona) to

strangle; (MED) to strangulate

estratagema [estrata'xema] nf (MIL) stratagem; (astucia) cunning

estrategia [estra'texja] nf strategy; **estratégico, a** adj strategic

estrato [es'trato] nm stratum, layer

estrechamente [es'tretʃamente] adv (íntimamente) closely, intimately; (pobremente: vivir) poorly

estrechar [estre'tʃar] vt (reducir) to narrow; (COSTURA) to take in; (abrazar) to hug, embrace; **~se** vr (reducirse) to narrow, grow narrow; (abrazarse) to embrace; **~ la mano** to shake hands

estrechez [estre'tʃeθ] nf narrowness; (de ropa) tightness; **estrecheces** nfpl (dificultades económicas) financial difficulties

estrecho, a [es'tretʃo, a] adj narrow; (apretado) tight; (íntimo) close, intimate; (miserable) mean ♦ nm strait; **~ de miras** narrow-minded

estrella [es'treʎa] nf star; **~ de mar** (ZOOL) starfish; **~ fugaz** shooting star; **estrellado, a** adj (forma) star-shaped; (cielo) starry

estrellar [estre'ʎar] vt (hacer añicos) to smash (to pieces); (huevos) to fry; **~se** vr to smash; (chocarse) to crash; (fracasar) to fail

estremecer [estreme'θer] vt to shake; **~se** vr to shake, tremble; **estremecimiento** nm (temblor) trembling, shaking

estrenar [estre'nar] vt (vestido) to wear for the first time; (casa) to move into; (película, obra de teatro) to première; **~se** vr (persona) to make one's début; **estreno** nm (CINE etc) première

estreñido, a [estre'ɲiðo, a] adj constipated

estreñimiento [estreɲi'mjento] nm constipation

estrépito [es'trepito] nm noise, racket; (fig) fuss; **estrepitoso, a** adj noisy; (fiesta) rowdy

estría [es'tria] nf groove

estribación [estriβa'θjon] nf (GEO) spur, foothill

estribar [estri'βar] vi: **~ en** to lie on

estribillo [estri'βiʎo] nm (LITERATURA) refrain; (MUS) chorus

estribo [es'triβo] nm (de jinete) stirrup; (de coche, tren) step; (de puente) support; (GEO) spur; **perder los ~s** to fly off the handle

estribor [estri'βor] nm (NAUT) starboard

estricto, a [es'trikto, a] adj (riguroso) strict; (severo) severe

estridente [estri'ðente] adj (color) loud; (voz) raucous

estropajo [estro'paxo] nm scourer

estropear [estrope'ar] vt to spoil; (dañar) to damage; **~se** vr (objeto) to get damaged; (persona: la piel etc) to be ruined

estructura [estruk'tura] nf structure

estruendo [es'trwendo] nm (ruido) racket, din; (fig) alboroto) uproar, turmoil

estrujar [estru'xar] vt (apretar) to squeeze; (aplastar) to crush; (fig) to drain, bleed

estuario [es'twarjo] nm estuary

estuche [es'tutʃe] nm box, case

estudiante [estu'ðjante] nm/f student; **estudiantil** adj student cpd

estudiar [estu'ðjar] vt to study

estudio [es'tuðjo] nm study; (CINE, ARTE, RADIO) studio; **~s** nmpl studies; (erudición) learning sg; **~so, a** adj studious

estufa [es'tufa] nf heater, fire

estupefaciente [estupefa'θjente] nm drug, narcotic

estupefacto, a [estupe'fakto, a] adj speechless, thunderstruck

estupendo, a [estu'pendo, a] adj wonderful, terrific; (fam) great; **¡~!** that's great!, fantastic!

estupidez [estupi'ðeθ] nf (torpeza) stupidity; (acto) stupid thing (to do)

estúpido, a [es'tupiðo, a] adj stupid, silly

estupor [estu'por] nm stupor; (fig) astonishment, amazement

estuve etc vb ver **estar**

esvástica [es'βastika] nf swastika

ETA ['eta] (ESP) nf abr (= Euskadi ta

Askatasuna) ETA

etapa [e'tapa] *nf* (*de viaje*) stage; (*DEPORTE*) leg; (*parada*) stopping place; (*fase*) stage, phase

etarra [e'tarra] *nm/f* member of ETA

etc. *abr* (= *etcétera*) etc

etcétera [et'θetera] *adv* etcetera

eternidad [eterni'ðað] *nf* eternity; **eterno, a** *adj* eternal, everlasting

ética ['etika] *nf* ethics *pl*

ético, a ['etiko, a] *adj* ethical

etiqueta [eti'keta] *nf* (*modales*) etiquette; (*rótulo*) label, tag

Eucaristía [eukaris'tia] *nf* Eucharist

eufemismo [eufe'mismo] *nm* euphemism

euforia [eu'forja] *nf* euphoria

euro ['euro] *nm* (*moneda*) euro

eurodiputado, a [eurodipu'taðo, a] *nm/f* Euro MP, MEP

Europa [eu'ropa] *nf* Europe; **europeo, a** *adj, nm/f* European

Euskadi [eus'kaði] *nm* the Basque Country *o* Provinces *pl*

euskera [eus'kera] *nm* (*LING*) Basque

evacuación [eßakwa'θjon] *nf* evacuation

evacuar [eßa'kwar] *vt* to evacuate

evadir [eßa'ðir] *vt* to evade, avoid; **~se** *vr* to escape

evaluar [eßa'lwar] *vt* to evaluate

evangelio [eßan'xeljo] *nm* gospel

evaporar [eßapo'rar] *vt* to evaporate; **~se** *vr* to vanish

evasión [eßa'sjon] *nf* escape, flight; (*fig*) evasion; **~ de capitales** flight of capital

evasiva [eßa'sißa] *nf* (*pretexto*) excuse

evasivo, a [eßa'sißo, a] *adj* evasive, non-committal

evento [e'ßento] *nm* event

eventual [eßen'twal] *adj* possible, conditional (upon circumstances); (*trabajador*) casual, temporary

evidencia [eßi'ðenθja] *nf* evidence, proof; **evidenciar** *vt* (*hacer patente*) to make evident; (*probar*) to prove, show; **evidenciarse** *vr* to be evident

evidente [eßi'ðente] *adj* obvious, clear

evitar [eßi'tar] *vt* (*evadir*) to avoid; (*impedir*) to prevent

evocar [eßo'kar] *vt* to evoke, call forth

evolución [eßolu'θjon] *nf* (*desarrollo*) evolution, development; (*cambio*) change; (*MIL*) manoeuvre; **evolucionar** *vi* to evolve; to manoeuvre

ex [eks] *adj* ex-; **el ~ ministro** the former minister, the ex-minister

exacerbar [eksaθer'ßar] *vt* to irritate, annoy

exactamente [eksakta'mente] *adv* exactly

exactitud [eksakti'tuð] *nf* exactness; (*precisión*) accuracy; (*puntualidad*) punctuality; **exacto, a** *adj* exact; accurate; punctual; **¡exacto!** exactly!

exageración [eksaxera'θjon] *nf* exaggeration

exagerar [eksaxe'rar] *vt, vi* to exaggerate

exaltado, a [eksal'taðo, a] *adj* (*apasionado*) over-excited, worked-up; (*POL*) extreme

exaltar [eksal'tar] *vt* to exalt, glorify; **~se** *vr* (*excitarse*) to get excited *o* worked-up

examen [ek'samen] *nm* examination

examinar [eksami'nar] *vt* to examine; **~se** *vr* to be examined, take an examination

exasperar [eksaspe'rar] *vt* to exasperate; **~se** *vr* to get exasperated, lose patience

Exca. *abr* = **Excelencia**

excavadora [ekskaßa'ðora] *nf* excavator

excavar [ekska'ßar] *vt* to excavate

excedencia [eksθe'ðenθja] *nf*: **estar en ~** to be on leave; **pedir** *o* **solicitar la ~** to ask for leave

excedente [eksθe'ðente] *adj, nm* excess, surplus

exceder [eksθe'ðer] *vt* to exceed, surpass; **~se** *vr* (*extralimitarse*) to go too far

excelencia [eksθe'lenθja] *nf* excellence; **E~** Excellency; **excelente** *adj* excellent

excentricidad [eksθentriθi'ðað] *nf* eccentricity; **excéntrico, a** *adj, nm/f* eccentric

excepción [eksθep'θjon] *nf* exception; **excepcional** *adj* exceptional

excepto [eks'θepto] *adv* excepting, except (for)

exceptuar [eksθep'twar] *vt* to except, exclude

excesivo, a [eksθe'siβo, a] *adj* excessive

exceso [eks'θeso] *nm* (*gen*) excess; (*COM*) surplus; **~ de equipaje/peso** excess luggage/weight

excitación [eksθita'θjon] *nf* (*sensación*) excitement; (*acción*) excitation

excitado, a [eksθi'taðo, a] *adj* excited; (*emociones*) aroused

excitar [eksθi'tar] *vt* to excite; (*incitar*) to urge; **~se** *vr* to get excited

exclamación [eksklama'θjon] *nf* exclamation

exclamar [ekskla'mar] *vi* to exclaim

excluir [eksklu'ir] *vt* to exclude; (*dejar fuera*) to shut out; (*descartar*) to reject; **exclusión** *nf* exclusion

exclusiva [eksklu'siβa] *nf* (*PRENSA*) exclusive, scoop; (*COM*) sole right

exclusivo, a [eksklu'siβo, a] *adj* exclusive; **derecho ~** sole *o* exclusive right

Excmo. *abr* = **excelentísmo**

excomulgar [ekskomul'ɣar] *vt* (*REL*) to excommunicate

excomunión [ekskomu'njon] *nf* excommunication

excursión [ekskur'sjon] *nf* excursion, outing; **excursionista** *nm/f* (*turista*) sightseer

excusa [eks'kusa] *nf* excuse; (*disculpa*) apology

excusar [eksku'sar] *vt* to excuse; **~se** *vr* (*disculparse*) to apologize

exhalar [eksa'lar] *vt* to exhale, breathe out; (*olor etc*) to give off; (*suspiro*) to breathe, heave

exhaustivo, a [eksaus'tiβo, a] *adj* (*análisis*) thorough; (*estudio*) exhaustive

exhausto, a [ek'sausto, a] *adj* exhausted

exhibición [eksiβi'θjon] *nf* exhibition, display, show

exhibir [eksi'ßir] *vt* to exhibit, display, show

exhortar [eksor'tar] *vt*: **~ a** to exhort to

exigencia [eksi'xenθja] *nf* demand, requirement; **exigente** *adj* demanding

exigir [eksi'xir] *vt* (*gen*) to demand, require; **~ el pago** to demand payment

exiliado, a [eksi'ljaðo, a] *adj* exiled
♦ *nm/f* exile

exilio [ek'siljo] *nm* exile

eximir [eksi'mir] *vt* to exempt

existencia [eksis'tenθja] *nf* existence; **~s** *nfpl* stock(s) (*pl*)

existir [eksis'tir] *vi* to exist, be

éxito ['eksito] *nm* (*triunfo*) success; (*MUS etc*) hit; **tener ~** to be successful

exonerar [eksone'rar] *vt* to exonerate; **~ de una obligación** to free from an obligation

exorbitante [eksorßi'tante] *adj* (*precio*) exorbitant; (*cantidad*) excessive

exorcizar [eksorθi'θar] *vt* to exorcize

exótico, a [ek'sotiko, a] *adj* exotic

expandir [ekspan'dir] *vt* to expand

expansión [ekspan'sjon] *nf* expansion

expansivo, a [ekspan'siβo, a] *adj*: **onda ~a** shock wave

expatriarse [ekspa'trjarse] *vr* to emigrate; (*POL*) to go into exile

expectativa [ekspekta'tiβa] *nf* (*espera*) expectation; (*perspectiva*) prospect

expedición [ekspeði'θjon] *nf* (*excursión*) expedition

expediente [ekspe'ðjente] *nm* expedient; (*JUR: procedimento*) action, proceedings *pl*; (: *papeles*) dossier, file, record

expedir [ekspe'ðir] *vt* (*despachar*) to send, forward; (*pasaporte*) to issue

expendedor, a [ekspende'ðor, a] *nm/f* (*vendedor*) dealer

expensas [eks'pensas] *nfpl*: **a ~ de** at the expense of

experiencia [ekspe'rjenθja] *nf* experience

experimentado, a [eksperimen'taðo, a] *adj* experienced

experimentar [eksperimen'tar] *vt* (*en laboratorio*) to experiment with; (*probar*) to test, try out; (*notar, observar*) to experience; (*deterioro, pérdida*) to suffer; **experimento** *nm* experiment

experto, a [eks'perto, a] *adj* expert, skilled
♦ *nm/f* expert

expiar [ekspi'ar] *vt* to atone for

expirar [ekspi'rar] *vi* to expire

explanada [ekspla'naða] *nf (llano)* plain

explayarse [ekspla'jarse] *vr (en discurso)* to speak at length; **~ con uno** to confide in sb

explicación [eksplika'θjon] *nf* explanation

explicar [ekspli'kar] *vt* to explain; **~se** *vr* to explain (o.s.)

explícito, a [eks'pliθito, a] *adj* explicit

explique *etc vb ver* **explicar**

explorador, a [eksplora'ðor, a] *nm/f (pionero)* explorer; *(MIL)* scout ♦ *nm (MED)* probe; *(TEC)* (radar) scanner

explorar [eksplo'rar] *vt* to explore; *(MED)* to probe; *(radar)* to scan

explosión [eksplo'sjon] *nf* explosion; **explosivo, a** *adj* explosive

explotación [eksplota'θjon] *nf* exploitation; *(de planta etc)* running

explotar [eksplo'tar] *vt* to exploit; to run, operate ♦ *vi* to explode

exponer [ekspo'ner] *vt* to expose; *(cuadro)* to display; *(vida)* to risk; *(idea)* to explain; **~se** *vr*: **~se a (hacer) algo** to run the risk of (doing) sth

exportación [eksporta'θjon] *nf (acción)* export; *(mercancías)* exports *pl*

exportar [ekspor'tar] *vt* to export

exposición [eksposi'θjon] *nf (gen)* exposure; *(de arte)* show, exhibition; *(explicación)* explanation; *(declaración)* account, statement

expresamente [ekspresa'mente] *adv (decir)* clearly; *(a propósito)* expressly

expresar [ekspre'sar] *vt* to express; **expresión** *nf* expression

expresivo, a [ekspre'siβo, a] *adj (persona, gesto, palabras)* expressive; *(cariñoso)* affectionate

expreso, a [eks'preso, a] *pp de* **expresar** ♦ *adj (explícito)* express; *(claro)* specific, clear; *(tren)* fast ♦ *adv*: **mandar ~** to send by express (delivery)

express [eks'pres] *(AM) adv*: **enviar algo ~** to send sth special delivery

exprimidor [eksprimi'ðor] *nm* squeezer

exprimir [ekspri'mir] *vt (fruta)* to squeeze; *(zumo)* to squeeze out

expropiar [ekspro'pjar] *vt* to expropriate

expuesto, a [eks'pwesto, a] *pp de* **exponer** ♦ *adj* exposed; *(cuadro etc)* on show, on display

expulsar [ekspul'sar] *vt (echar)* to eject, throw out; *(alumno)* to expel; *(despedir)* to sack, fire; *(DEPORTE)* to send off; **expulsión** *nf* expulsion; sending-off

exquisito, a [ekski'sito, a] *adj* exquisite; *(comida)* delicious

éxtasis ['ekstasis] *nm* ecstasy

extender [eksten'der] *vt* to extend; *(los brazos)* to stretch out, hold out; *(mapa, tela)* to spread (out), open (out); *(mantequilla)* to spread; *(certificado)* to issue; *(cheque, recibo)* to make out; *(documento)* to draw up; **~se** *vr (gen)* to extend; *(persona: en el suelo)* to stretch out; *(epidemia)* to spread; **extendido, a** *adj (abierto)* spread out, open; *(brazos)* outstretched; *(costumbre)* widespread

extensión [eksten'sjon] *nf (de terreno, mar)* expanse, stretch; *(de tiempo)* length, duration; *(TEL)* extension; **en toda la ~ de la palabra** in every sense of the word

extenso, a [eks'tenso, a] *adj* extensive

extenuar [ekste'nwar] *vt (debilitar)* to weaken

exterior [ekste'rjor] *adj (de fuera)* external; *(afuera)* outside, exterior; *(apariencia)* outward; *(deuda, relaciones)* foreign ♦ *nm (gen)* exterior, outside; *(aspecto)* outward appearance; *(DEPORTE)* wing(er); *(países extranjeros)* abroad; **en el ~** abroad; **al ~** outwardly, on the surface

exterminar [ekstermi'nar] *vt* to exterminate; **exterminio** *nm* extermination

externo, a [eks'terno, a] *adj (exterior)* external, outside; *(superficial)* outward ♦ *nm/f* day pupil

extinguir [ekstin'gir] *vt (fuego)* to extinguish, put out; *(raza, población)* to wipe out; **~se** *vr (fuego)* to go out; *(BIO)* to die out, become extinct

extinto, a [eks'tinto, a] *adj* extinct
extintor [ekstin'tor] *nm* (fire) extinguisher
extirpar [ekstir'par] *vt* (*MED*) to remove (surgically)
extorsión [ekstor'sjon] *nf* extorsion
extra ['ekstra] *adj inv* (*tiempo*) extra; (*chocolate, vino*) good-quality ♦ *nm/f* extra ♦ *nm* extra; (*bono*) bonus
extracción [ekstrak'θjon] *nf* extraction; (*en lotería*) draw
extracto [eks'trakto] *nm* extract
extradición [ekstraði'θjon] *nf* extradition
extraer [ekstra'er] *vt* to extract, take out
extraescolar [ekstraesko'lar] *adj*: **actividad ~** extracurricular activity
extralimitarse [ekstralimi'tarse] *vr* to go too far
extranjero, a [ekstran'xero, a] *adj* foreign ♦ *nm/f* foreigner ♦ *nm* foreign countries *pl*; **en el ~** abroad
extrañar [ekstra'ɲar] *vt* (*sorprender*) to find strange *o* odd; (*echar de menos*) to miss; **~se** *vr* (*sorprenderse*) to be amazed, be surprised
extrañeza [ekstra'ɲeθa] *nf* (*rareza*) strangeness, oddness; (*asombro*) amazement, surprise
extraño, a [eks'traɲo, a] *adj* (*extranjero*) foreign; (*raro, sorprendente*) strange, odd
extraordinario, a [ekstraorði'narjo, a] *adj* extraordinary; (*edición, número*) special ♦ *nm* (*de periódico*) special edition; **horas extraordinarias** overtime *sg*
extrarradio [ekstra'rraðjo] *nm* suburbs
extravagancia [ekstraβa'ğanθja] *nf* oddness; outlandishness; **extravagante** *adj* (*excéntrico*) eccentric; (*estrafalario*) outlandish
extraviado, a [ekstra'βjaðo, a] *adj* lost, missing
extraviar [ekstra'βjar] *vt* (*persona: desorientar*) to mislead, misdirect; (*perder*) to lose, misplace; **~se** *vr* to lose one's way, get lost; **extravío** *nm* loss; (*fig*) deviation
extremar [ekstre'mar] *vt* to carry to extremes; **~se** *vr* to do one's utmost, make every effort
extremaunción [ekstremaun'θjon] *nf* extreme unction
extremidad [ekstremi'ðað] *nf* (*punta*) extremity; **~es** *nfpl* (*ANAT*) extremities
extremo, a [eks'tremo, a] *adj* extreme; (*último*) last ♦ *nm* end; (*límite, grado sumo*) extreme; **en último ~** as a last resort
extrovertido, a [ekstroßer'tiðo, a] *adj, nm/f* extrovert
exuberancia [eksuße'ranθja] *nf* exuberance; **exuberante** *adj* exuberant; (*fig*) luxuriant, lush
eyacular [ejaku'lar] *vt, vi* to ejaculate

F, f

f.a.b. *abr* (= *franco a bordo*) f.o.b.
fabada [fa'βaða] *nf* bean and sausage stew
fábrica ['faßrika] *nf* factory; **marca de ~** trademark; **precio de ~** factory price
fabricación [faßrika'θjon] *nf* (*manufactura*) manufacture; (*producción*) production; **de ~ casera** home-made; **~ en serie** mass production
fabricante [faßri'kante] *nm/f* manufacturer
fabricar [faßri'kar] *vt* (*manufacturar*) to manufacture, make; (*construir*) to build; (*cuento*) to fabricate, devise
fábula ['faßula] *nf* (*cuento*) fable; (*chisme*) rumour; (*mentira*) fib
fabuloso, a [faßu'loso, a] *adj* (*oportunidad, tiempo*) fabulous, great
facción [fak'θjon] *nf* (*POL*) faction; **facciones** *nfpl* (*del rostro*) features
faceta [fa'θeta] *nf* facet
facha ['fatʃa] (*fam*) *nf* (*aspecto*) look; (*cara*) face
fachada [fa'tʃaða] *nf* (*ARQ*) façade, front
fácil ['faθil] *adj* (*simple*) easy; (*probable*) likely
facilidad [faθili'ðað] *nf* (*capacidad*) ease; (*sencillez*) simplicity; (*de palabra*) fluency; **~es** *nfpl* facilities

facilitar [faθili'tar] vt (hacer fácil) to make easy; (proporcionar) to provide

fácilmente ['faθilmente] adv easily

facsímil [fak'simil] nm facsimile, fax

factible [fak'tiβle] adj feasible

factor [fak'tor] nm factor

factura [fak'tura] nf (cuenta) bill; **facturación** nf (de equipaje) check-in; **facturar** vt (COM) to invoice, charge for; (equipaje) to check in

facultad [fakul'taθ] nf (aptitud, ESCOL etc) faculty; (poder) power

faena [fa'ena] nf (trabajo) work; (quehacer) task, job

faisán [fai'san] nm pheasant

faja ['faxa] nf (para la cintura) sash; (de mujer) corset; (de tierra) strip

fajo ['faxo] nm (de papeles) bundle; (de billetes) wad

falacia [fa'laθja] nf fallacy

falda ['falda] nf (prenda de vestir) skirt

falla ['faʎa] nf (defecto) fault, flaw

fallar [fa'ʎar] vt (JUR) to pronounce sentence on ♦ vi (memoria) to fail; (motor) to miss

fallecer [faʎe'θer] vi to pass away, die; **fallecimiento** nm decease, demise

fallido, a [fa'ʎiðo, a] adj (gen) frustrated, unsuccessful

fallo ['faʎo] nm (JUR) verdict, ruling; (fracaso) failure; **~ cardíaco** heart failure

falsedad [false'ðað] nf falseness; (hipocresía) hypocrisy; (mentira) falsehood

falsificar [falsifi'kar] vt (firma etc) to forge; (moneda) to counterfeit

falso, a ['falso, a] adj false; (documento, moneda etc) fake; **en ~** falsely

falta ['falta] nf (defecto) fault, flaw; (privación) lack, want; (ausencia) absence; (carencia) shortage; (equivocación) mistake; (DEPORTE) foul; **echar en ~** to miss; **hacer ~ hacer algo** to be necessary to do sth; **me hace ~ una pluma** I need a pen; **~ de educación** bad manners pl

faltar [fal'tar] vi (escasear) to be lacking, be wanting; (ausentarse) to be absent, be missing; **faltan 2 horas para llegar** there are 2 hours to go till arrival; **~ al respeto a uno** to be disrespectful to sb; **¡no faltaba más!** (no hay de qué) don't mention it

fama ['fama] nf (renombre) fame; (reputación) reputation

famélico, a [fa'meliko, a] adj starving

familia [fa'milja] nf family; **~ política** in-laws pl

familiar [fami'ljar] adj (relativo a la familia) family cpd; (conocido, informal) familiar ♦ nm relative, relation; **~idad** nf (gen) familiarity; (informalidad) homeliness; **~izarse** vr: **~izarse con** to familiarize o.s. with

famoso, a [fa'moso, a] adj (renombrado) famous

fanático, a [fa'natiko, a] adj fanatical ♦ nm/f fanatic; (CINE, DEPORTE) fan; **fanatismo** nm fanaticism

fanfarrón, ona [fanfa'rron, ona] adj boastful

fango ['fango] nm mud; **~so, a** adj muddy

fantasía [fanta'sia] nf fantasy, imagination; **joyas de ~** imitation jewellery sg

fantasma [fan'tasma] nm (espectro) ghost, apparition; (fanfarrón) show-off

fantástico, a [fan'tastiko, a] adj fantastic

farmacéutico, a [farma'θeutiko, a] adj pharmaceutical ♦ nm/f chemist (BRIT), pharmacist

farmacia [far'maθja] nf chemist's (shop)

(*BRIT*), pharmacy; **~ de turno** duty chemist; **~ de guardia** all-night chemist

fármaco ['farmako] *nm* drug

faro ['faro] *nm* (*NAUT: torre*) lighthouse; (*AUTO*) headlamp; **~s antiniebla** fog lamps; **~s delanteros/traseros** headlights/rear lights

farol [fa'rol] *nm* lantern, lamp

farola [fa'rola] *nf* street lamp (*BRIT*) *o* light (*US*)

farsa ['farsa] *nf* (*gen*) farce

farsante [far'sante] *nm/f* fraud, fake

fascículo [fas'θikulo] *nm* (*de revista*) part, instalment

fascinar [fasθi'nar] *vt* (*gen*) to fascinate

fascismo [fas'θismo] *nm* fascism; **fascista** *adj, nm/f* fascist

fase ['fase] *nf* phase

fastidiar [fasti'ðjar] *vt* (*molestar*) to annoy, bother; (*estropear*) to spoil; **~se** *vr*: **¡que se fastidie!** (*fam*) he'll just have to put up with it!

fastidio [fas'tiðjo] *nm* (*molestia*) annoyance; **~so, a** *adj* (*molesto*) annoying

fastuoso, a [fas'twoso, a] *adj* (*banquete, boda*) lavish; (*acto*) pompous

fatal [fa'tal] *adj* (*gen*) fatal; (*desgraciado*) ill-fated; (*fam: malo, pésimo*) awful; **~idad** *nf* (*destino*) fate; (*mala suerte*) misfortune

fatiga [fa'tiɣa] *nf* (*cansancio*) fatigue, weariness

fatigar [fati'ɣar] *vt* to tire, weary; **~se** *vr* to get tired

fatigoso, a [fati'ɣoso, a] *adj* (*cansador*) tiring

fatuo, a ['fatwo, a] *adj* (*vano*) fatuous; (*presuntuoso*) conceited

favor [fa'ßor] *nm* favour; **estar a ~ de** to be in favour of; **haga el ~ de...** would you be so good as to..., kindly...; **por ~** please; **~able** *adj* favourable

favorecer [faßore'θer] *vt* to favour; (*vestido etc*) to become, flatter; **este peinado le favorece** this hairstyle suits him

favorito, a [faßo'rito, a] *adj, nm/f*

favourite

fax [faks] *nm inv* fax; **mandar por ~** to fax

faz [faθ] *nf* face; **la ~ de la tierra** the face of the earth

fe [fe] *nf* (*REL*) faith; (*documento*) certificate; **prestar ~ a** to believe, credit; **actuar con buena/mala ~** to act in good/bad faith; **dar ~ de** to bear witness to

fealdad [feal'daθ] *nf* ugliness

febrero [fe'ßrero] *nm* February

febril [fe'ßril] *adj* (*fig: actividad*) hectic; (*mente, mirada*) feverish

fecha ['fetʃa] *nf* date; **~ de caducidad** (*de producto alimenticio*) sell-by date; (*de contrato etc*) expiry date; **con ~ adelantada** postdated; **en ~ próxima** soon; **hasta la ~** to date, so far; **poner ~** to date; **fechar** *vt* to date

fecundar [fekun'dar] *vt* (*generar*) to fertilize, make fertile; **fecundo, a** *adj* (*fértil*) fertile; (*fig*) prolific; (*productivo*) productive

federación [feðera'θjon] *nf* federation

felicidad [feliθi'ðaθ] *nf* happiness; **~es** *nfpl* (*felicitaciones*) best wishes, congratulations

felicitación [feliθita'θjon] *nf*: **¡felicitaciones!** congratulations!

felicitar [feliθi'tar] *vt* to congratulate

feligrés, esa [feli'ɣres, esa] *nm/f* parishioner

feliz [fe'liθ] *adj* happy

felpudo [fel'puðo] *nm* doormat

femenino, a [feme'nino, a] *adj, nm* feminine

feminista [femi'nista] *adj, nm/f* feminist

fenómeno [fe'nomeno] *nm* phenomenon (*fig*) freak, accident ♦ *adj* great ♦ *excl* great!, marvellous!; **fenomenal** *adj* = **fenómeno**

feo, a ['feo, a] *adj* (*gen*) ugly; (*desagradable*) bad, nasty

féretro ['feretro] *nm* (*ataúd*) coffin; (*sarcófago*) bier

feria ['ferja] *nf* (*gen*) fair; (*descanso*) holiday, rest day; (*AM: mercado*) village market; (*: cambio*) loose *o* small change

nentar [fermen'tar] *vi* to ferment

cidad [feroθi'ðað] *nf* fierceness, ocity

z [fe'roθ] *adj* (*cruel*) cruel; (*salvaje*) rce

eo, a ['ferreo, a] *adj* iron

etería [ferrete'ria] *nf* (*tienda*) nmonger's (shop) (*BRIT*), hardware re

ocarril [ferroka'rril] *nm* railway

oviario, a [ferro'ßjarjo, a] *adj* rail *cpd*

il ['fertil] *adj* (*productivo*) fertile; (*rico*) h; **fertilidad** *nf* (*gen*) fertility; roductividad) fruitfulness

iente [fer'ßjente] *adj* fervent

or [fer'ßor] *nm* fervour; **~oso, a** *adj* vent

ejar [feste'xar] *vt* (*celebrar*) to celebrate

ejo [fes'texo] *nm* celebration; **festejos** pl (*fiestas*) festivals

in [fes'tin] *nm* feast, banquet

ival [festi'ßal] *nm* festival

ividad [festißi'ðað] *nf* festivity

ivo, a [fes'tißo, a] *adj* (*de fiesta*) tive; (*CINE, LITERATURA*) humorous; **día ~** liday

do, a ['fetiðo, a] *adj* foul-smelling ['feto] *nm* foetus

le ['fjaßle] *adj* (*persona*) trustworthy; áquina) reliable

or, a [fia'ðor, a] *nm/f* (*JUR*) surety, arantor; (*COM*) backer; **salir ~ por uno** stand bail for sb

bre ['fjambre] *nm* cold meat

za ['fianθa] *nf* surety; (*JUR*): **libertad jo ~** release on bail

[fi'ar] *vt* (*salir garante de*) to guarantee; nder a crédito) to sell on credit; creto): **~ a** to confide (to) ♦ *vi* to trust; e *vr* to trust (in), rely on; **~se de uno** rely on sb

a ['fißra] *nf* fibre; **~ óptica** optical fibre

ión [fik'θjon] *nf* fiction

a ['fitʃa] *nf* (*TEL*) token; (*en juegos*) unter, marker; (*tarjeta*) (index) card; **har** *vt* (*archivar*) to file, index; EPORTE) to sign; **estar fichado** to have a record; **fichero** *nm* box file; (*INFORM*) file

ficticio, a [fik'tiθjo, a] *adj* (*imaginario*) fictitious; (*falso*) fabricated

fidelidad [fiðeli'ðað] *nf* (*lealtad*) fidelity, loyalty; **alta ~** high fidelity, hi-fi

fideos [fi'ðeos] *nmpl* noodles

fiebre ['fjeßre] *nf* (*MED*) fever; (*fig*) fever, excitement; **~ amarilla/del heno** yellow/ hay fever; **~ palúdica** malaria; **tener ~** to have a temperature

fiel [fjel] *adj* (*leal*) faithful, loyal; (*fiable*) reliable; (*exacto*) accurate, faithful ♦ *nm*: **los ~es** the faithful

fieltro [fjeltro] *nm* felt

fiera ['fjera] *nf* (*animal feroz*) wild animal o beast; (*fig*) dragon; *ver tb* **fiero**

fiero, a ['fjero, a] *adj* (*cruel*) cruel; (*feroz*) fierce; (*duro*) harsh

fiesta ['fjesta] *nf* party; (*de pueblo*) festival; (*vacaciones, tb*: **~s**) holiday *sg*; (*REL*): **~ de guardar** day of obligation

---
Fiestas

ℹ️ **Fiestas** *can be official public holidays or holidays set by each autonomous region, many of which coincide with religious festivals. There are also many* **fiestas** *all over Spain for a local patron saint or the Virgin Mary. These often last several days and can include religious processions, carnival parades, bullfights and dancing.*

---

figura [fi'ɣura] *nf* (*gen*) figure; (*forma, imagen*) shape, form; (*NAIPES*) face card

figurar [fiɣu'rar] *vt* (*representar*) to represent; (*fingir*) to figure ♦ *vi* to figure; **~se** *vr* (*imaginarse*) to imagine; (*suponer*) to suppose

fijador [fixa'ðor] *nm* (*FOTO etc*) fixative; (*de pelo*) gel

fijar [fi'xar] *vt* (*gen*) to fix; (*estampilla*) to affix, stick (on); **~se** *vr*: **~se en** to notice

fijo, a ['fixo, a] *adj* (*gen*) fixed; (*firme*) firm; (*permanente*) permanent ♦ *adv*: **mirar ~** to stare

fila ['fila] *nf* row; (MIL) rank; **ponerse en ~** to line up, get into line

filántropo, a [fi'lantropo, a] *nm/f* philanthropist

filatelia [fila'telja] *nf* philately, stamp collecting

filete [fi'lete] *nm* (carne) fillet steak; (pescado) fillet

filiación [filja'θjon] *nf* (POL) affiliation

filial [fi'ljal] *adj* filial ♦ *nf* subsidiary

Filipinas [fili'pinas] *nfpl*: **las ~** the Philippines; **filipino, a** *adj*, *nm/f* Philippine

filmar [fil'mar] *vt* to film, shoot

filo ['filo] *nm* (gen) edge; **sacar ~ a** to sharpen; **al ~ del mediodía** at about midday; **de doble ~** double-edged

filón [fi'lon] *nm* (MINERÍA) vein, lode; (fig) goldmine

filosofía [filoso'fia] *nf* philosophy; **filósofo, a** *nm/f* philosopher

filtrar [fil'trar] *vt*, *vi* to filter, strain; **~se** *vr* to filter; **filtro** *nm* (TEC, utensilio) filter

fin [fin] *nm* end; (objetivo) aim, purpose; **al ~ y al cabo** when all's said and done; **a ~ de** in order to; **por ~** finally; **en ~** in short; **~ de semana** weekend

final [fi'nal] *adj* final ♦ *nm* end, conclusion ♦ *nf* final; **~idad** *nf* (propósito) purpose, intention; **~ista** *nm/f* finalist; **~izar** *vt* to end, finish; (INFORM) to log out *o* off ♦ *vi* to end, come to an end

financiar [finan'θjar] *vt* to finance; **financiero, a** *adj* financial ♦ *nm/f* financier

finca ['finka] *nf* (bien inmueble) property, land; (casa de campo) country house; (AM) farm

fingir [fin'xir] *vt* (simular) to simulate, feign ♦ *vi* (aparentar) to pretend

finlandés, esa [finlan'des, esa] *adj* Finnish ♦ *nm/f* Finn ♦ *nm* (LING) Finnish

Finlandia [fin'landja] *nf* Finland

fino, a ['fino, a] *adj* fine; (delgado) slender; (de buenas maneras) polite, refined; (jerez) fino, dry

firma ['firma] *nf* signature; (COM) firm, company

firmamento [firma'mento] *nm* firmament

firmar [fir'mar] *vt* to sign

firme ['firme] *adj* firm; (estable) stable; (sólido) solid; (constante) steady; (decidido) resolute ♦ *nm* road (surface); **~mente** *adv* firmly; **~za** *nf* firmness; (constancia) steadiness; (solidez) solidity

fiscal [fis'kal] *adj* fiscal ♦ *nm/f* public prosecutor; **año ~** tax *o* fiscal year

fisco ['fisko] *nm* (hacienda) treasury, exchequer (BRIT)

fisgar [fis'var] *vt* to pry into

fisgonear [fisvone'ar] *vt* to poke one's nose into ♦ *vi* to pry, spy

física ['fisika] *nf* physics *sg*; *ver tb* **físico**

físico, a ['fisiko, a] *adj* physical ♦ *nm* physique ♦ *nm/f* physicist

fisura [fi'sura] *nf* crack; (MED) fracture

flác(c)ido, a ['fla(k)θiðo, a] *adj* flabby

flaco, a ['flako, a] *adj* (muy delgado) skinny, thin; (débil) weak, feeble

flagrante [fla'vrante] *adj* flagrant

flamante [fla'mante] (fam) *adj* brilliant; (nuevo) brand-new

flamenco, a [fla'menko, a] *adj* (de Flandes) Flemish; (baile, música) flamenco ♦ *nm* (baile, música) flamenco

flan [flan] *nm* creme caramel

flaqueza [fla'keθa] *nf* (delgadez) thinness, leanness; (fig) weakness

flash [flaʃ] (pl **~s** *o* **~es**) *nm* (FOTO) flash

flauta ['flauta] *nf* (MUS) flute

flecha ['fletʃa] *nf* arrow

flechazo [fle'tʃaθo] *nm* love at first sight

fleco ['fleko] *nm* fringe

flema ['flema] *nm* phlegm

flequillo [fle'kiʎo] *nm* (pelo) fringe

flexible [flek'siβle] *adj* flexible

flexión [flek'sjon] *nf* press-up

flexo ['flekso] *nm* adjustable table-lamp

flojera [flo'xera] (AM: fam) *nf*: **me da ~** I can't be bothered

flojo, a ['floxo, a] *adj* (gen) loose; (sin fuerzas) limp; (débil) weak

flor [flor] *nf* flower; **a ~ de** on the surface of; **~ecer** *vi* (BOT) to flower, bloom; (fig) to flourish; **~eciente** adj (BOT) in flower, flowering; (fig) thriving; **~ero** nm vase; **~istería** nf florist's (shop)

flota ['flota] nf fleet

flotador [flota'ðor] nm (gen) float; (para nadar) rubber ring

flotar [flo'tar] vi (gen) to float; **flote** nm: **a flote** afloat; **salir a flote** (fig) to get back on one's feet

fluctuar [fluk'twar] vi (oscilar) to fluctuate

fluidez [flui'ðeθ] nf fluidity; (fig) fluency

fluido, a ['fluiðo, a] adj, nm fluid

fluir [flu'ir] vi to flow

flujo ['fluxo] nm flow; **~ y reflujo** ebb and flow

flúor ['fluor] nm fluoride

fluvial [fluβi'al] adj (navegación, cuenca) fluvial, river cpd

foca ['foka] nf seal

foco ['foko] nm focus; (ELEC) floodlight; (AM) (light) bulb

fofo, a ['fofo, a] adj soft, spongy; (carnes) flabby

fogata [fo'ɣata] nf bonfire

fogón [fo'ɣon] nm (de cocina) ring, burner

fogoso, a [fo'ɣoso, a] adj spirited

folio ['foljo] nm folio, page

follaje [fo'ʎaxe] nm foliage

folletín [foʎe'tin] nm newspaper serial

folleto [fo'ʎeto] nm (POL) pamphlet

follón [fo'ʎon] (fam) nm (lío) mess; (conmoción) fuss; **armar un ~** to kick up a row

fomentar [fomen'tar] vt (MED) to foment; **fomento** nm (promoción) promotion

fonda ['fonda] nf inn

fondo ['fondo] nm (de mar) bottom; (de noche, sala) back; (ARTE etc) background; (reserva) fund; **~s** nmpl (COM) funds, resources; **una investigación a ~** a thorough investigation; **en el ~** at bottom, deep down

fonobuzón [fonoβu'θon] nm voice mail

fontanería [fontane'ria] nf plumbing; **fontanero** a, nm/f plumber

footing ['futin] nm jogging; **hacer ~** to jog, go jogging

forastero, a [foras'tero, a] nm/f stranger

forcejear [forθexe'ar] vi (luchar) to struggle

forense [fo'rense] nm/f pathologist

forjar [for'xar] vt to forge

forma ['forma] nf (figura) form, shape; (MED) fitness; (método) way, means; **las ~s** the conventions; **estar en ~** to be fit

formación [forma'θjon] nf (gen) formation; (educación) education; **~ profesional** vocational training

formal [for'mal] adj (gen) formal; (fig: serio) serious; (: de fiar) reliable; **~idad** nf formality; seriousness; **~izar** vt (JUR) to formalize; (situación) to put in order, regularize; **~izarse** vr (situación) to be put in order, to be regularized

formar [for'mar] vt (componer) to form, shape; (constituir) to make up, constitute; (ESCOL) to train, educate; **~se** vr (ESCOL) to be trained, educated; (cobrar forma) to form, take form; (desarrollarse) to develop

formatear [formate'ar] vt to format

formativo, a [forma'tiβo, a] adj (lecturas, años) formative

formato [for'mato] nm format

formidable [formi'ðaβle] adj (temible) formidable; (estupendo) tremendous

fórmula ['formula] nf formula

formular [formu'lar] vt (queja) to make, lodge; (petición) to draw up; (pregunta) to pose

formulario [formu'larjo] nm form

fornido, a [for'niðo, a] adj well-built

forrar [fo'rrar] vt (abrigo) to line; (libro) to cover; **forro** nm (de cuaderno) cover; (COSTURA) lining; (de sillón) upholstery

fortalecer [fortale'θer] vt to strengthen

fortaleza [forta'leθa] nf (MIL) fortress, stronghold; (fuerza) strength; (determinación) resolution

fortuito, a [for'twito, a] adj accidental

fortuna [for'tuna] nf (suerte) fortune, (good) luck; (riqueza) fortune, wealth

forzar [for'θar] vt (puerta) to force (open); (compeler) to compel

forzoso, a [for'θoso, a] adj necessary

fosa ['fosa] nf (sepultura) grave; (en tierra)

pit; **~s nasales** nostrils

fósforo ['fosforo] nm (QUÍM) phosphorus; (cerilla) match

foso ['foso] nm ditch; (TEATRO) pit; (AUTO): **~ de reconocimiento** inspection pit

foto ['foto] nf photo, snap(shot); **sacar una ~** to take a photo o picture

fotocopia [foto'kopja] nf photocopy; **fotocopiadora** nf photocopier; **fotocopiar** vt to photocopy

fotografía [fotoɣra'fia] nf (ARTE) photography; (una ~) photograph; **fotografiar** vt to photograph

fotógrafo, a [fo'toɣrafo, a] nm/f photographer

fracasar [fraka'sar] vi (gen) to fail

fracaso [fra'kaso] nm failure

fracción [frak'θjon] nf fraction; **fraccionamiento** (AM) nm housing estate

fractura [frak'tura] nf fracture, break

fragancia [fra'ɣanθja] nf (olor) fragrance, perfume

frágil ['fraxil] adj (débil) fragile; (COM) breakable

fragmento [fraɣ'mento] nm (pedazo) fragment

fragua ['fraɣwa] nf forge; **fraguar** vt to forge; (fig) to concoct ♦ vi to harden

fraile ['fraile] nm (REL) friar; (: monje) monk

frambuesa [fram'bwesa] nf raspberry

francamente [franka'mente] adv (hablar, decir) frankly; (realmente) really

francés, esa [fran'θes, esa] adj French ♦ nm/f Frenchman/woman ♦ nm (LING) French

Francia ['franθja] nf France

franco, a ['franko, a] adj (cándido) frank, open; (COM: exento) free ♦ nm (moneda) franc

francotirador, a [frankotira'ðor, a] nm/f sniper

franela [fra'nela] nf flannel

franja ['franxa] nf fringe

franquear [franke'ar] vt (camino) to clear; (carta, paquete postal) to frank, stamp; (obstáculo) to overcome

franqueo [fran'keo] nm postage

franqueza [fran'keθa] nf (candor) frankness

frasco ['frasko] nm bottle, flask; **~ al vacío** (vacuum) flask

frase ['frase] nf sentence; **~ hecha** set phrase; (pey) stock phrase

fraterno, a [fra'terno, a] adj brotherly, fraternal

fraude ['frauðe] nm (cualidad) dishonesty; (acto) fraud; **fraudulento, a** adj fraudulent

frazada [fra'saða] (AM) nf blanket

frecuencia [fre'kwenθja] nf frequency; **con ~** frequently, often

frecuentar [frekwen'tar] vt to frequent

fregadero [freɣa'ðero] nm (kitchen) sink

fregar [fre'ɣar] vt (frotar) to scrub; (platos) to wash (up); (AM) to annoy

fregona [fre'ɣona] nf mop

freír [fre'ir] vt to fry

frenar [fre'nar] vt to brake; (fig) to check

frenazo [fre'naθo] nm: **dar un ~** to brake sharply

frenesí [frene'si] nm frenzy; **frenético, a** adj frantic

freno ['freno] nm (TEC, AUTO) brake; (de cabalgadura) bit; (fig) check

frente ['frente] nm (ARQ, POL) front; (de objeto) front part ♦ nf forehead, brow; **~ a** in front of; (en situación opuesta de) opposite; **al ~ de** (fig) at the head of; **chocar de ~** to crash head-on; **hacer ~ a** to face up to

fresa ['fresa] (ESP) nf strawberry

fresco, a ['fresko, a] adj (nuevo) fresh; (frío) cool; (descarado) cheeky ♦ nm (aire) fresh air; (ARTE) fresco; (AM: jugo) fresh drink ♦ nm/f (fam): **ser un ~** to have a nerve; **tomar el ~** to get some fresh air; **frescura** nf freshness; (descaro) cheek, nerve

frialdad [frial'dað] nf (gen) coldness; (indiferencia) indifference

fricción [frik'θjon] nf (gen) friction; (acto) rub(bing); (MED) massage

gidez [frixi'ðeθ] *nf* frigidity

jorífico [frivo'rifiko] *nm* refrigerator

ol [fri'xol] *nm* kidney bean

o, a *etc* ['frio, a] *vb ver* **freír** ♦ *adj* cold; **indiferente**) indifferent ♦ *nm* cold; **difference**; **hace ~** it's cold; **tener ~** to **e** cold

to, a ['frito, a] *adj* fried; **me trae ~ ese ombre** I'm sick and tired of that man; **ritos** *nmpl* fried food

volo, a ['friβolo, a] *adj* frivolous

ntal [fron'tal] *adj* frontal; **choque ~** **ead-on collision**

ntera [fron'tera] *nf* frontier; **ronterizo, a** *adj* frontier *cpd*; (*contiguo*) **ordering**

ntón [fron'ton] *nm* (DEPORTE: *cancha*) **elota court**; (: *juego*) pelota

tar [fro'tar] *vt* to rub; **~se** *vr*: **~se las anos** to rub one's hands

ctífero, a [fruk'tifero, a] *adj* fruitful

ncir [frun'θir] *vt* to pucker; (COSTURA) to **leat**; **~ el ceño** to knit one's brow

strar [frus'trar] *vt* to frustrate

ta ['fruta] *nf* fruit; **frutería** *nf* fruit **hop**; **frutero, a** *adj* fruit *cpd* ♦ *nm/f* **uiterer** ♦ *nm* fruit bowl

tilla [fru'tiʎa] (AM) *nf* strawberry

to ['fruto] *nm* fruit; (*fig: resultado*) result; **beneficio**) benefit; **~s secos** nuts; **pasas etc**) dried fruit *sg*

e *vb ver* **ser**, **ir**

ego ['fweɣo] *nm* (*gen*) fire; **a ~ lento** on **low heat**; **¿tienes ~?** have you (got) a **ght?**; **~s artificiales** o **de artificio fireworks**

ente ['fwente] *nf* fountain; (*manantial*, **g**) spring; (*origen*) source; (*plato*) large **lish**

era *etc* ['fwera] *vb ver* **ser, ir** ♦ *adv* **ut(side)**; (*en otra parte*) away; (*excepto*, **alvo**) except, save ♦ *prep*: **~ de** outside; **fig**) besides; **~ de sí** beside o.s.; **por ~ n** the outside

era-borda [fwera'ßorða] *nm* speedboat

erte ['fwerte] *adj* strong; (*golpe*) hard; **uido**) loud; (*comida*) rich; (*lluvia*) heavy;

(*dolor*) intense ♦ *adv* strongly; hard; loud(ly)

fuerza *etc* ['fwerθa] *vb ver* **forzar** ♦ *nf* (*fortaleza*) strength; (TEC, ELEC) power; (*coacción*) force; (MIL: *tb*: **~s**) forces *pl*; **a ~ de** by dint of; **cobrar ~s** to recover one's strength; **tener ~s para** to have the strength to; **a la ~** forcibly, by force; **por ~** of necessity; **~ de voluntad** willpower

fuga ['fuɣa] *nf* (*huida*) flight, escape; (*de gas etc*) leak

fugarse [fu'ɣarse] *vr* to flee, escape

fugaz [fu'ɣaθ] *adj* fleeting

fugitivo, a [fuxi'tiβo, a] *adj, nm/f* fugitive

fui *vb ver* **ser**; **ir**

fulano, a [fu'lano, a] *nm/f* so-and-so, what's-his-name/what's-her-name

fulminante [fulmi'nante] *adj* (*fig: mirada*) fierce; (MED: *enfermedad, ataque*) sudden; (*fam: éxito, golpe*) sudden

fumador, a [fuma'ðor, a] *nm/f* smoker

fumar [fu'mar] *vt, vi* to smoke; **~ en pipa** to smoke a pipe

función [fun'θjon] *nf* function; (*en trabajo*) duties *pl*; (*espectáculo*) show; **entrar en funciones** to take up one's duties

funcionar [funθjo'nar] *vi* (*gen*) to function; (*máquina*) to work; **"no funciona"** "out of order"

funcionario, a [funθjo'narjo, a] *nm/f* civil servant

funda ['funda] *nf* (*gen*) cover; (*de almohada*) pillowcase

fundación [funda'θjon] *nf* foundation

fundamental [fundamen'tal] *adj* fundamental, basic

fundamentar [fundamen'tar] *vt* (*poner base*) to lay the foundations of; (*establecer*) to found; (*fig*) to base; **fundamento** *nm* (*base*) foundation

fundar [fun'dar] *vt* to found; **~se** *vr*: **~se en** to be founded on

fundición [fundi'θjon] *nf* fusing; (*fábrica*) foundry

fundir [fun'dir] *vt* (*gen*) to fuse; (*metal*) to smelt, melt down; (*nieve etc*) to melt; (COM) to merge; (*estatua*) to cast; **~se** *vr* (*colores etc*) to merge, blend; (*unirse*) to fuse together; (ELEC: *fusible, lámpara etc*) to fuse, blow; (*nieve etc*) to melt

fúnebre [ˈfuneβre] *adj* funeral *cpd*, funereal

funeral [funeˈral] *nm* funeral; **funeraria** *nf* undertaker's

funesto, a [fuˈnesto, a] *adj* (*día*) ill-fated; (*decisión*) fatal

furgón [furˈɣon] *nm* wagon; **furgoneta** *nf* (AUTO, COM) (transit) van (BRIT), pick-up (truck) (US)

furia [ˈfurja] *nf* (*ira*) fury; (*violencia*) violence; **furibundo, a** *adj* furious; **furioso, a** *adj* (*iracundo*) furious; (*violento*) violent; **furor** *nm* (*cólera*) rage

furtivo, a [furˈtiβo, a] *adj* furtive ♦ *nm* poacher

fusible [fuˈsiβle] *nm* fuse

fusil [fuˈsil] *nm* rifle; ~**ar** *vt* to shoot

fusión [fuˈsjon] *nf* (*gen*) melting; (*unión*) fusion; (COM) merger

fútbol [ˈfutβol] *nm* football; **futbolín** *nm* table football; **futbolista** *nm* footballer

futuro, a [fuˈturo, a] *adj, nm* future

G, g

gabardina [gaβarˈðina] *nf* raincoat, gabardine

gabinete [gaβiˈnete] *nm* (POL) cabinet; (*estudio*) study; (*de abogados etc*) office

gaceta [gaˈθeta] *nf* gazette

gachas [ˈgatʃas] *nfpl* porridge *sg*

gafas [ˈgafas] *nfpl* glasses; ~ **de sol** sunglasses

gafe [ˈgafe] *nm* jinx

gaita [ˈgaita] *nf* bagpipes *pl*

gajes [ˈgaxes] *nmpl*: **los ~ del oficio** occupational hazards

gajo [ˈgaxo] *nm* (*de naranja*) segment

gala [ˈgala] *nf* (*traje de etiqueta*) full dress; ~**s** *nfpl* (*ropa*) finery *sg*; **estar de ~** to be in one's best clothes; **hacer ~ de** to display

galante [gaˈlante] *adj* gallant; **galantería**

nf (*caballerosidad*) gallantry; (*cumplido*) politeness; (*comentario*) compliment

galápago [gaˈlapaɣo] *nm* (ZOOL) turtle

galardón [galarˈðon] *nm* award, prize

galaxia [gaˈlaksja] *nf* galaxy

galera [gaˈlera] *nf* (*nave*) galley; (*carro*) wagon; (IMPRENTA) galley

galería [galeˈria] *nf* (*gen*) gallery; (*balcón*) veranda(h); (*pasillo*) corridor

Gales [ˈgales] *nm* (*tb*: **País de ~**) Wales; **galés, esa** *adj* Welsh ♦ *nm/f* Welshman/woman ♦ *nm* (LING) Welsh

galgo, a [ˈgalɣo, a] *nm/f* greyhound

galimatías [galimaˈtias] *nmpl* (*lenguaje*) gibberish *sg*, nonsense *sg*

gallardía [gaʎarˈðia] *nf* (*valor*) bravery

gallego, a [gaˈʎeɣo, a] *adj, nm/f* Galician

galleta [gaˈʎeta] *nf* biscuit (BRIT), cookie (US)

gallina [gaˈʎina] *nf* hen ♦ *nm/f* (*fam: cobarde*) chicken; **gallinero** *nm* henhouse; (TEATRO) top gallery

gallo [ˈgaʎo] *nm* cock, rooster

galón [gaˈlon] *nm* (MIL) stripe; (COSTURA) braid; (*medida*) gallon

galopar [galoˈpar] *vi* to gallop

gama [ˈgama] *nf* (*fig*) range

gamba [ˈgamba] *nf* prawn (BRIT), shrimp (US)

gamberro, a [gamˈberro, a] *nm/f* hooligan, lout

gamuza [gaˈmuθa] *nf* chamois

gana [ˈgana] *nf* (*deseo*) desire, wish; (*apetito*) appetite; (*voluntad*) will; (*añoranza*) longing; **de buena ~** willingly; **de mala ~** reluctantly; **me da ~s de** I feel like, I want to; **no me da la ~** I don't feel like it; **tener ~s de** to feel like

ganadería [ganaðeˈria] *nf* (*ganado*) livestock; (*ganado vacuno*) cattle *pl*; (*cría, comercio*) cattle raising

ganado [gaˈnaðo] *nm* livestock; ~ **lanar** sheep *pl*; ~ **mayor** cattle *pl*; ~ **porcino** pigs *pl*

ganador, a [ganaˈðor, a] *adj* winning ♦ *nm/f* winner

ganancia [gaˈnanθja] *nf* (*lo ganado*) gain;

(aumento) increase; (beneficio) profit; **~s**
nfpl (ingresos) earnings; (beneficios) profit
sg, winnings
ganar [ga'nar] vt (obtener) to get, obtain;
(sacar ventaja) to gain; (salario etc) to
earn; (DEPORTE, premio) to win; (derrotar
a) to beat; (alcanzar) to reach ♦ vi
(DEPORTE) to win; **~se** vr: **~se la vida** to
earn one's living
ganchillo [gan'tʃiʎo] nm crochet
gancho ['gantʃo] nm (gen) hook;
(colgador) hanger
gandul, a [gan'dul, a] adj, nm/f good-
for-nothing, layabout
ganga ['ganga] nf bargain
gangrena [gan'grena] nf gangrene
ganso, a ['ganso, a] nm/f (ZOOL) goose;
(fam) idiot
ganzúa [gan'θua] nf skeleton key
garabatear [garaβate'ar] vi, vt (al escribir)
to scribble, scrawl
garabato [gara'βato] nm (escritura) scrawl,
scribble
garaje [ga'raxe] nm garage
garante [ga'rante] adj responsible ♦ nm/f
guarantor
garantía [garan'tia] nf guarantee
garantizar [garanti'θar] vt to guarantee
garbanzo [gar'βanθo] nm chickpea (BRIT),
garbanzo (US)
garbo ['garβo] nm grace, elegance
garfio ['garfjo] nm grappling iron
garganta [gar'ɣanta] nf (ANAT) throat; (de
botella) neck; **gargantilla** nf necklace
gárgaras ['garɣaras] nfpl: **hacer ~** to
gargle
garita [ga'rita] nf cabin, hut; (MIL) sentry
box
garra ['garra] nf (de gato, TEC) claw; (de
ave) talon; (fam: mano) hand, paw
garrafa [ga'rrafa] nf carafe, decanter
garrapata [garra'pata] nf tick
garrote [ga'rrote] nm (palo) stick; (porra)
cudgel; (suplicio) garrotte
garza ['garθa] nf heron
gas [gas] nm gas
gasa ['gasa] nf gauze

gaseosa [gase'osa] nf lemonade
gaseoso, a [gase'oso, a] adj gassy, fizzy
gasoil [ga'soil] nm diesel (oil)
gasóleo [ga'soleo] nm = **gasoil**
gasolina [gaso'lina] nf petrol, gas(oline)
(US); **gasolinera** nf petrol (BRIT) o gas
(US) station
gastado, a [gas'taðo, a] adj (dinero) spent;
(ropa) worn out; (usado: frase etc) trite
gastar [gas'tar] vt (dinero, tiempo) to
spend; (fuerzas) to use up; (desperdiciar)
to waste; (llevar) to wear; **~se** vr to wear
out; (estropearse) to waste; **~ en** to spend
on; **~ bromas** to crack jokes; **¿qué
número gastas?** what size (shoe) do you
take?
gasto ['gasto] nm (desembolso)
expenditure, spending; (consumo, uso)
use; **~s** nmpl (desembolsos) expenses;
(cargos) charges, costs
gastronomía [gastrono'mia] nf
gastronomy
gatear [gate'ar] vi (andar a gatas) to go
on all fours
gatillo [ga'tiʎo] nm (de arma de fuego)
trigger; (de dentista) forceps
gato, a ['gato, a] nm/f cat ♦ nm (TEC) jack;
andar a gatas to go on all fours
gaviota [ga'βjota] nf seagull
gay [ge] adj inv, nm gay, homosexual
gazpacho [gaθ'patʃo] nm gazpacho
gel [xel] nm (tb: **~ de baño/ducha**) gel
gelatina [xela'tina] nf jelly; (polvos etc)
gelatine
gema ['xema] nf gem
gemelo, a [xe'melo, a] adj, nm/f twin; **~s**
nmpl (de camisa) cufflinks; (prismáticos)
field glasses, binoculars
gemido [xe'miðo] nm (quejido) moan,
groan; (aullido) howl
Géminis ['xeminis] nm Gemini
gemir [xe'mir] vi (quejarse) to moan,
groan; (aullar) to howl
generación [xenera'θjon] nf generation
general [xene'ral] adj general ♦ nm
general; **por lo** o **en ~** in general; G**~itat**
nf Catalan parliament; **~izar** vt to

generalize; **~izarse** vr to become
generalized, spread; **~mente** adv
generally

generar [xene'rar] vt to generate

género ['xenero] nm (clase) kind, sort;
(tipo) type; (BIO) genus; (LING) gender;
(COM) material; **~ humano** human race

generosidad [xenerosi'ðað] nf generosity;
generoso, a adj generous

genial [xe'njal] adj inspired; (idea) brilliant;
(afable) genial

genio ['xenjo] nm (carácter) nature,
disposition; (humor) temper; (facultad
creadora) genius; **de mal ~** bad-tempered

genital [xeni'tal] adj genital; **genitales**
nmpl genitals

gente ['xente] nf (personas) people pl;
(parientes) relatives pl

gentil [xen'til] adj (elegante) graceful;
(encantador) charming; **~eza** nf grace;
charm; (cortesía) courtesy

gentío [xen'tio] nm crowd, throng

genuino, a [xe'nwino, a] adj genuine

geografía [xeoxra'fia] nf geography

geología [xeolo'xia] nf geology

geometría [xeome'tria] nf geometry

gerencia [xe'renθja] nf management;
gerente nm/f (supervisor) manager; (jefe)
director

geriatría [xeria'tria] nf (MED) geriatrics sg

germen ['xermen] nm germ

germinar [xermi'nar] vi to germinate

gesticular [xestiku'lar] vi to gesticulate;
(hacer muecas) to grimace;
gesticulación nf gesticulation; (mueca)
grimace

gestión [xes'tjon] nf management;
(diligencia, acción) negotiation;
gestionar vt (lograr) to try to arrange;
(dirigir) to manage

gesto ['xesto] nm (mueca) grimace;
(ademán) gesture

Gibraltar [xiβral'tar] nm Gibraltar;
gibraltareño, a adj, nm/f Gibraltarian

gigante [xi'γante] adj, nm/f giant;
gigantesco, a adj gigantic

gilipollas [xili'poλas] (fam) adj inv daft

♦ nm/f inv wally

gimnasia [xim'nasja] nf gymnastics pl;
gimnasio nm gymnasium; **gimnasta**
nm/f gymnast

gimotear [ximote'ar] vi to whine,
whimper

ginebra [xi'neβra] nf gin

ginecólogo, a [xine'koloγo, a] nm/f
gynaecologist

gira ['xira] nf tour, trip

girar [xi'rar] vt (dar la vuelta) to turn
(around); (: rápidamente) to spin; (COM:
giro postal) to draw; (: letra de cambio) to
issue ♦ vi to turn (round); (rápido) to spin

girasol [xira'sol] nm sunflower

giratorio, a [xira'torjo, a] adj revolving

giro ['xiro] nm (movimiento) turn,
revolution; (LING) expression; (COM) draft;
~ bancario/postal bank giro/postal order

gis [xis] (AM) nm chalk

gitano, a [xi'tano, a] adj, nm/f gypsy

glacial [gla'θjal] adj icy, freezing

glaciar [gla'θjar] nm glacier

glándula ['glandula] nf gland

global [glo'βal] adj global

globo ['gloβo] nm (esfera) globe, sphere;
(aerostato, juguete) balloon

glóbulo ['gloβulo] nm globule; (ANAT)
corpuscle

gloria ['glorja] nf glory

glorieta [glo'rjeta] nf (de jardín) bower,
arbour; (plazoleta) roundabout (BRIT),
traffic circle (US)

glorificar [glorifi'kar] vt (enaltecer) to
glorify, praise

glorioso, a [glo'rjoso, a] adj glorious

glotón, ona [glo'ton, ona] adj gluttonous,
greedy ♦ nm/f glutton

glucosa [glu'kosa] nf glucose

gobernador, a [goβerna'ðor, a] adj
governing ♦ nm/f governor;
gobernante adj governing

gobernar [goβer'nar] vt (dirigir) to guide,
direct; (POL) to rule, govern ♦ vi to
govern; (NAUT) to steer

gobierno etc [go'βjerno] vb ver **gobernar**
♦ nm (POL) government; (dirección)

guidance, direction; (NAUT) steering

goce etc ['goθe] vb ver **gozar** ♦ nm enjoyment

gol [gol] nm goal

golf [golf] nm golf

golfa ['golfa] (fam!) nf (mujer) slut, whore

golfo, a ['golfo, a] nm (GEO) gulf ♦ nm/f (fam: niño) urchin; (gamberro) lout

golondrina [golon'drina] nf swallow

golosina [golo'sina] nf (dulce) sweet; **goloso, a** adj sweet-toothed

golpe ['golpe] nm blow; (de puño) punch; (de mano) smack; (de remo) stroke; (fig: choque) clash; **no dar ~** to be bone idle; **de un ~** with one blow; **de ~** suddenly; **~ (de estado)** coup (d'état); **golpear** vt, vi to strike, knock; (asestar) to beat; (de puño) to punch; (golpetear) to tap

goma ['goma] nf (caucho) rubber; (elástico) elastic; (una ~) elastic band; **~ espuma** foam rubber; **~ de pegar** gum, glue; **~ de borrar** eraser, rubber (BRIT)

gomina [go'mina] nf hair gel

gordo, a ['gorðo, a] adj (gen) fat; (fam) enormous; **el (premio) ~** (en lotería) first prize; **gordura** nf fat; (corpulencia) fatness, stoutness

gorila [go'rila] nm gorilla

gorjear [gorxe'ar] vi to twitter, chirp

gorra ['gorra] nf cap; (de niño) bonnet; (militar) bearskin; **entrar de ~** (fam) to gatecrash; **ir de ~** to sponge

gorrión [go'rrjon] nm sparrow

gorro ['gorro] nm (gen) cap; (de niño, mujer) bonnet

gorrón, ona [go'rron, ona] nm/f scrounger; **gorronear** (fam) vi to scrounge

gota ['gota] nf (gen) drop; (de sudor) bead; (MED) gout; **gotear** vi to drip; (lloviznar) to drizzle; **gotera** nf leak

gozar [go'θar] vi to enjoy o.s.; **~ de** (disfrutar) to enjoy; (poseer) to possess

gozne ['goθne] nm hinge

gozo ['goθo] nm (alegría) joy; (placer) pleasure

gr. abr (= gramo, gramos) g

grabación [graβa'θjon] nf recording

grabado [gra'βaðo] nm print, engraving

grabadora [graβa'ðora] nf tape-recorder

grabar [gra'βar] vt to engrave; (discos, cintas) to record

gracia ['graθja] nf (encanto) grace, gracefulness; (humor) humour, wit; **¡(muchas) ~s!** thanks (very much)!; **~s a** thanks to; **tener ~** (chiste etc) to be funny; **no me hace ~** I am not keen; **gracioso, a** adj (divertido) funny, amusing; (cómico) comical ♦ nm/f (TEATRO) comic character

grada ['graða] nf (de escalera) step; (de anfiteatro) tier, row; **~s** nfpl (DEPORTE: de estadio) terraces

gradería [graðe'ria] nf (gradas) (flight of) steps pl; (de anfiteatro) tiers pl, rows pl; (DEPORTE: de estadio) terraces pl; **~ cubierta** covered stand

grado ['graðo] nm degree; (de aceite, vino) grade; (grada) step; (MIL) rank; **de buen ~** willingly

graduación [graðwa'θjon] nf (del alcohol) proof, strength; (ESCOL) graduation; (MIL) rank

gradual [gra'ðwal] adj gradual

graduar [gra'ðwar] vt (gen) to graduate; (MIL) to commission; **~se** vr to graduate; **~se la vista** to have one's eyes tested

gráfica ['grafika] nf graph

gráfico, a ['grafiko, a] adj graphic ♦ nm diagram; **~s** nmpl (INFORM) graphics

grajo ['graxo] nm rook

Gral abr (= General) Gen.

gramática [gra'matika] nf grammar

gramo ['gramo] nm gramme (BRIT), gram (US)

gran [gran] adj ver **grande**

grana ['grana] nf (color, tela) scarlet

granada [gra'naða] nf pomegranate; (MIL) grenade

granate [gra'nate] adj deep red

Gran Bretaña [-bre'taɲa] nf Great Britain

grande ['grande] (antes de nmsg: **gran**) adj (de tamaño) big, large; (alto) tall; (distinguido) great; (impresionante) grand

♦ nm grandee; **grandeza** nf greatness
grandioso, a [gran'djoso, a] adj
magnificent, grand
granel [gra'nel]: **a ~** adv (COM) in bulk
granero [gra'nero] nm granary, barn
granito [gra'nito] nm (AGR) small grain;
(roca) granite
granizado [grani'θaðo] nm iced drink
granizar [grani'θar] vi to hail; **granizo**
nm hail
granja ['granxa] nf (gen) farm; **granjear**
vt to win, gain; **granjearse** vr to win,
gain; **granjero, a** nm/f farmer
grano ['grano] nm grain; (semilla) seed; (de
café) bean; (MED) pimple, spot
granuja [gra'nuxa] nm/f rogue; (golfillo)
urchin
grapa ['grapa] nf staple; (TEC) clamp;
grapadora nf stapler
grasa ['grasa] nf (gen) grease; (de cocinar)
fat, lard; (sebo) suet; (mugre) filth;
grasiento, a adj greasy; (de aceite) oily;
graso, a adj (leche, queso, carne) fatty;
(pelo, piel) greasy
gratificación [gratifika'θjon] nf (bono)
bonus; (recompensa) reward
gratificar [gratifi'kar] vt to reward
gratinar [grati'nar] vt to cook au gratin
gratis ['gratis] adv free
gratitud [grati'tuð] nf gratitude
grato, a ['grato, a] adj (agradable)
pleasant, agreeable
gratuito, a [gra'twito, a] adj (gratis) free;
(sin razón) gratuitous
gravamen [gra'ßamen] nm (impuesto) tax
gravar [gra'ßar] vt to tax
grave ['graße] adj heavy; (serio) grave,
serious; **~dad** nf gravity
gravilla [gra'ßiʎa] nf gravel
gravitar [graßi'tar] vi to gravitate; **~ sobre**
to rest on
graznar [graθ'nar] vi (cuervo) to squawk;
(pato) to quack; (hablar ronco) to croak
Grecia ['greθja] nf Greece
gremio ['gremjo] nm trade, industry
greña ['greɲa] nf (cabellos) shock of hair
gresca ['greska] nf uproar

griego, a ['grjeʁo, a] adj, nm/f Greek
grieta ['grjeta] nf crack
grifo ['grifo] nm tap; (AM: AUTO) petrol
(BRIT) o gas (US) station
grilletes [gri'ʎetes] nmpl fetters
grillo ['griʎo] nm (ZOOL) cricket
gripe ['gripe] nf flu, influenza
gris [gris] adj (color) grey
gritar [gri'tar] vt, vi to shout, yell; **grito**
nm shout, yell; (de horror) scream
grosella [gro'seʎa] nf (red)currant; **~
negra** blackcurrant
grosería [grose'ria] nf (actitud) rudeness;
(comentario) vulgar comment; **grosero,
a** adj (poco cortés) rude, bad-mannered;
(ordinario) vulgar, crude
grosor [gro'sor] nm thickness
grotesco, a [gro'tesko, a] adj grotesque
grúa ['grua] nf (TEC) crane; (de petróleo)
derrick
grueso, a ['grweso, a] adj thick; (persona)
stout ♦ nm bulk; **el ~ de** the bulk of
grulla ['gruʎa] nf crane
grumo ['grumo] nm clot, lump
gruñido [gru'ɲiðo] nm grunt; (de persona)
grumble
gruñir [gru'ɲir] vi (animal) to growl;
(persona) to grumble
grupa ['grupa] nf (ZOOL) rump
grupo ['grupo] nm group; (TEC) unit, set
gruta ['gruta] nf grotto
guadaña [gwa'ðaɲa] nf scythe
guagua [gwa'ɣwa] (AM) nf (niño) baby;
(bus) bus
guante ['gwante] nm glove; **~ra** nf glove
compartment
guapo, a ['gwapo, a] adj good-looking,
attractive; (elegante) smart
guarda ['gwarða] nm/f (persona) guard,
keeper ♦ nf (acto) guarding; (custodia)
custody; **~bosques** nm inv
gamekeeper; **~costas** nm inv
coastguard vessel ♦ nm/f guardian,
protector; **~espaldas** nm/f inv
bodyguard; **~meta** nm/f goalkeeper;
guardar vt (gen) to keep; (vigilar) to
guard, watch over; (dinero: ahorrar) to

save; **guardarse** vr (preservarse) to protect o.s.; (evitar) to avoid; **guardar cama** to stay in bed; **~rropa** nm (armario) wardrobe; (en establecimiento público) cloakroom

guardería [gwarðe'ria] nf nursery

guardia ['gwarðja] nf (MIL) guard; (cuidado) care, custody ♦ nm/f guard; (policía) policeman/woman; **estar de ~** to be on guard; **montar ~** to mount guard; **G~ Civil** Civil Guard; **G~ Nacional** National Guard

guardián, ana [gwar'ðjan, ana] nm/f (gen) guardian, keeper

guarecer [gware'θer] vt (proteger) to protect; (abrigar) to shelter; **~se** vr to take refuge

guarida [gwa'riða] nf (de animal) den, lair; (refugio) refuge

guarnecer [gwarne'θer] vt (equipar) to provide; (adornar) to adorn; (TEC) to reinforce; **guarnición** nf (de vestimenta) trimming; (de piedra) mount; (CULIN) garnish; (arneses) harness; (MIL) garrison

guarro, a ['gwarro, a] nm/f pig

guasa ['gwasa] nf joke; (bromista) joking ♦ nm/f wit; joker

Guatemala [gwate'mala] nf Guatemala

guay [gwai] (fam) adj super, great

gubernativo, a [guβerna'tiβo, a] adj governmental

guerra ['gerra] nf war; **~ civil** civil war; **~ fría** cold war; **dar ~** to annoy; **guerrear** vi to wage war; **guerrero, a** adj fighting; (carácter) warlike ♦ nm/f warrior

guerrilla [ge'rriʎa] nf guerrilla warfare; (tropas) guerrilla band o group

guía etc ['gia] vb ver **guiar** ♦ nm/f (persona) guide ♦ nf (libro) guidebook; **~ de ferrocarriles** railway timetable; **~ telefónica** telephone directory

guiar [gi'ar] vt to guide, direct; (AUTO) to steer; **~se** vr: **~se por** to be guided by

guijarro [gi'xarro] nm pebble

guillotina [giʎo'tina] nf guillotine

guinda ['ginda] nf morello cherry

guindilla [gin'diʎa] nf chilli pepper

guiñapo [gi'ɲapo] nm (harapo) rag; (persona) reprobate, rogue

guiñar [gi'ɲar] vt to wink

guión [gi'on] nm (LING) hyphen, dash; (CINE) script; **guionista** nm/f scriptwriter

guiri ['giri] (fam: pey) nm/f foreigner

guirnalda [gir'nalda] nf garland

guisado [gi'saðo] nm stew

guisante [gi'sante] nm pea

guisar [gi'sar] vt, vi to cook; **guiso** nm cooked dish

guitarra [gi'tarra] nf guitar

gula ['gula] nf gluttony, greed

gusano [gu'sano] nm worm; (lombriz) earthworm

gustar [gus'tar] vt to taste, sample ♦ vi to please, be pleasing; **~ de algo** to like o enjoy sth; **me gustan las uvas** I like grapes; **le gusta nadar** she likes o enjoys swimming

gusto ['gusto] nm (sentido, sabor) taste; (placer) pleasure; **tiene ~ a menta** it tastes of mint; **tener buen ~** to have good taste; **sentirse a ~** to feel at ease; **mucho ~ (en conocerle)** pleased to meet you; **el ~ es mío** the pleasure is mine; **con ~** willingly, gladly; **~so, a** adj (sabroso) tasty; (agradable) pleasant

H, h

ha vb ver **haber**

haba ['aβa] nf bean

Habana [a'βana] nf: **la ~** Havana

habano [a'βano] nm Havana cigar

habéis vb ver **haber**

PALABRA CLAVE
---

haber [a'βer] vb aux 1 (tiempos compuestos) to have; **había comido** I had eaten; **antes/después de ~lo visto** before seeing/after seeing o having seen it

2: **¡~lo dicho antes!** you should have said so before!

3: **~ de: he de hacerlo** I have to do it;

ha de llegar mañana it should arrive
tomorrow
♦ *vb impers* **1** (*existencia: sg*) there is;
(: *pl*) there are; **hay un hermano/dos
hermanos** there is one brother/there are
two brothers; **¿cuánto hay de aquí a
Sucre?** how far is it from here to Sucre?
2 (*obligación*): **hay que hacer algo**
something must be done; **hay que
apuntarlo para acordarse** you have to
write it down to remember
3: **¡hay que ver!** well I never!
4: **¡no hay de** *o* **por** (*AM*) **qué!** don't
mention it!, not at all!
5: **¿qué hay?** (*¿qué pasa?*) what's up?,
what's the matter?; (*¿qué tal?*) how's it
going?
♦ **~se** *vr*: **habérselas con uno** to have it
out with sb
♦ *vt*: **he aquí unas sugerencias** here are
some suggestions; **no hay cintas blancas
pero sí las hay rojas** there aren't any
white ribbons but there are some red
ones
♦ *nm* (*en cuenta*) credit side; **~es** *nmpl*
assets; **¿cuánto tengo en el ~?** how
much do I have in my account?; **tiene
varias novelas en su ~** he has several
novels to his credit

habichuela [aβi'tʃwela] *nf* kidney bean
hábil ['aβil] *adj* (*listo*) clever, smart;
(*capaz*) fit, capable; (*experto*) expert; **día
~** working day; **habilidad** *nf* skill, ability
habilitar [aβili'tar] *vt* (*capacitar*) to enable;
(*dar instrumentos*) to equip; (*financiar*) to
finance
hábilmente [aβil'mente] *adv* skilfully,
expertly
habitación [aβita'θjon] *nf* (*cuarto*) room;
(*BIO: morada*) habitat; **~ sencilla** *o*
individual single room; **~ doble** *o* **de
matrimonio** double room
habitante [aβi'tante] *nm/f* inhabitant
habitar [aβi'tar] *vt* (*residir en*) to inhabit;
(*ocupar*) to occupy ♦ *vi* to live
hábito ['aβito] *nm* habit

habitual [aβi'twal] *adj* usual
habituar [aβi'twar] *vt* to accustom; **~se** *vr*:
~se a to get used to
habla ['aβla] *nf* (*capacidad de hablar*)
speech; (*idioma*) language; (*dialecto*)
dialect; **perder el ~** to become
speechless; **de ~ francesa** French-
speaking; **estar al ~** to be in contact;
(*TEL*) to be on the line; **¡González al ~!**
(*TEL*) González speaking!
hablador, a [aβla'ðor, a] *adj* talkative
♦ *nm/f* chatterbox
habladuría [aβlaðu'ria] *nf* rumour; **~s** *nfpl*
gossip *sg*
hablante [a'βlante] *adj* speaking ♦ *nm/f*
speaker
hablar [a'βlar] *vt* to speak, talk ♦ *vi* to
speak; **~se** *vr* to speak to each other; **~
con** to speak to; **~ de** to speak of *o*
about; **"se habla inglés"** "English
spoken here"; **¡ni ~!** it's out of the
question!
habré *etc vb ver* **haber**
hacendoso, a [aθen'doso, a] *adj*
industrious

PALABRA CLAVE

hacer [a'θer] *vt* **1** (*fabricar, producir*) to
make; (*construir*) to build; **~ una
película/un ruido** to make a film/noise;
el guisado lo hice yo I made *o* cooked
the stew
2 (*ejecutar: trabajo etc*) to do; **~ la colada**
to do the washing; **~ la comida** to do
the cooking; **¿qué haces?** what are you
doing?; **~ el malo** *o* **el papel del malo**
(*TEATRO*) to play the villain
3 (*estudios, algunos deportes*) to do; **~
español/económicas** to do *o* study
Spanish/economics; **~ yoga/gimnasia** to
do yoga/go to gym
4 (*transformar, incidir en*): **esto lo hará
más difícil** this will make it more difficult;
salir te hará sentir mejor going out will
make you feel better
5 (*cálculo*): **2 y 2 hacen 4** 2 and 2 make
4; **éste hace 100** this one makes 100

6 (+*subjun*): **esto hará que ganemos** this will make us win; **harás que no quiera venir** you'll stop him wanting to come
7 (*como sustituto de vb*) to do; **él bebió y yo hice lo mismo** he drank and I did likewise
8: **no hace más que criticar** all he does is criticize
♦ *vb semi-aux*: **hacer +infin 1** (*directo*): **les hice venir** I made *o* had them come; **~ trabajar a los demás** to get others to work
2 (*por intermedio de otros*): **~ reparar algo** to get sth repaired
♦ *vi* **1**: **haz como que no lo sabes** act as if you don't know
2 (*ser apropiado*): **si os hace** if it's alright with you
3: **~ de**: **~ de madre para uno** to be like a mother to sb; (*TEATRO*): **~ de Otelo** to play Othello
♦ *vb impers* **1**: **hace calor/frío** it's hot/cold; *ver tb* **bueno**; **sol**; **tiempo**
2 (*tiempo*): **hace 3 años** 3 years ago; **hace un mes que voy/no voy** I've been going/I haven't been for a month
3: **¿cómo has hecho para llegar tan rápido?** how did you manage to get here so quickly?
♦ **~se** *vr* **1** (*volverse*) to become; **se hicieron amigos** they became friends
2 (*acostumbrarse*): **~se a** to get used to
3: **se hace con huevos y leche** it's made out of eggs and milk; **eso no se hace** that's not done
4 (*obtener*): **~se de** *o* **con algo** to get hold of sth
5 (*fingirse*): **~se el sueco** to turn a deaf ear

hacha ['atʃa] *nf* axe; (*antorcha*) torch
hachís [a'tʃis] *nm* hashish
hacia ['aθja] *prep* (*en dirección de*) towards; (*cerca de*) near; (*actitud*) towards; **~ arriba/abajo** up(wards)/down(wards); **~ mediodía** about noon
hacienda [a'θjenda] *nf* (*propiedad*)

property; (*finca*) farm; (*AM*) ranch; **~ pública** public finance; **(Ministerio de) H~** Exchequer (*BRIT*), Treasury Department (*US*)
hada ['aða] *nf* fairy
hago *etc vb ver* **hacer**
Haití [ai'ti] *nm* Haiti
halagar [ala'var] *vt* to flatter
halago [a'laxo] *nm* flattery; **halagüeño, a** *adj* flattering
halcón [al'kon] *nm* falcon, hawk
hallar [a'ʎar] *vt* (*gen*) to find; (*descubrir*) to discover; (*toparse con*) to run into; **~se** *vr* to be (situated); **hallazgo** *nm* discovery; (*cosa*) find
halterofilia [altero'filja] *nf* weightlifting
hamaca [a'maka] *nf* hammock
hambre ['ambre] *nf* hunger; (*plaga*) famine; (*deseo*) longing; **tener ~** to be hungry; **hambriento, a** *adj* hungry, starving
hamburguesa [ambur'vesa] *nf* hamburger; **hamburguesería** *nf* burger bar
han *vb ver* **haber**
harapiento, a [ara'pjento, a] *adj* tattered, in rags
harapos [a'rapos] *nmpl* rags
haré *etc vb ver* **hacer**
harina [a'rina] *nf* flour
hartar [ar'tar] *vt* to satiate, glut; (*fig*) to tire, sicken; **~se** *vr* (*de comida*) to fill o.s., gorge o.s.; (*cansarse*) to get fed up (*de* with); **hartazgo** *nm* surfeit, glut; **harto, a** *adj* (*lleno*) full; (*cansado*) fed up ♦ *adv* (*bastante*) enough; (*muy*) very; **estar harto de** to be fed up with
has *vb ver* **haber**
hasta ['asta] *adv* even ♦ *prep* (*alcanzando a*) as far as; up to; down to; (*de tiempo: a tal hora*) till, until; (*antes de*) before ♦ *conj*: **~ que** until; **~ luego/el sábado** see you soon/on Saturday
hastiar [as'tjar] *vt* (*gen*) to weary; (*aburrir*) to bore; **~se** *vr*: **~se de** to get fed up with; **hastío** *nm* weariness; boredom
hatillo [a'tiʎo] *nm* belongings *pl*, kit;

(*montón*) bundle, heap

hay *vb ver* **haber**

Haya ['aja] *nf*: **la ~** The Hague

haya *etc* ['aja] *vb ver* **haber** ♦ *nf* beech tree

haz [aθ] *vb ver* **hacer** ♦ *nm* (*de luz*) beam

hazaña [a'θaɲa] *nf* feat, exploit

hazmerreír [aθmerre'ir] *nm inv* laughing stock

he *vb ver* **haber**

hebilla [e'ßiʎa] *nf* buckle, clasp

hebra ['eßra] *nf* thread; (*BOT: fibra*) fibre, grain

hebreo, a [e'ßreo, a] *adj, nm/f* Hebrew ♦ *nm* (*LING*) Hebrew

hechizar [etʃi'θar] *vt* to cast a spell on, bewitch

hechizo [e'tʃiθo] *nm* witchcraft, magic; (*acto de magía*) spell, charm

hecho, a ['etʃo, a] *pp de* **hacer** ♦ *adj* (*carne*) done; (*COSTURA*) ready-to-wear ♦ *nm* deed, act; (*dato*) fact; (*cuestión*) matter; (*suceso*) event ♦ *excl* agreed!, done!; **¡bien ~!** well done!; **de ~** in fact, as a matter of fact

hechura [e'tʃura] *nf* (*forma*) form, shape; (*de persona*) build

hectárea [ek'tarea] *nf* hectare

heder [e'ðer] *vi* to stink, smell

hediondo, a [e'ðjondo, a] *adj* stinking

hedor [e'ðor] *nm* stench

helada [e'laða] *nf* frost

heladera [ela'ðera] (*AM*) *nf* (*refrigerador*) refrigerator

helado, a [e'laðo, a] *adj* frozen; (*glacial*) icy; (*fig*) chilly, cold ♦ *nm* ice cream

helar [e'lar] *vt* to freeze, ice (up); (*dejar atónito*) to amaze; (*desalentar*) to discourage ♦ *vi* to freeze; **~se** *vr* to freeze

helecho [e'letʃo] *nm* fern

hélice ['eliθe] *nf* (*TEC*) propeller

helicóptero [eli'koptero] *nm* helicopter

hembra ['embra] *nf* (*BOT, ZOOL*) female; (*mujer*) woman; (*TEC*) nut

hemorragia [emo'rraxja] *nf* haemorrhage

hemorroides [emo'rroiðes] *nfpl* haemorrhoids, piles

hemos *vb ver* **haber**

hendidura [endi'ðura] *nf* crack, split

heno ['eno] *nm* hay

herbicida [erßi'θiða] *nm* weedkiller

heredad [ere'ðað] *nf* landed property; (*granja*) farm

heredar [ere'ðar] *vt* to inherit; **heredero, a** *nm/f* heir(ess)

hereje [e'rexe] *nm/f* heretic

herencia [e'renθja] *nf* inheritance

herida [e'riða] *nf* wound, injury; *ver tb* **herido**

herido, a [e'riðo, a] *adj* injured, wounded ♦ *nm/f* casualty

herir [e'rir] *vt* to wound, injure; (*fig*) to offend

hermanastro, a [erma'nastro, a] *nm/f* stepbrother/sister

hermandad [erman'dað] *nf* brotherhood

hermano, a [er'mano, a] *nm/f* brother/sister; **~ gemelo** twin brother; **hermana gemela** twin sister; **~ político** brother-in-law; **hermana política** sister-in-law

hermético, a [er'metiko, a] *adj* hermetic; (*fig*) watertight

hermoso, a [er'moso, a] *adj* beautiful, lovely; (*estupendo*) splendid; (*guapo*) handsome; **hermosura** *nf* beauty

hernia ['ernja] *nf* hernia

héroe ['eroe] *nm* hero

heroína [ero'ina] *nf* (*mujer*) heroine; (*droga*) heroin

heroísmo [ero'ismo] *nm* heroism

herradura [erra'ðura] *nf* horseshoe

herramienta [erra'mjenta] *nf* tool

herrero [e'rrero] *nm* blacksmith

herrumbre [e'rrumbre] *nf* rust

hervidero [erßi'ðero] *nm* (*fig*) swarm; (*POL etc*) hotbed

hervir [er'ßir] *vi* to boil; (*burbujear*) to bubble; (*fig*): **~ de** to teem with; **~ a fuego lento** to simmer; **hervor** *nm* boiling; (*fig*) ardour, fervour

heterosexual [eterosek'swal] *adj* heterosexual

hice *etc vb ver* **hacer**

hidratante [iðra'tante] *adj*: **crema ~**

moisturizing cream, moisturizer; **hidratar** vt (piel) to moisturize; **hidrato** nm: **hidratos de carbono** carbohydrates

hidráulica [i'ðraulika] nf hydraulics sg

hidráulico, a [i'ðrauliko, a] adj hydraulic

hidro... [iðro] prefijo hydro..., water-...; **~eléctrico, a** adj hydroelectric; **~fobia** nf hydrophobia, rabies; **hidrógeno** nm hydrogen

hiedra ['jeðra] nf ivy

hiel [jel] nf gall, bile; (fig) bitterness

hiela etc vb ver **helar**

hielo ['jelo] nm (gen) ice; (escarcha) frost; (fig) coldness, reserve

hiena ['jena] nf hyena

hierba ['jerßa] nf (pasto) grass; (CULIN, MED: planta) herb; **mala ~** weed; (fig) evil influence; **~buena** nf mint

hierro ['jerro] nm (metal) iron; (objeto) iron object

hígado ['iɣaðo] nm liver

higiene [i'xjene] nf hygiene; **higiénico, a** adj hygienic

higo ['iɣo] nm fig; **higuera** nf fig tree

hijastro, a [i'xastro, a] nm/f stepson/daughter

hijo, a ['ixo, a] nm/f son/daughter, child; **~s** nmpl children, sons and daughters; **~ de papá/mamá** daddy's/mummy's boy; **~ de puta** (fam!) bastard (!), son of a bitch (!)

hilar [i'lar] vt to spin; **~ fino** to split hairs

hilera [i'lera] nf row, file

hilo ['ilo] nm thread; (BOT) fibre; (metal) wire; (de agua) trickle, thin stream

hilvanar [ilßa'nar] vt (COSTURA) to tack (BRIT), baste (US); (fig) to do hurriedly

himno ['imno] nm hymn; **~ nacional** national anthem

hincapié [inka'pje] nm: **hacer ~ en** to emphasize

hincar [in'kar] vt to drive (in), thrust (in); **~se** vr: **~se de rodillas** to kneel down

hincha ['intʃa] (fam) nm/f fan

hinchado, a [in'tʃaðo, a] adj (gen) swollen; (persona) pompous

hinchar [in'tʃar] vt (gen) to swell; (inflar)

to blow up, inflate; (fig) to exaggerate; **~se** vr (inflarse) to swell up; (fam: de comer) to stuff o.s.; **hinchazón** nf (MED) swelling; (altivez) arrogance

hinojo [i'noxo] nm fennel

hipermercado [ipermer'kaðo] nm hypermarket, superstore

hípico, a ['ipiko, a] adj horse cpd

hipnotismo [ipno'tismo] nm hypnotism; **hipnotizar** vt to hypnotize

hipo ['ipo] nm hiccups pl

hipocresía [ipokre'sia] nf hypocrisy; **hipócrita** adj hypocritical ♦ nm/f hypocrite

hipódromo [i'poðromo] nm racetrack

hipopótamo [ipo'potamo] nm hippopotamus

hipoteca [ipo'teka] nf mortgage

hipótesis [i'potesis] nf inv hypothesis

hiriente [i'rjente] adj offensive, wounding

hispánico, a [is'paniko, a] adj Hispanic

hispano, a [is'pano, a] adj Hispanic, Spanish, Hispano- ♦ nm/f Spaniard; **H~américa** nf Latin America; **~americano, a** adj, nm/f Latin American

histeria [is'terja] nf hysteria

historia [is'torja] nf history; (cuento) story, tale; **~s** nfpl (chismes) gossip sg; **dejarse de ~s** to come to the point; **pasar a la ~** to go down in history; **~dor, a** nm/f historian; **historial** nm (profesional) curriculum vitae, C.V.; (MED) case history; **histórico, a** adj historical; (memorable) historic

historieta [isto'rjeta] nf tale, anecdote; (dibujos) comic strip

hito ['ito] nm (fig) landmark

hizo vb ver **hacer**

Hnos abr (= Hermanos) Bros.

hocico [o'θiko] nm snout

hockey ['xoki] nm hockey; **~ sobre hielo** ice hockey

hogar [o'ɣar] nm fireplace, hearth; (casa) home; (vida familiar) home life; **~eño, a** adj home cpd; (persona) home-loving

hoguera [o'ɣera] nf (gen) bonfire

hoja ['oxa] *nf* (*gen*) leaf; (*de flor*) petal; (*de papel*) sheet; (*página*) page; **~ de afeitar** razor blade

hojalata [oxa'lata] *nf* tin(plate)

hojaldre [o'xaldre] *nm* (*CULIN*) puff pastry

hojear [oxe'ar] *vt* to leaf through, turn the pages of

hola ['ola] *excl* hello!

Holanda [o'landa] *nf* Holland; **holandés, esa** *adj* Dutch ♦ *nm/f* Dutchman/woman ♦ *nm* (*LING*) Dutch

holgado, a [ol'xaðo, a] *adj* (*ropa*) loose, baggy; (*rico*) comfortable

holgar [ol'xar] *vi* (*descansar*) to rest; (*sobrar*) to be superfluous; **huelga decir que** it goes without saying that

holgazán, ana [olxa'θan, ana] *adj* idle, lazy ♦ *nm/f* loafer

holgura [ol'xura] *nf* looseness, bagginess; (*TEC*) play, free movement; (*vida*) comfortable living

hollín [o'ʎin] *nm* soot

hombre ['ombre] *nm* (*gen*) man; (*raza humana*): **el ~** man(kind) ♦ *excl*: **¡sí ~!** (*claro*) of course!; (*para énfasis*) man, old boy; **~ de negocios** businessman; **~ de pro** honest man; **~-rana** frogman

hombrera [om'brera] *nf* shoulder strap

hombro ['ombro] *nm* shoulder

hombruno, a [om'bruno, a] *adj* mannish

homenaje [ome'naxe] *nm* (*gen*) homage; (*tributo*) tribute

homicida [omi'θiða] *adj* homicidal ♦ *nm/f* murderer; **homicidio** *nm* murder, homicide

homologar [omolo'ðar] *vt* (*COM: productos, tamaños*) to standardize; **homólogo, a** *nm/f*: **su** *etc* **homólogo** his *etc* counterpart *o* opposite number

homosexual [omosek'swal] *adj, nm/f* homosexual

hondo, a ['ondo, a] *adj* deep; **lo ~** the depth(s) (*pl*), the bottom; **~nada** *nf* hollow, depression; (*cañón*) ravine

Honduras [on'duras] *nf* Honduras

hondureño, a [ondu'reɲo, a] *adj, nm/f* Honduran

honestidad [onesti'ðað] *nf* purity, chastity; (*decencia*) decency; **honesto, a** *adj* chaste; decent, honest; (*justo*) just

hongo ['ongo] *nm* (*BOT: gen*) fungus; (: *comestible*) mushroom; (: *venenoso*) toadstool

honor [o'nor] *nm* (*gen*) honour; **en ~ a la verdad** to be fair; **~able** *adj* honourable

honorario, a [ono'rarjo, a] *adj* honorary; **~s** *nmpl* fees

honra ['onra] *nf* (*gen*) honour; (*renombre*) good name; **~dez** *nf* honesty; (*de persona*) integrity; **~do, a** *adj* honest, upright

honrar [on'rar] *vt* to honour; **~se** *vr*: **~se con algo/de hacer algo** to be honoured by sth/to do sth

honroso, a [on'roso, a] *adj* (*honrado*) honourable; (*respetado*) respectable

hora ['ora] *nf* (*una ~*) hour; (*tiempo*) time; **¿qué ~ es?** what time is it?; **¿a qué ~?** at what time?; **media ~** half an hour; **a la ~ de recreo** at playtime; **a primera ~** first thing (in the morning); **a última ~** at the last moment; **a altas ~s** in the small hours; **¡a buena ~!** about time, too!; **dar la ~** to strike the hour; **~s de oficina/de trabajo** office/working hours; **~s de visita** visiting times; **~s extras** *o* **extraordinarias** overtime *sg*; **~s punta** rush hours

horadar [ora'ðar] *vt* to drill, bore

horario, a [o'rarjo, a] *adj* hourly, hour *cpd* ♦ *nm* timetable; **~ comercial** business hours *pl*

horca ['orka] *nf* gallows *sg*

horcajadas [orka'xaðas]: **a ~** *adv* astride

horchata [or'tʃata] *nf* cold drink made from tiger nuts and water, tiger nut milk

horizontal [oriθon'tal] *adj* horizontal

horizonte [ori'θonte] *nm* horizon

horma ['orma] *nf* mould

hormiga [or'miɣa] *nf* ant; **~s** *nfpl* (*MED*) pins and needles

hormigón [ormi'ɣon] *nm* concrete; **~ armado/pretensado** reinforced/prestressed concrete

hormigueo [ormi'ɣeo] nm (comezón) itch

hormona [or'mona] nf hormone

hornada [or'naða] nf batch (of loaves etc)

hornillo [or'niʎo] nm (cocina) portable stove

horno ['orno] nm (CULIN) oven; (TEC) furnace; **alto ~** blast furnace

horóscopo [o'roskopo] nm horoscope

horquilla [or'kiʎa] nf hairpin; (AGR) pitchfork

horrendo, a [o'rrendo, a] adj horrendous, frightful

horrible [o'rriβle] adj horrible, dreadful

horripilante [orripi'lante] adj hair-raising, horrifying

horror [o'rror] nm horror, dread; (atrocidad) atrocity; **¡qué ~!** (fam) how awful!; **~izar** vt to horrify, frighten; **~izarse** vr to be horrified; **~oso, a** adj horrifying, ghastly

hortaliza [orta'liθa] nf vegetable

hortelano, a [orte'lano, a] nm/f (market) gardener

hortera [or'tera] (fam) adj tacky

hosco, a ['osko, a] adj sullen, gloomy

hospedar [ospe'ðar] vt to put up; **~se** vr to stay, lodge

hospital [ospi'tal] nm hospital

hospitalario, a [ospita'larjo, a] adj (acogedor) hospitable; **hospitalidad** nf hospitality

hostal [os'tal] nm small hotel

hostelería [ostele'ria] nf hotel business o trade

hostia ['ostja] nf (REL) host, consecrated wafer; (fam!: golpe) whack, punch ♦ excl (fam!): **¡~(s)!** damn!

hostigar [osti'ɣar] vt to whip; (fig) to harass, pester

hostil [os'til] adj hostile; **~idad** nf hostility

hotel [o'tel] nm hotel; **~ero, a** adj hotel cpd ♦ nm/f hotelier

---

hotel

ⓘ *In Spain you can choose from the following categories of accommodation, in descending order of quality and price:*
hotel (from 5 stars to 1), **hostal, pensión, casa de huéspedes, fonda.** *The State also runs luxury hotels called* **paradores,** *which are usually sited in places of particular historical interest and are often historic buildings themselves.*

---

hoy [oi] adv (este día) today; (la actualidad) now(adays) ♦ nm present time; **~ (en) día** now(adays)

hoyo ['ojo] nm hole, pit; **hoyuelo** nm dimple

hoz [oθ] nf sickle

hube etc vb ver **haber**

hucha ['utʃa] nf money box

hueco, a ['weko, a] adj (vacío) hollow, empty; (resonante) booming ♦ nm hollow, cavity

huelga etc ['welɣa] vb ver **holgar** ♦ nf strike; **declararse en ~** to go on strike, come out on strike; **~ de hambre** hunger strike

huelguista [wel'ɣista] nm/f striker

huella ['weʎa] nf (pisada) tread; (marca del paso) footprint, footstep; (: de animal, máquina) track; **~ digital** fingerprint

huelo etc vb ver **oler**

huérfano, a ['werfano, a] adj orphan(ed) ♦ nm/f orphan

huerta ['werta] nf market garden; (en Murcia y Valencia) irrigated region

huerto ['werto] nm kitchen garden; (de árboles frutales) orchard

hueso ['weso] nm (ANAT) bone; (de fruta) stone

huésped, a ['wespeð, a] nm/f guest

huesudo, a [we'suðo, a] adj bony, big-boned

hueva ['weβa] nf roe

huevera [we'βera] nf eggcup

huevo ['weβo] nm egg; **~ duro/escalfado/frito** (ESP) o **estrellado** (AM)/**pasado por agua** hard-boiled/poached/fried/soft-boiled egg; **~s revueltos** scrambled eggs

huida [u'iða] nf escape, flight

huidizo, a [ui'ðiθo, a] adj shy

huir [u'ir] *vi (escapar)* to flee, escape; *(evitar)* to avoid; **~se** *vr (escaparse)* to escape

hule ['ule] *nm* oilskin

humanidad [umani'ðað] *nf (género humano)* man(kind); *(cualidad)* humanity

humanitario, a [umani'tarjo, a] *adj* humanitarian

humano, a [u'mano, a] *adj (gen)* human; *(humanitario)* humane ♦ *nm* human; **ser ~** human being

humareda [uma'reða] *nf* cloud of smoke

humedad [ume'ðað] *nf (del clima)* humidity; *(de pared etc)* dampness; **a prueba de ~** damp-proof; **humedecer** *vt* to moisten, wet; **humedecerse** *vr* to get wet

húmedo, a ['umeðo, a] *adj (mojado)* damp, wet; *(tiempo etc)* humid

humildad [umil'dað] *nf* humility, humbleness; **humilde** *adj* humble, modest

humillación [umiʎa'θjon] *nf* humiliation; **humillante** *adj* humiliating

humillar [umi'ʎar] *vt* to humiliate; **~se** *vr* to humble o.s., grovel

humo ['umo] *nm (de fuego)* smoke; *(gas nocivo)* fumes *pl*; *(vapor)* steam, vapour; **~s** *nmpl (fig)* conceit *sg*

humor [u'mor] *nm (disposición)* mood, temper; *(lo que divierte)* humour; **de buen/mal ~** in a good/bad mood; **~ista** *nm/f* comic; **~ístico, a** *adj* funny, humorous

hundimiento [undi'mjento] *nm (gen)* sinking; *(colapso)* collapse

hundir [un'dir] *vt* to sink; *(edificio, plan)* to ruin, destroy; **~se** *vr* to sink, collapse

húngaro, a ['ungaro, a] *adj, nm/f* Hungarian

Hungría [un'gria] *nf* Hungary

huracán [ura'kan] *nm* hurricane

huraño, a [u'raɲo, a] *adj (antisocial)* unsociable

hurgar [ur'var] *vt* to poke, jab; *(remover)* to stir (up); **~se** *vr*: **~se (las narices)** to pick one's nose

hurón, ona [u'ron, ona] *nm (ZOOL)* ferret

hurtadillas [urta'ðiʎas]: **a ~** *adv* stealthily, on the sly

hurtar [ur'tar] *vt* to steal; **hurto** *nm* theft, stealing

husmear [usme'ar] *vt (oler)* to sniff out, scent; *(fam)* to pry into

huyo *etc vb ver* **huir**

I, i

iba *etc vb ver* **ir**

ibérico, a [i'ßeriko, a] *adj* Iberian

iberoamericano, a [ißeroameri'kano, a] *adj, nm/f* Latin American

Ibiza [i'ßiθa] *nf* Ibiza

iceberg [iße'ßer] *nm* iceberg

icono [i'kono] *nm* ikon, icon

iconoclasta [ikono'klasta] *adj* iconoclastic ♦ *nm/f* iconoclast

ictericia [ikte'riθja] *nf* jaundice

I + D *abr (= Investigación y Desarrollo)* R & D

ida ['iða] *nf* going, departure; **~ y vuelta** round trip, return

idea [i'ðea] *nf* idea; **no tengo la menor ~** I haven't a clue

ideal [iðe'al] *adj, nm* ideal; **~ista** *nm/f* idealist; **~izar** *vt* to idealize

idear [iðe'ar] *vt* to think up; *(aparato)* to invent; *(viaje)* to plan

ídem ['iðem] *pron* ditto

idéntico, a [i'ðentiko, a] *adj* identical

identidad [iðenti'ðað] *nf* identity

identificación [iðentifika'θjon] *nf* identification

identificar [iðentifi'kar] *vt* to identify; **~se** *vr*: **~se con** to identify with

ideología [iðeolo'xia] *nf* ideology

idilio [i'ðiljo] *nm* love-affair

idioma [i'ðjoma] *nm (gen)* language

idiota [i'ðjota] *adj* idiotic ♦ *nm/f* idiot; **idiotez** *nf* idiocy

ídolo ['iðolo] *nm (tb fig)* idol

idóneo, a [i'ðoneo, a] *adj* suitable

iglesia [i'ɣlesja] *nf* church

ignorancia [iɣnoˈranθja] *nf* ignorance; **ignorante** *adj* ignorant, uninformed ♦ *nm/f* ignoramus

ignorar [iɣnoˈrar] *vt* not to know, be ignorant of; (*no hacer caso a*) to ignore

igual [iˈɣwal] *adj* (*gen*) equal; (*similar*) like, similar; (*mismo*) (the) same; (*constante*) constant; (*temperatura*) even ♦ *nm/f* equal; **~ que** like, the same as; **me da** *o* **es ~** I don't care; **son ~es** they're the same; **al ~ que** *prep, conj* like, just like

igualada [iɣwaˈlaða] *nf* equaliser

igualar [iɣwaˈlar] *vt* (*gen*) to equalize, make equal; (*allanar, nivelar*) to level (off), even (out); **~se** *vr* (*platos de balanza*) to balance out

igualdad [iɣwalˈdað] *nf* equality; (*similaridad*) sameness; (*uniformidad*) uniformity

igualmente [iɣwalˈmente] *adv* equally; (*también*) also, likewise ♦ *excl* the same to you!

ikurriña [ikuˈrriɲa] *nf* Basque flag

ilegal [ileˈɣal] *adj* illegal

ilegítimo, a [ileˈxitimo, a] *adj* illegitimate

ileso, a [iˈleso, a] *adj* unhurt

ilícito, a [iˈliθito, a] *adj* illicit

ilimitado, a [ilimiˈtaðo, a] *adj* unlimited

ilógico, a [iˈloxiko, a] *adj* illogical

iluminación [iluminaˈθjon] *nf* illumination; (*alumbrado*) lighting

iluminar [ilumiˈnar] *vt* to illuminate, light (up); (*fig*) to enlighten

ilusión [iluˈsjon] *nf* illusion; (*quimera*) delusion; (*esperanza*) hope; **hacerse ilusiones** to build up one's hopes; **ilusionado, a** *adj* excited; **ilusionar** *vi*: **le ilusiona ir de vacaciones** he's looking forward to going on holiday; **ilusionarse** *vr*: **ilusionarse (con)** to get excited (about)

ilusionista [ilusjoˈnista] *nm/f* conjurer

iluso, a [iˈluso, a] *adj* easily deceived ♦ *nm/f* dreamer

ilusorio, a [iluˈsorjo, a] *adj* (*de ilusión*) illusory, deceptive; (*esperanza*) vain

ilustración [ilustraˈθjon] *nf* illustration;

(*saber*) learning, erudition; **la I~** the Enlightenment; **ilustrado, a** *adj* illustrated; learned

ilustrar [ilusˈtrar] *vt* to illustrate; (*instruir*) to instruct; (*explicar*) to explain, make clear; **~se** *vr* to acquire knowledge

ilustre [iˈlustre] *adj* famous, illustrious

imagen [iˈmaxen] *nf* (*gen*) image; (*dibujo*) picture

imaginación [imaxinaˈθjon] *nf* imagination

imaginar [imaxiˈnar] *vt* (*gen*) to imagine; (*idear*) to think up; (*suponer*) to suppose; **~se** *vr* to imagine; **~io, a** *adj* imaginary; **imaginativo, a** *adj* imaginative

imán [iˈman] *nm* magnet

imbécil [imˈbeθil] *nm/f* imbecile, idiot

imitación [imitaˈθjon] *nf* imitation

imitar [imiˈtar] *vt* to imitate; (*parodiar, remedar*) to mimic, ape

impaciencia [impaˈθjenθja] *nf* impatience; **impaciente** *adj* impatient; (*nervioso*) anxious

impacto [imˈpakto] *nm* impact

impar [imˈpar] *adj* odd

imparcial [imparˈθjal] *adj* impartial, fair

impartir [imparˈtir] *vt* to impart, give

impasible [impaˈsißle] *adj* impassive

impecable [impeˈkaßle] *adj* impeccable

impedimento [impeðiˈmento] *nm* impediment, obstacle

impedir [impeˈðir] *vt* (*obstruir*) to impede, obstruct; (*estorbar*) to prevent

impenetrable [impeneˈtraßle] *adj* impenetrable; (*fig*) incomprehensible

imperar [impeˈrar] *vi* (*reinar*) to rule, reign; (*fig*) to prevail, reign; (*precio*) to be current

imperativo, a [imperaˈtißo, a] *adj* (*urgente*, LING) imperative

imperceptible [imperθepˈtißle] *adj* imperceptible

imperdible [imperˈðißle] *nm* safety pin

imperdonable [imperðoˈnaßle] *adj* unforgivable, inexcusable

imperfección [imperfekˈθjon] *nf* imperfection

imperfecto, a [imper'fekto, a] *adj* imperfect

imperial [impe'rjal] *adj* imperial; **~ismo** *nm* imperialism

imperio [im'perjo] *nm* empire; (*autoridad*) rule, authority; (*fig*) pride, haughtiness; **~so, a** *adj* imperious; (*urgente*) urgent; (*imperativo*) imperative

impermeable [imperme'aßle] *adj* waterproof ♦ *nm* raincoat, mac (*BRIT*)

impersonal [imperso'nal] *adj* impersonal

impertinencia [imperti'nenθja] *nf* impertinence; **impertinente** *adj* impertinent

imperturbable [impertur'ßaßle] *adj* imperturbable

ímpetu ['impetu] *nm* (*impulso*) impetus, impulse; (*impetuosidad*) impetuosity; (*violencia*) violence

impetuoso, a [impe'twoso, a] *adj* impetuous; (*río*) rushing; (*acto*) hasty

impío, a [im'pio, a] *adj* impious, ungodly

implacable [impla'kaßle] *adj* implacable

implantar [implan'tar] *vt* to introduce

implicar [impli'kar] *vt* to involve; (*entrañar*) to imply

implícito, a [im'pliθito, a] *adj* (*tácito*) implicit; (*sobreentendido*) implied

implorar [implo'rar] *vt* to beg, implore

imponente [impo'nente] *adj* (*impresionante*) impressive, imposing; (*solemne*) grand

imponer [impo'ner] *vt* (*gen*) to impose; (*exigir*) to exact; **~se** *vr* to assert o.s.; (*prevalecer*) to prevail; **imponible** *adj* (*COM*) taxable

impopular [impopu'lar] *adj* unpopular

importación [importa'θjon] *nf* (*acto*) importing; (*mercancías*) imports *pl*

importancia [impor'tanθja] *nf* importance; (*valor*) value, significance; (*extensión*) size, magnitude; **importante** *adj* important; valuable, significant

importar [impor'tar] *vt* (*del extranjero*) to import; (*costar*) to amount to ♦ *vi* to be important, matter; **me importa un rábano** I couldn't care less; **no importa** it

doesn't matter; **¿le importa que fume?** do you mind if I smoke?

importe [im'porte] *nm* (*total*) amount; (*valor*) value

importunar [importu'nar] *vt* to bother, pester

imposibilidad [imposißili'ðað] *nf* impossibility; **imposibilitar** *vt* to make impossible, prevent

imposible [impo'sißle] *adj* (*gen*) impossible; (*insoportable*) unbearable, intolerable

imposición [imposi'θjon] *nf* imposition; (*COM: impuesto*) tax; (: *inversión*) deposit

impostor, a [impos'tor, a] *nm/f* impostor

impotencia [impo'tenθja] *nf* impotence; **impotente** *adj* impotent

impracticable [imprakti'kaßle] *adj* (*irrealizable*) impracticable; (*intransitable*) impassable

impreciso, a [impre'θiso, a] *adj* imprecise, vague

impregnar [imprev'nar] *vt* to impregnate; **~se** *vr* to become impregnated

imprenta [im'prenta] *nf* (*acto*) printing; (*aparato*) press; (*casa*) printer's; (*letra*) print

imprescindible [impresθin'dißle] *adj* essential, vital

impresión [impre'sjon] *nf* (*gen*) impression; (*IMPRENTA*) printing; (*edición*) edition; (*FOTO*) print; (*marca*) imprint; **~ digital** fingerprint

impresionable [impresjo'naßle] *adj* (*sensible*) impressionable

impresionante [impresjo'nante] *adj* impressive; (*tremendo*) tremendous; (*maravilloso*) great, marvellous

impresionar [impresjo'nar] *vt* (*conmover*) to move; (*afectar*) to impress, strike; (*película fotográfica*) to expose; **~se** *vr* to be impressed; (*conmoverse*) to be moved

impreso, a [im'preso, a] *pp de* **imprimir** ♦ *adj* printed; **~s** *nmpl* printed matter; **impresora** *nf* printer

imprevisto, a [impre'ßisto, a] *adj* (*gen*) unforeseen; (*inesperado*) unexpected

imprimir [impri'mir] *vt* to imprint,
impress, stamp; (*textos*) to print; (*INFORM*)
to output, print out
improbable [impro'ßaßle] *adj*
improbable; (*inverosímil*) unlikely
improcedente [improθe'ðente] *adj*
inappropriate
improductivo, a [improðuk'tißo, a] *adj*
unproductive
improperio [impro'perjo] *nm* insult
impropio, a [im'propjo, a] *adj* improper
improvisado, a [improßi'saðo, a] *adj*
improvised
improvisar [improßi'sar] *vt* to improvise
improviso, a [impro'ßiso, a] *adj*: **de ~**
unexpectedly, suddenly
imprudencia [impru'ðenθja] *nf*
imprudence; (*indiscreción*) indiscretion;
(*descuido*) carelessness; **imprudente** *adj*
unwise, imprudent; (*indiscreto*) indiscreet
impúdico, a [im'puðiko, a] *adj* shameless;
(*lujurioso*) lecherous
impuesto, a [im'pwesto, a] *adj* imposed
♦ *nm* tax; **~ sobre el valor añadido**
value added tax
impugnar [impuɣ'nar] *vt* to oppose,
contest; (*refutar*) to refute, impugn
impulsar [impul'sar] *vt* to drive;
(*promover*) to promote, stimulate
impulsivo, a [impul'sißo, a] *adj*
impulsive; **impulso** *nm* impulse; (*fuerza,
empuje*) thrust, drive; (*fig: sentimiento*)
urge, impulse
impune [im'pune] *adj* unpunished
impureza [impu're θa] *nf* impurity;
impuro, a *adj* impure
imputar [impu'tar] *vt* to attribute
inacabable [inaka'ßaßle] *adj* (*infinito*)
endless; (*interminable*) interminable
inaccesible [inakθe'sißle] *adj* inaccessible
inacción [inak'θjon] *nf* inactivity
inaceptable [inaθep'taßle] *adj*
unacceptable
inactividad [inaktißi'ðað] *nf* inactivity;
(*COM*) dullness; **inactivo, a** *adj* inactive
inadecuado, a [inaðe'kwaðo, a] *adj*
(*insuficiente*) inadequate; (*inapto*)

unsuitable
inadmisible [inaðmi'sißle] *adj*
inadmissible
inadvertido, a [inaðßer'tiðo, a] *adj* (*no
visto*) unnoticed
inagotable [inaɣo'taßle] *adj* inexhaustible
inaguantable [inaɣwan'taßle] *adj*
unbearable
inalterable [inalte'raßle] *adj* immutable,
unchangeable
inanición [inani'θjon] *nf* starvation
inanimado, a [inani'maðo, a] *adj*
inanimate
inapreciable [inapre'θjaßle] *adj* (*cantidad,
diferencia*) imperceptible; (*ayuda, servicio*)
invaluable
inaudito, a [inau'ðito, a] *adj* unheard-of
inauguración [inauɣura'θjon] *nf*
inauguration; opening
inaugurar [inauɣu'rar] *vt* to inaugurate;
(*exposición*) to open
inca ['inka] *nm/f* Inca
incalculable [inkalku'laßle] *adj*
incalculable
incandescente [inkandes'θente] *adj*
incandescent
incansable [inkan'saßle] *adj* tireless,
untiring
incapacidad [inkapaθi'ðað] *nf* incapacity;
(*incompetencia*) incompetence; **~ física/
mental** physical/mental disability
incapacitar [inkapaθi'tar] *vt* (*inhabilitar*)
to incapacitate, render unfit; (*descalificar*)
to disqualify
incapaz [inka'paθ] *adj* incapable
incautación [inkauta'θjon] *nf* confiscation
incautarse [inkau'tarse] *vr*: **~ de** to seize,
confiscate
incauto, a [in'kauto, a] *adj* (*imprudente*)
incautious, unwary
incendiar [inθen'djar] *vt* to set fire to;
(*fig*) to inflame; **~se** *vr* to catch fire; **~io,
a** *adj* incendiary
incendio [in'θendjo] *nm* fire
incentivo [inθen'tißo] *nm* incentive
incertidumbre [inθerti'ðumbre] *nf*
(*inseguridad*) uncertainty; (*duda*) doubt

incesante [inθe'sante] *adj* incessant
incesto [in'θesto] *nm* incest
incidencia [inθi'ðenθja] *nf* (*MAT*)
incidence
incidente [inθi'ðente] *nm* incident
incidir [inθi'ðir] *vi* (*influir*) to influence;
(*afectar*) to affect; **~ en un error** to fall
into error
incienso [in'θjenso] *nm* incense
incierto, a [in'θjerto, a] *adj* uncertain
incineración [inθinera'θjon] *nf*
incineration; (*de cadáveres*) cremation
incinerar [inθine'rar] *vt* to burn;
(*cadáveres*) to cremate
incipiente [inθi'pjente] *adj* incipient
incisión [inθi'sjon] *nf* incision
incisivo, a [inθi'siβo, a] *adj* sharp,
cutting; (*fig*) incisive
incitar [inθi'tar] *vt* to incite, rouse
inclemencia [inkle'menθja] *nf* (*severidad*)
harshness, severity; (*del tiempo*)
inclemency
inclinación [inklina'θjon] *nf* (*gen*)
inclination; (*de tierras*) slope, incline; (*de
cabeza*) nod, bow; (*fig*) leaning, bent
inclinar [inkli'nar] *vt* to incline; (*cabeza*)
to nod, bow ♦ *vi* to lean, slope; **~se** *vr* to
bow; (*encorvarse*) to stoop; **~se a**
(*parecerse a*) to take after, resemble; **~se
ante** to bow down to; **me inclino a
pensar que** I'm inclined to think that
incluir [inklu'ir] *vt* to include; (*incorporar*)
to incorporate; (*meter*) to enclose
inclusive [inklu'siβe] *adv* inclusive ♦ *prep*
including
incluso [in'kluso] *adv* even
incógnita [in'koɣnita] *nf* (*MAT*) unknown
quantity
incógnito [in'koɣnito] *nm*: **de ~** incognito
incoherente [inkoe'rente] *adj* incoherent
incoloro, a [inko'loro, a] *adj* colourless
incólume [in'kolume] *adj* unhurt,
unharmed
incomodar [inkomo'ðar] *vt* to
inconvenience; (*molestar*) to bother,
trouble; (*fastidiar*) to annoy; **~se** *vr* to put
o.s. out; (*fastidiarse*) to get annoyed

incomodidad [inkomoði'ðað] *nf*
inconvenience; (*fastidio, enojo*)
annoyance; (*de vivienda*) discomfort
incómodo, a [in'komoðo, a] *adj*
(*inconfortable*) uncomfortable; (*molesto*)
annoying; (*inconveniente*) inconvenient
incomparable [inkompa'raβle] *adj*
incomparable
incompatible [inkompa'tiβle] *adj*
incompatible
incompetencia [inkompe'tenθja] *nf*
incompetence; **incompetente** *adj*
incompetent
incompleto, a [inkom'pleto, a] *adj*
incomplete, unfinished
incomprensible [inkompren'siβle] *adj*
incomprehensible
incomunicado, a [inkomuni'kaðo, a] *adj*
(*aislado*) cut off, isolated; (*confinado*) in
solitary confinement
inconcebible [inkonθe'βiβle] *adj*
inconceivable
incondicional [inkondiθjo'nal] *adj*
unconditional; (*apoyo*) wholehearted;
(*partidario*) staunch
inconexo, a [inko'nekso, a] *adj* (*gen*)
unconnected; (*desunido*) disconnected
inconfundible [inkonfun'diβle] *adj*
unmistakable
incongruente [inkon'ɣrwente] *adj*
incongruous
inconsciencia [inkons'θjenθja] *nf*
unconsciousness; (*fig*) thoughtlessness;
inconsciente *adj* unconscious;
thoughtless
inconsecuente [inkonse'kwente] *adj*
inconsistent
inconsiderado, a [inkonsiðe'raðo, a] *adj*
inconsiderate
inconsistente [inkonsis'tente] *adj* weak;
(*tela*) flimsy
inconstancia [inkon'stanθja] *nf*
inconstancy; (*inestabilidad*) unsteadiness;
inconstante *adj* inconstant
incontable [inkon'taβle] *adj* countless,
innumerable
incontestable [inkontes'taβle] *adj*

unanswerable; (*innegable*) undeniable

incontinencia [inkonti'nenθja] *nf* incontinence

inconveniencia [inkombe'njenθja] *nf* unsuitability, inappropriateness; (*descortesía*) impoliteness;
inconveniente *adj* unsuitable; impolite ♦ *nm* obstacle; (*desventaja*) disadvantage; **el inconveniente es que ...** the trouble is that ...

incordiar [inkor'ðjar] (*fam*) *vt* to bug, annoy

incorporación [inkorpora'θjon] *nf* incorporation

incorporar [inkorpo'rar] *vt* to incorporate; **~se** *vr* to sit up

incorrección [inkorrek'θjon] *nf* (*gen*) incorrectness, inaccuracy; (*descortesía*) bad-mannered behaviour; **incorrecto, a** *adj* (*gen*) incorrect, wrong; (*comportamiento*) bad-mannered

incorregible [inkorre'xiβle] *adj* incorrigible

incredulidad [inkreðuli'ðað] *nf* incredulity; (*escepticismo*) scepticism; **incrédulo, a** *adj* incredulous, unbelieving; sceptical

increíble [inkre'iβle] *adj* incredible

incremento [inkre'mento] *nm* increment; (*aumento*) rise, increase

increpar [inkre'par] *vt* to reprimand

incruento, a [in'krwento, a] *adj* bloodless

incrustar [inkrus'tar] *vt* to incrust; (*piedras: en joya*) to inlay

incubar [inku'βar] *vt* to incubate

inculcar [inkul'kar] *vt* to inculcate

inculpar [inkul'par] *vt* (*acusar*) to accuse; (*achacar, atribuir*) to charge, blame

inculto, a [in'kulto, a] *adj* (*persona*) uneducated; (*grosero*) uncouth ♦ *nm/f* ignoramus

incumplimiento [inkumpli'mjento] *nm* non-fulfilment; **~ de contrato** breach of contract

incurrir [inku'rrir] *vi*: **~ en** to incur; (*crimen*) to commit; **~ en un error** to make a mistake

indagación [indava'θjon] *nf* investigation; (*búsqueda*) search; (*JUR*) inquest

indagar [inda'var] *vt* to investigate; to search; (*averiguar*) to ascertain

indecente [inde'θente] *adj* indecent, improper; (*lascivo*) obscene

indecible [inde'θiβle] *adj* unspeakable; (*indescriptible*) indescribable

indeciso, a [inde'θiso, a] *adj* (*por decidir*) undecided; (*vacilante*) hesitant

indefenso, a [inde'fenso, a] *adj* defenceless

indefinido, a [indefi'niðo, a] *adj* indefinite; (*vago*) vague, undefined

indeleble [inde'leβle] *adj* indelible

indemne [in'demne] *adj* (*objeto*) undamaged; (*persona*) unharmed, unhurt

indemnizar [indemni'θar] *vt* to indemnify; (*compensar*) to compensate

independencia [independ'denθja] *nf* independence

independiente [independ'djente] *adj* (*libre*) independent; (*autónomo*) self-sufficient

indeterminado, a [indetermi'naðo, a] *adj* indefinite; (*desconocido*) indeterminate

India ['indja] *nf*: **la ~** India

indicación [indika'θjon] *nf* indication; (*señal*) sign; (*sugerencia*) suggestion, hint

indicado, a [indi'kaðo, a] *adj* (*momento, método*) right; (*tratamiento*) appropriate; (*solución*) likely

indicador [indika'ðor] *nm* indicator; (*TEC*) gauge, meter

indicar [indi'kar] *vt* (*mostrar*) to indicate, show; (*termómetro etc*) to read, register; (*señalar*) to point to

índice ['indiθe] *nm* index; (*catálogo*) catalogue; (*ANAT*) index finger, forefinger

indicio [in'diθjo] *nm* indication, sign; (*en pesquisa etc*) clue

indiferencia [indife'renθja] *nf* indifference; (*apatía*) apathy; **indiferente** *adj* indifferent

indígena [in'dixena] *adj* indigenous, native ♦ *nm/f* native

indigencia [indi'xenθja] *nf* poverty, need

indigestión [indixes'tjon] *nf* indigestion
indigesto, a [indi'xesto, a] *adj* (*alimento*) indigestible; (*fig*) turgid
indignación [indiɣna'θjon] *nf* indignation
indignar [indiɣ'nar] *vt* to anger, make indignant; **~se** *vr:* **~se por** to get indignant about
indigno, a [in'diɣno, a] *adj* (*despreciable*) low, contemptible; (*inmerecido*) unworthy
indio, a ['indjo, a] *adj, nm/f* Indian
indirecta [indi'rekta] *nf* insinuation, innuendo; (*sugerencia*) hint
indirecto, a [indi'rekto, a] *adj* indirect
indiscreción [indiskre'θjon] *nf* (*imprudencia*) indiscretion; (*irreflexión*) tactlessness; (*acto*) gaffe, faux pas
indiscreto, a [indis'kreto, a] *adj* indiscreet
indiscriminado, a [indiskrimi'naðo, a] *adj* indiscriminate
indiscutible [indisku'tiβle] *adj* indisputable, unquestionable
indispensable [indispen'saβle] *adj* indispensable, essential
indisponer [indispo'ner] *vt* to spoil, upset; (*salud*) to make ill; **~se** *vr* to fall ill; **~se con uno** to fall out with sb
indisposición [indisposi'θjon] *nf* indisposition
indispuesto, a [indis'pwesto, a] *adj* (*enfermo*) unwell, indisposed
indistinto, a [indis'tinto, a] *adj* indistinct; (*vago*) vague
individual [indiβi'ðwal] *adj* individual; (*habitación*) single ♦ *nm* (*DEPORTE*) singles *sg*
individuo, a [indi'βiðwo, a] *adj, nm* individual
índole ['indole] *nf* (*naturaleza*) nature; (*clase*) sort, kind
indómito, a [in'domito, a] *adj* indomitable
inducir [indu'θir] *vt* to induce; (*inferir*) to infer; (*persuadir*) to persuade
indudable [indu'ðaβle] *adj* undoubted; (*incuestionable*) unquestionable
indulgencia [indul'xenθja] *nf* indulgence
indultar [indul'tar] *vt* (*perdonar*) to

pardon, reprieve; (*librar de pago*) to exempt; **indulto** *nm* pardon; exemption
industria [in'dustrja] *nf* industry; (*habilidad*) skill; **industrial** *adj* industrial ♦ *nm* industrialist
inédito, a [in'eðito, a] *adj* (*texto*) unpublished; (*nuevo*) new
inefable [ine'faβle] *adj* ineffable, indescribable
ineficaz [inefi'kaθ] *adj* (*inútil*) ineffective; (*ineficiente*) inefficient
ineludible [inelu'ðiβle] *adj* inescapable, unavoidable
ineptitud [inepti'tuð] *nf* ineptitude, incompetence; **inepto, a** *adj* inept, incompetent
inequívoco, a [ine'kiβoko, a] *adj* unequivocal; (*inconfundible*) unmistakable
inercia [in'erθja] *nf* inertia; (*pasividad*) passivity
inerme [in'erme] *adj* (*sin armas*) unarmed; (*indefenso*) defenceless
inerte [in'erte] *adj* inert; (*inmóvil*) motionless
inesperado, a [inespe'raðo, a] *adj* unexpected, unforeseen
inestable [ines'taβle] *adj* unstable
inevitable [ineβi'taβle] *adj* inevitable
inexactitud [ineksakti'tuð] *nf* inaccuracy; **inexacto, a** *adj* inaccurate; (*falso*) untrue
inexperto, a [inek'sperto, a] *adj* (*novato*) inexperienced
infalible [infa'liβle] *adj* infallible; (*plan*) foolproof
infame [in'fame] *adj* infamous; (*horrible*) dreadful; **infamia** *nf* infamy; (*deshonra*) disgrace
infancia [in'fanθja] *nf* infancy, childhood
infantería [infante'ria] *nf* infantry
infantil [infan'til] *adj* (*pueril, aniñado*) infantile; (*cándido*) childlike; (*literatura, ropa etc*) children's
infarto [in'farto] *nm* (*tb:* **~ de miocardio**) heart attack
infatigable [infati'βaβle] *adj* tireless, untiring

infección [infek'θjon] *nf* infection;
infeccioso, a *adj* infectious
infectar [infek'tar] *vt* to infect; **~se** *vr* to
become infected
infeliz [infe'liθ] *adj* unhappy, wretched
♦ *nm/f* wretch
inferior [infe'rjor] *adj* inferior; (*situación*)
lower ♦ *nm/f* inferior, subordinate
inferir [infe'rir] *vt* (*deducir*) to infer,
deduce; (*causar*) to cause
infestar [infes'tar] *vt* to infest
infidelidad [infiðeli'ðað] *nf* (*gen*)
infidelity, unfaithfulness
infiel [in'fjel] *adj* unfaithful, disloyal;
(*erróneo*) inaccurate ♦ *nm/f* infidel,
unbeliever
infierno [in'fjerno] *nm* hell
infiltrarse [infil'trarse] *vr*: **~ en** to infiltrate
in(to); (*persona*) to work one's way in(to)
ínfimo, a ['infimo, a] *adj* (*más bajo*)
lowest; (*despreciable*) vile, mean
infinidad [infini'ðað] *nf* infinity;
(*abundancia*) great quantity
infinito, a [infi'nito, a] *adj, nm* infinite
inflación [infla'θjon] *nf* (*hinchazón*)
swelling; (*monetaria*) inflation; (*fig*)
conceit; **inflacionario, a** *adj* inflationary
inflamar [infla'mar] *vt* (*MED, fig*) to
inflame; **~se** *vr* to catch fire; to become
inflamed
inflar [in'flar] *vt* (*hinchar*) to inflate, blow
up; (*fig*) to exaggerate; **~se** *vr* to swell
(up); (*fig*) to get conceited
inflexible [inflek'sißle] *adj* inflexible; (*fig*)
unbending
infligir [infli'xir] *vt* to inflict
influencia [influ'enθja] *nf* influence;
influenciar *vt* to influence
influir [influ'ir] *vt* to influence
influjo [in'fluxo] *nm* influence
influya *etc vb ver* **influir**
influyente [influ'jente] *adj* influential
información [informa'θjon] *nf*
information; (*noticias*) news *sg*; (*JUR*)
inquiry; **I~** (*oficina*) Information Office;
(*mostrador*) Information Desk; (*TEL*)
Directory Enquiries

informal [infor'mal] *adj* (*gen*) informal
informar [infor'mar] *vt* (*gen*) to inform;
(*revelar*) to reveal, make known ♦ *vi* (*JUR*)
to plead; (*denunciar*) to inform; (*dar
cuenta de*) to report on; **~se** *vr* to find
out; **~se de** to inquire into
informática [infor'matika] *nf* computer
science, information technology
informe [in'forme] *adj* shapeless ♦ *nm*
report
infortunio [infor'tunjo] *nm* misfortune
infracción [infrak'θjon] *nf* infraction,
infringement
infranqueable [infranke'aßle] *adj*
impassable; (*fig*) insurmountable
infravalorar [infrabalo'rar] *vt* to
undervalue, underestimate
infringir [infrin'xir] *vt* to infringe,
contravene
infructuoso, a [infruk'twoso, a] *adj*
fruitless, unsuccessful
infundado, a [infun'daðo, a] *adj*
groundless, unfounded
infundir [infun'dir] *vt* to infuse, instil
infusión [infu'sjon] *nf* infusion; **~ de
manzanilla** camomile tea
ingeniar [inxe'njar] *vt* to think up, devise;
~se *vr*: **~se para** to manage to
ingeniería [inxenje'ria] *nf* engineering; **~
genética** genetic engineering;
ingeniero, a *nm/f* engineer; **ingeniero
de caminos/de sonido** civil engineer/
sound engineer
ingenio [in'xenjo] *nm* (*talento*) talent;
(*agudeza*) wit; (*habilidad*) ingenuity,
inventiveness; **~ azucarero** (*AM*) sugar
refinery
ingenioso, a [inxe'njoso, a] *adj*
ingenious, clever; (*divertido*) witty
ingenuidad [inxenwi'ðað] *nf*
ingenuousness; (*sencillez*) simplicity;
ingenuo, a *adj* ingenuous
ingerir [inxe'rir] *vt* to ingest; (*tragar*) to
swallow; (*consumir*) to consume
Inglaterra [ingla'terra] *nf* England
ingle ['ingle] *nf* groin
inglés, esa [in'gles, esa] *adj* English

♦ *nm/f* Englishman/woman ♦ *nm* (LING)
English

ngratitud [ingrati'tuð] *nf* ingratitude;
ingrato, a *adj* (gen) ungrateful

ngrediente [ingre'ðjente] *nm* ingredient

ngresar [ingre'sar] *vt* (dinero) to deposit
♦ *vi* to come in; ~ **en un club** to join a
club; ~ **en el hospital** to go into hospital

ingreso [in'greso] *nm* (entrada) entry;
(: en hospital etc) admission; ~**s** *nmpl*
(dinero) income *sg*; (: COM) takings *pl*

inhabitable [inaβi'taβle] *adj* uninhabitable

inhalar [ina'lar] *vt* to inhale

inherente [ine'rente] *adj* inherent

inhibir [ini'βir] *vt* to inhibit

inhóspito, a [i'nospito, a] *adj* (región,
paisaje) inhospitable

inhumano, a [inu'mano, a] *adj* inhuman

inicial [ini'θjal] *adj, nf* initial

iniciar [ini'θjar] *vt* (persona) to initiate;
(empezar) to begin, commence;
(conversación) to start up

iniciativa [iniθja'tiβa] *nf* initiative; **la ~
privada** private enterprise

ininterrumpido, a [ininterrum'piðo, a]
adj uninterrupted

injerencia [inxe'renθja] *nf* interference

injertar [inxer'tar] *vt* to graft; **injerto** *nm*
graft

injuria [in'xurja] *nf* (agravio, ofensa)
offence; (insulto) insult; **injuriar** *vt* to
insult; **injurioso, a** *adj* offensive;
insulting

injusticia [inxus'tiθja] *nf* injustice

injusto, a [in'xusto, a] *adj* unjust, unfair

inmadurez [inmaðu're θ] *nf* immaturity

inmediaciones [inmeðja'θjones] *nfpl*
neighbourhood *sg*, environs

inmediato, a [inme'ðjato, a] *adj*
immediate; (contiguo) adjoining; (rápido)
prompt; (próximo) neighbouring, next; **de
~** immediately

inmejorable [inmexo'raβle] *adj*
unsurpassable; (precio) unbeatable

inmenso, a [in'menso, a] *adj* immense,
huge

inmerecido, a [inmere'θiðo, a] *adj*
undeserved

inmigración [inmiɣra'θjon] *nf*
immigration

inmiscuirse [inmisku'irse] *vr* to interfere,
meddle

inmobiliaria [inmoβi'ljarja] *nf* estate
agency

inmobiliario, a [inmoβi'ljarjo, a] *adj*
real-estate *cpd*, property *cpd*

inmolar [inmo'lar] *vt* to immolate,
sacrifice

inmoral [inmo'ral] *adj* immoral

inmortal [inmor'tal] *adj* immortal; ~**izar**
vt to immortalize

inmóvil [in'moβil] *adj* immobile

inmueble [in'mweβle] *adj*: **bienes ~s** real
estate, landed property ♦ *nm* property

inmundicia [inmun'diθja] *nf* filth;
inmundo, a *adj* filthy

inmune [in'mune] *adj*: ~ **(a)** (MED)
immune (to)

inmunidad [inmuni'ðað] *nf* immunity

inmutarse [inmu'tarse] *vr* to turn pale; **no
se inmutó** he didn't turn a hair

innato, a [in'nato, a] *adj* innate

innecesario, a [inneθe'sarjo, a] *adj*
unnecessary

innoble [in'noβle] *adj* ignoble

innovación [innoβa'θjon] *nf* innovation

innovar [inno'βar] *vt* to introduce

inocencia [ino'θenθja] *nf* innocence

inocentada [inoθen'taða] *nf* practical joke

inocente [ino'θente] *adj* (ingenuo) naive,
innocent; (inculpable) innocent; (sin
malicia) harmless ♦ *nm/f* simpleton

Día de los Santos Inocentes

i The 28th December, **el día de los
(Santos) Inocentes**, is when the
Church commemorates the story of Herod's
slaughter of the innocent children of
Judaea. On this day Spaniards play
inocentadas (practical jokes) on each
other, much like our April Fool's Day
pranks.

---

inodoro [ino'ðoro] *nm* toilet, lavatory

(BRIT)

inofensivo, a [inofen'siβo, a] *adj* inoffensive, harmless

inolvidable [inolβi'ðaβle] *adj* unforgettable

inopinado, a [inopi'naðo, a] *adj* unexpected

inoportuno, a [inopor'tuno, a] *adj* untimely; (*molesto*) inconvenient

inoxidable [inoksi'ðaβle] *adj*: **acero ~** stainless steel

inquebrantable [inkeβran'taβle] *adj* unbreakable

inquietar [inkje'tar] *vt* to worry, trouble; **~se** *vr* to worry, get upset; **inquieto, a** *adj* anxious, worried; **inquietud** *nf* anxiety, worry

inquilino, a [inki'lino, a] *nm/f* tenant

inquirir [inki'rir] *vt* to enquire into, investigate

insaciable [insa'θjaβle] *adj* insatiable

insalubre [insa'luβre] *adj* unhealthy

inscribir [inskri'βir] *vt* to inscribe; **~ a uno en** (*lista*) to put sb on; (*censo*) to register sb on

inscripción [inskrip'θjon] *nf* inscription; (*ESCOL etc*) enrolment; (*censo*) registration

insecticida [insekti'θiða] *nm* insecticide

insecto [in'sekto] *nm* insect

inseguridad [inseɣuri'ðað] *nf* insecurity

inseguro, a [inse'ɣuro, a] *adj* insecure; (*inconstante*) unsteady; (*incierto*) uncertain

insensato, a [insen'sato, a] *adj* foolish, stupid

insensibilidad [insensiβili'ðað] *nf* (*gen*) insensitivity; (*dureza de corazón*) callousness

insensible [insen'siβle] *adj* (*gen*) insensitive; (*movimiento*) imperceptible; (*sin sentido*) numb

insertar [inser'tar] *vt* to insert

inservible [inser'βiβle] *adj* useless

insidioso, a [insi'ðjoso, a] *adj* insidious

insignia [in'siɣnja] *nf* (*señal distintiva*) badge; (*estandarte*) flag

insignificante [insiɣnifi'kante] *adj* insignificant

insinuar [insi'nwar] *vt* to insinuate, imply

insípido, a [in'sipiðo, a] *adj* insipid

insistencia [insis'tenθja] *nf* insistence

insistir [insis'tir] *vi* to insist; **~ en algo** to insist on sth; (*enfatizar*) to stress sth

insolación [insola'θjon] *nf* (*MED*) sunstroke

insolencia [inso'lenθja] *nf* insolence; **insolente** *adj* insolent

insólito, a [in'solito, a] *adj* unusual

insoluble [inso'luβle] *adj* insoluble

insolvencia [insol'βenθja] *nf* insolvency

insomnio [in'somnjo] *nm* insomnia

insondable [inson'daβle] *adj* bottomless; (*fig*) impenetrable

insonorizado, a [insonori'θaðo, a] *adj* (*cuarto etc*) soundproof

insoportable [insopor'taβle] *adj* unbearable

insospechado, a [insospe'tʃaðo, a] *adj* (*inesperado*) unexpected

inspección [inspek'θjon] *nf* inspection, check; **inspeccionar** *vt* (*examinar*) to inspect, examine; (*controlar*) to check

inspector, a [inspek'tor, a] *nm/f* inspector

inspiración [inspira'θjon] *nf* inspiration

inspirar [inspi'rar] *vt* to inspire; (*MED*) to inhale; **~se** *vr*: **~se en** to be inspired by

instalación [instala'θjon] *nf* (*equipo*) fittings *pl*, equipment; **~ eléctrica** wiring

instalar [insta'lar] *vt* (*establecer*) to instal; (*erguir*) to set up, erect; **~se** *vr* to establish o.s.; (*en una vivienda*) to move into

instancia [ins'tanθja] *nf* (*JUR*) petition; (*ruego*) request; **en última ~** as a last resort

instantánea [instan'tanea] *nf* snap(shot)

instantáneo, a [instan'taneo, a] *adj* instantaneous; **café ~** instant coffee

instante [ins'tante] *nm* instant, moment

instar [ins'tar] *vt* to press, urge

instaurar [instau'rar] *vt* (*costumbre*) to establish; (*normas, sistema*) to bring in, introduce; (*gobierno*) to instal

instigar [insti'ɣar] *vt* to instigate

instinto [ins'tinto] *nm* instinct; **por ~**

instinctively

nstitución [institu'θjon] *nf* institution, establishment

nstituir [institu'ir] *vt* to establish; (*fundar*) to found; **instituto** *nm* (*gen*) institute; (*ESP: ESCOL*) ≈ comprehensive (*BRIT*) *o* high (*US*) school

nstitutriz [institu'triθ] *nf* governess

nstrucción [instruk'θjon] *nf* instruction

nstructivo, a [instruk'tiβo, a] *adj* instructive

nstruir [instru'ir] *vt* (*gen*) to instruct; (*enseñar*) to teach, educate

nstrumento [instru'mento] *nm* (*gen*) instrument; (*herramienta*) tool, implement

nsubordinarse [insuβorδi'narse] *vr* to rebel

nsuficiencia [insufi'θjenθja] *nf* (*carencia*) lack; (*inadecuación*) inadequacy; **insuficiente** *adj* (*gen*) insufficient; (*ESCOL: calificación*) unsatisfactory

insufrible [insu'friβle] *adj* insufferable

insular [insu'lar] *adj* insular

insultar [insul'tar] *vt* to insult; **insulto** *nm* insult

insumiso, a [insu'miso, a] *nm/f* (*POL*) *person who refuses to do military service or its substitute, community service*

insuperable [insupe'raβle] *adj* (*excelente*) unsurpassable; (*problema etc*) insurmountable

insurgente [insur'xente] *adj*, *nm/f* insurgent

insurrección [insurrek'θjon] *nf* insurrection, rebellion

intachable [inta'tʃaβle] *adj* irreproachable

intacto, a [in'takto, a] *adj* intact

integral [inte'γral] *adj* integral; (*completo*) complete; **pan ~** wholemeal (*BRIT*) *o* wholewheat (*US*) bread

integrar [inte'γrar] *vt* to make up, compose; (*MAT*, *fig*) to integrate

integridad [inteγri'δaδ] *nf* wholeness; (*carácter*) integrity; **íntegro, a** *adj* whole, entire; (*honrado*) honest

intelectual [intelek'twal] *adj*, *nm/f* intellectual

inteligencia [inteli'xenθja] *nf* intelligence; (*ingenio*) ability; **inteligente** *adj* intelligent

inteligible [inteli'xiβle] *adj* intelligible

intemperie [intem'perje] *nf*: **a la ~** out in the open, exposed to the elements

intempestivo, a [intempes'tiβo, a] *adj* untimely

intención [inten'θjon] *nf* (*gen*) intention, purpose; **con segundas intenciones** maliciously; **con ~** deliberately

intencionado, a [intenθjo'naδo, a] *adj* deliberate; **bien ~** well-meaning; **mal ~** ill-disposed, hostile

intensidad [intensi'δaδ] *nf* (*gen*) intensity; (*ELEC*, *TEC*) strength; **llover con ~** to rain hard

intenso, a [in'tenso, a] *adj* intense; (*sentimiento*) profound, deep

intentar [inten'tar] *vt* (*tratar*) to try, attempt; **intento** *nm* attempt

interactivo, a [interak'tiβo, a] *adj* (*INFORM*) interactive

intercalar [interka'lar] *vt* to insert

intercambio [inter'kambjo] *nm* exchange, swap

interceder [interθe'δer] *vi* to intercede

interceptar [interθep'tar] *vt* to intercept

intercesión [interθe'sjon] *nf* intercession

interés [inte'res] *nm* (*gen*) interest; (*parte*) share, part; (*pey*) self-interest; **intereses creados** vested interests

interesado, a [intere'saδo, a] *adj* interested; (*prejuiciado*) prejudiced; (*pey*) mercenary, self-seeking

interesante [intere'sante] *adj* interesting

interesar [intere'sar] *vt*, *vi* to interest, be of interest to; **~se** *vr*: **~se en** *o* **por** to take an interest in

interferir [interfe'rir] *vt* to interfere with; (*TEL*) to jam ♦ *vi* to interfere

interfono [inter'fono] *nm* intercom

interino, a [inte'rino, a] *adj* temporary ♦ *nm/f* temporary holder of a post; (*MED*) locum; (*ESCOL*) supply teacher

interior [inte'rjor] *adj* inner, inside; (*COM*) domestic, internal ♦ *nm* interior, inside;

(fig) soul, mind; **Ministerio del I~**
≈ Home Office *(BRIT)*, ≈ Department of
the Interior *(US)*

interjección [interxek'θjon] *nf* interjection

interlocutor, a [interloku'tor, a] *nm/f*
speaker

intermedio, a [inter'meðjo, a] *adj*
intermediate ♦ *nm* interval

interminable [intermi'naβle] *adj* endless

intermitente [intermi'tente] *adj*
intermittent ♦ *nm (AUTO)* indicator

internacional [internaθjo'nal] *adj*
international

internado [inter'naðo] *nm* boarding
school

internar [inter'nar] *vt* to intern; *(en un
manicomio)* to commit; **~se** *vr (penetrar)*
to penetrate

Internet [inter'net] *nm o nf:* **el** *o* **la ~** the
Internet

interno, a [in'terno, a] *adj* internal,
interior; *(POL etc)* domestic ♦ *nm/f*
(alumno) boarder

interponer [interpo'ner] *vt* to interpose,
put in; **~se** *vr* to intervene

interpretación [interpreta'θjon] *nf*
interpretation

interpretar [interpre'tar] *vt* to interpret;
(TEATRO, MUS) to perform, play;
intérprete *nm/f (LING)* interpreter,
translator; *(MUS, TEATRO)* performer,
artist(e)

interrogación [interroɣa'θjon] *nf*
interrogation; *(LING: tb:* **signo de ~)**
question mark

interrogar [interro'ɣar] *vt* to interrogate,
question

interrumpir [interrum'pir] *vt* to interrupt

interrupción [interrup'θjon] *nf*
interruption

interruptor [interrup'tor] *nm (ELEC)*
switch

intersección [intersek'θjon] *nf*
intersection

interurbano, a [interur'ßano, a] *adj:*
llamada interurbana long-distance call

intervalo [inter'ßalo] *nm* interval;

(descanso) break; **a ~s** at intervals, every
now and then

intervenir [interße'nir] *vt (controlar)* to
control, supervise; *(MED)* to operate on
♦ *vi (participar)* to take part, participate;
(mediar) to intervene

interventor, a [interßen'tor, a] *nm/f*
inspector; *(COM)* auditor

intestino [intes'tino] *nm* intestine

intimar [inti'mar] *vi* to become friendly

intimidad [intimi'ðað] *nf* intimacy;
(familiaridad) familiarity; *(vida privada)*
private life; *(JUR)* privacy

íntimo, a ['intimo, a] *adj* intimate

intolerable [intole'raßle] *adj* intolerable,
unbearable

intoxicación [intoksika'θjon] *nf* poisoning

intranet [intra'net] *nf* intranet

intranquilizarse [intrankili'θarse] *vr* to
get worried *o* anxious; **intranquilo, a**
adj worried

intransitable [intransi'taßle] *adj*
impassable

intrépido, a [in'trepiðo, a] *adj* intrepid

intriga [in'triɣa] *nf* intrigue; *(plan)* plot;
intrigar *vt, vi* to intrigue

intrincado, a [intrin'kaðo, a] *adj* intricate

intrínseco, a [in'trinseko, a] *adj* intrinsic

introducción [introðuk'θjon] *nf*
introduction

introducir [introðu'θir] *vt (gen)* to
introduce; *(moneda etc)* to insert;
(INFORM) to input, enter

intromisión [intromi'sjon] *nf* interference,
meddling

introvertido, a [introßer'tiðo, a] *adj, nm/f*
introvert

intruso, a [in'truso, a] *adj* intrusive
♦ *nm/f* intruder

intuición [intwi'θjon] *nf* intuition

inundación [inunda'θjon] *nf* flood(ing);
inundar *vt* to flood; *(fig)* to swamp,
inundate

inusitado, a [inusi'taðo, a] *adj* unusual,
rare

inútil [in'util] *adj* useless; *(esfuerzo)* vain,
fruitless; **inutilidad** *nf* uselessness

inutilizar [inutili'θar] *vt* to make *o* render useless; **~se** *vr* to become useless

invadir [imba'ðir] *vt* to invade

inválido, a [im'baliðo, a] *adj* invalid ♦ *nm/f* invalid

invariable [imba'rjaßle] *adj* invariable

invasión [imba'sjon] *nf* invasion

invasor, a [imba'sor, a] *adj* invading ♦ *nm/f* invader

invención [imben'θjon] *nf* invention

inventar [imben'tar] *vt* to invent

inventario [imben'tarjo] *nm* inventory

inventiva [imben'tißa] *nf* inventiveness

invento [im'bento] *nm* invention

inventor, a [imben'tor, a] *nm/f* inventor

invernadero [imberna'ðero] *nm* greenhouse

inverosímil [imbero'simil] *adj* implausible

inversión [imber'sjon] *nf* (COM) investment

inverso, a [im'berso, a] *adj* inverse, opposite; **en el orden ~** in reverse order; **a la inversa** inversely, the other way round

inversor, a [imber'sor, a] *nm/f* (COM) investor

invertir [imber'tir] *vt* (COM) to invest; (*volcar*) to turn upside down; (*tiempo etc*) to spend

investigación [imbestiɣa'θjon] *nf* investigation; (ESCOL) research; **~ de mercado** market research

investigar [imbesti'ɣar] *vt* to investigate; (ESCOL) to do research into

invierno [im'bjerno] *nm* winter

invisible [imbi'sißle] *adj* invisible

invitado, a [imbi'taðo, a] *nm/f* guest

invitar [imbi'tar] *vt* to invite; (*incitar*) to entice; (*pagar*) to buy, pay for

invocar [imbo'kar] *vt* to invoke, call on

involucrar [imbolu'krar] *vt*: **~ en** to involve in; **~se** *vr* (*persona*): **~ en** to get mixed up in

involuntario, a [imbolun'tarjo, a] *adj* (*movimiento, gesto*) involuntary; (*error*) unintentional

inyección [injek'θjon] *nf* injection

inyectar [injek'tar] *vt* to inject

PALABRA CLAVE

ir [ir] *vi* **1** to go; (*a pie*) to walk; (*viajar*) to travel; **~ caminando** to walk; **fui en tren** I went *o* travelled by train; **¡(ahora) voy!** (I'm just) coming!

2: **~ (a) por**: **~ (a) por el médico** to fetch the doctor

3 (*progresar: persona, cosa*) to go; **el trabajo va muy bien** work is going very well; **¿cómo te va?** how are things going?; **me va muy bien** I'm getting on very well; **le fue fatal** it went awfully badly for him

4 (*funcionar*): **el coche no va muy bien** the car isn't running very well

5: **te va estupendamente ese color** that colour suits you fantastically well

6 (*locuciones*): **¿vino? - ¡que va!** did he come? - of course not!; **vamos, no llores** come on, don't cry; **¡vaya coche!** what a car!, that's some car!

7: **no vaya a ser: tienes que correr, no vaya a ser que pierdas el tren** you'll have to run so as not to miss the train

8 (+*pp*): **iba vestido muy bien** he was very well dressed

9: **no me** *etc* **va ni me viene** I *etc* don't care

♦ *vb aux* **1**: **~ a: voy/iba a hacerlo hoy** I am/was going to do it today

2 (+*gerundio*): **iba anocheciendo** it was getting dark; **todo se me iba aclarando** everything was gradually becoming clearer to me

3 (+*pp* = *pasivo*): **van vendidos 300 ejemplares** 300 copies have been sold so far

♦ **~se** *vr* **1**: **¿por dónde se va al zoológico?** which is the way to the zoo?

2 (*marcharse*) to leave; **ya se habrán ido** they must already have left *o* gone

ira ['ira] *nf* anger, rage

Irak [i'rak] *nm* = **Iraq**

Irán [i'ran] *nm* Iran; **iraní** *adj, nm/f*

Iranian

Iraq [i'rak] nm Iraq; **iraquí** adj, nm/f Iraqui

iris ['iris] nm inv (tb: **arco ~**) rainbow; (ANAT) iris

Irlanda [ir'landa] nf Ireland; **irlandés, esa** adj Irish ♦ nm/f Irishman/woman; **los irlandeses** the Irish

ironía [iro'nia] nf irony; **irónico, a** adj ironic(al)

IRPF ['i 'erre 'pe 'efe] nm abr (=Impuesto sobre la Renta de las Personas Físicas) (personal) income tax

irreal [irre'al] adj unreal

irrecuperable [irrekupe'raßle] adj irrecoverable, irretrievable

irreflexión [irreflek'sjon] nf thoughtlessness

irregular [irrexu'lar] adj (gen) irregular; (situación) abnormal

irremediable [irreme'ðjaßle] adj irremediable; (vicio) incurable

irreparable [irrepa'raßle] adj (daños) irreparable; (pérdida) irrecoverable

irresoluto, a [irreso'luto, a] adj irresolute, hesitant

irrespetuoso, a [irrespe'twoso, a] adj disrespectful

irresponsable [irrespon'saßle] adj irresponsible

irreversible [irreßer'sible] adj irreversible

irrigar [irri'var] vt to irrigate

irrisorio, a [irri'sorjo, a] adj derisory, ridiculous

irritar [irri'tar] vt to irritate, annoy

irrupción [irrup'θjon] nf irruption; (invasión) invasion

isla ['isla] nf island

islandés, esa [islan'des, esa] adj Icelandic ♦ nm/f Icelander

Islandia [is'landja] nf Iceland

isleño, a [is'leɲo, a] adj island cpd ♦ nm/f islander

Israel [isra'el] nm Israel; **israelí** adj, nm/f Israeli

istmo ['istmo] nm isthmus

Italia [i'talja] nf Italy; **italiano, a** adj,

nm/f Italian

itinerario [itine'rarjo] nm itinerary, route

IVA ['ißa] nm abr (= impuesto sobre el valor añadido) VAT

izar [i'θar] vt to hoist

izdo, a abr (= izquierdo, a) l.

izquierda [iθ'kjerda] nf left; (POL) left (wing); **a la ~** (estar) on the left; (torcer etc) (to the) left

izquierdista [iθkjer'ðista] nm/f left-winger, leftist

izquierdo, a [iθ'kjerðo, a] adj left

J, j

jabalí [xaßa'li] nm wild boar

jabalina [xaßa'lina] nf javelin

jabón [xa'ßon] nm soap; **jabonar** vt to soap

jaca ['xaka] nf pony

jacinto [xa'θinto] nm hyacinth

jactarse [xak'tarse] vr to boast, brag

jadear [xaðe'ar] vi to pant, gasp for breath; **jadeo** nm panting, gasping

jaguar [xa'ɣwar] nm jaguar

jalea [xa'lea] nf jelly

jaleo [xa'leo] nm racket, uproar; **armar un ~** to kick up a racket

jalón [xa'lon] (AM) nm tug

jamás [xa'mas] adv never

jamón [xa'mon] nm ham; **~ dulce, ~ de York** cooked ham; **~ serrano** cured ham

Japón [xa'pon] nm: **el ~** Japan; **japonés, esa** adj, nm/f Japanese ♦ nm (LING) Japanese

jaque ['xake] nm: **~ mate** checkmate

jaqueca [xa'keka] nf (very bad) headache, migraine

jarabe [xa'raße] nm syrup

jarcia ['xarθja] nf (NAUT) ropes pl, rigging

jardín [xar'ðin] nm garden; **~ de infancia** (ESP) o **de niños** (AM) nursery (school); **jardinería** nf gardening; **jardinero, a** nm/f gardener

jarra ['xarra] nf jar; (jarro) jug

jarro ['xarro] nm jug

jarrón [xa'rron] nm vase
jaula ['xaula] nf cage
jauría [xau'ria] nf pack of hounds
jazmín [xaθ'min] nm jasmine
J. C. abr (= Jesucristo) J.C.
jefa ['xefa] nf ver **jefe**
jefatura [xefa'tura] nf: ~ **de policía** police headquarters sg
jefe, a ['xefe, a] nm/f (gen) chief; head; (patrón) boss; ~ **de cocina** chef; ~ **de estación** stationmaster; ~ **de estado** head of state
jengibre [xen'xiβre] nm ginger
jeque ['xeke] nm sheik
jerarquía [xerar'kia] nf (orden) hierarchy; (rango) rank; **jerárquico, a** adj hierarchic(al)
jerez [xe'reθ] nm sherry
jerga ['xerxa] nf jargon
jeringa [xe'ringa] nf syringe; (AM) annoyance, bother; ~ **de engrase** grease gun; **jeringar** vt (fam) to annoy, bother; **jeringuilla** nf syringe
jeroglífico [xero'ɣlifiko] nm hieroglyphic
jersey [xer'sei] (pl ~s) nm jersey, pullover, jumper
Jerusalén [xerusa'len] n Jerusalem
Jesucristo [xesu'kristo] nm Jesus Christ
jesuita [xe'swita] adj, nm Jesuit
Jesús [xe'sus] nm Jesus; ¡~! good heavens!; (al estornudar) bless you!
jinete, a [xi'nete, a] nm/f horseman/woman, rider
jipijapa [xipi'xapa] (AM) nm straw hat
jirafa [xi'rafa] nf giraffe
jirón [xi'ron] nm rag, shred
jocoso, a [xo'koso, a] adj humorous, jocular
joder [xo'ðer] (fam!) vt, vi to fuck(!)
jofaina [xo'faina] nf washbasin
jornada [xor'naða] nf (viaje de un día) day's journey; (camino o viaje entero) journey; (día de trabajo) working day
jornal [xor'nal] nm (day's) wage; **~ero** nm (day) labourer
joroba [xo'roβa] nf hump, hunched back; **~do, a** adj hunchbacked ♦ nm/f hunchback

jota ['xota] nf (the letter) J; (danza) Aragonese dance; **no saber ni** ~ to have no idea
joven ['xoβen] (pl **jóvenes**) adj young ♦ nm young man, youth ♦ nf young woman, girl
jovial [xo'βjal] adj cheerful, jolly
joya ['xoja] nf jewel, gem; (fig: persona) gem; **joyería** nf (joyas) jewellery; (tienda) jeweller's (shop); **joyero** nm (persona) jeweller; (caja) jewel case
juanete [xwa'nete] nm (del pie) bunion
jubilación [xuβila'θjon] nf (retiro) retirement
jubilado, a [xuβi'laðo, a] adj retired ♦ nm/f pensioner (BRIT), senior citizen
jubilar [xuβi'lar] vt to pension off, retire; (fam) to discard; **~se** vr to retire
júbilo ['xuβilo] nm joy, rejoicing; **jubiloso, a** adj jubilant
judía [xu'ðia] nf (CULIN) bean; ~ **verde** French bean; ver tb **judío**
judicial [xuði'θjal] adj judicial
judío, a [xu'ðio, a] adj Jewish ♦ nm/f Jew(ess)
judo ['juðo] nm judo
juego etc ['xweɣo] vb ver **jugar** ♦ nm (gen) play; (pasatiempo, partido) game; (en casino) gambling; (conjunto) set; **fuera de** ~ (DEPORTE) offside; (: pelota) out of play; **J~s Olímpicos** Olympic Games
juerga ['xwerɣa] nf binge; (fiesta) party; **ir de** ~ to go out on a binge
jueves ['xweβes] nm inv Thursday
juez [xweθ] nm/f judge; ~ **de línea** linesman; ~ **de salida** starter
jugada [xu'ɣaða] nf play; **buena** ~ good move/shot/stroke etc
jugador, a [xuɣa'ðor, a] nm/f player; (en casino) gambler
jugar [xu'ɣar] vt, vi to play; (en casino) to gamble; (apostar) to bet; ~ **al fútbol** to play football
juglar [xu'ɣlar] nm minstrel
jugo ['xuɣo] nm (BOT) juice; (fig) essence, substance; ~ **de fruta** (AM) fruit juice;

~so, a adj juicy; (fig) substantial, important

iguete [xu'xete] nm toy; ~ar vi to play; ~ría nf toyshop

iguetón, ona [xuxe'ton, ona] adj playful

iicio ['xwiθjo] nm judgement; (razón) sanity, reason; (opinión) opinion; ~so, a adj wise, sensible

ilio ['xuljo] nm July

inco ['xunko] nm rush, reed

ingla ['xungla] nf jungle

inio ['xunjo] nm June

inta ['xunta] nf (asamblea) meeting, assembly; (comité, consejo) board, council, committee; (TEC) joint

intar [xun'tar] vt to join, unite; (maquinaria) to assemble, put together; (dinero) to collect; ~se vr to join, meet; (reunirse: personas) to meet, assemble; (arrimarse) to approach, draw closer; ~se con uno to join sb

into, a ['xunto, a] adj joined; (unido) united; (anexo) near, close; (contiguo, próximo) next, adjacent ♦ adv: todo ~ all at once; ~s together; ~ a near (to), next to

urado [xu'raðo] nm (JUR: individuo) juror; (: grupo) jury; (de concurso: grupo) panel (of judges); (: individuo) member of a panel

uramento [xura'mento] nm oath; (maldición) oath, curse; prestar ~ to take the oath; tomar ~ a to swear in, administer the oath to

urar [xu'rar] vt, vi to swear; ~ en falso to commit perjury; jurárselas a uno to have it in for sb

urídico, a [xu'riðiko, a] adj legal

urisdicción [xurisðik'θjon] nf (poder, autoridad) jurisdiction; (territorio) district

urisprudencia [xurispru'ðenθja] nf jurisprudence

urista [xu'rista] nm/f jurist

ustamente [xusta'mente] adv justly, fairly; (precisamente) just, exactly

usticia [xus'tiθja] nf justice; (equidad) fairness, justice; justiciero, a adj just

justificación [xustifika'θjon] nf justification; justificar vt to justify

justo, a ['xusto, a] adj (equitativo) just, fair, right; (preciso) exact, correct; (ajustado) tight ♦ adv (precisamente) exactly, precisely; (AM: apenas a tiempo) just in time

juvenil [xuße'nil] adj youthful

juventud [xußen'tuð] nf (adolescencia) youth; (jóvenes) young people pl

juzgado [xuθ'xaðo] nm tribunal; (JUR) court

juzgar [xuθ'xar] vt to judge; a ~ por ... to judge by ..., judging by ...

K, k

kg abr (= kilogramo) kg

kilo ['kilo] nm kilo ♦ pref: ~gramo nm kilogramme; ~metraje nm distance in kilometres, ≈ mileage; kilómetro nm kilometre; ~vatio nm kilowatt

kiosco ['kjosko] nm = quiosco

km abr (= kilómetro) km

Kosovo [ko'soßo] nm Kosovo

kv abr (= kilovatio) kw

L, l

l abr (= litro) l

la [la] art def the ♦ pron her; (Ud.) you; (cosa) it ♦ nm (MUS) la; ~ del sombrero rojo the girl in the red hat; tb ver el

laberinto [laße'rinto] nm labyrinth

labia ['laßja] nf fluency; (pey) glib tongue

labio ['laßjo] nm lip

labor [la'ßor] nf labour; (AGR) farm work; (tarea) job, task; (COSTURA) needlework; ~able adj (AGR) workable; día ~able working day; ~al adj (accidente) at work; (jornada) working

laboratorio [laßora'torjo] nm laboratory

laborioso, a [laßo'rjoso, a] adj (persona) hard-working; (trabajo) tough

laborista [laßo'rista] adj: Partido L~

Labour Party

labrado, a [la'ßraðo, a] *adj* worked; (*madera*) carved; (*metal*) wrought

labrador, a [laßra'ðor, a] *adj* farming *cpd* ♦ *nm/f* farmer

labranza [la'ßranθa] *nf* (*AGR*) cultivation

labrar [la'ßrar] *vt* (*gen*) to work; (*madera etc*) to carve; (*fig*) to cause, bring about

labriego, a [la'ßrjeɣo, a] *nm/f* peasant

laca ['laka] *nf* lacquer

lacayo [la'kajo] *nm* lackey

lacio, a ['laθjo, a] *adj* (*pelo*) lank, straight

lacón [la'kon] *nm* shoulder of pork

lacónico, a [la'koniko, a] *adj* laconic

lacra ['lakra] *nf* (*fig*) blot; **lacrar** *vt* (*cerrar*) to seal (with sealing wax); **lacre** *nm* sealing wax

lactancia [lak'tanθja] *nf* lactation

lactar [lak'tar] *vt, vi* to suckle

lácteo, a ['lakteo, a] *adj*: **productos ~s** dairy products

ladear [laðe'ar] *vt* to tip, tilt ♦ *vi* to tilt; **~se** *vr* to lean

ladera [la'ðera] *nf* slope

lado ['laðo] *nm* (*gen*) side; (*fig*) protection; (*MIL*) flank; **al ~ de** beside; **poner de ~ to** put on its side; **poner a un ~ to** put aside; **por todos ~s** on all sides, all round (*BRIT*)

ladrar [la'ðrar] *vi* to bark; **ladrido** *nm* bark, barking

ladrillo [la'ðriʎo] *nm* (*gen*) brick; (*azulejo*) tile

ladrón, ona [la'ðron, ona] *nm/f* thief

lagartija [laɣar'tixa] *nf* (*ZOOL*) (small) lizard

lagarto [la'ɣarto] *nm* (*ZOOL*) lizard

lago ['laɣo] *nm* lake

lágrima ['laɣrima] *nf* tear

laguna [la'ɣuna] *nf* (*lago*) lagoon; (*hueco*) gap

laico, a ['laiko, a] *adj* lay

lamentable [lamen'taßle] *adj* lamentable, regrettable; (*miserable*) pitiful

lamentar [lamen'tar] *vt* (*sentir*) to regret; (*deplorar*) to lament; **lo lamento mucho** I'm very sorry; **~se** *vr* to lament;

lamento *nm* lament

lamer [la'mer] *vt* to lick

lámina ['lamina] *nf* (*plancha delgada*) sheet; (*para estampar, estampa*) plate

lámpara ['lampara] *nf* lamp; **~ de alcohol/gas** spirit/gas lamp; **~ de pie** standard lamp

lamparón [lampa'ron] *nm* grease spot

lana ['lana] *nf* wool

lancha ['lantʃa] *nf* launch; **~ de pesca** fishing boat; **~ salvavidas/torpedera** lifeboat/torpedo boat

langosta [lan'gosta] *nf* (*crustáceo*) lobster; (: *de río*) crayfish; **langostino** *nm* Dublin Bay prawn

languidecer [langiðe'θer] *vi* to languish; **languidez** *nf* languor; **lánguido, a** *adj* (*gen*) languid; (*sin energía*) listless

lanilla [la'niʎa] *nf* nap

lanza ['lanθa] *nf* (*arma*) lance, spear

lanzamiento [lanθa'mjento] *nm* (*gen*) throwing; (*NAUT, COM*) launch, launching; **~ de peso** putting the shot

lanzar [lan'θar] *vt* (*gen*) to throw; (*DEPORTE: pelota*) to bowl; (*NAUT, COM*) to launch; (*JUR*) to evict; **~se** *vr* to throw o.s.

lapa ['lapa] *nf* limpet

lapicero [lapi'θero] *nm* pencil; (*AM: bolígrafo*) Biro ®

lápida ['lapiða] *nf* stone; **~ mortuoria** headstone; **~ conmemorativa** memorial stone; **lapidario, a** *adj, nm* lapidary

lápiz ['lapiθ] *nm* pencil; **~ de color** coloured pencil; **~ de labios** lipstick

lapón, ona [la'pon, ona] *nm/f* Laplander, Lapp

lapso ['lapso] *nm* (*de tiempo*) interval; (*error*) error

lapsus ['lapsus] *nm inv* error, mistake

largar [lar'ɣar] *vt* (*soltar*) to release; (*aflojar*) to loosen; (*lanzar*) to launch; (*fam*) to let fly; (*velas*) to unfurl; (*AM*) to throw; **~se** *vr* (*fam*) to beat it; **~se a** (*AM*) to start to

largo, a ['larɣo, a] *adj* (*longitud*) long; (*tiempo*) lengthy; (*fig*) generous ♦ *nm* length; (*MUS*) largo; **dos años ~s** two long years; **tiene 9 metros de ~** it is 9 metres long; **a lo ~ de** along; (*tiempo*) all through, throughout; **~metraje** *nm* feature film

laringe [la'rinxe] *nf* larynx; **laringitis** *nf* laryngitis

larva ['larßa] *nf* larva

las [las] *art def* the ♦ *pron* them; **~ que cantan** the ones/women/girls who sing; *tb ver* **el**

lascivo, a [las'θißo, a] *adj* lewd

láser ['laser] *nm* laser

lástima ['lastima] *nf* (*pena*) pity; **dar ~** to be pitiful; **es una ~ que** it's a pity that; **¡qué ~!** what a pity!; **ella está hecha una ~** she looks pitiful

lastimar [lasti'mar] *vt* (*herir*) to wound; (*ofender*) to offend; **~se** *vr* to hurt o.s.; **lastimero, a** *adj* pitiful, pathetic

lastre ['lastre] *nm* (*TEC, NAUT*) ballast; (*fig*) dead weight

lata ['lata] *nf* (*metal*) tin; (*caja*) tin (*BRIT*), can; (*fam*) nuisance; **en ~** tinned (*BRIT*), canned; **dar (la) ~** to be a nuisance

latente [la'tente] *adj* latent

lateral [late'ral] *adj* side *cpd*, lateral ♦ *nm* (*TEATRO*) wings

latido [la'tiðo] *nm* (*del corazón*) beat

latifundio [lati'fundjo] *nm* large estate; **latifundista** *nm/f* owner of a large estate

latigazo [lati'yaθo] *nm* (*golpe*) lash; (*sonido*) crack

látigo ['latiyo] *nm* whip

latín [la'tin] *nm* Latin

latino, a [la'tino, a] *adj* Latin; **~americano, a** *adj, nm/f* Latin-American

latir [la'tir] *vi* (*corazón, pulso*) to beat

latitud [lati'tuð] *nf* (*GEO*) latitude

latón [la'ton] *nm* brass

latoso, a [la'toso, a] *adj* (*molesto*) annoying; (*aburrido*) boring

laúd [la'uð] *nm* lute

laurel [lau'rel] *nm* (*BOT*) laurel; (*CULIN*) bay

lava ['laßa] *nf* lava

lavabo [la'ßaßo] *nm* (*pila*) washbasin; (*tb:*

~s) toilet

lavado [la'ßaðo] *nm* washing; (*de ropa*) laundry; (*ARTE*) wash; **~ de cerebro** brainwashing; **~ en seco** dry-cleaning

lavadora [laßa'ðora] *nf* washing machine

lavanda [la'ßanda] *nf* lavender

lavandería [laßande'ria] *nf* laundry; (*automática*) launderette

lavaplatos [laßa'platos] *nm inv* dishwasher

lavar [la'ßar] *vt* to wash; (*borrar*) to wipe away; **~se** *vr* to wash o.s.; **~se las manos** to wash one's hands; **~se los dientes** to brush one's teeth; **~ y marcar** (*pelo*) to shampoo and set; **~ en seco** to dry-clean; **~ los platos** to wash the dishes

lavavajillas [laßaßa'xiʎas] *nm inv* dishwasher

laxante [lak'sante] *nm* laxative

lazada [la'θaða] *nf* bow

lazarillo [laθa'riʎo] *nm*: **perro ~** guide dog

lazo ['laθo] *nm* knot; (*lazada*) bow; (*para animales*) lasso; (*trampa*) snare; (*vínculo*) tie

le [le] *pron* (*directo*) him (*o* her); (: *usted*) you; (*indirecto*) to him (*o* her *o* it); (: *usted*) to you

leal [le'al] *adj* loyal; **~tad** *nf* loyalty

lección [lek'θjon] *nf* lesson

leche ['letʃe] *nf* milk; **tiene mala ~** (*fam!*) he's a swine (*!*); **~ condensada/en polvo** condensed/powdered milk; **~ desnatada** skimmed milk; **~ra** *nf* (*vendedora*) milkmaid; (*recipiente*) (milk) churn; (*AM*) cow; **~ro, a** *adj* dairy

lecho ['letʃo] *nm* (*cama, de río*) bed; (*GEO*) layer

lechón [le'tʃon] *nm* sucking (*BRIT*) *o* suckling (*US*) pig

lechoso, a [le'tʃoso, a] *adj* milky

lechuga [le'tʃuɣa] *nf* lettuce

lechuza [le'tʃuθa] *nf* owl

lector, a [lek'tor, a] *nm/f* reader ♦ *nm*: **~ de discos compactos** CD player

lectura [lek'tura] *nf* reading

leer [le'er] *vt* to read

legado [le'ɣaðo] *nm* (*don*) bequest;

(herencia) legacy; *(enviado)* legate

legajo [le'xaxo] *nm* file

legal [le'val] *adj (gen)* legal; *(persona)* trustworthy; **~idad** *nf* legality

legalizar [levali'θar] *vt* to legalize; *(documento)* to authenticate

legaña [le'vaɲa] *nf* sleep *(in eyes)*

legar [le'var] *vt* to bequeath, leave

legendario, a [lexen'darjo, a] *adj* legendary

legión [le'xjon] *nf* legion; **legionario, a** *adj* legionary ♦ *nm* legionnaire

legislación [lexisla'θjon] *nf* legislation

legislar [lexis'lar] *vi* to legislate

legislatura [lexisla'tura] *nf (POL)* period of office

legitimar [lexiti'mar] *vt* to legitimize; **legítimo, a** *adj (genuino)* authentic; *(legal)* legitimate

lego, a ['levo, a] *adj (REL)* secular; *(ignorante)* ignorant ♦ *nm* layman

legua ['lewwa] *nf* league

legumbres [le'vumbres] *nfpl* pulses

leído, a [le'iðo, a] *adj* well-read

lejanía [lexa'nia] *nf* distance; **lejano, a** *adj* far-off; *(en el tiempo)* distant; *(fig)* remote

lejía [le'xia] *nf* bleach

lejos ['lexos] *adv* far, far away; **a lo ~** in the distance; **de** *o* **desde ~** from afar; **~ de** far from

lelo, a ['lelo, a] *adj* silly ♦ *nm/f* idiot

lema ['lema] *nm* motto; *(POL)* slogan

lencería [lenθe'ria] *nf* linen, drapery

lengua ['lengwa] *nf* tongue; *(LING)* language; **morderse la ~** to hold one's tongue

lenguado [len'gwaðo] *nm* sole

lenguaje [len'gwaxe] *nm* language

lengüeta [len'gweta] *nf (ANAT)* epiglottis; *(zapatos)* tongue, *(MUS)* reed

lente ['lente] *nf* lens; *(lupa)* magnifying glass; **~s** *nfpl (gafas)* glasses; **~s de contacto** contact lenses

lenteja [len'texa] *nf* lentil; **lentejuela** *nf* sequin

lentilla [len'tiʎa] *nf* contact lens

lentitud [lenti'tuð] *nf* slowness; **con ~** slowly

lento, a ['lento, a] *adj* slow

leña ['leɲa] *nf* firewood; **~dor, a** *nm/f* woodcutter

leño ['leɲo] *nm (trozo de árbol)* log; *(madera)* timber; *(fig)* blockhead

Leo ['leo] *nm* Leo

león [le'on] *nm* lion; **~ marino** sea lion

leopardo [leo'parðo] *nm* leopard

leotardos [leo'tarðos] *nmpl* tights

lepra ['lepra] *nf* leprosy; **leproso, a** *nm/f* leper

lerdo, a ['lerðo, a] *adj (lento)* slow; *(patoso)* clumsy

les [les] *pron (directo)* them; *(: ustedes)* you; *(indirecto)* to them; *(: ustedes)* to you

lesbiana [les'ßjana] *adj, nf* lesbian

lesión [le'sjon] *nf* wound, lesion; *(DEPORTE)* injury; **lesionado, a** *adj* injured ♦ *nm/f* injured person

letal [le'tal] *adj* lethal

letanía [leta'nia] *nf* litany

letargo [le'tarvo] *nm* lethargy

letra ['letra] *nf* letter; *(escritura)* handwriting; *(MUS)* lyrics *pl*; **~ de cambio** bill of exchange; **~ de imprenta** print; **~do, a** *adj* learned ♦ *nm/f* lawyer; **letrero** *nm (cartel)* sign; *(etiqueta)* label

letrina [le'trina] *nf* latrine

leucemia [leu'θemja] *nf* leukaemia

levadizo [leßa'ðiθo] *adj*: **puente ~** drawbridge

levadura [leßa'ðura] *nf (para el pan)* yeast; *(de la cerveza)* brewer's yeast

levantamiento [leßanta'mjento] *nm* raising, lifting; *(rebelión)* revolt, uprising; **~ de pesos** weight-lifting

levantar [leßan'tar] *vt (gen)* to raise; *(del suelo)* to pick up; *(hacia arriba)* to lift (up); *(plan)* to make, draw up; *(mesa)* to clear; *(campamento)* to strike; *(fig)* to cheer up, hearten; **~se** *vr* to get up; *(enderezarse)* to straighten up; *(rebelarse)* to rebel; **~ el ánimo** to cheer up

levante [le'ßante] *nm* east coast; **el L~** *region of Spain extending from Castellón* to Murcia

levar [le'ßar] *vt* to weigh

leve ['leße] *adj* light; (*fig*) trivial; **~dad** *nf* lightness

levita [le'ßita] *nf* frock coat

léxico ['leksiko] *nm* (*vocabulario*) vocabulary

ley [lei] *nf* (*gen*) law; (*metal*) standard

leyenda [le'jenda] *nf* legend

leyó *etc vb ver* **leer**

liar [li'ar] *vt* to tie (up); (*unir*) to bind; (*envolver*) to wrap (up); (*enredar*) to confuse; (*cigarrillo*) to roll; **~se** *vr* (*fam*) to get involved; **~se a palos** to get involved in a fight

Líbano ['lißano] *nm*: **el ~** (the) Lebanon

libelo [li'ßelo] *nm* satire, lampoon

libélula [li'ßelula] *nf* dragonfly

liberación [lißera'θjon] *nf* liberation; (*de la cárcel*) release

liberal [liße'ral] *adj*, *nm/f* liberal; **~idad** *nf* liberality, generosity

liberar [liße'rar] *vt* to liberate

libertad [lißer'tað] *nf* liberty, freedom; **~ de culto/de prensa/de comercio** freedom of worship/of the press/of trade; **~ condicional** probation; **~ bajo palabra** parole; **~ bajo fianza** bail

libertar [lißer'tar] *vt* (*preso*) to set free; (*de una obligación*) to release; (*eximir*) to exempt

libertino, a [lißer'tino, a] *adj* permissive ♦ *nm/f* permissive person

libra ['lißra] *nf* pound; (*ASTROLOGÍA*): **L~** Libra; **~ esterlina** pound sterling

librar [li'ßrar] *vt* (*de peligro*) to save; (*batalla*) to wage, fight; (*de impuestos*) to exempt; (*cheque*) to make out; (*JUR*) to exempt; **~se** *vr*: **~se de** to escape from, free o.s. from

libre ['lißre] *adj* free; (*lugar*) unoccupied; (*asiento*) vacant; (*de deudas*) free of debts; **~ de impuestos** free of tax; **tiro ~** free kick; **los 100 metros ~** the 100 metres free-style (race); **al aire ~** in the open air

librería [lißre'ria] *nf* (*tienda*) bookshop; **librero, a** *nm/f* bookseller

libreta [li'ßreta] *nf* notebook; **~ de ahorros** savings book

libro ['lißro] *nm* book; **~ de bolsillo** paperback; **~ de caja** cashbook; **~ de cheques** chequebook (*BRIT*), checkbook (*US*); **~ de texto** textbook

Lic. *abr* = **licenciado, a**

licencia [li'θenθja] *nf* (*gen*) licence; (*permiso*) permission; **~ por enfermedad** sick leave; **~ de caza** game licence; **~do, a** *adj* licensed ♦ *nm/f* graduate; **licenciar** *vt* (*empleado*) to dismiss; (*permitir*) to permit, allow; (*soldado*) to discharge; (*estudiante*) to confer a degree upon; **licenciarse** *vr*: **licenciarse en letras** to graduate in arts

licencioso, a [liθen'θjoso, a] *adj* licentious

licitar [liθi'tar] *vt* to bid for; (*AM*) to sell by auction

lícito, a ['liθito, a] *adj* (*legal*) lawful; (*justo*) fair, just; (*permisible*) permissible

licor [li'kor] *nm* spirits *pl* (*BRIT*), liquor (*US*); (*de frutas etc*) liqueur

licuadora [likwa'ðora] *nf* blender

licuar [li'kwar] *vt* to liquidize

líder ['liðer] *nm/f* leader; **liderato** *nm* leadership; **liderazgo** *nm* leadership

lidia ['liðja] *nf* bullfighting; (*una ~*) bullfight; **toros de ~** fighting bulls; **lidiar** *vt*, *vi* to fight

liebre ['ljeßre] *nf* hare

lienzo ['ljenθo] *nm* linen; (*ARTE*) canvas; (*ARQ*) wall

liga ['liɣa] *nf* (*de medias*) garter, suspender; (*AM: gomita*) rubber band; (*confederación*) league

ligadura [liɣa'ðura] *nf* bond, tie; (*MED, MUS*) ligature

ligamento [liɣa'mento] *nm* ligament

ligar [li'ɣar] *vt* (*atar*) to tie; (*unir*) to join; (*MED*) to bind up; (*MUS*) to slur ♦ *vi* to mix, blend; (*fam*): (**él**) **liga mucho** he pulls a lot of women; **~se** *vr* to commit o.s.

ligereza [lixe're θa] *nf* lightness; (*rapidez*) swiftness; (*agilidad*) agility; (*superficialidad*) flippancy

ligero, a [li'xero, a] *adj* (*de peso*) light; (*tela*) thin; (*rápido*) swift, quick; (*ágil*) agile, nimble; (*de importancia*) slight; (*de carácter*) flippant, superficial ♦ *adv*: **a la ligera** superficially

liguero [li'vero] *nm* suspender (*BRIT*) o garter (*US*) belt

lija ['lixa] *nf* (*ZOOL*) dogfish; (*tb*: **papel de ~**) sandpaper

lila ['lila] *nf* lilac

lima ['lima] *nf* file; (*BOT*) lime; **~ de uñas** nailfile; **limar** *vt* to file

limitación [limita'θjon] *nf* limitation, limit; **~ de velocidad** speed limit

limitar [limi'tar] *vt* to limit; (*reducir*) to reduce, cut down ♦ *vi*: **~ con** to border on; **~se** *vr*: **~se a** to limit o.s. to

límite ['limite] *nm* (*gen*) limit; (*fin*) end; (*frontera*) border; **~ de velocidad** speed limit

limítrofe [li'mitrofe] *adj* neighbouring

limón [li'mon] *nm* lemon ♦ *adj*: **amarillo ~** lemon-yellow; **limonada** *nf* lemonade

limosna [li'mosna] *nf* alms *pl*; **vivir de ~** to live on charity

limpiaparabrisas [limpjapara'ßrisas] *nm inv* windscreen (*BRIT*) o windshield (*US*) wiper

limpiar [lim'pjar] *vt* to clean; (*con trapo*) to wipe; (*quitar*) to wipe away; (*zapatos*) to shine, polish; (*fig*) to clean up

limpieza [lim'pjeθa] *nf* (*estado*) cleanliness; (*acto*) cleaning; (: *de las calles*) cleansing; (: *de zapatos*) polishing; (*habilidad*) skill; (*fig*: *POLICÍA*) clean-up; (*pureza*) purity; (*MIL*): **operación de ~** mopping-up operation; **~ en seco** dry cleaning

limpio, a ['limpjo, a] *adj* clean; (*moralmente*) pure; (*COM*) clear, net; (*fam*) honest ♦ *adv*: **jugar ~** to play fair; **pasar a** (*ESP*) **o en** (*AM*) **~** to make a clean copy

linaje [li'naxe] *nm* lineage, family

lince ['linθe] *nm* lynx

linchar [lin'tʃar] *vt* to lynch

lindar [lin'dar] *vi* to adjoin; **~ con** to border on; **linde** *nm* o *f* boundary; **lindero, a** *adj* adjoining ♦ *nm* boundary

lindo, a ['lindo, a] *adj* pretty, lovely ♦ *adv*: **nos divertimos de lo ~** we had a marvellous time; **canta muy ~** (*AM*) he sings beautifully

línea ['linea] *nf* (*gen*) line; **en ~** (*INFORM*) on line; **~ aérea** airline; **~ de meta** goal line; (*de carrera*) finishing line; **~ recta** straight line

lingote [lin'gote] *nm* ingot

lingüista [lin'gwista] *nm/f* linguist; **lingüística** *nf* linguistics *sg*

lino ['lino] *nm* linen; (*BOT*) flax

linóleo [li'noleo] *nm* lino, linoleum

linterna [lin'terna] *nf* torch (*BRIT*), flashlight (*US*)

lío ['lio] *nm* bundle; (*fam*) fuss; (*desorden*) muddle, mess; **armar un ~** to make a fuss

liquen ['liken] *nm* lichen

liquidación [likiða'θjon] *nf* liquidation; **venta de ~** clearance sale

liquidar [liki'ðar] *vt* (*mercancías*) to liquidate; (*deudas*) to pay off; (*empresa*) to wind up

líquido, a ['likiðo, a] *adj* liquid; (*ganancia*) net ♦ *nm* liquid; **~ imponible** net taxable income

lira ['lira] *nf* (*MUS*) lyre; (*moneda*) lira

lírico, a ['liriko, a] *adj* lyrical

lirio ['lirjo] *nm* (*BOT*) iris

lirón [li'ron] *nm* (*ZOOL*) dormouse; (*fig*) sleepyhead

Lisboa [lis'ßoa] *n* Lisbon

lisiado, a [li'sjaðo, a] *adj* injured ♦ *nm/f* cripple

lisiar [li'sjar] *vt* to maim; **~se** *vr* to injure o.s.

liso, a ['liso, a] *adj* (*terreno*) flat; (*cabello*) straight; (*superficie*) even; (*tela*) plain

lisonja [li'sonxa] *nf* flattery

lista ['lista] *nf* list; (*de alumnos*) school register; (*de libros*) catalogue; (*de platos*) menu; (*de precios*) price list; **pasar ~** to call the roll; **~ de correos** poste restante; **~ de espera** waiting list; **tela de ~s** striped material; **listín** *nm*: **~ (telefónico)**

telephone directory

listo, a ['listo, a] *adj (perspicaz)* smart, clever; *(preparado)* ready

listón [lis'ton] *nm (de madera, metal)* strip

litera [li'tera] *nf (en barco, tren)* berth; *(en dormitorio)* bunk, bunk bed

literal [lite'ral] *adj* literal

literario, a [lite'rarjo, a] *adj* literary

literato, a [lite'rato, a] *adj* literary ♦ *nm/f* writer

literatura [litera'tura] *nf* literature

litigar [liti'var] *vt* to fight ♦ *vi (JUR)* to go to law; *(fig)* to dispute, argue

litigio [li'tixjo] *nm (JUR)* lawsuit; *(fig)*: **en ~ con** in dispute with

litografía [litovra'fia] *nf* lithography; *(una ~)* lithograph

litoral [lito'ral] *adj* coastal ♦ *nm* coast, seaboard

litro ['litro] *nm* litre

liviano, a [li'ßjano, a] *adj (cosa, objeto)* trivial

lívido, a ['lißiðo, a] *adj* livid

llaga ['ʎava] *nf* wound

llama ['ʎama] *nf* flame; *(ZOOL)* llama

llamada [ʎa'maða] *nf* call; **~ al orden** call to order; **~ a pie de página** reference note

llamamiento [ʎama'mjento] *nm* call

llamar [ʎa'mar] *vt* to call; *(atención)* to attract ♦ *vi (por teléfono)* to telephone; *(a la puerta)* to knock *(o* ring); *(por señas)* to beckon; *(MIL)* to call up; **~se** *vr* to be called, be named; **¿cómo se llama usted?** what's your name?

llamarada [ʎama'raða] *nf (llamas)* blaze; *(rubor)* flush

llamativo, a [ʎama'tißo, a] *adj* showy; *(color)* loud

llano, a ['ʎano, a] *adj (superficie)* flat; *(persona)* straightforward; *(estilo)* clear ♦ *nm* plain, flat ground

llanta ['ʎanta] *nf (wheel)* rim; *(AM)*: **~ (de goma)** tyre; *(: cámara)* inner *(tube)*

llanto ['ʎanto] *nm* weeping

llanura [ʎa'nura] *nf* plain

llave ['ʎaße] *nf* key; *(del agua)* tap;

(MECÁNICA) spanner; *(de la luz)* switch; *(MUS)* key; **~ inglesa** monkey wrench; **~ maestra** master key; **~ de contacto** *(AUTO)* ignition key; **~ de paso** stopcock; **echar la ~ a** to lock up; **~ro** *nm* keyring

llegada [ʎe'vaða] *nf* arrival

llegar [ʎe'var] *vi* to arrive; *(alcanzar)* to reach; *(bastar)* to be enough; **~se** *vr*: **~se a** to approach; **~ a** to manage to, succeed in; **~ a saber** to find out; **~ a ser** to become; **~ a las manos de** to come into the hands of

llenar [ʎe'nar] *vt* to fill; *(espacio)* to cover; *(formulario)* to fill in *o* up; *(fig)* to heap

lleno, a ['ʎeno, a] *adj* full, filled; *(repleto)* full up ♦ *nm (TEATRO)* full house; **dar de ~ contra un muro** to hit a wall head-on

llevadero, a [ʎeßa'ðero, a] *adj* bearable, tolerable

llevar [ʎe'ßar] *vt* to take; *(ropa)* to wear; *(cargar)* to carry; *(quitar)* to take away; *(en coche)* to drive; *(transportar)* to transport; *(traer: dinero)* to carry; *(conducir)* to lead; *(MAT)* to carry ♦ *vi (suj: camino etc)*: **~ a** to lead to; **~se** *vr* to carry off, take away; **llevamos dos días aquí** we have been here for two days; **él me lleva 2 años** he's 2 years older than me; *(COM)*: **~ los libros** to keep the books; **~se bien** to get on well *(together)*

llorar [ʎo'rar] *vt, vi* to cry, weep; **~ de risa** to cry with laughter

lloriquear [ʎorike'ar] *vi* to snivel, whimper

lloro ['ʎoro] *nm* crying, weeping; **llorón, ona** *adj* tearful ♦ *nm/f* cry-baby; **~so, a** *adj (gen)* weeping, tearful; *(triste)* sad, sorrowful

llover [ʎo'ßer] *vi* to rain

llovizna [ʎo'ßiθna] *nf* drizzle; **lloviznar** *vi* to drizzle

llueve *etc vb ver* **llover**

lluvia ['ʎußja] *nf* rain; **~ radioactiva** *(radioactive)* fallout; **lluvioso, a** *adj* rainy

lo [lo] *art def*: **~ bello** the beautiful, what is beautiful, that which is beautiful ♦ *pron (persona)* him; *(cosa)* it; *tb ver* **el**

loable [lo'aβle] *adj* praiseworthy; **loar** *vt* to praise

lobo ['loβo] *nm* wolf; **~ de mar** (*fig*) sea dog; **~ marino** seal

lóbrego, a ['loβreɣo, a] *adj* dark; (*fig*) gloomy

lóbulo ['loβulo] *nm* lobe

local [lo'kal] *adj* local ♦ *nm* place, site; (*oficinas*) premises *pl*; **~idad** *nf* (*barrio*) locality; (*lugar*) location; (*TEATRO*) seat, ticket; **~izar** *vt* (*ubicar*) to locate, find; (*restringir*) to localize; (*situar*) to place

loción [lo'θjon] *nf* lotion

loco, a ['loko, a] *adj* mad ♦ *nm/f* lunatic, mad person

locomotora [lokomo'tora] *nf* engine, locomotive

locuaz [lo'kwaθ] *adj* loquacious

locución [loku'θjon] *nf* expression

locura [lo'kura] *nf* madness; (*acto*) crazy act

locutor, a [loku'tor, a] *nm/f* (*RADIO*) announcer; (*comentarista*) commentator; (*TV*) newsreader

locutorio [loku'torjo] *nm* (*en telefónica*) telephone booth

lodo ['loðo] *nm* mud

lógica ['loxika] *nf* logic

lógico, a ['loxiko, a] *adj* logical

login ['loɣin] *nm* login

logística [lo'xistika] *nf* logistics *sg*

logotipo [loðo'tipo] *nm* logo

logrado, a [lo'ðraðo, a] *adj* (*interpretación, reproducción*) polished, excellent

lograr [lo'ɣrar] *vt* to achieve; (*obtener*) to get, obtain; **~ hacer** to manage to do; **~ que uno venga** to manage to get sb to come

logro ['loɣro] *nm* achievement, success

loma ['loma] *nf* hillock (*BRIT*), small hill

lombriz [lom'briθ] *nf* worm

lomo ['lomo] *nm* (*de animal*) back; (*CULIN: de cerdo*) pork loin; (*: de vaca*) rib steak; (*de libro*) spine

lona ['lona] *nf* canvas

loncha ['lontʃa] *nf* = **lonja**

lonche ['lontʃe] (*AM*) *nm* lunch; **~ría** (*AM*)

nf snack bar, diner (*US*)

Londres ['londres] *n* London

longaniza [longa'niθa] *nf* pork sausage

longitud [lonxi'tuð] *nf* length; (*GEO*) longitude; **tener 3 metros de ~** to be 3 metres long; **~ de onda** wavelength

lonja ['lonxa] *nf* slice; (*de tocino*) rasher; **~ de pescado** fish market

loro ['loro] *nm* parrot

los [los] *art def* the ♦ *pron* them; (*ustedes*) you; **mis libros y ~ tuyos** my books and yours; *tb ver* **el**

losa ['losa] *nf* stone; **~ sepulcral** gravestone

lote ['lote] *nm* portion; (*COM*) lot

lotería [lote'ria] *nf* lottery; (*juego*) lotto

Lotería
---

i Millions of pounds are spent on *lotteries* each year in Spain, two of which are state-run: the **Lotería Primitiva** and the **Lotería Nacional**, with money raised going directly to the government. One of the most famous lotteries is run by the wealthy and influential society for the blind, "la ONCE".

---

loza ['loθa] *nf* crockery

lubina [lu'βina] *nf* sea bass

lubricante [luβri'kante] *nm* lubricant

lubricar [luβri'kar] *vt* to lubricate

lucha ['lutʃa] *nf* fight, struggle; **~ de clases** class struggle; **~ libre** wrestling; **luchar** *vi* to fight

lucidez [luθi'ðeθ] *nf* lucidity

lúcido, a ['luθiðo, a] *adj* (*persona*) lucid; (*mente*) logical; (*idea*) crystal-clear

luciérnaga [lu'θjernaɣa] *nf* glow-worm

lucir [lu'θir] *vt* to illuminate, light (up); (*ostentar*) to show off ♦ *vi* (*brillar*) to shine; **~se** *vr* to make a fool of o.s.

lucro ['lukro] *nm* profit, gain

lúdico, a ['luðiko, a] *adj* (*aspecto, actividad*) play *cpd*

luego ['lweɣo] *adv* (*después*) next; (*más tarde*) later, afterwards

lugar [luˈɣar] nm place; (sitio) spot; **en ~ de** instead of; **hacer ~** to make room; **fuera de ~** out of place; **tener ~** to take place; **~ común** commonplace

lugareño, a [luɣaˈreɲo, a] adj village cpd ♦ nm/f villager

lugarteniente [luɣarteˈnjente] nm deputy

lúgubre [ˈluɣuβre] adj mournful

lujo [ˈluxo] nm luxury; (fig) profusion, abundance; **~so, a** adj luxurious

lujuria [luˈxurja] nf lust

lumbre [ˈlumbre] nf fire; (para cigarrillo) light

lumbrera [lumˈbrera] nf luminary

luminoso, a [lumiˈnoso, a] adj luminous, shining

luna [ˈluna] nf moon; (de un espejo) glass; (de gafas) lens; (fig) crescent; **~ llena/nueva** full/new moon; **estar en la ~** to have one's head in the clouds; **~ de miel** honeymoon

lunar [luˈnar] adj lunar ♦ nm (ANAT) mole; **tela de ~es** spotted material

lunes [ˈlunes] nm inv Monday

lupa [ˈlupa] nf magnifying glass

lustrar [lusˈtrar] vt (mueble) to polish; (zapatos) to shine; **lustre** nm polish; (fig) lustre; **dar lustre a** to polish; **lustroso, a** adj shining

luto [ˈluto] nm mourning; **llevar el** o **vestirse de ~** to be in mourning

Luxemburgo [luksemˈburɣo] nm Luxemburgo

luz [luθ] (pl **luces**) nf light; **dar a ~ un niño** to give birth to a child; **sacar a la ~** to bring to light; **dar** o **encender** (ESP) o **prender** (AM)/**apagar la ~** to switch the light on/off; **a todas luces** by any reckoning; **tener pocas luces** to be dim o stupid; **~ roja/verde** red/green light; **~ de freno** brake light; **luces de tráfico** traffic lights; **traje de luces** bullfighter's costume

M, m

m abr (= metro) m; (= minuto) m

macarrones [makaˈrrones] nmpl macaroni sg

macedonia [maθeˈðonja] nf: **~ de frutas** fruit salad

macerar [maθeˈrar] vt to macerate

maceta [maˈθeta] nf (de flores) pot of flowers; (para plantas) flowerpot

machacar [matʃaˈkar] vt to crush, pound ♦ vi (insistir) to go on, keep on

machete [maˈtʃete] (AM) nm machete, (large) knife

machismo [maˈtʃismo] nm male chauvinism; **machista** adj, nm sexist

macho [ˈmatʃo] adj male; (fig) virile ♦ nm male; (fig) he-man

macizo, a [maˈθiθo, a] adj (grande) massive; (fuerte, sólido) solid ♦ nm mass, chunk

madeja [maˈðexa] nf (de lana) skein, hank; (de pelo) mass, mop

madera [maˈðera] nf wood; (fig) nature, character; **una ~** a piece of wood

madero [maˈðero] nm beam

madrastra [maˈðrastra] nf stepmother

madre [ˈmaðre] adj mother cpd; (AM) tremendous ♦ nf mother; (de vino etc) dregs pl; **~ política/soltera** mother-in-law/unmarried mother

Madrid [maˈðrið] n Madrid

madriguera [maðriˈɣera] nf burrow

madrileño, a [maðriˈleɲo, a] adj of o from Madrid ♦ nm/f native of Madrid

madrina [maˈðrina] nf godmother; (ARQ) prop, shore; (TEC) brace; (de boda) bridesmaid

madrugada [maðruˈɣaða] nf early morning; (alba) dawn, daybreak

madrugador, a [maðruɣaˈðor, a] adj early-rising

madrugar [maðruˈɣar] vi to get up early; (fig) to get ahead

madurar [maðuˈrar] vt, vi (fruta) to ripen;

(fig) to mature; **madurez** *nf* ripeness; maturity; **maduro, a** *adj* ripe; mature

maestra [ma'estra] *nf ver* **maestro**

maestría [maes'tria] *nf* mastery; *(habilidad)* skill, expertise

maestro, a [ma'estro, a] *adj* masterly; *(principal)* main ♦ *nm/f* master/mistress; *(profesor)* teacher ♦ *nm (autoridad)* authority; *(MUS)* maestro; *(AM)* skilled workman; **~ albañil** master mason

magdalena [mayða'lena] *nf* fairy cake

magia ['maxja] *nf* magic; **mágico, a** *adj* magic(al) ♦ *nm/f* magician

magisterio [maxis'terjo] *nm (enseñanza)* teaching; *(profesión)* teaching profession; *(maestros)* teachers *pl*

magistrado [maxis'traðo] *nm* magistrate

magistral [maxis'tral] *adj* magisterial; *(fig)* masterly

magnánimo, a [may'nanimo, a] *adj* magnanimous

magnate [may'nate] *nm* magnate, tycoon

magnético, a [may'netiko, a] *adj* magnetic; **magnetizar** *vt* to magnetize

magnetofón [maxneto'fon] *nm* tape recorder; **magnetofónico, a** *adj*: **cinta magnetofónica** recording tape

magnetófono [mayne'tofono] *nm* = **magnetofón**

magnífico, a [may'nifiko, a] *adj* splendid, magnificent

magnitud [mayni'tuð] *nf* magnitude

mago, a ['mayo, a] *nm/f* magician; **los Reyes M~s** the Magi, the Three Wise Men

magro, a ['mayro, a] *adj (carne)* lean

maguey [ma'yei] *nm* agave

magullar [mayu'ʎar] *vt (amoratar)* to bruise; *(dañar)* to damage

mahometano, a [maome'tano, a] *adj* Mohammedan

mahonesa [mao'nesa] *nf* mayonnaise

maíz [ma'iθ] *nm* maize *(BRIT)*, corn *(US)*; sweet corn

majadero, a [maxa'ðero, a] *adj* silly, stupid

majestad [maxes'tað] *nf* majesty;

majestuoso, a *adj* majestic

majo, a ['maxo, a] *adj* nice; *(guapo)* attractive, good-looking; *(elegante)* smart

mal [mal] *adv* badly; *(equivocadamente)* wrongly ♦ *adj* = **malo** ♦ *nm* evil; *(desgracia)* misfortune; *(daño)* harm, damage; *(MED)* illness; **~ que bien** rightly or wrongly; **ir de ~ en peor** to get worse and worse

malabarismo [malaßa'rismo] *nm* juggling; **malabarista** *nm/f* juggler

malaria [ma'larja] *nf* malaria

malcriado, a [mal'krjaðo, a] *adj* spoiled

maldad [mal'dað] *nf* evil, wickedness

maldecir [malde'θir] *vt* to curse ♦ *vi*: **~ de** to speak ill of

maldición [maldi'θjon] *nf* curse

maldito, a [mal'dito, a] *adj (condenado)* damned; *(perverso)* wicked; **¡~ sea!** damn it!

maleante [male'ante] *nm/f* criminal, crook

maledicencia [maleði'θenθja] *nf* slander, scandal

maleducado, a [maleðu'kaðo, a] *adj* bad-mannered, rude

malentendido [malenten'diðo] *nm* misunderstanding

malestar [males'tar] *nm (gen)* discomfort; *(fig: inquietud)* uneasiness; *(POL)* unrest

maleta [ma'leta] *nf* case, suitcase; *(AUTO)* boot *(BRIT)*, trunk *(US)*; **hacer las ~s** to pack; **maletera** *(AM) nf*, **maletero** *nm* *(AUTO)* boot *(BRIT)*, trunk *(US)*; **maletín** *nm* small case, bag

malévolo, a [ma'leßolo, a] *adj* malicious, spiteful

maleza [ma'leθa] *nf (hierbas malas)* weeds *pl*; *(arbustos)* thicket

malgastar [malyas'tar] *vt (tiempo, dinero)* to waste; *(salud)* to ruin

malhechor, a [male'tʃor, a] *nm/f* delinquent

malhumorado, a [malumo'raðo, a] *adj* bad-tempered

malicia [ma'liθja] *nf (maldad)* wickedness; *(astucia)* slyness, guile; *(mala intención)* malice, spite; *(carácter travieso)*

mischievousness; **malicioso, a** *adj*
wicked, evil; sly, crafty; malicious, spiteful;
mischievous
maligno, a [ma'liɣno, a] *adj* evil;
(*malévolo*) malicious; (*MED*) malignant
malla ['maʎa] *nf* mesh; (*de baño*) swimsuit;
(*de ballet, gimnasia*) leotard; **~s** *nfpl*
tights; **~ de alambre** wire mesh
Mallorca [ma'ʎorka] *nf* Majorca
malo, a ['malo, a] *adj* bad; (*falso*) false
♦ *nm/f* villain; **estar ~** to be ill
malograr [malo'ɣrar] *vt* to spoil; (*plan*) to
upset; (*ocasión*) to waste; **~se** *vr* (*plan
etc*) to fail, come to grief; (*persona*) to die
before one's time
malparado, a [malpa'raðo, a] *adj*: **salir ~**
to come off badly
malpensado, a [malpen'saðo, a] *adj*
nasty
malsano, a [mal'sano, a] *adj* unhealthy
malteada [malte'aða] (*AM*) *nf* milk shake
maltratar [maltra'tar] *vt* to ill-treat,
mistreat
maltrecho, a [mal'tretʃo, a] *adj* battered,
damaged
malvado, a [mal'ßaðo, a] *adj* evil,
villainous
malversar [malßer'sar] *vt* to embezzle,
misappropriate
Malvinas [mal'ßinas]: **Islas ~** *nfpl*
Falkland Islands
malvivir [malßi'ßir] *vi* to live poorly
mama ['mama] *nf* (*de animal*) teat; (*de
mujer*) breast
mamá [ma'ma] (*pl* **~s**) (*fam*) *nf* mum,
mummy
mamar [ma'mar] *vt, vi* to suck
mamarracho [mama'rratʃo] *nm* sight,
mess
mamífero [ma'mifero] *nm* mammal
mampara [mam'para] *nf* (*entre
habitaciones*) partition; (*biombo*) screen
mampostería [mamposte'ria] *nf* masonry
manada [ma'naða] *nf* (*ZOOL*) herd; (*: de
leones*) pride; (*: de lobos*) pack
manantial [manan'tjal] *nm* spring
manar [ma'nar] *vi* to run, flow

mancha ['mantʃa] *nf* stain, mark; (*ZOOL*)
patch; **manchar** *vt* (*gen*) to stain, mark;
(*ensuciar*) to soil, dirty
manchego, a [man'tʃeɣo, a] *adj* of o
from La Mancha
manco, a ['manko, a] *adj* (*de un brazo*)
one-armed; (*de una mano*) one-handed;
(*fig*) defective, faulty
mancomunar [mankomu'nar] *vt* to unite,
bring together; (*recursos*) to pool; (*JUR*) to
make jointly responsible;
mancomunidad *nf* union, association;
(*comunidad*) community; (*JUR*) joint
responsibility
mandamiento [manda'mjento] *nm*
(*orden*) order, command; (*REL*)
commandment; **~ judicial** warrant
mandar [man'dar] *vt* (*ordenar*) to order;
(*dirigir*) to lead, command; (*enviar*) to
send; (*pedir*) to order, ask for ♦ *vi* to be
in charge; (*pey*) to be bossy; **¿mande?**
pardon?, excuse me?; **~ hacer un traje** to
have a suit made
mandarina [manda'rina] *nf* tangerine,
mandarin (orange)
mandato [man'dato] *nm* (*orden*) order;
(*POL: período*) term of office; (*: territorio*)
mandate; **~ judicial** (search) warrant
mandíbula [man'dißula] *nf* jaw
mandil [man'dil] *nm* apron
mando ['mando] *nm* (*MIL*) command; (*de
país*) rule; (*el primer lugar*) lead; (*POL*)
term of office; (*TEC*) control; **~ a la
izquierda** left-hand drive
mandón, ona [man'don, ona] *adj* bossy,
domineering
manejable [mane'xaßle] *adj* manageable
manejar [mane'xar] *vt* to manage;
(*máquina*) to work, operate; (*caballo etc*)
to handle; (*casa*) to run, manage; (*AM:
AUTO*) to drive; **~se** *vr* (*comportarse*) to
act, behave; (*arreglárselas*) to manage;
manejo *nm* management; handling;
running; driving; (*facilidad de trato*) ease,
confidence; **manejos** *nmpl* (*intrigas*)
intrigues
manera [ma'nera] *nf* way, manner,

fashion; **~s** *nfpl* (*modales*) manners; **su ~
de ser** the way he is; (*aire*) his manner;
de ninguna ~ no way, by no means; **de
otra ~** otherwise; **de todas ~s** at any
rate; **no hay ~ de persuadirle** there's no
way of convincing him

manga ['manga] *nf* (*de camisa*) sleeve; (*de
riego*) hose

mangar [man'gar] (*fam*) *vt* to pinch, nick

mango ['mango] *nm* handle; (*BOT*) mango

mangonear [mangone'ar] *vi* (*meterse*) to
meddle, interfere; (*ser mandón*) to boss
people about

manguera [man'gera] *nf* hose

manía [ma'nia] *nf* (*MED*) mania; (*fig:
moda*) rage, craze; (*disgusto*) dislike;
(*malicia*) spite; **maníaco, a** *adj*
maniac(al) ♦ *nm/f* maniac

maniatar [manja'tar] *vt* to tie the hands of

maniático, a [ma'njatiko, a] *adj*
maniac(al) ♦ *nm/f* maniac

manicomio [mani'komjo] *nm* mental
hospital (*BRIT*), insane asylum (*US*)

manifestación [manifesta'θjon] *nf*
(*declaración*) statement, declaration; (*de
emoción*) show, display; (*POL: desfile*)
demonstration; (: *concentración*) mass
meeting

manifestar [manifes'tar] *vt* to show,
manifest; (*declarar*) to state, declare;
manifiesto, a *adj* clear, manifest ♦ *nm*
manifiesto

manillar [mani'ʎar] *nm* handlebars *pl*

maniobra [ma'njoβra] *nf* manœuvre; **~s**
nfpl (*MIL*) manœuvres; **maniobrar** *vt* to
manœuvre

manipulación [manipula'θjon] *nf*
manipulation

manipular [manipu'lar] *vt* to manipulate;
(*manejar*) to handle

maniquí [mani'ki] *nm* dummy ♦ *nm/f*
model

manirroto, a [mani'rroto, a] *adj* lavish,
extravagant ♦ *nm/f* spendthrift

manivela [mani'βela] *nf* crank

manjar [man'xar] *nm* (tasty) dish

mano ['mano] *nf* hand; (*ZOOL*) foot, paw;

(*de pintura*) coat; (*serie*) lot, series; **a ~** by
hand; **a ~ derecha/izquierda** on the
right(-hand side)/left(-hand side); **de
primera ~** (at) first hand; **de segunda ~**
(at) second hand; **robo a ~ armada**
armed robbery; **~ de obra** labour,
manpower; **estrechar la ~ a uno** to
shake sb's hand

manojo [ma'noxo] *nm* handful, bunch; **~
de llaves** bunch of keys

manopla [ma'nopla] *nf* mitten

manoseado, a [manose'aðo, a] *adj* well-
worn

manosear [manose'ar] *vt* (*tocar*) to
handle, touch; (*desordenar*) to mess up,
rumple; (*insistir en*) to overwork; (*AM*) to
caress, fondle

manotazo [mano'taθo] *nm* slap, smack

mansalva [man'salβa]: **a ~** *adv*
indiscriminately

mansedumbre [manse'ðumbre] *nf*
gentleness, meekness

mansión [man'sjon] *nf* mansion

manso, a ['manso, a] *adj* gentle, mild;
(*animal*) tame

manta ['manta] *nf* blanket; (*AM: poncho*)
poncho

manteca [man'teka] *nf* fat; (*AM*) butter; **~
de cacahuete/cacao** peanut/cocoa
butter; **~ de cerdo** lard

mantecado [mante'kaðo] (*AM*) *nm* ice
cream

mantel [man'tel] *nm* tablecloth

mantendré *etc vb ver* **mantener**

mantener [mante'ner] *vt* to support,
maintain; (*alimentar*) to sustain;
(*conservar*) to keep; (*TEC*) to maintain,
service; **~se** *vr* (*seguir de pie*) to be still
standing; (*no ceder*) to hold one's
ground; (*subsistir*) to sustain o.s., keep
going; **mantenimiento** *nm*
maintenance; sustenance; (*sustento*)
support

mantequilla [mante'kiʎa] *nf* butter

mantilla [man'tiʎa] *nf* mantilla; **~s** *nfpl*
(*de bebé*) baby clothes

manto ['manto] *nm* (*capa*) cloak; (*de*

ceremonia) robe, gown

mantuve *etc vb ver* **mantener**

manual [maˈnwal] *adj* manual ♦ *nm* manual, handbook

manufactura [manufakˈtura] *nf* manufacture; (*fábrica*) factory; **manufacturado, a** *adj* (*producto*) manufactured

manuscrito, a [manusˈkrito, a] *adj* handwritten ♦ *nm* manuscript

manutención [manutenˈθjon] *nf* maintenance; (*sustento*) support

manzana [manˈθana] *nf* apple; (*ARQ*) block (of houses)

manzanilla [manθaˈniʎa] *nf* (*planta*) camomile; (*infusión*) camomile tea

manzano [manˈθano] *nm* apple tree

maña [ˈmaɲa] *nf* (*gen*) skill, dexterity; (*pey*) guile; (*destreza*) trick, knack

mañana [maˈɲana] *adv* tomorrow ♦ *nm* future ♦ *nf* morning; **de** *o* **por la ~** in the morning; **¡hasta ~!** see you tomorrow!; **~ por la ~** tomorrow morning

mañoso, a [maˈɲoso, a] *adj* (*hábil*) skilful; (*astuto*) smart, clever

mapa [ˈmapa] *nm* map

maqueta [maˈketa] *nf* (scale) model

maquillaje [makiˈʎaxe] *nm* make-up; (*acto*) making up

maquillar [makiˈʎar] *vt* to make up; **~se** *vr* to put on (some) make-up

máquina [ˈmakina] *nf* machine; (*de tren*) locomotive, engine; (*FOTO*) camera; (*AM: coche*) car; (*fig*) machinery; **escrito a ~** typewritten; **~ de escribir** typewriter; **~ de coser/lavar** sewing/washing machine

maquinación [makinaˈθjon] *nf* machination, plot

maquinal [makiˈnal] *adj* (*fig*) mechanical, automatic

maquinaria [makiˈnarja] *nf* (*máquinas*) machinery; (*mecanismo*) mechanism, works *pl*

maquinilla [makiˈniʎa] *nf*: **~ de afeitar** razor

maquinista [makiˈnista] *nm/f* (*de tren*) engine driver; (*TEC*) operator; (*NAUT*) engineer

mar [mar] *nm o f* sea; **~ adentro** *o* **afuera** out at sea; **en alta ~** on the high seas; **la ~ de** (*fam*) lots of; **el M~ Negro/Báltico** the Black/Baltic Sea

maraña [maˈraɲa] *nf* (*maleza*) thicket; (*confusión*) tangle

maravilla [maraˈβiʎa] *nf* marvel, wonder; (*BOT*) marigold; **maravillar** *vt* to astonish, amaze; **maravillarse** *vr* to be astonished, be amazed; **maravilloso, a** *adj* wonderful, marvellous

marca [ˈmarka] *nf* (*gen*) mark; (*sello*) stamp; (*COM*) make, brand; **de ~** excellent, outstanding; **~ de fábrica** trademark; **~ registrada** registered trademark

marcado, a [marˈkaðo, a] *adj* marked, strong

marcador [markaˈðor] *nm* (*DEPORTE*) scoreboard; (: *persona*) scorer

marcapasos [markaˈpasos] *nm inv* pacemaker

marcar [marˈkar] *vt* (*gen*) to mark; (*número de teléfono*) to dial; (*gol*) to score; (*números*) to record, keep a tally of; (*pelo*) to set ♦ *vi* (*DEPORTE*) to score; (*TEL*) to dial

marcha [ˈmartʃa] *nf* march; (*TEC*) running, working; (*AUTO*) gear; (*velocidad*) speed; (*fig*) progress; (*dirección*) course; **poner en ~** to put into gear; (*fig*) to set in motion, get going; **dar ~ atrás** to reverse, put into reverse; **estar en ~** to be under way, be in motion

marchar [marˈtʃar] *vi* (*ir*) to go; (*funcionar*) to work, go; **~se** *vr* to go (away), leave

marchitar [martʃiˈtar] *vt* to wither, dry up; **~se** *vr* (*BOT*) to wither; (*fig*) to fade away; **marchito, a** *adj* withered, faded; (*fig*) in decline

marcial [marˈθjal] *adj* martial, military

marciano, a [marˈθjano, a] *adj, nm/f* Martian

marco [ˈmarko] *nm* frame; (*moneda*) mark; (*fig*) framework

marea [maˈrea] *nf* tide

marear [mare'ar] *vt* (*fig*) to annoy, upset; (*MED*): ~ **a uno** to make sb feel sick; **~se** *vr* (*tener náuseas*) to feel sick; (*desvanecerse*) to feel faint; (*aturdirse*) to feel dizzy; (*fam: emborracharse*) to get tipsy

maremoto [mare'moto] *nm* tidal wave

mareo [ma'reo] *nm* (*náusea*) sick feeling; (*en viaje*) travel sickness; (*aturdimiento*) dizziness; (*fam: lata*) nuisance

marfil [mar'fil] *nm* ivory

margarina [marɣa'rina] *nf* margarine

margarita [marɣa'rita] *nf* (*BOT*) daisy; **(rueda) ~** daisywheel

margen ['marxen] *nm* (*borde*) edge, border; (*fig*) margin, space ♦ *nf* (*de río etc*) bank; **dar ~ para** to give an opportunity for; **mantenerse al ~** to keep out of (of things)

marginar [marxi'nar] *vt* (*socialmente*) to marginalize, ostracize

marica [ma'rika] (*fam*) *nm* sissy

maricón [mari'kon] (*fam*) *nm* queer

marido [ma'riðo] *nm* husband

marihuana [mari'wana] *nf* marijuana, cannabis

marina [ma'rina] *nf* navy; **~ mercante** merchant navy

marinero, a [mari'nero, a] *adj* sea *cpd* ♦ *nm* sailor, seaman

marino, a [ma'rino, a] *adj* sea *cpd*, marine ♦ *nm* sailor

marioneta [marjo'neta] *nf* puppet

mariposa [mari'posa] *nf* butterfly

mariquita [mari'kita] *nf* ladybird (*BRIT*), ladybug (*US*)

mariscos [ma'riskos] *nmpl* shellfish *inv*, seafood(s)

marítimo, a [ma'ritimo, a] *adj* sea *cpd*, maritime

mármol ['marmol] *nm* marble

marqués, esa [mar'kes, esa] *nm/f* marquis/marchioness

marrón [ma'rron] *adj* brown

marroquí [marro'ki] *adj*, *nm/f* Moroccan ♦ *nm* Morocco (leather)

Marruecos [ma'rrwekos] *nm* Morocco

martes ['martes] *nm inv* Tuesday

Martes y Trece

ℹ️ *According to Spanish superstition Tuesday is an unlucky day, even more so if it falls on the 13th of the month.*

---

martillo [mar'tiʎo] *nm* hammer; **~ neumático** pneumatic drill (*BRIT*), jackhammer

mártir ['martir] *nm/f* martyr; **martirio** *nm* martyrdom; (*fig*) torture, torment

marxismo [mark'sismo] *nm* Marxism; **marxista** *adj*, *nm/f* Marxist

marzo ['marθo] *nm* March

PALABRA CLAVE

más [mas] *adj*, *adv* **1**: **~ (que/de)** (*compar*) more (than), ...+er (than); **~ grande/inteligente** bigger/more intelligent; **trabaja ~ (que yo)** he works more (than me); *ver tb* **cada**
2 (*superl*): **el ~** the most, ...+est; **el ~ grande/inteligente (de)** the biggest/most intelligent (in)
3 (*negativo*): **no tengo ~ dinero** I haven't got any more money; **no viene ~ por aquí** he doesn't come round here any more
4 (*adicional*): **no le veo ~ solución que ...** I see no other solution than to ...; **¿quién ~?** anybody else?
5 (+*adj: valor intensivo*): **¡qué perro ~ sucio!** what a filthy dog!; **¡es ~ tonto!** he's so stupid!
6 (*locuciones*): **~ o menos** more or less; **los ~** most people; **es ~** furthermore; **~ bien** rather; **¡qué ~ da!** what does it matter!; *ver tb* **no**
7: **por ~: por ~ que te esfuerces** no matter how hard you try; **por ~ que quisiera ...** much as I should like to ...
8: **de ~: veo que aquí estoy de ~** I can see I'm not needed here; **tenemos uno de ~** we've got one extra
♦ *prep*: **2 ~ 2 son 4** 2 *and o* plus 2 are 4
♦ *nm inv*: **este trabajo tiene sus ~ y**

sus menos this job's got its good points and its bad points

mas [mas] *conj* but
masa ['masa] *nf* (*mezcla*) dough; (*volumen*) volume, mass; (*FÍSICA*) mass; **en ~** en masse; **las ~s** (*POL*) the masses
masacre [ma'sakre] *nf* massacre
masaje [ma'saxe] *nm* massage
máscara ['maskara] *nf* mask; **mascarilla** *nf* (*de belleza, MED*) mask
masculino, a [masku'lino, a] *adj* masculine; (*BIO*) male
masía [ma'sia] *nf* farmhouse
masificación [masifika'θjon] *nf* overcrowding
masivo, a [ma'siβo, a] *adj* mass *cpd*
masón [ma'son] *nm* (free)mason
masoquista [maso'kista] *nm/f* masochist
masticar [masti'kar] *vt* to chew
mástil ['mastil] *nm* (*de navío*) mast; (*de guitarra*) neck
mastín [mas'tin] *nm* mastiff
masturbación [masturβa'θjon] *nf* masturbation
masturbarse [mastur'βarse] *vr* to masturbate
mata ['mata] *nf* (*arbusto*) bush, shrub; (*de hierba*) tuft
matadero [mata'ðero] *nm* slaughterhouse, abattoir
matador, a [mata'ðor, a] *adj* killing ♦ *nm/f* killer ♦ *nm* (*TAUR*) matador, bullfighter
matamoscas [mata'moskas] *nm inv* (*palo*) fly swat
matanza [ma'tanθa] *nf* slaughter
matar [ma'tar] *vt, vi* to kill; **~se** *vr* (*suicidarse*) to kill o.s., commit suicide; (*morir*) to be *o* get killed; **~ el hambre** to stave off hunger
matasellos [mata'seʎos] *nm inv* postmark
mate ['mate] *adj* matt ♦ *nm* (*en ajedrez*) (check)mate; (*AM: hierba*) maté; (: *vasija*) gourd
matemáticas [mate'matikas] *nfpl* mathematics; **matemático, a** *adj*

mathematical ♦ *nm/f* mathematician
materia [ma'terja] *nf* (*gen*) matter; (*TEC*) material; (*ESCOL*) subject; **en ~ de** on the subject of; **~ prima** raw material;
material *adj* material ♦ *nm* material; (*TEC*) equipment; **materialismo** *nm* materialism; **materialista** *adj* materialist(ic); **materialmente** *adv* materially; (*fig*) absolutely
maternal [mater'nal] *adj* motherly, maternal
maternidad [materni'ðað] *nf* motherhood, maternity; **materno, a** *adj* maternal; (*lengua*) mother *cpd*
matinal [mati'nal] *adj* morning *cpd*
matiz [ma'tiθ] *nm* shade; **~ar** *vt* (*variar*) to vary; (*ARTE*) to blend; **~ar de** to tinge with
matón [ma'ton] *nm* bully
matorral [mato'rral] *nm* thicket
matraca [ma'traka] *nf* rattle
matrícula [ma'trikula] *nf* (*registro*) register; (*AUTO*) registration number; (: *placa*) number plate; **matricular** *vt* to register, enrol
matrimonial [matrimo'njal] *adj* matrimonial
matrimonio [matri'monjo] *nm* (*pareja*) (married) couple; (*unión*) marriage
matriz [ma'triθ] *nf* (*ANAT*) womb; (*TEC*) mould; **casa ~** (*COM*) head office
matrona [ma'trona] *nf* (*persona de edad*) matron; (*comadrona*) midwife
maullar [mau'ʎar] *vi* to mew, miaow
maxilar [maksi'lar] *nm* jaw(bone)
máxima ['maksima] *nf* maxim
máxime ['maksime] *adv* especially
máximo, a ['maksimo, a] *adj* maximum; (*más alto*) highest; (*más grande*) greatest ♦ *nm* maximum
mayo ['majo] *nm* May
mayonesa [majo'nesa] *nf* mayonnaise
mayor [ma'jor] *adj* main, chief; (*adulto*) adult; (*de edad avanzada*) elderly; (*MUS*) major; (*compar: de tamaño*) bigger; (: *de edad*) older; (*superl: de tamaño*) biggest; (: *de edad*) oldest ♦ *nm* (*adulto*) adult; **al**

por ~ wholesale; **~ de edad** adult; **~es** *nmpl (antepasados)* ancestors

mayoral [majo'ral] *nm* foreman

mayordomo [major'ðomo] *nm* butler

mayoría [majo'ria] *nf* majority, greater part

mayorista [majo'rista] *nm/f* wholesaler

mayoritario, a [majori'tarjo, a] *adj* majority *cpd*

mayúscula [ma'juskula] *nf* capital letter

mayúsculo, a [ma'juskulo, a] *adj (fig)* big, tremendous

mazapán [maθa'pan] *nm* marzipan

mazo ['maθo] *nm (martillo)* mallet; *(de flores)* bunch; *(DEPORTE)* bat

me [me] *pron (directo)* me; *(indirecto)* (to) me; *(reflexivo)* (to) myself; **¡dámelo!** give it to me!

mear [me'ar] *(fam) vi* to pee, piss *(!)*

mecánica [me'kanika] *nf (ESCOL)* mechanics *sg; (mecanismo)* mechanism; *ver tb* **mecánico**

mecánico, a [me'kaniko, a] *adj* mechanical ♦ *nm/f* mechanic

mecanismo [meka'nismo] *nm* mechanism; *(marcha)* gear

mecanografía [mekanoɣra'fia] *nf* typewriting; **mecanógrafo, a** *nm/f* typist

mecate [me'kate] *(AM) nm* rope

mecedora [meθe'ðora] *nf* rocking chair

mecer [me'θer] *vt (cuna)* to rock; **~se** *vr* to rock; *(ramo)* to sway

mecha ['metʃa] *nf (de vela)* wick; *(de bomba)* fuse

mechero [me'tʃero] *nm (cigarette)* lighter

mechón [me'tʃon] *nm (gen)* tuft; *(de pelo)* lock

medalla [me'ðaʎa] *nf* medal

media ['meðja] *nf (ESP)* stocking; *(AM)* sock; *(promedio)* average

mediado, a [me'ðjaðo, a] *adj* half-full; *(trabajo)* half-completed; **a ~s de** in the middle of, halfway through

mediano, a [me'ðjano, a] *adj (regular)* medium, average; *(mediocre)* mediocre

medianoche [meðja'notʃe] *nf* midnight

mediante [me'ðjante] *adv* by (means of), through

mediar [me'ðjar] *vi (interceder)* to mediate, intervene

medicación [meðika'θjon] *nf* medication, treatment

medicamento [meðika'mento] *nm* medicine, drug

medicina [meði'θina] *nf* medicine

medición [meði'θjon] *nf* measurement

médico, a [me'ðiko, a] *adj* medical ♦ *nm/f* doctor

medida [me'ðiða] *nf* measure; *(medición)* measurement; *(prudencia)* prudence; **en cierta/gran ~** up to a point/to a great extent; **un traje a la ~** made-to-measure suit; **~ de cuello** collar size; **a ~ de** in proportion to; *(de acuerdo con)* in keeping with; **a ~ que** *(conforme)* as

medio, a ['meðjo, a] *adj* half (a); *(punto)* mid, middle; *(promedio)* average ♦ *adv* half ♦ *nm (centro)* middle, centre; *(promedio)* average; *(método)* means, way; *(ambiente)* environment; **~s** *nmpl* means, resources; **~ litro** half a litre; **las tres y media** half past three; **medio ambiente** environment; **M~ Oriente** Middle East; **a ~ terminar** half finished; **pagar a medias** to share the cost; **~ambiental** *adj (política, efectos)* environmental

mediocre [me'ðjokre] *adj* mediocre

mediodía [meðjo'ðia] *nm* midday, noon

medir [me'ðir] *vt, vi (gen)* to measure

meditar [meði'tar] *vt* to ponder, think over, meditate on; *(planear)* to think out

mediterráneo, a [meðite'rraneo, a] *adj* Mediterranean ♦ *nm*: **el M~** the Mediterranean (Sea)

médula ['meðula] *nf (ANAT)* marrow; **~ espinal** spinal cord

medusa [me'ðusa] *(ESP) nf* jellyfish

megafonía [meɣafo'nia] *nf* public address system, PA system; **megáfono** *nm* megaphone

megalómano, a [meɣa'lomano, a] *nm/f* megalomaniac

mejicano, a [mexi'kano, a] *adj, nm/f* Mexican

Méjico ['mexiko] *nm* Mexico

mejilla [me'xiʎa] *nf* cheek

mejillón [mexi'ʎon] *nm* mussel

mejor [me'xor] *adj, adv (compar)* better; *(superl)* best; **a lo ~** probably; *(quizá)* maybe; **~ dicho** rather; **tanto ~** so much the better

mejora [me'xora] *nf* improvement; **mejorar** *vt* to improve, make better ♦ *vi* to improve, get better; **mejorarse** *vr* to improve, get better

melancólico, a [melan'koliko, a] *adj (triste)* sad, melancholy; *(soñador)* dreamy

melena [me'lena] *nf (de persona)* long hair; *(ZOOL)* mane

mellizo, a [me'ʎiθo, a] *adj, nm/f* twin; **~s** *nmpl (AM)* cufflinks

melocotón [meloko'ton] *(ESP) nm* peach

melodía [melo'ðia] *nf* melody, tune

melodrama [melo'ðrama] *nm* melodrama; **melodramático, a** *adj* melodramatic

melón [me'lon] *nm* melon

membrillo [mem'briʎo] *nm* quince; **carne de ~** quince jelly

memorable [memo'raβle] *adj* memorable

memoria [me'morja] *nf (gen)* memory; **~s** *nfpl (de autor)* memoirs; **memorizar** *vt* to memorize

menaje [me'naxe] *nm:* **~ de cocina** kitchenware

mencionar [menθjo'nar] *vt* to mention

mendigar [mendi'ɣar] *vt* to beg (for)

mendigo, a [men'diɣo, a] *nm/f* beggar

mendrugo [men'druɣo] *nm* crust

menear [mene'ar] *vt* to move; **~se** *vr* to shake; *(balancearse)* to sway; *(moverse)* to move; *(fig)* to get a move on

menestra [me'nestra] *nf:* **~ de verduras** vegetable stew

menguante [men'gwante] *adj* decreasing, diminishing

menguar [men'gwar] *vt* to lessen, diminish ♦ *vi* to diminish, decrease

menopausia [meno'pausja] *nf* menopause

menor [me'nor] *adj (más pequeño: compar)* smaller; *(: superl)* smallest; *(más joven: compar)* younger; *(: superl)* youngest; *(MUS)* minor ♦ *nm/f (joven)* young person, juvenile; **no tengo la ~ idea** I haven't the faintest idea; **al por ~** retail; **~ de edad** person under age

Menorca [me'norka] *nf* Minorca

PALABRA CLAVE
---

menos [menos] *adj* 1: **~ (que/de)** *(compar: cantidad)* less (than); *(: número)* fewer (than); **con ~ entusiasmo** with less enthusiasm; **~ gente** fewer people; *ver tb* **cada**

2 *(superl)*: **es el que ~ culpa tiene** he is the least to blame

♦ *adv* 1 *(compar)*: **~ (que, de)** less (than); **me gusta ~ que el otro** I like it less than the other one

2 *(superl)*: **es el ~ listo (de su clase)** he's the least bright in his class; **de todas ellas es la que ~ me agrada** out of all of them she's the one I like least; **(por) lo ~** at the (very) least

3 *(locuciones)*: **no quiero verle y ~ visitarle** I don't want to see him let alone visit him; **tenemos 7 de ~** we're seven short

♦ *prep* except; *(cifras)* minus; **todos ~ él** everyone except (for) him; **5 ~ 2** 5 minus 2

♦ *conj:* **a ~ que: a ~ que venga mañana** unless he comes tomorrow

---

menospreciar [menospre'θjar] *vt* to underrate, undervalue; *(despreciar)* to scorn, despise

mensaje [men'saxe] *nm* message; **~ de texto** text message; **~ro, a** *nm/f* messenger

menstruación [menstrua'θjon] *nf* menstruation

menstruar [mens'trwar] *vi* to menstruate

mensual [men'swal] *adj* monthly; **1000 ptas ~es** 1000 ptas a month; **~idad** *nf (salario)* monthly salary; *(COM)* monthly payment, monthly instalment

menta ['menta] *nf* mint

mental [men'tal] *adj* mental; **~idad** *nf* mentality; **~izar** *vt* (*sensibilizar*) to make aware; (*convencer*) to convince; (*padres*) to prepare (mentally); **~izarse** *vr* (*concienciarse*) to become aware; **~izarse (de)** to get used to the idea (of); **~izarse de que ...** (*convencerse*) to get it into one's head that ...

mentar [men'tar] *vt* to mention, name

mente ['mente] *nf* mind

mentir [men'tir] *vi* to lie

mentira [men'tira] *nf* (*una ~*) lie; (*acto*) lying; (*invención*) fiction; **parece ~ que ...** it seems incredible that ..., I can't believe that ...

mentiroso, a [menti'roso, a] *adj* lying ♦ *nm/f* liar

menú [me'nu] (*pl* **~s**) *nm* menu; (*AM*) set meal; **~ del día** set menu

menudo, a [me'nuðo, a] *adj* (*pequeño*) small, tiny; (*sin importancia*) petty, insignificant; **¡~ negocio!** (*fam*) some deal!; **a ~** often, frequently

meñique [me'ɲike] *nm* little finger

meollo [me'oʎo] *nm* (*fig*) core

mercado [mer'kaðo] *nm* market

mercancía [merkan'θia] *nf* commodity; **~s** *nfpl* goods, merchandise *sg*

mercantil [merkan'til] *adj* mercantile, commercial

mercenario, a [merθe'narjo, a] *adj*, *nm* mercenary

mercería [merθe'ria] *nf* haberdashery (*BRIT*), notions (*US*); (*tienda*) haberdasher's (*BRIT*), notions store (*US*); (*AM*) drapery

mercurio [mer'kurjo] *nm* mercury

merecer [mere'θer] *vt* to deserve, merit ♦ *vi* to be deserving, be worthy; **merece la pena** it's worthwhile; **merecido, a** *adj* (well) deserved; **llevar su merecido** to get one's deserts

merendar [meren'dar] *vt* to have for tea ♦ *vi* to have tea; (*en el campo*) to have a picnic; **merendero** *nm* open-air cafe

merengue [me'renge] *nm* meringue

meridiano [meri'ðjano] *nm* (*GEO*) meridian

merienda [me'rjenda] *nf* (light) tea, afternoon snack; (*de campo*) picnic

mérito ['merito] *nm* merit; (*valor*) worth, value

merluza [mer'luθa] *nf* hake

merma ['merma] *nf* decrease; (*pérdida*) wastage; **mermar** *vt* to reduce, lessen ♦ *vi* to decrease, dwindle

mermelada [merme'laða] *nf* jam

mero, a ['mero, a] *adj* mere; (*AM: fam*) very

merodear [meroðe'ar] *vi*: **~ por** to prowl about

mes [mes] *nm* month

mesa ['mesa] *nf* table; (*de trabajo*) desk; (*GEO*) plateau; **~ directiva** board; **~ redonda** (*reunión*) round table; **poner/ quitar la ~** to lay/clear the table; **mesero, a** (*AM*) *nm/f* waiter/waitress

meseta [me'seta] *nf* (*GEO*) meseta, tableland

mesilla [me'siʎa] *nf*: **~ (de noche)** bedside table

mesón [me'son] *nm* inn

mestizo, a [mes'tiθo, a] *adj* half-caste, of mixed race ♦ *nm/f* half-caste

mesura [me'sura] *nf* moderation, restraint

meta ['meta] *nf* goal; (*de carrera*) finish

metabolismo [metaβo'lismo] *nm* metabolism

metáfora [me'tafora] *nf* metaphor

metal [me'tal] *nm* (*materia*) metal; (*MUS*) brass; **metálico, a** *adj* metallic; (*de metal*) metal ♦ *nm* (*dinero contante*) cash

metalurgia [meta'lurxja] *nf* metallurgy

meteoro [mete'oro] *nm* meteor; **~logía** *nf* meteorology

meter [me'ter] *vt* (*colocar*) to put, place; (*introducir*) to put in, insert; (*involucrar*) to involve; (*causar*) to make, cause; **~se** *vr*: **~se en** to go into, enter; (*fig*) to interfere in, meddle in; **~se a** to start; **~se a escritor** to become a writer; **~se con uno** to provoke sb, pick a quarrel with sb

meticuloso, a [metiku'loso, a] *adj*

meticulous, thorough

metódico, a [me'toðiko, a] *adj* methodical

método ['metoðo] *nm* method

metralleta [metra'ʎeta] *nf* sub-machine-gun

métrico, a ['metriko, a] *adj* metric

metro ['metro] *nm* metre; (*tren*) underground (*BRIT*), subway (*US*)

México ['mexiko] *nm* Mexico; **Ciudad de ~** Mexico City

mezcla ['meθkla] *nf* mixture; **mezclar** *vt* to mix (up); **mezclarse** *vr* to mix, mingle; **mezclarse en** to get mixed up in, get involved in

mezquino, a [meθ'kino, a] *adj* mean

mezquita [meθ'kita] *nf* mosque

mg. *abr* (= *miligramo*) mg

mi [mi] *adj* my ♦ *nm* (*MUS*) E

mí [mi] *pron* me; myself

mía ['mia] *pron ver* **mío**

miaja ['mjaxa] *nf* crumb

michelín [mitʃe'lin] (*fam*) *nm* (*de grasa*) spare tyre

micro ['mikro] (*AM*) *nm* minibus

microbio [mi'kroßjo] *nm* microbe

micrófono [mi'krofono] *nm* microphone

microondas [mikro'ondas] *nm inv* (*tb:* **horno ~**) microwave (oven)

microscopio [mikro'skopjo] *nm* microscope

miedo ['mjeðo] *nm* fear; (*nerviosismo*) apprehension, nervousness; **tener ~** to be afraid; **de ~** wonderful, marvellous; **hace un frío de ~** (*fam*) it's terribly cold; **~so, a** *adj* fearful, timid

miel [mjel] *nf* honey

miembro ['mjembro] *nm* limb; (*socio*) member; **~ viril** penis

mientras ['mjentras] *conj* while; (*duración*) as long as ♦ *adv* meanwhile; **~ tanto** meanwhile; **~ más tiene, más quiere** the more he has, the more he wants

miércoles ['mjerkoles] *nm inv* Wednesday

mierda ['mjerða] (*fam!*) *nf* shit (*!*)

miga ['miɣa] *nf* crumb; (*fig: meollo*) essence; **hacer buenas ~s** (*fam*) to get

on well

mil [mil] *num* thousand; **dos ~ libras** two thousand pounds

milagro [mi'laɣro] *nm* miracle; **~so, a** *adj* miraculous

milésima [mi'lesima] *nf* (*de segundo*) thousandth

mili ['mili] (*fam*) *nf*: **hacer la ~** to do one's military service

milicia [mi'liθja] *nf* militia; (*servicio militar*) military service

milímetro [mi'limetro] *nm* millimetre

militante [mili'tante] *adj* militant

militar [mili'tar] *adj* military ♦ *nm/f* soldier ♦ *vi* (*MIL*) to serve; (*en un partido*) to be a member

milla ['miʎa] *nf* mile

millar [mi'ʎar] *nm* thousand

millón [mi'ʎon] *num* million; **millonario, a** *nm/f* millionaire

mimar [mi'mar] *vt* to spoil, pamper

mimbre ['mimbre] *nm* wicker

mímica ['mimika] *nf* (*para comunicarse*) sign language; (*imitación*) mimicry

mimo ['mimo] *nm* (*caricia*) caress; (*de niño*) spoiling; (*TEATRO*) mime; (*: actor*) mime artist

mina ['mina] *nf* mine; **minar** *vt* to mine; (*fig*) to undermine

mineral [mine'ral] *adj* mineral ♦ *nm* (*GEO*) mineral; (*mena*) ore

minero, a [mi'nero, a] *adj* mining *cpd* ♦ *nm/f* miner

miniatura [minja'tura] *adj inv, nf* miniature

minidisco [mini'disko] *nm* Minidisc ®

minifalda [mini'falda] *nf* miniskirt

mínimo, a ['minimo, a] *adj, nm* minimum

minino, a [mi'nino, a] (*fam*) *nm/f* puss, pussy

ministerio [minis'terjo] *nm* Ministry; **M~ de Hacienda/de Asuntos Exteriores** Treasury (*BRIT*), Treasury Department (*US*)/Foreign Office (*BRIT*), State Department (*US*)

ministro, a [mi'nistro, a] *nm/f* minister

minoría [mino'ria] *nf* minority

minucioso, a [minu'θjoso, a] *adj* thorough, meticulous; (*prolijo*) very detailed

minúscula [mi'nuskula] *nf* small letter

minúsculo, a [mi'nuskulo, a] *adj* tiny, minute

minusválido, a [minus'ßaliðo, a] *adj* (physically) handicapped ♦ *nm/f* (physically) handicapped person

minuta [mi'nuta] *nf* (*de comida*) menu

minutero [minu'tero] *nm* minute hand

minuto [mi'nuto] *nm* minute

mío, a ['mio, a] *pron*: **el ~/la mía** mine; **un amigo ~** a friend of mine; **lo ~** what is mine

miope [mi'ope] *adj* short-sighted

mira ['mira] *nf* (*de arma*) sight(s) (*pl*); (*fig*) aim, intention

mirada [mi'raða] *nf* look, glance; (*expresión*) look, expression; **clavar la ~ en** to stare at; **echar una ~ a** to glance at

mirado, a [mi'raðo, a] *adj* (*sensato*) sensible; (*considerado*) considerate; **bien/ mal ~** well/not well thought of; **bien ~** all things considered

mirador [mira'ðor] *nm* viewpoint, vantage point

mirar [mi'rar] *vt* to look at; (*observar*) to watch; (*considerar*) to consider, think over; (*vigilar, cuidar*) to watch, look after ♦ *vi* to look; (*ARQ*) to face; **~se** *vr* (*dos personas*) to look at each other; **~ bien/ mal** to think highly of/have a poor opinion of; **~se al espejo** to look at o.s. in the mirror

mirilla [mi'riʎa] *nf* spyhole, peephole

mirlo ['mirlo] *nm* blackbird

misa ['misa] *nf* mass

miserable [mise'raßle] *adj* (*avaro*) mean, stingy; (*nimio*) miserable, paltry; (*lugar*) squalid; (*fam*) vile, despicable ♦ *nm/f* (*malvado*) rogue

miseria [mi'serja] *nf* (*pobreza*) poverty; (*tacañería*) meanness, stinginess; (*condiciones*) squalor; **una ~** a pittance

misericordia [miseri'korðja] *nf*

(*compasión*) compassion, pity; (*piedad*) mercy

misil [mi'sil] *nm* missile

misión [mi'sjon] *nf* mission; **misionero, a** *nm/f* missionary

mismo, a ['mismo, a] *adj* (*semejante*) same; (*después de pron*) -self; (*para enfásis*) very ♦ *adv*: **aquí/hoy ~** right here/this very day; **ahora ~** right now ♦ *conj*: **lo ~ que** just like, just as; **el ~ traje** the same suit; **en ese ~ momento** at that very moment; **vino el ~ Ministro** the minister himself came; **yo ~ lo vi** I saw it myself; **lo ~** the same (thing); **da lo ~** it's all the same; **quedamos en las mismas** we're no further forward; **por lo ~** for the same reason

misterio [mis'terjo] *nm* mystery; **~so, a** *adj* mysterious

mitad [mi'tað] *nf* (*medio*) half; (*centro*) middle; **a ~ de precio** (at) half-price; **en *o* a ~ del camino** halfway along the road; **cortar por la ~** to cut through the middle

mitigar [miti'var] *vt* to mitigate; (*dolor*) to ease; (*sed*) to quench

mitin ['mitin] (*pl* **mítines**) *nm* meeting

mito ['mito] *nm* myth

mixto, a ['miksto, a] *adj* mixed

ml. *abr* (= *mililitro*) ml

mm. *abr* (= *milímetro*) mm

mobiliario [moßi'ljarjo] *nm* furniture

mochila [mo'tʃila] *nf* rucksack (*BRIT*), back-pack

moción [mo'θjon] *nf* motion

moco ['moko] *nm* mucus; **~s** *nmpl* (*fam*) snot; **limpiarse los ~s de la nariz** (*fam*) to wipe one's nose

moda ['moða] *nf* fashion; (*estilo*) style; **a la *o* de ~** in fashion, fashionable; **pasado de ~** out of fashion

modales [mo'ðales] *nmpl* manners

modalidad [moðali'ðað] *nf* kind, variety

modelar [moðe'lar] *vt* to model

modelo [mo'ðelo] *adj inv*, *nm/f* model

módem ['moðem] *nm* (*INFORM*) modem

moderado, a [moðe'raðo, a] *adj*

moderate

oderar [moðe'rar] vt to moderate; (violencia) to restrain, control; (velocidad) to reduce; **~se** vr to restrain o.s., control o.s.

odernizar [moðerni'θar] vt to modernize

oderno, a [mo'ðerno, a] adj modern; (actual) present-day

odestia [mo'ðestja] nf modesty; **modesto, a** adj modest

ódico, a ['moðiko, a] adj moderate, reasonable

odificar [moðifi'kar] vt to modify

odisto, a [mo'ðisto, a] nm/f (diseñador) couturier, designer; (que confecciona) dressmaker

odo ['moðo] nm way, manner; (MUS) mode; **~s** nmpl manners; **de ningún ~** in no way; **de todos ~s** at any rate; **~ de empleo** directions pl (for use)

odorra [mo'ðorra] nf drowsiness

ofa ['mofa] nf: **hacer ~ de** to mock; **mofarse** vr: **mofarse de** to mock, scoff at

ogollón [moɣo'ʎon] (fam) adv a hell of a lot

oho ['moo] nm mould, mildew; (en metal) rust; **~so, a** adj mouldy; rusty

ojar [mo'xar] vt to wet; (humedecer) to damp(en), moisten; (calar) to soak; **~se** vr to get wet

ojón [mo'xon] nm boundary stone

olde ['molde] nm mould; (COSTURA) pattern; (fig) model; **~ado** nm soft perm; **~ar** vt to mould

ole ['mole] nf mass, bulk; (edificio) pile

oler [mo'ler] vt to grind, crush

olestar [moles'tar] vt to bother; (fastidiar) to annoy; (incomodar) to inconvenience, put out ♦ vi to be a nuisance; **~se** vr to bother; (incomodarse) to go to trouble; (ofenderse) to take offence; **¿(no) te molesta si ...?** do you mind if ...?

olestia [mo'lestja] nf bother, trouble; (incomodidad) inconvenience; (MED)

discomfort; **es una ~** it's a nuisance; **molesto, a** adj (que fastidia) annoying; (incómodo) inconvenient; (inquieto) uncomfortable, ill at ease; (enfadado) annoyed

molido, a [mo'liðo, a] adj: **estar ~** (fig) to be exhausted o dead beat

molinillo [moli'niʎo] nm: **~ de carne/café** mincer/coffee grinder

molino [mo'lino] nm (edificio) mill; (máquina) grinder

momentáneo, a [momen'taneo, a] adj momentary

momento [mo'mento] nm moment; **de ~** at the moment, for the moment

momia ['momja] nf mummy

monarca [mo'narka] nm/f monarch, ruler; **monarquía** nf monarchy; **monárquico, a** nm/f royalist, monarchist

monasterio [monas'terjo] nm monastery

mondar [mon'dar] vt to peel; **~se** vr: **~se de risa** (fam) to split one's sides laughing

moneda [mo'neða] nf (tipo de dinero) currency, money; (pieza) coin; **una ~ de 5 pesetas** a 5 peseta piece; **monedero** nm purse; **monetario, a** adj monetary, financial

monitor, a [moni'tor, a] nm/f instructor, coach ♦ nm (TV) set; (INFORM) monitor

monja ['monxa] nf nun

monje ['monxe] nm monk

mono, a ['mono, a] adj (bonito) lovely, pretty; (gracioso) nice, charming ♦ nm/f monkey, ape ♦ nm dungarees pl; (overoles) overalls pl

monopatín [monopa'tin] nm skateboard

monopolio [mono'poljo] nm monopoly; **monopolizar** vt to monopolize

monotonía [monoto'nia] nf (sonido) monotone; (fig) monotony

monótono, a [mo'notono, a] adj monotonous

monstruo ['monstrwo] nm monster ♦ adj inv fantastic; **~so, a** adj monstrous

montaje [mon'taxe] nm assembly; (TEATRO) décor; (CINE) montage

montaña [mon'taɲa] *nf* (*monte*) mountain; (*sierra*) mountains *pl*, mountainous area; (*AM: selva*) forest; **~ rusa** roller coaster; **montañero, a** *nm/f* mountaineer; **montañés, esa** *nm/f* highlander; **montañismo** *nm* mountaineering

montar [mon'tar] *vt* (*subir a*) to mount, get on; (*TEC*) to assemble, put together; (*negocio*) to set up; (*arma*) to cock; (*colocar*) to lift on to; (*CULIN*) to beat ♦ *vi* to mount, get on; (*sobresalir*) to overlap; **~ en cólera** to get angry; **~ a caballo** to ride, go horseriding

monte ['monte] *nm* (*montaña*) mountain; (*bosque*) woodland; (*área sin cultivar*) wild area, wild country; **M~ de Piedad** pawnshop

montón [mon'ton] *nm* heap, pile; (*fig*): **un ~ de** heaps of, lots of

monumento [monu'mento] *nm* monument

monzón [mon'θon] *nm* monsoon

moño ['moɲo] *nm* bun

moqueta [mo'keta] *nf* fitted carpet

mora ['mora] *nf* blackberry; *ver tb* **moro**

morada [mo'raða] *nf* (*casa*) dwelling, abode

morado, a [mo'raðo, a] *adj* purple, violet ♦ *nm* bruise

moral [mo'ral] *adj* moral ♦ *nf* (*ética*) ethics *pl*; (*moralidad*) morals *pl*, morality; (*ánimo*) morale

moraleja [mora'lexa] *nf* moral

moralidad [morali'ðað] *nf* morals *pl*, morality

morboso, a [mor'ßoso, a] *adj* morbid

morcilla [mor'θiʎa] *nf* blood sausage, ≈ black pudding (*BRIT*)

mordaz [mor'ðaθ] *adj* (*crítica*) biting, scathing

mordaza [mor'ðaθa] *nf* (*para la boca*) gag; (*TEC*) clamp

morder [mor'ðer] *vt* to bite; (*fig: consumir*) to eat away, eat into; **mordisco** *nm* bite

moreno, a [mo'reno, a] *adj* (*color*) (dark) brown; (*de tez*) dark; (*de pelo ~*) dark-

haired; (*negro*) black

morfina [mor'fina] *nf* morphine

moribundo, a [mori'ßundo, a] *adj* dying

morir [mo'rir] *vi* to die; (*fuego*) to die down; (*luz*) to go out; **~se** *vr* to die; (*fig*) to be dying; **murió en un accidente** he was killed in an accident; **~se por algo** to be dying for sth

moro, a ['moro, a] *adj* Moorish ♦ *nm/f* Moor

moroso, a [mo'roso, a] *nm/f* bad debtor, defaulter

morral [mo'rral] *nm* haversack

morro ['morro] *nm* (*ZOOL*) snout, nose; (*AUTO, AVIAT*) nose

morsa ['morsa] *nf* walrus

mortadela [morta'ðela] *nf* mortadella

mortaja [mor'taxa] *nf* shroud

mortal [mor'tal] *adj* mortal; (*golpe*) deadly; **~idad** *nf* mortality

mortero [mor'tero] *nm* mortar

mortífero, a [mor'tifero, a] *adj* deadly, lethal

mortificar [mortifi'kar] *vt* to mortify

mosca ['moska] *nf* fly

Moscú [mos'ku] *n* Moscow

mosquearse [moske'arse] (*fam*) *vr* (*enojarse*) to get cross; (*ofenderse*) to take offence

mosquitero [moski'tero] *nm* mosquito net

mosquito [mos'kito] *nm* mosquito

mostaza [mos'taθa] *nf* mustard

mosto ['mosto] *nm* (unfermented) grape juice

mostrador [mostra'ðor] *nm* (*de tienda*) counter; (*de café*) bar

mostrar [mos'trar] *vt* to show; (*exhibir*) to display, exhibit; (*explicar*) to explain; **~se** *vr*: **~se amable** to be kind; to prove to be kind; **no se muestra muy inteligente** he doesn't seem (to be) very intelligent

mota ['mota] *nf* speck, tiny piece; (*en diseño*) dot

mote ['mote] *nm* nickname

motín [mo'tin] *nm* (*del pueblo*) revolt, rising; (*del ejército*) mutiny

otivar [moti'ßar] vt (causar) to cause, motivate; (explicar) to explain, justify; **motivo** nm motive, reason

oto ['moto] (fam) nf = **motocicleta**

otocicleta [motoθi'kleta] nf motorbike (BRIT), motorcycle

otor [mo'tor] nm motor, engine; **~ a chorro/de reacción/de explosión** jet engine/internal combustion engine

otora [mo'tora] nf motorboat

ovedizo, a [moße'δiθo, a] adj ver **arena**

over [mo'ßer] vt to move; (cabeza) to shake; (accionar) to drive; (fig) to cause, provoke; **~se** vr to move; (fig) to get a move on

óvil ['moßil] adj mobile; (pieza de máquina) moving; (mueble) movable ♦ nm motive; **movilidad** nf mobility; **movilizar** vt to mobilize

ovimiento [moßi'mjento] nm movement; (TEC) motion; (actividad) activity

ozo, a ['moθo, a] adj (joven) young ♦ nm/f youth, young man/girl

uchacho, a [mu'tʃatʃo, a] nm/f (niño) boy/girl; (criado) servant; (criada) maid

uchedumbre [mutʃe'δumbre] nf crowd

ucho, a ['mutʃo, a] adj **1** (cantidad) a lot of, much; (número) lots of, a lot of, many; **~ dinero** a lot of money; **hace ~ calor** it's very hot; **muchas amigas** lots o a lot of friends
2 (sg: grande): **ésta es mucha casa para él** this house is much too big for him
♦ pron: **tengo ~ que hacer** I've got a lot to do; **~s dicen que ...** a lot of people say that ...; ver tb **tener**
♦ adv **1**: **me gusta ~** I like it a lot; **lo siento ~** I'm very sorry; **come ~** he eats a lot; **¿te vas a quedar ~?** are you going to be staying long?
2 (respuesta) very; **¿estás cansado? – ¡~!** are you tired? – very!
3 (locuciones): **como ~** at (the) most; **con ~: el mejor con ~** by far the best; **ni ~**

menos: no es rico ni ~ menos he's far from being rich
4: **por ~ que: por ~ que le creas** no matter how o however much you believe her

muda ['muδa] nf change of clothes

mudanza [mu'δanθa] nf (de casa) move

mudar [mu'δar] vt to change; (ZOOL) to shed ♦ vi to change; **~se** vr (la ropa) to change; **~se de casa** to move house

mudo, a ['muδo, a] adj dumb; (callado, CINE) silent

mueble ['mweßle] nm piece of furniture; **~s** nmpl furniture sg

mueca ['mweka] nf face, grimace; **hacer ~s a** to make faces at

muela ['mwela] nf (back) tooth

muelle ['mweʎe] nm spring; (NAUT) wharf; (malecón) pier

muero etc vb ver **morir**

muerte ['mwerte] nf death; (homicidio) murder; **dar ~ a** to kill

muerto, a ['mwerto, a] pp de **morir** ♦ adj dead ♦ nm/f dead man/woman; (difunto) deceased; (cadáver) corpse; **estar ~ de cansancio** to be dead tired

muestra ['mwestra] nf (señal) indication, sign; (demostración) demonstration; (prueba) proof; (estadística) sample; (modelo) model, pattern; (testimonio) token

muestreo [mwes'treo] nm sample, sampling

muestro etc vb ver **mostrar**

muevo etc vb ver **mover**

mugir [mu'xir] vi (vaca) to moo

mugre ['muxre] nf dirt, filth; **mugriento, a** adj dirty, filthy

mujer [mu'xer] nf woman; (esposa) wife; **~iego** nm womanizer

mula ['mula] nf mule

muleta [mu'leta] nf (para andar) crutch; (TAUR) stick with red cape attached

mullido, a [mu'ʎiδo, a] adj (cama) soft; (hierba) soft, springy

multa ['multa] nf fine; **poner una ~ a** to

fine; **multar** *vt* to fine

multicines [multi'θines] *nmpl* multiscreen cinema

multinacional [multinaθjo'nal] *nf* multinational

múltiple ['multiple] *adj* multiple; (*pl*) many, numerous

multiplicar [multipli'kar] *vt* (*MAT*) to multiply; (*fig*) to increase; **~se** *vr* (*BIO*) to multiply; (*fig*) to be everywhere at once

multitud [multi'tuð] *nf* (*muchedumbre*) crowd; **~ de** lots of

mundano, a [mun'dano, a] *adj* worldly

mundial [mun'djal] *adj* world-wide, universal; (*guerra, récord*) world *cpd*

mundo ['mundo] *nm* world; **todo el ~** everybody; **tener ~** to be experienced, know one's way around

munición [muni'θjon] *nf* ammunition

municipal [muniθi'pal] *adj* municipal, local

municipio [muni'θipjo] *nm* (*ayuntamiento*) town council, corporation; (*territorio administrativo*) town, municipality

muñeca [mu'ɲeka] *nf* (*ANAT*) wrist; (*juguete*) doll

muñeco [mu'ɲeko] *nm* (*figura*) figure; (*marioneta*) puppet; (*fig*) puppet, pawn

mural [mu'ral] *adj* mural, wall *cpd* ♦ *nm* mural

muralla [mu'raʎa] *nf* (city) wall(s) (*pl*)

murciélago [mur'θjelaɣo] *nm* bat

murmullo [mur'muʎo] *nm* murmur(ing); (*cuchicheo*) whispering

murmuración [murmura'θjon] *nf* gossip; **murmurar** *vi* to murmur, whisper; (*cotillear*) to gossip

muro ['muro] *nm* wall

muscular [musku'lar] *adj* muscular

músculo ['muskulo] *nm* muscle

museo [mu'seo] *nm* museum; **~ de arte** art gallery

musgo ['musɣo] *nm* moss

música ['musika] *nf* music; *ver tb* **músico**

músico, a ['musiko, a] *adj* musical ♦ *nm/f* musician

muslo ['muslo] *nm* thigh

mustio, a ['mustjo, a] *adj* (*persona*) depressed, gloomy; (*planta*) faded, withered

musulmán, ana [musul'man, ana] *nm/f* Moslem

mutación [muta'θjon] *nf* (*BIO*) mutation; (*cambio*) (sudden) change

mutilar [muti'lar] *vt* to mutilate; (*a una persona*) to maim

mutismo [mu'tismo] *nm* (*de persona*) uncommunicativeness; (*de autoridades*) silence

mutuamente [mutwa'mente] *adv* mutually

mutuo, a ['mutwo, a] *adj* mutual

muy [mwi] *adv* very; (*demasiado*) too; **M~ Señor mío** Dear Sir; **~ de noche** very late at night; **eso es ~ de él** that's just like him

N, n

N *abr* (= *norte*) N

nabo ['naβo] *nm* turnip

nácar ['nakar] *nm* mother-of-pearl

nacer [na'θer] *vi* to be born; (*de huevo*) to hatch; (*vegetal*) to sprout; (*río*) to rise; **nací en Barcelona** I was born in Barcelona; **nació una sospecha en su mente** a suspicion formed in her mind; **nacido, a** *adj* born; **recién nacido** newborn; **naciente** *adj* new, emerging; (*sol*) rising; **nacimiento** *nm* birth; (*de Navidad*) Nativity; (*de río*) source

nación [na'θjon] *nf* nation; **nacional** *adj* national; **nacionalismo** *nm* nationalism; **nacionalista** *nm/f* nationalist; **nacionalizar** *vt* to nationalize; **nacionalizarse** *vr* (*persona*) to become naturalized

nada ['naða] *pron* nothing ♦ *adv* not at all, in no way; **no decir ~** to say nothing, not to say anything; **~ más** nothing else; **de ~** don't mention it

nadador, a [naða'ðor, a] *nm/f* swimmer

nadar [na'ðar] *vi* to swim

nadie ['naðje] *pron* nobody, no-one; **~ habló** nobody spoke; **no había ~** there was nobody there, there wasn't anybody there

nado ['naðo]: **a ~** *adv*: **pasar a ~** to swim across

nafta ['nafta] (*AM*) *nf* petrol (*BRIT*), gas (*US*)

naipe ['naipe] *nm* (playing) card; **~s** *nmpl* cards

nalgas ['nalɣas] *nfpl* buttocks

nana ['nana] *nf* lullaby

naranja [na'ranxa] *adj inv, nf* orange; **media ~** (*fam*) better half; **naranjada** *nf* orangeade; **naranjo** *nm* orange tree

narciso [nar'θiso] *nm* narcissus

narcótico, a [nar'kotiko, a] *adj, nm* narcotic; **narcotizar** *vt* to drug; **narcotráfico** *nm* drug trafficking o running

nardo ['narðo] *nm* lily

narigudo, a [nari'ɣuðo, a] *adj* big-nosed

nariz [na'riθ] *nf* nose

narración [narra'θjon] *nf* narration; **narrador, a** *nm/f* narrator

narrar [na'rrar] *vt* to narrate, recount; **narrativa** *nf* narrative

nata ['nata] *nf* cream

natación [nata'θjon] *nf* swimming

natal [na'tal] *adj*: **ciudad ~** home town; **~idad** *nf* birth rate

natillas [na'tiʎas] *nfpl* custard *sg*

nativo, a [na'tiβo, a] *adj, nm/f* native

nato, a ['nato, a] *adj* born; **un músico ~** a born musician

natural [natu'ral] *adj* natural; (*fruta etc*) fresh ♦ *nm/f* native ♦ *nm* (*disposición*) nature

naturaleza [natura'leθa] *nf* nature; (*género*) nature, kind; **~ muerta** still life

naturalidad [naturali'ðað] *nf* naturalness

naturalmente [natural'mente] *adv* (*de modo natural*) in a natural way; **¡~!** of course!

naufragar [naufra'ɣar] *vi* to sink; **naufragio** *nm* shipwreck; **náufrago, a** *nm/f* castaway, shipwrecked person

nauseabundo, a [nausea'ßundo, a] *adj* nauseating, sickening

náuseas ['nauseas] *nfpl* nausea *sg*; **me da ~** it makes me feel sick

náutico, a ['nautiko, a] *adj* nautical

navaja [na'ßaxa] *nf* knife; (*de barbero, peluquero*) razor

naval [na'ßal] *adj* naval

Navarra [na'ßarra] *n* Navarre

nave ['naße] *nf* (*barco*) ship, vessel; (*ARQ*) nave; **~ espacial** spaceship

navegación [naßeɣa'θjon] *nf* navigation; (*viaje*) sea journey; **~ aérea** air traffic; **~ costera** coastal shipping; **navegador** *nm* (*INFORM*) browser; **navegante** *nm/f* navigator; **navegar** *vi* (*barco*) to sail; (*avión*) to fly

Navidad [naßi'ðað] *nf* Christmas; **~es** *nfpl* Christmas time; **Feliz N~** Merry Christmas; **navideño, a** *adj* Christmas *cpd*

navío [na'ßio] *nm* ship

nazca *etc vb ver* **nacer**

nazi ['naθi] *adj, nm/f* Nazi

NE *abr* (= *nor(d)este*) NE

neblina [ne'ßlina] *nf* mist

nebulosa [neßu'losa] *nf* nebula

necesario, a [neθe'sarjo, a] *adj* necessary

neceser [neθe'ser] *nm* toilet bag; (*bolsa grande*) holdall

necesidad [neθesi'ðað] *nf* need; (*lo inevitable*) necessity; (*miseria*) poverty, need; **en caso de ~** in case of need o emergency; **hacer sus ~es** to relieve o.s.

necesitado, a [neθesi'taðo, a] *adj* needy, poor; **~ de** in need of

necesitar [neθesi'tar] *vt* to need, require

necio, a ['neθjo, a] *adj* foolish

necrópolis [ne'kropolis] *nf inv* cemetery

nectarina [nekta'rina] *nf* nectarine

nefasto, a [ne'fasto, a] *adj* ill-fated, unlucky

negación [neɣa'θjon] *nf* negation; (*rechazo*) refusal, denial

negar [ne'ɣar] *vt* (*renegar, rechazar*) to refuse; (*prohibir*) to refuse, deny; (*desmentir*) to deny; **~se** *vr*: **~se a** to refuse to

negativa [neɣa'tißa] *nf* negative; (*rechazo*)

refusal, denial

negativo, a [neɣa'tiβo, a] *adj, nm* negative

negligencia [neɣli'xenθja] *nf* negligence; **negligente** *adj* negligent

negociado [neɣo'θjaðo] *nm* department, section

negociante [neɣo'θjante] *nm/f* businessman/woman

negociar [neɣo'θjar] *vt, vi* to negotiate; ~ **en** to deal in, trade in

negocio [ne'ɣoθjo] *nm* (COM) business; (*asunto*) affair, business; (*operación comercial*) deal, transaction; (AM) firm; (*lugar*) place of business; **los ~s** business *sg*; **hacer ~** to do business

negra ['neɣra] *nf* (MUS) crotchet; *ver tb* **negro**

negro, a ['neɣro, a] *adj* black; (*suerte*) awful ♦ *nm* black ♦ *nm/f* black man/woman

nene, a ['nene, a] *nm/f* baby, small child

nenúfar [ne'nufar] *nm* water lily

neologismo [neolo'xismo] *nm* neologism

neón [ne'on] *nm*: **luces/lámpara de ~** neon lights/lamp

neoyorquino, a [neojor'kino, a] *adj* (of) New York

nervio ['nerβjo] *nm* nerve; **nerviosismo** *nm* nervousness, nerves *pl*; **~so, a** *adj* nervous

neto, a ['neto, a] *adj* net

neumático, a [neu'matiko, a] *adj* pneumatic ♦ *nm* (ESP) tyre (BRIT), tire (US); ~ **de recambio** spare tyre

neurasténico, a [neuras'teniko, a] *adj* (*fig*) hysterical

neurólogo, a [neu'roloɣo, a] *nm/f* neurologist

neurona [neu'rona] *nf* nerve cell

neutral [neu'tral] *adj* neutral; **~izar** *vt* to neutralize; (*contrarrestar*) to counteract

neutro, a ['neutro, a] *adj* (BIO, LING) neuter

neutrón [neu'tron] *nm* neutron

nevada [ne'βaða] *nf* snowstorm; (*caída de nieve*) snowfall

nevar [ne'βar] *vi* to snow

nevera [ne'βera] (ESP) *nf* refrigerator (BRIT), icebox (US)

nevería [neβe'ria] (AM) *nf* ice-cream parlour

nexo ['nekso] *nm* link, connection

ni [ni] *conj* nor, neither; (*tb*: **~ siquiera**) not ... even; **~ aunque que** not even if; **~ blanco ~ negro** neither white nor black

Nicaragua [nika'raɣwa] *nf* Nicaragua; **nicaragüense** *adj, nm/f* Nicaraguan

nicho ['nitʃo] *nm* niche

nicotina [niko'tina] *nf* nicotine

nido ['niðo] *nm* nest

niebla ['njeβla] *nf* fog; (*neblina*) mist

niego *etc vb ver* **negar**

nieto, a ['njeto, a] *nm/f* grandson/daughter; **~s** *nmpl* grandchildren

nieve *etc* ['njeβe] *vb ver* **nevar** ♦ *nf* snow; (AM) icecream

N.I.F. *nm abr* (= *Número de Identificación Fiscal*) *personal identification number used for financial and tax purposes*

nimiedad [nimje'ðað] *nf* triviality

nimio, a ['nimjo, a] *adj* trivial, insignificant

ninfa ['ninfa] *nf* nymph

ningún [nin'gun] *adj ver* **ninguno**

ninguno, a [nin'guno, a] (*delante de nm*: **ningún**) *adj* no ♦ *pron* (*nadie*) nobody; (*ni uno*) none, not one; (*ni uno ni otro*) neither; **de ninguna manera** by no means, not at all

niña ['nina] *nf* (ANAT) pupil; *ver tb* **niño**

niñera [ni'nera] *nf* nursemaid, nanny; **niñería** *nf* childish act

niñez [ni'neθ] *nf* childhood; (*infancia*) infancy

niño, a ['nino, a] *adj* (*joven*) young; (*inmaduro*) immature ♦ *nm/f* child, boy/girl

nipón, ona [ni'pon, ona] *adj, nm/f* Japanese

níquel ['nikel] *nm* nickel; **niquelar** *vt* (TEC) to nickel-plate

níspero ['nispero] *nm* medlar

nitidez [niti'ðeθ] *nf* (*claridad*) clarity; (: *de imagen*) sharpness; **nítido, a** *adj* clear;

sharp

nitrato [ni'trato] *nm* nitrate

nitrógeno [ni'troxeno] *nm* nitrogen

nivel [ni'ßel] *nm* (GEO) level; (*norma*) level, standard; (*altura*) height; **~ de aceite** oil level; **~ de aire** spirit level; **~ de vida** standard of living; **~ar** *vt* to level out; (*fig*) to even up; (COM) to balance

NN. UU. *nfpl abr* (= Naciones Unidas) UN *sg*

no [no] *adv* no; not; (*con verbo*) not ♦ *excl* no!; **~ tengo nada** I don't have anything, I have nothing; **~ es el mío** it's not mine; **ahora ~** not now; **¿~ lo sabes?** don't you know?; **~ mucho** not much; **~ bien termine, lo entregaré** as soon as I finish I'll hand it over; **~ más: ayer ~ más** just yesterday; **¡pase ~ más!** come in!; **¡a que ~ lo sabes!** I bet you don't know!; **¡cómo ~!** of course!; **los países ~ alineados** the non-aligned countries; **la ~ intervención** non-intervention

noble ['noßle] *adj*, *nm/f* noble; **~za** *nf* nobility

noche ['notʃe] *nf* night, night-time; (*la tarde*) evening; **de ~, por la ~** at night; **es de ~** it's dark

Noche de San Juan

The **Noche de San Juan** on the 24th June is a *fiesta* coinciding with the summer solstice and which has taken the place of other ancient pagan festivals. Traditionally fire plays a major part in these festivities with celebrations and dancing taking place around bonfires in towns and villages across the country.

Nochebuena [notʃe'ßwena] *nf* Christmas Eve

Nochebuena

Traditional Christmas celebrations in Spanish-speaking countries mainly take place on the night of **Nochebuena**, Christmas Eve. Families gather together for large meal and the more religiously

inclined attend Midnight Mass. While presents are traditionally given by **los Reyes Magos** on the 6th January, more and more people are exchanging gifts on Christmas Eve.

nochevieja [notʃe'ßjexa] *nf* New Year's Eve

noción [no'θjon] *nf* notion

nocivo, a [no'θiβo, a] *adj* harmful

noctámbulo, a [nok'tambulo, a] *nm/f* sleepwalker

nocturno, a [nok'turno, a] *adj* (*de la noche*) nocturnal, night *cpd*; (*de la tarde*) evening *cpd* ♦ *nm* nocturne

nodriza [no'ðriθa] *nf* wet nurse; **buque** *o* **nave ~** supply ship

nogal [no'ɣal] *nm* walnut tree

nómada ['nomaða] *adj* nomadic ♦ *nm/f* nomad

nombramiento [nombra'mjento] *nm* naming; (*a un empleo*) appointment

nombrar [nom'brar] *vt* (*designar*) to name; (*mencionar*) to mention; (*dar puesto a*) to appoint

nombre ['nombre] *nm* name; (*sustantivo*) noun; **~ y apellidos** name in full; **~ común/propio** common/proper noun; **~ de pila/de soltera** Christian/maiden name; **poner ~ a** to call, name

nómina ['nomina] *nf* (*lista*) payroll; (*hoja*) payslip

nominal [nomi'nal] *adj* nominal

nominar [nomi'nar] *vt* to nominate

nominativo, a [nomina'tiβo, a] *adj* (COM): **cheque ~ a X** cheque made out to X

nono, a ['nono, a] *adj* ninth

nordeste [nor'ðeste] *adj* north-east, north-eastern, north-easterly ♦ *nm* north-east

nórdico, a ['norðiko, a] *adj* Nordic

noreste [no'reste] *adj*, *nm* = **nordeste**

noria ['norja] *nf* (AGR) waterwheel; (*de carnaval*) big (BRIT) *o* Ferris (US) wheel

norma ['norma] *nf* rule (of thumb)

normal [nor'mal] *adj* (*corriente*) normal;

(*habitual*) usual, natural; **~idad** *nf* normality; **restablecer la ~idad** to restore order; **~izar** *vt* (*reglamentar*) to normalize; (*TEC*) to standardize; **~izarse** *vr* to return to normal; **~mente** *adv* normally

normando, a [nor'mando, a] *adj*, *nm/f* Norman

normativa [norma'tiβa] *nf* (set of) rules *pl*, regulations *pl*

noroeste [noro'este] *adj* north-west, north-western, north-westerly ♦ *nm* north-west

norte ['norte] *adj* north, northern, northerly ♦ *nm* north; (*fig*) guide

norteamericano, a [norteameri'kano, a] *adj*, *nm/f* (North) American

Noruega [no'rweɣa] *nf* Norway

noruego, a [no'rweɣo, a] *adj*, *nm/f* Norwegian

nos [nos] *pron* (*directo*) us; (*indirecto*) us; to us; for us; from us; (*reflexivo*) (to) ourselves; (*recíproco*) (to) each other; **~ levantamos a las 7** we get up at 7

nosotros, as [no'sotros, as] *pron* (*sujeto*) we; (*después de prep*) us

nostalgia [nos'talxja] *nf* nostalgia

nota ['nota] *nf* note; (*ESCOL*) mark

notable [no'taβle] *adj* notable; (*ESCOL*) outstanding

notar [no'tar] *vt* to notice, note; **~se** *vr* to be obvious; **se nota que ...** one observes that ...

notarial [nota'rjal] *adj*: **acta ~** affidavit

notario [no'tarjo] *nm* notary

noticia [no'tiθja] *nf* (*información*) piece of news; **las ~s** the news *sg*; **tener ~s de alguien** to hear from sb

noticiero [noti'θjero] (*AM*) *nm* news bulletin

notificación [notifika'θjon] *nf* notification; **notificar** *vt* to notify, inform

notoriedad [notorje'ðað] *nf* fame, renown; **notorio, a** *adj* (*público*) well-known; (*evidente*) obvious

novato, a [no'βato, a] *adj* inexperienced ♦ *nm/f* beginner, novice

novecientos, as [noβe'θjentos, as] *num* nine hundred

novedad [noβe'ðað] *nf* (*calidad de nuevo*) newness; (*noticia*) piece of news; (*cambio*) change, (new) development

novel [no'βel] *adj* new; (*inexperto*) inexperienced ♦ *nm/f* beginner

novela [no'βela] *nf* novel

noveno, a [no'βeno, a] *adj* ninth

noventa [no'βenta] *num* ninety

novia ['noβja] *nf ver* **novio**

noviazgo [no'βjaθɣo] *nm* engagement

novicio, a [no'βiθjo, a] *nm/f* novice

noviembre [no'βjembre] *nm* November

novillada [noβi'ʎaða] *nf* (*TAUR*) bullfight with young bulls; **novillero** *nm* novice bullfighter; **novillo** *nm* young bull, bullock; **hacer novillos** (*fam*) to play truant

novio, a ['noβjo, a] *nm/f* boyfriend/girlfriend; (*prometido*) fiancé/fiancée; (*recién casado*) bridegroom/bride; **los ~s** the newly-weds

nubarrón [nuβa'rron] *nm* storm cloud

nube ['nuβe] *nf* cloud

nublado, a [nu'βlaðo, a] *adj* cloudy; **nublarse** *vr* to grow dark

nubosidad [nuβosi'ðað] *nf* cloudiness; **había mucha ~** it was very cloudy

nuca ['nuka] *nf* nape of the neck

nuclear [nukle'ar] *adj* nuclear

núcleo ['nukleo] *nm* (*centro*) core; (*FÍSICA*) nucleus

nudillo [nu'ðiʎo] *nm* knuckle

nudista [nu'ðista] *adj* nudist

nudo ['nuðo] *nm* knot; **~so, a** *adj* knotty

nuera ['nwera] *nf* daughter-in-law

nuestro, a ['nwestro, a] *adj* our ♦ *pron* ours; **~ padre** our father; **un amigo ~** a friend of ours; **es el ~** it's ours

nueva ['nweβa] *nf* piece of news

nuevamente [nweβa'mente] *adv* (*otra vez*) again; (*de nuevo*) anew

Nueva York [-'jɔrk] *n* New York

Nueva Zelanda [-θe'landa] *nf* New Zealand

nueve ['nweβe] *num* nine

evo, a ['nweßo, a] adj (gen) new; de ~
gain

ez [nweθ] nf walnut; ~ de Adán Adam's
ple; ~ moscada nutmeg

idad [nuli'ðað] nf (incapacidad)
competence; (abolición) nullity

o, a ['nulo, a] adj (inepto, torpe)
seless; (inválido) (null and) void;
DEPORTE) drawn, tied

m. abr (= número) no

meración [numera'θjon] nf (cifras)
umbers pl; (arábiga, romana etc)
umerals pl

meral [nume'ral] nm numeral

merar [nume'rar] vt to number

mero ['numero] nm (gen) number;
amaño: de zapato) size; (ejemplar: de
ario) number, issue; sin ~ numberless,
nnumbered; ~ de matrícula/de
eléfono registration/telephone number;
atrasado back number

meroso, a [nume'roso, a] adj
umerous

nca ['nunka] adv (jamás) never; ~ lo
ensé I never thought it; no viene ~ he
ever comes; ~ más never again; más
ue ~ more than ever

pcias ['nupθjas] nfpl wedding sg,
uptials

tria ['nutrja] nf otter

trición [nutri'θjon] nf nutrition

krido, a [nu'triðo, a] adj (alimentado)
ourished; (fig: grande) large; (abundante)
undant

krir [nu'trir] vt (alimentar) to nourish;
lar de comer) to feed; (fig) to strengthen;
utritivo, a adj nourishing, nutritious

on [ni'lon] nm nylon

Ñ, ñ

to, a ['nato, a] (AM) adj snub-nosed

ñería [noɲe'ria] nf insipidness

ño, a ['noɲo, a] adj (AM: tonto) silly,
upid; (soso) insipid; (persona) spineless

O, o

O abr (= oeste) W

o [o] conj or

o/ abr (= orden) o.

oasis [o'asis] nm inv oasis

obcecarse [oßθe'karse] vr to get o
become stubborn

obedecer [oßeðe'θer] vt to obey;
obediencia nf obedience; obediente
adj obedient

obertura [oßer'tura] nf overture

obesidad [oßesi'ðað] nf obesity; obeso,
a adj obese

obispo [o'ßispo] nm bishop

objeción [oßxe'θjon] nf objection; poner
objeciones to raise objections

objetar [oßxe'tar] vt, vi to object

objetivo, a [oßxe'tißo, a] adj, nm
objective

objeto [oß'xeto] nm (cosa) object; (fin)
aim

objetor, a [oßxe'tor, a] nm/f objector

oblicuo, a [o'ßlikwo, a] adj oblique;
(mirada) sidelong

obligación [oßliγa'θjon] nf obligation;
(COM) bond

obligar [oßli'γar] vt to force; ~se vr to
bind o.s.; obligatorio, a adj
compulsory, obligatory

oboe [o'ßoe] nm oboe

obra ['oßra] nf work; (ARQ) construction,
building; (TEATRO) play; ~ maestra
masterpiece; ~s públicas public works;
por ~ de thanks to (the efforts of); obrar
vt to work; (tener efecto) to have an effect
on ♦ vi to act, behave; (tener efecto) to
have an effect; la carta obra en su
poder the letter is in his/her possession

obrero, a [o'ßrero, a] adj (clase) working;
(movimiento) labour cpd ♦ nm/f (gen)
worker; (sin oficio) labourer

obscenidad [oßsθeni'ðað] nf obscenity;
obsceno, a adj obscene

obscu... = oscu...

obsequiar [oβse'kjar] vt (*ofrecer*) to present with; (*agasajar*) to make a fuss of, lavish attention on; **obsequio** nm (*regalo*) gift; (*cortesía*) courtesy, attention
observación [oβserβa'θjon] nf observation; (*reflexión*) remark
observador, a [oβserβa'ðor, a] nm/f observer
observar [oβser'βar] vt to observe; (*anotar*) to notice; **~se** vr to keep to, observe
obsesión [oβse'sjon] nf obsession; **obsesivo, a** adj obsessive
obsoleto, a [oβso'leto, a] adj obsolete
obstáculo [oβs'takulo] nm obstacle; (*impedimento*) hindrance, drawback
obstante [oβs'tante]: **no ~** adv nevertheless
obstinado, a [oβsti'naðo, a] adj obstinate, stubborn
obstinarse [oβsti'narse] vr to be obstinate; **~ en** to persist in
obstrucción [oβstruk'θjon] nf obstruction; **obstruir** vt to obstruct
obtener [oβte'ner] vt (*gen*) to obtain; (*premio*) to win
obturador [oβtura'ðor] nm (FOTO) shutter
obvio, a ['oβßjo, a] adj obvious
oca ['oka] nf (*animal*) goose; (*juego*) ≈ snakes and ladders
ocasión [oka'sjon] nf (*oportunidad*) opportunity, chance; (*momento*) occasion, time; (*causa*) cause; **de ~** secondhand; **ocasionar** vt to cause
ocaso [o'kaso] nm (fig) decline
occidente [okθi'ðente] nm west
OCDE nf abr (= *Organización de Cooperación y Desarrollo Económico*) OECD
océano [o'θeano] nm ocean; **el ~ Índico** the Indian Ocean
ochenta [o'tʃenta] num eighty
ocho ['otʃo] num eight; **~ días** a week
ocio ['oθjo] nm (*tiempo*) leisure; (*pey*) idleness; **~so, a** adj (*inactivo*) idle; (*inútil*) useless
octavilla [okta'viʎa] nf leaflet, pamphlet
octavo, a [ok'taβo, a] adj eighth

octubre [ok'tuβre] nm October
ocular [oku'lar] adj ocular, eye cpd; **testigo ~** eyewitness
oculista [oku'lista] nm/f oculist
ocultar [okul'tar] vt (*esconder*) to hide; (*callar*) to conceal; **oculto, a** adj hidden; (fig) secret
ocupación [okupa'θjon] nf occupation
ocupado, a [oku'paðo, a] adj (*persona*) busy; (*plaza*) occupied, taken; (*teléfono*) engaged; **ocupar** vt (*gen*) to occupy; **ocuparse** vr: **ocuparse de o en** (*gen*) to concern o.s. with; (*cuidar*) to look after
ocurrencia [oku'rrenθja] nf (*idea*) bright idea
ocurrir [oku'rrir] vi to happen; **~se** vr: **se me ocurrió que ...** it occurred to me that ...
odiar [o'ðjar] vt to hate; **odio** nm hate, hatred; **odioso, a** adj (*gen*) hateful; (*malo*) nasty
odontólogo, a [oðon'tolovo, a] nm/f dentist, dental surgeon
OEA nf abr (= *Organización de Estados Americanos*) OAS
oeste [o'este] nm west; **una película del ~** a western
ofender [ofen'der] vt (*agraviar*) to offend; (*insultar*) to insult; **~se** vr to take offence; **ofensa** nf offence; **ofensiva** nf offensive; **ofensivo, a** adj offensive
oferta [o'ferta] nf offer; (*propuesta*) proposal; **la ~ y la demanda** supply and demand; **artículos en ~** goods on offer
oficial [ofi'θjal] adj official ♦ nm (MIL) officer
oficina [ofi'θina] nf office; **~ de correos** post office; **~ de turismo** tourist office; **oficinista** nm/f clerk
oficio [o'fiθjo] nm (*profesión*) profession; (*puesto*) post; (REL) service; **ser del ~** to be an old hand; **tener mucho ~** to have a lot of experience; **~ de difuntos** funeral service
oficioso, a [ofi'θjoso, a] adj (pey) officious; (*no oficial*) unofficial, informal
ofimática [ofi'matika] nf office

automation

ofrecer [ofre'θer] *vt* (*dar*) to offer; (*proponer*) to propose; **~se** *vr* (*persona*) to offer o.s., volunteer; (*situación*) to present itself; **¿qué se le ofrece?, ¿se le ofrece algo?** what can I do for you?, can I get you anything?

ofrecimiento [ofreθi'mjento] *nm* offer

oftalmólogo, a [oftal'moloɣo, a] *nm/f* ophthalmologist

ofuscar [ofus'kar] *vt* (*por pasión*) to blind; (*por luz*) to dazzle

oída [o'iða] *nf*: **de ~s** by hearsay

oído [o'iðo] *nm* (ANAT) ear; (*sentido*) hearing

oigo *etc vb ver* **oír**

oír [o'ir] *vt* (*gen*) to hear; (*atender a*) to listen to; **¡oiga!** listen!; **~ misa** to attend mass

OIT *nf abr* (= *Organización Internacional del Trabajo*) ILO

ojal [o'xal] *nm* buttonhole

ojalá [oxa'la] *excl* if only (it were so)!, some hope! ♦ *conj* if only ...!, would that ...!; **~ (que) venga hoy** I hope he comes today

ojeada [oxe'aða] *nf* glance

ojera [o'xera] *nf*: **tener ~s** to have bags under one's eyes

ojeriza [oxe'riθa] *nf* ill-will

ojeroso, a [oxe'roso, a] *adj* haggard

ojo [o'xo] *nm* eye; (*de puente*) span; (*de cerradura*) keyhole ♦ *excl* careful!; **tener ~ para** to have an eye for; **~ de buey** porthole

okupa [o'kupa] (*fam*) *nm/f* squatter

ola ['ola] *nf* wave

olé [o'le] *excl* bravo!, olé!

oleada [ole'aða] *nf* big wave, swell; (*fig*) wave

oleaje [ole'axe] *nm* swell

óleo ['oleo] *nm* oil; **oleoducto** *nm* (oil) pipeline

oler [o'ler] *vt* (*gen*) to smell; (*inquirir*) to pry into; (*fig: sospechar*) to sniff out ♦ *vi* to smell; **~ a** to smell of

olfatear [olfate'ar] *vt* to smell; (*inquirir*) to

pry into; **olfato** *nm* sense of smell

oligarquía [oliɣar'kia] *nf* oligarchy

olimpíada [olim'piaða] *nf*: **las O~s** the Olympics; **olímpico, a** [o'limpiko, a] *adj* Olympic

oliva [o'liβa] *nf* (*aceituna*) olive; **aceite de ~** olive oil; **olivo** *nm* olive tree

olla ['oʎa] *nf* pan; (*comida*) stew; **~ a presión** *o* **exprés** pressure cooker; **~ podrida** *type of Spanish stew*

olmo ['olmo] *nm* elm (tree)

olor [o'lor] *nm* smell; **~oso, a** *adj* scented

olvidar [olβi'ðar] *vt* to forget; (*omitir*) to omit; **~se** *vr* (*fig*) to forget o.s.; **se me olvidó** I forgot

olvido [ol'βiðo] *nm* oblivion; (*despiste*) forgetfulness

ombligo [om'bliɣo] *nm* navel

omisión [omi'sjon] *nf* (*abstención*) omission; (*descuido*) neglect

omiso, a [o'miso, a] *adj*: **hacer caso ~ de** to ignore, pass over

omitir [omi'tir] *vt* to omit

omnipotente [omnipo'tente] *adj* omnipotent

omóplato [o'moplato] *nm* shoulder blade

OMS *nf abr* (= *Organización Mundial de la Salud*) WHO

once ['onθe] *num* eleven; **~s** (AM) *nfpl* tea break

onda ['onda] *nf* wave; **~ corta/larga/media** short/long/medium wave; **ondear** *vt, vi* to wave; (*tener ondas*) to be wavy; (*agua*) to ripple; **ondearse** *vr* to swing, sway

ondulación [ondula'θjon] *nf* undulation; **ondulado, a** *adj* wavy

ondular [ondu'lar] *vt* (*el pelo*) to wave ♦ *vi* to undulate; **~se** *vr* to undulate

ONG *nf abr* (= *organización no gubernamental*) NGO

ONU ['onu] *nf abr* (= *Organización de las Naciones Unidas*) UNO

opaco, a [o'pako, a] *adj* opaque

opción [op'θjon] *nf* (*gen*) option; (*derecho*) right, option

OPEP ['opep] *nf abr* (= *Organización de*

Países Exportadores de Petróleo) OPEC

ópera ['opera] *nf* opera; **~ bufa** *o* **cómica** comic opera

operación [opera'θjon] *nf* (*GEN*) operation; (*COM*) transaction, deal

operador, a [opera'ðor, a] *nm/f* operator; (*CINE: proyección*) projectionist; (*: rodaje*) cameraman

operar [ope'rar] *vt* (*producir*) to produce, bring about; (*MED*) to operate on ♦ *vi* (*COM*) to operate, deal; **~se** *vr* to occur; (*MED*) to have an operation

opereta [ope'reta] *nf* operetta

opinar [opi'nar] *vt* to think ♦ *vi* to give one's opinion; **opinión** *nf* (*creencia*) belief; (*criterio*) opinion

opio ['opjo] *nm* opium

oponente [opo'nente] *nm/f* opponent

oponer [opo'ner] *vt* (*resistencia*) to put up, offer; **~se** *vr* (*objetar*) to object; (*estar frente a frente*) to be opposed; (*dos personas*) to oppose each other; **~ A a B** to set A against B; **me opongo a pensar que ...** I refuse to believe *o* think that ...

oportunidad [oportuni'ðað] *nf* (*ocasión*) opportunity; (*posibilidad*) chance

oportuno, a [opor'tuno, a] *adj* (*en su tiempo*) opportune, timely; (*respuesta*) suitable; **en el momento ~** at the right moment

oposición [oposi'θjon] *nf* opposition; **oposiciones** *nfpl* (*ESCOL*) public examinations

opositor, a [oposi'tor, a] *nm/f* (*adversario*) opponent; (*candidato*): **~ (a)** candidate (for)

opresión [opre'sjon] *nf* oppression; **opresivo, a** *adj* oppressive; **opresor, a** *nm/f* oppressor

oprimir [opri'mir] *vt* to squeeze; (*fig*) to oppress

optar [op'tar] *vi* (*elegir*) to choose; **~ por** to opt for; **optativo, a** *adj* optional

óptico, a ['optiko, a] *adj* optic(al) ♦ *nm/f* optician; **óptica** *nf* optician's (shop); **desde esta óptica** from this point of view

optimismo [opti'mismo] *nm* optimism; **optimista** *nm/f* optimist

óptimo, a ['optimo, a] *adj* (*el mejor*) very best

opuesto, a [o'pwesto, a] *adj* (*contrario*) opposite; (*antagónico*) opposing

opulencia [opu'lenθja] *nf* opulence; **opulento, a** *adj* opulent

oración [ora'θjon] *nf* (*REL*) prayer; (*LING*) sentence

orador, a [ora'ðor, a] *nm/f* (*conferenciante*) speaker, orator

oral [o'ral] *adj* oral

orangután [orangu'tan] *nm* orangutan

orar [o'rar] *vi* to pray

oratoria [ora'torja] *nf* oratory

órbita ['orßita] *nf* orbit

orden ['orðen] *nm* (*gen*) order ♦ *nf* (*gen*) order; (*INFORM*) command; **~ del día** agenda; **de primer ~** first-rate; **en ~ de prioridad** in order of priority

ordenado, a [orðe'naðo, a] *adj* (*metódico*) methodical; (*arreglado*) orderly

ordenador [orðena'ðor] *nm* computer; **~ central** mainframe computer

ordenanza [orðe'nanθa] *nf* ordinance

ordenar [orðe'nar] *vt* (*mandar*) to order; (*poner orden*) to put in order, arrange; **~se** *vr* (*REL*) to be ordained

ordeñar [orðe'ɲar] *vt* to milk

ordinario, a [orði'narjo, a] *adj* (*común*) ordinary, usual; (*vulgar*) vulgar, common

orégano [o'reɣano] *nm* oregano

oreja [o'rexa] *nf* ear; (*MECÁNICA*) lug, flange

orfanato [orfa'nato] *nm* orphanage

orfandad [orfan'dað] *nf* orphanhood

orfebrería [orfeßre'ria] *nf* gold/silver work

orgánico, a [or'ɣaniko, a] *adj* organic

organigrama [orɣani'ɣrama] *nm* flow chart

organismo [orɣa'nismo] *nm* (*BIO*) organism; (*POL*) organization

organización [orɣaniθa'θjon] *nf* organization; **organizar** *vt* to organize

órgano ['orɣano] *nm* organ

orgasmo [or'ɣasmo] *nm* orgasm

rgía [orˈxia] nf orgy

rgullo [orˈɣuʎo] nm pride; **orgulloso, a** adj (gen) proud; (altanero) haughty

rientación [orjentaˈθjon] nf (posición) position; (dirección) direction

riental [orjenˈtal] adj eastern; (del Lejano Oriente) oriental

rientar [orjenˈtar] vt (situar) to orientate; (señalar) to point; (dirigir) to direct; (guiar) to guide; **~se** vr to get one's bearings

riente [oˈrjente] nm east; **Cercano/Medio/Lejano O~** Near/Middle/Far East

rigen [oˈrixen] nm origin

riginal [orixiˈnal] adj (nuevo) original; (extraño) odd, strange; **~idad** nf originality

riginar [orixiˈnar] vt to start, cause; **~se** vr to originate; **~io, a** adj original; **~io de** native of

rilla [oˈriʎa] nf (borde) border; (de río) bank; (de bosque, tela) edge; (de mar) shore

rina [oˈrina] nf urine; **orinal** nm (chamber) pot; **orinar** vi to urinate; **orinarse** vr to wet o.s.; **orines** nmpl urine

riundo, a [oˈrjundo, a] adj: **~ de** native of

rnitología [ornitoloˈxia] nf ornithology, bird-watching

ro [ˈoro] nm gold; **~s** nmpl (NAIPES) hearts

ropel [oroˈpel] nm tinsel

rquesta [orˈkesta] nf orchestra; **~ de cámara/sinfónica** chamber/symphony orchestra

rquídea [orˈkiðea] nf orchid

rtiga [orˈtiɣa] nf nettle

rtodoxo, a [ortoˈðokso, a] adj orthodox

rtografía [ortoɣraˈfia] nf spelling

rtopedia [ortoˈpeðja] nf orthopaedics sg; **ortopédico, a** adj orthopaedic

ruga [oˈruɣa] nf caterpillar

rzuelo [orˈθwelo] nm stye

s [os] pron (gen) you; (a vosotros) to you

sa [ˈosa] nf (she-)bear; **O~ Mayor/Menor** Great/Little Bear

osadía [osaˈðia] nf daring

osar [oˈsar] vi to dare

oscilación [osθilaˈθjon] nf (movimiento) oscillation; (fluctuación) fluctuation

oscilar [osθiˈlar] vi to oscillate; to fluctuate

oscurecer [oskureˈθer] vt to darken ♦ vi to grow dark; **~se** vr to grow o get dark

oscuridad [oskuriˈðað] nf obscurity; (tinieblas) darkness

oscuro, a [osˈkuro, a] adj dark; (fig) obscure; **a oscuras** in the dark

óseo, a [ˈoseo, a] adj bone cpd

oso [ˈoso] nm bear; **~ de peluche** teddy bear; **~ hormiguero** anteater

ostentación [ostentaˈθjon] nf (gen) ostentation; (acto) display

ostentar [ostenˈtar] vt (gen) to show; (pey) to flaunt, show off; (poseer) to have, possess

ostra [ˈostra] nf oyster

OTAN [ˈotan] nf abr (= Organización del Tratado del Atlántico Norte) NATO

otear [oteˈar] vt to observe; (fig) to look into

otitis [oˈtitis] nf earache

otoñal [otoˈɲal] adj autumnal

otoño [oˈtoɲo] nm autumn

otorgar [otorˈɣar] vt (conceder) to concede; (dar) to grant

otorrino, a [otoˈrrino, a], **otorrinolaringólogo, a** [otorrinolarinˈɡoloɣo, a] nm/f ear, nose and throat specialist

---

PALABRA CLAVE

otro, a [ˈotro, a] adj 1 (distinto: sg) another; (: pl) other; **con ~s amigos** with other o different friends
2 (adicional): **tráigame ~ café (más), por favor** can I have another coffee please; **~s 10 días más** another ten days
♦ pron 1: **el ~** the other one; **(los) ~s** (the) others; **de ~** somebody else's; **que lo haga ~** let somebody else do it
2 (recíproco): **se odian (la) una a (la) otra** they hate one another o each other
3: **~ tanto: comer ~ tanto** to eat the

same *o* as much again; **recibió una
decena de telegramas y otras tantas
llamadas** he got about ten telegrams
and as many calls

ovación [oβa'θjon] *nf* ovation
oval [o'βal] *adj* oval; **~ado, a** *adj* oval;
óvalo *nm* oval
ovario [o'βarjo] *nm* ovary
oveja [o'βexa] *nf* sheep
overol [oβe'rol] (*AM*) *nm* overalls *pl*
ovillo [o'βiʎo] *nm* (*de lana*) ball of wool;
hacerse un ~ to curl up
OVNI ['oβni] *nm abr* (= *objeto volante no
identificado*) UFO
ovulación [oβula'θjon] *nf* ovulation;
óvulo *nm* ovum
oxidación [oksiða'θjon] *nf* rusting
oxidar [oksi'ðar] *vt* to rust; **~se** *vr* to go
rusty
óxido ['oksiðo] *nm* oxide
oxigenado, a [oksixe'naðo, a] *adj* (*QUÍM*)
oxygenated; (*pelo*) bleached
oxígeno [ok'sixeno] *nm* oxygen
oyente [o'jente] *nm/f* listener, hearer
oyes *etc vb ver* **oír**
ozono [o'θono] *nm* ozone

P, p

P *abr* (= *padre*) Fr.
pabellón [paβe'ʎon] *nm* bell tent; (*ARQ*)
pavilion; (*de hospital etc*) block, section;
(*bandera*) flag
pacer [pa'θer] *vi* to graze
paciencia [pa'θjenθja] *nf* patience
paciente [pa'θjente] *adj, nm/f* patient
pacificación [paθifika'θjon] *nf*
pacification
pacificar [paθifi'kar] *vt* to pacify;
(*tranquilizar*) to calm
pacífico, a [pa'θifiko, a] *adj* (*persona*)
peaceable; (*existencia*) peaceful; **el
(océano) P~** the Pacific (Ocean)
pacifismo [paθi'fismo] *nm* pacifism;

pacifista *nm/f* pacifist
pacotilla [pako'tiʎa] *nf*: **de ~** (*actor,
escritor*) third-rate; (*mueble etc*) cheap
pactar [pak'tar] *vt* to agree to *o* on ♦ *vi* to
come to an agreement
pacto ['pakto] *nm* (*tratado*) pact; (*acuerdo*)
agreement
padecer [paðe'θer] *vt* (*sufrir*) to suffer;
(*soportar*) to endure, put up with;
padecimiento *nm* suffering
padrastro [pa'ðrastro] *nm* stepfather
padre ['paðre] *nm* father ♦ *adj* (*fam*): **un
éxito ~** a tremendous success; **~s** *nmpl*
parents
padrino [pa'ðrino] *nm* (*REL*) godfather; (*tb:
~ de boda*) best man; (*fig*) sponsor,
patron; **~s** *nmpl* godparents
padrón [pa'ðron] *nm* (*censo*) census, roll
paella [pa'eʎa] *nf* paella, *dish of rice with
meat, shellfish etc*
paga ['paɣa] *nf* (*pago*) payment; (*sueldo*)
pay, wages *pl*
pagano, a [pa'ɣano, a] *adj, nm/f* pagan,
heathen
pagar [pa'ɣar] *vt* to pay; (*las compras,
crimen*) to pay for; (*fig: favor*) to repay
♦ *vi* to pay; **~ al contado/a plazos** to
pay (in) cash/in instalments
pagaré [paɣa're] *nm* I.O.U.
página ['paxina] *nf* page; **~ de inicio**
(*INFORM*) home page
pago ['paɣo] *nm* (*dinero*) payment; **~
anticipado/a cuenta/contra reembolso**
advance payment/payment on account/
cash on delivery; **en ~ de** in return
for
pág(s). *abr* (= *página(s)*) p(p).
pague *etc vb ver* **pagar**
país [pa'is] *nm* (*gen*) country; (*región*) land;
los P~es Bajos the Low Countries; **el P~
Vasco** the Basque Country
paisaje [pai'saxe] *nm* landscape, scenery
paisano, a [pai'sano, a] *adj* of the same
country ♦ *nm/f* (*compatriota*) fellow
countryman/woman; **vestir de ~**
(*soldado*) to be in civvies; (*guardia*) to be
in plain clothes

aja ['paxa] nf straw; (fig) rubbish (BRIT), trash (US)

ajarita [paxa'rita] nf (corbata) bow tie

ájaro ['paxaro] nm bird; ~ carpintero woodpecker

ajita [pa'xita] nf (drinking) straw

ala ['pala] nf spade, shovel; (raqueta etc) bat; (: de tenis) racquet; (CULIN) slice; ~ matamoscas fly swat

alabra [pa'laßra] nf word; (facultad) (power of) speech; (derecho de hablar) right to speak; tomar la ~ (en mitin) to take the floor

alta ['palta] (AM) nf avocado (pear)

alabrota [pala'brota] nf swearword

alacio [pa'laθjo] nm palace; (mansión) mansion, large house; ~ de justicia courthouse; ~ municipal town/city hall

aladar [pala'ðar] nm palate; paladear vt to taste

alanca [pa'lanka] nf lever; (fig) pull, influence

alangana [palan'gana] nf washbasin

alco ['palko] nm box

alestina [pales'tina] nf Palestine; palestino, a nm/f Palestinian

aleta [pa'leta] nf (de pintor) palette; (de albañil) trowel; (de ping-pong) bat; (AM) ice lolly

aleto, a [pa'leto, a] (fam, pey) nm/f yokel

aliar [pa'ljar] vt (mitigar) to mitigate, alleviate; paliativo nm palliative

alidecer [paliðe'θer] vi to turn pale; palidez nf paleness; pálido, a adj pale

alillo [pa'liʎo] nm (mondadientes) toothpick; (para comer) chopstick

aliza [pa'liθa] nf beating, thrashing

alma ['palma] nf (ANAT) palm; (árbol) palm tree; batir o dar ~s to clap, applaud; ~da nf slap; ~das nfpl clapping sg, applause sg

almar [pal'mar] (fam) vi (tb: ~la) to die, kick the bucket

almear [palme'ar] vi to clap

almera [pal'mera] nf (BOT) palm tree

almo ['palmo] nm (medida) span; (fig) small amount; ~ a ~ inch by inch

alo ['palo] nm stick; (poste) post; (de

tienda de campaña) pole; (mango) handle, shaft; (golpe) blow, hit; (de golf) club; (de béisbol) bat; (NAUT) mast; (NAIPES) suit

paloma [pa'loma] nf dove, pigeon

palomitas [palo'mitas] nfpl popcorn sg

palpar [pal'par] vt to touch, feel

palpitación [palpita'θjon] nf palpitation

palpitante [palpi'tante] adj palpitating; (fig) burning

palpitar [palpi'tar] vi to palpitate; (latir) to beat

palta ['palta] (AM) nf avocado (pear)

paludismo [palu'ðismo] nm malaria

pamela [pa'mela] nf picture hat, sun hat

pampa ['pampa] (AM) nf pampas, prairie

pan [pan] nm bread; (una barra) loaf; ~ integral wholemeal (BRIT) o wholewheat (US) bread; ~ rallado breadcrumbs pl

pana ['pana] nf corduroy

panadería [panaðe'ria] nf baker's (shop); panadero, a nm/f baker

Panamá [pana'ma] nm Panama; panameño, a adj Panamanian

pancarta [paŋ'karta] nf placard, banner

panda ['panda] nm (ZOOL) panda

pandereta [pande'reta] nf tambourine

pandilla [pan'diʎa] nf set, group; (de criminales) gang; (pey: camarilla) clique

panecillo [pane'θiʎo] nm (bread) roll

panel [pa'nel] nm panel; ~ solar solar panel

panfleto [pan'fleto] nm pamphlet

pánico ['paniko] nm panic

panorama [pano'rama] nm panorama; (vista) view

pantalla [pan'taʎa] nf (de cine) screen; (de lámpara) lampshade

pantalón [panta'lon] nm trousers; pantalones nmpl trousers

pantano [pan'tano] nm (ciénaga) marsh, swamp; (depósito: de agua) reservoir; (fig) jam, difficulty

panteón [pante'on] nm: ~ familiar family tomb

pantera [pan'tera] nf panther

panti(e)s ['pantis] nmpl tights

pantomima [panto'mima] nf pantomime

pantorrilla [panto'rriʎa] *nf* calf (of the leg)

pantufla [pan'tufla] *nf* slipper

panty(s) ['panti(s)] *nm(pl)* tights

panza ['panθa] *nf* belly, paunch

pañal [pa'ɲal] *nm* nappy (*BRIT*), diaper (*US*); **~es** *nmpl* (*fig*) early stages, infancy *sg*

paño ['paɲo] *nm* (*tela*) cloth; (*pedazo de tela*) (piece of) cloth; (*trapo*) duster, rag; **~ higiénico** sanitary towel; **~s menores** underclothes

pañuelo [pa'ɲwelo] *nm* handkerchief, hanky (*fam*); (*para la cabeza*) (head)scarf

papa ['papa] *nm*: **el P~** the Pope ♦ *nf* (*AM*) potato

papá [pa'pa] (*pl* **~s**) (*fam*) *nm* dad(dy), pa (*US*)

papada [pa'paða] *nf* double chin

papagayo [papa'yajo] *nm* parrot

papanatas [papa'natas] (*fam*) *nm inv* simpleton

paparrucha [papa'rrutʃa] *nf* piece of nonsense

papaya [pa'paja] *nf* papaya

papear [pape'ar] (*fam*) *vt, vi* to scoff

papel [pa'pel] *nm* paper; (*hoja de ~*) sheet of paper; (*TEATRO, fig*) role; **~ de calco / carbón / de cartas** tracing paper/carbon paper/stationery; **~ de envolver / pintado** wrapping paper/wallpaper; **~ de aluminio / higiénico** aluminium (*BRIT*) o aluminum (*US*) foil/toilet paper; **~ de estaño** o **plata** tinfoil; **~ de lija** sandpaper; **~ moneda** paper money; **~ secante** blotting paper

papeleo [pape'leo] *nm* red tape

papelera [pape'lera] *nf* wastepaper basket; (*en la calle*) litter bin

papelería [papele'ria] *nf* stationer's (shop)

papeleta [pape'leta] *nf* (*POL*) ballot paper; (*ESCOL*) report

paperas [pa'peras] *nfpl* mumps *sg*

papilla [pa'piʎa] *nf* (*para niños*) baby food

paquete [pa'kete] *nm* (*de cigarrillos etc*) packet; (*CORREOS etc*) parcel; (*AM*) package tour; (: *fam*) nuisance

par [par] *adj* (*igual*) like, equal; (*MAT*) even ♦ *nm* equal; (*de guantes*) pair; (*de veces*) couple; (*POL*) peer; (*GOLF, COM*) par; **abrir de ~ en ~** to open wide

para ['para] *prep* for; **no es ~ comer** it's not for eating; **decir ~ sí** to say to o.s.; **¿~ qué lo quieres?** what do you want it for?; **se casaron ~ separarse otra vez** they married only to separate again; **lo tendré ~ mañana** I'll have it (for) tomorrow; **ir ~ casa** to go home, head for home; **~ profesor es muy estúpido** he's very stupid for a teacher; **¿quién es usted ~ gritar así?** who are you to shout like that?; **tengo bastante ~ vivir** I have enough to live on; *ver tb* **con**

parabién [para'βjen] *nm* congratulations *pl*

parábola [pa'raβola] *nf* parable; (*MAT*) parabola; **parabólica** *nf* (*tb*: **antena ~**) satellite dish

parabrisas [para'βrisas] *nm inv* windscreen (*BRIT*), windshield (*US*)

paracaídas [paraka'iðas] *nm inv* parachute; **paracaidista** *nm/f* parachutist; (*MIL*) paratrooper

parachoques [para'tʃokes] *nm inv* (*AUTO*) bumper; (*MECÁNICA etc*) shock absorber

parada [pa'raða] *nf* stop; (*acto*) stopping; (*de industria*) shutdown, stoppage; (*lugar*) stopping place; **~ de autobús** bus stop

paradero [para'ðero] *nm* stopping-place; (*situación*) whereabouts

parado, a [pa'raðo, a] *adj* (*persona*) motionless, standing still; (*fábrica*) closed, at a standstill; (*coche*) stopped; (*AM*) standing (up); (*sin empleo*) unemployed, idle

paradoja [para'ðoxa] *nf* paradox

parador [para'ðor] *nm* parador, state-run hotel

paráfrasis [pa'rafrasis] *nf inv* paraphrase

paraguas [pa'raxwas] *nm inv* umbrella

Paraguay [para'ɣwai] *nm*: **el ~** Paraguay; **paraguayo, a** *adj, nm/f* Paraguayan

paraíso [para'iso] *nm* paradise, heaven

paraje [pa'raxe] *nm* place, spot

aralelo, a [para'lelo, a] adj parallel

arálisis [pa'ralisis] nf inv paralysis;

paralítico, a adj, nm/f paralytic

aralizar [parali'θar] vt to paralyse; ~se vr to become paralysed; (fig) to come to a standstill

aramilitar [paramili'tar] adj paramilitary

aramo ['paramo] nm bleak plateau

arangón [paran'gon] nm: **sin ~** incomparable

aranoico, a [para'noiko, a] nm/f paranoiac

arapente [para'pente] nm (deporte) paragliding; (aparato) paraglider

arapléjico, a [para'plexiko, a] adj, nm/f paraplegic

arar [pa'rar] vt to stop; (golpe) to ward off ♦ vi to stop; ~se vr to stop; (AM) to stand up; **ha parado de llover** it has stopped raining; **van a ir a ~ a comisaría** they're going to end up in the police station; ~se en to pay attention to

ararrayos [para'rrajos] nm inv lightning conductor

arásito, a [pa'rasito, a] nm/f parasite

arcela [par'θela] nf plot, piece of ground

arche ['partʃe] nm (gen) patch

archís [par'tʃis] nm ludo

arcial [par'θjal] adj (pago) part-; (eclipse) partial; (JUR) prejudiced, biased; (POL) partisan; ~**idad** nf prejudice, bias

ardillo, a [par'ðiʎo, a] (pey) adj yokel

arecer [pare'θer] nm (opinión) opinion, view; (aspecto) looks pl ♦ vi (tener apariencia) to seem, look; (asemejarse) to look o seem like; (aparecer, llegar) to appear; ~se vr to look alike, resemble each other; ~se a to look like, resemble; **según parece** evidently, apparently; **me parece que** I think (that), it seems to me that

arecido, a [pare'θiðo, a] adj similar ♦ nm similarity, likeness, resemblance; **bien ~** good-looking, nice-looking

ared [pa'reð] nf wall

areja [pa'rexa] nf (par) pair; (dos personas) couple; (otro: de un par) other

one (of a pair); (persona) partner

parentela [paren'tela] nf relations pl

parentesco [paren'tesko] nm relationship

paréntesis [pa'rentesis] nm inv parenthesis; (en escrito) bracket

parezco etc vb ver **parecer**

pariente, a [pa'rjente, a] nm/f relative, relation

parir [pa'rir] vt to give birth to ♦ vi (mujer) to give birth, have a baby

París [pa'ris] n Paris

parking ['parkin] nm car park (BRIT), parking lot (US)

parlamentar [parlamen'tar] vi to parley

parlamentario, a [parlamen'tarjo, a] adj parliamentary ♦ nm/f member of parliament

parlamento [parla'mento] nm parliament

parlanchín, ina [parlan'tʃin, ina] adj indiscreet ♦ nm/f chatterbox

parlar [par'lar] vi to chatter (away)

paro ['paro] nm (huelga) stoppage (of work), strike; (desempleo) unemployment; **subsidio de ~** unemployment benefit

parodia [pa'roðja] nf parody; **parodiar** vt to parody

parpadear [parpaðe'ar] vi (ojos) to blink; (luz) to flicker

párpado ['parpaðo] nm eyelid

parque ['parke] nm (lugar verde) park; ~ **de atracciones/infantil/zoológico** fairground/playground/zoo

parqué [par'ke] nm parquet (flooring)

parquímetro [par'kimetro] nm parking meter

parra ['parra] nf (grape)vine

párrafo ['parrafo] nm paragraph; **echar un ~** (fam) to have a chat

parranda [pa'rranda] (fam) nf spree, binge

parrilla [pa'rriʎa] nf (CULIN) grill; (de coche) grille; **(carne a la) ~** barbecue; ~**da** nf barbecue

párroco ['parroko] nm parish priest

parroquia [pa'rrokja] nf parish; (iglesia) parish church; (COM) clientele, customers pl; ~**no, a** nm/f parishioner; client, customer

parsimonia [parsi'monja] *nf* calmness, level-headedness

parte ['parte] *nm* message; (*informe*) report ♦ *nf* part; (*lado, cara*) side; (*de reparto*) share; (*JUR*) party; **en alguna ~ de Europa** somewhere in Europe; **en/por todas ~s** everywhere; **en gran ~** to a large extent; **la mayor ~ de los españoles** most Spaniards; **de un tiempo a esta ~** for some time past; **de ~ de alguien** on sb's behalf; **¿de ~ de quién?** (*TEL*) who is speaking?; **por ~ de** on the part of; **yo por mí ~** I for my part; **por otra ~** on the other hand; **dar ~** to inform; **tomar ~** to take part

partición [parti'θjon] *nf* division, sharing-out; (*POL*) partition

participación [partiθipa'θjon] *nf* (*acto*) participation, taking part; (*parte, COM*) share; (*de lotería*) shared prize; (*aviso*) notice, notification

participante [partiθi'pante] *nm/f* participant

participar [partiθi'par] *vt* to notify, inform ♦ *vi* to take part, participate

partícipe [par'tiθipe] *nm/f* participant

particular [partiku'lar] *adj* (*especial*) particular, special; (*individual, personal*) private, personal ♦ *nm* (*punto, asunto*) particular, point; (*individuo*) individual; **tiene coche** ~ he has a car of his own

partida [par'tiða] *nf* (*salida*) departure; (*COM*) entry, item; (*juego*) game; (*grupo de personas*) band, group; **mala ~** dirty trick; **~ de nacimiento / matrimonio / defunción** birth/marriage/death certificate

partidario, a [parti'ðarjo, a] *adj* partisan ♦ *nm/f* supporter, follower

partido [par'tiðo] *nm* (*POL*) party; (*DEPORTE*) game, match; **sacar ~ de** to profit *o* benefit from; **tomar ~** to take sides

partir [par'tir] *vt* (*dividir*) to split, divide; (*compartir, distribuir*) to share (out), distribute; (*romper*) to break open, split open; (*rebanada*) to cut (off) ♦ *vi* (*ponerse*

en camino) to set off *o* out; (*comenzar*) to start (off *o* out); **~se** *vr* to crack *o* split *o* break (in two *etc*); **a ~ de** (starting) from

partitura [parti'tura] *nf* (*MUS*) score

parto ['parto] *nm* birth; (*fig*) product, creation; **estar de ~** to be in labour

pasa ['pasa] *nf* raisin; **~ de Corinto / de Esmirna** currant/sultana

pasada [pa'saða] *nf* passing, passage; **de ~** in passing, incidentally; **una mala ~** a dirty trick

pasadizo [pasa'ðiθo] *nm* (*pasillo*) passage, corridor; (*callejuela*) alley

pasado, a [pa'saðo, a] *adj* past; (*malo: comida, fruta*) bad; (*muy cocido*) overdone; (*anticuado*) out of date ♦ *nm* past; **~ mañana** the day after tomorrow; **el mes ~** last month

pasador [pasa'ðor] *nm* (*cerrojo*) bolt; (*de pelo*) hair slide; (*horquilla*) grip

pasaje [pa'saxe] *nm* passage; (*pago de viaje*) fare; (*los pasajeros*) passengers *pl*; (*pasillo*) passageway

pasajero, a [pasa'xero, a] *adj* passing; (*situación, estado*) temporary; (*amor, enfermedad*) brief ♦ *nm/f* passenger

pasamontañas [pasamon'taɲas] *nm inv* balaclava helmet

pasaporte [pasa'porte] *nm* passport

pasar [pa'sar] *vt* to pass; (*tiempo*) to spend; (*desgracias*) to suffer, endure; (*noticia*) to give, pass on; (*río*) to cross; (*barrera*) to pass through; (*falta*) to overlook, tolerate; (*contrincante*) to surpass, do better than; (*coche*) to overtake; (*CINE*) to show; (*enfermedad*) to give, infect with ♦ *vi* (*gen*) to pass; (*terminarse*) to be over; (*ocurrir*) to happen; **~se** *vr* (*flores*) to fade; (*comida*) to go bad *o* off; (*fig*) to overdo it, go too far; **~ de** to go beyond, exceed; **~ por** (*AM*) to fetch; **~lo bien/mal** to have a good/bad time; **¡pase!** come in!; **hacer ~** to show in; **~se al enemigo** to go over to the enemy; **se me pasó** I forgot; **no se le pasa nada** he misses nothing; **pase lo que pase** come what may; **¿qué**

pasa? what's going on?, what's up?;
¿qué te pasa? what's wrong?
pasarela [pasaˈrela] *nf* footbridge; *(en barco)* gangway
pasatiempo [pasaˈtjempo] *nm* pastime, hobby
Pascua [ˈpaskwa] *nf*: ~ **(de Resurrección)** Easter; ~ **de Navidad** Christmas; ~**s** *nfpl* Christmas (time); **¡felices ~s!** Merry Christmas!
pase [ˈpase] *nm* pass; *(CINE)* performance, showing
pasear [paseˈar] *vt* to take for a walk; *(exhibir)* to parade, show off ♦ *vi* to walk, go for a walk; ~**se** *vr* to walk, go for a walk; ~ **en coche** to go for a drive; **paseo** *nm (avenida)* avenue; *(distancia corta)* walk, stroll; **dar un** *o* **ir de paseo** to go for a walk
pasillo [paˈsiʎo] *nm* passage, corridor
pasión [paˈsjon] *nf* passion
pasivo, a [paˈsiβo, a] *adj* passive; *(inactivo)* inactive ♦ *nm (COM)* liabilities *pl*, debts *pl*
pasmar [pasˈmar] *vt (asombrar)* to amaze, astonish; **pasmo** *nm* amazement, astonishment; *(resfriado)* chill; *(fig)* wonder, marvel; **pasmoso, a** *adj* amazing, astonishing
paso, a [ˈpaso, a] *adj* dried ♦ *nm* step; *(modo de andar)* walk; *(huella)* footprint; *(rapidez)* speed, pace, rate; *(camino accesible)* way through, passage; *(cruce)* crossing; *(pasaje)* passing, passage; *(GEO)* pass; *(estrecho)* strait; ~ **a nivel** *(FERRO)* level-crossing; ~ **de peatones** pedestrian crossing; **a ese** ~ *(fig)* at that rate; **salir al** ~ **de** *o* **a** to waylay; **estar de** ~ to be passing through; ~ **elevado** flyover; **prohibido el** ~ no entry; **ceda el** ~ give way
pasota [paˈsota] *(fam) adj, nmf* ≈ dropout; **ser un (tipo)** ~ to be a bit of a dropout; *(ser indiferente)* not to care about anything
pasta [ˈpasta] *nf* paste; *(CULIN: masa)* dough; *(: de bizcochos etc)* pastry; *(fam)*

dough; ~**s** *nfpl (bizcochos)* pastries, small cakes; *(fideos, espaguetis etc)* pasta; ~ **de dientes** *o* **dentífrica** toothpaste
pastar [pasˈtar] *vt, vi* to graze
pastel [pasˈtel] *nm (dulce)* cake; *(ARTE)* pastel; ~ **de carne** meat pie; ~**ería** *nf* cake shop
pasteurizado, a [pasteuriˈθaðo, a] *adj* pasteurized
pastilla [pasˈtiʎa] *nf (de jabón, chocolate)* bar; *(píldora)* tablet, pill
pasto [ˈpasto] *nm (hierba)* grass; *(lugar)* pasture, field
pastor, a [pasˈtor, a] *nm/f* shepherd/ess ♦ *nm (REL)* clergyman, pastor; ~ **alemán** Alsatian
pata [ˈpata] *nf (pierna)* leg; *(pie)* foot; *(de muebles)* leg; ~**s arriba** upside down; **metedura de** ~ *(fam)* gaffe; **meter la** ~ *(fam)* to put one's foot in it; *(TEC)*: ~ **de cabra** crowbar; **tener buena/mala** ~ to be lucky/unlucky; ~**da** *nf* kick; *(en el suelo)* stamp
patalear [pataleˈar] *vi (en el suelo)* to stamp one's feet
patata [paˈtata] *nf* potato; ~**s fritas** chips, French fries; *(de bolsa)* crisps
paté [paˈte] *nm* pâté
patear [pateˈar] *vt (pisar)* to stamp on, trample (on); *(pegar con el pie)* to kick ♦ *vi* to stamp (with rage), stamp one's feet
patentar [patenˈtiar] *vt* to patent
patente [paˈtente] *adj* obvious, evident; *(COM)* patent ♦ *nf* patent
paternal [paterˈnal] *adj* fatherly, paternal; **paterno, a** *adj* paternal
patético, a [paˈtetiko, a] *adj* pathetic, moving
patilla [paˈtiʎa] *nf (de gafas)* side(piece); ~**s** *nfpl* sideburns
patín [paˈtin] *nm* skate; *(de trineo)* runner; **patinaje** *nm* skating; **patinar** *vi* to skate; *(resbalarse)* to skid, slip; *(fam)* to slip up, blunder
patio [ˈpatjo] *nm (de casa)* patio, courtyard; ~ **de recreo** playground

pato ['pato] *nm* duck; **pagar el ~** (*fam*) to take the blame, carry the can

patológico, a [pato'loxiko, a] *adj* pathological

patoso, a [pa'toso, a] (*fam*) *adj* clumsy

patraña [pa'traɲa] *nf* story, fib

patria ['patrja] *nf* native land, mother country

patrimonio [patri'monjo] *nm* inheritance; (*fig*) heritage

patriota [pa'trjota] *nm/f* patriot; **patriotismo** *nm* patriotism

patrocinar [patroθi'nar] *vt* to sponsor; **patrocinio** *nm* sponsorship

patrón, ona [pa'tron, ona] *nm/f* (*jefe*) boss, chief, master/mistress; (*propietario*) landlord/lady; (*REL*) patron saint ♦ *nm* (*TEC, COSTURA*) pattern

patronal [patro'nal] *adj*: **la clase ~** management

patronato [patro'nato] *nm* sponsorship; (*acto*) patronage; (*fundación benéfica*) trust, foundation

patrulla [pa'truʎa] *nf* patrol

pausa ['pausa] *nf* pause, break

pausado, a [pau'saðo, a] *adj* slow, deliberate

pauta ['pauta] *nf* line, guide line

pavimento [paβi'mento] *nm* (*con losas*) pavement, paving

pavo ['paβo] *nm* turkey; **~ real** peacock

pavor [pa'βor] *nm* dread, terror

payaso [pa'jaso] *nm/f* clown

payo, a [pa'jo, a] *nm/f* non-gipsy

paz [paθ] *nf* peace; (*tranquilidad*) peacefulness, tranquillity; **hacer las paces** to make peace; (*fig*) to make up

pazo ['paθo] *nm* country house

P.D. *abr* (= *posdata*) P.S., p.s.

peaje [pe'axe] *nm* toll

peatón [pea'ton] *nm* pedestrian

peca ['peka] *nf* freckle

pecado [pe'kaðo] *nm* sin; **pecador, a** *adj* sinful ♦ *nm/f* sinner

pecaminoso, a [pekami'noso, a] *adj* sinful

pecar [pe'kar] *vi* (*REL*) to sin; **peca de**

generoso he is generous to a fault

pecera [pe'θera] *nf* fish tank; (*redondo*) goldfish bowl

pecho ['petʃo] *nm* (*ANAT*) chest; (*de mujer*) breast; **dar el ~ a** to breast-feed; **tomar algo a ~** to take sth to heart

pechuga [pe'tʃuɣa] *nf* breast

peculiar [peku'ljar] *adj* special, peculiar; (*característico*) typical, characteristic; **~idad** *nf* peculiarity; special feature, characteristic

pedal [pe'ðal] *nm* pedal; **~ear** *vi* to pedal

pedante [pe'ðante] *adj* pedantic ♦ *nm/f* pedant; **~ría** *nf* pedantry

pedazo [pe'ðaθo] *nm* piece, bit; **hacerse ~s** to smash, shatter

pedernal [peðer'nal] *nm* flint

pediatra [pe'ðjatra] *nm/f* paediatrician

pedido [pe'ðiðo] *nm* (*COM*) order; (*petición*) request

pedir [pe'ðir] *vt* to ask for, request; (*comida, COM: mandar*) to order; (*necesitar*) to need, demand, require ♦ *vi* to ask; **me pidió que cerrara la puerta** he asked me to shut the door; **¿cuánto piden por el coche?** how much are they asking for the car?

pedo ['peðo] (*fam!*) *nm* fart

pega ['peɣa] *nf* snag; **poner ~s (a)** to complain (about)

pegadizo, a [peɣa'ðiθo, a] *adj* (*MUS*) catchy

pegajoso, a [peɣa'xoso, a] *adj* sticky, adhesive

pegamento [peɣa'mento] *nm* gum, glue

pegar [pe'ɣar] *vt* (*papel, sellos*) to stick (on); (*cartel*) to stick up; (*coser*) to sew (on); (*unir: partes*) to join, fix together; (*MED*) to give, infect with; (*dar: golpe*) to give, deal ♦ *vi* (*adherirse*) to stick, adhere; (*ir juntos: colores*) to match, go together; (*golpear*) to hit; (*quemar: el sol*) to strike hot, burn (*fig*); **~se** *vr* (*gen*) to stick; (*dos personas*) to hit each other, fight; (*fam*): **~ un grito** to let out a yell; **~ un salto** to jump (with fright); **~ en** to touch; **~se un tiro** to shoot o.s.

pegatina [peɣaˈtina] nf sticker

pegote [peˈɣote] (fam) nm eyesore, sight

peinado [peiˈnaðo] nm hairstyle

peinar [peiˈnar] vt to comb; (hacer estilo) to style; ~**se** vr to comb one's hair

peine [ˈpeine] nm comb; ~**ta** nf ornamental comb

p.ej. abr (= por ejemplo) e.g.

Pekín [peˈkin] n Pekin(g)

pelado, a [peˈlaðo, a] adj (fruta, patata etc) peeled; (cabeza) shorn; (campo, fig) bare; (fam: sin dinero) broke

pelaje [peˈlaxe] nm (ZOOL) fur, coat; (fig) appearance

pelar [peˈlar] vt (fruta, patatas etc) to peel; (cortar el pelo a) to cut the hair of; (quitar la piel: animal) to skin; ~**se** vr (la piel) to peel off; **voy a ~me** I'm going to get my hair cut

peldaño [pelˈdaɲo] nm step

pelea [peˈlea] nf (lucha) fight; (discusión) quarrel, row

peleado, a [peleˈaðo, a] adj: **estar ~ (con uno)** to have fallen out (with sb)

pelear [peleˈar] vi to fight; ~**se** vr to fight; (reñirse) to fall out, quarrel

peletería [peleteˈria] nf furrier's, fur shop

pelícano [peˈlikano] nm pelican

película [peˈlikula] nf film; (cobertura ligera) thin covering; (FOTO: rollo) roll o reel of film

peligro [peˈliɣro] nm danger; (riesgo) risk; **correr ~ de** to run the risk of; ~**so, a** adj dangerous; risky

pelirrojo, a [peliˈrroxo, a] adj red-haired, red-headed ♦ nm/f redhead

pellejo [peˈʎexo] nm (de animal) skin, hide

pellizcar [peʎiθˈkar] vt to pinch, nip

pelma [ˈpelma] (fam) nm/f pain (in the neck)

pelmazo [pelˈmaθo] (fam) nm = **pelma**

pelo [ˈpelo] nm (cabellos) hair; (de barba, bigote) whisker; (de animal: pellejo) hair, fur, coat; **al ~** just right; **venir al ~** to be exactly what one needs; **un hombre de ~ en pecho** a brave man; **por los ~s** by the skin of one's teeth; **no tener ~s en la**

lengua to be outspoken, not mince words; **tomar el ~ a uno** to pull sb's leg

pelota [peˈlota] nf ball; **en ~** stark naked; **hacer la ~ (a uno)** (fam) to creep (to sb); ~ **vasca** pelota

pelotari [peloˈtari] nm pelota player

pelotón [peloˈton] nm (MIL) squad, detachment

peluca [peˈluka] nf wig

peluche [peˈlutʃe] nm: **oso/muñeco de ~** teddy bear/soft toy

peludo, a [peˈluðo, a] adj hairy, shaggy

peluquería [pelukeˈria] nf hairdresser's; **peluquero, a** nm/f hairdresser

pelusa [peˈlusa] nf (BOT) down; (en tela) fluff

pena [ˈpena] nf (congoja) grief, sadness; (remordimiento) regret; (dificultad) trouble; (dolor) pain; (JUR) sentence; **merecer** o **valer la ~** to be worthwhile; **a duras ~s** with great difficulty; ~ **de muerte** death penalty; ~ **pecuniaria** fine; **¡qué ~!** what a shame!

penal [peˈnal] adj penal ♦ nm (cárcel) prison

penalidad [penaliˈðað] nf (problema, dificultad) trouble, hardship; (JUR) penalty, punishment; ~**es** nfpl trouble, hardship

penalti, penalty [peˈnalti] (pl ~s o ~es) nm penalty (kick)

pendiente [penˈdjente] adj pending, unsettled ♦ nm earring ♦ nf hill, slope

pene [ˈpene] nm penis

penetración [penetraˈθjon] nf (acto) penetration; (agudeza) sharpness, insight

penetrante [peneˈtrante] adj (herida) deep; (persona, arma) sharp; (sonido) penetrating, piercing; (mirada) searching; (viento, ironía) biting

penetrar [peneˈtrar] vt to penetrate, pierce; (entender) to grasp ♦ vi to penetrate, go in; (entrar) to enter, go in; (líquido) to soak in; (fig) to pierce

penicilina [peniθiˈlina] nf penicillin

península [peˈninsula] nf peninsula; **peninsular** adj peninsular

penique [peˈnike] nm penny

penitencia [peni'tenθja] *nf* penance

penoso, a [pe'noso, a] *adj* (*lamentable*) distressing; (*difícil*) arduous, difficult

pensador, a [pensa'ðor, a] *nm/f* thinker

pensamiento [pensa'mjento] *nm* thought; (*mente*) mind; (*idea*) idea

pensar [pen'sar] *vt* to think; (*considerar*) to think over, think out; (*proponerse*) to intend, plan; (*imaginarse*) to think up, invent ♦ *vi* to think; ~ **en** to aim at, aspire to; **pensativo, a** *adj* thoughtful, pensive

pensión [pen'sjon] *nf* (*casa*) boarding *o* guest house; (*dinero*) pension; (*cama y comida*) board and lodging; ~ **completa** full board; **media** ~ half-board; **pensionista** *nm/f* (*jubilado*) (old-age) pensioner; (*huésped*) lodger

penúltimo, a [pe'nultimo, a] *adj* penultimate, last but one

penumbra [pe'numbra] *nf* half-light

penuria [pe'nurja] *nf* shortage, want

peña ['peɲa] *nf* (*roca*) rock; (*cuesta*) cliff, crag; (*grupo*) group, circle; (*AM: club*) folk club

peñasco [pe'ɲasko] *nm* large rock, boulder

peñón [pe'ɲon] *nm* wall of rock; **el P~** the Rock (of Gibraltar)

peón [pe'on] *nm* labourer; (*AM*) farm labourer, farmhand; (*AJEDREZ*) pawn

peonza [pe'onθa] *nf* spinning top

peor [pe'or] *adj* (*comparativo*) worse; (*superlativo*) worst ♦ *adv* worse; worst; **de mal en ~** from bad to worse

pepinillo [pepi'niʎo] *nm* gherkin

pepino [pe'pino] *nm* cucumber; **(no) me importa un ~** I don't care one bit

pepita [pe'pita] *nf* (*BOT*) pip; (*MINERÍA*) nugget

pepito [pe'pito] *nm*: ~ **(de ternera)** steak sandwich

pequeñez [peke'ɲeθ] *nf* smallness, littleness; (*trivialidad*) trifle, triviality

pequeño, a [pe'keɲo, a] *adj* small, little

pera ['pera] *nf* pear; **peral** *nm* pear tree

percance [per'kanθe] *nm* setback, misfortune

percatarse [perka'tarse] *vr*: ~ **de** to notice, take note of

percebe [per'θeβe] *nm* barnacle

percepción [perθep'θjon] *nf* (*vista*) perception; (*idea*) notion, idea

percha ['pertʃa] *nf* (coat)hanger; (*ganchos*) coat hooks *pl*; (*de ave*) perch

percibir [perθi'βir] *vt* to perceive, notice; (*COM*) to earn, get

percusión [perku'sjon] *nf* percussion

perdedor, a [perðe'ðor, a] *adj* losing ♦ *nm/f* loser

perder [per'ðer] *vt* to lose; (*tiempo, palabras*) to waste; (*oportunidad*) to lose, miss; (*tren*) to miss ♦ *vi* to lose; ~**se** *vr* (*extraviarse*) to get lost; (*desaparecer*) to disappear, be lost to view; (*arruinarse*) to be ruined; **echar a ~** (*comida*) to spoil, ruin; (*oportunidad*) to waste

perdición [perði'θjon] *nf* perdition, ruin

pérdida ['perðiða] *nf* loss; (*de tiempo*) waste; ~**s** *nfpl* (*COM*) losses

perdido, a [per'ðiðo, a] *adj* lost

perdiz [per'ðiθ] *nf* partridge

perdón [per'ðon] *nm* (*disculpa*) pardon, forgiveness; (*clemencia*) mercy; **¡~!** sorry!, I beg your pardon!; **perdonar** *vt* to pardon, forgive; (*la vida*) to spare; (*excusar*) to exempt, excuse; **¡perdone (usted)!** sorry!, I beg your pardon!

perdurar [perðu'rar] *vi* (*resistir*) to last, endure; (*seguir existiendo*) to stand, still exist

perecedero, a [pereθe'ðero, a] *adj* perishable

perecer [pere'θer] *vi* to perish, die

peregrinación [pereɣrina'θjon] *nf* (*REL*) pilgrimage

peregrino, a [pere'ɣrino, a] *adj* (*idea*) strange, absurd ♦ *nm/f* pilgrim

perejil [pere'xil] *nm* parsley

perenne [pe'renne] *adj* everlasting, perennial

pereza [pe'reθa] *nf* laziness, idleness; **perezoso, a** *adj* lazy, idle

perfección [perfek'θjon] *nf* perfection;

perfeccionar *vt* to perfect; (*mejorar*) to improve; (*acabar*) to complete, finish

perfectamente [perfekta'mente] *adv* perfectly

perfecto, a [per'fekto, a] *adj* perfect; (*total*) complete

perfil [per'fil] *nm* profile; (*contorno*) silhouette, outline; (ARQ) (cross) section; **~es** *nmpl* features; **~ar** *vt* (*trazar*) to outline; (*fig*) to shape, give character to

perforación [perfora'θjon] *nf* perforation; (*con taladro*) drilling; **perforadora** *nf* punch

perforar [perfo'rar] *vt* to perforate; (*agujero*) to drill, bore; (*papel*) to punch a hole in ♦ *vi* to drill, bore

perfume [per'fume] *nm* perfume, scent

pericia [pe'riθja] *nf* skill, expertise

periferia [peri'ferja] *nf* periphery; (*de ciudad*) outskirts *pl*

periférico [peri'feriko] (AM) *nm* ring road (BRIT), beltway (US)

perímetro [pe'rimetro] *nm* perimeter

periódico, a [pe'rjoðiko, a] *adj* periodic(al) ♦ *nm* newspaper

periodismo [perjo'ðismo] *nm* journalism; **periodista** *nm/f* journalist

periodo [pe'rjoðo] *nm* period

período [pe'rioðo] *nm* = **periodo**

periquito [peri'kito] *nm* budgerigar, budgie

perito, a [pe'rito, a] *adj* (*experto*) expert; (*diestro*) skilled, skilful ♦ *nm/f* expert; skilled worker; (*técnico*) technician

perjudicar [perxuði'kar] *vt* (*gen*) to damage, harm; **perjudicial** *adj* damaging, harmful; (*en detrimento*) detrimental; **perjuicio** *nm* damage, harm

perjurar [perxu'rar] *vi* to commit perjury

perla ['perla] *nf* pearl; **me viene de ~s** it suits me fine

permanecer [permane'θer] *vi* (*quedarse*) to stay, remain; (*seguir*) to continue to be

permanencia [perma'nenθja] *nf* permanence; (*estancia*) stay

permanente [perma'nente] *adj* permanent, constant ♦ *nf* perm

permiso [per'miso] *nm* permission; (*licencia*) permit, licence; **con ~** excuse me; **estar de ~** (MIL) to be on leave; **~ de conducir** driving licence (BRIT), driver's license (US)

permitir [permi'tir] *vt* to permit, allow

pernera [per'nera] *nf* trouser leg

pernicioso, a [perni'θjoso, a] *adj* pernicious

pero ['pero] *conj* but; (*aún*) yet ♦ *nm* (*defecto*) flaw, defect; (*reparo*) objection

perpendicular [perpendiku'lar] *adj* perpendicular

perpetrar [perpe'trar] *vt* to perpetrate

perpetuar [perpe'twar] *vt* to perpetuate; **perpetuo, a** *adj* perpetual

perplejo, a [per'plexo, a] *adj* perplexed, bewildered

perra ['perra] *nf* (ZOOL) bitch; **estar sin una ~** to be flat broke

perrera [pe'rrera] *nf* kennel

perrito [pe'rrito] *nm*: **~ caliente** hot dog

perro ['perro] *nm* dog

persa ['persa] *adj, nm/f* Persian

persecución [perseku'θjon] *nf* pursuit, chase; (REL, POL) persecution

perseguir [perse'vir] *vt* to pursue, hunt; (*cortejar*) to chase after; (*molestar*) to pester, annoy; (REL, POL) to persecute

perseverante [perseβe'rante] *adj* persevering, persistent

perseverar [perseβe'rar] *vi* to persevere, persist

persiana [per'sjana] *nf* (Venetian) blind

persignarse [persiɣ'narse] *vr* to cross o.s.

persistente [persis'tente] *adj* persistent

persistir [persis'tir] *vi* to persist

persona [per'sona] *nf* person; **~ mayor** elderly person

personaje [perso'naxe] *nm* important person, celebrity; (TEATRO etc) character

personal [perso'nal] *adj* (*particular*) personal; (*para una persona*) single, for one person ♦ *nm* personnel, staff; **~idad** *nf* personality

personarse [perso'narse] *vr* to appear in

person
personificar [personifi'kar] *vt* to personify
perspectiva [perspek'tiβa] *nf* perspective;
   (*vista, panorama*) view, panorama;
   (*posibilidad futura*) outlook, prospect
perspicacia [perspi'kaθja] *nf* discernment,
   perspicacity
perspicaz [perspi'kaθ] *adj* shrewd
persuadir [perswa'ðir] *vt* (*gen*) to
   persuade; (*convencer*) to convince; ~se *vr*
   to become convinced; **persuasión** *nf*
   persuasion; **persuasivo, a** *adj*
   persuasive; convincing
pertenecer [pertene'θer] *vi* to belong;
   (*fig*) to concern; **perteneciente** *adj*:
   perteneciente a belonging to;
   pertenencia *nf* ownership;
   pertenencias *nfpl* (*bienes*) possessions,
   property *sg*
pertenezca *etc vb ver* **pertenecer**
pértiga ['pertiɣa] *nf*: **salto de ~** pole vault
pertinente [perti'nente] *adj* relevant,
   pertinent; (*apropiado*) appropriate; **~ a**
   concerning, relevant to
perturbación [perturßa'θjon] *nf* (*POL*)
   disturbance; (*MED*) upset, disturbance
perturbado, a [pertur'ßaðo, a] *adj*
   mentally unbalanced
perturbar [pertur'ßar] *vt* (*el orden*) to
   disturb; (*MED*) to upset, disturb;
   (*mentalmente*) to perturb
Perú [pe'ru] *nm*: **el ~** Peru; **peruano, a**
   adj, nm/f Peruvian
perversión [perßer'sjon] *nf* perversion;
   perverso, a *adj* perverse; (*depravado*)
   depraved
pervertido, a [perßer'tiðo, a] *adj*
   perverted ♦ *nm/f* pervert
pervertir [perßer'tir] *vt* to pervert, corrupt
pesa ['pesa] *nf* weight; (*DEPORTE*) shot
pesadez [pesa'ðeθ] *nf* (*peso*) heaviness;
   (*lentitud*) slowness; (*aburrimiento*)
   tediousness
pesadilla [pesa'ðiʎa] *nf* nightmare, bad
   dream
pesado, a [pe'saðo, a] *adj* heavy; (*lento*)
   slow; (*difícil, duro*) tough, hard; (*aburrido*)
boring, tedious; (*tiempo*) sultry
pésame ['pesame] *nm* expression of
   condolence, message of sympathy; **dar el**
   ~ to express one's condolences
pesar [pe'sar] *vt* to weigh ♦ *vi* to weigh;
   (*ser pesado*) to weigh a lot, be heavy;
   (*fig: opinión*) to carry weight; **no pesa**
   mucho it is not very heavy ♦ *nm*
   (*arrepentimiento*) regret; (*pena*) grief,
   sorrow; **a ~ de** *o* **pese a (que)** in spite
   of, despite
pesca ['peska] *nf* (*acto*) fishing; (*lo*
   pescado) catch; **ir de ~** to go fishing
pescadería [peskaðe'ria] *nf* fish shop,
   fishmonger's (*BRIT*)
pescadilla [peska'ðiʎa] *nf* whiting
pescado [pes'kaðo] *nm* fish
pescador, a [peska'ðor, a] *nm/f*
   fisherman/woman
pescar [pes'kar] *vt* (*tomar*) to catch;
   (*intentar tomar*) to fish for; (*conseguir:*
   trabajo) to manage to get ♦ *vi* to fish, go
   fishing
pescuezo [pes'kweθo] *nm* neck
pesebre [pe'seßre] *nm* manger
peseta [pe'seta] *nf* peseta
pesimista [pesi'mista] *adj* pessimistic
   ♦ *nm/f* pessimist
pésimo, a ['pesimo, a] *adj* awful, dreadful
peso ['peso] *nm* weight; (*balanza*) scales
   pl; (*moneda*) peso; **~ bruto/neto** gross/
   net weight; **vender al ~** to sell by weight
pesquero, a [pes'kero, a] *adj* fishing *cpd*
pesquisa [pes'kisa] *nf* inquiry,
   investigation
pestaña [pes'taɲa] *nf* (*ANAT*) eyelash;
   (*borde*) rim; **pestañear** *vi* to blink
peste ['peste] *nf* plague; (*mal olor*) stink,
   stench
pesticida [pesti'θiða] *nm* pesticide
pestillo [pes'tiʎo] *nm* (*cerrojo*) bolt;
   (*picaporte*) doorhandle
petaca [pe'taka] *nf* (*de cigarros*) cigarette
   case; (*de pipa*) tobacco pouch; (*AM:*
   maleta) suitcase
pétalo ['petalo] *nm* petal
petardo [pe'tardo] *nm* firework, firecracker

petición [peti'θjon] *nf (pedido)* request, plea; *(memorial)* petition; *(JUR)* plea

petrificar [petrifi'kar] *vt* to petrify

petróleo [pe'troleo] *nm* oil, petroleum; **petrolero, a** *adj* petroleum *cpd* ♦ *nm* (oil) tanker

peyorativo, a [pejora'tiβo, a] *adj* pejorative

pez [peθ] *nm* fish

pezón [pe'θon] *nm* teat, nipple

pezuña [pe'θuɲa] *nf* hoof

piadoso, a [pja'ðoso, a] *adj (devoto)* pious, devout; *(misericordioso)* kind, merciful

pianista [pja'nista] *nm/f* pianist

piano ['pjano] *nm* piano

piar [pjar] *vi* to cheep

pibe, a ['piβe, a] *(AM) nm/f* boy/girl

picadero [pika'ðero] *nm* riding school

picadillo [pika'ðiʎo] *nm* mince, minced meat

picado, a [pi'kaðo, a] *adj* pricked, punctured; *(CULIN)* minced, chopped; *(mar)* choppy; *(diente)* bad; *(tabaco)* cut; *(enfadado)* cross

picador [pika'ðor] *nm (TAUR)* picador; *(minero)* faceworker

picadura [pika'ðura] *nf (pinchazo)* puncture; *(de abeja)* sting; *(de mosquito)* bite; *(tabaco picado)* cut tobacco

picante [pi'kante] *adj* hot; *(comentario)* racy, spicy

picaporte [pika'porte] *nm (manija)* doorhandle; *(pestillo)* latch

picar [pi'kar] *vt (aguijerear, perforar)* to prick, puncture; *(abeja)* to sting; *(mosquito, serpiente)* to bite; *(CULIN)* to mince, chop; *(incitar)* to incite, goad; *(dañar, irritar)* to annoy, bother; *(quemar: lengua)* to burn, sting ♦ *vi (pez)* to bite, take the bait; *(sol)* to burn, scorch; *(abeja, MED)* to sting; *(mosquito)* to bite; **~se** *vr (agriarse)* to turn sour, go off; *(ofenderse)* to take offence

picardía [pikar'ðia] *nf* villainy; *(astucia)* slyness, craftiness; *(una ~)* dirty trick; *(palabra)* rude/bad word *o* expression

pícaro, a ['pikaro, a] *adj (malicioso)* villainous; *(travieso)* mischievous ♦ *nm (astuto)* crafty sort; *(sinvergüenza)* rascal, scoundrel

pichón [pi'tʃon] *nm* young pigeon

pico ['piko] *nm (de ave)* beak; *(punta)* sharp point; *(TEC)* pick, pickaxe; *(GEO)* peak, summit; **y ~** and a bit

picor [pi'kor] *nm* itch

picotear [pikote'ar] *vt* to peck ♦ *vi* to nibble, pick

picudo, a [pi'kuðo, a] *adj* pointed, with a point

pidió *etc vb ver* **pedir**

pido *etc vb ver* **pedir**

pie [pje] *(pl ~s) nm* foot; *(fig: motivo)* motive, basis; *(: fundamento)* foothold; **ir a ~** to go on foot, walk; **estar de ~** to be standing (up); **ponerse de ~** to stand up; **de ~s a cabeza** from top to bottom; **al ~ de la letra** *(citar)* literally, verbatim; *(copiar)* exactly, word for word; **en ~ de guerra** on a war footing; **dar ~ a** to give cause for; **hacer ~** *(en el agua)* to touch (the) bottom

piedad [pje'ðað] *nf (lástima)* pity, compassion; *(clemencia)* mercy; *(devoción)* piety, devotion

piedra ['pjeðra] *nf* stone; *(roca)* rock; *(de mechero)* flint; *(METEOROLOGÍA)* hailstone

piel [pjel] *nf (ANAT)* skin, hide, fur; *(cuero)* leather; *(BOT)* skin, peel

pienso *etc vb ver* **pensar**

pierdo *etc vb ver* **perder**

pierna ['pjerna] *nf* leg

pieza ['pjeθa] *nf* piece; *(habitación)* room; **~ de recambio** *o* **repuesto** spare (part)

pigmeo, a [piɣ'meo, a] *adj, nm/f* pigmy

pijama [pi'xama] *nm* pyjamas *pl*

pila ['pila] *nf (ELEC)* battery; *(montón)* heap, pile; *(lavabo)* sink

píldora ['pilðora] *nf* pill; **la ~ (anticonceptiva)** the (contraceptive) pill

pileta [pi'leta] *nf* basin, bowl; *(AM)* swimming pool

pillaje [pi'ʎaxe] *nm* pillage, plunder

pillar [pi'ʎar] *vt (saquear)* to pillage,

plunder; (*fam: coger*) to catch; (: *agarrar*)
to grasp, seize; (: *entender*) to grasp,
catch on to; **~se** *vr*: **~se un dedo con la
puerta** to catch one's finger in the door

pillo, a ['piʎo, a] *adj* villainous; (*astuto*) sly,
crafty ♦ *nm/f* rascal, rogue, scoundrel

piloto [pi'loto] *nm* pilot; (*de aparato*)
(pilot) light; (*AUTO: luz*) tail *o* rear light;
(: *conductor*) driver

pimentón [pimen'ton] *nm* paprika

pimienta [pi'mjenta] *nf* pepper

pimiento [pi'mjento] *nm* pepper,
pimiento

pin [pin] (*pl* **pins**) *nm* badge

pinacoteca [pinako'teka] *nf* art gallery

pinar [pi'nar] *nm* pine forest (*BRIT*), pine
grove (*US*)

pincel [pin'θel] *nm* paintbrush

pinchadiscos [pintʃa'ðiskos] *nm/f inv*
disc-jockey, DJ

pinchar [pin'tʃar] *vt* (*perforar*) to prick,
pierce; (*neumático*) to puncture; (*fig*) to
prod

pinchazo [pin'tʃaθo] *nm* (*perforación*)
prick; (*de neumático*) puncture; (*fig*) prod

pincho ['pintʃo] *nm* savoury (snack); **~
moruno** shish kebab; **~ de tortilla** small
slice of omelette

ping-pong ['pin'pon] *nm* table tennis

pingüino [pin'gwino] *nm* penguin

pino ['pino] *nm* pine (tree)

pinta ['pinta] *nf* spot; (*de líquidos*) spot,
drop; (*aspecto*) appearance, look(s) (*pl*);
~do, a *adj* spotted; (*de colores*)
colourful; **~das** *nfpl* graffiti *sg*

pintar [pin'tar] *vt* to paint ♦ *vi* to paint;
(*fam*) to count, be important; **~se** *vr* to
put on make-up

pintor, a [pin'tor, a] *nm/f* painter

pintoresco, a [pinto'resko, a] *adj*
picturesque

pintura [pin'tura] *nf* painting; **~ a la
acuarela** watercolour; **~ al óleo** oil
painting

pinza ['pinθa] *nf* (*ZOOL*) claw; (*para colgar
ropa*) clothes peg; (*TEC*) pincers *pl*; **~s**
nfpl (*para depilar etc*) tweezers *pl*

piña ['piɲa] *nf* (*fruto del pino*) pine cone;
(*fruta*) pineapple; (*fig*) group

piñón [pi'ɲon] *nm* (*fruto*) pine nut; (*TEC*)
pinion

pío, a ['pio, a] *adj* (*devoto*) pious, devout;
(*misericordioso*) merciful

piojo ['pjoxo] *nm* louse

pionero, a [pjo'nero, a] *adj* pioneering
♦ *nm/f* pioneer

pipa ['pipa] *nf* pipe; **~s** *nfpl* (*BOT*) (edible)
sunflower seeds

pipí [pi'pi] (*fam*) *nm*: **hacer ~** to have a
wee(-wee) (*BRIT*), have to go (wee-wee)
(*US*)

pique ['pike] *nm* (*resentimiento*) pique,
resentment; (*rivalidad*) rivalry,
competition; **irse a ~** to sink; (*esperanza,
familia*) to be ruined

piqueta [pi'keta] *nf* pick(axe)

piquete [pi'kete] *nm* (*MIL*) squad, party;
(*de obreros*) picket

pirado, a [pi'raðo, a] (*fam*) *adj* round the
bend ♦ *nm/f* nutter

piragua [pi'raxwa] *nf* canoe; **piragüismo**
nm canoeing

pirámide [pi'ramiðe] *nf* pyramid

pirata [pi'rata] *adj*, *nm* pirate ♦ *nm/f*: **~
informático/a** hacker

Pirineo(s) [piri'neo(s)] *nm(pl)* Pyrenees *pl*

pirómano, a [pi'romano, a] *nm/f* (*MED,
JUR*) arsonist

piropo [pi'ropo] *nm* compliment, (piece
of) flattery

pirueta [pi'rweta] *nf* pirouette

pis [pis] (*fam*) *nm* pee, piss; **hacer ~** to
have a pee; (*para niños*) to wee-wee

pisada [pi'saða] *nf* (*paso*) footstep; (*huella*)
footprint

pisar [pi'sar] *vt* (*caminar sobre*) to walk on,
tread on; (*apretar con el pie*) to press; (*fig*)
to trample on, walk all over ♦ *vi* to tread,
step, walk

piscina [pis'θina] *nf* swimming pool

Piscis ['pisθis] *nm* Pisces

piso ['piso] *nm* (*suelo, planta*) floor;
(*apartamento*) flat (*BRIT*), apartment;
primer ~ (*ESP*) first floor; (*AM*) ground

floor

pisotear [pisote'ar] *vt* to trample (on *o* underfoot)

pista ['pista] *nf* track, trail; (*indicio*) clue; **~ de aterrizaje** runway; **~ de baile** dance floor; **~ de hielo** ice rink; **~ de tenis** tennis court

pistola [pis'tola] *nf* pistol; (*TEC*) spray-gun; **pistolero, a** *nm/f* gunman/woman, gangster

pistón [pis'ton] *nm* (*TEC*) piston; (*MUS*) key

pitar [pi'tar] *vt* (*silbato*) to blow; (*rechiflar*) to whistle at, boo ♦ *vi* to whistle; (*AUTO*) to sound *o* toot one's horn; (*AM*) to smoke

pitillo [pi'tiʎo] *nm* cigarette

pito ['pito] *nm* whistle; (*de coche*) horn

pitón [pi'ton] *nm* (*ZOOL*) python

pitonisa [pito'nisa] *nf* fortune-teller

pitorreo [pito'rreo] *nm* joke; **estar de ~** to be joking

pizarra [pi'θarra] *nf* (*piedra*) slate; (*encerado*) blackboard

pizca ['piθka] *nf* pinch, spot; (*fig*) spot, speck; **ni ~** not a bit

placa ['plaka] *nf* plate; (*distintivo*) badge, insignia; **~ de matrícula** number plate

placentero, a [plaθen'tero, a] *adj* pleasant, agreeable

placer [pla'θer] *nm* pleasure ♦ *vt* to please

plácido, a ['plaθiðo, a] *adj* placid

plaga ['plaɣa] *nf* pest; (*MED*) plague; (*abundancia*) abundance; **plagar** *vt* to infest, plague; (*llenar*) to fill

plagio ['plaxjo] *nm* plagiarism

plan [plan] *nm* (*esquema, proyecto*) plan; (*idea, intento*) idea, intention; **tener ~** (*fam*) to have a date; **tener un ~** (*fam*) to have an affair; **en ~ económico** (*fam*) on the cheap; **vamos en ~ de turismo** we're going as tourists; **si te pones en ese ~ ...** if that's your attitude ...

plana ['plana] *nf* sheet (of paper), page; (*TEC*) trowel; **en primera ~** on the front page; **~ mayor** staff

plancha ['plantʃa] *nf* (*para planchar*) iron; (*rótulo*) plate, sheet; (*NAUT*) gangway; **a la ~** (*CULIN*) grilled; **~do** *nm* ironing; **planchar** *vt* to iron ♦ *vi* to do the ironing

planeador [planea'ðor] *nm* glider

planear [plane'ar] *vt* to plan ♦ *vi* to glide

planeta [pla'neta] *nm* planet

planicie [pla'niθje] *nf* plain

planificación [planifika'θjon] *nf* planning; **~ familiar** family planning

plano, a ['plano, a] *adj* flat, level, even ♦ *nm* (*MAT, TEC*) plane; (*FOTO*) shot; (*ARQ*) plan; (*GEO*) map; (*de ciudad*) street plan; **primer ~** close-up; **caer de ~** to fall flat

planta ['planta] *nf* (*BOT, TEC*) plant; (*ANAT*) sole of the foot, foot; (*piso*) floor; (*AM: personal*) staff; **~ baja** ground floor

plantación [planta'θjon] *nf* (*AGR*) plantation; (*acto*) planting

plantar [plan'tar] *vt* (*BOT*) to plant; (*levantar*) to erect, set up; **~se** *vr* to stand firm; **~ a uno en la calle** to throw sb out; **dejar plantado a uno** (*fam*) to stand sb up

plantear [plante'ar] *vt* (*problema*) to pose; (*dificultad*) to raise

plantilla [plan'tiʎa] *nf* (*de zapato*) insole; (*personal*) personnel; **ser de ~** to be on the staff

plantón [plan'ton] *nm* (*MIL*) guard, sentry; (*fam*) long wait; **dar (un) ~ a uno** to stand sb up

plasmar [plas'mar] *vt* (*dar forma*) to mould, shape; (*representar*) to represent; **~se** *vr*: **~se en** to take the form of

plasta ['plasta] (*fam*) *adj inv* boring ♦ *nm/f* bore

plástico, a ['plastiko, a] *adj* plastic ♦ *nm* plastic

Plastilina ® [plasti'lina] *nf* Plasticine ®

plata ['plata] *nf* (*metal*) silver; (*cosas hechas de ~*) silverware; (*AM*) cash, dough; **hablar en ~** to speak bluntly *o* frankly

plataforma [plata'forma] *nf* platform; **~ de lanzamiento/perforación** launch(ing) pad/drilling rig

plátano ['platano] *nm* (*fruta*) banana;

(*árbol*) plane tree; banana tree

platea [pla'tea] *nf* (*TEATRO*) pit

plateado, a [plate'aðo, a] *adj* silver; (*TEC*) silver-plated

plática ['platika] *nf* talk, chat; **platicar** *vi* to talk, chat

platillo [pla'tiʎo] *nm* saucer; ~**s** *nmpl* (*MUS*) cymbals; ~ **volador** *o* **volante** flying saucer

platino [pla'tino] *nm* platinum; ~**s** *nmpl* (*AUTO*) contact points

plato ['plato] *nm* plate, dish; (*parte de comida*) course; (*comida*) dish; ~ **combinado** set main course (*served on one plate*); ~ **fuerte** main course; **primer** ~ first course

playa ['plaja] *nf* beach; (*costa*) seaside; ~ **de estacionamiento** (*AM*) car park

playera [pla'jera] *nf* (*AM: camiseta*) T-shirt; ~**s** *nfpl* (*zapatos*) canvas shoes

plaza ['plaθa] *nf* square; (*mercado*) market(place); (*sitio*) room, space; (*en vehículo*) seat, place; (*colocación*) post, job; ~ **de toros** bullring

plazo ['plaθo] *nm* (*lapso de tiempo*) time, period; (*fecha de vencimiento*) expiry date; (*pago parcial*) instalment; **a corto/largo** ~ short-/long-term; **comprar algo a** ~**s** to buy sth on hire purchase (*BRIT*) *o* on time (*US*)

plazoleta [plaθo'leta] *nf* small square

pleamar [plea'mar] *nf* high tide

plebe ['pleße] *nf*: **la** ~ the common people *pl*, the masses *pl*; (*pey*) the plebs *pl*; ~**yo, a** *adj* plebeian; (*pey*) coarse, common

plebiscito [pleßis'θito] *nm* plebiscite

plegable [ple'xaßle] *adj* collapsible; (*silla*) folding

plegar [ple'xar] *vt* (*doblar*) to fold, bend; (*COSTURA*) to pleat; ~**se** *vr* to yield, submit

pleito ['pleito] *nm* (*JUR*) lawsuit, case; (*fig*) dispute, feud

plenilunio [pleni'lunjo] *nm* full moon

plenitud [pleni'tuð] *nf* plenitude, fullness; (*abundancia*) abundance

pleno, a ['pleno, a] *adj* full; (*completo*) complete ♦ *nm* plenum; **en** ~ **día** in broad daylight; **en** ~ **verano** at the height of summer; **en plena cara** full in the face

pliego *etc* ['pljexo] *vb ver* **plegar** ♦ *nm* (*hoja*) sheet (of paper); (*carta*) sealed letter/document; ~ **de condiciones** details *pl*, specifications *pl*

pliegue *etc* ['pljexe] *vb ver* **plegar** ♦ *nm* fold, crease; (*de vestido*) pleat

plomero [plo'mero] *nm* (*AM*) plumber

plomo ['plomo] *nm* (*metal*) lead; (*ELEC*) fuse; **sin** ~ unleaded

pluma ['pluma] *nf* feather; (*para escribir*): ~ (**estilográfica**) ink pen; ~ **fuente** (*AM*) fountain pen

plumero [plu'mero] *nm* (*para el polvo*) feather duster

plumón [plu'mon] *nm* (*de ave*) down; (*AM: fino*) felt-tip pen; (: *ancho*) marker

plural [plu'ral] *adj* plural; ~**idad** *nf* plurality

pluriempleo [pluriem'pleo] *nm* having more than one job

plus [plus] *nm* bonus; ~**valía** *nf* (*COM*) appreciation

población [poßla'θjon] *nf* population; (*pueblo, ciudad*) town, city

poblado, a [po'blaðo, a] *adj* inhabited ♦ *nm* (*aldea*) village; (*pueblo*) (small) town; **densamente** ~ densely populated

poblador, a [poßla'ðor, a] *nm/f* settler, colonist

poblar [po'ßlar] *vt* (*colonizar*) to colonize; (*fundar*) to found; (*habitar*) to inhabit

pobre ['poßre] *adj* poor ♦ *nm/f* poor person; ~**za** *nf* poverty

pocilga [po'θilxa] *nf* pigsty

pócima ['poθima] *nf* potion

PALABRA CLAVE
---

poco, a ['poko, a] *adj* **1** (*sg*) little, not much; ~ **tiempo** little *o* not much time; **de** ~ **interés** of little interest, not very interesting; **poca cosa** not much

2 (*pl*) few, not many; **unos** ~**s** a few, some; ~**s niños comen lo que les**

conviene few children eat what they should

♦ *adv* 1 little, not much; **cuesta ~** it doesn't cost much

2 (+*adj*: = *negativo, antónimo*): **~ amable/inteligente** not very nice/intelligent

3: **por ~ me caigo** I almost fell

4: **a ~: a ~ de haberse casado** shortly after getting married

5: **~ a ~** little by little

♦ *nm* a little, a bit; **un ~ triste/de dinero** a little sad/money

podar [po'ðar] *vt* to prune

PALABRA CLAVE

poder [po'ðer] *vi* 1 (*capacidad*) can, be able to; **no puedo hacerlo** I can't do it, I'm unable to do it

2 (*permiso*) can, may, be allowed to; **¿se puede?** may I (*o* we)?; **puedes irte ahora** you may go now; **no se puede fumar en este hospital** smoking is not allowed in this hospital

3 (*posibilidad*) may, might, could; **puede llegar mañana** he may *o* might arrive tomorrow; **pudiste haberte hecho daño** you might *o* could have hurt yourself; **¡podías habérmelo dicho antes!** you might have told me before!

4: **puede ser: puede ser** perhaps; **puede ser que lo sepa Tomás** Tomás may *o* might know

5: **¡no puedo más!** I've had enough!; **no pude menos que dejarlo** I couldn't help but leave it; **es tonto a más no ~** he's as stupid as they come

6: **~ con: no puedo con este crío** this kid's too much for me

♦ *nm* power; **~ adquisitivo** purchasing power; **detentar** *o* **ocupar** *o* **estar en el ~** to be in power

poderoso, a [poðe'roso, a] *adj* (*político, país*) powerful

podio ['poðjo] *nm* (DEPORTE) podium

podium ['poðjum] = **podio**

podrido, a [po'ðriðo, a] *adj* rotten, bad; (*fig*) rotten, corrupt

podrir [po'ðrir] = **pudrir**

poema [po'ema] *nm* poem

poesía [poe'sia] *nf* poetry

poeta [poe'eta] *nm/f* poet; **poético, a** *adj* poetic(al)

poetisa [poe'tisa] *nf* (woman) poet

póker ['poker] *nm* poker

polaco, a [po'lako, a] *adj* Polish ♦ *nm/f* Pole

polar [po'lar] *adj* polar; **~idad** *nf* polarity; **~izarse** *vr* to polarize

polea [po'lea] *nf* pulley

polémica [po'lemika] *nf* polemics *sg*; (*una ~*) controversy, polemic

polen ['polen] *nm* pollen

policía [poli'θia] *nm/f* policeman/woman ♦ *nf* police; **~co, a** *adj* police *cpd*; **novela policíaca** detective story; **policial** *adj* police *cpd*

polideportivo [poliðepor'tiβo] *nm* sports centre *o* complex

poligamia [poli'ɣamja] *nf* polygamy

polígono [po'liɣono] *nm* (MAT) polygon; **~ industrial** industrial estate

polilla [po'liʎa] *nf* moth

polio ['poljo] *nf* polio

política [po'litika] *nf* politics *sg*; (*económica, agraria etc*) policy; *ver tb* **político**

político, a [po'litiko, a] *adj* political; (*discreto*) tactful; (*de familia*) -in-law ♦ *nm/f* politician; **padre ~** father-in-law

póliza ['poliθa] *nf* certificate, voucher; (*impuesto*) tax stamp; **~ de seguros** insurance policy

polizón [poli'θon] *nm* stowaway

pollera [po'ʎera] (AM) *nf* skirt

pollería [poʎe'ria] *nf* poulterer's (shop)

pollo ['poʎo] *nm* chicken

polo ['polo] *nm* (GEO, ELEC) pole; (*helado*) ice lolly; (DEPORTE) polo; (*suéter*) polo-neck; **~ Norte/Sur** North/South Pole

Polonia [po'lonja] *nf* Poland

poltrona [pol'trona] *nf* easy chair

polución [polu'θjon] *nf* pollution
polvera [pol'ßera] *nf* powder compact
polvo ['polßo] *nm* dust; (*QUÍM, CULIN, MED*) powder; **~s** *nmpl* (*maquillaje*) powder *sg*; **quitar el ~** to dust; **~ de talco** talcum powder; **estar hecho ~** (*fam*) to be worn out o exhausted
pólvora ['polßora] *nf* gunpowder; (*fuegos artificiales*) fireworks *pl*
polvoriento, a [polßo'rjento, a] *adj* (*superficie*) dusty; (*sustancia*) powdery
pomada [po'maða] *nf* cream, ointment
pomelo [po'melo] *nm* grapefruit
pómez ['pomeθ] *nf*: **piedra ~** pumice stone
pomo ['pomo] *nm* doorknob
pompa ['pompa] *nf* (*burbuja*) bubble; (*bomba*) pump; (*esplendor*) pomp, splendour; **pomposo, a** *adj* splendid, magnificent; (*pey*) pompous
pómulo ['pomulo] *nm* cheekbone
pon [pon] *vb ver* **poner**
ponche ['pontʃe] *nm* punch
poncho ['pontʃo] *nm* poncho
ponderar [ponde'rar] *vt* (*considerar*) to weigh up, consider; (*elogiar*) to praise highly, speak in praise of
pondré *etc vb ver* **poner**

PALABRA CLAVE
---

poner [po'ner] *vt* **1** (*colocar*) to put; (*telegrama*) to send; (*obra de teatro*) to put on; (*película*) to show; **ponlo más fuerte** turn it up; **¿qué ponen en el Excelsior?** what's on at the Excelsior?
2 (*tienda*) to open; (*instalar: gas etc*) to put in; (*radio, TV*) to switch o turn on
3 (*suponer*): **pongamos que ...** let's suppose that ...
4 (*contribuir*): **el gobierno ha puesto otro millón** the government has contributed another million
5 (*TELEC*): **póngame con el Sr. López** can you put me through to Mr. López?
6: **~ de**: **le han puesto de director general** they've appointed him general manager

7 (*+adj*) to make; **me estás poniendo nerviosa** you're making me nervous
8 (*dar nombre*): **al hijo le pusieron Diego** they called their son Diego
♦ *vi* (*gallina*) to lay
♦ **~se** *vr* **1** (*colocarse*): **se puso a mi lado** he came and stood beside me; **tú ponte en esa silla** you go and sit on that chair
2 (*vestido, cosméticos*) to put on; **¿por qué no te pones el vestido nuevo?** why don't you put on o wear your new dress?
3 (*+adj*) to turn; to get, become; **se puso muy serio** he got very serious; **después de lavarla la tela se puso azul** after washing it the material turned blue
4: **~se a**: **se puso a llorar** he started to cry; **tienes que ~te a estudiar** you must get down to studying
5: **~se a bien con uno** to make it up with sb; **~se a mal con uno** to get on the wrong side of sb

---

pongo *etc vb ver* **poner**
poniente [po'njente] *nm* (*occidente*) west; (*viento*) west wind
pontífice [pon'tifiθe] *nm* pope, pontiff
popa ['popa] *nf* stern
popular [popu'lar] *adj* popular; (*cultura*) of the people, folk *cpd*; **~idad** *nf* popularity; **~izarse** *vr* to become popular

---
PALABRA CLAVE
---

por [por] *prep* **1** (*objetivo*) for; **luchar ~ la patria** to fight for one's country
2 (*+infin*): **~ no llegar tarde** so as not to arrive late; **~ citar unos ejemplos** to give a few examples
3 (*causa*) out of, because of; **~ escasez de fondos** through o for lack of funds
4 (*tiempo*): **~ la mañana/noche** in the morning/at night; **se queda ~ una semana** she's staying (for) a week
5 (*lugar*): **pasar ~ Madrid** to pass through Madrid; **ir a Guayaquil ~ Quito** to go to Guayaquil via Quito; **caminar ~ la calle** to walk along the street; *ver tb*

todo
6 (*cambio, precio*): **te doy uno nuevo ~ el que tienes** I'll give you a new one (in return) for the one you've got
7 (*valor distributivo*): **550 pesetas ~ hora/cabeza** 550 pesetas an *o* per hour/ a *o* per head
8 (*modo, medio*) by; **~ correo/avión** by post/air; **día ~ día** day by day; **entrar ~ la entrada principal** to go in through the main entrance
9: 10 ~ 10 son 100 10 times 10 is 100
10 (*en lugar de*): **vino él ~ su jefe** he came instead of his boss
11: ~ mí que revienten as far as I'm concerned they can drop dead
12: ¿~ qué? why?; **¿~ qué no?** why not?

porcelana [porθe'lana] *nf* porcelain; (*china*) china
porcentaje [porθen'taxe] *nm* percentage
porción [por'θjon] *nf* (*parte*) portion, share; (*cantidad*) quantity, amount
pordiosero, a [pordjo'sero, a] *nm/f* beggar
porfiar [por'fjar] *vi* to persist, insist; (*disputar*) to argue stubbornly
pormenor [porme'nor] *nm* detail, particular
pornografía [pornoɣra'fia] *nf* pornography
poro ['poro] *nm* pore; **~so, a** *adj* porous
porque ['porke] *conj* (*a causa de*) because; (*ya que*) since; (*con el fin de*) so that, in order that
porqué [por'ke] *nm* reason, cause
porquería [porke'ria] *nf* (*suciedad*) filth, dirt; (*acción*) dirty trick; (*objeto*) small thing, trifle; (*fig*) rubbish
porra ['porra] *nf* (*arma*) stick, club
porrazo [po'rraθo] *nm* blow, bump
porro ['porro] *nm* (*fam*) (*droga*) joint (*fam*)
porrón [po'rron] *nm* glass wine jar with a *long spout*
portaaviones [porta'(a)βjones] *nm inv* aircraft carrier

portada [por'taða] *nf* (*de revista*) cover
portador, a [porta'ðor, a] *nm/f* carrier, bearer; (*COM*) bearer, payee
portaequipajes [portaeki'paxes] *nm inv* (*AUTO: maletero*) boot; (*: baca*) luggage rack
portal [por'tal] *nm* (*entrada*) vestibule, hall; (*portada*) porch, doorway; (*puerta de entrada*) main door
portamaletas [portama'letas] *nm inv* (*AUTO: maletero*) boot; (*: baca*) roof rack
portarse [por'tarse] *vr* to behave, conduct o.s.
portátil [por'tatil] *adj* portable
portavoz [porta'βoθ] *nm/f* spokesman/ woman
portazo [por'taθo] *nm*: **dar un ~** to slam the door
porte ['porte] *nm* (*COM*) transport; (*precio*) transport charges *pl*
portento [por'tento] *nm* marvel, wonder; **~so, a** *adj* marvellous, extraordinary
porteño, a [por'teɲo, a] *adj* of *o* from Buenos Aires
portería [porte'ria] *nf* (*oficina*) porter's office; (*DEPORTE*) goal
portero, a [por'tero, a] *nm/f* porter; (*conserje*) caretaker; (*ujier*) doorman; (*DEPORTE*) goalkeeper; **~ automático** intercom
pórtico ['portiko] *nm* (*patio*) portico, porch; (*fig*) gateway; (*arcada*) arcade
portorriqueño, a [portorri'keɲo, a] *adj* Puerto Rican
Portugal [portu'ɣal] *nm* Portugal; **portugués, esa** *adj, nm/f* Portuguese
♦ *nm* (*LING*) Portuguese
porvenir [porβe'nir] *nm* future
pos [pos] *prep*: **en ~ de** after, in pursuit of
posada [po'saða] *nf* (*refugio*) shelter, lodging; (*mesón*) guest house; **dar ~ a** to give shelter to, take in
posaderas [posa'ðeras] *nfpl* backside *sg*, buttocks
posar [po'sar] *vt* (*en el suelo*) to lay down, put down; (*la mano*) to place, put gently
♦ *vi* (*modelo*) to sit, pose; **~se** *vr* to

settle; (*pájaro*) to perch; (*avión*) to land, come down

posavasos [posa'basos] *nm inv* coaster; (*para cerveza*) beermat

posdata [pos'ðata] *nf* postscript

pose ['pose] *nf* pose

poseedor, a [posee'ðor, a] *nm/f* owner, possessor; (*de récord, puesto*) holder

poseer [pose'er] *vt* to possess, own; (*ventaja*) to enjoy; (*récord, puesto*) to hold

posesión [pose'sjon] *nf* possession; **posesionarse** *vr*: **posesionarse de** to take possession of, take over

posesivo, a [pose'siβo, a] *adj* possessive

posgrado [pos'graðo] *nm*: **curso de ~** postgraduate course

posibilidad [posiβili'ðað] *nf* possibility; (*oportunidad*) chance; **posibilitar** *vt* to make possible; (*hacer realizable*) to make feasible

posible [po'siβle] *adj* possible; (*realizable*) feasible; **de ser ~** if possible; **en lo ~** as far as possible

posición [posi'θjon] *nf* position; (*rango social*) status

positivo, a [posi'tiβo, a] *adj* positive

poso ['poso] *nm* sediment; (*heces*) dregs *pl*

posponer [pospo'ner] *vt* (*relegar*) to put behind/below; (*aplazar*) to postpone

posta ['posta] *nf*: **a ~** deliberately, on purpose

postal [pos'tal] *adj* postal ♦ *nf* postcard

poste ['poste] *nm* (*de telégrafos etc*) post, pole; (*columna*) pillar

póster ['poster] (*pl* **pósteres, pósters**) *nm* poster

postergar [poster'var] *vt* to postpone, delay

posteridad [posteri'ðað] *nf* posterity

posterior [poste'rjor] *adj* back, rear; (*siguiente*) following, subsequent; (*más tarde*) later; **~idad** *nf*: **con ~idad** later, subsequently

postgrado [post'graðo] *nm* = **posgrado**

postizo, a [pos'tiθo, a] *adj* false, artificial ♦ *nm* hairpiece

postor, a [pos'tor, a] *nm/f* bidder

postre ['postre] *nm* sweet, dessert

postrero, a [pos'trero, a] (*delante de nmsg*: **postrer**) *adj* (*último*) last; (*que viene detrás*) rear

postulado [postu'laðo] *nm* postulate

póstumo, a ['postumo, a] *adj* posthumous

postura [pos'tura] *nf* (*del cuerpo*) posture, position; (*fig*) attitude, position

potable [po'taβle] *adj* drinkable; **agua ~** drinking water

potaje [po'taxe] *nm* thick vegetable soup

pote ['pote] *nm* pot, jar

potencia [po'tenθja] *nf* power; **~l** [poten'θjal] *adj, nm* potential; **~r** *vt* to boost

potente [po'tente] *adj* powerful

potro, a ['potro, a] *nm/f* (*ZOOL*) colt/filly ♦ *nm* (*de gimnasia*) vaulting horse

pozo ['poθo] *nm* well; (*de río*) deep pool; (*de mina*) shaft

P.P. *abr* (= *porte pagado*) CP

práctica ['praktika] *nf* practice; (*método*) method; (*arte, capacidad*) skill; **en la ~** in practice

practicable [prakti'kaβle] *adj* practicable; (*camino*) passable

practicante [prakti'kante] *nm/f* (*MED*: *ayudante de doctor*) medical assistant; (*: enfermero*) nurse; (*quien practica algo*) practitioner ♦ *adj* practising

practicar [prakti'kar] *vt* to practise; (*DEPORTE*) to play; (*realizar*) to carry out, perform

práctico, a ['praktiko, a] *adj* practical; (*instruido*: *persona*) skilled, expert

practique *etc vb ver* **practicar**

pradera [pra'ðera] *nf* meadow; (*US etc*) prairie

prado ['praðo] *nm* (*campo*) meadow, field; (*pastizal*) pasture

Praga ['prava] *n* Prague

pragmático, a [prav'matiko, a] *adj* pragmatic

preámbulo [pre'ambulo] *nm* preamble, introduction

precario, a [pre'karjo, a] *adj* precarious

precaución [prekau'θjon] *nf* (*medida preventiva*) preventive measure, precaution; (*prudencia*) caution, wariness

precaver [preka'ßer] *vt* to guard against; (*impedir*) to forestall; **~se** *vr*: **~se de** *o* **contra algo** to (be on one's) guard against sth; **precavido, a** *adj* cautious, wary

precedente [preθe'ðente] *adj* preceding; (*anterior*) former ♦ *nm* precedent

preceder [preθe'ðer] *vt, vi* to precede, go before, come before

precepto [pre'θepto] *nm* precept

preciado, a [pre'θjaðo, a] *adj* (*estimado*) esteemed, valuable

preciarse [pre'θjarse] *vr* to boast; **~se de** to pride o.s. on, boast of being

precinto [pre'θinto] *nm* (*tb*: **~ de garantía**) seal

precio ['preθjo] *nm* price; (*costo*) cost; (*valor*) value, worth; (*de viaje*) fare; **~ al contado/de coste/de oportunidad** cash/cost/bargain price; **~ al detalle** *o* **al por menor** retail price; **~ tope** top price

preciosidad [preθjosi'ðað] *nf* (*valor*) (high) value, (great) worth; (*encanto*) charm; (*cosa bonita*) beautiful thing; **es una ~** it's lovely, it's really beautiful

precioso, a [pre'θjoso, a] *adj* precious; (*de mucho valor*) valuable; (*fam*) lovely, beautiful

precipicio [preθi'piθjo] *nm* cliff, precipice; (*fig*) abyss

precipitación [preθipita'θjon] *nf* haste; (*lluvia*) rainfall

precipitado, a [preθipi'taðo, a] *adj* (*conducta*) hasty, rash; (*salida*) hasty, sudden

precipitar [preθipi'tar] *vt* (*arrojar*) to hurl down, throw; (*apresurar*) to hasten; (*acelerar*) to speed up, accelerate; **~se** *vr* to throw o.s.; (*apresurarse*) to rush; (*actuar sin pensar*) to act rashly

precisamente [preθisa'mente] *adv* precisely; (*exactamente*) precisely, exactly

precisar [preθi'sar] *vt* (*necesitar*) to need, require; (*fijar*) to determine exactly, fix;

(*especificar*) to specify

precisión [preθi'sjon] *nf* (*exactitud*) precision

preciso, a [pre'θiso, a] *adj* (*exacto*) precise; (*necesario*) necessary, essential

preconcebido, a [prekonθe'ßiðo, a] *adj* preconceived

precoz [pre'koθ] *adj* (*persona*) precocious; (*calvicie etc*) premature

precursor, a [prekur'sor, a] *nm/f* predecessor, forerunner

predecir [preðe'θir] *vt* to predict, forecast

predestinado, a [preðesti'naðo, a] *adj* predestined

predicar [preði'kar] *vt, vi* to preach

predicción [preðik'θjon] *nf* prediction

predilecto, a [preði'lekto, a] *adj* favourite

predisponer [preðispo'ner] *vt* to predispose; (*pey*) to prejudice; **predisposición** *nf* inclination; prejudice, bias

predominante [preðomi'nante] *adj* predominant

predominar [preðomi'nar] *vt* to dominate ♦ *vi* to predominate; (*prevalecer*) to prevail; **predominio** *nm* predominance; prevalence

preescolar [pre(e)sko'lar] *adj* preschool

prefabricado, a [prefaßri'kaðo, a] *adj* prefabricated

prefacio [pre'faθjo] *nm* preface

preferencia [prefe'renθja] *nf* preference; **de ~** preferably, for preference

preferible [prefe'rißle] *adj* preferable

preferir [prefe'rir] *vt* to prefer

prefiero *etc vb ver* **preferir**

prefijo [pre'fixo] *nm* (*TELEC*) (dialling) code

pregonar [preyo'nar] *vt* to proclaim, announce

pregunta [pre'yunta] *nf* question; **hacer una ~** to ask a question

preguntar [preyun'tar] *vt* to ask; (*cuestionar*) to question ♦ *vi* to ask; **~se** *vr* to wonder; **~ por alguien** to ask for sb

preguntón, ona [preyun'ton, ona] *adj* inquisitive

prehistórico, a [preis'toriko, a] *adj*

prehistoric

prejuicio [pre'xwiθjo] *nm* (*acto*) prejudgement; (*idea preconcebida*) preconception; (*parcialidad*) prejudice, bias

preliminar [prelimi'nar] *adj* preliminary

preludio [pre'luðjo] *nm* prelude

prematuro, a [prema'turo, a] *adj* premature

premeditación [premeðita'θjon] *nf* premeditation

premeditar [premeði'tar] *vt* to premeditate

premiar [pre'mjar] *vt* to reward; (*en un concurso*) to give a prize to

premio ['premjo] *nm* reward; prize; (*COM*) premium

premonición [premoni'θjon] *nf* premonition

prenatal [prena'tal] *adj* antenatal, prenatal

prenda ['prenda] *nf* (*ropa*) garment, article of clothing; (*garantía*) pledge; **~s** *nfpl* (*talentos*) talents, gifts

prendedor [prende'ðor] *nm* brooch

prender [pren'der] *vt* (*captar*) to catch, capture; (*detener*) to arrest; (*COSTURA*) to pin, attach; (*sujetar*) to fasten ♦ *vi* to catch; (*arraigar*) to take root; **~se** *vr* (*encenderse*) to catch fire

prendido, a [pren'diðo, a] (*AM*) *adj* (*luz etc*) on

prensa ['prensa] *nf* press; **la ~** the press; **prensar** *vt* to press

preñado, a [pre'naðo, a] *adj* pregnant; **~ de** pregnant with, full of

preocupación [preokupa'θjon] *nf* worry, concern; (*ansiedad*) anxiety

preocupado, a [preoku'paðo, a] *adj* worried, concerned; (*ansioso*) anxious

preocupar [preoku'par] *vt* to worry; **~se** *vr* to worry; **~se de algo** (*hacerse cargo*) to take care of sth

preparación [prepara'θjon] *nf* (*acto*) preparation; (*estado*) readiness; (*entrenamiento*) training

preparado, a [prepa'raðo, a] *adj* (*dispuesto*) prepared; (*CULIN*) ready (to serve) ♦ *nm* preparation

preparar [prepa'rar] *vt* (*disponer*) to prepare, get ready; (*TEC: tratar*) to prepare, process; (*entrenar*) to teach, train; **~se** *vr*: **~se a** *o* **para** to prepare to *o* for, get ready to *o* for; **preparativo, a** *adj* preparatory, preliminary; **preparativos** *nmpl* preparations; **preparatoria** (*AM*) *nf* sixth-form college (*BRIT*), senior high school (*US*)

prerrogativa [prerroʀa'tiβa] *nf* prerogative, privilege

presa ['presa] *nf* (*cosa apresada*) catch; (*víctima*) victim; (*de animal*) prey; (*de agua*) dam

presagiar [presa'xjar] *vt* to presage, forebode; **presagio** *nm* omen

prescindir [presθin'dir] *vi*: **~ de** (*privarse de*) to do without, go without; (*descartar*) to dispense with

prescribir [preskri'βir] *vt* to prescribe; **prescripción** *nf* prescription

presencia [pre'senθja] *nf* presence; **presencial** *adj*: **testigo presencial** eyewitness; **presenciar** *vt* to be present at; (*asistir a*) to attend; (*ver*) to see, witness

presentación [presenta'θjon] *nf* presentation; (*introducción*) introduction

presentador, a [presenta'ðor, a] *nm/f* presenter, compère

presentar [presen'tar] *vt* to present; (*ofrecer*) to offer; (*mostrar*) to show, display; (*a una persona*) to introduce; **~se** *vr* (*llegar inesperadamente*) to appear, turn up; (*ofrecerse como candidato*) to run, stand; (*aparecer*) to show, appear; (*solicitar empleo*) to apply

presente [pre'sente] *adj* present ♦ *nm* present; **hacer ~** to state, declare; **tener ~** to remember, bear in mind

presentimiento [presenti'mjento] *nm* premonition, presentiment

presentir [presen'tir] *vt* to have a premonition of

preservación [preserβa'θjon] *nf* protection, preservation

preservar [preser'ßar] vt to protect,
preserve; **preservativo** nm sheath,
condom
presidencia [presi'ðenθja] nf presidency;
(de comité) chairmanship
presidente [presi'ðente] nm/f president;
(de comité) chairman/woman
presidiario [presi'ðjarjo] nm convict
presidio [pre'sidjo] nm prison,
penitentiary
presidir [presi'ðir] vt (dirigir) to preside at,
preside over; (: comité) to take the chair
at; (dominar) to dominate, rule ♦ vi to
preside; to take the chair
presión [pre'sjon] nf pressure; **presionar**
vt to press; (fig) to press, put pressure on
♦ vi: **presionar para** to press for
preso, a [ˈpreso, a] nm/f prisoner; **tomar**
o **llevar ~ a uno** to arrest sb, take sb
prisoner
prestación [presta'θjon] nf service;
(subsidio) benefit; **prestaciones** nfpl
(TEC, AUT) performance features
prestado, a [pres'taðo, a] adj on loan;
pedir ~ to borrow
prestamista [presta'mista] nm/f
moneylender
préstamo [ˈprestamo] nm loan; ~
hipotecario mortgage
prestar [pres'tar] vt to lend, loan;
(atención) to pay; (ayuda) to give
presteza [pres'teθa] nf speed, promptness
prestigio [pres'tixjo] nm prestige; **~so, a**
adj (honorable) prestigious; (famoso,
renombrado) renowned, famous
presto, a [ˈpresto, a] adj (rápido) quick,
prompt; (dispuesto) ready ♦ adv at once,
right away.
presumido, a [presu'miðo, a] adj
(persona) vain
presumir [presu'mir] vt to presume ♦ vi
(tener aires) to be conceited; **según cabe**
~ as may be presumed, presumably;
presunción nf presumption;
presunto, a adj (supuesto) supposed,
presumed; (así llamado) so-called;
presuntuoso, a adj conceited,
presumptuous
presuponer [presupo'ner] vt to
presuppose
presupuesto [presu'pwesto] pp de
presuponer ♦ nm (FINANZAS) budget;
(estimación: de costo) estimate
pretencioso, a [preten'θjoso, a] adj
pretentious
pretender [preten'der] vt (intentar) to try
to, seek to; (reivindicar) to claim; (buscar)
to seek, try for; (cortejar) to woo, court; ~
que to expect that; **pretendiente** nm/f
(amante) suitor; (al trono) pretender
pretensión nf (aspiración) aspiration;
(reivindicación) claim; (orgullo) pretension
pretexto [pre'teksto] nm pretext; (excusa)
excuse
prevalecer [preßale'θer] vi to prevail
prevención [preßen'θjon] nf prevention;
(precaución) precaution
prevenido, a [preße'niðo, a] adj
prepared, ready; (cauteloso) cautious
prevenir [preße'nir] vt (impedir) to
prevent; (predisponer) to prejudice, bias;
(avisar) to warn; (preparar) to prepare,
get ready; **~se** vr to get ready, prepare;
~se contra to take precautions against;
preventivo, a adj preventive,
precautionary
prever [pre'ßer] vt to foresee
previo, a [ˈpreßjo, a] adj (anterior)
previous; (preliminar) preliminary ♦ prep:
~ acuerdo de los otros subject to the
agreement of the others
previsión [preßi'sjon] nf (perspicacia)
foresight; (predicción) forecast; **previsto,**
a adj anticipated, forecast
prima [ˈprima] nf (COM) bonus; **~ de**
seguro insurance premium; ver tb **primo**
primacía [prima'θia] nf primacy
primario, a [pri'marjo, a] adj primary
primavera [prima'ßera] nf spring(-time)
primera [pri'mera] nf (AUTO) first gear;
(FERRO: tb: **~ clase**) first class; **de ~** (fam)
first-class, first-rate
primero, a [pri'mero, a] (delante de nmsg:
primer) adj first; (principal) prime ♦ adv

first; (más bien) sooner, rather; **primera plana** front page

primicia [pri'miθja] nf (tb: ~ **informativa**) scoop

primitivo, a [primi'tiβo, a] adj primitive; (original) original

primo, a ['primo, a] adj prime ♦ nm/f cousin; (fam) fool, idiot; ~ **hermano** first cousin; **materias primas** raw materials

primogénito, a [primo'xenito, a] adj first-born

primordial [primor'ðjal] adj basic, fundamental

primoroso, a [primo'roso, a] adj exquisite, delicate

princesa [prin'θesa] nf princess

principal [prinθi'pal] adj principal, main ♦ nm (jefe) chief, principal

príncipe ['prinθipe] nm prince

principiante [prinθi'pjante] nm/f beginner

principio [prin'θipjo] nm (comienzo) beginning, start; (origen) origin; (primera etapa) rudiment, basic idea; (moral) principle; **a ~s de** at the beginning of

pringoso, a [prin'yoso, a] adj (grasiento) greasy; (pegajoso) sticky

pringue ['pringe] nm (grasa) grease, fat, dripping

prioridad [priori'ðað] nf priority

prisa ['prisa] nf (apresuramiento) hurry, haste; (rapidez) speed; (urgencia) (sense of) urgency; **a o de** ~ quickly; **correr** ~ to be urgent; **darse** ~ to hurry up; **estar de o tener** ~ to be in a hurry

prisión [pri'sjon] nf (cárcel) prison; (período de cárcel) imprisonment; **prisionero, a** nm/f prisoner

prismáticos [pris'matikos] nmpl binoculars

privación [priβa'θjon] nf deprivation; (falta) want, privation

privado, a [pri'βaðo, a] adj private

privar [pri'βar] vt to deprive; **privativo, a** adj exclusive

privilegiado, a [priβile'xjaðo, a] adj privileged; (memoria) very good

privilegiar [priβile'xjar] vt to grant a privilege to; (favorecer) to favour

privilegio [priβi'lexjo] nm privilege; (concesión) concession

pro [pro] nm o f profit, advantage ♦ prep: **asociación ~ ciegos** association for the blind ♦ prefijo: ~ **soviético/americano** pro-Soviet/American; **en ~ de** on behalf of, for; **los ~s y los contras** the pros and cons

proa ['proa] nf bow, prow; **de** ~ bow cpd, fore

probabilidad [proβaβili'ðað] nf probability, likelihood; (oportunidad, posibilidad) chance, prospect; **probable** adj probable, likely

probador [proβa'ðor] nm (en tienda) fitting room

probar [pro'βar] vt (demostrar) to prove; (someter a prueba) to test, try out; (ropa) to try on; (comida) to taste ♦ vi to try; ~**se un traje** to try on a suit

probeta [pro'βeta] nf test tube

problema [pro'βlema] nm problem

procedente [proθe'ðente] adj (razonable) reasonable; (conforme a derecho) proper, fitting; ~ **de** coming from, originating in

proceder [proθe'ðer] vi (avanzar) to proceed; (actuar) to act; (ser correcto) to be right (and proper), be fitting ♦ nm (comportamiento) behaviour, conduct; ~ **de** to come from, originate in; **procedimiento** nm procedure; (proceso) process; (método) means pl, method

procesado, a [proθe'saðo, a] nm/f accused

procesador [proθesa'ðor] nm: ~ **de textos** word processor

procesar [proθe'sar] vt to try, put on trial

procesión [proθe'sjon] nf procession

proceso [pro'θeso] nm process; (JUR) trial

proclamar [prokla'mar] vt to proclaim

procreación [prokrea'θjon] nf procreation

procrear [prokre'ar] vt, vi to procreate

procurador, a [prokura'ðor, a] nm/f attorney

procurar [proku'rrar] *vt* (*intentar*) to try, endeavour; (*conseguir*) to get, obtain; (*asegurar*) to secure; (*producir*) to produce

prodigio [pro'ðixjo] *nm* prodigy; (*milagro*) wonder, marvel; **~so, a** *adj* prodigious, marvellous

pródigo, a ['proðiɣo, a] *adj*: **hijo ~** prodigal son

producción [proðuk'θjon] *nf* (*gen*) production; (*producto*) output; **~ en serie** mass production

producir [proðu'θir] *vt* to produce; (*causar*) to cause, bring about; **~se** *vr* (*cambio*) to come about; (*accidente*) to take place; (*problema etc*) to arise; (*hacerse*) to be produced, be made; (*estallar*) to break out

productividad [proðuktiβi'ðað] *nf* productivity; **productivo, a** *adj* productive; (*provechoso*) profitable

producto [pro'ðukto] *nm* product

productor, a [proðuk'tor, a] *adj* productive, producing ♦ *nm/f* producer

proeza [pro'eθa] *nf* exploit, feat

profanar [profa'nar] *vt* to desecrate, profane; **profano, a** *adj* profane ♦ *nm/f* layman/woman

profecía [profe'θia] *nf* prophecy

proferir [profe'rir] *vt* (*palabra, sonido*) to utter; (*injuria*) to hurl, let fly

profesión [profe'sjon] *nf* profession; **profesional** *adj* professional

profesor, a [profe'sor, a] *nm/f* teacher; **~ado** *nm* teaching profession

profeta [pro'feta] *nm/f* prophet; **profetizar** *vt*, *vi* to prophesy

prófugo, a ['profuxo, a] *nm/f* fugitive; (*MIL: desertor*) deserter

profundidad [profundi'ðað] *nf* depth; **profundizar** *vi*: **profundizar en** to go deeply into; **profundo, a** *adj* deep; (*misterio, pensador*) profound

progenitor [proxeni'tor] *nm* ancestor; **~es** *nmpl* (*padres*) parents

programa [pro'ɣrama] *nm* programme (*BRIT*), program (*US*); **~ción** *nf* programming; **~dor, a** *nm/f*

programmer; **programar** *vt* to program

progresar [proɣre'sar] *vi* to progress, make progress; **progresista** *adj, nm/f* progressive; **progresivo, a** *adj* progressive; (*gradual*) gradual; (*continuo*) continuous; **progreso** *nm* progress

prohibición [proiβi'θjon] *nf* prohibition, ban

prohibir [proi'βir] *vt* to prohibit, ban, forbid; **se prohibe fumar, prohibido fumar** no smoking; **"prohibido el paso"** "no entry"

prójimo, a ['proximo, a] *nm/f* fellow man; (*vecino*) neighbour

proletariado [proleta'rjaðo] *nm* proletariat

proletario, a [prole'tarjo, a] *adj, nm/f* proletarian

proliferación [prolifera'θjon] *nf* proliferation

proliferar [prolife'rar] *vi* to proliferate; **prolífico, a** *adj* prolific

prólogo ['proloxo] *nm* prologue

prolongación [prolonga'θjon] *nf* extension; **prolongado, a** *adj* (*largo*) long; (*alargado*) lengthy

prolongar [prolon'var] *vt* to extend; (*reunión etc*) to prolong; (*calle, tubo*) to extend

promedio [pro'meðjo] *nm* average; (*de distancia*) middle, mid-point

promesa [pro'mesa] *nf* promise

prometer [prome'ter] *vt* to promise ♦ *vi* to show promise; **~se** *vr* (*novios*) to get engaged; **prometido, a** *adj* promised; engaged ♦ *nm/f* fiancé/fiancée

prominente [promi'nente] *adj* prominent

promiscuo, a [pro'miskwo, a] *adj* promiscuous

promoción [promo'θjon] *nf* promotion

promotor [promo'tor] *nm* promoter; (*instigador*) instigator

promover [promo'βer] *vt* to promote; (*causar*) to cause; (*instigar*) to instigate, stir up

promulgar [promul'var] *vt* to promulgate; (*anunciar*) to proclaim

pronombre [pro'nombre] *nm* pronoun

pronosticar [pronosti'kar] *vt* to predict, foretell, forecast; **pronóstico** *nm* prediction, forecast; **pronóstico del tiempo** weather forecast

pronto, a ['pronto, a] *adj (rápido)* prompt, quick; *(preparado)* ready ♦ *adv* quickly, promptly; *(en seguida)* at once, right away; *(dentro de poco)* soon; *(temprano)* early ♦ *nm*: **tener ~s de enojo** to be quick-tempered; **de ~** suddenly; **por lo ~** meanwhile, for the present

pronunciación [pronunθja'θjon] *nf* pronunciation

pronunciar [pronun'θjar] *vt* to pronounce; *(discurso)* to make, deliver; **~se** *vr* to revolt, rebel; *(declararse)* to declare o.s.

propagación [propaɣa'θjon] *nf* propagation

propaganda [propa'ɣanda] *nf (política)* propaganda; *(comercial)* advertising

propagar [propa'ɣar] *vt* to propagate

propensión [propen'sjon] *nf* inclination, propensity; **propenso, a** *adj* inclined to; **ser propenso a** to be inclined to, have a tendency to

propicio, a [pro'piθjo, a] *adj* favourable, propitious

propiedad [propje'ðað] *nf* property; *(posesión)* possession, ownership; **~ particular** private property

propietario, a [propje'tarjo, a] *nm/f* owner, proprietor

propina [pro'pina] *nf* tip

propio, a ['propjo, a] *adj* own, of one's own; *(característico)* characteristic, typical; *(debido)* proper; *(mismo)* selfsame, very; **el ~ ministro** the minister himself; **¿tienes casa propia?** have you a house of your own?

proponer [propo'ner] *vt* to propose, put forward; *(problema)* to pose; **~se** *vr* to propose, intend

proporción [propor'θjon] *nf* proportion; *(MAT)* ratio; **proporciones** *nfpl (dimensiones)* dimensions; *(fig)* size *sg*; **proporcionado, a** *adj* proportionate;

(regular) medium, middling; *(justo)* just right; **proporcionar** *vt (dar)* to give, supply, provide

proposición [proposi'θjon] *nf* proposition; *(propuesta)* proposal

propósito [pro'posito] *nm* purpose; *(intento)* aim, intention ♦ *adv*: **a ~** by the way, incidentally; *(a posta)* on purpose, deliberately; **a ~ de** about, with regard to

propuesta [pro'pwesta] *vb ver* **proponer** ♦ *nf* proposal

propulsar [propul'sar] *vt* to drive, propel; *(fig)* to promote, encourage; **propulsión** *nf* propulsion; **propulsión a chorro** *o* **por reacción** jet propulsion

prórroga ['prorroɣa] *nf* extension; *(JUR)* stay; *(COM)* deferment; *(DEPORTE)* extra time; **prorrogar** *vt (período)* to extend; *(decisión)* to defer, postpone

prorrumpir [prorrum'pir] *vi* to burst forth, break out

prosa ['prosa] *nf* prose

proscrito, a [pro'skrito, a] *adj* banned

proseguir [prose'ɣir] *vt* to continue, carry on ♦ *vi* to continue, go on

prospección [prospek'θjon] *nf* exploration; *(del oro)* prospecting

prospecto [pros'pekto] *nm* prospectus

prosperar [prospe'rar] *vi* to prosper, thrive, flourish; **prosperidad** *nf* prosperity; *(éxito)* success; **próspero, a** *adj* prosperous, flourishing; *(que tiene éxito)* successful

prostíbulo [pros'tiβulo] *nm* brothel *(BRIT)*, house of prostitution *(US)*

prostitución [prostitu'θjon] *nf* prostitution

prostituir [prosti'twir] *vt* to prostitute; **~se** *vr* to prostitute o.s., become a prostitute

prostituta [prosti'tuta] *nf* prostitute

protagonista [protaɣo'nista] *nm/f* protagonist

protagonizar [protaɣoni'θar] *vt* to take the chief rôle in

protección [protek'θjon] *nf* protection

protector, a [protek'tor, a] *adj* protective, protecting ♦ *nm/f* protector

proteger [prote'xer] vt to protect; **protegido, a** nm/f protégé/protégée

proteína [prote'ina] nf protein

protesta [pro'testa] nf protest; (declaración) protestation

protestante [protes'tante] adj Protestant

protestar [protes'tar] vt to protest, declare ♦ vi to protest

protocolo [proto'kolo] nm protocol

prototipo [proto'tipo] nm prototype

prov. abr (= provincia) prov

provecho [pro'βetʃo] nm advantage, benefit; (FINANZAS) profit; **¡buen ~!** bon appétit!; **en ~ de** to the benefit of; **sacar ~ de** to benefit from, profit by

proveer [proβe'er] vt to provide, supply ♦ vi: **~ a** to provide for

provenir [proβe'nir] vi: **~ de** to come from, stem from

proverbio [pro'βerβjo] nm proverb

providencia [proβi'ðenθja] nf providence

provincia [pro'βinθja] nf province; **~no, a** adj provincial; (del campo) country cpd

provisión [proβi'sjon] nf provision; (abastecimiento) provision, supply; (medida) measure, step

provisional [proβisjo'nal] adj provisional

provocación [proβoka'θjon] nf provocation

provocar [proβo'kar] vt to provoke; (alentar) to tempt, invite; (causar) to bring about, lead to; (promover) to promote; (estimular) to rouse, stimulate; **¿te provoca un café?** (AM) would you like a coffee?; **provocativo, a** adj provocative

próximamente [proksima'mente] adv shortly, soon

proximidad [proksimi'ðað] nf closeness, proximity; **próximo, a** adj near, close; (vecino) neighbouring; (siguiente) next

proyectar [projek'tar] vt (objeto) to hurl, throw; (luz) to cast, shed; (CINE) to screen, show; (planear) to plan

proyectil [projek'til] nm projectile, missile

proyecto [pro'jekto] nm plan; (estimación de costo) detailed estimate

proyector [projek'tor] nm (CINE) projector

prudencia [pru'ðenθja] nf (sabiduría) wisdom; (cuidado) care; **prudente** adj sensible, wise; (conductor) careful

prueba etc ['prweβa] vb ver **probar** ♦ nf proof; (ensayo) test, trial; (degustación) tasting, sampling; (de ropa) fitting; **a ~** on trial; **a ~ de** proof against; **a ~ de agua/fuego** waterproof/fireproof; **someter a ~** to put to the test

prurito [pru'rito] nm itch; (de bebé) nappy (BRIT) o diaper (US) rash

psico... [siko] prefijo psycho...; **~análisis** nm inv psychoanalysis; **~logía** nf psychology; **~lógico, a** adj psychological; **psicólogo, a** nm/f psychologist; **psicópata** nm/f psychopath; **~sis** nf inv psychosis

psiquiatra [si'kjatra] nm/f psychiatrist; **psiquiátrico, a** adj psychiatric

psíquico, a ['sikiko, a] adj psychic(al)

PSOE [pe'soe] nm abr = **Partido Socialista Obrero Español**

pta(s) abr = **peseta(s)**

pts abr = **pesetas**

púa ['pua] nf (BOT, ZOOL) prickle, spine; (para guitarra) plectrum (BRIT), pick (US); **alambre de ~** barbed wire

pubertad [puβer'tað] nf puberty

publicación [puβlika'θjon] nf publication

publicar [puβli'kar] vt (editar) to publish; (hacer público) to publicize; (divulgar) to make public, divulge

publicidad [puβliθi'ðað] nf publicity; (COM: propaganda) advertising; **publicitario, a** adj publicity cpd; advertising cpd

público, a ['puβliko, a] adj public ♦ nm public; (TEATRO etc) audience

puchero [pu'tʃero] nm (CULIN: guiso) stew; (: olla) cooking pot; **hacer ~s** to pout

pude etc vb ver **poder**

púdico, a ['puðiko, a] adj modest

pudiente [pu'ðjente] adj (rico) wealthy, well-to-do

pudiera etc vb ver **poder**

pudor [pu'ðor] nm modesty

pudrir [pu'ðrir] *vt* to rot; **~se** *vr* to rot, decay
pueblo ['pweβlo] *nm* people; (*nación*) nation; (*aldea*) village
puedo *etc vb ver* **poder**
puente ['pwente] *nm* bridge; **hacer ~** (*inf*) to take extra days off work between 2 public holidays; to take a long weekend; **~ aéreo** shuttle service; **~ colgante** suspension bridge

---

hacer puente

i When a public holiday in Spain falls on a Tuesday or Thursday it is common practice for employers to make the Monday or Friday a holiday as well and to give everyone a four-day weekend. This is known as **hacer puente**. When a named public holiday such as the **Día de la Constitución** falls on a Tuesday or Thursday, people refer to the whole holiday period as e.g. the **puente de la Constitución**.

---

puerco, a ['pwerko, a] *nm/f* pig/sow ♦ *adj* (*sucio*) dirty, filthy; (*obsceno*) disgusting; **~ de mar** marino dolphin
pueril [pwe'ril] *adj* childish
puerro ['pwerro] *nm* leek
puerta ['pwerta] *nf* door; (*de jardín*) gate; (*portal*) doorway; (*fig*) gateway; (*portería*) goal; **a la ~** at the door; **a ~ cerrada** behind closed doors; **~ giratoria** revolving door
puerto ['pwerto] *nm* port; (*paso*) pass; (*fig*) haven, refuge
Puerto Rico [pwerto'riko] *nm* Puerto Rico; **puertorriqueño, a** *adj, nm/f* Puerto Rican
pues [pwes] *adv* (*entonces*) then; (*bueno*) well, well then; (*así que*) so ♦ *conj* (*ya que*) since; **¡~!** (*sí*) yes!, certainly!
puesta ['pwesta] *nf* (*apuesta*) bet, stake; **~ en marcha** starting; **~ del sol** sunset
puesto, a ['pwesto, a] *pp de* **poner** ♦ *adj*: **tener algo ~** to have sth on, be wearing sth ♦ *nm* (*lugar, posición*) place; (*trabajo*)

post, job; (*COM*) stall ♦ *conj*: **~ que** since, as
púgil ['puxil] *nm* boxer
pugna ['puɣna] *nf* battle, conflict; **pugnar** *vi* (*luchar*) to struggle, fight; (*pelear*) to fight
pujar [pu'xar] *vi* (*en subasta*) to bid; (*esforzarse*) to struggle, strain
pulcro, a ['pulkro, a] *adj* neat, tidy
pulga ['pulɣa] *nf* flea
pulgada [pul'ɣaða] *nf* inch
pulgar [pul'ɣar] *nm* thumb
pulir [pu'lir] *vt* to polish; (*alisar*) to smooth; (*fig*) to polish up, touch up
pulla ['puʎa] *nf* cutting remark
pulmón [pul'mon] *nm* lung; **pulmonía** *nf* pneumonia
pulpa ['pulpa] *nf* pulp; (*de fruta*) flesh, soft part
pulpería [pulpe'ria] (*AM*) *nf* (*tienda*) small grocery store
púlpito ['pulpito] *nm* pulpit
pulpo ['pulpo] *nm* octopus
pulsación [pulsa'θjon] *nf* beat; **pulsaciones** pulse rate
pulsar [pul'sar] *vt* (*tecla*) to touch, tap; (*MUS*) to play; (*botón*) to press, push ♦ *vi* to pulsate; (*latir*) to beat, throb; (*MED*): **~ a uno** to take sb's pulse
pulsera [pul'sera] *nf* bracelet
pulso ['pulso] *nm* (*ANAT*) pulse; (*fuerza*) strength; (*firmeza*) steadiness, steady hand
pulverizador [pulβeriθa'ðor] *nm* spray, spray gun
pulverizar [pulβeri'θar] *vt* to pulverize; (*líquido*) to spray
puna ['puna] (*AM*) *nf* mountain sickness
punitivo, a [puni'tiβo, a] *adj* punitive
punta ['punta] *nf* point, tip; (*extremidad*) end; (*fig*) touch, trace; **horas ~s** peak hours, rush hours; **sacar ~ a** to sharpen
puntada [pun'taða] *nf* (*COSTURA*) stitch
puntal [pun'tal] *nm* prop, support
puntapié [punta'pje] *nm* kick
puntear [punte'ar] *vt* to tick, mark
puntería [punte'ria] *nf* (*de arma*) aim,

aiming; (*destreza*) marksmanship

puntero, a [pun'tero, a] *adj* leading ♦ *nm* (*palo*) pointer

puntiagudo, a [puntja'ɣuðo, a] *adj* sharp, pointed

puntilla [pun'tiʎa] *nf* (*encaje*) lace edging *o* trim; **(andar) de ~s** (to walk) on tiptoe

punto ['punto] *nm* (*gen*) point; (*señal diminuta*) spot, dot; (COSTURA, MED) stitch; (*lugar*) spot, place; (*momento*) point, moment; **a ~** ready; **estar a ~ de** to be on the point of *o* about to; **en ~** on the dot; **~ muerto** dead centre; (AUTO) neutral (gear); **~ final** full stop (BRIT), period (US); **~ y coma** semicolon; **~ de interrogación** question mark; **~ de vista** point of view, viewpoint; **hacer ~** (*tejer*) to knit

puntuación [puntwa'θjon] *nf* punctuation; (*puntos: en examen*) mark(s) (*pl*); (: DEPORTE) score

puntual [pun'twal] *adj* (*a tiempo*) punctual; (*exacto*) exact, accurate; **~idad** *nf* punctuality; exactness, accuracy; **~izar** *vt* to fix, specify

puntuar [pun'twar] *vi* (DEPORTE) to score, count

punzada [pun'θaða] *nf* (*de dolor*) twinge

punzante [pun'θante] *adj* (*dolor*) shooting, sharp; (*herramienta*) sharp; **punzar** *vt* to prick, pierce ♦ *vi* to shoot, stab

puñado [pu'ɲaðo] *nm* handful

puñal [pu'ɲal] *nm* dagger; **~ada** *nf* stab

puñetazo [puɲe'taθo] *nm* punch

puño ['puɲo] *nm* (ANAT) fist; (*cantidad*) fistful, handful; (COSTURA) cuff; (*de herramienta*) handle

pupila [pu'pila] *nf* pupil

pupitre [pu'pitre] *nm* desk

puré [pu're] *nm* puree; (*sopa*) (thick) soup; **~ de patatas** mashed potatoes

pureza [pu'reθa] *nf* purity

purga ['purɣa] *nf* purge; **purgante** *adj*, *nm* purgative; **purgar** *vt* to purge

purgatorio [purɣa'torjo] *nm* purgatory

purificar [purifi'kar] *vt* to purify; (*refinar*) to refine

puritano, a [puri'tano, a] *adj* (*actitud*) puritanical; (*iglesia, tradición*) puritan ♦ *nm/f* puritan

puro, a ['puro, a] *adj* pure; (*verdad*) simple, plain ♦ *adv*: **de ~ cansado** out of sheer tiredness ♦ *nm* cigar

púrpura ['purpura] *nf* purple; **purpúreo, a** *adj* purple

pus [pus] *nm* pus

puse *etc vb ver* **poner**

pusiera *etc vb ver* **poner**

pústula ['pustula] *nf* pimple, sore

puta ['puta] (*fam!*) *nf* whore, prostitute

putrefacción [putrefak'θjon] *nf* rotting, putrefaction

PVP *abr* (ESP: = *precio venta al público*) RRP

pyme, PYME ['pime] *nf abr* (= *Pequeña y Mediana Empresa*) SME

Q, q

que [ke] *conj* **1** (*con oración subordinada: muchas veces no se traduce*): that; **dijo ~ vendría** he said (that) he would come; **espero ~ lo encuentres** I hope (that) you find it; *ver tb* **el**

2 (*en oración independiente*): **¡~ entre!** send him in; **¡~ se mejore tu padre!** I hope your father gets better

3 (*enfático*): **¿me quieres? - ¡~ sí!** do you love me? – of course!

4 (*consecutivo: muchas veces no se traduce*) that; **es tan grande ~ no lo puedo levantar** it's so big (that) I can't lift it

5 (*comparaciones*) than; **yo ~ tú/él** if I were you/him; *ver tb* **más; menos; mismo**

6 (*valor disyuntivo*): **~ le guste o no** whether he likes it or not; **~ venga o ~ no venga** whether he comes or not

7 (*porque*): **no puedo, ~ tengo ~ quedarme en casa** I can't, I've got to

stay in
♦ *pron* **1** (*cosa*) that, which; (+*prep*)
which; **el sombrero ~ te compraste** the
hat (that *o* which) you bought; **la cama
en ~ dormí** the bed (that *o* which) I slept
in
2 (*persona: suj*) that, who; (: *objeto*) that,
whom; **el amigo ~ me acompañó al
museo** the friend that *o* who went to the
museum with me: **la chica ~ invité** the
girl (that *o* whom) I invited

qué [ke] *adj* what?, which? ♦ *pron* what?;
¡~ divertido! how funny!; **¿~ edad
tienes?** how old are you?; **¿de ~ me
hablas?** what are you saying to me?; **¿~
tal?** how are you?, how are things?; **¿~
hay (de nuevo)?** what's new?
quebradizo, a [keβra'ðiθo, a] *adj* fragile;
(*persona*) frail
quebrado, a [ke'βraðo, a] *adj* (*roto*)
broken ♦ *nm/f* bankrupt ♦ *nm* (*MAT*)
fraction
quebrantar [keβran'tar] *vt* (*infringir*) to
violate, transgress; **~se** *vr* (*persona*) to fail
in health
quebranto [ke'βranto] *nm* damage, harm;
(*dolor*) grief, pain
quebrar [ke'βrar] *vt* to break, smash ♦ *vi*
to go bankrupt; **~se** *vr* to break, get
broken; (*MED*) to be ruptured
quedar [ke'ðar] *vi* to stay, remain;
(*encontrarse: sitio*) to be; (*haber aún*) to
remain, be left; **~se** *vr* to remain, stay
(behind); **~se (con) algo** to keep sth; **~
en** (*acordar*) to agree on/to; **~ en nada**
to come to nothing; **~ por hacer** to be
still to be done; **~ ciego/mudo** to be left
blind/dumb; **no te queda bien ese
vestido** that dress doesn't suit you; **eso
queda muy lejos** that's a long way
(away); **quedamos a las seis** we agreed
to meet at six
quedo, a ['keðo, a] *adj* still ♦ *adv* softly,
gently
quehacer [kea'θer] *nm* task, job; **~es
(domésticos)** *nmpl* household chores

queja ['kexa] *nf* complaint; **quejarse** *vr*
(*enfermo*) to moan, groan; (*protestar*) to
complain; **quejarse de que** to complain
(about the fact) that; **quejido** *nm* moan
quemado, a [ke'maðo, a] *adj* burnt
quemadura [kema'ðura] *nf* burn, scald
quemar [ke'mar] *vt* to burn; (*fig:
malgastar*) to burn up, squander ♦ *vi* to
be burning hot; **~se** *vr* (*consumirse*) to
burn (up); (*del sol*) to get sunburnt
quemarropa [kema'rropa]: **a ~** *adv*
point-blank
quepo *etc vb ver* **caber**
querella [ke'reʎa] *nf* (*JUR*) charge;
(*disputa*) dispute; **~rse** *vr* (*JUR*) to file a
complaint

┌─────────────────────────┐
│ *PALABRA CLAVE* │
└─────────────────────────┘

querer [ke'rer] *vt* **1** (*desear*) to want;
quiero más dinero I want more money;
quisiera *o* **querría un té** I'd like a tea;
sin ~ unintentionally; **quiero ayudar/que
vayas** I want to help/you to go
2 (*preguntas: para pedir algo*): **¿quiere
abrir la ventana?** could you open the
window?; **¿quieres echarme una mano?**
can you give me a hand?
3 (*amar*) to love; (*tener cariño a*) to be
fond of; **quiere mucho a sus hijos** he's
very fond of his children
4 (*requerir*): **esta planta quiere más luz**
this plant needs more light
5: **le pedí que me dejara ir pero no
quiso** I asked him to let me go but he
refused

querido, a [ke'riðo, a] *adj* dear ♦ *nm/f*
darling; (*amante*) lover
queso ['keso] *nm* cheese
quicio ['kiθjo] *nm* hinge; **sacar a uno de
~** to get on sb's nerves
quiebra ['kjeβra] *nf* break, split; (*COM*)
bankruptcy; (*ECON*) slump
quiebro ['kjeβro] *nm* (*del cuerpo*) swerve
quien [kjen] *pron* who; **hay ~ piensa que**
there are those who think that; **no hay ~
lo haga** no-one will do it

quién [kjen] *pron* who, whom; ¿~ **es?** who's there?

quienquiera [kjen'kjera] (*pl* **quienesquiera**) *pron* whoever

quiero *etc vb ver* **querer**

quieto, a ['kjeto, a] *adj* still; (*carácter*) placid; **quietud** *nf* stillness

quilate [ki'late] *nm* carat

quilla ['kiʎa] *nf* keel

quimera [ki'mera] *nf* chimera; **quimérico, a** *adj* fantastic

químico, a ['kimiko, a] *adj* chemical ♦ *nm/f* chemist ♦ *nf* chemistry

quincalla [kin'kaʎa] *nf* hardware, ironmongery (*BRIT*)

quince ['kinθe] *num* fifteen; ~ **días** a fortnight; ~**añero, a** *nm/f* teenager; ~**na** *nf* fortnight; (*pago*) fortnightly pay; ~**nal** *adj* fortnightly

quiniela [ki'njela] *nf* football pools *pl*; ~**s** *nfpl* (*impreso*) pools coupon *sg*

quinientos, as [ki'njentos, as] *adj, num* five hundred

quinina [ki'nina] *nf* quinine

quinto, a ['kinto, a] *adj* fifth ♦ *nf* country house; (*MIL*) call-up, draft

quiosco ['kjosko] *nm* (*de música*) bandstand; (*de periódicos*) news stand

quirófano [ki'rofano] *nm* operating theatre

quirúrgico, a [ki'rurxiko, a] *adj* surgical

quise *etc vb ver* **querer**

quisiera *etc vb ver* **querer**

quisquilloso, a [kiski'ʎoso, a] *adj* (*susceptible*) touchy; (*meticuloso*) pernickety

quiste ['kiste] *nm* cyst

quitaesmalte [kitaes'malte] *nm* nail-polish remover

quitamanchas [kita'mantʃas] *nm inv* stain remover

quitanieves [kita'njeβes] *nm inv* snowplough (*BRIT*), snowplow (*US*)

quitar [ki'tar] *vt* to remove, take away; (*ropa*) to take off; (*dolor*) to relieve; ¡**quita de ahí!** get away!; ~**se** *vr* to withdraw; (*ropa*) to take off; **se quitó el sombrero** he took off his hat

quite ['kite] *nm* (*esgrima*) parry; (*evasión*) dodge

Quito ['kito] *n* Quito

quizá(s) [ki'θa(s)] *adv* perhaps, maybe

R, r

rábano ['raβano] *nm* radish; **me importa un ~** I don't give a damn

rabia ['raβja] *nf* (*MED*) rabies *sg*; (*ira*) fury, rage; **rabiar** *vi* to have rabies; to rage, be furious **rabiar por algo** to long for sth

rabieta [ra'βjeta] *nf* tantrum, fit of temper

rabino [ra'βino] *nm* rabbi

rabioso, a [ra'βjoso, a] *adj* rabid; (*fig*) furious

rabo ['raβo] *nm* tail

racha ['ratʃa] *nf* gust of wind: **buena/ mala ~** spell of good/bad luck

racial [ra'θjal] *adj* racial, race *cpd*

racimo [ra'θimo] *nm* bunch

raciocinio [raθjo'θinjo] *nm* reason

ración [ra'θjon] *nf* portion; **raciones** *nfpl* rations

racional [raθjo'nal] *adj* (*razonable*) reasonable; (*lógico*) rational; ~**izar** *vt* to rationalize

racionar [raθjo'nar] *vt* to ration (out)

racismo [ra'θismo] *nm* racism; **racista** *adj, nm/f* racist

radar [ra'ðar] *nm* radar

radiactivo, a [raðiak'tiβo, a] *adj* = **radioactivo**

radiador [raðja'ðor] *nm* radiator

radiante [ra'ðjante] *adj* radiant

radical [raði'kal] *adj, nm/f* radical

radicar [raði'kar] *vi*: ~ **en** (*dificultad, problema*) to lie in; (*solución*) to consist in; ~**se** *vr* to establish o.s., put down (one's) roots

radio ['raðjo] *nf* radio; (*aparato*) radio (set) ♦ *nm* (*MAT*) radius; (*QUÍM*) radium; ~**actividad** *nf* radioactivity; ~**activo, a** *adj* radioactive; ~**difusión** *nf* broadcasting; ~**emisora** *nf* transmitter,

radio station; **~escucha** *nm/f* listener;
~grafía *nf* X-ray; **~grafiar** *vt* to X-ray;
~terapia *nf* radiotherapy; **~yente** *nm/f*
listener

ráfaga ['rafaɣa] *nf* gust; (*de luz*) flash; (*de
tiros*) burst

raído, a [ra'iðo, a] *adj* (*ropa*) threadbare

raigambre [rai'ɣambre] *nf* (*BOT*) roots *pl*;
(*fig*) tradition

raíz [ra'iθ] *nf* root; **~ cuadrada** square
root; **a ~ de** as a result of

raja ['raxa] *nf* (*de melón etc*) slice; (*grieta*)
crack; **rajar** *vt* to split; (*fam*) to slash;
rajarse *vr* to split, crack; **rajarse de** to
back out of

rajatabla [raxa'taβla]: **a ~** *adv*
(*estrictamente*) strictly, to the letter

rallador [raʎa'ðor] *nm* grater

rallar [ra'ʎar] *vt* to grate

rama ['rama] *nf* branch; **~je** *nm* branches
pl, foliage; **ramal** (*de cuerda*) strand;
(*FERRO*) branch line (*BRIT*); (*AUTO*) branch
(*road*) (*BRIT*)

rambla ['rambla] *nf* (*avenida*) avenue

ramificación [ramifika'θjon] *nf*
ramification

ramificarse [ramifi'karse] *vr* to branch
out

ramillete [rami'ʎete] *nm* bouquet

ramo ['ramo] *nm* branch; (*sección*)
department, section

rampa ['rampa] *nf* ramp

ramplón, ona [ram'plon, ona] *adj*
uncouth, coarse

rana ['rana] *nf* frog; **salto de ~** leapfrog

ranchero [ran'tʃero] *nm* (*AM*) rancher;
smallholder

rancho ['rantʃo] *nm* (*grande*) ranch;
(*pequeño*) small farm

rancio, a ['ranθjo, a] *adj* (*comestibles*)
rancid; (*vino*) aged, mellow; (*fig*) ancient

rango ['rango] *nm* rank, standing

ranura [ra'nura] *nf* groove; (*de teléfono
etc*) slot

rapar [ra'par] *vt* to shave; (*los cabellos*) to
crop

rapaz [ra'paθ] (*nf*: **rapaza**) *nm/f* young

boy/girl ♦ *adj* (*ZOOL*) predatory

rape ['rape] *nm* (*pez*) monkfish; **al ~**
cropped

rapé [ra'pe] *nm* snuff

rapidez [rapi'ðeθ] *nf* speed, rapidity;
rápido, a *adj* fast, quick ♦ *adv* quickly
♦ *nm* (*FERRO*) express; **rápidos** *nmpl*
rapids

rapiña [ra'piɲa] *nm* robbery; **ave de ~**
bird of prey

raptar [rap'tar] *vt* to kidnap; **rapto** *nm*
kidnapping; (*impulso*) sudden impulse;
(*éxtasis*) ecstasy, rapture

raqueta [ra'keta] *nf* racquet

raquítico, a [ra'kitiko, a] *adj* stunted; (*fig*)
poor, inadequate; **raquitismo** *nm*
rickets *sg*

rareza [ra'reθa] *nf* rarity; (*fig*) eccentricity

raro, a ['raro, a] *adj* (*poco común*) rare;
(*extraño*) odd, strange; (*excepcional*)
remarkable

ras [ras] *nm*: **a ~ de** level with; **a ~ de
tierra** at ground level

rasar [ra'sar] *vt* (*igualar*) to level

rascacielos [raska'θjelos] *nm inv*
skyscraper

rascar [ras'kar] *vt* (*con las uñas etc*) to
scratch; (*raspar*) to scrape; **~se** *vr* to
scratch (*o.s.*)

rasgar [ras'ɣar] *vt* to tear, rip (up)

rasgo ['rasɣo] *nm* (*con pluma*) stroke; **~s**
nmpl (*facciones*) features, characteristics;
a grandes ~s in outline, broadly

rasguñar [rasɣu'ɲar] *vt* to scratch;
rasguño *nm* scratch

raso, a ['raso, a] *adj* (*liso*) flat, level; (*a
baja altura*) very low ♦ *nm* satin; **cielo ~**
clear sky

raspadura [raspa'ðura] *nf* (*acto*) scrape,
scraping; (*marca*) scratch; **~s** *nfpl* (*de
papel etc*) scrapings

raspar [ras'par] *vt* to scrape; (*arañar*) to
scratch; (*limar*) to file

rastra ['rastra] *nf* (*AGR*) rake; **a ~s** by
dragging; (*fig*) unwillingly

rastreador [rastrea'ðor] *nm* tracker; **~ de
minas** minesweeper

rastrear [rastre'ar] *vt* (*seguir*) to track
rastrero, a [ras'trero, a] *adj* (BOT, ZOOL) creeping; (*fig*) despicable, mean
rastrillo [ras'triλo] *nm* rake
rastro ['rastro] *nm* (AGR) rake; (*pista*) track, trail; (*vestigio*) trace; **el R~** the Madrid fleamarket
rastrojo [ras'troxo] *nm* stubble
rasurador [rasura'ðor] (AM) *nm* electric shaver
rasuradora [rasura'ðora] (AM) *nf* = **rasurador**
rasurarse [rasu'rarse] *vr* to shave
rata ['rata] *nf* rat
ratear [rate'ar] *vt* (*robar*) to steal
ratero, a [ra'tero, a] *adj* light-fingered ♦ *nm/f* (*carterista*) pickpocket; (AM: *de casas*) burglar
ratificar [ratifi'kar] *vt* to ratify
rato ['rato] *nm* while, short time; **a ~s** from time to time; **hay para ~** there's still a long way to go; **al poco ~** soon afterwards; **pasar el ~** to kill time; **pasar un buen/mal ~** to have a good/rough time; **en mis ~s libres** in my spare time
ratón [ra'ton] *nm* mouse; **ratonera** *nf* mousetrap
raudal [rau'ðal] *nm* torrent; **a ~es** in abundance
raya ['raja] *nf* line; (*marca*) scratch; (*en tela*) stripe; (*de pelo*) parting; (*límite*) boundary; (*pez*) ray; (*puntuación*) dash; **a ~s** striped; **pasarse de la ~** to go too far: **tener a ~** to keep in check; **rayar** *vt* to line; to scratch; (*subrayar*) to underline ♦ *vi*: **rayar en** *o* **con** to border on
rayo ['rajo] *nm* (*del sol*) ray, beam; (*de luz*) shaft; (*en una tormenta*) (flash of) lightning; **~s X** X-rays
raza ['raθa] *nf* race; **~ humana** human race
razón [ra'θon] *nf* reason; (*justicia*) right, justice; (*razonamiento*) reasoning; (*motivo*) reason, motive; (MAT) ratio; **a ~ de 10 cada día** at the rate of 10 a day; **"~: ..."** "inquiries to ..."; **en ~ de** with regard to; **dar ~ a uno** to agree that sb is right; **tener ~** to be right; **~ directa/inversa**

direct/inverse proportion; **~ de ser** raison d'être; **razonable** *adj* reasonable; (*justo, moderado*) fair; **razonamiento** *nm* (*juicio*) judg(e)ment; (*argumento*) reasoning; **razonar** *vt*, *vi* to reason, argue
reacción [reak'θjon] *nf* reaction; **avión a ~** jet plane; **~ en cadena** chain reaction; **reaccionar** *vi* to react; **reaccionario, a** *adj* reactionary
reacio, a [re'aθjo, a] *adj* stubborn
reactivar [reakti'ßar] *vt* to revitalize
reactor [reak'tor] *nm* reactor
readaptación [reaðapta'θjon] *nf*: **~ profesional** industrial retraining
reajuste [rea'xuste] *nm* readjustment
real [re'al] *adj* real; (*del rey*, *fig*) royal
realce [re'alθe] *nm* (*lustre*, *fig*) splendour; **poner de ~** to emphasize
realidad [reali'ðað] *nf* reality, fact; (*verdad*) truth
realista [rea'lista] *nm/f* realist
realización [realiθa'θjon] *nf* fulfilment
realizador, a [realiθa'ðor, a] *nm/f* filmmaker
realizar [reali'θar] *vt* (*objetivo*) to achieve; (*plan*) to carry out; (*viaje*) to make, undertake; **~se** *vr* to come about, come true
realmente [real'mente] *adv* really, actually
realquilar [realki'lar] *vt* to sublet
realzar [real'θar] *vt* to enhance; (*acentuar*) to highlight
reanimar [reani'mar] *vt* to revive; (*alentar*) to encourage; **~se** *vr* to revive
reanudar [reanu'ðar] *vt* (*renovar*) to renew; (*historia*, *viaje*) to resume
reaparición [reapari'θjon] *nf* reappearance
rearme [re'arme] *nm* rearmament
rebaja [re'ßaxa] *nf* (COM) reduction; (: *descuento*) discount; **~s** *nfpl* (COM) sale; **rebajar** *vt* (*bajar*) to lower; (*reducir*) to reduce; (*disminuir*) to lessen; (*humillar*) to humble
rebanada [reßa'naða] *nf* slice
rebañar [reßa'nar] *vt* (*comida*) to scrape

up; (*plato*) to scrape clean
rebaño [re'βaɲo] *nm* herd; (*de ovejas*) flock
rebasar [reβa'sar] *vt* (*tb:* **~ de**) to exceed
rebatir [reβa'tir] *vt* to refute
rebeca [re'βeka] *nf* cardigan
rebelarse [reβe'larse] *vr* to rebel, revolt
rebelde [re'βelde] *adj* rebellious; (*niño*) unruly ♦ *nm/f* rebel; **rebeldía** *nf* rebelliousness; (*desobediencia*) disobedience
rebelión [reβe'ljon] *nf* rebellion
reblandecer [reβlande'θer] *vt* to soften
rebobinar [reβoβi'nar] *vt* (*cinta, película de video*) to rewind
rebosante [reβo'sante] *adj* overflowing
rebosar [reβo'sar] *vi* (*líquido, recipiente*) to overflow; (*abundar*) to abound, be plentiful
rebotar [reβo'tar] *vt* to bounce; (*rechazar*) to repel ♦ *vi* (*pelota*) to bounce; (*bala*) to ricochet; **rebote** *nm* rebound; **de rebote** on the rebound
rebozado, a [reβo'θaðo, a] *adj* fried in batter *o* breadcrumbs
rebozar [reβo'θar] *vt* to wrap up; (*CULIN*) to fry in batter *o* breadcrumbs
rebuscado, a [reβus'kaðo, a] *adj* (*amanerado*) affected; (*palabra*) recherché; (*idea*) far-fetched
rebuscar [reβus'kar] *vi*: **~ (en/por)** to search carefully (in/for)
rebuznar [reβuθ'nar] *vi* to bray
recado [re'kaðo] *nm* (*mensaje*) message; (*encargo*) errand; **tomar un ~** (*TEL*) to take a message
recaer [reka'er] *vi* to relapse; **~ en** to fall to *o* on; (*criminal etc*) to fall back into, relapse into; **recaída** *nf* relapse
recalcar [rekal'kar] *vt* (*fig*) to stress, emphasize
recalcitrante [rekalθi'trante] *adj* recalcitrant
recalentar [rekalen'tar] *vt* (*volver a calentar*) to reheat; (*calentar demasiado*) to overheat
recámara [re'kamara] (*AM*) *nf* bedroom

recambio [re'kambjo] *nm* spare; (*de pluma*) refill
recapacitar [rekapaθi'tar] *vi* to reflect
recargado, a [rekar'γaðo, a] *adj* overloaded
recargar [rekar'γar] *vt* to overload; (*batería*) to recharge; **recargo** *nm* surcharge; (*aumento*) increase
recatado, a [reka'taðo, a] *adj* (*modesto*) modest, demure; (*prudente*) cautious
recato [re'kato] *nm* (*modestia*) modesty, demureness; (*cautela*) caution
recaudación [rekauða'θjon] *nf* (*acción*) collection; (*cantidad*) takings *pl*; (*en deporte*) gate; **recaudador, a** *nm/f* tax collector
recelar [reθe'lar] *vt*: **~ que** (*sospechar*) to suspect that; (*temer*) to fear that ♦ *vi*: **~ de** to distrust; **recelo** *nm* distrust, suspicion; **receloso, a** *adj* distrustful, suspicious
recepción [reθep'θjon] *nf* reception; **recepcionista** *nm/f* receptionist
receptáculo [reθep'takulo] *nm* receptacle
receptivo, a [reθep'tiβo, a] *adj* receptive
receptor, a [reθep'tor, a] *nm/f* recipient ♦ *nm* (*TEL*) receiver
recesión [reθe'sjon] *nf* (*COM*) recession
receta [re'θeta] *nf* (*CULIN*) recipe; (*MED*) prescription
rechazar [retʃa'θar] *vt* to reject; (*oferta*) to turn down; (*ataque*) to repel
rechazo [re'tʃaθo] *nm* rejection
rechifla [re'tʃifla] *nf* hissing, booing; (*fig*) derision
rechinar [retʃi'nar] *vi* to creak; (*dientes*) to grind
rechistar [retʃis'tar] *vi*: **sin ~** without a murmur
rechoncho, a [re'tʃontʃo, a] (*fam*) *adj* thickset (*BRIT*), heavy-set (*US*)
rechupete [retʃu'pete]: **de ~** (*comida*) delicious, scrumptious
recibidor, a [reθiβi'ðor, a] *nm* entrance hall
recibimiento [reθiβi'mjento] *nm* reception, welcome

recibir [reθi'ßir] *vt* to receive; (*dar la bienvenida*) to welcome ♦ *vi* to entertain; **~se** *vr*: **~se de** to qualify as; **recibo** *nm* receipt

reciclar [reθi'klar] *vt* to recycle

recién [re'θjen] *adv* recently, newly; **los ~ casados** the newly-weds; **el ~ llegado** the newcomer; **el ~ nacido** the newborn child

reciente [re'θjente] *adj* recent; (*fresco*) fresh; **~mente** *adv* recently

recinto [re'θinto] *nm* enclosure; (*área*) area, place

recio, a ['reθjo, a] *adj* strong, tough; (*voz*) loud ♦ *adv* hard; loud(ly)

recipiente [reθi'pjente] *nm* receptacle

reciprocidad [reθiproθi'ðað] *nf* reciprocity; **recíproco, a** *adj* reciprocal

recital [reθi'tal] *nm* (*MUS*) recital; (*LITERATURA*) reading

recitar [reθi'tar] *vt* to recite

reclamación [reklama'θjon] *nf* claim, demand; (*queja*) complaint

reclamar [rekla'mar] *vt* to claim, demand ♦ *vi*: **~ contra** to complain about; **~ a uno en justicia** to take sb to court; **reclamo** *nm* (*anuncio*) advertisement; (*tentación*) attraction

reclinar [rekli'nar] *vt* to recline, lean; **~se** *vr* to lean back

recluir [reklu'ir] *vt* to intern, confine

reclusión [reklu'sjon] *nf* (*prisión*) prison; (*refugio*) seclusion; **~ perpetua** life imprisonment

recluta [re'kluta] *nm/f* recruit ♦ *nf* recruitment; **reclutar** *vt* (*datos*) to collect; (*dinero*) to collect up; **~miento** [rekluta'mjento] *nm* recruitment

recobrar [reko'ßrar] *vt* (*salud*) to recover; (*rescatar*) to get back; **~se** *vr* to recover

recodo [re'koðo] *nm* (*de río, camino*) bend

recogedor [rekoxe'ðor] *nm* dustpan

recoger [reko'xer] *vt* to collect; (*AGR*) to harvest; (*levantar*) to pick up; (*juntar*) to gather; (*pasar a buscar*) to come for, get; (*dar asilo*) to give shelter to; (*faldas*) to gather up; (*pelo*) to put up; **~se** *vr*

(*retirarse*) to retire; **recogido, a** *adj* (*lugar*) quiet, secluded; (*pequeño*) small ♦ *nf* (*CORREOS*) collection; (*AGR*) harvest

recolección [rekolek'θjon] *nf* (*AGR*) harvesting; (*colecta*) collection

recomendación [rekomenda'θjon] *nf* (*sugerencia*) suggestion, recommendation; (*referencia*) reference

recomendar [rekomen'dar] *vt* to suggest, recommend; (*confiar*) to entrust

recompensa [rekom'pensa] *nf* reward, recompense; **recompensar** *vt* to reward, recompense

recomponer [rekompo'ner] *vt* to mend

reconciliación [rekonθilja'θjon] *nf* reconciliation

reconciliar [rekonθi'ljar] *vt* to reconcile; **~se** *vr* to become reconciled

recóndito, a [re'kondito, a] *adj* (*lugar*) hidden, secret

reconfortar [rekonfor'tar] *vt* to comfort

reconocer [rekono'θer] *vt* to recognize; (*registrar*) to search; (*MED*) to examine; **reconocido, a** *adj* recognized; (*agradecido*) grateful; **reconocimiento** *nm* recognition; search; examination; gratitude; (*confesión*) admission

reconquista [rekon'kista] *nf* reconquest; **la R~** the Reconquest (of Spain)

reconstituyente [rekonstitu'jente] *nm* tonic

reconstruir [rekonstru'ir] *vt* to reconstruct

reconversión [rekonßer'sjon] *nf*: **~ industrial** industrial rationalization

recopilación [rekopila'θjon] *nf* (*resumen*) summary; (*compilación*) compilation; **recopilar** *vt* to compile

récord ['rekorð] (*pl* **~s**) *adj inv, nm* record

recordar [rekor'ðar] *vt* (*acordarse de*) to remember; (*acordar a otro*) to remind ♦ *vi* to remember

recorrer [reko'rrer] *vt* (*país*) to cross, travel through; (*distancia*) to cover; (*registrar*) to search; (*repasar*) to look over; **recorrido** *nm* run, journey; **tren de largo recorrido** main-line train

recortado, a [rekor'taðo, a] *adj* uneven,

irregular

recortar [rekor'tar] *vt* to cut out; **recorte** *nm* (*acción, de prensa*) cutting; (*de telas, chapas*) trimming; **recorte presupuestario** budget cut

recostado, a [rekos'taðo, a] *adj* leaning; **estar ~** to be lying down

recostar [rekos'tar] *vt* to lean; **~se** *vr* to lie down

recoveco [reko'ßeko] *nm* (*de camino, río etc*) bend; (*en casa*) cubby hole

recreación [rekrea'θjon] *nf* recreation

recrear [rekre'ar] *vt* (*entretener*) to entertain; (*volver a crear*) to recreate; **recreativo, a** *adj* recreational; **recreo** *nm* recreation; (*ESCOL*) break, playtime

recriminar [rekrimi'nar] *vt* to reproach ♦ *vi* to recriminate; **~se** *vr* to reproach each other

recrudecer [rekruðe'θer] *vt, vi* to worsen; **~se** *vr* to worsen

recrudecimiento [rekruðeθi'mjento] *nm* upsurge

recta ['rekta] *nf* straight line

rectángulo, a [rek'tangulo, a] *adj* rectangular ♦ *nm* rectangle

rectificar [rektifi'kar] *vt* to rectify; (*volverse recto*) to straighten ♦ *vi* to correct o.s.

rectitud [rekti'tuð] *nf* straightness; (*fig*) rectitude

recto, a ['rekto, a] *adj* straight; (*persona*) honest, upright ♦ *nm* rectum

rector, a [rek'tor, a] *adj* governing

recuadro [re'kwaðro] *nm* box; (*TIPOGRAFÍA*) inset

recubrir [reku'ßrir] *vt*: **~ (con)** (*pintura, crema*) to cover (with)

recuento [re'kwento] *nm* inventory; **hacer el ~ de** to count o reckon up

recuerdo [re'kwerðo] *nm* souvenir; **~s** *nmpl* (*memorias*) memories; **¡~s a tu madre!** give my regards to your mother!

recular [reku'lar] *vi* to back down

recuperable [rekupe'raßle] *adj* recoverable

recuperación [rekupera'θjon] *nf* recovery

recuperar [rekupe'rar] *vt* to recover;

(*tiempo*) to make up; **~se** *vr* to recuperate

recurrir [reku'rrir] *vi* (*JUR*) to appeal; **~ a** to resort to; (*persona*) to turn to;

recurso *nm* resort; (*medios*) means *pl*, resources *pl*; (*JUR*) appeal

recusar [reku'sar] *vt* to reject, refuse

red [reð] *nf* net, mesh; (*FERRO etc*) network; (*trampa*) trap; **la R~** (*Internet*) the Net

redacción [reðak'θjon] *nf* (*acción*) editing; (*personal*) editorial staff; (*ESCOL*) essay, composition

redactar [reðak'tar] *vt* to draw up, draft; (*periódico*) to edit

redactor, a [reðak'tor, a] *nm/f* editor

redada [re'ðaða] *nf*: **~ policial** police raid, round-up

rededor [reðe'ðor] *nm*: **al** *o* **en ~** around, round about

redención [reðen'θjon] *nf* redemption

redicho, a [re'ðitʃo, a] *adj* affected

redil [re'ðil] *nm* sheepfold

redimir [reði'mir] *vt* to redeem

rédito ['reðito] *nm* interest, yield

redoblar [reðo'ßlar] *vt* to redouble ♦ *vi* (*tambor*) to roll

redomado, a [reðo'maðo, a] *adj* (*astuto*) sly, crafty; (*perfecto*) utter

redonda [re'ðonda] *nf*: **a la ~** around, round about

redondear [reðonde'ar] *vt* to round, round off

redondel [reðon'del] *nm* (*círculo*) circle; (*TAUR*) bullring, arena

redondo, a [re'ðondo, a] *adj* (*circular*) round; (*completo*) complete

reducción [reðuk'θjon] *nf* reduction

reducido, a [reðu'θiðo, a] *adj* reduced; (*limitado*) limited; (*pequeño*) small

reducir [reðu'θir] *vt* to reduce; to limit; **~se** *vr* to diminish

redundancia [reðun'danθja] *nf* redundancy

reembolsar [re(e)mbol'sar] *vt* (*persona*) to reimburse; (*dinero*) to repay, pay back; (*depósito*) to refund; **reembolso** *nm* reimbursement; refund

reemplazar [re(e)mpla'θar] *vt* to replace;

reemplazo *nm* replacement; **de reemplazo** (*MIL*) reserve

reencuentro [re(e)n'kwentro] *nm* reunion

referencia [refe'renθja] *nf* reference; **con ~ a** with reference to

referéndum [refe'rendum] (*pl* ~**s**) *nm* referendum

referente [refe'rente] *adj*: ~ **a** concerning, relating to

referir [refe'rir] *vt* (*contar*) to tell, recount; (*relacionar*) to refer, relate; ~**se** *vr*: ~**se a** to refer to

refilón [refi'lon]: **de ~** *adv* obliquely

refinado, a [refi'naðo, a] *adj* refined

refinamiento [refina'mjento] *nm* refinement

refinar [refi'nar] *vt* to refine; **refinería** *nf* refinery

reflejar [refle'xar] *vt* to reflect; **reflejo, a** *adj* reflected; (*movimiento*) reflex ♦ *nm* reflection; (*ANAT*) reflex

reflexión [reflek'sjon] *nf* reflection; **reflexionar** *vt* to reflect on ♦ *vi* to reflect; (*detenerse*) to pause (to think)

reflexivo, a [reflek'sißo, a] *adj* thoughtful; (*LING*) reflexive

reflujo [re'fluxo] *nm* ebb

reforma [re'forma] *nf* reform; (*ARQ etc*) repair; ~ **agraria** agrarian reform

reformar [refor'mar] *vt* to reform; (*modificar*) to change, alter; (*ARQ*) to repair; ~**se** *vr* to mend one's ways

reformatorio [reforma'torjo] *nm* reformatory

reforzar [refor'θar] *vt* to strengthen; (*ARQ*) to reinforce; (*fig*) to encourage

refractario, a [refrak'tarjo, a] *adj* (*TEC*) heat-resistant

refrán [re'fran] *nm* proverb, saying

refregar [refre'ɣar] *vt* to scrub

refrenar [refre'nar] *vt* to check, restrain

refrendar [refren'dar] *vt* (*firma*) to endorse, countersign; (*ley*) to approve

refrescante [refres'kante] *adj* refreshing, cooling

refrescar [refres'kar] *vt* to refresh ♦ *vi* to cool down; ~**se** *vr* to get cooler; (*tomar*

aire fresco) to go out for a breath of fresh air; (*beber*) to have a drink

refresco [re'fresko] *nm* soft drink, cool drink; "~**s**" "refreshments"

refriega [re'frjeɣa] *nf* scuffle, brawl

refrigeración [refrixera'θjon] *nf* refrigeration; (*de sala*) air-conditioning

refrigerador [refrixera'ðor] *nm* refrigerator (*BRIT*), icebox (*US*)

refrigerar [refrixe'rar] *vt* to refrigerate; (*sala*) to air-condition

refuerzo [re'fwerθo] *nm* reinforcement; (*TEC*) support

refugiado, a [refu'xjaðo, a] *nm/f* refugee

refugiarse [refu'xjarse] *vr* to take refuge, shelter

refugio [re'fuxjo] *nm* refuge; (*protección*) shelter

refunfuñar [refunfu'nar] *vi* to grunt, growl; (*quejarse*) to grumble

refutar [refu'tar] *vt* to refute

regadera [reɣa'ðera] *nf* watering can

regadío [reɣa'ðio] *nm* irrigated land

regalado, a [reɣa'laðo, a] *adj* comfortable, luxurious; (*gratis*) free, for nothing

regalar [reɣa'lar] *vt* (*dar*) to give (as a present); (*entregar*) to give away; (*mimar*) to pamper, make a fuss of

regaliz [reɣa'liθ] *nm* liquorice

regalo [re'ɣalo] *nm* (*obsequio*) gift, present; (*gusto*) pleasure

regañadientes [reɣaɲa'ðjentes]: **a ~** *adv* reluctantly

regañar [reɣa'nar] *vt* to scold ♦ *vi* to grumble; **regañón, ona** *adj* nagging

regar [re'ɣar] *vt* to water, irrigate; (*fig*) to scatter, sprinkle

regatear [reɣate'ar] *vt* (*COM*) to bargain over; (*escatimar*) to be mean with ♦ *vi* to bargain, haggle; (*DEPORTE*) to dribble; **regateo** *nm* bargaining; dribbling; (*del cuerpo*) swerve, dodge

regazo [re'ɣaθo] *nm* lap

regeneración [rexenera'θjon] *nf* regeneration

regenerar [rexene'rar] *vt* to regenerate

regentar [rexen'tar] *vt* to direct, manage; **regente** *nm* (*COM*) manager; (*POL*) regent

régimen ['reximen] (*pl* **regímenes**) *nm* regime; (*MED*) diet

regimiento [rexi'mjento] *nm* regiment

regio, a ['rexjo, a] *adj* royal, regal; (*fig: suntuoso*) splendid; (*AM: fam*) great, terrific

región [re'xjon] *nf* region

regir [re'xir] *vt* to govern, rule; (*dirigir*) to manage, run ♦ *vi* to apply, be in force

registrar [rexis'trar] *vt* (*buscar*) to search; (: *en cajón*) to look through; (*inspeccionar*) to inspect; (*anotar*) to register, record; (*INFORM*) to log; **~se** *vr* to register; (*ocurrir*) to happen

registro [re'xistro] *nm* (*acto*) registration; (*MUS, libro*) register; (*inspección*) inspection, search; **~ civil** registry office

regla ['rexla] *nf* (*ley*) rule, regulation; (*de medir*) ruler, rule; (*MED: período*) period

reglamentación [rexlamenta'θjon] *nf* (*acto*) regulation; (*lista*) rules *pl*

reglamentar [rexlamen'tar] *vt* to regulate; **reglamentario, a** *adj* statutory; **reglamento** *nm* rules *pl*, regulations *pl*

regocijarse [reɣoθi'xarse] *vr*: **~ de** to rejoice at, be happy about; **regocijo** *nm* joy, happiness

regodearse [reɣoðe'arse] *vr* to be glad, be delighted; **regodeo** *nm* delight

regresar [reɣre'sar] *vi* to come back, go back, return; **regresivo, a** *adj* backward; (*fig*) regressive; **regreso** *nm* return

reguero [re'ɣero] *nm* (*de sangre etc*) trickle; (*de humo*) trail

regulador [reɣula'ðor] *nm* regulator; (*de radio etc*) knob, control

regular [reɣu'lar] *adj* regular; (*normal*) normal, usual; (*común*) ordinary; (*organizado*) regular, orderly; (*mediano*) average; (*fam*) not bad, so-so ♦ *adv* so-so, alright ♦ *vt* (*controlar*) to control, regulate; (*TEC*) to adjust; **por lo ~** as a rule; **~idad** *nf* regularity; **~izar** *vt* to regularize

regusto [re'ɣusto] *nm* aftertaste

rehabilitación [reaßilita'θjon] *nf* rehabilitation; (*ARQ*) restoration

rehabilitar [reaßili'tar] *vt* to rehabilitate; (*ARQ*) to restore; (*reintegrar*) to reinstate

rehacer [rea'θer] *vt* (*reparar*) to mend, repair; (*volver a hacer*) to redo, repeat; **~se** *vr* (*MED*) to recover

rehén [re'en] *nm* hostage

rehuir [reu'ir] *vt* to avoid, shun

rehusar [reu'sar] *vt, vi* to refuse

reina ['reina] *nf* queen; **~do** *nm* reign

reinante [rei'nante] *adj* (*fig*) prevailing

reinar [rei'nar] *vi* to reign

reincidir [reinθi'ðir] *vi* to relapse

reincorporarse [reinkorpo'rarse] *vr*: **~ a** to rejoin

reino ['reino] *nm* kingdom; **el R~ Unido** the United Kingdom

reintegrar [reinte'ɣrar] *vt* (*reconstituir*) to reconstruct; (*persona*) to reinstate; (*dinero*) to refund, pay back; **~se** *vr*: **~se a** to return to

reír [re'ir] *vi* to laugh; **~se** *vr* to laugh; **~se de** to laugh at

reiterar [reite'rar] *vt* to reiterate

reivindicación [reißindika'θjon] *nf* (*demanda*) claim, demand; (*justificación*) vindication

reivindicar [reißindi'kar] *vt* to claim

reja ['rexa] *nf* (*de ventana*) grille, bars *pl*; (*en la calle*) grating

rejilla [re'xiʎa] *nf* grating, grille; (*muebles*) wickerwork; (*de ventilación*) vent; (*de coche etc*) luggage rack

rejoneador [rexonea'ðor] *nm* mounted bullfighter

rejuvenecer [rexußene'θer] *vt, vi* to rejuvenate

relación [rela'θjon] *nf* relation, relationship; (*MAT*) ratio; (*narración*) report; **relaciones públicas** public relations; **con ~ a, en ~ con** in relation to; **relacionar** *vt* to relate, connect; **relacionarse** *vr* to be connected, be linked

relajación [relaxa'θjon] *nf* relaxation
relajado, a [rela'xaðo, a] *adj* (*disoluto*)
loose; (*cómodo*) relaxed; (*MED*) ruptured
relajar [rela'xar] *vt* to relax; **~se** *vr* to relax
relamerse [rela'merse] *vr* to lick one's lips
relamido, a [rela'miðo, a] *adj* (*pulcro*)
overdressed; (*afectado*) affected
relámpago [re'lampaxo] *nm* flash of
lightning; **visita/huelga ~** lightning visit/
strike; **relampaguear** *vi* to flash
relatar [rela'tar] *vt* to tell, relate
relativo, a [rela'tiβo, a] *adj* relative; **en lo
~ a** concerning
relato [re'lato] *nm* (*narración*) story, tale
relegar [rele'xar] *vt* to relegate
relevante [rele'βante] *adj* eminent,
outstanding
relevar [rele'βar] *vt* (*sustituir*) to relieve;
~se *vr* to relay; **~ a uno de un cargo** to
relieve sb of his post
relevo [re'leβo] *nm* relief; **carrera de ~s**
relay race
relieve [re'ljeβe] *nm* (*ARTE, TEC*) relief; (*fig*)
prominence, importance; **bajo ~** bas-relief
religión [reli'xjon] *nf* religion; **religioso,
a** *adj* religious ♦ *nm/f* monk/nun
relinchar [relin'tʃar] *vi* to neigh; **relincho**
nm neigh; (*acto*) neighing
reliquia [re'likja] *nf* relic; **~ de familia**
heirloom
rellano [re'ʎano] *nm* (*ARQ*) landing
rellenar [reʎe'nar] *vt* (*llenar*) to fill up;
(*CULIN*) to stuff; (*COSTURA*) to pad;
relleno, a *adj* full up; stuffed ♦ *nm*
stuffing; (*de tapicería*) padding
reloj [re'lo(x)] *nm* clock; **~ (de pulsera)**
wristwatch; **~ despertador** alarm (clock);
poner el ~ to set one's watch (*o* the
clock); **~ero, a** *nm/f* clockmaker;
watchmaker
reluciente [relu'θjente] *adj* brilliant,
shining
relucir [relu'θir] *vi* to shine; (*fig*) to excel
relumbrar [relum'brar] *vi* to dazzle, shine
brilliantly
remachar [rema'tʃar] *vt* to rivet; (*fig*) to
hammer home, drive home; **remache**

nm rivet
remanente [rema'nente] *nm* remainder;
(*COM*) balance; (*de producto*) surplus
remangar [reman'gar] *vt* to roll up
remanso [re'manso] *nm* pool
remar [re'mar] *vi* to row
rematado, a [rema'taðo, a] *adj* complete,
utter
rematar [rema'tar] *vt* to finish off; (*COM*)
to sell off cheap ♦ *vi* to end, finish off;
(*DEPORTE*) to shoot
remate [re'mate] *nm* end, finish; (*punta*)
tip; (*DEPORTE*) shot; (*ARQ*) top; **de** *o* **para
~** to crown it all (*BRIT*), to top it off
remedar [reme'ðar] *vt* to imitate
remediar [reme'ðjar] *vt* to remedy;
(*subsanar*) to make good, repair; (*evitar*)
to avoid
remedio [re'meðjo] *nm* remedy; (*alivio*)
relief, help; (*JUR*) recourse, remedy; **poner
~ a** to correct, stop; **no tener más ~** to
have no alternative; **¡qué ~!** there's no
choice!; **sin ~** hopeless
remedo [re'meðo] *nm* imitation; (*pey*)
parody
remendar [remen'dar] *vt* to repair; (*con
parche*) to patch
remesa [re'mesa] *nf* remittance; (*COM*)
shipment
remiendo [re'mjendo] *nm* mend; (*con
parche*) patch; (*cosido*) darn
remilgado, a [remil'xaðo, a] *adj* prim;
(*afectado*) affected
remilgo [re'milxo] *nm* primness;
(*afectación*) affectation
reminiscencia [reminis'θenθja] *nf*
reminiscence
remiso, a [re'miso, a] *adj* slack, slow
remite [re'mite] *nm* (*en sobre*) name and
address of sender
remitir [remi'tir] *vt* to remit, send ♦ *vi* to
slacken; (*en carta*): **remite: X** sender: X;
remitente *nm/f* sender
remo ['remo] *nm* (*de barco*) oar; (*DEPORTE*)
rowing
remojar [remo'xar] *vt* to steep, soak;
(*galleta etc*) to dip, dunk

remojo [reˈmoxo] *nm*: **dejar la ropa en ~** to leave clothes to soak

remolacha [remoˈlatʃa] *nf* beet, beetroot

remolcador [remolkaˈðor] *nm* (*NAUT*) tug; (*AUTO*) breakdown lorry

remolcar [remolˈkar] *vt* to tow

remolino [remoˈlino] *nm* eddy; (*de agua*) whirlpool; (*de viento*) whirlwind; (*de gente*) crowd

remolque [reˈmolke] *nm* tow, towing; (*cuerda*) towrope; **llevar a ~** to tow

remontar [remonˈtar] *vt* to mend; **~se** *vr* to soar; **~se a** (*COM*) to amount to; **~ el vuelo** to soar

remorder [remorˈðer] *vt* to distress, disturb; **~le la conciencia a uno** to have a guilty conscience; **remordimiento** *nm* remorse

remoto, a [reˈmoto, a] *adj* remote

remover [remoˈβer] *vt* to stir; (*tierra*) to turn over; (*objetos*) to move round

remozar [remoˈθar] *vt* (*ARQ*) to refurbish

remuneración [remuneraˈθjon] *nf* remuneration

remunerar [remuneˈrar] *vt* to remunerate; (*premiar*) to reward

renacer [renaˈθer] *vi* to be reborn; (*fig*) to revive; **renacimiento** *nm* rebirth; **el Renacimiento** the Renaissance

renacuajo [renaˈkwaxo] *nm* (*ZOOL*) tadpole

renal [reˈnal] *adj* renal, kidney *cpd*

rencilla [renˈθiʎa] *nf* quarrel

rencor [renˈkor] *nm* rancour, bitterness; **~oso, a** *adj* spiteful

rendición [rendiˈθjon] *nf* surrender

rendido, a [renˈdiðo, a] *adj* (*sumiso*) submissive; (*cansado*) worn-out, exhausted

rendija [renˈdixa] *nf* (*hendedura*) crack, cleft

rendimiento [rendiˈmjento] *nm* (*producción*) output; (*TEC, COM*) efficiency

rendir [renˈdir] *vt* (*vencer*) to defeat; (*producir*) to produce; (*dar beneficio*) to yield; (*agotar*) to exhaust ♦ *vi* to pay; **~se** *vr* (*someterse*) to surrender; (*cansarse*) to

wear o.s. out; **~ homenaje** *o* **culto a** to pay homage to

renegar [reneˈxar] *vi* (*renunciar*) to renounce; (*blasfemar*) to blaspheme; (*quejarse*) to complain

RENFE [ˈrenfe] *nf abr* (= *Red Nacional de los Ferrocarriles Españoles*) ≈ BR (*BRIT*)

renglón [renˈglon] *nm* (*línea*) line; (*COM*) item, article; **a ~ seguido** immediately after

renombrado, a [renomˈbraðo, a] *adj* renowned

renombre [reˈnombre] *nm* renown

renovación [renoβaˈθjon] *nf* (*de contrato*) renewal; (*ARQ*) renovation

renovar [renoˈβar] *vt* to renew; (*ARQ*) to renovate

renta [ˈrenta] *nf* (*ingresos*) income; (*beneficio*) profit; (*alquiler*) rent; **~ vitalicia** annuity; **rentable** *adj* profitable; **rentar** *vt* to produce, yield

renuncia [reˈnunθja] *nf* resignation

renunciar [renunˈθjar] *vt* to renounce; (*tabaco, alcohol etc*): **~ a** to give up; (*oferta, oportunidad*) to turn down; (*puesto*) to resign ♦ *vi* to resign

reñido, a [reˈɲiðo, a] *adj* (*batalla*) bitter, hard-fought; **estar ~ con uno** to be on bad terms with sb

reñir [reˈɲir] *vt* (*regañar*) to scold ♦ *vi* (*estar peleado*) to quarrel, fall out; (*combatir*) to fight

reo [ˈreo] *nm/f* culprit, offender; **~ de muerte** prisoner condemned to death

reojo [reˈoxo] *nm*: **de ~** *adv* out of the corner of one's eye

reparación [reparaˈθjon] *nf* (*acto*) mending, repairing; (*TEC*) repair; (*fig*) amends, reparation

reparar [repaˈrar] *vt* to repair; (*fig*) to make amends for; (*observar*) to observe ♦ *vi*: **~ en** (*darse cuenta de*) to notice; (*prestar atención a*) to pay attention to

reparo [reˈparo] *nm* (*advertencia*) observation; (*duda*) doubt; (*dificultad*) difficulty; **poner ~s (a)** to raise objections (to)

repartición [reparti'θjon] *nf* distribution; (*división*) division; **repartidor, a** *nm/f* distributor

repartir [repar'tir] *vt* to distribute, share out; (*CORREOS*) to deliver; **reparto** *nm* distribution; delivery; (*TEATRO, CINE*) cast; (*AM: urbanización*) housing estate (*BRIT*), real estate development (*US*)

repasar [repa'sar] *vt* (*ESCOL*) to revise; (*MECÁNICA*) to check, overhaul; (*COSTURA*) to mend; **repaso** *nm* revision; overhaul; checkup; mending

repatriar [repa'trjar] *vt* to repatriate

repecho [re'petʃo] *nm* steep incline

repelente [repe'lente] *adj* repellent, repulsive

repeler [repe'ler] *vt* to repel

repensar [repen'sar] *vt* to reconsider

repente [re'pente] *nm*: **de ~** suddenly; **~ de ira** fit of anger

repentino, a [repen'tino, a] *adj* sudden

repercusión [reperku'sjon] *nf* repercussion

repercutir [reperku'tir] *vi* (*objeto*) to rebound; (*sonido*) to echo; **~ en** (*fig*) to have repercussions on

repertorio [reper'torjo] *nm* list; (*TEATRO*) repertoire

repetición [repeti'θjon] *nf* repetition

repetir [repe'tir] *vt* to repeat; (*plato*) to have a second helping of ♦ *vi* to repeat; (*sabor*) to come back; **~se** *vr* (*volver sobre un tema*) to repeat o.s.

repetitivo, a [repeti'tiβo, a] *adj* repetitive, repetitious

repicar [repi'kar] *vt* (*campanas*) to ring

repique [re'pike] *nm* pealing, ringing; **~teo** *nm* pealing; (*de tambor*) drumming

repisa [re'pisa] *nf* ledge, shelf; (*de ventana*) windowsill; **~ de chimenea** mantelpiece

repito *etc vb ver* **repetir**

replantearse [replante'arse] *vr*: **~ un problema** to reconsider a problem

replegarse [reple'xarse] *vr* to fall back, retreat

repleto, a [re'pleto, a] *adj* replete, full up

réplica ['replika] *nf* answer; (*ARTE*) replica

replicar [repli'kar] *vi* to answer; (*objetar*) to argue, answer back

repliegue [re'pljeɣe] *nm* (*MIL*) withdrawal

repoblación [repoβla'θjon] *nf* repopulation; (*de río*) restocking; **~ forestal** reafforestation

repoblar [repo'βlar] *vt* to repopulate; (*con árboles*) to reafforest

repollo [re'poʎo] *nm* cabbage

reponer [repo'ner] *vt* to replace, put back; (*TEATRO*) to revive; **~se** *vr* to recover; **~ que** to reply that

reportaje [repor'taxe] *nm* report, article

reportero, a [repor'tero, a] *nm/f* reporter

reposacabezas [reposaka'βeθas] *nm inv* headrest

reposado, a [repo'saðo, a] *adj* (*descansado*) restful; (*tranquilo*) calm

reposar [repo'sar] *vi* to rest, repose

reposición [reposi'θjon] *nf* replacement; (*CINE*) remake

reposo [re'poso] *nm* rest

repostar [repos'tar] *vt* to replenish; (*AUTO*) to fill up (with petrol (*BRIT*) *o* gasoline (*US*))

repostería [reposte'ria] *nf* confectioner's (shop); **repostero, a** *nm/f* confectioner

reprender [repren'der] *vt* to reprimand

represa [re'presa] *nf* dam; (*lago artificial*) lake, pool

represalia [repre'salja] *nf* reprisal

representación [representa'θjon] *nf* representation; (*TEATRO*) performance; **representante** *nm/f* representative; performer

representar [represen'tar] *vt* to represent; (*TEATRO*) to perform; (*edad*) to look; **~se** *vr* to imagine; **representativo, a** *adj* representative

represión [repre'sjon] *nf* repression

reprimenda [repri'menda] *nf* reprimand, rebuke

reprimir [repri'mir] *vt* to repress

reprobar [repro'βar] *vt* to censure, reprove

reprochar [repro'tʃar] *vt* to reproach; **reproche** *nm* reproach

reproducción [reproðuk'θjon] *nf*
reproduction

reproducir [reproðu'θir] *vt* to reproduce;
~se *vr* to breed; (*situación*) to recur

reproductor, a [reproðuk'tor, a] *adj*
reproductive

reptil [rep'til] *nm* reptile

república [re'puβlika] *nf* republic; **R~
Dominicana** Dominican Republic;
republicano, a *adj, nm/f* republican

repudiar [repu'ðjar] *vt* to repudiate; (*fe*) to
renounce

repuesto [re'pwesto] *nm* (*pieza de
recambio*) spare (part); (*abastecimiento*)
supply; **rueda de ~** spare wheel

repugnancia [repuɣ'nanθja] *nf*
repugnance; **repugnante** *adj*
repugnant, repulsive

repugnar [repuɣ'nar] *vt* to disgust

repulsa [re'pulsa] *nf* rebuff

repulsión [repul'sjon] *nf* repulsion,
aversion; **repulsivo, a** *adj* repulsive

reputación [reputa'θjon] *nf* reputation

requemado, a [reke'maðo, a] *adj*
(*quemado*) scorched; (*bronceado*) tanned

requerimiento [rekeri'mjento] *nm*
request; (*JUR*) summons

requerir [reke'rir] *vt* (*pedir*) to ask,
request; (*exigir*) to require; (*llamar*) to
send for, summon

requesón [reke'son] *nm* cottage cheese

requete... [re'kete] *prefijo* extremely

réquiem ['rekjem] (*pl* **~s**) *nm* requiem

requisito [reki'sito] *nm* requirement,
requisite

res [res] *nf* beast, animal

resaca [re'saka] *nf* (*en el mar*) undertow,
undercurrent; (*fam*) hangover

resaltar [resal'tar] *vi* to project, stick out;
(*fig*) to stand out

resarcir [resar'θir] *vt* to compensate; **~se**
vr to make up for

resbaladizo, a [resβala'ðiθo, a] *adj*
slippery

resbalar [resβa'lar] *vi* to slip, slide; (*fig*) to
slip (up); **~se** *vr* to slip, slide; to slip (up);
resbalón *nm* (*acción*) slip

rescatar [reska'tar] *vt* (*salvar*) to save,
rescue; (*objeto*) to get back, recover;
(*cautivos*) to ransom

rescate [res'kate] *nm* rescue; (*de objeto*)
recovery; **pagar un ~** to pay a ransom

rescindir [resθin'dir] *vt* to rescind

rescisión [resθi'sjon] *nf* cancellation

rescoldo [res'koldo] *nm* embers *pl*

resecar [rese'kar] *vt* to dry thoroughly;
(*MED*) to cut out, remove; **~se** *vr* to dry
up

reseco, a [re'seko, a] *adj* very dry; (*fig*)
skinny

resentido, a [resen'tiðo, a] *adj* resentful

resentimiento [resenti'mjento] *nm*
resentment, bitterness

resentirse [resen'tirse] *vr* (*debilitarse*:
persona) to suffer; **~ de** (*consecuencias*) to
feel the effects of; **~ de** (*o* **por**) **algo** to
resent sth, be bitter about sth

reseña [re'seɲa] *nf* (*cuenta*) account;
(*informe*) report; (*LITERATURA*) review

reseñar [rese'ɲar] *vt* to describe;
(*LITERATURA*) to review

reserva [re'serβa] *nf* reserve; (*reservación*)
reservation; **a ~ de que ...** unless ...; **con
toda ~** in strictest confidence

reservado, a [reser'βaðo, a] *adj* reserved;
(*retraído*) cold, distant ♦ *nm* private room

reservar [reser'βar] *vt* (*guardar*) to keep;
(*habitación, entrada*) to reserve; **~se** *vr* to
save o.s.; (*callar*) to keep to o.s.

resfriado [resfri'aðo] *nm* cold; **resfriarse**
vr to cool; (*MED*) to catch (a) cold

resguardar [resɣwar'ðar] *vt* to protect,
shield; **~se** *vr*: **~se de** to guard against;
resguardo *nm* defence; (*vale*) voucher;
(*recibo*) receipt, slip

residencia [resi'ðenθja] *nf* residence; **~l**
nf (*urbanización*) housing estate

residente [resi'ðente] *adj, nm/f* resident

residir [resi'ðir] *vi* to reside, live; **~ en** to
reside in, lie in

residuo [re'siðwo] *nm* residue

resignación [resiɣna'θjon] *nf* resignation;
resignarse *vr*: **resignarse a** *o* **con** to
resign o.s. to, be resigned to

resina [re'sina] *nf* resin
resistencia [resis'tenθja] *nf* (*dureza*) endurance, strength; (*oposición, ELEC*) resistance; **resistente** *adj* strong, hardy; resistant
resistir [resis'tir] *vt* (*soportar*) to bear; (*oponerse a*) to resist, oppose; (*aguantar*) to put up with ♦ *vi* to resist; (*aguantar*) to last, endure; **~se** *vr*: **~se a** to refuse to, resist
resolución [resolu'θjon] *nf* resolution; (*decisión*) decision; **resoluto, a** *adj* resolute
resolver [resol'ßer] *vt* to resolve; (*solucionar*) to solve, resolve; (*decidir*) to decide, settle; **~se** *vr* to make up one's mind
resonancia [reso'nanθja] *nf* (*del sonido*) resonance; (*repercusión*) repercussion
resonar [reso'nar] *vi* to ring, echo
resoplar [reso'plar] *vi* to snort; **resoplido** *nm* heavy breathing
resorte [re'sorte] *nm* spring; (*fig*) lever
respaldar [respal'dar] *vt* to back (up), support; **~se** *vr* to lean back; **~se con** *o* **en** (*fig*) to take one's stand on; **respaldo** *nm* (*de sillón*) back; (*fig*) support, backing
respectivo, a [respek'tißo, a] *adj* respective; **en lo ~ a** with regard to
respecto [res'pekto] *nm*: **al ~** on this matter; **con ~ a, ~ de** with regard to, in relation to
respetable [respe'taßle] *adj* respectable
respetar [respe'tar] *vt* to respect; **respeto** *nm* respect; (*acatamiento*) deference; **respetos** *nmpl* respects; **respetuoso, a** *adj* respectful
respingo [res'pingo] *nm* start, jump
respiración [respira'θjon] *nf* breathing; (*MED*) respiration; (*ventilación*) ventilation
respirar [respi'rar] *vi* to breathe; **respiratorio, a** *adj* respiratory; **respiro** *nm* breathing; (*fig: descanso*) respite
resplandecer [resplande'θer] *vi* to shine; **resplandeciente** *adj* resplendent, shining; **resplandor** *nm* brilliance,

brightness; (*de luz, fuego*) blaze
responder [respon'der] *vt* to answer ♦ *vi* to answer; (*fig*) to respond; (*pey*) to answer back; **~ de** *o* **por** to answer for; **respondón, ona** *adj* cheeky
responsabilidad [responsaßili'ðað] *nf* responsibility
responsabilizarse [responsaßili'θarse] *vr* to make o.s. responsible, take charge
responsable [respon'saßle] *adj* responsible
respuesta [res'pwesta] *nf* answer, reply
resquebrajar [reskeßra'xar] *vt* to crack, split; **~se** *vr* to crack, split
resquemor [reske'mor] *nm* resentment
resquicio [res'kiθjo] *nm* chink; (*hendedura*) crack
resta ['resta] *nf* (*MAT*) remainder
restablecer [restaßle'θer] *vt* to re-establish, restore; **~se** *vr* to recover
restallar [resta'ʎar] *vi* to crack
restante [res'tante] *adj* remaining; **lo ~** the remainder
restar [res'tar] *vt* (*MAT*) to subtract; (*fig*) to take away ♦ *vi* to remain, be left
restauración [restaura'θjon] *nf* restoration
restaurante [restau'rante] *nm* restaurant
restaurar [restau'rar] *vt* to restore
restitución [restitu'θjon] *nf* return, restitution
restituir [restitu'ir] *vt* (*devolver*) to return, give back; (*rehabilitar*) to restore
resto ['resto] *nm* (*residuo*) rest, remainder; (*apuesta*) stake; **~s** *nmpl* remains
restregar [restre'xar] *vt* to scrub, rub
restricción [restrik'θjon] *nf* restriction
restrictivo, a [restrik'tißo, a] *adj* restrictive
restringir [restrin'xir] *vt* to restrict, limit
resucitar [resuθi'tar] *vt, vi* to resuscitate, revive
resuello [re'sweʎo] *nm* (*aliento*) breath; **estar sin ~** to be breathless
resuelto, a [re'swelto, a] *pp de* **resolver** ♦ *adj* resolute, determined
resultado [resul'taðo] *nm* result; (*conclusión*) outcome; **resultante** *adj*

resulting, resultant

resultar [resul'tar] *vi* (*ser*) to be; (*llegar a ser*) to turn out to be; (*salir bien*) to turn out well; (*COM*) to amount to; ~ **de** to stem from; **me resulta difícil hacerlo** it's difficult for me to do it

resumen [re'sumen] (*pl* **resúmenes**) *nm* summary, résumé; **en** ~ in short

resumir [resu'mir] *vt* (*cortar*) to abridge, cut down; (*condensar*) to summarize

resurgir [resur'xir] *vi* (*reaparecer*) to reappear

resurrección [resurre(k)'θjon] *nf* resurrection

retablo [re'taßlo] *nm* altarpiece

retaguardia [reta'ɣwarðja] *nf* rearguard

retahíla [reta'ila] *nf* series, string

retal [re'tal] *nm* remnant

retar [re'tar] *vt* to challenge; (*desafiar*) to defy, dare

retardar [retar'ðar] *vt* (*demorar*) to delay; (*hacer más lento*) to slow down; (*retener*) to hold back

retazo [re'taðo] *nm* snippet (*BRIT*), fragment

retener [rete'ner] *vt* (*intereses*) to withhold

reticente [reti'θente] *adj* (*tono*) insinuating; (*postura*) reluctant; **ser** ~ **a hacer algo** to be reluctant *o* unwilling to do sth

retina [re'tina] *nf* retina

retintín [retin'tin] *nm* jangle, jingle

retirada [reti'raða] *nf* (*MIL, refugio*) retreat; (*de dinero*) withdrawal; (*de embajador*) recall; **retirado, a** *adj* (*lugar*) remote; (*vida*) quiet; (*jubilado*) retired

retirar [reti'rar] *vt* to withdraw; (*quitar*) to remove; (*jubilar*) to retire, pension off; ~**se** *vr* to retreat, withdraw; to retire; (*acostarse*) to retire, go to bed; **retiro** *nm* retreat; retirement; (*pago*) pension

reto ['reto] *nm* dare, challenge

retocar [reto'kar] *vt* (*fotografía*) to touch up, retouch

retoño [re'toɲo] *nm* sprout, shoot; (*fig*) offspring, child

retoque [re'toke] *nm* retouching

retorcer [retor'θer] *vt* to twist; (*manos, lavado*) to wring; ~**se** *vr* to become twisted; (*mover el cuerpo*) to writhe

retorcido, a [retor'θiðo, a] *adj* (*persona*) devious

retórica [re'torika] *nf* rhetoric; (*pey*) affectedness; **retórico, a** *adj* rhetorical

retornar [retor'nar] *vt* to return, give back ♦ *vi* to return, go/come back; **retorno** *nm* return

retortijón [retorti'xon] *nm* twist, twisting

retozar [reto'θar] *vi* (*juguetear*) to frolic, romp; (*saltar*) to gambol; **retozón, ona** *adj* playful

retracción [retrak'θjon] *nf* retraction

retractarse [retrak'tarse] *vr* to retract; **me retracto** I take that back

retraerse [retra'erse] *vr* to retreat, withdraw; **retraído, a** *adj* shy, retiring; **retraimiento** *nm* retirement; (*timidez*) shyness

retransmisión [retransmi'sjon] *nf* repeat (broadcast)

retransmitir [retransmi'tir] *vt* (*mensaje*) to relay; (*TV etc*) to repeat, retransmit; (: *en vivo*) to broadcast live

retrasado, a [retra'saðo, a] *adj* late; (*MED*) mentally retarded; (*país etc*) backward, underdeveloped

retrasar [retra'sar] *vt* (*demorar*) to postpone, put off; (*retardar*) to slow down ♦ *vi* (*atrasarse*) to be late; (*reloj*) to be slow; (*producción*) to fall (off); (*quedarse atrás*) to lag behind; ~**se** *vr* to be late; to be slow; to fall (off); to lag behind

retraso [re'traso] *nm* (*demora*) delay; (*lentitud*) slowness; (*tardanza*) lateness; (*atraso*) backwardness; ~**s** (*FINANZAS*) *nmpl* arrears; **llegar con** ~ to arrive late; ~ **mental** mental deficiency

retratar [retra'tar] *vt* (*ARTE*) to paint the portrait of; (*fotografiar*) to photograph; (*fig*) to depict, describe; ~**se** *vr* to have one's portrait painted; to have one's photograph taken; **retrato** *nm* portrait;

(fig) likeness; **retrato-robot** nm Identikit
® picture

etreta [re'treta] nf retreat

etrete [re'trete] nm toilet

etribución [retriβu'θjon] nf (recompensa)
reward; (pago) pay, payment

etribuir [retri'βwir] vt (recompensar) to
reward; (pagar) to pay

etro... ['retro] prefijo retro...

etroactivo, a [retroak'tiβo, a] adj
retroactive, retrospective

etroceder [retroθe'ðer] vi (echarse atrás)
to move back(wards); (fig) to back down

etroceso [retro'θeso] nm backward
movement; (MED) relapse; (fig) backing
down

etrógrado, a [re'troɣraðo, a] adj
retrograde, retrogressive; (POL) reactionary

etrospectivo, a [retrospek'tiβo, a] adj
retrospective

etrovisor [retroβi'sor] nm (tb: **espejo ~**)
rear-view mirror

etumbar [retum'bar] vi to echo, resound

euma [re'uma], **reuma** ['reuma] nm
rheumatism

umatismo [reuma'tismo] nm = **reúma**

unificar [reunifi'kar] vt to reunify

unión [reu'njon] nf (asamblea) meeting;
(fiesta) party

unir [reu'nir] vt (juntar) to reunite, join
(together); (recoger) to gather (together);
(personas) to get together; (cualidades) to
combine; **~se** vr (personas: en asamblea)
to meet, gather

validar [reβali'ðar] vt (ratificar) to
confirm, ratify

valorizar [reβalori'θar] vt to revalue,
reassess

vancha [re'βantʃa] nf revenge

velación [reβela'θjon] nf revelation

velado [reβe'laðo] nm developing

velar [reβe'lar] vt to reveal; (FOTO) to
develop

venta [re'βenta] nf (de entradas: para
concierto) touting

ventar [reβen'tar] vt to burst, explode

ventón [reβen'ton] nm (AUTO) blow-out

(BRIT), flat (US)

reverencia [reβe'renθja] nf reverence;
reverenciar vt to revere

reverendo, a [reβe'rendo, a] adj reverend

reverente [reβe'rente] adj reverent

reversible [reβer'siβle] adj (prenda)
reversible

reverso [re'βerso] nm back, other side; (de
moneda) reverse

revertir [reβer'tir] vi to revert

revés [re'βes] nm back, wrong side; (fig)
reverse, setback; (DEPORTE) backhand; **al ~**
the wrong way round; (de arriba abajo)
upside down; (ropa) inside out; **volver
algo del ~** to turn sth round; (ropa) to
turn sth inside out

revestir [reβes'tir] vt (cubrir) to cover, coat

revisar [reβi'sar] vt (examinar) to check;
(texto etc) to revise; **revisión** nf revision

revisor, a [reβi'sor, a] nm/f inspector;
(FERRO) ticket collector

revista [re'βista] nf magazine, review;
(TEATRO) revue; (inspección) inspection;
pasar ~ a to review, inspect

revivir [reβi'βir] vi to revive

revocación [reβoka'θjon] nf repeal

revocar [reβo'kar] vt to revoke

revolcarse [reβol'karse] vr to roll about

revolotear [reβolote'ar] vi to flutter

revoltijo [reβol'tixo] nm mess, jumble

revoltoso, a [reβol'toso, a] adj (travieso)
naughty, unruly

revolución [reβolu'θjon] nf revolution;
revolucionar vt to revolutionize;
revolucionario, a adj, nm/f
revolutionary

revolver [reβol'βer] vt (desordenar) to
disturb, mess up; (mover) to move about
♦ vi: **~ en** to go through, rummage
(about) in; **~se** vr (volver contra) to turn
on o against

revólver [re'βolβer] nm revolver

revuelo [re'βwelo] nm fluttering; (fig)
commotion

revuelta [re'βwelta] nf (motín) revolt;
(agitación) commotion

revuelto, a [re'βwelto, a] pp de **revolver**

♦ adj (mezclado) mixed-up, in disorder

rey [rei] nm king; **Día de R~es** Twelfth Night

Reyes Magos

i On the night before the 6th January (the Epiphany), children go to bed expecting **los Reyes Magos** (the Three Wise Men) to bring them presents. Twelfth Night processions, known as **cabalgatas**, take place that evening when 3 people dressed as **los Reyes Magos** arrive in the town by land or sea to the delight of the children.

---

reyerta [re'jerta] nf quarrel, brawl
rezagado, a [reθa'yaðo, a] nm/f straggler
rezagar [reθa'yar] vt (dejar atrás) to leave behind; (retrasar) to delay, postpone
rezar [re'θar] vi to pray; **~ con** (fam) to concern, have to do with; **rezo** nm prayer
rezongar [reθon'gar] vi to grumble
rezumar [reθu'mar] vt to ooze
ría ['ria] nf estuary
riada [ri'aða] nf flood
ribera [ri'ßera] nf (de río) bank; (: área) riverside
ribete [ri'ßete] nm (de vestido) border; (fig) addition; **~ar** vt to edge, border
ricino [ri'θino] nm: **aceite de ~** castor oil
rico, a ['riko, a] adj rich; (adinerado) wealthy, rich; (lujoso) luxurious; (comida) delicious; (niño) lovely, cute ♦ nm/f rich person
rictus ['riktus] nm (mueca) sneer, grin
ridiculez [riðiku'leθ] nf absurdity
ridiculizar [riðikuli'θar] vt to ridicule
ridículo, a [ri'ðikulo, a] adj ridiculous; **hacer el ~** to make a fool of o.s.; **poner a uno en ~** to make a fool of sb
riego ['rjeyo] nm (aspersión) watering; (irrigación) irrigation
riel [rjel] nm rail
rienda ['rjenda] nf rein; **dar ~ suelta a** to give free rein to
riesgo ['rjesyo] nm risk; **correr el ~ de** to

run the risk of
rifa ['rifa] nf (lotería) raffle; **rifar** vt to raffle
rifle ['rifle] nm rifle
rigidez [rixi'ðeθ] nf rigidity, stiffness; (fig) strictness; **rígido, a** adj rigid, stiff; strict, inflexible
rigor [ri'vor] nm strictness, rigour; (inclemencia) harshness; **de ~** de rigueur, essential; **riguroso, a** adj rigorous; harsh; (severo) severe
rimar [ri'mar] vi to rhyme
rimbombante [rimbom'bante] adj pompous
rímel ['rimel] nm mascara
rímmel ['rimel] nm = **rímel**
rincón [rin'kon] nm corner (inside)
rinoceronte [rinoθe'ronte] nm rhinoceros
riña ['rina] nf (disputa) argument; (pelea) brawl
riñón [ri'non] nm kidney
río etc ['rio] vb ver **reír** ♦ nm river; (fig) torrent, stream; **~ abajo/arriba** downstream/upstream; **~ de la Plata** River Plate
rioja [ri'oxa] nm (vino) rioja (wine)
rioplatense [riopla'tense] adj of o from the River Plate region
riqueza [ri'keθa] nf wealth, riches pl; (cualidad) richness
risa ['risa] nf laughter; (una ~) laugh; **¡qué ~!** what a laugh!
risco ['risko] nm crag, cliff
risible [ri'sißle] adj ludicrous, laughable
risotada [riso'taða] nf guffaw, loud laugh
ristra ['ristra] nf string
risueño, a [ri'sweno, a] adj (sonriente) smiling; (contento) cheerful
ritmo ['ritmo] nm rhythm; **a ~ lento** slowly; **trabajar a ~ lento** to go slow
rito ['rito] nm rite
ritual [ri'twal] adj, nm ritual
rival [ri'ßal] adj, nm/f rival; **~idad** nf rivalry; **~izar** vi: **~izar con** to rival, vie with
rizado, a [ri'θaðo, a] adj curly ♦ nm curls pl
rizar [ri'θar] vt to curl; **~se** vr (pelo) to

curl; (*agua*) to ripple; **rizo** *nm* curl; ripple
RNE *nf abr* = **Radio Nacional de España**
robar [ro'ßar] *vt* to rob; (*objeto*) to steal; (*casa etc*) to break into; (*NAIPES*) to draw
roble ['roßle] *nm* oak; **~dal** *nm* oakwood
robo ['roßo] *nm* robbery, theft
robot [ro'ßot] *nm* robot; **~ (de cocina)** food processor
robustecer [roßuste'θer] *vt* to strengthen
robusto, a [ro'ßusto, a] *adj* robust, strong
roca ['roka] *nf* rock
roce ['roθe] *nm* (*caricia*) brush; (*TEC*) friction; (*en la piel*) graze; **tener ~ con** to be in close contact with
rociar [ro'θjar] *vt* to spray
rocín [ro'θin] *nm* nag, hack
rocío [ro'θio] *nm* dew
rocoso, a [ro'koso, a] *adj* rocky
rodaballo [roða'baʎo] *nm* turbot
rodado, a [ro'ðaðo, a] *adj* (*con ruedas*) wheeled
rodaja [ro'ðaxa] *nf* slice
rodaje [ro'ðaxe] *nm* (*CINE*) shooting, filming; (*AUTO*) running in
rodar [ro'ðar] *vt* (*vehículo*) to wheel (along); (*escalera*) to roll down; (*viajar por*) to travel (over) ♦ *vi* to roll; (*coche*) to go, run; (*CINE*) to shoot, film
rodear [roðe'ar] *vt* to surround ♦ *vi* to go round; **~se** *vr*: **~se de amigos** to surround o.s. with friends
rodeo [ro'ðeo] *nm* (*ruta indirecta*) detour; (*evasión*) evasion; (*AM*) rodeo; **hablar sin ~s** to come to the point, speak plainly
rodilla [ro'ðiʎa] *nf* knee; **de ~s** kneeling; **ponerse de ~s** to kneel (down)
rodillo [ro'ðiʎo] *nm* roller; (*CULIN*) rolling-pin
roedor, a [roe'ðor, a] *adj* gnawing ♦ *nm* rodent
roer [ro'er] *vt* (*masticar*) to gnaw; (*corroer, fig*) to corrode
rogar [ro'xar] *vt, vi* (*pedir*) to ask for; (*suplicar*) to beg, plead; **se ruega no fumar** please do not smoke
rojizo, a [ro'xiθo, a] *adj* reddish
rojo, a ['roxo, a] *adj, nm* red; **al ~ vivo**

red-hot
rol [rol] *nm* list, roll; (*papel*) role
rollito [ro'ʎito] *nm*: **~ de primavera** spring roll
rollizo, a [ro'ʎiθo, a] *adj* (*objeto*) cylindrical; (*persona*) plump
rollo ['roʎo] *nm* roll; (*de cuerda*) coil; (*madera*) log; (*fam*) bore; **¡qué ~!** what a carry-on!
Roma ['roma] *n* Rome
romance [ro'manθe] *nm* (*amoroso*) romance; (*LITERATURA*) ballad
romano, a [ro'mano, a] *adj, nm/f* Roman; **a la romana** in batter
romanticismo [romanti'θismo] *nm* romanticism
romántico, a [ro'mantiko, a] *adj* romantic
rombo ['rombo] *nm* (*GEOM*) rhombus
romería [rome'ria] *nf* (*REL*) pilgrimage; (*excursión*) trip, outing

---
Romería

i Originally a pilgrimage to a shrine or church to express devotion to the Virgin Mary or a local Saint, the **romería** has also become a rural festival which accompanies the pilgrimage. People come from all over to attend, bringing their own food and drink, and spend the day in celebration.

---

romero, a [ro'mero, a] *nm/f* pilgrim ♦ *nm* rosemary
romo, a ['romo, a] *adj* blunt; (*fig*) dull
rompecabezas [rompeka'ßeθas] *nm inv* riddle, puzzle; (*juego*) jigsaw (puzzle)
rompeolas [rompe'olas] *nm inv* breakwater
romper [rom'per] *vt* to break; (*hacer pedazos*) to smash; (*papel, tela etc*) to tear, rip ♦ *vi* (*olas*) to break; (*sol, diente*) to break through; **~ un contrato** to break a contract; **~ a** (*empezar a*) to start (suddenly) to; **~ a llorar** to burst into tears; **~ con uno** to fall out with sb
ron [ron] *nm* rum
roncar [ron'kar] *vi* to snore

ronco, a ['ronko, a] *adj (afónico)* hoarse; *(áspero)* raucous

ronda ['ronda] *nf (gen)* round; *(patrulla)* patrol; **rondar** *vt* to patrol ♦ *vi* to patrol; *(fig)* to prowl round

ronquido [ron'kiðo] *nm* snore, snoring

ronronear [ronrone'ar] *vi* to purr; **ronroneo** *nm* purr

roña ['rona] *nf (VETERINARIA)* mange; *(mugre)* dirt, grime; *(óxido)* rust

roñoso, a [ro'noso, a] *adj (mugriento)* filthy; *(tacaño)* mean

ropa ['ropa] *nf* clothes *pl,* clothing; **~ blanca** linen; **~ de cama** bed linen; **~ interior** underwear; **~ para lavar** washing; **~je** *nm* gown, robes *pl*

ropero [ro'pero] *nm* linen cupboard; *(guardarropa)* wardrobe

rosa ['rosa] *adj* pink ♦ *nf* rose; **~ de los vientos** the compass

rosado, a [ro'saðo, a] *adj* pink ♦ *nm* rosé

rosal [ro'sal] *nm* rosebush

rosario [ro'sarjo] *nm (REL)* rosary; **rezar el ~** to say the rosary

rosca ['roska] *nf (de tornillo)* thread; *(de humo)* coil, spiral; *(pan, postre)* ring-shaped roll/pastry

rosetón [rose'ton] *nm* rosette; *(ARQ)* rose window

rosquilla [ros'kiʎa] *nf* doughnut-shaped fritter

rostro ['rostro] *nm (cara)* face

rotación [rota'θjon] *nf* rotation; **~ de cultivos** crop rotation

rotativo, a [rota'tiβo, a] *adj* rotary

roto, a ['roto, a] *pp de* **romper** ♦ *adj* broken

rotonda [ro'tonda] *nf* roundabout

rótula ['rotula] *nf* kneecap; *(TEC)* ball-and-socket joint

rotulador [rotula'ðor] *nm* felt-tip pen

rotular [rotu'lar] *vt (carta, documento)* to head, entitle; *(objeto)* to label; **rótulo** *nm* heading, title; label; *(letrero)* sign

rotundamente [rotunda'mente] *adv (negar)* flatly; *(responder, afirmar)* emphatically; **rotundo, a** *adj* round;

(enfático) emphatic

rotura [ro'tura] *nf (acto)* breaking; *(MED)* fracture

roturar [rotu'rar] *vt* to plough

rozadura [roθa'ðura] *nf* abrasion, graze

rozar [ro'θar] *vt (frotar)* to rub; *(arañar)* to scratch; *(tocar ligeramente)* to shave, touch lightly; **~se** *vr* to rub (together); **~se con** *(fam)* to rub shoulders with

rte. *abr* (= *remite, remitente*) sender

RTVE *nf abr* = **Radiotelevisión Española**

rubí [ru'βi] *nm* ruby; *(de reloj)* jewel

rubio, a ['ruβjo, a] *adj* fair-haired, blond(e) ♦ *nm/f* blond/blonde; **tabaco ~** Virginia tobacco

rubor [ru'βor] *nm (sonrojo)* blush; *(timidez)* bashfulness; **~izarse** *vr* to blush

rúbrica ['ruβrika] *nf (de la firma)* flourish; **rubricar** *vt (firmar)* to sign with a flourish; *(concluir)* to sign and seal

rudimentario, a [ruðimen'tarjo, a] *adj* rudimentary; **rudimento** *nm* rudiment

rudo, a ['ruðo, a] *adj (sin pulir)* unpolished; *(grosero)* coarse; *(violento)* violent; *(sencillo)* simple

rueda ['rweða] *nf* wheel; *(círculo)* ring, circle; *(rodaja)* slice, round; **~ delantera/trasera/de repuesto** front/back/spare wheel; **~ de prensa** press conference

ruedo ['rweðo] *nm (círculo)* circle; *(TAUR)* arena, bullring

ruego *etc* ['rwexo] *vb ver* **rogar** ♦ *nm* request

rufián [ru'fjan] *nm* scoundrel

rugby ['ruxβi] *nm* rugby

rugido [ru'xiðo] *nm* roar

rugir [ru'xir] *vi* to roar

rugoso, a [ru'xoso, a] *adj (arrugado)* wrinkled; *(áspero)* rough; *(desigual)* ridged

ruido ['rwiðo] *nm* noise; *(sonido)* sound; *(alboroto)* racket, row; *(escándalo)* commotion, rumpus; **~so, a** *adj* noisy, loud; *(fig)* sensational

ruin [rwin] *adj* contemptible, mean

ruina ['rwina] *nf* ruin; *(colapso)* collapse; *(de persona)* ruin, downfall

ruindad [rwin'dað] *nf* lowness, meanness;

(acto) low o mean act

ruinoso, a [rwi'noso, a] adj ruinous; (destartalado) dilapidated, tumbledown; (COM) disastrous

ruiseñor [rwise'ɲor] nm nightingale

ruleta [ru'leta] nf roulette

rulo ['rulo] nm (para el pelo) curler

Rumanía [ruma'nia] nf Rumania

rumba ['rumba] nf rumba

rumbo ['rumbo] nm (ruta) route, direction; (ángulo de dirección) course, bearing; (fig) course of events; **ir con ~ a** to be heading for

rumboso, a [rum'boso, a] adj generous

rumiante [ru'mjante] nm ruminant

rumiar [ru'mjar] vt to chew; (fig) to chew over ♦ vi to chew the cud

rumor [ru'mor] nm (ruido sordo) low sound; (murmuración) murmur, buzz

rumorearse [rumore'arse] vr: **se rumorea que** it is rumoured that

runrún [run'run] nm (voces) murmur, sound of voices; (fig) rumour

rupestre [ru'pestre] adj rock cpd

ruptura [rup'tura] nf rupture

rural [ru'ral] adj rural

Rusia ['rusja] nf Russia; **ruso, a** adj, nm/f Russian

rústica ['rustika] nf: **libro en ~** paperback (book); ver tb **rústico**

rústico, a ['rustiko, a] adj rustic; (ordinario) coarse, uncouth ♦ nm/f yokel

ruta ['ruta] nf route

rutina [ru'tina] nf routine; **~rio, a** adj routine

S, s

s abr (= santo, a) St; (= sur) S

s. abr (= siglo) C.; (= siguiente) foll

S.A. abr (= Sociedad Anónima) Ltd. (BRIT), Inc. (US)

sábado ['saβaðo] nm Saturday

sábana ['saβana] nf sheet

sabandija [saβan'dixa] nf bug, insect

sabañón [saβa'ɲon] nm chilblain

saber [sa'βer] vt to know; (llegar a conocer) to find out, learn; (tener capacidad de) to know how to ♦ vi: **~ a** to taste of, taste like ♦ nm knowledge, learning; **a ~** namely; **¿sabes conducir/nadar?** can you drive/swim?; **¿sabes francés?** do you speak French?; **~ de memoria** to know by heart; **hacer ~ algo a uno** to inform sb of sth, let sb know sth

sabiduría [saβiðu'ria] nf (conocimientos) wisdom; (instrucción) learning

sabiendas [sa'βjendas]: **a ~** adv knowingly

sabio, a ['saβjo, a] adj (docto) learned; (prudente) wise, sensible

sabor [sa'βor] nm taste, flavour; **~ear** vt to taste, savour; (fig) to relish

sabotaje [saβo'taxe] nm sabotage

saboteador, a [saβotea'ðor, a] nm/f saboteur

sabotear [saβote'ar] vt to sabotage

sabré etc vb ver **saber**

sabroso, a [sa'βroso, a] adj tasty; (fig: fam) racy, salty

sacacorchos [saka'kortʃos] nm inv corkscrew

sacapuntas [saka'puntas] nm inv pencil sharpener

sacar [sa'kar] vt to take out; (fig: extraer) to get (out); (quitar) to remove, get out; (hacer salir) to bring out; (conclusión) to draw; (novela etc) to publish, bring out; (ropa) to take off; (obra) to make; (premio) to receive; (entradas) to get; (TENIS) to serve; **~ adelante** (niño) to bring up; (negocio) to carry on, go on with; **~ a uno a bailar** to get sb up to dance; **~ una foto** to take a photo; **~ la lengua** to stick out one's tongue; **~ buenas/malas notas** to get good/bad marks

sacarina [saka'rina] nf saccharin(e)

sacerdote [saθer'ðote] nm priest

saciar [sa'θjar] vt (hambre, sed) to satisfy; **~se** vr (de comida) to get full up; **comer hasta ~se** to eat one's fill

saco ['sako] nm bag; (grande) sack; (su

contenido) bagful; (*AM*) jacket; ~ **de
dormir** sleeping bag
sacramento [sakra'mento] *nm* sacrament
sacrificar [sakrifi'kar] *vt* to sacrifice;
sacrificio *nm* sacrifice
sacrilegio [sakri'lexjo] *nm* sacrilege;
sacrílego, a *adj* sacrilegious
sacristía [sakris'tia] *nf* sacristy
sacro, a ['sakro, a] *adj* sacred
sacudida [saku'ðiða] *nf* (*agitación*) shake,
shaking; (*sacudimiento*) jolt, bump; ~
eléctrica electric shock
sacudir [saku'ðir] *vt* to shake; (*golpear*) to
hit
sádico, a ['saðiko, a] *adj* sadistic ♦ *nm/f*
sadist; **sadismo** *nm* sadism
saeta [sa'eta] *nf* (*flecha*) arrow
sagacidad [saɣaθi'ðað] *nf* shrewdness,
cleverness; **sagaz** *adj* shrewd, clever
sagitario [saxi'tarjo] *nm* Sagittarius
sagrado, a [sa'ɣraðo, a] *adj* sacred, holy
Sáhara ['saara] *nm*: **el** ~ the Sahara
(desert)
sal [sal] *vb ver* **salir** ♦ *nf* salt
sala ['sala] *nf* room; (~ **de estar**) living
room; (*TEATRO*) house, auditorium; (*de
hospital*) ward; ~ **de apelación** court; ~
de espera waiting room; ~ **de estar**
living room; ~ **de fiestas** dance hall
salado, a [sa'laðo, a] *adj* salty; (*fig*) witty,
amusing; **agua salada** salt water
salar [sa'lar] *vt* to salt, add salt to
salarial [sala'rjal] *adj* (*aumento, revisión*)
wage *cpd*, salary *cpd*
salario [sa'larjo] *nm* wage, pay
salchicha [sal'tʃitʃa] *nf* (*pork*) sausage;
salchichón *nm* (*salami-type*) sausage
saldar [sal'dar] *vt* to pay; (*vender*) to sell
off; (*fig*) to settle, resolve; **saldo** *nm*
(*pago*) settlement; (*de una cuenta*)
balance; (*lo restante*) remnant(s) (*pl*),
remainder; **saldos** *nmpl* (*en tienda*) sale
saldré *etc vb ver* **salir**
salero [sa'lero] *nm* salt cellar
salgo *etc vb ver* **salir**
salida [sa'liða] *nf* (*puerta etc*) exit, way
out; (*acto*) leaving, going out; (*de tren,*

AVIAT) departure; (*TEC*) output, production; (*fig*) way out; (*COM*) opening;
(*GEO, válvula*) outlet; (*de gas*) leak; **calle
sin** ~ cul-de-sac; ~ **de incendios** fire
escape
saliente [sa'ljente] *adj* (*ARQ*) projecting;
(*sol*) rising; (*fig*) outstanding

┌─────────────────────┐
│ **PALABRA CLAVE** │
└─────────────────────┘

salir [sa'lir] *vi* 1 (*partir: tb:* ~ **de**) to leave;
Juan ha salido Juan is out; **salió de la
cocina** he came out of the kitchen
2 (*aparecer*) to appear; (*disco, libro*) to
come out; **anoche salió en la tele** she
appeared *o* was on TV last night; **salió en
todos los periódicos** it was in all the
papers
3 (*resultar*): **la muchacha nos salió muy
trabajadora** the girl turned out to be a
very hard worker; **la comida te ha salido
exquisita** the food was delicious; **sale
muy caro** it's very expensive
4: ~**le a uno algo: la entrevista que
hice me salió bien/mal** the interview I
did went *o* turned out well/badly
5: ~ **adelante: no sé como haré para** ~
adelante I don't know how I'll get by
♦ ~**se** *vr* (*líquido*) to spill; (*animal*) to
escape

saliva [sa'liβa] *nf* saliva
salmo ['salmo] *nm* psalm
salmón [sal'mon] *nm* salmon
salmonete [salmo'nete] *nm* red mullet
salmuera [sal'mwera] *nf* pickle, brine
salón [sa'lon] *nm* (*de casa*) living room,
lounge; (*muebles*) lounge suite; ~ **de
belleza** beauty parlour; ~ **de baile** dance
hall
salpicadero [salpika'ðero] *nm* (*AUTO*)
dashboard
salpicar [salpi'kar] *vt* (*rociar*) to sprinkle,
spatter; (*esparcir*) to scatter
salpicón [salpi'kon] *nm*: ~ **de mariscos**
seafood salad
salsa ['salsa] *nf* sauce; (*con carne asada*)
gravy; (*fig*) spice

saltamontes [salta'montes] *nm inv* grasshopper

saltar [sal'tar] *vt* to jump (over), leap (over); (*dejar de lado*) to skip, miss out ♦ *vi* to jump, leap; (*pelota*) to bounce; (*al aire*) to fly up; (*quebrarse*) to break; (*al agua*) to dive; (*fig*) to explode, blow up

salto ['salto] *nm* jump, leap; (*al agua*) dive; **~ de agua** waterfall; **~ de altura** high jump

saltón, ona [sal'ton, ona] *adj* (*ojos*) bulging, popping; (*dientes*) protruding

salud [sa'luð] *nf* health; **¡(a su) ~!** cheers!, good health!; **~able** *adj* (*de buena ~*) healthy; (*provechoso*) good, beneficial

saludar [salu'ðar] *vt* to greet; (*MIL*) to salute; **saludo** *nm* greeting; **"saludos"** (*en carta*) "best wishes", "regards"

salva ['salßa] *nf*: **~ de aplausos** ovation

salvación [salßa'θjon] *nf* salvation; (*rescate*) rescue

salvado [sal'ßaðo] *nm* bran

salvaguardar [salßaɣwar'ðar] *vt* to safeguard

salvajada [salßa'xaða] *nf* atrocity

salvaje [sal'ßaxe] *adj* wild; (*tribu*) savage; **salvajismo** *nm* savagery

salvamento [salßa'mento] *nm* rescue

salvapantallas [salßa'pantaʎas] *nm* (*INFORM*) screen saver

salvar [sal'ßar] *vt* (*rescatar*) to save, rescue; (*resolver*) to overcome, resolve; (*cubrir distancias*) to cover, travel; (*hacer excepción*) to except, exclude; (*barco*) to salvage

salvavidas [salßa'ßiðas] *adj inv*: **bote/ chaleco/cinturón ~** lifeboat/life jacket/life belt

salvo, a ['salßo, a] *adj* safe ♦ *adv* except (for), save; **a ~** out of danger; **~ que** unless; **~conducto** *nm* safe-conduct

san [san] *adj* saint; **S~ Juan** St John

sanar [sa'nar] *vt* (*herida*) to heal; (*persona*) to cure ♦ *vi* (*persona*) to get well, recover; (*herida*) to heal

sanción [san'θjon] *nf* sanction; **sancionar** *vt* to sanction

sandalia [san'dalja] *nf* sandal

sandez [san'deθ] *nf* foolishness

sandía [san'dia] *nf* watermelon

sandwich ['sandwitʃ] (*pl* **~s**, **~es**) *nm* sandwich

saneamiento [sanea'mjento] *nm* sanitation

sanear [sane'ar] *vt* to clean up; (*terreno*) to drain

Sanfermines

i The **Sanfermines** *is a week-long festival in Pamplona made famous by Ernest Hemingway. From the 7th July, the feast of "San Fermín", crowds of mainly young people take to the streets drinking, singing and dancing. Early in the morning bulls are released along the narrow streets leading to the bullring, and young men risk serious injury to show their bravery by running out in front of them, a custom which is also typical of many Spanish villages.*

---

sangrar [san'grar] *vt, vi* to bleed; **sangre** *nf* blood

sangría [san'gria] *nf* sangria

sangriento, a [san'grjento, a] *adj* bloody

sanguijuela [sangi'xwela] *nf* (*ZOOL*, *fig*) leech

sanguinario, a [sangi'narjo, a] *adj* bloodthirsty

sanguíneo, a [san'gineo, a] *adj* blood *cpd*

sanidad [sani'ðað] *nf*: **~ (pública)** public health

San Isidro

i **San Isidro** *is the patron saint of Madrid, and gives his name to the week-long festivities which take place around the 15th May. Originally an 18th-century trade fair, the* **San Isidro** *celebrations now include music, dance, a famous* **romería**, *theatre and bullfighting.*

---

sanitario, a [sani'tarjo, a] *adj* health *cpd*; **~s** *nmpl* toilets (*BRIT*), washroom (*US*)

sano, a ['sano, a] *adj* healthy; *(sin daños)*
  sound; *(comida)* wholesome; *(entero)*
  whole, intact; **~ y salvo** safe and sound
Santiago [san'tjaɣo] *nm:* **~ (de Chile)**
  Santiago
santiamén [santja'men] *nm:* **en un ~** in
  no time at all
santidad [santi'ðað] *nf* holiness, sanctity
santiguarse [santi'ɣwarse] *vr* to make the
  sign of the cross
santo, a ['santo, a] *adj* holy; *(fig)*
  wonderful, miraculous ♦ *nm/f* saint ♦ *nm*
  saint's day; **~ y seña** password
santuario [san'twarjo] *nm* sanctuary,
  shrine
saña ['saɲa] *nf* rage, fury
sapo ['sapo] *nm* toad
saque ['sake] *nm* (TENIS) service, serve;
  (FÚTBOL) throw-in; **~ de esquina** corner
  (kick)
saquear [sake'ar] *vt* (MIL) to sack; *(robar)*
  to loot, plunder; *(fig)* to ransack; **saqueo**
  nm sacking; looting, plundering;
  ransacking
sarampión [saram'pjon] *nm* measles *sg*
sarcasmo [sar'kasmo] *nm* sarcasm;
  sarcástico, a *adj* sarcastic
sardina [sar'ðina] *nf* sardine
sargento [sar'xento] *nm* sergeant
sarmiento [sar'mjento] *nm* (BOT) vine
  shoot
sarna ['sarna] *nf* itch; *(MED)* scabies
sarpullido [sarpu'ʎiðo] *nm* (MED) rash
sarro ['sarro] *nm* (en dientes) tartar, plaque
sartén [sar'ten] *nf* frying pan
sastre ['sastre] *nm* tailor; **~ría** *nf* (arte)
  tailoring; *(tienda)* tailor's (shop)
Satanás [sata'nas] *nm* Satan
satélite [sa'telite] *nm* satellite
sátira ['satira] *nf* satire
satisfacción [satisfak'θjon] *nf* satisfaction
satisfacer [satisfa'θer] *vt* to satisfy;
  (gastos) to meet; *(pérdida)* to make good;
  ~se *vr* to satisfy o.s., be satisfied;
  (vengarse) to take revenge; **satisfecho,**
  a *adj* satisfied; *(contento)* content(ed),
  happy; *(tb:* **satisfecho de sí mismo)**

self-satisfied, smug
saturar [satu'rar] *vt* to saturate; **~se** *vr*
  (mercado, aeropuerto) to reach saturation
  point
sauce ['sauθe] *nm* willow; **~ llorón**
  weeping willow
sauna ['sauna] *nf* sauna
savia ['saβja] *nf* sap
saxofón [sakso'fon] *nm* saxophone
sazonar [saθo'nar] *vt* to ripen; *(CULIN)* to
  flavour, season
SE *abr (= sudeste)* SE

PALABRA CLAVE

se [se] *pron* 1 *(reflexivo: sg: m)* himself; *(: f)*
  herself; *(: pl)* themselves; *(: cosa)* itself;
  (: de Vd) yourself; *(: de Vds)* yourselves; **~**
  está preparando she's preparing herself;
  para usos léxicos del pron ver el vb en
  cuestión, p.ej. **arrepentirse**
  2 *(con complemento indirecto)* to him; to
  her; to them; to it; to you; **a usted ~ lo**
  dije ayer I told you yesterday; **~ compró**
  un sombrero he bought himself a hat; **~**
  rompió la pierna he broke his leg
  3 *(uso recíproco)* each other, one another;
  ~ miraron (el uno al otro) they looked at
  each other *o* one another
  4 *(en oraciones pasivas):* **se han vendido**
  muchos libros a lot of books have been
  sold
  5 *(impers):* **~ dice que** people say that, it
  is said that; **allí ~ come muy bien** the
  food there is very good, you can eat very
  well

sé *vb ver* **saber; ser**
sea *etc vb ver* **ser**
sebo ['seβo] *nm* fat, grease
secador [seka'ðor] *nm:* **~ de pelo** hair-
  dryer
secadora [seka'ðora] *nf* tumble dryer
secar [se'kar] *vt* to dry; **~se** *vr* to dry (off);
  (río, planta) to dry up
sección [sek'θjon] *nf* section
seco, a ['seko, a] *adj* dry; *(carácter)* cold;
  (respuesta) sharp, curt; **habrá pan a**

secas there will be just bread; **decir algo a secas** to say sth curtly; **parar en ~** to stop dead

secretaría [sekreta'ria] nf secretariat

secretario, a [sekre'tarjo, a] nm/f secretary

secreto, a [se'kreto, a] adj secret; (persona) secretive ♦ nm secret; (calidad) secrecy

secta ['sekta] nf sect; **~rio, a** adj sectarian

sector [sek'tor] nm sector

secuela [se'kwela] nf consequence

secuencia [se'kwenθja] nf sequence

secuestrar [sekwes'trar] vt to kidnap; (bienes) to seize, confiscate; **secuestro** nm kidnapping; seizure, confiscation

secular [seku'lar] adj secular

secundar [sekun'dar] vt to second, support

secundario, a [sekun'darjo, a] adj secondary

sed [seð] nf thirst; **tener ~** to be thirsty

seda ['seða] nf silk

sedal [se'ðal] nm fishing line

sedante [se'ðante] nm sedative

sede ['seðe] nf (de gobierno) seat; (de compañía) headquarters pl; **Santa S~** Holy See

sedentario, a [seðen'tarjo, a] adj sedentary

sediento, a [se'ðjento, a] adj thirsty

sedimento [seði'mento] nm sediment

sedoso, a [se'ðoso, a] adj silky, silken

seducción [seðuk'θjon] nf seduction

seducir [seðu'θir] vt to seduce; (cautivar) to charm, fascinate; (atraer) to attract; **seductor, a** adj seductive; charming, fascinating; attractive ♦ nm/f seducer

segar [se'ɣar] vt (mies) to reap, cut; (hierba) to mow, cut

seglar [se'ɣlar] adj secular, lay

segregación [seɣreɣa'θjon] nf segregation. **~ racial** racial segregation

segregar [seɣre'ɣar] vt to segregate, separate

seguida [se'ɣiða] nf: **en ~** at once, right away

seguido, a [se'ɣiðo, a] adj (continuo) continuous, unbroken; (recto) straight ♦ adv (directo) straight (on); (después) after; (AM: a menudo) often; **~s** consecutive, successive; **5 días ~s** 5 days running, 5 days in a row

seguimiento [seɣi'mjento] nm chase, pursuit; (continuación) continuation

seguir [se'ɣir] vt to follow; (venir después) to follow on, come after; (proseguir) to continue; (perseguir) to chase, pursue ♦ vi (gen) to follow; (continuar) to continue, carry o go on; **~se** vr to follow; **sigo sin comprender** I still don't understand; **sigue lloviendo** it's still raining

según [se'ɣun] prep according to ♦ adv: **¿irás? – ~** are you going? — it all depends ♦ conj as; **~ caminamos** while we walk

segundo, a [se'ɣundo, a] adj second ♦ nm second ♦ nf second meaning; **de segunda mano** second-hand; **segunda (clase)** second class; **segunda enseñanza** secondary education; **segunda (marcha)** (AUT) second (gear)

seguramente [seɣura'mente] adv surely; (con certeza) for sure, with certainty

seguridad [seɣuri'ðað] nf safety; (del estado, de casa etc) security; (certidumbre) certainty; (confianza) confidence; (estabilidad) stability; **~ social** social security

seguro, a [se'ɣuro, a] adj (cierto) sure, certain; (fiel) trustworthy; (libre de peligro) safe; (bien defendido, firme) secure ♦ adv for sure, certainly ♦ nm (COM) insurance; **~ contra terceros/a todo riesgo** third party/comprehensive insurance; **~s sociales** social security sg

seis [seis] num six

seísmo [se'ismo] nm tremor, earthquake

selección [selek'θjon] nf selection; **seleccionar** vt to pick, choose, select

selectividad [selektiβi'ðað] (ESP) nf university entrance examination

selecto, a [se'lekto, a] adj select, choice; (escogido) selected

sellar [se'ʎar] vt (documento oficial) to seal; (pasaporte, visado) to stamp

sello ['seʎo] nm stamp; (precinto) seal

selva ['selβa] nf (bosque) forest, woods pl; (jungla) jungle

semáforo [se'maforo] nm (AUTO) traffic lights pl; (FERRO) signal

semana [se'mana] nf week; **entre ~** during the week; **S~ Santa** Holy Week; **semanal** adj weekly; **~rio** nm weekly magazine

---
Semana Santa

i In Spain celebrations for **Semana Santa** (Holy Week) are often spectacular. "Viernes Santo", "Sábado Santo" and "Domingo de Resurrección" (Good Friday, Holy Saturday, Easter Sunday) are all national public holidays, with additional days being given as local holidays. There are fabulous **procesiones** all over the country, with members of "cofradías" (brotherhoods) dressing in hooded robes and parading their "pasos" (religious floats and sculptures) through the streets. Seville has the most famous Holy Week processions.

---

semblante [sem'blante] nm face; (fig) look

sembrar [sem'brar] vt to sow; (objetos) to sprinkle, scatter about; (noticias etc) to spread

semejante [seme'xante] adj (parecido) similar ♦ nm fellow man, fellow creature; **~s** alike, similar; **nunca hizo cosa ~** he never did any such thing; **semejanza** nf similarity, resemblance

semejar [seme'xar] vi to seem like, resemble; **~se** vr to look alike, be similar

semen ['semen] nm semen

semestral [semes'tral] adj half-yearly, bi-annual

semicírculo [semi'θirkulo] nm semicircle

semidesnatado, a [semiðesna'taðo, a] adj semi-skimmed

semifinal [semifi'nal] nf semifinal

semilla [se'miʎa] nf seed

seminario [semi'narjo] nm (REL) seminary; (ESCOL) seminar

sémola ['semola] nf semolina

Sena ['sena] nm: **el ~** the (river) Seine

senado [se'naðo] nm senate; **senador, a** nm/f senator

sencillez [senθi'ʎeθ] nf simplicity; (de persona) naturalness; **sencillo, a** adj simple; natural, unaffected

senda ['senda] nf path, track

senderismo [sende'rismo] nm hiking

sendero [sen'dero] nm path, track

sendos, as ['sendos, as] adj pl: **les dio ~ golpes** he hit both of them

senil [se'nil] adj senile

seno ['seno] nm (ANAT) bosom, bust; (fig) bosom; **~s** breasts

sensación [sensa'θjon] nf sensation; (sentido) sense; (sentimiento) feeling; **sensacional** adj sensational

sensato, a [sen'sato, a] adj sensible

sensible [sen'sible] adj sensitive; (apreciable) perceptible, appreciable; (pérdida) considerable; **~ro, a** adj sentimental

sensitivo, a [sensi'tiβo, a] adj sense cpd

sensorial [senso'rjal] adj sensory

sensual [sen'swal] adj sensual

sentada [sen'taða] nf sitting; (protesta) sit-in

sentado, a [sen'taðo, a] adj: **estar ~** to sit, be sitting (down); **dar por ~** to take for granted, assume

sentar [sen'tar] vt to sit, seat; (fig) to establish ♦ vi (vestido) to suit; (alimento): **~ bien/mal a** to agree/disagree with; **~se** vr (persona) to sit, sit down; (los depósitos) to settle

sentencia [sen'tenθja] nf (máxima) maxim, saying; (JUR) sentence; **sentenciar** vt to sentence

sentido, a [sen'tiðo, a] adj (pérdida) regrettable; (carácter) sensitive ♦ nm sense; (sentimiento) feeling; (significado) sense, meaning; (dirección) direction; **mi más ~ pésame** my deepest sympathy; **~**

del humor sense of humour; **~ único** one-way (street); **tener ~** to make sense

sentimental [sentimen'tal] *adj* sentimental; **vida ~** love life

sentimiento [senti'mjento] *nm* feeling

sentir [sen'tir] *vt* to feel; *(percibir)* to perceive, sense; *(lamentar)* to regret, be sorry for ♦ *vi (tener la sensación)* to feel; *(lamentarse)* to feel sorry ♦ *nm* opinion, judgement; **~se bien/mal** to feel well/ill; **lo siento** I'm sorry

seña ['seɲa] *nf* sign; *(MIL)* password; **~s** *nfpl (dirección)* address *sg*; **~s personales** personal description *sg*

señal [se'ɲal] *nf* sign; *(síntoma)* symptom; *(FERRO, TELEC)* signal; *(marca)* mark; *(COM)* deposit; **en ~ de** as a token of, as a sign of; **~ar** *vt* to mark; *(indicar)* to point out, indicate

señor [se'ɲor] *nm (hombre)* man; *(caballero)* gentleman; *(dueño)* owner, master; *(trato: antes de nombre propio)* Mr; *(: hablando directamente)* sir; **muy ~ mío** Dear Sir; **el ~ alcalde/presidente** the mayor/president

señora [se'ɲora] *nf (dama)* lady; *(trato: antes de nombre propio)* Mrs; *(: hablando directamente)* madam; *(esposa)* wife; **Nuestra S~** Our Lady

señorita [seɲo'rita] *nf (con nombre y/o apellido)* Miss; *(mujer joven)* young lady

señorito [seɲo'rito] *nm* young gentleman; *(pey)* rich kid

señuelo [se'ɲwelo] *nm* decoy

sepa *etc vb ver* **saber**

separación [separa'θjon] *nf* separation; *(división)* division; *(hueco)* gap

separar [sepa'rar] *vt* to separate; *(dividir)* to divide; **~se** *vr (parte)* to come away; *(partes)* to come apart; *(persona)* to leave, go away; *(matrimonio)* to separate; **separatismo** *nm* separatism

sepia ['sepja] *nf* cuttlefish

septentrional [septentrjo'nal] *adj* northern

septiembre [sep'tjembre] *nm* September

séptimo, a ['septimo, a] *adj, nm* seventh

sepulcral [sepul'kral] *adj (fig: silencio, atmósfera)* deadly; **sepulcro** *nm* tomb, grave

sepultar [sepul'tar] *vt* to bury; **sepultura** *nf (acto)* burial; *(tumba)* grave, tomb

sequedad [seke'ðað] *nf* dryness; *(fig)* brusqueness, curtness

sequía [se'kia] *nf* drought

séquito ['sekito] *nm (de rey etc)* retinue; *(seguidores)* followers *pl*

PALABRA CLAVE

ser [ser] *vi* 1 *(descripción)* to be; **es médica/muy alta** she's a doctor/very tall; **la familia es de Cuzco** his *(o her etc)* family is from Cuzco; **soy Ana** *(TELEC)* Ana speaking *o* here

2 *(propiedad)*: **es de Joaquín** it's Joaquín's, it belongs to Joaquín

3 *(horas, fechas, números)*: **es la una** it's one o'clock; **son las seis y media** it's half-past six; **es el 1 de junio** it's the first of June; **somos/son seis** there are six of us/them

4 *(en oraciones pasivas)*: **ha sido descubierto ya** it's already been discovered

5: **es de esperar que ...** it is to be hoped *o* I *etc* hope that ...

6 *(locuciones con sub)*: **o sea** that is to say; **sea él sea su hermana** either him or his sister

7: **a no ~ por él ...** but for him ...

8: **a no ~ que: a no ~ que tenga uno ya** unless he's got one already

♦ *nm* being; **~ humano** human being

serenarse [sere'narse] *vr* to calm down

sereno, a [se'reno, a] *adj (persona)* calm, unruffled; *(el tiempo)* fine, settled; *(ambiente)* calm, peaceful ♦ *nm* night watchman

serial [ser'jal] *nm* serial

serie ['serje] *nf* series; *(cadena)* sequence, succession; **fuera de ~** out of order; *(fig)* special, out of the ordinary; **fabricación en ~** mass production

seriedad [serje'ðað] *nf* seriousness; (*formalidad*) reliability; **serio, a** *adj* serious; reliable, dependable; grave, serious; **en serio** *adv* seriously

serigrafía [seriɣra'fia] *nf* silk-screen printing

sermón [ser'mon] *nm* (*REL*) sermon

seropositivo, a [seroposi'tiβo, a] *adj* HIV positive

serpentear [serpente'ar] *vi* to wriggle; (*camino, río*) to wind, snake

serpentina [serpen'tina] *nf* streamer

serpiente [ser'pjente] *nf* snake; **~ de cascabel** rattlesnake

serranía [serra'nia] *nf* mountainous area

serrar [se'rrar] *vt* = **aserrar**

serrín [se'rrin] *nm* = **aserrín**

serrucho [se'rrutʃo] *nm* saw

servicio [ser'βiθjo] *nm* service; **~s** *nmpl* toilet(s); **~ incluido** service charge included; **~ militar** military service

servidumbre [serβi'ðumbre] *nf* (*sujeción*) servitude; (*criados*) servants *pl*, staff

servil [ser'βil] *adj* servile

servilleta [serβi'ʎeta] *nf* serviette, napkin

servir [ser'βir] *vt* to serve ♦ *vi* to serve; (*tener utilidad*) to be of use, be useful; **~se** *vr* to serve *o* help o.s.; **~se de algo** to make use of sth, use sth; **sírvase pasar** please come in

sesenta [se'senta] *num* sixty

sesgo [ˈsesɣo] *nm* slant; (*fig*) slant, twist

sesión [se'sjon] *nf* (*POL*) session, sitting; (*CINE*) showing

seso [ˈseso] *nm* brain; **sesudo, a** *adj* sensible, wise

seta [ˈseta] *nf* mushroom; **~ venenosa** toadstool

setecientos, as [sete'θjentos, as] *adj*, *num* seven hundred

setenta [se'tenta] *num* seventy

seto [ˈseto] *nm* hedge

seudónimo [seu'ðonimo] *nm* pseudonym

severidad [seβeri'ðað] *nf* severity; **severo, a** *adj* severe

Sevilla [se'βiʎa] *n* Seville; **sevillano, a** *adj* of *o* from Seville ♦ *nm/f* native *o* inhabitant of Seville

sexo [ˈsekso] *nm* sex

sexto, a [ˈseksto, a] *adj*, *nm* sixth

sexual [sek'swal] *adj* sexual; **vida ~** sex life

si [si] *conj* if; **me pregunto ~ ...** I wonder if *o* whether ...

sí [si] *adv* yes ♦ *nm* consent ♦ *pron* (*uso impersonal*) oneself; (*sg: m*) himself; (: *f*) herself; (: *de cosa*) itself; (*de usted*) yourself; (*pl*) themselves; (*de ustedes*) yourselves; (*recíproco*) each other; **él no quiere pero yo ~** he doesn't want to but I do; **ella ~ vendrá** she will certainly come, she is sure to come; **claro que ~** of course; **creo que ~** I think so

siamés, esa [sja'mes, esa] *adj*, *nm/f* Siamese

SIDA [ˈsiða] *nm abr* (= *Síndrome de Inmunodeficiencia Adquirida*) AIDS

siderúrgico, a [siðe'rurxico, a] *adj* iron and steel *cpd*

sidra [ˈsiðra] *nf* cider

siembra [ˈsjembra] *nf* sowing

siempre [ˈsjempre] *adv* always; (*todo el tiempo*) all the time; **~ que** (*cada vez*) whenever; (*dado que*) provided that; **como ~** as usual; **para ~** for ever

sien [sjen] *nf* temple

siento *etc vb ver* **sentar**; **sentir**

sierra [ˈsjerra] *nf* (*TEC*) saw; (*cadena de montañas*) mountain range

siervo, a [ˈsjerβo, a] *nm/f* slave

siesta [ˈsjesta] *nf* siesta, nap; **echar la ~** to have an afternoon nap *o* a siesta

siete [ˈsjete] *num* seven

sífilis [ˈsifilis] *nf* syphilis

sifón [si'fon] *nm* syphon; **whisky con ~** whisky and soda

sigla [ˈsiɣla] *nf* abbreviation; acronym

siglo [ˈsiɣlo] *nm* century; (*fig*) age

significación [siɣnifika'θjon] *nf* significance

significado [siɣnifi'kaðo] *nm* (*de palabra etc*) meaning

significar [siɣnifi'kar] *vt* to mean, signify; (*notificar*) to make known, express; **significativo, a** *adj* significant

signo ['sivno] nm sign; ~ **de admiración** o **exclamación** exclamation mark; ~ **de interrogación** question mark

sigo etc vb ver **seguir**

siguiente [si'vjente] adj next, following

siguió etc vb ver **seguir**

sílaba ['silaßa] nf syllable

silbar [sil'ßar] vt, vi to whistle; **silbato** nm whistle; **silbido** nm whistle, whistling

silenciador [silenθja'ðor] nm silencer

silenciar [silen'θjar] vt (persona) to silence; (escándalo) to hush up; **silencio** nm silence, quiet; **silencioso, a** adj silent, quiet

silla ['siʎa] nf (asiento) chair; (tb: ~ **de montar**) saddle; ~ **de ruedas** wheelchair

sillón [si'ʎon] nm armchair, easy chair

silueta [si'lweta] nf silhouette; (de edificio) outline; (figura) figure

silvestre [sil'ßestre] adj wild

simbólico, a [sim'boliko, a] adj symbolic(al)

simbolizar [simboli'θar] vt to symbolize

símbolo ['simbolo] nm symbol

simetría [sime'tria] nf symmetry

simiente [si'mjente] nf seed

similar [simi'lar] adj similar

simio ['simjo] nm ape

simpatía [simpa'tia] nf liking; (afecto) affection; (amabilidad) kindness; **simpático, a** adj nice, pleasant; kind

simpatizante [simpati'θante] nm/f sympathizer

simpatizar [simpati'θar] vi: ~ **con** to get on well with

simple ['simple] adj simple; (elemental) simple, easy; (mero) mere; (puro) pure, sheer ♦ nm/f simpleton; ~**za** nf simpleness; (necedad) silly thing; **simplificar** vt to simplify

simposio [sim'posjo] nm symposium

simular [simu'lar] vt to simulate

simultáneo, a [simul'taneo, a] adj simultaneous

sin [sin] prep without; **la ropa está ~ lavar** the clothes are unwashed; ~ **que** without;

~ **embargo** however, still

sinagoga [sina'voya] nf synagogue

sinceridad [sinθeri'ðað] nf sincerity; **sincero, a** adj sincere

sincronizar [sinkroni'θar] vt to synchronize

sindical [sindi'kal] adj union cpd, trade-union cpd; ~**ista** adj, nm/f trade unionist

sindicato [sindi'kato] nm (de trabajadores) trade(s) union; (de negociantes) syndicate

síndrome ['sindrome] nm (MED) syndrome; ~ **de abstinencia** (MED) withdrawal symptoms

sinfín [sin'fin] nm: **un ~ de** a great many, no end of

sinfonía [sinfo'nia] nf symphony

singular [singu'lar] adj singular; (fig) outstanding, exceptional; (raro) peculiar, odd; ~**idad** nf singularity, peculiarity; ~**izarse** vr to distinguish o.s., stand out

siniestro, a [si'njestro, a] adj sinister ♦ nm (accidente) accident

sinnúmero [sin'numero] nm = **sinfín**

sino ['sino] nm fate, destiny ♦ conj (pero) but; (salvo) except, save

sinónimo, a [si'nonimo, a] adj synonymous ♦ nm synonym

síntesis ['sintesis] nf synthesis; **sintético, a** adj synthetic

sintetizar [sinteti'θar] vt to synthesize

sintió vb ver **sentir**

síntoma ['sintoma] nm symptom

sintonía [sinto'nia] nf (RADIO, MUS: de programa) tuning; **sintonizar** vt (RADIO: emisora) to tune (in)

sinvergüenza [simber'ɣwenθa] nm/f rogue, scoundrel; ¡**es un ~**! he's got a nerve!

siquiera [si'kjera] conj even if, even though ♦ adv at least; **ni ~** not even

sirena [si'rena] nf siren

Siria ['sirja] nf Syria

sirviente, a [sir'ßjente, a] nm/f servant

sirvo etc vb ver **servir**

sisear [sise'ar] vt, vi to hiss

sistema [sis'tema] nm system; (método) method; **sistemático, a** adj systematic

---

sistema educativo

i The reform of the Spanish **sistema educativo** (education system) begun in the early 90s has replaced the courses **EGB, BUP** and **COU** with the following: "*Primaria*" a compulsory 6 years; "*Secundaria*" a compulsory 4 years and "*Bachillerato*" an optional 2-year secondary school course, essential for those wishing to go on to higher education.

---

sitiar [si'tjar] *vt* to besiege, lay siege to

sitio ['sitjo] *nm* (*lugar*) place; (*espacio*) room, space; (*MIL*) siege; **~ Web** (*INFORM*) website

situación [sitwa'θjon] *nf* situation, position; (*estatus*) position, standing

situado, a [situ'aðo] *adj* situated, placed

situar [si'twar] *vt* to place, put; (*edificio*) to locate, situate

slip [slip] *nm* pants *pl*, briefs *pl*

smoking ['smokin, es'mokin] (*pl* **~s**) *nm* dinner jacket (*BRIT*), tuxedo (*US*)

snob [es'nob] = **esnob**

SO *abr* (= **suroeste**) SW

sobaco [so'βako] *nm* armpit

sobar [so'βar] *vt* (*ropa*) to rumple; (*comida*) to play around with

soberanía [soβera'nia] *nf* sovereignty; **soberano, a** *adj* sovereign; (*fig*) supreme ♦ *nm/f* sovereign

soberbia [so'βerβja] *nf* pride; haughtiness, arrogance; magnificence

soberbio, a [so'βerβjo, a] *adj* (*orgulloso*) proud; (*altivo*) haughty, arrogant; (*estupendo*) magnificent, superb

sobornar [soβor'nar] *vt* to bribe; **soborno** *nm* bribe

sobra ['soβra] *nf* excess, surplus; **~s** *nfpl* left-overs, scraps; **de ~** surplus, extra; **tengo de ~** I've more than enough; **~do, a** *adj* (*más que suficiente*) more than enough; (*superfluo*) excessive; **sobrante** *adj* remaining, extra ♦ *nm* surplus

sobrar [so'βrar] *vt* to exceed, surpass ♦ *vi* (*tener de más*) to be more than enough;

(*quedar*) to remain, be left (over)

sobrasada [soβra'saða] *nf* pork sausage spread

sobre ['soβre] *prep* (*gen*) on; (*encima*) on (top of); (*por encima de, arriba de*) over, above; (*más que*) more than; (*además*) in addition to, besides; (*alrededor de*) about ♦ *nm* envelope; **~ todo** above all

sobrecama [soβre'kama] *nf* bedspread

sobrecargar [soβrekar'xar] *vt* (*camión*) to overload; (*COM*) to surcharge

sobredosis [soβre'ðosis] *nf inv* overdose

sobreentender [soβre(e)nten'der] *vt* to deduce, infer; **~se** *vr*: **se sobreentiende que ...** it is implied that ...

sobrehumano, a [soβreu'mano, a] *adj* superhuman

sobrellevar [soβreλe'βar] *vt* to bear, endure

sobremesa [soβre'mesa] *nf*: **durante la ~** after dinner; **ordenador de ~** desktop computer

sobrenatural [soβrenatu'ral] *adj* supernatural

sobrenombre [soβre'nombre] *nm* nickname

sobrepasar [soβrepa'sar] *vt* to exceed, surpass

sobreponerse [soβrepo'nerse] *vr*: **~ a** to overcome

sobresaliente [soβresa'ljente] *adj* outstanding, excellent

sobresalir [soβresa'lir] *vi* to project, jut out; (*fig*) to stand out, excel

sobresaltar [soβresal'tar] *vt* (*asustar*) to scare, frighten; (*sobrecoger*) to startle; **sobresalto** *nm* (*movimiento*) start; (*susto*) scare; (*turbación*) sudden shock

sobretodo [soβre'toðo] *nm* overcoat

sobrevenir [soβreβe'nir] *vi* (*ocurrir*) to happen (unexpectedly); (*resultar*) to follow, ensue

sobreviviente [soβreβi'βjente] *adj* surviving ♦ *nm/f* survivor

sobrevivir [soβreβi'βir] *vi* to survive

sobrevolar [soβreβo'lar] *vt* to fly over

sobriedad [so'βrje'ðað] *nf* sobriety,

soberness; (*moderación*) moderation, restraint

sobrino, a [so'ßrino, a] *nm/f* nephew/niece

sobrio, a ['soßrjo, a] *adj* sober; (*moderado*) moderate, restrained

socarrón, ona [soka'rron, ona] *adj* (*sarcástico*) sarcastic, ironic(al)

socavar [soka'ßar] *vt* (*tb fig*) to undermine

socavón [soka'ßon] *nm* (*hoyo*) hole

sociable [so'θjaßle] *adj* (*persona*) sociable, friendly; (*animal*) social

social [so'θjal] *adj* social; (*COM*) company *cpd*

socialdemócrata [soθjalde'mokrata] *nm/f* social democrat

socialista [soθja'lista] *adj, nm/f* socialist

socializar [soθjali'θar] *vt* to socialize

sociedad [soθje'ðað] *nf* society; (*COM*) company; **~ anónima** limited company; **~ de consumo** consumer society

socio, a ['soθjo, a] *nm/f* (*miembro*) member; (*COM*) partner

sociología [soθjolo'xia] *nf* sociology; **sociólogo, a** *nm/f* sociologist

socorrer [soko'rrer] *vt* to help; **socorrista** *nm/f* first aider; (*en piscina, playa*) lifeguard; **socorro** *nm* (*ayuda*) help, aid; (*MIL*) relief; **¡socorro!** help!

soda ['soða] *nf* (*sosa*) soda; (*bebida*) soda (water)

sofá [so'fa] (*pl* **~s**) *nm* sofa, settee; **~-cama** *nm* studio couch; sofa bed

sofisticación [sofistika'θjon] *nf* sophistication

sofocar [sofo'kar] *vt* to suffocate; (*apagar*) to smother, put out; **~se** *vr* to suffocate; (*fig*) to blush, feel embarrassed; **sofoco** *nm* suffocation; embarrassment

sofreír [sofre'ir] *vt* (*CULIN*) to fry lightly

soga ['soxa] *nf* rope

sois *vb ver* **ser**

soja ['soxa] *nf* soya

sol [sol] *nm* sun; (*luz*) sunshine, sunlight; **hace ~** it is sunny

solamente [sola'mente] *adv* only, just

solapa [so'lapa] *nf* (*de chaqueta*) lapel; (*de*

libro) jacket

solapado, a [sola'paðo, a] *adj* (*intenciones*) underhand; (*gestos, movimiento*) sly

solar [so'lar] *adj* solar, sun *cpd*

solaz [so'laθ] *nm* recreation, relaxation; **~ar** *vt* (*divertir*) to amuse

soldado [sol'daðo] *nm* soldier; **~ raso** private

soldador [solda'ðor] *nm* soldering iron; (*persona*) welder

soldar [sol'dar] *vt* to solder, weld

soleado, a [sole'aðo, a] *adj* sunny

soledad [sole'ðað] *nf* solitude; (*estado infeliz*) loneliness

solemne [so'lemne] *adj* solemn; **solemnidad** *nf* solemnity

soler [so'ler] *vi* to be in the habit of, be accustomed to; **suele salir a las ocho** she usually goes out at 8 o'clock

solfeo [sol'feo] *nm* solfa

solicitar [soliθi'tar] *vt* (*permiso*) to ask for, seek; (*puesto*) to apply for; (*votos*) to canvass for; (*atención*) to attract

solícito, a [so'liθito, a] *adj* (*diligente*) diligent; (*cuidadoso*) careful; **solicitud** *nf* (*calidad*) great care; (*petición*) request; (*a un puesto*) application

solidaridad [soliðari'ðað] *nf* solidarity; **solidario, a** *adj* (*participación*) joint, common; (*compromiso*) mutually binding

solidez [soli'ðeθ] *nf* solidity; **sólido, a** *adj* solid

soliloquio [soli'lokjo] *nm* soliloquy

solista [so'lista] *nm/f* soloist

solitario, a [soli'tarjo, a] *adj* (*persona*) lonely, solitary; (*lugar*) lonely, desolate ♦ *nm/f* (*reclusa*) recluse; (*en la sociedad*) loner ♦ *nm* solitaire

sollozar [soʎo'θar] *vi* to sob; **sollozo** *nm* sob

solo, a ['solo, a] *adj* (*único*) single, sole; (*sin compañía*) alone; (*solitario*) lonely; **hay una sola dificultad** there is just one difficulty; **a solas** alone, by oneself

sólo ['solo] *adv* only, just

solomillo [solo'miʎo] *nm* sirloin

soltar [sol'tar] vt (dejar ir) to let go of; (desprender) to unfasten, loosen; (librar) to release, set free; (risa etc) to let out

soltero, a [sol'tero, a] adj single, unmarried ♦ nm/f bachelor/single woman; **solterón, ona** nm/f old bachelor/spinster

soltura [sol'tura] nf looseness, slackness; (de los miembros) agility, ease of movement; (en el hablar) fluency, ease

soluble [so'luβle] adj (QUÍM) soluble; (problema) solvable; ~ **en agua** soluble in water

solución [solu'θjon] nf solution; **solucionar** vt (problema) to solve; (asunto) to settle, resolve

solventar [solβen'tar] vt (pagar) to settle, pay; (resolver) to resolve; **solvente** adj (ECON: empresa, persona) solvent

sombra ['sombra] nf shadow; (como protección) shade; **~s** nfpl (oscuridad) darkness sg, shadows; **tener buena/mala ~** to be lucky/unlucky

sombrero [som'brero] nm hat

sombrilla [som'briʎa] nf parasol, sunshade

sombrío, a [som'brio, a] adj (oscuro) dark; (triste) sombre, sad; (persona) gloomy

somero, a [so'mero, a] adj superficial

someter [some'ter] vt (país) to conquer; (persona) to subject to one's will; (informe) to present, submit; **~se** vr to give in, yield, submit; **~ a** to subject to

somier [so'mjer] (pl **somiers**) n spring mattress

somnífero [som'nifero] nm sleeping pill

somnolencia [somno'lenθja] nf sleepiness, drowsiness

somos vb ver **ser**

son [son] vb ver **ser** ♦ nm sound; **en ~ de broma** as a joke

sonajero [sona'xero] nm (baby's) rattle

sonambulismo [sonambu'lismo] nm sleepwalking; **sonámbulo, a** nm/f sleepwalker

sonar [so'nar] vt to ring ♦ vi to sound; (hacer ruido) to make a noise; (pronunciarse) to be sounded, be pronounced; (ser conocido) to sound familiar; (campana) to ring; (reloj) to strike, chime; **~se** vr: **~se (las narices)** to blow one's nose; **me suena ese nombre** that name rings a bell

sonda ['sonda] nf (NAUT) sounding; (TEC) bore, drill; (MED) probe

sondear [sonde'ar] vt to sound; to bore (into), drill; to probe, sound; (fig) to sound out; **sondeo** nm sounding; boring, drilling; (fig) poll, enquiry

sonido [so'niðo] nm sound

sonoro, a [so'noro, a] adj sonorous; (resonante) loud, resonant

sonreír [sonre'ir] vi to smile; **~se** vr to smile; **sonriente** adj smiling; **sonrisa** nf smile

sonrojarse [sonro'xarse] vr to blush, go red; **sonrojo** nm blush

soñador, a [soɲa'ðor, a] nm/f dreamer

soñar [so'ɲar] vt, vi to dream; **~ con** to dream about o of

soñoliento, a [soɲo'ljento, a] adj sleepy, drowsy

sopa ['sopa] nf soup

sopesar [sope'sar] vt to consider, weigh up

soplar [so'plar] vt (polvo) to blow away, blow off; (inflar) to blow up; (vela) to blow out ♦ vi to blow; **soplo** nm blow, puff; (de viento) puff, gust

soplón, ona [so'plon, ona] (fam), nm/f (niño) telltale; (de policía) grass (fam)

sopor [so'por] nm drowsiness

soporífero [sopo'rifero] nm sleeping pill

soportable [sopor'taβle] adj bearable

soportar [sopor'tar] vt to bear, carry; (fig) to bear, put up with; **soporte** nm support; (fig) pillar, support

soprano [so'prano] nf soprano

sorber [sor'βer] vt (chupar) to sip; (absorber) to soak up, absorb

sorbete [sor'βete] nm iced fruit drink

sorbo ['sorβo] nm (trago: grande) gulp, swallow; (: pequeño) sip

sordera [sor'ðera] nf deafness

sórdido, a ['sorðiðo, a] adj dirty, squalid

sordo, a ['sorðo, a] adj (persona) deaf
♦ nm/f deaf person; ~mudo, a adj deaf
and dumb

sorna ['sorna] nf sarcastic tone

soroche [so'rotʃe] (AM) nm mountain
sickness

sorprendente [sorpren'dente] adj
surprising

sorprender [sorpren'der] vt to surprise;
sorpresa nf surprise

sortear [sorte'ar] vt to draw lots for; (rifar)
to raffle; (dificultad) to avoid; sorteo nm
(en lotería) draw; (rifa) raffle

sortija [sor'tixa] nf ring; (rizo) ringlet, curl

sosegado, a [sose'ɣaðo, a] adj quiet,
calm

sosegar [sose'ɣar] vt to quieten, calm; (el
ánimo) to reassure ♦ vi to rest; sosiego
nm quiet(ness), calm(ness)

soslayo [sos'lajo]: de ~ adv obliquely,
sideways

soso, a ['soso, a] adj (CULIN) tasteless;
(aburrido) dull, uninteresting

sospecha [sos'petʃa] nf suspicion;
sospechar vt to suspect;
sospechoso, a adj suspicious;
(testimonio, opinión) suspect ♦ nm/f
suspect

sostén [sos'ten] nm (apoyo) support;
(sujetador) bra; (alimentación) sustenance,
food

sostener [soste'ner] vt to support;
(mantener) to keep up, maintain;
(alimentar) to sustain, keep going; ~se vr
to support o.s.; (seguir) to continue,
remain; sostenido, a adj continuous,
sustained; (prolongado) prolonged

sotana [so'tana] nf (REL) cassock

sótano ['sotano] nm basement

soviético, a [so'βjetiko, a] adj Soviet; los
~s the Soviets

soy vb ver ser

Sr. abr (= Señor) Mr

Sra. abr (= Señora) Mrs

S.R.C. abr (= se ruega contestación)
R.S.V.P.

Sres. abr (= Señores) Messrs

Srta. abr (= Señorita) Miss

Sta. abr (= Santa) St

status ['status, e'status] nm inv status

Sto. abr (= Santo) St

su [su] pron (de él) his; (de ella) her; (de
una cosa) its; (de ellos, ellas) their; (de
usted, ustedes) your

suave ['swaβe] adj gentle; (superficie)
smooth; (trabajo) easy; (música, voz) soft,
sweet; suavidad nf gentleness;
smoothness; softness, sweetness;
suavizante nm (de ropa) softener; (del
pelo) conditioner; suavizar vt to soften;
(quitar la aspereza) to smooth (out)

subalimentado, a [suβalimen'taðo, a]
adj undernourished

subasta [su'βasta] nf auction; subastar
vt to auction (off)

subcampeón, ona [suβkampe'on, ona]
nm/f runner-up

subconsciente [suβkon'sθjente] adj, nm
subconscious

subdesarrollado, a [suβðesarro'ʎaðo, a]
adj underdeveloped

subdesarrollo [suβðesa'rroʎo] nm
underdevelopment

subdirector, a [suβðirek'tor, a] nm/f
assistant director

súbdito, a ['suβðito, a] nm/f subject

subestimar [suβesti'mar] vt to
underestimate, underrate

subida [su'βiða] nf (de montaña etc)
ascent, climb; (de precio) rise, increase;
(pendiente) slope, hill

subir [su'βir] vt (objeto) to raise, lift up;
(cuesta, calle) to go up; (colina, montaña)
to climb; (precio) to raise, put up ♦ vi to
go up, come up; (a un coche) to get in;
(a un autobús, tren o avión) to get on,
board; (precio) to rise, go up; (río, marea)
to rise; ~se vr to get up, climb

súbito, a ['suβito, a] adj (repentino)
sudden; (imprevisto) unexpected

subjetivo, a [suβxe'tiβo, a] adj subjective

sublevación [suβleβa'θjon] nf revolt,
rising

sublevar [suβle'βar] vt to rouse to revolt;

~se *vr* to revolt, rise

sublime [su'ßlime] *adj* sublime

submarinismo [sußmari'nismo] *nm* scuba diving

submarino, a [sußma'rino, a] *adj* underwater ♦ *nm* submarine

subnormal [sußnor'mal] *adj* subnormal ♦ *nm/f* subnormal person

subordinado, a [sußorði'naðo, a] *adj*, *nm/f* subordinate

subrayar [sußra'jar] *vt* to underline

subsanar [sußsa'nar] *vt* to recitfy

subscribir [sußskri'ßir] *vt* = **suscribir**

subsidio [sußsiðjo] *nm* (*ayuda*) aid, financial help; (*subvención*) subsidy, grant; (*de enfermedad, paro etc*) benefit, allowance

subsistencia [sußsis'tenθja] *nf* subsistence

subsistir [sußsis'tir] *vi* to subsist; (*sobrevivir*) to survive, endure

subterráneo, a [sußte'rraneo, a] *adj* underground, subterranean ♦ *nm* underpass, underground passage

subtítulo [sußtitulo] *nm* (*CINE*) subtitle

suburbano, a [sußur'ßano, a] *adj* suburban

suburbio [su'ßurßjo] *nm* (*barrio*) slum quarter

subvención [sußßen'θjon] *nf* (*ECON*) subsidy, grant; **subvencionar** *vt* to subsidize

subversión [sußßer'sjon] *nf* subversion; **subversivo, a** *adj* subversive

subyugar [sußju'ɣar] *vt* (*país*) to subjugate, subdue; (*enemigo*) to overpower; (*voluntad*) to dominate

sucedáneo, a [suθe'ðaneo, a] *adj* substitute ♦ *nm* substitute (food)

suceder [suθe'ðer] *vt*, *vi* to happen; (*seguir*) to succeed, follow; **lo que sucede es que ...** the fact is that ...; **sucesión** *nf* succession; (*serie*) sequence, series

sucesivamente [suθesißa'mente] *adv*: **y así ~** and so on

sucesivo, a [suθe'sißo, a] *adj* successive,

following; **en lo ~** in future, from now on

suceso [su'θeso] *nm* (*hecho*) event, happening; (*incidente*) incident

suciedad [suθje'ðað] *nf* (*estado*) dirtiness; (*mugre*) dirt, filth

sucinto, a [su'θinto, a] *adj* (*conciso*) succinct, concise

sucio, a ['suθjo, a] *adj* dirty

suculento, a [suku'lento, a] *adj* succulent

sucumbir [sukum'bir] *vi* to succumb

sucursal [sukur'sal] *nf* branch (office)

sudadera [suða'ðera] *nf* sweatshirt

Sudáfrica [suð'afrika] *nf* South Africa

Sudamérica [suða'merika] *nf* South America; **sudamericano, a** *adj*, *nm/f* South American

sudar [su'ðar] *vt*, *vi* to sweat

sudeste [su'ðeste] *nm* south-east

sudoeste [suðo'este] *nm* south-west

sudor [su'ðor] *nm* sweat; **~oso, a** *adj* sweaty, sweating

Suecia ['sweθja] *nf* Sweden; **sueco, a** *adj* Swedish ♦ *nm/f* Swede

suegro, a ['sweɣro, a] *nm/f* father-/ mother-in-law

suela ['swela] *nf* sole

sueldo ['sweldo] *nm* pay, wage(s) (*pl*)

suele *etc vb ver* **soler**

suelo ['swelo] *nm* (*tierra*) ground; (*de casa*) floor

suelto, a ['swelto, a] *adj* loose; (*libre*) free; (*separado*) detached; (*ágil*) quick, agile ♦ *nm* (*loose*) change, small change

sueño *etc vb ver* **soñar** ♦ *nm* sleep; (*somnolencia*) sleepiness, drowsiness; (*lo soñado, fig*) dream; **tener ~** to be sleepy

suero ['swero] *nm* (*MED*) serum; (*de leche*) whey

suerte ['swerte] *nf* (*fortuna*) luck; (*azar*) chance; (*destino*) fate, destiny; (*especie*) sort, kind; **tener ~** to be lucky; **de otra ~** otherwise, if not; **de ~ que** so that, in such a way that

suéter ['sweter] *nm* sweater

suficiente [sufi'θjente] *adj* enough, sufficient ♦ *nm* (*ESCOL*) pass

sufragio [su'fraxjo] *nm* (*voto*) vote; (*derecho de voto*) suffrage

sufrido, a [su'friðo, a] *adj* (*persona*) tough; (*paciente*) long-suffering, patient

sufrimiento [sufri'mjento] *nm* (*dolor*) suffering

sufrir [su'frir] *vt* (*padecer*) to suffer; (*soportar*) to bear, put up with; (*apoyar*) to hold up, support ♦ *vi* to suffer

sugerencia [suxe'renθja] *nf* suggestion

sugerir [suxe'rir] *vt* to suggest; (*sutilmente*) to hint

sugestión [suxes'tjon] *nf* suggestion; (*sutil*) hint; **sugestionar** *vt* to influence

sugestivo, a [suxes'tißo, a] *adj* stimulating; (*fascinante*) fascinating

suicida [sui'θiða] *adj* suicidal ♦ *nm/f* suicidal person; (*muerto*) suicide, person who has committed suicide; **suicidarse** *vr* to commit suicide, kill o.s.; **suicidio** *nm* suicide

Suiza ['swiθa] *nf* Switzerland; **suizo, a** *adj, nm/f* Swiss

sujeción [suxe'θjon] *nf* subjection

sujetador [suxeta'ðor] *nm* (*sostén*) bra

sujetar [suxe'tar] *vt* (*fijar*) to fasten; (*detener*) to hold down; **~se** *vr* to subject o.s.; **sujeto, a** *adj* fastened, secure ♦ *nm* subject; (*individuo*) individual; **sujeto a** subject to

suma ['suma] *nf* (*cantidad*) total, sum; (*de dinero*) sum; (*acto*) adding (up), addition; **en ~** in short

sumamente [suma'mente] *adv* extremely, exceedingly

sumar [su'mar] *vt* to add (up) ♦ *vi* to add up

sumario, a [su'marjo, a] *adj* brief, concise ♦ *nm* summary

sumergir [sumer'xir] *vt* to submerge; (*hundir*) to sink

suministrar [sumini'strar] *vt* to supply, provide; **suministro** *nm* supply; (*acto*) supplying, providing

sumir [su'mir] *vt* to sink, submerge; (*fig*) to plunge

sumisión [sumi'sjon] *nf* (*acto*) submission;

(*calidad*) submissiveness, docility; **sumiso, a** *adj* submissive, docile

sumo, a ['sumo, a] *adj* great, extreme; (*autoridad*) highest, supreme

suntuoso, a [sun'twoso, a] *adj* sumptuous, magnificent

supe *etc vb ver* **saber**

supeditar [supeði'tar] *vt*: **~ algo a algo** to subordinate sth to sth

super... [super] *prefijo* super..., over...; **~bueno** *adj* great, fantastic

súper ['super] *nf* (*gasolina*) three-star (petrol)

superar [supe'rar] *vt* (*sobreponerse a*) to overcome; (*rebasar*) to surpass, do better than; (*pasar*) to go beyond; **~se** *vr* to excel o.s.

superávit [supe'raßit] *nm inv* surplus

superficial [superfi'θjal] *adj* superficial; (*medida*) surface *cpd*, of the surface

superficie [super'fiθje] *nf* surface; (*área*) area

superfluo, a [su'perflwo, a] *adj* superfluous

superior [supe'rjor] *adj* (*piso, clase*) upper; (*temperatura, número, nivel*) higher; (*mejor: calidad, producto*) superior, better ♦ *nm/f* superior; **~idad** *nf* superiority

supermercado [supermer'kaðo] *nm* supermarket

superponer [superpo'ner] *vt* to superimpose

supersónico, a [super'soniko, a] *adj* supersonic

superstición [supersti'θjon] *nf* superstition; **supersticioso, a** *adj* superstitious

supervisar [superßi'sar] *vt* to supervise

supervivencia [superßi'ßenθja] *nf* survival

superviviente [superßi'ßjente] *adj* surviving

supiera *etc vb ver* **saber**

suplantar [suplan'tar] *vt* to supplant

suplemento [suple'mento] *nm* supplement

suplente [su'plente] *adj, nm/f* substitute

supletorio, a [suple'torjo, a] *adj*

supplementary ♦ *nm* supplement;
teléfono ~ extension

súplica ['suplika] *nf* request; (*JUR*) petition

suplicar [supli'kar] *vt* (*cosa*) to beg (for),
plead for; (*persona*) to beg, plead with

suplicio [su'pliθjo] *nm* torture

suplir [su'plir] *vt* (*compensar*) to make
good, make up for; (*reemplazar*) to
replace, substitute ♦ *vi*: ~ **a** to take the
place of, substitute for

supo *etc vb ver* **saber**

suponer [supo'ner] *vt* to suppose;
suposición *nf* supposition

supremacía [suprema'θia] *nf* supremacy

supremo, a [su'premo, a] *adj* supreme

supresión [supre'sjon] *nf* suppression; (*de
derecho*) abolition; (*de palabra etc*)
deletion; (*de restricción*) cancellation,
lifting

suprimir [supri'mir] *vt* to suppress;
(*derecho, costumbre*) to abolish; (*palabra
etc*) to delete; (*restricción*) to cancel, lift

supuesto, a [su'pwesto, a] *pp de* **suponer**
♦ *adj* (*hipotético*) supposed ♦ *nm*
assumption, hypothesis; ~ **que** since; **por**
~ of course

sur [sur] *nm* south

surcar [sur'kar] *vt* to plough; **surco** *nm*
(*en metal, disco*) groove; (*AGR*) furrow

surgir [sur'xir] *vi* to arise, emerge;
(*dificultad*) to come up, crop up

suroeste [suro'este] *nm* south-west

surtido, a [sur'tiðo, a] *adj* mixed, assorted
♦ *nm* (*selección*) selection, assortment;
(*abastecimiento*) supply, stock; ~**r** *nm* (*tb:*
~**r de gasolina**) petrol pump (*BRIT*), gas
pump (*US*)

surtir [sur'tir] *vt* to supply, provide ♦ *vi* to
spout, spurt

susceptible [susθep'tiβle] *adj* susceptible;
(*sensible*) sensitive; ~ **de** capable of

suscitar [susθi'tar] *vt* to cause, provoke;
(*interés, sospechas*) to arouse

suscribir [suskri'βir] *vt* (*firmar*) to sign;
(*respaldar*) to subscribe to, endorse; ~**se**
vr to subscribe; **suscripción** *nf*
subscription

susodicho, a [suso'ðitʃo, a] *adj* above-
mentioned

suspender [suspen'der] *vt* (*objeto*) to
hang (up), suspend; (*trabajo*) to stop,
suspend; (*ESCOL*) to fail; (*interrumpir*) to
adjourn; (*atrasar*) to postpone;
suspensión *nf* suspension; (*fig*)
stoppage, suspension

suspenso, a [sus'penso, a] *adj* hanging,
suspended; (*ESCOL*) failed ♦ *nm* (*ESCOL*)
fail; **quedar** *o* **estar en** ~ to be pending

suspicacia [suspi'kaθja] *nf* suspicion,
mistrust; **suspicaz** *adj* suspicious,
distrustful

suspirar [suspi'rar] *vi* to sigh; **suspiro**
nm sigh

sustancia [sus'tanθja] *nf* substance

sustentar [susten'tar] *vt* (*alimentar*) to
sustain, nourish; (*objeto*) to hold up,
support; (*idea, teoría*) to maintain,
uphold; (*fig*) to sustain, keep going;
sustento *nm* support; (*alimento*)
sustenance, food

sustituir [sustitu'ir] *vt* to substitute,
replace; **sustituto, a** *nm/f* substitute,
replacement

susto ['susto] *nm* fright, scare

sustraer [sustra'er] *vt* to remove, take
away; (*MAT*) to subtract

susurrar [susu'rrar] *vi* to whisper;
susurro *nm* whisper

sutil [su'til] *adj* (*aroma, diferencia*) subtle;
(*tenue*) thin; (*inteligencia, persona*) sharp;
~**eza** *nf* subtlety; thinness

suyo, a ['sujo, a] (*con artículo o después
del verbo* **ser**) *adj* (*de él*) his; (*de ella*)
hers; (*de ellos, ellas*) theirs; (*de Ud, Uds*)
yours; **un amigo** ~ a friend of his (*o* hers
o theirs *o* yours)

T, t

tabacalera [taßaka'lera] *nf*: **T~** Spanish state tobacco monopoly

tabaco [ta'ßako] *nm* tobacco; (*fam*) cigarettes *pl*

taberna [ta'ßerna] *nf* bar, pub (*BRIT*)

tabique [ta'ßike] *nm* partition (wall)

tabla ['taßla] *nf* (*de madera*) plank; (*estante*) shelf; (*de vestido*) pleat; (*ARTE*) panel; **~s** *nfpl*: **estar** *o* **quedar en ~s** to draw; **~do** *nm* (*plataforma*) platform; (*TEATRO*) stage

tablao [ta'ßlao] *nm* (*tb*: **~ flamenco**) flamenco show

tablero [ta'ßlero] *nm* (*de madera*) plank, board; (*de ajedrez, damas*) board; **~ de anuncios** notice (*BRIT*) *o* bulletin (*US*) board

tableta [ta'ßleta] *nf* (*MED*) tablet; (*de chocolate*) bar

tablón [ta'ßlon] *nm* (*de suelo*) plank; (*de techo*) beam; **~ de anuncios** notice board (*BRIT*), bulletin board (*US*)

tabú [ta'ßu] *nm* taboo

tabular [taßu'lar] *vt* to tabulate

taburete [taßu'rete] *nm* stool

tacaño, a [ta'kaɲo, a] *adj* mean

tacha ['tatʃa] *nf* flaw; (*TEC*) stud; **tachar** *vt* (*borrar*) to cross out; **tachar de** to accuse of

tácito, a ['taθito, a] *adj* tacit

taciturno, a [taθi'turno, a] *adj* silent

taco ['tako] *nm* (*BILLAR*) cue; (*libro de billetes*) book; (*AM: de zapato*) heel; (*tarugo*) peg; (*palabrota*) swear word

tacón [ta'kon] *nm* heel; **de ~ alto** high-heeled; **taconeo** *nm* (*heel*) stamping

táctica ['taktika] *nf* tactics *pl*

táctico, a ['taktiko, a] *adj* tactical

tacto ['takto] *nm* touch; (*fig*) tact

taimado, a [tai'maðo, a] *adj* (*astuto*) sly

tajada [ta'xaða] *nf* slice

tajante [ta'xante] *adj* sharp

tajo ['taxo] *nm* (*corte*) cut; (*GEO*) cleft

tal [tal] *adj* such; **~ vez** perhaps ♦ *pron* (*persona*) someone, such a one; (*cosa*) something, such a thing; **~ como** such as; **~ para cual** (*dos iguales*) two of a kind ♦ *adv*: **~ como** (*igual*) just as; **~ cual** (*como es*) just as it is; **¿qué ~?** how are things?; **¿qué ~ te gusta?** how do you like it? ♦ *conj*: **con ~ de que** provided that

taladrar [tala'ðrar] *vt* to drill; **taladro** *nm* drill

talante [ta'lante] *nm* (*humor*) mood; (*voluntad*) will, willingness

talar [ta'lar] *vt* to fell, cut down; (*devastar*) to devastate

talco ['talko] *nm* (*polvos*) talcum powder

talego [ta'leɣo] *nm* sack

talento [ta'lento] *nm* talent; (*capacidad*) ability

TALGO ['talɣo] (*ESP*) *nm abr* (= *tren articulado ligero Goicoechea-Oriol*) ≈ HST (*BRIT*)

talismán [talis'man] *nm* talisman

talla ['taʎa] *nf* (*estatura, fig, MED*) height, stature; (*palo*) measuring rod; (*ARTE*) carving; (*medida*) size

tallado, a [ta'ʎaðo, a] *adj* carved ♦ *nm* carving

tallar [ta'ʎar] *vt* (*madera*) to carve; (*metal etc*) to engrave; (*medir*) to measure

tallarines [taʎa'rines] *nmpl* noodles

talle ['taʎe] *nm* (*ANAT*) waist; (*fig*) appearance

taller [ta'ʎer] *nm* (*TEC*) workshop; (*de artista*) studio

tallo ['taʎo] *nm* (*de planta*) stem; (*de hierba*) blade; (*brote*) shoot

talón [ta'lon] *nm* (*ANAT*) heel; (*COM*) counterfoil; (*cheque*) cheque (*BRIT*), check (*US*)

talonario [talo'narjo] *nm* (*de cheques*) chequebook (*BRIT*), checkbook (*US*); (*de recibos*) receipt book

tamaño, a [ta'maɲo, a] *adj* (*tan grande*) such a big; (*tan pequeño*) such a small ♦ *nm* size; **de ~ natural** full-size

tamarindo [tama'rindo] *nm* tamarind

tambalearse [tambale'arse] *vr* (*persona*) to stagger; (*vehículo*) to sway

también [tam'bjen] *adv* (*igualmente*) also, too, as well; (*además*) besides

tambor [tam'bor] *nm* drum; (*ANAT*) eardrum; **~ del freno** brake drum

tamiz [ta'miθ] *nm* sieve; **~ar** *vt* to sieve

tampoco [tam'poko] *adv* nor, neither; **yo ~ lo compré** I didn't buy it either

tampón [tam'pon] *nm* tampon

tan [tan] *adv* so; **~ es así que ...** so much so that ....

tanda ['tanda] *nf* (*gen*) series; (*turno*) shift

tangente [tan'xente] *nf* tangent

Tánger ['tanxer] *n* Tangier(s)

tangible [tan'xiβle] *adj* tangible

tanque ['tanke] *nm* (*cisterna, MIL*) tank; (*AUTO*) tanker

tantear [tante'ar] *vt* (*calcular*) to reckon (up); (*medir*) to take the measure of; (*probar*) to test, try out; (*tomar la medida: persona*) to take the measurements of; (*situación*) to weigh up; (*persona: opinión*) to sound out ♦ *vi* (*DEPORTE*) to score; **tanteo** *nm* (*cálculo*) (rough) calculation; (*prueba*) test, trial; (*DEPORTE*) scoring

tanto, a ['tanto, a] *adj* (*cantidad*) so much, as much; **~s** so many, as many; **20 y ~s** 20-odd ♦ *adv* (*cantidad*) so much, as much; (*tiempo*) so long, as long ♦ *conj*: **en ~ que** while; **hasta ~ (que)** until such time as ♦ *nm* (*suma*) certain amount; (*proporción*) so much; (*punto*) point; (*gol*) goal; **un ~ perezoso** somewhat lazy ♦ *pron*: **cada uno paga ~** each one pays so much; **~ tú como yo** both you and I; **~ como eso** as much as that; **~ más ... cuanto que** all the more ... because; **~ mejor/peor** so much the better/the worse; **~ si viene como si va** whether he comes or whether he goes; **~ es así que** so much so that; **por o por lo ~** therefore; **me he vuelto ronco de o con ~ hablar** I have become hoarse with so much talking; **a ~s de agosto** on such and such a day in August

tapa ['tapa] *nf* (*de caja, olla*) lid; (*de*

botella) top; (*de libro*) cover; (*comida*) snack

tapadera [tapa'ðera] *nf* lid, cover

tapar [ta'par] *vt* (*cubrir*) to cover; (*envolver*) to wrap o cover up; (*la vista*) to obstruct; (*persona, falta*) to conceal; (*AM*) to fill; **~se** *vr* to wrap o.s. up

taparrabo [tapa'rraβo] *nm* loincloth

tapete [ta'pete] *nm* table cover

tapia ['tapja] *nf* (garden) wall; **tapiar** *vt* to wall in

tapicería [tapiθe'ria] *nf* tapestry; (*para muebles*) upholstery; (*tienda*) upholsterer's (shop)

tapiz [ta'piθ] *nm* (*alfombra*) carpet; (*tela tejida*) tapestry; **~ar** *vt* (*muebles*) to upholster

tapón [ta'pon] *nm* (*de botella*) top; (*de lavabo*) plug; **~ de rosca** screw-top

taquigrafía [takivra'fia] *nf* shorthand; **taquígrafo, a** *nm/f* shorthand writer, stenographer

taquilla [ta'kiʎa] *nf* (*donde se compra*) booking office; (*suma recogida*) takings *pl*; **taquillero, a** *adj*: **función taquillera** box office success ♦ *nm/f* ticket clerk

tara ['tara] *nf* (*defecto*) defect; (*COM*) tare

tarántula [ta'rantula] *nf* tarantula

tararear [tarare'ar] *vi* to hum

tardar [tar'ðar] *vi* (*tomar tiempo*) to take a long time; (*llegar tarde*) to be late; (*demorar*) to delay; **¿tarda mucho el tren?** does the train take (very) long?; **a más ~** at the latest; **no tardes en venir** come soon

tarde ['tarðe] *adv* late ♦ *nf* (*de día*) afternoon; (*al anochecer*) evening; **de ~ en ~** from time to time; **¡buenas ~s!** good afternoon!; **a o por la ~** in the afternoon; in the evening

tardío, a [tar'ðio, a] *adj* (*retrasado*) late; (*lento*) slow (to arrive)

tarea [ta'rea] *nf* task; (*faena*) chore; (*ESCOL*) homework

tarifa [ta'rifa] *nf* (*lista de precios*) price list; (*precio*) tariff

tarima [ta'rima] *nf* (*plataforma*) platform

tarjeta [tar'xeta] nf card; **~ postal/de crédito/de Navidad** postcard/credit card/Christmas card

tarro ['tarro] nm jar, pot

tarta ['tarta] nf (pastel) cake; (de base dura) tart

tartamudear [tartamuðe'ar] vi to stammer; **tartamudo, a** adj stammering ♦ nm/f stammerer

tártaro, a ['tartaro, a] adj: **salsa tártara** tartar(e) sauce

tasa ['tasa] nf (precio) (fixed) price, rate; (valoración) valuation; (medida, norma) measure, standard; **~ de cambio/interés** exchange/interest rate; **~s universitarias** university fees; **~s de aeropuerto** airport tax; **~ción** nf valuation; **~dor, a** nm/f valuer

tasar [ta'sar] vt (arreglar el precio) to fix a price for; (valorar) to value, assess

tasca ['taska] (fam) nf pub

tatarabuelo, a [tatara'ßwelo, a] nm/f great-great-grandfather/mother

tatuaje [ta'twaxe] nm (dibujo) tattoo; (acto) tattooing

tatuar [ta'twar] vt to tattoo

taurino, a [tau'rino, a] adj bullfighting cpd

Tauro ['tauro] nm Taurus

tauromaquia [tauro'makja] nf tauromachy, (art of) bullfighting

taxi ['taksi] nm taxi

taxista [tak'sista] nm/f taxi driver

taza ['taθa] nf cup; (de retrete) bowl; **~ para café** coffee cup; **tazón** nm (taza grande) mug, large cup; (de fuente) basin

te [te] pron (complemento de objeto) you; (complemento indirecto) (to) you; (reflexivo) (to) yourself; **¿~ duele mucho el brazo?** does your arm hurt a lot?; **~ equivocas** you're wrong; **¡cálma~!** calm down!

té [te] nm tea

tea ['tea] nf torch

teatral [tea'tral] adj theatre cpd; (fig) theatrical

teatro [te'atro] nm theatre; (LITERATURA) plays pl, drama

tebeo [te'ßeo] nm comic

techo ['tetʃo] nm (externo) roof; (interno) ceiling; **~ corredizo** sunroof

tecla ['tekla] nf key; **~do** nm keyboard; **teclear** vi (MUS) to strum; (con los dedos) to tap ♦ vt (INFORM) to key in

técnica ['teknika] nf technique; (tecnología) technology; ver tb **técnico**

técnico, a ['tekniko, a] adj technical ♦ nm/f technician; (experto) expert

tecnología [teknolo'xia] nf technology; **tecnológico, a** adj technological

tedio ['teðjo] nm boredom, tedium; **~so, a** adj boring, tedious

teja ['texa] nf tile; (BOT) lime (tree); **~do** nm (tiled) roof

tejemaneje [texema'nexe] nm (lío) fuss; (intriga) intrigue

tejer [te'xer] vt to weave; (hacer punto) to knit; (fig) to fabricate; **tejido** nm (tela) material, fabric; (telaraña) web; (ANAT) tissue

tel [tel] abr (= teléfono) tel

tela ['tela] nf (tejido) material; (telaraña) web; (en líquido) skin; **telar** nm (máquina) loom

telaraña [tela'raɲa] nf cobweb

tele ['tele] (fam) nf telly (BRIT), tube (US)

tele... ['tele] prefijo tele...; **~comunicación** nf telecommunication; **~control** nm remote control; **~diario** nm television news; **~difusión** nf (television) broadcast; **~dirigido, a** adj remote-controlled

teléf abr (= teléfono) tel

teleférico [tele'feriko] nm (de esquí) ski-lift

telefonear [telefone'ar] vi to telephone

telefónico, a [tele'foniko, a] adj telephone cpd

telefonillo [telefo'niʎo] nm (de puerta) intercom

telefonista [telefo'nista] nm/f telephonist

teléfono [te'lefono] nm (tele)phone; **estar hablando al ~** to be on the phone; **llamar a uno por ~** to ring sb (up) o phone sb (up); **~ móvil** car phone; **~ portátil** mobile phone

telegrafía [teleɣra'fia] *nf* telegraphy
telégrafo [te'leɣrafo] *nm* telegraph
telegrama [tele'ɣrama] *nm* telegram
tele: **~impresor** *nm* teleprinter (*BRIT*), teletype (*US*); **~novela** *nf* soap (opera); **~objetivo** *nm* telephoto lens; **~patía** *nf* telepathy; **~pático, a** *adj* telepathic; **~scópico, a** *adj* telescopic; **~scopio** *nm* telescope; **~silla** *nm* chairlift; **~spectador, a** *nm/f* viewer; **~squí** *nm* ski-lift; **~tarjeta** *nf* phonecard; **~tipo** *nm* teletype; **~ventas** *nfpl* telesales
televidente [teleßi'ðente] *nm/f* viewer
televisar [teleßi'sar] *vt* to televise
televisión [teleßi'sjon] *nf* television; **~ digital** digital television
televisor [teleßi'sor] *nm* television set
télex ['teleks] *nm inv* telex
telón [te'lon] *nm* curtain; **~ de acero** (*POL*) iron curtain; **~ de fondo** backcloth, background
tema ['tema] *nm* (*asunto*) subject, topic; (*MUS*) theme; **temática** *nf* (*social, histórica, artística*) range of topics; **temático, a** *adj* thematic
temblar [tem'blar] *vi* to shake, tremble; (*de frío*) to shiver; **temblón, ona** *adj* shaking; **temblor** *nm* trembling; (*de tierra*) earthquake; **tembloroso, a** *adj* trembling
temer [te'mer] *vt* to fear ♦ *vi* to be afraid; **temo que llegue tarde** I am afraid he may be late
temerario, a [teme'rarjo, a] *adj* (*descuidado*) reckless; (*irreflexivo*) hasty; **temeridad** *nf* (*imprudencia*) rashness; (*audacia*) boldness
temeroso, a [teme'roso, a] *adj* (*miedoso*) fearful; (*que inspira temor*) frightful
temible [te'mißle] *adj* fearsome
temor [te'mor] *nm* (*miedo*) fear; (*duda*) suspicion
témpano ['tempano] *nm*: **~ de hielo** ice-floe
temperamento [tempera'mento] *nm* temperament
temperatura [tempera'tura] *nf* temperature

tempestad [tempes'taŏ] *nf* storm; **tempestuoso, a** *adj* stormy
templado, a [tem'plaŏo, a] *adj* (*moderado*) moderate; (*frugal*) frugal; (*agua*) lukewarm; (*clima*) mild; (*MUS*) well-tuned; **templanza** *nf* moderation; mildness
templar [tem'plar] *vt* (*moderar*) to moderate; (*furia*) to restrain; (*calor*) to reduce; (*afinar*) to tune (up); (*acero*) to temper; (*tuerca*) to tighten up; **temple** *nm* (*ajuste*) tempering; (*afinación*) tuning; (*pintura*) tempera
templo ['templo] *nm* (*iglesia*) church; (*pagano etc*) temple
temporada [tempo'raŏa] *nf* time, period; (*estación*) season
temporal [tempo'ral] *adj* (*no permanente*) temporary; (*REL*) temporal ♦ *nm* storm
tempranero, a [tempra'nero, a] *adj* (*BOT*) early; (*persona*) early-rising
temprano, a [tem'prano, a] *adj* early; (*demasiado pronto*) too soon, too early
ten *vb ver* **tener**
tenaces [te'naθes] *adj pl ver* **tenaz**
tenacidad [tenaθi'ðaŏ] *nf* tenacity; (*dureza*) toughness; (*terquedad*) stubbornness
tenacillas [tena'θiʎas] *nfpl* tongs; (*para el pelo*) curling tongs (*BRIT*) o iron *sg* (*US*); (*MED*) forceps
tenaz [te'naθ] *adj* (*material*) tough; (*persona*) tenacious; (*creencia, resistencia*) stubborn
tenaza(s) [te'naθa(s)] *nf(pl)* (*MED*) forceps; (*TEC*) pliers; (*ZOOL*) pincers
tendedero [tende'ðero] *nm* (*para ropa*) drying place; (*cuerda*) clothes line
tendencia [ten'denθja] *nf* tendency; **tener ~ a** to tend to, have a tendency to; **tendencioso, a** *adj* tendentious
tender [ten'der] *vt* (*extender*) to spread out; (*colgar*) to hang out; (*vía férrea, cable*) to lay; (*estirar*) to stretch ♦ *vi*: **~ a** to tend to, have a tendency towards; **~se** *vr* to lie down; **~ la cama/la mesa** (*AM*)

to make the bed/lay (BRIT) o set (US) the table

enderete [tende'rete] nm (puesto) stall; (exposición) display of goods

endero, a [ten'dero, a] nm/f shopkeeper

endido, a [ten'diðo, a] adj (acostado) lying down, flat; (colgado) hanging ♦ nm (TAUR) front rows of seats; **a galope ~** flat out

endón [ten'don] nm tendon

endré etc vb ver **tener**

enebroso, a [tene'ßroso, a] adj (oscuro) dark; (fig) gloomy

enedor [tene'ðor] nm (CULIN) fork; **~ de libros** book-keeper

enencia [te'nenθja] nf (de casa) tenancy; (de oficio) tenure; (de propiedad) possession

---

PALABRA CLAVE

ener [te'ner] vt **1** (poseer, gen) to have; (en la mano) to hold; **¿tienes un boli?** have you got a pen?; **va a ~ un niño** she's going to have a baby; **¡ten (o tenga)!, ¡aquí tienes (o tiene)!** here you are!

2 (edad, medidas) to be; **tiene 7 años** she's 7 (years old); **tiene 15 cm de largo** it's 15 cm long; ver **calor; hambre** etc

3 (considerar): **lo tengo por brillante** I consider him to be brilliant; **~ en mucho a uno** to think very highly of sb

4 (+pp: = pretérito): **tengo terminada ya la mitad del trabajo** I've done half the work already

5: ~ que hacer algo to have to do sth; **tengo que acabar este trabajo hoy** I have to finish this job today

6: ¿qué tienes, estás enfermo? what's the matter with you, are you ill?

♦ **~se** vr **1: ~se en pie** to stand up

2: ~se por to think o.s.; **se tiene por muy listo** he thinks himself very clever

---

engo etc vb ver **tener**

enia ['tenja] nf tapeworm

eniente [te'njente] nm (rango) lieutenant; (ayudante) deputy

tenis ['tenis] nm tennis; **~ de mesa** table tennis; **~ta** nm/f tennis player

tenor [te'nor] nm (sentido) meaning; (MUS) tenor; **a ~ de** on the lines of

tensar [ten'sar] vt to tighten; (arco) to draw

tensión [ten'sjon] nf tension; (TEC) stress; (MED): **~ arterial** blood pressure; **tener la ~ alta** to have high blood pressure

tenso, a ['tenso, a] adj tense

tentación [tenta'θjon] nf temptation

tentáculo [ten'takulo] nm tentacle

tentador, a [tenta'ðor, a] adj tempting

tentar [ten'tar] vt to tempt; (atraer) to attract; **tentativa** nf attempt; **tentativa de asesinato** attempted murder

tentempié [tentem'pje] nm snack

tenue ['tenwe] adj (delgado) thin, slender; (neblina) light; (lazo, vínculo) slight

teñir [te'ɲir] vt to dye; (fig) to tinge; **~se** vr to dye; **~se el pelo** to dye one's hair

teología [teolo'xia] nf theology

teoría [teo'ria] nf theory; **en ~** in theory; **teóricamente** adv theoretically; **teórico, a** adj theoretic(al) ♦ nm/f theoretician, theorist; **teorizar** vi to theorize

terapéutico, a [tera'peutiko, a] adj therapeutic

terapia [te'rapja] nf therapy

tercer [ter'θer] adj ver **tercero**

tercermundista [terθermun'dista] adj Third World cpd

tercero, a [ter'θero, a] adj (delante de nmsg: **tercer**) third ♦ nm (JUR) third party

terceto [ter'θeto] nm trio

terciar [ter'θjar] vi (participar) to take part; (hacer de árbitro) to mediate; **~se** vr to come up; **~io, a** adj tertiary

tercio ['terθjo] nm third

terciopelo [terθjo'pelo] nm velvet

terco, a ['terko, a] adj obstinate

tergal ® [ter'val] nm type of polyester

tergiversar [terxißer'sar] vt to distort

termal [ter'mal] adj thermal

termas ['termas] *nfpl* hot springs
térmico, a ['termiko, a] *adj* thermal
terminación [termina'θjon] *nf* (*final*) end; (*conclusión*) conclusion, ending
terminal [termi'nal] *adj, nm, nf* terminal
terminante [termi'nante] *adj* (*final*) final, definitive; (*tajante*) categorical; **~mente** *adv*: **~mente prohibido** strictly forbidden
terminar [termi'nar] *vt* (*completar*) to complete, finish; (*concluir*) to end ♦ *vi* (*llegar a su fin*) to end; (*parar*) to stop; (*acabar*) to finish; **~se** *vr* to come to an end; **~ por hacer algo** to end up (by) doing sth
término ['termino] *nm* end, conclusion; (*parada*) terminus; (*límite*) boundary; **~ medio** average; (*fig*) middle way; **en último ~** (*a fin de cuentas*) in the last analysis; (*como último recurso*) as a last resort
terminología [terminolo'xia] *nf* terminology
termodinámico, a [termoði'namiko, a] *adj* thermodynamic
termómetro [ter'mometro] *nm* thermometer
termonuclear [termonukle'ar] *adj* thermonuclear
termo(s) ® ['termo(s)] *nm* Thermos ® (flask)
termostato [termo'stato] *nm* thermostat
ternero, a [ter'nero, a] *nm/f* (*animal*) calf ♦ *nf* (*carne*) veal
ternura [ter'nura] *nf* (*trato*) tenderness; (*palabra*) endearment; (*cariño*) fondness
terquedad [terke'ðað] *nf* obstinacy
terrado [te'rraðo] *nm* terrace
terraplén [terra'plen] *nm* embankment
terrateniente [terrate'njente] *nm/f* landowner
terraza [te'rraθa] *nf* (*balcón*) balcony; (*tejado*) (flat) roof; (*AGR*) terrace
terremoto [terre'moto] *nm* earthquake
terrenal [terre'nal] *adj* earthly
terreno [te'rreno] *nm* (*tierra*) land; (*parcela*) plot; (*suelo*) soil; (*fig*) field; **un ~** a piece of land

terrestre [te'rrestre] *adj* terrestrial; (*ruta*) land *cpd*
terrible [te'rriβle] *adj* terrible, awful
territorio [terri'torjo] *nm* territory
terrón [te'rron] *nm* (*de azúcar*) lump; (*de tierra*) clod, lump
terror [te'rror] *nm* terror; **~ífico, a** *adj* terrifying; **~ista** *adj, nm/f* terrorist
terso, a ['terso, a] *adj* (*liso*) smooth; (*pulido*) polished; **tersura** *nf* smoothness
tertulia [ter'tulja] *nf* (*reunión informal*) social gathering; (*grupo*) group, circle
tesis ['tesis] *nf inv* thesis
tesón [te'son] *nm* (*firmeza*) firmness; (*tenacidad*) tenacity
tesorero, a [teso'rero, a] *nm/f* treasurer
tesoro [te'soro] *nm* treasure; (*COM, POL*) treasury
testaferro [testa'ferro] *nm* figurehead
testamentario, a [testamen'tarjo, a] *adj* testamentary ♦ *nm/f* executor/executrix
testamento [testa'mento] *nm* will
testar [tes'tar] *vi* to make a will
testarudo, a [testa'ruðo, a] *adj* stubborn
testículo [tes'tikulo] *nm* testicle
testificar [testifi'kar] *vt* to testify; (*fig*) to attest ♦ *vi* to give evidence
testigo [tes'tiγo] *nm/f* witness; **~ de cargo/descargo** witness for the prosecution/defence; **~ ocular** eye witness
testimoniar [testimo'njar] *vt* to testify to; (*fig*) to show; **testimonio** *nm* testimony
teta ['teta] *nf* (*de biberón*) teat; (*ANAT: fam*) breast
tétanos ['tetanos] *nm* tetanus
tetera [te'tera] *nf* teapot
tétrico, a ['tetriko, a] *adj* gloomy, dismal
textil [teks'til] *adj* textile
texto ['teksto] *nm* text; **textual** *adj* textual
textura [teks'tura] *nf* (*de tejido*) texture
tez [teθ] *nf* (*cutis*) complexion
ti [ti] *pron* you; (*reflexivo*) yourself
tía ['tia] *nf* (*pariente*) aunt; (*fam*) chick, bird
tibieza [ti'βjeθa] *nf* (*temperatura*) tepidness; (*actitud*) coolness; **tibio, a** *adj* lukewarm
tiburón [tiβu'ron] *nm* shark

tic [tik] *nm* (*ruido*) click; (*de reloj*) tick; (*MED*): ~ **nervioso** nervous tic

tictac [tik'tak] *nm* (*de reloj*) tick tock

tiempo ['tjempo] *nm* time; (*época, período*) age, period; (*METEOROLOGÍA*) weather; (*LING*) tense; (*DEPORTE*) half; **a** ~ in time; **a un** *o* **al mismo** ~ at the same time; **al poco** ~ very soon (after); **se quedó poco** ~ he didn't stay very long; **hace poco** ~ not long ago; **mucho** ~ a long time; **de** ~ **en** ~ from time to time; **hace buen/mal** ~ the weather is fine/bad; **estar a** ~ to be in time; **hace** ~ some time ago; **hacer** ~ to while away the time; **motor de 2 ~s** two-stroke engine; **primer** ~ first half

tienda ['tjenda] *nf* shop, store; ~ **(de campaña)** tent; ~ **de alimentación** *o* **comestibles** grocer's (*BRIT*), grocery store (*US*)

tienes *etc vb ver* **tener**

tienta *etc* ['tjenta] *vb ver* **tentar** ♦ *nf*: **andar a ~s** to grope one's way along

tiento ['tjento] *vb ver* **tentar** ♦ *nm* (*tacto*) touch; (*precaución*) wariness

tierno, a ['tjerno, a] *adj* (*blando*) tender; (*fresco*) fresh; (*amable*) sweet

tierra ['tjerra] *nf* earth; (*suelo*) soil; (*mundo*) earth, world; (*país*) country, land; ~ **adentro** inland

tieso, a ['tjeso, a] *adj* (*rígido*) rigid; (*duro*) stiff; (*fam: orgulloso*) conceited

tiesto ['tjesto] *nm* flowerpot

tifoidea [tifoi'ðea] *nf* typhoid

tifón [ti'fon] *nm* typhoon

tifus ['tifus] *nm* typhus

tigre ['tivre] *nm* tiger

tijera [ti'xera] *nf* scissors *pl*; (*ZOOL*) claw; **~s** *nfpl* scissors; (*para plantas*) shears

tijeretear [tixere'tear] *vt* to snip

tila ['tila] *nf* lime blossom tea

tildar [til'dar] *vt*: ~ **de** to brand as

tilde ['tilde] *nf* (*TIP*) tilde

tilín [ti'lin] *nm* tinkle

tilo ['tilo] *nm* lime tree

timar [ti'mar] *vt* (*estafar*) to swindle

timbal [tim'bal] *nm* small drum

timbrar [tim'brar] *vt* to stamp

timbre ['timbre] *nm* (*sello*) stamp; (*campanilla*) bell; (*tono*) timbre; (*COM*) stamp duty

timidez [timi'ðeθ] *nf* shyness; **tímido, a** *adj* shy

timo ['timo] *nm* swindle

timón [ti'mon] *nm* helm, rudder; **timonel** *nm* helmsman

tímpano ['timpano] *nm* (*ANAT*) eardrum; (*MUS*) small drum

tina ['tina] *nf* tub; (*baño*) bath(tub); **tinaja** *nf* large jar

tinglado [tin'glaðo] *nm* (*cobertizo*) shed; (*fig: truco*) trick; (*intriga*) intrigue

tinieblas [ti'njeßlas] *nfpl* darkness *sg*; (*sombras*) shadows

tino ['tino] *nm* (*habilidad*) skill; (*juicio*) insight

tinta ['tinta] *nf* ink; (*TEC*) dye; (*ARTE*) colour

tinte ['tinte] *nm* dye

tintero [tin'tero] *nm* inkwell

tintinear [tintine'ar] *vt* to tinkle

tinto ['tinto] *nm* red wine

tintorería [tintore'ria] *nf* dry cleaner's

tintura [tin'tura] *nf* (*QUÍM*) dye; (*farmacéutico*) tincture

tío ['tio] *nm* (*pariente*) uncle; (*fam: individuo*) bloke (*BRIT*), guy

tiovivo [tio'ßißo] *nm* merry-go-round

típico, a ['tipiko, a] *adj* typical

tipo ['tipo] *nm* (*clase*) type, kind; (*hombre*) fellow; (*ANAT: de hombre*) build; (: *de mujer*) figure; (*IMPRENTA*) type; ~ **bancario/de descuento/de interés/de cambio** bank/discount/interest/exchange rate

tipografía [tipovra'fia] *nf* printing *cpd*; **tipográfico, a** *adj* printing *cpd*

tíquet ['tiket] (*pl* **~s**) *nm* ticket; (*en tienda*) cash slip

tiquismiquis [tikis'mikis] *nm inv* fussy person ♦ *nmpl* (*querellas*) squabbling *sg*; (*escrúpulos*) silly scruples

tira ['tira] *nf* strip; (*fig*) abundance; ~ **y afloja** give and take

tirabuzón [tiraßu'θon] *nm* (*rizo*) curl

tirachinas [tira'tʃinas] *nm inv* catapult

tirada [ti'raða] *nf* (*acto*) cast, throw; (*serie*) series; (*TIP*) printing, edition; **de una ~** at one go

tirado, a [ti'raðo, a] *adj* (*barato*) dirt-cheap; (*fam: fácil*) very easy

tirador [tira'ðor] *nm* (*mango*) handle

tiranía [tira'nia] *nf* tyranny; **tirano, a** *adj* tyrannical ♦ *nm/f* tyrant

tirante [ti'rante] *adj* (*cuerda etc*) tight, taut; (*relaciones*) strained ♦ *nm* (*ARQ*) brace; (*TEC*) stay; **~s** *nmpl* (*de pantalón*) braces (*BRIT*), suspenders (*US*); **tirantez** *nf* tightness; (*fig*) tension

tirar [ti'rar] *vt* to throw; (*dejar caer*) to drop; (*volcar*) to upset; (*derribar*) to knock down *o* over; (*desechar*) to throw out *o* away; (*dinero*) to squander; (*imprimir*) to print ♦ *vi* (*disparar*) to shoot; (*de la puerta etc*) to pull; (*fam: andar*) to go; (*tender a, buscar realizar*) to tend to; (*DEPORTE*) to shoot; **~se** *vr* to throw o.s.; **~ abajo** to bring down, destroy; **tira más a su padre** he takes more after his father; **ir tirando** to manage; **a todo ~** at the most

tirita [ti'rita] *nf* (sticking) plaster (*BRIT*), bandaid (*US*)

tiritar [tiri'tar] *vi* to shiver

tiro ['tiro] *nm* (*lanzamiento*) throw; (*disparo*) shot; (*DEPORTE*) shot; (*GOLF, TENIS*) drive; (*alcance*) range; **~ al blanco** target practice; **caballo de ~** cart-horse; **andar de ~s largos** to be all dressed up; **al ~** (*AM*) at once

tirón [ti'ron] *nm* (*sacudida*) pull, tug; **de un ~** in one go, all at once

tiroteo [tiro'teo] *nm* exchange of shots, shooting

tísico, a ['tisiko, a] *adj* consumptive

tisis ['tisis] *nf inv* consumption, tuberculosis

títere ['titere] *nm* puppet

titiritero, a [titiri'tero, a] *nm/f* puppeteer

titubeante [tituße'ante] *adj* (*al andar*) shaky, tottering; (*al hablar*) stammering; (*dudoso*) hesitant

titubear [tituße'ar] *vi* to stagger; to

stammer; (*fig*) to hesitate; **titubeo** *nm* staggering; stammering; hesitation

titulado, a [titu'laðo, a] *adj* (*libro*) entitled; (*persona*) titled

titular [titu'lar] *adj* titular ♦ *nm/f* holder ♦ *nm* headline ♦ *vt* to title; **~se** *vr* to be entitled; **título** *nm* title; (*de diario*) headline; (*certificado*) professional qualification; (*universitario*) (university) degree; **a título de** in the capacity of

tiza ['tiθa] *nf* chalk

tiznar [tiθ'nar] *vt* to blacken

tizón [ti'θon] *nm* brand

toalla [to'aʎa] *nf* towel

tobillo [to'βiʎo] *nm* ankle

tobogán [toβo'ɣan] *nm* (*montaña rusa*) roller-coaster; (*de niños*) chute, slide

tocadiscos [toka'ðiskos] *nm inv* record player

tocado, a [to'kaðo, a] *adj* (*fam*) touched ♦ *nm* headdress

tocador [toka'ðor] *nm* (*mueble*) dressing table; (*cuarto*) boudoir; (*fam*) ladies' toilet (*BRIT*) *o* room (*US*)

tocante [to'kante]: **~ a** *prep* with regard to

tocar [to'kar] *vt* to touch; (*MUS*) to play; (*referirse a*) to allude to; (*timbre*) to ring ♦ *vi* (*a la puerta*) to knock (on *o* at the door); (*ser de turno*) to fall to, be the turn of; (*ser hora*) to be due; **~se** *vr* (*cubrirse la cabeza*) to cover one's head; (*tener contacto*) to touch (each other); **por lo que a mí me toca** as far as I am concerned; **te toca a tí** it's your turn

tocayo, a [to'kajo, a] *nm/f* namesake

tocino [to'θino] *nm* bacon

todavía [toða'βia] *adv* (*aun*) even; (*aún*) still, yet; **~ más** yet more; **~ no** not yet

---

todo, a ['toðo, a] *adj* 1 (*con artículo sg*) all; **toda la carne** all the meat; **toda la noche** all night, the whole night; **~ el libro** the whole book; **toda una botella** a whole bottle; **~ lo contrario** quite the opposite; **está toda sucia** she's all dirty; **por ~ el país** throughout the whole

todopoderoso → torear

country

2 (*con artículo pl*) all; every; **~s los libros** all the books; **todas las noches** every night; **~s los que quieran salir** all those who want to leave

♦ *pron* **1** everything, all; **~s** everyone, everybody; **lo sabemos ~** we know everything; **~s querían más tiempo** everybody *o* everyone wanted more time; **nos marchamos ~s** all of us left

2: **con ~**: **con ~ él me sigue gustando** even so I still like him

♦ *adv* all; **vaya ~ seguido** keep straight on *o* ahead

♦ *nm*: **como un ~** as a whole; **del ~: no me agrada del ~** I don't entirely like it

todopoderoso, a [toðopoðe'roso, a] *adj* all powerful; (*REL*) almighty

toga ['toɣa] *nf* toga; (*ESCOL*) gown

Tokio ['tokjo] *n* Tokyo

toldo ['toldo] *nm* (*para el sol*) sunshade (*BRIT*), parasol; (*tienda*) marquee

tolerancia [tole'ranθja] *nf* tolerance; **tolerante** *adj* (*sociedad*) liberal; (*persona*) open-minded

tolerar [tole'rar] *vt* to tolerate; (*resistir*) to endure

toma ['toma] *nf* (*acto*) taking; (*MED*) dose; **~ (de corriente)** socket

tomar [to'mar] *vt* to take; (*aspecto*) to take on; (*beber*) to drink ♦ *vi* to take; (*AM*) to drink; **~se** *vr* to take; **~se por** to consider o.s. to be; **~ a bien/a mal** to take well/ badly; **~ en serio** to take seriously; **~ el pelo a alguien** to pull sb's leg; **~la con uno** to pick a quarrel with sb; **¡tome!** here you are!; **~ el sol** to sunbathe

tomate [to'mate] *nm* tomato

tomillo [to'miʎo] *nm* thyme

tomo ['tomo] *nm* (*libro*) volume

ton [ton] *abr* = **tonelada** ♦ *nm*: **sin ~ ni son** without rhyme or reason

tonada [to'naða] *nf* tune

tonalidad [tonali'ðað] *nf* tone

tonel [to'nel] *nm* barrel

tonelada [tone'laða] *nf* ton; **tonelaje** *nm* tonnage

tónica ['tonika] *nf* (*MUS*) tonic; (*fig*) keynote

tónico, a ['toniko, a] *adj* tonic ♦ *nm* (*MED*) tonic

tonificar [tonifi'kar] *vt* to tone up

tono ['tono] *nm* tone; **fuera de ~** inappropriate; **darse ~** to put on airs

tontería [tonte'ria] *nf* (*estupidez*) foolishness; (*cosa*) stupid thing; (*acto*) foolish act; **~s** *nfpl* (*disparates*) rubbish *sg*, nonsense *sg*

tonto, a ['tonto, a] *adj* stupid, silly ♦ *nm/f* fool

topar [to'par] *vi*: **~ contra** *o* **en** to run into; **~ con** to run up against

tope ['tope] *adj* maximum ♦ *nm* (*fin*) end; (*límite*) limit; (*FERRO*) buffer; (*AUTO*) bumper; **al ~** end to end

tópico, a ['topiko, a] *adj* topical ♦ *nm* platitude

topo ['topo] *nm* (*ZOOL*) mole; (*fig*) blunderer

topografía [topoɣra'fia] *nf* topography; **topógrafo, a** *nm/f* topographer

toque *etc* ['toke] *vb ver* **tocar** ♦ *nm* touch; (*MUS*) beat; (*de campana*) peal; **dar un ~ a** to warn; **~ de queda** curfew

toqué *vb ver* **tocar**

toquetear [tokete'ar] *vt* to finger

toquilla [to'kiʎa] *nf* (*pañuelo*) headscarf; (*chal*) shawl

tórax ['toraks] *nm* thorax

torbellino [torbe'ʎino] *nm* whirlwind; (*fig*) whirl

torcedura [torθe'ðura] *nf* twist; (*MED*) sprain

torcer [tor'θer] *vt* to twist; (*la esquina*) to turn; (*MED*) to sprain ♦ *vi* (*desviar*) to turn off; **~se** *vr* (*ladearse*) to bend; (*desviarse*) to go astray; (*fracasar*) to go wrong; **torcido, a** *adj* twisted; (*fig*) crooked ♦ *nm* curl

tordo, a ['torðo, a] *adj* dappled ♦ *nm* thrush

torear [tore'ar] *vt* (*fig: evadir*) to avoid; (*jugar con*) to tease ♦ *vi* to fight bulls;

toreo nm bullfighting; **torero, a** nm/f bullfighter

tormenta [tor'menta] nf storm; (fig: confusión) turmoil

tormento [tor'mento] nm torture; (fig) anguish

tornar [tor'nar] vt (devolver) to return, give back; (transformar) to transform ♦ vi to go back; **~se** vr (ponerse) to become

tornasolado, a [tornaso'laðo, a] adj (brillante) iridescent; (reluciente) shimmering

torneo [tor'neo] nm tournament

tornillo [tor'niʎo] nm screw

torniquete [torni'kete] nm (MED) tourniquet

torno ['torno] nm (TEC) winch; (tambor) drum; **en ~ (a)** round, about

toro ['toro] nm bull; (fam) he-man; **los ~s** bullfighting

toronja [to'ronxa] nf grapefruit

torpe ['torpe] adj (poco hábil) clumsy, awkward; (necio) dim; (lento) slow

torpedo [tor'peðo] nm torpedo

torpeza [tor'peθa] nf (falta de agilidad) clumsiness; (lentitud) slowness; (error) mistake

torre ['torre] nf tower; (de petróleo) derrick

torrefacto, a [torre'fakto, a] adj roasted

torrente [to'rrente] nm torrent

tórrido, a ['torriðo, a] adj torrid

torrija [to'rrixa] nf French toast

torsión [tor'sjon] nf twisting

torso ['torso] nm torso

torta ['torta] nf cake; (fam) slap

tortícolis [tor'tikolis] nm inv stiff neck

tortilla [tor'tiʎa] nf omelette; (AM) maize pancake; **~ francesa/española** plain/ potato omelette

tórtola ['tortola] nf turtledove

tortuga [tor'tuxa] nf tortoise

tortuoso, a [tor'twoso, a] adj winding

tortura [tor'tura] nf torture; **torturar** vt to torture

tos [tos] nf cough; **~ ferina** whooping cough

tosco, a ['tosko, a] adj coarse

toser [to'ser] vi to cough

tostada [tos'taða] nf piece of toast; **tostado, a** adj toasted; (por el sol) dark brown; (piel) tanned

tostador [tosta'ðor] nm toaster

tostar [tos'tar] vt to toast; (café) to roast; (persona) to tan; **~se** vr to get brown

total [to'tal] adj total ♦ adv in short; (al fin y al cabo) when all is said and done ♦ nm total; **~ que** to cut (BRIT) o make (US) a long story short

totalidad [totali'ðað] nf whole

totalitario, a [totali'tarjo, a] adj totalitarian

tóxico, a ['toksiko, a] adj toxic ♦ nm poison; **toxicómano, a** nm/f drug addict

toxina [to'ksina] nf toxin

tozudo, a [to'θuðo, a] adj obstinate

traba ['traβa] nf bond, tie; (cadena) shackle

trabajador, a [traβaxa'ðor, a] adj hard-working ♦ nm/f worker

trabajar [traβa'xar] vt to work; (AGR) to till; (empeñarse en) to work at; (convencer) to persuade ♦ vi to work; (esforzarse) to strive; **trabajo** nm work; (tarea) task; (POL) labour; (fig) effort; **tomarse el trabajo de** to take the trouble to; **trabajo por turno/a destajo** shift work/ piecework; **trabajoso, a** adj hard

trabalenguas [traβa'lengwas] nm inv tongue twister

trabar [tra'βar] vt (juntar) to join, unite; (atar) to tie down, fetter; (agarrar) to seize; (amistad) to strike up; **~se** vr to become entangled; **trabársele a uno la lengua** to be tongue-tied

tracción [trak'θjon] nf traction; **~ delantera/trasera** front-wheel/rear-wheel drive

tractor [trak'tor] nm tractor

tradición [traði'θjon] nf tradition; **tradicional** adj traditional

traducción [traðuk'θjon] nf translation

traducir [traðu'θir] vt to translate; **traductor, a** nm/f translator traer [tra'er] *vt* to bring; (*llevar*) to carry; (*llevar puesto*) to wear; (*incluir*) to carry; (*causar*) to cause; ~se *vr*: ~se algo to be up to sth

traficar [trafi'kar] *vi* to trade

tráfico ['trafiko] *nm* (COM) trade; (AUTO) traffic

tragaluz [traɣa'luθ] *nm* skylight

tragaperras [traɣa'perras] *nm o f inv* slot machine

tragar [tra'ɣar] *vt* to swallow; (*devorar*) to devour, bolt down; ~se *vr* to swallow

tragedia [tra'xeðja] *nf* tragedy; trágico, a *adj* tragic

trago ['traɣo] *nm* (*líquido*) drink; (*bocado*) gulp; (*fam: de bebida*) swig; (*desgracia*) blow

traición [trai'θjon] *nf* treachery; (JUR) treason; (*una* ~) act of treachery; traicionar *vt* to betray

traicionero, a [traiθjo'nero, a] *adj* treacherous

traidor, a [trai'ðor, a] *adj* treacherous ♦ *nm/f* traitor

traigo *etc vb ver* traer

traje ['traxe] *vb ver* traer ♦ *nm* (*de hombre*) suit; (*de mujer*) dress; (*vestido típico*) costume; ~ de baño swimsuit; ~ de luces bullfighter's costume

trajera *etc vb ver* traer

trajín [tra'xin] *nm* (*fam*) bustle; trajinar *vi* (*moverse*) to bustle about

trama ['trama] *nf* (*intriga*) plot; (*de tejido*) weft (BRIT), woof (US); tramar *vt* to plot; (TEC) to weave

tramitar [trami'tar] *vt* (*asunto*) to transact; (*negociar*) to negotiate

trámite ['tramite] *nm* (*paso*) step; (JUR) transaction; ~s *nmpl* (*burocracia*) procedure *sg*; (JUR) proceedings

tramo ['tramo] *nm* (*de tierra*) plot; (*de escalera*) flight; (*de vía*) section

tramoya [tra'moja] *nf* (TEATRO) piece of stage machinery; tramoyista *nm/f* scene shifter; (*fig*) trickster

trampa ['trampa] *nf* trap; (*en el suelo*) trapdoor; (*truco*) trick; (*engaño*) fiddle;

trampear *vt, vi* to cheat

trampolín [trampo'lin] *nm* (*de piscina etc*) diving board

tramposo, a [tram'poso, a] *adj* crooked, cheating ♦ *nm/f* crook, cheat

tranca ['tranka] *nf* (*palo*) stick; (*de puerta, ventana*) bar; trancar *vt* to bar

trance ['tranθe] *nm* (*momento difícil*) difficult moment *o* juncture; (*estado hipnotizado*) trance

tranquilidad [trankili'ðað] *nf* (*calma*) calmness, stillness; (*paz*) peacefulness

tranquilizar [trankili'θar] *vt* to calm (down); (*asegurar*) to reassure; ~se *vr* to calm down; tranquilo, a *adj* (*calmado*) calm; (*apacible*) peaceful; (*mar*) calm; (*mente*) untroubled

transacción [transak'θjon] *nf* transaction

transbordador [transβorða'ðor] *nm* ferry

transbordar [transβor'ðar] *vt* to transfer; transbordo *nm* transfer; hacer transbordo to change (trains *etc*)

transcurrir [transku'rrir] *vi* (*tiempo*) to pass; (*hecho*) to take place

transcurso [trans'kurso] *nm*: ~ del tiempo lapse (of time)

transeúnte [transe'unte] *nm/f* passer-by

transferencia [transfe'renθja] *nf* transference; (COM) transfer

transferir [transfe'rir] *vt* to transfer

transformador [transforma'ðor] *nm* (ELEC) transformer

transformar [transfor'mar] *vt* to transform; (*convertir*) to convert

tránsfuga [trans'fuɣa] *nm/f* (MIL) deserter; (POL) turncoat

transfusión [transfu'sjon] *nf* transfusion

transgénico, a [trans'xeniko, a] *adj* genetically modified, GM

transición [transi'θjon] *nf* transition

transigir [transi'xir] *vi* to compromise, make concessions

transitar [transi'tar] *vi* to go (from place to place); tránsito *nm* transit; (AUTO) traffic; transitorio, a *adj* transitory

transmisión [transmi'sjon] *nf* (TEC) transmission; (*transferencia*) transfer; ~ en

directo/exterior live/outside broadcast
transmitir [transmi'tir] *vt* to transmit; (*RADIO, TV*) to broadcast
transparencia [transpa'renθja] *nf* transparency; (*claridad*) clearness, clarity; (*foto*) slide
transparentar [transparen'tar] *vt* to reveal ♦ *vi* to be transparent; **transparente** *adj* transparent; (*claro*) clear
transpirar [transpi'rar] *vi* to perspire
transportar [transpor'tar] *vt* to transport; (*llevar*) to carry; **transporte** *nm* transport; (*COM*) haulage
transversal [transßer'sal] *adj* transverse, cross
tranvía [tram'bia] *nm* tram
trapecio [tra'peθjo] *nm* trapeze; **trapecista** *nm/f* trapeze artist
trapero, a [tra'pero, a] *nm/f* ragman
trapicheo [trapi'tʃeo] (*fam*) *nm* scheme, fiddle
trapo ['trapo] *nm* (*tela*) rag; (*de cocina*) cloth
tráquea ['trakea] *nf* windpipe
traqueteo [trake'teo] *nm* rattling
tras [tras] *prep* (*detrás*) behind; (*después*) after
trasatlántico [trasat'lantiko] *nm* (*barco*) (cabin) cruiser
trascendencia [trasθen'denθja] *nf* (*importancia*) importance; (*FILOSOFÍA*) transcendence
trascendental [trasθenden'tal] *adj* important; (*FILOSOFÍA*) transcendental
trascender [trasθen'der] *vi* (*noticias*) to come out; (*suceso*) to have a wide effect
trasero, a [tra'sero, a] *adj* back, rear ♦ *nm* (*ANAT*) bottom
trasfondo [tras'fondo] *nm* background
trasgredir [trasγre'ðir] *vt* to contravene
trashumante [trasu'mante] *adj* (*animales*) migrating
trasladar [trasla'ðar] *vt* to move; (*persona*) to transfer; (*postergar*) to postpone; (*copiar*) to copy; **~se** *vr* (*mudarse*) to move; **traslado** *nm* move; (*mudanza*) move, removal

traslucir [traslu'θir] *vt* to show; **~se** *vr* to be translucent; (*fig*) to be revealed
trasluz [tras'luθ] *nm* reflected light; **al ~** against *o* up to the light
trasnochador, a [trasnotʃa'ðor, a] *nm/f* night owl
trasnochar [trasno'tʃar] *vi* (*acostarse tarde*) to stay up late
traspapelar [traspape'lar] *vt* (*document, carta*) to mislay, misplace
traspasar [traspa'sar] *vt* (*suj: bala etc*) to pierce, go through; (*propiedad*) to sell, transfer; (*calle*) to cross over; (*límites*) to go beyond; (*ley*) to break; **traspaso** *nm* (*venta*) transfer, sale
traspié [tras'pje] *nm* (*tropezón*) trip; (*error*) blunder
trasplantar [trasplan'tar] *vt* to transplant
traste ['traste] *nm* (*MUS*) fret; **dar al ~ con algo** to ruin sth
trastero [tras'tero] *nm* storage room
trastienda [tras'tjenda] *nf* back of shop
trasto ['trasto] (*pey*) *nm* (*cosa*) piece of junk; (*persona*) dead loss
trastornado, a [trastor'naðo, a] *adj* (*loco*) mad, crazy
trastornar [trastor'nar] *vt* (*fig: planes*) to disrupt; (: *nervios*) to shatter; (: *persona*) to drive crazy; **~se** *vr* (*volverse loco*) to go mad *o* crazy; **trastorno** *nm* (*acto*) overturning; (*confusión*) confusion
tratable [tra'taßle] *adj* friendly
tratado [tra'taðo] *nm* (*POL*) treaty; (*COM*) agreement
tratamiento [trata'mjento] *nm* treatment; **~ de textos** (*INFORM*) word processing *cpd*
tratar [tra'tar] *vt* (*ocuparse de*) to treat; (*manejar, TEC*) to handle; (*MED*) to treat; (*dirigirse a: persona*) to address ♦ *vi*: **~ de** (*hablar sobre*) to deal with, be about; (*intentar*) to try to; **~se** *vr* to treat each other; **~ con** (*COM*) to trade in; (*negociar*) to negotiate with; (*tener contactos*) to have dealings with; **¿de qué se trata?** what's it about?; **trato** *nm* dealings *pl*; (*relaciones*) relationship; (*comportamiento*)

manner; (*COM*) agreement

trauma ['trauma] *nm* trauma

través [tra'ßes] *nm* (*fig*) reverse; **al ~** across, crossways; **a ~ de** across; (*sobre*) over; (*por*) through

travesaño [traße'saɲo] *nm* (*ARQ*) crossbeam; (*DEPORTE*) crossbar

travesía [traße'sia] *nf* (*calle*) cross-street; (*NAUT*) crossing

travesura [traße'sura] *nf* (*broma*) prank; (*ingenio*) wit

traviesa [tra'ßjesa] *nf* (*ARQ*) crossbeam

travieso, a [tra'ßjeso, a] *adj* (*niño*) naughty

trayecto [tra'jekto] *nm* (*ruta*) road, way; (*viaje*) journey; (*tramo*) stretch; **~ria** *nf* trajectory; (*fig*) path

traza ['traθa] *nf* (*aspecto*) looks *pl*; (*señal*) sign; **~do, a** *adj*: **bien ~do** shapely, well-formed ♦ *nm* (*ARQ*) plan, design; (*fig*) outline

trazar [tra'θar] *vt* (*ARQ*) to plan; (*ARTE*) to sketch; (*fig*) to trace; (*plan*) to draw up; **trazo** *nm* (*línea*) line; (*bosquejo*) sketch

trébol ['treßol] *nm* (*BOT*) clover

trece ['treθe] *num* thirteen

trecho ['tretʃo] *nm* (*distancia*) distance; (*de tiempo*) while; **de ~ en ~** at intervals

tregua ['treɣwa] *nf* (*MIL*) truce; (*fig*) respite

treinta ['treinta] *num* thirty

tremendo, a [tre'mendo, a] *adj* (*terrible*) terrible; (*imponente: cosa*) imposing; (*fam: fabuloso*) tremendous

trémulo, a ['tremulo, a] *adj* quivering

tren [tren] *nm* train; **~ de aterrizaje** undercarriage

trenca ['trenka] *nf* duffel coat

trenza ['trenθa] *nf* (*de pelo*) plait (*BRIT*), braid (*US*); **trenzar** *vt* (*pelo*) to plait, braid; **trenzarse** *vr* (*AM*) to become involved

trepadora [trepa'ðora] *nf* (*BOT*) climber

trepar [tre'par] *vt, vi* to climb

trepidante [trepi'ðante] *adj* (*acción*) fast; (*ritmo*) hectic

tres [tres] *num* three

tresillo [tre'siʎo] *nm* three-piece suite;

(*MUS*) triplet

treta ['treta] *nf* trick

triángulo ['trjangulo] *nm* triangle

tribu ['trißu] *nf* tribe

tribuna [tri'ßuna] *nf* (*plataforma*) platform; (*DEPORTE*) (grand)stand

tribunal [trißu'nal] *nm* (*JUR*) court; (*comisión, fig*) tribunal

tributar [trißu'tar] *vt* (*gen*) to pay; **tributo** *nm* (*COM*) tax

tricotar [triko'tar] *vi* to knit

trigal [tri'ɣal] *nm* wheat field

trigo ['triɣo] *nm* wheat

trigueño, a [tri'ɣeɲo, a] *adj* (*pelo*) corn-coloured

trillado, a [tri'ʎaðo, a] *adj* threshed; (*asunto*) trite, hackneyed; **trilladora** *nf* threshing machine

trillar [tri'ʎar] *vt* (*AGR*) to thresh

trimestral [trimes'tral] *adj* quarterly; (*ESCOL*) termly

trimestre [tri'mestre] *nm* (*ESCOL*) term

trinar [tri'nar] *vi* (*pájaros*) to sing; (*rabiar*) to fume, be angry

trinchar [trin'tʃar] *vt* to carve

trinchera [trin'tʃera] *nf* (*fosa*) trench

trineo [tri'neo] *nm* sledge

trinidad [trini'ðað] *nf* trio; (*REL*): **la T~** the Trinity

trino ['trino] *nm* trill

tripa ['tripa] *nf* (*ANAT*) intestine; (*fam: tb: ~s*) insides *pl*

triple ['triple] *adj* triple

triplicado, a [tripli'kaðo, a] *adj*: **por ~** in triplicate

tripulación [tripula'θjon] *nf* crew

tripulante [tripu'lante] *nm/f* crewman/woman

tripular [tripu'lar] *vt* (*barco*) to man; (*AUTO*) to drive

triquiñuela [triki'ɲwela] *nf* trick

tris [tris] *nm inv* crack; **en un ~** in an instant

triste ['triste] *adj* sad; (*lamentable*) sorry, miserable; **~za** *nf* (*aflicción*) sadness; (*melancolía*) melancholy

triturar [tritu'rar] *vt* (*moler*) to grind;

(*mascar*) to chew

triunfar [trjun'far] *vi* (*tener éxito*) to triumph; (*ganar*) to win; **triunfo** *nm* triumph

trivial [tri'ßjal] *adj* trivial; **~izar** *vt* to minimize, play down

triza ['triθa] *nf*: **hacer ~s** to smash to bits; (*papel*) to tear to shreds

trocar [tro'kar] *vt* to exchange

trocear [troθe'ar] *vt* (*carne, manzana*) to cut up, cut into pieces

trocha ['trotʃa] *nf* short cut

troche ['trotʃe]: **a ~ y moche** *adv* helter-skelter, pell-mell

trofeo [tro'feo] *nm* (*premio*) trophy; (*éxito*) success

tromba ['tromba] *nf* downpour

trombón [trom'bon] *nm* trombone

trombosis [trom'bosis] *nf inv* thrombosis

trompa ['trompa] *nf* horn; (*trompo*) humming top; (*hocico*) snout; (*fam*): **cogerse una ~** to get tight

trompazo [trom'paθo] *nm* bump, bang

trompeta [trom'peta] *nf* trumpet; (*clarín*) bugle

trompicón [trompi'kon]: **a ~es** *adv* in fits and starts

trompo ['trompo] *nm* spinning top

trompón [trom'pon] *nm* bump

tronar [tro'nar] *vt* (*AM*) to shoot ♦ *vi* to thunder; (*fig*) to rage

tronchar [tron'tʃar] *vt* (*árbol*) to chop down; (*fig: vida*) to cut short; (: *esperanza*) to shatter; (*persona*) to tire out; **~se** *vr* to fall down

tronco ['tronko] *nm* (*de árbol, ANAT*) trunk

trono ['trono] *nm* throne

tropa ['tropa] *nf* (*MIL*) troop; (*soldados*) soldiers *pl*

tropel [tro'pel] *nm* (*muchedumbre*) crowd

tropezar [trope'θar] *vi* to trip, stumble; (*error*) to slip up; **~ con** to run into; (*topar con*) to bump into; **tropezón** *nm* trip; (*fig*) blunder

tropical [tropi'kal] *adj* tropical

trópico ['tropiko] *nm* tropic

tropiezo [tro'pjeθo] *vb ver* **tropezar** ♦ *nm*

(*error*) slip, blunder; (*desgracia*) misfortune; (*obstáculo*) snag

trotamundos [trota'mundos] *nm inv* globetrotter

trotar [tro'tar] *vi* to trot; **trote** *nm* trot; (*fam*) travelling; **de mucho trote** hard-wearing

trozo ['troθo] *nm* bit, piece

trucha ['trutʃa] *nf* trout

truco ['truko] *nm* (*habilidad*) knack; (*engaño*) trick

trueno ['trweno] *nm* thunder; (*estampido*) bang

trueque *etc* ['trweke] *vb ver* **trocar** ♦ *nm* exchange; (*COM*) barter

trufa ['trufa] *nf* (*BOT*) truffle

truhán, ana [tru'an, ana] *nm/f* rogue

truncar [trun'kar] *vt* (*cortar*) to truncate; (*fig: la vida etc*) to cut short; (: *el desarrollo*) to stunt

tu [tu] *adj* your

tú [tu] *pron* you

tubérculo [tu'ßerkulo] *nm* (*BOT*) tuber

tuberculosis [tußerku'losis] *nf inv* tuberculosis

tubería [tuße'ria] *nf* pipes *pl*; (*conducto*) pipeline

tubo ['tußo] *nm* tube, pipe; **~ de ensayo** test tube; **~ de escape** exhaust (pipe)

tuerca ['twerka] *nf* nut

tuerto, a ['twerto, a] *adj* blind in one eye ♦ *nm/f* one-eyed person

tuerza *etc vb ver* **torcer**

tuétano ['twetano] *nm* marrow; (*BOT*) pith

tufo ['tufo] *nm* (*hedor*) stench

tul [tul] *nm* tulle

tulipán [tuli'pan] *nm* tulip

tullido, a [tu'ʎiðo, a] *adj* crippled

tumba ['tumba] *nf* (*sepultura*) tomb

tumbar [tum'bar] *vt* to knock down; **~se** *vr* (*echarse*) to lie down; (*extenderse*) to stretch out

tumbo ['tumbo] *nm*: **dar ~s** to stagger

tumbona [tum'bona] *nf* (*butaca*) easy chair; (*de playa*) deckchair (*BRIT*), beach chair (*US*)

tumor [tu'mor] *nm* tumour

tumulto [tuˈmulto] *nm* turmoil

tuna [ˈtuna] *nf* (*MUS*) student music group; *ver tb* **tuno**

---
tuna

A **tuna** *is a musical group made up of university students or former students who dress up in costumes from the "Edad de Oro", the Spanish Golden Age. These groups go through the town playing their guitars, lutes and tambourines and serenade the young ladies in the halls of residence or make impromptu appearances at weddings or parties singing traditional Spanish songs for a few* **pesetas**.

---

tunante [tuˈnante] *nm/f* rascal

tunda [ˈtunda] *nf* (*golpeo*) beating

túnel [ˈtunel] *nm* tunnel

Túnez [ˈtuneθ] *nm* Tunisia; (*ciudad*) Tunis

tuno, a [ˈtuno, a] *nm/f* (*fam*) rogue ♦ *nm* member of student music group

tupido, a [tuˈpiðo, a] *adj* (*denso*) dense; (*tela*) close-woven

turba [ˈturßa] *nf* crowd

turbante [turˈßante] *nm* turban

turbar [turˈßar] *vt* (*molestar*) to disturb; (*incomodar*) to upset; **~se** *vr* to be disturbed

turbina [turˈßina] *nf* turbine

turbio, a [ˈturßjo, a] *adj* cloudy; (*tema etc*) confused

turbulencia [turßuˈlenθja] *nf* turbulence; (*fig*) restlessness; **turbulento, a** *adj* turbulent; (*fig: intranquilo*) restless; (: *ruidoso*) noisy

turco, a [ˈturko, a] *adj* Turkish ♦ *nm/f* Turk

turismo [tuˈrismo] *nm* tourism; (*coche*) car; **turista** *nm/f* tourist; **turístico, a** *adj* tourist *cpd*

turnar [turˈnar] *vi* to take (it in) turns; **~se** *vr* to take (it in) turns; **turno** *nm* (*de trabajo*) shift; (*juegos etc*) turn

turquesa [turˈkesa] *nf* turquoise

Turquía [turˈkia] *nf* Turkey

turrón [tuˈrron] *nm* (*dulce*) nougat

tutear [tuteˈar] *vt* to address as familiar "tú"; **~se** *vr* to be on familiar terms

tutela [tuˈtela] *nf* (*legal*) guardianship; **tutelar** *adj* tutelary ♦ *vt* to protect

tutor, a [tuˈtor, a] *nm/f* (*legal*) guardian; (*ESCOL*) tutor

tuve *etc vb ver* **tener**

tuviera *etc vb ver* **tener**

tuyo, a [ˈtujo, a] *adj* yours, of yours ♦ *pron* yours; **un amigo ~** a friend of yours; **los ~s** (*fam*) your relations, your family

TV [ˈteˈße] *nf abr* (= *televisión*) TV

TVE *nf abr* = **Televisión Española**

U, u

u [u] *conj* or

ubicar [ußiˈkar] *vt* to place, situate; (*AM: encontrar*) to find; **~se** *vr* to lie, be located

ubre [ˈußre] *nf* udder

UCI *nf abr* (= *Unidad de Cuidados Intensivos*) ICU

Ud(s) *abr* = **usted(es)**

UE *nf abr* (= *Unión Europea*) EU

ufanarse [ufaˈnarse] *vr* to boast; **~ de** to pride o.s. on; **ufano, a** *adj* (*arrogante*) arrogant; (*presumido*) conceited

UGT *nf abr* = **Unión General de Trabajadores**

ujier [uˈxjer] *nm* usher; (*portero*) doorkeeper

úlcera [ˈulθera] *nf* ulcer

ulcerar [ulθeˈrar] *vt* to make sore; **~se** *vr* to ulcerate

ulterior [ulteˈrjor] *adj* (*más allá*) farther, further; (*subsecuente, siguiente*) subsequent

últimamente [ˈultimamente] *adv* (*recientemente*) lately, recently

ultimar [ultiˈmar] *vt* to finish; (*finalizar*) to finalize; (*AM: rematar*) to finish off

ultimátum [ultiˈmatum] (*pl* **~s**) ultimatum

último, a [ˈultimo, a] *adj* last; (*más reciente*) latest, most recent; (*más bajo*) bottom; (*más alto*) top; **en las últimas**

on one's last legs; **por ~** finally
ultra ['ultra] *adj* ultra ♦ *nm/f* extreme
right-winger
ultrajar [ultra'xar] *vt* (*ofender*) to outrage;
(*insultar*) to insult, abuse; **ultraje** *nm*
outrage; insult
ultramar [ultra'mar] *nm*: **de** *o* **en ~**
abroad, overseas
ultramarinos [ultrama'rinos] *nmpl*
groceries; **tienda de ~** grocer's (shop)
ultranza [ul'tranθa]: **a ~** *adv* (*a todo
trance*) at all costs; (*completo*) outright
ultratumba [ultra'tumba] *nf*: **la vida de ~**
the next life
umbral [um'bral] *nm* (*gen*) threshold
umbrío, a [um'brio, a] *adj* shady

PALABRA CLAVE

un, una [un, 'una] *art indef* a; (*antes de
vocal*) an; **una mujer/naranja** a woman/
an orange
♦ *adj*: **unos** (*o* **unas**): **hay unos regalos
para ti** there are some presents for you;
hay unas cervezas en la nevera there
are some beers in the fridge

---

unánime [u'nanime] *adj* unanimous;
unanimidad *nf* unanimity
undécimo, a [un'deθimo, a] *adj* eleventh
ungir [un'xir] *vt* to anoint
ungüento [un'gwento] *nm* ointment
únicamente ['unikamente] *adv* solely,
only
único, a ['uniko, a] *adj* only, sole; (*sin par*)
unique
unidad [uni'ðað] *nf* unity; (*COM, TEC etc*)
unit
unido, a [u'niðo, a] *adj* joined, linked; (*fig*)
united
unificar [unifi'kar] *vt* to unite, unify
uniformar [unifor'mar] *vt* to make
uniform, level up; (*persona*) to put into
uniform
uniforme [uni'forme] *adj* uniform, equal;
(*superficie*) even ♦ *nm* uniform;
uniformidad *nf* uniformity; (*de terreno*)
levelness, evenness

unilateral [unilate'ral] *adj* unilateral
unión [u'njon] *nf* union; (*acto*) uniting,
joining; (*unidad*) unity; (*TEC*) joint; **la U~
Europea** the European Union; **la U~
Soviética** the Soviet Union
unir [u'nir] *vt* (*juntar*) to join, unite; (*atar*)
to tie, fasten; (*combinar*) to combine; **~se**
vr to join together, unite; (*empresas*) to
merge
unísono [u'nisono] *nm*: **al ~** in unison
universal [uniβer'sal] *adj* universal;
(*mundial*) world *cpd*
universidad [uniβersi'ðað] *nf* university
universitario, a [uniβersi'tarjo, a] *adj*
university *cpd* ♦ *nm/f* (*profesor*) lecturer;
(*estudiante*) (university) student;
(*graduado*) graduate
universo [uni'βerso] *nm* universe

PALABRA CLAVE

uno, a ['uno, a] *adj* one; **es todo ~** it's all
one and the same; **~s pocos** a few; **~s
cien** about a hundred
♦ *pron* 1 one; **quiero sólo ~** I only want
one; **~ de ellos** one of them
2 (*alguien*) somebody, someone; **conozco
a ~ que se te parece** I know somebody
o someone who looks like you; **~ mismo**
oneself; **~s querían quedarse** some
(people) wanted to stay
3: **(los) ~s ... (los) otros ...** some ...
others; **una y otra son muy agradables**
they're both very nice
♦ *nf* one; **es la una** it's one o'clock
♦ *nm* (*number*) one

---

untar [un'tar] *vt* (*mantequilla*) to spread;
(*engrasar*) to grease, oil
uña ['uɲa] *nf* (*ANAT*) nail; (*garra*) claw;
(*casco*) hoof; (*arrancaclavos*) claw
uranio [u'ranjo] *nm* uranium
urbanidad [urβani'ðað] *nf* courtesy,
politeness
urbanismo [urβa'nismo] *nm* town
planning
urbanización [urβaniθa'θjon] *nf* (*barrio,
colonia*) housing estate

urbanizar [urβani'θar] vt (zona) to develop, urbanize

urbano, a [ur'βano, a] adj (de ciudad) urban; (cortés) courteous, polite

urbe ['urβe] nf large city

urdimbre [ur'ðimbre] nf (de tejido) warp; (intriga) intrigue

urdir [ur'ðir] vt to warp; (complot) to plot, contrive

urgencia [ur'xenθja] nf urgency; (prisa) haste, rush; (emergencia) emergency; servicios de ~ emergency services; "Urgencias" "Casualty"; urgente adj urgent

urgir [ur'xir] vi to be urgent; me urge I'm in a hurry for it

urinario, a [uri'narjo, a] adj urinary ♦ nm urinal

urna ['urna] nf urn; (POL) ballot box

urraca [u'rraka] nf magpie

URSS nf: la ~ the USSR

Uruguay [uru'ɣwai] nm: el ~ Uruguay; uruguayo, a adj, nm/f Uruguayan

usado, a [u'saðo, a] adj used; (de segunda mano) secondhand

usar [u'sar] vt to use; (ropa) to wear; (tener costumbre) to be in the habit of; ~se vr to be used; uso nm use; wear; (costumbre) usage, custom; (moda) fashion; al uso in keeping with custom; al uso de in the style of

usted [us'teð] pron (sg) you sg; (pl): ~es you pl

usual [u'swal] adj usual

usuario, a [usu'arjo, a] nm/f user

usura [u'sura] nf usury; usurero, a nm/f usurer

usurpar [usur'par] vt to usurp

utensilio [uten'siljo] nm tool; (CULIN) utensil

útero ['utero] nm uterus, womb

útil ['util] adj useful ♦ nm tool; utilidad nf usefulness; (COM) profit; utilizar vt to use, utilize

utopía [uto'pia] nf Utopia; utópico, a adj Utopian

uva ['uβa] nf grape

---

las uvas

In Spain **las uvas** *play a big part on New Year's Eve* **(Nochevieja)***, when on the stroke of midnight people gather at home, in restaurants or in the* **plaza mayor** *and eat a grape for each stroke of the clock of the* **Puerta del Sol** *in Madrid. It is said to bring luck for the following year.*

V, v

v abr (= voltio) v

va vb ver ir

vaca ['baka] nf (animal) cow; carne de ~ beef

vacaciones [baka'θjones] nfpl holidays

vacante [ba'kante] adj vacant, empty ♦ nf vacancy

vaciar [ba'θjar] vt to empty out; (ahuecar) to hollow out; (moldear) to cast; ~se vr to empty

vacilante [baθi'lante] adj unsteady; (habla) faltering; (dudoso) hesitant

vacilar [baθi'lar] vi to be unsteady; (al hablar) to falter; (dudar) to hesitate, waver; (memoria) to fail

vacío, a [ba'θio, a] adj empty; (puesto) vacant; (desocupado) idle; (vano) vain ♦ nm emptiness; (FÍSICA) vacuum; (un ~) (empty) space

vacuna [ba'kuna] nf vaccine; vacunar vt to vaccinate

vacuno, a [ba'kuno, a] adj cow cpd; ganado ~ cattle

vacuo, a ['bakwo, a] adj empty

vadear [baðe'ar] vt (río) to ford; vado nm ford

vagabundo, a [baɣa'βundo, a] adj wandering ♦ nm tramp

vagamente [baɣa'mente] adv vaguely

vagancia [ba'ɣanθja] nf (pereza) idleness, laziness

vagar [ba'ɣar] vi to wander; (no hacer

nada) to idle

vagina [ba'xina] *nf* vagina

vago, a ['baɣo, a] *adj* vague; (*perezoso*) lazy ♦ *nm/f* (*vagabundo*) tramp; (*flojo*) lazybones *sg*, idler

vagón [ba'ɣon] *nm* (FERRO: *de pasajeros*) carriage; (: *de mercancías*) wagon

vaguedad [baɣe'ðað] *nf* vagueness

vaho ['bao] *nm* (*vapor*) vapour, steam; (*respiración*) breath

vaina ['baina] *nf* sheath

vainilla [bai'niʎa] *nf* vanilla

vainita [bai'nita] (AM) *nf* green *o* French bean

vais *vb ver* ir

vaivén [bai'βen] *nm* to-and-fro movement; (*de tránsito*) coming and going; **vaivenes** *nmpl* (*fig*) ups and downs

vajilla [ba'xiʎa] *nf* crockery, dishes *pl*; **lavar la ~** to do the washing-up (BRIT), wash the dishes (US)

valdré *etc vb ver* valer

vale ['bale] *nm* voucher; (*recibo*) receipt; (*pagaré*) IOU

valedero, a [bale'ðero, a] *adj* valid

valenciano, a [balen'θjano, a] *adj* Valencian

valentía [balen'tia] *nf* courage, bravery

valer [ba'ler] *vt* to be worth; (MAT) to equal; (*costar*) to cost ♦ *vi* (*ser útil*) to be useful; (*ser válido*) to be valid; **~se** *vr* to take care of oneself; **~se de** to make use of, take advantage of; **~ la pena** to be worthwhile; **¿vale?** (ESP) OK?

valeroso, a [bale'roso, a] *adj* brave, valiant

valgo *etc vb ver* valer

valía [ba'lia] *nf* worth, value

validar [bali'ðar] *vt* to validate; validez *nf* validity; válido, a *adj* valid

valiente [ba'ljente] *adj* brave, valiant ♦ *nm* hero

valioso, a [ba'ljoso, a] *adj* valuable

valla ['baʎa] *nf* fence; (DEPORTE) hurdle; **~ publicitaria** hoarding; **vallar** *vt* to fence in

valle ['baʎe] *nm* valley

valor [ba'lor] *nm* value, worth; (*precio*) price; (*valentía*) valour, courage; (*importancia*) importance; **~es** *nmpl* (COM) securities; **~ar** *vt* to value

vals [bals] *nm inv* waltz

válvula ['balβula] *nf* valve

vamos *vb ver* ir

vampiro, resa [bam'piro, 'resa] *nm/f* vampire

van *vb ver* ir

vanagloriarse [banaɣlo'rjarse] *vr* to boast

vandalismo [banda'lismo] *nm* vandalism; vándalo, a *nm/f* vandal

vanguardia [ban'gwardja] *nf* vanguard; (ARTE *etc*) avant-garde

vanidad [bani'ðað] *nf* vanity; vanidoso, a *adj* vain, conceited

vano, a ['bano, a] *adj* vain

vapor [ba'por] *nm* vapour; (*vaho*) steam; **al ~** (CULIN) steamed; **~izador** *nm* atomizer; **~izar** *vt* to vaporize; **~oso, a** *adj* vaporous

vapulear [bapule'ar] *vt* to beat, thrash

vaquero, a [ba'kero, a] *adj* cattle *cpd* ♦ *nm* cowboy; **~s** *nmpl* (*pantalones*) jeans

vaquilla [ba'kiʎa] *nf* (ZOOL) heifer

vara ['bara] *nf* stick; (TEC) rod; **~ mágica** magic wand

variable [ba'rjaβle] *adj, nf* variable

variación [baria'θjon] *nf* variation

variar [bar'jar] *vt* to vary; (*modificar*) to modify; (*cambiar de posición*) to switch around ♦ *vi* to vary

varicela [bari'θela] *nf* chickenpox

varices [ba'riθes] *nfpl* varicose veins

variedad [barje'ðað] *nf* variety

varilla [ba'riʎa] *nf* stick; (BOT) twig; (TEC) rod; (*de rueda*) spoke

vario, a ['barjo, a] *adj* varied; **~s** various, several

varita [ba'rita] *nf*: **~ mágica** magic wand

varón [ba'ron] *nm* male, man; varonil *adj* manly, virile

Varsovia [bar'soβja] *n* Warsaw

vas *vb ver* ir

vasco, a ['basko, a] *adj, nm/f* Basque

vascongado, a [baskon'gaðo, a] *adj* Basque; **las Vascongadas** the Basque Country

vascuence [bas'kwenθe] *adj* = **vascongado**

vaselina [base'lina] *nf* Vaseline ®

vasija [ba'sixa] *nf* container, vessel

vaso ['baso] *nm* glass, tumbler; (*ANAT*) vessel

vástago ['bastaɣo] *nm* (*BOT*) shoot; (*TEC*) rod; (*fig*) offspring

vasto, a ['basto, a] *adj* vast, huge

Vaticano [bati'kano] *nm:* **el ~** the Vatican

vatio ['batjo] *nm* (*ELEC*) watt

vaya *etc vb ver* **ir**

Vd(s) *abr* = **usted(es)**

ve *vb ver* **ir; ver**

vecindad [beθin'dað] *nf* neighbourhood; (*habitantes*) residents *pl*

vecindario [beθin'darjo] *nm* neighbourhood; residents *pl*

vecino, a [be'θino, a] *adj* neighbouring ♦ *nm/f* neighbour; (*residente*) resident

veda ['beða] *nf* prohibition

vedar [be'ðar] *vt* (*prohibir*) to ban, prohibit; (*impedir*) to stop, prevent

vegetación [bexeta'θjon] *nf* vegetation

vegetal [bexe'tal] *adj, nm* vegetable

vegetariano, a [bexeta'rjano, a] *adj, nm/f* vegetarian

vehemencia [be(e)'menθja] *nf* vehemence; **vehemente** *adj* vehement

vehículo [be'ikulo] *nm* vehicle; (*MED*) carrier

veía *etc vb ver* **ver**

veinte ['beinte] *num* twenty

vejación [bexa'θjon] *nf* vexation; (*humillación*) humiliation

vejar [be'xar] *vt* (*irritar*) to annoy, vex; (*humillar*) to humiliate

vejez [be'xeθ] *nf* old age

vejiga [be'xiɣa] *nf* (*ANAT*) bladder

vela ['bela] *nf* (*de cera*) candle; (*NAUT*) sail; (*insomnio*) sleeplessness; (*vigilia*) vigil; (*MIL*) sentry duty; **estar a dos ~s** (*fam: sin dinero*) to be skint

velado, a [be'laðo, a] *adj* veiled; (*sonido*) muffled; (*FOTO*) blurred ♦ *nf* soirée

velar [be'lar] *vt* (*vigilar*) to keep watch over ♦ *vi* to stay awake; **~ por** to watch over, look after

velatorio [bela'torjo] *nm* (funeral) wake

veleidad [belei'ðað] *nf* (*ligereza*) fickleness; (*capricho*) whim

velero [be'lero] *nm* (*NAUT*) sailing ship; (*AVIAT*) glider

veleta [be'leta] *nf* weather vane

veliz [be'lis] (*AM*) *nm* suitcase

vello ['beʎo] *nm* down, fuzz

velo ['belo] *nm* veil

velocidad [beloθi'ðað] *nf* speed; (*TEC, AUTO*) gear

velocímetro [belo'θimetro] *nm* speedometer

veloz [be'loθ] *adj* fast

ven *vb ver* **venir**

vena ['bena] *nf* vein

venado [be'naðo] *nm* deer

vencedor, a [benθe'ðor, a] *adj* victorious ♦ *nm/f* victor, winner

vencer [ben'θer] *vt* (*dominar*) to defeat, beat; (*derrotar*) to vanquish; (*superar, controlar*) to overcome, master ♦ *vi* (*triunfar*) to win (through), triumph; (*plazo*) to expire; **vencido, a** *adj* (*derrotado*) defeated, beaten; (*COM*) due ♦ *adv:* **pagar vencido** to pay in arrears; **vencimiento** *nm* (*COM*) maturity

venda ['benda] *nf* bandage; **vendaje** *nm* bandage, dressing; **vendar** *vt* to bandage; **vendar los ojos** to blindfold

vendaval [benda'βal] *nm* (*viento*) gale

vendedor, a [bende'ðor, a] *nm/f* seller

vender [ben'der] *vt* to sell; **~ al contado/ al por mayor/al por menor** to sell for cash/wholesale/retail

vendimia [ben'dimja] *nf* grape harvest

vendré *etc vb ver* **venir**

veneno [be'neno] *nm* poison; (*de serpiente*) venom; **~so, a** *adj* poisonous; venomous

venerable [bene'raβle] *adj* venerable; **venerar** *vt* (*respetar*) to revere; (*adorar*) to worship venéreo, a [be'nereo, a] *adj*: **enfermedad venérea** venereal disease

venezolano, a [beneθo'lano, a] *adj* Venezuelan

Venezuela [bene'θwela] *nf* Venezuela

venganza [beŋ'ganθa] *nf* vengeance, revenge; vengar *vt* to avenge; **vengarse** *vr* to take revenge; vengativo, a *adj* (*persona*) vindictive

vengo *etc vb ver* venir

venia ['benja] *nf* (*perdón*) pardon; (*permiso*) consent

venial [be'njal] *adj* venial

venida [be'niða] *nf* (*llegada*) arrival; (*regreso*) return

venidero, a [beni'ðero, a] *adj* coming, future

venir [be'nir] *vi* to come; (*llegar*) to arrive; (*ocurrir*) to happen; (*fig*): ~ **de** to stem from; ~ **bien/mal** to be suitable/unsuitable; **el año que viene** next year; **~se abajo** to collapse

venta ['benta] *nf* (*COM*) sale; ~ **a plazos** hire purchase; ~ **al contado/al por mayor/al por menor** *o* **al detalle** cash sale/wholesale/retail; ~ **con derecho a retorno** sale or return; **"en ~"** "for sale"

ventaja [ben'taxa] *nf* advantage; ventajoso, a *adj* advantageous

ventana [ben'tana] *nf* window; ventanilla *nf* (*de taquilla*) window (*of booking office etc*)

ventilación [bentila'θjon] *nf* ventilation; (*corriente*) draught

ventilador [bentila'ðor] *nm* fan

ventilar [benti'lar] *vt* to ventilate; (*para secar*) to put out to dry; (*asunto*) to air, discuss

ventisca [ben'tiska] *nf* blizzard

ventrílocuo, a [ben'trilokwo, a] *nm/f* ventriloquist

ventura [ben'tura] *nf* (*felicidad*) happiness; (*buena suerte*) luck; (*destino*) fortune; **a la (buena)** ~ at random; venturoso, a *adj* happy; (*afortunado*) lucky, fortunate

veo *etc vb ver* ver

ver [ber] *vt* to see; (*mirar*) to look at, watch; (*entender*) to understand; (*investigar*) to look into; ♦ *vi* to see; to understand; **~se** *vr* (*encontrarse*) to meet; (*dejarse* ~) to be seen; (*hallarse: en un apuro*) to find o.s., be; **a** ~ let's see; **no tener nada que** ~ **con** to have nothing to do with; **a mi modo de** ~ as I see it

vera ['bera] *nf* edge, verge; (*de río*) bank

veracidad [beraθi'ðað] *nf* truthfulness

veranear [berane'ar] *vi* to spend the summer; veraneo *nm* summer holiday; veraniego, a *adj* summer *cpd*

verano [be'rano] *nm* summer

veras ['beras] *nfpl* truth *sg*; **de** ~ really, truly

veraz [be'raθ] *adj* truthful

verbal [ber'βal] *adj* verbal

verbena [ber'βena] *nf* (*baile*) open-air dance

verbo ['berβo] *nm* verb; ~so, a *adj* verbose

verdad [ber'ðað] *nf* truth; (*fiabilidad*) reliability; **de** ~ real, proper; **a decir** ~ to tell the truth; ~ero, a *adj* (*veraz*) true, truthful; (*fiable*) reliable; (*fig*) real

verde ['berðe] *adj* green; (*chiste*) blue, dirty ♦ *nm* green; **viejo** ~ dirty old man; ~ar *vi* to turn green; verdor *nm* greenness

verdugo [ber'ðuxo] *nm* executioner

verdulero, a [berðu'lero, a] *nm/f* greengrocer

verduras [ber'ðuras] *nfpl* (*CULIN*) greens

vereda [be'reða] *nf* path; (*AM*) pavement (*BRIT*), sidewalk (*US*)

veredicto [bere'ðikto] *nm* verdict

vergonzoso, a [berɣon'θoso, a] *adj* shameful; (*tímido*) timid, bashful

vergüenza [ber'ɣwenθa] *nf* shame, sense of shame; (*timidez*) bashfulness; (*pudor*) modesty; **me da** ~ I'm ashamed

verídico, a [be'riðiko, a] *adj* true, truthful

verificar [berifi'kar] *vt* to check; (*corroborar*) to verify; (*llevar a cabo*) to carry out; **~se** *vr* (*predicción*) to prove to be true

verja ['berxa] *nf* (*cancela*) iron gate; (*valla*)

iron railings pl; (de ventana) grille
vermut [ber'mut] (pl ~s) nm vermouth
verosímil [bero'simil] adj likely, probable;
(relato) credible
verruga [be'rruɣa] nf wart
versado, a [ber'saðo, a] adj: ~ en versed
in
versátil [ber'satil] adj versatile
versión [ber'sjon] nf version
verso ['berso] nm verse; un ~ a line of
poetry
vértebra ['berteβra] nf vertebra
verter [ber'ter] vt (líquido: adrede) to
empty, pour (out); (: sin querer) to spill;
(basura) to dump ♦ vi to flow
vertical [berti'kal] adj vertical
vértice ['bertiθe] nm vertex, apex
vertidos [ber'tiðos] nmpl waste sg
vertiente [ber'tjente] nf slope; (fig) aspect
vertiginoso, a [bertixi'noso, a] adj giddy,
dizzy
vértigo ['bertiɣo] nm vertigo; (mareo)
dizziness
vesícula [be'sikula] nf blister
vespino ® [bes'pino] nm o nf moped
vestíbulo [bes'tiβulo] nm hall; (de teatro)
foyer
vestido [bes'tiðo] pp de **vestir**; ~ de
azul/marinero dressed in blue/as a sailor
♦ nm (ropa) clothes pl, clothing; (de
mujer) dress, frock
vestigio [bes'tixjo] nm (huella) trace; ~s
nmpl (restos) remains
vestimenta [besti'menta] nf clothing
vestir [bes'tir] vt (poner: ropa) to put on;
(llevar: ropa) to wear; (proveer de ropa a)
to clothe; (suj: sastre) to make clothes for
♦ vi to dress; (verse bien) to look good;
~se vr to get dressed, dress o.s.
vestuario [bes'twarjo] nm clothes pl,
wardrobe; (TEATRO: cuarto) dressing room;
(DEPORTE) changing room
veta ['beta] nf (vena) vein, seam; (en carne)
streak; (de madera) grain
vetar [be'tar] vt to veto
veterano, a [bete'rano, a] adj, nm veteran
veterinaria [beteri'narja] nf veterinary

science; ver tb **veterinario**
veterinario, a [beteri'narjo, a] nm/f
vet(erinary surgeon)
veto ['beto] nm veto
vez [beθ] nf time; (turno) turn; a la ~ que
at the same time as; a su ~ in its turn;
otra ~ again; una ~ once; de una ~ in
one go; de una ~ para siempre once
and for all; en ~ de instead of; a o
algunas veces sometimes; una y otra ~
repeatedly; de ~ en cuando from time to
time; 7 veces 9 7 times 9; hacer las
veces de to stand in for; tal ~ perhaps
vía ['bia] nf track, route; (FERRO) line; (fig)
way; (ANAT) passage, tube ♦ prep via, by
way of; por ~ judicial by legal means;
por ~ oficial through official channels; en
~s de in the process of; ~ aérea airway;
V~ Láctea Milky Way; ~ pública public
road o thoroughfare
viable ['bjaβle] adj (solución, plan,
alternativa) feasible
viaducto [bja'ðukto] nm viaduct
viajante [bja'xante] nm commercial
traveller
viajar [bja'xar] vi to travel; **viaje** nm
journey; (gira) tour; (NAUT) voyage; **estar
de viaje** to be on a trip; **viaje de ida y
vuelta** round trip; **viaje de novios**
honeymoon; **viajero**, a adj travelling;
(ZOOL) migratory ♦ nm/f (quien viaja)
traveller; (pasajero) passenger
vial [bjal] adj road cpd, traffic cpd
víbora ['biβora] nf viper; (AM) poisonous
snake
vibración [biβra'θjon] nf vibration
vibrar [bi'βrar] vt, vi to vibrate
vicario [bi'karjo] nm curate
vicepresidente [biθepresi'ðente] nm/f
vice-president
viceversa [biθe'βersa] adv vice versa
viciado, a [bi'θjaðo, a] adj (corrompido)
corrupt; (contaminado) foul,
contaminated; **viciar** vt (pervertir) to
pervert; (JUR) to nullify; (estropear) to
spoil; **viciarse** vr to become corrupted
vicio ['biθjo] nm vice; (mala costumbre)

bad habit; **~so, a** adj (muy malo)
vicious; (corrompido) depraved ♦ nm/f
depraved person
vicisitud [biθisi'tuð] nf vicissitude
víctima ['biktima] nf victim
victoria [bik'torja] nf victory; **victorioso,
a** adj victorious
vid [bið] nf vine
vida ['biða] nf (gen) life; (duración) lifetime;
de por ~ for life; **en la/mi ~** never; **estar
con ~** to be still alive; **ganarse la ~** to
earn one's living
vídeo ['bideo] nm video ♦ adj inv:
película ~ video film; **videocámara** nf
camcorder; **videocasete** nm video cassette; **videoclub** nm video
club; **videojuego** nm video game
vidriero, a [bi'ðrjero, a] nm/f glazier ♦ nf
(ventana) stained-glass window; (AM: de
tienda) shop window; (puerta) glass door
vidrio ['biðrjo] nm glass
vieira ['bjeira] nf scallop
viejo, a ['bjexo, a] adj old ♦ nm/f old
man/woman; **hacerse ~** to get old
Viena ['bjena] n Vienna
vienes etc vb ver **venir**
vienés, esa [bje'nes, esa] adj Viennese
viento ['bjento] nm wind; **hacer ~** to be
windy
vientre ['bjentre] nm belly; (matriz) womb
viernes ['bjernes] nm inv Friday; **V~
Santo** Good Friday
Vietnam [bjet'nam] nm: **el ~** Vietnam;
vietnamita adj Vietnamese
viga ['biɣa] nf beam, rafter; (de metal)
girder
vigencia [bi'xenθja] nf validity; **estar en ~**
to be in force; **vigente** adj valid, in
force; (imperante) prevailing
vigésimo, a [bi'xesimo, a] adj twentieth
vigía [bi'xia] nm look-out
vigilancia [bixi'lanθja] nf: **tener a uno
bajo ~** to keep watch on sb
vigilar [bixi'lar] vt to watch over ♦ vi (gen)
to be vigilant; (hacer guardia) to keep
watch; **~ por** to take care of
vigilia [vi'xilja] nf wakefulness, being

awake; (REL) fast
vigor [bi'ɣor] nm vigour, vitality; **en ~** in
force; **entrar/poner en ~** to come/put
into effect; **~oso, a** adj vigorous
VIH nm abr (= virus de la
inmunodeficiencia humana) HIV; **~
positivo/negativo** HIV-positive/-negative
vil [bil] adj vile, low; **~eza** nf vileness;
(acto) base deed
vilipendiar [bilipen'djar] vt to vilify, revile
villa ['biʎa] nf (casa) villa; (pueblo) small
town; (municipalidad) municipality; **~
miseria** (AM) shantytown
villancico [biʎan'θiko] nm (Christmas)
carol
villorrio [bi'ʎorrjo] nm shantytown
vilo ['bilo]: **en ~** adv in the air, suspended;
(fig) on tenterhooks, in suspense
vinagre [bi'naɣre] nm vinegar
vinagreta [bina'ɣreta] nf vinaigrette,
French dressing
vinculación [binkula'θjon] nf (lazo) link,
bond; (acción) linking
vincular [binku'lar] vt to link, bind;
vínculo nm link, bond
vine etc vb ver **venir**
vinicultura [binikul'tura] nf wine growing
viniera etc vb ver **venir**
vino ['bino] vb ver **venir** ♦ nm wine; **~
blanco/tinto** white/red wine
viña ['bina] nf vineyard; **viñedo** nm
vineyard
viola ['bjola] nf viola
violación [bjola'θjon] nf violation; **~
(sexual)** rape
violar [bjo'lar] vt to violate; (sexualmente)
to rape
violencia [bjo'lenθja] nf violence, force;
(incomodidad) embarrassment; (acto
injusto) unjust act; **violentar** vt to force;
(casa) to break into; (agredir) to assault;
(violar) to violate; **violento, a** adj
violent; (furioso) furious; (situación)
embarrassing; (acto) forced, unnatural
violeta [bjo'leta] nf violet
violín [bjo'lin] nm violin
violón [bjo'lon] nm double bass

viraje [bi'raxe] *nm* turn; (*de vehículo*) swerve; (*fig*) change of direction; **virar** *vi* to change direction

virgen ['birxen] *adj, nf* virgin

Virgo ['birxo] *nm* Virgo

viril [bi'ril] *adj* virile; **~idad** *nf* virility

virtud [bir'tuð] *nf* virtue; **en ~ de** by virtue of; **virtuoso, a** *adj* virtuous ♦ *nm/f* virtuoso

viruela [bi'rwela] *nf* smallpox

virulento, a [biru'lento, a] *adj* virulent

virus ['birus] *nm inv* virus

visa ['bisa] (*AM*) *nf* = **visado**

visado [bi'saðo] *nm* visa

víscera ['bisθera] (*ANAT, ZOOL*) gut, bowel; **~s** *nfpl* entrails

visceral [bisθe'ral] *adj* (*odio*) intense; **reacción ~** gut reaction

viscoso, a [bis'koso, a] *adj* viscous

visera [bi'sera] *nf* visor

visibilidad [bisiβili'ðað] *nf* visibility; **visible** *adj* visible; (*fig*) obvious

visillos [bi'siʎos] *nmpl* lace curtains

visión [bi'sjon] *nf* (*ANAT*) vision, (eye)sight; (*fantasía*) vision, fantasy

visita [bi'sita] *nf* call, visit; (*persona*) visitor; **hacer una ~** to pay a visit

visitar [bisi'tar] *vt* to visit, call on

vislumbrar [bislum'brar] *vt* to glimpse, catch a glimpse of

viso ['biso] *nm* (*del metal*) glint, gleam; (*de tela*) sheen; (*aspecto*) appearance

visón [bi'son] *nm* mink

visor [bi'sor] *nm* (*FOTO*) viewfinder

víspera ['bispera] *nf*: **la ~ de ...** the day before ...

vista ['bista] *nf* sight, vision; (*capacidad de ver*) (eye)sight; (*mirada*) look(s) (*pl*); **a primera ~** at first glance; **hacer la ~ gorda** to turn a blind eye; **volver la ~** to look back; **está a la ~ que** it's obvious that; **en ~ de** in view of; **en ~ de que** in view of the fact that; **¡hasta la ~!** so long!, see you!; **con ~s a** with a view to; **~zo** *nm* glance; **dar o echar un ~zo a** to glance at

visto, a ['bisto, a] *pp de* **ver** ♦ *vb ver tb*

vestir ♦ *adj* seen; (*considerado*) considered ♦ *nm*: **~ bueno** approval; **"~ bueno"** "approved"; **por lo ~** apparently; **está ~ que** it's clear that; **está bien/mal ~** it's acceptable/unacceptable; **~ que** since, considering that

vistoso, a [bis'toso, a] *adj* colourful

visual [bi'swal] *adj* visual

vital [bi'tal] *adj* life *cpd*, living *cpd*; (*fig*) vital; (*persona*) lively, vivacious; **~icio, a** *adj* for life; **~idad** *nf* (*de persona, negocio*) energy; (*de ciudad*) liveliness

vitamina [bita'mina] *nf* vitamin

viticultor, a [bitikul'tor, a] *nm/f* wine grower; **viticultura** *nf* wine growing

vitorear [bitore'ar] *vt* to cheer, acclaim

vitrina [bi'trina] *nf* show case; (*AM*) shop window

viudez [bju'ðeθ] *nf* widowhood

viudo, a ['bjuðo, a] *nm/f* widower/widow

viva ['biβa] *excl* hurrah!; **¡~ el rey!** long live the king!

vivacidad [biβaθi'ðað] *nf* (*vigor*) vigour; (*vida*) liveliness

vivaracho, a [biβa'ratʃo, a] *adj* jaunty, lively; (*ojos*) bright, twinkling

vivaz [bi'βaθ] *adj* lively

víveres ['biβeres] *nmpl* provisions

vivero [bi'βero] *nm* (*para plantas*) nursery; (*para peces*) fish farm; (*fig*) hotbed

viveza [bi'βeθa] *nf* liveliness; (*agudeza: mental*) sharpness

vivienda [bi'βjenda] *nf* housing; (*una ~*) house; (*piso*) flat (*BRIT*), apartment (*US*)

viviente [bi'βjente] *adj* living

vivir [bi'βir] *vt, vi* to live ♦ *nm* life, living

vivo, a ['biβo, a] *adj* living, alive; (*fig: descripción*) vivid; (*persona: astuto*) smart, clever; **en ~** (*transmisión etc*) live

vocablo [bo'kaβlo] *nm* (*palabra*) word; (*término*) term

vocabulario [bokaβu'larjo] *nm* vocabulary

vocación [boka'θjon] *nf* vocation; **vocacional** (*AM*) *nf* ≈ technical college

vocal [bo'kal] *adj* vocal ♦ *nf* vowel; **~izar** *vt* to vocalize

vocear [boθe'ar] *vt* (*para vender*) to cry;

(*aclamar*) to acclaim; (*fig*) to proclaim
♦ *vi* to yell; **vocerío** *nm* shouting
vocero [boˈθero] *nm/f* spokesman/woman
voces [ˈboθes] *pl de* **voz**
vociferar [boθifeˈrar] *vt* to shout ♦ *vi* to
yell
vodka [ˈboðka] *nm o f* vodka
vol *abr* = **volumen**
volador, a [bolaˈðor, a] *adj* flying
volandas [boˈlandas]: **en ~** *adv* in the air
volante [boˈlante] *adj* flying ♦ *nm* (*de
coche*) steering wheel; (*de reloj*) balance
volar [boˈlar] *vt* (*edificio*) to blow up ♦ *vi*
to fly
volátil [boˈlatil] *adj* volatile
volcán [bolˈkan] *nm* volcano; **~ico, a** *adj*
volcanic
volcar [bolˈkar] *vt* to upset, overturn;
(*tumbar, derribar*) to knock over; (*vaciar*)
to empty out ♦ *vi* to overturn; **~se** *vr* to
tip over
voleibol [boleiˈβol] *nm* volleyball
volqué *etc vb ver* **volcar**
voltaje [bolˈtaxe] *nm* voltage
voltear [bolteˈar] *vt* to turn over; (*volcar*)
to turn upside down
voltereta [bolteˈreta] *nf* somersault
voltio [ˈboltjo] *nm* volt
voluble [boˈluβle] *adj* fickle
volumen [boˈlumen] (*pl* **volúmenes**) *nm*
volume; **voluminoso, a** *adj*
voluminous; (*enorme*) massive
voluntad [bolunˈtað] *nf* will; (*resolución*)
willpower; (*deseo*) desire, wish
voluntario, a [bolunˈtarjo, a] *adj*
voluntary ♦ *nm/f* volunteer
voluntarioso, a [boluntaˈrjoso, a] *adj*
headstrong
voluptuoso, a [bolupˈtwoso, a] *adj*
voluptuous
volver [bolˈβer] *vt* (*gen*) to turn; (*dar
vuelta a*) to turn (over); (*voltear*) to turn
round, turn upside down; (*poner al revés*)
to turn inside out; (*devolver*) to return
♦ *vi* to return, go back, come back; **~se**
vr to turn round; **~ la espalda** to turn
one's back; **~ triste** *etc* **a uno** to make sb

sad *etc*; **~ a hacer** to do again; **~ en sí** to
come to; **~se insoportable/muy caro** to
get *o* become unbearable/very expensive;
~se loco to go mad
vomitar [bomiˈtar] *vt, vi* to vomit;
vómito *nm* vomit
voraz [boˈraθ] *adj* voracious
vos [bos] (*AM*) *pron* you
vosotros, as [boˈsotros, as] *pron* you;
(*reflexivo*): **entre/para ~** among/for
yourselves
votación [botaˈθjon] *nf* (*acto*) voting;
(*voto*) vote
votar [boˈtar] *vi* to vote; **voto** *nm* vote;
(*promesa*) vow; **votos** (*good*) wishes
voy *vb ver* **ir**
voz [boθ] *nf* voice; (*grito*) shout; (*rumor*)
rumour; (*LING*) word; **dar voces** to shout,
yell; **a media ~** in a low voice; **a ~ en
cuello** *o* **en grito** at the top of one's
voice; **de viva ~** verbally; **en ~ alta** aloud;
~ de mando command
vuelco [ˈbwelko] *vb ver* **volcar** ♦ *nm* spill,
overturning
vuelo [ˈbwelo] *vb ver* **volar** ♦ *nm* flight;
(*encaje*) lace, frill; **coger al ~** to catch in
flight; **~ charter/regular** charter/
scheduled flight; **~ libre** (*DEPORTE*) hang-
gliding
vuelque *etc vb ver* **volcar**
vuelta [ˈbwelta] *nf* (*gen*) turn; (*curva*)
bend, curve; (*regreso*) return; (*revolución*)
revolution; (*de circuito*) lap; (*de papel,
tela*) reverse; (*cambio*) change; **a la ~** on
one's return; **a ~ de correo** by return of
post; **dar ~s** (*suj: cabeza*) to spin; **dar ~s
a una idea** to turn over an idea (in one's
head); **estar de ~** to be back; **dar una ~**
to go for a walk; (*en coche*) to go for a
drive; **~ ciclista** (*DEPORTE*) (cycle) tour
vuelto *pp de* **volver**
vuelvo *etc vb ver* **volver**
vuestro, a [ˈbwestro, a] *adj* your; **un
amigo ~** a friend of yours ♦ *pron*: **el ~/la
vuestra, los ~s/las vuestras** yours
vulgar [bulˈvar] *adj* (*ordinario*) vulgar;
(*común*) common; **~idad** *nf*

commonness; (*acto*) vulgarity; (*expresión*) coarse expression; **~izar** *vt* to popularize
vulgo ['bulxo] *nm* common people
vulnerable [bulne'raßle] *adj* vulnerable
vulnerar [bulne'rar] *vt* (*ley, acuerdo*) to violate, breach; (*derechos, intimidad*) to violate; (*reputación*) to damage

W, w

Walkman ® [wak'man] *nm* Walkman ®
wáter ['bater] *nm* toilet
whisky ['wiski] *nm* whisky, whiskey

X, x

xenofobia [kseno'foßja] *nf* xenophobia
xilófono [ksi'lofono] *nm* xylophone

Y, y

y [i] *conj* and
ya [ja] *adv* (*gen*) already; (*ahora*) now; (*en seguida*) at once; (*pronto*) soon ♦ *excl* all right! ♦ *conj* (*ahora que*) now that; **~ lo sé** I know; **~ que** since
yacer [ja'θer] *vi* to lie
yacimiento [jaθi'mjento] *nm* (*de mineral*) deposit; (*arqueológico*) site
yanqui ['janki] *adj, nm/f* Yankee
yate ['jate] *nm* yacht
yazco *etc vb ver* **yacer**
yedra ['jeðra] *nf* ivy
yegua ['jexwa] *nf* mare
yema ['jema] *nf* (*del huevo*) yolk; (*BOT*) leaf bud; (*fig*) best part; **~ del dedo** fingertip
yergo *etc vb ver* **erguir**
yermo, a ['jermo, a] *adj* (*estéril, fig*) barren ♦ *nm* wasteland
yerno ['jerno] *nm* son-in-law
yerro *etc vb ver* **errar**
yeso ['jeso] *nm* plaster
yo [jo] *pron* I; **soy ~** it's me, it is I

yodo ['joðo] *nm* iodine
yoga ['joxa] *nm* yoga
yogur(t) [jo'xur(t)] *nm* yoghurt
yugo ['juxo] *nm* yoke
Yugoslavia [juxos'laßja] *nf* Yugoslavia
yugular [juxu'lar] *adj* jugular
yunque ['junke] *nm* anvil
yunta ['junta] *nf* yoke
yuxtaponer [jukstapo'ner] *vt* to juxtapose; **yuxtaposición** *nf* juxtaposition

Z, z

zafar [θa'far] *vt* (*soltar*) to untie; (*superficie*) to clear; **~se** *vr* (*escaparse*) to escape; (*TEC*) to slip off
zafio, a ['θafjo, a] *adj* coarse
zafiro [θa'firo] *nm* sapphire
zaga ['θaxa] *nf*: **a la ~** behind, in the rear
zaguán [θa'xwan] *nm* hallway
zaherir [θae'rir] *vt* (*criticar*) to criticize
zaino, a ['θaino, a] *adj* (*caballo*) chestnut
zalamería [θalame'ria] *nf* flattery; **zalamero, a** *adj* flattering; (*cobista*) suave
zamarra [θa'marra] *nf* (*chaqueta*) sheepskin jacket
zambullirse [θambu'ʎirse] *vr* to dive
zampar [θam'par] *vt* to gobble down
zanahoria [θana'orja] *nf* carrot
zancada [θan'kaða] *nf* stride
zancadilla [θanka'ðiʎa] *nf* trip
zanco ['θanko] *nm* stilt
zancudo, a [θan'kuðo, a] *adj* long-legged ♦ *nm* (*AM*) mosquito
zángano ['θangano] *nm* drone
zanja ['θanxa] *nf* ditch; **zanjar** *vt* (*resolver*) to resolve
zapata [θa'pata] *nf* (*MECÁNICA*) shoe
zapatear [θapate'ar] *vi* to tap with one's feet
zapatería [θapate'ria] *nf* (*oficio*) shoemaking; (*tienda*) shoe shop; (*fábrica*) shoe factory; **zapatero, a** *nm/f*

shoemaker

zapatilla [θapa'tiʎa] *nf* slipper; ~ **de deporte** training shoe

zapato [θa'pato] *nm* shoe

zapping ['θapin] *nm* channel-hopping; **hacer ~** to flick through the channels

zar [θar] *nm* tsar, czar

zarandear [θarande'ar] *(fam) vt* to shake vigorously

zarpa ['θarpa] *nf (garra)* claw

zarpar [θar'par] *vi* to weigh anchor

zarza ['θarθa] *nf (BOT)* bramble; **zarzal** *nm (matorral)* bramble patch

zarzamora [θarθa'mora] *nf* blackberry

zarzuela [θar'θwela] *nf* Spanish light opera

zigzag [θiɣ'θaɣ] *nm* zigzag; **zigzaguear** *vi* to zigzag

zinc [θink] *nm* zinc

zócalo ['θokalo] *nm (ARQ)* plinth, base

zodíaco [θo'ðiako] *nm (ASTRO)* zodiac

zona ['θona] *nf* zone; ~ **fronteriza** border area; ~ **(del) euro** Euroland

zoo ['θoo] *nm* zoo

zoología [θoolo'xia] *nf* zoology; **zoológico, a** *adj* zoological ♦ *nm (tb:* **parque ~)** zoo; **zoólogo, a** *nm/f* zoologist

zoom [θum] *nm* zoom lens

zopilote [θopi'lote] *(AM) nm* buzzard

zoquete [θo'kete] *nm (fam)* blockhead

zorro, a ['θorro, a] *adj* crafty ♦ *nm/f* fox/vixen

zozobra [θo'θoßra] *nf (fig)* anxiety; **zozobrar** *vi (hundirse)* to capsize; *(fig)* to fail

zueco ['θweko] *nm* clog

zumbar [θum'bar] *vt (golpear)* to hit ♦ *vi* to buzz; **zumbido** *nm* buzzing

zumo ['θumo] *nm* juice

zurcir [θur'θir] *vt (coser)* to darn

zurdo, a ['θurðo, a] *adj (persona)* left-handed

zurrar [θu'rrar] *(fam) vt* to wallop

USING YOUR COLLINS POCKET DICTIONARY

Supplement by
Roy Simon
reproduced by kind permission of
Tayside Region Education Department

USING YOUR COLLINS POCKET DICTIONARY

Introduction

We are delighted that you have decided to invest in this Collins Pocket Dictionary! Whether you intend to use it in school, at home, on holiday or at work, we are sure that you will find it very useful.

The purpose of this supplement is to help you become aware of the wealth of vocabulary and grammatical information your dictionary contains, to explain how this information is presented and also to point out some of the traps one can fall into when using a Spanish-English English-Spanish dictionary.

In the pages which follow you will find explanations and wordgames (not too difficult!) designed to give you practice in exploring the dictionary's contents and in retrieving information for a variety of purposes. Answers are provided at the end. If you spend a little time on these pages you should be able to use your dictionary more efficiently and effectively. Have fun!

Contents

i

HOW INFORMATION IS PRESENTED IN YOUR DICTIONARY

A great deal of information is packed into your Collins Pocket Dictionary using colour, various typefaces, sizes of type, symbols, abbreviations and brackets. The purpose of this section is to acquaint you with the conventions used in presenting information.

Headwords

A headword is the word you look up in a dictionary. Headwords are listed in alphabetical order throughout the dictionary. They are printed in colour so that they stand out clearly from all the other words on the dictionary page.

Note that at the top of each page two headwords appear. These tell you which is the first and last word dealt with on the page in question. They are there to help you scan through the dictionary more quickly.

The Spanish alphabet consists of 27 letters: the same 26 letters as the English alphabet, in the same order, plus 'ñ', which comes after letter 'n'. You will need to remember that words containing this letter will be listed slightly differently from what you would expect according to English alphabetical order: thus 'caña' does not come immediately after 'cana', but follows the last word beginning with 'can-' in the list, namely 'canuto'.

Where two Spanish words are distinguished only by an accent, the accented form follows the unaccented, e.g. 'de', 'dé'.

A dictionary entry

An entry is made up of a headword and all the information about that headword. Entries will be short or long depending on how frequently a word is used in either English or Spanish and how many meanings it has. Inevitably, the fuller the dictionary entry the more care is needed in sifting through it to find the information you require.

Meanings

The translations of a headword are given in ordinary type. Where there is more than one meaning or usage, a semi-colon separates one from the other.

completo, a [kom'pleto, a] *adj* complete; (*perfecto*) perfect; (*lleno*) full ♦ *nm* full complement

complicado, a [kompli'kaðo, a] *adj* complicated; **estar ~ en** to be mixed up in

cómplice ['kompliθe] *nm/f* accomplice

complot [kom'plo(t)] (*pl* **~s**) *nm* plot

aiming; (*destreza*) marksmanship

puntero, a [pun'tero, a] *adj* leading ♦ *nm* (*palo*) pointer

puntiagudo, a [puntja'ɣuðo, a] *adj* sharp, pointed

puntilla [pun'tiʎa] *nf* (*encaje*) lace edging

puritano, a [puri'tano, a] *adj* (*actitud*) puritanical; (*iglesia, tradición*) puritan ♦ *nm/f* puritan

puro, a ['puro, a] *adj* pure; (*verdad*) simple, plain ♦ *adv*: **de ~ cansado** out of sheer tiredness ♦ *nm* cigar

nevar [ne'ɣar] *vi* to snow

cuenta *etc* ['kwenta] *vb ver* **contar** ♦ *nf* (*cálculo*) count, counting; (*en café, restaurante*) bill (*BRIT*), check (*US*); (*COM*) account; (*de collar*) bead; **a fin de ~s** in the end; **caer en la ~** to catch on; **darse ~ de** to realize; **tener en ~** to bear in mind; **echar ~s** to take stock; **~ corriente/de ahorros** current/savings account; **~ atrás** countdown; **~kilómetros** *nm inv* ≈ milometer; (*de velocidad*) speedometer

titubear [titu'ße'ar] *vi* to stagger; to stammer; (*fig*) to hesitate; **titubeo** *nm* staggering; stammering; hesitation

iii

In addition, you will often find other words appearing in *italics* in brackets before the translations. These either give some notion of the contexts in which the headword might appear (as with 'lane' opposite – 'lane in the country', 'lane in a race', etc.) or else they provide synonyms (as with 'hit' opposite – 'strike', 'reach', etc.).

Phonetic spellings

The phonetic spelling of each headword – i.e. its pronunciation – is given in square brackets immediately after it. The phonetic transcription of Spanish and English vowels and consonants is given on pages viii to xi at the front of your dictionary.

Additional information about headwords

Information about the usage or form of certain headwords is given in brackets between the phonetics and the translation or translations. Have a look at the entries for 'COU', 'cuenca', 'mast', 'R.S.V.P.' and 'burro' opposite.

This information is usually given in abbreviated form. A helpful list of abbreviations is given on pages vi and vii at the front of your dictionary.

You should be particularly careful with colloquial words or phrases. Words labelled (*fam*) would not normally be used in formal speech, while those labelled (*fam!*) would be considered offensive.

Careful consideration of such style labels will help indicate the degree of formality and appropriateness of a word and could help you avoid many an embarrassing situation when using Spanish!

Expressions in which the headword appears

An entry will often feature certain common expressions in which the headword appears. These expressions are in **bold** type, but in black as opposed to colour. A swung dash (~) is used instead of repeating a headword in an entry. 'Tono' and 'mano' opposite illustrate this point.

Related words

In the Pocket Dictionary words related to certain headwords are sometimes given at the end of an entry, as with 'ambición' and 'accept' opposite. These are easily picked out as they are also in colour. To help you find these words, they are placed in alphabetical order after the headword to which they belong: cf. 'accept', 'general' opposite.

lane [leɪn] *n* (*in country*) camino; (*AUT*) carril *m*; (*in race*) calle *f*

hit [hɪt] (*pt, pp* **hit**) *vt* (*strike*) golpear, pegar; (*reach: target*) alcanzar; (*collide with: car*) chocar contra; (*fig: affect*) afectar ♦ *n* golpe *m*; (*success*) éxito; **to ~ it off with sb** llevarse bien con uno; **~-and-run driver** *n* conductor(a) que atropella y huye

embrollar [embro'ʎar] *vt* (*el asunto*) to confuse, complicate; (*implicar*) to involve, embroil; **~se** *vr* (*confundirse*) to get into a muddle *o* mess

repoblación [repoβla'θjon] *nf* repopulation; (*de río*) restocking; **~ forestal** reafforestation

COU [kou] (*ESP*) *nm abr* (= *Curso de Orientación Universitaria*) 1 *year course leading to final school-leaving certificate and university entrance examinations*

cuenca ['kwenka] *nf* (*ANAT*) eye socket; (*GEO*) bowl, deep valley

mast [mɑ:st] *n* (*NAUT*) mástil *m*; (*RADIO etc*) torre *f*

R.S.V.P. *abbr* (= *répondez s'il vous plaît*) SRC

burro, a ['burro, a] *nm/f* donkey/she-donkey; (*fig*) ass, idiot

menudo, a [me'nuðo, a] *adj* (*pequeño*) small, tiny; (*sin importancia*) petty, insignificant; **¡~ negocio!** (*fam*) some deal!; **a ~** often, frequently

bocazas [bo'kaθas] (*fam*) *nm inv* bigmouth

cabrón [ka'βron] *nm* cuckold; (*fam!*) bastard (!)

mano ['mano] *nf* hand; (*ZOOL*) foot, paw; (*de pintura*) coat; (*serie*) lot, series; **a ~** by hand; **a ~ derecha/izquierda** on the right(-hand side)/left(-hand side); **de primera ~** (at) first hand; **de segunda ~** (at) second hand; **robo a ~ armada** armed robbery; **~ de obra** labour, manpower; **estrechar la ~ a uno** to shake sb's hand

tono ['tono] *nm* tone; **fuera de ~** inappropriate; **darse ~** to put on airs

ambición [ambi'θjon] *nf* ambition; **ambicionar** *vt* to aspire to; **ambicioso, a** *adj* ambitious

accept [ək'sept] *vt* aceptar; (*responsibility, blame*) admitir; **~able** *adj* acceptable; **~ance** *n* aceptación *f*

general [xene'ral] *adj* general ♦ *nm* general; **por lo** *o* **en ~** in general; **G~itat** *nf* Catalan parliament; **~ize** *vt* to generalize; **~izarse** *vr* to become generalized, spread; **~mente** *adv* generally

'Key' words

Your Collins Pocket Dictionary gives special status to certain Spanish and English words which can be looked on as 'key' words in each language. These are words which have many different usages. 'Poder', 'menos' and 'se' opposite are typical examples in Spanish. You are likely to become familiar with them in your day-to-day language studies.

There will be occasions, however, when you want to check on a particular usage. Your dictionary can be very helpful here. Note how with 'poder', for example, different parts of speech and different usages are clearly indicated by a combination of lozenges - ♦ - and numbers. In addition, further guides to usage are given in the language of the user who needs them. These are bracketed and in italics.

poder [po'ðer] *vi* **1** (*capacidad*) can, be able to; **no puedo hacerlo** I can't do it, I'm unable to do it

2 (*permiso*) can, may, be allowed to; **¿se puede?** may I (o we)?; **puedes irte ahora** you may go now; **no se puede fumar en este hospital** smoking is not allowed in this hospital

3 (*posibilidad*) may, might, could; **puede llegar mañana** he may *o* might arrive tomorrow; **pudiste haberte hecho daño** you might *o* could have hurt yourself; **¡podías habérmelo dicho antes!** you might have told me before!

4: puede ser: puede ser perhaps; **puede ser que lo sepa Tomás** Tomás may *o* might know

5: ¡no puedo más! I've had enough!; **no pude menos que dejarlo** I couldn't help but leave it; **es tonto a más no ~** he's as stupid as they come

6: ~ con: no puedo con este crío this kid's too much for me

♦ *nm* power; **~ adquisitivo** purchasing power; **detentar** *o* **ocupar** *o* **estar en el ~** to be in power

se [se] *pron* **1** (*reflexivo: sg: m*) himself; (*: f*) herself; (*: pl*) themselves; (*: cosa*) itself; (*: de Vd*) yourself; (*: de Vds*) yourselves; **~ está preparando** she's preparing herself; *para usos léxicos del pron ver el vb en cuestión, p.ej.* **arrepentirse**

2 (*con complemento indirecto*) to him; to her; to it; to you; **a usted ~ lo dije ayer** I told you yesterday; **~ compró un sombrero** he bought himself a hat; **~ rompió la pierna** he broke his leg

3 (*uso recíproco*) each other, one another; **~ miraron (el uno al otro)** they looked at each other *o* one another

4 (*en oraciones pasivas*): **se han vendido muchos libros** a lot of books have been sold

5 (*impers*): **~ dice que** people say that, it is said that; **allí ~ come muy bien** the food there is very good, you can eat very well there

menos [menos] *adj* **1: ~ (que/de)** (*compar: cantidad*) less (than); (*: número*) fewer (than); **con ~ entusiasmo** with less enthusiasm; **~ gente** fewer people; *ver tb* **cada**

2 (*superl*): **es el que ~ culpa tiene** he is the least to blame

♦ *adv* **1** (*compar*): **~ (que, de)** less (than); **me gusta ~ que el otro** I like it less than the other one

2 (*superl*): **es el ~ listo (de su clase)** he's the least bright in his class; **de todas ellas es la que ~ me agrada** out of all of them she's the one I like least; **(por) lo ~** at (the very) least

3 (*locuciones*): **no quiero verle y ~ visitarle** I don't want to see him let alone visit him; **tenemos 7 de ~** we're seven short

♦ *prep* except; (*cifras*) minus; **todos ~ él** everyone except (for) him; **5 ~ 2** 5 minus 2

♦ *conj*: **a ~ que: a ~ que venga mañana** unless he comes tomorrow

WORDGAME 1

HEADWORDS

Study the following sentences. In each sentence a wrong word spelt very similarly to the correct word has deliberately been put in and the sentence doesn't make sense. This word is shaded each time. Write out each sentence again, putting in the <u>correct</u> word which you will find in your dictionary near the wrong word.

> Example: Aparcar aquí no es delirio.
>
> ['Delirio' (= delirium) is the wrong word and should be replaced by 'delito' (= offence)]

1. El mecánico se negó a arrebatarme el coche.

2. El baúl estaba cubierto de pólvora.

3. Es muy caro reventar las fotos en esa tienda.

4. Les gusta mucho dar pasillos a caballo.

5. Para ayunar a su madre pone la mesa todos los días.

6. La ballesta es el animal más grande del mundo.

7. Mientras esquiábamos nos cayó una nevera tremenda.

8. No me gustó el último capota del libro.

9. Tuvimos un pincho y hubo que parar el coche.

10. Hay que cerrar la puerta con candidato.

WORDGAME 2

DICTIONARY ENTRIES

Complete the crossword below by looking up the English words in the list and finding the correct Spanish translations. There is a slight catch, however! All the English words can be translated several ways into Spanish, but only one translation will fit correctly into each part of the crossword. So look carefully through the entries in the English-Spanish section of your dictionary.

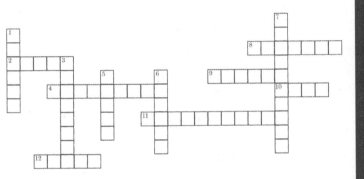

1. HORN
2. THROW
3. REMEMBER
4. PERFORMANCE
5. SPEECH
6. WHOLE

7. AMUSE
8. OLD
9. BELL
10. MATERIAL
11. ENDING
12. PART

WORDGAME 3

FINDING MEANINGS

In this list there are eight pairs of words that have some sort of connection with each other. For example, **'curso'** (= 'course') and **'estudiante'** (= 'student') are linked. Find the other pairs by looking up the words in your dictionary.

1. bata
2. nido
3. cuero
4. zapatillas
5. campanario
6. estudiante
7. libro
8. bolso
9. pasarela
10. aleta
11. curso
12. estante
13. urraca
14. barco
15. veleta
16. tiburón

WORDGAME 4

SYNONYMS

Complete the crossword by supplying SYNONYMS of the words below. You will sometimes find the synonym you are looking for in italics bracketed at the entries for the words listed below. Sometimes you will have to turn to the English-Spanish section for help.

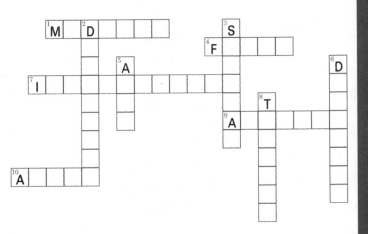

1. maneras
2. desilusión
3. exceder
4. incendio
5. cariño

6. vencer
7. inacabable
8. éxito
9. complacer
10. aeroplano

WORDGAME 5

SPELLING

You will often use your dictionary to check spellings. The person who has compiled this list of ten Spanish words has made <u>three</u> spelling mistakes. Find the three words which have been misspelt and write them out correctly.

1. pájaro
2. acienda
3. oleaje
4. gigante
5. avarrotar
6. peregil
7. ahora
8. velocidad
9. quinientos
10. abridor

WORDGAME 6

ANTONYMS

Complete the crossword by supplying ANTONYMS (i.e. opposites) in Spanish of the words below. Use your dictionary to help.

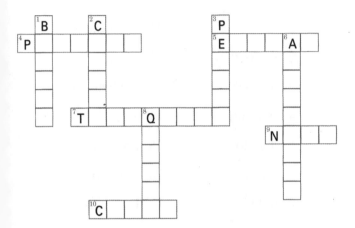

1. feo
2. abrir
3. ligero
4. riqueza
5. salir

6. engordar
7. inquieto
8. poner
9. todo
10. oscuro

WORDGAME 7

PHONETIC SPELLINGS

The phonetic transcriptions of twenty Spanish words are given below. If you study pages viii and ix at the front of your dictionary you should be able to work out what the words are.

1. 'aɣwa
2. θju'ðað
3. alreðe'ðor
4. mu'tʃatʃo
5. 'bjento
6. 'niɲo
7. bol'βer
8. 'kaʎe
9. θiɣ'θaɣ
10. 'xenjo

11. 'gwarða
12. 'tʃoke
13. em'bjar
14. ka'βaʎo
15. aβo'ɣaðo
16. korre'xir
17. ko'mjenθo
18. 'eʎos
19. xer'sei
20. i'ɣwal

WORDGAME 8

EXPRESSIONS IN WHICH THE HEADWORD APPEARS

If you look up the headword 'mismo' in the Spanish-English section of your dictionary you will find that the word can have many meanings. Study the entry carefully and translate the following sentences into English.

1. Ahora mismo se lo llevo.

2. A mí me da lo mismo.

3. Lo mismo que tú estudias francés yo estudio español.

4. En ese mismo momento llegó la policía.

5. Acudió el mismo Presidente.

6. Todos los domingos se ponía el mismo traje.

7. Lo hice yo mismo.

8. Era un hipócrita, y por lo mismo despreciado por todos.

9. Tenemos que empezar hoy mismo.

10. Lo vi aquí mismo.

WORDGAME 9

RELATED WORDS

Fill in the blanks in the pairs of sentences below. The missing words are related to the headwords on the left. Choose the correct 'relative' each time. You will find it in your dictionary near the headword provided.

HEADWORD	RELATED WORDS
estudiante	1. Realiza sus _____ en la Universidad.
	2. Hay que _____ bien el texto.
pertenecer	3. Estos son los terrenos _____ al Ayuntamiento.
	4. Recogió todas sus _____ y se fue.
empleo	5. Es _____ de banco.
	6. Voy a _____ todos los medios a mi alcance.
atractivo	7. Esa perspectiva no me _____ nada.
	8. Aquella mujer ejercía una gran _____ sobre él.
terminante	9. Al _____ de la reunión todos se fueron a tomar café.
	10. No le dejaron _____ lo que estaba diciendo.
falsedad	11. Lo que estás diciendo es completamente _____
	12. Se dedicaban a _____ billetes de banco.

WORDGAME 10

'KEY' WORDS

Study carefully the entry **'hacer'** in your dictionary and find translations for the following:

1. it's cold

2. I made them come

3. to study Economics

4. this will make it more difficult

5. to do the cooking

6. they became friends

7. I've been going for a month

8. to turn a deaf ear

9. if it's alright with you

10. to get hold of something

THE DICTIONARY AND GRAMMAR

While it is true that a dictionary can never be a substitute for a detailed grammar reference book, it nevertheless provides a great deal of grammatical information. If you know how to extract this information you will be able to use Spanish more accurately both in speech and in writing.

The Collins Pocket Dictionary presents grammatical information as follows.

Parts of speech

Parts of speech are given in italics immediately after the phonetic spellings of headwords. Abbreviated forms are used. Abbreviations can be checked on pages vi and vii.

Changes in parts of speech within an entry – for example, from adjective to adverb to noun, or from noun to intransitive verb to transitive verb – are indicated by means of lozenges - ♦ - as with the Spanish 'derecho' and the English 'act' opposite.

Genders of Spanish nouns

The gender of each noun in the Spanish-English section of the dictionary is indicated in the following way:

> *nm* = nombre masculino
> *nf* = nombre femenino

You will occasionally see *nm/f* beside an entry. This indicates that a noun – 'habitante', for example – can be either masculine or feminine.

Feminine forms of nouns are shown, as with 'ministro' opposite: the feminine ending is substituted for the masculine, so that 'ministro' becomes 'ministra' in the feminine.

In the English-Spanish section of the dictionary, genders are not shown for masculine nouns ending in '-o' or feminine nouns ending in '-a'. Otherwise, the gender immediately follows the translation. If a noun can be either masculine or feminine, this is shown by '*m/f*' if the form of the noun does not change, or by the feminine ending if it does change, as with 'graduate' and 'dentist' opposite. Note that when an ending is added on to a word rather than substituted for another ending it appears in brackets.

It is most important that you know the correct gender of a Spanish noun, since it is going to determine the form of both adjectives and past participles. If you are in any doubt as to the gender of a noun, it is always best to check it in your dictionary.

estría [es'tria] *nf* groove

tenue ['tenwe] *adj* (*delgado*) thin, slender; (*neblina*) light; (*lazo, vínculo*) slight

derecho, a [de'retʃo, a] *adj* right, right-hand ♦ *nm* (*privilegio*) right; (*lado*) right(-hand) side; (*leyes*) law ♦ *adv* straight, directly; **~s** *nmpl* (*de aduana*) duty *sg*; (*de autor*) royalties; **tener ~ a** to have a right to

act [ækt] *n* acto, acción *f*; (*of play*) acto; (*in music hall etc*) número; (*LAW*) decreto, ley *f* ♦ *vi* (*behave*) comportarse; (*have effect*: *drug, chemical*) hacer efecto; (*THEATRE*) actuar; (*pretend*) fingir; (*take action*) obrar ♦ *vt* (*part*) hacer el papel de; **in the ~ of**: **to catch sb in the ~ of ...** pillar a uno en el momento en que ...; **to ~ as** actuar *or* hacer de; **~ing** *adj* suplente ♦ *n* (*activity*) actuación *f*; (*profession*) profesión *f* de actor

criterio [kri'terjo] *nm* criterion; (*juicio*) judgement

manguera [man'gera] *nf* hose

habitante [aßi'tante] *nm/f* inhabitant

ministro, a [mi'nistro, a] *nm/f* minister

graduate [*n* 'grædjuit, *vb* 'grædjueit] *n* (*US: of high school*) graduado/a; (*of university*) licenciado/a ♦ *vi* graduarse; licenciarse; **graduation** [-'eiʃən] *n* (*ceremony*) entrega del título

dentist ['dentist] *n* dentista *m/f*

Adjectives

Adjectives are given in both their masculine and feminine forms, where these are different. The usual rule is to drop the 'o' of the masculine form and add an 'a' to make an adjective feminine, as with 'negro' opposite.

Some adjectives have identical masculine and feminine forms. Where this occurs, there is no 'a' beside the basic masculine form.

Adverbs

The normal 'rule' for forming adverbs in Spanish is to add '-mente' to the feminine form of the adjective. Thus:

$$seguro > segura > seguramente$$

The '-mente' ending is often the equivalent of the English '-ly':

> seguramente – surely
> lentamente – slowly

In your dictionary Spanish adverbs are not generally given, since the English translation can usually be derived from the relevant translation of the adjective headword. Usually the translation can be formed by adding '-ly' to the relevant adjective translation: e.g.

> fiel – faithful
> fielmente – faithfully

In cases where the basic translation for the adverb cannot be derived from those for the adjective, the adverb is likely to be listed as a headword in alphabetical order. This means it may not be immediately adjacent to the adjective headword: see 'actual' and 'actualmente' opposite.

Information about verbs

A major problem facing language learners is that the form of a verb will change according to the subject and/or the tense being used. A typical Spanish verb can take many different forms – too many to list in a dictionary entry.

negro, a ['neɣro, a] *adj* black; (*suerte*) awful ♦ *nm* black ♦ *nm/f* black man/woman

valiente [ba'ljente] *adj* brave, valiant ♦ *nm* hero

seguramente [seɣura'mente] *adv* surely; (*con certeza*) for sure, with certainty

actual [ak'twal] *adj* present(-day), current; **~idad** *nf* present; **~idades** *nfpl* (*noticias*) news *sg*; **en la ~idad** at present; (*hoy día*) nowadays
actualizar [aktwali'θar] *vt* to update, modernize
actualmente [aktwal'mente] *adv* at present; (*hoy día*) nowadays

Yet, although verbs are listed in your dictionary in their infinitive forms only, this does not mean that the dictionary is of limited value when it comes to handling the verb system of the Spanish language. On the contrary, it contains much valuable information.

First of all, your dictionary will help you with the meanings of unfamiliar verbs. If you came across the word 'decidió' in a text and looked it up in your dictionary you wouldn't find it. What you must do is assume that it is part of a verb and look for the infinitive form. Thus you will deduce that 'decidió' is a form of the verb 'decidir'. You now have the basic meaning of the word you are concerned with – something to do with English verb 'decide' – and this should be enough to help you understand the text you are reading.

It is usually an easy task to make the connection between the form of a verb and the infinitive. For example, 'decidieran', 'decidirá', 'decidimos' and 'decidido' are all recognisable as parts of the infinitive 'decidir'. However, sometimes it is less obvious – for example, 'pueda', 'podrán' and 'pude' are all parts of 'poder'. The only real solution to this problem is to learn the various forms of the main Spanish regular and irregular verbs.

And this is the second source of help offered by your dictionary as far as verbs are concerned. The verb tables on page xii of the Collins Pocket Dictionary provide a summary of some of the main forms of the main tenses of regular and irregular verbs. Consider the verb 'poder' below where the following information is given:

1 pudiendo	– Present Participle
2 puede	– Imperative
3 puedo, puedes, puede, pueden	– Present Tense forms
4 pude, pudiste, pudo, pudimos, pudisteis, pudieron	– Preterite forms
5 podré *etc*	– 1st Person Singular of the Future Tense
6 pueda, puedas, pueda, puedan	– Present Subjunctive forms
7 pudiera *etc*	– 1st Person Singular of the Imperfect Subjunctive

The regular '-ar', '-er', and '-ir' verbs – 'hablar', 'comer' and 'vivir' – are presented in greater detail. The main tenses and the different endings are given in full. This information can be transferred and applied to all verbs in the list. In addition, the main parts of the most common irregular verbs are listed in the body of the dictionary.

HABLAR

1 hablando
2 habla, hablad
3 hablo, hablas, habla, hablamos, habláis, hablan
4 hablé, hablaste, habló, hablamos, hablasteis, hablaron
5 hablaré, hablarás, hablará, hablaremos, hablaréis, hablarán
6 hable, hables, hable, hablemos, habléis, hablen
7 hablara, hablaras, hablara, habláramos, hablarais, hablaran
8 hablado
9 hablaba, hablabas, hablaba, hablábamos, hablabais, hablaban

In order to make maximum use of the information contained in these pages, a good working knowledge of the various rules affecting Spanish verbs is required. You will acquire this in the course of your Spanish studies and your Collins dictionary will serve as a useful reminder. If you happen to forget how to form the second person singular form of the Future Tense of 'poder' (i.e. how to translate 'you will be able to'), there will be no need to panic – your dictionary contains the information!

WORDGAME 11

PARTS OF SPEECH

In each sentence below a word has been shaded. Put a tick in the appropriate box to indicate the <u>part of speech</u> each time.

SENTENCE	Noun	Adj	Adv	Verb
1. Es estudiante de derecho.				
2. No hables tan alto.				
3. No tiene mucho dinero en su haber.				
4. Es un escrito muy largo.				
5. Vaya todo seguido.				
6. Es un dicho muy frecuente.				
7. Llegamos a casa muy tarde.				
8. Le gusta mucho andar por el campo.				
9. Lo hacemos por tu bien.				
10. A mi parecer es una buena película.				

WORDGAME 12

MEANING CHANGING WITH GENDER

Some Spanish nouns change meaning according to their gender, i.e. according to whether they are masculine or feminine. Look at the pairs of sentences below and fill in the blanks with either 'un', 'una', 'el' or 'la'. Use your dictionary to help.

1. No podía comprender _____ cólera de su padre.

   _____ cólera hace estragos en las regiones tropicales.

2. Perdí _____ pendiente en su casa.

   El coche no podía subir por _____ pendiente.

3. Los niños jugaban con _____ cometa.

   Dicen que en abril caerá _____ cometa.

4. Vimos _____ policía dentro de su coche.

   _____ policía ha descubierto una red de traficantes de droga.

5. Hay que cambiar _____ order de los números.

   En cuanto recibió _____ orden se puso en camino.

6. ¿Ha llegado _____ parte de la policía?

   _____ parte de atrás de la casa es muy sombría.

7. Pasó dos días en _____ coma profundo.

   Tienes que poner _____ coma ahí.

8. Los soldados están todavía en _____ frente.

   El pelo le cubría _____ frente.

WORDGAME 13

ADVERBS

Translate the following Spanish adverbs into English (generally by adding **-ly** to the adjective).

1. recientemente
2. lamentablemente
3. constantemente
4. mensualmente
5. pesadamente
6. inconscientemente
7. inmediatamente
8. ampliamente
9. tenazmente
10. brillantemente

WORDGAME 14

VERB TENSES

Use your dictionary to help you fill in the blanks in the table below.
(Remember the important pages at the front of your dictionary.)

INFINITIVE	PRESENT SUBJUNCTIVE	PRETERITE	FUTURE
tener		yo	
hacer			yo
poder			yo
decir		yo	
agradecer	yo		
saber			yo
reír	yo		
querer		yo	
caber	yo		
ir	yo		
salir			yo
ser		yo	

WORDGAME 15

IRREGULAR VERBS

Use your dictionary to find the <u>first person</u> present indicative of these verbs.

INFINITIVE	PRESENT INDICATIVE
conocer	
saber	
estar	
ofrecer	
poder	
ser	
poner	
divertir	
traer	
decir	
preferir	
negar	
dar	
instruir	

WORDGAME 16

IDENTIFYING INFINITIVES

In the sentences below you will see various Spanish verbs shaded. Use your dictionary to help you find the **infinitive** form of each verb.

1. Cuando erá pequeño dormía en la misma habitación que mi hermano.

2. Mis amigos vienen conmigo.

3. No cupieron todos los libros en el estante.

4. ¿Es que no veías lo que pasaba?

5. El sábado saldremos todos juntos.

6. Ya hemos visto la casa.

7. ¿Quieres que lo ponga aquí?

8. Le dije que viniera a las ocho.

9. Nos han escrito tres cartas ya.

10. No sabían qué hacer.

11. Tuvimos que salir temprano.

12. En cuanto supe lo de su padre la llamé por teléfono.

13. ¿Por qué no trajiste el dinero?

14. Prefiero quedarme en casa.

15. Quiero que conozcas a mi padre.

MORE ABOUT MEANING

In this section we will consider some of the problems associated with using a bilingual dictionary.

Overdependence on your dictionary

That the dictionary is an invaluable tool for the language learner is beyond dispute. Nevertheless, it is possible to become overdependent on your dictionary, turning to it in an almost automatic fashion every time you come up against a new word or phrase in a Spanish text. Tackling an unfamiliar text in this way will turn reading in Spanish into an extremely tedious activity. It is possible to argue that if you stop to look up every new word you may actually be *hindering* your ability to read in Spanish – you are so concerned with the individual words that you pay no attention to the text as a whole and to the context which gives them meaning. It is therefore important to develop appropriate reading skills – using clues such as titles, headlines, illustrations, etc., understanding relations within a sentence, etc. to predict or infer what a text is about.

A detailed study of the development of reading skills is not within the scope of this supplement; we are concerned with knowing how to use a dictionary, which is only one of several important skills involved in reading. Nevertheless, it may be instructive to look at one example. You see the following text in a Spanish newspaper and are interested in working out what it is about.

Contextual clues here include the heading in large type, which indicates that this is some sort of announcement, and the names. The verb 'recibir' is very much like the English 'receive' and you will also know 'form' words such as 'una', 'y' and so forth from your general studies in Spanish, as well as essential vocabulary such as 'niña', 'hijos', 'nombre'. Given that this extract appeared in a newspaper,

> **Natalicios**
> La señora de García Rodríguez (don Alfonso), de soltera Laura Montes de la Torre, ha dado a luz una niña, cuarta de sus hijos, que recibirá el nombre de Beatriz y tendrá como padrinos a doña Mercedes Sánchez Serrano y don Felipe Gómez Morales.

you will probably have worked out by now that this is an announcement placed in the 'Personal Column'.

So you have used contextual and word-formation clues to get you to the point where you have understood that this notice has been placed in the personal column because something has happened to señora de García Rodríguez and that somebody is going to be given the name of 'Beatriz'. And you have reached this point *without* opening your dictionary once. Common sense and your knowledge of newspaper contents in this country will suggest that this must be an announcement of someone's birth or death. Thus 'dar a luz' ('to give birth') and 'padrinos' ('godparents') become the only words that you need to look up in order to confirm that this is indeed a birth announcement.

When learning Spanish we are helped considerably by the fact that many Spanish and English words look and sound alike and have exactly the same meaning. Such words are called 'COGNATES'. Many words which look similar in Spanish and English come from a common Latin root. Other words are the same or nearly the same in both languages because the Spanish language has borrowed a word from English or vice versa. The dictionary will often not be necessary where cognates are concerned – provided you know the English word that the Spanish word resembles!

Words with more than one meaning

The need to examine with care *all* the information contained in a dictionary entry must be stressed. This is particularly important with the many Spanish words which have more than one meaning. For example, the Spanish 'destino' can mean 'destiny' as well as 'destination'. How you translated the word would depend on the context in which you found it.

Similarly, if you were trying to translate a phrase such as 'sigo sin saber', you would have to look through the whole entry for 'seguir' to get the right translation. If you restricted your search to the first line of the entry and saw that the first meaning given is 'to follow', you might be tempted to assume that the phrase meant 'I follow without knowing'. But if you examined the entry closely you would see that 'seguir sin ...' means 'to still do ... or 'to still be ...'. So 'sigo sin saber' means 'I still don't know'.

The same need for care applies when you are using the English-Spanish section of your dictionary to translate a word from English into Spanish. Watch out in particular for the lozenges indicating changes in parts of speech.

The noun 'sink' is 'fregadero', while the verb is 'hundir'. If you don't watch what you are doing, you could end up with ridiculous non-Spanish e.g. 'Dejó los platos en el hundir'!

Phrasal verbs

Another potential source of difficulty is English phrasal verbs. These consist of a common verb ('make', 'get', etc.) plus an adverb and/or a preposition to give English expressions such as 'to make out', 'to get on', etc. Entries for such verbs tend to be fairly full, so close examination of the contents is required. Note how these verbs appear in colour within the entry.

sink [sɪŋk] (*pt* **sank**, *pp* **sunk**) *n* fregadero ♦ *vt* (*ship*) hundir, echar a pique; (*foundations*) excavar ♦ *vi* (*gen*) hundirse; **to ~ sth into** hundir algo en; **~ in** *vi* (*fig*) penetrar, calar

make [meɪk] (*pt*, *pp* **made**) *vt* hacer; (*manufacture*) fabricar; (*mistake*) cometer; (*speech*) pronunciar; (*cause to be*): **to ~ sb sad** poner triste a alguien; (*force*): **to ~ sb do sth** obligar a alguien a hacer algo; (*earn*) ganar; (*equal*): **2 and 2 ~ 4** 2 y 2 son 4 ♦ *n* marca; **to ~ the bed** hacer la cama; **to ~ a fool of sb** poner a alguien en ridículo; **to ~ a profit/loss** obtener ganancias/sufrir pérdidas; **to ~ it** (*arrive*) llegar; (*achieve sth*) tener éxito; **what time do you ~ it?** ¿qué hora tienes?; **to ~ do with** contentarse con; **~ for** *vt fus* (*place*) dirigirse a; **~ out** *vt* (*decipher*) descifrar; (*understand*) entender; (*see*) distinguir; (*cheque*) extender; **~ up** *vt* (*invent*) inventar; (*prepare*) hacer; (*constitute*) constituir ♦ *vi* reconciliarse;

Falsos amigos

We noted above that many Spanish and English words have similar forms *and* meanings. There are, however, many Spanish words which *look* like English words but have a completely *different* meaning. For example, 'la carpeta' means 'the folder'; 'sensible' means 'sensitive'. This can easily lead to serious mistranslations.

Sometimes the meaning of the Spanish word is quite close to the English. For example, 'la moneda' means 'coin' rather than 'money'; 'simpático' means 'nice' rather than 'sympathetic'. But some Spanish words which look similar to English words have two meanings, one the same as the English, the other completely different! 'El plato' can mean 'course' (in a meal) as well as 'plate'; 'la cámara' can mean 'camera', but also 'chamber'.

Such words are often referred to as FALSOS AMIGOS ('false friends'). You will have to look at the context in which they appear to arrive at the correct meaning. If they seem to fit in with the sense of the passage as a whole, you will probably not need to look them up. If they don't make sense, however, you may well be dealing with 'falsos amigos'.

WORDGAME 17

WORDS IN CONTEXT

Study the sentences below. Translations of the shaded words are given at the bottom. Match the number of the sentence and the letter of the translation correctly each time.

1. Tendremos que atarlo con una cuerda.
2. La cuerda del reloj se ha roto.
3. Iremos al cine para entretener a los niños.
4. No me entretengas, que llegaré tarde.
5. Le dieron una patada en la espinilla.
6. Tenía una espinilla enorme en la nariz.
7. Siempre le da mucho sueño después de comer.
8. Anoche me desperté sobresaltada por un mal sueño.
9. El niño tocaba todo lo que veía.
10. Su padre tocaba muy bien la guitarra.
11. Tuvo un acceso de tos.
12. Todas las vías de acceso estaban cerradas.
13. Me gustaría estudiar la carrera de Derecho.
14. Todos querían participar en la carrera.
15. He quebrado el plato sin darme cuenta.
16. No sabían que esa empresa había quebrado.

a. touched   e. fit   i. rope   m. gone bankrupt
b. shin(bone)   f. course   j. hold up   n. played
c. entertain   g. sleepiness   k. entry   o. dream
d. spring   h. blackhead   l. race   p. broken

WORDGAME 18

WORDS WITH MORE THAN ONE MEANING

Look at the advertisements below. The words which are shaded can have more than one meaning. Use your dictionary to help you work out the correct translation in the context.

1

El Pescador
RESTAURANTE

Mariscos de viveros propios
Teléfono 406 12 80 – MADRID 6

P FÁCIL
APARCAMIENTO

2

Restaurante
LOS CEREZOS

ALTA COCINA REGIONAL
Para amantes de lo tradicional
RESERVAS: 574 34 11/12

3

INTERLANGUE
ANUNCIA CURSO MASTER DE
INGLÉS JURÍDICO PARA
PROFESIONALES DEL DERECHO
Inicio: 20 de octubre

4

¡¡¡BUTACAS PIEL A MEDIDA!!!

APROVECHE GRANDES REBAJAS EN OCTUBRE

¡En fábrica, más calidad y menor precio!

Horario continuado de 9,30 a 20,30 –
incluso sábados

GRANDES ALMACENES "EL CONDOR"
IMPORTANTES REBAJAS DE FIN DE TEMPORADA

5

6

Guía **TELEVISION**
JUEVES, 19
19.00. – Partido adelantado de la
JORNADA DE LIGA de PRIMERA DIVISION:
Atlético de Madrid – Barcelona (TV-2)

Bar-restaurante **"La Ballena"**

platos combinados desde 300 ptas.
helados, postres nuestra especialidad

7

8

ULTIMAS VIVIENDAS
de 2 y 3 dormitorios con
plaza de garaje opcional
Lunes a Viernes mañanas de 11 a 13,30.
Tardes de 16,30 a 19,30.

9

Calle de
ISABEL LA CATOLICA
N.ºs 50 - 56

PISOS EXTERIORES
DE 80 m^2

FINANCIACION A 11 AÑOS
13 Y 13,5% CON LA CAJA DE BARCELONA

WORDGAME 19

FALSE FRIENDS

Look at the advertisements below. The words which are shaded resemble English words but have different meanings here. Find a correct translation for each word in the context.

1

LA MAYOR COLECCION DE
**ALFOMBRAS
PERSAS Y
ORIENTALES**
*¡¡¡VENTA DE LIQUIDACION
POR CAMBIO DE DOMICILIO!!!*

2

Teatro Nacional:
"El Alcalde de Zalamea"
Localidades en venta a partir de mañana

3

PRODUCTOS BENGOLEA
**¡NO RECURRA A
LA COMPETENCIA!**
Visite nuestro local en Castellana 500

4

OFERTA ESPECIAL
cubiertos de acero inoxidable de
primerísima calidad en planta baja

HAVE FUN WITH YOUR DICTIONARY

Here are some word games for you to try. You will find your dictionary helpful as you attempt the activities.

WORDGAME 20

CODED WORDS

In the boxes below the letters of eight Spanish words have been replaced by numbers. A number represents the same letter each time (though an accent may be required sometimes).

Try to crack the code and find the eight words. If you need help, use your dictionary.

Here is a clue: all the words you are looking for have something to do with TRANSPORT.

1. | C¹ | A² | M³ | 4 | 5 | 6 |

2. | 2 | 7 | 8 | 5 | 9 | 7 | 10 |

3. | 1 | 5 | 1 | 11 | 12 |

4. | 9 | 4 | 1 | 4 | 1 | 13 | 12 | 8 | 2 |

5. | 8 | 14 | 12 | 6 |

6. | 11 | 12 | 13 | 4 | 1 | 5 | 15 | 8 | 12 | 14 | 5 |

7. | 2 | 3 | 9 | 7 | 13 | 2 | 6 | 1 | 4 | 2 |

8. | 3 | 5 | 8 | 5 |

WORDGAME 21

BEHEADED WORDS

If you 'behead' certain Spanish words, i.e. take away their first letter, you are left with another Spanish word. For example, if you behead **'aplomo'** (= 'self-assurance'), you get **'plomo'** (= 'lead'), and **'bala'** (= 'bullet') gives **'ala'** (= 'wing').

The following words have their heads chopped off, i.e. the first letter has been removed. Use your dictionary to help you form a new Spanish word by adding one letter to the start of each word below. You will find that some of them can have more than one answer. Write down the new Spanish word and its meaning.

1. bajo (= low)
2. oler (= to smell)
3. año (= year)
4. oro (= gold)
5. reparar (= to repair)
6. ama (= owner)
7. rendido (= worn-out)
8. cuerdo (= sane)
9. ave (= bird)
10. batir (= to beat)
11. resto (= rest)
12. precio (= price)
13. cera (= wax)
14. hora (= hour)
15. pinar (= pine forest)

WORDGAME 22

PALABRAS CRUZADAS

Complete this crossword by looking up the words listed below in the English-Spanish section of your dictionary. Remember to read through the entry carefully to find the word that will fit.

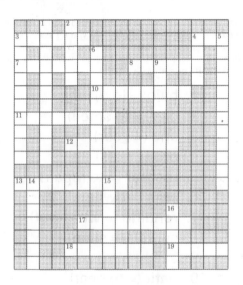

ACROSS

3. to bark
4. wing
7. lie
8. above
10. to work out
11. to lighten
12. to need
13. usual
17. cornet
18. to stink
19. radius

DOWN

1. to identify
2. to go out
3. regrettable
4. to love
5. streamlined
6. heating
9. expensive
14. to oblige
15. tricks
16. now

WORDGAME 23

There are twelve Spanish words hidden in the grid below. Each word is made up of five letters but has been split into two parts.

Find the Spanish words. Each group of letters can only be used once.

Use your dictionary to help you.

bla	lir	bu	ma	que	go
gor	ar	ver	vi	asi	jor
cal	me	ha	jo	lar	so
bo	jía	lo	vol	sa	eno

WORDGAME 24

Here is a list of Spanish words for things you will find in the kitchen. Unfortunately, they have all been jumbled up. Try to work out what each word is and put the word in the boxes on the right. You will see that there are seven shaded boxes below. With the seven letters in the shaded boxes make up <u>another</u> Spanish word for an object you can find in the kitchen.

1. azta   ¿Quieres una ____ de café?

2. eanevr   ¡Mete la mantequilla en la ____!

3. asme   ¡La comida está en la ____!

4. zoac   Su madre está calentando la leche en el ____

5. roegcanldo   ¡No saques el helado del ____ todavía!

6. uclclohi   ¿Dónde has puesto el ____ del queso?

7. rgoif   ¿Puedes cerrar ya el ____ del agua caliente?

The word you are looking for is:

WORDGAME 25

PALABRAS CRUZADAS

Take the four letters given each time and put them in the four empty boxes in the centre of each grid. Arrange them in such a way that you form four six-letter words. Use your dictionary to check the words.

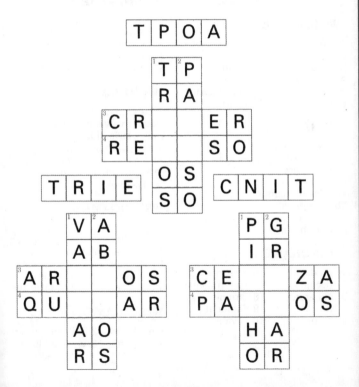

xliii

ANSWERS

WORDGAME 1

1	arreglarme	6	ballena
2	polvo	7	nevada
3	revelar	8	capítulo
4	paseos	9	pinchazo
5	ayudar	10	candado

WORDGAME 2

1	cuerno	7	entretener
2	echar	8	antiguo
3	recordar	9	timbre
4	actuación	10	tela
5	habla	11	terminación
6	entero	12	parte

WORDGAME 3

bata + zapatillas
nido + urraca
cuero + bolso
campanario + veleta
estudiante + curso
libro + estante
pasarela + barco
aleta + tiburón

WORDGAME 4

1	modales	6	derrotar
2	decepción	7	interminable
3	superar	8	triunfo
4	fuego	9	agradar
5	amor	10	avión

WORDGAME 5

2	hacienda
5	abalorios
6	perejil

WORDGAME 6

1	bonito	6	adelgazar
2	cerrar	7	tranquilo
3	pesado	8	quitar
4	pobreza	9	nada
5	entrar	10	claro

WORDGAME 7

agua, ciudad, alrededor,
muchacho, viento, niño,
volver, calle, zigzag,
genio, guarda, choque,
enviar, caballo, abogado,
corregir, comienzo, ellos,
jersey, igual

WORDGAME 9

1	estudios	7	atrae
2	estudiar	8	atracción
3	pertenecientes	9	término
4	pertenencias	10	terminar
5	empleado	11	falso
6	emplear	12	falsificar

WORDGAME 11

1 n	2 adv	3 n	4 n	5 adv
6 n	7 adv	8 v	9 n	10 n

WORDGAME 12

1	la; El	5	el; la
2	el; la	6	el; La
3	una; un	7	un; una
4	un; La	8	el; la

WORDGAME 14

tuve	ría
haré	quise
podré	quepa
dije	vaya
agradezca	saldré
sabré	fui

WORDGAME 15

conozco	divierto
sé	traigo
estoy	digo
ofrezco	prefiero
puedo	niego
soy	doy
pongo	instruyo

WORDGAME 16

1	dormir	9	escribir
2	venir	10	saber
3	caber	11	tener
4	ver	12	saber
5	salir	13	traer
6	ver	14	preferir
7	poner	15	conocer
8	venir		

WORDGAME 17

1	i	5	b	9	a	13	f
2	d	6	h	10	n	14	l
3	c	7	g	11	e	15	p
4	j	8	o	12	k	16	m

WORDGAME 18

1 fish farm
2 cuisine
3 law
4 leather
5 significant
6 league
7 set main course
8 space
9 savings bank

WORDGAME 19

1 clearance sale;
   home (Here; address)
2 tickets
3 competition
4 cutlery
5 retirement
6 small hotel; rooms
7 guest house
8 premises
9 address

WORDGAME 20

1	camión	5	tren
2	autobús	6	helicóptero
3	coche	7	ambulancia
4	bicicleta	8	moto

WORDGAME 21

1	abajo	7	prendido
2	doler; moler;	8	acuerdo
	soler	9	nave
3	baño; paño;	10	abatir
	daño; caño	11	presto
4	coro; loro;	12	aprecio
	moro; poro	13	acera
5	preparar	14	ahora
6	cama; dama;	15	opinar
	fama; gama;		
	mama; rama		

WORDGAME 22

ACROSS:
3 ladrar
4 ala
7 mentira
8 encima
10 elaborar
11 aligerar
12 necesitar
13 corriente
17 cucurucho
18 apestar
19 radio

DOWN:
1 identificar
2 salir
3 lamentable
4 amar
5 aerodinámico
6 calefacción
9 caro
14 obligar
15 trucos
16 ahora

WORDGAME 23

enojo	verbo
queso	calma
salir	asilo
volar	largo
vigor	mejor
bujía	habla

WORDGAME 24

1	taza	5	congelador
2	nevera	6	cuchillo
3	mesa	7	grifo
4	cazo		

Missing word – ARMARIO

WORDGAME 25

1)	1	trapos	2	patoso
	3	cráter	4	reposo
2)	1	variar	2	abetos
	3	arreos	4	quitar
3)	1	pincho	2	gritar
	3	ceniza	4	pactos

ENGLISH – SPANISH
INGLÉS – ESPAÑOL

A, a

A [eɪ] *n* (MUS) la *m*

a [ə] *indef art* (*before vowel or silent h:* an)
1 un(a); **~ book** un libro; **an apple** una manzana; **she's ~ doctor** (ella) es médica
2 (*instead of the number "one"*) un(a); **~ year ago** hace un año; **~ hundred/thousand** *etc* **pounds** cien/mil *etc* libras
3 (*in expressing ratios, prices etc*): **3 ~ day/week** 3 al día/a la semana; **10 km an hour** 10 km por hora; **£5 ~ person** £5 por persona; **30p ~ kilo** 30p el kilo

A.A. *n abbr* (= *Automobile Association:* BRIT) ≈ RACE *m* (SP); (= *Alcoholics Anonymous*) Alcohólicos Anónimos

A.A.A. (US) *n abbr* (= *American Automobile Association*) ≈ RACE *m* (SP)

aback [əˈbæk] *adv*: **to be taken ~** quedar desconcertado

abandon [əˈbændən] *vt* abandonar; (*give up*) renunciar a

abate [əˈbeɪt] *vi* (*storm*) amainar; (*anger*) aplacarse; (*terror*) disminuir

abattoir [ˈæbətwɑː*] (BRIT) *n* matadero

abbey [ˈæbɪ] *n* abadía

abbot [ˈæbət] *n* abad *m*

abbreviation [əˌbriːvɪˈeɪʃən] *n* abreviatura

abdicate [ˈæbdɪkeɪt] *vt* renunciar a ♦ *vi* abdicar

abdomen [ˈæbdəmən] *n* abdomen *m*

abduct [æbˈdʌkt] *vt* raptar, secuestrar

abeyance [əˈbeɪəns] *n*: **in ~** (*law*) en desuso; (*matter*) en suspenso

abide [əˈbaɪd] *vt*: **I can't ~ it/him** no lo/le puedo ver; **~ by** *vt fus* atenerse a

ability [əˈbɪlɪtɪ] *n* habilidad *f*, capacidad *f*; (*talent*) talento

abject [ˈæbdʒɛkt] *adj* (*poverty*) miserable; (*apology*) rastrero

ablaze [əˈbleɪz] *adj* en llamas, ardiendo

able [ˈeɪbl] *adj* capaz; (*skilled*) hábil; **to be ~ to do sth** poder hacer algo; **~-bodied** *adj* sano; **ably** *adv* hábilmente

abnormal [æbˈnɔːməl] *adj* anormal

aboard [əˈbɔːd] *adv* a bordo ♦ *prep* a bordo de

abode [əˈbəud] *n*: **of no fixed ~** sin domicilio fijo

abolish [əˈbɒlɪʃ] *vt* suprimir, abolir

aborigine [æbəˈrɪdʒɪnɪ] *n* aborigen *m/f*

abort [əˈbɔːt] *vt*, *vi* abortar; **~ion** [əˈbɔːʃən] *n* aborto; **to have an ~ion** abortar, hacerse abortar; **~ive** *adj* malogrado

about [əˈbaut] *adv* 1 (*approximately*) más o menos, aproximadamente; **~ a hundred/thousand** *etc* unos(unas) cien/mil *etc*; **it takes ~ 10 hours** se tarda unas *or* más o menos 10 horas; **at ~ 2 o'clock** sobre las dos; **I've just ~ finished** casi he terminado
2 (*referring to place*) por todas partes; **to leave things lying ~** dejar las cosas (tiradas) por ahí; **to run ~** correr por todas partes; **to walk ~** pasearse, ir y venir
3: **to be ~ to do sth** estar a punto de hacer algo
♦ *prep* 1 (*relating to*) de, sobre, acerca de; **a book ~ London** un libro sobre *or* acerca de Londres; **what is it ~?** ¿de qué se trata?, ¿qué pasa?; **we talked ~ it** hablamos de eso *or* ello; **what** *or* **how doing this?** ¿qué tal si hacemos esto?
2 (*referring to place*) por; **to walk ~ the town** caminar por la ciudad

above [ə'bʌv] adv encima, por encima, arriba ♦ prep encima de; (*greater than: in number*) más de; (: *in rank*) superior a; **mentioned** ~ susodicho; ~ **all** sobre todo; ~ **board** adj legítimo

abrasive [ə'breɪzɪv] adj abrasivo; (*manner*) brusco

abreast [ə'brest] adv de frente; **to keep** ~ **of** (*fig*) mantenerse al corriente de

abroad [ə'brɔːd] adv (*to be*) en el extranjero; (*to go*) al extranjero

abrupt [ə'brʌpt] adj (*sudden*) brusco; (*curt*) áspero

abruptly [ə'brʌptlɪ] adv (*leave*) repentinamente; (*speak*) bruscamente

abscess ['æbsɪs] n absceso

abscond [əb'skɒnd] vi (*thief*): **to** ~ **with** fugarse con; (*prisoner*): **to** ~ (**from**) escaparse (de)

absence ['æbsəns] n ausencia

absent ['æbsənt] adj ausente; ~**ee** [-'tiː] n ausente m/f; ~-**minded** adj distraído

absolute ['æbsəluːt] adj absoluto; ~**ly** [-'luːtlɪ] adv (*totally*) totalmente; (*certainly!*) ¡por supuesto (que sí)!

absolve [əb'zɒlv] vt: **to** ~ **sb** (**from**) absolver a alguien (de)

absorb [əb'zɔːb] vt absorber; **to be** ~**ed in a book** estar absorto en un libro; ~**ent cotton** (*US*) n algodón m hidrófilo; ~**ing** adj absorbente

absorption [əb'zɔːpʃən] n absorción f

abstain [əb'steɪn] vi: **to** ~ (**from**) abstenerse (de)

abstinence ['æbstɪnəns] n abstinencia

abstract ['æbstrækt] adj abstracto

absurd [əb'sɜːd] adj absurdo

abundance [ə'bʌndəns] n abundancia

abuse [n ə'bjuːs, vb ə'bjuːz] n (*insults*) insultos mpl, injurias fpl; (*ill-treatment*) malos tratos mpl; (*misuse*) abuso ♦ vt insultar; maltratar; abusar de; **abusive** adj ofensivo

abysmal [ə'bɪzməl] adj pésimo; (*failure*) garrafal; (*ignorance*) supino

abyss [ə'bɪs] n abismo

AC abbr (= *alternating current*) corriente f

alterna

academic [ækə'demɪk] adj académico, universitario; (*pej: issue*) puramente teórico ♦ n estudioso/a; profesor(a) m/f universitario/a

academy [ə'kædəmɪ] n (*learned body*) academia; (*school*) instituto, colegio; ~ **of music** conservatorio

accelerate [æk'seləreɪt] vt, vi acelerar; **accelerator** (*BRIT*) n acelerador m

accent ['æksent] n acento; (*fig*) énfasis m

accept [ək'sept] vt aceptar; (*responsibility, blame*) admitir; ~**able** adj aceptable; ~**ance** n aceptación f

access ['ækses] n acceso; **to have** ~ **to** tener libre acceso a; ~**ible** [-'sesəbl] adj (*place, person*) accesible; (*knowledge etc*) asequible

accessory [æk'sesərɪ] n accesorio; (*LAW*): ~ **to** cómplice de

accident ['æksɪdənt] n accidente m; (*chance event*) casualidad f; **by** ~ (*unintentionally*) sin querer; (*by chance*) por casualidad; ~**al** [-'dentl] adj accidental, fortuito; ~**ally** [-'dentəlɪ] adv sin querer; por casualidad; ~ **insurance** n seguro contra accidentes; ~-**prone** adj propenso a los accidentes

acclaim [ə'kleɪm] vt aclamar, aplaudir ♦ n aclamación f, aplausos mpl

acclimatize [ə'klaɪmətaɪz] (*US* **acclimate**) vt: **to become** ~**d** aclimatarse

accommodate [ə'kɒmədeɪt] vt (*subj: person*) alojar, hospedar; (: *car, hotel etc*) tener cabida para; (*oblige, help*) complacer; **accommodating** adj servicial, complaciente

accommodation [əkɒmə'deɪʃən] n (*US* **accommodations** npl) alojamiento

accompany [ə'kʌmpənɪ] vt acompañar

accomplice [ə'kʌmplɪs] n cómplice m/f

accomplish [ə'kʌmplɪʃ] vt (*finish*) concluir; (*achieve*) lograr; ~**ed** adj experto, hábil; ~**ment** n (*skill: gen pl*) talento; (*completion*) realización f

accord [ə'kɔːd] n acuerdo ♦ vt conceder;

of his own ~ espontáneamente; ~ance *n*: **in ~ance with** de acuerdo con; ~ing: **~ing to** *prep* según; (*in accordance with*) conforme a; ~ingly *adv* (*appropriately*) de acuerdo con esto; (*as a result*) en consecuencia

accordion [əˈkɔːdɪən] *n* acordeón *m*

accost [əˈkɔst] *vt* abordar, dirigirse a

account [əˈkaunt] *n* (COMM) cuenta; (*report*) informe *m*; ~**s** *npl* (COMM) cuentas *fpl*; **of no ~** de ninguna importancia; **on ~** a cuenta; **on no ~** bajo ningún concepto; **on ~ of** a causa de, por motivo de; **to take into ~, take ~ of** tener en cuenta; **~ for** *vt fus* (*explain*) explicar; (*represent*) representar; ~**able** *adj*: **~able (to)** responsable (ante); ~**ancy** *n* contabilidad *f*; ~**ant** *n* contable *m/f*, contador(a) *m/f*; ~ **number** *n* (*at bank etc*) número de cuenta

accrued interest [əˈkruːd-] *n* interés *m* acumulado

accumulate [əˈkjuːmjuleɪt] *vt* acumular ♦ *vi* acumularse

accuracy [ˈækjurəsɪ] *n* (*of total*) exactitud *f*; (*of description etc*) precisión *f*

accurate [ˈækjurɪt] *adj* (*total*) exacto; (*description*) preciso; (*person*) cuidadoso; (*device*) de precisión; ~**ly** *adv* con precisión

accusation [ækjuˈzeɪʃən] *n* acusación *f*

accuse [əˈkjuːz] *vt*: **to ~ sb (of sth)** acusar a uno (de algo); ~**d** *n* (LAW) acusado/a

accustom [əˈkʌstəm] *vt* acostumbrar; ~**ed** *adj*: **~ed to** acostumbrado a

ace [eɪs] *n* as *m*

ache [eɪk] *n* dolor *m* ♦ *vi* doler; **my head ~s** me duele la cabeza

achieve [əˈtʃiːv] *vt* (*aim, result*) alcanzar; (*success*) lograr, conseguir; ~**ment** *n* (*completion*) realización *f*; (*success*) éxito

acid [ˈæsɪd] *adj* ácido; (*taste*) agrio ♦ *n* (CHEM, *inf: LSD*) ácido; ~ **rain** *n* lluvia ácida

acknowledge [əkˈnɔlɪdʒ] *vt* (*letter: also*: ~ **receipt of**) acusar recibo de; (*fact, situation, person*) reconocer; ~**ment** *n*

acuse *m* de recibo

acne [ˈæknɪ] *n* acné *m*

acorn [ˈeɪkɔːn] *n* bellota

acoustic [əˈkuːstɪk] *adj* acústico; ~**s** *n, npl* acústica *sg*

acquaint [əˈkweɪnt] *vt*: **to ~ sb with sth** (*inform*) poner a uno al corriente de algo; **to be ~ed with** conocer; ~**ance** *n* (*person*) conocido/a; (*with person, subject*) conocimiento

acquire [əˈkwaɪə*] *vt* adquirir; **acquisition** [ækwɪˈzɪʃən] *n* adquisición *f*

acquit [əˈkwɪt] *vt* absolver, exculpar; **to ~ o.s. well** salir con éxito

acre [ˈeɪkə*] *n* acre *m*

acrid [ˈækrɪd] *adj* acre

acrobat [ˈækrəbæt] *n* acróbata *m/f*

across [əˈkrɔs] *prep* (*on the other side of*) al otro lado de, del otro lado de; (*crosswise*) a través de ♦ *adv* de un lado a otro, de una parte a otra; a través, al través; (*measurement*): **the road is 10m ~** la carretera tiene 10m de ancho; **to run/ swim ~** atravesar corriendo/nadando; ~ **from** enfrente de

acrylic [əˈkrɪlɪk] *adj* acrílico ♦ *n* acrílica

act [ækt] *n* acto, acción *f*; (*of play*) acto; (*in music hall etc*) número; (LAW) decreto, ley *f* ♦ *vi* (*behave*) comportarse; (*have effect: drug, chemical*) hacer efecto; (THEATRE) actuar; (*pretend*) fingir; (*take action*) obrar ♦ *vt* (*part*) hacer el papel de; **in the ~ of**: **to catch sb in the ~ of ...** pillar a uno en el momento en que ...; **to ~ as** actuar *or* hacer de; ~**ing** *adj* suplente ♦ *n* (*activity*) actuación *f*; (*profession*) profesión *f* de actor

action [ˈækʃən] *n* acción *f*, acto; (MIL) acción *f*, batalla; (LAW) proceso, demanda; **out of ~** (*person*) fuera de combate; (*thing*) estropeado; **to take ~** tomar medidas; ~ **replay** *n* (TV) repetición *f*

activate [ˈæktɪveɪt] *vt* activar

active [ˈæktɪv] *adj* activo, enérgico; (*volcano*) en actividad; ~**ly** *adv* (*participate*) activamente; (*discourage,* *dislike*) enérgicamente; **activity** [-'tɪvɪtɪ] *n* actividad *f*; **activity holiday** *n* *vacaciones fpl con actividades organizadas*

actor ['æktə*] *n* actor *m*

actress ['æktrɪs] *n* actriz *f*

actual ['æktjuəl] *adj* verdadero, real; (*emphatic use*) propiamente dicho; **~ly** *adv* realmente, en realidad; (*even*) incluso

acumen ['ækjumən] *n* perspicacia

acute [ə'kjuːt] *adj* agudo

ad [æd] *n abbr* = **advertisement**

A.D. *adv abbr* (= *anno Domini*) A.C.

adamant ['ædəmənt] *adj* firme, inflexible

adapt [ə'dæpt] *vt* adaptar ♦ *vi*: **to ~ (to)** adaptarse (a), ajustarse (a); **~able** *adj* adaptable; **~er, ~or** *n* (ELEC) adaptador *m*

add [æd] *vt* añadir, agregar; (*figures: also: ~ up*) sumar ♦ *vi*: **to ~ to** (*increase*) aumentar, acrecentar; **it doesn't ~ up** (*fig*) no tiene sentido

adder ['ædə*] *n* víbora

addict ['ædɪkt] *n* adicto/a; (*enthusiast*) entusiasta *m/f*; **~ed** [ə'dɪktɪd] *adj*: **to be ~ed to** ser adicto a; (*football etc*) ser fanático de; **~ion** [ə'dɪkʃən] *n* (*to drugs etc*) adicción *f*; **~ive** [ə'dɪktɪv] *adj* que causa adicción

addition [ə'dɪʃən] *n* (*adding up*) adición *f*; (*thing added*) añadidura, añadido; **in ~** además, por añadidura; **in ~ to** además de; **~al** *adj* adicional

additive ['ædɪtɪv] *n* aditivo

address [ə'drɛs] *n* dirección *f*, señas *fpl*; (*speech*) discurso ♦ *vt* (*letter*) dirigir; (*speak to*) dirigirse a, dirigir la palabra a; (*problem*) tratar

adept ['ædept] *adj*: **~ at** experto *or* hábil en

adequate ['ædɪkwɪt] *adj* (*satisfactory*) adecuado; (*enough*) suficiente

adhere [əd'hɪə*] *vi*: **to ~ to** (*stick to*) pegarse a; (*fig: abide by*) observar; (: *belief etc*) ser partidario de

adhesive [əd'hiːzɪv] *n* adhesivo; **~ tape** *n* (BRIT) cinta adhesiva; (US: MED)

esparadrapo

ad hoc [æd'hɔk] *adj* ad hoc

adjacent [ə'dʒeɪsənt] *adj*: **~ to** contiguo a, inmediato a

adjective ['ædʒektɪv] *n* adjetivo

adjoining [ə'dʒɔɪnɪŋ] *adj* contiguo, vecino

adjourn [ə'dʒəːn] *vt* aplazar ♦ *vi* suspenderse

adjudicate [ə'dʒuːdɪkeɪt] *vi* sentenciar

adjust [ə'dʒʌst] *vt* (*change*) modificar; (*clothing*) arreglar; (*machine*) ajustar ♦ *vi*: **to ~ (to)** adaptarse (a); **~able** *adj* ajustable; **~ment** *n* adaptación *f*; (*to machine, prices*) ajuste *m*

ad-lib [æd'lɪb] *vt, vi* improvisar; **ad lib** *adv* de forma improvisada

administer [əd'mɪnɪstə*] *vt* administrar; **administration** [-'treɪʃən] *n* (*management*) administración *f*; (*government*) gobierno; **administrative** [-trətɪv] *adj* administrativo

admiral ['ædmərəl] *n* almirante *m*; **A~ty** (BRIT) *n* Ministerio de Marina, Almirantazgo

admiration [ædmə'reɪʃən] *n* admiración *f*

admire [əd'maɪə*] *vt* admirar; **~r** *n* (*fan*) admirador(a) *m/f*

admission [əd'mɪʃən] *n* (*to university, club*) ingreso; (*entry fee*) entrada; (*confession*) confesión *f*

admit [əd'mɪt] *vt* (*confess*) confesar; (*permit to enter*) dejar entrar, dar entrada a; (*to club, organization*) admitir; (*accept: defeat*) reconocer; **to be ~ted to hospital** ingresar en el hospital; **~ to** *vt fus* confesarse culpable de; **~tance** *n* entrada *f*; **~tedly** *adv* es cierto *or* verdad que

admonish [əd'mɔnɪʃ] *vt* amonestar

ad nauseam [æd'nɔːsɪæm] *adv* hasta el cansancio

ado [ə'duː] *n*: **without (any) more ~** sin más (ni más)

adolescent [ædəu'lesnt] *adj, n* adolescente *m/f*

adopt [ə'dɔpt] *vt* adoptar; **~ed** *adj* adoptivo; **~ion** [ə'dɔpʃən] *n* adopción *f*

adore [əˈdɔː*] vt adorar
Adriatic [eɪdrɪˈætɪk] n: **the ~ (Sea)** el (Mar) Adriático
adrift [əˈdrɪft] adv a la deriva
adult [ˈædʌlt] n adulto/a ♦ adj (grown-up) adulto; (for adults) para adultos
adultery [əˈdʌltərɪ] n adulterio
advance [ədˈvɑːns] n (progress) adelanto, progreso; (money) anticipo, préstamo; (MIL) avance m ♦ adj: **~ booking** venta anticipada; **~ notice**, **~ warning** previo aviso ♦ vt (money) anticipar; (theory, idea) proponer (para la discusión) ♦ vi avanzar, adelantarse; **to make ~s (to sb)** hacer proposiciones (a alguien); **in ~** por adelantado; **~d** adj avanzado; (SCOL: studies) adelantado
advantage [ədˈvɑːntɪdʒ] n (also TENNIS) ventaja; **to take ~ of** (person) aprovecharse de; (opportunity) aprovechar
Advent [ˈædvənt] n (REL) Adviento
adventure [ədˈventʃə*] n aventura; **adventurous** [-tʃərəs] adj atrevido, aventurero
adverb [ˈædvəːb] n adverbio
adverse [ˈædvəːs] adj adverso, contrario
adversity [ədˈvəːsɪtɪ] n infortunio
advert [ˈædvəːt] (BRIT) n abbr = advertisement
advertise [ˈædvətaɪz] vi (in newspaper etc) anunciar, hacer publicidad; **to ~ for** (staff, accommodation etc) buscar por medio de anuncios ♦ vt anunciar; **~ment** [ədˈvəːtɪsmənt] n (COMM) anuncio; **~r** n anunciante m/f; **advertising** n publicidad f, anuncios mpl; (industry) industria publicitaria
advice [ədˈvaɪs] n consejo, consejos mpl; (notification) aviso; **a piece of ~** un consejo; **to take legal ~** consultar con un abogado
advisable [ədˈvaɪzəbl] adj aconsejable, conveniente
advise [ədˈvaɪz] vt aconsejar; (inform): **to ~ sb of sth** informar a uno de algo; **to ~ sb against sth/doing sth** desaconsejar algo a uno/aconsejar a uno que no haga algo;

~dly [ədˈvaɪzɪdlɪ] adv (deliberately) deliberadamente; **~r** n = advisor; **advisor** n consejero/a; (consultant) asesor(a) m/f; **advisory** adj consultivo
advocate [ˈædvəkeɪt] vt abogar por ♦ n [-kɪt] (lawyer) abogado/a; (supporter): **~ of** defensor(a) m/f de
Aegean [iːˈdʒiːən] n: **the ~ (Sea)** el (Mar) Egeo
aerial [ˈɛərɪəl] n antena ♦ adj aéreo
aerobics [ɛəˈrəubɪks] n aerobic m
aeroplane [ˈɛərəpleɪn] (BRIT) n avión m
aerosol [ˈɛərəsɒl] n aerosol m
aesthetic [iːsˈθetɪk] adj estético
afar [əˈfɑː*] adv: **from ~** desde lejos
affair [əˈfɛə*] n asunto; (also: **love ~**) aventura (amorosa)
affect [əˈfekt] vt (influence) afectar, influir en; (afflict, concern) afectar; (move) conmover; **~ed** adj afectado
affection [əˈfekʃən] n afecto, cariño; **~ate** adj afectuoso, cariñoso
affinity [əˈfɪnɪtɪ] n (bond, rapport): **to feel an ~ with** sentirse identificado con; (resemblance) afinidad f
afflict [əˈflɪkt] vt afligir
affluence [ˈæfluəns] n opulencia, riqueza
affluent [ˈæfluənt] adj (wealthy) acomodado; **the ~ society** la sociedad opulenta
afford [əˈfɔːd] vt (provide) proporcionar; **can we ~ (to buy) it?** ¿tenemos bastante dinero para comprarlo?
Afghanistan [æfˈɡænɪstæn] n Afganistán m
afield [əˈfiːld] adv: **far ~** muy lejos
afloat [əˈfləut] adv (floating) a flote
afoot [əˈfut] adv: **there is something ~** algo se está tramando
afraid [əˈfreɪd] adj: **to be ~ of** (person) tener miedo a; (thing) tener miedo de; **to be ~ to** tener miedo de, temer; **I am ~ that** me temo que; **I am ~ not/so** lo siento, pero no/es así
afresh [əˈfreʃ] adv de nuevo, otra vez
Africa [ˈæfrɪkə] n África; **~n** adj, n africano/a m/f

after ['ɑːftə*] *prep* (*time*) después de; (*place, order*) detrás de, tras ♦ *adv* después ♦ *conj* después (de) que; **what/who are you ~?** ¿qué/a quién busca usted?; **~ having done/he left** después de haber hecho/después de que se marchó; **to name sb ~ sb** llamar a uno por uno; **it's twenty ~ eight** (*US*) son las ocho y veinte; **to ask ~ sb** preguntar por alguien; **~ all** después de todo, al fin y al cabo; **~ you!** ¡pase usted!; **~-effects** *npl* consecuencias *fpl*, efectos *mpl*; **~math** *n* consecuencias *fpl*, resultados *mpl*; **~noon** *n* tarde *f*; **~s** (*inf*) *n* (*dessert*) postre *m*; **~-sales service** (*BRIT*) *n* servicio de asistencia pos-venta; **~-shave (lotion)** *n* aftershave *m*; **~sun (lotion/cream)** *n* loción *f*/crema para después del sol, aftersun *m*; **~thought** *n* ocurrencia (tardía); **~wards** (*US* **~ward**) *adv* después, más tarde

again [ə'gen] *adv* otra vez, de nuevo; **to do sth ~** volver a hacer algo; **~ and ~** una y otra vez

against [ə'genst] *prep* (*in opposition to*) en contra de; (*leaning on, touching*) contra, junto a

age [eɪdʒ] *n* edad *f*; (*period*) época ♦ *vi* envejecer(se) ♦ *vt* envejecer; **she is 20 years of ~** tiene 20 años; **to come of ~** llegar a la mayoría de edad; **it's been ~s since I saw you** hace siglos que no te veo; **~d 10** de 10 años de edad; **the ~d** ['eɪdʒɪd] *npl* los ancianos; **~ group** *n*: **to be in the same ~ group** tener la misma edad; **~ limit** *n* edad *f* mínima (*or* máxima)

agency ['eɪdʒənsɪ] *n* agencia

agenda [ə'dʒɛndə] *n* orden *m* del día

agent ['eɪdʒənt] *n* agente *m/f*; (*COMM: holding concession*) representante *m/f*, delegado/a; (*CHEM, fig*) agente *m*

aggravate ['ægrəveɪt] *vt* (*situation*) agravar; (*person*) irritar

aggregate ['ægrɪgeɪt] *n* conjunto

aggressive [ə'gresɪv] *adj* (*belligerent*) agresivo; (*assertive*) enérgico

aggrieved [ə'griːvd] *adj* ofendido, agraviado

aghast [ə'gɑːst] *adj* horrorizado

agile ['ædʒaɪl] *adj* ágil

agitate ['ædʒɪteɪt] *vt* (*trouble*) inquietar ♦ *vi*: **to ~ for/against** hacer campaña pro *or* en favor de/en contra de

AGM *n abbr* (= *annual general meeting*) asamblea anual

ago [ə'gəu] *adv*: **2 days ~** hace 2 días; **not long ~** hace poco; **how long ~?** ¿hace cuánto tiempo?

agog [ə'gɒg] *adj* (*eager*) ansioso; (*excited*) emocionado

agonizing ['ægənaɪzɪŋ] *adj* (*pain*) atroz; (*decision, wait*) angustioso

agony ['ægənɪ] *n* (*pain*) dolor *m* agudo; (*distress*) angustia; **to be in ~** retorcerse de dolor

agree [ə'griː] *vt* (*price, date*) acordar, quedar en ♦ *vi* (*have same opinion*): **to ~ (with/that)** estar de acuerdo (con/que); (*correspond*) coincidir, concordar; (*consent*) acceder; **to ~ with** (*subj: person*) estar de acuerdo con, ponerse de acuerdo con; (: *food*) sentar bien a; (*LING*) concordar con; **to ~ to sth/to do sth** consentir en algo/aceptar hacer algo; **to ~ that** (*admit*) estar de acuerdo en que; **~able** *adj* (*sensation*) agradable; (*person*) simpático; (*willing*) de acuerdo, conforme; **~d** *adj* (*time, place*) convenido; **~ment** *n* acuerdo; (*contract*) contrato; **in ~ment** de acuerdo, conforme

agricultural [ægrɪ'kʌltʃərəl] *adj* agrícola

agriculture ['ægrɪkʌltʃə*] *n* agricultura

aground [ə'graund] *adv*: **to run ~** (*NAUT*) encallar, embarrancar

ahead [ə'hed] *adv* (*in front*) delante; (*into the future*): **she had no time to think ~** no tenía tiempo de hacer planes para el futuro; **~ of** delante de; (*in advance of*) antes de; **~ of time** antes de la hora; **go right** *or* **straight ~** (*direction*) siga adelante; (*permission*) hazlo (*or* hágalo)

aid [eɪd] *n* ayuda, auxilio; (*device*) aparato ♦ *vt* ayudar, auxiliar; **in ~ of** a beneficio de

aide [eɪd] n (person, also MIL) ayudante m/f

AIDS [eɪdz] n abbr (= acquired immune deficiency syndrome) SIDA m

ailment ['eɪlmənt] n enfermedad f, achaque m

aim [eɪm] vt (gun, camera) apuntar; (missile, remark) dirigir; (blow) asestar ♦ vi (also: **take ~**) apuntar ♦ n (in shooting: skill) puntería; (objective) propósito, meta; **to ~ at** (with weapon) apuntar a; (objective) aspirar a, pretender; **to ~ to do** tener la intención de hacer; **~less** adj sin propósito, sin objeto

ain't [eɪnt] (inf) = am not; aren't; isn't

air [ɛə*] n aire m; (appearance) aspecto ♦ vt (room) ventilar; (clothes, ideas) airear ♦ cpd aéreo; **to throw sth into the ~** (ball etc) lanzar algo al aire; **by ~** (travel) en avión; **to be on the ~** (RADIO, TV) estar en antena; **~bed** (BRIT) n colchón m neumático; **~-conditioned** adj climatizado; **~ conditioning** n aire acondicionado; **~craft** n inv avión m; **~craft carrier** n porta(a)viones m inv; **~field** n campo de aviación; **A~ Force** n fuerzas fpl aéreas, aviación f; **~ freshener** n ambientador m; **~gun** n escopeta de aire comprimido; **~ hostess** (BRIT) n azafata; **~ letter** (BRIT) n carta aérea; **~lift** n puente m aéreo; **~line** n línea aérea; **~liner** n avión m de pasajeros; **~mail** n: **by ~mail** por avión; **~plane** (US) n avión m; **~port** n aeropuerto; **~ raid** n ataque m aéreo; **~sick** adj: **to be ~sick** marearse (en avión); **~space** n espacio aéreo; **~tight** adj hermético; **~-traffic controller** n controlador(a) m/f aéreo/a; **~y** adj (room) bien ventilado; (fig: manner) desenfadado

aisle [aɪl] n (of church) nave f; (of theatre, supermarket) pasillo; **~ seat** n (on plane) asiento de pasillo

ajar [ə'dʒɑː*] adj entreabierto

alarm [ə'lɑːm] n (in shop, bank) alarma; (anxiety) inquietud f ♦ vt asustar,

inquietar; **~ call** n (in hotel etc) alarma; **~ clock** n despertador m

alas [ə'læs] adv desgraciadamente

albeit [ɔːl'biːt] conj aunque

album ['ælbəm] n álbum m; (L.P.) elepé m

alcohol ['ælkəhɒl] n alcohol m; **~ic** [-'hɒlɪk] adj, n alcohólico/a m/f

ale [eɪl] n cerveza

alert [ə'lɜːt] adj (attentive) atento; (to danger, opportunity) alerta ♦ n alerta m, alarma ♦ vt poner sobre aviso; **to be on the ~** (also MIL) estar alerta or sobre aviso

algebra ['ældʒɪbrə] n álgebra

Algeria [æl'dʒɪərɪə] n Argelia

alias ['eɪlɪəs] adv alias, conocido por ♦ n (of criminal) apodo; (of writer) seudónimo

alibi ['ælɪbaɪ] n coartada

alien ['eɪlɪən] n (foreigner) extranjero/a; (extraterrestrial) extraterrestre m/f ♦ adj: **~ to** ajeno a; **~ate** vt enajenar, alejar

alight [ə'laɪt] adj ardiendo; (eyes) brillante ♦ vi (person) apearse, bajar; (bird) posarse

align [ə'laɪn] vt alinear

alike [ə'laɪk] adj semejantes, iguales ♦ adv igualmente, del mismo modo; **to look ~** parecerse

alimony ['ælɪmənɪ] n manutención f

alive [ə'laɪv] adj vivo; (lively) alegre

KEYWORD

all [ɔːl] adj (sg) todo/a; (pl) todos/as; **~ day** todo el día; **~ night** toda la noche; **~ men** todos los hombres; **~ five came** vinieron los cinco; **~ the books** todos los libros; **~ his life** toda su vida

♦ pron 1 todo; **I ate it ~, I ate ~ of it** me lo comí todo; **~ of us went** fuimos todos; **~ the boys went** fueron todos los chicos; **is that ~?** ¿eso es todo?, ¿algo más?; (in shop) ¿algo más?, ¿alguna cosa más?

2 (in phrases): **above ~** sobre todo; **after ~** después de todo; **at ~: not at ~** (in answer to question) en absoluto; (in answer to thanks) ¡de nada!, ¡no hay de qué!; **I'm not at ~ tired** no estoy nada cansado/a; **anything at ~ will do** cualquier cosa viene bien; **~ in ~** a fin

de cuentas
♦ *adv*: ~ **alone** completamente solo/a;
it's not as hard as ~ that no es tan
difícil como lo pintas; **~ the more/the
better** tanto más/mejor; **~ but** casi; **the
score is 2 ~** están empatados a 2

all clear *n* (*after attack etc*) fin *m* de la
alerta; (*fig*) luz *f* verde
allege [ə'ledʒ] *vt* pretender; **~dly**
[ə'ledʒɪdlɪ] *adv* supuestamente, según se
afirma
allegiance [ə'li:dʒəns] *n* lealtad *f*
allergy ['ælədʒɪ] *n* alergia
alleviate [ə'li:vɪeɪt] *vt* aliviar
alley ['ælɪ] *n* callejuela
alliance [ə'laɪəns] *n* alianza
allied ['ælaɪd] *adj* aliado
alligator ['ælɪgeɪtə*] *n* (*ZOOL*) caimán *m*
all-in (*BRIT*) *adj*, *adv* (*charge*) todo incluido
all-night *adj* (*café, shop*) abierto toda la
noche; (*party*) que dura toda la noche
allocate ['æləkeɪt] *vt* (*money etc*) asignar
allot [ə'lɔt] *vt* asignar; **~ment** *n* ración *f*;
(*garden*) parcela
all-out *adj* (*effort etc*) supremo; **all out**
adv con todas las fuerzas
allow [ə'lau] *vt* permitir, dejar; (*a claim*)
admitir; (*sum, time etc*) dar, conceder;
(*concede*): **to ~ that** reconocer que; **to ~
sb to do** permitir a alguien hacer; **he is
~ed to ...** se le permite ...; **~ for** *vt fus*
tener en cuenta; **~ance** *n* subvención *f*;
(*welfare payment*) subsidio, pensión *f*;
(*pocket money*) dinero de bolsillo; (*tax
~ance*) desgravación *f*; **to make ~ances
for** (*person*) disculpar a; (*thing*) tener en
cuenta
alloy ['ælɔɪ] *n* mezcla
all: ~ **right** *adv* bien; (*as answer*)
¡conforme!, ¡está bien!; **~-rounder** *n*:
he's a good ~-rounder se le da bien
todo; **~-time** *adj* (*record*) de todos los
tiempos
alluring [ə'ljuərɪŋ] *adj* atractivo,
tentador(a)
ally ['ælaɪ] *n* aliado/a ♦ *vt*: **to ~ o.s. with**

aliarse con
almighty [ɔːl'maɪtɪ] *adj* todopoderoso;
(*row etc*) imponente
almond ['ɑːmənd] *n* almendra
almost ['ɔːlməust] *adv* casi
alone [ə'ləun] *adj*, *adv* solo; **to leave sb ~**
dejar a uno en paz; **to leave sth ~** no
tocar algo, dejar algo sin tocar; **let ~ ...** y
mucho menos ...
along [ə'lɔŋ] *prep* a lo largo de, por ♦ *adv*:
is he coming ~ with us? ¿viene con
nosotros?; **he was limping ~** iba
cojeando; **~ with** junto con; **all ~** (*all the
time*) desde el principio; **~side** *prep* al
lado de ♦ *adv* al lado
aloof [ə'luːf] *adj* reservado ♦ *adv*: **to stand
~** mantenerse apartado
aloud [ə'laud] *adv* en voz alta
alphabet ['ælfəbet] *n* alfabeto
Alps [ælps] *npl*: **the ~** los Alpes
already [ɔːl'redɪ] *adv* ya
alright [ɔːl'raɪt] (*BRIT*) *adv* = **all right**
Alsatian [æl'seɪʃən] *n* (*dog*) pastor *m*
alemán
also ['ɔːlsəu] *adv* también, además
altar ['ɔltə*] *n* altar *m*
alter ['ɔltə*] *vt* cambiar, modificar ♦ *vi*
cambiar; **~ation** [ɔltə'reɪʃən] *n* cambio; (*to
clothes*) arreglo; (*to building*) arreglos *mpl*
alternate [*adj* ɔl'tə:nɪt, *vb* 'ɔltə:neɪt] *adj*
(*actions etc*) alternativo; (*events*) alterno;
(*US*) = **alternative** ♦ *vi*: **to ~ (with)**
alternar (con); **on ~ days** un día sí y otro
no; **alternating current** [-neɪtɪŋ] *n*
corriente *f* alterna
alternative [ɔl'tə:nətɪv] *adj* alternativo ♦ *n*
alternativa; ~ **medicine** medicina
alternativa; **~ly** *adv*: **~ly one could ...**
por otra parte se podría ...
although [ɔːl'ðəu] *conj* aunque
altitude ['æltɪtjuːd] *n* altura
alto ['æltəu] *n* (*female*) contralto *f*; (*male*)
alto
altogether [ɔːltə'geðə*] *adv*
completamente, del todo; (*on the whole*)
en total, en conjunto
aluminium [ælju'mɪnɪəm] (*BRIT*),

aluminum [ə'lu:mɪnəm] (US) n aluminio
always ['ɔ:lweɪz] adv siempre
Alzheimer's (disease) ['æltshaɪməz-] n
enfermedad f de Alzheimer
AM n abbr (= Assembly Member)
parlamentario/a m/f
am [æm] vb see **be**
a.m. adv abbr (= ante meridiem) de la
mañana
amalgamate [ə'mælgəmeɪt] vi
amalgamarse ♦ vt amalgamar, unir
amateur ['æmətə*] n aficionado/a,
amateur m/f; **~ish** adj inexperto
amaze [ə'meɪz] vt asombrar, pasmar; **to
be ~d (at)** quedar pasmado (de); **~ment**
n asombro, sorpresa; **amazing** adj
extraordinario; (fantastic) increíble
Amazon ['æməzən] n (GEO) Amazonas m
ambassador [æm'bæsədə*] n
embajador(a) m/f
amber ['æmbə*] n ámbar m; **at ~** (BRIT:
AUT) en el amarillo
ambiguous [æm'bɪgjuəs] adj ambiguo
ambition [æm'bɪʃən] n ambición f;
ambitious [-ʃəs] adj ambicioso
ambulance ['æmbjuləns] n ambulancia
ambush ['æmbuʃ] n emboscada ♦ vt
tender una emboscada a
amenable [ə'mi:nəbl] adj: **to be ~ to**
dejarse influir por
amend [ə'mend] vt enmendar; **to make
~s** dar cumplida satisfacción
amenities [ə'mi:nɪtɪz] npl comodidades
fpl
America [ə'merɪkə] n (USA) Estados mpl
Unidos; **~n** adj, n norteamericano/a m/f;
estadounidense m/f
amiable ['eɪmɪəbl] adj amable, simpático
amicable ['æmɪkəbl] adj amistoso,
amigable
amid(st) [ə'mɪd(st)] prep entre, en medio
de
amiss [ə'mɪs] adv: **to take sth ~** tomar algo a mal; **there's something ~** pasa algo
ammonia [ə'məunɪə] n amoníaco
ammunition [æmju'nɪʃən] n municiones
fpl

amnesty ['æmnɪstɪ] n amnistía
amok [ə'mɔk] adv: **to run ~** enloquecerse,
desbocarse
among(st) [ə'mʌŋ(st)] prep entre, en
medio de
amorous ['æmərəs] adj amoroso
amount [ə'maunt] n (gen) cantidad f; (of
bill etc) suma, importe m ♦ vi: **to ~ to**
sumar; (be same as) equivaler a, significar
amp(ère) ['æmp(eə*)] n amperio
ample ['æmpl] adj (large) grande;
(abundant) abundante; (enough) bastante,
suficiente
amplifier ['æmplɪfaɪə*] n amplificador m
amuse [ə'mju:z] vt divertir; (distract)
distraer, entretener; **~ment** n diversión f;
(pastime) pasatiempo; (laughter) risa;
~ment arcade n salón m de juegos;
~ment park n parque m de atracciones
an [æn] indef art see **a**
anaemic [ə'ni:mɪk] (US **anemic**) adj
anémico; (fig) soso, insípido
anaesthetic [ænɪs'θetɪk] n (US
anesthetic) anestesia
analog(ue) ['ænəlɔg] adj (computer,
watch) analógico
analyse ['ænəlaɪz] (US **analyze**) vt analizar;
analysis [ə'næləsɪs] (pl **analyses**) n
análisis m inv; **analyst** [-lɪst] n (political
analyst, psychoanalyst) analista m/f
analyze ['ænəlaɪz] (US) vt = **analyse**
anarchist ['ænəkɪst] n anarquista m/f
anatomy [ə'nætəmɪ] n anatomía
ancestor ['ænsɪstə*] n antepasado
anchor ['æŋkə*] n ancla, áncora ♦ vi (also:
to drop ~) anclar ♦ vt anclar; **to weigh ~**
levar anclas
anchovy ['æntʃəvɪ] n anchoa
ancient ['eɪnʃənt] adj antiguo
ancillary [æn'sɪlərɪ] adj auxiliar
and [ænd] conj y; (before i-, hi- +consonant)
e; **men ~ women** hombres y mujeres;
father ~ son padre e hijo; **trees ~ grass**
árboles y hierba; **~ so on** etcétera, y así
sucesivamente; **try ~ come** procura venir;
he talked ~ talked habló sin parar;
better ~ better cada vez mejor

Andes ['ændi:z] *npl*: **the ~** los Andes
anemic *etc* [ə'ni:mɪk] (*US*) = **anaemic** *etc*
anesthetic *etc* [ænɪs'θetɪk] (*US*) = **anaesthetic** *etc*
anew [ə'nju:] *adv* de nuevo, otra vez
angel ['eɪndʒəl] *n* ángel *m*
anger ['æŋgə*] *n* cólera
angina [æn'dʒaɪnə] *n* angina (del pecho)
angle ['æŋgl] *n* ángulo; **from their ~** desde su punto de vista
angler ['æŋglə*] *n* pescador(a) *m/f* (de caña)
Anglican ['æŋglɪkən] *adj, n* anglicano/a *m/f*
angling ['æŋglɪŋ] *n* pesca con caña
Anglo... ['æŋgləu] *prefix* anglo...
angrily ['æŋgrɪlɪ] *adv* coléricamente, airadamente
angry ['æŋgrɪ] *adj* enfadado, airado; (*wound*) inflamado; **to be ~ with sb/at sth** estar enfadado con alguien/por algo; **to get ~** enfadarse, enojarse
anguish ['æŋgwɪʃ] *n* (*physical*) tormentos *mpl*; (*mental*) angustia
animal ['ænɪməl] *n* animal *m*; (*pej: person*) bestia ♦ *adj* animal
animate ['ænɪmɪt] *adj* vivo; **~d** [-meɪtɪd] *adj* animado
aniseed ['ænɪsi:d] *n* anís *m*
ankle ['æŋkl] *n* tobillo *m*; **~ sock** *n* calcetín *m* corto
annex [*n* 'æneks, *vb* ə'neks] *n* (*also*: BRIT: *annexe*) (*building*) edificio anexo ♦ *vt* (*territory*) anexionar
annihilate [ə'naɪəleɪt] *vt* aniquilar
anniversary [ænɪ'və:sərɪ] *n* aniversario
announce [ə'nauns] *vt* anunciar; **~ment** *n* anuncio; (*official*) declaración *f*; **~r** *n* (RADIO) locutor(a) *m/f*; (TV) presentador(a) *m/f*
annoy [ə'nɔɪ] *vt* molestar, fastidiar; **don't get ~ed!** ¡no se enfade!; **~ance** *n* enojo; **~ing** *adj* molesto, fastidioso; (*person*) pesado
annual ['ænjuəl] *adj* anual ♦ *n* (BOT) anual *m*; (*book*) anuario; **~ly** *adv* anualmente, cada año

annul [ə'nʌl] *vt* anular
annum ['ænəm] *n see* **per**
anonymous [ə'nɔnɪməs] *adj* anónimo
anorak ['ænəræk] *n* anorak *m*
anorexia [ænə'reksɪə] *n* (MED: *also*: **~ nervosa**) anorexia
another [ə'nʌðə*] *adj* (*one more, a different one*) otro ♦ *pron* otro; *see* **one**
answer ['ɑ:nsə*] *n* contestación *f*, respuesta; (*to problem*) solución *f* ♦ *vi* contestar, responder ♦ *vt* (*reply to*) contestar a, responder a; (*problem*) resolver; (*prayer*) escuchar; **in ~ to your letter** contestando *or* en contestación a su carta; **to ~ the phone** contestar *or* coger el teléfono; **to ~ the bell** *or* **the door** acudir a la puerta; **~ back** *vi* replicar, ser respondón/ona; **~ for** *vt fus* responder de *or* por; **~ to** *vt fus* (*description*) corresponder a; **~able** *adj*: **~able to sb for sth** responsable ante uno de algo; **~ing machine** *n* contestador *m* automático
ant [ænt] *n* hormiga
antagonism [æn'tægənɪzm] *n* antagonismo, hostilidad *f*
antagonize [æn'tægənaɪz] *vt* provocar la enemistad de
Antarctic [ænt'ɑ:ktɪk] *n*: **the ~** el Antártico
antelope ['æntɪləup] *n* antílope *m*
antenatal ['æntɪ'neɪtl] *adj* antenatal, prenatal; **~ clinic** *n* clínica prenatal
anthem ['ænθəm] *n*: **national ~** himno nacional
anthropology [ænθrə'pɔlədʒɪ] *n* antropología
anti... [æntɪ] *prefix* anti...; **~-aircraft** [-'eəkrɑ:ft] *adj* antiaéreo; **~biotic** [-baɪ'ɔtɪk] *n* antibiótico; **~body** ['æntɪbɔdɪ] *n* anticuerpo
anticipate [æn'tɪsɪpeɪt] *vt* prever; (*expect*) esperar, contar con; (*look forward to*) esperar con ilusión; (*do first*) anticiparse a, adelantarse a; **anticipation** [-'peɪʃən] *n* (*expectation*) previsión *f*; (*eagerness*) ilusión *f*, expectación *f*
anticlimax [æntɪ'klaɪmæks] *n* decepción *f*

anticlockwise [æntɪ'klɔkwaɪz] (*BRIT*) *adv* en dirección contraria a la de las agujas del reloj

antics ['æntɪks] *npl* gracias *fpl*

anticyclone [æntɪ'saɪkləun] *n* anticiclón *m*

antidepressant ['æntɪdɪ'presnt] *n* antidepressivo

antidote ['æntɪdəut] *n* antídoto

antifreeze ['æntɪfriːz] *n* anticongelante *m*

antihistamine [æntɪ'hɪstəmiːn] *n* antihistamínico

antiquated ['æntɪkweɪtɪd] *adj* anticuado

antique [æn'tiːk] *n* antigüedad *f* ♦ *adj* antiguo; ~ **dealer** *n* anticuario/a; ~ **shop** *n* tienda de antigüedades

antiquity [æn'tɪkwɪtɪ] *n* antigüedad *f*

antiseptic [æntɪ'septɪk] *adj, n* antiséptico

antlers ['æntləz] *npl* cuernas *fpl*, cornamenta *sg*

anus ['eɪnəs] *n* ano

anvil ['ænvɪl] *n* yunque *m*

anxiety [æŋ'zaɪətɪ] *n* inquietud *f*; (*MED*) ansiedad *f*; ~ **to do** deseo de hacer

anxious ['æŋkʃəs] *adj* inquieto, preocupado; (*worrying*) preocupante; (*keen*): **to be ~ to do** tener muchas ganas de hacer

KEYWORD

any ['enɪ] *adj* 1 (*in questions etc*) algún/alguna; **have you ~ butter/children?** ¿tienes mantequilla/hijos?; **if there are ~ tickets left** si quedan billetes, si queda algún billete

2 (*with negative*): **I haven't ~ money/books** no tengo dinero/libros

3 (*no matter which*) cualquier; ~ **excuse will do** valdrá *or* servirá cualquier excusa; **choose ~ book you like** escoge el libro que quieras; ~ **teacher you ask will tell you** cualquier profesor al que preguntes te lo dirá

4 (*in phrases*): **in ~ case** de todas formas, en cualquier caso; ~ **day now** cualquier día (de estos); **at ~ moment** en cualquier momento, de un momento a otro; **at ~ rate** en todo caso; ~ **time: come (at) ~**

time ven cuando quieras; **he might come (at) ~ time** podría llegar de un momento a otro

♦ *pron* 1 (*in questions etc*): **have you got ~?** ¿tienes alguno(s)/a(s)?; **can ~ of you sing?** ¿sabe cantar alguno de vosotros/ustedes?

2 (*with negative*): **I haven't ~ (of them)** no tengo ninguno

3 (*no matter which one(s)*): **take ~ of those books (you like)** toma el libro que quieras de ésos

♦ *adv* 1 (*in questions etc*): **do you want ~ more soup/sandwiches?** ¿quieres más sopa/bocadillos?; **are you feeling ~ better?** ¿te sientes algo mejor?

2 (*with negative*): **I can't hear him ~ more** ya no le oigo; **don't wait ~ longer** no esperes más

anybody ['enɪbɔdɪ] *pron* cualquiera; (*in interrogative sentences*) alguien; (*in negative sentences*): **I don't see ~** no veo a nadie; **if ~ should phone ...** si llama alguien ...

anyhow ['enɪhau] *adv* (*at any rate*) de todos modos, de todas formas; (*haphazard*): **do it ~ you like** hazlo como quieras; **she leaves things just ~** deja las cosas como quiera *or* de cualquier modo; **I shall go ~** de todos modos iré

anyone ['enɪwʌn] *pron* = **anybody**

anything ['enɪθɪŋ] *pron* (*in questions etc*) algo, alguna cosa; (*with negative*) nada; **can you see ~?** ¿ves algo?; **if ~ happens to me ...** si algo me ocurre ...; (*no matter what*): **you can say ~ you like** puedes decir lo que quieras; ~ **will do** vale todo *or* cualquier cosa; **he'll eat ~** come de todo *or* lo que sea

anyway ['enɪweɪ] *adv* (*at any rate*) de todos modos, de todas formas; **I shall go ~** iré de todos modos; (*besides*): **~, I couldn't come even if I wanted to** además, no podría venir aunque quisiera; **why are you phoning, ~?** ¿entonces, por qué llamas?, ¿por qué llamas, pues?

anywhere ['ɛnɪwɛə*] adv (in questions etc):
can you see him ~? ¿le ves por algún
lado?; **are you going ~?** ¿vas a algún
sitio?; (with negative): **I can't see him ~**
no le veo por ninguna parte; **~ in the
world** (no matter where) en cualquier
parte (del mundo); **put the books down
~** deja los libros donde quieras

apart [ə'pɑːt] adv (aside) aparte; (situation):
~ (from) separado (de); (movement): **to
pull ~** separar; **10 miles ~** separados por
10 millas; **to take ~** desmontar; **~ from**
prep aparte de

apartheid [ə'pɑːteɪt] n apartheid m

apartment [ə'pɑːtmənt] n (US) piso (SP),
departamento (AM), apartamento; (room)
cuarto; **~ building** (US) n edificio de
apartamentos

apathetic [æpə'θɛtɪk] adj apático,
indiferente

ape [eɪp] n mono ♦ vt imitar, remedar

aperitif [ə'pɛrɪtɪf] n aperitivo

aperture ['æpətʃjuə*] n rendija, resquicio;
(PHOT) abertura

APEX ['eɪpɛks] n abbr (= Advanced
Purchase Excursion Fare) tarifa APEX f

apex n ápice m; (fig) cumbre f

apiece [ə'piːs] adv cada uno

aplomb [ə'plɔm] n aplomo

apologetic [əpɔlə'dʒɛtɪk] adj de disculpa;
(person) arrepentido

apologize [ə'pɔlədʒaɪz] vi: **to ~ (for sth to
sb)** disculparse (con alguien de algo)

apology [ə'pɔlədʒɪ] n disculpa, excusa

apostrophe [ə'pɔstrəfɪ] n apóstrofo m

appal [ə'pɔːl] vt horrorizar, espantar; **~ling**
adj espantoso; (awful) pésimo

apparatus [æpə'reɪtəs] n (equipment)
equipo; (organization) aparato; (in
gymnasium) aparatos mpl

apparel [ə'pærl] (US) n ropa

apparent [ə'pærənt] adj aparente;
(obvious) evidente; **~ly** adv por lo visto,
al parecer

appeal [ə'piːl] vi (LAW) apelar ♦ n (LAW)
apelación f; (request) llamamiento; (plea)
petición f; (charm) atractivo; **to ~ for**

reclamar; **to ~ to** (be attractive to) atraer;
it doesn't ~ to me no me atrae, no me
llama la atención; **~ing** adj (attractive)
atractivo

appear [ə'pɪə*] vi aparecer, presentarse;
(LAW) comparecer; (publication) salir (a
luz), publicarse; (seem) parecer; **to ~ on
TV/in "Hamlet"** salir por la tele/hacer
un papel en "Hamlet"; **it would ~ that**
parecería que; **~ance** n aparición f;
(look) apariencia, aspecto

appease [ə'piːz] vt (pacify) apaciguar;
(satisfy) satisfacer

appendices [ə'pɛndɪsiːz] npl of **appendix**

appendicitis [əpɛndɪ'saɪtɪs] n apendicitis f

appendix [ə'pɛndɪks] (pl **appendices**) n
apéndice m

appetite ['æpɪtaɪt] n apetito; (fig) deseo,
anhelo

appetizer ['æpɪtaɪzə*] n (drink) aperitivo;
(food) tapas fpl (SP)

applaud [ə'plɔːd] vt, vi aplaudir

applause [ə'plɔːz] n aplausos mpl

apple ['æpl] n manzana; **~ tree** n
manzano

appliance [ə'plaɪəns] n aparato

applicable [ə'plɪkəbl] adj (relevant): **to be
~ (to)** referirse (a)

applicant ['æplɪkənt] n candidato/a;
solicitante m/f

application [æplɪ'keɪʃən] n aplicación f;
(for a job etc) solicitud f, petición f; **~
form** n solicitud f

applied [ə'plaɪd] adj aplicado

apply [ə'plaɪ] vt (paint etc) poner; (law etc:
put into practice) poner en vigor ♦ vi: **to
~ to** (ask) dirigirse a; (be applicable) ser
aplicable a; **to ~ for** (permit, grant, job)
solicitar; **to ~ o.s. to** aplicarse a,
dedicarse a

appoint [ə'pɔɪnt] vt (to post) nombrar;
~ed adj: **at the ~ed time** a la hora
señalada; **~ment** n (with client) cita; (act)
nombramiento; (post) puesto; (at
hairdresser etc): **to have an ~ment** tener
hora; **to make an ~ment (with sb)** citarse
(con uno)

appraisal [əˈpreɪzl] n valoración f

appreciate [əˈpriːʃieɪt] vt apreciar, tener en mucho; (be grateful for) agradecer; (be aware of) comprender ♦ vi (COMM) aumentar(se) en valor; **appreciation** [-ˈeɪʃən] n apreciación f; (gratitude) reconocimiento, agradecimiento; (COMM) aumento en valor

appreciative [əˈpriːʃiətɪv] adj apreciativo; (comment) agradecido

apprehensive [æprɪˈhensɪv] adj aprensivo

apprentice [əˈprentɪs] n aprendiz/a m/f; **~ship** n aprendizaje m

approach [əˈprəʊtʃ] vi acercarse ♦ vt acercarse a; (ask, apply to) dirigirse a; (situation, problem) abordar ♦ n acercamiento; (access) acceso; (to problem, situation): ~ (to) actitud f (ante); **~able** adj (person) abordable; (place) accesible

appropriate [adj əˈprəʊprɪɪt, vb əˈprəʊprɪeɪt] adj apropiado, conveniente ♦ vt (take) apropiarse de

approval [əˈpruːvəl] n aprobación f, visto bueno; (permission) consentimiento; **on ~** (COMM) a prueba

approve [əˈpruːv] vt aprobar; **~ of** vt fus (thing) aprobar; (person): **they don't ~ of her** (ella) no les parece bien

approximate [əˈprɒksɪmɪt] adj aproximado; **~ly** adv aproximadamente, más o menos

apricot [ˈeɪprɪkɒt] n albaricoque m (SP), damasco (AM)

April [ˈeɪprəl] n abril m; **~ Fools' Day** n el primero de abril; ≈ día m de los Inocentes (28 December)

apron [ˈeɪprən] n delantal m

apt [æpt] adj acertado, apropiado; (likely): **~ to do** propenso a hacer

aquarium [əˈkweərɪəm] n acuario

Aquarius [əˈkweərɪəs] n Acuario

Arab [ˈærəb] adj, n árabe m/f

Arabian [əˈreɪbɪən] adj árabe

Arabic [ˈærəbɪk] adj árabe; (numerals) arábigo ♦ n árabe m

arable [ˈærəbl] adj cultivable

Aragon [ˈærəgən] n Aragón m

arbitrary [ˈɑːbɪtrərɪ] adj arbitrario

arbitration [ɑːbɪˈtreɪʃən] n arbitraje m

arcade [ɑːˈkeɪd] n (round a square) soportales mpl; (shopping mall) galería comercial

arch [ɑːtʃ] n arco; (of foot) arco del pie ♦ vt arquear

archaeologist [ɑːkɪˈɒlədʒɪst] (US **archeologist**) n arqueólogo/a

archaeology [ɑːkɪˈɒlədʒɪ] (US **archeology**) n arqueología

archbishop [ɑːtʃˈbɪʃəp] n arzobispo

archeology etc [ɑːkɪˈɒlədʒɪ] (US) = **archaeology** etc

archery [ˈɑːtʃərɪ] n tiro al arco

architect [ˈɑːkɪtekt] n arquitecto/a; **~ure** n arquitectura

archives [ˈɑːkaɪvz] npl archivo

Arctic [ˈɑːktɪk] adj ártico ♦ n: **the ~** el Ártico

ardent [ˈɑːdənt] adj ardiente, apasionado

arduous [ˈɑːdjuəs] adj (task) arduo; (journey) agotador(a)

are [ɑː*] vb see **be**

area [ˈeərɪə] n área, región f; (part of place) zona; (MATH etc) área, superficie f; (in room: e.g. dining ~) parte f; (of knowledge, experience) campo

arena [əˈriːnə] n estadio; (of circus) pista

aren't [ɑːnt] = **are not**

Argentina [ɑːdʒənˈtiːnə] n Argentina; **Argentinian** [-ˈtɪnɪən] adj, n argentino/a m/f

arguably [ˈɑːgjuəblɪ] adv posiblemente

argue [ˈɑːgjuː] vi (quarrel) discutir, pelearse; (reason) razonar, argumentar; **to ~ that** sostener que

argument [ˈɑːgjumənt] n discusión f, pelea; (reasons) argumento; **~ative** [-ˈmentətɪv] adj discutidor(a)

Aries [ˈeərɪz] n Aries m

arise [əˈraɪz] (pt **arose**, pp **arisen**) vi surgir, presentarse

arisen [əˈrɪzn] pp of **arise**

aristocrat [ˈærɪstəkræt] n aristócrata m/f

arithmetic [əˈrɪθmətɪk] n aritmética

ark [ɑːk] *n*: **Noah's A~** el Arca *f* de Noé

arm [ɑːm] *n* brazo ♦ *vt* armar; **~s** *npl* armas *fpl*; **~ in ~** cogidos del brazo

armaments ['ɑːməmənts] *npl* armamento

armchair ['ɑːmtʃeə*] *n* sillón *m*, butaca

armed [ɑːmd] *adj* armado; **~ robbery** *n* robo a mano armada

armour ['ɑːmə*] (*US* **armor**) *n* armadura; (*MIL: tanks*) blindaje *m*; **~ed car** *n* coche *m* (*SP*) *or* carro (*AM*) blindado

armpit ['ɑːmpɪt] *n* sobaco, axila

armrest ['ɑːmrest] *n* apoyabrazos *m inv*

army ['ɑːmɪ] *n* ejército *m*, (*fig*) multitud *f*

aroma [ə'rəumə] *n* aroma *m*, fragancia; **~therapy** *n* aromaterapia

arose [ə'rəuz] *pt of* **arise**

around [ə'raund] *adv* alrededor; (*in the area*): **there is no one else ~** no hay nadie más por aquí ♦ *prep* alrededor de

arouse [ə'rauz] *vt* despertar; (*anger*) provocar

arrange [ə'reɪndʒ] *vt* arreglar, ordenar; (*organize*) organizar; **to ~ to do sth** quedar en hacer algo; **~ment** *n* arreglo; (*agreement*) acuerdo; **~ments** *npl* (*preparations*) preparativos *mpl*

array [ə'reɪ] *n*: **~ of** (*things*) serie *f* de; (*people*) conjunto de

arrears [ə'rɪəz] *npl* atrasos *mpl*; **to be in ~ with one's rent** estar retrasado en el pago del alquiler

arrest [ə'rest] *vt* detener; (*sb's attention*) llamar ♦ *n* detención *f*; **under ~** detenido

arrival [ə'raɪvəl] *n* llegada; **new ~** recién llegado/a; (*baby*) recién nacido

arrive [ə'raɪv] *vi* llegar; (*baby*) nacer

arrogant ['ærəgənt] *adj* arrogante

arrow ['ærəu] *n* flecha

arse [ɑːs] (*BRIT: inf!*) *n* culo, trasero

arson ['ɑːsn] *n* incendio premeditado

art [ɑːt] *n* arte *m*; (*skill*) destreza; **A~s** *npl* (*SCOL*) Letras *fpl*

artery ['ɑːtərɪ] *n* arteria

art gallery *n* pinacoteca; (*saleroom*) galería de arte

arthritis [ɑː'θraɪtɪs] *n* artritis *f*

artichoke ['ɑːtɪtʃəuk] *n* alcachofa;
Jerusalem ~ aguaturma

article ['ɑːtɪkl] *n* artículo; (*BRIT: LAW: training*): **~s** *npl* contrato de aprendizaje; **~ of clothing** prenda de vestir

articulate [*adj* ɑː'tɪkjulɪt, *vb* ɑː'tɪkjuleɪt] *adj* claro, bien expresado ♦ *vt* expresar; **~d lorry** (*BRIT*) *n* trailer *m*

artificial [ɑːtɪ'fɪʃəl] *adj* artificial; (*affected*) afectado

artillery [ɑː'tɪlərɪ] *n* artillería

artisan ['ɑːtɪzæn] *n* artesano

artist ['ɑːtɪst] *n* artista *m/f*; (*MUS*) intérprete *m/f*; **~ic** [ɑː'tɪstɪk] *adj* artístico; **~ry** *n* arte *m*, habilidad *f* (artística)

art school *n* escuela de bellas artes

KEYWORD
---

as [æz] *conj* **1** (*referring to time*) cuando, mientras; a medida que; **~ the years went by** con el paso de los años; **he came in ~ I was leaving** entró cuando me marchaba; **~ from tomorrow** desde *or* a partir de mañana

2 (*in comparisons*): **~ big ~** tan grande como; **twice ~ big ~** el doble de grande que; **~ much money/many books ~** tanto dinero/tantos libros como; **~ soon ~** en cuanto

3 (*since, because*) como, ya que; **he left early ~ he had to be home by 10** se fue temprano ya que tenía que estar en casa a las 10

4 (*referring to manner, way*): **do ~ you wish** haz lo que quieras; **~ she said** como dijo; **he gave it to me ~ a present** me lo dio de regalo

5 (*in the capacity of*): **he works ~ a barman** trabaja de barman; **~ chairman of the company, he ...** como presidente de la compañía, ...

6 (*concerning*): **~ for** *or* **to that** por *or* en lo que respecta a eso

7: **~ if** *or* **though** como si; **he looked ~ if he was ill** parecía como si estuviera enfermo, tenía aspecto de enfermo; *see also* **long**; **such**; **well**

a.s.a.p. *abbr* (= *as soon as possible*) cuanto antes

asbestos [æz'bestəs] *n* asbesto, amianto

ascend [ə'send] *vt* subir; (*throne*) ascender *or* subir a

ascent [ə'sent] *n* subida; (*slope*) cuesta, pendiente *f*

ascertain [æsə'teɪn] *vt* averiguar

ash [æʃ] *n* ceniza; (*tree*) fresno

ashamed [ə'ʃeɪmd] *adj* avergonzado, apenado (*AM*); **to be ~ of** avergonzarse de

ashore [ə'ʃɔː*] *adv* en tierra; (*swim etc*) a tierra

ashtray ['æʃtreɪ] *n* cenicero

Ash Wednesday *n* miércoles *m* de Ceniza

Asia ['eɪʃə] *n* Asia; **~n** *adj, n* asiático/a *m/f*

aside [ə'saɪd] *adv* a un lado ♦ *n* aparte *m*

ask [ɑːsk] *vt* (*question*) preguntar; (*invite*) invitar; **to ~ sb sth/to do sth** preguntar algo a alguien/pedir a alguien que haga algo; **to ~ sb about sth** preguntar algo a alguien; **to ~ (sb) a question** hacer una pregunta (a alguien); **to ~ sb out to dinner** invitar a cenar a uno; **~ after** *vt fus* preguntar por; **~ for** *vt fus* pedir; (*trouble*) buscar

asking price *n* precio inicial

asleep [ə'sliːp] *adj* dormido; **to fall ~** dormirse, quedarse dormido

asparagus [əs'pærəgəs] *n* (*plant*) espárrago; (*food*) espárragos *mpl*

aspect ['æspekt] *n* aspecto, apariencia; (*direction in which a building etc faces*) orientación *f*

aspersions [əs'pəːʃənz] *npl*: **to cast ~ on** difamar a, calumniar a

asphyxiation [æsfɪksɪ'eɪʃən] *n* asfixia

aspire [əs'paɪə*] *vi*: **to ~ to** aspirar a, ambicionar

aspirin ['æsprɪn] *n* aspirina

ass [æs] *n* asno, burro; (*inf: idiot*) imbécil *m/f*; (*US: inf!*) culo, trasero

assailant [ə'seɪlənt] *n* asaltador(a) *m/f*, agresor(a) *m/f*

assassinate [ə'sæsɪneɪt] *vt* asesinar;

assassination [əsæsɪ'neɪʃən] *n* asesinato

assault [ə'sɔːlt] *n* asalto; (*LAW*) agresión *f* ♦ *vt* asaltar, atacar; (*sexually*) violar

assemble [ə'sembl] *vt* reunir, juntar; (*TECH*) montar ♦ *vi* reunirse, juntarse

assembly [ə'semblɪ] *n* reunión *f*, asamblea; (*parliament*) parlamento *m*; (*construction*) montaje *m*; **~ line** *n* cadena de montaje

assent [ə'sent] *n* asentimiento, aprobación *f*

assert [ə'səːt] *vt* afirmar; (*authority*) hacer valer; **~ion** [-[ən] *n* afirmación *f*

assess [ə'ses] *vt* valorar, calcular; (*tax, damages*) fijar; (*for tax*) gravar; **~ment** *n* valoración *f*; (*for tax*) gravamen *m*; **~or** *n* asesor(a) *m/f*

asset ['æset] *n* ventaja; **~s** *npl* (*COMM*) activo; (*property, funds*) fondos *mpl*

assign [ə'saɪn] *vt*: **to ~ (to)** (*date*) fijar (para); (*task*) asignar (a); (*resources*) destinar (a); **~ment** *n* tarea

assist [ə'sɪst] *vt* ayudar; **~ance** *n* ayuda, auxilio; **~ant** *n* ayudante *m/f*; (*BRIT: also:* **shop ~ant**) dependiente/a *m/f*

associate [*adj, n* ə'səʊʃɪɪt, *vb* ə'səʊʃɪeɪt] *adj* asociado ♦ *n* (*at work*) colega *m/f* ♦ *vt* asociar; (*ideas*) relacionar ♦ *vi*: **to ~ with sb** tratar con alguien

association [əsəʊsɪ'eɪʃən] *n* asociación *f*

assorted [ə'sɔːtɪd] *adj* surtido, variado

assortment [ə'sɔːtmənt] *n* (*of shapes, colours*) surtido; (*of books*) colección *f*; (*of people*) mezcla

assume [ə'sjuːm] *vt* suponer; (*responsibilities*) asumir; (*attitude*) adoptar, tomar

assumption [ə'sʌmpʃən] *n* suposición *f*, presunción *f*; (*of power etc*) toma

assurance [ə'ʃuərəns] *n* garantía, promesa; (*confidence*) confianza, aplomo; (*insurance*) seguro

assure [ə'ʃuə*] *vt* asegurar

asthma ['æsmə] *n* asma

astonish [ə'stɒnɪʃ] *vt* asombrar, pasmar; **~ment** *n* asombro, sorpresa

astound [ə'staund] *vt* asombrar, pasmar

astray [ə'streɪ] *adv:* **to go ~** extraviarse; **to lead ~** (*morally*) llevar por mal camino

astride [ə'straɪd] *prep* a caballo *or* horcajadas sobre

astrology [æs'trɒlədʒɪ] *n* astrología

astronaut ['æstrənɔːt] *n* astronauta *m/f*

astronomy [æs'trɒnəmɪ] *n* astronomía

asylum [ə'saɪləm] *n* (*refuge*) asilo; (*mental hospital*) manicomio

---KEYWORD---

at [æt] *prep* **1** (*referring to position*) en; (*direction*) a; **~ the top** en lo alto; **~ home/school** en casa/la escuela; **to look ~ sth/sb** mirar algo/a uno
2 (*referring to time*): **~ 4 o'clock** a las 4; **~ night** por la noche; **~ Christmas** en Navidad; **~ times** a veces
3 (*referring to rates, speed etc*): **~ £1 a kilo** a una libra el kilo; **two ~ a time** de dos en dos; **~ 50 km/h** a 50 km/h
4 (*referring to manner*): **~ a stroke** de un golpe; **~ peace** en paz
5 (*referring to activity*): **to be ~ work** estar trabajando; (*in the office etc*) estar en el trabajo; **to play ~ cowboys** jugar a los vaqueros; **to be good ~ sth** ser bueno en algo
6 (*referring to cause*): **shocked/surprised/annoyed ~ sth** asombrado/sorprendido/fastidiado por algo; **I went ~ his suggestion** fui a instancias suyas

ate [eɪt] *pt of* **eat**

atheist ['eɪθɪɪst] *n* ateo/a

Athens ['æθɪnz] *n* Atenas

athlete ['æθliːt] *n* atleta *m/f*

athletic [æθ'letɪk] *adj* atlético; **~s** *n* atletismo

Atlantic [ət'læntɪk] *adj* atlántico ♦ *n:* **the ~ (Ocean)** el (Océano) Atlántico

atlas ['ætləs] *n* atlas *m*

A.T.M. *n abbr* (= *automated telling machine*) cajero automático

atmosphere ['ætməsfɪə*] *n* atmósfera; (*of place*) ambiente *m*

atom ['ætəm] *n* átomo; **~ic** [ə'tɒmɪk] *adj*

atómico; **~(ic) bomb** *n* bomba atómica; **~izer** ['ætəmaɪzə*] *n* atomizador *m*

atone [ə'təun] *vi:* **~ for** expiar

atrocious [ə'trəuʃəs] *adj* atroz

attach [ə'tætʃ] *vt* (*fasten*) atar; (*join*) unir, sujetar; (*document, letter*) adjuntar; (*importance etc*) dar, conceder; **to be ~ed to sb/sth** (*to like*) tener cariño a alguien/algo

attaché case [ə'tæʃeɪ-] *n* maletín *m*

attachment [ə'tætʃmənt] *n* (*tool*) accesorio; (*love*): **~ (to)** apego (a)

attack [ə'tæk] *vt* (MIL) atacar; (*subj: criminal*) agredir, asaltar; (*criticize*) criticar; (*task*) emprender ♦ *n* ataque *m*, asalto; (*on sb's life*) atentado; (*fig: criticism*) crítica; (*of illness*) ataque *m*; **heart ~** infarto (de miocardio); **~er** *n* agresor(a) *m/f*, asaltante *m/f*

attain [ə'teɪn] *vt* (*also:* **~ to**) alcanzar; (*achieve*) lograr, conseguir

attempt [ə'tempt] *n* tentativa, intento; (*attack*) atentado ♦ *vt* intentar; **~ed** *adj:* **~ed burglary/murder/suicide** tentativa *or* intento de robo/asesinato/suicidio

attend [ə'tend] *vt* asistir a; (*patient*) atender; **~ to** *vt fus* ocuparse de; (*customer, patient*) atender a; **~ance** *n* asistencia, presencia; (*people present*) concurrencia; **~ant** *n* ayudante *m/f*; (*in garage etc*) encargado/a ♦ *adj* (*dangers*) concomitante

attention [ə'tenʃən] *n* atención *f*; (*care*) atenciones *fpl* ♦ *excl* (MIL) ¡firme(s)!; **for the ~ of ...** (ADMIN) atención ...

attentive [ə'tentɪv] *adj* atento

attic ['ætɪk] *n* desván *m*

attitude ['ætɪtjuːd] *n* actitud *f*; (*disposition*) disposición *f*

attorney [ə'tɜːnɪ] *n* (*lawyer*) abogado/a; **A~ General** (BRIT) ≈ Presidente *m* del Consejo del Poder Judicial (SP); (US) ≈ ministro de justicia

attract [ə'trækt] *vt* atraer; (*sb's attention*) llamar; **~ion** [ə'trækʃən] *n* encanto; (*gen pl: amusements*) diversiones *fpl*; (PHYSICS) atracción *f*; (*fig: towards sb, sth*) atractivo;

~ive adj guapo; (interesting) atrayente
attribute [n 'ætrɪbjuːt, vb ə'trɪbjuːt] n
atributo ♦ vt: **to ~ sth to** atribuir algo a
attrition [ə'trɪʃən] n: **war of ~** guerra de
agotamiento
aubergine ['əubəʒiːn] (BRIT) n berenjena;
(colour) morado
auburn ['ɔːbən] adj color castaño rojizo
auction ['ɔːkʃən] n (also: sale by ~) subasta
♦ vt subastar; **~eer** [-'nɪə*] n
subastador(a) m/f
audible ['ɔːdɪbl] adj audible, que se puede
oír
audience ['ɔːdɪəns] n público; (RADIO)
radioescuchas mpl; (TV) telespectadores
mpl; (interview) audiencia
audio-visual [ɔːdɪəu'vɪzjuəl] adj
audiovisual; **~ aid** n ayuda audiovisual
audit ['ɔːdɪt] vt revisar, intervenir
audition [ɔː'dɪʃən] n audición f
auditor ['ɔːdɪtə*] n interventor(a) m/f,
censor(a) m/f de cuentas
augment [ɔːg'ment] vt aumentar
augur ['ɔːgə*] vi: **it ~s well** es un buen
augurio
August ['ɔːgəst] n agosto
aunt [ɑːnt] n tía; **~ie** n diminutive of
aunt; **~y** n diminutive of **aunt**
au pair ['əu'peə*] n (also: ~ **girl**) (chica) au
pair f
auspicious [ɔːs'pɪʃəs] adj propicio, de
buen augurio
Australia [ɔs'treɪlɪə] n Australia; **~n** adj, n
australiano/a m/f
Austria ['ɔstrɪə] n Austria; **~n** adj, n
austríaco/a m/f
authentic [ɔː'θentɪk] adj auténtico
author ['ɔːθə] n autor(a) m/f
authoritarian [ɔːθɔrɪ'teərɪən] adj
autoritario
authoritative [ɔː'θɔrɪtətɪv] adj autorizado;
(manner) autoritario
authority [ɔː'θɔrɪtɪ] n autoridad f; (official
permission) autorización f; **the authorities**
npl las autoridades
authorize ['ɔːθəraɪz] vt autorizar
auto ['ɔːtəu] (US) n coche m (SP), carro

(AM), automóvil m
auto: ~biography [ɔːtəbar'ɔgrəfɪ] n
autobiografía; **~graph** ['ɔːtəgrɑːf] n
autógrafo ♦ vt (photo etc) dedicar;
(programme) firmar; **~mated** ['ɔːtəmeɪtɪd]
adj automatizado; **~matic** [ɔːtə'mætɪk] adj
automático ♦ n (gun) pistola automática;
(car) coche m automático; **~matically**
adv automáticamente; **~mation**
[ɔː'tɔmeɪʃən] n reconversión f; **~mobile**
['ɔːtəməbiːl] (US) n coche m (SP), carro
(AM), automóvil m; **~nomy** [ɔː'tɔnəmɪ] n
autonomía
autumn ['ɔːtəm] n otoño
auxiliary [ɔːg'zɪlɪərɪ] adj, n auxiliar m/f
avail [ə'veɪl] vt: **to ~ o.s. of** aprovechar(se)
de ♦ n: **to no ~** en vano, sin resultado
available [ə'veɪləbl] adj disponible;
(unoccupied) libre; (person: unattached)
soltero y sin compromiso
avalanche ['ævəlɑːnʃ] n alud m,
avalancha
avant-garde ['ævɑ̃'gɑːd] adj de
vanguardia
Ave. abbr = **avenue**
avenge [ə'vendʒ] vt vengar
avenue ['ævənjuː] n avenida; (fig) camino
average ['ævərɪdʒ] n promedio, término
medio ♦ adj medio, de término medio;
(ordinary) regular, corriente ♦ vt sacar un
promedio de; **on ~** por regla general; **~
out** vi: **to ~ out at** salir en un promedio
de
averse [ə'vɜːs] adj: **to be ~ to sth/doing**
sentir aversión or antipatía por algo/por
hacer
avert [ə'vɜːt] vt prevenir; (blow) desviar;
(one's eyes) apartar
aviary ['eɪvɪərɪ] n pajarera, avería
avocado [ævə'kɑːdəu] n (also: BRIT: ~
pear) aguacate m (SP), palta (AM)
avoid [ə'vɔɪd] vt evitar, eludir
await [ə'weɪt] vt esperar, aguardar
awake [ə'weɪk] (pt awoke, pp awoken or
awaked) adj despierto ♦ vt despertar
♦ vi despertarse; **to be ~** estar despierto;
~ning n el despertar

award [ə'wɔːd] *n* premio; (*LAW: damages*) indemnización *f* ♦ *vt* otorgar, conceder; (*LAW: damages*) adjudicar

aware [ə'wɛə*] *adj*: ~ **(of)** consciente (de); **to become ~ of/that** (*realize*) darse cuenta de/de que; (*learn*) enterarse de/de que; **~ness** *n* conciencia; (*knowledge*) conocimiento

away [ə'weɪ] *adv* fuera; (*movement*): **she went ~** se marchó; (*far ~*) lejos; **two kilometres ~** a dos kilómetros de distancia; **two hours ~ by car** a dos horas en coche; **the holiday was two weeks ~** faltaban dos semanas para las vacaciones; **he's ~ for a week** estará ausente una semana; **to take ~ (from)** quitar (a); (*subtract*) substraer (de); **to work/pedal ~** seguir trabajando/pedaleando; **to fade ~** (*colour*) desvanecerse; (*sound*) apagarse; ~ **game** *n* (*SPORT*) partido de fuera

awe [ɔː] *n* admiración *f* respetuosa; **~-inspiring** *adj* imponente

awful ['ɔːfəl] *adj* horroroso; (*quantity*): **an ~ lot (of)** cantidad (de); **~ly** *adv* (*very*) terriblemente

awkward ['ɔːkwəd] *adj* desmañado, torpe; (*shape*) incómodo; (*embarrassing*) delicado, difícil

awning ['ɔːnɪŋ] *n* (*of tent, caravan, shop*) toldo

awoke [ə'wəuk] *pt of* **awake**

awoken [ə'wəukən] *pp of* **awake**

awry [ə'raɪ] *adv*: **to be ~** estar descolocado *or* mal puesto

axe [æks] (*US* **ax**) *n* hacha ♦ *vt* (*project*) cortar; (*jobs*) reducir

axes ['æksiːz] *npl of* **axis**

axis ['æksɪs] (*pl* **axes**) *n* eje *m*

axle ['æksl] *n* eje *m*, árbol *m*

ay(e) [aɪ] *excl* sí

B, b

B [biː] *n* (*MUS*) si *m*

B.A. *abbr* = **Bachelor of Arts**

baby ['beɪbɪ] *n* bebé *m/f*; (*US: inf: darling*) mi amor; ~ **carriage** (*US*) *n* cochecito; **~-sit** *vi* hacer de canguro; **~-sitter** *n* canguro/a; ~ **wipe** *n* toallita húmeda (*para bebés*)

bachelor ['bætʃələ*] *n* soltero; **B~ of Arts/Science** licenciado/a en Filosofía y Letras/Ciencias

back [bæk] *n* (*of person*) espalda; (*of animal*) lomo; (*of hand*) dorso; (*as opposed to front*) parte *f* de atrás; (*of chair*) respaldo; (*of page*) reverso; (*of book*) final *m*; (*FOOTBALL*) defensa *m*; (*of crowd*): **the ones at the ~** los del fondo ♦ *vt* (*candidate: also:* ~ **up**) respaldar, apoyar; (*horse: at races*) apostar a; (*car*) dar marcha atrás a *or* con ♦ *vi* (*car etc*) ir (*or* salir *or* entrar) marcha atrás ♦ *adj* (*payment, rent*) atrasado; (*seats, wheels*) de atrás ♦ *adv* (*not forward*) (hacia) atrás; (*returned*): **he's ~** está de vuelta, ha vuelto; **he ran ~** volvió corriendo; (*restitution*): **throw the ball ~** devuelve la pelota; **can I have it ~?** ¿me lo devuelve?; (*again*): **he called ~** llamó de nuevo; ~ **down** *vi* echarse atrás; ~ **out** *vi* (*of promise*) volverse atrás; ~ **up** *vt* (*person*) apoyar, respaldar; (*theory*) defender; (*COMPUT*) hacer una copia preventiva *or* de reserva; **~bencher** (*BRIT*) *n* miembro del parlamento sin cargo relevante; **~bone** *n* columna vertebral; **~date** *vt* (*pay rise*) dar efecto retroactivo a; (*letter*) poner fecha atrasada a; **~drop** *n* telón *m* de fondo; **~fire** *vi* (*AUT*) petardear; (*plans*) fallar, salir mal; **~ground** *n* fondo; (*of events*) antecedentes *mpl*; (*basic knowledge*) bases *fpl*; (*experience*) conocimientos *mpl*, educación *f*; **family ~ground** origen *m*, antecedentes *mpl*; **~hand** *n* (*TENNIS*:

also: **~hand stroke**) revés *m*; **~hander**
(*BRIT*) *n* (*bribe*) soborno; **~ing** *n* (*fig*)
apoyo, respaldo; **~lash** *n* reacción *f*;
~log *n*: **~log of work** trabajo atrasado; **~
number** *n* (*of magazine etc*) número
atrasado; **~pack** *n* mochila; **~packer** *n*
mochilero/a; **~ pay** *n* pago atrasado;
~side (*inf*) *n* trasero, culo; **~stage** *adv*
entre bastidores; **~stroke** *n* espalda;
~up *adj* suplementario; (*COMPUT*) de
reserva ♦ *n* (*support*) apoyo; (*also*: **~-up
file**) copia preventiva *or* de reserva;
~ward *adj* (*person, country*) atrasado;
~wards *adv* hacia atrás; (*read a list*) al
revés; (*fall*) de espaldas; **~yard** *n*
traspatio

bacon ['beɪkən] *n* tocino, beicon *m*

bad [bæd] *adj* malo; (*mistake, accident*)
grave; (*food*) podrido, pasado; **his ~ leg**
su pierna lisiada; **to go ~** (*food*) pasarse

badge [bædʒ] *n* insignia; (*policeman's*)
chapa, placa

badger ['bædʒə*] *n* tejón *m*

badly ['bædlɪ] *adv* mal; **to reflect ~ on sb**
influir negativamente en la reputación de
uno; **~ wounded** gravemente herido; **he
needs it ~** le hace gran falta; **to be ~ off
(for money)** andar mal de dinero

badminton ['bædmɪntən] *n* bádminton *m*

bad-tempered *adj* de mal genio *or*
carácter; (*temporarily*) de mal humor

bag [bæg] *n* bolsa; (*handbag*) bolso;
(*satchel*) mochila; (*case*) maleta; **~s of**
(*inf*) un montón de; **~gage** *n* equipaje
m; **~gage allowance** *n* límite *m* de
equipaje; **~gage reclaim** *n* recogida de
equipajes; **~gy** *adj* amplio; **~pipes** *npl*
gaita

Bahamas [bə'hɑːməz] *npl*: **the ~** las Islas
Bahamas

bail [beɪl] *n* fianza ♦ *vt* (*prisoner: gen: grant
~ to*) poner en libertad bajo fianza; (*boat:
also: ~ out*) achicar; **on ~** (*prisoner*) bajo
fianza; **to ~ sb out** obtener la libertad de
uno bajo fianza; *see also* **bale**

bailiff ['beɪlɪf] *n* alguacil *m*

bait [beɪt] *n* cebo ♦ *vt* poner cebo en;

(*tease*) tomar el pelo a

bake [beɪk] *vt* cocer (al horno) ♦ *vi*
cocerse; **~d beans** *npl* judías *fpl* en salsa
de tomate; **~d potato** *n* patata al horno;
~r *n* panadero; **~ry** *n* panadería; (*for
cakes*) pastelería; **baking** *n* (*act*) amasar
m; (*batch*) hornada; **baking powder** *n*
levadura (en polvo)

balance ['bæləns] *n* equilibrio; (*COMM:
sum*) balance *m*; (*remainder*) resto; (*scales*)
balanza ♦ *vt* equilibrar; (*budget*) nivelar;
(*account*) saldar; (*make equal*) equilibrar; **~
of trade/payments** balanza de
comercio/pagos; **~d** *adj* (*personality, diet*)
equilibrado; (*report*) objetivo; **~ sheet** *n*
balance *m*

balcony ['bælkənɪ] *n* (*open*) balcón *m*;
(*closed*) galería; (*in theatre*) anfiteatro

bald [bɔːld] *adj* calvo; (*tyre*) liso

bale [beɪl] *n* (*AGR*) paca, fardo; (*of papers
etc*) fajo; **~ out** *vi* lanzarse en paracaídas

Balearics [bælɪ'ærɪks] *npl*: **the ~** las
Baleares

ball [bɔːl] *n* pelota; (*football*) balón *m*; (*of
wool, string*) ovillo; (*dance*) baile *m*; **to
play ~** (*fig*) cooperar

ballast ['bæləst] *n* lastre *m*

ball bearings *npl* cojinetes *mpl* de bolas

ballerina [bælə'riːnə] *n* bailarina

ballet ['bæleɪ] *n* ballet *m*; **~ dancer** *n*
bailarín/ina *m/f*

balloon [bə'luːn] *n* globo

ballot ['bælət] *n* votación *f*; **~ paper** *n*
papeleta (para votar)

ballpoint (pen) ['bɔːlpɔɪnt-] *n* bolígrafo

ballroom ['bɔːlrum] *n* salón *m* de baile

Baltic ['bɔːltɪk] *n*: **the ~ (Sea)** el (Mar)
Báltico

ban [bæn] *n* prohibición *f*, proscripción *f*
♦ *vt* prohibir, proscribir

banal [bə'nɑːl] *adj* banal, vulgar

banana [bə'nɑːnə] *n* plátano (*SP*), banana
(*AM*)

band [bænd] *n* grupo; (*strip*) faja, tira;
(*stripe*) lista; (*MUS: jazz*) orquesta; (: *rock*)
grupo; (: *MIL*) banda; **~ together** *vi*
juntarse, asociarse

bandage ['bændɪdʒ] n venda, vendaje m
♦ vt vendar
Bandaid ® ['bændeɪd] (US) n tirita
bandit ['bændɪt] n bandido
bandy-legged ['bændɪ'legd] adj estevado
bang [bæŋ] n (of gun, exhaust) estallido,
detonación f; (of door) portazo; (blow)
golpe m ♦ vt (door) cerrar de golpe;
(one's head) golpear ♦ vi estallar; (door)
cerrar de golpe
Bangladesh [bæŋglə'deʃ] n Bangladesh m
bangs [bæŋz] (US) npl flequillo
banish ['bænɪʃ] vt desterrar
banister(s) ['bænɪstə(z)] n(pl) barandilla,
pasamanos m inv
bank [bæŋk] n (COMM) banco; (of river,
lake) ribera, orilla; (of earth) terraplén m
♦ vi (AVIAT) ladearse; ~ **on** vt fus contar
con; ~ **account** n cuenta de banco; ~
card n tarjeta bancaria; ~**er** n banquero;
~**er's card** (BRIT) n = ~ **card**; **B~
holiday** (BRIT) n día m festivo; ~**ing** n
banca; ~**note** n billete m de banco; ~
rate n tipo de interés bancario

---
bank holiday
---

*El término bank holiday se aplica en
el Reino Unido a todo día festivo
oficial en el que cierran bancos y
comercios. Los más importantes son en
Navidad, Semana Santa, finales de mayo
y finales de agosto y, al contrario que en
los países de tradición católica, no
coinciden necesariamente con una
celebración religiosa.*

bankrupt ['bæŋkrʌpt] adj quebrado,
insolvente; **to go ~** hacer bancarrota; **to
be ~** estar en quiebra; ~**cy** n quiebra
bank statement n balance m or detalle
m de cuenta
banner ['bænə*] n pancarta
bannister(s) ['bænɪstə(z)] n(pl)
= **banister(s)**
baptism ['bæptɪzəm] n bautismo; (act)
bautizo
bar [bɑː*] n (pub) bar m; (counter)

mostrador m; (rod) barra; (of window,
cage) reja; (of soap) pastilla; (of chocolate)
tableta; (fig: hindrance) obstáculo;
(prohibition) proscripción f; (MUS) barra
♦ vt (road) obstruir; (person) excluir;
(activity) prohibir; **the B~** (LAW) la
abogacía; **behind ~s** entre rejas; ~ **none**
sin excepción
barbaric [bɑː'bærɪk] adj bárbaro
barbecue ['bɑːbɪkjuː] n barbacoa
barbed wire ['bɑːbd-] n alambre m de
púas
barber ['bɑːbə*] n peluquero, barbero
bar code n código de barras
bare [beə*] adj desnudo; (trees) sin hojas;
(necessities etc) básico ♦ vt desnudar;
(teeth) enseñar; ~**back** adv a pelo, sin
silla; ~**faced** adj descarado; ~**foot** adj,
adv descalzo; ~**ly** adv apenas
bargain ['bɑːgɪn] n pacto, negocio; (good
buy) ganga ♦ vi negociar; (haggle)
regatear; **into the ~** además, por
añadidura; ~ **for** vt fus: **he got more
than he ~ed for** le resultó peor de lo que
esperaba
barge [bɑːdʒ] n barcaza; ~ **in** vi irrumpir;
(interrupt: conversation) interrumpir
bark [bɑːk] n (of tree) corteza; (of dog)
ladrido ♦ vi ladrar
barley ['bɑːlɪ] n cebada
barmaid ['bɑːmeɪd] n camarera
barman ['bɑːmən] n camarero, barman m
barn [bɑːn] n granero
barometer [bə'rɒmɪtə*] n barómetro
baron ['bærən] n barón m; (press ~ etc)
magnate m; ~**ess** n baronesa
barracks ['bærəks] npl cuartel m
barrage ['bærɑːʒ] n (MIL) descarga,
bombardeo; (dam) presa; (of criticism)
lluvia, aluvión m
barrel ['bærəl] n barril m; (of gun) cañón
m
barren ['bærən] adj estéril
barricade [bærɪ'keɪd] n barricada
barrier ['bærɪə*] n barrera
barring ['bɑːrɪŋ] prep excepto, salvo
barrister ['bærɪstə*] (BRIT) n abogado/a

barrow ['bærəu] n (cart) carretilla (de mano)

bartender ['bɑːtendə*] (US) n camarero, barman m

barter ['bɑːtə*] vt: **to ~ sth for sth** trocar algo por algo

base [beɪs] n base f ♦ vt: **to ~ sth on** basar or fundar algo en ♦ adj bajo, infame

baseball ['beɪsbɔːl] n béisbol m

basement ['beɪsmənt] n sótano

bases¹ ['beɪsiːz] npl of **basis**

bases² ['beɪsɪz] npl of **base**

bash [bæʃ] (inf) vt golpear

bashful ['bæʃful] adj tímido, vergonzoso

basic ['beɪsɪk] adj básico; **~ally** adv fundamentalmente, en el fondo; (simply) sencillamente; **~s** npl: **the ~s** los fundamentos

basil ['bæzl] n albahaca

basin ['beɪsn] n (concave, tazón m; (GEO) cuenca; (also: **wash~**) lavabo

basis ['beɪsɪs] (pl **bases**) n base f; **on a part-time/trial ~** a tiempo parcial/a prueba

bask [bɑːsk] vi: **to ~ in the sun** tomar el sol

basket ['bɑːskɪt] n cesta, cesto; canasta; **~ball** n baloncesto

Basque [bæsk] adj, n vasco/a m/f; **~ Country** n Euskadi m, País m Vasco

bass [beɪs] n (MUS: instrument) bajo; (double ~) contrabajo; (singer) bajo

bassoon [bə'suːn] n fagot m

bastard ['bɑːstəd] n bastardo; (inf!) hijo de puta (!)

bat [bæt] n (ZOOL) murciélago; (for ball games) palo; (BRIT: for table tennis) pala ♦ vt: **he didn't ~ an eyelid** ni pestañeó

batch [bætʃ] n (of bread) hornada; (of letters etc) lote m

bated ['beɪtɪd] adj: **with ~ breath** sin respirar

bath [bɑːθ, pl bɑːðz] n (action) baño; (~tub) baño (SP), bañera (SP), tina (AM) ♦ vt bañar; **to have a ~** bañarse, tomar un baño; see also **baths**

bathe [beɪð] vi bañarse ♦ vt (wound) lavar; **~r** n bañista m/f

bathing ['beɪðɪŋ] n el bañarse; **~ costume** (US = **suit**) n traje m de baño

bath: ~robe n (man's) batín m; (woman's) bata; **~room** n (cuarto de) baño; **~s** [bɑːðz] npl (also: **swimming ~s**) piscina; **~ towel** n toalla de baño

baton ['bætən] n (MUS) batuta; (ATHLETICS) testigo; (weapon) porra

batter ['bætə*] vt maltratar; (subj: rain etc) azotar ♦ n masa (para rebozar); **~ed** adj (hat, pan) estropeado

battery ['bætərɪ] n (AUT) batería; (of torch) pila

battle ['bætl] n batalla; (fig) lucha ♦ vi luchar; **~ship** n acorazado

bawl [bɔːl] vi chillar, gritar; (child) berrear

bay [beɪ] n (GEO) bahía; **B~ of Biscay** ≈ mar Cantábrico; **to hold sb at ~** mantener a alguien a raya; **~ leaf** n hoja de laurel

bay window n ventana salediza

bazaar [bə'zɑː*] n bazar m; (fete) venta con fines benéficos

B. & B. n abbr (= bed and breakfast) cama y desayuno

BBC n abbr (= British Broadcasting Corporation) cadena de radio y televisión estatal británica

B.C. adv abbr (= before Christ) a. de C.

KEYWORD

be [biː] (pt **was, were**, pp **been**) aux vb **1** (with present participle: forming continuous tenses): **what are you doing?** ¿qué estás haciendo?, ¿qué haces?; **they're coming tomorrow** vienen mañana; **I've been waiting for you for hours** llevo horas esperándote

2 (with pp: forming passives) ser (but often replaced by active or reflective constructions); **to ~ murdered** ser asesinado; **the box had been opened** habían abierto la caja; **the thief was nowhere to ~ seen** no se veía al ladrón por ninguna parte

3 (*in tag questions*): **it was fun, wasn't it?** fue divertido, ¿no? *or* ¿verdad?; **he's good-looking, isn't he?** es guapo, ¿no te parece?; **she's back again, is she?** entonces, ¿ha vuelto?

4 (+*to* +*infin*): **the house is to ~ sold** (*necessity*) hay que vender la casa; (*future*) van a vender la casa; **he's not to open it** no tiene que abrirlo

♦ *vb* +*complement* **1** (*with n or num complement, but see also* **3, 4, 5** *and impers vb below*) ser; **he's a doctor** es médico; **2 and 2 are 4** 2 y 2 son 4

2 (*with adj complement: expressing permanent or inherent quality*) ser; (*: expressing state seen as temporary or reversible*) estar; **I'm English** soy inglés/esa; **she's tall/pretty** es alta/bonita; **he's young** es joven; **~ careful/good/quiet** ten cuidado/pórtate bien/cállate; **I'm tired** estoy cansado/a; **it's dirty** está sucio/a

3 (*of health*) estar; **how are you?** ¿cómo estás?; **he's very ill** está muy enfermo; **I'm better now** ya estoy mejor

4 (*of age*) tener; **how old are you?** ¿cuántos años tienes?; **I'm sixteen (years old)** tengo dieciséis años

5 (*cost*) costar; ser; **how much was the meal?** ¿cuánto fue *or* costó la comida?; **that'll ~ £5.75, please** son £5.75, por favor; **this shirt is £17** esta camisa cuesta £17

♦ *vi* **1** (*exist, occur etc*) existir, haber; **the best singer that ever was** el mejor cantante que existió jamás; **is there a God?** ¿hay un Dios?, ¿existe Dios?; **~ that as it may** sea como sea; **so ~ it** así sea

2 (*referring to place*) estar; **I won't ~ here tomorrow** no estaré aquí mañana

3 (*referring to movement*): **where have you been?** ¿dónde has estado?

♦ *impers vb* **1** (*referring to time*): **it's 5 o'clock** son las 5; **it's the 28th of April** estamos a 28 de abril

2 (*referring to distance*): **it's 10 km to the village** el pueblo está a 10 km

3 (*referring to the weather*): **it's too hot/cold** hace demasiado calor/frío; **it's windy today** hace viento hoy

4 (*emphatic*): **it's me** soy yo; **it was Maria who paid the bill** fue María la que pagó la cuenta

beach [biːtʃ] *n* playa ♦ *vt* varar
beacon ['biːkən] *n* (*lighthouse*) faro; (*marker*) guía
bead [biːd] *n* cuenta; (*of sweat etc*) gota
beak [biːk] *n* pico
beaker ['biːkə*] *n* vaso de plástico
beam [biːm] *n* (*ARCH*) viga, travesaño; (*of light*) rayo, haz *m* de luz ♦ *vi* brillar; (*smile*) sonreír
bean [biːn] *n* judía; **runner/broad ~** habichuela/haba; **coffee ~** grano de café; **~sprouts** *npl* brotes *mpl* de soja
bear [bɛə*] (*pt* bore, *pp* borne) *n* oso ♦ *vt* (*weight etc*) llevar; (*cost*) pagar; (*responsibility*) tener; (*endure*) soportar, aguantar; (*children*) parir, tener; (*fruit*) dar ♦ *vi*: **to ~ right/left** torcer a la derecha/izquierda; **~ out** (*suspicions*) corroborar, confirmar; (*person*) dar la razón a; **~ up** *vi* (*remain cheerful*) mantenerse animado
beard [bɪəd] *n* barba; **~ed** *adj* con barba, barbudo
bearer ['bɛərə*] *n* portador(a) *m/f*
bearing ['bɛərɪŋ] *n* porte *m*, comportamiento; (*connection*) relación *f*; **~s** *npl* (*also:* **ball ~s**) cojinetes *mpl* a bolas; **to take a ~** tomar marcaciones; **to find one's ~s** orientarse
beast [biːst] *n* bestia; (*inf*) bruto, salvaje *m*; **~ly** (*inf*) *adj* horrible
beat [biːt] (*pt* beat, *pp* beaten) *n* (*of heart*) latido; (*MUS*) ritmo, compás *m*; (*of policeman*) ronda ♦ *vt* pegar, golpear; (*eggs*) batir; (*defeat: opponent*) vencer, derrotar; (*: record*) sobrepasar ♦ *vi* (*heart*) latir; (*drum*) redoblar; (*rain, wind*) azotar; **off the ~en track** aislado; **to ~ it** (*inf*) largarse; **~ off** *vt* rechazar; **~ up** *vt* (*attack*) dar una paliza a; **~ing** *n* paliza

beautiful ['bjuːtɪful] *adj* precioso, hermoso, bello; **~ly** *adv* maravillosamente

beauty ['bjuːtɪ] *n* belleza; **~ salon** *n* salón *m* de belleza; **~ spot** *n* (*TOURISM*) lugar *m* pintoresco

beaver ['biːvəʳ] *n* castor *m*

became [bɪ'keɪm] *pt of* **become**

because [bɪ'kɔz] *conj* porque; **~ of** debido a, a causa de

beckon ['bɛkən] *vt* (*also*: **~ to**) llamar con señas

become [bɪ'kʌm] (*irreg*: *like* **come**) *vt* (*suit*) favorecer, sentar bien a ♦ *vi* (+*n*) hacerse, llegar a ser; (+*adj*) ponerse, volverse; **to ~ fat** engordar

becoming [bɪ'kʌmɪŋ] *adj* (*behaviour*) decoroso; (*clothes*) favorecedor(a)

bed [bed] *n* cama; (*of flowers*) macizo; (*of coal, clay*) capa; (*of river*) lecho; (*of sea*) fondo; **to go to ~** acostarse; **~ and breakfast** *n* (*place*) pensión *f*; (*terms*) cama y desayuno; **~clothes** *npl* ropa de cama; **~ding** *n* ropa de cama

---
bed and breakfast

ⓘ *Se llama* **bed and breakfast** *a una forma de alojamiento, en el campo o la ciudad, que ofrece cama y desayuno a precios inferiores a los de un hotel. El servicio se suele anunciar con carteles en los que a menudo se usa únicamente la abreviatura* **B. & B.**

---

bedraggled [bɪ'drægld] *adj* (*untidy*: *person*) desastrado; (*clothes, hair*) desordenado

bed: **~ridden** *adj* postrado (en cama); **~room** *n* dormitorio; **~side** *n*: **at the ~side of** a la cabecera de; **~sit(ter)** (*BRIT*) *n* estudio (*SP*), suite *m* (*AM*); **~spread** *n* cubrecama *m*, colcha; **~time** *n* hora de acostarse

bee [biː] *n* abeja

beech [biːtʃ] *n* haya

beef [biːf] *n* carne *f* de vaca; **roast ~** rosbif *m*; **~burger** *n* hamburguesa; **B~eater** *n* alabardero de la Torre de Londres

beehive ['biːhaɪv] *n* colmena

beeline ['biːlaɪn] *n*: **to make a ~ for** ir derecho a

been [biːn] *pp of* **be**

beer [bɪəʳ] *n* cerveza

beet [biːt] (*US*) *n* (*also*: **red ~**) remolacha

beetle ['biːtl] *n* escarabajo

beetroot ['biːtruːt] (*BRIT*) *n* remolacha

before [bɪ'fɔːʳ] *prep* (*of time*) antes de; (*of space*) delante de ♦ *conj* antes (de) que ♦ *adv* antes, anteriormente; delante, adelante; **~ going** antes de marcharse; **~ she goes** antes de que se vaya; **the week ~** la semana anterior; **I've never seen it ~** no lo he visto nunca; **~hand** *adv* de antemano, con anticipación

beg [beg] *vi* pedir limosna ♦ *vt* pedir, rogar; (*entreat*) suplicar; **to ~ sb to do sth** rogar a uno que haga algo; *see also* **pardon**

began [bɪ'gæn] *pt of* **begin**

beggar ['begəʳ] *n* mendigo/a

begin [bɪ'gɪn] (*pt* **began**, *pp* **begun**) *vt, vi* empezar, comenzar; **to ~ doing** *or* **to do sth** empezar a hacer algo; **~ner** *n* principiante *m/f*; **~ning** *n* principio, comienzo

begun [bɪ'gʌn] *pp of* **begin**

behalf [bɪ'hɑːf] *n*: **on ~ of** en nombre de, por; (*for benefit of*) en beneficio de; **on my/his ~** por mí/él

behave [bɪ'heɪv] *vi* (*person*) portarse, comportarse; (*well*: *also*: **~ o.s.**) portarse bien; **behaviour** (*US* **behavior**) *n* comportamiento, conducta

behind [bɪ'haɪnd] *prep* detrás de; (*supporting*): **to be ~ sb** apoyar a alguien ♦ *adv* detrás, por detrás, atrás ♦ *n* trasero; **to be ~ (schedule)** ir retrasado; **~ the scenes** (*fig*) entre bastidores

behold [bɪ'həʊld] (*irreg*: *like* **hold**) *vt* contemplar

beige [beɪʒ] *adj* color beige

Beijing ['beɪ'dʒɪŋ] *n* Pekín *m*

being ['biːɪŋ] *n* ser *m*; (*existence*): **in ~** existente; **to come into ~** aparecer

Beirut [beɪ'ruːt] *n* Beirut *m*

Belarus [belǝ'rus] *n* Bielorrusia
belated [bɪ'leɪtɪd] *adj* atrasado, tardío
belch [beltʃ] *vi* eructar ♦ *vt* (*gen*: ~ **out**: *smoke etc*) arrojar
Belgian ['beldʒǝn] *adj*, *n* belga *m/f*
Belgium ['beldʒǝm] *n* Bélgica *f*
belief [bɪ'liːf] *n* opinión *f*; (*faith*) fe *f*
believe [bɪ'liːv] *vt*, *vi* creer; **to ~ in** creer en; **~r** *n* partidario/a; (*REL*) creyente *m/f*, fiel *m/f*
belittle [bɪ'lɪtl] *vt* quitar importancia a
bell [bel] *n* campana; (*small*) campanilla; (*on door*) timbre *m*
belligerent [bɪ'lɪdʒǝrǝnt] *adj* agresivo
bellow ['belǝu] *vi* bramar; (*person*) rugir
belly ['belɪ] *n* barriga, panza
belong [bɪ'lɒŋ] *vi*: **to ~ to** pertenecer a; (*club etc*) ser socio de; **this book ~s here** este libro va aquí; **~ings** *npl* pertenencias *fpl*
beloved [bɪ'lʌvɪd] *adj* querido/a
below [bɪ'lǝu] *prep* bajo, debajo de; (*less than*) inferior a ♦ *adv* abajo, (por) debajo; **see ~** véase más abajo
belt [belt] *n* cinturón *m*; (*TECH*) correa, cinta ♦ *vt* (*thrash*) pegar con correa; **~way** (*US*) *n* (*AUT*) carretera de circunvalación
bench [bentʃ] *n* banco; (*BRIT*: *POL*): **the Government/Opposition ~es** (los asientos de) los miembros del Gobierno/ de la Oposición; **the B~** (*LAW*: *judges*) magistratura
bend [bend] (*pt*, *pp* **bent**) *vt* doblar ♦ *vi* inclinarse ♦ *n* (*BRIT*: *in road, river*) curva; (*in pipe*) codo; ~ **down** *vi* inclinarse, doblarse; ~ **over** *vi* inclinarse
beneath [bɪ'niːθ] *prep* bajo, debajo de; (*unworthy of*) indigno de ♦ *adv* abajo, (por) debajo
benefactor ['benɪfæktǝ*] *n* bienhechor *m*
beneficial [benɪ'fɪʃǝl] *adj* beneficioso
benefit ['benɪfɪt] *n* beneficio; (*allowance of money*) subsidio ♦ *vt* beneficiar ♦ *vi*: **he'll ~ from it** le sacará provecho
benevolent [bɪ'nevǝlǝnt] *adj* (*person*) benévolo

benign [bɪ'naɪn] *adj* benigno; (*smile*) afable
bent [bent] *pt*, *pp of* **bend** ♦ *n* inclinación *f* ♦ *adj*: **to be ~ on** estar empeñado en
bequest [bɪ'kwest] *n* legado
bereaved [bɪ'riːvd] *npl*: **the ~** *los íntimos de una persona afligidos por su muerte*
beret ['bereɪ] *n* boina
Berlin [bǝː'lɪn] *n* Berlín
berm [bǝːm] (*US*) *n* (*AUT*) arcén *m*
Bermuda [bǝː'mjuːdǝ] *n* las Bermudas
berry ['berɪ] *n* baya
berserk [bǝ'sǝːk] *adj*: **to go ~** perder los estribos
berth [bǝːθ] *n* (*bed*) litera; (*cabin*) camarote *m*; (*for ship*) amarradero ♦ *vi* atracar, amarrar
beseech [bɪ'siːtʃ] (*pt*, *pp* **besought**) *vt* suplicar
beset [bɪ'set] (*pt*, *pp* **beset**) *vt* (*person*) acosar
beside [bɪ'saɪd] *prep* junto a, al lado de; **to be ~ o.s. with anger** estar fuera de sí; **that's ~ the point** eso no tiene nada que ver; ~**s** *adv* además ♦ *prep* además de
besiege [bɪ'siːdʒ] *vt* sitiar; (*fig*) asediar
best [best] *adj* (el/la) mejor ♦ *adv* (lo) mejor; **the ~ part of** (*quantity*) la mayor parte de; **at ~** en el mejor de los casos; **to make the ~ of sth** sacar el mejor partido de algo; **to do one's ~** hacer todo lo posible; **to the ~ of my knowledge** que yo sepa; **to the ~ of my ability** como mejor puedo; ~**-before date** *n* fecha de consumo preferente; ~ **man** *n* padrino de boda
bestow [bɪ'stǝu] *vt* (*title*) otorgar
bestseller ['best'selǝ*] *n* éxito de librería, bestseller *m*
bet [bet] (*pt*, *pp* **bet** *or* **betted**) *n* apuesta ♦ *vt*: **to ~ money on** apostar dinero por; **to ~ sb sth** apostar algo a uno ♦ *vi* apostar
betray [bɪ'treɪ] *vt* traicionar; (*trust*) faltar a; ~**al** *n* traición *f*
better ['betǝ*] *adj*, *adv* mejor ♦ *vt* superar ♦ *n*: **to get the ~ of sb** quedar por

encima de alguien; **you had ~ do it** más vale que lo hagas; **he thought ~ of it** cambió de parecer; **to get ~** (MED) mejorar(se); **~ off** adj mejor; (wealthier) más acomodado

betting ['betɪŋ] n juego, el apostar; **~ shop** (BRIT) n agencia de apuestas

between [bɪ'twiːn] prep entre ♦ adv (time) mientras tanto; (place) en medio

beverage ['bevərɪdʒ] n bebida

beware [bɪ'weə*] vi: **to ~ (of)** tener cuidado (con); **"~ of the dog"** "perro peligroso"

bewildered [bɪ'wɪldəd] adj aturdido, perplejo

beyond [bɪ'jɔnd] prep más allá de; (past: understanding) fuera de; (after: date) después de, más allá de; (above) superior a ♦ adv (in space) más allá; (in time) posteriormente; **~ doubt** fuera de toda duda; **~ repair** irreparable

bias ['baɪəs] n (prejudice) prejuicio, pasión f; (preference) predisposición f; **~(s)ed** adj parcial

bib [bɪb] n babero

Bible ['baɪbl] n Biblia

bicarbonate of soda [baɪ'kɑːbənɪt-] n bicarbonato sódico

bicker ['bɪkə*] vi pelearse

bicycle ['baɪsɪkl] n bicicleta

bid [bɪd] (pt **bade** or **bid**, pp **bidden** or **bid**) n oferta, postura; (in tender) licitación f; (attempt) tentativa, conato ♦ vi hacer una oferta ♦ vt (offer) ofrecer; **to ~ sb good day** dar a uno los buenos días; **~der** n: **the highest ~der** el mejor postor; **~ding** n (at auction) ofertas fpl

bide [baɪd] vt: **to ~ one's time** esperar el momento adecuado

bifocals [baɪ'fəʊklz] npl gafas fpl (SP) or anteojos mpl (AM) bifocales

big [bɪg] adj grande; (brother, sister) mayor

bigheaded ['bɪg'hedɪd] adj engreído

bigot ['bɪgət] n fanático/a, intolerante m/f; **~ed** adj fanático, intolerante; **~ry** n fanatismo, intolerancia

big top n (at circus) carpa

bike [baɪk] n bici f

bikini [bɪ'kiːnɪ] n bikini m

bilingual [baɪ'lɪŋgwəl] adj bilingüe

bill [bɪl] n cuenta; (invoice) factura; (POL) proyecto de ley; (US: banknote) billete m; (of bird) pico; (of show) programa m; **"post no ~s"** "prohibido fijar carteles"; **to fit** or **fill the ~** (fig) cumplir con los requisitos; **~board** (US) n cartelera

billet ['bɪlɪt] n alojamiento

billfold ['bɪlfəʊld] (US) n cartera

billiards ['bɪljədz] n billar m

billion ['bɪljən] n (BRIT) billón m (millón de millones); (US) mil millones mpl

bimbo ['bɪmbəʊ] (inf) n tía buena sin seso

bin [bɪn] n (for rubbish) cubo (SP) or bote m (AM) de la basura; (container) recipiente m

bind [baɪnd] (pt, pp **bound**) vt atar; (book) encuadernar; (oblige) obligar ♦ n (inf: nuisance) lata; **~ing** adj (contract) obligatorio

binge [bɪndʒ] (inf) n: **to go on a ~** ir de juerga

bingo ['bɪŋgəʊ] n bingo m

binoculars [bɪ'nɔkjuləz] npl prismáticos mpl

bio... [baɪə] prefix: **~chemistry** n bioquímica; **~degradable** [baɪəʊdɪ'greɪdəbl] adj biodegradable; **~graphy** [baɪ'ɔgrəfɪ] n biografía; **~logical** adj biológico; **~logy** [baɪ'ɔlədʒɪ] n biología

birch [bəːtʃ] n (tree) abedul m

bird [bəːd] n ave f, pájaro; (BRIT: inf: girl) chica; **~'s eye view** n (aerial view) vista de pájaro; (overview) visión f de conjunto; **~ watcher** n ornitólogo/a

Biro ® ['baɪrəʊ] n bolígrafo

birth [bəːθ] n nacimiento; **to give ~ to** parir, dar a luz; **~ certificate** n partida de nacimiento; **~ control** n (policy) control m de natalidad; (methods) métodos mpl anticonceptivos; **~day** n cumpleaños m inv ♦ cpd (cake, card etc) de cumpleaños; **~place** n lugar m de nacimiento; **~ rate** n (tasa de) natalidad *f*

biscuit ['bɪskɪt] (*BRIT*) *n* galleta, bizcocho (*AM*)

bisect [baɪ'sɛkt] *vt* bisecar

bishop ['bɪʃəp] *n* obispo; (*CHESS*) alfil *m*

bit [bɪt] *pt of* **bite** ♦ *n* trozo, pedazo, pedacito; (*COMPUT*) bit *m*, bitio; (*for horse*) freno, bocado; **a ~ of** un poco de; **a ~ mad** un poco loco; **~ by ~** poco a poco

bitch [bɪtʃ] *n* perra; (*infl: woman*) zorra (!)

bite [baɪt] (*pt* **bit**, *pp* **bitten**) *vt*, *vi* morder; (*insect etc*) picar ♦ *n* (*insect ~*) picadura; (*mouthful*) bocado; **to ~ one's nails** comerse las uñas; **let's have a ~ (to eat)** (*inf*) vamos a comer algo

bitter ['bɪtə*] *adj* amargo; (*wind*) cortante, penetrante; (*battle*) encarnizado ♦ *n* (*BRIT: beer*) cerveza típica británica a base de lúpulos; **~ness** *n* lo amargo, amargura; (*anger*) rencor *m*

bizarre [bɪ'zɑː*] *adj* raro, extraño

black [blæk] *adj* negro; (*tea, coffee*) solo ♦ *n* color *m* negro; (*person*): **B~** negro/a ♦ *vt* (*BRIT: INDUSTRY*) boicotear; **to give sb a ~ eye** ponerle a uno el ojo morado; **~ and blue** (*bruised*) amoratado; **to be in the ~** (*bank account*) estar en números negros; **~berry** *n* zarzamora; **~bird** *n* mirlo; **~board** *n* pizarra; **~ coffee** *n* café *m* solo; **~currant** *n* grosella negra; **~en** *vt* (*fig*) desacreditar; **~ ice** *n* hielo invisible en la carretera; **~leg** (*BRIT*) *n* esquirol *m*, rompehuelgas *m inv*; **~list** *n* lista negra; **~mail** *n* chantaje *m* ♦ *vt* chantajear; **~ market** *n* mercado negro; **~out** *n* (*MIL*) oscurecimiento; (*power cut*) apagón *m*; (*TV, RADIO*) interrupción *f* de programas; (*fainting*) desvanecimiento; **B~ Sea** *n*: **the B~ Sea** el Mar Negro; **~ sheep** *n* (*fig*) oveja negra; **~smith** *n* herrero; **~ spot** *n* (*AUT*) lugar *m* peligroso; (*for unemployment etc*) punto negro

bladder ['blædə*] *n* vejiga

blade [bleɪd] *n* hoja; (*of propeller*) paleta; **a ~ of grass** una brizna de hierba

blame [bleɪm] *n* culpa ♦ *vt*: **to ~ sb for sth** echar a uno la culpa de algo; **to be to ~** tener la culpa de

bland [blænd] *adj* (*music, taste*) soso

blank [blæŋk] *adj* en blanco; (*look*) sin expresión ♦ *n* (*of memory*): **my mind is a ~** no puedo recordar nada; (*on form*) blanco, espacio en blanco; (*cartridge*) cartucho sin bala *or* de fogueo; **~ cheque** *n* cheque *m* en blanco

blanket ['blæŋkɪt] *n* manta (*SP*), cobija (*AM*); (*of snow*) capa; (*of fog*) manto

blare [blɛə*] *vi* sonar estrepitosamente

blasé ['blɑːzeɪ] *adj* hastiado

blast [blɑːst] *n* (*of wind*) ráfaga, soplo; (*of explosive*) explosión ♦ *vt* (*blow up*) volar; **~-off** *n* (*SPACE*) lanzamiento

blatant ['bleɪtənt] *adj* descarado

blaze [bleɪz] *n* (*fire*) fuego; (*fig: of colour*) despliegue *m*; (: *of glory*) esplendor *m* ♦ *vi* arder en llamas; (*fig*) brillar ♦ *vt*: **to ~ a trail** (*fig*) abrir (un) camino; **in a ~ of publicity** con gran publicidad

blazer ['bleɪzə*] *n* chaqueta de uniforme de colegial o de socio de club

bleach [bliːtʃ] *n* (*also*: **household ~**) lejía ♦ *vt* blanquear; **~ed** *adj* (*hair*) teñido (de rubio); **~ers** (*US*) *npl* (*SPORT*) gradas *fpl* al sol

bleak [bliːk] *adj* (*countryside*) desierto; (*prospect*) poco prometedor(a); (*weather*) crudo; (*smile*) triste

bleat [bliːt] *vi* balar

bleed [bliːd] (*pt*, *pp* **bled**) *vt*, *vi* sangrar; **my nose is ~ing** me está sangrando la nariz

bleeper ['bliːpə*] *n* busca *m*

blemish ['blɛmɪʃ] *n* marca, mancha; (*on reputation*) tacha

blend [blɛnd] *n* mezcla ♦ *vt* mezclar; (*colours etc*) combinar, mezclar ♦ *vi* (*colours etc: also*: **~ in**) combinarse, mezclarse

bless [blɛs] (*pt*, *pp* **blessed** *or* **blest**) *vt* bendecir; **~ you!** (*after sneeze*) ¡Jesús!; **~ing** *n* (*approval*) aprobación *f*; (*godsend*) don *m* del cielo, bendición *f*; (*advantage*) beneficio, ventaja

blew [bluː] *pt of* **blow**

blind [blaɪnd] *adj* ciego; (*fig*): ~ **(to)** ciego
(a) ♦ *n* (*for window*) persiana ♦ *vt* cegar;
(*dazzle*) deslumbrar; (*deceive*): **to ~ sb to
...** cegar a uno a ...; **the ~** *npl* los ciegos;
~ **alley** *n* callejón *m* sin salida; ~
corner (*BRIT*) *n* esquina escondida;
~**fold** *n* venda ♦ *adv* con los ojos
vendados ♦ *vt* vendar los ojos a; ~**ly** *adv*
a ciegas, ciegamente; ~**ness** *n* ceguera;
~ **spot** *n* (*AUT*) ángulo ciego

blink [blɪŋk] *vi* parpadear, pestañear;
(*light*) oscilar; ~**ers** *npl* anteojeras *fpl*

bliss [blɪs] *n* felicidad *f*

blister ['blɪstə*] *n* ampolla ♦ *vi* (*paint*)
ampollarse

blizzard ['blɪzəd] *n* ventisca

bloated ['bləʊtɪd] *adj* hinchado; (*person:
full*) ahíto

blob [blɔb] *n* (*drop*) gota; (*indistinct object*)
bulto

bloc [blɔk] *n* (*POL*) bloque *m*

block [blɔk] *n* bloque *m*; (*in pipes*)
obstáculo; (*of buildings*) manzana (*SP*),
cuadra (*AM*) ♦ *vt* obstruir, cerrar;
(*progress*) estorbar; ~ **of flats** (*BRIT*)
bloque *m* de pisos; **mental ~** bloqueo
mental; ~**ade** [-'keɪd] *n* bloqueo ♦ *vt*
bloquear; ~**age** *n* estorbo, obstrucción *f*;
~**buster** *n* (*book*) bestseller *m*; (*film*)
éxito de público; ~ **letters** *npl* letras *fpl*
de molde

bloke [bləʊk] (*BRIT: inf*) *n* tipo, tío

blond(e) [blɔnd] *adj*, *n* rubio/a *m/f*

blood [blʌd] *n* sangre *f*; ~ **donor** *n*
donante *m/f* de sangre; ~ **group** *n*
grupo sanguíneo; ~**hound** *n* sabueso; ~
poisoning *n* envenenamiento de la
sangre; ~ **pressure** *n* presión *f*
sanguínea; ~**shed** *n* derramamiento de
sangre; ~**shot** *adj* inyectado en sangre;
~**stream** *n* corriente *f* sanguínea; ~ **test**
n análisis *m inv* de sangre; ~**thirsty** *adj*
sanguinario; ~ **vessel** *n* vaso sanguíneo;
~**y** *adj* sangriento; (*nose etc*) lleno de
sangre; (*BRIT: inf!*): **this ~y...** este

condenado *o* puñetero ... (!) ♦ *adv*: ~**y
strong/good** (*BRIT: inf!*) terriblemente
fuerte/bueno; ~**y-minded** (*BRIT: inf*) *adj*
puñetero (!)

bloom [bluːm] *n* flor *f* ♦ *vi* florecer

blossom ['blɔsəm] *n* flor *f* ♦ *vi* (*also fig*)
florecer

blot [blɔt] *n* borrón *m*; (*fig*) mancha ♦ *vt*
(*stain*) manchar; ~ **out** *vt* (*view*) tapar

blotchy ['blɔtʃi] *adj* (*complexion*) lleno de
manchas

blotting paper ['blɔtɪŋ-] *n* papel *m*
secante

blouse [blauz] *n* blusa

blow [bləʊ] (*pt* **blew**, *pp* **blown**) *n* golpe
m; (*with sword*) espadazo ♦ *vi* soplar;
(*dust, sand etc*) volar; (*fuse*) fundirse ♦ *vt*
(*subj: wind*) llevarse; (*fuse*) quemar;
(*instrument*) tocar; **to ~ one's nose**
sonarse; ~ **away** *vt* llevarse, arrancar; ~
down *vt* derribar; ~ **off** *vt* arrebatar; ~
out *vi* apagarse; ~ **over** *vi* amainar; ~
up *vi* estallar ♦ *vt* volar; (*tyre*) inflar;
(*PHOT*) ampliar; ~**-dry** *n* moldeado (con
secador); ~**lamp** (*BRIT*) *n* soplete *m*,
lámpara de soldar; ~**-out** *n* (*of tyre*)
pinchazo; ~**torch** *n* = ~**lamp**

blue [bluː] *adj* azul; (*depressed*) deprimido;
~ **film/joke** película/chiste *m* verde; **out
of the ~** (*fig*) de repente; ~**bell** *n*
campanilla, campánula azul; ~**bottle** *n*
moscarda, mosca azul; ~**print** *n* (*fig*)
anteproyecto

bluff [blʌf] *vi* tirarse un farol, farolear ♦ *n*
farol *m*; **to call sb's ~** coger a uno la
palabra

blunder ['blʌndə*] *n* patinazo, metedura
de pata ♦ *vi* cometer un error, meter la
pata

blunt [blʌnt] *adj* (*pencil*) despuntado;
(*knife*) desafilado, romo; (*person*) franco,
directo

blur [bləː*] *n* (*shape*): **to become a ~**
hacerse borroso ♦ *vt* (*vision*) enturbiar;
(*distinction*) borrar

blush [blʌʃ] *vi* ruborizarse, ponerse
colorado ♦ *n* rubor *m*

blustery ['blʌstərɪ] *adj* (*weather*)
tempestuoso, tormentoso
boar [bɔː*] *n* verraco, cerdo
board [bɔːd] *n* (*card~*) cartón *m*; (*wooden*)
tabla, tablero; (*on wall*) tablón *m*; (*for
chess etc*) tablero; (*committee*) junta,
consejo; (*in firm*) mesa *or* junta directiva;
(*NAUT, AVIAT*): **on ~** a bordo ♦ *vt* (*ship*)
embarcarse en; (*train*) subir a; **full ~** (*BRIT*)
pensión completa; **half ~** (*BRIT*) media
pensión; **to go by the ~** (*fig*) ser
abandonado *or* olvidado; **~ up** *vt* (*door*)
tapiar; **~ and lodging** *n* casa y comida;
~er *n* (*SCOL*) interno/a; **~ing card** (*BRIT*)
n tarjeta de embarque; **~ing house** *n*
casa de huéspedes; **~ing pass** (*US*) *n* =
~ing card; **~ing school** *n* internado; **~
room** *n* sala de juntas
boast [bəʊst] *vi*: **to ~ (about *or* of)**
alardear (de)
boat [bəʊt] *n* barco, buque *m*; (*small*)
barca, bote *m*
bob [bɔb] *vi* (*also*: **~ up and down**)
menearse, balancearse; **~ up** *vi*
(re)aparecer de repente
bobby ['bɔbɪ] (*BRIT: inf*) *n* poli *m*
bobsleigh ['bɔbsleɪ] *n* bob *m*
bode [bəʊd] *vi*: **to ~ well/ill (for)** ser
prometedor/poco prometedor (para)
bodily ['bɔdɪlɪ] *adj* corporal ♦ *adv* (*move:
person*) en peso
body ['bɔdɪ] *n* cuerpo; (*corpse*) cadáver *m*;
(*of car*) caja, carrocería; (*fig: group*) grupo;
(*: organization*) organismo; **~-building** *n*
culturismo; **~guard** *n* guardaespaldas *m
inv*; **~work** *n* carrocería
bog [bɔg] *n* pantano, ciénaga ♦ *vt*: **to get
~ged down** (*fig*) empantanarse, atascarse
bogus ['bəʊgəs] *adj* falso, fraudulento
boil [bɔɪl] *vt* (*water*) hervir; (*eggs*) pasar por
agua, cocer ♦ *vi* hervir; (*fig: with anger*)
estar furioso; (*: with heat*) asfixiarse ♦ *n*
(*MED*) furúnculo, divieso; **to come to the
~, to come to a ~** (*US*) comenzar a
hervir; **to ~ down to** (*fig*) reducirse a; **~
over** *vi* salirse, rebosar; (*anger etc*) llegar
al colmo; **~ed egg** *n* huevo cocido (*SP*)

or pasado (*AM*); **~ed potatoes** *npl*
patatas *fpl* (*SP*) *or* papas *fpl* (*AM*) hervidas;
~er *n* caldera; **~er suit** (*BRIT*) *n* mono;
~ing point *n* punto de ebullición
boisterous ['bɔɪstərəs] *adj* (*noisy*)
bullicioso; (*excitable*) exuberante; (*crowd*)
tumultuoso
bold [bəʊld] *adj* valiente, audaz; (*pej*)
descarado; (*colour*) llamativo
Bolivia [bə'lɪvɪə] *n* Bolivia; **~n** *adj*, *n*
boliviano/a *m/f*
bollard ['bɔləd] (*BRIT*) *n* (*AUT*) poste *m*
bolt [bəʊlt] *n* (*lock*) cerrojo; (*with nut*)
perno, tornillo ♦ *adv*: **~ upright** rígido,
erguido ♦ *vt* (*door*) echar el cerrojo a;
(*also*: **~ together**) sujetar con tornillos;
(*food*) engullir ♦ *vi* fugarse; (*horse*)
desbocarse
bomb [bɔm] *n* bomba ♦ *vt* bombardear; **~
disposal** *n* desmontaje *m* de explosivos;
~er *n* (*AVIAT*) bombardero; **~shell** *n* (*fig*)
bomba
bond [bɔnd] *n* (*promise*) fianza; (*FINANCE*)
bono; (*link*) vínculo, lazo; (*COMM*): **in ~** en
depósito bajo fianza
bondage ['bɔndɪdʒ] *n* esclavitud *f*
bone [bəʊn] *n* hueso; (*of fish*) espina ♦ *vt*
deshuesar; quitar las espinas a; **~ idle** *adj*
gandul; **~ marrow** *n* médula
bonfire ['bɔnfaɪə*] *n* hoguera, fogata
bonnet ['bɔnɪt] *n* gorra; (*BRIT: of car*) capó
m
bonus ['bəʊnəs] *n* (*payment*) paga
extraordinaria, plus *m*; (*fig*) bendición *f*
bony ['bəʊnɪ] *adj* (*arm, face*) huesudo;
(*MED: tissue*) óseo; (*meat*) lleno de huesos;
(*fish*) lleno de espinas
boo [buː] *excl* ¡uh! ♦ *vt* abuchear, rechiflar
booby trap ['buːbɪ-] *n* trampa explosiva
book [bʊk] *n* libro; (*of tickets*) taco; (*of
stamps etc*) librito ♦ *vt* (*ticket*) sacar; (*seat,
room*) reservar; **~s** *npl* (*COMM*) cuentas
fpl, contabilidad *f*; **~case** *n* librería,
estante *m* para libros; **~ing office** *n*
(*BRIT: RAIL*) despacho de billetes (*SP*) *or*
boletos (*AM*); (*THEATRE*) taquilla (*SP*),
boletería (*AM*); **~-keeping** *n* contabilidad

f; ~let n folleto; ~maker n corredor m de apuestas; ~seller n librero; ~shop, ~store n librería

oom [bu:m] n (noise) trueno, estampido; (in prices etc) alza rápida; (ECON, in population) boom m ♦ vi (cannon) hacer gran estruendo, retumbar; (ECON) estar en alza

oon [bu:n] n favor m, beneficio

oost [bu:st] n estímulo, empuje m ♦ vt estimular, empujar; ~er n (MED) reinyección f

oot [bu:t] n bota; (BRIT: of car) maleta, maletero ♦ vt (COMPUT) arrancar; to ~ (in addition) además, por añadidura

ooth [bu:ð] n (telephone ~, voting ~) cabina

ooze [bu:z] (inf) n bebida

order ['bɔ:də*] n borde m, margen m; (of a country) frontera; (for flowers) arriate m ♦ vt (road) bordear; (another country: also: ~ on) lindar con; B~s n: the B~s región fronteriza entre Escocia e Inglaterra; ~ on vt fus (insanity etc) rayar en; ~line n: on the ~line en el límite; ~line case n caso dudoso

ore [bɔ:*] pt of bear ♦ vt (hole) hacer un agujero en; (well) perforar; (person) aburrir ♦ n (person) pelmazo, pesado; (of gun) calibre m; to be ~d estar aburrido; ~dom n aburrimiento

oring ['bɔ:rɪŋ] adj aburrido

orn [bɔ:n] adj: to be ~ nacer; I was ~ in 1960 nací en 1960

orne [bɔ:n] pp of bear

orough ['bʌrə] n municipio

orrow ['bɔrəu] vt: to ~ sth (from sb) tomar algo prestado (a alguien)

osnia(-Herzegovina) ['bɔsnɪə(herzə'gəuvi:nə)] n Bosnia (-Herzegovina)

osom ['buzəm] n pecho

oss [bɔs] n jefe m ♦ vt (also: ~ about or around) mangonear; ~y adj mandón/ona

osun ['bausn] n contramaestre m

otany ['bɔtənɪ] n botánica

otch [bɔtʃ] vt (also: ~ up) arruinar,

estropear

both [bəuθ] adj, pron ambos/as, los/las dos; ~ of us went, we ~ went fuimos los dos, ambos fuimos ♦ adv: ~ A and B tanto A como B

bother ['bɔðə*] vt (worry) preocupar; (disturb) molestar, fastidiar ♦ vi (also: ~ o.s.) molestarse ♦ n (trouble) dificultad f; (nuisance) molestia, lata; to ~ doing tomarse la molestia de hacer

bottle ['bɔtl] n botella; (small) frasco; (baby's) biberón m ♦ vt embotellar; ~ up vt suprimir; ~ bank n contenedor m de vidrio; ~neck n (AUT) embotellamiento; (in supply) obstáculo; ~-opener n abrebotellas m inv

bottom ['bɔtəm] n (of box, sea) fondo; (buttocks) trasero, culo; (of page) pie m; (of list) final m; (of class) último/a ♦ adj (lowest) más bajo; (last) último

bough [bau] n rama

bought [bɔ:t] pt, pp of buy

boulder ['bəuldə*] n canto rodado

bounce [bauns] vi (ball) (re)botar; (cheque) ser rechazado ♦ vt hacer (re)botar ♦ n (rebound) (re)bote m; ~r (inf) n gorila m (que echa a los alborotadores de un bar, club etc)

bound [baund] pt, pp of bind ♦ n (leap) salto; (gen pl: limit) límite m ♦ vi (leap) saltar ♦ vt (border) rodear ♦ adj: ~ by rodeado de; to be ~ to do sth (obliged) tener el deber de hacer algo; he's ~ to come es seguro que vendrá; out of ~s prohibido el paso; ~ for con destino a

boundary ['baundrɪ] n límite m

bouquet ['bukeɪ] n (of flowers) ramo

bourgeois ['buəʒwɑ:] adj burgués/esa m/f

bout [baut] n (of malaria etc) ataque m; (of activity) período; (BOXING etc) combate m, encuentro

bow¹ [bau] n (knot) lazo; (weapon, MUS) arco

bow² [bau] n (of the head) reverencia; (NAUT: also: ~s) proa ♦ vi inclinarse, hacer una reverencia; (yield): to ~ to or before ceder ante, someterse a

bowels [bauəlz] *npl* intestinos *mpl*, vientre *m*; (*fig*) entrañas *fpl*

bowl [bəul] *n* tazón *m*, cuenco; (*ball*) bola ♦ *vi* (CRICKET) arrojar la pelota; *see also* **bowls**

bow-legged ['bəu'legɪd] *adj* estevado

bowler ['bəulə*] *n* (CRICKET) lanzador *m* (de la pelota); (BRIT: *also:* **~ hat**) hongo, bombín *m*

bowling ['bəulɪŋ] *n* (*game*) bochas *fpl*, bolos *mpl*; **~ alley** *n* bolera; **~ green** *n* pista para bochas

bowls [bəulz] *n* juego de las bochas, bolos *mpl*

bow tie ['bəu-] *n* corbata de lazo, pajarita

box [bɔks] *n* (*also:* **cardboard ~**) caja, cajón *m*; (THEATRE) palco ♦ *vt* encajonar ♦ *vi* (SPORT) boxear; **~er** ['bɔksə*] *n* (*person*) boxeador *m*; **~ing** ['bɔksɪŋ] *n* (SPORT) boxeo; **B~ing Day** (BRIT) *n* día en que se dan los aguinaldos, 26 de diciembre; **~ing gloves** *npl* guantes *mpl* de boxeo; **~ing ring** *n* ring *m*, cuadrilátero; **~ office** *n* taquilla (SP), boletería (AM); **~room** *n* trastero

```
Boxing Day
```

ℹ️ *El día 26 de diciembre se conoce como* **Boxing Day** *y es día festivo en todo el Reino Unido. En el siglo XIX era tradición entregar "Christmas boxes" (aguinaldos) a empleados, carteros y otros proveedores en este día, y de ahí el nombre.*

boy [bɔɪ] *n* (*young*) niño; (*older*) muchacho, chico; (*son*) hijo

boycott ['bɔɪkɔt] *n* boicot *m* ♦ *vt* boicotear

boyfriend ['bɔɪfrend] *n* novio

boyish ['bɔɪʃ] *adj* juvenil; (*girl*) con aspecto de muchacho

B.R. *n abbr* (*formerly = British Rail*) ≈ RENFE *f* (SP)

bra [brɑː] *n* sostén *m*, sujetador *m*

brace [breɪs] *n* (BRIT: *also:* **~s**: *on teeth*) corrector *m*, aparato; (*tool*) berbiquí *m*

♦ *vt* (*knees, shoulders*) tensionar; **~s** *npl* (BRIT) tirantes *mpl*; **to ~ o.s.** (*fig*) prepararse

bracelet ['breɪslɪt] *n* pulsera, brazalete *m*

bracing ['breɪsɪŋ] *adj* vigorizante, tónico

bracket ['brækɪt] *n* (TECH) soporte *m*, puntal *m*; (*group*) clase *f*, categoría; (*also:* **brace ~**) soporte *m*, abrazadera; (*also:* **round ~**) paréntesis *m*; (*also:* **square ~**) corchete *m* ♦ *vt* (*word etc*) poner entre paréntesis

brag [bræg] *vi* jactarse

braid [breɪd] *n* (*trimming*) galón *m*; (*of hair*) trenza

brain [breɪn] *n* cerebro; **~s** *npl* sesos *mpl*; **she's got ~s** es muy lista; **~wash** *vt* lavar el cerebro; **~wave** *n* idea luminosa; **~y** *adj* muy inteligente

braise [breɪz] *vt* cocer a fuego lento

brake [breɪk] *n* (*on vehicle*) freno ♦ *vi* frenar; **~ light** *n* luz *f* de frenado

bran [bræn] *n* salvado

branch [brɑːntʃ] *n* rama; (COMM) sucursal *f*; **~ out** *vi* (*fig*) extenderse

brand [brænd] *n* marca; (*fig: type*) tipo ♦ *vt* (*cattle*) marcar con hierro candente; **~-new** *adj* flamante, completamente nuevo

brandy ['brændɪ] *n* coñac *m*

brash [bræʃ] *adj* (*forward*) descarado

brass [brɑːs] *n* latón *m*; **the ~** (MUS) los cobres; **~ band** *n* banda de metal

brat [bræt] (*pej*) *n* mocoso/a

brave [breɪv] *adj* valiente, valeroso ♦ *vt* (*face up to*) desafiar; **~ry** *n* valor *m*, valentía

brawl [brɔːl] *n* pelea, reyerta

brazen ['breɪzn] *adj* descarado, cínico ♦ *vt*: **to ~ it out** echarle cara

Brazil [brə'zɪl] *n* (el) Brasil; **~ian** *adj, n* brasileño/a *m/f*

breach [briːtʃ] *vt* abrir brecha en ♦ *n* (*gap*) brecha; (*breaking*): **~ of contract** infracción *f* de contrato; **~ of the peace** perturbación *f* del órden público

bread [bred] *n* pan *m*; **~ and butter** *n* pan con mantequilla; (*fig*) pan (de cada día); ~**bin** n panera; ~**crumbs** npl migajas fpl; (CULIN) pan rallado; ~**line** n: **on the ~line** en la miseria

readth [brɛtθ] n anchura; (fig) amplitud f

readwinner ['brɛdwɪnə*] n sustento m de la familia

reak [breɪk] (pt **broke**, pp **broken**) vt romper; (promise) faltar a; (law) violar, infringir; (record) batir ♦ vi romperse, quebrarse; (storm) estallar; (weather) cambiar; (dawn) despuntar; (news etc) darse a conocer ♦ n (gap) abertura; (fracture) fractura; (time) intervalo; (: at school) (período de) recreo; (chance) oportunidad f; **to ~ the news to sb** comunicar la noticia a uno; ~ **down** vt (figures, data) analizar, descomponer ♦ vi (machine) estropearse; (AUT) averiarse; (person) romper a llorar; (talks) fracasar; ~ **even** vi cubrir los gastos; ~ **free** or **loose** vi escaparse; ~ **in** vt (horse etc) domar ♦ vi (burglar) forzar una entrada; (interrupt) interrumpir; ~ **into** vt fus (house) forzar; ~ **off** vi (speaker) pararse, detenerse; (branch) partir; ~ **open** vt (door etc) abrir por la fuerza, forzar; ~ **out** vi estallar; (prisoner) escaparse; **to ~ out in spots** salirle a uno granos; ~ **up** vi (ship) hacerse pedazos; (crowd, meeting) disolverse; (marriage) deshacerse; (SCOL) terminar (el curso) ♦ vt (rocks etc) partir; (journey) partir; (fight etc) acabar con; ~**age** n rotura; ~**down** n (AUT) avería; (in communications) interrupción f; (MED: also: **nervous ~down**) colapso, crisis f nerviosa; (of marriage, talks) fracaso; (of statistics) análisis m inv; ~**down van** (BRIT) n (camión m) grúa; ~**er** n (ola) rompiente f

reakfast ['brɛkfəst] n desayuno

reak: ~-**in** n robo con allanamiento de morada; ~**ing and entering** n (LAW) violación f de domicilio, allanamiento de morada; ~**through** n (also fig) avance m; ~**water** n rompeolas m inv

reast [brɛst] n (of woman) pecho, seno; (chest) pecho; (of bird) pechuga; ~-**feed**

(irreg: like **feed**) vt, vi amamantar, criar a los pechos; ~-**stroke** n braza (de pecho)

breath [brɛθ] n aliento, respiración f; **to take a deep ~** respirar hondo; **out of ~** sin aliento, sofocado

Breathalyser ® ['brɛθəlaɪzə*] (BRIT) n alcoholímetro m

breathe [briːð] vt, vi respirar; ~ **in** vt, vi aspirar; ~ **out** vt, vi espirar; ~**r** n respiro; **breathing** n respiración f

breath: ~**less** adj sin aliento, jadeante; ~**taking** (gap) adj imponente, pasmoso

breed [briːd] (pt, pp **bred**) vt criar ♦ vi reproducirse, procrear ♦ n (ZOOL) raza, casta; (type) tipo; ~**ing** n (of person) educación f

breeze [briːz] n brisa

breezy ['briːzɪ] adj de mucho viento, ventoso; (person) despreocupado

brevity ['brɛvɪtɪ] n brevedad f

brew [bruː] vt (tea) hacer; (beer) elaborar ♦ vi (fig: trouble) prepararse; (storm) amenazar; ~**ery** n fábrica de cerveza, cervecería

bribe [braɪb] n soborno ♦ vt sobornar, cohechar; ~**ry** n soborno, cohecho

bric-a-brac ['brɪkəbræk] n inv baratijas fpl

brick [brɪk] n ladrillo; ~**layer** n albañil m

bridal ['braɪdl] adj nupcial

bride [braɪd] n novia; ~**groom** n novio; ~**smaid** n dama de honor

bridge [brɪdʒ] n puente m; (NAUT) puente m de mando; (of nose) caballete m; (CARDS) bridge m ♦ vt (fig): **to ~ a gap** llenar un vacío

bridle ['braɪdl] n brida, freno; ~ **path** n camino de herradura

brief [briːf] adj breve, corto ♦ n (LAW) escrito; (task) cometido, encargo ♦ vt informar; ~**s** npl (for men) calzoncillos mpl; (for women) bragas fpl; ~**case** n cartera (SP), portafolio (AM); ~**ing** n (PRESS) informe m; ~**ly** adv (glance) fugazmente; (say) en pocas palabras

brigadier [brɪgə'dɪə*] n general m de brigada

bright [braɪt] adj brillante; (room)

luminoso; (*day*) de sol; (*person: clever*) listo, inteligente; (: *lively*) alegre; (*colour*) vivo; (*future*) prometedor(a); ~**en** (*also:* **~en up**) vt (*room*) hacer más alegre; (*event*) alegrar ♦ vi (*weather*) despejarse; (*person*) animarse, alegrarse; (*prospects*) mejorar

brilliance ['brɪljəns] n brillo, brillantez f; (*of talent etc*) brillantez

brilliant ['brɪljənt] adj brillante; (*inf*) fenomenal

brim [brɪm] n borde m; (*of hat*) ala

brine [braɪn] n (*CULIN*) salmuera

bring [brɪŋ] (*pt, pp* **brought**) vt (*thing, person: with you*) traer; (: *to sb*) llevar, conducir; (*trouble, satisfaction*) causar; ~ **about** vt ocasionar, producir; ~ **back** vt volver a traer; (*return*) devolver; ~ **down** vt (*government, plane*) derribar; (*price*) rebajar; ~ **forward** vt adelantar; ~ **off** vt (*task, plan*) lograr, conseguir; ~ **out** vt sacar; (*book etc*) publicar; (*meaning*) subrayar; ~ **round** vt (*unconscious person*) hacer volver en sí; ~ **up** vt subir; (*person*) educar, criar; (*question*) sacar a colación; (*food: vomit*) devolver, vomitar

brink [brɪŋk] n borde m

brisk [brɪsk] adj (*abrupt: tone*) brusco; (*person*) enérgico, vigoroso; (*pace*) rápido; (*trade*) activo

bristle ['brɪsl] n cerda ♦ vi: **to ~ in anger** temblar de rabia

Britain ['brɪtən] n (*also:* **Great ~**) Gran Bretaña

British ['brɪtɪʃ] adj británico ♦ npl: **the ~** los británicos; ~ **Isles** npl: **the ~ Isles** las Islas Británicas; ~ **Rail** n ≈ RENFE f (SP)

Briton ['brɪtən] n británico/a

brittle ['brɪtl] adj quebradizo, frágil

broach [brəʊtʃ] vt (*subject*) abordar

broad [brɔːd] adj ancho; (*range*) amplio; (*smile*) abierto; (*general: outlines etc*) general; (*accent*) cerrado; **in ~ daylight** en pleno día; ~**cast** (*irreg: like* **cast**) n emisión f ♦ vt (*RADIO*) emitir; (*TV*) transmitir ♦ vi emitir; transmitir; ~**en** vt ampliar ♦ vi ensancharse; **to ~en one's**

mind hacer más tolerante a uno; ~**ly** adv en general; ~~**-minded** adj tolerante, liberal

broccoli ['brɔkəlɪ] n brécol m

brochure ['brəʊʃjʊə*] n folleto

broil [brɔɪl] vt (*CULIN*) asar a la parrilla

broke [brəʊk] pt of **break** ♦ adj (*inf*) pelado, sin blanca

broken ['brəʊkən] pp of **break** ♦ adj roto; (*machine: also:* **~ down**) averiado; **~ leg** pierna rota; **in ~ English** en un inglés imperfecto; ~~**-hearted** adj con el corazón partido

broker ['brəʊkə*] n agente m/f, bolsista m/f; (*insurance ~*) agente de seguros

brolly ['brɔlɪ] n (*BRIT: inf*) paraguas m inv

bronchitis [brɒŋ'kaɪtɪs] n bronquitis f

bronze [brɒnz] n bronce m

brooch [brəʊtʃ] n prendedor m, broche m

brood [bruːd] n camada, cría ♦ vi (*person*) dejarse obsesionar

broom [brum] n escoba; (*BOT*) retama

Bros. abbr (= *Brothers*) Hnos

broth [brɒθ] n caldo

brothel ['brɒθl] n burdel m

brother ['brʌðə*] n hermano; ~~**-in-law** n cuñado

brought [brɔːt] pt, pp of **bring**

brow [brau] n (*forehead*) frente m; (*eye~*) ceja; (*of hill*) cumbre f

brown [braun] adj (*colour*) marrón; (*hair*) castaño; (*tanned*) bronceado, moreno ♦ n (*colour*) color m marrón or pardo ♦ vt (*CULIN*) dorar; ~ **bread** n pan integral

Brownie ['braunɪ] n niña exploradora; b~ (*US: cake*) pastel de chocolate con nueces

brown paper n papel m de estraza

brown sugar n azúcar m terciado

browse [brauz] vi (*through book*) hojear; (*in shop*) mirar; ~**r** n (*COMPUT*) navegador m

bruise [bruːz] n cardenal m (SP), moretón m (AM) ♦ vt magullar

brunch [brʌnʃ] n desayuno-almuerzo

brunette [bruː'net] n morena

brunt [brʌnt] n: **to bear the ~ of** llevar el peso de

brush [brʌʃ] n cepillo; (*for painting,*

shaving etc) brocha; (artist's) pincel m;
(with police etc) roce m ♦ vt (sweep)
barrer; (groom) cepillar; (also: ~ against)
rozar al pasar; ~ aside vt rechazar, no
hacer caso a; ~ up vt (knowledge)
repasar, refrescar; ~wood n (sticks) leña

Brussels ['brʌslz] n Bruselas; ~ sprout n
col f de Bruselas

brute [bruːt] n bruto; (person) bestia ♦ adj:
by ~ force a fuerza bruta

B.Sc. abbr (= Bachelor of Science)
licenciado en Ciencias

BSE n abbr (= bovine spongiform
encephalopathy) encefalopatía
espongiforme bovina

BTW abbr (= by the way) por cierto

bubble ['bʌbl] n burbuja ♦ vi burbujear,
borbotar; ~ **bath** n espuma para el
baño; ~ **gum** n chicle m de globo

buck [bʌk] n (rabbit) conejo macho; (deer)
gamo; (US: inf) dólar m ♦ vi corcovear; **to
pass the ~ (to sb)** echar (a uno) el
muerto; ~ **up** vi (cheer up) animarse,
cobrar ánimo

┌─────────────────────────────┐
│ **Buckingham Palace** │
└─────────────────────────────┘

ⓘ **Buckingham Palace** *es la residencia
oficial del monarca británico en
Londres. El palacio se concluyó en 1703 y
fue residencia del Duque de Buckingham
hasta que, en 1762, pasó a manos de
Jorge III. Fue reconstruido en el siglo XIX
y posteriormente reformado a principios de
este siglo. Una parte del palacio está
actualmente abierta al público.*

bucket ['bʌkɪt] n cubo, balde m

buckle ['bʌkl] n hebilla ♦ vt abrochar con
hebilla ♦ vi combarse

bud [bʌd] n (of plant) brote m, yema; (of
flower) capullo ♦ vi brotar, echar brotes

Buddhism ['budɪzm] n Budismo

budding ['bʌdɪŋ] adj en ciernes, en
embrión

buddy ['bʌdɪ] n (US) compañero,
compinche m

budge [bʌdʒ] vt mover; (fig) hacer ceder

♦ vi moverse, ceder

budgerigar ['bʌdʒərɪgaː*] n periquito

budget ['bʌdʒɪt] n presupuesto ♦ vi: **to ~
for sth** presupuestar algo

budgie ['bʌdʒɪ] n = **budgerigar**

buff [bʌf] adj (colour) color de ante ♦ n
(inf: enthusiast) entusiasta m/f

buffalo ['bʌfələu] (pl ~ or ~es) n (BRIT)
búfalo; (US: bison) bisonte m

buffer ['bʌfə*] n (COMPUT) memoria
intermedia; (RAIL) tope m

buffet[1] ['bufeɪ] n (BRIT: in station) bar m,
cafetería; (food) buffet m; ~ **car** (BRIT) n
(RAIL) coche-comedor m

buffet[2] ['bʌfɪt] vt golpear

bug [bʌg] n (esp US: insect) bicho,
sabandija; (COMPUT) error m; (germ)
microbio, bacilo; (spy device) micrófono
oculto ♦ vt (inf: annoy) fastidiar

buggy ['bʌgɪ] n cochecito de niño

bugle ['bjuːgl] n corneta, clarín m

build [bɪld] (pt, pp **built**) n (of person) tipo
♦ vt construir, edificar; ~ **up** vt (morale,
forces, production) acrecentar; (stocks)
acumular; ~er n (contractor) contratista
m/f; ~ing n construcción f; (structure)
edificio; ~ing society (BRIT) n sociedad f
inmobiliaria

built [bɪlt] pt, pp of **build** ♦ adj: ~-**in**
(wardrobe etc) empotrado; ~-**up area** n
zona urbanizada

bulb [bʌlb] n (BOT) bulbo; (ELEC) bombilla
(SP), foco (AM)

Bulgaria [bʌl'geərɪə] n Bulgaria; ~n adj, n
búlgaro/a m/f

bulge [bʌldʒ] n bulto, protuberancia ♦ vi
bombearse, pandearse; (pocket etc): **to ~
(with)** rebosar (de)

bulk [bʌlk] n masa, mole f; **in ~** (COMM) a
granel; **the ~ of** la mayor parte de; ~y
adj voluminoso, abultado

bull [bul] n toro; (male elephant, whale)
macho; ~**dog** n dogo

bulldozer ['buldəuzə*] n bulldozer m

bullet ['bulɪt] n bala

bulletin ['bulɪtɪn] n anuncio, parte m;
(journal) boletín m; ~ **board** n (US)

tablón *m* de anuncias; (*COMPUT*) tablero de noticias

bulletproof ['bulɪtpruːf] *adj* a prueba de balas

bullfight ['bulfaɪt] *n* corrida de toros; ~**er** *n* torero; ~**ing** *n* los toros, el toreo

bullion ['buljən] *n* oro (*or* plata) en barras

bullock ['bulək] *n* novillo

bullring ['bulrɪŋ] *n* plaza de toros

bull's-eye *n* centro del blanco

bully ['bulɪ] *n* valentón *m*, matón *m* ♦ *vt* intimidar, tiranizar

bum [bʌm] *n* (*inf: backside*) culo; (*esp US: tramp*) vagabundo

bumblebee ['bʌmblbiː] *n* abejorro

bump [bʌmp] *n* (*blow*) tope *m*, choque *m*; (*jolt*) sacudida; (*on road etc*) bache *m*; (*on head etc*) chichón *m* ♦ *vt* (*strike*) chocar contra; ~ **into** *vt fus* chocar contra, tropezar con; (*person*) topar con; ~**er** *n* (*AUT*) parachoques *m inv* ♦ *adj*: ~**er crop/harvest** cosecha abundante; ~**er cars** *npl* coches *mpl* de choque; ~**y** *adj* (*road*) lleno de baches

bun [bʌn] *n* (*BRIT: cake*) pastel *m*; (*US: bread*) bollo; (*of hair*) moño

bunch [bʌntʃ] *n* (*of flowers*) ramo; (*of keys*) manojo; (*of bananas*) piña; (*of people*) grupo; ~**es** *npl* (*in hair*) coletas *fpl*

bundle ['bʌndl] *n* bulto, fardo; (*of sticks*) haz *m*; (*of papers*) legajo ♦ *vt* (*also: ~ up*) atar, envolver; **to ~ sth/sb into** meter algo/a alguien precipitadamente en

bungalow ['bʌŋɡələu] *n* bungalow *m*, chalé *m*

bungle ['bʌŋɡl] *vt* hacer mal

bunion ['bʌnjən] *n* juanete *m*

bunk [bʌŋk] *n* litera; ~ **beds** *npl* literas *fpl*

bunker ['bʌŋkə*] *n* (*coal store*) carbonera; (*MIL*) refugio; (*GOLF*) bunker *m*

bunny ['bʌnɪ] *n* (*also: ~ rabbit*) conejito

buoy [bɔɪ] *n* boya; ~**ant** *adj* (*ship*) capaz de flotar; (*economy*) boyante; (*person*) optimista

burden ['bəːdn] *n* carga ♦ *vt* cargar

bureau [bjuə'rəu] *n* (*pl* **bureaux**) *n* (*BRIT:*

writing desk) escritorio, buró *m*; (*US: chest of drawers*) cómoda; (*office*) oficina, agencia

bureaucracy [bjuə'rɔkrəsɪ] *n* burocracia

burglar ['bəːglə*] *n* ladrón/ona *m/f*; ~ **alarm** *n* alarma *f* antirrobo; ~**y** *n* robo con allanamiento, robo de una casa

burial ['berɪəl] *n* entierro

burly ['bəːlɪ] *adj* fornido, membrudo

Burma ['bəːmə] *n* Birmania

burn [bəːn] (*pt, pp* **burned** *or* **burnt**) *vt* quemar; (*house*) incendiar ♦ *vi* quemarse, arder; incendiarse; (*sting*) escocer ♦ *n* quemadura; ~ **down** *vt* incendiar; ~**er** *n* (*on cooker etc*) quemador *m*; ~**ing** *adj* (*building etc*) en llamas; (*hot: sand etc*) abrasador(a); (*ambition*) ardiente

burrow ['bʌrəu] *n* madriguera ♦ *vi* hacer una madriguera; (*rummage*) hurgar

bursary ['bəːsərɪ] (*BRIT*) *n* beca

burst [bəːst] (*pt, pp* **burst**) *vt* reventar; (*subj: river: banks etc*) romper ♦ *vi* reventarse; (*tyre*) pincharse ♦ *n* (*of gunfire*) ráfaga; (*also: ~ pipe*) reventón *m*; **a ~ of energy/speed/enthusiasm** una explosión de energía/un ímpetu de velocidad/un arranque de entusiasmo; **to ~ into flames** estallar en llamas; **to ~ into tears** deshacerse en lágrimas; **to ~ out laughing** soltar la carcajada; **to ~ open** abrirse de golpe; **to be ~ing with** (*subj: container*) estar lleno a rebosar de; (*person*) reventar por *or* de; ~ **into** *vt fus* (*room etc*) irrumpir en

bury ['berɪ] *vt* enterrar; (*body*) enterrar, sepultar

bus [bʌs] (*pl* ~**es**) *n* autobús *m*

bush [buʃ] *n* arbusto; (*scrub land*) monte *m*; **to beat about the ~** andar(se) con rodeos

bushy [buʃɪ] *adj* (*thick*) espeso, poblado

busily ['bɪzɪlɪ] *adv* afanosamente

business ['bɪznɪs] *n* (*matter*) asunto; (*trading*) comercio, negocios *mpl*; (*firm*) empresa, casa; (*occupation*) oficio; **to be away on ~** estar en viaje de negocios; **it's my ~ to ...** me toca *or* corresponde ...;

it's none of my ~ yo no tengo nada que ver; he means ~ habla en serio; ~like *adj* eficiente; ~man *n* hombre *m* de negocios; ~ trip *n* viaje *m* de negocios; ~woman *n* mujer *f* de negocios

usker ['bʌskə*] (BRIT) *n* músico/a ambulante

us: ~ shelter *n* parada cubierta; ~ station *n* estación *f* de autobuses; ~-stop *n* parada de autobús

ust [bʌst] *n* (ANAT) pecho; (*sculpture*) busto ♦ *adj* (*inf: broken*) roto, estropeado; to go ~ quebrar

ustle ['bʌsl] *n* bullicio, movimiento ♦ *vi* menearse, apresurarse; bustling *adj* (*town*) animado, bullicioso

usy ['bɪzɪ] *adj* ocupado, atareado; (*shop, street*) concurrido, animado; (TEL: *line*) comunicando ♦ *vt*: to ~ o.s. with ocuparse en; ~body *n* entrometido/a; ~ signal (US) *n* (TEL) señal *f* de comunicando

KEYWORD

ut [bʌt] *conj* 1 pero; he's not very bright, ~ he's hard-working no es muy inteligente, pero es trabajador
2 (*in direct contradiction*) sino; he's not English ~ French no es inglés sino francés; he didn't sing ~ he shouted no cantó sino que gritó
3 (*showing disagreement, surprise etc*): ~ that's far too expensive! ¡pero eso es carísimo!; ~ it does work! ¡(pero) sí que funciona!
♦ *prep* (*apart from, except*) menos, salvo; we've had nothing ~ trouble no hemos tenido más que problemas; no-one ~ him can do it nadie más que él puede hacerlo; who ~ a lunatic would do such a thing? ¡sólo un loco haría una cosa así!; ~ for you/your help no fuera por ti/tu ayuda; anything ~ that cualquier cosa menos eso
♦ *adv* (*just, only*): she's ~ a child no es más que una niña; had I ~ known si lo hubiera sabido; I can ~ try al menos lo

puedo intentar; it's all ~ finished está casi acabado

butcher ['butʃə*] *n* carnicero ♦ *vt* hacer una carnicería con; (*cattle etc*) matar; ~'s (shop) *n* carnicería

butler ['bʌtlə*] *n* mayordomo

butt [bʌt] *n* (*barrel*) tonel *m*; (*of gun*) culata; (*of cigarette*) colilla; (BRIT: *fig: target*) blanco ♦ *vt* dar cabezadas contra, top(et)ar; ~ in *vi* (*interrupt*) interrumpir

butter ['bʌtə*] *n* mantequilla ♦ *vt* untar con mantequilla; ~cup *n* botón *m* de oro

butterfly ['bʌtəflaɪ] *n* mariposa; (SWIMMING: *also*: ~ stroke) braza de mariposa

buttocks ['bʌtəks] *npl* nalgas *fpl*

button ['bʌtn] *n* botón *m*; (US) placa, chapa ♦ *vt* (*also*: ~ up) abotonar, abrochar ♦ *vi* abrocharse

buttress ['bʌtrɪs] *n* contrafuerte *m*

buy [baɪ] (*pt, pp* bought) *vt* comprar ♦ *n* compra; to ~ sb sth/sth from sb comprarle algo a alguien; to ~ sb a drink invitar a alguien a tomar algo; ~er *n* comprador(a) *m/f*

buzz [bʌz] *n* zumbido; (*inf: phone call*) llamada (por teléfono) ♦ *vi* zumbar; ~er *n* timbre *m*; ~ word *n* palabra que está de moda

KEYWORD

by [baɪ] *prep* 1 (*referring to cause, agent*) por; de; killed ~ lightning muerto por un relámpago; a painting ~ Picasso un cuadro de Picasso
2 (*referring to method, manner, means*): ~ bus/car/train en autobús/coche/tren; to pay ~ cheque pagar con un cheque; ~ moonlight/candlelight a la luz de la luna/una vela; ~ saving hard, he ... ahorrando, ...
3 (*via, through*) por; we came ~ Dover vinimos por Dover
4 (*close to, past*): the house ~ the river la casa junto al río; she rushed ~ me

pasó a mi lado como una exhalación; **I go ~ the post office every day** paso por delante de Correos todos los días
5 (*time: not later than*) para; (: *during*): **~ daylight** de día; **~ 4 o'clock** para las cuatro; **~ this time tomorrow** mañana a estas horas; **~ the time I got here it was too late** cuando llegué ya era demasiado tarde
6 (*amount*): **~ the metre/kilo** por metro/kilo; **paid ~ the hour** pagado por hora
7 (*MATH, measure*): **to divide/multiply ~ 3** dividir/multiplicar por 3; **a room 3 metres ~ 4** una habitación de 3 metros por 4; **it's broader ~ a metre** es un metro más ancho
8 (*according to*) según, de acuerdo con; **it's 3 o'clock ~ my watch** según mi reloj, son las tres; **it's all right ~ me** por mí, está bien
9: (**all**) **~ oneself** *etc* todo solo; **he did it (all) ~ himself** lo hizo él solo; **he was standing (all) ~ himself in a corner** estaba de pie solo en un rincón
10: **~ the way** a propósito, por cierto; **this wasn't my idea, ~ the way** pues, no fue idea mía
♦ *adv* 1 *see* go; pass *etc*
2: **~ and ~** finalmente; **they'll come back ~ and ~** acabarán volviendo; **~ and large** en líneas generales, en general

bye(-bye) ['baɪ('baɪ)] *excl* adiós, hasta luego
by(e)-law *n* ordenanza municipal
by: **~-election** (*BRIT*) *n* elección *f* parcial; **~gone** ['baɪɡɔn] *adj* pasado, del pasado ♦ *n*: **let ~gones be ~gones** lo pasado, pasado está; **~pass** ['baɪpɑːs] *n* carretera de circunvalación; (*MED*) (operación *f* de) by-pass *m* ♦ *vt* evitar; **~-product** *n* subproducto, derivado (*of situation*) consecuencia; **~stander** ['baɪstændə*] *n* espectador(a) *m/f*
byte [baɪt] *n* (*COMPUT*) byte *m*, octeto
byword ['baɪwɜːd] *n*: **to be a ~ for** ser conocidísimo por

C, c

C [siː] *n* (*MUS*) do *m*
C. *abbr* (= *centigrade*) C.
C.A. *abbr* = **chartered accountant**
cab [kæb] *n* taxi *m*; (*of truck*) cabina
cabbage ['kæbɪdʒ] *n* col *f*, berza
cabin ['kæbɪn] *n* cabaña; (*on ship*) camarote *m*; (*on plane*) cabina; **~ crew** *n* tripulación *f* de cabina; **~ cruiser** *n* yate *m* de motor
cabinet ['kæbɪnɪt] *n* (*POL*) consejo de ministros; (*furniture*) armario; (*also*: **display ~**) vitrina
cable ['keɪbl] *n* cable *m* ♦ *vt* cablegrafiar; **~-car** *n* teleférico; **~ television** *n* televisión *f* por cable
cache [kæʃ] *n* (*of arms, drugs etc*) alijo
cackle ['kækl] *vi* lanzar risotadas; (*hen*) cacarear
cactus ['kæktəs] (*pl* **cacti**) *n* cacto
cadge [kædʒ] (*inf*) *vt* gorronear
Caesarean [siːˈzɛərɪən] *adj*: **~ (section)** cesárea
café ['kæfeɪ] *n* café *m*
cafeteria [kæfɪˈtɪərɪə] *n* cafetería
cage [keɪdʒ] *n* jaula
cagey ['keɪdʒɪ] (*inf*) *adj* cauteloso, reservado
cagoule [kəˈɡuːl] *n* chubasquero
cajole [kəˈdʒəʊl] *vt* engatusar
cake [keɪk] *n* (*CULIN: large*) tarta; (: *small*) pastel *m*; (*of soap*) pastilla; **~d** *adj*: **~d with** cubierto de
calculate ['kælkjuleɪt] *vt* calcular; **calculation** [-'leɪʃən] *n* cálculo, cómputo; **calculator** *n* calculadora
calendar ['kæləndə*] *n* calendario; **~ month/year** *n* mes *m*/año civil
calf [kɑːf] (*pl* **calves**) *n* (*of cow*) ternero, becerro; (*of other animals*) cría; (*also*: **~skin**) piel *f* de becerro; (*ANAT*) pantorrilla
calibre ['kælɪbə*] (*US* **caliber**) *n* calibre *m*
call [kɔːl] *vt* llamar; (*meeting*) convocar

♦ *vi* (*shout*) llamar; (*TEL*) llamar (por teléfono), telefonear (*esp AM*); (*visit: also*: ~ **in**, ~ **round**) hacer una visita ♦ *n* llamada; (*of bird*) canto; **to be ~ed** llamarse; (*of duty*) de guardia; ~ **back** *vi* (*return*) volver; (*TEL*) volver a llamar; ~ **for** *vt fus* (*demand*) pedir, exigir; (*fetch*) venir por (*SP*), pasar por (*AM*); ~ **off** *vt* (*cancel: meeting, race*) cancelar; (: *deal*) anular; (: *strike*) desconvocar; ~ **on** *vt fus* (*visit*) visitar; (*turn to*) acudir a; ~ **out** *vi* gritar; ~ **up** *vt* (*MIL*) llamar al servicio militar; (*TEL*) llamar; ~**box** (*BRIT*) *n* cabina telefónica; ~ **centre** *n* (*BRIT*) centro de atención al cliente; ~**er** *n* visita; (*TEL*) usuario/a; ~ **girl** *n* prostituta; ~-**in** (*US*) *n* (*programa m*) coloquio (por teléfono); ~**ing** *n* vocación *f*; (*occupation*) profesión *f*; ~**ing card** (*US*) *n* tarjeta de visita

callous ['kæləs] *adj* insensible, cruel

calm [kɑːm] *adj* tranquilo; (*sea*) liso, en calma ♦ *n* calma, tranquilidad *f* ♦ *vt* calmar, tranquilizar; ~ **down** *vi* calmarse, tranquilizarse ♦ *vt* calmar, tranquilizar

Calor gas ® ['kælə•-] *n* butano

calorie ['kælərɪ] *n* caloría

calves [kɑːvz] *npl of* **calf**

Cambodia [kæm'bəudjə] *n* Camboya

camcorder ['kæmkɔːdə•] *n* videocámara

came [keɪm] *pt of* **come**

camel ['kæməl] *n* camello

camera ['kæmərə] *n* máquina fotográfica; (*CINEMA*, *TV*) cámara; **in ~** (*LAW*) a puerta cerrada; ~**man** *n* cámara *m*

camouflage ['kæməflɑːʒ] *n* camuflaje *m* ♦ *vt* camuflar

camp [kæmp] *n* campamento, camping *m*; (*MIL*) campamento; (*for prisoners*) campo; (*fig: faction*) bando ♦ *vi* acampar ♦ *adj* afectado, afeminado

campaign [kæm'peɪn] *n* (*MIL, POL etc*) campaña ♦ *vi* hacer campaña

camp: ~**bed** (*BRIT*) *n* cama de campaña; ~**er** *n* campista *m/f*; (*vehicle*) caravana; ~**ing** *n* camping *m*; **to go ~ing** hacer camping; ~**site** *n* camping *m*

campus ['kæmpəs] *n* ciudad *f* universitaria

can¹ [kæn] *n* (*of oil, water*) bidón *m*; (*tin*) lata, bote *m* ♦ *vt* enlatar

---

KEYWORD

---

can² [kæn] (*negative* **cannot**, **can't**; *conditional and pt* **could**) *aux vb* **1** (*be able to*) poder; **you ~ do it if you try** puedes hacerlo si lo intentas; **I ~'t see you** no te veo

2 (*know how to*) saber; **I ~ swim/play tennis/drive** sé nadar/jugar al tenis/conducir; **~ you speak French?** ¿hablas *or* sabes hablar francés?

3 (*may*) poder; **~ I use your phone?** ¿me dejas *or* puedo usar tu teléfono?

4 (*expressing disbelief, puzzlement etc*): **it ~'t be true!** ¡no puede ser (verdad)!; **what CAN he want?** ¿qué querrá?

5 (*expressing possibility, suggestion etc*): **he could be in the library** podría estar en la biblioteca; **she could have been delayed** pudo haberse retrasado

---

Canada ['kænədə] *n* (el) Canadá; **Canadian** [kə'neɪdɪən] *adj, n* canadiense *m/f*

canal [kə'næl] *n* canal *m*

canary [kə'neərɪ] *n* canario; **the C~ Islands** *npl* las (Islas) Canarias

cancel ['kænsəl] *vt* cancelar; (*train*) suprimir; (*cross out*) tachar, borrar; ~**lation** [-'leɪʃən] *n* cancelación *f*; supresión *f*

cancer ['kænsə•] *n* cáncer *m*; **C~** (*ASTROLOGY*) Cáncer *m*

candid ['kændɪd] *adj* franco, abierto

candidate ['kændɪdeɪt] *n* candidato/a

candle ['kændl] *n* vela; (*in church*) cirio; ~**light** *n*: **by ~light** a la luz de una vela; ~**stick** *n* (*single*) candelero; (*low*) palmatoria; (*bigger, ornate*) candelabro

candour ['kændə•] (*US* **candor**) *n* franqueza

candy ['kændɪ] *n* azúcar *m* cande; (*US*) caramelo; ~**floss** (*BRIT*) *n* algodón *m* (azucarado)

cane [keɪn] *n* (*BOT*) caña; (*stick*) vara,

palmeta; (*for furniture*) mimbre *f* ♦ (*BRIT*) *vt* (*SCOL*) castigar (con vara)

canister ['kænɪstə*] *n* bote *m*, lata; (*of gas*) bombona

cannabis ['kænəbɪs] *n* marijuana

canned [kænd] *adj* en lata, de lata

cannon ['kænən] (*pl* ~ *or* ~**s**) *n* cañón *m*

cannot ['kænɔt] = **can not**

canoe [kə'nuː] *n* canoa; (*SPORT*) piragua; ~**ing** *n* piragüismo

canon ['kænən] *n* (*clergyman*) canónigo; (*standard*) canon *m*

can-opener *n* abrelatas *m inv*

canopy ['kænəpɪ] *n* dosel *m*; toldo

can't [kænt] = **can not**

canteen [kæn'tiːn] *n* (*eating place*) cantina; (*BRIT: of cutlery*) juego

canter ['kæntə*] *vi* ir a medio galope

canvas ['kænvəs] *n* (*material*) lona; (*painting*) lienzo; (*NAUT*) velas *fpl*

canvass ['kænvəs] *vi* (*POL*): **to ~ for** solicitar votos por ♦ *vt* (*COMM*) sondear

canyon ['kænjən] *n* cañón *m*

cap [kæp] *n* (*hat*) gorra; (*of pen*) capuchón *m*; (*of bottle*) tapa, tapón *m*; (*contraceptive*) diafragma *m*; (*for toy gun*) cápsula ♦ *vt* (*outdo*) superar; (*limit*) recortar

capability [keɪpə'bɪlɪtɪ] *n* capacidad *f*

capable ['keɪpəbl] *adj* capaz

capacity [kə'pæsɪtɪ] *n* capacidad *f*; (*position*) calidad *f*

cape [keɪp] *n* capa; (*GEO*) cabo

caper ['keɪpə*] *n* (*CULIN: gen:* ~**s**) alcaparra; (*prank*) broma

capital ['kæpɪtl] *n* (*also:* ~ **city**) capital *f*; (*money*) capital *m*; (*also:* ~ **letter**) mayúscula; ~ **gains tax** *n* impuesto sobre las ganancias de capital; ~**ism** *n* capitalismo; ~**ist** *adj, n* capitalista *m/f*; ~**ize on** *vt fus* aprovechar; ~ **punishment** *n* pena de muerte

Capitol

ⓘ *El Capitolio (Capitol) es el edificio del Congreso (Congress) de los Estados Unidos, situado en la ciudad de Washington. Por extensión, también se suele llamar así al edificio en el que tienen lugar las sesiones parlamentarias de la cámara de representantes de muchos de los estados.*

Capricorn ['kæprɪkɔːn] *n* (*ASTROLOGY*) Capricornio

capsize [kæp'saɪz] *vt* volcar, hacer zozobrar ♦ *vi* volcarse, zozobrar

capsule ['kæpsjuːl] *n* cápsula

captain ['kæptɪn] *n* capitán *m*

caption ['kæpʃən] *n* (*heading*) título; (*to picture*) leyenda

captive ['kæptɪv] *adj, n* cautivo/a *m/f*

capture ['kæptʃə*] *vt* prender, apresar; (*animal, COMPUT*) capturar; (*place*) tomar; (*attention*) captar, llamar ♦ *n* apresamiento; captura; toma; (*data ~*) formulación *f* de datos

car [kɑː*] *n* coche *m*, carro (*AM*), automóvil *m*; (*US: RAIL*) vagón *m*

carafe [kə'ræf] *n* jarra

carat ['kærət] *n* quilate *m*

caravan ['kærəvæn] *n* (*BRIT*) caravana, ruló *f*; (*in desert*) caravana; ~**ning** *n*: **to go** ~**ning** ir de vacaciones en caravana, viajar en caravana; ~ **site** (*BRIT*) *n* camping *m* para caravanas

carbohydrate [kɑːbəu'haɪdreɪt] *n* hidrato de carbono; (*food*) fécula

carbon ['kɑːbən] *n* carbono; ~ **paper** *n* papel *m* carbón

car boot sale *n mercadillo organizado en un aparcamiento, en el que se exponen las mercancías en el maletero del coche*

carburettor [kɑːbju'retə*] (*US* **carburetor**) *n* carburador *m*

card [kɑːd] *n* (*material*) cartulina; (*index ~ etc*) ficha; (*playing ~*) carta, naipe *m*; (*visiting ~, greetings ~ etc*) tarjeta; ~**board** *n* cartón *m*

cardiac ['kɑːdɪæk] *adj* cardíaco

cardigan ['kɑːdɪgən] *n* rebeca

cardinal ['kɑːdɪnl] *adj* cardinal; (*importance, principal*) esencial ♦ *n* cardenal *m*

card index *n* fichero

care [keə*] *n* cuidado; *(worry)* inquietud *f*; *(charge)* cargo, custodia ♦ *vi*: **to ~ about** *(person, animal)* tener cariño a; *(thing, idea)* preocuparse por; **~ of** en casa de, al cuidado de *m*; **in sb's ~** a cargo de uno; **to take ~ to** cuidarse de, tener cuidado de; **to take ~ of** cuidar; *(problem etc)* ocuparse de; **I don't ~** no me importa; **I couldn't ~ less** eso me trae sin cuidado; **~ for** *vt fus* cuidar a; *(like)* querer

career [kə'rɪə*] *n* profesión *f*; *(in work, school)* carrera ♦ *vi (also: ~ along)* correr a toda velocidad; **~ woman** *n* mujer *f* dedicada a su profesión

care: ~free *adj* despreocupado; **~ful** *adj* cuidadoso; *(cautious)* cauteloso; **(be) ~ful!** ¡tenga cuidado!; **~fully** *adv* con cuidado, cuidadosamente; con cautela; **~less** *adj* descuidado; *(heedless)* poco atento; **~lessness** *n* descuido; falta de atención; **~r** ['keərə*] *n* enfermero/a *m/f* *(official)*; *(unpaid)* persona que cuida a un pariente o vecino

caress [kə'res] *n* caricia ♦ *vt* acariciar

caretaker ['keəteikə*] *n* portero/a, conserje *m/f*

car-ferry *n* transbordador *m* para coches

cargo ['kɑːgəu] *(pl ~es) n* cargamento, carga

car hire *n* alquiler *m* de automóviles

Caribbean [kærɪ'biːən] *n*: **the ~ (Sea)** el (Mar) Caribe

caring ['keərɪŋ] *adj* humanitario; *(behaviour)* afectuoso

carnation [kɑː'neɪʃən] *n* clavel *m*

carnival ['kɑːnɪvəl] *n* carnaval *m*; *(US: funfair)* parque *m* de atracciones

carol ['kærəl] *n*: **(Christmas) ~** villancico

carp [kɑːp] *n (fish)* carpa

car park *(BRIT) n* aparcamiento, parking *m*

carpenter ['kɑːpɪntə*] *n* carpintero/a

carpet ['kɑːpɪt] *n* alfombra; *(fitted)* moqueta ♦ *vt* alfombrar

car phone *n* teléfono movil

car rental *(US) n* alquiler *m* de coches

carriage ['kærɪdʒ] *n (BRIT: RAIL)* vagón *m*; *(horse-drawn)* coche *m*; *(of goods)* transporte *m*; *(: cost)* porte *m*, flete *m*; **~way** *(BRIT) n (part of road)* calzada

carrier ['kærɪə*] *n (transport company)* transportista, empresa de transportes; *(MED)* portador *m*; **~ bag** *(BRIT) n* bolsa de papel *or* plástico

carrot ['kærət] *n* zanahoria

carry ['kærɪ] *vt (subj: person)* llevar; *(transport)* transportar; *(involve: responsibilities etc)* entrañar, implicar; *(MED)* ser portador de ♦ *vi (sound)* oírse; **to get carried away** *(fig)* entusiasmarse; **~ on** *vi (continue)* seguir (adelante), continuar ♦ *vt* proseguir, continuar; **~ out** *vt (orders)* cumplir; *(investigation)* llevar a cabo, realizar; **~ cot** *(BRIT) n* cuna portátil; **~on** *(inf) n (fuss)* lío

cart [kɑːt] *n* carro, carreta ♦ *vt (inf: transport)* acarrear

carton ['kɑːtən] *n (box)* caja (de cartón); *(of milk etc)* bote *m*; *(of yogurt)* tarrina

cartoon [kɑː'tuːn] *n (PRESS)* caricatura; *(comic strip)* tira cómica; *(film)* dibujos *mpl* animados

cartridge ['kɑːtrɪdʒ] *n* cartucho; *(of pen)* recambio; *(of record player)* cápsula

carve [kɑːv] *vt (meat)* trinchar; *(wood, stone)* cincelar, esculpir; *(initials etc)* grabar; **~ up** *vt* dividir, repartir; **carving** *n (object)* escultura; *(design)* talla; *(art)* tallado; **carving knife** *n* trinchante *m*

car wash *n* lavado de coches

case [keɪs] *n (container)* caja; *(MED)* caso; *(for jewels etc)* estuche *m*; *(LAW)* causa, proceso; *(BRIT: also: suit~)* maleta; **in ~ of** en caso de; **in any ~** en todo caso; **just in ~** por si acaso

cash [kæʃ] *n* dinero en efectivo, dinero contante ♦ *vt* cobrar, hacer efectivo; **to pay (in) ~** pagar al contado; **~ on delivery** cóbrese al entregar; **~book** *n* libro de caja; **~ card** *n* tarjeta *f* dinero; **~ desk** *(BRIT) n* caja; **~ dispenser** *n* cajero automático

cashew [kæ'ʃuː] *n (also: ~ nut)* anacardo

cash flow n flujo de fondos, cash-flow m
cashier [kæˈʃɪə*] n cajero/a
cashmere [ˈkæʃmɪə*] n cachemira
cash register n caja
casing [ˈkeɪsɪŋ] n revestimiento
casino [kəˈsiːnəʊ] n casino
casket [ˈkɑːskɪt] n cofre m, estuche m;
(US: coffin) ataúd m
casserole [ˈkæsərəʊl] n (food, pot) cazuela
cassette [kæˈset] n cassette f; ~ **player/
recorder** n tocacassettes m inv, cassette
m
cast [kɑːst] (pt, pp **cast**) vt (throw) echar,
arrojar, lanzar; (glance, eyes) dirigir;
(THEATRE): **to ~ sb as Othello** dar a uno el
papel de Otelo ♦ vi (FISHING) lanzar ♦ n
(THEATRE) reparto; (also: **plaster ~**) vaciado;
to ~ one's vote votar; **to ~ doubt on**
suscitar dudas acerca de; **~ off** vi (NAUT)
desamarrar; (KNITTING) cerrar (los puntos);
~ on vi (KNITTING) poner los puntos
castanets [kæstəˈnets] npl castañuelas fpl
castaway [ˈkɑːstəweɪ] n náufrago/a
caster sugar [ˈkɑːstə*-] (BRIT) n azúcar m
extrafino
Castile [kæsˈtiːl] n Castilla; **Castilian** adj,
n castellano/a m/f
casting vote [ˈkɑːstɪŋ-] (BRIT) n voto
decisivo
cast iron n hierro fundido
castle [ˈkɑːsl] n castillo; (CHESS) torre f
castor oil [ˈkɑːstə*-] n aceite m de ricino
casual [ˈkæʒjʊl] adj fortuito; (irregular:
work etc) eventual, temporero;
(unconcerned) despreocupado; (clothes) de
sport; **~ly** adv de manera despreocupada;
(dress) de sport
casualty [ˈkæʒjʊltɪ] n víctima, herido;
(dead) muerto; (MED: department)
urgencias fpl
cat [kæt] n gato; (big ~) felino
Catalan [ˈkætəlæn] adj, n catalán/ana m/f
catalogue [ˈkætəlɒg] (US **catalog**) n
catálogo ♦ vt catalogar
Catalonia [kætəˈləʊnɪə] n Cataluña
catalyst [ˈkætəlɪst] n catalizador m
catalytic convertor [kætəˈlɪtɪk kənˈvɜːtə*]

n catalizador m
catapult [ˈkætəpʌlt] n tirachinas m inv
catarrh [kəˈtɑː*] n catarro
catastrophe [kəˈtæstrəfɪ] n catástrofe f
catch [kætʃ] (pt, pp **caught**) vt coger (SP),
agarrar (AM); (arrest) detener; (grasp) asir;
(breath) contener; (surprise: person)
sorprender; (attract: attention) captar;
(hear) oír; (MED) contagiarse de, coger;
(also: **~ up**) alcanzar ♦ vi (fire)
encenderse; (in branches etc) enredarse
♦ n (fish etc) pesca; (act of catching)
cogida; (hidden problem) dificultad f;
(game) pilla-pilla; (of lock) pestillo,
cerradura; **to ~ fire** encenderse; **to ~
sight of** divisar; **~ on** vi (understand) caer
en la cuenta; (grow popular) hacerse
popular; **~ up** vi (fig) ponerse al día;
~ing [ˈkætʃɪŋ] adj (MED) contagioso;
~ment area [ˈkætʃmənt-] (BRIT) n zona
de captación; **~phrase** [ˈkætʃfreɪz] n lema
m, eslogan m; **~y** [ˈkætʃɪ] adj (tune)
pegadizo
category [ˈkætɪɡərɪ] n categoría, clase f
cater [ˈkeɪtə*] vi: **to ~ for** (BRIT) abastecer
a; (needs) atender a; (COMM: parties etc)
proveer comida a; **~er** n abastecedor(a)
m/f, proveedor(a) m/f; **~ing** n (trade)
hostelería
caterpillar [ˈkætəpɪlə*] n oruga, gusano
cathedral [kəˈθiːdrəl] n catedral f
catholic [ˈkæθəlɪk] adj (tastes etc) amplio;
C~ adj, n (REL) católico/a m/f
CAT scan [kæt-] n TAC f, tomografía
Catseye ® [ˈkætsˈaɪ] (BRIT) n (AUT)
catafoto
cattle [ˈkætl] npl ganado
catty [ˈkætɪ] adj malicioso, rencoroso
caucus [ˈkɔːkəs] n (POL) camarilla política;
(: US: to elect candidates) comité m
electoral
caught [kɔːt] pt, pp of **catch**
cauliflower [ˈkɒlɪflaʊə*] n coliflor f
cause [kɔːz] n causa, motivo, razón f;
(principle: also: POL) causa ♦ vt causar
caution [ˈkɔːʃən] n cautela, prudencia;
(warning) advertencia, amonestación f

♦ vt amonestar; **cautious** adj cauteloso, prudente, precavido

avalry ['kævəlrɪ] n caballería

ave [keɪv] n cueva, caverna; ~ **in** vi (roof etc) derrumbarse, hundirse

aviar(e) ['kævɪɑ:*] n caviar m

B n abbr (= Citizens' Band (Radio)) banda ciudadana

BI n abbr (= Confederation of British Industry) ≈ C.E.O.E. f (SP)

c abbr = **cubic centimetres**; = **carbon copy**

CTV n abbr (= closed-circuit television) circuito cerrado de televisión

CD n abbr (= compact disc) DC m; (player) (reproductor de) disco compacto; ~ **player** n lector m de discos compactos, **~-ROM** [si:di:'rɔm] n abbr CD-ROM m

ease [si:s] vt, vi cesar; **~fire** n alto m el fuego; **~less** adj incesante

edar ['si:də*] n cedro

eiling ['si:lɪŋ] n techo; (fig) límite m

elebrate ['sɛlɪbreɪt] vt celebrar ♦ vi divertirse; **~d** adj célebre; **celebration** [-'breɪʃən] n fiesta, celebración f

elery ['sɛlərɪ] n apio

ell [sɛl] n celda; (BIOL) célula

ellar ['sɛlə*] n sótano; (for wine) bodega

ello ['tʃɛləu] n violoncelo

ellophane ® ['sɛləfeɪn] n celofán m

ellphone ['sɛlfəun] n teléfono celular

elt [kɛlt, sɛlt] adj, n celta m/f; **~ic** adj celta

ement [sə'mɛnt] n cemento; ~ **mixer** n hormigonera

emetery ['sɛmɪtrɪ] n cementerio

ensor ['sɛnsə*] n censor m ♦ vt (cut) censurar; **~ship** n censura

ensure ['sɛnʃə*] vt censurar

ensus ['sɛnsəs] n censo

ent [sɛnt] n (unit of dollar) centavo, céntimo; (unit of euro) céntimo; see also **per**

entenary [sɛn'ti:nərɪ] n centenario

enter ['sɛntə*] (US) = **centre**

enti... [sɛntɪ] prefix: **~grade** adj centígrado; **~litre** (US **~liter**) n centilitro;

~metre (US **~meter**) n centímetro

centipede ['sɛntɪpi:d] n ciempiés m inv

central ['sɛntrəl] adj central; (of house etc) céntrico; **C~ America** n Centroamérica; ~ **heating** n calefacción f central; **~ize** vt centralizar

centre ['sɛntə*] (US **center**) n centro; (fig) núcleo ♦ vt centrar; **~-forward** n (SPORT) delantero centro; **~-half** n (SPORT) medio centro

century ['sɛntjurɪ] n siglo; **20th ~** siglo veinte

ceramic [sɪ'ræmɪk] adj cerámico; **~s** n cerámica

cereal ['si:rɪəl] n cereal m

ceremony ['sɛrɪmənɪ] n ceremonia; **to stand on ~** hacer ceremonias, estar de cumplido

certain ['sə:tən] adj seguro; (person): **a ~ Mr Smith** un tal Sr Smith; (particular, some) cierto; **for ~** a ciencia cierta; **~ly** adv (undoubtedly) ciertamente; (of course) desde luego, por supuesto; **~ty** n certeza, certidumbre f, seguridad f; (inevitability) certeza

certificate [sə'tɪfɪkɪt] n certificado

certified ['sə:tɪfaɪd]: ~ **mail** (US) n correo certificado; ~ **public accountant** (US) n contable m/f diplomado/a

certify ['sə:tɪfaɪ] vt certificar; (award diploma to) conceder un diploma a; (declare insane) declarar loco

cervical ['sə:vɪkl] adj cervical

cervix ['sə:vɪks] n cuello del útero

cf. abbr (= compare) cfr

CFC n abbr (= chlorofluorocarbon) CFC m

ch. abbr (= chapter) cap

chain [tʃeɪn] n cadena; (of mountains) cordillera; (of events) sucesión f ♦ vt (also: ~ **up**) encadenar; ~ **reaction** n reacción f en cadena; **~-smoke** vi fumar un cigarrillo tras otro; ~ **store** n tienda de una cadena, ≈ gran almacén

chair [tʃɛə*] n silla; (armchair) sillón m, butaca; (of university) cátedra; (of meeting etc) presidencia ♦ vt (meeting) presidir; **~lift** n telesilla; **~man** n presidente m

chalk [tʃɔːk] n (GEO) creta; (for writing) tiza (SP), gis m (AM)

challenge ['tʃælɪndʒ] n desafío, reto ♦ vt desafiar, retar; (statement, right) poner en duda; **to ~ sb to do sth** retar a uno a que haga algo; **challenging** adj exigente; (tone) de desafío

chamber ['tʃeɪmbə*] n cámara, sala; (POL) cámara; (BRIT: LAW: gen pl) despacho; **~ of commerce** cámara de comercio; **~maid** n camarera

chamois ['ʃæmwɑː] n gamuza

champagne [ʃæm'peɪn] n champaña m, champán m

champion ['tʃæmpɪən] n campeón/ona m/f; (of cause) defensor(a) m/f; **~ship** n campeonato

chance [tʃɑːns] n (opportunity) ocasión f, oportunidad f; (likelihood) posibilidad f; (risk) riesgo ♦ vt arriesgar, probar ♦ adj fortuito, casual; **to ~ it** arriesgarse, intentarlo; **to take a ~** arriesgarse; **by ~** por casualidad

chancellor ['tʃɑːnsələ*] n canciller m; **C~ of the Exchequer** (BRIT) n Ministro de Hacienda

chandelier [ʃændə'lɪə*] n araña (de luces)

change [tʃeɪndʒ] vt cambiar; (replace) cambiar, reemplazar; (gear, clothes, job) cambiar de; (transform) transformar ♦ vi cambiar(se); (trains) hacer transbordo; (traffic lights) cambiar de color; (be transformed): **to ~ into** transformarse en ♦ n cambio; (alteration) modificación f, transformación f; (of clothes) muda; (coins) suelto, sencillo; (money returned) vuelta; **to ~ gear** (AUT) cambiar de marcha; **to ~ one's mind** cambiar de opinión or idea; **for a ~** para variar; **~able** adj (weather) cambiable; **~ machine** n máquina de cambio; **~over** n (to new system) cambio; **changing** adj cambiante; **changing room** (BRIT) n vestuario

channel ['tʃænl] n (TV) canal m; (of river) cauce m; (groove) conducto; (fig: medium) medio ♦ vt (river etc) encauzar; **the**

(English) C~ el Canal (de la Mancha); **the C~ Islands** las Islas Normandas; **the C~ Tunnel** el túnel del Canal de la Mancha, el Eurotúnel; **~-hopping** n (TV) zapping m

chant [tʃɑːnt] n (of crowd) gritos mpl; (REL) canto ♦ vt (slogan, word) repetir a gritos

chaos ['keɪɔs] n caos m

chap [tʃæp] (BRIT: inf) n (man) tío, tipo

chapel ['tʃæpəl] n capilla

chaperone ['ʃæpərəʊn] n carabina

chaplain ['tʃæplɪn] n capellán m

chapped [tʃæpt] adj agrietado

chapter ['tʃæptə*] n capítulo

char [tʃɑː*] vt (burn) carbonizar, chamuscar

character ['kærɪktə*] n carácter m, naturaleza, índole f; (moral strength, personality) carácter; (in novel, film) personaje m; **~istic** [-'rɪstɪk] adj característico ♦ n característica

charcoal ['tʃɑːkəʊl] n carbón m vegetal; (ART) carboncillo

charge [tʃɑːdʒ] n (LAW) cargo, acusación f; (cost) precio, coste m; (responsibility) cargo ♦ vt (LAW): **to ~ (with)** acusar (de); (battery) cargar; (price) pedir; (customer) cobrar ♦ vi precipitarse; (MIL) cargar, atacar; **~s** npl: **to reverse the ~s** (BRIT: TEL) revertir el cobro; **to take ~ of** hacerse cargo de, encargarse de; **to be in ~ of** estar encargado de; (business) mandar; **how much do you ~?** ¿cuánto cobra usted?; **to ~ an expense (up) to sb's account** cargar algo a cuenta de alguien; **~ card** n tarjeta de cuenta

charity ['tʃærɪtɪ] n caridad f; (organization) sociedad f benéfica; (money, gifts) limosnas fpl

charm [tʃɑːm] n encanto, atractivo; (talisman) hechizo; (on bracelet) dije m ♦ vt encantar; **~ing** adj encantador(a)

chart [tʃɑːt] n (diagram) cuadro; (graph) gráfica; (map) carta de navegación ♦ vt (course) trazar; (progress) seguir; **~s** npl (Top 40): **the ~s** ≈ los 40 principales (SP)

charter ['tʃɑːtə*] vt (plane) alquilar; (ship) fletar ♦ n (document) carta; (of university, *company)* estatutos *mpl*; **~ed accountant** (*BRIT*) *n* contable *m/f* diplomado/a; **~ flight** *n* vuelo chárter

chase [tʃeɪs] *vt* (*pursue*) perseguir; (*also:* **~ away**) ahuyentar ♦ *n* persecución *f*

chasm [ˈkæzəm] *n* sima

chassis [ˈʃæsɪ] *n* chasis *m*

chat [tʃæt] *vi* (*also:* **have a ~**) charlar ♦ *n* charla; **~ show** (*BRIT*) *n* programa *m* de entrevistas

chatter [ˈtʃætəʳ] *vi* (*person*) charlar; (*teeth*) castañetear ♦ *n* (*of birds*) parloteo; (*of people*) charla, cháchara; **~box** (*inf*) *n* parlanchín/ina *m/f*

chatty [ˈtʃætɪ] *adj* (*style*) informal; (*person*) hablador(a)

chauffeur [ˈʃəʊfəʳ] *n* chófer *m*

chauvinist [ˈʃəʊvɪnɪst] *n* (*male ~*) machista *m*; (*nationalist*) chovinista *m/f*

cheap [tʃiːp] *adj* barato; (*joke*) de mal gusto; (*poor quality*) de mala calidad ♦ *adv* barato; **~ day return** *n* billete *m* de ida y vuelta el mismo día; **~er** *adj* más barato; **~ly** *adv* barato, a bajo precio

cheat [tʃiːt] *vi* hacer trampa ♦ *vt*: **to ~ sb (out of sth)** estafar (algo) a uno ♦ *n* (*person*) tramposo/a

check [tʃek] *vt* (*examine*) controlar; (*facts*) comprobar; (*halt*) parar, detener; (*restrain*) refrenar, restringir ♦ *n* (*inspection*) control *m*, inspección *f*; (*curb*) freno; (*US: bill*) nota, cuenta; (*US*) = **cheque**; (*pattern: gen pl*) cuadro ♦ *adj* (*also:* **~ed**: *pattern, cloth*) a cuadros; **~ in** *vi* (*at hotel*) firmar el registro; (*at airport*) facturar el equipaje ♦ *vt* (*luggage*) facturar; **~ out** *vi* (*of hotel*) marcharse; **~ up** *vi*: **to ~ up on sth** comprobar algo; **to ~ up on sb** investigar a alguien; **~ered** (*US*) *adj* = **check; chequered**; **~ers** (*US*) *n* juego de damas; **~-in (desk)** *n* mostrador *m* de facturación; **~ing account** (*US*) *n* cuenta corriente; **~mate** *n* jaque *m* mate; **~out** *n* caja; **~point** *n* (punto de) control *m*; **~room** (*US*) *n* consigna; **~up** *n* (*MED*) reconocimiento

general

cheek [tʃiːk] *n* mejilla; (*impudence*) descaro; **what a ~!** ¡qué cara!; **~bone** *n* pómulo; **~y** *adj* fresco, descarado

cheep [tʃiːp] *vi* piar

cheer [tʃɪəʳ] *vt* vitorear, aplaudir; (*gladden*) alegrar, animar ♦ *vi* dar vivas ♦ *n* viva *m*; **~s** *npl* aplausos *mpl*; **~s!** ¡salud!; **~ up** *vi* animarse ♦ *vt* alegrar, animar; **~ful** *adj* alegre

cheerio [tʃɪərɪˈəʊ] (*BRIT*) *excl* ¡hasta luego!

cheese [tʃiːz] *n* queso; **~board** *n* tabla de quesos

cheetah [ˈtʃiːtə] *n* leopardo cazador

chef [ʃef] *n* jefe/a *m/f* de cocina

chemical [ˈkemɪkəl] *adj* químico ♦ *n* producto químico

chemist [ˈkemɪst] *n* (*BRIT: pharmacist*) farmacéutico/a; (*scientist*) químico/a; **~ry** *n* química; **~'s (shop)** (*BRIT*) *n* farmacia

cheque [tʃek] (*US* **check**) *n* cheque *m*; **~book** *n* talonario de cheques (*SP*), chequera (*AM*); **~ card** *n* tarjeta de cheque

chequered [ˈtʃekəd] (*US* **checkered**) *adj* (*fig*) accidentado

cherish [ˈtʃerɪʃ] *vt* (*love*) querer, apreciar; (*protect*) cuidar; (*hope etc*) abrigar

cherry [ˈtʃerɪ] *n* cereza; (*also:* **~ tree**) cerezo

chess [tʃes] *n* ajedrez *m*; **~board** *n* tablero (de ajedrez)

chest [tʃest] *n* (*ANAT*) pecho; (*box*) cofre *m*, cajón *m*; **~ of drawers** *n* cómoda

chestnut [ˈtʃesnʌt] *n* castaña; **~ (tree)** *n* castaño

chew [tʃuː] *vt* mascar, masticar; **~ing gum** *n* chicle *m*

chic [ʃiːk] *adj* elegante

chick [tʃɪk] *n* pollito, polluelo; (*inf: girl*) chica

chicken [ˈtʃɪkɪn] *n* gallina, pollo; (*food*) pollo; (*inf: coward*) gallina *m/f*; **~ out** (*inf*) *vi* rajarse; **~pox** *n* varicela

chicory [ˈtʃɪkərɪ] *n* (*for coffee*) achicoria; (*salad*) escarola

chief [tʃiːf] *n* jefe/a *m/f* ♦ *adj* principal; **~**

executive n director(a) m/f general; **~ly** adv principalmente

chilblain ['tʃɪlbleɪn] n sabañón m

child [tʃaɪld] (pl **children**) n niño/a; (offspring) hijo/a; **~birth** n parto; **~hood** n niñez f, infancia; **~ish** adj pueril, aniñado; **~like** adj de niño; **~ minder** (BRIT) n madre f de día; **~ren** ['tʃɪldrən] npl of **child**

Chile ['tʃɪlɪ] n Chile m; **~an** adj, n chileno/a m/f

chill [tʃɪl] n frío; (MED) resfriado ♦ vt enfriar; (CULIN) congelar

chil(l)i ['tʃɪlɪ] (BRIT) n chile m (SP), ají m (AM)

chilly ['tʃɪlɪ] adj frío

chime [tʃaɪm] n repique m; (of clock) campanada ♦ vi repicar; sonar

chimney ['tʃɪmnɪ] n chimenea; **~ sweep** n deshollinador m

chimpanzee [tʃɪmpæn'ziː] n chimpancé m

chin [tʃɪn] n mentón m, barbilla

china ['tʃaɪnə] n porcelana; (crockery) loza

China ['tʃaɪnə] n China; **Chinese** [tʃaɪ'niːz] adj chino ♦ n inv chino/a; (LING) chino

chink [tʃɪŋk] n (opening) grieta, hendedura; (noise) tintineo

chip [tʃɪp] n (gen pl: CULIN: BRIT) patata (SP) or papa (AM) frita; (: US: also: **potato ~**) patata or papa frita; (of wood) astilla; (of glass, stone) lasca; (at poker) ficha; (COMPUT) chip m ♦ vt (cup, plate) desconchar

---
⎡ **chip shop** ⎤

ⓘ Se denomina **chip shop** o "fish-and-chip shop" a un establecimiento en el que se sirven algunas especialidades de comida rápida, muy populares entre los británicos, sobre todo pescado rebozado y patatas fritas.

---

chiropodist [kɪ'rɔpədɪst] (BRIT) n pedicuro/a, callista m/f

chirp [tʃəːp] vi (bird) gorjear, piar

chisel ['tʃɪzl] n (for wood) escoplo; (for stone) cincel m

chit [tʃɪt] n nota

chitchat ['tʃɪttʃæt] n chismes mpl, habladurías fpl

chivalry ['ʃɪvəlrɪ] n caballerosidad f

chives [tʃaɪvz] npl cebollinos mpl

chlorine ['klɔːriːn] n cloro

chock-a-block ['tʃɔkə'blɔk] adj atestado

chock-full ['tʃɔk'ful] adj atestado

chocolate ['tʃɔklɪt] n chocolate m; (sweet) bombón m

choice [tʃɔɪs] n elección f, selección f; (option) opción f; (preference) preferencia ♦ adj escogido

choir ['kwaɪə*] n coro; **~boy** n niño de coro

choke [tʃəuk] vi ahogarse; (on food) atragantarse ♦ vt estrangular, ahogar; (block): **to be ~d with** estar atascado de ♦ n (AUT) estárter m

cholesterol [kə'lestərɔl] n colesterol m

choose [tʃuːz] (pt **chose**, pp **chosen**) vt escoger, elegir; (team) seleccionar; **to ~ to do sth** optar por hacer algo

choosy ['tʃuːzɪ] adj delicado

chop [tʃɔp] vt (wood) cortar, tajar; (CULIN: also: **~ up**) picar ♦ n (CULIN) chuleta; **~s** npl (jaws) boca, labios mpl

chopper ['tʃɔpə*] n (helicopter) helicóptero

choppy ['tʃɔpɪ] adj (sea) picado, agitado

chopsticks ['tʃɔpstɪks] npl palillos mpl

chord [kɔːd] n (MUS) acorde m

chore [tʃɔː*] n faena, tarea; (routine task) trabajo rutinario

chorus ['kɔːrəs] n coro; (repeated part of song) estribillo

chose [tʃəuz] pt of **choose**

chosen ['tʃəuzn] pp of **choose**

chowder ['tʃaudə*] n (esp US) sopa de pescado

Christ [kraɪst] n Cristo

christen ['krɪsn] vt bautizar

Christian ['krɪstɪən] adj, n cristiano/a m/f; **~ity** [-'ænɪtɪ] n cristianismo; **~ name** n nombre m de pila

Christmas ['krɪsməs] n Navidad f; **Merry ~!** ¡Felices Pascuas!; **~ card** n crismas m inv, tarjeta de Navidad; **~ Day** n día m

de Navidad; ~ **Eve** n Nochebuena; ~
tree n árbol m de Navidad
chrome [krəum] n cromo
chronic ['krɒnɪk] adj crónico
chronological [krɒnə'lɒdʒɪkəl] adj
cronológico
chubby ['tʃʌbɪ] adj regordete
chuck [tʃʌk] (inf) vt lanzar, arrojar; (BRIT:
also: ~ **up**) abandonar; ~ **out** vt (person)
echar (fuera); (rubbish etc) tirar
chuckle ['tʃʌkl] vi reírse entre dientes
chug [tʃʌg] vi resoplar; (car, boat: also: ~
along) avanzar traqueteando
chum [tʃʌm] n compañero/a
chunk [tʃʌŋk] n pedazo, trozo
church [tʃəːtʃ] n iglesia; ~**yard** n
cementerio
churn [tʃəːn] n (for butter) mantequera;
(for milk) lechera; ~ **out** vt producir en
serie
chute [ʃuːt] n (also: **rubbish** ~) vertedero;
(for coal etc) rampa de caída
chutney ['tʃʌtnɪ] n condimento a base de
frutas de la India
CIA (US) n abbr (= Central Intelligence
Agency) CIA f
CID (BRIT) n abbr (= Criminal Investigation
Department) ≈ B.I.C. f (SP)
cider ['saɪdə*] n sidra
cigar [sɪ'gɑː*] n puro
cigarette [sɪgə'rɛt] n cigarrillo (SP), cigarro
(AM); pitillo; ~ **case** n pitillera; ~ **end** n
colilla
Cinderella [sɪndə'rɛlə] n Cenicienta
cinders ['sɪndəz] npl cenizas fpl
cine camera ['sɪnɪ-] (BRIT) n cámara
cinematográfica
cinema ['sɪnəmə] n cine m
cinnamon ['sɪnəmən] n canela
circle ['səːkl] n círculo; (in theatre)
anfiteatro ♦ vi dar vueltas ♦ vt (surround)
rodear, cercar; (move round) dar la vuelta
a
circuit ['səːkɪt] n circuito; (tour) gira;
(track) pista; (lap) vuelta; ~**ous**
[səː'kjuɪtəs] adj indirecto
circular ['səːkjulə*] adj circular ♦ n circular

f
circulate ['səːkjuleɪt] vi circular; (person: at
party etc) hablar con los invitados ♦ vt
poner en circulación; **circulation**
[-'leɪʃən] n circulación f; (of newspaper)
tirada
circumstances ['səːkəmstənsɪz] npl
circunstancias fpl; (financial condition)
situación f económica
circus ['səːkəs] n circo
CIS n abbr (= Commonwealth of
Independent States) CEI f
cistern ['sɪstən] n tanque m, depósito; (in
toilet) cisterna
citizen ['sɪtɪzn] n (POL) ciudadano/a; (of
city) vecino/a, habitante m/f; ~**ship** n
ciudadanía
citrus fruits ['sɪtrəs-] npl agrios mpl
city ['sɪtɪ] n ciudad f; **the C~** centro
financiero de Londres
civic ['sɪvɪk] adj cívico; (authorities)
municipal; ~ **centre** (BRIT) n centro
público
civil ['sɪvɪl] adj civil; (polite) atento, cortés;
~ **engineer** n ingeniero de caminos(,
canales y puertos); ~**ian** [sɪ'vɪlɪən] adj civil
(no militar) ♦ n civil m/f, paisano/a
civilization [sɪvɪlaɪ'zeɪʃən] n civilización f
civilized ['sɪvɪlaɪzd] adj civilizado
civil: ~ **law** n derecho civil; ~ **servant** n
funcionario/a del Estado; **C~ Service** n
administración f pública; ~ **war** n guerra
civil
claim [kleɪm] vt exigir, reclamar; (rights
etc) reivindicar; (assert) pretender ♦ vi (for
insurance) reclamar ♦ n reclamación f;
pretensión f; ~**ant** n demandante m/f
clairvoyant [klɛə'vɔɪənt] n clarividente m/f
clam [klæm] n almeja
clamber ['klæmbə*] vi trepar
clammy ['klæmɪ] adj frío y húmedo
clamour ['klæmə*] (US **clamor**) vi: **to ~ for**
clamar por, pedir a voces
clamp [klæmp] n abrazadera, grapa ♦ vt
(2 things together) cerrar fuertemente;
(one thing on another) afianzar (con
abrazadera); (AUT: wheel) poner el cepo a;

~ **down on** vt fus (subj: government, police) reforzar la lucha contra

clang [klæŋ] vi sonar, hacer estruendo

clap [klæp] vi aplaudir; **~ping** n aplausos mpl

claret ['klærət] n burdeos m inv

clarify ['klærɪfaɪ] vt aclarar

clarinet [klærɪ'net] n clarinete m

clash [klæʃ] n enfrentamiento; choque m; desacuerdo; estruendo ♦ vi (fight) enfrentarse; (beliefs) chocar; (disagree) estar en desacuerdo; (colours) desentonar; (two events) coincidir

clasp [klɑːsp] n (hold) apretón m; (fastener) cierre m ♦ vt apretar; abrazar

class [klɑːs] n clase f ♦ vt clasificar

classic ['klæsɪk] adj, n clásico; **~al** adj clásico

classified ['klæsɪfaɪd] adj (information) reservado; **~ advertisement** n anuncio por palabras

classmate ['klɑːsmeɪt] n compañero/a de clase

classroom ['klɑːsrum] n aula

clatter ['klætə*] n estrépito ♦ vi hacer ruido or estrépito

clause [klɔːz] n cláusula; (LING) oración f

claw [klɔː] n (of cat) uña; (of bird of prey) garra; (of lobster) pinza

clay [kleɪ] n arcilla

clean [kliːn] adj limpio; (record, reputation) bueno, intachable; (joke) decente ♦ vt limpiar; (hands etc) lavar; ~ **out** vt limpiar; ~ **up** vt limpiar, asear; **~-cut** adj (person) bien parecido; **~er** n (person) asistenta; (substance) producto para la limpieza; **~er's** n tintorería; **~ing** n limpieza; **~liness** ['klɛnlɪnɪs] n limpieza

cleanse [klɛnz] vt limpiar; **~r** n (for face) crema limpiadora

clean-shaven adj sin barba, afeitado

cleansing department (BRIT) n departamento de limpieza

clear [klɪə*] adj claro; (road, way) libre; (conscience) limpio, tranquilo; (skin) terso; (sky) despejado ♦ vt (space) despejar, limpiar; (LAW: suspect) absolver; (obstacle)

salvar, saltar por encima de; (cheque) aceptar ♦ vi (fog etc) despejarse ♦ adv: ~ **of** a distancia de; **to ~ the table** recoger or levantar la mesa; ~ **up** vt limpiar; (mystery) aclarar, resolver; **~ance** n (removal) despeje m; (permission) acreditación f; **~-cut** adj bien definido, nítido; **~ing** n (in wood) claro; **~ing bank** (BRIT) n cámara de compensación; **~ly** adv claramente; (evidently) sin duda; **~way** (BRIT) n carretera donde no se puede parar

clef [klef] n (MUS) clave f

cleft [kleft] n (in rock) grieta, hendedura

clench [klentʃ] vt apretar, cerrar

clergy ['klɜːdʒɪ] n clero; **~man** n clérigo

clerical ['klerɪkəl] adj de oficina; (REL) clerical

clerk [klɑːk, (US) klɜːrk] n (BRIT) oficinista m/f; (US) dependiente/a m/f

clever ['klevə*] adj (intelligent) inteligente, listo; (skilful) hábil; (device, arrangement) ingenioso

click [klɪk] vt (tongue) chasquear; (heels) taconear ♦ vi (COMPUT) hacer clic; **to ~ on an icon** hacer clic en un icono

client ['klaɪənt] n cliente m/f

cliff [klɪf] n acantilado

climate ['klaɪmɪt] n clima m

climax ['klaɪmæks] n (of battle, career) apogeo; (of film, book) punto culminante; (sexual) orgasmo

climb [klaɪm] vi subir; (plant) trepar; (move with effort): **to ~ over a wall/into a car** trepar a una tapia/subir a un coche ♦ vt (stairs) subir; (tree) trepar a; (mountain) escalar ♦ n subida; **~-down** n vuelta atrás; **~er** n alpinista m/f (SP), andinista m/f (AM); **~ing** n alpinismo (SP), andinismo (AM)

clinch [klɪntʃ] vt (deal) cerrar; (argument) remachar

cling [klɪŋ] (pt, pp **clung**) vi: **to ~ to** agarrarse a; (clothes) pegarse a

clinic ['klɪnɪk] n clínica; **~al** adj clínico; (fig) frío

clink [klɪŋk] *vi* tintinar

clip [klɪp] *n* (*for hair*) horquilla; (*also:*
paper ~) sujetapapeles *m inv*, clip *m*; (*TV,*
CINEMA) fragmento ♦ *vt* (*cut*) cortar; (*also:*
~ together) unir; **~pers** *npl* (*for*
gardening) tijeras *fpl*; **~ping** *n*
(*newspaper*) recorte *m*

cloak [kləuk] *n* capa, manto ♦ *vt* (*fig*)
encubrir, disimular; **~room** *n*
guardarropa; (*BRIT: WC*) lavabo (*SP*), aseos
mpl (*SP*), baño (*AM*)

clock [klɔk] *n* reloj *m*; **~ in** *or* **on** *vi*
fichar, picar; **~ off** *or* **out** *vi* fichar *or*
picar la salida; **~wise** *adv* en el sentido
de las agujas del reloj; **~work** *n* aparato
de relojería ♦ *adj* (*toy*) de cuerda

clog [klɔg] *n* zueco, chanclo ♦ *vt* atascar
♦ *vi* (*also:* **~ up**) atascarse

cloister ['klɔɪstə*] *n* claustro

clone [kləun] *n* clon *m* ♦ *vt* clonar

close¹ [kləus] *adj* (*near*): **~ (to)** cerca (de);
(*friend*) íntimo; (*connection*) estrecho;
(*examination*) detallado, minucioso;
(*weather*) bochornoso; **to have a ~ shave**
(*fig*) escaparse por un pelo ♦ *adv* cerca; **~
by**, **~ at hand** muy cerca; **~ to** *prep* cerca
de

close² [kləuz] *vt* (*shut*) cerrar; (*end*)
concluir, terminar ♦ *vi* (*shop etc*) cerrarse;
(*end*) concluirse, terminarse ♦ *n* (*end*) fin
m, final *m*, conclusión *f*; **~ down** *vi*
cerrarse definitivamente; **~d** *adj* (*shop*
etc) cerrado; **~d shop** *n* taller *m* gremial

close-knit [kləus'nɪt] *adj* (*fig*) muy unido

closely ['kləuslɪ] *adv* (*study*) con detalle;
(*watch*) de cerca; (*resemble*)
estrechamente

closet ['klɔzɪt] *n* armario

close-up ['kləusʌp] *n* primer plano

closure ['kləuʒə*] *n* cierre *m*

clot [klɔt] *n* (*gen:* **blood ~**) coágulo; (*inf:*
idiot) imbécil *m/f* ♦ *vi* (*blood*) coagularse

cloth [klɔθ] *n* (*material*) tela, paño; (*rag*)
trapo

clothe [kləuð] *vt* vestir; **~s** *npl* ropa; **~s
brush** *n* cepillo (para la ropa); **~s line** *n*
cuerda (para tender la ropa); **~s peg** (*US*

~s pin) *n* pinza

clothing ['kləuðɪŋ] *n* = **clothes**

cloud [klaud] *n* nube *f*; **~burst** *n*
aguacero; **~y** *adj* nublado, nublosos;
(*liquid*) turbio

clout [klaut] *vt* dar un tortazo a

clove [kləuv] *n* clavo; **~ of garlic** diente *m*
de ajo

clover ['kləuvə*] *n* trébol *m*

clown [klaun] *n* payaso ♦ *vi* (*also:* **~
about, ~ around**) hacer el payaso

cloying ['klɔɪɪŋ] *adj* empalagoso

club [klʌb] *n* (*society*) club *m*; (*weapon*)
porra, cachiporra; (*also:* **golf ~**) palo ♦ *vt*
aporrear ♦ *vi*: **to ~ together** (*for gift*)
comprar entre todos; **~s** *npl* (*CARDS*)
tréboles *mpl*; **~ class** *n* (*AVIAT*) clase *f*
preferente; **~house** *n local social, sobre
todo en clubs deportivos*

cluck [klʌk] *vi* cloquear

clue [klu:] *n* pista; (*in crosswords*)
indicación *f*; **I haven't a ~** no tengo ni
idea

clump [klʌmp] *n* (*of trees*) grupo

clumsy ['klʌmzɪ] *adj* (*person*) torpe,
desmañado; (*tool*) difícil de manejar;
(*movement*) desgarbado

clung [klʌŋ] *pt, pp of* **cling**

cluster ['klʌstə*] *n* grupo ♦ *vi* agruparse,
apiñarse

clutch [klʌtʃ] *n* (*AUT*) embrague *m*; (*grasp*):
~es garras *fpl* ♦ *vt* asir; agarrar

clutter ['klʌtə*] *vt* atestar

cm *abbr* (= *centimetre*) cm

CND *n abbr* (= *Campaign for Nuclear
Disarmament*) plataforma pro desarme
nuclear

Co. *abbr* = **county**; **company**

c/o *abbr* (= *care of*) c/a, a/c

coach [kəutʃ] *n* autocar *m* (*SP*), coche *m*
de línea; (*horse-drawn*) coche *m*; (*of train*)
vagón *m*, coche *m*; (*SPORT*) entrenador(a)
m/f, instructor(a) *m/f*; (*tutor*) profesor(a)
m/f particular ♦ *vt* (*SPORT*) entrenar;
(*student*) preparar, enseñar; **~ trip** *n*
excursión *f* en autocar

coal [kəul] *n* carbón *m*; **~ face** *n* frente *m*

de carbón; **~field** *n* yacimiento de carbón

coalition [kəʊə'lɪʃən] *n* coalición *f*

coalman ['kəʊlmən] (*irreg*) *n* carbonero

coalmine ['kəʊlmaɪn] *n* mina de carbón

coarse [kɔ:s] *adj* basto, burdo; (*vulgar*) grosero, ordinario

coast [kəʊst] *n* costa, litoral *m* ♦ *vi* (*AUT*) ir en punto muerto; **~al** *adj* costero, costanero; **~guard** *n* guardacostas *m inv*; **~line** *n* litoral *m*

coat [kəʊt] *n* abrigo; (*of animal*) pelaje *m*, lana; (*of paint*) mano *f*, capa ♦ *vt* cubrir, revestir; **~ of arms** *n* escudo de armas; **~ hanger** *n* percha (*SP*), gancho (*AM*); **~ing** *n* capa, baño

coax [kəʊks] *vt* engatusar

cobbler ['kɔblə] *n* zapatero (remendón)

cobbles ['kɔblz] *npl*, **cobblestones** ['kɔblstəʊnz] *npl* adoquines *mpl*

cobweb ['kɔbweb] *n* telaraña

cocaine [kə'keɪn] *n* cocaína

cock [kɔk] *n* (*rooster*) gallo; (*male bird*) macho ♦ *vt* (*gun*) amartillar; **~erel** *n* gallito

cockle ['kɔkl] *n* berberecho

cockney ['kɔknɪ] *n* habitante de ciertos barrios de Londres

cockpit ['kɔkpɪt] *n* cabina

cockroach ['kɔkrəʊtʃ] *n* cucaracha

cocktail ['kɔkteɪl] *n* coctel *m*, cóctel *m*; **~ cabinet** *n* mueble-bar *m*; **~ party** *n* coctel *m*, cóctel *m*

cocoa ['kəʊkəʊ] *n* cacao; (*drink*) chocolate *m*

coconut ['kəʊkənʌt] *n* coco

cod [kɔd] *n* bacalao

C.O.D. *abbr* (= *cash on delivery*) C.A.E.

code [kəʊd] *n* código; (*cipher*) clave *f*; (*dialling* ~) prefijo; (*post* ~) código postal

cod-liver oil ['kɔdlɪvər-] *n* aceite *m* de hígado de bacalao

coercion [kəʊ'ə:ʃən] *n* coacción *f*

coffee ['kɔfɪ] *n* café *m*; **~ bar** (*BRIT*) *n* cafetería; **~ bean** *n* grano de café; **~ break** *n* descanso (para tomar café); **~pot** *n* cafetera; **~ table** *n* mesita (para servir el café)

coffin ['kɔfɪn] *n* ataúd *m*

cog [kɔg] *n* (*wheel*) rueda dentada; (*tooth*) diente *m*

cogent ['kəʊdʒənt] *adj* convincente

cognac ['kɔnjæk] *n* coñac *m*

coil [kɔɪl] *n* rollo; (*ELEC*) bobina, carrete *m*; (*contraceptive*) espiral *f* ♦ *vt* enrollar

coin [kɔɪn] *n* moneda ♦ *vt* (*word*) inventar, idear; **~age** *n* moneda; **~-box** (*BRIT*) *n* cabina telefónica

coincide [kəʊɪn'saɪd] *vi* coincidir; (*agree*) estar de acuerdo; **coincidence** [kəʊ'ɪnsɪdəns] *n* casualidad *f*

Coke ® [kəʊk] *n* Coca-Cola ®

coke [kəʊk] *n* (*coal*) coque *m*

colander ['kɔləndə*] *n* colador *m*, escurridor *m*

cold [kəʊld] *adj* frío ♦ *n* frío; (*MED*) resfriado; **it's ~** hace frío; **to be ~** (*person*) tener frío; **to catch ~** enfriarse; **to catch a ~** resfriarse, acatarrarse; **in ~ blood** a sangre fría; **~-shoulder** *vt* dar *or* volver la espalda a; **~ sore** *n* herpes *mpl or fpl*

coleslaw ['kəʊlslɔ:] *n* especie de ensalada de col

colic ['kɔlɪk] *n* cólico

collapse [kə'læps] *vi* hundirse, derrumbarse; (*MED*) sufrir un colapso ♦ *n* hundimiento, derrumbamiento; (*MED*) colapso; **collapsible** *adj* plegable

collar ['kɔlə*] *n* (*of coat, shirt*) cuello; (*of dog etc*) collar; **~bone** *n* clavícula

collateral [kɔ'lætərəl] *n* garantía colateral

colleague ['kɔli:g] *n* colega *m/f*; (*at work*) compañero, a

collect [kə'lekt] *vt* (*litter, mail etc*) recoger; (*as a hobby*) coleccionar; (*BRIT: call and pick up*) recoger; (*debts, subscriptions etc*) recaudar ♦ *vi* reunirse; (*dust*) acumularse; **to call ~** (*US: TEL*) llamar a cobro revertido; **~ion** [kə'lekʃən] *n* colección *f*; (*of mail, for charity*) recogida; **~or** *n* coleccionista *m/f*

college ['kɔlɪdʒ] *n* colegio mayor; (*of agriculture, technology*) escuela universitaria

collide [kə'laɪd] vi chocar
colliery ['kɒlɪərɪ] (BRIT) n mina de carbón
collision [kə'lɪʒən] n choque m
colloquial [kə'ləukwɪəl] adj familiar, coloquial
Colombia [kə'lɒmbɪə] n Colombia; ~n adj, n colombiano/a
colon ['kəulən] n (sign) dos puntos; (MED) colon m
colonel ['kɜːnl] n coronel m
colonial [kə'ləunɪəl] adj colonial
colony ['kɒlənɪ] n colonia
colour ['kʌlə*] (US **color**) n color m ♦ vt color(e)ar; (dye) teñir; (fig: account) adornar; (: judgement) distorsionar ♦ vi (blush) sonrojarse; ~**s** npl (of party, club) colores mpl; **in ~** en color; ~ **in** vt colorear; ~ **bar** n segregación f racial; ~~**blind** adj daltónico; ~**ed** adj de color; (photo) en color; ~ **film** n película en color; ~**ful** adj lleno de color; (story) fantástico; (person) excéntrico; ~**ing** n (complexion) tez f; (in food) colorante m; ~ **scheme** n combinación f de colores; ~ **television** n televisión f en color
colt [kəult] n potro
column ['kɒləm] n columna; ~**ist** ['kɒləmnɪst] n columnista m/f
coma ['kəumə] n coma m
comb [kəum] n peine m; (ornamental) peineta ♦ vt (hair) peinar; (area) registrar a fondo
combat ['kɒmbæt] n combate m ♦ vt combatir
combination [kɒmbɪ'neɪʃən] n combinación f
combine [vb kəm'baɪn, n 'kɒmbaɪn] vt combinar; (qualities) reunir ♦ vi combinarse ♦ n (ECON) cartel m; ~ **(harvester)** n cosechadora

---
KEYWORD
---

come [kʌm] (pt **came**, pp **come**) vi **1** (movement towards) venir; **to ~ running** venir corriendo
2 (arrive) llegar; **he's ~ here to work** ha venido aquí para trabajar; **to ~ home**

volver a casa
3 (reach): **to ~ to** llegar a; **the bill came to £40** la cuenta ascendía a cuarenta libras
4 (occur): **an idea came to me** se me ocurrió una idea
5 (be, become): **to ~ loose/undone** etc aflojarse/desabrocharse, desatarse etc; **I've ~ to like him** por fin ha llegado a gustarme
come about vi suceder, ocurrir
come across vt fus (person) topar con; (thing) dar con
come away vi (leave) marcharse; (become detached) desprenderse
come back vi (return) volver
come by vt fus (acquire) conseguir
come down vi (price) bajar; (tree, building) ser derribado
come forward vi presentarse
come from vt fus (place, source) ser de
come in vi (visitor) entrar; (train, report) llegar; (fashion) ponerse de moda; (on deal etc) entrar
come in for vt fus (criticism etc) recibir
come into vt fus (money) heredar; (be involved) tener que ver con; **to ~ into fashion** ponerse de moda
come off vi (button) soltarse, desprenderse; (attempt) salir bien
come on vi (pupil) progresar; (work, project) desarrollarse; (lights) encenderse; (electricity) volver; **~ on!** ¡vamos!
come out vi (fact) salir a la luz; (book, sun) salir; (stain) quitarse
come round vi (after faint, operation) volver en sí
come to vi (wake) volver en sí
come up vi (sun) salir; (problem) surgir; (event) aproximarse; (in conversation) mencionarse
come up against vt fus (resistance etc) tropezar con
come up with vt fus (idea) sugerir; (money) conseguir
come upon vt fus (find) dar con

comeback ['kʌmbæk] *n*: **to make a ~** (*THEATRE*) volver a las tablas

comedian [kə'mi:dɪən] *n* cómico; **comedienne** [-'ɛn] *n* cómica

comedy ['kɒmɪdɪ] *n* comedia; (*humour*) comicidad *f*

comet ['kɒmɪt] *n* cometa *m*

comeuppance [kʌm'ʌpəns] *n*: **to get one's ~** llevar su merecido

comfort ['kʌmfət] *n* bienestar *m*; (*relief*) alivio ♦ *vt* consolar; **~s** *npl* (*of home etc*) comodidades *fpl*; **~able** *adj* cómodo; (*financially*) acomodado; (*easy*) fácil; **~ably** *adv* cómodamente; (*live*) holgadamente; **~ station** (*US*) *n* servicios *mpl*

comic ['kɒmɪk] *adj* (*also*: **~al**) cómico ♦ *n* (*comedian*) cómico; (*BRIT: for children*) tebeo; (*BRIT: for adults*) comic *m*; **~ strip** *n* tira cómica

coming ['kʌmɪŋ] *n* venida, llegada ♦ *adj* que viene; **~(s) and going(s)** *n(pl)* ir y venir *m*, ajetreo

comma ['kɒmə] *n* coma

command [kə'mɑ:nd] *n* orden *f*, mandato; (*MIL: authority*) mando; (*mastery*) dominio ♦ *vt* (*troops*) mandar; (*give orders to*): **to ~ sb to do** mandar *or* ordenar a uno hacer; **~eer** [kɒmən'dɪə*] *vt* requisar; **~er** *n* (*MIL*) comandante *m/f*, jefe/a *m/f*

commemorate [kə'mɛmərət] *vt* conmemorar

commence [kə'mɛns] *vt*, *vi* comenzar, empezar

commend [kə'mɛnd] *vt* elogiar, alabar; (*recommend*) recomendar

commensurate [kə'mɛnʃərɪt] *adj*: **~ with** en proporción a, que corresponde a

comment ['kɒmɛnt] *n* comentario ♦ *vi*: **to ~ on** hacer comentarios sobre; **"no ~"** (*written*) "sin comentarios"; (*spoken*) "no tengo nada que decir"; **~ary** ['kɒməntərɪ] *n* comentario; **~ator** ['kɒməntertə*] *n* comentarista *m/f*

commerce ['kɒmə:s] *n* comercio

commercial [kə'mə:ʃəl] *adj* comercial ♦ *n* (*TV, RADIO*) anuncio

commiserate [kə'mɪzəreɪt] *vi*: **to ~ with** compadecerse de, condolerse de

commission [kə'mɪʃən] *n* (*committee, fee*) comisión *f* ♦ *vt* (*work of art*) encargar; **out of ~** fuera de servicio; **~aire** [kəmɪʃə'nɛə*] (*BRIT*) *n* portero; **~er** *n* (*POLICE*) comisario de policía

commit [kə'mɪt] *vt* (*act*) cometer; (*resources*) dedicar; (*to sb's care*) entregar; **to ~ o.s. (to do)** comprometerse (a hacer); **to ~ suicide** suicidarse; **~ment** *n* compromiso; (*to ideology etc*) entrega

committee [kə'mɪtɪ] *n* comité *m*

commodity [kə'mɒdɪtɪ] *n* mercancía

common ['kɒmən] *adj* común; (*pej*) ordinario ♦ *n* campo común; **the C~s** *npl* (*BRIT*) (la Cámara de) los Comunes *mpl*; **in ~** en común; **~er** *n* plebeyo; **~ law** *n* ley *f* consuetudinaria; **~ly** *adv* comúnmente; **C~ Market** *n* Mercado Común; **~place** *adj* de lo más común; **~room** *n* sala común; **~ sense** *n* sentido común; **the C~wealth** *n* la Commonwealth

commotion [kə'məʊʃən] *n* tumulto, confusión *f*

commune [*n* 'kɒmju:n, *vb* kə'mju:n] *n* (*group*) comuna ♦ *vi*: **to ~ with** comulgar *or* conversar con

communicate [kə'mju:nɪkeɪt] *vt* comunicar ♦ *vi*: **to ~ (with)** comunicarse (con); (*in writing*) estar en contacto (con)

communication [kəmju:nɪ'keɪʃən] *n* comunicación *f*; **~ cord** (*BRIT*) *n* timbre *m* de alarma

communion [kə'mju:nɪən] *n* (*also*: **Holy C~**) comunión *f*

communiqué [kə'mju:nɪkeɪ] *n* comunicado, parte *f*

communism ['kɒmjunɪzəm] *n* comunismo; **communist** *adj*, *n* comunista *m/f*

community [kə'mju:nɪtɪ] *n* comunidad *f*; (*large group*) colectividad *f*; **~ centre** *n* centro social; **~ chest** (*US*) *n* arca comunitaria, fondo común

commutation ticket [kɔmju'teɪʃən-] (*US*) *n* billete *m* de abono

commute [kə'mju:t] *vi viajar a diario de la casa al trabajo* ♦ *vt* conmutar; **~r** *n* persona (que viaja ... *see vi*)

compact [*adj* kəm'pækt, *n* 'kɔmpækt] *adj* compacto ♦ *n* (*also*: **powder ~**) polvera; **~ disc** *n compact disc m;* **~ disc player** *n* reproductor *m* de disco compacto, compact disc *m*

companion [kəm'pænɪən] *n* compañero/a; **~ship** *n* compañerismo

company ['kʌmpənɪ] *n* compañía; (*COMM*) sociedad *f*, compañía; **to keep sb ~** acompañar a uno; **~ secretary** (*BRIT*) *n* secretario/a de compañía

comparative [kəm'pærətɪv] *adj* relativo; (*study*) comparativo; **~ly** *adv* (*relatively*) relativamente

compare [kəm'pɛə*] *vt*: **to ~ sth/sb with/to** comparar algo/a uno con ♦ *vi*: **to ~ (with)** compararse (con); **comparison** [-'pærɪsn] *n* comparación *f*

compartment [kəm'pɑ:tmənt] *n* (*also*: *RAIL*) compartim(i)ento

compass ['kʌmpəs] *n* brújula; **~es** *npl* (*MATH*) compás *m*

compassion [kəm'pæʃən] *n* compasión *f*; **~ate** *adj* compasivo

compatible [kəm'pætɪbl] *adj* compatible

compel [kəm'pel] *vt* obligar

compensate ['kɔmpənseɪt] *vt* compensar ♦ *vi*: **to ~ for** compensar; **compensation** [-'seɪʃən] *n* (*for loss*) indemnización *f*

compère ['kɔmpɛə*] *n* presentador *m*

compete [kəm'pi:t] *vi* (*take part*) tomar parte, concurrir; (*vie with*): **to ~ with** competir con, hacer competencia a

competent ['kɔmpɪtənt] *adj* competente, capaz

competition [kɔmpɪ'tɪʃən] *n* (*contest*) concurso; (*rivalry*) competencia

competitive [kəm'petɪtɪv] *adj* (*ECON, SPORT*) competitivo

competitor [kəm'petɪtə*] *n* (*rival*) competidor(a) *m/f*; (*participant*)

concursante *m/f*

complacency [kəm'pleɪsnsɪ] *n* autosatisfacción *f*

complacent [kəm'pleɪsnt] *adj* autocomplaciente

complain [kəm'pleɪn] *vi* quejarse; (*COMM*) reclamar; **~t** *n* queja; reclamación *f*; (*MED*) enfermedad *f*

complement [*n* 'kɔmplɪmənt, *vb* 'kɔmplɪment] *n* complemento; (*esp of ship's crew*) dotación *f* ♦ *vt* (*enhance*) complementar; **~ary** [kɔmplɪ'mentərɪ] *adj* complementario

complete [kəm'pli:t] *adj* (*full*) completo; (*finished*) acabado ♦ *vt* (*fulfil*) completar; (*finish*) acabar; (*a form*) llenar; **~ly** *adv* completamente; **completion** [-'pli:ʃən] *n* terminación *f*; (*of contract*) realización *f*

complex ['kɔmpleks] *adj*, *n* complejo

complexion [kəm'plekʃən] *n* (*of face*) tez *f*, cutis *m*

compliance [kəm'plaɪəns] *n* (*submission*) sumisión *f*; (*agreement*) conformidad *f*; **in ~ with** de acuerdo con

complicate ['kɔmplɪkeɪt] *vt* complicar; **~d** *adj* complicado; **complication** [-'keɪʃən] *n* complicación *f*

compliment [*n* 'kɔmplɪmənt] *n* (*formal*) cumplido ♦ *vt* felicitar; **~s** *npl* (*regards*) saludos *mpl*; **to pay sb a ~** hacer cumplidos a uno; **~ary** [-'mentərɪ] *adj* lisonjero; (*free*) de favor

comply [kəm'plaɪ] *vi*: **to ~ with** cumplir con

component [kəm'pəunənt] *adj* componente ♦ *n* (*TECH*) pieza

compose [kəm'pəuz] *vt*: **to be ~d of** componerse de; (*music etc*) componer; **to ~ o.s.** tranquilizarse; **~d** *adj* sosegado; **~r** *n* (*MUS*) compositor(a) *m/f*; **composition** [kɔmpə'zɪʃən] *n* composición *f*

compost ['kɔmpɔst] *n* abono (vegetal)

composure [kəm'pəuʒə*] *n* serenidad *f*, calma

compound ['kɔmpaund] *n* (*CHEM*) compuesto; (*LING*) palabra compuesta;

(*enclosure*) recinto ♦ *adj* compuesto;
(*fracture*) complicado
comprehend [kɔmprɪ'hend] *vt*
comprender; **comprehension** [-'henʃən]
n comprensión *f*
comprehensive [kɔmprɪ'hensɪv] *adj*
exhaustivo; (*INSURANCE*) contra todo
riesgo; ~ **(school)** *n* centro estatal de
enseñanza secundaria; ≈ Instituto
Nacional de Bachillerato (*SP*)
compress [*vb* kəm'pres, *n* 'kɔmpres] *vt*
comprimir; (*information*) condensar ♦ *n*
(*MED*) compresa
comprise [kəm'praɪz] *vt* (*also*: **be ~d of**)
comprender, constar de; (*constitute*)
constituir
compromise ['kɔmprəmaɪz] *n* (*agreement*)
arreglo ♦ *vt* comprometer ♦ *vi* transigir
compulsion [kəm'pʌlʃən] *n* compulsión *f*;
(*force*) obligación *f*
compulsive [kəm'pʌlsɪv] *adj* compulsivo;
(*viewing, reading*) obligado
compulsory [kəm'pʌlsərɪ] *adj* obligatorio
computer [kəm'pju:tə*] *n* ordenador *m*,
computador *m*, computadora; ~ **game** *n*
juego para ordenador; ~-**generated** *adj*
realizado por ordenador, creado por
ordenador; ~**ize** *vt* (*data*) computerizar;
(*system*) informatizar; ~ **programmer** *n*
programador(a) *m/f*; ~ **programming** *n*
programación *f*; ~ **science** *n*
informática; **computing** [kəm'pju:tɪŋ] *n*
(*activity, science*) informática
comrade ['kɔmrɪd] *n* (*POL, MIL*) camarada;
(*friend*) compañero/a; ~**ship** *n*
camaradería, compañerismo
con [kɔn] *vt* (*deceive*) engañar; (*cheat*)
estafar ♦ *n* estafa
conceal [kən'si:l] *vt* ocultar
conceit [kən'si:t] *n* presunción *f*; ~**ed** *adj*
presumido
conceive [kən'si:v] *vt, vi* concebir
concentrate ['kɔnsəntreɪt] *vi* concentrarse
♦ *vt* concentrar
concentration [kɔnsən'treɪʃən] *n*
concentración *f*
concept ['kɔnsept] *n* concepto

concern [kən'sə:n] *n* (*matter*) asunto;
(*COMM*) empresa; (*anxiety*) preocupación *f*
♦ *vt* (*worry*) preocupar; (*involve*) afectar;
(*relate to*) tener que ver con; **to be ~ed**
(about) interesarse (por), preocuparse
(por); ~**ing** *prep* sobre, acerca de
concert ['kɔnsət] *n* concierto; ~**ed**
[kən'sə:təd] *adj* (*efforts etc*) concertado; ~
hall *n* sala de conciertos
concerto [kən'tʃə:təu] *n* concierto
concession [kən'seʃən] *n* concesión *f*; **tax**
~ privilegio fiscal
conclude [kən'klu:d] *vt* concluir; (*treaty*
etc) firmar; (*agreement*) llegar a; (*decide*)
llegar a la conclusión de; **conclusion**
[-'klu:ʒən] *n* conclusión *f*; firma;
conclusive [-'klu:sɪv] *adj* decisivo,
concluyente
concoct [kən'kɔkt] *vt* confeccionar; (*plot*)
tramar; ~**ion** [-'kɔkʃən] *n* mezcla
concourse ['kɔŋkɔ:s] *n* vestíbulo
concrete ['kɔnkri:t] *n* hormigón *m* ♦ *adj*
de hormigón; (*fig*) concreto
concur [kən'kə:*] *vi* estar de acuerdo,
asentir
concurrently [kən'kʌrntlɪ] *adv* al mismo
tiempo
concussion [kən'kʌʃən] *n* conmoción *f*
cerebral
condemn [kən'dem] *vt* condenar;
(*building*) declarar en ruina
condense [kən'dens] *vi* condensarse ♦ *vt*
condensar, abreviar; ~**d milk** *n* leche *f*
condensada
condition [kən'dɪʃən] *n* condición *f*,
estado; (*requirement*) condición *f* ♦ *vt*
condicionar; **on ~ that** a condición (de)
que; ~**er** *n* suavizante
condolences [kən'dəulənsɪz] *npl* pésame
m
condom ['kɔndəm] *n* condón *m*
condone [kən'dəun] *vt* condonar
conducive [kən'dju:sɪv] *adj*: ~ **to**
conducente a
conduct [*n* 'kɔndʌkt, *vb* kən'dʌkt] *n*
conducta, comportamiento ♦ *vt* (*lead*)
conducir; (*manage*) llevar a cabo, dirigir;

(*MUS*) dirigir; **to ~ o.s.** comportarse; ~ed
tour (*BRIT*) n visita acompañada; ~or n
(*of orchestra*) director m; (*US: on train*)
revisor(a) m/f; (*on bus*) cobrador m; (*ELEC*)
conductor m; ~ress n (*on bus*)
cobradora

cone [kəun] n cono; (*pine ~*) piña; (*on
road*) pivote m; (*for ice-cream*) cucurucho

confectioner [kən'fekʃənə*] n repostero/a;
~'s **(shop)** n confitería; ~y n dulces mpl

confer [kən'fə:*] vt: **to ~ sth on** otorgar
algo a ♦ vi conferenciar

conference ['kɔnfərns] n (*meeting*)
reunión f; (*convention*) congreso

confess [kən'fes] vt confesar ♦ vi admitir;
~**ion** [-'feʃən] n confesión f

confetti [kən'feti] n confeti m

confide [kən'faid] vi: **to ~ in** confiar en

confidence ['kɔnfidns] n (*also:* **self-~**)
confianza; (*secret*) confidencia; **in ~**
(*speak, write*) en confianza; ~ **trick** n
timo; **confident** adj seguro de sí mismo;
(*certain*) seguro; **confidential**
[kɔnfi'denʃəl] adj confidencial

confine [kən'fain] vt (*limit*) limitar; (*shut
up*) encerrar; ~d adj (*space*) reducido;
~ment n (*prison*) prisión f; ~s ['kɔnfainz]
npl confines mpl

confirm [kən'fə:m] vt confirmar; ~ation
[kɔnfə'meiʃən] n confirmación f; ~ed adj
empedernido

confiscate ['kɔnfiskeit] vt confiscar

conflict [n 'kɔnflikt, vb kən'flikt] n conflicto
♦ vi (*opinions*) chocar; ~ing adj
contradictorio

conform [kən'fɔ:m] vi conformarse; **to ~
to** ajustarse a

confound [kən'faund] vt confundir

confront [kən'frʌnt] vt (*problems*) hacer
frente a; (*enemy, danger*) enfrentarse con;
~ation [kɔnfrən'teiʃən] n enfrentamiento

confuse [kən'fju:z] vt (*perplex*) aturdir,
desconcertar; (*mix up*) confundir;
(*complicate*) complicar; ~d adj confuso;
(*person*) perplejo; **confusing** adj
confuso; **confusion** [-'fju:ʒən] n
confusión f

congeal [kən'dʒi:l] vi (*blood*) coagularse;
(*sauce etc*) cuajarse

congested [kən'dʒestid] adj
congestionado; **congestion** n
congestión f

congratulate [kən'grætjuleit] vt: **to ~ sb
(on)** felicitar a uno (por);
congratulations [-'leiʃənz] npl
felicitaciones fpl; **congratulations!**
¡enhorabuena!

congregate ['kɔngrigeit] vi congregarse;
congregation [-'geiʃən] n (*of a church*)
feligreses mpl

congress ['kɔngres] n congreso; (*US*): **C~**
Congreso; **C~man** (*irreg*) (*US*) n
miembro del Congreso

conifer ['kɔnifə*] n conífera

conjunctivitis [kəndʒʌŋkti'vaitis] n
conjuntivitis f

conjure ['kʌndʒə*] vi hacer juegos de
manos; ~ **up** vt (*ghost, spirit*) hacer
aparecer; (*memories*) evocar; ~r n
ilusionista m/f

con man ['kɔn-] n estafador m

connect [kə'nekt] vt juntar, unir; (*ELEC*)
conectar; (*TEL: subscriber*) poner; (: *caller*)
poner al habla; (*fig*) relacionar, asociar
♦ vi: **to ~ with** (*train*) enlazar con; **to be
~ed with** (*associated*) estar relacionado
con; ~**ion** [-ʃən] n juntura, unión f; (*ELEC*)
conexión f; (*RAIL*) enlace m f; (*TEL*)
comunicación f; (*fig*) relación f

connive [kə'naiv] vi: **to ~ at** hacer la vista
gorda a

connoisseur [kɔni'sə*] n experto/a,
entendido/a

conquer ['kɔŋkə*] vt (*territory*) conquistar;
(*enemy, feelings*) vencer; ~or n
conquistador m

conquest ['kɔŋkwest] n conquista

cons [kɔnz] npl see **convenience**; **pro**

conscience ['kɔnʃəns] n conciencia

conscientious [kɔnʃi'enʃəs] adj
concienzudo; (*objection*) de conciencia

conscious ['kɔnʃəs] adj (*deliberate*)
deliberado; (*awake, aware*) consciente;
~**ness** n conciencia; (*MED*) conocimiento

conscript [ˈkɒnskrɪpt] *n* recluta *m*; **~ion** [kənˈskrɪpʃən] *n* servicio militar (obligatorio)

consensus [kənˈsensəs] *n* consenso

consent [kənˈsent] *n* consentimiento ♦ *vi*: **to ~ (to)** consentir (en)

consequence [ˈkɒnsɪkwəns] *n* consecuencia; (*significance*) importancia

consequently [ˈkɒnsɪkwəntlɪ] *adv* por consiguiente

conservation [kɒnsəˈveɪʃən] *n* conservación *f*

conservative [kənˈsɜːvətɪv] *adj* conservador(a); (*estimate etc*) cauteloso; **C~** (*BRIT*) *adj*, *n* (*POL*) conservador(a) *m/f*

conservatory [kənˈsɜːvətrɪ] *n* invernadero; (*MUS*) conservatorio

conserve [kənˈsɜːv] *vt* conservar ♦ *n* conserva

consider [kənˈsɪdə*] *vt* considerar; (*take into account*) tener en cuenta; (*study*) estudiar, examinar; **to ~ doing sth** pensar en (la posibilidad de) hacer algo; **~able** *adj* considerable; **~ably** *adv* notablemente; **~ate** *adj* considerado; **consideration** [-ˈreɪʃən] *n* consideración *f*; (*factor*) factor *m*; **to give sth further consideration** estudiar algo más a fondo; **~ing** *prep* teniendo en cuenta

consign [kənˈsaɪn] *vt*: **to ~ to** (*sth unwanted*) relegar a; (*person*) destinar a; **~ment** *n* envío

consist [kənˈsɪst] *vi*: **to ~ of** consistir en

consistency [kənˈsɪstənsɪ] *n* (*of argument etc*) coherencia; consecuencia; (*thickness*) consistencia

consistent [kənˈsɪstənt] *adj* (*person*) consecuente; (*argument etc*) coherente

consolation [kɒnsəˈleɪʃən] *n* consuelo

console¹ [kənˈsəul] *vt* consolar

console² [ˈkɒnsəul] *n* consola

consonant [ˈkɒnsənənt] *n* consonante *f*

consortium [kənˈsɔːtɪəm] *n* consorcio

conspicuous [kənˈspɪkjuəs] *adj* (*visible*) visible

conspiracy [kənˈspɪrəsɪ] *n* conjura, complot *m*

constable [ˈkʌnstəbl] (*BRIT*) *n* policía *m/f*; **chief ~** ≈ jefe *m* de policía

constabulary [kənˈstæbjulərɪ] *n* ≈ policía

constant [ˈkɒnstənt] *adj* constante; **~ly** *adv* constantemente

constipated [ˈkɒnstɪpeɪtəd] *adj* estreñido; **constipation** [kɒnstɪˈpeɪʃən] *n* estreñimiento

constituency [kənˈstɪtjuənsɪ] *n* (*POL: area*) distrito electoral; (: *electors*) electorado; **constituent** [-ənt] *n* (*POL*) elector(a) *m/f*; (*part*) componente *m*

constitution [kɒnstɪˈtjuːʃən] *n* constitución *f*; **~al** *adj* constitucional

constraint [kənˈstreɪnt] *n* obligación *f*; (*limit*) restricción *f*

construct [kənˈstrʌkt] *vt* construir; **~ion** [-ʃən] *n* construcción *f*; **~ive** *adj* constructivo

consul [ˈkɒnsl] *n* cónsul *m/f*; **~ate** [ˈkɒnsjulɪt] *n* consulado

consult [kənˈsʌlt] *vt* consultar; **~ant** *n* (*BRIT: MED*) especialista *m/f*; (*other specialist*) asesor(a) *m/f*; **~ation** [kɒnsəlˈteɪʃən] *n* consulta; **~ing room** (*BRIT*) *n* consultorio

consume [kənˈsjuːm] *vt* (*eat*) comerse; (*drink*) beberse; (*fire etc*, *COMM*) consumir; **~r** *n* consumidor(a) *m/f*; **~r goods** *npl* bienes *mpl* de consumo

consummate [ˈkɒnsʌmeɪt] *vt* consumar

consumption [kənˈsʌmpʃən] *n* consumo

cont. *abbr* (= *continued*) sigue

contact [ˈkɒntækt] *n* contacto; (*person*) contacto; (: *pej*) enchufe *m* ♦ *vt* ponerse en contacto con; **~ lenses** *npl* lentes *fpl* de contacto

contagious [kənˈteɪdʒəs] *adj* contagioso

contain [kənˈteɪn] *vt* contener; **to ~ o.s.** contenerse; **~er** *n* recipiente *m*; (*for shipping etc*) contenedor *m*

contaminate [kənˈtæmɪneɪt] *vt* contaminar

cont'd *abbr* (= *continued*) sigue

contemplate [ˈkɒntəmpleɪt] *vt* contemplar; (*reflect upon*) considerar

contemporary [kənˈtempərərɪ] *adj*, *n*

contemporáneo/a *m/f*

contempt [kən'tɛmpt] *n* desprecio; **~ of court** (*LAW*) desacato (a los tribunales); **~ible** *adj* despreciable; **~uous** *adj* desdeñoso

contend [kən'tɛnd] *vt* (*argue*) afirmar ♦ *vi*: **to ~ with/for** luchar contra/por; **~er** *n* (*SPORT*) contendiente *m/f*

content [*adj, vb* kən'tɛnt, *n* 'kɔntɛnt] *adj* (*happy*) contento; (*satisfied*) satisfecho ♦ *vt* contentar; satisfacer ♦ *n* contenido; **~s** *npl* contenido; **(table of) ~s** índice *m* de materias; **~ed** *adj* contento; satisfecho

contention [kən'tɛnʃən] *n* (*assertion*) aseveración *f*; (*disagreement*) discusión *f*

contest [*n* 'kɔntɛst, *vb* kən'tɛst] *n* lucha; (*competition*) concurso ♦ *vt* (*dispute*) impugnar; (*POL*) presentarse como candidato/a en; **~ant** [kən'tɛstənt] *n* concursante *m/f*; (*in fight*) contendiente *m/f*

context ['kɔntɛkst] *n* contexto

continent ['kɔntɪnənt] *n* continente *m*; **the C~** (*BRIT*) el continente europeo; **~al** [-'nɛntl] *adj* continental; **~al breakfast** *n* desayuno estilo europeo; **~al quilt** (*BRIT*) *n* edredón *m*

contingency [kən'tɪndʒənsɪ] *n* contingencia

continual [kən'tɪnjuəl] *adj* continuo; **~ly** *adv* constantemente

continuation [kəntɪnju'eɪʃən] *n* prolongación *f*; (*after interruption*) reanudación *f*

continue [kən'tɪnju:] *vi, vt* seguir, continuar

continuous [kən'tɪnjuəs] *adj* continuo

contort [kən'tɔːt] *vt* retorcer

contour ['kɔntuə*] *n* contorno; (*also:* **~ line**) curva de nivel

contraband ['kɔntrəbænd] *n* contrabando

contraceptive [kɔntrə'sɛptɪv] *adj, n* anticonceptivo

contract [*n* 'kɔntrækt, *vb* kən'trækt] *n* contrato ♦ *vi* (*COMM*): **to ~ to do sth** comprometerse por contrato a hacer algo; (*become smaller*) contraerse,

encogerse ♦ *vt* contraer; **~ion** [kən'trækʃən] *n* contracción *f*; **~or** *n* contratista *m/f*

contradict [kɔntrə'dɪkt] *vt* contradecir; **~ion** [-ʃən] *n* contradicción *f*

contraption [kən'træpʃən] (*pej*) *n* artilugio *m*

contrary¹ ['kɔntrərɪ] *adj* contrario ♦ *n* lo contrario; **on the ~** al contrario; **unless you hear to the ~** a no ser que le digan lo contrario

contrary² [kən'trɛərɪ] *adj* (*perverse*) terco

contrast [*n* 'kɔntrɑːst, *vt* kən'trɑːst] *n* contraste *m* ♦ *vt* comparar; **in ~ to** en contraste con

contravene [kɔntrə'viːn] *vt* infringir

contribute [kən'trɪbjuːt] *vi* contribuir ♦ *vt*: **to ~ £10/an article to** contribuir con 10 libras/un artículo a; **to ~ to** (*charity*) donar a; (*newspaper*) escribir para; (*discussion*) intervenir en; **contribution** [kɔntrɪ'bjuːʃən] *n* (*donation*) donativo; (*BRIT: for social security*) cotización *f*; (*to debate*) intervención *f*; (*to journal*) colaboración *f*; **contributor** *n* contribuyente *m/f*; (*to newspaper*) colaborador(a) *m/f*

contrive [kən'traɪv] *vt* (*invent*) idear ♦ *vi*: **to ~ to do** lograr hacer

control [kən'trəul] *vt* controlar; (*process etc*) dirigir; (*machinery*) manejar; (*temper*) dominar; (*disease*) contener ♦ *n* control *m*; **~s** *npl* (*of vehicle*) instrumentos *mpl* de mando; (*of radio*) controles *mpl*; (*governmental*) medidas *fpl* de control; **under ~** bajo control; **to be in ~ of** tener el mando de; **the car went out of ~** se perdió el control del coche; **~led substance** *n* sustancia controlada; **~ panel** *n* tablero de instrumentos; **~ room** *n* sala de mando; **~ tower** *n* (*AVIAT*) torre *f* de control

controversial [kɔntrə'vəːʃl] *adj* polémico

controversy ['kɔntrəvəːsɪ] *n* polémica

convalesce [kɔnvə'lɛs] *vi* convalecer

convector [kən'vɛktə*] *n* calentador *m* de aire

convene [kən'vi:n] *vt* convocar ♦ *vi* reunirse

convenience [kən'vi:nɪəns] *n* (*easiness*) comodidad *f*; (*suitability*) idoneidad *f*; (*advantage*) ventaja; **at your ~** cuando le sea conveniente; **all modern ~s, all mod cons** (*BRIT*) todo confort

convenient [kən'vi:nɪənt] *adj* (*useful*) útil; (*place, time*) conveniente

convent ['kɔnvənt] *n* convento

convention [kən'venʃən] *n* convención *f*; (*meeting*) asamblea; (*agreement*) convenio; **~al** *adj* convencional

converge [kən'və:dʒ] *vi* convergir; (*people*): **to ~ on** dirigirse todos a

conversant [kən'və:snt] *adj*: **to be ~ with** estar al tanto de

conversation [kɔnvə'seɪʃən] *n* conversación *f*; **~al** *adj* familiar; **~al skill** facilidad *f* de palabra

converse [*n* 'kɔnvə:s, *vb* kən'və:s] *n* inversa ♦ *vi* conversar; **~ly** [-'və:slɪ] *adv* a la inversa

conversion [kən'və:ʃən] *n* conversión *f*

convert [*vb* kən'və:t, *n* 'kɔnvə:t] *vt* (*REL, COMM*) convertir; (*alter*): **to ~ sth into/to** transformar algo en/convertir algo a ♦ *n* converso/a; **~ible** *adj* convertible ♦ *n* descapotable *m*

convey [kən'veɪ] *vt* llevar; (*thanks*) comunicar; (*idea*) expresar; **~or belt** *n* cinta transportadora

convict [*vb* kən'vɪkt, *n* 'kɔnvɪkt] *vt* (*find guilty*) declarar culpable a ♦ *n* presidiario/a; **~ion** [-ʃən] *n* condena; (*belief, certainty*) convicción *f*

convince [kən'vɪns] *vt* convencer; **~d** *adj*: **~d of/that** convencido de/de que; **convincing** *adj* convincente

convoluted ['kɔnvəlu:tɪd] *adj* (*argument etc*) enrevesado

convoy ['kɔnvɔɪ] *n* convoy *m*

convulse [kən'vʌls] *vt*: **to be ~d with laughter** desternillarse de risa; **convulsion** [-'vʌlʃən] *n* convulsión *f*

cook [kuk] *vt* (*stew etc*) guisar; (*meal*) preparar ♦ *vi* cocer; (*person*) cocinar ♦ *n*

cocinero/a; **~ book** *n* libro de cocina; **~er** *n* cocina; **~ery** *n* cocina; **~ery book** (*BRIT*) *n* = **~ book**; **~ie** (*US*) *n* galleta; **~ing** *n* cocina

cool [ku:l] *adj* fresco; (*not afraid*) tranquilo; (*unfriendly*) frío ♦ *vt* enfriar ♦ *vi* enfriarse; **~ness** *n* frescura; tranquilidad *f*; (*indifference*) falta de entusiasmo

coop [ku:p] *n* gallinero ♦ *vt*: **to ~ up** (*fig*) encerrar

cooperate [kəu'ɔpəreɪt] *vi* cooperar, colaborar; **cooperation** [-'reɪʃən] *n* cooperación *f*, colaboración *f*; **cooperative** [-rətɪv] *adj* (*business*) cooperativo; (*person*) servicial ♦ *n* cooperativa

coordinate [*vb* kəu'ɔ:dɪneɪt, *n* kəu'ɔ:dɪnət] *vt* coordinar ♦ *n* (*MATH*) coordenada; **~s** *npl* (*clothes*) coordinados *mpl*; **coordination** [-'neɪʃən] *n* coordinación *f*

co-ownership [kəu'əunəʃɪp] *n* co-propiedad *f*

cop [kɔp] (*inf*) *n* poli *m* (*SP*), tira *m* (*AM*)

cope [kəup] *vi*: **to ~ with** (*problem*) hacer frente a

copper ['kɔpə*] *n* (*metal*) cobre *m*; (*BRIT: inf*) poli *m*; **~s** *npl* (*money*) calderilla (*SP*), centavos *mpl* (*AM*)

copulate ['kɔpjuleɪt] *vi* copularse

copy ['kɔpɪ] *n* copia; (*of book etc*) ejemplar *m* ♦ *vt* copiar; **~right** *n* derechos *mpl* de autor

coral ['kɔrəl] *n* coral *m*

cord [kɔ:d] *n* cuerda; (*ELEC*) cable *m*; (*fabric*) pana

cordial ['kɔ:dɪəl] *adj* cordial ♦ *n* cordial *m*

cordon ['kɔ:dn] *n* cordón *m*; **~ off** *vt* acordonar

corduroy ['kɔ:dərɔɪ] *n* pana

core [kɔ:*] *n* centro, núcleo; (*of fruit*) corazón *m*; (*of problem*) meollo ♦ *vt* quitar el corazón de

coriander [kɔrɪ'ændə*] *n* culantro

cork [kɔ:k] *n* corcho; (*tree*) alcornoque *m*; **~screw** *n* sacacorchos *m inv*

corn [kɔ:n] *n* (*BRIT: cereal crop*) trigo; (*US: maize*) maíz *m*; (*on foot*) callo; **~ on the**

cob (CULIN) maíz en la mazorca (SP), choclo (AM)

corned beef ['kɔ:nd-] n carne f acecinada (en lata)

corner ['kɔ:nə*] n (outside) esquina; (inside) rincón m; (in road) curva; (FOOTBALL) córner m; (BOXING) esquina ♦ vt (trap) arrinconar; (COMM) acaparar ♦ vi (in car) tomar las curvas; ~**stone** n (also fig) piedra angular

cornet ['kɔ:nɪt] n (MUS) corneta; (BRIT: of ice-cream) cucurucho

cornflakes ['kɔ:nfleɪks] npl copos mpl de maíz, cornflakes mpl

cornflour ['kɔ:nflauə*] (BRIT), **cornstarch** ['kɔ:nstɑ:tʃ] (US) n harina de maíz

Cornwall ['kɔ:nwəl] n Cornualles m

corny ['kɔ:nɪ] (inf) adj gastado

coronary ['kɔrənərɪ] n (also: ~ **thrombosis**) infarto

coronation [kɔrə'neɪʃən] n coronación f

coroner ['kɔrənə*] n juez m (de instrucción)

corporal ['kɔ:pərl] n cabo ♦ adj: ~ **punishment** castigo corporal

corporate ['kɔ:pərɪt] adj (action, ownership) colectivo; (finance, image) corporativo

corporation [kɔ:pə'reɪʃən] n (of town) ayuntamiento; (COMM) corporación f

corps [kɔ:*, pl kɔ:z] n inv cuerpo; **diplomatic** ~ cuerpo diplomático; **press** ~ gabinete m de prensa

corpse [kɔ:ps] n cadáver m

correct [kə'rekt] adj justo, exacto; (proper) correcto ♦ vt corregir; (exam) corregir, calificar; ~**ion** [-ʃən] n (act) corrección f; (instance) rectificación f

correspond [kɔrɪs'pɔnd] vi (write): **to** ~ (**with**) escribirse (con); (be equivalent to): **to** ~ (**to**) corresponder (a); (be in accordance): **to** ~ (**with**) corresponder (con); ~**ence** n correspondencia; ~**ence course** n curso por correspondencia; ~**ent** n corresponsal m/f

corridor ['kɔrɪdɔ:*] n pasillo

corrode [kə'rəud] vt corroer ♦ vi corroerse

corrugated ['kɔrəgeɪtɪd] adj ondulado; ~ **iron** n chapa ondulada

corrupt [kə'rʌpt] adj (person) corrupto; (COMPUT) corrompido ♦ vt corromper; (COMPUT) degradar

Corsica ['kɔ:sɪkə] n Córcega

cosmetic [kɔz'metɪk] adj, n cosmético

cosmopolitan [kɔzmə'pɔlɪtn] adj cosmopolita

cost [kɔst] (pt, pp **cost**) n (price) precio; ~**s** npl (COMM) costes mpl; (LAW) costas fpl ♦ vt costar, valer ♦ vt preparar el presupuesto de; **how much does it** ~? ¿cuánto cuesta?; **to** ~ **sb time/effort** costarle a uno tiempo/esfuerzo; **it** ~ **him his life** le costó la vida; **at all** ~**s** cueste lo que cueste

co-star ['kəustɑ:*] n coprotagonista m/f

Costa Rica ['kɔstə'ri:kə] n Costa Rica; ~**n** adj, n costarriqueño/a m/f

cost-effective [kɔstɪ'fektɪv] adj rentable

costly ['kɔstlɪ] adj costoso

cost-of-living [kɔstəv'lɪvɪŋ] adj: ~ **allowance** plus m de carestía de vida; ~ **index** índice m del costo de vida

cost price (BRIT) n precio de coste

costume ['kɔstju:m] n traje m; (BRIT: also: **swimming** ~) traje de baño; ~ **jewellery** n bisutería

cosy ['kəuzɪ] (US **cozy**) adj (person) cómodo; (room) acogedor(a)

cot [kɔt] n (BRIT: child's) cuna; (US: campbed) cama de campaña

cottage ['kɔtɪdʒ] n casita de campo; (rustic) barraca; ~ **cheese** n requesón m

cotton ['kɔtn] n algodón m; (thread) hilo; ~ **on to** (inf) vt fus caer en la cuenta de; ~ **candy** (US) n algodón m (azucarado); ~ **wool** (BRIT) n algodón m (hidrófilo)

couch [kautʃ] n sofá m; (doctor's etc) diván m

couchette [ku:'ʃet] n litera

cough [kɔf] vi toser ♦ n tos f; ~ **drop** n pastilla para la tos

could [kud] pt of **can²**; ~**n't** = **could not**

council ['kaunsl] n consejo; **city** or **town** ~ consejo municipal; ~ **estate** (BRIT) n urbanización f de viviendas municipales de alquiler; **~ house** (BRIT) n vivienda municipal de alquiler; **~lor** n concejal(a) m/f

counsel ['kaunsl] n (advice) consejo; (lawyer) abogado/a ♦ vt aconsejar; **~lor** n consejero/a; **~or** (US) n abogado/a

count [kaunt] vt contar; (include) incluir ♦ vi contar ♦ n cuenta; (of votes) escrutinio; (level) nivel m; (nobleman) conde m; **~ on** vt fus contar con; **~down** n cuenta atrás

countenance ['kauntinəns] n semblante m, rostro ♦ vt (tolerate) aprobar, tolerar

counter ['kauntə*] n (in shop) mostrador m; (in games) ficha f ♦ vt contrarrestar ♦ adv: **to run ~ to** ser contrario a, ir en contra de; **~act** vt contrarrestar

counterfeit ['kauntəfit] n falsificación f, simulación f ♦ vt falsificar ♦ adj falso, falsificado

counterfoil ['kauntəfɔil] n talón m

counterpart ['kauntəpɑːt] n homólogo/a

counter-productive [kauntəprə'dʌktiv] adj contraproducente

countersign ['kauntəsain] vt refrendar

countess ['kauntis] n condesa

countless ['kauntlis] adj innumerable

country ['kʌntri] n país m; (native land) patria; (as opposed to town) campo; (region) región f, tierra; **~ dancing** (BRIT) n baile m regional; **~ house** n casa de campo; **~man** n (irreg) (compatriot) compatriota m; (rural) campesino, paisano; **~side** n campo

county ['kaunti] n condado

coup [kuː] (pl **~s**) n (also: **~ d'état**) golpe m (de estado); (achievement) éxito

couple ['kʌpl] n (of things) par m; (of people) pareja; (married ~) matrimonio; **a ~ of** un par de

coupon ['kuːpɔn] n cupón m; (voucher) valé m

courage ['kʌrɪdʒ] n valor m, valentía; **~ous** [kə'reɪdʒəs] adj valiente

courgette [kuə'ʒet] (BRIT) n calabacín m (SP), calabacita (AM)

courier ['kuriə*] n mensajero/a; (for tourists) guía m/f (de turismo)

course [kɔːs] n (direction) dirección f; (of river, SCOL) curso; (process) transcurso; (MED): **~ of treatment** tratamiento; (of ship) rumbo; (part of meal) plato; (GOLF) campo; **of ~** desde luego, naturalmente; **of ~!** ¡claro!

court [kɔːt] n (royal) corte f; (LAW) tribunal m, juzgado; (TENNIS etc) pista, cancha ♦ vt (woman) cortejar a; **to take to ~** demandar

courteous ['kəːtiəs] adj cortés

courtesy ['kəːtəsi] n cortesía; **(by) ~ of** por cortesía de; **~ bus, ~ coach** n autobús m gratuito

court-house ['kɔːthaus] (US) n palacio de justicia

courtier ['kɔːtiə*] n cortesano

court-martial (pl **courts-martial**) n consejo de guerra

courtroom ['kɔːtrum] n sala de justicia

courtyard ['kɔːtjɑːd] n patio

cousin ['kʌzn] n primo/a; **first ~** primo/a carnal, primo/a hermano/a

cove [kəuv] n cala, ensenada

covenant ['kʌvənənt] n pacto

cover ['kʌvə*] vt cubrir; (feelings, mistake) ocultar; (with lid) tapar; (book etc) forrar; (distance) recorrer; (include) abarcar; (protect: also: INSURANCE) cubrir; (PRESS) investigar; (discuss) tratar ♦ n cubierta; (lid) tapa; (for chair etc) funda; (envelope) sobre m; (for book) forro; (of magazine) portada; (shelter) abrigo; (INSURANCE) cobertura; (of spy) cobertura; **~s** npl (on bed) sábanas; mantas; **to take ~** (shelter) protegerse, resguardarse; **under ~** (indoors) bajo techo; **under ~ of darkness** al amparo de la oscuridad; **under separate ~** (COMM) por separado; **~ up** vi: **to ~ up for sb** encubrir a uno; **~age** n (TV, PRESS) cobertura; **~alls** (US) npl mono; **~ charge** n precio del cubierto; **~ing** n capa; **~ing letter** (US **~ letter**) n carta de explicación; **~ note** n (INSURANCE) póliza provisional

covert ['kʌvət] *adj* secreto, encubierto

cover-up *n* encubrimiento

cow [kau] *n* vaca; (*inf: woman*) bruja ♦ *vt* intimidar

coward ['kauəd] *n* cobarde *m/f*; **~ice** [-ɪs] *n* cobardía; **~ly** *adj* cobarde

cowboy ['kaubɔɪ] *n* vaquero

cower ['kauə*] *vi* encogerse (de miedo)

coy [kɔɪ] *adj* tímido

cozy ['kəuzɪ] (*US*) *adj* = **cosy**

CPA (*US*) *n abbr* = **certified public accountant**

crab [kræb] *n* cangrejo; **~ apple** *n* manzana silvestre

crack [kræk] *n* grieta; (*noise*) crujido; (*drug*) crack *m* ♦ *vt* agrietar, romper; (*nut*) cascar; (*solve: problem*) resolver; (*: code*) descifrar; (*whip etc*) chasquear; (*knuckles*) crujir; (*joke*) contar ♦ *adj* (*expert*) de primera; **~ down on** *vt fus* adoptar fuertes medidas contra; **~ up** *vi* (*MED*) sufrir una crisis nerviosa; **~er** *n* (*biscuit*) cráquer *m*; (*Christmas ~er*) petardo sorpresa

crackle ['krækl] *vi* crepitar

cradle ['kreɪdl] *n* cuna

craft [krɑ:ft] *n* (*skill*) arte *m*; (*trade*) oficio; (*cunning*) astucia; (*boat: pl inv*) barco; (*plane: pl inv*) avión *m*

craftsman ['krɑ:ftsmən] *n* artesano; **~ship** *n* (*quality*) destreza

crafty ['krɑ:ftɪ] *adj* astuto

crag [kræg] *n* peñasco

cram [kræm] *vt* (*fill*): **to ~ sth with** llenar algo (a reventar) de; (*put*): **to ~ sth into** meter algo a la fuerza en ♦ *vi* (*for exams*) empollar

cramp [kræmp] *n* (*MED*) calambre *m*; **~ed** *adj* apretado, estrecho

cranberry ['krænbərɪ] *n* arándano agrio

crane [kreɪn] *n* (*TECH*) grúa; (*bird*) grulla

crank [kræŋk] *n* manivela; (*person*) chiflado

cranny ['krænɪ] *n see* **nook**

crash [kræʃ] *n* (*noise*) estrépito; (*of cars etc*) choque *m*; (*of plane*) accidente *m* de aviación; (*COMM*) quiebra ♦ *vt* (*car, plane*) estrellar ♦ *vi* (*car, plane*) estrellarse; (*two*

cars) chocar; (*COMM*) quebrar; **~ course** *n* curso acelerado; **~ helmet** *n* casco (protector); **~ landing** *n* aterrizaje *m* forzado

crass [kræs] *adj* grosero, maleducado

crate [kreɪt] *n* cajón *m* de embalaje; (*for bottles*) caja

cravat(e) [krə'væt] *n* pañuelo

crave [kreɪv] *vt, vi*: **to ~ (for)** ansiar, anhelar

crawl [krɔ:l] *vi* (*drag o.s.*) arrastrarse; (*child*) andar a gatas, gatear; (*vehicle*) avanzar (lentamente) ♦ *n* (*SWIMMING*) crol *m*

crayfish ['kreɪfɪʃ] *n inv* (*freshwater*) cangrejo de río; (*saltwater*) cigala

crayon ['kreɪən] *n* lápiz *m* de color

craze [kreɪz] *n* (*fashion*) moda

crazy ['kreɪzɪ] *adj* (*person*) loco; (*idea*) disparatado; (*inf: keen*): **~ about sb/sth** loco por uno/algo

creak [kri:k] *vi* (*floorboard*) crujir; (*hinge etc*) chirriar, rechinar

cream [kri:m] *n* (*of milk*) nata, crema; (*lotion*) crema; (*fig*) flor *f* y nata ♦ *adj* (*colour*) color crema; **~ cake** *n* pastel *m* de nata; **~ cheese** *n* queso blanco; **~y** *adj* cremoso; (*colour*) color crema

crease [kri:s] *n* (*fold*) pliegue *m*; (*in trousers*) raya; (*wrinkle*) arruga ♦ *vt* (*wrinkle*) arrugar ♦ *vi* (*wrinkle up*) arrugarse

create [kri:'eɪt] *vt* crear; **creation** [-ʃən] *n* creación *f*; **creative** *adj* creativo; **creator** *n* creador(a) *m/f*

creature ['kri:tʃə*] *n* (*animal*) animal *m*, bicho; (*person*) criatura

crèche [kreʃ] *n* guardería (infantil)

credence ['kri:dəns] *n*: **to lend** *or* **give ~ to** creer en, dar crédito a

credentials [krɪ'denʃlz] *npl* (*references*) referencias *fpl*; (*identity papers*) documentos *mpl* de identidad

credible ['kredɪbl] *adj* creíble; (*trustworthy*) digno de confianza

credit ['kredɪt] *n* crédito; (*merit*) honor *m*, mérito ♦ *vt* (*COMM*) abonar; (*believe: also:*

give ~ to) creer, prestar fe a ♦ *adj* crediticio; **~s** *npl* (*CINEMA*) fichas *fpl* técnicas; **to be in ~** (*person*) tener saldo a favor; **to ~ sb with** (*fig*) reconocer a uno el mérito de; **~ card** *n* tarjeta de crédito; **~or** *n* acreedor(a) *m/f*
creed [kri:d] *n* credo
creek [kri:k] *n* cala, ensenada; (*US*) riachuelo
creep [kri:p] *n* arrastrarse; **~er** *n* enredadera; **~y** *adj* (*frightening*) horripilante
cremate [krɪ'meɪt] *vt* incinerar
crematorium [kremə'tɔ:rɪəm] (*pl* **crematoria**) *n* crematorio
crêpe [kreɪp] *n* (*fabric*) crespón *m*; (*also:* **~ rubber**) crepé *m*; **~ bandage** (*BRIT*) *n* venda de crepé
crept [krept] *pt, pp of* **creep**
crescent ['kresnt] *n* media luna; (*street*) calle *f* (en forma de semicírculo)
cress [kres] *n* berro
crest [krest] *n* (*of bird*) cresta; (*of hill*) cima, cumbre *f*; (*of coat of arms*) blasón *m*; **~fallen** *adj* alicaído
crevice ['krevɪs] *n* grieta, hendedura
crew [kru:] *n* (*of ship etc*) tripulación *f*; (*TV, CINEMA*) equipo; **~-cut** *n* corte *m* al rape; **~-neck** *n* cuello a la caja
crib [krɪb] *n* cuna ♦ *vt* (*inf*) plagiar
crick [krɪk] *n* (*in neck*) tortícolis *f*
cricket ['krɪkɪt] *n* (*insect*) grillo; (*game*) críquet *m*
crime [kraɪm] *n* (*no pl: illegal activities*) crimen *m*; (*illegal action*) delito; **criminal** ['krɪmɪnl] *n* criminal *m/f*, delincuente *m/f* ♦ *adj* criminal; (*illegal*) delictivo; (*law*) penal
crimson ['krɪmzn] *adj* carmesí
cringe [krɪndʒ] *vi* agacharse, encogerse
crinkle ['krɪŋkl] *vt* arrugar
cripple ['krɪpl] *n* lisiado/a, cojo/a ♦ *vt* lisiar, mutilar
crisis ['kraɪsɪs] (*pl* **crises**) *n* crisis *f inv*
crisp [krɪsp] *adj* fresco; (*vegetables etc*) crujiente; (*manner*) seco; **~s** (*BRIT*) *npl* patatas *fpl* (*SP*) or papas *fpl* (*AM*) fritas

crisscross ['krɪskrɔs] *adj* entrelazado
criterion [kraɪ'tɪərɪən] (*pl* **criteria**) *n* criterio
critic ['krɪtɪk] *n* crítico/a; **~al** *adj* crítico; (*illness*) grave; **~ally** *adv* (*speak etc*) en tono crítico; (*ill*) gravemente; **~ism** ['krɪtɪsɪzm] *n* crítica; **~ize** ['krɪtɪsaɪz] *vt* criticar
croak [krəuk] *vi* (*frog*) croar; (*raven*) graznar; (*person*) gruñir
Croatia [krəu'eɪʃə] *n* Croacia
crochet ['krəuʃeɪ] *n* ganchillo
crockery ['krɔkərɪ] *n* loza, vajilla
crocodile ['krɔkədaɪl] *n* cocodrilo
crocus ['krəukəs] *n* croco, crocus *m*
croft [krɔft] *n* granja pequeña
crony ['krəunɪ] (*inf: pej*) *n* compinche *m/f*
crook [kruk] *n* ladrón/ona *m/f*; (*of shepherd*) cayado; **~ed** ['krukɪd] *adj* torcido; (*dishonest*) nada honrado
crop [krɔp] *n* (*produce*) cultivo; (*amount produced*) cosecha; (*riding ~*) látigo de montar ♦ *vt* cortar, recortar; **~ up** *vi* surgir, presentarse
cross [krɔs] *n* cruz *f*; (*hybrid*) cruce *m* ♦ *vt* (*street etc*) cruzar, atravesar ♦ *adj* de mal humor, enojado; **~ out** *vt* tachar; **~ over** *vi* cruzar; **~bar** *n* travesaño; **~-country (race)** *n* carrera a campo traviesa, cross *m*; **~-examine** *vt* interrogar; **~-eyed** *adj* bizco; **~fire** *n* fuego cruzado; **~ing** *n* (*sea passage*) travesía; (*also:* **pedestrian ~ing**) paso para peatones; **~ing guard** (*US*) *n* persona encargada de ayudar a los niños a cruzar la calle; **~ purposes** *npl*: **to be at ~ purposes** no comprenderse uno a otro; **~-reference** *n* referencia, llamada; **~roads** *n* cruce *m*, encrucijada; **~ section** *n* corte *m* transversal; (*of population*) muestra (representativa); **~walk** (*US*) *n* paso de peatones; **~wind** *n* viento de costado; **~word** *n* crucigrama *m*
crotch [krɔtʃ] *n* (*ANAT, of garment*) entrepierna
crotchet ['krɔtʃɪt] *n* (*MUS*) negra
crouch [krautʃ] *vi* agacharse, acurrucarse

crow [krəʊ] *n* (*bird*) cuervo; (*of cock*) canto, cacareo ♦ *vi* (*cock*) cantar
crowbar ['krəʊbɑ:*] *n* palanca
crowd [kraʊd] *n* muchedumbre *f*, multitud *f* ♦ *vt* (*fill*) llenar ♦ *vi* (*gather*): **to ~ round** reunirse en torno a; (*cram*): **to ~ in** entrar en tropel; **~ed** *adj* (*full*) atestado; (*densely populated*) superpoblado
crown [kraʊn] *n* corona; (*of head*) coronilla; (*for tooth*) funda; (*of hill*) cumbre *f* ♦ *vt* coronar; (*fig*) completar, rematar; **~ jewels** *npl* joyas *fpl* reales; **~ prince** *n* príncipe *m* heredero
crow's feet *npl* patas *fpl* de gallo
crucial ['kru:ʃl] *adj* decisivo
crucifix ['kru:sɪfɪks] *n* crucifijo; **~ion** [-'fɪkʃən] *n* crucifixión *f*
crude [kru:d] *adj* (*materials*) bruto; (*fig: basic*) tosco; (: *vulgar*) ordinario; **~ (oil)** *n* (*petróleo*) crudo
cruel ['kruəl] *adj* cruel; **~ty** *n* crueldad *f*
cruise [kru:z] *n* crucero ♦ *vi* (*ship*) hacer un crucero; (*car*) ir a velocidad de crucero; **~r** *n* (*motorboat*) yate *m* de motor; (*warship*) crucero
crumb [krʌm] *n* miga, migaja
crumble ['krʌmbl] *vt* desmenuzar ♦ *vi* (*building, also fig*) desmoronarse; **crumbly** *adj* que se desmigaja fácilmente
crumpet ['krʌmpɪt] *n* ≈ bollo para tostar
crumple ['krʌmpl] *vt* (*paper*) estrujar; (*material*) arrugar
crunch [krʌntʃ] *vt* (*with teeth*) mascar; (*underfoot*) hacer crujir ♦ *n* (*fig*) hora *or* momento de la verdad; **~y** *adj* crujiente
crusade [kru:'seɪd] *n* cruzada
crush [krʌʃ] *n* (*crowd*) aglomeración *f*; (*infatuation*): **to have a ~ on sb** estar loco por uno; (*drink*): **lemon ~** limonada ♦ *vt* aplastar; (*paper*) estrujar; (*cloth*) arrugar; (*fruit*) exprimir; (*opposition*) aplastar; (*hopes*) destruir
crust [krʌst] *n* corteza; (*of snow, ice*) costra
crutch [krʌtʃ] *n* muleta
crux [krʌks] *n*: **the ~ of** lo esencial de, el quid de

cry [kraɪ] *vi* llorar; (*shout: also:* **~ out**) gritar ♦ *n* (*shriek*) chillido; (*shout*) grito; **~ off** *vi* echarse atrás
cryptic ['krɪptɪk] *adj* enigmático, secreto
crystal ['krɪstl] *n* cristal *m*; **~-clear** *adj* claro como el agua
cub [kʌb] *n* cachorro; (*also:* **~ scout**) niño explorador
Cuba ['kju:bə] *n* Cuba; **~n** *adj*, *n* cubano/a *m/f*
cube [kju:b] *n* cubo ♦ *vt* (MATH) cubicar; **cubic** *adj* cúbico
cubicle ['kju:bɪkl] *n* (*at pool*) caseta; (*for bed*) cubículo
cuckoo ['kuku:] *n* cuco; **~ clock** *n* reloj *m* de cucú
cucumber ['kju:kʌmbə*] *n* pepino
cuddle ['kʌdl] *vt* abrazar ♦ *vi* abrazarse
cue [kju:] *n* (*snooker ~*) taco; (THEATRE *etc*) señal *f*
cuff [kʌf] *n* (*of sleeve*) puño; (*US: of trousers*) vuelta; (*blow*) bofetada; **off the ~** *adv* de improviso; **~links** *npl* gemelos *mpl*
cuisine [kwɪ'zi:n] *n* cocina
cul-de-sac ['kʌldəsæk] *n* callejón *m* sin salida
cull [kʌl] *vt* (*idea*) sacar ♦ *n* (*of animals*) matanza selectiva
culminate ['kʌlmɪneɪt] *vi*: **to ~ in** terminar en; **culmination** [-'neɪʃən] *n* culminación *f*, colmo
culottes [ku:'lɔts] *npl* falda pantalón *f*
culprit ['kʌlprɪt] *n* culpable *m/f*
cult [kʌlt] *n* culto
cultivate ['kʌltɪveɪt] *vt* (*also fig*) cultivar; **~d** *adj* culto; **cultivation** [-'veɪʃən] *n* cultivo
cultural ['kʌltʃərəl] *adj* cultural
culture ['kʌltʃə*] *n* (*also fig*) cultura; (BIO) cultivo; **~d** *adj* culto
cumbersome ['kʌmbəsəm] *adj* de mucho bulto, voluminoso; (*process*) enrevesado
cunning ['kʌnɪŋ] *n* astucia ♦ *adj* astuto
cup [kʌp] *n* taza; (*as prize*) copa
cupboard ['kʌbəd] *n* armario; (*kitchen*) alacena

cup tie (*BRIT*) *n* partido de copa

curate ['kjuərɪt] *n* cura *m*

curator [kjuə'reɪtə*] *n* director(a) *m/f*

curb [kə:b] *vt* refrenar; (*person*) reprimir ♦ *n* freno; (*US*) bordillo

curdle ['kə:dl] *vi* cuajarse

cure [kjuə*] *vt* curar ♦ *n* cura, curación *f*; (*fig: solution*) remedio

curfew ['kə:fju:] *n* toque *m* de queda

curiosity [kjuərɪ'ɔsɪtɪ] *n* curiosidad *f*

curious ['kjuərɪəs] *adj* curioso; (*person: interested*): **to be ~** sentir curiosidad

curl [kə:l] *n* rizo ♦ *vt* (*hair*) rizar ♦ *vi* rizarse; **~ up** *vi* (*person*) hacerse un ovillo; **~er** *n* rulo; **~y** *adj* rizado

currant ['kʌrnt] *n* pasa (de Corinto); (*black~, red~*) grosella

currency ['kʌrnsɪ] *n* moneda; **to gain ~** (*fig*) difundirse

current ['kʌrnt] *n* corriente *f* ♦ *adj* (*accepted*) corriente; (*present*) actual; **~ account** (*BRIT*) *n* cuenta corriente; **~ affairs** *npl* noticias *fpl* de actualidad; **~ly** *adv* actualmente

curriculum [kə'rɪkjuləm] (*pl* **~s** or **curricula**) *n* plan *m* de estudios; **~ vitae** *n* currículum *m*

curry ['kʌrɪ] *n* curry *m* ♦ *vt*: **to ~ favour with** buscar favores con; **~ powder** *n* curry *m* en polvo

curse [kə:s] *vi* soltar tacos ♦ *vt* maldecir ♦ *n* maldición *f*; (*swearword*) palabrota, taco

cursor ['kə:sə*] *n* (*COMPUT*) cursor *m*

cursory ['kə:sərɪ] *adj* rápido, superficial

curt [kə:t] *adj* corto, seco

curtail [kə:'teɪl] *vt* (*visit etc*) acortar; (*freedom*) restringir; (*expenses etc*) reducir

curtain ['kə:tn] *n* cortina; (*THEATRE*) telón *m*

curts(e)y ['kə:tsɪ] *vi* hacer una reverencia

curve [kə:v] *n* curva ♦ *vi* (*road*) hacer una curva; (*line etc*) curvarse

cushion ['kuʃən] *n* cojín *m*; (*of air*) colchón *m* ♦ *vt* (*shock*) amortiguar

custard ['kʌstəd] *n* natillas *fpl*

custody ['kʌstədɪ] *n* custodia; **to take into ~** detener

custom ['kʌstəm] *n* costumbre *f*; (*COMM*) clientela; **~ary** *adj* acostumbrado

customer ['kʌstəmə*] *n* cliente *m/f*

customized ['kʌstəmaɪzd] *adj* (*car etc*) hecho a encargo

custom-made *adj* hecho a la medida

customs ['kʌstəmz] *npl* aduana; **~ officer** *n* aduanero/a

cut [kʌt] (*pt, pp* **cut**) *vt* cortar; (*price*) rebajar; (*text, programme*) acortar; (*reduce*) reducir ♦ *vi* cortar ♦ *n* (*of garment*) corte *m*; (*in skin*) cortadura; (*in salary etc*) rebaja; (*in spending*) reducción *f*, recorte *m*; (*slice of meat*) tajada; **to ~ a tooth** echar un diente; **~ down** *vt* (*tree*) derribar; (*reduce*) reducir; **~ off** *vt* cortar; (*person, place*) aislar; (*TEL*) desconectar; **~ out** *vt* (*shape*) recortar; (*stop: activity etc*) dejar; (*remove*) quitar; **~ up** *vt* cortar (en pedazos); **~back** *n* reducción *f*

cute [kju:t] *adj* mono

cuticle ['kju:tɪkl] *n* cutícula

cutlery ['kʌtlərɪ] *n* cubiertos *mpl*

cutlet ['kʌtlɪt] *n* chuleta; (*nut etc ~*) plato vegetariano hecho con nueces y verdura en forma de chuleta

cut: ~out *n* (*switch*) dispositivo de seguridad, disyuntor *m*; (*cardboard ~out*) recortable *m*; **~-price** (*US* **~-rate**) *adj* a precio reducido; **~throat** *adj* feroz

cutting ['kʌtɪŋ] *adj* (*remark*) mordaz ♦ *n* (*BRIT: from newspaper*) recorte *m*; (*from plant*) esqueje *m*

CV *n abbr* = **curriculum vitae**

cwt *abbr* = **hundredweight(s)**

cyanide ['saɪənaɪd] *n* cianuro

cybercafé ['saɪbəkæfeɪ] *n* cibercafé *m*

cycle ['saɪkl] *n* ciclo; (*bicycle*) bicicleta ♦ *vi* ir en bicicleta; **~ lane** *n* carril-bici *m*; **~ path** *n* carril-bici *m*; **cycling** *n* ciclismo; **cyclist** *n* ciclista *m/f*

cyclone ['saɪkləun] *n* ciclón *m*

cygnet ['sɪgnɪt] *n* pollo de cisne

cylinder ['sɪlɪndə*] *n* cilindro; (*of gas*) bombona; **~-head gasket** *n* junta de culata

cymbals ['sɪmblz] npl platillos mpl
cynic ['sɪnɪk] n cínico/a; ~al adj cínico;
~ism ['sɪnɪsɪzəm] n cinismo
Cyprus ['saɪprəs] n Chipre f
cyst [sɪst] n quiste m; ~itis [-'taɪtɪs] n
cistitis f
czar [zɑː*] n zar m
Czech [tʃɛk] adj, n checo/a m/f; ~
Republic n la República Checa

D, d

D [diː] n (MUS) re m
dab [dæb] vt (eyes, wound) tocar
(ligeramente); (paint, cream) poner un
poco de
dabble ['dæbl] vi: to ~ in ser algo
aficionado a
dad [dæd] n = daddy
daddy ['dædɪ] n papá m
daffodil ['dæfədɪl] n narciso
daft [dɑːft] adj tonto
dagger ['dægə*] n puñal m, daga
daily ['deɪlɪ] adj diario, cotidiano ♦ adv
todos los días, cada día
dainty ['deɪntɪ] adj delicado
dairy ['dɛərɪ] n (shop) lechería; (on farm)
vaquería; ~ farm n granja; ~ products
npl productos mpl lácteos; ~ store (US)
n lechería
daisy ['deɪzɪ] n margarita
dale [deɪl] n valle m
dam [dæm] n presa ♦ vt construir una
presa sobre, represar
damage ['dæmɪdʒ] n lesión f; daño; (dents
etc) desperfectos mpl; (fig) perjuicio ♦ vt
dañar, perjudicar; (spoil, break) estropear;
~s npl (LAW) daños mpl y perjuicios
damn [dæm] vt condenar; (curse) maldecir
♦ n (inf): I don't give a ~ me importa un
pito ♦ adj (inf: also: ~ed) maldito; ~ (it)!
¡maldito sea!; ~ing adj (evidence)
irrecusable
damp [dæmp] adj húmedo, mojado ♦ n
humedad f ♦ vt (also: ~en: cloth, rag)
mojar; (: enthusiasm) enfriar

damson ['dæmzən] n ciruela damascena
dance [dɑːns] n baile m ♦ vi bailar; ~ hall
n salón m de baile; ~r n bailador(a) m/f;
(professional) bailarín/ina m/f; dancing n
baile m
dandelion ['dændɪlaɪən] n diente m de
león
dandruff ['dændrəf] n caspa
Dane [deɪn] n danés/esa m/f
danger ['deɪndʒə*] n peligro; (risk) riesgo;
~! (on sign) ¡peligro de muerte!; to be in
~ of correr riesgo de; ~ous adj peligroso;
~ously adv peligrosamente
dangle ['dæŋgl] vt colgar ♦ vi pender,
colgar
Danish ['deɪnɪʃ] adj danés/esa ♦ n (LING)
danés m
dare [dɛə*] vt: to ~ sb to do desafiar a
uno a hacer ♦ vi: to ~ (to) do sth
atreverse a hacer algo; I ~ say (I suppose)
puede ser (que); daring adj atrevido,
osado ♦ n atrevimiento, osadía
dark [dɑːk] adj oscuro; (hair, complexion)
moreno ♦ n: in the ~ a oscuras; to be in
the ~ about (fig) no saber nada de; after
~ después del anochecer; ~en vt (colour)
hacer más oscuro ♦ vi oscurecerse; ~
glasses npl gafas fpl negras (SP),
anteojos mpl negros (AM); ~ness n
oscuridad f; ~room n cuarto oscuro
darling ['dɑːlɪŋ] adj, n querido/a m/f
darn [dɑːn] vt zurcir
dart [dɑːt] n dardo; (in sewing) sisa ♦ vi
precipitarse; ~ away/along vi salir/
marchar disparado; ~board n diana; ~s
n dardos mpl
dash [dæʃ] n (small quantity: of liquid)
gota, chorrito; (: of solid) pizca; (sign)
raya ♦ vt (throw) tirar; (hopes) defraudar
♦ vi precipitarse, ir de prisa; ~ away or
off vi marcharse apresuradamente
dashboard ['dæʃbɔːd] n (AUT) salpicadero
dashing ['dæʃɪŋ] adj gallardo
data ['deɪtə] npl datos mpl; ~base n base
f de datos; ~ processing n proceso de
datos
date [deɪt] n (day) fecha; (with friend) cita;

(*fruit*) dátil *m* ♦ *vt* fechar; (*person*) salir con; **~ of birth** fecha de nacimiento; **to ~** *adv* hasta la fecha; **~d** *adj* anticuado; **~ rape** *n* violación ocurrida durante una cita con un conocido

daub [dɔːb] *vt* embadurnar

daughter ['dɔːtə*] *n* hija; **~-in-law** *n* nuera, hija política

daunting ['dɔːntɪŋ] *adj* desalentador(a)

dawdle ['dɔːdl] *vi* (*go slowly*) andar muy despacio

dawn [dɔːn] *n* alba, amanecer *m*; (*fig*) nacimiento ♦ *vi* (*day*) amanecer; (*fig*): **it ~ed on him that …** cayó en la cuenta de que …

day [deɪ] *n* día *m*; (*working ~*) jornada; (*hey-~*) tiempos *mpl*, días *mpl*; **the ~ before/after** el día anterior/siguiente; **the ~ after tomorrow** pasado mañana; **the ~ before yesterday** anteayer; **the following ~** el día siguiente; **by ~** de día; **~break** *n* amanecer *m*; **~dream** *vi* soñar despierto; **~light** *n* luz *f* (del día); **~ return** (BRIT) *n* billete *m* de ida y vuelta (en un día); **~time** *n* día *m*; **~-to-~** *adj* cotidiano

daze [deɪz] *vt* (*stun*) aturdir ♦ *n*: **in a ~** aturdido

dazzle ['dæzl] *vt* deslumbrar

DC *abbr* (= *direct current*) corriente *f* continua

dead [ded] *adj* muerto; (*limb*) dormido; (*telephone*) cortado; (*battery*) agotado ♦ *adv* (*completely*) totalmente; (*exactly*) exactamente; **to shoot sb ~** matar a uno a tiros; **~ tired** muerto (de cansancio); **to stop ~** parar en seco; **the ~** *npl* los muertos; **to be a ~ loss** (*inf*: *person*) ser un inútil; **~en** *vt* (*blow, sound*) amortiguar; (*pain etc*) aliviar; **~ end** *n* callejón *m* sin salida; **~ heat** *n* (SPORT) empate *m*; **~line** *n* fecha (*or* hora) tope; **~lock** *n*: **to reach ~lock** llegar a un punto muerto; **~ly** *adj* mortal, fatal; **~pan** *adj* sin expresión; **the D~ Sea** *n* el Mar Muerto

deaf [def] *adj* sordo; **~en** *vt* ensordecer; **~ness** *n* sordera

deal [diːl] (*pt, pp* **dealt**) *n* (*agreement*) pacto, convenio; (*business ~*) trato ♦ *vt* dar; (*card*) repartir; **a great ~ (of)** bastante, mucho; **~ in** *vt fus* tratar en, comerciar en; **~ with** *vt fus* (*people*) tratar con; (*problem*) ocuparse de; (*subject*) tratar de; **~ings** *npl* (COMM) transacciones *fpl*; (*relations*) relaciones *fpl*

dealt [delt] *pt, pp of* **deal**

dean [diːn] *n* (REL) deán *m*; (SCOL: BRIT) decano; (: US) decano; rector *m*

dear [dɪə*] *adj* querido; (*expensive*) caro ♦ *n*: **my ~** mi querido/a ♦ *excl*: **~ me!** ¡Dios mío!; **D~ Sir/Madam** (*in letter*) Muy Señor Mío, Estimado Señor/Estimada Señora; **D~ Mr/Mrs X** Estimado/a Señor(a) X; **~ly** *adv* (*love*) mucho; (*pay*) caro

death [deθ] *n* muerte *f*; **~ certificate** *n* partida de defunción; **~ly** *adj* (*white*) como un muerto; (*silence*) sepulcral; **~ penalty** *n* pena de muerte; **~ rate** *n* mortalidad *f*; **~ toll** *n* número de víctimas

debacle [deɪˈbɑːkl] *n* desastre *m*

debase [dɪˈbeɪs] *vt* degradar

debatable [dɪˈbeɪtəbl] *adj* discutible

debate [dɪˈbeɪt] *n* debate *m* ♦ *vt* discutir

debit ['debɪt] *n* debe *m* ♦ *vt*: **to ~ a sum to sb** *or* **sb's account** cargar una suma en cuenta a alguien

debris ['debriː] *n* escombros *mpl*

debt [det] *n* deuda; **to be in ~** tener deudas; **~or** *n* deudor(a) *m/f*

début ['deɪbjuː] *n* presentación *f*

decade ['dekeɪd] *n* decenio, década

decadence ['dekədəns] *n* decadencia

decaff ['diːkæf] (*inf*) *n* descafeinado

decaffeinated [dɪˈkæfɪneɪtɪd] *adj* descafeinado

decanter [dɪˈkæntə*] *n* garrafa

decay [dɪˈkeɪ] *n* (*of building*) desmoronamiento; (*of tooth*) caries *f inv* ♦ *vi* (*rot*) pudrirse

deceased [dɪˈsiːst] *n*: **the ~** el/la difunto/a

deceit [dɪˈsiːt] *n* engaño; **~ful** *adj* engañoso; **deceive** [dɪˈsiːv] *vt* engañar

December [dɪ'sembə*] *n* diciembre *m*

decent ['diːsənt] *adj* (*proper*) decente; (*person: kind*) amable, bueno

deception [dɪ'sepʃən] *n* engaño

deceptive [dɪ'septɪv] *adj* engañoso

decibel ['desɪbel] *n* decibel(io) *m*

decide [dɪ'saɪd] *vt* (*person*) decidir; (*question, argument*) resolver ♦ *vi* decidir; **to ~ to do/that** decidir hacer/que; **to ~ on sth** decidirse por algo; **~d** *adj* (*resolute*) decidido; (*clear, definite*) indudable; **~dly** [-dɪdlɪ] *adv* decididamente; (*emphatically*) con resolución

deciduous [dɪ'sɪdjuəs] *adj* de hoja caduca

decimal ['desɪməl] *adj* decimal ♦ *n* decimal *m*; **~ point** *n* coma decimal

decipher [dɪ'saɪfə*] *vt* descifrar

decision [dɪ'sɪʒən] *n* decisión *f*

decisive [dɪ'saɪsɪv] *adj* decisivo; (*person*) decidido

deck [dek] *n* (NAUT) cubierta; (*of bus*) piso; (*record ~*) platina; (*of cards*) baraja; **~chair** *n* tumbona

declaration [deklə'reɪʃən] *n* declaración *f*

declare [dɪ'kleə*] *vt* declarar

decline [dɪ'klaɪn] *n* disminución *f*, descenso ♦ *vt* rehusar ♦ *vi* (*person, business*) decaer; (*strength*) disminuir

decoder [diː'kəudə*] *n* (TV) decodificador *m*

décor ['deɪkɔ:*] *n* decoración *f*; (THEATRE) decorado

decorate ['dekəreɪt] *vt* (*adorn*): **to ~ (with)** adornar (de), decorar (de); (*paint*) pintar; (*paper*) empapelar; **decoration** [-'reɪʃən] *n* adorno; (*act*) decoración *f*; (*medal*) condecoración *f*; **decorator** *n* (*workman*) pintor *m* (decorador)

decorum [dɪ'kɔ:rəm] *n* decoro

decoy ['diːkɔɪ] *n* señuelo

decrease [*n* 'diːkriːs, *vb* diː'kriːs] *n*: **~ (in)** disminución *f* (de) ♦ *vt* disminuir, reducir ♦ *vi* reducirse

decree [dɪ'kriː] *n* decreto; **~ nisi** *n* sentencia provisional de divorcio

dedicate ['dedɪkeɪt] *vt* dedicar;

dedication [-'keɪʃən] *n* (*devotion*) dedicación *f*; (*in book*) dedicatoria

deduce [dɪ'djuːs] *vt* deducir

deduct [dɪ'dʌkt] *vt* restar; descontar; **~ion** [dɪ'dʌkʃən] *n* (*amount deducted*) descuento; (*conclusion*) deducción *f*, conclusión *f*

deed [diːd] *n* hecho, acto; (*feat*) hazaña; (LAW) escritura

deep [diːp] *adj* profundo; (*expressing measurements*) de profundidad; (*voice*) bajo; (*breath*) profundo; (*colour*) intenso ♦ *adv*: **the spectators stood 20 ~** los espectadores se formaron de 20 en fondo; **to be 4 metres ~** tener 4 metros de profundidad; **~en** *vt* ahondar, profundizar ♦ *vi* aumentar, crecer; **~-freeze** *n* congelador *m*; **~-fry** *vt* freír en aceite abundante; **~ly** *adv* (*breathe*) a pleno pulmón; (*interested, moved, grateful*) profundamente, hondamente; **~-sea diving** *n* buceo de altura; **~-seated** *adj* (*beliefs*) (profundamente) arraigado

deer [dɪə*] *n inv* ciervo

deface [dɪ'feɪs] *vt* (*wall, surface*) estropear, pintarrajear

default [dɪ'fɔ:lt] *n*: **by ~** (*win*) por incomparecencia ♦ *adj* (COMPUT) por defecto

defeat [dɪ'fiːt] *n* derrota ♦ *vt* derrotar, vencer; **~ist** *adj, n* derrotista *m/f*

defect [*n* 'diːfekt, *vb* dɪ'fekt] *n* defecto ♦ *vi*: **to ~ to the enemy** pasarse al enemigo; **~ive** [dɪ'fektɪv] *adj* defectuoso

defence [dɪ'fens] (US **defense**) *n* defensa; **~less** *adj* indefenso

defend [dɪ'fend] *vt* defender; **~ant** *n* acusado/a; (*in civil case*) demandado/a; **~er** *n* defensor(a) *m/f*; (SPORT) defensa *m/f*

defense [dɪ'fens] (US) *n* = **defence**

defensive [dɪ'fensɪv] *adj* defensivo ♦ *n*: **on the ~** a la defensiva

defer [dɪ'fə:*] *vt* aplazar

defiance [dɪ'faɪəns] *n* desafío; **in ~ of** en contra de; **defiant** [dɪ'faɪənt] *adj* *(challenging)* desafiante, retador(a)

deficiency [dɪˈfɪʃənsɪ] *n (lack)* falta; *(defect)* defecto; **deficient** [dɪˈfɪʃənt] *adj* deficiente

deficit [ˈdɛfɪsɪt] *n* déficit *m*

define [dɪˈfaɪn] *vt (word etc)* definir; *(limits etc)* determinar

definite [ˈdɛfɪnɪt] *adj (fixed)* determinado; *(obvious)* claro; *(certain)* indudable; **he was ~ about it** no dejó lugar a dudas (sobre ello); **~ly** *adv* desde luego, por supuesto

definition [dɛfɪˈnɪʃən] *n* definición *f*; *(clearness)* nitidez *f*

deflate [diːˈfleɪt] *vt* desinflar

deflect [dɪˈflɛkt] *vt* desviar

defraud [dɪˈfrɔːd] *vt:* **to ~ sb of sth** estafar algo a uno

defrost [diːˈfrɔst] *vt* descongelar; **~er** *(US)* *n (demister)* eliminador *m* de vaho

deft [dɛft] *adj* diestro, hábil

defunct [dɪˈfʌŋkt] *adj* difunto; *(organization etc)* ya no existe

defuse [diːˈfjuːz] *vt* desactivar; *(situation)* calmar

defy [dɪˈfaɪ] *vt (resist)* oponerse a; *(challenge)* desafiar; *(fig)*: **it defies description** resulta imposible describirlo

degenerate [*vb* dɪˈdʒɛnəreɪt, *adj* dɪˈdʒɛnərɪt] *vi* degenerar ♦ *adj* degenerado

degree [dɪˈɡriː] *n* grado; *(SCOL)* título; **to have a ~ in maths** tener una licenciatura en matemáticas; **by ~s** *(gradually)* poco a poco, por etapas; **to some ~** hasta cierto punto

dehydrated [diːhaɪˈdreɪtɪd] *adj* deshidratado; *(milk)* en polvo

de-ice [diːˈaɪs] *vt* deshelar

deign [deɪn] *vi:* **to ~ to do** dignarse hacer

dejected [dɪˈdʒɛktɪd] *adj* abatido, desanimado

delay [dɪˈleɪ] *vt* demorar, aplazar; *(person)* entretener; *(train)* retrasar ♦ *vi* tardar ♦ *n* demora, retraso; **to be ~ed** retrasarse; **without ~** en seguida, sin tardar

delectable [dɪˈlɛktəbl] *adj (person)*

encantador(a); *(food)* delicioso

delegate [*n* ˈdɛlɪɡɪt, *vb* ˈdɛlɪɡeɪt] *n* delegado/a ♦ *vt (person)* delegar en; *(task)* delegar

delete [dɪˈliːt] *vt* suprimir, tachar

deliberate [*adj* dɪˈlɪbərɪt, *vb* dɪˈlɪbəreɪt] *adj (intentional)* intencionado; *(slow)* pausado, lento ♦ *vi* deliberar; **~ly** *adv (on purpose)* a propósito

delicacy [ˈdɛlɪkəsɪ] *n* delicadeza; *(choice food)* manjar *m*

delicate [ˈdɛlɪkɪt] *adj* delicado; *(fragile)* frágil

delicatessen [dɛlɪkəˈtɛsn] *n* ultramarinos *mpl* finos

delicious [dɪˈlɪʃəs] *adj* delicioso

delight [dɪˈlaɪt] *n (feeling)* placer *m*, deleite *m*; *(person, experience etc)* encanto, delicia ♦ *vt* encantar, deleitar; **to take ~ in** deleitarse en; **~ed** *adj* **(at** *or* **with/ to do)** encantado (con/de hacer); **~ful** *adj* encantador(a), delicioso

delinquent [dɪˈlɪŋkwənt] *adj, n* delincuente *m/f*

delirious [dɪˈlɪrɪəs] *adj:* **to be ~** delirar, desvariar; **to be ~ with** estar loco de

deliver [dɪˈlɪvə*] *vt (distribute)* repartir; *(hand over)* entregar; *(message)* comunicar; *(speech)* pronunciar; *(MED)* asistir al parto de; **~y** *n* reparto; entrega; *(of speaker)* modo de expresarse; *(MED)* parto, alumbramiento; **to take ~y of** recibir

delude [dɪˈluːd] *vt* engañar

deluge [ˈdɛljuːdʒ] *n* diluvio

delusion [dɪˈluːʒən] *n* ilusión *f*, engaño

de luxe [dəˈlʌks] *adj* de lujo

demand [dɪˈmɑːnd] *vt (gen)* exigir; *(rights)* reclamar ♦ *n* exigencia; *(claim)* reclamación *f*; *(ECON)* demanda; **to be in ~** ser muy solicitado; **on ~** a solicitud; **~ing** *adj (boss)* exigente; *(work)* absorbente

demean [dɪˈmiːn] *vt:* **to ~ o.s.** rebajarse

demeanour [dɪˈmiːnə*] *(US* **demeanor)** *n* porte *m*, conducta

demented [dɪˈmɛntɪd] *adj* demente

demise [dɪ'maɪz] n (*death*) fallecimiento

demister [diː'mɪstə*] n (AUT) eliminador m de vaho

demo ['dɛməʊ] (*inf*) n abbr
(= *demonstration*) manifestación f

democracy [dɪ'mɒkrəsɪ] n democracia;
democrat ['dɛməkræt] n demócrata m/f;
democratic [dɛmə'krætɪk] adj
democrático; (US) demócrata

demolish [dɪ'mɒlɪʃ] vt derribar, demoler;
(*fig: argument*) destruir

demon ['diːmən] n (*evil spirit*) demonio

demonstrate ['dɛmənstreɪt] vt demostrar;
(*skill, appliance*) mostrar ♦ vi manifestarse;
demonstration [-'streɪʃən] n (POL)
manifestación f; (*proof, exhibition*)
demostración f; **demonstrator** n (POL)
manifestante m/f; (COMM) demostrador(a)
m/f; vendedor(a) m/f

demote [dɪ'məʊt] vt degradar

demure [dɪ'mjʊə*] adj recatado

den [dɛn] n (*of animal*) guarida; (*room*)
habitación f

denial [dɪ'naɪəl] n (*refusal*) negativa; (*of
report etc*) negación f

denim ['dɛnɪm] n tela vaquera; ~**s** npl
vaqueros mpl

Denmark ['dɛnmɑːk] n Dinamarca

denomination [dɪnɒmɪ'neɪʃən] n valor m;
(REL) confesión f

denounce [dɪ'naʊns] vt denunciar

dense [dɛns] adj (*crowd*) denso; (*thick*)
espeso; (: *foliage etc*) tupido; (*inf: stupid*)
torpe; ~**ly** adv: ~**ly populated** con una
alta densidad de población

density ['dɛnsɪtɪ] n densidad f; **single/
double-~ disk** n (COMPUT) disco de
densidad sencilla/doble densidad

dent [dɛnt] n abolladura ♦ vt (*also*: **make
a ~ in**) abollar

dental ['dɛntl] adj dental; ~ **surgeon** n
odontólogo/a

dentist ['dɛntɪst] n dentista m/f

dentures ['dɛntʃəz] npl dentadura
(postiza)

deny [dɪ'naɪ] vt negar; (*charge*) rechazar

deodorant [diː'əʊdərənt] n desodorante m

depart [dɪ'pɑːt] vi irse, marcharse; (*train*)
salir; **to ~ from** (*fig: differ from*) apartarse
de

department [dɪ'pɑːtmənt] n (COMM)
sección f; (SCOL) departamento; (POL)
ministerio; ~ **store** n gran almacén m

departure [dɪ'pɑːtʃə*] n partida, ida; (*of
train*) salida; (*of employee*) marcha; **a new
~** un nuevo rumbo; ~ **lounge** n (*at
airport*) sala de embarque

depend [dɪ'pend] vi: **to ~ on** depender de;
(*rely on*) contar con; **it ~s** depende,
según; ~**ing on the result** según el
resultado; ~**able** adj (*person*) formal,
serio; (*watch*) exacto; (*car*) seguro; ~**ant**
n dependiente m/f; ~**ent** adj: **to be ~ent
on** depender de ♦ n = **dependant**

depict [dɪ'pɪkt] vt (*in picture*) pintar;
(*describe*) representar

depleted [dɪ'pliːtɪd] adj reducido

deploy [dɪ'plɔɪ] vt desplegar

deport [dɪ'pɔːt] vt deportar

deposit [dɪ'pɒzɪt] n depósito; (CHEM)
sedimento; (*of ore, oil*) yacimiento ♦ vt
(*gen*) depositar; ~ **account** (BRIT) n
cuenta de ahorros

depot ['dɛpəʊ] n (*storehouse*) depósito; (*for
vehicles*) parque m; (US) estación f

depreciate [dɪ'priːʃɪeɪt] vi depreciarse,
perder valor

depress [dɪ'pres] vt deprimir; (*wages etc*)
hacer bajar; (*press down*) apretar; ~**ed**
adj deprimido; ~**ing** adj deprimente;
~**ion** [dɪ'preʃən] n depresión f

deprivation [deprɪ'veɪʃən] n privación f

deprive [dɪ'praɪv] vt: **to ~ sb of** privar a
uno de; ~**d** adj necesitado

depth [depθ] n profundidad f; (*of
cupboard*) fondo; **to be in the ~s of
despair** sentir la mayor desesperación; **to
be out of one's ~** (*in water*) no hacer
pie; (*fig*) sentirse totalmente perdido

deputize ['depjutaɪz] vi: **to ~ for sb** suplir
a uno

deputy ['depjutɪ] adj: ~ **head**
subdirector(a) m/f ♦ n sustituto/a,
suplente m/f; (US: POL) diputado/a; (US:

also: ~ **sheriff**) agente *m* (del sheriff)
derail [dɪˈreɪl] *vt*: **to be ~ed** descarrilarse
deranged [dɪˈreɪndʒd] *adj* trastornado
derby [ˈdɑːbɪ] (*US*) *n* (*hat*) hongo
derelict [ˈderɪlɪkt] *adj* abandonado
derisory [dɪˈraɪzərɪ] *adj* (*sum*) irrisorio
derive [dɪˈraɪv] *vt* (*benefit etc*) obtener
♦ *vi*: **to ~ from** derivarse de
derogatory [dɪˈrɔgətərɪ] *adj* despectivo
descend [dɪˈsend] *vt*, *vi* descender, bajar;
to ~ from descender de; **to ~ to** rebajarse
a; **~ant** *n* descendiente *m/f*
descent [dɪˈsent] *n* descenso; (*origin*)
descendencia
describe [dɪsˈkraɪb] *vt* describir;
description [-ˈkrɪpʃən] *n* descripción *f*;
(*sort*) clase *f*, género
desecrate [ˈdesɪkreɪt] *vt* profanar
desert [*n* ˈdezət, *vb* dɪˈzɜːt] *n* desierto ♦ *vt*
abandonar ♦ *vi* (*MIL*) desertar; **~er**
[dɪˈzɜːtə*] *n* desertor(a) *m/f*; **~ion**
[dɪˈzɜːʃən] *n* deserción *f*; (*LAW*) abandono;
~ **island** *n* isla desierta; **~s** [dɪˈzɜːts] *npl*:
to get one's just ~s llevar su merecido
deserve [dɪˈzɜːv] *vt* merecer, ser digno de;
deserving *adj* (*person*) digno; (*action*,
cause) meritorio
design [dɪˈzaɪn] *n* (*sketch*) bosquejo;
(*layout*, *shape*) diseño; (*pattern*) dibujo;
(*intention*) intención *f* ♦ *vt* diseñar
designate [*vb* ˈdezɪgneɪt, *adj* ˈdezɪgnɪt] *vt*
(*appoint*) nombrar; (*destine*) designar
♦ *adj* designado
designer [dɪˈzaɪnə*] *n* diseñador(a) *m/f*;
(*fashion* ~) modisto/a, diseñador(a) *m/f*
de moda
desirable [dɪˈzaɪərəbl] *adj* (*proper*)
deseable; (*attractive*) atractivo
desire [dɪˈzaɪə*] *n* deseo ♦ *vt* desear
desk [desk] *n* (*in office*) escritorio; (*for
pupil*) pupitre *m*; (*in hotel*, *at airport*)
recepción *f*; (*BRIT: in shop*, *restaurant*) caja
desk-top publishing [ˈdesktɔp-] *n*
autoedición *f*
desolate [ˈdesəlɪt] *adj* (*place*) desierto;
(*person*) afligido
despair [dɪsˈpeə*] *n* desesperación *f* ♦ *vi*:

to ~ of perder la esperanza de
despatch [dɪsˈpætʃ] *n*, *vt* = **dispatch**
desperate [ˈdespərɪt] *adj* desesperado;
(*fugitive*) peligroso; **to be ~ for sth/to do**
necesitar urgentemente algo/hacer; **~ly**
adv desesperadamente; (*very*)
terriblemente, gravemente
desperation [despəˈreɪʃən] *n*
desesperación *f*; **in (sheer) ~**
(absolutamente) desesperado
despicable [dɪsˈpɪkəbl] *adj* vil,
despreciable
despise [dɪsˈpaɪz] *vt* despreciar
despite [dɪsˈpaɪt] *prep* a pesar de, pese a
despondent [dɪsˈpɔndənt] *adj* deprimido,
abatido
dessert [dɪˈzɜːt] *n* postre *m*; **~spoon** *n*
cuchara (de postre)
destination [destɪˈneɪʃən] *n* destino
destiny [ˈdestɪnɪ] *n* destino
destitute [ˈdestɪtjuːt] *adj* desamparado,
indigente
destroy [dɪsˈtrɔɪ] *vt* destruir; (*animal*)
sacrificar; **~er** *n* (*NAUT*) destructor *m*
destruction [dɪsˈtrʌkʃən] *n* destrucción *f*
detach [dɪˈtætʃ] *vt* separar; (*unstick*)
despegar; **~ed** *adj* (*attitude*) objetivo,
imparcial; **~ed house** *n* ≈ chalé *m*,
≈ chalet *m*; **~ment** *n* (*aloofness*) frialdad
f; (*MIL*) destacamento
detail [ˈdiːteɪl] *n* detalle *m*; (*no pl: in
picture etc*) detalles *mpl*; (*trifle*) pequeñez
f ♦ *vt* detallar; (*MIL*) destacar; **in ~**
detalladamente; **~ed** *adj* detallado
detain [dɪˈteɪn] *vt* retener; (*in captivity*)
detener
detect [dɪˈtekt] *vt* descubrir; (*MED*, *POLICE*)
identificar; (*MIL*, *RADAR*, *TECH*) detectar;
~ion [dɪˈtekʃən] *n* descubrimiento;
identificación *f*; **~ive** *n* detective *m/f*;
~ive story *n* novela policíaca; **~or** *n*
detector *m*
detention [dɪˈtenʃən] *n* detención *f*,
arresto; (*SCOL*) castigo
deter [dɪˈtɜː*] *vt* (*dissuade*) disuadir
detergent [dɪˈtɜːdʒənt] *n* detergente *m*
deteriorate [dɪˈtɪərɪəreɪt] *vi* deteriorarse;

deterioration [-'reɪʃən] n deterioro
determination [dɪtəːmɪ'neɪʃən] n resolución f
determine [dɪ'təːmɪn] vt determinar; ~d adj (person) resuelto, decidido; ~d to do resuelto a hacer
deterrent [dɪ'tɛrənt] n (MIL) fuerza de disuasión
detest [dɪ'tɛst] vt aborrecer
detonate ['dɛtəneɪt] vi estallar ♦ vt hacer detonar
detour ['diːtuə•] n (gen, US: AUT) desviación f
detract [dɪ'trækt] vt: to ~ from quitar mérito a, desvirtuar
detriment ['dɛtrɪmənt] n: to the ~ of en perjuicio de; ~al [dɛtrɪ'mɛntl] adj: ~al (to) perjudicial (a)
devaluation [dɪvæljuː'eɪʃən] n devaluación f
devalue [diː'væljuː] vt (currency) devaluar; (fig) quitar mérito a
devastate ['dɛvəsteɪt] vt devastar; (fig): to be ~d by quedar destrozado por; devastating adj devastador(a); (fig) arrollador(a)
develop [dɪ'vɛləp] vt desarrollar; (PHOT) revelar; (disease) coger; (habit) adquirir; (fault) empezar a tener ♦ vi desarrollarse; (advance) progresar; (facts, symptoms) aparecer; ~er n promotor m; ~ing country n país m en (vías de) desarrollo; ~ment n desarrollo; (advance) progreso; (of affair, case) desenvolvimiento; (of land) urbanización f
deviation [diːvɪ'eɪʃən] n desviación f
device [dɪ'vaɪs] n (apparatus) aparato, mecanismo
devil ['dɛvl] n diablo, demonio
devious ['diːvɪəs] adj taimado
devise [dɪ'vaɪz] vt idear, inventar
devoid [dɪ'vɔɪd] adj: ~ of desprovisto de
devolution [diːvə'luːʃən] n (POL) descentralización f
devote [dɪ'vəut] vt: to ~ sth to dedicar algo a; ~d adj (loyal) leal, fiel; to be ~d to sb querer con devoción a alguien; the

book is ~d to politics el libro trata de la política; ~e [dɛvəu'tiː] n entusiasta m/f; (REL) devoto/a; devotion n dedicación f; (REL) devoción f
devour [dɪ'vauə•] vt devorar
devout [dɪ'vaut] adj devoto
dew [djuː] n rocío
diabetes [daɪə'biːtiːz] n diabetes f; diabetic [-'bɛtɪk] adj, n diabético/a m/f
diabolical [daɪə'bɔlɪkəl] (inf) adj (weather, behaviour) pésimo
diagnosis [daɪəg'nəusɪs] (pl -ses) n diagnóstico
diagonal [daɪ'ægənl] adj, n diagonal f
diagram ['daɪəgræm] n diagrama m, esquema m
dial ['daɪəl] n esfera, cuadrante m, cara (AM); (on radio etc) selector m; (of phone) disco ♦ vt (number) marcar
dialling ['daɪəlɪŋ]: ~ code n prefijo; ~ tone (US dial tone) n (BRIT) señal f or tono de marcar
dialogue ['daɪəlɔg] (US dialog) n diálogo
diameter [daɪ'æmɪtə•] n diámetro
diamond ['daɪəmənd] n diamante m; (shape) rombo; ~s npl (CARDS) diamantes mpl
diaper ['daɪəpə•] (US) n pañal m
diaphragm ['daɪəfræm] n diafragma m
diarrhoea [daɪə'riːə] (US diarrhea) n diarrea
diary ['daɪərɪ] n (daily account) diario; (book) agenda
dice [daɪs] n inv dados mpl ♦ vt (CULIN) cortar en cuadritos
Dictaphone ® ['dɪktəfəun] n dictáfono ®
dictate [dɪk'teɪt] vt dictar; (conditions) imponer; dictation [-'teɪʃən] n dictado; (giving of orders) órdenes fpl
dictator [dɪk'teɪtə•] n dictador m; ~ship n dictadura
dictionary ['dɪkʃənrɪ] n diccionario
did [dɪd] pt of do
didn't ['dɪdənt] = did not
die [daɪ] vi morir; (fig: fade) desvanecerse, desaparecer; to be dying for sth/to do sth morirse por algo/de ganas de hacer

algo; **~ away** _vi_ (_sound, light_) perderse;
~ down _vi_ apagarse; (_wind_) amainar; **~
out** _vi_ desaparecer
diesel ['di:zǝl] _n_ vehículo con motor
Diesel; **~ engine** _n_ motor _m_ Diesel; **~
(oil)** _n_ gasoil _m_
diet ['daɪət] _n_ dieta; (_restricted food_)
régimen _m_ ♦ _vi_ (_also_: **be on a ~**) estar a
dieta, hacer régimen
differ ['dɪfǝ*] _vi_: **to ~ (from)** (_be different_)
ser distinto (a), diferenciarse (de);
(_disagree_) discrepar (de); **~ence** _n_
diferencia; (_disagreement_) desacuerdo;
~ent _adj_ diferente, distinto; **~entiate**
[-'renʃɪeɪt] _vi_: **to ~entiate (between)**
distinguir (entre); **~ently** _adv_ de otro
modo, en forma distinta
difficult ['dɪfɪkǝlt] _adj_ difícil; **~y** _n_
dificultad _f_
diffident ['dɪfɪdǝnt] _adj_ tímido
dig [dɪg] (_pt, pp_ **dug**) _vt_ (_hole, ground_)
cavar ♦ _n_ (_prod_) empujón _m_;
(_archaeological_) excavación _f_; (_remark_)
indirecta; **to ~ one's nails into** clavar las
uñas en; **~ into** _vt fus_ (_savings_)
consumir; **~ up** _vt_ (_information_)
desenterrar; (_plant_) desarraigar
digest [_vb_ daɪ'dʒest, _n_ 'daɪdʒest] _vt_ (_food_)
digerir; (_facts_) asimilar ♦ _n_ resumen _m_;
~ion [dɪ'dʒestʃǝn] _n_ digestión _f_
digit ['dɪdʒɪt] _n_ (_number_) dígito; (_finger_)
dedo; **~al** _adj_ digital; **~al camera** _n_
cámara digital; **~al TV** _n_ televisión _f_
digital
dignified ['dɪgnɪfaɪd] _adj_ grave, solemne
dignity ['dɪgnɪtɪ] _n_ dignidad _f_
digress [daɪ'gres] _vi_: **to ~ from** apartarse
de
digs [dɪgz] (_BRIT: inf_) _npl_ pensión _f_,
alojamiento
dilapidated [dɪ'læpɪdeɪtɪd] _adj_
desmoronado, ruinoso
dilemma [daɪ'lemǝ] _n_ dilema _m_
diligent ['dɪlɪdʒǝnt] _adj_ diligente
dilute [daɪ'lu:t] _vt_ diluir
dim [dɪm] _adj_ (_light_) débil; (_outline_)
indistinto; (_room_) oscuro; (_inf: stupid_)

lerdo ♦ _vt_ (_light_) bajar
dime [daɪm] (_US_) _n_ _moneda de diez
centavos_
dimension [dɪ'menʃǝn] _n_ dimensión _f_
diminish [dɪ'mɪnɪʃ] _vt, vi_ disminuir
diminutive [dɪ'mɪnjʊtɪv] _adj_ diminuto ♦ _n_
(_LING_) diminutivo
dimmers ['dɪmǝz] (_US_) _npl_ (_AUT: dipped
headlights_) luces _fpl_ cortas; (: _parking
lights_) luces _fpl_ de posición
dimple ['dɪmpl] _n_ hoyuelo
din [dɪn] _n_ estruendo, estrépito
dine [daɪn] _vi_ cenar; **~r** _n_ (_person_)
comensal _m/f_
dinghy ['dɪŋgɪ] _n_ bote _m_; (_also_: **rubber ~**)
lancha (neumática)
dingy ['dɪndʒɪ] _adj_ (_room_) sombrío; (_colour_)
sucio
dining car ['daɪnɪŋ-] (_BRIT_) _n_ (_RAIL_) coche-
comedor _m_
dining room _n_ comedor _m_
dinner ['dɪnǝ*] _n_ (_evening meal_) cena;
(_lunch_) comida; (_public_) cena, banquete
_m_; **~ jacket** _n_ smoking _m_; **~ party** _n_
cena; **~ time** _n_ (_evening_) hora de cenar;
(_midday_) hora de comer
dinosaur ['daɪnǝsɔ:*] _n_ dinosaurio
dip [dɪp] _n_ (_slope_) pendiente _m_; (_in sea_)
baño; (_CULIN_) salsa ♦ _vt_ (_in water_) mojar;
(_ladle etc_) meter; (_BRIT: AUT_): **to ~ one's
lights** poner luces de cruce ♦ _vi_ (_road etc_)
descender, bajar
diploma [dɪ'plǝumǝ] _n_ diploma _m_
diplomacy [dɪ'plǝuměsɪ] _n_ diplomacia
diplomat ['dɪplǝmæt] _n_ diplomático/a; **~ic**
[dɪplǝ'mætɪk] _adj_ diplomático
diprod ['dɪprɔd] (_US_) _n_ = **dipstick**
dipstick ['dɪpstɪk] (_BRIT_) _n_ (_AUT_) varilla de
nivel (del aceite)
dipswitch ['dɪpswɪtʃ] (_BRIT_) _n_ (_AUT_)
interruptor _m_
dire [daɪǝ*] _adj_ calamitoso
direct [daɪ'rekt] _adj_ directo; (_challenge_)
claro; (_person_) franco ♦ _vt_ dirigir; (_order_):
to ~ sb to do sth mandar a uno hacer
algo ♦ _adv_ derecho; **can you ~ me to...?**
¿puede indicarme dónde está...?; **~ debit**

(*BRIT*) *n* domiciliación *f* bancaria de recibos

direction [dɪ'rɛkʃən] *n* dirección *f*; **sense of ~** sentido de la dirección; **~s** *npl* (*instructions*) instrucciones *fpl*; **~s for use** modo de empleo

directly [dɪ'rɛktlɪ] *adv* (*in straight line*) directamente; (*at once*) en seguida

director [dɪ'rɛktə*] *n* director(a) *m/f*

directory [dɪ'rɛktərɪ] *n* (*TEL*) guía (telefónica); (*COMPUT*) directorio; **~ enquiries**, **~ assistance** (*US*) *n* (servicio de) información *f*

dirt [dəːt] *n* suciedad *f*; (*earth*) tierra; **~-cheap** *adj* baratísimo; **~y** *adj* sucio; (*joke*) verde (*SP*), colorado (*AM*) ♦ *vt* ensuciar; (*stain*) manchar; **~y trick** *n* juego sucio

disability [dɪsə'bɪlɪtɪ] *n* incapacidad *f*

disabled [dɪs'eɪbld] *adj*: **to be physically ~** ser minusválido/a; **to be mentally ~** ser deficiente mental

disadvantage [dɪsəd'vɑːntɪdʒ] *n* desventaja, inconveniente *m*

disagree [dɪsə'griː] *vi* (*differ*) discrepar; **to ~ (with)** no estar de acuerdo (con); **~able** *adj* desagradable; (*person*) antipático; **~ment** *n* desacuerdo

disallow [dɪsə'lau] *vt* (*goal*) anular; (*claim*) rechazar

disappear [dɪsə'pɪə*] *vi* desaparecer; **~ance** *n* desaparición *f*

disappoint [dɪsə'pɔɪnt] *vt* decepcionar, defraudar; **~ed** *adj* decepcionado; **~ing** *adj* decepcionante; **~ment** *n* decepción *f*

disapproval [dɪsə'pruːvəl] *n* desaprobación *f*

disapprove [dɪsə'pruːv] *vi*: **to ~ of** ver mal

disarmament [dɪs'ɑːməmənt] *n* desarme *m*

disarray [dɪsə'reɪ] *n*: **in ~** (*army*, *organization*) desorganizado; (*hair*, *clothes*) desarreglado

disaster [dɪ'zɑːstə*] *n* desastre *m*

disband [dɪs'bænd] *vt* disolver ♦ *vi* desbandarse

disbelief [dɪsbə'liːf] *n* incredulidad *f*

disc [dɪsk] *n* disco; (*COMPUT*) = **disk**

discard [dɪs'kɑːd] *vt* (*old things*) tirar; (*fig*) descartar

discern [dɪ'səːn] *vt* percibir, discernir; (*understand*) comprender; **~ing** *adj* perspicaz

discharge [*vb* dɪs'tʃɑːdʒ, *n* 'dɪstʃɑːdʒ] *vt* (*task*, *duty*) cumplir; (*waste*) verter; (*patient*) dar de alta; (*employee*) despedir; (*soldier*) licenciar; (*defendant*) poner en libertad ♦ *n* (*ELEC*) descarga; (*MED*) supuración *f*; (*dismissal*) despedida; (*of duty*) desempeño; (*of debt*) pago, descargo

discipline ['dɪsɪplɪn] *n* disciplina ♦ *vt* disciplinar; (*punish*) castigar

disc jockey *n* pinchadiscos *m/f inv*

disclaim [dɪs'kleɪm] *vt* negar

disclose [dɪs'kləuz] *vt* revelar; **disclosure** [-'kləuʒə*] *n* revelación *f*

disco ['dɪskəu] *n abbr* = **discothèque**

discomfort [dɪs'kʌmfət] *n* incomodidad *f*; (*unease*) inquietud *f*; (*physical*) malestar *m*

disconcert [dɪskən'səːt] *vt* desconcertar

disconnect [dɪskə'nɛkt] *vt* separar; (*ELEC etc*) desconectar

discontent [dɪskən'tɛnt] *n* descontento; **~ed** *adj* descontento

discontinue [dɪskən'tɪnjuː] *vt* interrumpir; (*payments*) suspender; **"~d"** (*COMM*) "ya no se fabrica"

discord ['dɪskɔːd] *n* discordia; (*MUS*) disonancia

discothèque ['dɪskəutɛk] *n* discoteca

discount [*n* 'dɪskaunt, *vb* dɪs'kaunt] *n* descuento ♦ *vt* descontar

discourage [dɪs'kʌrɪdʒ] *vt* desalentar; (*advise against*): **to ~ sb from doing** disuadir a uno de hacer

discover [dɪs'kʌvə*] *vt* descubrir; (*error*) darse cuenta de; **~y** *n* descubrimiento

discredit [dɪs'krɛdɪt] *vt* desacreditar

discreet [dɪ'skriːt] *adj* (*tactful*) discreto; (*careful*) circunspecto, prudente

discrepancy [dɪ'skrɛpənsɪ] *n* diferencia

discretion [dɪ'skrɛʃən] *n* (*tact*) discreción

f; **at the ~ of** a criterio de
discriminate [dɪ'skrɪmɪneɪt] *vi*: **to ~ between** distinguir entre; **to ~ against** discriminar contra; **discriminating** *adj* entendido; **discrimination** [-'neɪʃən] *n* (*discernment*) perspicacia; (*bias*) discriminación *f*
discuss [dɪ'skʌs] *vt* discutir; (*a theme*) tratar; **~ion** [dɪ'skʌʃən] *n* discusión *f*
disdain [dɪs'deɪn] *n* desdén *m*
disease [dɪ'ziːz] *n* enfermedad *f*
disembark [dɪsɪm'bɑːk] *vt, vi* desembarcar
disentangle [dɪsɪn'tæŋgl] *vt* soltar; (*wire, thread*) desenredar
disfigure [dɪs'fɪgə*] *vt* (*person*) desfigurar; (*object*) afear
disgrace [dɪs'greɪs] *n* ignominia; (*shame*) vergüenza, escándalo ♦ *vt* deshonrar; **~ful** *adj* vergonzoso
disgruntled [dɪs'grʌntld] *adj* disgustado, descontento
disguise [dɪs'gaɪz] *n* disfraz *m* ♦ *vt* disfrazar; **in ~** disfrazado
disgust [dɪs'gʌst] *n* repugnancia ♦ *vt* repugnar, dar asco a; **~ing** *adj* repugnante, asqueroso; (*behaviour etc*) vergonzoso
dish [dɪʃ] *n* (*gen*) plato; **to do** *or* **wash the ~es** fregar los platos; **~ out** *vt* repartir; **~ up** *vt* servir; **~cloth** *n* estropajo
dishearten [dɪs'hɑːtn] *vt* desalentar
dishevelled [dɪ'ʃevəld] (*US* **disheveled**) *adj* (*hair*) despeinado; (*appearance*) desarreglado
dishonest [dɪs'ɒnɪst] *adj* (*person*) poco honrado, tramposo; (*means*) fraudulento; **~y** *n* falta de honradez
dishonour [dɪs'ɒnə*] (*US* **dishonor**) *n* deshonra; **~able** *adj* deshonroso
dishtowel [dɪʃtəuəl] (*US*) *n* estropajo
dishwasher ['dɪʃwɒʃə*] *n* lavaplatos *m inv*
disillusion [dɪsɪ'luːʒən] *vt* desilusionar
disinfect [dɪsɪn'fekt] *vt* desinfectar; **~ant** *n* desinfectante *m*
disintegrate [dɪs'ɪntɪgreɪt] *vi* disgregarse, desintegrarse
disinterested [dɪs'ɪntrəstɪd] *adj*

desinteresado
disjointed [dɪs'dʒɔɪntɪd] *adj* inconexo
disk [dɪsk] *n* (*esp US*) = **disc**; (*COMPUT*) disco, disquete *m*; **single-/double-sided ~** disco de una cara/dos caras; **~ drive** *n* disc drive *m*; **~ette** *n* = **disk**
dislike [dɪs'laɪk] *n* antipatía, aversión *f* ♦ *vt* tener antipatía a
dislocate ['dɪsləkeɪt] *vt* dislocar
dislodge [dɪs'lɒdʒ] *vt* sacar
disloyal [dɪs'lɔɪəl] *adj* desleal
dismal ['dɪzml] *adj* (*gloomy*) deprimente, triste; (*very bad*) malísimo, fatal
dismantle [dɪs'mæntl] *vt* desmontar, desarmar
dismay [dɪs'meɪ] *n* consternación *f* ♦ *vt* consternar
dismiss [dɪs'mɪs] *vt* (*worker*) despedir; (*pupils*) dejar marchar; (*soldiers*) dar permiso para irse; (*idea, LAW*) rechazar; (*possibility*) descartar; **~al** *n* despido
dismount [dɪs'maunt] *vi* apearse
disobedient [dɪsə'biːdɪənt] *adj* desobediente
disobey [dɪsə'beɪ] *vt* desobedecer
disorder [dɪs'ɔːdə*] *n* desorden *m*; (*rioting*) disturbios *mpl*; (*MED*) trastorno; **~ly** *adj* desordenado; (*meeting*) alborotado; (*conduct*) escandaloso
disorientated [dɪs'ɔːrɪenteɪtəd] *adj* desorientado
disown [dɪs'əun] *vt* (*action*) renegar de; (*person*) negar cualquier tipo de relación con
disparaging [dɪs'pærɪdʒɪŋ] *adj* despreciativo
dispassionate [dɪs'pæʃənɪt] *adj* (*unbiased*) imparcial
dispatch [dɪs'pætʃ] *vt* enviar ♦ *n* (*sending*) envío; (*PRESS*) informe *m*; (*MIL*) parte *m*
dispel [dɪs'pel] *vt* disipar
dispense [dɪs'pens] *vt* (*medicines*) preparar; **~ with** *vt fus* prescindir de; **~r** *n* (*container*) distribuidor *m* automático; **dispensing chemist** (*BRIT*) *n* farmacia
disperse [dɪs'pəːs] *vt* dispersar ♦ *vi* dispersarse

dispirited [dɪ'spɪrɪtɪd] *adj* desanimado, desalentado

displace [dɪs'pleɪs] *vt* desplazar, reemplazar; **~d person** *n* (POL) desplazado/a

display [dɪs'pleɪ] *n* (*in shop window*) escaparate *m*; (*exhibition*) exposición *f*; (COMPUT) visualización *f*; (*of feeling*) manifestación *f* ♦ *vt* exponer; manifestar; (*ostentatiously*) lucir

displease [dɪs'pliːz] *vt* (*offend*) ofender; (*annoy*) fastidiar; **~d** *adj*: **~d with** disgustado con; **displeasure** [-'pleʒə*] *n* disgusto

disposable [dɪs'pəuzəbl] *adj* desechable; (*income*) disponible; **~ nappy** *n* pañal *m* desechable

disposal [dɪs'pəuzl] *n* (*of rubbish*) destrucción *f*; **at one's ~** a su disposición

dispose [dɪs'pəuz] *vi*: **to ~ of** (*unwanted goods*) deshacerse de; (*problem etc*) resolver; **~d** *adj*: **~d to do** dispuesto a hacer; **to be well-~d towards sb** estar bien dispuesto hacia uno; **disposition** [dɪspə'zɪʃən] *n* (*nature*) temperamento *m*; (*inclination*) propensión *f*

disprove [dɪs'pruːv] *vt* refutar

dispute [dɪs'pjuːt] *n* disputa; (*also*: **industrial ~**) conflicto (laboral) ♦ *vt* (*argue*) disputar, discutir; (*question*) cuestionar

disqualify [dɪs'kwɔlɪfaɪ] *vt* (SPORT) desclasificar; **to ~ sb for sth/from doing sth** incapacitar a alguien para algo/hacer algo

disquiet [dɪs'kwaɪət] *n* preocupación *f*, inquietud *f*

disregard [dɪsrɪ'gɑːd] *vt* (*ignore*) no hacer caso de

disrepair [dɪsrɪ'pɛə*] *n*: **to fall into ~** (*building*) desmoronarse

disreputable [dɪs'repjutəbl] *adj* (*person*) de mala fama; (*behaviour*) vergonzoso

disrespectful [dɪsrɪ'spektful] *adj* irrespetuoso

disrupt [dɪs'rʌpt] *vt* (*plans*) desbaratar, trastornar; (*conversation*) interrumpir

dissatisfaction [dɪssætɪs'fækʃən] *n* disgusto, descontento

dissect [dɪ'sekt] *vt* disecar

dissent [dɪ'sent] *n* disensión *f*

dissertation [dɪsə'teɪʃən] *n* tesina

disservice [dɪs'sɜːvɪs] *n*: **to do sb a ~** perjudicar a alguien

dissimilar [dɪ'sɪmɪlə*] *adj* distinto

dissipate ['dɪsɪpeɪt] *vt* disipar; (*waste*) desperdiciar

dissolve [dɪ'zɔlv] *vt* disolver ♦ *vi* disolverse; **to ~ in(to) tears** deshacerse en lágrimas

dissuade [dɪ'sweɪd] *vt*: **to ~ sb (from)** disuadir a uno (de)

distance ['dɪstəns] *n* distancia; **in the ~** a lo lejos

distant ['dɪstənt] *adj* lejano; (*manner*) reservado, frío

distaste [dɪs'teɪst] *n* repugnancia; **~ful** *adj* repugnante, desagradable

distended [dɪ'stendɪd] *adj* (*stomach*) hinchado

distil [dɪs'tɪl] (US **distill**) *vt* destilar; **~lery** *n* destilería

distinct [dɪs'tɪŋkt] *adj* (*different*) distinto; (*clear*) claro; (*unmistakeable*) inequívoco; **as ~ from** a diferencia de; **~ion** [dɪs'tɪŋkʃən] *n* distinción *f*; (*honour*) honor *m*; (*in exam*) sobresaliente *m*; **~ive** *adj* distintivo

distinguish [dɪs'tɪŋgwɪʃ] *vt* distinguir; **to ~ o.s.** destacarse; **~ed** *adj* (*eminent*) distinguido; **~ing** *adj* (*feature*) distintivo

distort [dɪs'tɔːt] *vt* distorsionar; (*shape, image*) deformar; **~ion** [dɪs'tɔːʃən] *n* distorsión *f*; deformación *f*

distract [dɪs'trækt] *vt* distraer; **~ed** *adj* distraído; **~ion** [dɪs'trækʃən] *n* distracción *f*; (*confusion*) aturdimiento

distraught [dɪs'trɔːt] *adj* loco de inquietud

distress [dɪs'tres] *n* (*anguish*) angustia, aflicción *f* ♦ *vt* afligir; **~ing** *adj* angustioso; doloroso; **~ signal** *n* señal *f* de socorro

distribute [dɪs'trɪbjuːt] *vt* distribuir; (*share out*) repartir; **distribution** [-'bjuːʃən] *n* distribución f, reparto; **distributor** n (AUT) distribuidor m; (COMM) distribuidora

district ['dɪstrɪkt] n (of country) zona, región f; (of town) barrio; (ADMIN) distrito; ~ **attorney** (US) n fiscal m/f; ~ **nurse** (BRIT) n enfermera que atiende a pacientes a domicilio

distrust [dɪs'trʌst] n desconfianza ♦ vt desconfiar de

disturb [dɪs'tə:b] vt (person: bother, interrupt) molestar; (: upset) perturbar, inquietar; (disorganize) alterar; ~**ance** n (upheaval) perturbación f; (political etc: gen pl) disturbio; (of mind) trastorno; ~**ed** adj (worried, upset) preocupado, angustiado; **emotionally** ~**ed** trastornado; (childhood) inseguro; ~**ing** adj inquietante, perturbador(a)

disuse [dɪs'ju:s] n: **to fall into** ~ caer en desuso

disused [dɪs'ju:zd] adj abandonado

ditch [dɪtʃ] n zanja; (irrigation ~) acequia ♦ vt (inf: partner) deshacerse de; (: plan, car etc) abandonar

dither ['dɪðə*] (pej) vi vacilar

ditto ['dɪtəu] adv ídem, lo mismo

divan [dɪ'væn] n (also: ~ **bed**) cama turca

dive [daɪv] n (from board) salto; (underwater) buceo; (of submarine) sumersión f ♦ vi (swimmer: into water) saltar; (: under water) zambullirse, bucear; (fish, submarine) sumergirse; (bird) lanzarse en picado; **to** ~ **into** (bag etc) meter la mano en; (place) meterse de prisa en; ~**r** n (underwater) buzo

diverse [daɪ'və:s] adj diversos/as, varios/as

diversion [daɪ'və:ʃən] n (BRIT: AUT) desviación f; (distraction, MIL) diversión f; (of funds) distracción f

divert [daɪ'və:t] vt (turn aside) desviar

divide [dɪ'vaɪd] vt dividir; (separate) separar ♦ vi dividirse; (road) bifurcarse; ~**d highway** (US) n carretera de doble calzada

dividend ['dɪvɪdend] n dividendo; (fig): **to pay** ~**s** proporcionar beneficios

divine [dɪ'vaɪn] adj (also fig) divino

diving ['daɪvɪŋ] n (SPORT) salto; (underwater) buceo; ~ **board** n trampolín m

divinity [dɪ'vɪnɪtɪ] n divinidad f; (SCOL) teología

division [dɪ'vɪʒən] n división f; (sharing out) reparto; (disagreement) diferencias fpl; (COMM) sección f

divorce [dɪ'vɔ:s] n divorcio ♦ vt divorciarse de; ~**d** adj divorciado; ~**e** [-'si:] n divorciado/a

divulge [daɪ'vʌldʒ] vt divulgar, revelar

D.I.Y. (BRIT) adj, n abbr = **do-it-yourself**

dizzy ['dɪzɪ] adj (spell) de mareo; **to feel** ~ marearse

DJ n abbr = **disc jockey**

---KEYWORD---

do [du:] (pt **did**, pp **done**) n (inf: party etc): **we're having a little** ~ **on Saturday** damos una fiestecita el sábado; **it was rather a grand** ~ fue un acontecimiento a lo grande
♦ aux vb 1 (in negative constructions: not translated) **I don't understand** no entiendo
2 (to form questions: not translated) **didn't you know?** ¿no lo sabías?; **what** ~ **you think?** ¿qué opinas?
3 (for emphasis, in polite expressions): **people** ~ **make mistakes sometimes** sí que se cometen errores a veces; **she does seem rather late** a mí también me parece que se ha retrasado; ~ **sit down/ help yourself** siéntate/sírvete por favor; ~ **take care!** ¡ten cuidado(, te pido)!
4 (used to avoid repeating vb): **she sings better than I** ~ canta mejor que yo; ~ **you agree? – yes, I** ~/**no, I don't** ¿estás de acuerdo? — sí (lo estoy)/no (lo estoy); **she lives in Glasgow – so** ~ **I** vive en Glasgow — yo también; **he didn't like it and neither did we** no le gustó y a nosotros tampoco; **who made this mess?** ¿quién hizo esta chapuza? — yo; **he asked me to help him and I did** me pidió que le ayudara y lo hice

5 (*in question tags*): **you like him, don't you?** te gusta, ¿verdad? *or* ¿no?; **I don't know him, ~ I?** creo que no le conozco ♦ *vt* **1** (*gen, carry out, perform etc*): **what are you ~ing tonight?** ¿qué haces esta noche?; **what can I ~ for you?** ¿en qué puedo servirle?; **to ~ the washing-up/cooking** fregar los platos/cocinar; **to ~ one's teeth/hair/nails** lavarse los dientes/arreglarse el pelo/arreglarse las uñas

2 (*AUT etc*): **the car was ~ing 100** el coche iba a 100; **we've done 200 km already** ya hemos hecho 200 km; **he can ~ 100 in that car** puede ir a 100 en ese coche ♦ *vi* **1** (*act, behave*) hacer; **~ as I ~** haz como yo

2 (*get on, fare*): **he's ~ing well/badly at school** va bien/mal en la escuela; **the firm is ~ing well** la empresa anda *or* va bien; **how ~ you ~?** mucho gusto; (*less formal*) ¿qué tal?

3 (*suit*): **will it ~?** ¿sirve?, ¿está *or* va bien?

4 (*be sufficient*) bastar; **will £10 ~?** ¿será bastante con £10?; **that'll ~** así está bien; **that'll ~!** (*in annoyance*) ¡ya está bien!, ¡basta ya!; **to make ~ (with)** arreglárselas (con)

do away with *vt fus* (*kill, disease*) eliminar; (*abolish: law etc*) abolir; (*withdraw*) retirar

do up *vt* (*laces*) atar; (*zip, dress, shirt*) abrochar; (*renovate: room, house*) renovar

do with *vt fus* (*need*): **I could ~ with a drink/some help** no me vendría mal un trago/un poco de ayuda; (*be connected*) tener que ver con; **what has it got to ~ with you?** ¿qué tiene que ver contigo?

do without *vi* pasar sin; **if you're late for tea then you'll ~ without** si llegas tarde tendrás que quedarte sin cenar ♦ *vt fus* pasar sin; **I can ~ without a car** puedo pasar sin coche

dock [dɔk] *n* (*NAUT*) muelle *m*; (*LAW*)

banquillo (de los acusados); **~s** *npl* (*NAUT*) muelles *mpl*, puerto *sg* ♦ *vi* (*enter ~*) atracar (la) muelle; (*SPACE*) acoplarse; **~er** *n* trabajador *m* portuario, estibador *m*; **~yard** *n* astillero

doctor ['dɔktə*] *n* médico/a; (*Ph.D. etc*) doctor(a) *m/f* ♦ *vt* (*drink etc*) adulterar; **D~ of Philosophy** *n* Doctor en Filosofía y Letras

document ['dɔkjumənt] *n* documento; **~ary** [-'mentəri] *adj* documental ♦ *n* documental *m*

dodge [dɔdʒ] *n* (*fig*) truco ♦ *vt* evadir; (*blow*) esquivar

dodgems ['dɔdʒəmz] (*BRIT*) *npl* coches *mpl* de choque

doe [dəu] *n* (*deer*) cierva, gama; (*rabbit*) coneja

does [dʌz] *vb see* **do**; **~n't** = **does not**

dog [dɔg] *n* perro ♦ *vt* seguir los pasos de; (*subj: bad luck*) perseguir; **~ collar** *n* collar *m* de perro; (*of clergyman*) alzacuellos *m inv*; **~-eared** *adj* sobado

dogged ['dɔgid] *adj* tenaz, obstinado

dogsbody ['dɔgzbɔdi] (*BRIT: inf*) *n* burro de carga

doings ['duiŋz] *npl* (*activities*) actividades *fpl*

do-it-yourself *n* bricolaje *m*

doldrums ['dɔldrəmz] *npl*: **to be in the ~** (*person*) estar abatido; (*business*) estar estancado

dole [dəul] (*BRIT*) *n* (*payment*) subsidio de paro; **on the ~** parado; **~ out** *vt* repartir

doll [dɔl] *n* muñeca; (*US: inf: woman*) muñeca, gachí *f*

dollar ['dɔlə*] *n* dólar *m*

dolled up (*inf*) *adj* arreglado

dolphin ['dɔlfin] *n* delfín *m*

domain [də'mein] *n* (*fig*) campo, competencia; (*land*) dominios *mpl*

dome [dəum] *n* (*ARCH*) cúpula

domestic [də'mestik] *adj* (*animal, duty*) doméstico; (*flight, policy*) nacional; **~ated** *adj* domesticado; (*home-loving*) casero, hogareño

dominate ['dɔmineit] *vt* dominar

domineering [dɔmɪˈnɪərɪŋ] *adj* dominante
dominion [dəˈmɪnɪən] *n* dominio
domino [ˈdɒmɪnəu] (*pl* **~es**) *n* ficha de dominó; **~es** *n* (*game*) dominó
don [dɒn] (*BRIT*) *n* profesor(a) *m/f* universitario/a
donate [dəˈneɪt] *vt* donar; **donation** [dəˈneɪʃən] *n* donativo
done [dʌn] *pp of* **do**
donkey [ˈdɒŋkɪ] *n* burro
donor [ˈdəunə*] *n* donante *m/f*; **~ card** *n* carnet *m* de donante
don't [dəunt] = **do not**
donut [ˈdəunʌt] (*US*) *n* = **doughnut**
doodle [ˈduːdl] *vi* hacer dibujitos *or* garabatos
doom [duːm] *n* (*fate*) suerte *f* ♦ *vt*: **to be ~ed to failure** estar condenado al fracaso
door [dɔː*] *n* puerta; **~bell** *n* timbre *m*; **~handle** *n* tirador *m*; (*of car*) manija; **~man** (*irreg*) *n* (*in hotel*) portero; **~mat** *n* felpudo, estera; **~step** *n* peldaño; **~to~** *adj* de puerta en puerta; **~way** *n* entrada, puerta
dope [dəup] *n* (*inf: drug*) droga; (: *person*) imbécil *m/f* ♦ *vt* (*horse etc*) drogar
dormant [ˈdɔːmənt] *adj* inactivo
dormitory [ˈdɔːmɪtrɪ] *n* (*BRIT*) dormitorio; (*US*) colegio mayor
dormouse [ˈdɔːmaus] (*pl* **-mice**) *n* lirón *m*
DOS *n abbr* (= *disk operating system*) DOS *m*
dosage [ˈdəusɪdʒ] *n* dosis *f inv*
dose [dəus] *n* dósis *f inv*
doss house [ˈdɒss-] (*BRIT*) *n* pensión *f* de mala muerte
dossier [ˈdɒsɪeɪ] *n* expediente *m*, dosier *m*
dot [dɒt] *n* punto ♦ *vi*: **~ted with** salpicado de; **on the ~** en punto
double [ˈdʌbl] *adj* doble ♦ *adv* (*twice*): **to cost ~** costar el doble ♦ *n* doble *m* ♦ *vt* doblar ♦ *vi* doblarse; **on the ~, at the ~** (*BRIT*) corriendo; **~ bass** *n* contrabajo; **~ bed** *n* cama de matrimonio; **~ bend** *n* (*BRIT*) doble curva; **~-breasted** *adj* cruzado; **~-click** *vi* (*COMPUT*) hacer doble clic; **~cross** *vt* (*trick*) engañar;

(*betray*) traicionar; **~decker** *n* autobús *m* de dos pisos; **~ glazing** (*BRIT*) *n* doble acristalamiento; **~ room** *n* habitación *f* doble; **~s** *n* (*TENNIS*) juego de dobles; **doubly** *adv* doblemente
doubt [daut] *n* duda ♦ *vt* dudar; (*suspect*) dudar de; **to ~ that** dudar que; **~ful** *adj* dudoso; (*person*): **to be ~ful about sth** tener dudas sobre algo; **~less** *adv* sin duda
dough [dəu] *n* masa, pasta; **~nut** (*US* **donut**) *n* ≈ rosquilla
dove [dʌv] *n* paloma
dovetail [ˈdʌvteɪl] *vi* (*fig*) encajar
dowdy [ˈdaudɪ] *adj* (*person*) mal vestido; (*clothes*) pasado de moda
down [daun] *n* (*feathers*) plumón *m*, flojel *m* ♦ *adv* (*~wards*) abajo, hacia abajo; (*on the ground*) por *or* en tierra ♦ *prep* abajo ♦ *vt* (*inf: drink*) beberse; **~ with X!** ¡abajo X!; **~-and-out** *n* vagabundo/a; **~-at-heel** *adj* venido a menos; (*appearance*) desaliñado; **~cast** *adj* abatido; **~fall** *n* caída, ruina; **~hearted** *adj* desanimado; **~hill** *adv*: **to go ~hill** (*also fig*) ir cuesta abajo; **~load** *vt* (*COMPUT*) bajar; **~ payment** *n* entrada, pago al contado; **~pour** *n* aguacero; **~right** *adj* (*nonsense, lie*) manifiesto; (*refusal*) terminante; **~size** *vi* (*ECON: company*) reducir la plantilla de

---

Downing Street

i **Downing Street** *es la calle de Londres en la que están las residencias oficiales del Presidente del Gobierno (Prime Minister), tradicionalmente en el No. 10, y del Ministro de Economía (Chancellor of the Exchequer). La calle está situada en el céntrico barrio londinense de Westminster y está cerrada al tráfico de peatones y vehículos. En lenguaje periodístico, se usa también* **Downing Street** *para referirse al primer ministro o al Gobierno.*

Down's syndrome [ˈdaunz-] *n* síndrome *m* de Down
down: **~stairs** *adv* (*below*) (en la casa de)

abajo; (~wards) escaleras abajo; ~stream adv aguas or río abajo; ~-to-earth adj práctico; ~town adv en el centro de la ciudad; ~ under adv en Australia (or Nueva Zelanda); ~ward [-wəd] adj, adv hacia abajo; ~wards [-wədz] adv hacia abajo

dowry ['dauri] n dote f

doz. abbr = dozen

doze [dəuz] vi dormitar; ~ off vi quedarse medio dormido

dozen ['dʌzn] n docena; a ~ books una docena de libros; ~s of cantidad de

Dr. abbr = doctor; drive

drab [dræb] adj gris, monótono

draft [drɑːft] n (first copy) borrador m; (POL: of bill) anteproyecto; (US: call-up) quinta ♦ vt (plan) preparar; (write roughly) hacer un borrador de; see also draught

draftsman ['drɑːftsmən] (US) n = draughtsman

drag [dræg] vt arrastrar; (river) dragar, rastrear ♦ vi (time) pasar despacio; (play, film etc) hacerse pesado ♦ n (inf) lata; (women's clothing): in ~ vestido de travesti; ~ on vi ser interminable; ~ and drop vt (COMPUT) arrastrar y soltar

dragon ['drægən] n dragón m

dragonfly ['drægənflaɪ] n libélula

drain [dreɪn] n desaguadero; (in street) sumidero; (source of loss): to be a ~ on consumir, agotar ♦ vt (land, marshes) desaguar; (reservoir) desecar; (vegetables) escurrir ♦ vi escurrirse; ~age n (act) desagüe m; (MED, AGR) drenaje m; (sewage) alcantarillado; ~ing board (US ~board) n escurridera, escurridor m; ~pipe n tubo de desagüe

drama ['drɑːmə] n (art) teatro; (play) drama m; (excitement) emoción f; ~tic [drə'mætɪk] adj dramático; (sudden, marked) espectacular; ~tist ['dræmətɪst] n dramaturgo/a; ~tize ['dræmətaɪz] vt (events) dramatizar

drank [dræŋk] pt of drink

drape [dreɪp] vt (cloth) colocar; (flag) colgar; ~s (US) npl cortinas fpl

drastic ['dræstɪk] adj (measure) severo; (change) radical, drástico

draught [drɑːft] (US draft) n (of air) corriente f de aire; (NAUT) calado; on ~ (beer) de barril; ~ beer n cerveza de barril; ~board (BRIT) n tablero de damas; ~s (BRIT) n (game) juego de damas

draughtsman ['drɑːftsmən] (US draftsman) (irreg) n delineante m

draw [drɔː] (pt drew, pp drawn) vt (picture) dibujar; (cart) tirar de; (curtain) correr; (take out) sacar; (attract) atraer; (money) retirar; (wages) cobrar ♦ vi (SPORT) empatar ♦ n (SPORT) empate m; (lottery) sorteo; ~ near vi acercarse; ~ out vi (lengthen) alargarse ♦ vt sacar; ~ up vi (stop) pararse ♦ vt (chair) acercar; (document) redactar; ~back n inconveniente m, desventaja; ~bridge n puente m levadizo

drawer [drɔː*] n cajón m

drawing ['drɔːɪŋ] n dibujo; ~ board n tablero (de dibujante); ~ pin (BRIT) n chincheta; ~ room n salón m

drawl [drɔːl] n habla lenta y cansina

drawn [drɔːn] pp of draw

dread [dred] n pavor m, terror m ♦ vt temer, tener miedo or pavor a; ~ful adj horroroso

dream [driːm] (pt, pp dreamed or dreamt) n sueño ♦ vt, vi soñar; ~y adj (distracted) soñador(a), distraído; (music) suave

dreary ['drɪərɪ] adj monótono

dredge [dredʒ] vt dragar

dregs [dregz] npl posos mpl; (of humanity) hez f

drench [drentʃ] vt empapar

dress [dres] n vestido; (clothing) ropa ♦ vt vestir; (wound) vendar ♦ vi vestirse; to get ~ed vestirse; ~ up vi vestirse de etiqueta; (in fancy dress) disfrazarse; ~ circle (BRIT) n principal m; ~er n (furniture) aparador m; (: US) cómoda (con espejo); ~ing n (MED) vendaje m; (CULIN) aliño; ~ing gown (BRIT) n bata; ~ing room n (THEATRE) camarín m;

(*SPORT*) vestuario; **~ing table** *n* tocador *m*; **~maker** *n* modista, costurera; **~ rehearsal** *n* ensayo general

drew [druː] *pt of* **draw**

dribble ['drɪbl] *vi* (*baby*) babear ♦ *vt* (*ball*) regatear

dried [draɪd] *adj* (*fruit*) seco; (*milk*) en polvo

drier ['draɪə*] *n* = **dryer**

drift [drɪft] *n* (*of current etc*) flujo; (*of snow*) ventisquero; (*meaning*) significado ♦ *vi* (*boat*) ir a la deriva; (*sand, snow*) amontonarse; **~wood** *n* madera de deriva

drill [drɪl] *n* (*~ bit*) broca; (*tool for DIY etc*) taladro; (*of dentist*) fresa; (*for mining etc*) perforadora, barrena; (*MIL*) instrucción *f* ♦ *vt* perforar, taladrar; (*troops*) enseñar la instrucción a ♦ *vi* (*for oil*) perforar

drink [drɪŋk] (*pt* **drank**, *pp* **drunk**) *n* bebida; (*sip*) trago ♦ *vt, vi* beber; **to have a ~** tomar algo; tomar una copa *or* un trago; **a ~ of water** un trago de agua; **~er** *n* bebedor(a) *m/f*; **~ing water** *n* agua potable

drip [drɪp] *n* (*act*) goteo; (*one ~*) gota; (*MED*) gota a gota *m* ♦ *vi* gotear; **~-dry** *adj* (*shirt*) inarrugable; **~ping** *n* (*animal fat*) pringue *m*

drive [draɪv] (*pt* **drove**, *pp* **driven**) *n* (*journey*) viaje *m* (en coche); (*also:* **~way**) entrada; (*energy*) energía, vigor *m*; (*COMPUT: also:* **disk ~**) drive *m* ♦ *vt* (*car*) conducir (*SP*), manejar (*AM*); (*nail*) clavar; (*push*) empujar; (*TECH: motor*) impulsar ♦ *vi* (*AUT: at controls*) conducir; (*: travel*) pasearse en coche; **left-/right-hand ~** conducción *f* a la izquierda/derecha; **to ~ sb mad** volverle loco a uno

drivel ['drɪvl] (*inf*) *n* tonterías *fpl*

driven ['drɪvn] *pp of* **drive**

driver ['draɪvə*] *n* conductor(a) *m/f* (*SP*), chofer *m* (*AM*); (*of taxi, bus*) chofer; **~'s license** (*US*) *n* carnet *m* de conducir

driveway ['draɪvweɪ] *n* entrada

driving ['draɪvɪŋ] *n* el conducir (*SP*), el manejar (*AM*); **~ instructor** *n*

instructor(a) *m/f* de conducción *or* manejo; **~ lesson** *n* clase *f* de conducción *or* manejo; **~ licence** (*BRIT*) *n* permiso de conducir; **~ school** *n* autoescuela; **~ test** *n* examen *m* de conducción *or* manejo

drizzle ['drɪzl] *n* llovizna

drool [druːl] *vi* babear

droop [druːp] *vi* (*flower*) marchitarse; (*shoulders*) encorvarse; (*head*) inclinarse

drop [drɒp] *n* (*of water*) gota; (*lessening*) baja; (*fall*) caída ♦ *vt* dejar caer; (*voice, eyes, price*) bajar; (*passenger*) dejar; (*omit*) omitir ♦ *vi* (*object*) caer; (*wind*) amainar; **~s** *npl* (*MED*) gotas *fpl*; **~ off** *vi* (*sleep*) dormirse ♦ *vt* (*passenger*) dejar; **~ out** *vi* (*withdraw*) retirarse; **~out** *n* marginado/a; (*SCOL*) estudiante que abandona los estudios; **~per** *n* cuentagotas *m inv*; **~pings** *npl* excremento

drought [draut] *n* sequía

drove [drəuv] *pt of* **drive**

drown [draun] *vt* ahogar ♦ *vi* ahogarse

drowsy ['drauzɪ] *adj* soñoliento; **to be ~** tener sueño

drug [drʌg] *n* medicamento; (*narcotic*) droga ♦ *vt* drogar; **to be on ~s** drogarse; **~ addict** *n* drogadicto/a; **~gist** (*US*) *n* farmacéutico; **~store** (*US*) *n* farmacia

drum [drʌm] *n* tambor *m*; (*for oil, petrol*) bidón *m*; **~s** *npl* batería; **~mer** *n* tambor *m*

drunk [drʌŋk] *pp of* **drink** ♦ *adj* borracho ♦ *n* (*also:* **~ard**) borracho/a; **~en** *adj* borracho; (*laughter, party*) de borrachos

dry [draɪ] *adj* seco; (*day*) sin lluvia; (*climate*) árido, seco ♦ *vt* secar; (*tears*) enjugarse ♦ *vi* secarse; **~ up** *vi* (*river*) secarse; **~-cleaner's** *n* tintorería; **~-cleaning** *n* lavado en seco; **~er** *n* (*for hair*) secador *m*; (*US: for clothes*) secadora; **~ rot** *n* putrefacción *f* fungoide

DSS *n abbr* = **Department of Social Security**

DTP *n abbr* (= *desk-top publishing*) autoedición *f*

dual ['djuəl] *adj* doble; **~ carriageway**

(BRIT) n carretera de doble calzada; ~-**purpose** adj de doble uso
dubbed [dʌbd] adj (CINEMA) doblado
dubious ['djuːbɪəs] adj indeciso; (reputation, company) sospechoso
duchess ['dʌtʃɪs] n duquesa
duck [dʌk] n pato ♦ vi agacharse; ~**ling** n patito
duct [dʌkt] n conducto, canal m
dud [dʌd] n (object, tool) engaño, engañifa ♦ adj: ~ **cheque** (BRIT) cheque m sin fondos
due [djuː] adj (owed): **he is ~ £10** se le deben 10 libras; (expected: event): **the meeting is ~ on Wednesday** la reunión tendrá lugar el miércoles; (: arrival) **the train is ~ at 8am** el tren tiene su llegada para las 8; (proper) debido ♦ n: **to give sb his** (or **her**) **~** ser justo con alguien ♦ adv: ~ **north** derecho al norte; ~**s** npl (for club, union) cuota; (in harbour) derechos mpl; **in ~ course** a su debido tiempo; ~ **to** debido a; **to be ~ to** deberse a
duet [djuːˈet] n dúo
duffel bag ['dʌfəl] n bolsa de lona
duffel coat n trenca, abrigo de tres cuartos
dug [dʌg] pt, pp of **dig**
duke [djuːk] n duque m
dull [dʌl] adj (light) débil; (stupid) torpe; (boring) pesado; (sound, pain) sordo; (weather, day) gris ♦ vt (pain, grief) aliviar; (mind, senses) entorpecer
duly ['djuːlɪ] adv debidamente; (on time) a su debido tiempo
dumb [dʌm] adj (mute) mudo; (pej: stupid) estúpido; ~**founded** [dʌmˈfaʊndɪd] adj pasmado
dummy ['dʌmɪ] n (tailor's ~) maniquí m; (mock-up) maqueta; (BRIT: for baby) chupete m ♦ adj falso, postizo
dump [dʌmp] n (also: **rubbish ~**) basurero, vertedero; (inf: place) cuchitril m ♦ vt (put down) dejar; (get rid of) deshacerse de; (COMPUT: data) transferir
dumpling ['dʌmplɪŋ] n bola de masa hervida

dumpy ['dʌmpɪ] adj regordete/a
dunce [dʌns] n zopenco
dung [dʌŋ] n estiércol m
dungarees [dʌŋgəˈriːz] npl mono
dungeon ['dʌndʒən] n calabozo
duplex ['djuːpleks] n dúplex m
duplicate [n 'djuːplɪkət, vb 'djuːplɪkeɪt] n duplicado ♦ vt duplicar; (photocopy) fotocopiar; (repeat) repetir; **in ~** por duplicado
durable ['djuərəbl] adj duradero
duration [djuəˈreɪʃən] n duración f
during ['djuərɪŋ] prep durante
dusk [dʌsk] n crepúsculo, anochecer m
dust [dʌst] n polvo ♦ vt quitar el polvo a, desempolvar; (cake etc): **to ~ with** espolvorear de; ~**bin** (BRIT) n cubo de la basura (SP), balde m (AM); ~**er** n paño, trapo; ~**man** (BRIT irreg) n basurero; ~**y** adj polvoriento
Dutch [dʌtʃ] adj holandés/esa ♦ n (LING) holandés m; **the ~** npl los holandeses; **to go ~** (inf) pagar cada uno lo suyo; ~**man/woman** (irreg) n holandés/esa m/f
duty ['djuːtɪ] n deber m; (tax) derechos mpl de aduana; **on ~** de servicio; (at night etc) de guardia; **off ~** libre (de servicio); ~**-free** adj libre de impuestos
duvet ['duːveɪ] (BRIT) n edredón m
DVD n abbr (= digital versatile (or) video disc) DVD m
dwarf [dwɔːf] (pl **dwarves**) n enano/a ♦ vt empequeñecer
dwell [dwel] (pt, pp **dwelt**) vi morar; ~ **on** vt fus explayarse en
dwindle ['dwɪndl] vi menguar, disminuir
dye [daɪ] n tinte m ♦ vt teñir
dying ['daɪɪŋ] adj moribundo, agonizante
dyke [daɪk] (BRIT) n dique m
dynamic [daɪˈnæmɪk] adj dinámico
dynamite ['daɪnəmaɪt] n dinamita
dynamo ['daɪnəməʊ] n dinamo f
dynasty ['dɪnəstɪ] n dinastía

E, e

E [iː] n (MUS) mi m

each [iːtʃ] adj (keen) cada inv ♦ pron cada uno; **~ other** el uno al otro; **they hate ~ other** se odian (entre ellos or mutuamente); **they have 2 books ~** tienen 2 libros por persona

eager ['iːgə*] adj (keen) entusiasmado; **to be ~ to do sth** tener muchas ganas de hacer algo, impacientarse por hacer algo; **to be ~ for** tener muchas ganas de

eagle ['iːgl] n águila

ear [ɪə*] n oreja; oído; (of corn) espiga; **~ache** n dolor m de oídos; **~drum** n tímpano

earl [əːl] n conde m

earlier ['əːlɪə*] adj anterior ♦ adv antes

early ['əːlɪ] adv temprano; (before time) con tiempo, con anticipación ♦ adj temprano; (settlers etc) primitivo; (death, departure) prematuro; (reply) pronto; **to have an ~ night** acostarse temprano; **in the ~** or **~ in the spring** a principios de primavera; **~ retirement** n jubilación f anticipada

earmark ['ɪəmɑːk] vt: **to ~ (for)** reservar (para), destinar (a)

earn [əːn] vt (salary) percibir; (interest) devengar; (praise) merecerse

earnest ['əːnɪst] adj (wish) fervoroso; (person) serio, formal; **in ~** en serio

earnings ['əːnɪŋz] npl (personal) sueldo, ingresos mpl; (company) ganancias fpl

ear: ~phones npl auriculares mpl; **~ring** n pendiente m, arete m; **~shot** n: **within ~shot** al alcance del oído

earth [əːθ] n tierra; (BRIT: ELEC) cable m de toma de tierra ♦ vt (BRIT: ELEC) conectar a tierra; **~enware** n loza (de barro); **~quake** n terremoto; **~y** adj (fig: vulgar) grosero

ease [iːz] n facilidad f; (comfort) comodidad f ♦ vt (lessen: problem) mitigar; (: pain) aliviar; (: tension) reducir; **to ~ sth in/out** meter/sacar algo con cuidado; **at ~!** (MIL)

¡descansen!; **~ off** or **up** vi (wind, rain) amainar; (slow down) aflojar la marcha

easel ['iːzl] n caballete m

easily ['iːzɪlɪ] adv fácilmente

east [iːst] n este m ♦ adj del este, oriental; (wind) este ♦ adv al este, hacia el este; **the E~** el Oriente; (POL) los países del Este

Easter ['iːstə*] n Pascua (de Resurrección); **~ egg** n huevo de Pascua

east: ~erly ['iːstəlɪ] adj (to the east) al este; (from the east) del este; **~ern** ['iːstən] adj del este, oriental; (oriental) oriental; **~ward(s)** ['iːstwəd(z)] adv hacia el este

easy ['iːzɪ] adj fácil; (simple) sencillo; (comfortable) holgado, cómodo; (relaxed) tranquilo ♦ adv: **to take it** or **things ~** (not worry) tomarlo con calma; (rest) descansar; **~ chair** n sillón m; **~-going** adj acomodadizo

eat [iːt] (pt **ate**, pp **eaten**) vt comer; **~ away at** vt fus corroer; mermar; **~ into** vt fus corroer; (savings) mermar

eaves [iːvz] npl alero

eavesdrop ['iːvzdrɔp] vi: **to ~ (on)** escuchar a escondidas

ebb [ɛb] n reflujo ♦ vi bajar; (fig: also: **~ away**) decaer

ebony ['ɛbənɪ] n ébano

EC n abbr (= European Community) CE f

ECB n abbr (= European Central Bank) BCE m

eccentric [ɪk'sɛntrɪk] adj, n excéntrico/a m/f

echo ['ɛkəu] (pl **~es**) n eco m ♦ vt (sound) repetir ♦ vi resonar, hacer eco

éclair [ɪ'klɛə*] n pastelillo relleno de crema y con chocolate por encima

eclipse [ɪ'klɪps] n eclipse m

ecology [ɪ'kɔlədʒɪ] n ecología

e-commerce n abbr (= electronic commerce) comercio electrónico

economic [iːkə'nɔmɪk] adj económico; (business etc) rentable; **~al** adj económico; **~s** n (SCOL) economía ♦ npl (of project etc) rentabilidad f

economize [ɪ'kɔnəmaɪz] vi economizar, ahorrar

economy [ɪ'kɒnəmɪ] n economía; ~ **class** n (AVIAT) clase f económica; ~ **size** n tamaño económico

ecstasy ['ɛkstəsɪ] n éxtasis m inv; (drug) éxtasis m inv; **ecstatic** [ɛks'tætɪk] adj extático

ECU ['eɪkjuː] n (= European Currency Unit) ECU m

Ecuador ['ɛkwədɔːr] n Ecuador m; **~ian** adj, n ecuatoriano/a m/f

eczema ['ɛksɪmə] n eczema m

edge [ɛdʒ] n (of knife etc) filo; (of object) borde, (of lake etc) orilla ♦ vt (SEWING) ribetear; **on** ~ (fig) = **edgy**; **to** ~ **away from** alejarse poco a poco de; **~ways** adv: **he couldn't get a word in ~ways** no pudo meter ni baza

edgy ['ɛdʒɪ] adj nervioso, inquieto

edible ['ɛdɪbl] adj comestible

Edinburgh ['ɛdɪnbərə] n Edimburgo

edit ['ɛdɪt] vt (be editor of) dirigir; (text, report) corregir, preparar; **~ion** [ɪ'dɪʃən] n edición f; **~or** n (of newspaper) director(a) m/f; (of column): **foreign/political ~or** encargado de la sección de extranjero/política; (of book) redactor(a) m/f; **~orial** [-'tɔːrɪəl] adj editorial ♦ n editorial m

educate ['ɛdjukeɪt] vt (gen) educar; (instruct) instruir

education [ɛdju'keɪʃən] n educación f; (schooling) enseñanza; (SCOL) pedagogía; **~al** adj (policy etc) educacional; (experience) docente; (toy) educativo

EEC n abbr (= European Economic Community) CEE f

eel [iːl] n anguila

eerie ['ɪərɪ] adj misterioso

effect [ɪ'fɛkt] n efecto ♦ vt efectuar, llevar a cabo; **to take** ~ (law) entrar en vigor or vigencia; (drug) surtir efecto; **in** ~ en realidad; **~ive** adj eficaz; (actual) verdadero; **~ively** adv eficazmente; (in reality) efectivamente; **~iveness** n eficacia

effeminate [ɪ'fɛmɪnɪt] adj afeminado

efficiency [ɪ'fɪʃənsɪ] n eficiencia; rendimiento

efficient [ɪ'fɪʃənt] adj eficiente; (machine) de buen rendimiento

effort ['ɛfət] n esfuerzo; **~less** adj sin ningún esfuerzo; (style) natural

effusive [ɪ'fjuːsɪv] adj efusivo

e.g. adv abbr (= exempli gratia) p. ej.

egg [ɛg] n huevo; **hard-boiled/soft-boiled** ~ huevo duro/pasado por agua; ~ **on** vt incitar; **~cup** n huevera, ~ **plant** (esp US) n berenjena; **~shell** n cáscara de huevo

ego ['iːgəu] n ego; **~tism** n egoísmo; **~tist** n egoísta m/f

Egypt ['iːdʒɪpt] n Egipto m; **~ian** [ɪ'dʒɪpʃən] adj, n egipcio/a m/f

eiderdown ['aɪdədaun] n edredón m

eight [eɪt] num ocho; **~een** num diez y ocho, dieciocho; **eighth** [eɪtθ] num octavo; **~y** num ochenta

Eire ['ɛərə] n Eire m

either ['aɪðər] adj cualquiera de los dos; (both, each) cada ♦ pron: ~ (of them) cualquiera (de los dos) ♦ adv tampoco; **on** ~ **side** en ambos lados; **I don't like** ~ no me gusta ninguno/a de los/las dos; **no, I don't** ~ no, yo tampoco ♦ conj: ~ **yes or no** o sí o no

eject [ɪ'dʒɛkt] vt echar, expulsar; (tenant) desahuciar; **~or seat** n asiento proyectable

elaborate [adj ɪ'læbərɪt, vb ɪ'læbəreɪt] adj (complex) complejo ♦ vt (expand) ampliar; (refine) refinar ♦ vi explicar con más detalles

elastic [ɪ'læstɪk] n elástico ♦ adj elástico; (fig) flexible; ~ **band** (BRIT) n gomita

elated [ɪ'leɪtɪd] adj: **to be** ~ regocijarse

elbow ['ɛlbəu] n codo

elder ['ɛldər] adj mayor ♦ n (tree) saúco; (person) mayor; **~ly** adj de edad, mayor ♦ npl: **the ~ly** los mayores

eldest ['ɛldɪst] adj, n el/la mayor

elect [ɪ'lɛkt] vt elegir ♦ adj: **the president** ~ el presidente electo; **to** ~ **to do** optar por hacer; **~ion** [ɪ'lɛkʃən] n elección f; **~ioneering** [ɪlɛkʃə'nɪərɪŋ] n campaña

electoral; **~or** n elector(a) m/f; **~oral** adj
electoral; **~orate** n electorado

electric [ɪ'lektrɪk] adj eléctrico; **~al** adj
eléctrico; **~ blanket** n manta eléctrica; **~
fire** n estufa eléctrica; **~ian** [ɪlek'trɪʃən] n
electricista m/f; **~ity** [ɪlek'trɪsɪtɪ] n
electricidad f; **electrify** [ɪ'lektrɪfaɪ] vt
(RAIL) electrificar; (fig: audience) electrizar

electronic [ɪlek'trɒnɪk] adj electrónico; **~
mail** n correo electrónico; **~s** n
electrónica

elegant ['elɪɡənt] adj elegante

element ['elɪmənt] n elemento; (of kettle
etc) resistencia; **~ary** [-'mentərɪ] adj
elemental; (primitive) rudimentario;
(school) primario

elephant ['elɪfənt] n elefante m

elevation [elɪ'veɪʃən] n elevación f;
(height) altura

elevator ['elɪveɪtə*] n (US) ascensor m; (in
warehouse etc) montacargas m inv

eleven [ɪ'levn] num once; **~ses** (BRIT) npl
café m de las once; **~th** num undécimo

elicit [ɪ'lɪsɪt] vt: **to ~ (from)** sacar (de)

eligible ['elɪdʒəbl] adj: **an ~ young man/
woman** un buen partido; **to be ~ for sth**
llenar los requisitos para algo

elm [elm] n olmo

elongated ['iːlɒŋɡeɪtɪd] adj alargado

elope [ɪ'ləup] vi fugarse (para casarse)

eloquent ['eləkwənt] adj elocuente

else [els] adv: **something ~** otra cosa;
somewhere ~ en otra parte; **everywhere
~** en todas partes menos aquí; **where ~?**
¿dónde más?, ¿en qué otra parte?; **there
was little ~ to do** apenas quedaba otra
cosa que hacer; **nobody ~ spoke** no
habló nadie más; **~where** adv (be) en
otra parte; (go) a otra parte

elude [ɪ'luːd] vt (subj: idea etc) escaparse a;
(capture) esquivar

elusive [ɪ'luːsɪv] adj esquivo; (quality)
difícil de encontrar

emaciated [ɪ'meɪsɪeɪtɪd] adj demacrado

E-mail, e-mail ['iːmeɪl] n abbr
(= electronic mail) correo electrónico, e-
mail m

emancipate [ɪ'mænsɪpeɪt] vt emancipar

embankment [ɪm'bæŋkmənt] n terraplén
m

embark [ɪm'bɑːk] vi embarcarse ♦ vt
embarcar; **to ~ on** (journey) emprender;
(course of action) lanzarse; **~ation**
[embɑː'keɪʃən] n (people) embarco; (goods)
embarque m

embarrass [ɪm'bærəs] vt avergonzar;
(government etc) dejar en mal lugar; **~ed**
adj (laugh, silence) embarazoso; **~ing** adj
(situation) violento; (question)
embarazoso; **~ment** n (shame)
vergüenza; (problem): **to be an ~ment for
sb** poner en un aprieto a uno

embassy ['embəsɪ] n embajada

embedded [ɪm'bedɪd] adj (object)
empotrado; (thorn etc) clavado

embellish [ɪm'belɪʃ] vt embellecer; (story)
adornar

embers ['embəz] npl rescoldo, ascua

embezzle [ɪm'bezl] vt desfalcar, malversar

embitter [ɪm'bɪtə*] vt (fig: sour) amargar

embody [ɪm'bɒdɪ] vt (spirit) encarnar;
(include) incorporar

embossed [ɪm'bɒst] adj realzado

embrace [ɪm'breɪs] vt abrazar, dar un
abrazo a; (include) abarcar ♦ vi abrazarse
♦ n abrazo

embroider [ɪm'brɔɪdə*] vt bordar; **~y** n
bordado

embryo ['embrɪəu] n embrión m

emerald ['emərəld] n esmeralda

emerge [ɪ'mɜːdʒ] vi salir; (arise) surgir

emergency [ɪ'mɜːdʒənsɪ] n crisis f inv; **in
an ~** en caso de urgencia; **state of ~**
estado de emergencia; **~ cord** (US) n
timbre m de alarma; **~ exit** n salida de
emergencia; **~ landing** n aterrizaje m
forzoso; **~ services** npl (fire, police,
ambulance) servicios mpl de urgencia or
emergencia

emery board ['emərɪ-] n lima de uñas

emigrate ['emɪɡreɪt] vi emigrar

emissions [ɪ'mɪʃənz] npl emisión f

emit [ɪ'mɪt] vt emitir; (smoke) arrojar;
(smell) despedir; (sound) producir

emotion [ɪ'məʊʃən] *n* emoción *f*; ~**al** *adj* (*needs*) emocional; (*person*) sentimental; (*scene*) conmovedor(a), emocionante; (*speech*) emocionado

emperor ['empərə*] *n* emperador *m*

emphasis ['emfəsɪs] (*pl* -**ses**) *n* énfasis *m inv*

emphasize ['emfəsaɪz] *vt* (*word, point*) subrayar, recalcar; (*feature*) hacer resaltar

emphatic [em'fætɪk] *adj* (*reply*) categórico; (*person*) insistente

empire ['empaɪə*] *n* (*also fig*) imperio *m*

employ [ɪm'plɔɪ] *vt* emplear; ~**ee** [-'iː] *n* empleado/a; ~**er** *n* patrón/ona *m/f*; empresario/a; ~**ment** *n* (*work*) trabajo; ~**ment agency** *n* agencia de colocaciones

empower [ɪm'paʊə*] *vt*: **to ~ sb to do sth** autorizar a uno para hacer algo

empress ['emprɪs] *n* emperatriz *f*

emptiness ['emptɪnɪs] *n* vacío *m*; (*of life etc*) vaciedad *f*

empty ['emptɪ] *adj* vacío; (*place*) desierto; (*house*) desocupado; (*threat*) vano ♦ *vt* vaciar; (*place*) dejar vacío ♦ *vi* vaciarse; (*house etc*) quedar desocupado; ~**-handed** *adj* con las manos vacías

EMU *n abbr* (= *European Monetary Union*) UME *f*

emulate ['emjuleɪt] *vt* emular

emulsion [ɪ'mʌlʃən] *n* emulsión *f*; (*also:* ~ **paint**) pintura emulsión

enable [ɪ'neɪbl] *vt*: **to ~ sb to do sth** permitir a uno hacer algo

enamel [ɪ'næməl] *n* esmalte *m*; (*also:* ~ **paint**) pintura esmaltada

enchant [ɪn'tʃɑːnt] *vt* encantar; ~**ing** *adj* encantador(a)

encl. *abbr* (= *enclosed*) adj

enclose [ɪn'kləʊz] *vt* (*land*) cercar; (*letter etc*) adjuntar; **please find ~d** le mandamos adjunto

enclosure [ɪn'kləʊʒə*] *n* cercado, recinto

encompass [ɪn'kʌmpəs] *vt* abarcar

encore [ɒŋ'kɔː*] *excl* ¡otra!, ¡bis! ♦ *n* bis *m*

encounter [ɪn'kaʊntə*] *n* encuentro ♦ *vt* encontrar, encontrarse con; (*difficulty*) tropezar con

encourage [ɪn'kʌrɪdʒ] *vt* alentar, animar; (*activity*) fomentar; (*growth*) estimular; ~**ment** *n* estímulo; (*of industry*) fomento

encroach [ɪn'krəʊtʃ] *vi*: **to ~ (up)on** invadir; (*rights*) usurpar; (*time*) adueñarse de

encyclop(a)edia [ensaɪkləʊ'piːdɪə] *n* enciclopedia

end [end] *n* (*gen, also aim*) fin *m*; (*of table*) extremo; (*of street*) final *m*; (*SPORT*) lado ♦ *vt* terminar, acabar; (*also:* **bring to an ~, put an ~ to**) acabar con ♦ *vi* terminar, acabar; **in the ~** al fin; **on ~** (*object*) de punta, de cabeza; **to stand on ~** (*hair*) erizarse; **for hours on ~** hora tras hora; ~ **up** *vi*: **to ~ up in** terminar en; (*place*) ir a parar en

endanger [ɪn'deɪndʒə*] *vt* poner en peligro; **an ~ed species** una especie en peligro de extinción

endearing [ɪn'dɪərɪŋ] *adj* simpático, atractivo

endeavour [ɪn'devə*] (*US* **endeavor**) *n* esfuerzo; (*attempt*) tentativa ♦ *vi*: **to ~ to do** esforzarse por hacer; (*try*) procurar hacer

ending ['endɪŋ] *n* (*of book*) desenlace *m*; (*LING*) terminación *f*

endive ['endaɪv] *n* (*chicory*) endibia; (*curly*) escarola

endless ['endlɪs] *adj* interminable, inacabable

endorse [ɪn'dɔːs] *vt* (*cheque*) endosar; (*approve*) aprobar; ~**ment** *n* (*on driving licence*) nota de inhabilitación

endure [ɪn'djʊə*] *vt* (*bear*) aguantar, soportar ♦ *vi* (*last*) durar

enemy ['enəmɪ] *adj, n* enemigo/a *m/f*

energetic [enə'dʒetɪk] *adj* enérgico

energy ['enədʒɪ] *n* energía

enforce [ɪn'fɔːs] *vt* (*LAW*) hacer cumplir

engage [ɪn'geɪdʒ] *vt* (*attention*) llamar; (*interest*) ocupar; (*in conversation*) abordar; (*worker*) contratar; **to ~ the clutch** embragar ♦ *vi* (*TECH*) engranar; **to ~ in** dedicarse a, ocuparse en; ~**d** adj (BRIT: busy, in use) ocupado; (betrothed) prometido; **to get ~d** prometerse; ~**d tone** (BRIT) n (TEL) señal f de comunicando; ~**ment** n (appointment) compromiso, cita; (booking) contratación f; (to marry) compromiso; (period) noviazgo; ~**ment ring** n anillo de prometida

engaging [ɪnˈɡeɪdʒɪŋ] adj atractivo

engine [ˈɛndʒɪn] n (AUT) motor m; (RAIL) locomotora f

engineer [ɛndʒɪˈnɪə*] n ingeniero; (BRIT: for repairs) mecánico; (on ship, US: RAIL) maquinista m; ~**ing** n ingeniería

England [ˈɪŋɡlənd] n Inglaterra

English [ˈɪŋɡlɪʃ] adj inglés/esa ♦ n (LING) inglés m; **the ~** npl los ingleses mpl; **the ~ Channel** n (el Canal de) la Mancha; ~**man/woman** (irreg) n inglés/esa m/f

engraving [ɪnˈɡreɪvɪŋ] n grabado

engrossed [ɪnˈɡrəʊst] adj: ~ **in** absorto en

engulf [ɪnˈɡʌlf] vt (subj: water) sumergir, hundir; (: fire) prender; (: fear) apoderarse de

enhance [ɪnˈhɑːns] vt (gen) aumentar; (beauty) realzar

enjoy [ɪnˈdʒɔɪ] vt (health, fortune) disfrutar de, gozar de; (like) gustarle a uno; **to ~ o.s.** divertirse; ~**able** adj agradable; (amusing) divertido; ~**ment** n (joy) placer m; (activity) diversión f

enlarge [ɪnˈlɑːdʒ] vt aumentar; (broaden) extender; (PHOT) ampliar ♦ vi: **to ~ on** (subject) tratar con más detalles; ~**ment** n (PHOT) ampliación f

enlighten [ɪnˈlaɪtn] vt (inform) informar; ~**ed** adj comprensivo; **the E~ment** n (HISTORY) ≈ la Ilustración, ≈ el Siglo de las Luces

enlist [ɪnˈlɪst] vt alistar; (support) conseguir ♦ vi alistarse

enmity [ˈɛnmɪtɪ] n enemistad f

enormous [ɪˈnɔːməs] adj enorme

enough [ɪˈnʌf] adj: ~ **time/books** bastante tiempo/bastantes libros ♦ pron bastante(s) ♦ adv: **big ~** bastante grande; **he has not worked ~** no ha trabajado

bastante; **have you got ~?** ¿tiene usted bastante(s)?; ~ **to eat** (lo) suficiente or (lo) bastante para comer; ~**!** ¡basta ya!; **that's ~, thanks** con eso basta, gracias; **I've had ~ of him** estoy harto de él; ... **which, funnily** or **oddly ~** ... ... lo que, por extraño que parezca ...

enquire [ɪnˈkwaɪə*] vt, vi = **inquire**

enrage [ɪnˈreɪdʒ] vt enfurecer

enrol [ɪnˈrəʊl] (US **enroll**) vt (members) inscribir; (SCOL) matricular ♦ vi inscribirse; matricularse; ~**ment** (US **enrollment**) n inscripción f; matriculación f

en route [ɔnˈruːt] adv durante el viaje

en suite [ɔnˈswiːt] adj: **with ~ bathroom** con baño

ensure [ɪnˈʃʊə*] vt asegurar

entail [ɪnˈteɪl] vt suponer

entangled [ɪnˈtæŋɡld] adj: **to become ~ (in)** quedarse enredado (en) or enmarañado (en)

enter [ˈɛntə*] vt (room) entrar en; (club) hacerse socio de; (army) alistarse en; (sb for a competition) inscribir; (write down) anotar, apuntar; (COMPUT) meter ♦ vi entrar; ~ **for** vt fus presentarse para; ~ **into** vt fus (discussion etc) entablar; (agreement) llegar a, firmar

enterprise [ˈɛntəpraɪz] n empresa; (spirit) iniciativa; **free ~** la libre empresa; **private ~** la iniciativa privada; **enterprising** adj emprendedor(a)

entertain [ɛntəˈteɪn] vt (amuse) divertir; (invite: guest) invitar (a casa); (idea) abrigar; ~**er** n artista m/f; ~**ing** adj divertido, entretenido; ~**ment** n (amusement) diversión f; (show) espectáculo

enthralled [ɪnˈθrɔːld] adj encantado

enthusiasm [ɪnˈθuːzɪæzəm] n entusiasmo

enthusiast [ɪnˈθuːzɪæst] n entusiasta m/f; ~**ic** [-ˈæstɪk] adj entusiasta; **to be ~ic about** entusiasmarse por

entire [ɪnˈtaɪə*] adj entero; ~**ly** adv totalmente, todo; ~**ty** [ɪnˈtaɪərətɪ] n: **in its ~ty** en su totalidad

entitle [ɪnˈtaɪtl] vt: **to ~ sb to sth** dar a

uno derecho a algo; **~d** *adj* (*book*) titulado; **to be ~d to do** tener derecho a hacer

ntrance [*n* 'entrəns, *vb* ɪn'trɑːns] *n* entrada ♦ *vt* encantar, hechizar; **to gain ~ to** (*university etc*) ingresar en; **~ examination** *n* examen *m* de ingreso; **~ fee** *n* cuota; **~ ramp** (*US*) *n* (*AUT*) rampa de acceso

ntrant ['entrənt] *n* (*in race, competition*) participante *m/f*; (*in examination*) candidato/a

ntrenched [en'trentʃd] *adj* inamovible

ntrepreneur [ɔntrəprə'nəː*] *n* empresario

ntrust [ɪn'trʌst] *vt*: **to ~ sth to sb** confiar algo a uno

ntry ['entrɪ] *n* entrada; (*in competition*) participación *f*; (*in register*) apunte *m*; (*in account*) partida; (*in reference book*) artículo; **"no ~"** "prohibido el paso"; (*AUT*) "dirección prohibida"; **~ form** *n* hoja de inscripción; **~ phone** *n* portero automático

nvelop [ɪn'veləp] *vt* envolver

nvelope ['envələup] *n* sobre *m*

nvious ['envɪəs] *adj* envidioso; (*look*) de envidia

nvironment [ɪn'vaɪərnmənt] *n* (*surroundings*) entorno; (*natural world*): **the ~** el medio ambiente; **~al** [-'mentl] *adj* ambiental; medioambiental; **~-friendly** *adj* no perjudicial para el medio ambiente

nvisage [ɪn'vɪzɪdʒ] *vt* prever

nvoy ['envɔɪ] *n* enviado

nvy ['envɪ] *n* envidia ♦ *vt* tener envidia a; **to ~ sb sth** envidiar algo a uno

pic ['epɪk] *n* épica ♦ *adj* épico

pidemic [epɪ'demɪk] *n* epidemia

pilepsy ['epɪlepsɪ] *n* epilepsia

pisode ['epɪsəud] *n* episodio

pitomize [ɪ'pɪtəmaɪz] *vt* epitomar, resumir

qual ['iːkwl] *adj* igual; (*treatment*) equitativo ♦ *n* igual *m/f* ♦ *vt* ser igual a; (*fig*) igualar; **to be ~ to** (*task*) estar a la altura de; **~ity** [iː'kwɔlɪtɪ] *n* igualdad *f*;

~ize *vi* (*SPORT*) empatar; **~ly** *adv* igualmente; (*share etc*) a partes iguales

equate [ɪ'kweɪt] *vt*: **to ~ sth with** equiparar algo con; **equation** [ɪ'kweɪʒən] *n* (*MATH*) ecuación *f*

equator [ɪ'kweɪtə*] *n* ecuador *m*

equilibrium [iːkwɪ'lɪbrɪəm] *n* equilibrio

equip [ɪ'kwɪp] *vt* equipar; (*person*) proveer; **to be well ~ped** estar bien equipado; **~ment** *n* equipo; (*tools*) avíos *mpl*

equities ['ekwɪtɪz] (*BRIT*) *npl* (*COMM*) derechos *mpl* sobre *or* en el activo

equivalent [ɪ'kwɪvələnt] *adj*: **~ (to)** equivalente (a) ♦ *n* equivalente *m*

era ['ɪərə] *n* era, época

eradicate [ɪ'rædɪkeɪt] *vt* erradicar

erase [ɪ'reɪz] *vt* borrar; **~r** *n* goma de borrar

erect [ɪ'rekt] *adj* erguido ♦ *vt* erigir, levantar; (*assemble*) montar; **~ion** [-ʃən] *n* construcción *f*; (*assembly*) montaje *m*; (*PHYSIOL*) erección *f*

ERM *n abbr* (= *Exchange Rate Mechanism*) tipo de cambio europeo

erode [ɪ'rəud] *vt* (*GEO*) erosionar; (*metal*) corroer, desgastar; (*fig*) desgastar

erotic [ɪ'rɔtɪk] *adj* erótico

errand ['ernd] *n* recado (*SP*), mandado (*AM*)

erratic [ɪ'rætɪk] *adj* desigual, poco uniforme

error ['erə*] *n* error *m*, equivocación *f*

erupt [ɪ'rʌpt] *vi* entrar en erupción; (*fig*) estallar; **~ion** [ɪ'rʌpʃən] *n* erupción *f*; (*of war*) estallido

escalate ['eskəleɪt] *vi* extenderse, intensificarse

escalator ['eskəleɪtə*] *n* escalera móvil

escapade [eskə'peɪd] *n* travesura

escape [ɪ'skeɪp] *n* fuga ♦ *vi* escaparse; (*flee*) huir, evadirse; (*leak*) fugarse ♦ *vt* (*responsibility etc*) evitar, eludir; (*consequences*) escapar a; (*elude*): **his name ~s me** no me sale su nombre; **to ~ from** (*place*) escaparse de; (*person*) escaparse a

escort [*n* 'eskɔːt, *vb* ɪ'skɔːt] *n* acompañante

m/f; (MIL) escolta ♦ *vt* acompañar
Eskimo ['eskɪməu] *n* esquimal *m/f*
especially [ɪ'speʃlɪ] *adv* (*above all*) sobre todo; (*particularly*) en particular, especialmente
espionage ['espɪənɑːʒ] *n* espionaje *m*
esplanade [espla'neɪd] *n* (*by sea*) paseo marítimo
Esquire [ɪ'skwaɪə] (*abbr* **Esq.**) *n*: **J. Brown, ~** Sr. D. J. Brown
essay ['eseɪ] *n* (LITERATURE) ensayo; (SCOL: *short*) redacción *f*; (: *long*) trabajo
essence ['esns] *n* esencia
essential [ɪ'senʃl] *adj* (*necessary*) imprescindible; (*basic*) esencial; **~s** *npl* lo imprescindible, lo esencial; **~ly** *adv* esencialmente
establish [ɪ'stæblɪʃ] *vt* establecer; (*prove*) demostrar; (*relations*) entablar; (*reputation*) ganarse; **~ed** *adj* (*business*) conocido; (*practice*) arraigado; **~ment** *n* establecimiento; **the E~ment** la clase dirigente
estate [ɪ'steɪt] *n* (*land*) finca, hacienda; (*inheritance*) herencia; (BRIT: *also*: **housing ~**) urbanización *f*; **~ agent** (BRIT) *n* agente *m/f* inmobiliario/a; **~ car** (BRIT) *n* furgoneta
esteem [ɪ'stiːm] *n*: **to hold sb in high ~** estimar en mucho a uno
esthetic [ɪs'θetɪk] (US) *adj* = **aesthetic**
estimate [*n* 'estɪmət, *vb* 'estɪmeɪt] *n* estimación *f*, apreciación *f*; (*assessment*) tasa, cálculo; (COMM) presupuesto ♦ *vt* estimar, tasar; calcular; **estimation** [-'meɪʃən] *n* opinión *f*, juicio; cálculo
estranged [ɪ'streɪndʒd] *adj* separado
estuary ['estjuərɪ] *n* estuario, ría
etc *abbr* (= *et cetera*) etc
eternal [ɪ'tɜːnl] *adj* eterno
eternity [ɪ'tɜːnɪtɪ] *n* eternidad *f*
ethical ['eθɪkl] *adj* ético; **ethics** ['eθɪks] *n* ética ♦ *npl* moralidad *f*
Ethiopia [iːθɪ'əupɪə] *n* Etiopia
ethnic ['eθnɪk] *adj* étnico; **~ minority** *n* minoría étnica
ethos ['iːθɒs] *n* genio, carácter *m*

etiquette ['etɪket] *n* etiqueta
EU *n abbr* (= *European Union*) UE *f*
euro ['juərəu] *n* euro
Eurocheque ['juərəutʃek] *n* Eurocheque *m*
Euroland [juərəulænd] *n* Eurolandia
Europe ['juərəp] *n* Europa; **~an** [-'piːən] *adj*, *n* europeo/a *m/f*; **~an Community** *n* Comunidad *f* Europea; **~an Union** *n* Unión *f* Europea
evacuate [ɪ'vækjueɪt] *vt* (*people*) evacuar; (*place*) desocupar
evade [ɪ'veɪd] *vt* evadir, eludir
evaporate [ɪ'væpəreɪt] *vi* evaporarse; (*fig*) desvanecerse; **~d milk** *n* leche *f* evaporada
evasion [ɪ'veɪʒən] *n* evasión *f*
eve [iːv] *n*: **on the ~ of** en vísperas de
even ['iːvn] *adj* (*level*) llano; (*smooth*) liso; (*speed, temperature*) uniforme; (*number*) par ♦ *adv* hasta, incluso; (*introducing a comparison*) aún, todavía; **~ if, ~ though** aunque *+sub*; **~ more** aun más; **~ so** aun así; **not ~** ni siquiera; **~ he was there** hasta él estuvo allí; **~ on Sundays** incluso los domingos; **to get ~ with sb** ajustar cuentas con uno
evening ['iːvnɪŋ] *n* tarde *f*; (*late*) noche *f*; **in the ~** por la tarde; **~ class** *n* clase *f* nocturna; **~ dress** *n* (*no pl: formal clothes*) traje *m* de etiqueta; (*woman's*) traje *m* de noche
event [ɪ'vent] *n* suceso, acontecimiento; (SPORT) prueba; **in the ~ of** en caso de; **~ful** *adj* (*life*) activo; (*day*) ajetreado
eventual [ɪ'ventʃuəl] *adj* final; **~ity** [-'ælɪtɪ] *n* eventualidad *f*; **~ly** *adv* (*finally*) finalmente; (*in time*) con el tiempo
ever ['evə] *adv* (*at any time*) nunca, jamás; (*at all times*) siempre; (*in question*): **why ~ not?** ¿y por qué no?; **the best ~** lo nunca visto; **have you ~ seen it?** ¿lo ha visto usted alguna vez?; **better than ~** mejor que nunca; **~ since** *adv* desde entonces ♦ *conj* después de que; **~green** *n* árbol *m* de hoja perenne; **~lasting** *adj* eterno, perpetuo

KEYWORD

every ['evrɪ] *adj* **1** (*each*) cada; **~ one of them** (*persons*) todos ellos/as; (*objects*) cada uno de ellos/as; **~ shop in the town was closed** todas las tiendas de la ciudad estaban cerradas
2 (*all possible*) todo/a; **I gave you ~ assistance** te di toda la ayuda posible; **I have ~ confidence in him** tiene toda mi confianza; **we wish you ~ success** te deseamos toda suerte de éxitos
3 (*showing recurrence*) todo/a; **~ day/ week** todos los días/todas las semanas; **~ other car had been broken into** habían forzado uno de cada dos coches; **she visits me ~ other/third day** me visita cada dos/tres días; **~ now and then** de vez en cuando

every: **~body** *pron* = **everyone**; **~day** *adj* (*daily*) cotidiano, de todos los días; (*usual*) acostumbrado; **~one** *pron* todos/ as, todo el mundo; **~thing** *pron* todo; **this shop sells ~thing** esta tienda vende de todo; **~where** *adv*: **I've been looking for you ~where** te he estado buscando por todas partes; **~where you go you meet ...** en todas partes encuentras ...

evict [ɪ'vɪkt] *vt* desahuciar; **~ion** [ɪ'vɪkʃən] *n* desahucio

evidence ['evɪdəns] *n* (*proof*) prueba; (*of witness*) testimonio; (*sign*) indicios *mpl*; **to give ~** prestar declaración, dar testimonio

evident ['evɪdənt] *adj* evidente, manifiesto; **~ly** *adv* por lo visto

evil ['iːvl] *adj* malo; (*influence*) funesto ♦ *n* mal *m*

evoke [ɪ'vəuk] *vt* evocar

evolution [iːvə'luːʃən] *n* evolución *f*

evolve [ɪ'vɔlv] *vt* desarrollar ♦ *vi* evolucionar, desarrollarse

ewe [juː] *n* oveja

ex- [eks] *prefix* ex

exact [ɪg'zækt] *adj* exacto; (*person*) meticuloso ♦ *vt*: **to ~ sth (from)** exigir algo (de); **~ing** *adj* exigente; (*conditions*) arduo; **~ly** *adv* exactamente; (*indicating agreement*) exacto

exaggerate [ɪg'zædʒəreɪt] *vt*, *vi* exagerar; **exaggeration** [-'reɪʃən] *n* exageración *f*

exalted [ɪg'zɔːltɪd] *adj* eminente

exam [ɪg'zæm] *n abbr* (SCOL) = **examination**

examination [ɪgzæmɪ'neɪʃən] *n* examen *m*; (MED) reconocimiento

examine [ɪg'zæmɪn] *vt* examinar; (*inspect*) inspeccionar, escudriñar; (MED) reconocer; **~r** *n* examinador(a) *m/f*

example [ɪg'zɑːmpl] *n* ejemplo; **for ~** por ejemplo

exasperate [ɪg'zɑːspəreɪt] *vt* exasperar, irritar; **exasperation** [-ʃən] *n* exasperación *f*, irritación *f*

excavate ['ekskəveɪt] *vt* excavar

exceed [ɪk'siːd] *vt* (*amount*) exceder; (*number*) pasar de; (*speed limit*) sobrepasar; (*powers*) excederse en; (*hopes*) superar; **~ingly** *adv* sumamente, sobremanera

excellent ['eksələnt] *adj* excelente

except [ɪk'sept] *prep* (*also*: **~ for, ~ing**) excepto, salvo ♦ *vt* exceptuar, excluir; **~ if/when** excepto si/cuando; **~ that** salvo que; **~ion** [ɪk'sepʃən] *n* excepción *f*; **to take ~ion to** ofenderse por; **~ional** [ɪk'sepʃənl] *adj* excepcional

excerpt ['eksɜːpt] *n* extracto

excess [ɪk'ses] *n* exceso; **~es** *npl* (*of cruelty etc*) atrocidades *fpl*; **~ baggage** *n* exceso de equipaje; **~ fare** *n* suplemento; **~ive** *adj* excesivo

exchange [ɪks'tʃeɪndʒ] *n* intercambio; (*conversation*) diálogo; (*also*: **telephone ~**) central *f* (telefónica) ♦ *vt*: **to ~ (for)** cambiar (por); **~ rate** *n* tipo de cambio

exchequer [ɪks'tʃekə*] (BRIT) *n*: **the E~** la Hacienda del Fisco

excise ['eksaɪz] *n* impuestos *mpl* sobre el alcohol y el tabaco

excite [ɪk'saɪt] *vt* (*stimulate*) estimular; (*arouse*) excitar; **~d** *adj*: **to get ~d** emocionarse; **~ment** *n* (*agitation*)

excitación *f*; (*exhilaration*) emoción *f*;
exciting *adj* emocionante
exclaim [ɪkˈskleɪm] *vi* exclamar;
exclamation [ɛkskləˈmeɪʃən] *n*
exclamación *f*; **exclamation mark** *n*
punto de admiración
exclude [ɪkˈskluːd] *vt* excluir; exceptuar
exclusive [ɪkˈskluːsɪv] *adj* exclusivo; (*club,
district*) selecto; **~ of tax** excluyendo
impuestos; **~ly** *adv* únicamente
excruciating [ɪkˈskruːʃieɪtɪŋ] *adj* (*pain*)
agudísimo, atroz; (*noise, embarrassment*)
horrible
excursion [ɪkˈskəːʃən] *n* (*tourist ~*)
excursión *f*
excuse [*n* ɪkˈskjuːs, *vb* ɪkˈskjuːz] *n* disculpa,
excusa; (*pretext*) pretexto ♦ *vt* (*justify*)
justificar; (*forgive*) disculpar, perdonar; **to
~ sb from doing sth** dispensar a uno de
hacer algo; **~ me!** (*attracting attention*)
¡por favor!; (*apologizing*) ¡perdón!; **if you
will ~ me** con su permiso
ex-directory [ˈɛksdɪˈrektərɪ] (*BRIT*) *adj* que
no consta en la guía
execute [ˈɛksɪkjuːt] *vt* (*plan*) realizar;
(*order*) cumplir; (*person*) ajusticiar,
ejecutar; **execution** [-ˈkjuːʃən] *n*
realización *f*; cumplimiento; ejecución *f*
executive [ɪgˈzɛkjutɪv] *n* (*person,
committee*) ejecutivo; (*POL: committee*)
poder *m* ejecutivo ♦ *adj* ejecutivo
exemplify [ɪgˈzɛmplɪfaɪ] *vt* ejemplificar;
(*illustrate*) ilustrar
exempt [ɪgˈzɛmpt] *adj*: **~ from** exento de
♦ *vt*: **to ~ sb from** eximir a uno de; **~ion**
[-ʃən] *n* exención *f*
exercise [ˈɛksəsaɪz] *n* ejercicio ♦ *vt*
(*patience*) usar de; (*right*) valerse de; (*dog*)
llevar de paseo; (*mind*) preocupar ♦ *vi*
(*also: to take ~*) hacer ejercicio(s); **~ bike**
n ciclostático ® *m*, bicicleta estática; **~
book** *n* cuaderno
exert [ɪgˈzəːt] *vt* ejercer; **to ~ o.s.**
esforzarse; **~ion** [-ʃən] *n* esfuerzo
exhale [ɛksˈheɪl] *vt* despedir ♦ *vi* exhalar
exhaust [ɪgˈzɔːst] *n* (*AUT: also:* **~ pipe**)
escape *m*; (: *fumes*) gases *mpl* de escape

♦ *vt* agotar; **~ed** *adj* agotado; **~ion**
[ɪgˈzɔːstʃən] *n* agotamiento; **nervous ~ion**
postración *f* nerviosa; **~ive** *adj*
exhaustivo
exhibit [ɪgˈzɪbɪt] *n* (*ART*) obra expuesta;
(*LAW*) objeto expuesto ♦ *vt* (*show:
emotions*) manifestar; (: *courage, skill*)
demostrar; (*paintings*) exponer; **~ion**
[ɛksɪˈbɪʃən] *n* exposición *f*; (*of talent etc*)
demostración *f*
exhilarating [ɪgˈzɪləreɪtɪŋ] *adj* estimulante,
tónico
exile [ˈɛksaɪl] *n* exilio; (*person*) exiliado/a
♦ *vt* desterrar, exiliar
exist [ɪgˈzɪst] *vi* existir; (*live*) vivir; **~ence** *n*
existencia; **~ing** *adj* existente, actual
exit [ˈɛksɪt] *n* salida ♦ *vi* (*THEATRE*) hacer
mutis; (*COMPUT*) salir (al sistema); **~ poll**
n encuesta a la salida de los colegios
electorales; **~ ramp** (*US*) *n* (*AUT*) vía de
acceso
exodus [ˈɛksədəs] *n* éxodo
exonerate [ɪgˈzɒnəreɪt] *vt*: **to ~ from**
exculpar de
exotic [ɪgˈzɒtɪk] *adj* exótico
expand [ɪkˈspænd] *vt* ampliar; (*number*)
aumentar ♦ *vi* (*population*) aumentar;
(*trade etc*) expandirse; (*gas, metal*)
dilatarse
expanse [ɪkˈspæns] *n* extensión *f*
expansion [ɪkˈspænʃən] *n* (*of population*)
aumento; (*of trade*) expansión *f*
expect [ɪkˈspekt] *vt* esperar; (*require*)
contar con; (*suppose*) suponer ♦ *vi*: **to be
~ing** (*pregnant woman*) estar embarazada;
~ancy *n* (*anticipation*) esperanza; **life
~ancy** esperanza de vida; **~ant mother**
n futura madre *f*; **~ation** [ɛkspekˈteɪʃən] *n*
(*hope*) esperanza; (*belief*) expectativa
expedient [ɪkˈspiːdɪənt] *adj* conveniente,
oportuno ♦ *n* recurso, expediente *m*
expedition [ɛkspəˈdɪʃən] *n* expedición *f*
expel [ɪkˈspel] *vt* arrojar; (*from place*)
expulsar
expend [ɪkˈspend] *vt* (*money*) gastar; (*time,
energy*) consumir; **~iture** *n* gastos *mpl*,
desembolso; consumo

expense [ɪk'spɛns] n gasto, gastos mpl; (high cost) costa; **~s** npl (COMM) gastos mpl; **at the ~ of** a costa de; **~ account** n cuenta de gastos

expensive [ɪk'spɛnsɪv] adj caro, costoso

experience [ɪk'spɪərɪəns] n experiencia ♦ vt experimentar; (suffer) sufrir; **~d** adj experimentado

experiment [ɪk'spɛrɪmənt] n experimento ♦ vi hacer experimentos

expert ['ɛkspə:t] adj experto, perito ♦ n experto/a, perito/a; (specialist) especialista m/f; **~ise** [-'ti:z] n pericia

expire [ɪk'spaɪə*] vi caducar, vencer; **expiry** n vencimiento

explain [ɪk'spleɪn] vt explicar; **explanation** [ɛksplə'neɪʃən] n explicación f; **explanatory** [ɪk'splænətrɪ] adj explicativo; aclaratorio

explicit [ɪk'splɪsɪt] adj explícito

explode [ɪk'spləud] vi estallar, explotar; (population) crecer rápidamente; (with anger) reventar

exploit [n 'ɛksplɔɪt, vb ɪk'splɔɪt] n hazaña ♦ vt explotar; **~ation** [-'teɪʃən] n explotación f

exploratory [ɪk'splɔrətrɪ] adj de exploración; (fig: talks) exploratorio, preliminar

explore [ɪk'splɔ:*] vt explorar; (fig) examinar; investigar; **~r** n explorador(a) m/f

explosion [ɪk'spləuʒən] n (also fig) explosión f; **explosive** [ɪks'pləusɪv] adj, n explosivo

exponent [ɪk'spəunənt] n (of theory etc) partidario/a; (of skill etc) exponente m/f

export [vb ɛk'spɔ:t, n 'ɛkspɔ:t] vt exportar ♦ n (process) exportación f; (product) producto de exportación ♦ cpd de exportación; **~er** n exportador m

expose [ɪk'spəuz] vt exponer; (unmask) desenmascarar; **~d** adj expuesto

exposure [ɪk'spəuʒə*] n exposición f; (publicity) publicidad f; (PHOT: speed) velocidad f de obturación; (: shot) fotografía f; **to die from ~** (MED) morir de frío; **~ meter** n fotómetro

express [ɪk'sprɛs] adj (definite) expreso, explícito; (BRIT: letter etc) urgente ♦ n (train) rápido ♦ vt expresar; **~ion** [ɪk'sprɛʃən] n expresión f; (of actor etc) sentimiento; **~ly** adv expresamente; **~way** (US) n (urban motorway) autopista

exquisite [ɛk'skwɪzɪt] adj exquisito

extend [ɪk'stɛnd] vt (visit, street) prolongar; (building) ampliar; (invitation) ofrecer ♦ vi (land) extenderse; (period of time) prolongarse

extension [ɪk'stɛnʃən] n extensión f; (building) ampliación f; (of time) prolongación f; (TEL: in private house) línea derivada; (: in office) extensión f

extensive [ɪk'stɛnsɪv] adj extenso; (damage) importante; (knowledge) amplio; **~ly** adv: **he's travelled ~ly** ha viajado por muchos países

extent [ɪk'stɛnt] n (breadth) extensión f; (scope) alcance m; **to some ~** hasta cierto punto; **to the ~ of...** hasta el punto de...; **to such an ~ that...** hasta tal punto que...; **to what ~?** ¿hasta qué punto?

extenuating [ɪk'stɛnjueɪtɪŋ] adj: **~ circumstances** circunstancias fpl atenuantes

exterior [ɛk'stɪərɪə*] adj exterior, externo ♦ n exterior m

external [ɛk'stə:nl] adj externo

extinct [ɪk'stɪŋkt] adj (volcano) extinguido; (race) extinto

extinguish [ɪk'stɪŋgwɪʃ] vt extinguir, apagar; **~er** n extintor m

extort [ɪk'stɔ:t] vt obtener por fuerza; **~ionate** adj excesivo, exorbitante

extra ['ɛkstrə] adj adicional ♦ adv (in addition) de más ♦ n (luxury, addition) extra m; (CINEMA, THEATRE) extra m/f, comparsa m/f

extra... ['ɛkstrə] prefix extra...

extract [vb ɪk'strækt, n 'ɛkstrækt] vt sacar; (tooth) extraer; (money, promise) obtener ♦ n extracto

extracurricular [ɛkstrəkə'rɪkjulə*] adj extraescolar, extra-académico

extradite ['ekstrədaıt] vt extraditar
extra: **~marital** adj extramatrimonial;
 ~mural [ekstrə'mjuərl] adj extraescolar;
 ~ordinary [ık'strɔːdnrı] adj
 extraordinario; (odd) raro
extravagance [ık'strævəgəns] n derroche
 m, despilfarro; (thing bought)
 extravagancia
extravagant [ık'strævəgənt] adj (lavish:
 person) pródigo; (: gift) (demasiado) caro;
 (wasteful) despilfarrador(a)
extreme [ık'striːm] adj extremo,
 extremado ♦ n extremo; **~ly** adv
 sumamente, extremadamente
extricate ['ekstrikeıt] vt: **to ~ sth/sb from**
 librar algo/a uno de
extrovert ['ekstrəvɜːt] n extrovertido/a
eye [aı] n ojo ♦ vt mirar de soslayo, ojear;
 to keep an ~ on vigilar; **~bath** n ojera;
 ~brow n ceja; **~drops** npl gotas fpl
 para los ojos, colino; **~lash** n pestaña;
 ~lid n párpado; **~liner** n lápiz m de
 ojos; **~-opener** n revelación f, gran
 sorpresa; **~shadow** n sombreador m de
 ojos; **~sight** n vista; **~sore** n
 monstruosidad f; **~ witness** n testigo
 m/f presencial

F, f

F [ef] n (MUS) fa m
F. abbr = **Fahrenheit**
fable ['feıbl] n fábula
fabric ['fæbrık] n tejido, tela
fabulous ['fæbjuləs] adj fabuloso
façade [fə'sɑːd] n fachada
face [feıs] n (ANAT) cara, rostro; (of clock)
 esfera (SP), cara (AM); (of mountain) cara,
 ladera; (of building) fachada ♦ vt
 (direction) estar de cara a; (situation) hacer
 frente a; (facts) aceptar; **~ down** (person,
 card) boca abajo; **to lose ~**
 desprestigiarse; **to make** or **pull a ~** hacer
 muecas; **in the ~ of** (difficulties etc) ante;
 on the ~ of it a primera vista; **~ to ~** cara
 a cara; **~ up to** vt fus hacer frente a,

arrostrar; **~ cloth** (BRIT) n manopla; **~
cream** n crema (de belleza); **~ lift** n
 estirado facial; (of building) renovación f;
 ~ powder n polvos mpl; **~-saving** adj
 para salvar las apariencias; **~ value** n (of
 stamp) valor m nominal; **to take sth at ~
 value** (fig) tomar algo en sentido literal
facilities [fə'sılıtız] npl (buildings)
 instalaciones fpl; (equipment) servicios
 mpl; **credit ~** facilidades fpl de crédito
facing ['feısıŋ] prep frente a
facsimile [fæk'sımılı] n (replica) facsímil(e)
 m; (machine) telefax m; (fax) fax m
fact [fækt] n hecho; **in ~** en realidad
factor ['fæktə*] n factor m
factory ['fæktərı] n fábrica
factual ['fæktjuəl] adj basado en los
 hechos
faculty ['fækəltı] n facultad f; (US: teaching
 staff) personal m docente
fad [fæd] n novedad f, moda
fade [feıd] vi desteñirse; (sound, smile)
 desvanecerse; (light) apagarse; (flower)
 marchitarse; (hope, memory) perderse
fag [fæg] (BRIT: inf) n (cigarette) pitillo (SP),
 cigarro
fail [feıl] vt (candidate) suspender; (exam)
 no aprobar (SP), reprobar (AM); (subj:
 memory etc) fallar a ♦ vi suspender; (be
 unsuccessful) fracasar; (strength, brakes)
 fallar; (light) acabarse; **to ~ to do sth**
 (neglect) dejar de hacer algo; (be unable)
 no poder hacer algo; **without ~** sin falta;
 ~ing n falta, defecto ♦ prep a falta de;
 ~ure ['feıljə*] n fracaso; (person)
 fracasado/a; (mechanical etc) fallo
faint [feınt] adj débil; (recollection) vago;
 (mark) apenas visible ♦ n desmayo ♦ vi
 desmayarse; **to feel ~** estar mareado,
 marearse
fair [fɛə*] adj justo; (hair, person) rubio;
 (weather) bueno; (good enough) regular;
 (considerable) considerable ♦ adv (play)
 limpio ♦ n feria; (BRIT: funfair) parque m
 de atracciones; **~ly** adv (justly) con
 justicia; (quite) bastante; **~ness** n justicia,
 imparcialidad f; **~ play** n juego limpio

fairy ['fɛərɪ] n hada; ~ **tale** n cuento de hadas

faith [feɪθ] n fe f; (trust) confianza; (sect) religión f; ~**ful** adj (loyal: troops etc) leal; (spouse) fiel; (account) exacto; ~**fully** adv fielmente; **yours** ~**fully** (BRIT: in letters) le saluda atentamente

fake [feɪk] n (painting etc) falsificación f; (person) impostor(a) m/f ♦ adj falso ♦ vt fingir; (painting etc) falsificar

falcon ['fɔːlkən] n halcón m

fall [fɔːl] (pt fell, pp fallen) n caída; (in price etc) descenso; (US) otoño ♦ vi caer(se); (price) bajar, descender; ~**s** npl (water~) cascada, salto de agua; **to** ~ **flat** (on one's face) caerse (boca abajo); (plan) fracasar; (joke, story) no hacer gracia; ~ **back** vi retroceder; ~ **back on** vt fus (remedy etc) recurrir a; ~ **behind** vi quedarse atrás; ~ **down** vi (person) caerse; (building, hopes) derrumbarse; ~ **for** vt fus (trick) dejarse engañar por; (person) enamorarse de; ~ **in** vi (roof) hundirse; (MIL) alinearse; ~ **off** vi caerse; (diminish) disminuir; ~ **out** vi (friends etc) reñir; (hair, teeth) caerse; ~ **through** vi (plan, project) fracasar

fallacy ['fæləsɪ] n error m

fallen ['fɔːlən] pp of **fall**

fallout ['fɔːlaut] n lluvia radioactiva

fallow ['fæləu] adj en barbecho

false [fɔːls] adj falso; **under** ~ **pretences** con engaños; ~ **alarm** n falsa alarma; ~ **teeth** (BRIT) npl dentadura postiza

falter ['fɔːltə*] vi vacilar; (engine) fallar

fame [feɪm] n fama

familiar [fə'mɪlɪə*] adj conocido, familiar; (tone) de confianza; **to be** ~ **with** (subject) conocer (bien)

family ['fæmɪlɪ] n familia; ~ **business** n negocio familiar; ~ **doctor** n médico/a de cabecera

famine ['fæmɪn] n hambre f, hambruna

famished ['fæmɪʃt] adj hambriento

famous ['feɪməs] adj famoso, célebre; ~**ly** adv (get on) estupendamente

fan [fæn] n abanico; (ELEC) ventilador m; (of pop star) fan m/f; (SPORT) hincha m/f ♦ vt abanicar; (fire, quarrel) atizar

fanatic [fə'nætɪk] n fanático/a

fan belt n correa del ventilador

fanciful ['fænsɪful] adj (design, name) fantástico

fancy ['fænsɪ] n (whim) capricho, antojo; (imagination) imaginación f ♦ adj (luxury) lujoso, de lujo ♦ vt (feel like, want) tener ganas de; (imagine) imaginarse; (think) creer; **to take a** ~ **to sb** tomar cariño a uno; **he fancies her** (inf) le gusta (ella) mucho; ~ **dress** n disfraz m; ~**-dress ball** n baile m de disfraces

fanfare ['fænfɛə*] n fanfarria (de trompeta)

fang [fæŋ] n colmillo

fantastic [fæn'tæstɪk] adj (enormous) enorme; (strange, wonderful) fantástico

fantasy ['fæntəzɪ] n (dream) sueño; (unreality) fantasía

far [fɑː*] adj (distant) lejano ♦ adv lejos; (much, greatly) mucho; ~ **away**, ~ **off** (a lo) lejos; ~ **better** mucho mejor; ~ **from** lejos de; **by** ~ con mucho; **go as** ~ **as the farm** vaya hasta la granja; **as** ~ **as I know** que yo sepa; **how** ~? ¿hasta dónde?; (fig) ¿hasta qué punto?; ~**away** adj remoto; (look) distraído

farce [fɑːs] n farsa

fare [fɛə*] n (on trains, buses) precio (del billete); (in taxi: cost) tarifa; (food) comida; **half** ~ medio pasaje m; **full** ~ pasaje completo

Far East n: **the** ~ el Extremo Oriente

farewell [fɛə'wel] excl, n adiós m

farm [fɑːm] n granja (SP), finca (AM), estancia (AM) ♦ vt cultivar; ~**er** n granjero (SP), estanciero (AM); ~**hand** n peón m; ~**house** n granja, casa de hacienda (AM); ~**ing** n agricultura; (of crops) cultivo; (of animals) cría; ~**land** n tierra de cultivo; ~ **worker** n = ~**hand**; ~**yard** n corral m

far-reaching [fɑː'riːtʃɪŋ] adj (reform, effect) de gran alcance

fart [fɑːt] (infl) vi tirarse un pedo (!)

farther ['fɑːðə*] adv más lejos, más allá

farthest adj más lejano
farthest ['fɑːðɪst] *superlative of* **far**
fascinate ['fæsɪneɪt] vt fascinar;
  fascination [-'neɪʃən] n fascinación f
fascism ['fæʃɪzəm] n fascismo
fashion ['fæʃən] n moda; (~ *industry*)
  industria de la moda; (*manner*) manera
  ♦ vt formar; **in ~** a la moda; **out of ~**
  pasado de moda; (*manner*) ~able adj de moda; ~
  show n desfile m de modelos
fast [fɑːst] adj rápido; (*dye, colour*)
  resistente; (*clock*): **to be ~** estar
  adelantado ♦ adv rápidamente, de prisa;
  (*stuck, held*) firmemente ♦ n ayuno ♦ vi
  ayunar; **~ asleep** profundamente
  dormido
fasten ['fɑːsn] vt atar, sujetar; (*coat, belt*)
  abrochar ♦ vi atarse; abrocharse; ~er,
  ~ing n cierre m; (*of door etc*) cerrojo
fast food n comida rápida, platos mpl
  preparados
fastidious [fæs'tɪdɪəs] adj (*fussy*)
  quisquilloso
fat [fæt] adj gordo; (*book*) grueso; (*profit*)
  grande, pingüe ♦ n grasa; (*on person*)
  carnes fpl; (*lard*) manteca
fatal ['feɪtl] adj (*mistake*) fatal; (*injury*)
  mortal; ~ity [fə'tælɪtɪ] n (*road death etc*)
  víctima f; ~ly adv fatalmente; mortalmente
fate [feɪt] n destino; (*of person*) suerte f;
  ~ful adj fatídico
father ['fɑːðə*] n padre m; ~-in-law n
  suegro; ~ly adj paternal
fathom ['fæðəm] n braza ♦ vt (*mystery*)
  desentrañar; (*understand*) lograr
  comprender
fatigue [fə'tiːg] n fatiga, cansancio
fatten ['fætn] vt, vi engordar
fatty ['fætɪ] adj (*food*) graso ♦ n (*inf*)
  gordito/a, gordinflón/ona m/f
fatuous ['fætjuəs] adj fatuo, necio
faucet ['fɔːsɪt] (*US*) n grifo (*SP*), llave f (*AM*)
fault [fɔːlt] n (*blame*) culpa; (*defect: in
  person, machine*) defecto; (*GEO*) falla ♦ vt
  criticar; **it's my ~** es culpa mía; **to find ~
  with** criticar, poner peros a; **at ~** culpable;
  ~y adj defectuoso

fauna ['fɔːnə] n fauna
favour ['feɪvə*] (*US* favor) n favor m;
  (*approval*) aprobación f ♦ vt (*proposition*)
  estar a favor de, aprobar; (*assist*) ser
  propicio a; **to do sb a ~** hacer un favor a
  uno; **to find ~ with sb** caer en gracia a
  uno; **in ~ of** a favor de; ~able adj
  favorable; ~ite ['feɪvrɪt] adj, n favorito,
  preferido
fawn [fɔːn] n cervato ♦ adj (*also*: ~-
  coloured) color de cervato, leonado ♦ vi:
  to ~ (up)on adular
fax [fæks] n (*document*) fax m; (*machine*)
  telefax m ♦ vt mandar por telefax
FBI (*US*) n abbr (= *Federal Bureau of
  Investigation*) ≈ BIC f (*SP*)
fear [fɪə*] n miedo, temor m ♦ vt tener
  miedo de, temer; **for ~ of** por si; ~ful adj
  temeroso, miedoso; (*awful*) terrible;
  ~less adj audaz
feasible ['fiːzəbl] adj factible
feast [fiːst] n banquete m; (*REL: also*: ~
  day) fiesta ♦ vi festejar
feat [fiːt] n hazaña
feather ['feðə*] n pluma
feature ['fiːtʃə*] n característica; (*article*)
  artículo de fondo ♦ vt (*subj: film*)
  presentar ♦ vi: **to ~ in** tener un papel
  destacado en; ~s npl (*of face*) facciones
  fpl; ~ **film** n largometraje m
February ['februəri] n febrero
fed [fed] pt, pp of **feed**
federal ['fedərəl] adj federal
fed up [fed'ʌp] adj: **to be ~ (with)** estar
  harto (de)
fee [fiː] n pago; (*professional*) derechos
  mpl, honorarios mpl; (*of club*) cuota;
  school ~s matrícula
feeble ['fiːbl] adj débil; (*joke*) flojo
feed [fiːd] (*pt, pp* fed) n comida; (*of
  animal*) pienso; (*on printer*) dispositivo de
  alimentación ♦ vt alimentar; (*BRIT: baby:
  breast~*) dar el pecho a; (*animal*) dar de
  comer a; (*data, information*): **to ~ into**
  meter en; ~ **on** vt fus alimentarse de;
  ~back n reacción f, feedback m
feel [fiːl] (*pt, pp* felt) n (*sensation*)

sensación f; (sense of touch) tacto; (impression): **to have the ~ of** parecerse a ♦ vt tocar; (pain etc) sentir; (think, believe) creer; **to ~ hungry/cold** tener hambre/frío; **to ~ lonely/better** sentirse solo/mejor; **I don't ~ well** no me siento bien; **it ~s soft** es suave al tacto; **to ~ like** (want) tener ganas de; **~ about** or **around** vi tantear; **~er** n (of insect) antena; **~ing** n (physical) sensación f; (foreboding) presentimiento; (emotion) sentimiento

feet [fiːt] npl of **foot**

feign [feɪn] vt fingir

fell [fɛl] pt of **fall** ♦ vt (tree) talar

fellow ['fɛləʊ] n tipo, tío (SP); (comrade) compañero; (of learned society) socio/a ♦ cpd: **~ citizen** n conciudadano/a; **~ countryman** (irreg) n compatriota m; **~ men** npl semejantes mpl; **~ship** n compañerismo; (grant) beca

felony ['fɛlənɪ] n crimen m

felt [fɛlt] pt, pp of **feel** ♦ n fieltro; **~-tip pen** n rotulador m

female ['fiːmeɪl] n (pej: woman) mujer f, tía; (ZOOL) hembra ♦ adj femenino; hembra

feminine ['fɛmɪnɪn] adj femenino

feminist ['fɛmɪnɪst] n feminista

fence [fɛns] n valla, cerca ♦ vt (also: **~ in**) cercar ♦ vi (SPORT) hacer esgrima; **fencing** n esgrima

fend [fɛnd] vi: **to ~ for o.s.** valerse por sí mismo; **~ off** vt (attack) rechazar; (questions) evadir

fender ['fɛndə*] n guardafuego; (US: AUT) parachoques m inv

ferment [vb fə'mɛnt, n 'fɜːmɛnt] vi fermentar ♦ n (fig) agitación f

fern [fɜːn] n helecho

ferocious [fə'rəʊʃəs] adj feroz

ferret ['fɛrɪt] n hurón m

ferry ['fɛrɪ] n (small) barca (de pasaje), balsa; (large: also: **~boat**) transbordador m (SP), embarcadero (AM) ♦ vt transportar

fertile ['fɜːtaɪl] adj fértil; (BIOL) fecundo;

fertilize ['fɜːtɪlaɪz] vt (BIOL) fecundar; (AGR) abonar; **fertilizer** n abono

fester ['fɛstə*] vi ulcerarse

festival ['fɛstɪvəl] n (REL) fiesta; (ART, MUS) festival m

festive ['fɛstɪv] adj festivo; **the ~ season** (BRIT: Christmas) las Navidades

festivities [fɛs'tɪvɪtɪz] npl fiestas fpl

festoon [fɛs'tuːn] vt: **to ~ with** engalanar de

fetch [fɛtʃ] vt ir a buscar; (sell for) venderse por

fête [feɪt] n fiesta

fetus ['fiːtəs] (US) n = **foetus**

feud [fjuːd] n (hostility) enemistad f; (quarrel) disputa

fever ['fiːvə*] n fiebre f; **~ish** adj febril

few [fjuː] adj (not many) pocos ♦ pron pocos; algunos; **a ~** adj unos pocos, algunos ♦ pron algunos; **~er** adj menos; **~est** adj los/las menos

fiancé [fɪ'ɑ̃ːŋseɪ] n novio, prometido; **~e** n novia, prometida

fib [fɪb] n mentirilla

fibre ['faɪbə*] (US **fiber**) n fibra; **~glass (Fiberglass** ® US) n fibra de vidrio

fickle ['fɪkl] adj inconstante

fiction ['fɪkʃən] n ficción f; **~al** adj novelesco; **fictitious** [fɪk'tɪʃəs] adj ficticio

fiddle ['fɪdl] n (MUS) violín m; (cheating) trampa ♦ vt (BRIT: accounts) falsificar; **~ with** vt fus juguetear con

fidget ['fɪdʒɪt] vi enredar; **stop ~ing!** ¡estáte quieto!

field [fiːld] n campo; (fig) campo, esfera; (SPORT) campo, cancha (AM); **~ marshal** n mariscal m; **~work** n trabajo de campo

fiend [fiːnd] n demonio

fierce [fɪəs] adj feroz; (wind, heat) fuerte; (fighting, enemy) encarnizado

fiery ['faɪərɪ] adj (burning) ardiente; (temperament) apasionado

fifteen [fɪf'tiːn] num quince

fifth [fɪfθ] num quinto

fifty ['fɪftɪ] num cincuenta; **~-~** adj (deal, split) a medias ♦ adv a medias, mitad por mitad

fig [fɪg] n higo
fight [faɪt] (pt, pp fought) n (gen) pelea; (MIL) combate m; (struggle) lucha ♦ vt luchar contra; (cancer, alcoholism) combatir; (election) intentar ganar; (emotion) resistir ♦ vi pelear, luchar; **~er** n combatiente m/f; (plane) caza m; **~ing** n combate m, pelea
figment ['fɪgmənt] n: **a ~ of the imagination** una quimera
figurative ['fɪgjʊrətɪv] adj (meaning) figurado; (style) figurativo
figure ['fɪgə*] n (DRAWING, GEOM) figura, dibujo; (number, cipher) cifra; (body, outline) tipo; (personality) figura ♦ vt (esp US) imaginar ♦ vi (appear) figurar; **~ out** vt (work out) resolver; **~head** n (NAUT) mascarón m de proa; (pej: leader) figura decorativa; **~ of speech** n figura retórica
file [faɪl] n (tool) lima; (dossier) expediente m; (folder) carpeta; (COMPUT) fichero; (row) fila ♦ vt limar; (LAW: claim) presentar; (store) archivar; **~ in/out** vi entrar/salir en fila; **filing cabinet** n fichero, archivador m
fill [fɪl] vt (space): **to ~ (with)** llenar (de); (vacancy, need) cubrir ♦ n: **to eat one's ~** llenarse; **~ in** vt rellenar; **~ up** vt llenar (hasta el borde) ♦ vi (AUT) poner gasolina
fillet ['fɪlɪt] n filete m; **~ steak** n filete m de ternera
filling ['fɪlɪŋ] n (CULIN) relleno; (for tooth) empaste m; **~ station** n estación f de servicio
film [fɪlm] n película ♦ vt (scene) filmar ♦ vi rodar (una película); **~ star** n astro, estrella de cine
filter ['fɪltə*] n filtro ♦ vt filtrar; **~ lane** (BRIT) n carril m de selección; **~-tipped** adj con filtro
filth [fɪlθ] n suciedad f; **~y** adj sucio; (language) obsceno
fin [fɪn] n (gen) aleta
final ['faɪnl] adj (last) final, último; (definitive) definitivo, terminante ♦ n (BRIT: SPORT) final f; **~s** npl (SCOL) examen m

final; (US: SPORT) final f
finale [fɪ'nɑːlɪ] n final m
final: ~ist n (SPORT) finalista m/f; **~ize** vt concluir, completar; **~ly** adv (lastly) por último, finalmente; (eventually) por fin
finance [faɪ'næns] n (money) fondos mpl; **~s** npl finanzas fpl; (personal ~s) situación f económica ♦ vt financiar; **financial** [-'nænʃəl] adj financiero
find [faɪnd] (pt, pp found) vt encontrar, hallar; (come upon) descubrir ♦ n hallazgo; descubrimiento; **to ~ sb guilty** (LAW) declarar culpable a uno; **~ out** vt averiguar; (truth, secret) descubrir; **to ~ out about** (subject) informarse sobre; (by chance) enterarse de; **~ings** npl (LAW) veredicto, fallo; (of report) recomendaciones fpl
fine [faɪn] adj excelente; (thin) fino ♦ adv (well) bien ♦ n (LAW) multa ♦ vt (LAW) multar; **to be ~** (person) estar bien; (weather) hacer buen tiempo; **~ arts** npl bellas artes fpl
finery ['faɪnərɪ] n adornos mpl
finger ['fɪŋgə*] n dedo ♦ vt (touch) manosear; **little/index ~** (dedo) meñique m/índice m; **~nail** n uña; **~print** n huella dactilar; **~tip** n yema del dedo
finish ['fɪnɪʃ] n (end) fin m; (SPORT) meta; (polish etc) acabado ♦ vt, vi terminar; **to ~ doing sth** acabar de hacer algo; **to ~ third** llegar el tercero; **~ off** vt acabar, terminar; (kill) acabar con; **~ up** vt acabar, terminar ♦ vi ir a parar, terminar; **~ing line** n línea de llegada or meta
finite ['faɪnaɪt] adj finito; (verb) conjugado
Finland ['fɪnlənd] n Finlandia
Finn [fɪn] n finlandés/esa m/f; **~ish** adj finlandés/esa ♦ n (LING) finlandés m
fir [fəː*] n abeto
fire ['faɪə*] n fuego; (in hearth) lumbre f; (accidental) incendio; (heater) estufa ♦ vt (gun) disparar; (interest) despertar; (inf: dismiss) despedir ♦ vi (shoot) disparar; **on ~** ardiendo, en llamas; **~ alarm** n alarma de incendios; **~arm** n arma de fuego; **~ brigade** (US ~ **department**) n (cuerpo

de) bomberos *mpl*; ~ **engine** *n* coche *m* de bomberos; ~ **escape** *n* escalera de incendios; ~ **extinguisher** *n* extintor *m* (de incendios); **~guard** *n* rejilla de protección; **~man** (*irreg*) *n* bombero; **~place** *n* chimenea; **~side** *n*: **by the ~side** al lado de la chimenea; ~ **station** *n* parque *m* de bomberos; **~wood** *n* leña; **~works** *npl* fuegos *mpl* artificiales

firing squad ['faɪrɪŋ-] *n* pelotón *m* de ejecución

firm [fə:m] *adj* firme; (*look, voice*) resuelto ♦ *n* firma, empresa; **~ly** *adv* firmemente; resueltamente

first [fə:st] *adj* primero ♦ *adv* (*before others*) primero; (*when listing reasons etc*) en primer lugar, primeramente ♦ *n* (*person: in race*) primero/a; (*AUT*) primera; (*BRIT: SCOL*) título de licenciado con calificación de sobresaliente; **at ~** al principio; **~ of all** ante todo; **~ aid** *n* primera ayuda, primeros auxilios *mpl*; **~-aid kit** *n* botiquín *m*; **~-class** *adj* (*excellent*) de primera (categoría); (*ticket etc*) de primera clase; **~-hand** *adj* de primera mano; **F~ Lady** (*esp US*) *n* primera dama; **~ly** *adv* en primer lugar; ~ **name** *n* nombre *m* (de pila); **~-rate** *adj* estupendo

fish [fɪʃ] *n inv* pez *m*; (*food*) pescado ♦ *vt, vi* pescar; **to go ~ing** ir de pesca; **~erman** (*irreg*) *n* pescador *m*; ~ **farm** *n* criadero de peces; ~ **fingers** (*BRIT*) *npl* croquetas *fpl* de pescado; **~ing boat** *n* barca de pesca; **~ing line** *n* sedal *m*; **~ing rod** *n* caña (de pescar); **~monger's (shop)** (*BRIT*) *n* pescadería; ~ **sticks** (*US*) *npl* = ~ **fingers**; **~y** (*inf*) *adj* sospechoso

fist [fɪst] *n* puño

fit [fɪt] *adj* (*healthy*) en (buena) forma; (*proper*) adecuado, apropiado ♦ *vt* (*subj: clothes*) estar *or* sentar bien a; (*instal*) poner; (*equip*) proveer, dotar; (*facts*) cuadrar *or* corresponder con ♦ *vi* (*clothes*) sentar bien; (*in space, gap*) caber; (*facts*) coincidir ♦ *n* (*MED*) ataque *m*; ~ **to** (*ready*)

a punto de; ~ **for** apropiado para; **a ~ of anger/pride** un arranque de cólera/ orgullo; **this dress is a good ~** este vestido me sienta bien; **by ~s and starts** a rachas; ~ **in** *vi* (*fig: person*) llevarse bien (con todos); **~ful** *adj* espasmódico, intermitente; **~ment** *n* módulo adosable; **~ness** *n* (*MED*) salud *f*; **~ted carpet** *n* moqueta; **~ted kitchen** *n* cocina amueblada; **~ter** *n* ajustador *m*; **~ting** *adj* apropiado ♦ *n* (*of dress*) prueba; (*of piece of equipment*) instalación *f*; **~ting room** *n* probador *m*; **~tings** *npl* instalaciones *fpl*

five [faɪv] *num* cinco; **~r** (*inf*) *n* (*BRIT*) billete *m* de cinco libras; (*US*) billete *m* de cinco dólares

fix [fɪks] *vt* (*secure*) fijar, asegurar; (*mend*) arreglar; (*prepare*) preparar ♦ *n*: **to be in a ~** estar en un aprieto; ~ **up** *vt* (*meeting*) arreglar; **to ~ sb up with sth** proveer a uno de algo; **~ation** [fɪk'seɪʃən] *n* obsesión *f*; **~ed** *adj* (*prices etc*) fijo; **~ture** *n* (*SPORT*) encuentro; **~tures** *npl* (*cupboards etc*) instalaciones *fpl* fijas

fizzy ['fɪzɪ] *adj* (*drink*) gaseoso

fjord [fjɔ:d] *n* fiordo

flabbergasted ['flæbəga:stɪd] *adj* pasmado, alucinado

flabby ['flæbɪ] *adj* gordo

flag [flæg] *n* bandera; (*stone*) losa ♦ *vi* decaer; **to ~ sb down** hacer señas a uno para que se pare; **~pole** *n* asta de bandera; **~ship** *n* buque *m* insignia; (*fig*) bandera

flair [fleə*] *n* aptitud *f* especial

flak [flæk] *n* (*MIL*) fuego antiaéreo; (*inf: criticism*) lluvia de críticas

flake [fleɪk] *n* (*of rust, paint*) escama; (*of snow, soap powder*) copo ♦ *vi* (*also:* ~ **off**) desconcharse

flamboyant [flæm'bɔɪənt] *adj* (*dress*) vistoso; (*person*) extravagante

flame [fleɪm] *n* llama

flamingo [flə'mɪŋɡəʊ] *n* flamenco

flammable ['flæməbl] *adj* inflamable

flan [flæn] (*BRIT*) *n* tarta

flank [flæŋk] n (of animal) ijar m; (of army) flanco ♦ vt flanquear

flannel ['flænl] n (BRIT: also: **face ~**) manopla; (fabric) franela

flap [flæp] n (of pocket, envelope) solapa ♦ vt (wings, arms) agitar ♦ vi (sail, flag) ondear

flare [flɛə*] n llamarada; (MIL) bengala; (in skirt etc) vuelo; ~ **up** vi encenderse; (fig: person) encolerizarse; (: revolt) estallar

flash [flæʃ] n relámpago; (also: **news ~**) noticias fpl de última hora; (PHOT) flash m ♦ vt (light, headlights) lanzar un destello con; (news, message) transmitir; (smile) lanzar ♦ vi brillar; (hazard light etc) lanzar destellos; **in a ~** en un instante; **he ~ed by** or **past** pasó como un rayo; **~back** n (CINEMA) flashback m; **~bulb** n bombilla fusible; **~ cube** n cubo de flash; **~light** n linterna

flashy ['flæʃi] (pej) adj ostentoso

flask [flɑːsk] n frasco; (also: **vacuum ~**) termo

flat [flæt] adj llano; (smooth) liso; (tyre) desinflado; (battery) descargado; (beer) muerto; (refusal etc) rotundo; (MUS) desafinado; (rate) fijo ♦ n (BRIT: apartment) piso (SP), departamento (AM), apartamento; (AUT) pinchazo; (MUS) bemol m; **to work ~ out** trabajar a toda mecha; **~ly** adv terminantemente, de plano; **~ten** vt (also: **~ten out**) allanar; (smooth out) alisar; (building, plants) arrasar

flatter ['flætə*] vt adular, halagar; **~ing** adj halagüeño; (dress) que favorece; **~y** n adulación f

flaunt [flɔːnt] vt ostentar, lucir

flavour ['fleɪvə*] (US **flavor**) n sabor m, gusto ♦ vt sazonar, condimentar; **strawberry-~ed** con sabor a fresa; **~ing** n (in product) aromatizante m

flaw [flɔː] n defecto; **~less** adj impecable

flax [flæks] n lino

flea [fliː] n pulga

fleck [flɛk] n (mark) mota

flee [fliː] (pt, pp **fled**) vt huir de ♦ vi huir,

fugarse

fleece [fliːs] n vellón m; (wool) lana ♦ vt (inf) desplumar

fleet [fliːt] n flota; (of lorries etc) escuadra

fleeting ['fliːtɪŋ] adj fugaz

Flemish ['flɛmɪʃ] adj flamenco

flesh [flɛʃ] n carne f; (skin) piel f; (of fruit) pulpa; **~ wound** n herida superficial

flew [fluː] pt of **fly**

flex [flɛks] n cordón m ♦ vt (muscles) tensar; **~ible** adj flexible

flick [flɪk] n capirotazo; chasquido ♦ vt (with hand) dar un capirotazo a; (whip etc) chasquear; (switch) accionar; **~ through** vt fus hojear

flicker ['flɪkə*] vi (light) parpadear; (flame) vacilar

flier ['flaɪə*] n aviador(a) m/f

flight [flaɪt] n vuelo; (escape) huida, fuga; (also: **~ of steps**) tramo (de escaleras); **~ attendant** (US) n camarero/azafata; **~ deck** n (AVIAT) cabina de mandos; (NAUT) cubierta de aterrizaje

flimsy ['flɪmzi] adj (thin) muy ligero; (building) endeble; (excuse) flojo

flinch [flɪntʃ] vi encogerse; **to ~ from** retroceder ante

fling [flɪŋ] (pt, pp **flung**) vt arrojar

flint [flɪnt] n pedernal m; (in lighter) piedra

flip [flɪp] vt dar la vuelta a; (switch: turn on) encender; (: turn off) apagar; (coin) echar a cara o cruz

flippant ['flɪpənt] adj poco serio

flipper ['flɪpə*] n aleta

flirt [flɜːt] vi coquetear, flirtear ♦ n coqueta

float [fləʊt] n flotador m; (in procession) carroza; (money) reserva ♦ vi flotar; (swimmer) hacer la plancha

flock [flɒk] n (of sheep) rebaño; (of birds) bandada ♦ vi: **to ~ to** acudir en tropel a

flog [flɒg] vt azotar

flood [flʌd] n inundación f; (of letters, imports etc) avalancha ♦ vt inundar ♦ vi (place) inundarse; (people): **to ~ into** inundar; **~ing** n inundaciones fpl; **~light** n foco

floor [flɔː*] n suelo; (storey) piso; (of sea)

fondo ♦ vt (subj: question) dejar sin respuesta; (: blow) derribar; **ground ~**, **first ~** (US) planta baja; **first ~, second ~** (US) primer piso; **~board** n tabla; **~ show** n cabaret m

flop [flɔp] n fracaso ♦ vi (fail) fracasar; (fall) derrumbarse; **~py** adj flojo ♦ n (COMPUT: also: **~py disk**) floppy m

flora [ˈflɔːrə] n flora

floral [ˈflɔːrl] adj (pattern) floreado

florid [ˈflɔrɪd] adj florido; (complexion) rubicundo

florist [ˈflɔrɪst] n florista m/f; **~'s (shop)** n florería

flounder [ˈflaundə*] vi (swimmer) patalear; (fig: economy) estar en dificultades ♦ n (ZOOL) platija

flour [ˈflauə*] n harina

flourish [ˈflʌrɪʃ] vi florecer ♦ n ademán m, movimiento (ostentado)

flout [flaut] vt burlarse de

flow [fləu] n (movement) flujo; (of traffic) circulación f; (tide) corriente f ♦ vi (river, blood) fluir; (traffic) circular; **~ chart** n organigrama m

flower [ˈflauə*] n flor f ♦ vi florecer; **~ bed** n macizo; **~pot** n tiesto; **~y** adj (fragrance) floral; (pattern) floreado; (speech) florido

flown [fləun] pp of **fly**

flu [fluː] n: **to have ~** tener la gripe

fluctuate [ˈflʌktjueɪt] vi fluctuar

fluent [ˈfluːənt] adj (linguist) que habla perfectamente; (speech) elocuente; **he speaks ~ French, he's ~ in French** domina el francés; **~ly** adv con fluidez

fluff [flʌf] n pelusa; **~y** adj de pelo suave

fluid [ˈfluːɪd] adj (movement) fluido, líquido; (situation) inestable ♦ n fluido, líquido

fluke [fluːk] (inf) n chiripa

flung [flʌŋ] pt, pp of **fling**

fluoride [ˈfluəraɪd] n fluoruro

flurry [ˈflʌrɪ] n (of snow) temporal m; **~ of activity** frenesí m de actividad

flush [flʌʃ] n rubor m; (fig: of youth etc) resplandor m ♦ vt limpiar con agua ♦ vi

ruborizarse ♦ adj: **~ with** a ras de; **to ~ the toilet** hacer funcionar la cisterna; **~ed** adj ruborizado

flustered [ˈflʌstəd] adj aturdido

flute [fluːt] n flauta

flutter [ˈflʌtə*] n (of wings) revoloteo, aleteo; **a ~ of panic/excitement** una oleada de pánico/excitación ♦ vi revolotear

flux [flʌks] n: **to be in a state of ~** estar continuamente cambiando

fly [flaɪ] (pt **flew**, pp **flown**) n mosca; (on trousers: also: **flies**) bragueta ♦ vt (plane) pilot(e)ar; (cargo) transportar (en avión); (distances) recorrer (en avión) ♦ vi volar; (passengers) ir en avión; (escape) evadirse; (flag) ondear; **~ away** or **off** vi emprender el vuelo; **~-drive** n: **~-drive holiday** vacaciones que incluyen vuelo y alquiler de coche; **~ing** n (activity) (el) volar; (action) vuelo ♦ adj: **~ing visit** visita relámpago; **with ~ing colours** con lucimiento; **~ing saucer** n platillo volante; **~ing start** n: **to get off to a ~ing start** empezar con buen pie; **~over** (BRIT) n paso a desnivel or superior; **~sheet** n (for tent) doble techo

foal [fəul] n potro

foam [fəum] n espuma ♦ vi hacer espuma; **~ rubber** n goma espuma

fob [fɔb] vt: **to ~ sb off with sth** despachar a uno con algo

focal point [ˈfəukl-] n (fig) centro de atención

focus [ˈfəukəs] (pl **~es**) n foco; (centre) centro ♦ vt (field glasses etc) enfocar ♦ vi: **to ~ (on)** enfocar (a); (issue etc) centrarse en; **in/out of ~** enfocado/desenfocado

fodder [ˈfɔdə*] n pienso

foetus [ˈfiːtəs] (US **fetus**) n feto

fog [fɔg] n niebla; **~gy** adj: **it's ~gy** hay niebla, está brumoso; **~ lamp** (US **~ light**) n (AUT) faro de niebla

foil [fɔɪl] vt frustrar ♦ n hoja; (kitchen ~) papel m (de) aluminio; (complement) complemento; (FENCING) florete m

fold [fəuld] n (bend, crease) pliegue m;

(*AGR*) redil *m* ♦ *vt* doblar; (*arms*) cruzar; ~ up *vi* plegarse, doblarse; (*business*) quebrar ♦ *vt* (*map etc*) plegar; ~er *n* (*for papers*) carpeta; (*COMPUT*) directorio; ~ing *adj* (*chair, bed*) plegable

foliage ['fəulɪdʒ] *n* follaje *m*

folk [fəuk] *npl* gente *f* ♦ *adj* popular, folklórico; ~s *npl* (*family*) familia *sg*, parientes *mpl*; ~lore ['fəuklɔ:ᵘ] *n* folklore *m*; ~ song *n* canción *f* popular *or* folklórica

follow ['fɒləu] *vt* seguir ♦ *vi* seguir; (*result*) resultar; **to ~ suit** hacer lo mismo; ~ up *vt* (*letter, offer*) responder a; (*case*) investigar; ~er *n* (*of person, belief*) partidario/a; ~ing *adj* siguiente ♦ *n* afición *f*, partidarios *mpl*

folly ['fɒlɪ] *n* locura

fond [fɒnd] *adj* (*memory, smile etc*) cariñoso; (*hopes*) ilusorio; **to be ~ of** tener cariño a; (*pastime, food*) ser aficionado a

fondle ['fɒndl] *vt* acariciar

font [fɒnt] *n* pila bautismal; (*TYP*) fundición *f*

food [fu:d] *n* comida; ~ mixer *n* batidora; ~ poisoning *n* intoxicación *f* alimenticia; ~ processor *n* robot *m* de cocina; ~stuffs *npl* comestibles *mpl*

fool [fu:l] *n* tonto/a; (*CULIN*) puré *m* de frutas con nata ♦ *vt* engañar ♦ *vi* (*gen*: ~ around*) bromear; ~hardy *adj* temerario; ~ish *adj* tonto; (*careless*) imprudente; ~proof *adj* (*plan etc*) infalible

foot [fut] (*pl* feet) *n* pie *m*; (*measure*) pie *m* (= 304 mm); (*of animal*) pata ♦ *vt* (*bill*) pagar; **on ~** a pie; ~age *n* (*CINEMA*) imágenes *fpl*; ~ball *n* balón *m*; (*game: BRIT*) fútbol *m*; (*: US*) fútbol *m* americano; ~ball player *n* (*BRIT: also:* ~baller) futbolista *m*; (*US*) jugador *m* de fútbol americano; ~brake *n* freno de pie; ~bridge *n* puente *m* para peatones; ~hills *npl* estribaciones *fpl*; ~hold *n* pie *m* firme; ~ing *n* (*fig*) posición *f*; **to lose one's ~ing** perder el pie; ~lights *npl* candilejas *fpl*; ~note *n* nota (al pie de la página); ~path *n* sendero; ~print *n*

huella, pisada; ~step *n* paso; ~wear *n* calzado

KEYWORD

for [fɔ:] *prep* **1** (*indicating destination, intention*) para; **the train ~ London** el tren con destino a *or* de Londres; **he left ~ Rome** marchó para Roma; **he went ~ the paper** fue por el periódico; **is this ~ me?** ¿es esto para mí?; **it's time ~ lunch** es la hora de comer

2 (*indicating purpose*) para; **what('s it) ~?** ¿para qué (es)?; **to pray ~ peace** rezar por la paz

3 (*on behalf of, representing*): **the MP ~ Hove** el diputado por Hove; **he works ~ the government/a local firm** trabaja para el gobierno/en una empresa local; **I'll ask him ~ you** se lo pediré por ti; **G ~ George** G de Gerona

4 (*because of*) por esta razón; ~ **fear of being criticized** por temor a ser criticado

5 (*with regard to*) para; **it's cold ~ July** hace frío para julio; **he has a gift ~ languages** tiene don de lenguas

6 (*in exchange for*) por; **I sold it ~ £5** lo vendí por £5; **to pay 50 pence ~ a ticket** pagar 50 peniques por un billete

7 (*in favour of*): **are you ~ or against us?** ¿estás con nosotros o contra nosotros?; **I'm all ~ it** estoy totalmente a favor; **vote ~ X** vote (a) X

8 (*referring to distance*): **there are roadworks ~ 5 km** hay obras en 5 km; **we walked ~ miles** caminamos kilómetros y kilómetros

9 (*referring to time*): **he was away ~ 2 years** estuvo fuera (durante) dos años; **it hasn't rained ~ 3 weeks** no ha llovido durante *or* en 3 semanas; **I have known her ~ years** la conozco desde hace años; **can you do it ~ tomorrow?** ¿lo podrás hacer para mañana?

10 (*with infinitive clauses*): **it is not ~ me to decide** la decisión no es cosa mía; **it would be best ~ you to leave** sería mejor que te fueras; **there is still time ~**

you to do it todavía te queda tiempo para hacerlo; ~ **this to be possible ...** para que esto sea posible ...
11 (*in spite of*) a pesar de; ~ **all his complaints** a pesar de sus quejas
♦ *conj* (*since, as: rather formal*) puesto que

forage ['fɒrɪdʒ] *vi* (*animal*) forrajear; (*person*): **to ~ for** hurgar en busca de
foray ['fɒreɪ] *n* incursión *f*
forbid [fə'bɪd] (*pt* **forbad(e)**, *pp* **forbidden**) *vt* prohibir; **to ~ sb to do sth** prohibir a uno hacer algo; ~**ding** *adj* amenazador(a)
force [fɔːs] *n* fuerza ♦ *vt* forzar; (*push*) meter a la fuerza; **to ~ o.s. to do** hacer un esfuerzo por hacer; **the F~s** *npl* (*BRIT*) las Fuerzas Armadas; **in ~** en vigor; ~**d** [fɔːst] *adj* forzado; ~**-feed** *vt* alimentar a la fuerza; ~**ful** *adj* enérgico
forcibly ['fɔːsəblɪ] *adv* a la fuerza; (*speak*) enérgicamente
ford [fɔːd] *n* vado
fore [fɔː*] *n*: **to come to the ~** empezar a destacar
fore: ~**arm** *n* antebrazo; ~**boding** *n* presentimiento; ~**cast** *n* pronóstico ♦ *vt* (*irreg: like* **cast**) pronosticar; ~**court** *n* patio; ~**finger** *n* (dedo) índice *m*; ~**front** *n*: **in the ~front of** en la vanguardia de
forego *vt* = **forgo**
foregone ['fɔːgɒn] *pp* of **forego** ♦ *adj*: **it's a ~ conclusion** es una conclusión evidente
foreground ['fɔːgraund] *n* primer plano
forehead ['fɒrɪd] *n* frente *f*
foreign ['fɒrɪn] *adj* extranjero; (*trade*) exterior; (*object*) extraño; ~**er** *n* extranjero/a; ~ **exchange** *n* divisas *fpl*; **F~ Office** *n* (*BRIT*) Ministerio de Asuntos Exteriores; **F~ Secretary** (*BRIT*) *n* Ministro de Asuntos Exteriores
fore: ~**leg** *n* pata delantera; ~**man** (*irreg*) *n* capataz *m*; (*in construction*) maestro de obras; ~**most** *adj* principal ♦ *adv*: **first**

and ~most ante todo
forensic [fə'rensɪk] *adj* forense
fore: ~**runner** *n* precursor(a) *m/f*; ~**see** (*pt* **foresaw**, *pp* **foreseen**) *vt* prever; ~**seeable** *adj* previsible; ~**shadow** *vt* prefigurar, anunciar; ~**sight** *n* previsión *f*
forest ['fɒrɪst] *n* bosque *m*
forestry ['fɒrɪstrɪ] *n* silvicultura
foretaste ['fɔːteɪst] *n* muestra
foretell [fɔː'tel] (*pt, pp* **foretold**) *vt* predecir, pronosticar
forever [fə'revə*] *adv* para siempre; (*endlessly*) constantemente
foreword ['fɔːwəːd] *n* prefacio
forfeit ['fɔːfɪt] *vt* perder
forgave [fə'geɪv] *pt of* **forgive**
forge [fɔːdʒ] *n* herrería ♦ *vt* (*signature, money*) falsificar; (*metal*) forjar; ~ **ahead** *vi* avanzar mucho; ~**ry** *n* falsificación *f*
forget [fə'get] (*pt* **forgot**, *pp* **forgotten**) *vt* olvidar ♦ *vi* olvidarse; ~**ful** *adj* despistado; ~**-me-not** *n* nomeolvides *f inv*
forgive [fə'gɪv] (*pt* **forgave**, *pp* **forgiven**) *vt* perdonar; **to ~ sb for sth** perdonar algo a uno; ~**ness** *n* perdón *m*
forgo [fɔː'gəu] (*pt* **forwent**, *pp* **forgone**) *vt* (*give up*) renunciar a; (*go without*) privarse de
forgot [fə'gɒt] *pt of* **forget**
forgotten [fə'gɒtn] *pp of* **forget**
fork [fɔːk] *n* (*for eating*) tenedor *m*; (*for gardening*) horca; (*of roads*) bifurcación *f* ♦ *vi* (*road*) bifurcarse; ~ **out** (*inf*) *vt* (*pay*) desembolsar; ~**-lift truck** *n* máquina elevadora
forlorn [fə'lɔːn] *adj* (*person*) triste, melancólico; (*place*) abandonado; (*attempt, hope*) desesperado
form [fɔːm] *n* forma; (*BRIT: SCOL*) clase *f*; (*document*) formulario ♦ *vt* formar; (*idea*) concebir; (*habit*) adquirir; **in top ~** en plena forma; **to ~ a queue** hacer cola
formal ['fɔːməl] *adj* (*offer, receipt*) por escrito; (*person etc*) correcto; (*occasion, dinner*) de etiqueta; (*dress*) correcto; (*garden*) (de estilo) clásico; ~**ity** [-'mælɪtɪ]

n (*procedure*) trámite *m*; corrección *f*;
etiqueta; **~ly** *adv* oficialmente
format ['fɔːmæt] *n* formato ♦ *vt* (*COMPUT*)
formatear
formative ['fɔːmətɪv] *adj* (*years*) de
formación; (*influence*) formativo
former ['fɔːmə*] *adj* anterior; (*earlier*)
antiguo; (*ex*) ex; **the ~ ... the latter ...**
aquél ... éste ...; **~ly** *adv* antes
formula ['fɔːmjulə] *n* fórmula
forsake [fə'seɪk] (*pt* **forsook**, *pp* **forsaken**)
vt (*gen*) abandonar; (*plan*) renunciar a
fort [fɔːt] *n* fuerte *m*
forte ['fɔːtɪ] *n* fuerte *m*
forth [fɔːθ] *adv*: **back and ~** de acá para
allá; **and so ~** y así sucesivamente;
~coming *adj* próximo, venidero; (*help,
information*) disponible; (*character*)
comunicativo; **~right** *adj* franco; **~with**
adv en el acto
fortify ['fɔːtɪfaɪ] *vt* (*city*) fortificar; (*person*)
fortalecer
fortitude ['fɔːtɪtjuːd] *n* fortaleza
fortnight ['fɔːtnaɪt] (*BRIT*) *n* quince días
mpl; quincena; **~ly** *adj* de cada quince
días, quincenal ♦ *adv* cada quince días,
quincenalmente
fortress ['fɔːtrɪs] *n* fortaleza
fortunate ['fɔːtʃənɪt] *adj* afortunado; **it is
~ that ...** (es una) suerte que ...; **~ly** *adv*
afortunadamente
fortune ['fɔːtʃən] *n* suerte *f*; (*wealth*)
fortuna; **~-teller** *n* adivino/a
forty ['fɔːtɪ] *num* cuarenta
forum ['fɔːrəm] *n* foro
forward ['fɔːwəd] *adj* (*movement, position*)
avanzado; (*front*) delantero; (*in time*)
adelantado; (*not shy*) atrevido ♦ *n* (*SPORT*)
delantero ♦ *vt* (*letter*) remitir; (*career*)
promocionar; **to move ~** avanzar; **~(s)**
adv (hacia) adelante
fossil ['fɔsl] *n* fósil *m*
foster ['fɔstə*] *vt* (*child*) acoger en una
familia; fomentar; **~ child** *n* hijo/a
adoptivo/a
fought [fɔːt] *pt*, *pp of* **fight**
foul [faul] *adj* sucio, puerco; (*weather, smell*

etc) asqueroso; (*language*) grosero;
(*temper*) malísimo ♦ *n* (*SPORT*) falta ♦ *vt*
(*dirty*) ensuciar; **~ play** *n* (*LAW*) muerte *f*
violenta
found [faund] *pt*, *pp of* **find** ♦ *vt* fundar;
~ation [-'deɪʃən] *n* (*act*) fundación *f*;
(*basis*) base *f*; (*also*: **~ation cream**) crema
base; **~ations** *npl* (*of building*) cimientos
mpl
founder ['faundə*] *n* fundador(a) *m/f* ♦ *vi*
hundirse
foundry ['faundrɪ] *n* fundición *f*
fountain ['fauntɪn] *n* fuente *f*; **~ pen** *n*
pluma (estilográfica) (*SP*), pluma-fuente *f*
(*AM*)
four [fɔː*] *num* cuatro; **on all ~s** a gatas;
~-poster (bed) *n* cama de dosel;
~teen *num* catorce; **~th** *num* cuarto
fowl [faul] *n* ave *f* (de corral)
fox [fɔks] *n* zorro ♦ *vt* confundir
foyer ['fɔɪeɪ] *n* vestíbulo
fraction ['frækʃən] *n* fracción *f*
fracture ['fræktʃə*] *n* fractura
fragile ['frædʒaɪl] *adj* frágil
fragment ['frægmənt] *n* fragmento
fragrant ['freɪgrənt] *adj* fragante, oloroso
frail [freɪl] *adj* frágil; (*person*) débil
frame [freɪm] *n* (*TECH*) armazón *m*; (*of
person*) cuerpo; (*of picture, door etc*)
marco; (*of spectacles*: *also*: **~s**) montura
♦ *vt* enmarcar; **~ of mind** *n* estado de
ánimo; **~work** *n* marco
France [frɑːns] *n* Francia
franchise ['fræntʃaɪz] *n* (*POL*) derecho de
votar, sufragio; (*COMM*) licencia,
concesión *f*
frank [fræŋk] *adj* franco ♦ *vt* (*letter*)
franquear; **~ly** *adv* francamente
frantic ['fræntɪk] *adj* (*distraught*)
desesperado; (*hectic*) frenético
fraternity [frə'tɜːnɪtɪ] *n* (*feeling*) fraternidad
f; (*group of people*) círculos *mpl*
fraud [frɔːd] *n* fraude *m*; (*person*)
impostor(a) *m/f*
fraught [frɔːt] *adj*: **~ with** lleno de
fray [freɪ] *vi* deshilacharse
freak [friːk] *n* (*person*) fenómeno; (*event*

suceso anormal

reckle ['frɛkl] n peca

ree [fri:] adj libre; (gratis) gratuito ♦ vt (prisoner etc) poner en libertad; (jammed object) soltar; **~ (of charge), for ~** gratis; **~dom** ['fri:dəm] n libertad f; **F~fone** ® ['fri:fəʊn] n número gratuito; **~-for-all** n riña general; **~ gift** n prima; **~hold** n propiedad f vitalicia; **~ kick** n tiro libre; **~lance** adj independiente ♦ adv por cuenta propia; **~ly** adv libremente; (liberally) generosamente; **F~mason** n francmasón m; **F~post** ® n porte m pagado; **~-range** adj (hen, eggs) de granja; **~ trade** n libre comercio; **~way** (US) n autopista; **~ will** n libre albedrío; **of one's own ~ will** por su propia voluntad

reeze [fri:z] (pt **froze**, pp **frozen**) vi (weather) helar; (liquid, pipe, person) helarse, congelarse ♦ vt helar; (food, prices, salaries) congelar ♦ n helada; (on arms, wages) congelación f; **~-dried** adj liofilizado; **~r** n congelador m (SP), congeladora (AM)

reezing ['fri:zɪŋ] adj helado; **3 degrees below ~** tres grados bajo cero; **~ point** n punto de congelación

eight [freɪt] n (goods) carga; (money charged) flete m; **~ train** (US) n tren m de mercancías

rench [frɛntʃ] adj francés/esa ♦ n (LING) francés m; **the ~** npl los franceses; **~ bean** n judía verde; **~ fried potatoes** npl patatas fpl (SP) or papas fpl (AM) fritas; **~ fries** (US) npl = **~ fried potatoes**; **~man/woman** (irreg) n francés/esa m/f; **~ window** n puerta de cristal

renzy ['frɛnzɪ] n frenesí m

requent [adj 'fri:kwənt, vb frɪ'kwɛnt] adj frecuente ♦ vt frecuentar; **~ly** [-əntlɪ] adv frecuentemente, a menudo

resh [freʃ] adj fresco; (bread) tierno; (new) nuevo; **~en** vi (wind, air) soplar más recio; **~en up** vi (person) arreglarse, lavarse; **~er** (BRIT: inf) n (UNIV) estudiante

m/f de primer año; **~ly** adv (made, painted etc) recién; **~man** (US irreg) n = **~er**; **~ness** n frescura; **~water** adj (fish) de agua dulce

fret [frɛt] vi inquietarse

friar ['fraɪə*] n fraile m; (before name) fray m

friction ['frɪkʃən] n fricción f

Friday ['fraɪdɪ] n viernes m inv

fridge [frɪdʒ] (BRIT) n nevera (SP), refrigeradora (AM)

fried [fraɪd] adj frito

friend [frɛnd] n amigo/a; **~ly** adj simpático; (government) amigo; (place) acogedor(a); (match) amistoso; **~ly fire** fuego amigo, disparos mpl del propio bando; **~ship** n amistad f

frieze [fri:z] n friso

fright [fraɪt] n (terror) terror m; (scare) susto; **to take ~** asustarse; **~en** vt asustar; **~ened** adj asustado; **~ening** adj espantoso; **~ful** adj espantoso, horrible

frill [frɪl] n volante m

fringe [frɪndʒ] n (BRIT: of hair) flequillo; (on lampshade etc) flecos mpl; (of forest etc) borde m, margen m; **~ benefits** npl beneficios mpl marginales

frisk [frɪsk] vt cachear, registrar

frisky ['frɪskɪ] adj juguetón/ona

fritter ['frɪtə*] n buñuelo; **~ away** vt desperdiciar

frivolous ['frɪvələs] adj frívolo

frizzy ['frɪzɪ] adj rizado

fro [frəʊ] see **to**

frock [frɒk] n vestido

frog [frɒg] n rana; **~man** n hombre-rana m

frolic ['frɒlɪk] vi juguetear

KEYWORD

from [frɒm] prep 1 (indicating starting place) de, desde; **where do you come ~?** ¿de dónde eres?; **~ London to Glasgow** de Londres a Glasgow; **to escape ~ sth/ sb** escaparse de algo/alguien

2 (indicating origin etc) de; **a letter/ telephone call ~ my sister** una carta/

llamada de mi hermana; **tell him ~ me
that ...** dígale de mi parte que ...
3 (*indicating time*): **~ one o'clock to** *or*
until *or* **till two** de(sde) la una a *or* hasta
las dos; **~ January (on)** a partir de enero
4 (*indicating distance*) de; **the hotel is 1
km ~ the beach** el hotel está a 1 km de
la playa
5 (*indicating price, number etc*) de; **prices
range ~ £10 to £50** los precios van
desde £10 a *or* hasta £50; **the interest
rate was increased ~ 9% to 10%** el tipo
de interés fue incrementado de un 9% a
un 10%
6 (*indicating difference*) de; **he can't tell
red ~ green** no sabe distinguir el rojo del
verde; **to be different ~ sb/sth** ser
diferente a algo/alguien
7 (*because of, on the basis of*): **~ what he
says** por lo que dice; **weak ~ hunger**
debilitado por el hambre

front [frʌnt] *n* (*foremost part*) parte *f*
delantera; (*of house*) fachada; (*of dress*)
delantero; (*promenade: also:* **sea ~**) paseo
marítimo; (*MIL, POL, METEOROLOGY*) frente
m; (*fig: appearances*) apariencias *fpl* ♦ *adj*
(*wheel, leg*) delantero; (*row, line*) primero;
in ~ (of) delante (de); **~ door** *n* puerta
principal; **~ier** [ˈfrʌntɪə*] *n* frontera; **~
page** *n* primera plana; **~ room** (*BRIT*) *n*
salón *m*, sala; **~-wheel drive** *n* tracción
f delantera
frost [frɔst] *n* helada; (*also:* **hoar-**)
escarcha; **~bite** *n* congelación *f*; **~ed** *adj*
(*glass*) deslustrado; **~y** *adj* (*weather*) de
helada; (*welcome etc*) glacial
froth [frɔθ] *n* espuma
frown [fraun] *vi* fruncir el ceño
froze [frəuz] *pt of* **freeze**
frozen [ˈfrəuzn] *pp of* **freeze**
fruit [fruːt] *n inv* fruta; fruto; (*fig*) fruto;
resultados *mpl*; **~erer** *n* frutero/a;
~erer's (shop) *n* frutería; **~ful** *adj*
provechoso; **~ion** [fruːˈɪʃən] *n*: **to come
to ~ion** realizarse; **~ juice** *n* zumo (*SP*) *or*
jugo (*AM*) de fruta; **~ machine** (*BRIT*) *n*

máquina *f* tragaperras; **~ salad** *n*
macedonia (*SP*) *or* ensalada (*AM*) de frutas
frustrate [frʌsˈtreɪt] *vt* frustrar
fry [fraɪ] (*pt, pp* **fried**) *vt* freír; **small ~**
gente *f* menuda; **~ing pan** *n* sartén *f*
ft. *abbr* = **foot; feet**
fudge [fʌdʒ] *n* (*CULIN*) caramelo blando
fuel [fjuəl] *n* (*for heating*) combustible *m*;
(*coal*) carbón *m*; (*wood*) leña; (*for engine*)
carburante *m*; **~ oil** *n* fuel oil *m*; **~ tank**
n depósito (de combustible)
fugitive [ˈfjuːdʒɪtɪv] *n* fugitivo/a
fulfil [fulˈfɪl] *vt* (*function*) cumplir con;
(*condition*) satisfacer; (*wish, desire*) realizar;
~ment (*US* **fulfillment**) *n* satisfacción *f*;
(*of promise, desire*) realización *f*
full [ful] *adj* lleno; (*fig*) pleno; (*complete*)
completo; (*maximum*) máximo;
(*information*) detallado; (*price*) íntegro;
(*skirt*) amplio ♦ *adv*: **to know ~ well** saber
perfectamente que; **I'm ~ (up)** no
puedo más; **~ employment** pleno
empleo; **a ~ two hours** dos horas
completas; **at ~ speed** a máxima
velocidad; **in ~** (*reproduce, quote*)
íntegramente; **~-length** *adj* (*novel etc*)
entero; (*coat*) largo; (*portrait*) de cuerpo
entero; **~ moon** *n* luna llena; **~-scale**
adj (*attack, war*) en gran escala; (*model*)
de tamaño natural; **~ stop** *n* punto; **~-
time** *adj* (*work*) de tiempo completo
♦ *adv*: **to work ~-time** trabajar a tiempo
completo; **~y** *adv* completamente; (*at
least*) por lo menos; **~y-fledged** *adj*
(*teacher, barrister*) diplomado
fumble [ˈfʌmbl] *vi*: **to ~ with** manejar
torpemente
fume [fjuːm] *vi* (*rage*) estar furioso; **~s** *npl*
humo, gases *mpl*
fun [fʌn] *n* (*amusement*) diversión *f*; **to
have ~** divertirse; **for ~** en broma; **to
make ~ of** burlarse de
function [ˈfʌŋkʃən] *n* función *f* ♦ *vi*
funcionar; **~al** *adj* (*operational*) en buen
estado; (*practical*) funcional
fund [fʌnd] *n* fondo; (*reserve*) reserva; **~s**
npl (*money*) fondos *mpl*

fundamental [fʌndə'mɛntl] *adj* fundamental

funeral ['fjuːnərəl] *n* (*burial*) entierro; (*ceremony*) funerales *mpl*; ~ **parlour** (*BRIT*) *n* funeraria; ~ **service** *n* misa de difuntos, funeral *m*

funfair ['fʌnfeə*] (*BRIT*) *n* parque *m* de atracciones

fungus ['fʌŋgəs] (*pl* **fungi**) *n* hongo; (*mould*) moho

funnel ['fʌnl] *n* embudo; (*of ship*) chimenea

funny ['fʌnɪ] *adj* gracioso, divertido; (*strange*) curioso, raro

fur [fəː*] *n* piel *f*; (*BRIT*: *in kettle etc*) sarro; ~ **coat** *n* abrigo de pieles

furious ['fjuərɪəs] *adj* furioso; (*effort*) violento

furlong ['fəːlɒŋ] *n* octava parte de una milla, = 201.17 m

furnace ['fəːnɪs] *n* horno

furnish ['fəːnɪʃ] *vt* amueblar; (*supply*) suministrar; (*information*) facilitar; ~**ings** *npl* muebles *mpl*

furniture ['fəːnɪtʃə*] *n* muebles *mpl*; **piece of** ~ mueble *m*

furrow ['fʌrəu] *n* surco

furry ['fəːrɪ] *adj* peludo

further ['fəːðə*] *adj* (*new*) nuevo, adicional ♦ *adv* más lejos; (*more*) más; (*moreover*) además ♦ *vt* promover, adelantar; ~ **education** *n* educación *f* superior; ~**more** [fəːðə'mɔː*] *adv* además

furthest ['fəːðɪst] *superlative of* **far**

fury ['fjuərɪ] *n* furia

fuse [fjuːz] (*US* **fuze**) *n* fusible *m*; (*for bomb etc*) mecha ♦ *vt* (*metal*) fundir; (*fig*) fusionar ♦ *vi* fundirse; fusionarse; (*BRIT*: *ELEC*): **to ~ the lights** fundir los plomos; ~ **box** *n* caja de fusibles

fuss [fʌs] *n* (*excitement*) conmoción *f*; (*trouble*) alboroto, jaleo; **to make a ~** armar un lío *or* jaleo; **to make a ~ of sb** mimar a uno; ~**y** *adj* (*person*) exigente; (*too ornate*) recargado

futile ['fjuːtaɪl] *adj* vano

future ['fjuːtʃə*] *adj* futuro; (*coming*)

venidero ♦ *n* futuro; (*prospects*) porvenir; **in ~** de ahora en adelante

fuze [fjuːz] (*US*) = **fuse**

fuzzy ['fʌzɪ] *adj* (*PHOT*) borroso; (*hair*) muy rizado

G, g

G [dʒiː] *n* (*MUS*) sol *m*

g. *abbr* (= *gram(s)*) gr.

G7 *abbr* (= *Group of Seven*) el grupo de los 7

gabble ['gæbl] *vi* hablar atropelladamente

gable ['geɪbl] *n* aguilón *m*

gadget ['gædʒɪt] *n* aparato

Gaelic ['geɪlɪk] *adj, n* (*LING*) gaélico

gag [gæg] *n* (*on mouth*) mordaza; (*joke*) chiste *m* ♦ *vt* amordazar

gaiety ['geɪtɪ] *n* alegría

gaily ['geɪlɪ] *adv* alegremente

gain [geɪn] *n*: ~ **(in)** aumento (de); (*profit*) ganancia ♦ *vt* ganar ♦ *vi* (*watch*) adelantarse; **to ~ from/by sth** sacar provecho de algo; **to ~ on sb** ganar terreno a uno; **to ~ 3 lbs** (*in weight*) engordar 3 libras

gal. *abbr* = **gallon**

gala ['gɑːlə] *n* fiesta

gale [geɪl] *n* (*wind*) vendaval *m*

gallant ['gælənt] *adj* valiente; (*towards ladies*) atento

gall bladder ['gɔːl-] *n* vesícula biliar

gallery ['gælərɪ] *n* (*also*: **art** ~: *public*) pinacoteca; (: *private*) galería de arte; (*for spectators*) tribuna

gallon ['gælən] *n* galón *m* (*BRIT* = 4,546 *litros*, *US* = 3,785 *litros*)

gallop ['gæləp] *n* galope *m* ♦ *vi* galopar

gallows ['gæləuz] *n* horca

gallstone ['gɔːlstəun] *n* cálculo biliario

galore [gə'lɔː*] *adv* en cantidad, en abundancia

gambit ['gæmbɪt] *n* (*fig*): **(opening)** ~ estrategia (inicial)

gamble ['gæmbl] *n* (*risk*) riesgo ♦ *vt* jugar, apostar ♦ *vi* (*take a risk*) jugársela; (*bet*)

apostar; **to ~ on** apostar a; (*success etc*)
contar con; ~r *n* jugador(a) *m/f*;
gambling *n* juego
game [geɪm] *n* juego; (*match*) partido; (*of
cards*) partida; (*HUNTING*) caza ♦ *adj*
(*willing*): **to be ~ for anything** atreverse a
todo; **big ~** caza mayor; **~keeper** *n*
guardabosques *m inv*
gammon ['gæmən] *n* (*bacon*) tocino
ahumado; (*ham*) jamón *m* ahumado
gamut ['gæmət] *n* gama
gang [gæŋ] *n* (*of criminals*) pandilla; (*of
friends etc*) grupo; (*of workmen*) brigada;
~ up *vi*: **to ~ up on sb** aliarse contra uno
gangster ['gæŋstə*] *n* gángster *m*
gangway ['gæŋweɪ] *n* (*on ship*) pasarela
gaol [dʒeɪl] (*BRIT*) *n, vt* = **jail**
gap [gæp] *n* vacío, hueco (*AM*); (*in trees,
traffic*) claro; (*in time*) intervalo;
(*difference*): **~ (between)** diferencia (*entre*)
gap year (*BRIT: SCH*) *n* año sabático (*antes
de empezar a estudiar en la universidad*)
gape [geɪp] *vi* mirar boquiabierto; (*shirt
etc*) abrirse (*completamente*); **gaping** *adj*
(*completamente*) abierto
garage ['gærɑːʒ] *n* garaje *m*; (*for repairs*)
taller *m*
garbage ['gɑːbɪdʒ] (*US*) *n* basura; (*inf:
nonsense*) tonterías *fpl*; **~ can** *n* cubo
(*SP*) *or* bote *m* (*AM*) de la basura
garbled ['gɑːbld] *adj* (*distorted*) falsificado,
amañado
garden ['gɑːdn] *n* jardín *m*; **~s** *npl* (*park*)
parque *m*; **~er** *n* jardinero/a; **~ing** *n*
jardinería
gargle ['gɑːgl] *vi* hacer gárgaras, gargarear
(*AM*)
garish ['gɛərɪʃ] *adj* chillón/ona
garland ['gɑːlənd] *n* guirnalda
garlic ['gɑːlɪk] *n* ajo
garment ['gɑːmənt] *n* prenda (de vestir)
garnish ['gɑːnɪʃ] *vt* (*CULIN*) aderezar
garrison ['gærɪsn] *n* guarnición *f*
garter ['gɑːtə*] *n* (*for sock*) liga; (*US*)
liguero
gas [gæs] *n* gas *m*; (*fuel*) combustible *m*;
(*US: gasoline*) gasolina ♦ *vt* asfixiar con

gas; **~ cooker** (*BRIT*) *n* cocina de gas; **~
cylinder** *n* bombona de gas; **~ fire** *n*
estufa de gas
gash [gæʃ] *n* raja; (*wound*) cuchillada ♦ *vt*
rajar; acuchillar
gasket ['gæskɪt] *n* (*AUT*) junta de culata
gas mask *n* careta antigás
gas meter *n* contador *m* de gas
gasoline ['gæsəliːn] (*US*) *n* gasolina
gasp [gɑːsp] *n* boqueada; (*of shock etc*)
grito sofocado ♦ *vi* (*pant*) jadear
gas station (*US*) *n* gasolinera
gastric ['gæstrɪk] *adj* gástrico
gate [geɪt] *n* puerta; (*iron ~*) verja; **~crash**
(*BRIT*) *vt* colarse en; **~way** *n* puerta
gather ['gæðə*] *vt* (*flowers, fruit*) coger
(*SP*), recoger; (*assemble*) reunir; (*pick up*)
recoger; (*SEWING*) fruncir; (*understand*)
entender ♦ *vi* (*assemble*) reunirse; **to ~
speed** ganar velocidad; **~ing** *n* reunión
f, asamblea
gaudy ['gɔːdɪ] *adj* chillón/ona
gauge [geɪdʒ] *n* (*instrument*) indicador *m*
♦ *vt* medir; (*fig*) juzgar
gaunt [gɔːnt] *adj* (*haggard*) demacrado;
(*stark*) desolado
gauntlet ['gɔːntlɪt] *n* (*fig*): **to run the ~ of**
exponerse a; **to throw down the ~** arrojar
el guante
gauze [gɔːz] *n* gasa
gave [geɪv] *pt of* **give**
gay [geɪ] *adj* (*homosexual*) gay; (*joyful*)
alegre; (*colour*) vivo
gaze [geɪz] *n* mirada fija ♦ *vi*: **to ~ at sth**
mirar algo fijamente
gazelle [gə'zɛl] *n* gacela
gazumping [gə'zʌmpɪŋ] (*BRIT*) *n la subida
del precio de una casa una vez que ya ha
sido apalabrado*
GB *abbr* = **Great Britain**
GCE *n abbr* (*BRIT*) = *General Certificate of
Education*
GCSE (*BRIT*) *n abbr* (= *General Certificate
of Secondary Education*) *examen de
reválida que se hace a los 16 años*
gear [gɪə*] *n* equipo, herramientas *fpl*;
(*TECH*) engranaje *m*; (*AUT*) velocidad *f*,

marcha ♦ *vt* (*fig: adapt*): **to ~ sth to**
adaptar *or* ajustar algo a; **top** *or* **high**
(*US*)/**low ~** cuarta/primera velocidad; **in ~**
en marcha; **~ box** *n* caja de cambios; **~**
lever *n* palanca de cambio; **~ shift** (*US*)
n = **~ lever**

geese [giːs] *npl of* **goose**

gel [dʒɛl] *n* gel *m*

gem [dʒɛm] *n* piedra preciosa

Gemini ['dʒɛmɪnaɪ] *n* Géminis *m*, Gemelos
mpl

gender ['dʒɛndə*] *n* género

gene [dʒiːn] *n* gen(e) *m*

general ['dʒɛnərl] *n* general *m* ♦ *adj*
general; **in ~** en general; **~ delivery** (*US*)
n lista de correos; **~ election** *n*
elecciones *fpl* generales; **~ly** *adv*
generalmente, en general; **~**
practitioner *n* médico general

generate ['dʒɛnəreɪt] *vt* (*ELEC*) generar;
(*jobs, profits*) producir

generation [dʒɛnə'reɪʃən] *n* generación *f*

generator ['dʒɛnəreɪtə*] *n* generador *m*

generosity [dʒɛnə'rɒsɪtɪ] *n* generosidad *f*

generous ['dʒɛnərəs] *adj* generoso

genetic [dʒɪ'nɛtɪk] *adj*: **~ engineering**
ingeniería genética; **~ fingerprinting**
identificación *f* genética

Geneva [dʒɪ'niːvə] *n* Ginebra

genial ['dʒiːnɪəl] *adj* afable, simpático

genitals ['dʒɛnɪtlz] *npl* (órganos *mpl*)
genitales *mpl*

genius ['dʒiːnɪəs] *n* genio

genteel [dʒɛn'tiːl] *adj* fino, elegante

gentle ['dʒɛntl] *adj* apacible, dulce;
(*animal*) manso; (*breeze, curve etc*) suave

gentleman ['dʒɛntlmən] (*irreg*) *n* señor *m*;
(*well-bred man*) caballero

gently ['dʒɛntlɪ] *adv* dulcemente,
suavemente

gentry ['dʒɛntrɪ] *n* alta burguesía

gents [dʒɛnts] *n* aseos *mpl* (de caballeros)

genuine ['dʒɛnjuɪn] *adj* auténtico; (*person*)
sincero

geography [dʒɪ'ɒɡrəfɪ] *n* geografía

geology [dʒɪ'ɒlədʒɪ] *n* geología

geometric(al) [dʒɪə'mɛtrɪk(l)] *adj*

geométrico

geranium [dʒɪ'reɪnjəm] *n* geranio

geriatric [dʒɛrɪ'ætrɪk] *adj, n* geriátrico/a
m/f

germ [dʒəːm] *n* (*microbe*) microbio,
bacteria; (*seed, fig*) germen *m*

German ['dʒəːmən] *adj* alemán/ana ♦ *n*
alemán/ana *m/f*; (*LING*) alemán *m*; **~**
measles *n* rubéola

Germany ['dʒəːmənɪ] *n* Alemania

gesture ['dʒɛstjə*] *n* gesto; (*symbol*)
muestra

KEYWORD

get [gɛt] (*pt, pp* **got**, *pp* **gotten** (*US*)) *vi* **1**
(*become, be*) ponerse, volverse; **to ~ old/**
tired envejecer/cansarse; **to ~ drunk**
emborracharse; **to ~ dirty** ensuciarse; **to ~**
married casarse; **when do I ~ paid?**
¿cuándo me pagan *or* se me paga?; **it's**
~ting late se está haciendo tarde
2 (*go*): **to ~ to/from** llegar a/de; **to ~**
home llegar a casa
3 (*begin*) empezar a; **to ~ to know sb**
(llegar a) conocer a uno; **I'm ~ting to like**
him me está empezando a gustar; **let's ~**
going *or* **started** ¡vamos (a empezar)!
4 (*modal aux vb*): **you've got to do it**
tienes que hacerlo
♦ *vt* **1**: **to ~ sth done** (*finish*) terminar
algo; (*have done*) mandar hacer algo; **to ~**
one's hair cut cortarse el pelo; **to ~ the**
car going *or* **to go** arrancar el coche; **to**
~ sb to do sth conseguir *or* hacer que
alguien haga algo; **to ~ sth/sb ready**
preparar algo/a alguien
2 (*obtain: money, permission, results*)
conseguir; (*find: job, flat*) encontrar;
(*fetch: person, doctor*) buscar; (*object*) ir a
buscar, traer; **to ~ sth for sb** conseguir
algo para alguien; **~ me Mr Jones,**
please (*TEL*) póngame *or* comuníqueme
(*AM*) con el Sr. Jones, por favor; **can I ~**
you a drink? ¿quieres algo de beber?
3 (*receive: present, letter*) recibir; (*acquire:*
reputation) alcanzar; (*: prize*) ganar; **what**
did you ~ for your birthday? ¿qué te

regalaron por tu cumpleaños?; **how much did you ~ for the painting?** ¿cuánto sacaste por el cuadro?
4 (*catch*) coger (*SP*), agarrar (*AM*); (*hit: target etc*) dar en; **to ~ sb by the arm/throat** coger *or* agarrar a uno por el brazo/cuello; **~ him!** ¡cógelo! (*SP*), ¡atrápalo! (*AM*); **the bullet got him in the leg** la bala le dio en la pierna
5 (*take, move*) llevar; **to ~ sth to sb** hacer llegar algo a alguien; **do you think we'll ~ it through the door?** ¿crees que lo podremos meter por la puerta?
6 (*catch, take: plane, bus etc*) coger (*SP*), tomar (*AM*); **where do I ~ the train for Birmingham?** ¿dónde se coge *or* se toma el tren para Birmingham?
7 (*understand*) entender; (*hear*) oír; **I've got it!** ¡ya lo tengo!, ¡eureka!; **I don't ~ your meaning** no te entiendo; **I'm sorry, I didn't ~ your name** lo siento, no cogí tu nombre
8 (*have, possess*): **to have got** tener
get about *vi* salir mucho; (*news*) divulgarse
get along *vi* (*agree*) llevarse bien; (*depart*) marcharse = **get by**
get at *vt fus* (*attack*) atacar; (*reach*) alcanzar
get away *vi* marcharse; (*escape*) escaparse
get away with *vt fus* hacer impunemente
get back *vi* (*return*) volver ♦ *vt* recobrar
get by *vi* (*pass*) (lograr) pasar; (*manage*) arreglárselas
get down *vi* bajarse ♦ *vt fus* bajar ♦ *vt* bajar; (*depress*) deprimir
get down to *vt fus* (*work*) ponerse a
get in *vi* entrar; (*train*) llegar; (*arrive home*) volver a casa, regresar
get into *vt fus* entrar en; (*vehicle*) subir a; **to ~ into a rage** enfadarse
get off *vi* (*from train etc*) bajar; (*depart: person, car*) marcharse ♦ *vt* (*remove*) quitar ♦ *vt fus* (*train, bus*) bajar de
get on *vi* (*at exam etc*): **how are you**

~ting on? ¿cómo te va?; (*agree*): **to ~ on (with)** llevarse bien (con) ♦ *vt fus* subir a
get out *vi* salir; (*of vehicle*) bajar ♦ *vt* sacar
get out of *vt fus* salir de; (*duty etc*) escaparse de
get over *vt fus* (*illness*) recobrarse de
get round *vt fus* rodear; (*fig: person*) engatusar a
get through *vi* (*TEL*) (lograr) comunicarse
get through to *vt fus* (*TEL*) comunicar con
get together *vi* reunirse ♦ *vt* reunir, juntar
get up *vi* (*rise*) levantarse ♦ *vt fus* subir
get up to *vt fus* (*reach*) llegar a; (*prank*) hacer

geyser ['giːzəʳ] *n* (*water heater*) calentador *m* de agua; (*GEO*) géiser *m*
ghastly ['gɑːstlɪ] *adj* horrible
gherkin ['gəːkɪn] *n* pepinillo
ghetto blaster ['gɛtəʊblɑːstəʳ] *n* cassette *m* portátil de gran tamaño
ghost [gəʊst] *n* fantasma *m*
giant ['dʒaɪənt] *n* gigante *m/f* ♦ *adj* gigantesco, gigante
gibberish ['dʒɪbərɪʃ] *n* galimatías *m*
giblets ['dʒɪblɪts] *npl* menudillos *mpl*
Gibraltar [dʒɪˈbrɔːltəʳ] *n* Gibraltar *m*
giddy ['gɪdɪ] *adj* mareado
gift [gɪft] *n* regalo; (*ability*) talento; **~ed** *adj* dotado; **~ token** *or* **voucher** *n* vale *m* canjeable por un regalo
gigantic [dʒaɪˈgæntɪk] *adj* gigantesco
giggle ['gɪgl] *vi* reírse tontamente
gill [dʒɪl] *n* (*measure*) = 0.25 pints (*BRIT* = 0.148l, *US* = 0.118l)
gills [gɪlz] *npl* (*of fish*) branquias *fpl*, agallas *fpl*
gilt [gɪlt] *adj, n* dorado; **~-edged** *adj* (*COMM*) de máxima garantía
gimmick ['gɪmɪk] *n* truco
gin [dʒɪn] *n* ginebra
ginger ['dʒɪndʒəʳ] *n* jengibre *m*; **~ ale** = **~ beer**; **~ beer** (*BRIT*) *n* gaseosa de

jengibre; **~bread** *n* pan *m* (*or* galleta) de jengibre

gingerly ['dʒɪndʒəlɪ] *adv* con cautela

gipsy ['dʒɪpsɪ] *n* = **gypsy**

giraffe [dʒɪ'rɑːf] *n* jirafa

girder ['gɜːdə*] *n* viga

girl [gɜːl] *n* (*small*) niña; (*young woman*) chica, joven *f*, muchacha; (*daughter*) hija; **an English ~** una (chica) inglesa; **~friend** *n* (*of girl*) amiga; (*of boy*) novia; **~ish** *adj* de niña

giro ['dʒaɪrəʊ] *n* (BRIT: *bank* ~) giro bancario; (*post office* ~) giro postal; (*state benefit*) *cheque quincenal del subsidio de desempleo*

gist [dʒɪst] *n* lo esencial

give [gɪv] (*pt* **gave**, *pp* **given**) *vt* dar; (*deliver*) entregar; (*as gift*) regalar ♦ *vi* (*break*) romperse; (*stretch: fabric*) dar de sí; **to ~ sb sth, ~ sth to sb** dar algo a uno; **~ away** *vt* (*give free*) regalar; (*betray*) traicionar; (*disclose*) revelar; **~ back** *vt* devolver; **~ in** *vi* ceder ♦ *vt* entregar; **~ off** *vt* despedir; **~ out** *vt* distribuir; **~ up** *vi* rendirse, darse por vencido ♦ *vt* renunciar a; **to ~ up smoking** dejar de fumar; **to ~ o.s. up** entregarse; **~ way** *vi* ceder; (BRIT: AUT) ceder el paso

glacier ['glæsɪə*] *n* glaciar *m*

glad [glæd] *adj* contento

gladly ['glædlɪ] *adv* con mucho gusto

glamorous ['glæmərəs] *adj* encantador(a), atractivo; **glamour** ['glæmə*] *n* encanto, atractivo

glance [glɑːns] *n* ojeada, mirada ♦ *vi*: **to ~ at** echar una ojeada a; **glancing** *adj* (*blow*) oblicuo

gland [glænd] *n* glándula

glare [gleə*] *n* (*of anger*) mirada feroz; (*of light*) deslumbramiento, brillo; **to be in the ~ of publicity** ser el foco de la atención pública ♦ *vi* deslumbrar; **to ~ at** mirar con odio a; **glaring** *adj* (*mistake*) manifiesto

glass [glɑːs] *n* vidrio, cristal *m*; (*for drinking*) vaso; (: *with stem*) copa; **~es** *npl*

(*spectacles*) gafas *fpl*; **~house** *n* invernadero; **~ware** *n* cristalería

glaze [gleɪz] *vt* (*window*) poner cristales a; (*pottery*) vidriar ♦ *n* vidriado; **glazier** ['gleɪzɪə*] *n* vidriero/a

gleam [gliːm] *vi* brillar

glean [gliːn] *vt* (*information*) recoger

glee [gliː] *n* alegría, regocijo

glen [glɛn] *n* cañada

glib [glɪb] *adj* de mucha labia; (*promise, response*) poco sincero

glide [glaɪd] *vi* deslizarse; (AVIAT, *birds*) planear; **~r** *n* (AVIAT) planeador *m*; **gliding** *n* (AVIAT) vuelo sin motor

glimmer ['glɪmə*] *n* luz *f* tenue; (*of interest*) muestra; (*of hope*) rayo

glimpse [glɪmps] *n* vislumbre *m* ♦ *vt* vislumbrar, entrever

glint [glɪnt] *vi* centellear

glisten ['glɪsn] *vi* relucir, brillar

glitter ['glɪtə*] *vi* relucir, brillar

gloat [gləʊt] *vi*: **to ~ over** recrearse en

global ['gləʊbl] *adj* mundial; **~ warming** (re)calentamiento global *or* de la tierra

globe [gləʊb] *n* globo; (*model*) globo terráqueo

gloom [gluːm] *n* tinieblas *fpl*, oscuridad *f*; (*sadness*) tristeza, melancolía; **~y** *adj* (*dark*) oscuro; (*sad*) triste; (*pessimistic*) pesimista

glorious ['glɔːrɪəs] *adj* glorioso; (*weather etc*) magnífico

glory ['glɔːrɪ] *n* gloria

gloss [glɒs] *n* (*shine*) brillo; (*paint*) pintura de aceite; **~ over** *vt fus* disimular

glossary ['glɒsərɪ] *n* glosario

glossy ['glɒsɪ] *adj* lustroso; (*magazine*) de lujo

glove [glʌv] *n* guante *m*; **~ compartment** *n* (AUT) guantera*

glow [gləʊ] *vi* brillar

glower ['glaʊə*] *vi*: **to ~ at** mirar con ceño

glue [gluː] *n* goma (de pegar), cemento ♦ *vt* pegar

glum [glʌm] *adj* (*person, tone*) melancólico

glut [glʌt] *n* superabundancia

glutton ['glʌtn] *n* glotón/ona *m/f*; **a ~ for**

work un(a) trabajador(a) incansable

GM *adj abbr* (= *genetically modified*) transgénico

GMO *n abbr* (= *genetically-modified organism*) organismo transgénico

gnat [næt] *n* mosquito

gnaw [nɔː] *vt* roer

gnome [nəum] *n* gnomo

go [gəu] (*pt* **went**, *pp* **gone**; *pl* ~**es**) *vi* ir; (*travel*) viajar; (*depart*) irse, marcharse; (*work*) funcionar, marchar; (*be sold*) venderse; (*time*) pasar; (*fit, suit*): **to ~ with** hacer juego con; (*become*) ponerse; (*break etc*) estropearse, romperse ♦ *n*: **to have a ~ (at)** probar suerte (con); **to be on the ~** no parar; **whose ~ is it?** ¿a quién le toca?; **he's going to do it** va a hacerlo; **to ~ for a walk** ir de paseo; **to ~ dancing** ir a bailar; **how did it ~?** ¿qué tal salió *or* resultó?, ¿cómo ha ido?; ~ **about** *vi* (*rumour*) propagarse ♦ *vt fus*: **how do I ~ about this?** ¿cómo me las arreglo para hacer esto?; ~ **ahead** *vi* seguir adelante; ~ **along** *vi* ir ♦ *vt fus* bordear; **to ~ along with** (*agree*) estar de acuerdo con; ~ **away** *vi* irse, marcharse; ~ **back** *vi* volver; ~ **back on** *vt fus* (*promise*) faltar a; ~ **by** *vi* (*time*) pasar ♦ *vt fus* guiarse por; ~ **down** *vi* bajar; (*ship*) hundirse; (*sun*) ponerse ♦ *vt fus* bajar; ~ **for** *vt fus* (*fetch*) ir por; (*like*) gustar; (*attack*) atacar; ~ **in** *vi* entrar; ~ **in for** *vt fus* (*competition*) presentarse a; ~ **into** *vt fus* entrar en; (*investigate*) investigar; (*embark on*) dedicarse a; ~ **off** *vi* irse, marcharse; (*food*) pasarse; (*explode*) estallar; (*event*) realizarse ♦ *vt fus* dejar de gustar; **I'm going off him/the idea** ya no me gusta tanto él/la idea; ~ **on** *vi* (*continue*) seguir, continuar; (*happen*) pasar, ocurrir; **to ~ on doing sth** seguir haciendo algo; ~ **out** *vi* salir; (*fire, light*) apagarse; ~ **over** *vi* (*ship*) zozobrar ♦ *vt fus* (*check*) revisar; ~ **through** *vt fus* (*town etc*) atravesar; ~ **up** *vi*, *vt fus* subir; ~ **without** *vt fus* pasarse sin

goad [gəud] *vt* aguijonear

go-ahead *adj* (*person*) dinámico; (*firm*) innovador(a) ♦ *n* luz *f* verde

goal [gəul] *n* meta; (*score*) gol *m*; ~**keeper** *n* portero; ~**post** *n* poste *m* (de la portería)

goat [gəut] *n* cabra

gobble ['gɔbl] *vt* (*also:* ~ **down**, ~ **up**) tragarse, engullir

go-between *n* intermediario/a

god [gɔd] *n* dios *m*; **G~** *n* Dios *m*; ~**child** *n* ahijado/a; ~**daughter** *n* ahijada; ~**dess** *n* diosa; ~**father** *n* padrino; ~**forsaken** *adj* dejado de la mano de Dios; ~**mother** *n* madrina; ~**send** *n* don *m* del cielo; ~**son** *n* ahijado

goggles ['gɔglz] *npl* gafas *fpl*

going ['gəuiŋ] *n* (*conditions*) estado del terreno ♦ *adj*: **the ~ rate** la tarifa corriente *or* en vigor

gold [gəuld] *n* oro ♦ *adj* de oro; ~**en** *adj* (*made of*) de oro; (~ *in colour*) dorado; ~**fish** *n* pez *m* de colores; ~**mine** *n* (*also fig*) mina de oro; ~**-plated** *adj* chapado en oro; ~**smith** *n* orfebre *m/f*

golf [gɔlf] *n* golf *m*; ~ **ball** *n* (*for game*) pelota de golf; ~ **club** *n* club *m* de golf; (*stick*) palo (de golf); ~ **course** *n* campo de golf; ~**er** *n* golfista *m/f*

gone [gɔn] *pp of* **go**

good [gud] *adj* bueno; (*pleasant*) agradable; (*kind*) bueno, amable; (*well-behaved*) educado ♦ *n* bien *m*, provecho; ~**s** *npl* (*COMM*) mercancías *fpl*; ~**!** ¡qué bien!; **to be ~ at** tener aptitud para; **to be ~ for** servir para; **it's ~ for you** te hace bien; **would you be ~ enough to ...?** ¿podría hacerme el favor de ...?, ¿sería tan amable de ...?; **a ~ deal (of)** mucho; **a ~ many** muchos; **to make ~** reparar; **it's no ~ complaining** no vale la pena (de) quejarse; **for ~** para siempre, definitivamente; ~ **morning/afternoon** ¡buenos días/buenas tardes!; ~ **evening!** ¡buenas noches!; ~ **night!** ¡buenas noches!; ~**bye!** ¡adiós!; **to say ~bye** despedirse; **G~ Friday** *n* Viernes *m* Santo; ~**-looking** *adj* guapo; ~**-natured**

adj amable, simpático; **~ness** *n* (*of person*) bondad *f*; **for ~ness sake!** ¡por Dios!; **~ness gracious!** ¡Dios mío!; **~s train** (*BRIT*) *n* tren *m* de mercancías; **~will** *n* buena voluntad *f*

goose [guːs] (*pl* **geese**) *n* ganso, oca

gooseberry ['guzbəɪ] *n* grosella espinosa; **to play ~** hacer de carabina

gooseflesh ['guːsfleʃ] *n* = **goose pimples**

goose pimples *npl* carne *f* de gallina

gore [gɔː*] *vt* cornear ♦ *n* sangre *f*

gorge [gɔːdʒ] *n* barranco ♦ *vr*: **to ~ o.s. (on)** atracarse (de)

gorgeous ['gɔːdʒəs] *adj* (*thing*) precioso; (*weather*) espléndido; (*person*) guapísimo

gorilla [gə'rɪlə] *n* gorila *m*

gorse [gɔːs] *n* tojo

gory ['gɔːrɪ] *adj* sangriento

go-slow (*BRIT*) *n* huelga de manos caídas

gospel ['gɔspl] *n* evangelio

gossip ['gɔsɪp] *n* (*scandal*) cotilleo, chismes *mpl*; (*chat*) charla; (*person*) cotilla *m/f*; (*chismoso/a* ♦ *vi* cotillear

got [gɔt] *pt, pp of* **get**; **~ten** (*US*) *pp of* **get**

gout [gaut] *n* gota

govern ['gʌvən] *vt* gobernar; (*influence*) dominar; **~ess** *n* institutriz *f*; **~ment** *n* gobierno; **~or** *n* gobernador(a) *m/f*; (*of school etc*) miembro del consejo; (*of jail*) director(a) *m/f*

gown [gaun] *n* traje *m*; (*of teacher, BRIT: of judge*) toga

G.P. *n abbr* = **general practitioner**

grab [græb] *vt* coger (*SP*) *or* agarrar (*AM*), arrebatar ♦ *vi*: **to ~ at** intentar agarrar

grace [greɪs] *n* gracia ♦ *vt* honrar; (*adorn*) adornar; **5 days' ~** un plazo de 5 días; **~ful** *adj* grácil; (*style, shape*) elegante, gracioso; **gracious** ['greɪʃəs] *adj* amable

grade [greɪd] *n* (*quality*) clase *f*, calidad *f*; (*in hierarchy*) grado; (*SCOL: mark*) nota; (*US: school class*) curso ♦ *vt* clasificar; **~ crossing** (*US*) *n* paso a nivel; **~ school** (*US*) *n* escuela primaria

gradient ['greɪdɪənt] *n* pendiente *f*

gradual ['grædjuəl] *adj* paulatino; **~ly** *adv*

paulatinamente

graduate [*n* 'grædjuɪt, *vb* 'grædjueɪt] *n* (*US: of high school*) graduado/a; (*of university*) licenciado/a ♦ *vi* graduarse; licenciarse; **graduation** [-'eɪʃən] *n* (*ceremony*) entrega del título

graffiti [grə'fiːtɪ] *n* pintadas *fpl*

graft [grɑːft] *n* (*AGR, MED*) injerto; (*BRIT: inf*) trabajo duro; (*bribery*) corrupción *f* ♦ *vt* injertar

grain [greɪn] *n* (*single particle*) grano; (*corn*) granos *mpl*, cereales *mpl*; (*of wood*) fibra

gram [græm] *n* gramo

grammar ['græmə*] *n* gramática; **~ school** (*BRIT*) *n* ≈ instituto de segunda enseñanza, liceo (*SP*)

grammatical [grə'mætɪkl] *adj* gramatical

gramme [græm] *n* = **gram**

gramophone ['græməfəun] (*BRIT*) *n* tocadiscos *m inv*

grand [grænd] *adj* magnífico, imponente; (*wonderful*) estupendo; (*gesture etc*) grandioso; **~children** *npl* nietos *mpl*; **~dad** (*inf*) *n* yayo, abuelito; **~daughter** *n* nieta; **~eur** ['grændjə*] *n* magnificencia, lo grandioso; **~father** *n* abuelo; **~ma** (*inf*) *n* yaya, abuelita; **~mother** *n* abuela; **~pa** (*inf*) *n* = **~dad**; **~parents** *npl* abuelos *mpl*; **~ piano** *n* piano de cola; **~son** *n* nieto; **~stand** *n* (*SPORT*) tribuna

granite ['grænɪt] *n* granito

granny ['grænɪ] (*inf*) *n* abuelita, yaya

grant [grɑːnt] *vt* (*concede*) conceder; (*admit*) reconocer ♦ *n* (*SCOL*) beca; (*ADMIN*) subvención *f*; **to take sth/sb for ~ed** dar algo por sentado/no hacer ningún caso a uno

granulated sugar ['grænjuːleɪtɪd-] (*BRIT*) *n* azúcar *m* blanquilla

grape [greɪp] *n* uva

grapefruit ['greɪpfruːt] *n* pomelo (*SP*), toronja (*AM*)

graph [grɑːf] *n* gráfica; **~ic** ['græfɪk] *adj* gráfico; **~ics** *n* artes *fpl* gráficas ♦ *npl* (*drawings*) dibujos *mpl*

grapple ['græpl] *vi*: **to ~ with sth/sb**

agarrar a algo/uno

grasp [grɑːsp] vt agarrar, asir; (understand) comprender ♦ n (grip) asimiento; (understanding) comprensión f; **~ing** adj (mean) avaro

grass [grɑːs] n hierba; (lawn) césped m; **~hopper** n saltamontes m inv; **~-roots** adj (fig) popular

grate [greit] n parrilla de chimenea ♦ vi: **to ~ (on)** chirriar (sobre) ♦ vt (CULIN) rallar

grateful ['greitful] adj agradecido

grater ['greitə*] n rallador m

gratifying ['grætifaiŋ] adj grato

grating ['greitiŋ] n (iron bars) reja ♦ adj (noise) áspero

gratitude ['grætitjuːd] n agradecimiento

gratuity [grə'tjuːiti] n gratificación f

grave [greiv] n tumba ♦ adj serio, grave

gravel ['grævl] n grava

gravestone ['greivstəun] n lápida

graveyard ['greivjɑːd] n cementerio

gravity ['græviti] n gravedad f

gravy ['greivi] n salsa de carne

gray [grei] adj = **grey**

graze [greiz] vi pacer ♦ vt (touch lightly) rozar; (scrape) raspar ♦ n (MED) abrasión f

grease [griːs] n (fat) grasa; (lubricant) lubricante m ♦ vt engrasar; lubrificar; **~proof paper** (BRIT) n papel m apergaminado; **greasy** adj grasiento

great [greit] adj grande; (inf) magnífico, estupendo, **G~ Britain** n Gran Bretaña; **~-grandfather** n bisabuelo; **~-grandmother** n bisabuela; **~ly** adv muy; (with verb) mucho; **~ness** n grandeza

Greece [griːs] n Grecia

greed [griːd] n (also: **~iness**) codicia, avaricia; (for food) gula; (for power etc) avidez f; **~y** adj avaro; (for food) glotón/ona

Greek [griːk] adj griego ♦ n griego/a; (LING) griego

green [griːn] adj (also POL) verde; (inexperienced) novato ♦ n verde m; (stretch of grass) césped m; (GOLF) green

m; **~s** npl (vegetables) verduras fpl; **~ belt** n zona verde; **~ card** n (AUT) carta verde; (US: work permit) permiso de trabajo para los extranjeros en EE. UU.; **~ery** n verdura; **~grocer** (BRIT) n verdulero/a; **~house** n invernadero; **~house effect** n efecto invernadero; **~house gas** n gases mpl de invernadero; **~ish** adj verdoso

Greenland ['griːnlənd] n Groenlandia

greet [griːt] vt (welcome) dar la bienvenida a; (receive: news) recibir; **~ing** n (welcome) bienvenida; **~ing(s) card** n tarjeta de felicitación

grenade [grə'neid] n granada

grew [gruː] pt of **grow**

grey [grei] adj gris; (weather) sombrío; **~-haired** adj canoso; **~hound** n galgo

grid [grid] n reja; (ELEC) red f; **~lock** n (traffic jam) retención f

grief [griːf] n dolor m, pena

grievance ['griːvəns] n motivo de queja, agravio

grieve [griːv] vi afligirse, acongojarse ♦ vt dar pena a; **to ~ for** llorar por

grievous ['griːvəs] adj: **~ bodily harm** (LAW) daños mpl corporales graves

grill [gril] n (on cooker) parrilla; (also: **mixed ~**) parillada ♦ vt (BRIT) asar a la parrilla; (inf: question) interrogar

grille [gril] n reja; (AUT) rejilla

grim [grim] adj (place) sombrío; (situation) triste; (person) ceñudo

grimace [gri'meis] n mueca ♦ vi hacer muecas

grime [graim] n mugre f, suciedad f

grin [grin] n sonrisa abierta ♦ vi sonreír abiertamente

grind [graind] (pt, pp **ground**) vt (coffee, pepper etc) moler; (US: meat) picar; (make sharp) afilar ♦ n (work) rutina

grip [grip] n (hold) asimiento; (control) control m, dominio; (of tyre etc): **to have a good/bad ~** agarrarse bien/mal; (handle) asidero; (holdall) maletín m ♦ vt agarrar; (viewer, reader) fascinar; **to get to ~s with** enfrentarse con; **~ping** adj absorbente

grisly ['grɪzlɪ] *adj* horripilante, horrible

gristle ['grɪsl] *n* ternilla

grit [grɪt] *n* gravilla; (*courage*) valor *m* ♦ *vt* (*road*) poner gravilla en; **to ~ one's teeth** apretar los dientes

groan [grəun] *n* gemido; quejido ♦ *vi* gemir; quejarse

grocer ['grəusə*] *n* tendero (de ultramarinos (*SP*)); **~ies** *npl* comestibles *mpl*; **~'s (shop)** *n* tienda de ultramarinos *or* de abarrotes (*AM*)

groin [grɔɪn] *n* ingle *f*

groom [gru:m] *n* mozo/a de cuadra; (*also*: **bride~**) novio ♦ *vt* (*horse*) almohazar; (*fig*): **to ~ sb for** preparar a uno para; **well-~ed** de buena presencia

groove [gru:v] *n* ranura, surco

grope [grəup]: **to ~ for** *vt fus* buscar a tientas

gross [grəus] *adj* (*neglect, injustice*) grave; (*vulgar: behaviour*) grosero; (: *appearance*) de mal gusto; (*COMM*) bruto; **~ly** *adv* (*greatly*) enormemente

grotto ['grɔtəu] *n* gruta

grotty ['grɔtɪ] (*inf*) *adj* horrible

ground [graund] *pt, pp of* **grind** ♦ *n* suelo, tierra; (*SPORT*) campo, terreno; (*reason: gen pl*) causa, razón *f*; (*US: also*: **~ wire**) tierra ♦ *vt* (*plane*) mantener en tierra; (*US: ELEC*) conectar con tierra; **~s** *npl* (*of coffee etc*) poso; (*gardens etc*) jardines *mpl*, parque *m*; **on the ~** en el suelo; **to the ~** al suelo; **to gain/lose ~** ganar/perder terreno; **~ cloth** (*US*) *n* = **~sheet**; **~ing** *n* (*in education*) conocimientos *mpl* básicos; **~less** *adj* infundado; **~sheet** (*BRIT*) *n* tela impermeable; suelo; **~ staff** *n* personal *m* de tierra; **~work** *n* preparación *f*

group [gru:p] *n* grupo; (*musical*) conjunto ♦ *vt* (*also*: **~ together**) agrupar ♦ *vi* (*also*: **~ together**) agruparse

grouse [graus] *n inv* (*bird*) urogallo ♦ *vi* (*complain*) quejarse

grove [grəuv] *n* arboleda

grovel ['grɔvl] *vi* (*fig*): **to ~ before** humillarse ante

grow [grəu] (*pt* **grew**, *pp* **grown**) *vi* crecer; (*increase*) aumentar; (*expand*) desarrollarse; (*become*) volverse; **to ~ rich/weak** enriquecerse/debilitarse ♦ *vt* cultivar; (*hair, beard*) dejar crecer; **~ up** *vi* crecer, hacerse hombre/mujer; **~er** *n* cultivador(a) *m/f*, productor(a) *m/f*; **~ing** *adj* creciente

growl [graul] *vi* gruñir

grown [grəun] *pp of* **grow**; **~-up** *n* adulto, mayor *m/f*

growth [grəuθ] *n* crecimiento, desarrollo; (*what has grown*) brote *m*; (*MED*) tumor *m*

grub [grʌb] *n* larva, gusano; (*inf: food*) comida

grubby ['grʌbɪ] *adj* sucio, mugriento

grudge [grʌdʒ] *n* (motivo de) rencor *m* ♦ *vt*: **to ~ sb sth** dar algo a uno de mala gana; **to bear sb a ~** guardar rencor a uno

gruelling ['gruəlɪŋ] (*US* **grueling**) *adj* penoso, duro

gruesome ['gru:səm] *adj* horrible

gruff [grʌf] *adj* (*voice*) ronco; (*manner*) brusco

grumble ['grʌmbl] *vi* refunfuñar, quejarse

grumpy ['grʌmpɪ] *adj* gruñón/ona

grunt [grʌnt] *vi* gruñir

G-string ['dʒi:strɪŋ] *n* taparrabo

guarantee [gærən'ti:] *n* garantía ♦ *vt* garantizar

guard [ga:d] *n* (*squad*) guardia; (*one man*) guardia *m*; (*BRIT: RAIL*) jefe *m* de tren; (*on machine*) dispositivo de seguridad; (*also*: **fire~**) rejilla de protección ♦ *vt* guardar; (*prisoner*) vigilar; **to be on one's ~** estar alerta; **~ against** *vt fus* (*prevent*) protegerse de; **~ed** *adj* (*fig*) cauteloso; **~ian** *n* guardián/ana *m/f*; (*of minor*) tutor(a) *m/f*; **~'s van** *n* (*BRIT: RAIL*) furgón *m*

Guatemala [gwætɪ'mɑ:lə] *n* Guatemala; **~n** *adj, n* guatemalteco/a *m/f*

guerrilla [gə'rɪlə] *n* guerrillero/a

guess [gɛs] *vi* adivinar; (*US*) suponer ♦ *vt*

adivinar; suponer ♦ n suposición f,
conjetura; **to take** or **have a ~** tratar de
adivinar; **~work** n conjeturas fpl
guest [gɛst] n invitado/a; (in hotel)
huésped(a) m/f; **~ house** n casa de
huéspedes, pensión f; **~ room** n cuarto
de huéspedes
guffaw [gʌˈfɔː] vi reírse a carcajadas
guidance ['gaɪdəns] n (advice) consejos
mpl
guide [gaɪd] n (person) guía m/f; (book,
fig) guía f ♦ vt (round museum etc) guiar;
(lead) conducir; (direct) orientar; **(girl) ~**
n exploradora; **~book** n guía f; **~ dog** n
perro m guía; **~lines** npl (advice)
directrices fpl
guild [gɪld] n gremio
guilt [gɪlt] n culpabilidad f; **~y** adj
culpable
guinea pig ['gɪnɪ-] n cobaya; (fig)
conejillo de Indias
guise [gaɪz] n: **in** or **under the ~ of** bajo
apariencia de
guitar [gɪˈtɑː*] n guitarra
gulf [gʌlf] n golfo; (abyss) abismo
gull [gʌl] n gaviota
gullible ['gʌlɪbl] adj crédulo
gully ['gʌlɪ] n barranco
gulp [gʌlp] vi tragar saliva ♦ vt (also: **~
down**) tragarse
gum [gʌm] n (ANAT) encía; (glue) goma,
cemento; (sweet) caramelo de goma;
(also: **chewing-~**) chicle m ♦ vt pegar
con goma; **~boots** (BRIT) npl botas fpl
de goma
gun [gʌn] n (small) pistola, revólver m;
(shotgun) escopeta; (rifle) fusil m;
(cannon) cañón m; **~boat** n cañonero;
~fire n disparos mpl; **~man** n pistolero;
~point n: **at ~point** a mano armada;
~powder n pólvora; **~shot** n
escopetazo
gurgle ['gəːgl] vi (baby) gorgotear; (water)
borbotear
gush [gʌʃ] vi salir a raudales; (person)
deshacerse en efusiones
gust [gʌst] n (of wind) ráfaga

gusto ['gʌstəu] n entusiasmo
gut [gʌt] n intestino; **~s** npl (ANAT) tripas
fpl; (courage) valor m
gutter ['gʌtə*] n (of roof) canalón m; (in
street) cuneta
guy [gaɪ] n (also: **~rope**) cuerda; (inf: man)
tío (SP), tipo; (figure) monigote m

Guy Fawkes' Night

i La noche del cinco de noviembre, **Guy
Fawkes' Night**, se celebra en el Reino
Unido el fracaso de la conspiración de la
pólvora ("Gunpowder Plot"), un intento
fallido de volar el parlamento de Jaime I
en 1605. Esa noche se lanzan fuegos
artificiales y se hacen hogueras en las que
se queman unos muñecos de trapo que
representan a **Guy Fawkes**, uno de los
cabecillas de la revuelta. Días antes, los
niños tienen por costumbre pedir a los
transeúntes "a penny for the guy", dinero
que emplean en comprar cohetes y
petardos.

---

guzzle ['gʌzl] vi tragar ♦ vt engullir
gym [dʒɪm] n (also: **gymnasium**)
gimnasio; (also: **gymnastics**) gimnasia; **~nast** n
gimnasta m/f; **~ shoes** npl zapatillas fpl
(de deporte); **~ slip** (BRIT) n túnica de
colegiala
gynaecologist [gaɪnɪˈkɔlədʒɪst] (US
gynecologist) n ginecólogo/a
gypsy ['dʒɪpsɪ] n gitano/a

H, h

haberdashery [hæbəˈdæʃərɪ] (BRIT) n
mercería
habit ['hæbɪt] n hábito, costumbre f; (drug
~) adicción f; (costume) hábito
habitual [həˈbɪtjuəl] adj acostumbrado,
habitual; (drinker, liar) empedernido
hack [hæk] vt (cut) cortar; (slice) tajar ♦ n
(pej: writer) escritor(a) m/f a sueldo; **~er**
n (COMPUT) pirata m/f informático/a
hackneyed ['hæknɪd] adj trillado

had [hæd] *pt, pp of* **have**
haddock ['hædək] (*pl* ~ *or* ~**s**) *n* especie de merluza
hadn't ['hædnt] = **had not**
haemorrhage ['hemərɪdʒ] (*US* **hemorrhage**) *n* hemorragia
haemorrhoids ['hemərɔɪdz] (*US* **hemorrhoids**) *npl* hemorroides *fpl*
haggle ['hægl] *vi* regatear
Hague [heɪg] *n*: **The ~** La Haya
hail [heɪl] *n* granizo; (*fig*) lluvia ♦ *vt* saludar; (*taxi*) llamar a; (*acclaim*) aclamar ♦ *vi* granizar; ~**stone** *n* (piedra de) granizo
hair [hɛə*] *n* pelo, cabellos *mpl*; (*one* ~) pelo, cabello; (*on legs etc*) vello; **to do one's ~** arreglarse el pelo; **to have grey ~** tener canas *fpl*; ~**brush** *n* cepillo (para el pelo); ~**cut** *n* corte *m* (de pelo); ~**do** *n* peinado; ~**dresser** *n* peluquero/a; ~**dresser's** *n* peluquería; ~ **dryer** *n* secador *m* de pelo; ~**grip** *n* horquilla; ~**net** *n* redecilla; ~**piece** *n* postizo; ~**pin** *n* horquilla; ~**pin bend** (*US* ~**pin curve**) *n* curva de horquilla; ~**raising** *adj* espeluznante; ~**removing cream** *n* crema depilatoria; ~ **spray** *n* laca; ~**style** *n* peinado; ~**y** *adj* peludo; velludo; (*inf: frightening*) espeluznante
hake [heɪk] (*pl inv or* ~**s**) *n* merluza
half [hɑːf] (*pl* **halves**) *n* mitad *f*; (*of beer*) ≈ caña (*SP*), media pinta; (*RAIL, BUS*) billete *m* de niño ♦ *adj* medio ♦ *adv* medio, a medias; **two and a ~** dos y media; **~ a dozen** media docena; **~ a pound** media libra; **to cut sth in ~** cortar algo por la mitad; ~**caste** ['hɑːfkɑːst] *n* mestizo/a; ~**hearted** *adj* indiferente, poco entusiasta; ~**hour** *n* media hora; ~**mast** *n*: **at ~mast** (*flag*) a media asta; ~**price** *adj, adv* a mitad de precio; ~ **term** (*BRIT*) *n* (*SCOL*) vacaciones *fpl* de mediados del trimestre; ~**time** *n* descanso; ~**way** *adv* a medio camino; (*in period of time*) a mitad de
hall [hɔːl] *n* (*for concerts*) sala; (*entrance way*) hall *m*; vestíbulo; ~ **of residence** (*BRIT*) *n* residencia
hallmark ['hɔːlmɑːk] *n* sello
hallo [hə'ləu] *excl* = **hello**
Hallowe'en [hæləu'iːn] *n* víspera de Todos los Santos

Hallowe'en

🛈 *La tradición anglosajona dice que en la noche del 31 de octubre,* **Hallowe'en,** *víspera de Todos los Santos, es posible ver a brujas y fantasmas. En este día los niños se disfrazan y van de puerta en puerta llevando un farol hecho con una calabaza en forma de cabeza humana. Cuando se les abre la puerta gritan "trick or treat", amenazando con gastar una broma a quien no les dé golosinas o algo de calderilla.*

---

hallucination [həluːsɪ'neɪʃən] *n* alucinación *f*
hallway ['hɔːlweɪ] *n* vestíbulo
halo ['heɪləu] *n* (*of saint*) halo, aureola
halt [hɔːlt] *n* (*stop*) alto, parada; interrumpir ♦ *vi* pararse
halve [hɑːv] *vt* partir por la mitad
halves [hɑːvz] *npl of* **half**
ham [hæm] *n* jamón *m* (cocido)
hamburger ['hæmbəːgə*] *n* hamburguesa
hamlet ['hæmlɪt] *n* aldea
hammer ['hæmə*] *n* martillo ♦ *vt* (*nail*) clavar; (*force*): **to ~ an idea into sb/a message across** meter una idea en la cabeza a uno/machacar una idea ♦ *vi* dar golpes
hammock ['hæmək] *n* hamaca
hamper ['hæmpə*] *vt* estorbar ♦ *n* cesto
hand [hænd] *n* mano *f*; (*of clock*) aguja; (*writing*) letra; (*worker*) obrero ♦ *vt* dar, pasar; **to give** *or* **lend sb a ~** echar una mano a uno, ayudar a uno; **at ~** a mano; **in ~** (*time*) libre; (*job etc*) entre manos; **on ~** (*person, services*) a mano, al alcance; **to ~** (*information etc*) a mano; **on the one ~ ..., on the other ~ ...** por una parte ... por otra (parte) ...; **~ in** *vt* entregar; **~ out** *vt* distribuir; **~ over** *vt* (*deliver*)

entregar; ~**bag** n bolso (*SP*), cartera (*AM*);
~**book** n manual m; ~**brake** n freno de
mano; ~**cuffs** npl esposas *fpl*; ~**ful** n
puñado
handicap ['hændɪkæp] n minusvalía;
(*disadvantage*) desventaja; (*SPORT*)
handicap m ♦ vt estorbar; **mentally/
physically ~ped** deficiente m/f (mental/
minusválido/a (físico/a)
handicraft ['hændɪkrɑːft] n artesanía;
(*object*) objeto de artesanía
handiwork ['hændɪwɜːk] n obra
handkerchief ['hæŋkətʃɪf] n pañuelo
handle ['hændl] n (*of door etc*) tirador m;
(*of cup etc*) asa; (*of knife etc*) mango; (*for
winding*) manivela ♦ vt (*touch*) tocar; (*deal
with*) encargarse de; (*treat: people*)
manejar; "**~ with care**" "(manéjese) con
cuidado"; **to fly off the ~** perder los
estribos; ~**bar(s)** n(pl) manillar m
hand: ~ luggage n equipaje m de mano;
~**made** adj hecho a mano; ~**out** n
(*money etc*) limosna; (*leaflet*) folleto; ~**rail**
n pasamanos m inv; ~**shake** n apretón
m de manos
handsome ['hænsəm] adj guapo;
(*building*) bello; (*fig: profit*) considerable
handwriting ['hændraɪtɪŋ] n letra
handy ['hændɪ] adj (*close at hand*) a la
mano; (*tool etc*) práctico; (*skilful*) hábil,
diestro
hang [hæŋ] (*pt, pp* hung) vt colgar;
(*criminal: pt, pp* hanged) ahorcar ♦ vi
(*painting, coat etc*) colgar; (*hair, drapery*)
caer; **to get the ~ of sth** (*inf*) lograr
dominar algo; ~ **about** or **around** vi
haraganear; ~ **on** vi (*wait*) esperar; ~ **up**
vi (*TEL*) colgar ♦ vt colgar
hanger ['hæŋə*] n percha; ~**-on** n
parásito
hang: ~-gliding ['-ɡlaɪdɪŋ] n vuelo libre;
~**over** n (*after drinking*) resaca; ~**-up** n
complejo
hanker ['hæŋkə*] vi: **to ~ after** añorar
hankie ['hæŋkɪ], **hanky** ['hæŋkɪ] n abbr =
handkerchief
haphazard [hæp'hæzəd] adj fortuito

happen ['hæpən] vi suceder, ocurrir;
(*chance*): **he ~ed to hear/see** dió la
casualidad de que oyó/vió; **as it ~s** da la
casualidad de que; ~**ing** n suceso,
acontecimiento
happily ['hæpɪlɪ] adv (*luckily*)
afortunadamente; (*cheerfully*) alegremente
happiness ['hæpɪnɪs] n felicidad f;
(*cheerfulness*) alegría
happy ['hæpɪ] adj feliz; (*cheerful*) alegre; **to
be ~ (with)** estar contento (con); **to be ~
to do** estar encantado de hacer; ~
birthday! ¡feliz cumpleaños!; ~**-go-lucky**
adj despreocupado; ~ **hour** n horas en
las que la bebida es más barata, happy
hour f
harass ['hærəs] vt acosar, hostigar;
~**ment** n persecución f
harbour ['hɑːbə*] (*US* **harbor**) n puerto
♦ vt (*fugitive*) dar abrigo a; (*hope etc*)
abrigar
hard [hɑːd] adj duro; (*difficult*) difícil;
(*work*) arduo; (*person*) severo; (*fact*)
innegable ♦ adv (*work*) mucho, duro;
(*think*) profundamente; **to look ~ at**
clavar los ojos en; **to try ~** esforzarse; **no
~ feelings!** ¡sin rencor(es)!; **to be ~ of
hearing** ser duro de oído; **to be ~ done
by** ser tratado injustamente; ~**back** n
libro en cartoné; ~ **cash** n dinero
contante; ~ **disk** n (*COMPUT*) disco duro
or rígido; ~**en** vt endurecer; (*fig*) curtir
♦ vi endurecerse; curtirse; ~**-headed** adj
realista; ~ **labour** n trabajos *mpl*
forzados
hardly ['hɑːdlɪ] adv apenas; ~ **ever** casi
nunca
hard: ~ship n privación f; ~ **shoulder**
(*BRIT*) n (*AUT*) arcén m; ~**-up** (*inf*) adj sin
un duro (*SP*), sin plata (*AM*); ~**ware** n
ferretería; (*COMPUT*) hardware m; (*MIL*)
armamento; ~**ware shop** n ferretería;
~**-wearing** adj resistente, duradero; ~**-
working** adj trabajador(a)
hardy ['hɑːdɪ] adj fuerte; (*plant*) resistente
hare [hɛə*] n liebre f; ~**-brained** adj
descabellado

harm [hɑːm] n daño, mal m ♦ vt (person) hacer daño a; (health, interests) perjudicar; (thing) dañar; out of ~'s way a salvo; ~ful adj dañino; ~less adj (person) inofensivo; (joke etc) inocente

harmony ['hɑːmənɪ] n armonía

harness ['hɑːnɪs] n arreos mpl; (for child) arnés m; (safety ~) arneses mpl ♦ vt (horse) enjaezar; (resources) aprovechar

harp [hɑːp] n arpa ♦ vi: to ~ on (about) machacar (con)

harrowing ['hærəʊɪŋ] adj angustioso

harsh [hɑːʃ] adj (cruel) duro, cruel; (severe) severo; (sound) áspero; (light) deslumbrador(a)

harvest ['hɑːvɪst] n (~ time) siega; (of cereals etc) cosecha; (of grapes) vendimia ♦ vt cosechar

has [hæz] vb see have

hash [hæʃ] n (CULIN) picadillo; (fig: mess) lío

hashish ['hæʃɪʃ] n hachís m

hasn't ['hæznt] = has not

hassle ['hæsl] (inf) n lata

haste [heɪst] n prisa; ~n ['heɪsn] vt acelerar ♦ vi darse prisa; hastily adv de prisa; precipitadamente; hasty adj apresurado; (rash) precipitado

hat [hæt] n sombrero

hatch [hætʃ] n (NAUT: also: ~way) escotilla; (also: service ~) ventanilla ♦ vi (bird) salir del cascarón ♦ vt incubar; (plot) tramar; 5 eggs have ~ed han salido 5 pollos

hatchback ['hætʃbæk] n (AUT) tres or cinco puertas m

hatchet ['hætʃɪt] n hacha

hate [heɪt] vt odiar, aborrecer ♦ n odio; ~ful adj odioso; hatred ['heɪtrɪd] n odio

haughty ['hɔːtɪ] adj altanero

haul [hɔːl] vt tirar ♦ n (of fish) redada; (of stolen goods etc) botín m; ~age (BRIT) n transporte m; (costs) gastos mpl de transporte; ~ier (US =~er) n transportista m/f

haunch [hɔːntʃ] n anca; (of meat) pierna

haunt [hɔːnt] vt (subj: ghost) aparecerse en; (obsess) obsesionar ♦ n guarida

KEYWORD

have [hæv] (pt, pp had) aux vb 1 (gen) haber; to ~ arrived/eaten haber llegado/comido; having finished or when he had finished, he left cuando hubo acabado, se fue

2 (in tag questions): you've done it, ~n't you? lo has hecho, ¿verdad? or ¿no?

3 (in short answers and questions): I ~n't no; so I ~ pues, es verdad; we ~n't paid — yes we ~! no hemos pagado — ¡sí que hemos pagado!; I've been there before, ~ you? he estado allí antes, ¿y tú?

♦ modal aux vb (be obliged): to ~ (got) to do sth tener que hacer algo; you ~n't to tell her no hay que or no debes decírselo

♦ vt 1 (possess): he has (got) blue eyes/dark hair tiene los ojos azules/el pelo negro

2 (referring to meals etc): to ~ breakfast/lunch/dinner desayunar/comer/cenar; to ~ a drink/a cigarette tomar algo/fumar un cigarrillo

3 (receive) recibir; (obtain) obtener; may I ~ your address? ¿puedes darme tu dirección?; you can ~ it for £5 te lo puedes quedar por £5; I must ~ it by tomorrow lo necesito para mañana; to ~ a baby tener un niño or bebé

4 (maintain, allow): I won't ~ it/this nonsense! ¡no lo permitiré!/¡no permitiré estas tonterías!; we can't ~ that no podemos permitir eso

5: to ~ sth done hacer or mandar hacer algo; to ~ one's hair cut cortarse el pelo; to ~ sb do sth hacer que alguien haga algo

6 (experience, suffer): to ~ a cold/flu tener un resfriado/la gripe; she had her bag stolen/her arm broken le robaron el bolso/se rompió un brazo; to ~ an operation operarse

7 (+noun): to ~ a swim/walk/bath/rest nadar/dar un paseo/darse un baño/descansar; let's ~ a look vamos a ver; to

~ **a meeting/party** celebrar una
reunión/una fiesta; **let me ~ a try** déjame
intentarlo
have out vt: **to ~ it out with sb** (settle a
problem etc) dejar las cosas en claro con
alguien

haven ['heɪvn] n puerto; (fig) refugio
haven't ['hævnt] = **have not**
havoc ['hævək] n estragos *mpl*
hawk [hɔːk] n halcón *m*
hay [heɪ] n heno; ~ **fever** n fiebre *f* del
heno; ~**stack** n almiar *m*
haywire ['heɪwaɪə*] (inf) adj: **to go ~**
(plan) embrollarse
hazard ['hæzəd] n peligro ♦ vt aventurar;
~**ous** adj peligroso; ~ **warning lights**
npl (AUT) señales *fpl* de emergencia
haze [heɪz] n neblina
hazelnut ['heɪzlnʌt] n avellana
hazy ['heɪzɪ] adj brumoso; (idea) vago
he [hiː] pron él; ~ **who ... él que ...,**
quien ...
head [hed] n cabeza; (leader) jefe/a *m/f*;
(of school) director(a) *m/f* ♦ vt (list)
encabezar; (group) capitanear; (company)
dirigir; ~**s (or tails)** cara (o cruz); ~ **first**
de cabeza; ~ **over heels** (in love)
perdidamente; **to ~ the ball** cabecear (la
pelota); ~ **for** vt fus dirigirse a; (disaster)
ir camino de; ~**ache** n dolor *m* de
cabeza; ~**dress** n tocado; ~**ing** n título;
~**lamp** (BRIT) n = ~**light**; ~**land** n
promontorio; ~**light** n faro; ~**line** n
titular *m*; ~**long** adv (fall) de cabeza;
(rush) precipitadamente; ~**master/
mistress** n director(a) *m/f* (de escuela);
~ **office** n oficina central, central *f*; ~~
on (collision) de frente; ~**phones** npl
auriculares *mpl*; ~**quarters** npl sede *f*
central; (MIL) cuartel *m* general; ~**rest** n
reposa-cabezas *m inv*; ~**room** n (in car)
altura interior; (under bridge) (límite *m* de)
altura; ~**scarf** n pañuelo; ~**strong** adj
testarudo; ~ **waiter** n maître *m*; ~**way**
n: **to make ~way** (fig) hacer progresos;
~**wind** n viento contrario; ~**y** adj

(experience, period) apasionante; (wine)
cabezón; (atmosphere) embriagador(a)
heal [hiːl] vt curar ♦ vi cicatrizarse
health [helθ] n salud *f*; ~ **food** n
alimentos *mpl* orgánicos; the **H~
Service** (BRIT) n el servicio de salud
pública; ≈ el Insalud (SP); ~**y** adj sano,
saludable
heap [hiːp] n montón *m* ♦ vt: **to ~ (up)**
amontonar; **to ~ sth with** llenar algo
hasta arriba de; ~**s of** un montón de
hear [hɪə*] (pt, pp **heard**) vt (also LAW) oír;
(news) saber de ♦ vi oír; **to ~ about** oír
hablar de; **to ~ from sb** tener noticias de
uno; ~**ing** n (sense) oído; (LAW) vista;
~**ing aid** n audífono; ~**say** n rumores
mpl, habillas *fpl*
hearse [hɜːs] n coche *m* fúnebre
heart [hɑːt] n corazón *m*; (fig) valor *m*; (of
lettuce) cogollo; ~**s** npl (CARDS) corazones
mpl; **to lose/take** ~ descorazonarse/
cobrar ánimo; **at** ~ en el fondo; **by** ~
(learn, know) de memoria; ~ **attack** n
infarto (de miocardio); ~**beat** n latido
(del corazón); ~**breaking** adj
desgarrador(a); ~**broken** adj: **she was
~broken about it** esto le partió el
corazón; ~**burn** n acedía; ~ **failure** n
fallo cardíaco; ~**felt** adj (deeply felt) más
sentido
hearth [hɑːθ] n (fireplace) chimenea
hearty ['hɑːtɪ] adj (person) campechano;
(laugh) sano; (dislike, support) absoluto
heat [hiːt] n calor *m*; (SPORT: also:
qualifying ~) prueba eliminatoria ♦ vt
calentar; ~ **up** vi calentarse ♦ vt calentar;
~**ed** adj caliente; (fig) acalorado; ~**er** n
estufa; (in car) calefacción *f*
heath [hiːθ] (BRIT) n brezal *m*
heather ['heðə*] n brezo
heating ['hiːtɪŋ] n calefacción *f*
heatstroke ['hiːtstrəuk] n insolación *f*
heatwave ['hiːtweɪv] n ola de calor
heave [hiːv] vt (pull) tirar; (push) empujar
con esfuerzo; (lift) levantar (con esfuerzo)
♦ vi (chest) palpitar; (retch) tener náuseas
♦ n tirón *m*; empujón *m*; **to ~ a sigh**

suspirar

heaven ['hɛvn] n cielo; (fig) una maravilla; ~**ly** adj celestial; (fig) maravilloso

heavily ['hɛvɪlɪ] adv pesadamente; (drink, smoke) con exceso; (sleep, sigh) profundamente; (depend) mucho

heavy ['hɛvɪ] adj pesado; (work, blow) duro; (sea, rain, meal) fuerte; (drinker, smoker) grande; (responsibility) grave; (schedule) ocupado; (weather) bochornoso; ~ **goods vehicle** n vehículo pesado; ~**weight** n (SPORT) peso pesado

Hebrew ['hi:bru:] adj, n (LING) hebreo

heckle ['hɛkl] vt interrumpir

hectic ['hɛktɪk] adj agitado

he'd [hi:d] = **he would**; **he had**

hedge [hɛdʒ] n seto ♦ vi contestar con evasivas; **to ~ one's bets** (fig) cubrirse

hedgehog ['hɛdʒhɔg] n erizo

heed [hi:d] vt (also: **take ~ of**) (pay attention to) hacer caso de; ~**less** adj: **to be ~less (of)** no hacer caso (de)

heel [hi:l] n talón m; (of shoe) tacón m ♦ vt (shoe) poner tacón a

hefty ['hɛftɪ] adj (person) fornido; (parcel, profit) gordo

heifer ['hɛfə*] n novilla, ternera

height [haɪt] n (of person) estatura; (of building) altura; (high ground) cerro; (altitude) altitud f; (fig: of season): **at the ~ of summer** en los días más calurosos del verano; (: of power etc) cúspide f; (: of stupidity etc) colmo; ~**en** vt elevar; (fig) aumentar

heir [ɛə*] n heredero; ~**ess** n heredera; ~**loom** n reliquia de familia

held [hɛld] pt, pp of **hold**

helicopter ['hɛlɪkɔptə*] n helicóptero

hell [hɛl] n infierno; ~**!** (inf) ¡demonios!

he'll [hi:l] = **he will**; **he shall**

hello [hə'ləu] excl ¡hola!; (to attract attention) ¡oiga!; (surprise) ¡caramba!

helm [hɛlm] n (NAUT) timón m

helmet ['hɛlmɪt] n casco

help [hɛlp] n ayuda; (cleaner etc) criada, asistenta ♦ vt ayudar; ~**!** ¡socorro!; ~

yourself sírvete; **he can't ~ it** no es culpa suya; ~**er** n ayudante m/f; ~**ful** adj útil; (person) servicial; (advice) útil; ~**ing** n ración f; ~**less** adj (incapable) incapaz; (defenceless) indefenso

hem [hɛm] n dobladillo ♦ vt poner or coser el dobladillo; ~ **in** vt cercar

hemorrhage ['hɛmərɪdʒ] (US) n = **haemorrhage**

hemorrhoids ['hɛmərɔɪdz] (US) npl = **haemorrhoids**

hen [hɛn] n gallina; (female bird) hembra

hence [hɛns] adv (therefore) por lo tanto; **2 years ~** de aquí a 2 años; ~**forth** adv de hoy en adelante

hepatitis [hɛpə'taɪtɪs] n hepatitis f

her [hə:*] pron (direct) la; (indirect) le; (stressed, after prep) ella ♦ adj su; see also **me**; **my**

herald ['hɛrəld] n heraldo ♦ vt anunciar; ~**ry** n heráldica

herb [hə:b] n hierba

herd [hə:d] n rebaño

here [hɪə*] adv aquí; (at this point) en este punto; ~**!** (present) ¡presente!; ~ **is/are** aquí está/están; ~ **she is** aquí está; ~**after** adv en el futuro; ~**by** adv (in letter) por la presente

heritage ['hɛrɪtɪdʒ] n patrimonio

hermit ['hə:mɪt] n ermitaño/a

hernia ['hə:nɪə] n hernia

hero ['hɪərəu] (pl ~**es**) n héroe m; (in book, film) protagonista m

heroin ['hɛrəuɪn] n heroína

heroine ['hɛrəuɪn] n heroína; (in book, film) protagonista

heron ['hɛrən] n garza

herring ['hɛrɪŋ] n arenque m

hers [hə:z] pron (el) suyo/(la) suya etc; see also **mine**[1]

herself [hə:'sɛlf] pron (reflexive) se; (emphatic) ella misma; (after prep) sí (misma); see also **oneself**

he's [hi:z] = **he is**; **he has**

hesitant ['hɛzɪtənt] adj vacilante

hesitate ['hɛzɪteɪt] vi vacilar; (in speech) titubear; (be unwilling) resistirse a;

hesitation ['-teɪʃən] n indecisión f; titubeo; dudas fpl

heterosexual [hetərəu'sɛksjuəl] adj heterosexual

heyday ['heɪdeɪ] n: **the ~ of** el apogeo de

HGV n abbr = **heavy goods vehicle**

hi [haɪ] excl ¡hola!; (to attract attention) ¡oiga!

hiatus [haɪ'eɪtəs] n vacío

hibernate ['haɪbəneɪt] vi invernar

hiccough ['hɪkʌp] = **hiccup**

hiccup ['hɪkʌp] vi hipar; **~s** npl hipo

hide [haɪd] (pt **hid**, pp **hidden**) n (skin) piel f ♦ vt esconder, ocultar ♦ vi: **to ~ (from sb)** esconderse or ocultarse (de uno); **~-and-seek** n escondite m

hideous ['hɪdɪəs] adj horrible

hiding ['haɪdɪŋ] n (beating) paliza; **to be in ~** (concealed) estar escondido

hierarchy ['haɪərɑːkɪ] n jerarquía

hi-fi ['haɪfaɪ] n estéreo, hifi m ♦ adj de alta fidelidad

high [haɪ] adj alto; (speed, number) grande; (price) elevado; (wind) fuerte; (voice) agudo ♦ adv alto, a gran altura; **it is 20 m ~** tiene 20 m de altura; **~ in the air** en las alturas; **~brow** adj intelectual; **~chair** n silla alta; **~er education** n educación f or enseñanza superior; **~-handed** adj despótico; **~-heeled** adj de tacón alto; **~ jump** n (SPORT) salto de altura; **the H~lands** npl las tierras altas de Escocia; **~light** n (fig: of event) punto culminante; (in hair) reflejo ♦ vt subrayar; **~ly** adv (paid) muy bien; (critical, confidential) sumamente; (a lot): **to speak/think ~ly of** hablar muy bien de/ tener en mucho a; **~ly strung** adj hipertenso; **~ness** n altura; **Her or His H~ness** Su Alteza; **~-pitched** adj agudo; **~-rise block** n torre f de pisos; **~ school** n ≈ Instituto Nacional de Bachillerato (SP); **~ season** n (BRIT) temporada alta; **~ street** n (BRIT) calle f mayor; **~way** n carretera; (US) carretera nacional; autopista; **H~way Code** (BRIT) n código de la circulación

hijack ['haɪdʒæk] vt secuestrar; **~er** n secuestrador(a) m/f

hike [haɪk] vi (go walking) ir de excursión (a pie) ♦ n caminata; **~r** n excursionista m/f; **hiking** n senderismo

hilarious [hɪ'lɛərɪəs] adj divertidísimo

hill [hɪl] n colina; (high) montaña; (slope) cuesta; **~side** n ladera; **~ walking** n senderismo (de montaña); **~y** adj montañoso

hilt [hɪlt] n (of sword) empuñadura; **to the ~** (fig: support) incondicionalmente

him [hɪm] pron (direct) le, lo; (indirect) le; (stressed, after prep) él; see also **me**; **~self** pron (reflexive) se; (emphatic) él mismo; (after prep) sí (mismo); see also **oneself**

hinder ['hɪndə*] vt estorbar, impedir; **hindrance** ['hɪndrəns] n estorbo

hindsight ['haɪndsaɪt] n: **with ~** en retrospectiva

Hindu ['hɪnduː] n hindú m/f

hinge [hɪndʒ] n bisagra, gozne m ♦ vi (fig): **to ~ on** depender de

hint [hɪnt] n indirecta; (advice) consejo; (sign) dejo ♦ vt: **to ~ that** insinuar que ♦ vi: **to ~ at** hacer alusión a

hip [hɪp] n cadera

hippopotamus [hɪpə'pɔtəməs] (pl **~es** or **hippopotami**) n hipopótamo

hire ['haɪə*] vt (BRIT: car, equipment) alquilar; (worker) contratar ♦ n alquiler m; **for ~** se alquila; (taxi) libre; **~(d) car** (BRIT) n coche m de alquiler; **~ purchase** (BRIT) n compra a plazos

his [hɪz] pron (el) suyo/(la) suya etc ♦ adj su; see also **mine**[1]; **my**

Hispanic [hɪs'pænɪk] adj hispánico

hiss [hɪs] vi silbar

historian [hɪ'stɔːrɪən] n historiador(a) m/f

historic(al) [hɪ'stɔrɪk(l)] adj histórico

history ['hɪstərɪ] n historia

hit [hɪt] (pt, pp **hit**) vt (strike) golpear, pegar; (reach: target) alcanzar; (collide with: car) chocar contra; (fig: affect) afectar ♦ n golpe m; (success) éxito; **to ~ it off with sb** llevarse bien con uno; **~-**

and-run driver n conductor(a) que atropella y huye

hitch [hɪtʃ] vt (fasten) atar, amarrar; (also: ~ **up**) remangar ♦ n (difficulty) dificultad f; **to ~ a lift** hacer autostop

hitch-hike vi hacer autostop; **~hiking** n autostop m

hi-tech [haɪˈtɛk] adj de alta tecnología

hitherto [ˈhɪðəˈtuː] adv hasta ahora

HIV n abbr (= human immunodeficiency virus) VIH m; **~-negative/positive** adj VIH negativo/positivo

hive [haɪv] n colmena

HMS abbr = His (Her) Majesty's Ship

hoard [hɔːd] n (treasure) tesoro; (stockpile) provisión f ♦ vt acumular; (goods) acaparar; **~ing** n (for posters) cartelera

hoarse [hɔːs] adj ronco

hoax [həʊks] n trampa

hob [hɔb] n quemador m

hobble [ˈhɔbl] vi cojear

hobby [ˈhɔbɪ] n pasatiempo, afición f

hobo [ˈhəʊbəʊ] (US) n vagabundo

hockey [ˈhɔkɪ] n hockey m

hog [hɔg] n cerdo, puerco ♦ vt (fig) acaparar; **to go the whole ~** poner toda la carne en el asador

hoist [hɔɪst] n (crane) grúa ♦ vt levantar, alzar; (flag, sail) izar

hold [həʊld] (pt, pp **held**) vt sostener; (contain) contener; (have: power, qualification) tener; (keep back) retener; (believe) sostener; (consider) considerar; (keep in position): **to ~ one's head up** mantener la cabeza alta; (meeting) celebrar ♦ vi (withstand pressure) resistir; (be valid) valer ♦ n (grasp) asimiento m; (fig) dominio; **~ the line!** (TEL) ¡no cuelgue!; **to ~ one's own** (fig) defenderse; **to catch** or **get (a) ~ of** agarrarse or asirse de; ~ **back** vt retener; (secret) ocultar; ~ **down** vt (person) sujetar; (job) mantener; ~ **off** vt (enemy) rechazar; ~ **on** vi agarrarse bien; (wait) esperar; ~ **on!** (TEL) ¡(espere) un momento!; ~ **on to** vt fus agarrarse a; (keep) guardar; ~ **out** vt ofrecer ♦ vi (resist) resistir; ~ **up** vt (raise)

levantar; (support) apoyar; (delay) retrasar; (rob) asaltar; **~all** (BRIT) n bolsa; **~er** n (container) receptáculo; (of ticket, record) poseedor(a) m/f; (of office, title etc) titular m/f; **~ing** n (share) interés m; (farmland) parcela; **~up** n (robbery) atraco; (delay) retraso; (BRIT: in traffic) embotellamiento

hole [həʊl] n agujero

holiday [ˈhɔlədɪ] n vacaciones fpl; (public ~) (día m de) fiesta, día m feriado; **on ~** de vacaciones; **~ camp** n (BRIT: also: ~ **centre**) centro de vacaciones; **~-maker** (BRIT) n turista m/f; **~ resort** n centro turístico

holiness [ˈhəʊlɪnɪs] n santidad f

Holland [ˈhɔlənd] n Holanda

hollow [ˈhɔləʊ] adj hueco; (claim) vacío; (eyes) hundido; (sound) sordo ♦ n hueco; (in ground) hoyo ♦ vt: **to ~ out** excavar

holly [ˈhɔlɪ] n acebo

holocaust [ˈhɔləkɔːst] n holocausto

holy [ˈhəʊlɪ] adj santo, sagrado; (water) bendito

homage [ˈhɔmɪdʒ] n homenaje m

home [həʊm] n casa; (country) patria; (institution) asilo ♦ cpd (domestic) casero, de casa; (ECON, POL) nacional ♦ adv (direction) a casa; (right in: nail etc) a fondo; **at ~** en casa; (in country) en el país; (fig) como pez en el agua; **to go/ come ~** ir/volver a casa; **make yourself at ~** ¡estás en tu casa!; ~ **address** n domicilio; **~land** n tierra natal; **~less** adj sin hogar, sin casa; **~ly** adj (simple) sencillo; **~-made** adj casero; **H~ Office** (BRIT) n Ministerio del Interior; ~ **page** n página de inicio; ~ **rule** n autonomía; **H~ Secretary** (BRIT) n Ministro del Interior; **~sick** adj: **to be ~sick** tener morriña, sentir nostalgia; ~ **town** n ciudad f natal; **~ward** [ˈhəʊmwəd] adj (journey) hacia casa; **~work** n deberes mpl

homoeopathic [həʊmɪəˈpæθɪk] (US **homeopathic**) adj homeopático

homosexual [hɔməʊˈsɛksjuəl] adj, n homosexual m/f

Honduran [hɒn'djuərən] *adj, n* hondureño/a *m/f*

Honduras [hɒn'djuərəs] *n* Honduras *f*

honest ['ɒnɪst] *adj* honrado; (*sincere*) franco, sincero; **~ly** *adv* honradamente; francamente; **~y** *n* honradez *f*

honey ['hʌnɪ] *n* miel *f*; **~comb** *n* panal *m*; **~moon** *n* luna de miel; **~suckle** *n* madreselva

honk [hɒŋk] *vi* (AUT) tocar el pito, pitar

honorary ['ɒnərərɪ] *adj* (*member, president*) de honor; (*title*) honorífico; **~ degree** doctorado honoris causa

honour ['ɒnə*] (US **honor**) *vt* honrar; (*commitment, promise*) cumplir con ♦ *n* honor *m*, honra; **~able** *adj* honorable; **~s degree** *n* (SCOL) título de licenciado con calificación alta

hood [hud] *n* capucha; (BRIT: AUT) capota; (US: AUT) capó *m*; (*of cooker*) campana de humos

hoof [hu:f] (*pl* **hooves**) *n* pezuña

hook [huk] *n* gancho; (*on dress*) corchete *m*, broche *m*; (*for fishing*) anzuelo ♦ *vt* enganchar; (*fish*) pescar

hooligan ['hu:lɪgən] *n* gamberro

hoop [hu:p] *n* aro

hooray [hu:'reɪ] *excl* = **hurray**

hoot [hu:t] (BRIT) *vi* (AUT) tocar el pito, pitar; (*siren*) sonar la sirena; (*owl*) ulular; **~er** (BRIT) *n* (AUT) pito, claxon *m*; (NAUT) sirena

Hoover ® ['hu:və*] (BRIT) *n* aspiradora ♦ *vt*: **h~** pasar la aspiradora por

hooves [hu:vz] *npl of* **hoof**

hop [hɒp] *vi* saltar, brincar; (*on one foot*) saltar con un pie

hope [həup] *vt, vi* esperar ♦ *n* esperanza; **I ~ so/not** espero que sí/no; **~ful** *adj* (*person*) optimista; (*situation*) prometedor(a); **~fully** *adv* con esperanza; (*one hopes*): **~fully he will recover** esperamos que se recupere; **~less** *adj* desesperado; (*person*): **to be ~less** ser un desastre

hops [hɒps] *npl* lúpulo

horizon [hə'raɪzn] *n* horizonte *m*; **~tal** [hɒrɪ'zɒntl] *adj* horizontal

hormone ['hɔ:məun] *n* hormona

horn [hɔ:n] *n* cuerno; (MUS: *also*: **French ~**) trompa; (AUT) pito, claxon *m*

hornet ['hɔ:nɪt] *n* avispón *m*

horoscope ['hɒrəskəup] *n* horóscopo

horrible ['hɒrɪbl] *adj* horrible

horrid ['hɒrɪd] *adj* horrible, horroroso

horrify ['hɒrɪfaɪ] *vt* horrorizar

horror ['hɒrə*] *n* horror *m*; **~ film** *n* película de horror

hors d'œuvre [ɔ:'də:vrə] *n* entremeses *mpl*

horse [hɔ:s] *n* caballo; **~back** *n*: **on ~back** a caballo; **~ chestnut** *n* (*tree*) castaño de Indias; (*nut*) castaña de Indias; **~man/woman** (*irreg*) *n* jinete/a *m/f*; **~power** *n* (*also*: de fuerza); **~racing** *n* carreras *fpl* de caballos; **~radish** *n* rábano picante; **~shoe** *n* herradura

hose [həuz] *n* (*also*: **~pipe**) manguera

hospitable [hɒs'pɪtəbl] *adj* hospitalario

hospital ['hɒspɪtl] *n* hospital *m*

hospitality [hɒspɪ'tælɪtɪ] *n* hospitalidad *f*

host [həust] *n* anfitrión *m*; (TV, RADIO) presentador *m*; (REL) hostia; (*large number*): **a ~ of** multitud de

hostage ['hɒstɪdʒ] *n* rehén *m*

hostel ['hɒstl] *n* hostal *m*; **(youth) ~** albergue *m* juvenil

hostess ['həustɪs] *n* anfitriona *f*; (BRIT: **air ~**) azafata; (TV, RADIO) presentadora

hostile ['hɒstaɪl] *adj* hostil

hot [hɒt] *adj* caliente; (*weather*) caluroso, de calor; (*as opposed to warm*) muy caliente; (*spicy*) picante; **to be ~** (*person*) tener calor; (*object*) estar caliente; (*weather*) hacer calor; **~bed** *n* (*fig*) semillero; **~ dog** *n* perro caliente

hotel [həu'tel] *n* hotel *m*

hot: ~house *n* invernadero; **~ line** *n* (POL) teléfono rojo; **~ly** *adv* con pasión, apasionadamente; **~-water bottle** *n* bolsa de agua caliente

hound [haund] *vt* acosar ♦ *n* perro (de caza)

hour ['auə*] *n* hora; **~ly** *adj* (de) cada hora

house [n haus, pl 'hauzɪz, vb hauz] n (gen, firm) casa; (POL) cámara; (THEATRE) sala ♦ vt (person) alojar; (collection) albergar; **on the ~** (fig) la casa invita; **~ arrest** n arresto domiciliario; **~boat** n casa flotante; **~bound** adj confinado en casa; **~breaking** n allanamiento de morada; **~hold** n familia; (home) casa; **~keeper** n ama de llaves; **~keeping** n (work) trabajos mpl domésticos; **~keeping** (money) n dinero para gastos domésticos; **~-warming party** n fiesta de estreno de una casa; **~wife** (irreg) n ama de casa; **~work** n faenas fpl (de la casa)

housing ['hauzɪŋ] n (act) alojamiento, (houses) viviendas fpl; **~ development**, **~ estate** (BRIT) n urbanización f

hovel ['hɔvl] n casucha

hover ['hɔvə*] vi flotar (en el aire); **~craft** n aerodeslizador m

how [hau] adv (in what way) cómo; **~ are you?** ¿cómo estás?; **~ much milk/many people?** ¿cuánta leche/gente?; **~ much does it cost?** ¿cuánto cuesta?; **~ long have you been here?** ¿cuánto hace que estás aquí?; **~ old are you?** ¿cuántos años tienes?; **~ tall is he?** ¿cómo es de alto?; **~ is school?** ¿cómo (te) va (en) la escuela?; **~ was the film?** ¿qué tal la película?; **~ lovely/awful!** ¡qué bonito/horror!

however [hau'ɛvə*] adv: **~ I do it** lo haga como lo haga; **~ cold it is** por mucho frío que haga; **~ fast he runs** por muy rápido que corra; **~ did you do it?** ¿cómo lo hiciste? ♦ conj sin embargo, no obstante

howl [haul] n aullido ♦ vi aullar; (person) dar alaridos; (wind) ulular

H.P. n abbr = **hire purchase**

h.p. abbr = **horse power**

HQ n abbr = **headquarters**

HTML n abbr (= hypertext markup language) lenguaje m de hipertexto

hub [hʌb] n (of wheel) cubo; (fig) centro

hubcap ['hʌbkæp] n tapacubos m inv

huddle ['hʌdl] vi: **to ~ together** acurrucarse

hue [hjuː] n color m, matiz m

huff [hʌf] n: **in a ~** enojado

hug [hʌg] vt abrazar; (thing) apretar con los brazos

huge [hjuːdʒ] adj enorme

hull [hʌl] n (of ship) casco

hullo [hə'ləu] excl = **hello**

hum [hʌm] vt tararear, canturrear ♦ vi tararear, canturrear; (insect) zumbar

human ['hjuːmən] adj, n humano; **~e** [hjuː'meɪn] adj humano, humanitario; **~itarian** [hjuːmænɪ'tɛərɪən] adj humanitario; **~ity** [hjuː'mænɪtɪ] n humanidad f

humble ['hʌmbl] adj humilde

humdrum ['hʌmdrʌm] adj (boring) monótono, aburrido

humid ['hjuːmɪd] adj húmedo

humiliate [hjuː'mɪlɪeɪt] vt humillar

humorous ['hjuːmərəs] adj gracioso, divertido

humour ['hjuːmə*] (US humor) n humorismo, sentido del humor; (mood) humor m ♦ vt (person) complacer

hump [hʌmp] n (in ground) montículo; (camel's) giba

hunch [hʌntʃ] n (premonition) presentimiento; **~back** n joroba m/f; **~ed** adj jorobado

hundred ['hʌndrəd] num ciento; (before n) cien; **~s of** centenares de; **~weight** n (BRIT) = 50.8 kg; 112 lb; (US) = 45.3 kg; 100 lb

hung [hʌŋ] pt, pp of **hang**

Hungarian [hʌŋ'gɛərɪən] adj, n húngaro/a m/f

Hungary ['hʌŋgərɪ] n Hungría

hunger ['hʌŋgə*] n hambre f ♦ vi: **to ~ for** (fig) tener hambre de, anhelar; **~ strike** n huelga de hambre

hungry ['hʌŋgrɪ] adj: **~ (for)** hambriento (de); **to be ~** tener hambre

hunk [hʌŋk] n (of bread etc) trozo, pedazo

hunt [hʌnt] vt (seek) buscar; (SPORT) cazar ♦ vi (search): **to ~ (for)** buscar; (SPORT) cazar ♦ n búsqueda; caza, cacería; **~er** n cazador(a) m/f; **~ing** n caza

hurdle ['həːdl] *n* (*SPORT*) valla; (*fig*) obstáculo

hurl [həːl] *vt* lanzar, arrojar

hurrah [huˈrɑː] *excl* = **hurray**

hurray [huˈreɪ] *excl* ¡viva!

hurricane ['hʌrɪkən] *n* huracán *m*

hurried ['hʌrɪd] *adj* (*rushed*) hecho de prisa; **~ly** *adv* con prisa, apresuradamente

hurry ['hʌrɪ] *n* prisa ♦ *vi* (*also*: ~ **up**) apresurarse, darse prisa ♦ *vt* (*also*: ~ **up**: *person*) dar prisa a; (: *work*) hacer de prisa; **to be in a ~** tener prisa

hurt [həːt] (*pt, pp* **hurt**) *vt* hacer daño a ♦ *vi* doler ♦ *adj* lastimado; **~ful** *adj* (*remark etc*) hiriente

hurtle ['həːtl] *vi*: **to ~ past** pasar como un rayo; **to ~ down** ir a toda velocidad

husband ['hʌzbənd] *n* marido

hush [hʌʃ] *n* silencio ♦ *vt* hacer callar; **~!** ¡chitón!, ¡cállate!; **~ up** *vt* encubrir

husk [hʌsk] *n* (*of wheat*) cáscara

husky ['hʌskɪ] *adj* ronco ♦ *n* perro esquimal

hustle ['hʌsl] *vt* (*hurry*) dar prisa a ♦ *n*: **~ and bustle** ajetreo

hut [hʌt] *n* cabaña; (*shed*) cobertizo

hutch [hʌtʃ] *n* conejera

hyacinth ['haɪəsɪnθ] *n* jacinto

hydrant ['haɪdrənt] *n* (*also*: **fire ~**) boca de incendios

hydraulic [haɪˈdrɔːlɪk] *adj* hidráulico

hydroelectric [haɪdrəʊˈlektrɪk] *adj* hidroeléctrico

hydrofoil ['haɪdrəfɔɪl] *n* aerodeslizador *m*

hydrogen ['haɪdrədʒən] *n* hidrógeno

hygiene ['haɪdʒiːn] *n* higiene *f*; **hygienic** [-'dʒiːnɪk] *adj* higiénico

hymn [hɪm] *n* himno

hype [haɪp] (*inf*) *n* bombardeo publicitario

hypermarket ['haɪpəmɑːkɪt] *n* hipermercado

hyphen ['haɪfn] *n* guión *m*

hypnotize ['hɪpnətaɪz] *vt* hipnotizar

hypocrisy [hɪˈpɔkrɪsɪ] *n* hipocresía

hypocrite ['hɪpəkrɪt] *n* hipócrita *m/f*; **hypocritical** [hɪpəˈkrɪtɪkl] *adj* hipócrita

hypothesis [haɪˈpɔθɪsɪs] (*pl* **hypotheses**)

n hipótesis *f inv*

hysteria [hɪˈstɪərɪə] *n* histeria; **hysterical** [-'sterɪkl] *adj* histérico; (*funny*) para morirse de risa; **hysterics** [-'sterɪks] *npl* histeria; **to be in hysterics** (*fig*) morirse de risa

I, i

I [aɪ] *pron* yo

ice [aɪs] *n* hielo; (~ *cream*) helado ♦ *vt* (*cake*) alcorzar ♦ *vi* (*also*: ~ **over**, ~ **up**) helarse; **~berg** *n* iceberg *m*; **~box** *n* (*BRIT*) congelador *m*; (*US*) nevera (*SP*), refrigeradora (*AM*); ~ **cream** *n* helado; ~ **cube** *n* cubito de hielo; **~d** *adj* (*cake*) escarchado; (*drink*) helado; ~ **hockey** *n* hockey *m* sobre hielo

Iceland ['aɪslənd] *n* Islandia

ice: ~ **lolly** (*BRIT*) *n* polo; ~ **rink** *n* pista de hielo; ~ **skating** *n* patinaje *m* sobre hielo

icicle ['aɪsɪkl] *n* carámbano

icing ['aɪsɪŋ] *n* (*CULIN*) alcorza; ~ **sugar** (*BRIT*) *n* azúcar *m* glas(eado)

icon ['aɪkɔn] *n* icono

icy ['aɪsɪ] *adj* helado

I'd [aɪd] = **I would**; **I had**

idea [aɪˈdɪə] *n* idea

ideal [aɪˈdɪəl] *n* ideal *m* ♦ *adj* ideal

identical [aɪˈdentɪkl] *adj* idéntico

identification [aɪdentɪfɪˈkeɪʃn] *n* identificación *f*; (**means of**) ~ documentos *mpl* personales

identify [aɪˈdentɪfaɪ] *vt* identificar

Identikit ® [aɪˈdentɪkɪt] *n*: ~ (**picture**) retrato-robot *m*

identity [aɪˈdentɪtɪ] *n* identidad *f*; ~ **card** *n* carnet *m* de identidad

ideology [aɪdɪˈɔlədʒɪ] *n* ideología

idiom ['ɪdɪəm] *n* modismo; (*style of speaking*) lenguaje *m*

idiosyncrasy [ɪdɪəʊˈsɪŋkrəsɪ] *n* idiosincrasia

idiot ['ɪdɪət] *n* idiota *m/f*; **~ic** [-'ɔtɪk] *adj* tonto

idle ['aɪdl] *adj* (*inactive*) ocioso; (*lazy*)

holgazán/ana; (*unemployed*) parado, desocupado; (*machinery etc*) parado; (*talk etc*) frívolo ♦ *vi* (*machine*) marchar en vacío

idol ['aɪdl] *n* ídolo; **~ize** *vt* idolatrar

i.e. *abbr* (= *that is*) esto es

if [ɪf] *conj* si; **~ necessary** si fuera necesario, si hiciese falta; **~ I were you** yo en tu lugar; **~ so/not** de ser así/si no; **~ only I could!** ¡ojalá pudiera!; *see also* **as; even**

igloo ['ɪɡluː] *n* iglú *m*

ignite [ɪɡ'naɪt] *vt* (*set fire to*) encender ♦ *vi* encenderse

ignition [ɪɡ'nɪʃən] *n* (*AUT: process*) ignición *f*; (: *mechanism*) encendido; **to switch on/off the ~** arrancar/apagar el motor; **~ key** *n* (*AUT*) llave *f* de contacto

ignorant ['ɪɡnərənt] *adj* ignorante; **to be ~ of** ignorar

ignore [ɪɡ'nɔː*] *vt* (*person, advice*) no hacer caso de; (*fact*) pasar por alto

I'll [aɪl] = **I will; I shall**

ill [ɪl] *adj* enfermo, malo ♦ *n* mal *m* ♦ *adv* mal; **to be taken ~** ponerse enfermo; **~-advised** *adj* (*decision*) imprudente; **~-at-ease** *adj* incómodo

illegal [ɪ'liːɡl] *adj* ilegal

illegible [ɪ'ledʒɪbl] *adj* ilegible

illegitimate [ɪlɪ'dʒɪtɪmət] *adj* ilegítimo

ill-fated *adj* malogrado

ill feeling *n* rencor *m*

illiterate [ɪ'lɪtərət] *adj* analfabeto

ill: **~-mannered** *adj* mal educado; **~ness** *n* enfermedad *f*; **~-treat** *vt* maltratar

illuminate [ɪ'luːmɪneɪt] *vt* (*room, street*) iluminar, alumbrar; **illumination** [-'neɪʃən] *n* alumbrado; **illuminations** *npl* (*decorative lights*) iluminaciones *fpl*, luces *fpl*

illusion [ɪ'luːʒən] *n* ilusión *f*; (*trick*) truco

illustrate ['ɪləstreɪt] *vt* ilustrar

illustration [ɪlə'streɪʃən] *n* (*act of illustrating*) ilustración *f*; (*example*) ejemplo, ilustración *f*; (*in book*) lámina

illustrious [ɪ'lʌstrɪəs] *adj* ilustre

I'm [aɪm] = **I am**

image ['ɪmɪdʒ] *n* imagen *f*; **~ry** [-ərɪ] *n* imágenes *fpl*

imaginary [ɪ'mædʒɪnərɪ] *adj* imaginario

imagination [ɪmædʒɪ'neɪʃən] *n* imaginación *f*; (*inventiveness*) inventiva

imaginative [ɪ'mædʒɪnətɪv] *adj* imaginativo

imagine [ɪ'mædʒɪn] *vt* imaginarse

imbalance [ɪm'bæləns] *n* desequilibrio

imitate ['ɪmɪteɪt] *vt* imitar; **imitation** [ɪmɪ'teɪʃən] *n* imitación *f*; (*copy*) copia

immaculate [ɪ'mækjulət] *adj* inmaculado

immaterial [ɪmə'tɪərɪəl] *adj* (*unimportant*) sin importancia

immature [ɪmə'tjuə*] *adj* (*person*) inmaduro

immediate [ɪ'miːdɪət] *adj* inmediato; (*pressing*) urgente, apremiante; (*nearest: family*) próximo; (: *neighbourhood*) inmediato; **~ly** *adv* (*at once*) en seguida; (*directly*) inmediatamente; **~ly next to** muy junto a

immense [ɪ'mɛns] *adj* inmenso, enorme; (*importance*) enorme

immerse [ɪ'məːs] *vt* (*submerge*) sumergir; **to be ~d in** (*fig*) estar absorto en

immersion heater [ɪ'məːʃən-] (*BRIT*) *n* calentador *m* de inmersión

immigrant ['ɪmɪɡrənt] *n* inmigrante *m/f*; **immigration** [ɪmɪ'ɡreɪʃən] *n* inmigración *f*

imminent ['ɪmɪnənt] *adj* inminente

immobile [ɪ'məubaɪl] *adj* inmóvil

immoral [ɪ'mɔrl] *adj* inmoral

immortal [ɪ'mɔːtl] *adj* inmortal

immune [ɪ'mjuːn] *adj*: **~ (to)** inmune (a); **immunity** *n* (*MED, of diplomat*) inmunidad *f*

immunize ['ɪmjunaɪz] *vt* inmunizar

impact ['ɪmpækt] *n* impacto

impair [ɪm'pɛə*] *vt* perjudicar

impart [ɪm'pɑːt] *vt* comunicar; (*flavour*) proporcionar

impartial [ɪm'pɑːʃl] *adj* imparcial

impassable [ɪm'pɑːsəbl] *adj* (*barrier*) infranqueable; (*river, road*) intransitable

impassive [ɪmˈpæsɪv] *adj* impasible
impatience [ɪmˈpeɪʃəns] *n* impaciencia
impatient [ɪmˈpeɪʃənt] *adj* impaciente; **to get** *or* **grow ~** impacientarse
impeccable [ɪmˈpekəbl] *adj* impecable
impede [ɪmˈpiːd] *vt* estorbar
impediment [ɪmˈpedɪmənt] *n* obstáculo, estorbo; (*also*: **speech ~**) defecto (del habla)
impending [ɪmˈpendɪŋ] *adj* inminente
imperative [ɪmˈperətɪv] *adj* (*tone*) imperioso; (*need*) imprescindible
imperfect [ɪmˈpəːfɪkt] *adj* (*goods etc*) defectuoso ♦ *n* (LING: *also*: **~ tense**) imperfecto
imperial [ɪmˈpɪərɪəl] *adj* imperial
impersonal [ɪmˈpəːsənl] *adj* impersonal
impersonate [ɪmˈpəːsəneɪt] *vt* hacerse pasar por; (THEATRE) imitar
impertinent [ɪmˈpəːtɪnənt] *adj* impertinente, insolente
impervious [ɪmˈpəːvɪəs] *adj* impermeable; (*fig*): **~ to** insensible a
impetuous [ɪmˈpetjuəs] *adj* impetuoso
impetus [ˈɪmpətəs] *n* ímpetu *m*; (*fig*) impulso
impinge [ɪmˈpɪndʒ]: **to ~ on** *vt fus* (*affect*) afectar a
implement [*n* ˈɪmplɪmənt, *vb* ˈɪmplɪment] *n* herramienta; (*for cooking*) utensilio ♦ *vt* (*regulation*) hacer efectivo; (*plan*) realizar
implicit [ɪmˈplɪsɪt] *adj* implícito; (*belief, trust*) absoluto
imply [ɪmˈplaɪ] *vt* (*involve*) suponer; (*hint*) dar a entender que
impolite [ɪmpəˈlaɪt] *adj* mal educado
import [*vb* ɪmˈpɔːt, *n* ˈɪmpɔːt] *vt* importar ♦ *n* (COMM) importación *f*; (: *article*) producto importado; (*meaning*) significado, sentido
importance [ɪmˈpɔːtəns] *n* importancia
important [ɪmˈpɔːtənt] *adj* importante; **it's not ~** no importa, no tiene importancia
importer [ɪmˈpɔːtə*] *n* importador(a) *m/f*
impose [ɪmˈpəuz] *vt* imponer ♦ *vi*: **to ~ on sb** abusar de uno; **imposing** *adj* imponente, impresionante

imposition [ɪmpəˈzɪʃn] *n* (*of tax etc*) imposición *f*; **to be an ~ on** (*person*) molestar a
impossible [ɪmˈpɔsɪbl] *adj* imposible; (*person*) insoportable
impotent [ˈɪmpətənt] *adj* impotente
impound [ɪmˈpaund] *vt* embargar
impoverished [ɪmˈpɔvərɪʃt] *adj* necesitado
impractical [ɪmˈpræktɪkl] *adj* (*person, plan*) poco práctico
imprecise [ɪmprɪˈsaɪs] *adj* impreciso
impregnable [ɪmˈpregnəbl] *adj* (*castle*) inexpugnable
impress [ɪmˈpres] *vt* impresionar; (*mark*) estampar; **to ~ sth on sb** hacer entender algo a uno
impression [ɪmˈpreʃən] *n* impresión *f*; (*imitation*) imitación *f*; **to be under the ~ that** tener la impresión de que; **~ist** *n* impresionista *m/f*
impressive [ɪmˈpresɪv] *adj* impresionante
imprint [ˈɪmprɪnt] *n* (*outline*) huella; (PUBLISHING) pie *m* de imprenta
imprison [ɪmˈprɪzn] *vt* encarcelar; **~ment** *n* encarcelamiento; (*term of ~ment*) cárcel *f*
improbable [ɪmˈprɔbəbl] *adj* improbable, inverosímil
improper [ɪmˈprɔpə*] *adj* (*unsuitable*: *conduct etc*) incorrecto; (: *activities*) deshonesto
improve [ɪmˈpruːv] *vt* mejorar; (*foreign language*) perfeccionar ♦ *vi* mejorarse; **~ment** *n* mejoramiento; perfección *f*; progreso
improvise [ˈɪmprəvaɪz] *vt*, *vi* improvisar
impulse [ˈɪmpʌls] *n* impulso; **to act on ~** obrar sin reflexión; **impulsive** [-ˈpʌlsɪv] *adj* irreflexivo
impure [ɪmˈpjuə*] *adj* (*adulterated*) adulterado; (*morally*) impuro; **impurity** *n* impureza

---
KEYWORD
---

in [ɪn] *prep* **1** (*indicating place, position, with place names*) en; **~ the house/garden** en (la) casa/el jardín; ~ **here/there** aquí/ahí *or* allí dentro; ~ **London/England** en Londres/Inglaterra

2 (*indicating time*) en; ~ **spring** en (la) primavera; ~ **the afternoon** por la tarde; **at 4 o'clock** ~ **the afternoon** a las 4 de la tarde; **I did it** ~ **3 hours/days** lo hice en 3 horas/días; **I'll see you** ~ **2 weeks** *or* ~ **2 weeks' time** te veré dentro de 2 semanas

3 (*indicating manner etc*) en; ~ **a loud/ soft voice** en voz alta/baja; ~ **pencil/ink** a lápiz/bolígrafo; **the boy** ~ **the blue shirt** el chico de la camisa azul

4 (*indicating circumstances*): ~ **the sun/ shade/rain** al sol/a la sombra/bajo la lluvia; **a change** ~ **policy** un cambio de política

5 (*indicating mood, state*): ~ **tears** en lágrimas, llorando; ~ **anger/despair** enfadado/desesperado; **to live** ~ **luxury** vivir lujosamente

6 (*with ratios, numbers*): **1** ~ **10 households, 1 household** ~ **10** una de cada 10 familias; **20 pence** ~ **the pound** 20 peniques por libra; **they lined up** ~ **twos** se alinearon de dos en dos

7 (*referring to people, works*) en; entre; **the disease is common** ~ **children** la enfermedad es común entre los niños; ~ **(the works of) Dickens** en (las obras de) Dickens

8 (*indicating profession etc*): **to be** ~ **teaching** estar en la enseñanza

9 (*after superlative*) de; **the best pupil** ~ **the class** el/la mejor alumno/a de la clase

10 (*with present participle*): ~ **saying this** al decir esto

♦ *adv*: **to be** ~ (*person: at home*) estar en casa; (*work*) estar; (*train, ship, plane*) haber llegado; (*in fashion*) estar de moda; **she'll be** ~ **later today** llegará más tarde hoy; **to ask sb** ~ hacer pasar a uno; **to run/limp** *etc* ~ entrar corriendo/cojeando *etc*

♦ *n*: **the ~s and outs** (*of proposal,*

situation etc) los detalles

in. *abbr* = **inch**
inability [ɪnə'bɪlɪtɪ] *n*: ~ **(to do)** incapacidad *f* (de hacer)
inaccurate [ɪn'ækjʊrət] *adj* inexacto, incorrecto
inadequate [ɪn'ædɪkwət] *adj* (*income, reply etc*) insuficiente; (*person*) incapaz
inadvertently [ɪnəd'vɜːtntlɪ] *adv* por descuido
inadvisable [ɪnəd'vaɪzəbl] *adj* poco aconsejable
inane [ɪ'neɪn] *adj* necio, fatuo
inanimate [ɪn'ænɪmət] *adj* inanimado
inappropriate [ɪnə'prəʊprɪət] *adj* inadecuado; (*improper*) poco oportuno
inarticulate [ɪnɑː'tɪkjʊlət] *adj* (*person*) incapaz de expresarse; (*speech*) mal pronunciado
inasmuch as [ɪnəz'mʌtʃ-] *conj* puesto que, ya que
inauguration [ɪnɔːgju'reɪʃən] *n* ceremonia de apertura
inborn [ɪn'bɔːn] *adj* (*quality*) innato
inbred [ɪn'brɛd] *adj* innato; (*family*) engendrado por endogamia
Inc. *abbr* (*US: = incorporated*) S.A.
incapable [ɪn'keɪpəbl] *adj* incapaz
incapacitate [ɪnkə'pæsɪteɪt] *vt*: **to** ~ **sb** incapacitar a uno
incense [*n* 'ɪnsɛns, *vb* ɪn'sɛns] *n* incienso
♦ *vt* (*anger*) indignar, encolerizar
incentive [ɪn'sɛntɪv] *n* incentivo, estímulo
incessant [ɪn'sɛsnt] *adj* incesante, continuo; ~**ly** *adv* constantemente
incest ['ɪnsɛst] *n* incesto
inch [ɪntʃ] *n* pulgada; **to be within an** ~ **of** estar a dos dedos de; **he didn't give an** ~ no dio concesión alguna
incident ['ɪnsɪdnt] *n* incidente *m*
incidental [ɪnsɪ'dɛntl] *adj* accesorio; ~ **to** relacionado con; ~**ly** [-'dɛntəlɪ] *adv* (*by the way*) a propósito
incite [ɪn'saɪt] *vt* provocar
inclination [ɪnklɪ'neɪʃən] *n* (*tendency*) tendencia, inclinación *f*; (*desire*) deseo;

(*disposition*) propensión *f*

incline [*n* 'ınklaın, *vb* ın'klaın] *n* pendiente *m*, cuesta ♦ *vt* (*head*) poner de lado ♦ *vi* inclinarse; to be ~d to (*tend*) ser propenso a

include [ın'klu:d] *vt* (*incorporate*) incluir; (*in letter*) adjuntar; including *prep* incluso, inclusive

inclusion [ın'klu:ʒən] *n* inclusión *f*

inclusive [ın'klusıv] *adj* inclusivo; ~ of tax incluidos los impuestos

income ['ınkʌm] *n* (*earned*) ingresos *mpl*; (*from property etc*) renta; (*from investment etc*) rédito; ~ tax *n* impuesto sobre la renta

incoming ['ınkʌmıŋ] *adj* (*flight, government etc*) entrante

incomparable [ın'kɔmpərəbl] *adj* incomparable, sin par

incompatible [ınkəm'pætıbl] *adj* incompatible

incompetent [ın'kɔmpıtənt] *adj* incompetente

incomplete [ınkəm'pli:t] *adj* (*partial: achievement etc*) incompleto; (*unfinished: painting etc*) inacabado

incongruous [ın'kɔŋgruəs] *adj* (*strange*) discordante; (*inappropriate*) incongruente

inconsiderate [ınkən'sıdərət] *adj* desconsiderado

inconsistent [ınkən'sıstənt] *adj* inconsecuente; (*contradictory*) incongruente; ~ with (que) no concuerda con

inconspicuous [ınkən'spıkjuəs] *adj* (*colour, building etc*) discreto; (*person*) que llama poco la atención

inconvenience [ınkən'vi:njəns] *n* inconvenientes *mpl*; (*trouble*) molestia, incomodidad *f* ♦ *vt* incomodar

inconvenient [ınkən'vi:njənt] *adj* incómodo, poco práctico; (*time, place, visitor*) inoportuno

incorporate [ın'kɔ:pəreıt] *vt* incorporar; (*contain*) comprender; (*add*) agregar; ~d *adj*: ~d company (*US*) ≈ sociedad *f* anónima

incorrect [ınkə'rekt] *adj* incorrecto

increase [*n* 'ınkri:s, *vb* ın'kri:s] *n* aumento ♦ *vi* aumentar; (*grow*) crecer; (*price*) subir ♦ *vt* aumentar; (*price*) subir; increasing *adj* creciente; increasingly *adv* cada vez más, más y más

incredible [ın'kredıbl] *adj* increíble

incubator ['ınkjubeıtə*] *n* incubadora

incumbent [ın'kʌmbənt] *adj*: it is ~ on him to ... le incumbe ...

incur [ın'kə:*] *vt* (*expenditure*) incurrir; (*loss*) sufrir; (*anger, disapproval*) provocar

indebted [ın'detıd] *adj*: to be ~ to sb estar agradecido a uno

indecent [ın'di:snt] *adj* indecente; ~ assault (*BRIT*) *n* atentado contra el pudor; ~ exposure *n* exhibicionismo

indecisive [ındı'saısıv] *adj* indeciso

indeed [ın'di:d] *adv* efectivamente, en realidad; (*in fact*) en efecto; (*furthermore*) es más; yes ~! ¡claro que sí!

indefinitely [ın'defınıtlı] *adv* (*wait*) indefinidamente

indemnity [ın'demnıtı] *n* (*insurance*) indemnidad *f*; (*compensation*) indemnización *f*

independence [ındı'pendns] *n* independencia

Independence Day
---

i El cuatro de julio es Independence Day, la fiesta nacional de Estados Unidos, que se celebra en conmemoración de la Declaración de Independencia, escrita por Thomas Jefferson y aprobada en 1776. En ella se proclamaba la independencia total de Gran Bretaña de las trece colonias americanas que serían el origen de los Estados Unidos de América.

---

independent [ındı'pendənt] *adj* independiente

index ['ındeks] (*pl* ~es) *n* (*in book*) índice *m*; (: *in library etc*) catálogo; (*pl* indices: *ratio, sign*) exponente *m*; ~ card *n* ficha; ~ed (*US*) *adj* = ~-linked; ~ finger *n* índice *m*; ~-linked (*BRIT*) *adj* vinculado al índice del coste de la vida

India ['ɪndɪə] n la India; **~n** adj, n indio/a m/f; **Red ~n** piel roja m/f; **~n Ocean** n: **the ~n Ocean** el Océano Índico

indicate ['ɪndɪkeɪt] vt indicar; **indication** [-'keɪʃən] n indicio, señal f; **indicative** [ɪn'dɪkətɪv] adj: **to be indicative of** indicar; **indicator** n indicador m; (AUT) intermitente m

indices ['ɪndɪsiːz] npl of **index**

indictment [ɪn'daɪtmənt] n acusación f

indifferent [ɪn'dɪfrənt] adj indiferente; (mediocre) regular

indigenous [ɪn'dɪdʒɪnəs] adj indígena

indigestion [ɪndɪ'dʒestʃən] n indigestión f

indignant [ɪn'dɪgnənt] adj: **to be ~ at sth/with sb** indignarse por algo/con uno

indigo ['ɪndɪgəʊ] adj de color añil ♦ n añil m

indirect [ɪndɪ'rekt] adj indirecto

indiscreet [ɪndɪ'skriːt] adj indiscreto, imprudente

indiscriminate [ɪndɪ'skrɪmɪnət] adj indiscriminado

indisputable [ɪndɪ'spjuːtəbl] adj incontestable

indistinct [ɪndɪ'stɪŋkt] adj (noise, memory etc) confuso

individual [ɪndɪ'vɪdjuəl] n individuo ♦ adj individual; (personal) personal; (particular) particular; **~ly** adv (singly) individualmente

indoctrinate [ɪn'dɔktrɪneɪt] vt adoctrinar

indoor ['ɪndɔː*] adj (swimming pool) cubierto; (plant) de interior; (sport) bajo cubierta; **~s** [ɪn'dɔːz] adv dentro

induce [ɪn'djuːs] vt inducir, persuadir; (bring about) producir; (birth) provocar; **~ment** n (incentive) incentivo; (pej: bribe) soborno

indulge [ɪn'dʌldʒ] vt (whim) satisfacer; (person) complacer; (child) mimar ♦ vi: **to ~ in** darse el gusto de; **~nce** n vicio; (leniency) indulgencia; **~nt** adj indulgente

industrial [ɪn'dʌstrɪəl] adj industrial; **~ action** n huelga; **~ estate** (BRIT) n polígono (SP) or zona (AM) industrial; **~ist**

n industrial m/f; **~ize** vt industrializar; **~ park** (US) n = **~ estate**

industrious [ɪn'dʌstrɪəs] adj trabajador(a); (student) aplicado

industry ['ɪndəstrɪ] n industria; (diligence) aplicación f

inebriated [ɪ'niːbrɪeɪtɪd] adj borracho

inedible [ɪn'edɪbl] adj incomible; (poisonous) no comestible

ineffective [ɪnɪ'fektɪv] adj ineficaz, inútil

ineffectual [ɪnɪ'fektʃuəl] adj = **ineffective**

inefficient [ɪnɪ'fɪʃənt] adj ineficaz, ineficiente

inept [ɪ'nept] adj incompetente

inequality [ɪnɪ'kwɔlɪtɪ] n desigualdad f

inert [ɪ'nɜːt] adj inerte, inactivo; (immobile) inmóvil

inescapable [ɪnɪ'skeɪpəbl] adj ineludible

inevitable [ɪn'evɪtəbl] adj inevitable; **inevitably** adv inevitablemente

inexcusable [ɪnɪks'kjuːzəbl] adj imperdonable

inexpensive [ɪnɪk'spensɪv] adj económico

inexperienced [ɪnɪk'spɪərɪənst] adj inexperto

infallible [ɪn'fælɪbl] adj infalible

infamous ['ɪnfəməs] adj infame

infancy ['ɪnfənsɪ] n infancia

infant ['ɪnfənt] n niño/a; (baby) niño pequeño, bebé m; (pej) aniñado

infantry ['ɪnfəntrɪ] n infantería

infant school (BRIT) n parvulario

infatuated [ɪn'fætjueɪtɪd] adj: **~ with** (in love) loco por

infatuation [ɪnfætʊ'eɪʃən] n enamoramiento, pasión f

infect [ɪn'fekt] vt (wound) infectar; (food) contaminar; (person, animal) contagiar; **~ion** [ɪn'fekʃən] n infección f; (fig) contagio; **~ious** [ɪn'fekʃəs] adj (also fig) contagioso

infer [ɪn'fɜː*] vt deducir, inferir

inferior [ɪn'fɪərɪə*] adj, n inferior m/f; **~ity** [-rɪ'ɔrətɪ] n inferioridad f

infertile [ɪn'fɜːtaɪl] adj estéril; (person) infecundo

infested [ɪn'festɪd] adj: **~ with** plagado de

in-fighting *n* (*fig*) lucha(s) *f(pl)* interna(s)

infinite ['ɪnfɪnɪt] *adj* infinito

infinitive [ɪn'fɪnɪtɪv] *n* infinitivo

infinity [ɪn'fɪnɪtɪ] *n* infinito; (*an ~*) infinidad *f*

infirmary [ɪn'fɜːmərɪ] *n* hospital *m*

inflamed [ɪn'fleɪmd] *adj*: **to become ~** inflamarse

inflammable [ɪn'flæməbl] *adj* inflamable

inflammation [ɪnflə'meɪʃən] *n* inflamación *f*

inflatable [ɪn'fleɪtəbl] *adj* (*ball, boat*) inflable

inflate [ɪn'fleɪt] *vt* (*tyre, price etc*) inflar; (*fig*) hinchar; **inflation** [ɪn'fleɪʃən] *n* (*ECON*) inflación *f*

inflexible [ɪn'fleksəbl] *adj* (*rule*) rígido; (*person*) inflexible

inflict [ɪn'flɪkt] *vt*: **to ~ sth on sb** infligir algo en uno

influence ['ɪnfluəns] *n* influencia ♦ *vt* influir en, influenciar; **under the ~ of alcohol** en estado de embriaguez; **influential** [-'enʃl] *adj* influyente

influenza [ɪnflu'enzə] *n* gripe *f*

influx ['ɪnflʌks] *n* afluencia

inform [ɪn'fɔːm] *vt*: **to ~ sb of sth** informar a uno sobre *or* de algo ♦ *vi*: **to ~ on sb** delatar a uno

informal [ɪn'fɔːməl] *adj* (*manner, tone*) familiar; (*dress, interview, occasion*) informal; (*visit, meeting*) extraoficial; **~ity** [-'mælɪtɪ] *n* informalidad *f*; sencillez *f*

informant [ɪn'fɔːmənt] *n* informante *m/f*

information [ɪnfə'meɪʃən] *n* información *f*; (*knowledge*) conocimientos *mpl*; **a piece of ~** un dato; **~ desk** *n* (mostrador *m* de) información *f*; **~ office** *n* información *f*

informative [ɪn'fɔːmətɪv] *adj* informativo

informer [ɪn'fɔːmə*] *n* (*also*: **police ~**) soplón-ona *m/f*

infra-red [ɪnfrə'red] *adj* infrarrojo

infrastructure ['ɪnfrəstrʌktʃə*] *n* (*of system etc*) infraestructura

infringe [ɪn'frɪndʒ] *vt* infringir, violar ♦ *vi*: **to ~ on** abusar de; **~ment** *n* infracción *f*;

(*of rights*) usurpación *f*

infuriating [ɪn'fjuərɪeɪtɪŋ] *adj* (*habit, noise*) enloquecedor(a)

ingenious [ɪn'dʒiːnjəs] *adj* ingenioso; **ingenuity** [-dʒɪ'njuːɪtɪ] *n* ingeniosidad *f*

ingenuous [ɪn'dʒenjuəs] *adj* ingenuo

ingot ['ɪŋgət] *n* lingote *m*, barra

ingrained [ɪn'greɪnd] *adj* arraigado

ingratiate [ɪn'greɪʃɪeɪt] *vt*: **to ~ o.s. with** congraciarse con

ingredient [ɪn'griːdɪənt] *n* ingrediente *m*

inhabit [ɪn'hæbɪt] *vt* vivir en; **~ant** *n* habitante *m/f*

inhale [ɪn'heɪl] *vt* inhalar ♦ *vi* (*breathe in*) aspirar; (*in smoking*) tragar

inherent [ɪn'hɪərənt] *adj*: **~ in** *or* **to** inherente a

inherit [ɪn'herɪt] *vt* heredar; **~ance** *n* herencia; (*fig*) patrimonio

inhibit [ɪn'hɪbɪt] *vt* inhibir, impedir; **~ed** *adj* (*PSYCH*) cohibido; **~ion** [-'bɪʃən] *n* cohibición *f*

inhospitable [ɪnhɔs'pɪtəbl] *adj* (*person*) inhospitalario; (*place*) inhóspito

inhuman [ɪn'hjuːmən] *adj* inhumano

initial [ɪ'nɪʃl] *adj* primero ♦ *n* inicial *f* ♦ *vt* firmar con las iniciales; **~s** *npl* (*as signature*) iniciales *fpl*; (*abbreviation*) siglas *fpl*; **~ly** *adv* al principio

initiate [ɪ'nɪʃɪeɪt] *vt* iniciar; **to ~ proceedings against sb** (*LAW*) entablar proceso contra uno

initiative [ɪ'nɪʃətɪv] *n* iniciativa

inject [ɪn'dʒekt] *vt* inyectar; **to ~ sb with sth** inyectar algo a uno; **~ion** [ɪn'dʒekʃən] *n* inyección *f*

injunction [ɪn'dʒʌŋkʃən] *n* interdicto

injure ['ɪndʒə*] *vt* (*hurt*) herir, lastimar; (*fig: reputation etc*) perjudicar; **~d** *adj* (*person, arm*) herido, lastimado; **injury** *n* herida, lesión *f*; (*wrong*) perjuicio, daño; **injury time** *n* (*SPORT*) (tiempo de) descuento

injustice [ɪn'dʒʌstɪs] *n* injusticia

ink [ɪŋk] *n* tinta

inkling ['ɪŋklɪŋ] *n* sospecha; (*idea*) idea

inlaid ['ɪnleɪd] *adj* (*with wood, gems etc*) incrustado

inland [*adj* 'inlənd, *adv* in'lænd] *adj* (*waterway, port etc*) interior ♦ *adv* tierra adentro; **I~ Revenue** (*BRIT*) *n* departamento de impuestos; ≈ Hacienda (*SP*)

in-laws *npl* suegros *mpl*

inlet ['inlɛt] *n* (*GEO*) ensenada, cala; (*TECH*) admisión *f*, entrada

inmate ['inmeɪt] *n* (*in prison*) preso/a; presidiario/a; (*in asylum*) internado/a

inn [in] *n* posada, mesón *m*

innate [ɪ'neɪt] *adj* innato

inner ['inə*] *adj* (*courtyard, calm*) interior; (*feelings*) íntimo; **~ city** *n* barrios deprimidos del centro de una ciudad; **~ tube** *n* (*of tyre*) cámara (*SP*), llanta (*AM*)

innings ['ininz] *n* (*CRICKET*) entrada, turno

innocent ['inəsnt] *adj* inocente

innocuous [ɪ'nɒkjuəs] *adj* inocuo

innovation [inəu'veɪʃən] *n* novedad *f*

innuendo [inju'ɛndəu] (*pl* **~es**) *n* indirecta

inoculation [inɒkju'leɪʃən] *n* inoculación *f*

in-patient *n* paciente *m/f* interno/a

input ['input] *n* entrada; (*of resources*) inversión *f*; (*COMPUT*) entrada de datos

inquest ['inkwɛst] *n* (*coroner's*) encuesta judicial

inquire [in'kwaɪə*] *vi* preguntar ♦ *vt*: **to ~ whether** preguntar si; **to ~ about** (*person*) preguntar por; (*fact*) informarse de; **~ into** *vt fus* investigar, indagar; **inquiry** *n* pregunta; (*investigation*) investigación *f*, pesquisa; **"Inquiries"** "Información"; **inquiry office** (*BRIT*) *n* oficina de información

inquisitive [in'kwizitiv] *adj* (*curious*) curioso

ins. *abbr* = **inches**

insane [in'sein] *adj* loco; (*MED*) demente

insanity [in'sæniti] *n* demencia, locura

inscription [in'skripʃən] *n* inscripción *f*; (*in book*) dedicatoria

inscrutable [in'skru:təbl] *adj* inescrutable, insondable

insect ['insɛkt] *n* insecto; **~icide** [in'sɛktɪsaɪd] *n* insecticida *m*; **~ repellent** *n* loción *f* contra insectos

insecure [insɪ'kjuə*] *adj* inseguro

insemination [insɛmɪ'neɪʃən] *n*: **artificial ~** inseminación *f* artificial

insensitive [in'sɛnsitiv] *adj* insensible

insert [*vb* in'sɜ:t, *n* 'insɜ:t] *vt* (*into sth*) introducir ♦ *n* encarte *m*; **~ion** [in'sɜ:ʃən] *n* inserción *f*

in-service ['insɜ:vis] *adj* (*training, course*) a cargo de la empresa

inshore [in'fɔ:*] *adj* de bajura ♦ *adv* (*be*) cerca de la orilla; (*move*) hacia la orilla

inside ['in'said] *n* interior *m* ♦ *adj* interior, interno ♦ *adv* (*be*) (por) dentro; (*go*) hacia dentro ♦ *prep* dentro de; (*of time*): **~ 10 minutes** en menos de 10 minutos; **~s** *npl* (*inf: stomach*) tripas *fpl*; **~ information** *n* información *f* confidencial; **~ lane** *n* (*AUT: in Britain*) carril *m* izquierdo; (: *in US, Europe etc*) carril *m* derecho; **~ out** *adv* (*turn*) al revés; (*know*) a fondo

insider dealing, insider trading *n* (*STOCK EXCHANGE*) abuso de información privilegiada

insight ['insait] *n* perspicacia

insignificant [insig'nifikmt] *adj* insignificante

insincere [insin'sɪə*] *adj* poco sincero

insinuate [in'sinjueit] *vt* insinuar

insipid [in'sipid] *adj* soso, insulso

insist [in'sist] *vi* insistir; **to ~ on** insistir en; **to ~ that** insistir en que; (*claim*) exigir que; **~ent** *adj* insistente; (*noise, action*) persistente

insole ['insəul] *n* plantilla

insolent ['insələnt] *adj* insolente, descarado

insomnia [in'sɒmniə] *n* insomnio

inspect [in'spɛkt] *vt* inspeccionar, examinar; (*troops*) pasar revista a; **~ion** [in'spɛkʃən] *n* inspección *f*, examen *m*; (*of troops*) revista; **~or** *n* inspector(a) *m/f*; (*BRIT: on buses, trains*) revisor(a) *m/f*

inspiration [inspə'reɪʃən] *n* inspiración *f*; **inspire** [in'spaɪə*] *vt* inspirar

instability [instə'biliti] *n* inestabilidad *f*

install [in'stɔ:l] *vt* instalar; (*official*)

nombrar; ~ation [ɪnstə'leɪʃən] *n*
instalación *f*

instalment [ɪn'stɔːlmənt] (*US* **installment**)
n plazo; (*of story*) entrega; (*of TV serial
etc*) capítulo; **in ~s** (*pay, receive*) a plazos

instance ['ɪnstəns] *n* ejemplo, caso; **for ~**
por ejemplo; **in the first ~** en primer
lugar

instant ['ɪnstənt] *n* instante *m*, momento
♦ *adj* inmediato; (*coffee etc*) instantáneo;
~ly *adv* en seguida

instead [ɪn'sted] *adv* en cambio; **~ of** en
lugar de, en vez de

instep ['ɪnstep] *n* empeine *m*

instil [ɪn'stɪl] *vt*: **to ~ sth into** inculcar algo
a

instinct ['ɪnstɪŋkt] *n* instinto

institute ['ɪnstɪtjuːt] *n* instituto;
(*professional body*) colegio ♦ *vt* (*begin*)
iniciar, empezar; (*proceedings*) entablar;
(*system, rule*) establecer

institution [ɪnstɪ'tjuːʃən] *n* institución *f*;
(*MED: home*) asilo; (: *asylum*) manicomio;
(*of system etc*) establecimiento; (*of
custom*) iniciación *f*

instruct [ɪn'strʌkt] *vt*: **to ~ sb in sth**
instruir a uno en *or* sobre algo; **to ~ sb to
do sth** dar instrucciones a uno de hacer
algo; **~ion** [ɪn'strʌkʃən] *n* (*teaching*)
instrucción *f*; **~ions** *npl* (*orders*) órdenes
fpl; **~ions (for use)** modo de empleo;
~or *n* instructor(a) *m/f*

instrument ['ɪnstrəmənt] *n* instrumento;
~al [-'mentl] *adj* (*MUS*) instrumental; **to
be ~al in** ser (el) artífice de; **~ panel** *n*
tablero (de instrumentos)

insufficient [ɪnsə'fɪʃənt] *adj* insuficiente

insular ['ɪnsjulə*] *adj* insular; (*person*)
estrecho de miras

insulate ['ɪnsjuleɪt] *vt* aislar; **insulation**
[-'leɪʃən] *n* aislamiento

insulin ['ɪnsjulɪn] *n* insulina

insult [*n* 'ɪnsʌlt, *vb* ɪn'sʌlt] *n* insulto ♦ *vt*
insultar; **~ing** *adj* insultante

insurance [ɪn'ʃuərəns] *n* seguro; **fire/life
~** seguro contra incendios/sobre la vida; **~
agent** *n* agente *m/f* de seguros; **~**

policy *n* póliza (de seguros)

insure [ɪn'ʃuə*] *vt* asegurar

intact [ɪn'tækt] *adj* íntegro; (*unharmed*)
intacto

intake ['ɪnteɪk] *n* (*of food*) ingestión *f*; (*of
air*) consumo; (*BRIT: SCOL*): **an ~ of 200 a
year** 200 matriculados al año

integral ['ɪntɪɡrəl] *adj* (*whole*) íntegro;
(*part*) integrante

integrate ['ɪntɪɡreɪt] *vt* integrar ♦ *vi*
integrarse

integrity [ɪn'tɛɡrɪtɪ] *n* honradez *f*, rectitud
f

intellect ['ɪntəlɛkt] *n* intelecto; **~ual**
[-'lɛktjuəl] *adj*, *n* intelectual *m/f*

intelligence [ɪn'tɛlɪdʒəns] *n* inteligencia

intelligent [ɪn'tɛlɪdʒənt] *adj* inteligente

intelligible [ɪn'tɛlɪdʒɪbl] *adj* inteligible,
comprensible

intend [ɪn'tɛnd] *vt* (*gift etc*): **to ~ sth for**
destinar algo a; **to ~ to do sth** tener
intención de *or* pensar hacer algo

intense [ɪn'tɛns] *adj* intenso; **~ly** *adv*
(*extremely*) sumamente

intensify [ɪn'tɛnsɪfaɪ] *vt* intensificar;
(*increase*) aumentar

intensive [ɪn'tɛnsɪv] *adj* intensivo; **~ care
unit** *n* unidad *f* de vigilancia intensiva

intent [ɪn'tɛnt] *n* propósito; (*LAW*)
premeditación *f* ♦ *adj* (*absorbed*) absorto;
(*attentive*) atento; **to all ~s and purposes**
prácticamente; **to be ~ on doing sth**
estar resuelto a hacer algo

intention [ɪn'tɛnʃən] *n* intención *f*,
propósito; **~al** *adj* deliberado; **~ally** *adv*
a propósito

intently [ɪn'tɛntlɪ] *adv* atentamente,
fijamente

interact [ɪntər'ækt] *vi* influirse
mutuamente; **~ive** *adj* (*COMPUT*)
interactivo

interchange ['ɪntətʃeɪndʒ] *n* intercambio;
(*on motorway*) intersección *f*; **~able** *adj*
intercambiable

intercom ['ɪntəkɔm] *n* interfono

intercourse ['ɪntəkɔːs] *n* (*sexual*)
relaciones *fpl* sexuales

interest ['ɪntrɪst] *n* (*also* COMM) interés *m*
♦ *vt* interesar; **to be ~ed in** interesarse por; ~**ing** *adj* interesante; ~ **rate** *n* tipo *or* tasa de interés

interface ['ɪntəfeɪs] *n* (COMPUT) junción *f*

interfere [ɪntə'fɪə*] *vi*: **to ~ in** entrometerse en; **to ~ with** (*hinder*) estorbar; (*damage*) estropear

interference [ɪntə'fɪərəns] *n* intromisión *f*; (RADIO, TV) interferencia

interim ['ɪntərɪm] *n*: **in the ~** en el ínterin ♦ *adj* provisional

interior [ɪn'tɪərɪə*] *n* interior *m* ♦ *adj* interior; ~ **designer** *n* interiorista *m/f*

interjection [ɪntə'dʒekʃən] *n* interposición *f*; (LING) interjección *f*

interlock [ɪntə'lɒk] *vi* entrelazarse

interlude ['ɪntəluːd] *n* intervalo; (THEATRE) intermedio

intermediate [ɪntə'miːdɪət] *adj* intermedio

intermission [ɪntə'mɪʃən] *n* intermisión *f*; (THEATRE) descanso

intern [*vb* ɪn'tɜːn, *n* 'ɪntɜːn] *vt* internar ♦ *n* (US) interno/a

internal [ɪn'tɜːnl] *adj* (*layout, pipes, security*) interior; (*injury, structure, memo*) internal; ~**ly** *adv* **"not to be taken ~ly"** "uso externo"; **I~ Revenue Service** (US) *n* departamento de impuestos; ≈ Hacienda (SP)

international [ɪntə'næʃənl] *adj* internacional ♦ *n* (BRIT: *match*) partido internacional

Internet ['ɪntənet] *n*: **the ~** Internet *m or f*; ~ **café** *n* cibercafé *m*; ~ **Service Provider** *n* proveedor *m* de (accesso a) Internet

interplay ['ɪntəpleɪ] *n* interacción *f*

interpret [ɪn'tɜːprɪt] *vt* interpretar; (*translate*) traducir; (*understand*) entender ♦ *vi* hacer de intérprete; ~**er** *n* intérprete *m/f*

interrogate [ɪn'terəugeɪt] *vt* interrogar; **interrogation** [-'geɪʃən] *n* interrogatorio

interrupt [ɪntə'rʌpt] *vt, vi* interrumpir; ~**ion** [-'rʌpʃən] *n* interrupción *f*

intersect [ɪntə'sekt] *vi* (*roads*) cruzarse;

~**ion** [-'sekʃən] *n* (*of roads*) cruce *m*

intersperse [ɪntə'spəːs] *vt*: **to ~ with** salpicar de

intertwine [ɪntə'twaɪn] *vt* entrelazarse

interval ['ɪntəvl] *n* intervalo; (BRIT: THEATRE, SPORT) descanso; (: SCOL) recreo; **at ~s** a ratos, de vez en cuando

intervene [ɪntə'viːn] *vi* intervenir; (*event*) interponerse; (*time*) transcurrir; **intervention** *n* intervención *f*

interview ['ɪntəvjuː] *n* entrevista ♦ *vt* entrevistarse con; ~**er** *n* entrevistador(a) *m/f*

intestine [ɪn'testɪn] *n* intestino

intimacy ['ɪntɪməsɪ] *n* intimidad *f*

intimate [*adj* 'ɪntɪmət, *vb* 'ɪntɪmeɪt] *adj* íntimo; (*friendship*) estrecho; (*knowledge*) profundo ♦ *vt* dar a entender

into ['ɪntuː] *prep* en; (*towards*) a; (*inside*) hacia el interior de; ~ **3 pieces/French** en 3 pedazos/al francés

intolerable [ɪn'tɒlərəbl] *adj* intolerable, insoportable

intolerant [ɪn'tɒlərənt] *adj*: ~ **(of)** intolerante (con *or* para)

intoxicated [ɪn'tɒksɪkeɪtɪd] *adj* embriagado

intractable [ɪn'træktəbl] *adj* (*person*) intratable; (*problem*) espinoso

intranet ['ɪntrənet] *n* intranet *f*

intransitive [ɪn'trænsɪtɪv] *adj* intransitivo

intravenous [ɪntrə'viːnəs] *adj* intravenoso

in-tray *n* bandeja de entrada

intricate ['ɪntrɪkət] *adj* (*design, pattern*) intrincado

intrigue [ɪn'triːg] *n* intriga ♦ *vt* fascinar; **intriguing** *adj* fascinante

intrinsic [ɪn'trɪnsɪk] *adj* intrínseco

introduce [ɪntrə'djuːs] *vt* introducir, meter; (*speaker, TV show etc*) presentar; **to ~ sb (to sb)** presentar uno (a otro); **to ~ sb to** (*pastime, technique*) introducir a uno a; **introduction** [-'dʌkʃən] *n* introducción *f*; (*of person*) presentación *f*; **introductory** [-'dʌktərɪ] *adj* introductorio; (*lesson, offer*) de introducción

introvert ['ɪntrəvɜːt] *n* introvertido/a ♦ *adj*
(*also*: **~ed**) introvertido

intrude [ɪn'truːd] *vi* (*person*) entrometerse;
to ~ on estorbar; **~r** *n* intruso/a;
intrusion [-ʒən] *n* invasión *f*

intuition [ɪntjuː'ɪʃən] *n* intuición *f*

inundate ['ɪnʌndeɪt] *vt*: **to ~ with** inundar
de

invade [ɪn'veɪd] *vt* invadir

invalid [*n* 'ɪnvəlɪd, *adj* ɪn'vælɪd] *n* (*MED*)
minusválido/a ♦ *adj* (*not valid*) inválido,
nulo

invaluable [ɪn'væljuəbl] *adj* inestimable

invariable [ɪn'vɛərɪəbl] *adj* invariable

invent [ɪn'vent] *vt* inventar; **~ion**
[ɪn'venʃən] *n* invento; (*lie*) ficción *f*,
mentira; **~ive** *adj* inventivo; **~or** *n*
inventor(a) *m/f*

inventory ['ɪnvəntrɪ] *n* inventario

invert [ɪn'vɜːt] *vt* invertir

inverted commas (*BRIT*) *npl* comillas
fpl

invest [ɪn'vest] *vt* invertir ♦ *vi*: **to ~ in**
(*company etc*) invertir dinero en; (*fig*: *sth
useful*) comprar

investigate [ɪn'vestɪɡeɪt] *vt* investigar;
investigation [-'ɡeɪʃən] *n* investigación *f*,
pesquisa

investment [ɪn'vestmənt] *n* inversión *f*

investor [ɪn'vestə*] *n* inversionista *m/f*

invigilator [ɪn'vɪdʒɪleɪtə*] *n* persona que
vigila en un examen

invigorating [ɪn'vɪɡəreɪtɪŋ] *adj* vigorizante

invisible [ɪn'vɪzɪbl] *adj* invisible

invitation [ɪnvɪ'teɪʃən] *n* invitación *f*

invite [ɪn'vaɪt] *vt* invitar; (*opinions etc*)
solicitar, pedir; **inviting** *adj* atractivo;
(*food*) apetitoso

invoice ['ɪnvɔɪs] *n* factura ♦ *vt* facturar

involuntary [ɪn'vɔləntrɪ] *adj* involuntario

involve [ɪn'vɔlv] *vt* suponer, implicar;
tener que ver con; (*concern, affect*)
corresponder; **to ~ sb (in sth)**
comprometer a uno (con algo); **~d** *adj*
complicado; **to be ~d in** (*take part*) tomar
parte en; (*be engrossed*) estar muy metido
en; **~ment** *n* participación *f*; dedicación *f*

inward ['ɪnwəd] *adj* (*movement*) interior,
interno; (*thought, feeling*) íntimo; **~(s)**
adv hacia dentro

I/O *abbr* (*COMPUT* = *input/output*)
entrada/salida

iodine ['aɪəudiːn] *n* yodo

ion ['aɪən] *n* ion *m*; **ioniser** ['aɪənaɪzə*] *n*
ionizador *m*

iota [aɪ'əutə] *n* jota, ápice *m*

IOU *n abbr* (= *I owe you*) pagaré *m*

IQ *n abbr* (= *intelligence quotient*) cociente
m intelectual

IRA *n abbr* (= *Irish Republican Army*) IRA
m

Iran [ɪ'rɑːn] *n* Irán *m*; **~ian** [ɪ'reɪnɪən] *adj*,
n iraní *m/f*

Iraq [ɪ'rɑːk] *n* Iraq; **~i** *adj*, *n* iraquí *m/f*

irate [aɪ'reɪt] *adj* enojado, airado

Ireland ['aɪələnd] *n* Irlanda

iris ['aɪrɪs] (*pl* **~es**) *n* (*ANAT*) iris *m*; (*BOT*)
lirio

Irish ['aɪrɪʃ] *adj* irlandés/esa ♦ *npl*: **the ~**
los irlandeses; **~man/woman** (*irreg*) *n*
irlandés/esa *m/f*; **~ Sea** *n*: **the ~ Sea** el
mar de Irlanda

iron ['aɪən] *n* hierro; (*for clothes*) plancha
♦ *cpd* de hierro ♦ *vt* (*clothes*) planchar; **~
out** *vt* (*fig*) allanar

ironic(al) [aɪ'rɔnɪk(l)] *adj* irónico

ironing ['aɪənɪŋ] *n* (*activity*) planchado;
(*clothes: ironed*) ropa planchada; (: *to be
ironed*) ropa por planchar; **~ board** *n*
tabla de planchar

ironmonger's (shop) ['aɪənmʌŋɡəz]
(*BRIT*) *n* ferretería, quincallería

irony ['aɪrənɪ] *n* ironía

irrational [ɪ'ræʃənl] *adj* irracional

irreconcilable [ɪrekən'saɪləbl] *adj* (*ideas*)
incompatible; (*enemies*) irreconciliable

irregular [ɪ'reɡjulə*] *adj* irregular; (*surface*)
desigual; (*action, event*) anómalo;
(*behaviour*) poco ortodoxo

irrelevant [ɪ'reləvənt] *adj* fuera de lugar,
inoportuno

irresolute [ɪ'rezəluːt] *adj* indeciso

irrespective [ɪrɪ'spektɪv]: **~ of** *prep* sin
tener en cuenta, no importa

irresponsible [ɪrɪˈspɒnsɪbl] adj (act)
irresponsable; (person) poco serio
irrigate [ˈɪrɪgeɪt] vt regar; irrigation
[-ˈgeɪʃən] n riego
irritable [ˈɪrɪtəbl] adj (person) de mal
humor
irritate [ˈɪrɪteɪt] vt fastidiar; (MED) picar;
irritating adj fastidioso; irritation
[-ˈteɪʃən] n fastidio; enfado; picazón f
IRS (US) n abbr = Internal Revenue
Service
is [ɪz] vb see be
Islam [ˈɪzlɑːm] n Islam m; ~ic [ɪzˈlæmɪk]
adj islámico
island [ˈaɪlənd] n isla; ~er n isleño/a
isle [aɪl] n isla
isn't [ˈɪznt] = is not
isolate [ˈaɪsəleɪt] vt aislar; ~d adj aislado;
isolation [-ˈleɪʃən] n aislamiento
ISP n abbr = Internet Service Provider
Israel [ˈɪzreɪl] n Israel m; ~i [ɪzˈreɪlɪ] adj, n
israelí m/f
issue [ˈɪsjuː] n (problem, subject) cuestión
f; (outcome) resultado; (of banknotes
etc) emisión f; (of newspaper etc)
edición f ♦ vt (rations, equipment)
distribuir, repartir; (orders) dar; (certificate,
passport) expedir; (decree) promulgar;
(magazine) publicar; (cheques) extender;
(banknotes, stamps) emitir; at ~ en
cuestión; to take ~ with sb (over)
estar en desacuerdo con uno (sobre); to
make an ~ of sth hacer una cuestión de
algo
Istanbul [ɪstænˈbuːl] n Estambul m

KEYWORD

it [ɪt] pron 1 (specific: subject: not generally
translated) él/ella; (: direct object) lo, la;
(: indirect object) le; (after prep) él/ella;
(abstract concept) ello; ~'s on the table
está en la mesa; I can't find ~ no lo (or
la) encuentro; give ~ to me dámelo (or
dámela); I spoke to him about ~ le hablé
del asunto; what did you learn from ~?
¿qué aprendiste de él (or ella)?; did you
go to ~? (party, concert etc) ¿fuiste?

2 (impersonal): ~'s raining llueve, está
lloviendo; ~'s 6 o'clock/the 10th of
August son las 6/es el 10 de agosto; how
far is ~? – ~'s 10 miles/2 hours on the
train ¿a qué distancia está? — a 10
millas/2 horas en tren; who is ~? — ~'s
me ¿quién es? — soy yo

Italian [ɪˈtæljən] adj italiano ♦ n italiano/a;
(LING) italiano
italics [ɪˈtælɪks] npl cursiva
Italy [ˈɪtəlɪ] n Italia
itch [ɪtʃ] n picazón f ♦ vi (part of body)
picar; to ~ to do sth rabiar por hacer
algo; ~y adj: my hand is ~y me pica la
mano
it'd [ˈɪtd] = it would; it had
item [ˈaɪtəm] n artículo; (on agenda) asunto
(a tratar); (also: news ~) noticia; ~ize vt
detallar
itinerary [aɪˈtɪnərərɪ] n itinerario
it'll [ˈɪtl] = it will; it shall
its [ɪts] adj su; sus pl
it's [ɪts] = it is; it has
itself [ɪtˈself] pron (reflexive) sí mismo/a;
(emphatic) él mismo/ella misma
ITV n abbr (BRIT: = Independent Television)
cadena de televisión comercial
independiente del Estado
I.U.D. n abbr (= intra-uterine device) DIU
m
I've [aɪv] = I have
ivory [ˈaɪvərɪ] n marfil m
ivy [ˈaɪvɪ] n (BOT) hiedra

J, j

jab [dʒæb] vt: to ~ sth into sth clavar algo
en algo ♦ n (inf) (MED) pinchazo
jack [dʒæk] n (AUT) gato; (CARDS) sota; ~
up vt (AUT) levantar con gato
jackal [ˈdʒækɔːl] n (ZOOL) chacal m
jacket [ˈdʒækɪt] n chaqueta, americana,
saco (AM); (of book) sobrecubierta
jack: ~-knife vi colear; ~ plug n (ELEC)
enchufe m de clavija; ~pot n premio

gordo

jaded ['dʒeɪdɪd] *adj* (*tired*) cansado; (*fed-up*) hastiado

jagged ['dʒægɪd] *adj* dentado

jail [dʒeɪl] *n* cárcel *f* ♦ *vt* encarcelar

jam [dʒæm] *n* mermelada; (*also*: **traffic ~**) embotellamiento; (*inf: difficulty*) apuro ♦ *vt* (*passage etc*) obstruir; (*mechanism, drawer etc*) atascar; (*RADIO*) interferir ♦ *vi* atascarse, trabarse; **to ~ sth into sth** meter algo a la fuerza en algo

Jamaica [dʒə'meɪkə] *n* Jamaica

jangle ['dʒæŋgl] *vi* entrechocar (ruidosamente)

janitor ['dʒænɪtə*] *n* (*caretaker*) portero, conserje *m*

January ['dʒænjuərɪ] *n* enero

Japan [dʒə'pæn] *n* (el) Japón; **~ese** [dʒæpə'niːz] *adj* japonés/esa ♦ *n inv* japonés/esa *m/f*; (*LING*) japonés *m*

jar [dʒɑː*] *n* tarro, bote *m* ♦ *vi* (*sound*) chirriar; (*colours*) desentonar

jargon ['dʒɑːgən] *n* jerga

jasmine ['dʒæzmɪn] *n* jazmín *m*

jaundice ['dʒɔːndɪs] *n* ictericia

jaunt [dʒɔːnt] *n* excursión *f*

javelin ['dʒævlɪn] *n* jabalina

jaw [dʒɔː] *n* mandíbula

jay [dʒeɪ] *n* (*ZOOL*) arrendajo

jaywalker ['dʒeɪwɔːkə*] *n* peatón/ona *m/f* imprudente

jazz [dʒæz] *n* jazz *m*; **~ up** *vt* (*liven up*) animar, avivar

jealous ['dʒeləs] *adj* celoso; (*envious*) envidioso; **~y** *n* celos *mpl*; envidia

jeans [dʒiːnz] *npl* vaqueros *mpl*, tejanos *mpl*

Jeep ® [dʒiːp] *n* jeep *m*

jeer [dʒɪə*] *vi*: **to ~ (at)** (*mock*) mofarse (de)

jelly ['dʒelɪ] *n* (*jam*) jalea; (*dessert etc*) gelatina; **~fish** *n inv* medusa (*SP*), aguaviva (*AM*)

jeopardy ['dʒepədɪ] *n*: **to be in ~** estar en peligro

jerk [dʒɜːk] *n* (*jolt*) sacudida; (*wrench*) tirón *m*; (*inf*) imbécil *m/f* ♦ *vt* tirar

bruscamente de ♦ *vi* (*vehicle*) traquetear

jersey ['dʒɜːzɪ] *n* jersey *m*; (*fabric*) (tejido de) punto

Jesus ['dʒiːzəs] *n* Jesús *m*

jet [dʒet] *n* (*of gas, liquid*) chorro; (*AVIAT*) avión *m* a reacción; **~-black** *adj* negro como el azabache; **~ engine** *n* motor *m* a reacción; **~ lag** *n* desorientación *f* después de un largo vuelo

jettison ['dʒetɪsn] *vt* desechar

jetty ['dʒetɪ] *n* muelle *m*, embarcadero

Jew [dʒuː] *n* judío

jewel ['dʒuːəl] *n* joya; (*in watch*) rubí *m*; **~ler** (*US* **~er**) *n* joyero/a; **~ler's (shop)** (*US* **~ry store**) *n* joyería; **~lery** (*US* **~ry**) *n* joyas *fpl*, alhajas *fpl*

Jewess ['dʒuːɪs] *n* judía

Jewish ['dʒuːɪʃ] *adj* judío

jibe [dʒaɪb] *n* mofa

jiffy ['dʒɪfɪ] (*inf*) *n*: **in a ~** en un santiamén

jigsaw ['dʒɪgsɔː] *n* (*also*: **~ puzzle**) rompecabezas *m inv*, puzle *m*

jilt [dʒɪlt] *vt* dejar plantado a

jingle ['dʒɪŋgl] *n* musiquilla ♦ *vi* tintinear

jinx [dʒɪŋks] *n*: **there's a ~ on it** está gafado

jitters ['dʒɪtəz] (*inf*) *npl*: **to get the ~** ponerse nervioso

job [dʒɔb] *n* (*task*) tarea; (*post*) empleo; **it's not my ~** no me incumbe a mí; **it's a good ~ that ...** menos mal que ...; **just the ~!** ¡estupendo!; **~ centre** (*BRIT*) *n* oficina estatal de colocaciones; **~less** *adj* sin trabajo

jockey ['dʒɔkɪ] *n* jockey *m/f* ♦ *vi*: **to ~ for position** maniobrar para conseguir una posición

jog [dʒɔg] *vt* empujar (ligeramente) ♦ *vi* (*run*) hacer footing; **to ~ sb's memory** refrescar la memoria a uno; **~ along** *vi* (*fig*) ir tirando; **~ging** *n* footing *m*

join [dʒɔɪn] *vt* (*things*) juntar, unir; (*club*) hacerse socio de; (*POL: party*) afiliarse a; (*queue*) ponerse en; (*meet: people*) reunirse con ♦ *vi* (*roads*) juntarse; (*rivers*) confluir ♦ *n* juntura; **~ in** *vi* tomar parte, participar ♦ *vt fus* tomar parte *or* participar en; ~ **up** vi reunirse; (MIL) alistarse

joiner ['dʒɔɪnə*] (BRIT) n carpintero/a; ~**y** n carpintería

joint [dʒɔɪnt] n (TECH) junta, unión f; (ANAT) articulación f; (BRIT: CULIN) pieza de carne (para asar); (inf: place) tugurio; (: of cannabis) porro ♦ adj (common) común; (combined) combinado; ~ **account** (with bank etc) cuenta común

joke [dʒəʊk] n chiste m; (also: **practical** ~) broma ♦ vi bromear; **to play a ~ on** gastar una broma a; ~**r** n (CARDS) comodín m

jolly ['dʒɔlɪ] adj (merry) alegre; (enjoyable) divertido ♦ adv (BRIT: inf) muy, terriblemente

jolt [dʒəʊlt] n (jerk) sacudida; (shock) susto ♦ vt (physically) sacudir; (emotionally) asustar

jostle ['dʒɔsl] vt dar empellones a, codear

jot [dʒɔt] n: **not one** ~ ni jota, ni pizca; ~ **down** vt apuntar; ~**ter** (BRIT) n bloc m

journal ['dʒə:nl] n (magazine) revista; (diary) periódico, diario; ~**ism** n periodismo; ~**ist** n periodista m/f, reportero/a

journey ['dʒə:nɪ] n viaje m; (distance covered) trayecto

jovial ['dʒəʊvɪəl] adj risueño, jovial

joy [dʒɔɪ] n alegría; ~**ful** adj alegre; ~**ous** adj alegre; ~ **ride** n (illegal) paseo en coche robado; ~**rider** n gamberro que roba un coche para dar una vuelta y luego abandonarlo; ~ **stick** n (AVIAT) palanca de mando; (COMPUT) palanca de control

JP n abbr = **Justice of the Peace**

Jr abbr = **junior**

jubilant ['dʒu:bɪlnt] adj jubiloso

judge [dʒʌdʒ] n juez m/f; (fig: expert) perito ♦ vt juzgar; (consider) considerar; **judg(e)ment** n juicio

judiciary [dʒu:'dɪʃɪərɪ] n poder m judicial

judicious [dʒu:'dɪʃəs] adj juicioso

judo ['dʒu:dəʊ] n judo

jug [dʒʌg] n jarra

juggernaut ['dʒʌgənɔ:t] (BRIT) n (huge truck) trailer m

juggle ['dʒʌgl] vi hacer juegos malabares; ~**r** n malabarista m/f

juice [dʒu:s] n zumo, jugo (esp AM); **juicy** adj jugoso

jukebox ['dʒu:kbɔks] n máquina de discos

July [dʒu:'laɪ] n julio

jumble ['dʒʌmbl] n revoltijo ♦ vt (also: ~ up) revolver; ~ **sale** (BRIT) n venta de objetos usados con fines benéficos

---
jumble sale

Los jumble sales son unos mercadillos que se organizan con fines benéficos en los locales de un colegio, iglesia u otro centro público. En ellos puede comprarse todo tipo de artículos baratos de segunda mano, sobre todo ropa, juguetes, libros, vajillas o muebles.

---

jumbo (jet) ['dʒʌmbəʊ-] n jumbo

jump [dʒʌmp] vi saltar, dar saltos; (with fear etc) pegar un bote; (increase) aumentar ♦ vt saltar ♦ n salto; aumento; **to ~ the queue** (BRIT)

jumper ['dʒʌmpə*] n (BRIT: pullover) suéter m, jersey m; (US: dress) mandil m; ~ **cables** (US) npl = **jump leads**

jump leads (BRIT) npl cables mpl puente de batería

jumpy ['dʒʌmpɪ] (inf) adj nervioso

Jun. abbr = **junior**

junction ['dʒʌŋkʃən] n (BRIT: of roads) cruce m; (RAIL) empalme m

juncture ['dʒʌŋktʃə*] n: **at this** ~ en este momento, en esta coyuntura

June [dʒu:n] n junio

jungle ['dʒʌŋgl] n selva, jungla

junior ['dʒu:nɪə*] adj (in age) menor, más joven; (brother/sister etc): **7 years her** ~ siete años menor que ella; (position) subalterno ♦ n menor m/f, joven m/f; ~ **school** (BRIT) n escuela primaria

junk [dʒʌŋk] n (cheap goods) baratijas fpl; (rubbish) basura; ~ **food** n alimentos preparados y envasados de escaso valor nutritivo

junkie ['dʒʌŋkı] (*inf*) *n* drogadicto/a, yonqui *m/f*

junk mail *n* propaganda de buzón

junk shop *n* tienda de objetos usados

Junr *abbr* = **junior**

juror ['dʒuərə*] *n* jurado

jury ['dʒuərɪ] *n* jurado

just [dʒʌst] *adj* justo ♦ *adv* (*exactly*) exactamente; (*only*) sólo, solamente; **he's ~ done it/left** acaba de hacerlo/irse; ~ **right** perfecto; ~ **two o'clock** las dos en punto; **she's ~ as clever as you** (ella) es tan lista como tú; ~ **as well that ...** menos mal que ...; ~ **as he was leaving** en el momento en que se marchaba; ~ **before/enough** justo antes/lo suficiente; ~ **here** aquí mismo; **he ~ missed** ha fallado por poco; ~ **listen to this** escucha esto un momento

justice ['dʒʌstɪs] *n* justicia; (*US: judge*) juez *m*; **to do ~ to** (*fig*) hacer justicia a; **J~ of the Peace** *n* juez *m* de paz

justify ['dʒʌstɪfaɪ] *vt* justificar; (*text*) alinear

jut [dʒʌt] *vi* (*also:* ~ **out**) sobresalir

juvenile ['dʒuːvənaɪl] *adj* (*court*) de menores; (*humour, mentality*) infantil ♦ *n* menor *m* de edad

K, k

K *abbr* (= *one thousand*) mil; (= *kilobyte*) kilobyte *m*, kiloocteto

kangaroo [kæŋgə'ruː] *n* canguro

karate [kə'rɑːtɪ] *n* karate *m*

kebab [kə'bæb] *n* pincho moruno

keel [kiːl] *n* quilla; **on an even ~** (*fig*) en equilibrio

keen [kiːn] *adj* (*interest, desire*) grande, vivo; (*eye, intelligence*) agudo; (*competition*) reñido; (*edge*) afilado; (*eager*) entusiasta; **to be ~ to do** *or* **on doing sth** tener muchas ganas de hacer algo; **to be ~ on sth/sb** interesarse por algo/uno

keep [kiːp] (*pt, pp* **kept**) *vt* (*preserve, store*)

guardar; (*hold back*) quedarse con; (*maintain*) mantener; (*detain*) detener; (*shop*) ser propietario de; (*feed: family etc*) mantener; (*promise*) cumplir; (*chickens, bees etc*) criar; (*accounts*) llevar; (*diary*) escribir; (*prevent*): **to ~ sb from doing sth** impedir a uno hacer algo ♦ *vi* (*food*) conservarse; (*remain*) seguir, continuar ♦ *n* (*of castle*) torreón *m*; (*food etc*) comida, subsistencia; (*inf*): **for ~s** para siempre; **to ~ doing sth** seguir haciendo algo; **to ~ sb happy** tener a uno contento; **to ~ a place tidy** mantener un lugar limpio; **to ~ sth to o.s.** guardar algo para sí mismo; **to ~ sth (back) from sb** ocultar algo a uno; **to ~ time** (*clock*) mantener la hora exacta; ~ **on** *vi*: **to ~ on doing** seguir *or* continuar haciendo; **to ~ on (about sth)** no parar de hablar (de algo); ~ **out** *vi* (*stay out*) permanecer fuera; **"~ out"** "prohibida la entrada"; ~ **up** *vt* mantener, conservar ♦ *vi* no retrasarse; **to ~ up with** (*pace*) ir al paso de; (*level*) mantenerse a la altura de; ~**er** *n* guardián/ana *m/f*; ~**-fit** *n* gimnasia (para mantenerse en forma); ~**ing** *n* (*care*) cuidado; **in ~ing with** de acuerdo con; ~**sake** *n* recuerdo

kennel ['kɛnl] *n* perrera; ~**s** *npl* residencia canina

Kenya ['kɛnjə] *n* Kenia

kept [kɛpt] *pt, pp of* **keep**

kerb [kəːb] (*BRIT*) *n* bordillo

kernel ['kəːnl] *n* (*nut*) almendra; (*fig*) meollo

ketchup ['kɛtʃəp] *n* salsa de tomate, catsup *m*

kettle ['kɛtl] *n* hervidor *m* de agua; ~ **drum** *n* (*MUS*) timbal *m*

key [kiː] *n* llave *f*; (*MUS*) tono; (*of piano, typewriter*) tecla ♦ *adj* (*issue etc*) clave *inv* ♦ *vt* (*also:* ~ **in**) teclear; ~**board** *n* teclado; ~**ed up** *adj* (*person*) nervioso; ~**hole** *n* ojo (de la cerradura); ~**hole surgery** *n* cirugía cerrada, cirugía no invasiva; ~**note** *n* (*MUS*) tónica; (*of speech*) punto principal *or* clave; ~**ring** *n* llavero

khaki ['kɑːkɪ] n caqui

kick [kɪk] vt dar una patada or un puntapié a; (inf: habit) quitarse de ♦ vi (horse) dar coces ♦ n patada; puntapié m; (of animal) coz f; (thrill): **he does it for ~s** lo hace por pura diversión; **~ off** vi (SPORT) hacer el saque inicial

kid [kɪd] n (inf: child) chiquillo/a; (animal) cabrito; (leather) cabritilla f ♦ vi (inf) bromear

kidnap ['kɪdnæp] vt secuestrar; **~per** n secuestrador(a) m/f; **~ping** n secuestro

kidney ['kɪdnɪ] n riñón m

kill [kɪl] vt matar; (murder) asesinar ♦ n matanza; **to ~ time** matar el tiempo; **~er** n asesino/a; **~ing** n (one) asesinato; (several) matanza; **to make a ~ing** (fig) hacer su agosto; **~joy** n (BRIT) aguafiestas m/f inv

kiln [kɪln] n horno

kilo ['kiːləʊ] n kilo; **~byte** n (COMPUT) kilobyte m, kilociteto; **~gram(me)** ['kɪləʊgræm] n kilo, kilogramo; **~metre** ['kɪləmiːtə*] (US **~meter**) n kilómetro; **~watt** ['kɪləʊwɒt] n kilovatio

kilt [kɪlt] n falda escocesa

kin [kɪn] n see **next**

kind [kaɪnd] adj amable, atento ♦ n clase f, especie f; (species) género; **in ~** (COMM) en especie; **a ~ of** una especie de; **to be two of a ~** ser tal para cual

kindergarten ['kɪndəgɑːtn] n jardín m de la infancia

kind-hearted adj bondadoso, de buen corazón

kindle ['kɪndl] vt encender; (arouse) despertar

kindly ['kaɪndlɪ] adj bondadoso; cariñoso ♦ adv bondadosamente, amablemente; **will you ~** ... sea usted tan amable de ...

kindness ['kaɪndnɪs] n (quality) bondad f, amabilidad f; (act) favor m

king [kɪŋ] n rey m; **~dom** n reino; **~fisher** n martín m pescador; **~-size** adj de tamaño extra

kiosk ['kiːɒsk] n quiosco; (BRIT: TEL) cabina

kipper ['kɪpə*] n arenque m ahumado

kiss [kɪs] n beso ♦ vt besar; **to ~ (each other)** besarse; **~ of life** n respiración f boca a boca

kit [kɪt] n (equipment) equipo; (tools etc) (caja de) herramientas fpl; (assembly ~) juego de armar

kitchen ['kɪtʃɪn] n cocina; **~ sink** n fregadero

kite [kaɪt] n (toy) cometa

kitten ['kɪtn] n gatito/a

kitty ['kɪtɪ] n (pool of money) fondo común

km abbr (= kilometre) km

knack [næk] n: **to have the ~ of doing sth** tener el don de hacer algo

knapsack ['næpsæk] n mochila

knead [niːd] vt amasar

knee [niː] n rodilla; **~cap** n rótula

kneel [niːl] (pt, pp **knelt**) vi (also: **~ down**) arrodillarse

knew [njuː] pt of **know**

knickers ['nɪkəz] (BRIT) npl bragas fpl

knife [naɪf] (pl **knives**) n cuchillo ♦ vt acuchillar

knight [naɪt] n caballero; (CHESS) caballo; **~hood** (BRIT) n (title): **to receive a ~hood** recibir el título de Sir

knit [nɪt] vt tejer, tricotar ♦ vi hacer punto, tricotar; (bones) soldarse; **to ~ one's brows** fruncir el ceño; **~ting** n labor f de punto; **~ting machine** n máquina de tricotar; **~ting needle** n aguja de hacer punto; **~wear** n prendas fpl de punto

knives [naɪvz] npl of **knife**

knob [nɒb] n (of door) tirador m; (of stick) puño; (on radio, TV) botón m

knock [nɒk] vt (strike) golpear; (bump into) chocar contra; (inf) criticar ♦ vi (at door etc): **to ~ at/on** llamar a ♦ n golpe m; (on door) llamada; **~ down** vt atropellar; **~ off** (inf) vi (finish) salir del trabajo ♦ vt (from price) descontar; (inf: steal) birlar; **~ out** vt dejar sin sentido; (BOXING) poner fuera de combate, dejar K.O.; (in competition) eliminar; **~ over** vt (object) tirar; (person) atropellar; **~er** n (on door) aldabón m; **~out** n (BOXING) K.O. m, knockout *m* ♦ *cpd* (*competition etc*) eliminatorio

knot [nɔt] *n* nudo ♦ *vt* anudar

know [nəu] (*pt* knew, *pp* known) *vt* (*facts*) saber; (*be acquainted with*) conocer; (*recognize*) reconocer, conocer; to ~ how to swim saber nadar; to ~ about *or* of sb/sth saber de uno/algo; ~-all *n* sabelotodo *m/f*; ~-how *n* conocimientos *mpl*; ~ing *adj* (*look*) de complicidad; ~ingly *adv* (*purposely*) adrede; (*smile, look*) con complicidad

knowledge ['nɔlɪdʒ] *n* conocimiento; (*learning*) saber *m*, conocimientos *mpl*; ~able *adj* entendido

knuckle ['nʌkl] *n* nudillo

Koran [kɔ'rɑːn] *n* Corán *m*

Korea [kə'rɪə] *n* Corea

kosher ['kəuʃə*] *adj* autorizado por la ley judía

Kosovo ['kɒsəvəu] *n* Kosovo *m*

L, l

L (*BRIT*) *abbr* = learner driver

l. *abbr* (= litre) l

lab [læb] *n abbr* = laboratory

label ['leɪbl] *n* etiqueta ♦ *vt* poner etiqueta a

labor *etc* ['leɪbə*] (*US*) = labour

laboratory [lə'bɔrətərɪ] *n* laboratorio

laborious [lə'bɔːrɪəs] *adj* penoso

labour ['leɪbə*] (*US* labor) *n* (*hard work*) trabajo; (~ *force*) mano *f* de obra; (*MED*): to be in ~ estar de parto ♦ *vi*: to ~ (at sth) trabajar (en algo) ♦ *vt*: to ~ a point insistir en un punto; L~, the L~ party (*BRIT*) el partido laborista, los laboristas *mpl*; ~ed *adj* (*breathing*) fatigoso; ~er *n* peón *m*; farm ~er peón *m*; (*day* ~er) jornalero

lace [leɪs] *n* encaje *m*; (*of shoe etc*) cordón *m* ♦ *vt* (*shoes: also*: ~ up) atarse (los zapatos)

lack [læk] *n* (*absence*) falta ♦ *vt* faltarle a uno, carecer de; through *or* for ~ of por

falta de; to be ~ing faltar, no haber; to be ~ing in sth faltarle a uno algo

lacquer ['lækə*] *n* laca

lad [læd] *n* muchacho, chico

ladder ['lædə*] *n* escalera (de mano); (*BRIT*: *in tights*) carrera

laden ['leɪdn] *adj*: ~ (with) cargado (de)

ladle ['leɪdl] *n* cucharón *m*

lady ['leɪdɪ] *n* señora; (*dignified*) dama; "ladies and gentlemen ..." "señoras y caballeros ..."; young ~ señorita; the ladies' (room) los servicios de señoras; ~bird (*US* ~bug) *n* mariquita; ~like *adj* fino; L~ship *n*: your L~ship su Señoría

lag [læg] *n* retraso ♦ *vi* (*also*: ~ behind) retrasarse, quedarse atrás ♦ *vt* (*pipes*) revestir

lager ['lɑːgə*] *n* cerveza (rubia)

lagoon [lə'guːn] *n* laguna

laid [leɪd] *pt*, *pp* of lay; ~ back (*inf*) *adj* relajado; ~ up *adj*: to be ~ up (with) tener que guardar cama (a causa de)

lain [leɪn] *pp* of lie

lake [leɪk] *n* lago

lamb [læm] *n* cordero; (*meat*) (carne *f* de) cordero; ~ chop *n* chuleta de cordero; lambswool *n* lana de cordero

lame [leɪm] *adj* cojo; (*excuse*) poco convincente

lament [lə'mɛnt] *n* quejo ♦ *vt* lamentarse de

laminated ['læmɪneɪtɪd] *adj* (*metal*) laminado; (*wood*) contrachapado; (*surface*) plastificado

lamp [læmp] *n* lámpara; ~post (*BRIT*) *n* (poste *m* de) farol *m*; ~shade *n* pantalla

lance [lɑːns] *vt* (*MED*) abrir con lanceta

land [lænd] *n* tierra; (*country*) país *m*; (*piece of* ~) terreno; (*estate*) tierras *fpl*, finca ♦ *vi* (*from ship*) desembarcar; (*AVIAT*) aterrizar; (*fig: fall*) caer, terminar ♦ *vt* (*passengers, goods*) desembarcar; to ~ sb with sth (*inf*) hacer cargar a uno con algo; ~ up *vi*: to ~ up in/at ir a parar a/ en; ~fill site ['lændfɪl-] *n* vertedero; ~ing *n* aterrizaje *m*; (*of staircase*) rellano; ~ing gear *n* (*AVIAT*) tren *m* de aterrizaje;

~lady n (of rented house, pub etc) dueña;
~lord n propietario; (of pub etc) patrón
m; ~mark n lugar m conocido; **to be a
~mark** (fig) marcar un hito histórico;
~owner n terrateniente m/f; ~scape n
paisaje m; ~scape gardener n
arquitecto de jardines; ~slide n (GEO)
corrimiento de tierras; (fig: POL) victoria
arrolladora
lane [leɪn] n (in country) camino; (AUT)
carril m; (in race) calle f
language ['læŋɡwɪdʒ] n lenguaje m;
(national tongue) idioma m, lengua; **bad
~** palabrotas fpl; **~ laboratory** n
laboratorio de idiomas
lank [læŋk] adj (hair) lacio
lanky ['læŋkɪ] adj larguirucho
lantern ['læntn] n linterna, farol m
lap [læp] n (of track) vuelta; (of body)
regazo; **to sit on sb's ~** sentarse en las
rodillas de uno ♦ vt (also: **~ up**) beber a
lengüetadas ♦ vi (waves) chapotear; **~ up**
vt (fig) tragarse
lapel [ləˈpel] n solapa
Lapland ['læplænd] n Laponia
lapse [læps] n fallo; (moral) desliz m; (of
time) intervalo ♦ vi (expire) caducar;
(time) pasar, transcurrir; **to ~ into bad
habits** caer en malos hábitos
laptop (computer) ['læptɒp-] n
(ordenador m) portátil m
larch [lɑːtʃ] n alerce m
lard [lɑːd] n manteca (de cerdo)
larder ['lɑːdə*] n despensa
large [lɑːdʒ] adj grande; **at ~** (free) en
libertad; (generally) en general; ~ly adv
(mostly) en su mayor parte; (introducing
reason) en gran parte; **~-scale** adj (map)
en gran escala; (fig) importante
lark [lɑːk] n (bird) alondra; (joke) broma
laryngitis [lærɪnˈdʒaɪtɪs] n laringitis f
laser ['leɪzə*] n láser m; **~ printer** n
impresora (por) láser
lash [læʃ] n latigazo; (also: **eye~**) pestaña
♦ vt azotar; (tie) atar/atar; **~ out** vi: **to ~
out (at sb)** (hit) arremeter (contra uno); **to ~ out against**

sb lanzar invectivas contra uno
lass [læs] (BRIT) n chica
lasso [læˈsuː] n lazo
last [lɑːst] adj último; (end: of series etc)
final ♦ adv (most recently) la última vez;
(finally) por último ♦ vi durar; (continue)
continuar, seguir; **~ night** anoche; **~
week** la semana pasada; **at ~** por fin; **~
but one** penúltimo; **~-ditch** adj
(attempt) último, desesperado; ~ing adj
duradero; ~ly adv por último, finalmente;
~-minute adj de última hora
latch [lætʃ] n pestillo
late [leɪt] adj (far on: in time, process etc) al
final de; (not on time) tarde, atrasado;
(dead) fallecido ♦ adv tarde; (behind time,
schedule) con retraso; **of ~** últimamente; **~
at night** a última hora de la noche; **in ~
May** hacia fines de mayo; **the ~ Mr X** el
difunto Sr X; **~comer** n recién llegado/a;
~ly adv últimamente; ~r adj (date etc)
posterior; (version etc) más reciente ♦ adv
más tarde, después; **~st** ['leɪtɪst] adj
último; **at the ~st** a más tardar
lathe [leɪð] n torno
lather ['lɑːðə*] n espuma (de jabón) ♦ vt
enjabonar
Latin ['lætɪn] n latín m ♦ adj latino; **~
America** n América latina; **~-
American** adj, n latinoamericano/a
latitude ['lætɪtjuːd] n latitud f; (fig) libertad
f
latter ['lætə*] adj último; (of two) segundo
♦ n: **the ~** el último, éste; ~ly adv
últimamente
laudable ['lɔːdəbl] adj loable
laugh [lɑːf] n risa ♦ vi reír(se); **(to do sth)
for a ~** (hacer algo) en broma; **~ at** vt
fus reírse de; **~ off** vt tomar algo a risa;
~able adj ridículo; ~ing stock n: **the
~ing stock of** el hazmerreír de; ~ter n
risa
launch [lɔːntʃ] n lanzamiento; (boat)
lancha ♦ vt (ship) botar; (rocket etc)
lanzar; (fig) comenzar; **~ into** vt fus
lanzarse a; **~(ing) pad** n plataforma de
lanzamiento

launder ['lɔ:ndə*] vt lavar
Launderette ® [lɔ:n'dret] (BRIT) n
lavandería (automática)
Laundromat ® ['lɔ:ndrəmæt] (US) n
= **Launderette**
laundry ['lɔ:ndrɪ] n (dirty) ropa sucia;
(clean) colada; (room) lavadero
lavatory ['lævətərɪ] n wáter m
lavender ['lævəndə*] n lavanda
lavish ['lævɪʃ] adj (amount) abundante;
(person): ~ **with** pródigo en ♦ vt: **to ~ sth
on sb** colmar a uno de algo
law [lɔ:] n ley f; (SCOL) derecho; (a rule)
regla; (professions connected with ~)
jurisprudencia; ~-**abiding** adj respetuoso
de la ley; ~ **and order** n orden m
público; ~ **court** n tribunal m (de
justicia); ~**ful** adj legítimo, lícito; ~**less**
adj (action) criminal
lawn [lɔ:n] n césped m; ~**mower** n
cortacésped m; ~ **tennis** n tenis m sobre
hierba
law school (US) n (SCOL) facultad f de
derecho
lawsuit ['lɔ:su:t] n pleito
lawyer ['lɔ:jə*] n abogado/a; (for sales,
wills etc) notario/a
lax [læks] adj laxo
laxative ['læksətɪv] n laxante m
lay [leɪ] (pt, pp **laid**) pt of **lie** ♦ adj laico;
(not expert) lego ♦ vt (place) colocar;
(eggs, table) poner; (cable) tender;
(carpet) extender; ~ **aside** or **by** vt dejar
a un lado; ~ **down** vt (pen etc) dejar;
(rules etc) establecer; **to ~ down the law**
(pej) imponer las normas; ~ **off** vt
(workers) despedir; ~ **on** vt (meal,
facilities) proveer; ~ **out** vt (spread out)
disponer, exponer; ~**about** (inf) n vago/
a; ~-**by** n (BRIT: AUT) área de
aparcamiento
layer ['leɪə*] n capa
layman ['leɪmən] (irreg) n lego
layout ['leɪaʊt] n (design) plan m, trazado;
(PRESS) composición f
laze [leɪz] vi (also: ~ **about**) holgazanear
lazy ['leɪzɪ] adj perezoso, vago; (movement)

lento
lb. abbr = **pound** (weight)
lead¹ [li:d] (pt, pp **led**) n (front position)
delantera; (clue) pista; (ELEC) cable m; (for
dog) correa; (THEATRE) papel m principal
♦ vt (walk etc in front of) ir a la cabeza
de; (guide): **to ~ sb somewhere** conducir
a uno a algún sitio; (be leader of) dirigir;
(start, guide: activity) protagonizar ♦ vi
(road, pipe etc) conducir a; (SPORT) ir
primero; **to be in the ~** (SPORT) llevar la
delantera; (fig) ir a la cabeza; **to ~ the
way** (also fig) llevar la delantera; ~ **away**
vt llevar; ~ **back** vt (person, route) llevar
de vuelta; ~ **on** vt (tease) engañar; ~ **to**
vt fus producir, provocar; ~ **up to** vt fus
(events) conducir a; (in conversation)
preparar el terreno para
lead² [led] n (metal) plomo; (in pencil)
mina; ~**ed petrol** n gasolina con plomo
leader ['li:də*] n jefe/a m/f, líder m;
(SPORT) líder m; ~**ship** n dirección f;
(position) mando; (quality) iniciativa
leading ['li:dɪŋ] adj (main) principal; (first)
primero; (front) delantero; ~ **lady** n
(THEATRE) primera actriz f; ~ **light** n
(person) figura principal; ~ **man** (irreg) n
(THEATRE) primer galán m
lead singer [li:d-] n cantante m/f
leaf [li:f] (pl **leaves**) n hoja ♦ vi: **to ~
through** hojear; **to turn over a new ~**
reformarse
leaflet ['li:flɪt] n folleto
league [li:g] n sociedad f; (FOOTBALL) liga;
to be in ~ with haberse confabulado con
leak [li:k] n (of liquid, gas) escape m, fuga;
(in pipe) agujero; (in roof) gotera; (in
security) filtración f ♦ vi (shoes, ship)
hacer agua; (pipe) tener (un) escape;
(roof) gotear; (liquid, gas) escaparse,
fugarse; (fig) divulgarse ♦ vt (fig) filtrar
lean [li:n] (pt, pp **leaned** or **leant**) adj
(thin) flaco; (meat) magro ♦ vt: **to ~ sth
on sth** apoyar algo en algo ♦ vi (slope)
inclinarse; **to ~ against** apoyarse contra;
to ~ on apoyarse en; ~ **back/forward**
vi inclinarse hacia atrás/adelante; ~ **out**

vi asomarse; **~ over** *vi* inclinarse; **~ing**
n: **~ing (towards)** inclinación *f* (hacia);
leant [lent] *pt, pp of* **lean**

leap [liːp] (*pt, pp* **leaped** or **leapt**) *n* salto
♦ *vi* saltar; **~frog** *n* pídola; **~ year** *n*
año bisiesto

learn [ləːn] (*pt, pp* **learned** or **learnt**) *vt*
aprender ♦ *vi* aprender; **to ~ about sth**
enterarse de algo; **to ~ to do sth**
aprender a hacer algo; **~ed** ['ləːnɪd] *adj*
erudito; **~er** *n* (*BRIT: also*: **~er driver**)
principiante *m/f*; **~ing** *n* el saber *m*,
conocimientos *mpl*

lease [liːs] *n* arriendo ♦ *vt* arrendar

leash [liːʃ] *n* correa

least [liːst] *adj*: **the ~** (*slightest*) el menor,
el más pequeño; (*smallest amount of*)
mínimo ♦ *adv* (*+vb*) menos; (*+adj*): **the ~
expensive** el/la menos costoso/a; **the ~
possible effort** el menor esfuerzo posible;
at ~ por lo menos, al menos; **you could
at ~ have written** por lo menos podías
haber escrito; **not in the ~** en absoluto

leather ['leðə*] *n* cuero

leave [liːv] (*pt, pp* **left**) *vt* dejar; (*go away
from*) abandonar; (*place etc: permanently*)
salir de ♦ *vi* irse; (*train etc*) salir ♦ *n*
permiso; **to ~ sth to sb** (*money etc*) legar
algo a uno; (*responsibility etc*) encargar a
uno de algo; **to be left** quedar, sobrar;
there's some milk left over sobra or
queda algo de leche; **on ~** de permiso; **~
behind** *vt* (*on purpose*) dejar;
(*accidentally*) dejarse; **~ out** *vt* omitir; **~
of absence** *n* permiso de ausentarse

leaves [liːvz] *npl of* **leaf**

Lebanon ['lebənən] *n*: **the ~** el Líbano

lecherous ['letʃərəs] (*pej*) *adj* lascivo

lecture ['lektʃə*] *n* conferencia; (*SCOL*)
clase *f* ♦ *vi* dar una clase ♦ *vt* (*scold*): **to
~ sb on** or **about sth** echar una
reprimenda a uno por algo; **to give a ~
on** dar una conferencia sobre; **~r** *n*
conferenciante *m/f*; (*BRIT: at university*)
profesor(a) *m/f*

led [led] *pt, pp of* **lead**

ledge [ledʒ] *n* repisa; (*of window*) alféizar

m; (*of mountain*) saliente *m*

ledger ['ledʒə*] *n* libro mayor

leech [liːtʃ] *n* sanguijuela

leek [liːk] *n* puerro

leer [lɪə*] *vi*: **to ~ at sb** mirar de manera
lasciva a uno

leeway ['liːweɪ] *n* (*fig*): **to have some ~**
tener cierta libertad de acción

left [left] *pt, pp of* **leave** ♦ *adj* izquierdo;
(*remaining*): **there are 2 ~** quedan dos
♦ *n* izquierda ♦ *adv* a la izquierda; **on** or
to the ~ a la izquierda; **the L~** (*POL*) la
izquierda; **~-handed** *adj* zurdo; **the ~-
hand side** *n* la izquierda; **~-luggage
(office)** (*BRIT*) *n* consigna; **~-overs** *npl*
sobras *fpl*; **~-wing** *adj* (*POL*) de
izquierdas, izquierdista

leg [leg] *n* pierna; (*of animal, chair*) pata;
(*trouser ~*) pernera; (*CULIN: of lamb*)
pierna; (*of chicken*) pata; (*of journey*)
etapa

legacy ['legəsɪ] *n* herencia

legal ['liːgl] *adj* (*permitted by law*) lícito; (*of
law*) legal; **~ holiday** (*US*) *n* fiesta oficial;
~ize *vt* legalizar; **~ly** *adv* legalmente; **~
tender** *n* moneda de curso legal

legend ['ledʒənd] *n* (*also fig: person*)
leyenda

legislation [ledʒɪs'leɪʃən] *n* legislación *f*

legislature ['ledʒɪslətʃə*] *n* cuerpo
legislativo

legitimate [lɪ'dʒɪtɪmət] *adj* legítimo

leg-room *n* espacio para las piernas

leisure ['leʒə*] *n* ocio, tiempo libre; **at ~**
con tranquilidad; **~ centre** *n* centro de
recreo; **~ly** *adj* sin prisa; lento

lemon ['lemən] *n* limón *m*; **~ade** *n* (*fizzy*)
gaseosa; **~ tea** *n* té *m* con limón

lend [lend] (*pt, pp* **lent**) *vt*: **to ~ sth to sb**
prestar algo a alguien; **~ing library** *n*
biblioteca de préstamo

length [leŋθ] *n* (*size*) largo, longitud *f*;
(*distance*): **the ~ of** todo lo largo de; (*of
swimming pool, cloth*) largo; (*of wood,
string*) trozo; (*amount of time*) duración *f*;
at ~ (*at last*) por fin, finalmente;
(*lengthily*) largamente; **~en** *vt* alargar

♦ *vi* alargarse; **~ways** *adv* a lo largo; **~y**
adj largo, extenso
lenient ['li:nɪənt] *adj* indulgente
lens [lenz] *n* (*of spectacles*) lente *f*; (*of
camera*) objetivo
Lent [lent] *n* Cuaresma
lent [lent] *pt, pp of* **lend**
lentil ['lentl] *n* lenteja
Leo ['li:əu] *n* Leo
leotard ['li:ətɑ:d] *n* mallas *fpl*
leprosy ['leprəsɪ] *n* lepra
lesbian ['lezbɪən] *n* lesbiana
less [les] *adj* (*in size, degree etc*) menor; (*in
quality*) menos ♦ *pron, adv* menos ♦ *prep*:
~ tax/10% discount menos impuestos/el
10 por ciento de descuento; **~ than half**
menos de la mitad; **~ than ever** menos
que nunca; **~ and ~** cada vez menos; **the
~ he works ...** cuanto menos trabaja ...;
~en *vi* disminuir, reducirse ♦ *vt*
disminuir, reducir; **~er** ['lesə*] *adj* menor;
to a ~er extent en menor grado
lesson ['lesn] *n* clase *f*; (*warning*) lección *f*
let [let] (*pt, pp* let) *vt* (*allow*) dejar,
permitir; (*BRIT: lease*) alquilar; **to ~ sb do
sth** dejar que uno haga algo; **to ~ sb
know sth** comunicar algo a uno; **~'s go**
¡vamos!; **~ him come** que venga; **"to ~"**
"se alquila"; **~ down** *vt* (*tyre*) desinflar;
(*disappoint*) defraudar; **~ go** *vi, vt* soltar;
~ in *vt* dejar entrar; (*visitor etc*) hacer
pasar; **~ off** *vt* (*culprit*) dejar escapar;
(*gun*) disparar; (*bomb*) accionar; (*firework*)
hacer estallar; **~ on** (*inf*) *vi* divulgar; **~
out** *vt* dejar salir; (*sound*) soltar; **~ up** *vi*
amainar, disminuir
lethal ['li:θl] *adj* (*weapon*) mortífero;
(*poison, wound*) mortal
letter ['letə*] *n* (*of alphabet*) letra;
(*correspondence*) carta; **~ bomb** *n* carta-
bomba; **~box** (*BRIT*) *n* buzón *m*; **~ing** *n*
letras *fpl*
lettuce ['letɪs] *n* lechuga
let-up *n* disminución *f*
leukaemia [lu:'ki:mɪə] (*US* **leukemia**) *n*
leucemia
level ['levl] *adj* (*flat*) llano ♦ *adv*: **to draw**

~ with llegar a la altura de ♦ *n* nivel *m*;
(*height*) altura ♦ *vt* nivelar; allanar;
(*destroy: building*) derribar; (*: forest*)
arrasar; **to be ~ with** estar a nivel de;
"A" ~s (*BRIT*) *npl* ≈ exámenes *mpl* de
bachillerato superior, B.U.P.; **"O" ~s**
(*BRIT*) *npl* ≈ exámenes *mpl* de octavo de
básica; **on the ~** (*fig: honest*) serio; **~ off**
or **out** *vi* (*prices etc*) estabilizarse; **~
crossing** (*BRIT*) *n* paso a nivel; **~-
headed** *adj* sensato
lever ['li:və*] *n* (*also fig*) palanca ♦ *vt*: **to ~
up** levantar con palanca; **~age** *n* (*using
bar etc*) apalancamiento; (*fig: influence*)
influencia
levy ['levɪ] *n* impuesto ♦ *vt* exigir, recaudar
lewd [lu:d] *adj* lascivo; (*joke*) obsceno,
colorado (*AM*)
liability [laɪə'bɪlətɪ] *n* (*pej: person, thing*)
estorbo, lastre *m*; (*JUR: responsibility*)
responsabilidad *f*; **liabilities** *npl* (*COMM*)
pasivo
liable ['laɪəbl] *adj* (*subject*): **~ to** sujeto a;
(*responsible*): **~ for** responsable de; (*likely*):
~ to do propenso a hacer
liaise [lɪ'eɪz] *vi*: **to ~ with** enlazar con;
liaison [li:'eɪzɔn] *n* (*coordination*) enlace
m; (*affair*) relaciones *fpl* amorosas
liar ['laɪə*] *n* mentiroso/a
libel ['laɪbl] *n* calumnia ♦ *vt* calumniar
liberal ['lɪbərəl] *adj* liberal; (*offer, amount
etc*) generoso
liberate ['lɪbəreɪt] *vt* (*people: from poverty
etc*) librar; (*prisoner*) libertar; (*country*)
liberar
liberty ['lɪbətɪ] *n* libertad *f*; (*criminal*): **to
be at ~** estar en libertad; **to be at ~ to
do** estar libre para hacer; **to take the ~ of
doing sth** tomarse la libertad de hacer
algo
Libra ['li:brə] *n* Libra
librarian [laɪ'breərɪən] *n* bibliotecario/a
library ['laɪbrərɪ] *n* biblioteca
libretto [lɪ'bretəu] *n* libreto
Libya ['lɪbɪə] *n* Libia; **~n** *adj, n* libio/a *m/f*
lice [laɪs] *npl of* **louse**
licence ['laɪsəns] (*US* **license**) *n* licencia.

(*permit*) permiso; (*also*: **driving ~**, (*US*) **driver's ~**) carnet *m* de conducir (*SP*), permiso (*AM*)

license [ˈlaɪsəns] *n* (*US*) = **licence** ♦ *vt* autorizar, dar permiso a; **~d** *adj* (*for alcohol*) autorizado para vender bebidas alcohólicas; (*car*) matriculado; **~ plate** (*US*) *n* placa (de matrícula)

lick [lɪk] *vt* lamer; (*inf*: *defeat*) dar una paliza a; **to ~ one's lips** relamerse

licorice [ˈlɪkərɪs] (*US*) *n* = **liquorice**

lid [lɪd] *n* (*of box, case*) tapa; (*of pan*) tapadera

lido [ˈlaɪdəu] *n* (*BRIT*) piscina

lie [laɪ] (*pt* **lay**, *pp* **lain**) *vi* (*rest*) estar echado, estar acostado; (*of object: be situated*) estar, encontrarse; (*tell lies: pt, pp* **lied**) mentir ♦ *n* mentira; **to ~ low** (*fig*) mantenerse a escondidas; **~ about** *or* **around** *vi* (*things*) estar tirado; (*BRIT: people*) estar tumbado; **~-down** (*BRIT*) *n*: **to have a ~-down** echarse (una siesta); **~-in** (*BRIT*) *n*: **to have a ~-in** quedarse en la cama

lieu [luː]: **in ~ of** *prep* en lugar de

lieutenant [lefˈtɛnənt, (*US*) luːˈtɛnənt] *n* (*MIL*) teniente *m*

life [laɪf] (*pl* **lives**) *n* vida; **to come to ~** animarse; **~ assurance** (*BRIT*) *n* seguro de vida; **~belt** (*BRIT*) *n* salvavidas *m inv*; **~boat** *n* lancha de socorro; **~guard** *n* vigilante *m/f*, socorrista *m/f*; **~ insurance** *n* = **~ assurance**; **~ jacket** *n* chaleco salvavidas; **~less** *adj* sin vida; (*dull*) soso; **~like** *adj* (*model etc*) que parece vivo; (*realistic*) realista; **~long** *adj* de toda la vida; **~ preserver** (*US*) *n* cinturón *m*/chaleco salvavidas; **~ sentence** *n* cadena perpetua; **~-size** *adj* de tamaño natural; **~ span** *n* vida; **~style** *n* estilo de vida; **~ support system** *n* (*MED*) sistema *m* de respiración asistida; **~time** *n* (*of person*) vida; (*of thing*) período de vida

lift [lɪft] *vt* levantar; (*end: ban, rule*) levantar, suprimir ♦ *vi* (*fog*) disiparse ♦ *n* (*BRIT: machine*) ascensor *m*; **to give sb a**

~ (*BRIT*) llevar a uno en el coche; **~-off** *n* despegue *m*

light [laɪt] (*pt, pp* **lighted** *or* **lit**) *n* luz *f*; (*lamp*) luz *f*, lámpara; (*AUT*) faro; (*for cigarette etc*): **have you got a ~?** ¿tienes fuego? ♦ *vt* (*candle, cigarette, fire*) encender (*SP*), prender (*AM*); (*room*) alumbrar ♦ *adj* (*colour*) claro; (*not heavy, also fig*) ligero; (*room*) con mucha luz; (*gentle, graceful*) ágil; **~s** *npl* (*traffic ~s*) semáforos *mpl*; **to come to ~** salir a luz; **in the ~ of** (*new evidence etc*) a la luz de; **~ up** *vi* (*smoke*) encender un cigarrillo; (*face*) iluminarse ♦ *vt* (*illuminate*) iluminar, alumbrar; (*set fire to*) encender; **~ bulb** *n* bombilla (*SP*), foco (*AM*); **~en** *vt* (*make less heavy*) aligerar; **~er** *n* (*also*: **cigarette ~er**) encendedor *m*, mechero; **~-headed** *adj* (*dizzy*) mareado; (*excited*) exaltado; **~-hearted** *adj* (*person*) alegre; (*remark etc*) divertido; **~house** *n* faro; **~ing** *n* (*system*) alumbrado; **~ly** *adv* ligeramente; (*not seriously*) con poca seriedad; **to get off ~ly** ser castigado con poca severidad; **~ness** *n* (*in weight*) ligereza

lightning [ˈlaɪtnɪŋ] *n* relámpago, rayo; **~ conductor** (*US* **~ rod**) *n* pararrayos *m inv*

light: ~ pen *n* lápiz *m* óptico; **~weight** *adj* (*suit*) ligero ♦ *n* (*BOXING*) peso ligero; **~ year** *n* año luz

like [laɪk] *vt* gustarle a uno ♦ *prep* como ♦ *adj* parecido, semejante ♦ *n*: **and the ~** y otros por el estilo; **his ~s and dislikes** sus gustos y aversiones; **I would ~, I'd ~** me gustaría; (*for purchase*) quisiera; **would you ~ a coffee?** ¿te apetece un café?; **I ~ swimming** me gusta nadar; **she ~s apples** le gustan las manzanas; **to be** *or* **look ~ sb/sth** parecerse a alguien/algo; **what does it look/taste/sound ~?** ¿cómo es/a qué sabe/cómo suena?; **that's just ~ him** es muy de él, es característico de él; **do it ~ this** hazlo así; **it is nothing ~ ...** no tiene parecido alguno con ...; **~able** *adj* simpático, agradable

likelihood [ˈlaɪklɪhud] n probabilidad f
likely [ˈlaɪklɪ] adj probable; **he's ~ to leave** es probable que se vaya; **not ~!** ¡ni hablar!
likeness [ˈlaɪknɪs] n semejanza, parecido; **that's a good ~** se parece mucho
likewise [ˈlaɪkwaɪz] adv igualmente; **to do ~** hacer lo mismo
liking [ˈlaɪkɪŋ] n: **~ (for)** (person) cariño (a); (thing) afición (a); **to be to sb's ~** ser del gusto de uno
lilac [ˈlaɪlək] n (tree) lilo; (flower) lila
lily [ˈlɪlɪ] n lirio, azucena; **~ of the valley** n lirio de los valles
limb [lɪm] n miembro
limber [ˈlɪmbə*]: **to ~ up** vi (SPORT) hacer ejercicios de calentamiento
limbo [ˈlɪmbəu] n: **to be in ~** (fig) quedar a la expectativa
lime [laɪm] n (tree) limero; (fruit) lima; (GEO) cal f
limelight [ˈlaɪmlaɪt] n: **to be in the ~** (fig) ser el centro de atención
limerick [ˈlɪmərɪk] n especie de poema humorístico
limestone [ˈlaɪmstəun] n piedra caliza
limit [ˈlɪmɪt] n límite m ♦ vt limitar; **~ed** adj limitado; **to be ~ed to** limitarse a; **~ed (liability) company** (BRIT) n sociedad f anónima
limousine [ˈlɪməziːn] n limusina
limp [lɪmp] n: **to have a ~** tener cojera ♦ vi cojear ♦ adj flojo; (material) fláccido
limpet [ˈlɪmpɪt] n lapa
line [laɪn] n línea; (rope) cuerda; (for fishing) sedal m; (wire) hilo; (row, series) fila, hilera; (of writing) renglón m, línea; (of song) verso; (on face) arruga; (RAIL) vía ♦ vt (road etc) llenar; (SEWING) forrar; **to ~ the streets** llenar las aceras; **in ~ with** alineado con; (according to) de acuerdo con; **~ up** vi hacer cola ♦ vt alinear; (prepare) preparar; organizar
lined [laɪnd] adj (face) arrugado; (paper) rayado
linen [ˈlɪnɪn] n ropa blanca; (cloth) lino
liner [ˈlaɪnə*] n vapor m de línea,

transatlántico; (for bin) bolsa (de basura)
linesman [ˈlaɪnzmən] n (SPORT) juez m de línea
line-up n (US: queue) cola; (SPORT) alineación f
linger [ˈlɪŋgə*] vi retrasarse, tardar en marcharse; (smell, tradition) persistir
lingerie [ˈlænʒəriː] n lencería
linguist [ˈlɪŋgwɪst] n lingüista m/f; **~ics** n lingüística
lining [ˈlaɪnɪŋ] n forro; (ANAT) (membrana) mucosa
link [lɪŋk] n (of a chain) eslabón m; (relationship) relación f, vínculo ♦ vt vincular, unir; (associate): **to ~ with** or **to** relacionar con; **~s** npl (GOLF) campo de golf; **~ up** vt acoplar ♦ vi unirse
lino [ˈlaɪnəu] n = **linoleum**
linoleum [lɪˈnəulɪəm] n linóleo
lion [ˈlaɪən] n león m; **~ess** n leona
lip [lɪp] n labio
liposuction [ˈlɪpəusʌkʃən] n liposucción f
lip: **~read** vi leer los labios; **~ salve** n crema protectora para labios; **~ service** n: **to pay ~ service to sth** (pej) prometer algo de boquilla; **~stick** n lápiz m de labios, carmín m
liqueur [lɪˈkjuə*] n licor m
liquid [ˈlɪkwɪd] adj, n líquido; **~ize** [-aɪz] vt (CULIN) licuar; **~izer** [-aɪzə*] n licuadora
liquor [ˈlɪkə*] n licor m, bebidas fpl alcohólicas
liquorice [ˈlɪkərɪs] (BRIT) n regaliz m
liquor store (US) n bodega, tienda de vinos y bebidas alcohólicas
Lisbon [ˈlɪzbən] n Lisboa
lisp [lɪsp] n ceceo m ♦ vi cecear
list [lɪst] n lista ♦ vt (mention) enumerar; (put on a list) poner en una lista; **~ed building** (BRIT) n monumento declarado de interés histórico-artístico
listen [ˈlɪsn] vi escuchar, oír; **to ~ to sb/sth** escuchar a uno/algo; **~er** n oyente m/f; (RADIO) radioyente m/f
listless [ˈlɪstlɪs] adj apático, indiferente
lit [lɪt] pt, pp of **light**
liter [ˈliːtə*] (US) n = **litre**

literacy ['lɪtərəsɪ] n capacidad f de leer y escribir

literal ['lɪtərl] adj literal

literary ['lɪtərərɪ] adj literario

literate ['lɪtərət] adj que sabe leer y escribir; (educated) culto

literature ['lɪtərɪtʃə*] n literatura; (brochures etc) folletos mpl

lithe [laɪð] adj ágil

litigation [lɪtɪ'geɪʃən] n litigio

litre ['liːtə*] (US **liter**) n litro

litter ['lɪtə*] n (rubbish) basura; (young animals) camada, cría; ~ **bin** n (BRIT) n papelera; ~ed adj: ~ed with (scattered) lleno de

little ['lɪtl] adj (small) pequeño; (not much) poco ♦ adv poco; **a** ~ un poco (de); ~ **house/bird** casita/pajarito; **a** ~ **bit** un poquito; ~ **by** ~ poco a poco; ~ **finger** n dedo meñique

live¹ [laɪv] adj (animal) vivo; (wire) conectado; (broadcast) en directo; (shell) cargado

live² [lɪv] vi vivir; ~ **down** vt hacer olvidar; ~ **on** vt fus (food, salary) vivir de; ~ **together** vi vivir juntos; ~ **up to** vt fus (fulfil) cumplir con

livelihood ['laɪvlɪhud] n sustento

lively ['laɪvlɪ] adj vivo; (interesting: place, book etc) animado

liven up ['laɪvn-] vt animar ♦ vi animarse

liver ['lɪvə*] n hígado

lives [laɪvz] npl of **life**

livestock ['laɪvstɔk] n ganado

livid ['lɪvɪd] adj lívido; (furious) furioso

living ['lɪvɪŋ] adj (alive) vivo ♦ n: **to earn** or **make a** ~ ganarse la vida; ~ **conditions** npl condiciones fpl de vida; ~ **room** n sala (de estar); ~ **standards** npl nivel m de vida; ~ **wage** n jornal m suficiente para vivir

lizard ['lɪzəd] n lagarto; (small) lagartija

load [ləud] n carga; (weight) peso ♦ vt (COMPUT) cargar; (also: ~ **up**): **to** ~ (**with**) cargar (con or de); **a** ~ **of rubbish** (inf) tonterías fpl; **a** ~ **of**, ~**s of** (fig) (gran) cantidad de, montones de; ~ed adj

(vehicle): **to be** ~ed **with** estar cargado de; (question) intencionado; (inf: rich) forrado (de dinero)

loaf [ləuf] (pl **loaves**) n (barra de) pan m

loan [ləun] n préstamo ♦ vt prestar; **on** ~ prestado

loath [ləuθ] adj: **to be** ~ **to do sth** estar poco dispuesto a hacer algo

loathe [ləuð] vt aborrecer; (person) odiar; **loathing** n aversión f; odio

loaves [ləuvz] npl of **loaf**

lobby ['lɔbɪ] n vestíbulo, sala de espera; (POL: pressure group) grupo de presión ♦ vt presionar

lobster ['lɔbstə*] n langosta

local ['ləukl] adj local ♦ n (pub) bar m; **the** ~**s** los vecinos, los del lugar; ~ **anaesthetic** n (MED) anestesia local; ~ **authority** n municipio, ayuntamiento (SP); ~ **call** n (TEL) llamada local; ~ **government** n gobierno municipal; ~**ity** [-'kælɪtɪ] n localidad f; ~**ly** [-kəlɪ] adv en la vecindad; por aquí

locate [ləu'keɪt] vt (find) localizar; (situate): **to be** ~d **in** estar situado en

location [ləu'keɪʃən] n situación f; **on** ~ (CINEMA) en exteriores

loch [lɔx] n lago

lock [lɔk] n (of door, box) cerradura; (of canal) esclusa; (of hair) mechón m ♦ vt (with key) cerrar (con llave) ♦ vi (door etc) cerrarse (con llave); (wheels) trabarse; ~ **in** vt encerrar; ~ **out** vt (person) cerrar la puerta a; ~ **up** vt (criminal) meter en la cárcel; (mental patient) encerrar; (house) cerrar (con llave) ♦ vi echar la llave

locker ['lɔkə*] n casillero

locket ['lɔkɪt] n medallón m

locksmith ['lɔksmɪθ] n cerrajero/a

lockup ['lɔkʌp] n (jail, cell) cárcel f

locum ['ləukəm] n (MED) (médico/a) interino/a

locust ['ləukəst] n langosta

lodge [lɔdʒ] n casita (del guarda) ♦ vi (person): **to** ~ (**with**) alojarse (en casa de); (bullet, bone) incrustarse ♦ vt (complaint) presentar; ~**r** n huésped(a) m/f

lodgings ['lɒdʒɪŋz] *npl* alojamiento
loft [lɒft] *n* desván *m*
lofty ['lɒftɪ] *adj* (*noble*) sublime; (*haughty*) altanero
log [lɒg] *n* (*of wood*) leño, tronco; (*written account*) diario ♦ *vt* anotar
logbook ['lɒgbuk] *n* (NAUT) diario de a bordo; (AVIAT) diario de vuelo; (*of car*) documentación *f* (del coche (SP) or carro (AM))
loggerheads ['lɒgəhedz] *npl*: **to be at ~ (with)** estar en desacuerdo (con)
logic ['lɒdʒɪk] *n* lógica; **~al** *adj* lógico
logo ['ləugəu] *n* logotipo
loin [lɔɪn] *n* (CULIN) lomo, solomillo
loiter ['lɔɪtə*] *vi* (*linger*) entretenerse
loll [lɒl] *vi* (*also*: **~ about**) repantigarse
lollipop ['lɒlɪpɒp] *n* pirulí *m*; **~ man/lady** (BRIT *irreg*) *n* persona encargada de ayudar a los niños a cruzar la calle

---
lollipop man/lollipop lady
---

i En el Reino Unido, se llama **lollipop man** o **lollipop lady** a la persona que se ocupa de parar el tráfico en los alrededores de los colegios para que los niños crucen sin peligro. Suelen ser personas ya jubiladas, vestidas con una gabardina de color llamativo y llevan una señal de stop portátil, la cual recuerda por su forma a una piruleta, y de ahí su nombre.

London ['lʌndən] *n* Londres; **~er** *n* londinense *m/f*
lone [ləun] *adj* solitario
loneliness ['ləunlɪnɪs] *n* soledad *f*; aislamiento
lonely ['ləunlɪ] *adj* (*situation*) solitario; (*person*) solo; (*place*) aislado
long [lɒŋ] *adj* largo ♦ *adv* mucho tiempo, largamente ♦ *vi*: **to ~ for sth** anhelar algo; **so** or **as ~ as** mientras, con tal que; **don't be ~!** ¡no tardes!, ¡vuelve pronto!; **how ~ is the street?** ¿cuánto tiene la calle de largo?; **how ~ is the lesson?**

¿cuánto dura la clase?; **6 metres ~** que mide 6 metros, de 6 metros de largo; **6 months ~** que dura 6 meses, de 6 meses de duración; **all night ~** toda la noche; **he no ~er comes** ya no viene; **~ before** mucho antes; **before ~** (+*future*) dentro de poco; (+*past*) poco tiempo después; **at ~ last** al fin, por fin; **~-distance** *adj* (*race*) de larga distancia; (*call*) interurbano; **~-haired** *adj* de pelo largo; **~hand** *n* escritura sin abreviaturas; **~ing** *n* anhelo, ansia; (*nostalgia*) nostalgia ♦ *adj* anhelante
longitude ['lɒŋgɪtjuːd] *n* longitud *f*
long: **~ jump** *n* salto de longitud; **~-life** *adj* (*batteries*) de larga duración; (*milk*) uperizado; **~-lost** *adj* desaparecido hace mucho tiempo; **~-range** *adj* (*plan*) de gran alcance; (*missile*) de largo alcance; **~-sighted** (BRIT) *adj* présbita; **~-standing** *adj* de mucho tiempo; **~-suffering** *adj* sufrido; **~-term** *adj* a largo plazo; **~ wave** *n* onda larga; **~-winded** *adj* prolijo
loo [luː] (BRIT: *inf*) *n* wáter *m*
look [luk] *vi* mirar; (*seem*) parecer; (*building etc*) **to ~ south/on to the sea** dar al sur/al mar ♦ *n* (*gen*): **to have a ~** mirar; (*glance*) mirada; (*appearance*) aire *m*, aspecto; **~s** *npl* (*good* ~*s*) belleza; **~ (here)!** (*expressing annoyance etc*) ¡oye!; **~!** (*expressing surprise*) ¡mira!; **~ after** *vt fus* (*care for*) cuidar a; (*deal with*) encargarse de; **~ at** *vt fus* mirar; (*read quickly*) echar un vistazo a; **~ back** *vi* mirar hacia atrás; **~ down on** *vt fus* (*fig*) despreciar, mirar con desprecio; **~ for** *vt fus* buscar; **~ forward to** *vt fus* esperar con ilusión; (*in letters*): **we ~ forward to hearing from you** quedamos a la espera de sus gratas noticias; **~ into** *vt* investigar; **~ on** *vi* mirar (como espectador); **~ out** *vi* (*beware*): **to ~ out (for)** tener cuidado (de); **~ out for** *vt fus* (*seek*) buscar; (*await*) esperar; **~ round** *vi* volver la cabeza; **~ through** *vt fus* (*examine*) examinar; **~ to** *vt fus* (*rely on*)

contar con; ~ **up** *vi* mirar hacia arriba; (*improve*) mejorar ♦ *vt* (*word*) buscar; ~ **up to** *vt fus* admirar; ~**-out** *n* (*tower etc*) puesto de observación; (*person*) vigía *m/f*; **to be on the ~-out for sth** estar al acecho de algo

oom [lu:m] *vi*: ~ **(up)** (*threaten*) surgir, amenazar; (*event: approach*) aproximarse

oony [ˈluːnɪ] (*inf*) *n*, *adj* loco/a *m/f*

oop [luːp] *n* lazo ♦ *vt*: **to ~ sth round sth** pasar algo alrededor de algo; ~**hole** *n* escapatoria

oose [luːs] *adj* suelto; (*clothes*) ancho; (*morals, discipline*) relajado; **to be on the ~** estar en libertad; **to be at a ~ end** *or* **at ~ ends** (*US*) no saber qué hacer; ~ **change** *n* cambio; ~ **chippings** *npl* (*on road*) gravilla suelta; ~**ly** *adv* libremente, aproximadamente; ~**n** *vt* aflojar

oot [luːt] *n* botín *m* ♦ *vt* saquear

op off [lɔp-] (*vt*) (*branches*) podar

op-sided *adj* torcido

ord [lɔːd] *n* señor *m*; **L~ Smith** Lord Smith; **the L~** el Señor; **my ~** (*to bishop*) Ilustrísima; (*to noble etc*) Señor; **good L~!** ¡Dios mío!; **the (House of) L~s** (*BRIT*) la Cámara de los Lores; ~**ship** *n*: **your L~ship** su Señoría

ore [lɔː*] *n* tradiciones *fpl*

orry [ˈlɔrɪ] (*BRIT*) *n* camión *m*; ~ **driver** *n* camionero/a

ose [luːz] (*pt, pp* **lost**) *vt* perder ♦ *vi* perder, ser vencido; **to ~ (time)** (*clock*) atrasarse; ~**r** *n* perdedor(a) *m/f*

oss [lɔs] *n* pérdida; **heavy ~es** (*MIL*) grandes pérdidas; **to be at a ~** no saber qué hacer; **to make a ~** sufrir pérdidas

ost [lɔst] *pt, pp of* **lose** ♦ *adj* perdido; ~ **property** (*US* = **and found**) *n* objetos *mpl* perdidos

ot [lɔt] *n* (*group: of things*) grupo; (*at auctions*) lote *m*; **the ~** el todo, todos; **a ~** (*large number: of books etc*) muchos; (*a great deal*) mucho, bastante; **a ~ of, ~s of** mucho(s) (*pl*); **I read a ~** leo bastante; **to draw ~s (for sth)** echar suertes (para

decidir algo)

lotion [ˈləʊʃən] *n* loción *f*

lottery [ˈlɔtərɪ] *n* lotería

loud [laud] *adj* (*voice, sound*) fuerte; (*laugh, shout*) estrepitoso; (*condemnation etc*) enérgico; (*gaudy*) chillón/ona ♦ *adv* (*speak etc*) fuerte; **out ~** en voz alta; ~**hailer** (*BRIT*) *n* megáfono; ~**ly** *adv* (*noisily*) fuerte; (*aloud*) en voz alta; ~**speaker** *n* altavoz *m*

lounge [laundʒ] *n* salón *m*, sala (de estar); (*at airport etc*) sala; (*BRIT: also*: ~**-bar**) salón-bar *m* ♦ *vi* (*also*: ~ **about** *or* **around**) reposar, holgazanear

louse [laus] (*pl* **lice**) *n* piojo

lousy [ˈlauzɪ] (*inf*) *adj* (*bad quality*) malísimo, asqueroso; (*ill*) fatal

lout [laut] *n* gamberro/a

lovable [ˈlʌvəbl] *adj* amable, simpático

love [lʌv] *n* (*romantic, sexual*) amor *m*; (*kind, caring*) cariño ♦ *vt* amar, querer; (*thing, activity*) encantarle a uno; **"~ from Anne"** (*on letter*) "un abrazo (de) Anne"; **to ~ to do** encantarle a uno hacer; **to be/fall in ~ with** estar enamorado/ enamorarse de; **to make ~** hacer el amor; **for the ~ of** por amor de; **"15 ~"** (*TENNIS*) "15 a cero"; **I ~ paella** me encanta la paella; ~ **affair** *n* aventura sentimental; ~ **letter** *n* carta de amor; ~ **life** *n* vida sentimental

lovely [ˈlʌvlɪ] *adj* (*delightful*) encantador(a); (*beautiful*) precioso

lover [ˈlʌvə*] *n* amante *m/f*; (*person in love*) enamorado; (*amateur*): **a ~ of** un(a) aficionado/a *or* un(a) amante de

loving [ˈlʌvɪŋ] *adj* amoroso, cariñoso; (*action*) tierno

low [ləʊ] *adj, ad* bajo ♦ *n* (*METEOROLOGY*) área de baja presión; **to be ~ on** (*supplies etc*) andar mal de; **to feel ~** sentirse deprimido; **to turn (down)** ~ bajar; ~**alcohol** *adj* de bajo contenido en alcohol; ~**-calorie** *adj* bajo en calorías; ~**-cut** *adj* (*dress*) escotado

lower [ˈləʊə*] *adj* más bajo; (*less important*) menos importante ♦ *vt* bajar;

(*reduce*) reducir ♦ *vr*: **to ~ o.s. to** (*fig*) rebajarse a
low: **~-fat** *adj* (*milk, yoghurt*) desnatado; (*diet*) bajo en calorías; **~lands** *npl* (*GEO*) tierras *fpl* bajas; **~ly** *adj* humilde, inferior; **~ season** *n* la temporada baja
loyal ['lɔɪəl] *adj* leal; **~ty** *n* lealtad *f*; **~ty card** *n* tarjeta cliente
lozenge ['lɔzɪndʒ] *n* (*MED*) pastilla
L.P. *n abbr* (= *long-playing record*) elepé *m*
L-plates ['el-] (*BRIT*) *npl* placas *fpl* de aprendiz de conductor

L-plates

i En el Reino Unido las personas que están aprendiendo a conducir deben llevar en la parte delantera y trasera de su vehículo unas placas blancas con una L en rojo conocidas como **L-plates** (*de* **learner**). No es necesario que asistan a clases teóricas sino que, desde el principio, se les entrega un carnet de conducir provisional ("*provisional driving licence*") para que realicen sus prácticas, aunque no pueden circular por las autopistas y deben ir siempre acompañadas por un conductor con carnet definitivo ("*full driving licence*").

Ltd *abbr* (= *limited company*) S.A.
lubricate ['lu:brɪkeɪt] *vt* lubricar, engrasar
luck [lʌk] *n* suerte *f*; **bad ~** mala suerte; **good ~!** ¡que tengas suerte!, ¡suerte!; **bad** *or* **hard** *or* **tough ~!** ¡qué penal!; **~ily** *adv* afortunadamente; **~y** *adj* afortunado; (*at cards etc*) con suerte; (*object*) que trae suerte
ludicrous ['lu:dɪkrəs] *adj* absurdo
lug [lʌg] *vt* (*drag*) arrastrar
luggage ['lʌgɪdʒ] *n* equipaje *m*; **~ rack** *n* (*on car*) baca, portaequipajes *m inv*
lukewarm ['lu:kwɔ:m] *adj* tibio
lull [lʌl] *n* tregua ♦ *vt*: **to ~ sb to sleep** arrullar a uno; **to ~ sb into a false sense of security** dar a alguien una falsa sensación de seguridad

lullaby ['lʌləbaɪ] *n* nana
lumbago [lʌm'beɪgəu] *n* lumbago
lumber ['lʌmbə*] *n* (*junk*) trastos *mpl* viejos; (*wood*) maderos *mpl*; **~ with** *vt*: **to be ~ed with** tener que cargar con algo; **~jack** *n* maderero
luminous ['lu:mɪnəs] *adj* luminoso
lump [lʌmp] *n* terrón *m*; (*fragment*) trozo; (*swelling*) bulto ♦ *vt* (*also*: **~ together**) juntar; **~ sum** *n* suma global; **~y** *adj* (*sauce*) lleno de grumos; (*mattress*) lleno de bultos
lunatic ['lu:nətɪk] *adj* loco
lunch [lʌntʃ] *n* almuerzo, comida ♦ *vi* almorzar
luncheon ['lʌntʃən] *n* almuerzo; **~ voucher** (*BRIT*) *n* vale *m* de comida
lunch time *n* hora de comer
lung [lʌŋ] *n* pulmón *m*
lunge [lʌndʒ] *vi* (*also*: **~ forward**) abalanzarse; **to ~ at** arremeter contra
lurch [lə:tʃ] *vi* dar sacudidas ♦ *n* sacudida; **to leave sb in the ~** dejar a uno plantado
lure [luə*] *n* (*attraction*) atracción *f* ♦ *vt* tentar
lurid ['luərɪd] *adj* (*colour*) chillón/ona; (*account*) espeluznante
lurk [lə:k] *vi* (*person, animal*) estar al acecho; (*fig*) acechar
luscious ['lʌʃəs] *adj* (*attractive: person, thing*) precioso; (*food*) delicioso
lush [lʌʃ] *adj* exuberante
lust [lʌst] *n* lujuria; (*greed*) codicia
lustre ['lʌstə*] (*US* **luster**) *n* lustre *m*, brillo
lusty ['lʌstɪ] *adj* robusto, fuerte
Luxembourg ['lʌksəmbə:g] *n* Luxemburgo
luxuriant [lʌg'zjuərɪənt] *adj* exuberante
luxurious [lʌg'zjuərɪəs] *adj* lujoso
luxury ['lʌkʃərɪ] *n* lujo ♦ *cpd* de lujo
lying ['laɪɪŋ] *n* mentiras *fpl* ♦ *adj* mentiroso
lyrical ['lɪrɪkl] *adj* lírico
lyrics ['lɪrɪks] *npl* (*of song*) letra

M, m

m. *abbr* = **metre; mile; million**

M.A. *abbr* = **Master of Arts**

mac [mæk] (*BRIT*) *n* impermeable *m*

macaroni [mækə'rəʊnɪ] *n* macarrones *mpl*

machine [mə'ʃiːn] *n* máquina ♦ *vt* (*dress etc*) coser a máquina; (*TECH*) hacer a máquina; **~ gun** *n* ametralladora; **~ language** *n* (*COMPUT*) lenguaje *m* máquina; **~ry** *n* maquinaria; (*fig*) mecanismo

macho ['mætʃəʊ] *adj* machista

mackerel ['mækrl] *n inv* caballa

mackintosh ['mækɪntɔʃ] (*BRIT*) *n* impermeable *m*

mad [mæd] *adj* loco; (*idea*) disparatado; (*angry*) furioso; (*keen*): **to be ~ about sth** volverle loco a uno algo

madam ['mædəm] *n* señora

madden ['mædn] *vt* volver loco

made [meɪd] *pt, pp of* **make**

Madeira [mə'dɪərə] *n* (*GEO*) Madera; (*wine*) vino de Madera

made-to-measure (*BRIT*) *adj* hecho a la medida

madly ['mædlɪ] *adv* locamente

madman ['mædmən] (*irreg*) *n* loco

madness ['mædnɪs] *n* locura

Madrid [mə'drɪd] *n* Madrid

magazine [mægə'ziːn] *n* revista; (*RADIO, TV*) programa *m* magazina

maggot ['mægət] *n* gusano

magic ['mædʒɪk] *n* magia ♦ *adj* mágico; **~ian** [mə'dʒɪʃən] *n* mago/a; (*conjurer*) prestidigitador(a) *m/f*

magistrate ['mædʒɪstreɪt] *n* juez *m/f* (municipal)

magnet ['mægnɪt] *n* imán *m*; **~ic** [-'netɪk] *adj* magnético; (*personality*) atrayente

magnificent [mæg'nɪfɪsənt] *adj* magnífico

magnify ['mægnɪfaɪ] *vt* (*object*) ampliar; (*sound*) aumentar; **~ing glass** *n* lupa

magpie ['mægpaɪ] *n* urraca

mahogany [mə'hɔgənɪ] *n* caoba

maid [meɪd] *n* criada; **old ~** (*pej*) solterona

maiden ['meɪdn] *n* doncella ♦ *adj* (*aunt etc*) solterona; (*speech, voyage*) inaugural; **~ name** *n* nombre *m* de soltera

mail [meɪl] *n* correo; (*letters*) cartas *fpl* ♦ *vt* echar al correo; **~box** (*US*) *n* buzón *m*; **~ing list** *n* lista de direcciones; **~-order** *n* pedido postal

maim [meɪm] *vt* mutilar, lisiar

main [meɪn] *adj* principal, mayor ♦ *n* (*pipe*) cañería maestra; (*US*) red *f* eléctrica; **the ~s** *npl* (*BRIT*: *ELEC*) la red eléctrica; **in the ~** en general; **~frame** *n* (*COMPUT*) ordenador *m* central; **~land** *n* tierra firme; **~ly** *adv* principalmente; **~ road** *n* carretera; **~stay** *n* (*fig*) pilar *m*; **~stream** *n* corriente *f* principal

maintain [meɪn'teɪn] *vt* mantener; **maintenance** ['meɪntənəns] *n* mantenimiento; (*LAW*) manutención *f*

maize [meɪz] (*BRIT*) *n* maíz *m* (*SP*), choclo (*AM*)

majestic [mə'dʒestɪk] *adj* majestuoso

majesty ['mædʒɪstɪ] *n* majestad *f*; (*title*): **Your M~** Su Majestad

major ['meɪdʒə*] *n* (*MIL*) comandante *m* ♦ *adj* principal; (*MUS*) mayor

Majorca [mə'jɔːkə] *n* Mallorca

majority [mə'dʒɒrɪtɪ] *n* mayoría

make [meɪk] (*pt, pp* **made**) *vt* hacer; (*manufacture*) fabricar; (*mistake*) cometer; (*speech*) pronunciar; (*cause to be*): **to ~ sb sad** poner triste a alguien; (*force*): **to ~ sb do sth** obligar a alguien a hacer algo; (*earn*) ganar; (*equal*): **2 and 2 ~ 4** 2 y 2 son 4 ♦ *n* marca; **to ~ the bed** hacer la cama; **to ~ a fool of sb** poner a alguien en ridículo; **to ~ a profit/loss** obtener ganancias/sufrir pérdidas; **to ~ it** (*arrive*) llegar; (*achieve sth*) tener éxito; **what time do you ~ it?** ¿qué hora tienes?; **to ~ do with** contentarse con; **~ for** *vt fus* (*place*) dirigirse a; **~ out** *vt* (*decipher*) descifrar; (*understand*) entender; (*see*) distinguir; (*cheque*) extender; **~ up** *vt* (*invent*) inventar; (*prepare*) hacer; (*constitute*) constituir ♦ *vi* reconciliarse;

(*with cosmetics*) maquillarse; ~ **up for** *vt fus* compensar; **~-believe** *n* ficción *f*, invención *f*; **~r** *n* fabricante *m/f*; (*of film, programme*) autor(a) *m/f*; **~shift** *adj* improvisado; **~-up** *n* maquillaje *m*; **~-up remover** *n* desmaquillador *m*

making ['meɪkɪŋ] *n* (*fig*): **in the ~** en vías de formación; **to have the ~s of** (*person*) tener madera de

Malaysia [mə'leɪzɪə] *n* Malasia, Malaysia

male [meɪl] *n* (BIOL) macho ♦ *adj* (*sex, attitude*) masculino; (*child etc*) varón

malfunction [mæl'fʌŋkʃən] *n* mal funcionamiento

malice ['mælɪs] *n* malicia; **malicious** [mə'lɪʃəs] *adj* malicioso; rencoroso

malignant [mə'lɪgnənt] *adj* (MED) maligno

mall [mɔːl] (US) *n* (*also*: **shopping ~**) centro comercial

mallet ['mælɪt] *n* mazo

malnutrition [mælnju:'trɪʃən] *n* desnutrición *f*

malpractice [mæl'præktɪs] *n* negligencia profesional

malt [mɔːlt] *n* malta; (*whisky*) whisky *m* de malta

Malta ['mɔːltə] *n* Malta; **Maltese** [-'tiːz] *adj, n inv* maltés/esa *m/f*

mammal ['mæml] *n* mamífero

mammoth ['mæməθ] *n* mamut *m* ♦ *adj* gigantesco

man [mæn] (*pl* **men**) *n* hombre *m*; (~*kind*) el hombre ♦ *vt* (NAUT) tripular; (MIL) guarnecer; (*operate: machine*) manejar; **an old ~** un viejo; **~ and wife** marido y mujer

manage ['mænɪdʒ] *vi* arreglárselas, ir tirando ♦ *vt* (*be in charge of*) dirigir; (*control: person*) manejar; (: *ship*) gobernar; **~able** *adj* manejable; **~ment** *n* dirección *f*; **~r** *n* director(a) *m/f*; (*of pop star*) mánayer *m/f*; (SPORT) entrenador *m/f*; **~ress** *n* directora, entrenadora; **~rial** [-ə'dʒɪərɪəl] *adj* directivo; **managing director** *n* director(a) *m/f* general

mandarin ['mændərɪn] *n* (*also*: **~ orange**)

mandarina; (*person*) mandarín *m*

mandatory ['mændətərɪ] *adj* obligatorio

mane [meɪn] *n* (*of horse*) crin *f*; (*of lion*) melena

maneuver [mə'nuːvə*] (US) = **manoeuvre**

manfully ['mænfəlɪ] *adv* valientemente

mangle ['mæŋgl] *vt* mutilar, destrozar

man: **~handle** *vt* maltratar; **~hole** *n* agujero de acceso; **~hood** *n* edad *f* viril; (*state*) virilidad *f*; **~-hour** *n* hora-hombre *f*; **~hunt** *n* (POLICE) búsqueda y captura

mania ['meɪnɪə] *n* manía; **~c** ['meɪnɪæk] *n* maníaco/a; (*fig*) maniático

manic ['mænɪk] *adj* frenético; **~-depressive** *n* maníaco/a depresivo/a

manicure ['mænɪkjuə*] *n* manicura

manifest ['mænɪfest] *vt* manifestar, mostrar ♦ *adj* manifiesto

manifesto [mænɪ'festəu] *n* manifiesto

manipulate [mə'nɪpjuleɪt] *vt* manipular

man: **~kind** [mæn'kaɪnd] *n* humanidad *f*, género humano; **~ly** *adj* varonil; **~-made** *adj* artificial

manner ['mænə*] *n* manera, modo; (*behaviour*) conducta, manera de ser; (*type*): **all ~ of things** toda clase de cosas; **~s** *npl* (*behaviour*) modales *mpl*; **bad ~s** mala educación; **~ism** *n* peculiaridad *f* de lenguaje (*or* de comportamiento)

manoeuvre [mə'nuːvə*] (US **maneuver**) *vt, vi* maniobrar ♦ *n* maniobra

manor ['mænə*] *n* (*also*: **~ house**) casa solariega

manpower ['mænpauə*] *n* mano *f* de obra

mansion ['mænʃən] *n* palacio, casa grande

manslaughter ['mænslɔːtə*] *n* homicidio no premeditado

mantelpiece ['mæntlpiːs] *n* repisa, chimenea

manual ['mænjuəl] *adj* manual ♦ *n* manual *m*

manufacture [mænju'fæktʃə*] *vt* fabricar ♦ *n* fabricación *f*; **~r** *n* fabricante *m/f*

manure [mə'njuə*] *n* estiércol *m*

manuscript ['mænjuskrɪpt] *n* manuscrito

many ['menɪ] *adj, pron* muchos/as; **a**

great ~ muchísimos, un buen número de; **~ a time** muchas veces

map [mæp] *n* mapa *m*; **to ~ out** *vt* proyectar

maple ['meɪpl] *n* arce *m* (*SP*), maple *m* (*AM*)

mar [mɑ:*] *vt* estropear

marathon ['mærəθən] *n* maratón *m*

marble ['mɑ:bl] *n* mármol *m*; (*toy*) canica *f*

March [mɑ:tʃ] *n* marzo

march [mɑ:tʃ] *vi* (*MIL*) marchar; (*demonstrators*) manifestarse ♦ *n* marcha; (*demonstration*) manifestación *f*

mare [meə*] *n* yegua

margarine [mɑ:dʒə'ri:n] *n* margarina

margin ['mɑ:dʒɪn] *n* margen *m*; (*COMM*: *profit ~*) margen *m* de beneficios; **~al** *adj* marginal; **~al seat** *n* (*POL*) escaño electoral difícil de asegurar

marigold ['mærɪɡəʊld] *n* caléndula

marijuana [mærɪ'wɑ:nə] *n* marijuana

marina [mə'ri:nə] *n* puerto deportivo

marinate ['mærɪneɪt] *vt* marinar

marine [mə'ri:n] *adj* marino ♦ *n* soldado de marina

marital ['mærɪtl] *adj* matrimonial; **~ status** estado civil

marjoram ['mɑ:dʒərəm] *n* mejorana

mark [mɑ:k] *n* marca, señal *f*; (*in snow, mud etc*) huella; (*stain*) mancha; (*BRIT*: *SCOL*) nota; (*currency*) marco ♦ *vt* marcar; manchar; (*damage: furniture*) rayar; (*indicate: place etc*) señalar; (*BRIT*: *SCOL*) calificar, corregir; **to ~ time** marcar el paso; (*fig*) marcar(se) un ritmo; **~ed** *adj* (*obvious*) marcado, acusado; **~er** *n* (*sign*) marcador *m*; (*bookmark*) señal *f* (de libro)

market ['mɑ:kɪt] *n* mercado ♦ *vt* (*COMM*) comercializar; **~ garden** (*BRIT*) *n* huerto; **~ing** *n* márketing *m*; **~place** *n* mercado; **~ research** *n* análisis *m inv* de mercados

marksman ['mɑ:ksmən] *n* tirador *m*

marmalade ['mɑ:məleɪd] *n* mermelada de naranja

maroon [mə'ru:n] *vt*: **to be ~ed** quedar aislado; (*fig*) quedar abandonado

marquee [mɑ:'ki:] *n* entoldado

marriage ['mærɪdʒ] *n* (*relationship, institution*) matrimonio; (*wedding*) boda; (*act*) casamiento; **~ certificate** *n* partida de casamiento

married ['mærɪd] *adj* casado; (*life, love*) conyugal

marrow ['mærəʊ] *n* médula; (*vegetable*) calabacín *m*

marry ['mæri] *vt* casarse con; (*subj: father, priest etc*) casar ♦ *vi* (*also*: **get married**) casarse

Mars [mɑ:z] *n* Marte *m*

marsh [mɑ:ʃ] *n* pantano; (*salt ~*) marisma

marshal ['mɑ:ʃl] *n* (*MIL*) mariscal *m*; (*at sports meeting etc*) oficial *m*; (*US*: *of police, fire department*) jefe/a *m/f* ♦ *vt* (*thoughts etc*) ordenar; (*soldiers*) formar

marshy ['mɑ:ʃi] *adj* pantanoso

martial law ['mɑ:ʃl-] *n* ley *f* marcial

martyr ['mɑ:tə*] *n* mártir *m/f*; **~dom** *n* martirio

marvel ['mɑ:vl] *n* maravilla, prodigio ♦ *vi*: **to ~ (at)** maravillarse (de); **~lous** (*US* **~ous**) *adj* maravilloso

Marxist ['mɑ:ksɪst] *adj*, *n* marxista *m/f*

marzipan ['mɑ:zɪpæn] *n* mazapán *m*

mascara [mæs'kɑ:rə] *n* rímel *m*

masculine ['mæskjʊlɪn] *adj* masculino

mash [mæʃ] *vt* machacar; **~ed potatoes** *npl* puré *m* de patatas (*SP*) *or* papas (*AM*)

mask [mɑ:sk] *n* máscara ♦ *vt* (*cover*): **to ~ one's face** ocultarse la cara; (*hide: feelings*) esconder

mason ['meɪsn] *n* (*also*: **stone~**) albañil *m*; (*also*: **free~**) masón *m*; **~ry** *n* (*in building*) mampostería

masquerade [mæskə'reɪd] *vi*: **to ~ as** disfrazarse de, hacerse pasar por

mass [mæs] *n* (*people*) muchedumbre *f*; (*of air, liquid etc*) masa; (*of detail, hair etc*) gran cantidad *f*; (*REL*) misa ♦ *vi* reunirse; concentrarse; **the ~es** *npl* las masas; **~es of** (*inf*) montones de

massacre ['mæsəkə*] *n* masacre *f*

massage ['mæsɑ:ʒ] *n* masaje *m* ♦ *vt* dar masaje en

masseur [mæ'sə:*] n masajista m
masseuse [mæ'sə:z] n masajista f
massive ['mæsɪv] adj enorme; (support, changes) masivo
mass media npl medios mpl de comunicación
mass production n fabricación f en serie
mast [mɑːst] n (NAUT) mástil m; (RADIO etc) torre f
master ['mɑːstə*] n (of servant) amo; (of situation) dueño, maestro; (in primary school) maestro; (in secondary school) profesor m; (title for boys): **M~ X** Señorito X ♦ vt dominar; **M~ of Arts/Science** n licenciatura superior en Letras/Ciencias; **~ly** adj magistral; **~mind** n inteligencia superior ♦ vt dirigir, planear; **~piece** n obra maestra; **~y** n maestría
mat [mæt] n estera; (also: **door~**) felpudo; (also: **table ~**) salvamanteles m inv, posavasos m inv ♦ adj = **matt**
match [mætʃ] n cerilla, fósforo; (game) partido; (equal) igual m/f ♦ vt (go well with) hacer juego con; (equal) igualar; (correspond to) corresponderse con; (pair: also: **~ up**) casar con ♦ vi hacer juego; **to be a good ~** hacer juego; **~box** n caja de cerillas; **~ing** adj que hace juego
mate [meɪt] n (work~) colega m/f; (inf: friend) amigo/a; (animal) macho m/ hembra f; (in merchant navy) segundo de a bordo ♦ vi acoplarse, aparearse ♦ vt aparear
material [mə'tɪərɪəl] n (substance) materia; (information) material m; (cloth) tela, tejido ♦ adj material; (important) esencial; **~s** npl materiales mpl
maternal [mə'tə:nl] adj maternal
maternity [mə'tə:nɪtɪ] n maternidad f; **~ dress** n vestido premamá
math [mæθ] (US) n = **mathematics**
mathematical [mæθə'mætɪkl] adj matemático
mathematician [mæθəmə'tɪʃən] n matemático/a
mathematics [mæθə'mætɪks] n

matemáticas fpl
maths [mæθs] (BRIT) n = **mathematics**
matinée ['mætɪneɪ] n sesión f de tarde
matrices ['meɪtrɪsiːz] npl of **matrix**
matriculation [mətrɪkju'leɪʃən] n (formalización f de) matrícula
matrimony ['mætrɪmənɪ] n matrimonio
matrix ['meɪtrɪks] (pl **matrices**) n matriz f
matron ['meɪtrən] n enfermera f jefe; (in school) ama de llaves
mat(t) [mæt] adj mate
matted ['mætɪd] adj enmarañado
matter ['mætə*] n cuestión f, asunto; (PHYSICS) sustancia, materia; (reading ~) material m; (MED: pus) pus m ♦ vi importar; **~s** npl (affairs) asuntos mpl, temas mpl; **it doesn't ~** no importa; **what's the ~?** ¿qué pasa?; **no ~ what** pase lo que pase; **as a ~ of course** por rutina; **as a ~ of fact** de hecho; **~-of-fact** adj prosaico, práctico
mattress ['mætrɪs] n colchón m
mature [mə'tjuə*] adj maduro ♦ vi madurar; **maturity** n madurez f
maul [mɔːl] vt magullar
mauve [məuv] adj de color malva (SP) or guinda (AM)
maximum ['mæksɪməm] (pl **maxima**) adj máximo ♦ n máximo
May [meɪ] n mayo
may [meɪ] (conditional: **might**) vi (indicating possibility): **he ~ come** puede que venga; (be allowed to): **~ I smoke?** ¿puedo fumar?; (wishes): **~ God bless you!** ¡que Dios le bendiga!; **you ~ as well go** bien puedes irte
maybe ['meɪbiː] adv quizá(s)
May Day n el primero de Mayo
mayhem ['meɪhɛm] n caos m total
mayonnaise [meɪə'neɪz] n mayonesa
mayor [mɛə*] n alcalde m; **~ess** n alcaldesa
maze [meɪz] n laberinto
M.D. abbr = **Doctor of Medicine**
me [miː] pron (direct) me; (stressed, after pron) mí; **can you hear ~?** ¿me oyes?; **he heard ME!** me oyó a mí; **it's ~** soy yo;

give them to ~ dámelos/las; **with/ without ~** conmigo/sin mí

meadow ['medəu] n prado, pradera

meagre ['mi:gə*] (US **meager**) adj escaso, pobre

meal [mi:l] n comida; (flour) harina; **~time** n hora de comer

mean [mi:n] (pt, pp **meant**) adj (with money) tacaño; (unkind) mezquino, malo; (shabby) humilde; (average) medio ♦ vt (signify) querer decir, significar; (refer to) referirse a; (intend): **to ~ to do sth** pensar or pretender hacer algo ♦ n medio, término medio; **~s** npl (way) medio, manera; (money) recursos mpl, por medio de; **by all ~s!** ¡naturalmente!, ¡claro que sí!; **do you ~ it?** ¿lo dices en serio?; **what do you ~?** ¿qué quiere decir?; **to be meant for sb/sth** ser para uno/algo

meander [mɪ'ændə*] vi (river) serpentear

meaning ['mi:nɪŋ] n significado, sentido; (purpose) sentido, propósito; **~ful** adj significativo; **~less** adj sin sentido

meanness ['mi:nnɪs] n (with money) tacañería; (unkindness) maldad f, mezquindad f; (shabbiness) humildad f

meant [ment] pt, pp of **mean**

meantime ['mi:ntaɪm] adv (also: **in the ~**) mientras tanto

meanwhile ['mi:nwaɪl] adv = **meantime**

measles ['mi:zlz] n sarampión m

measure ['meʒə*] vt, vi medir ♦ n medida; (ruler) regla; **~ments** npl medidas fpl

meat [mi:t] n carne f; **cold ~** fiambre m; **~ball** n albóndiga; **~ pie** n pastel m de carne

Mecca ['mekə] n La Meca

mechanic [mɪ'kænɪk] n mecánico/a; **~s** n mecánica ♦ npl mecanismo; **~al** adj mecánico

mechanism ['mekənɪzəm] n mecanismo

medal ['medl] n medalla; **~lion** [mɪ'dæliən] n medallón m; **~list** (US **~ist**) n (SPORT) medallista m/f

meddle ['medl] vi: **to ~ in** entrometerse

en; **to ~ with sth** manosear algo

media ['mi:dɪə] npl medios mpl de comunicación ♦ npl of **medium**

mediaeval [medɪ'i:vl] adj = **medieval**

mediate ['mi:dɪeɪt] vi mediar; **mediator** n intermediario/a, mediador(a) m/f

Medicaid ® ['medɪkeɪd] (US) n programa de ayuda médica para los pobres

medical ['medɪkl] adj médico ♦ n reconocimiento médico

Medicare ® ['medɪkeə*] (US) n programa de ayuda médica para los ancianos

medication [medɪ'keɪʃən] n medicación f

medicine ['medsɪn] n medicina; (drug) medicamento

medieval [medɪ'i:vl] adj medieval

mediocre [mi:dɪ'əukə*] adj mediocre

meditate ['medɪteɪt] vi meditar

Mediterranean [medɪtə'reɪnɪən] adj mediterráneo; **the ~ (Sea)** el (Mar) Mediterráneo

medium ['mi:dɪəm] (pl **media**) adj mediano, regular ♦ n (means) medio; (pl **mediums**: person) médium m/f; **~ wave** n onda media

meek [mi:k] adj manso, sumiso

meet [mi:t] (pt, pp **met**) vt encontrar; (accidentally) encontrarse con, tropezar con; (by arrangement) reunirse con; (for the first time) conocer; (go and fetch) ir a buscar; (opponent) enfrentarse con; (obligations) cumplir; (encounter: problem) hacer frente a; (need) satisfacer ♦ vi encontrarse; (in session) reunirse; (join: objects) unirse; (for the first time) conocerse; **~ with** vt fus (difficulty) tropezar con; **to ~ with success** tener éxito; **~ing** n encuentro; (arranged) cita, compromiso; (business ~ing) reunión f; (POL) mitin m

megabyte ['megəbaɪt] n (COMPUT) megabyte m, megaocteto

megaphone ['megəfəun] n megáfono

melancholy ['melənkəlɪ] n melancolía ♦ adj melancólico

mellow ['meləu] adj (wine) añejo; (sound, colour) suave ♦ vi (person) ablandar

melody ['mɛlədɪ] n melodía
melon ['mɛlən] n melón m
melt [mɛlt] vi (metal) fundirse; (snow)
derretirse ♦ vt fundir; ~down n (in
nuclear reactor) fusión f de un reactor
(nuclear); ~ing pot n (fig) crisol m
member ['mɛmbə*] n (gen, ANAT)
miembro; (of club) socio/a; M~ of
Parliament (BRIT) diputado/a; M~ of the
European Parliament (BRIT)
eurodiputado/a; M~ of the Scottish
Parliament (BRIT) diputado/a del
Parlamento escocés; ~ship n (members)
número de miembros; (state) filiación f;
~ship card n carnet m de socio
memento [mə'mɛntəu] n recuerdo
memo ['mɛməu] n apunte m, nota
memoirs ['mɛmwɑːz] npl memorias fpl
memorandum [mɛmə'rændəm] (pl
memoranda) n apunte m, nota; (official
note) acta
memorial [mɪ'mɔːrɪəl] n monumento
conmemorativo ♦ adj conmemorativo
memorize ['mɛməraɪz] vt aprender de
memoria
memory ['mɛmərɪ] n (also: COMPUT)
memoria; (instance) recuerdo; (of dead
person): in ~ of a la memoria de
men [mɛn] npl of man
menace ['mɛnəs] n amenaza ♦ vt
amenazar; menacing adj amenazador(a)
mend [mɛnd] vt reparar, arreglar; (darn)
zurcir ♦ vi reponerse ♦ n arreglo, reparación
f; zurcido ♦ n: to be on the ~ ir mejorando;
to ~ one's ways enmendarse; ~ing n
reparación f; (clothes) ropa por remendar
meningitis [mɛnɪn'dʒaɪtɪs] n meningitis f
menopause ['mɛnəupɔːz] n menopausia
menstruation [mɛnstru'eɪʃən] n
menstruación f
mental ['mɛntl] adj mental; ~ity [-'tælɪtɪ] n
mentalidad f
mention ['mɛnʃən] n mención f ♦ vt
mencionar; (speak of) hablar de; don't ~
it! ¡de nada!
menu ['mɛnjuː] n (set ~) menú m;
(printed) carta; (COMPUT) menú m

MEP n abbr = Member of the European
Parliament
merchandise ['mɜːtʃəndaɪz] n mercancías
fpl
merchant ['mɜːtʃənt] n comerciante m/f;
~ bank (BRIT) n banco comercial; ~
navy (US ~ marine) n marina mercante
merciful ['mɜːsɪful] adj compasivo;
(fortunate) afortunado
merciless ['mɜːsɪlɪs] adj despiadado
mercury ['mɜːkjurɪ] n mercurio
mercy ['mɜːsɪ] n compasión f; (REL)
misericordia; at the ~ of a la merced de
merely ['mɪəlɪ] adv simplemente, sólo
merge [mɜːdʒ] vt (join) unir ♦ vi unirse;
(COMM) fusionarse; (colours etc) fundirse;
~r n (COMM) fusión f
meringue [mə'ræŋ] n merengue m
merit ['mɛrɪt] n mérito ♦ vt merecer
mermaid ['mɜːmeɪd] n sirena
merry ['mɛrɪ] adj alegre; M~ Christmas!
¡Felices Pascuas!; ~-go-round n tiovivo
mesh [mɛʃ] n malla
mesmerize ['mɛzməraɪz] vt hipnotizar
mess [mɛs] n (muddle: of situation)
confusión f; (: of room) revoltijo; (dirt)
porquería; (MIL) comedor m; ~ about or
around (inf) vi perder el tiempo; (pass
the time) entretenerse; ~ about or
around with (inf) vt fus divertirse con;
~ up vt (spoil) estropear; (dirty) ensuciar
message ['mɛsɪdʒ] n recado, mensaje m
messenger ['mɛsɪndʒə*] n mensajero/a
Messrs abbr (on letters: = Messieurs) Sres
messy ['mɛsɪ] adj (dirty) sucio; (untidy)
desordenado
met [mɛt] pt, pp of meet
metal ['mɛtl] n metal m; ~lic [-'tælɪk] adj
metálico
metaphor ['mɛtəfə*] n metáfora
meteor ['miːtɪə*] n meteoro; ~ite [-aɪt] n
meteorito
meteorology [miːtɪə'rɔlədʒɪ] n
meteorología
meter ['miːtə*] n (instrument) contador m;
(US: unit) = metre ♦ vt (US: POST) franquear
method ['mɛθəd] n método

meths [mɛθs] (*BRIT*) *n*, **methylated spirit** ['mɛθɪleɪtɪd-] (*BRIT*) *n* alcohol *m* metilado *or* desnaturalizado

metre ['miːtə*] (*US* **meter**) *n* metro

metric ['mɛtrɪk] *adj* métrico

metropolitan [mɛtrə'pɒlɪtən] *adj* metropolitano; **the M~ Police** (*BRIT*) la policía londinense

mettle ['mɛtl] *n*: **to be on one's ~** estar dispuesto a mostrar todo lo que uno vale

mew [mjuː] *vi* (*cat*) maullar

mews [mjuːz] *n*: **~ flat** (*BRIT*) *piso acondicionado en antiguos establos o cocheras*

Mexican ['mɛksɪkən] *adj*, *n* mejicano/a *m/f*, mexicano/a *m/f*

Mexico ['mɛksɪkəʊ] *n* Méjico (*SP*), México (*AM*); **~ City** *n* Ciudad *f* de Méjico *or* México

miaow [miː'aʊ] *vi* maullar

mice [maɪs] *npl of* **mouse**

micro... [maɪkrəʊ] *prefix* micro...; **~chip** *n* microplaqueta; **~(computer)** *n* microordenador *m*; **~phone** *n* micrófono; **~processor** *n* microprocesador *m*; **~scope** *n* microscopio; **~wave** *n* (*also*: **~wave oven**) horno microondas

mid [mɪd] *adj*: **in ~ May** a mediados de mayo; **in ~ afternoon** a media tarde; **in ~ air** en el aire; **~day** *n* mediodía *m*

middle ['mɪdl] *n* centro; (*half-way point*) medio; (*waist*) cintura ♦ *adj* de en medio; (*course, way*) intermedio; **in the ~ of the night** en plena noche; **~-aged** *adj* de mediana edad; **the M~ Ages** *npl* la Edad Media; **~-class** *adj* de clase media; **the ~ class(es)** *n(pl)* la clase media; **M~ East** *n* Oriente *m* Medio; **~man** *n* intermediario; **~ name** *n* segundo nombre; **~-of-the-road** *adj* moderado; **~weight** *n* (*BOXING*) peso medio

middling ['mɪdlɪŋ] *adj* mediano

midge [mɪdʒ] *n* mosquito

midget ['mɪdʒɪt] *n* enano/a

Midlands ['mɪdləndz] *npl*: **the ~** *la región central de Inglaterra*

midnight ['mɪdnaɪt] *n* medianoche *f*

midst [mɪdst] *n*: **in the ~ of** (*crowd*) en medio de; (*situation, action*) en mitad de

midsummer [mɪd'sʌmə*] *n*: **in ~** en pleno verano

midway [mɪd'weɪ] *adj*, *adv*: **~ (between)** a medio camino (entre); **~ through** a la mitad (de)

midweek [mɪd'wiːk] *adv* entre semana

midwife ['mɪdwaɪf] (*pl* **midwives**) *n* comadrona, partera

might [maɪt] *vb see* **may** ♦ *n* fuerza, poder *m*; **~y** *adj* fuerte, poderoso

migraine ['miːgreɪn] *n* jaqueca

migrant ['maɪgrənt] *n adj* (*bird*) migratorio; (*worker*) emigrante

migrate [maɪ'greɪt] *vi* emigrar

mike [maɪk] *n abbr* (= *microphone*) micro

mild [maɪld] *adj* (*person*) apacible; (*climate*) templado; (*slight*) ligero; (*taste*) suave; (*illness*) leve; **~ly** *adv* ligeramente; suavemente; **to put it ~ly** para no decir más

mile [maɪl] *n* milla; **~age** *n* número de millas, ≈ kilometraje *m*; **~ometer** [maɪ'lɒmɪtə*] *n* ≈ cuentakilómetros *m inv*; **~stone** *n* mojón *m*

militant ['mɪlɪtnt] *adj*, *n* militante *m/f*

military ['mɪlɪtərɪ] *adj* militar

militia [mɪ'lɪʃə] *n* milicia

milk [mɪlk] *n* leche *f* ♦ *vt* (*cow*) ordeñar; (*fig*) chupar; **~ chocolate** *n* chocolate *m* con leche; **~man** (*irreg*) *n* lechero; **~ shake** *n* batido, malteada (*AM*); **~y** *adj* lechoso; **M~y Way** *n* Vía Láctea

mill [mɪl] *n* (*windmill etc*) molino; (*coffee ~*) molinillo; (*factory*) fábrica ♦ *vt* moler ♦ *vi* (*also*: **~ about**) arremolinarse

millennium [mɪ'lɛnɪəm] (*pl* **~s** *or* **millennia**) *n* milenio, milenario

miller ['mɪlə*] *n* molinero

milli... ['mɪlɪ] *prefix*: **~gram(me)** *n* miligramo; **~metre** (*US* **~meter**) *n* milímetro

million ['mɪljən] *n* millón *m*; **a ~ times** un millón de veces; **~aire** [-jə'nɛə*] *n* millonario/a

milometer [maɪ'lɒmɪtə*] (*BRIT*) *n*
= **mileometer**

mime [maɪm] *n* mímica; (*actor*) mimo/a
♦ *vt* remedar ♦ *vi* actuar de mimo

mimic ['mɪmɪk] *n* imitador(a) *m/f* ♦ *adj*
mímico ♦ *vt* remedar, imitar

min. *abbr* = **minimum; minute(s)**

mince [mɪns] *vt* picar ♦ *n* (*BRIT: CULIN*)
carne *f* picada; **~meat** *n* conserva de
fruta picada; (*US: meat*) carne *f* picada; **~
pie** *n* empanadilla rellena de fruta
picada; **~r** *n* picadora de carne

mind [maɪnd] *n* mente *f*; (*intellect*)
intelecto *m*; (*contrasted with matter*) espíritu
m ♦ *vt* (*attend to, look after*) ocuparse de,
cuidar; (*be careful of*) tener cuidado con;
(*object to*): **I don't ~ the noise** no me
molesta el ruido; **it is on my ~** me
preocupa; **to bear sth in ~** tomar *or*
tener algo en cuenta; **to make up one's
~** decidirse; **I don't ~** me es igual; **~ you,
...** te advierto que ...; **never ~!** ¡es igual!,
¡no importa!; (*don't worry*) ¡no te
preocupes!; **"~ the step"** "cuidado con
el escalón"; **~er** *n* guardaespaldas *m inv*;
(*child ~er*) ≈ niñera; **~ful** *adj*: **~ful of**
consciente de; **~less** *adj* (*crime*) sin
motivo; (*work*) de autómata

mine¹ [maɪn] *pron* el mío/la mía *etc*; **a
friend of ~** un(a) amigo/a mío/mía ♦ *adj*:
this book is ~ este libro es mío

mine² [maɪn] *n* mina ♦ *vt* (*coal*) extraer;
(*bomb: beach etc*) minar; **~field** *n* campo
de minas; **miner** *n* minero/a

mineral ['mɪnərəl] *adj* mineral ♦ *n* mineral
m; **~s** *npl* (*BRIT: soft drinks*) refrescos *mpl*;
~ water *n* agua mineral

mingle ['mɪŋgl] *vi*: **to ~ with** mezclarse
con

miniature ['mɪnətʃə*] *adj* (en) miniatura
♦ *n* miniatura

minibus ['mɪnɪbʌs] *n* microbús *m*

Minidisc ® ['mɪnɪdɪsk] *n* minidisco

minimal ['mɪnɪml] *adj* mínimo

minimize ['mɪnɪmaɪz] *vt* minimizar; (*play
down*) empequeñecer

minimum ['mɪnɪməm] (*pl* **minima**) *n*, *adj*
mínimo

mining ['maɪnɪŋ] *n* explotación *f* minera

miniskirt ['mɪnɪskɜ:t] *n* minifalda

minister ['mɪnɪstə*] *n* (*BRIT: POL*) ministro/a
(*SP*), secretario/a (*AM*); (*REL*) pastor *m*
♦ *vi*: **to ~ to** atender a

ministry ['mɪnɪstrɪ] *n* (*BRIT: POL*) ministerio
(*SP*), secretaría (*AM*); (*REL*) sacerdocio

mink [mɪŋk] *n* visón *m*

minnow ['mɪnəʊ] *n* pececillo (*de agua
dulce*)

minor ['maɪnə*] *adj* (*repairs, injuries*) leve;
(*poet, planet*) menor; (*MUS*) menor ♦ *n*
(*LAW*) menor *m* de edad

Minorca [mɪ'nɔ:kə] *n* Menorca

minority [maɪ'nɒrɪtɪ] *n* minoría

mint [mɪnt] *n* (*plant*) menta, hierbabuena;
(*sweet*) caramelo de menta ♦ *vt* (*coins*)
acuñar; **the (Royal) M~, the (US) M~** la
Casa de la Moneda; **in ~ condition** en
perfecto estado

minus ['maɪnəs] *n* (*also*: **~ sign**) signo de
menos ♦ *prep* menos; **12 ~ 6 equals 6**
12 menos 6 son 6; **~ 24°C** menos 24
grados

minute¹ ['mɪnɪt] *n* minuto; (*fig*)
momento; **~s** *npl* (*of meeting*) actas *fpl*;
at the last ~ a última hora

minute² [maɪ'nju:t] *adj* diminuto; (*search*)
minucioso

miracle ['mɪrəkl] *n* milagro

mirage ['mɪrɑ:ʒ] *n* espejismo

mirror ['mɪrə*] *n* espejo; (*in car*) retrovisor *m*

mirth [mɜ:θ] *n* alegría

misadventure [mɪsəd'ventʃə*] *n* desgracia

misapprehension [mɪsæprɪ'henʃən] *n*
equivocación *f*

misappropriate [mɪsə'prəʊprɪeɪt] *vt*
malversar

misbehave [mɪsbɪ'heɪv] *vi* portarse mal

miscalculate [mɪs'kælkjuleɪt] *vt* calcular
mal

miscarriage ['mɪskærɪdʒ] *n* (*MED*) aborto;
~ of justice error *m* judicial

miscellaneous [mɪsɪ'leɪnɪəs] *adj* varios/
as, diversos/as

mischief ['mɪstʃɪf] *n* travesuras *fpl*,

diabluras *fpl*; *(maliciousness)* malicia;
mischievous [-ʃɪvəs] *adj* travieso
misconception [mɪskən'sepʃən] *n* idea
equivocada; equivocación *f*
misconduct [mɪs'kɔndʌkt] *n* mala
conducta; **professional ~** falta profesional
misdemeanour [mɪsdɪ'miːnə*] *(US*
misdemeanor) *n* delito, ofensa
miser ['maɪzə*] *n* avaro/a
miserable ['mɪzərəbl] *adj (unhappy)* triste,
desgraciado; *(unpleasant, contemptible)*
miserable
miserly ['maɪzəlɪ] *adj* avariento, tacaño
misery ['mɪzərɪ] *n* tristeza; *(wretchedness)*
miseria, desdicha
misfire [mɪs'faɪə*] *vi* fallar
misfit ['mɪsfɪt] *n* inadaptado/a
misfortune [mɪs'fɔːtʃən] *n* desgracia
misgiving [mɪs'gɪvɪŋ] *n (apprehension)*
presentimiento; **to have ~s about sth**
tener dudas acerca de algo
misguided [mɪs'gaɪdɪd] *adj* equivocado
mishandle [mɪs'hændl] *vt (mismanage)*
manejar mal
mishap ['mɪshæp] *n* desgracia,
contratiempo
misinform [mɪsɪn'fɔːm] *vt* informar mal
misinterpret [mɪsɪn'tə:prɪt] *vt* interpretar
mal
misjudge [mɪs'dʒʌdʒ] *vt* juzgar mal
mislay [mɪs'leɪ] *(irreg) vt* extraviar, perder
mislead [mɪs'liːd] *(irreg) vt* llevar a
conclusiones erróneas; **~ing** *adj*
engañoso
mismanage [mɪs'mænɪdʒ] *vt* administrar
mal
misplace [mɪs'pleɪs] *vt* extraviar
misprint ['mɪsprɪnt] *n* errata, error *m* de
imprenta
Miss [mɪs] *n* Señorita
miss [mɪs] *vt (train etc)* perder; *(fail to hit:
target)* errar; *(regret the absence of)*: **I ~
him** (yo) le echo de menos *or* a faltar;
(fail to see): **you can't ~ it** no tiene
pérdida ♦ *vi* fallar ♦ *n (shot)* tiro fallido *or*
perdido; **~ out** *(BRIT) vt* omitir
misshapen [mɪs'ʃeɪpən] *adj* deforme

missile ['mɪsaɪl] *n (AVIAT)* mísil *m; (object
thrown)* proyectil *m*
missing ['mɪsɪŋ] *adj (pupil)* ausente;
(thing) perdido; *(MIL)*: **~ in action**
desaparecido en combate
mission ['mɪʃən] *n* misión *f; (official
representation)* delegación *f;* **~ary** *n*
misionero/a
mist [mɪst] *n (light)* neblina; *(heavy)* niebla;
(at sea) bruma ♦ *vi (eyes: also: ~ **over**, ~
up)* llenarse de lágrimas; *(BRIT: windows:
also: ~ **over**, ~ **up**)* empañarse
mistake [mɪs'teɪk] *(vt: irreg) n* error *m*
♦ *vt* entender mal; **by ~** por
equivocación; **to make a ~** equivocarse;
to ~ A for B confundir A con B;
mistaken *pp of* **mistake** ♦ *adj*
equivocado; **to be mistaken** equivocarse,
engañarse
mister ['mɪstə*] *(inf) n* señor *m; see* **Mr**
mistletoe ['mɪsltəu] *n* muérdago
mistook [mɪs'tuk] *pt of* **mistake**
mistress ['mɪstrɪs] *n (lover)* amante *f; (of
house)* señora (de la casa); *(BRIT: in
primary school)* maestra; *(in secondary
school)* profesora; *(of situation)* dueña
mistrust [mɪs'trʌst] *vt* desconfiar de
misty ['mɪstɪ] *adj (day)* de niebla; *(glasses
etc)* empañado
misunderstand [mɪsʌndə'stænd] *(irreg)*
vt, vi entender mal; **~ing** *n*
malentendido
misuse [*n* mɪs'juːs, *vb* mɪs'juːz] *n* mal uso;
(of power) abuso; *(of funds)* malversación *f*
♦ *vt* abusar de; malversar
mitt(en) ['mɪt(n)] *n* manopla
mix [mɪks] *vt* mezclar; *(combine)* unir ♦ *vi*
mezclarse; *(people)* llevarse bien ♦ *n*
mezcla; **~ up** *vt* mezclar; *(confuse)*
confundir; **~ed** *adj* mixto; *(feelings etc)*
encontrado; **~ed-up** *adj (confused)*
confuso, revuelto; **~er** *n (for food)*
licuadora; *(for drinks)* coctelera; *(person)*:
he's a good ~er tiene don de gentes;
~ture *n* mezcla; *(also:* **cough ~ture**)
jarabe *m;* **~up** *n* confusión *f*
mm *abbr (= millimetre)* mm

moan [məun] *n* gemido ♦ *vi* gemir; (*inf: complain*): **to ~ (about)** quejarse (de)
moat [məut] *n* foso
mob [mɔb] *n* multitud *f* ♦ *vt* acosar
mobile ['məubail] *adj* móvil ♦ *n* móvil *m*; **~ home** *n* caravana *f*; **~ phone** *n* teléfono portátil
mock [mɔk] *vt* (*ridicule*) ridiculizar; (*laugh at*) burlarse de ♦ *adj* fingido; **~ exam** *examen preparatorio antes de los exámenes oficiales*; **~ery** *n* burla; **~-up** *n* maqueta
mod [mɔd] *adj see* **convenience**
mode [məud] *n* modo
model ['mɔdl] *n* modelo; (*fashion ~, artist's ~*) modelo *m/f* ♦ *adj* modelo ♦ *vt* (*with clay etc*) modelar (*copy*): **to ~ o.s. on** tomar como modelo a ♦ *vi* ser modelo; **to ~ clothes** pasar modelos, ser modelo; **~ railway** *n* ferrocarril *m* de juguete
modem ['məudəm] *n* modem *m*
moderate [*adj* 'mɔdərət, *vb* 'mɔdəreit] *adj* moderado/a ♦ *vi* moderarse, calmarse ♦ *vt* moderar
modern ['mɔdən] *adj* moderno; **~ize** *vt* modernizar
modest ['mɔdist] *adj* modesto; (*small*) módico; **~y** *n* modestia
modify ['mɔdifai] *vt* modificar
mogul ['məugəl] *n* (*fig*) magnate *m*
mohair ['məuheə*] *n* mohair *m*
moist [mɔist] *adj* húmedo; **~en** ['mɔisn] *vt* humedecer; **~ure** ['mɔistʃə*] *n* humedad *f*; **~urizer** ['mɔistʃəraizə*] *n* crema hidratante
molar ['məulə*] *n* muela
mold [məuld] (*US*) *n, vt* = **mould**
mole [məul] *n* (*animal, spy*) topo; (*spot*) lunar *m*
molest [məu'lest] *vt* importunar; (*assault sexually*) abusar sexualmente
mollycoddle ['mɔlɪkɔdl] *vt* mimar
molt [məult] (*US*) *vi* = **moult**
molten ['məultən] *adj* fundido; (*lava*) líquido
mom [mɔm] (*US*) *n* = **mum**

moment ['məumənt] *n* momento; **at the ~** de momento, por ahora; **~ary** *adj* momentáneo; **~ous** [-'mentəs] *adj* trascendental, importante
momentum [məu'mentəm] *n* momento; (*fig*) ímpetu *m*; **to gather ~** cobrar velocidad; (*fig*) ganar fuerza
mommy ['mɔmi] (*US*) *n* = **mummy**
Monaco ['mɔnəkəu] *n* Mónaco
monarch ['mɔnək] *n* monarca *m/f*; **~y** *n* monarquía
monastery ['mɔnəstəri] *n* monasterio
Monday ['mʌndi] *n* lunes *m inv*
monetary ['mʌnitəri] *adj* monetario
money ['mʌni] *n* dinero; (*currency*) moneda; **to make ~** ganar dinero; **~ order** *n* giro; **~-spinner** (*inf*) *n*: **to be a ~-spinner** dar mucho dinero
mongrel ['mʌŋgrəl] *n* (*dog*) perro mestizo
monitor ['mɔnitə*] *n* (*SCOL*) monitor *m*; (*also*: **television ~**) receptor *m* de control; (*of computer*) monitor *m* ♦ *vt* controlar
monk [mʌŋk] *n* monje *m*
monkey ['mʌŋki] *n* mono; **~ nut** (*BRIT*) *n* cacahuete *m* (*SP*), maní *m* (*AM*); **~ wrench** *n* llave *f* inglesa
monopoly [mə'nɔpəli] *n* monopolio
monotone ['mɔnətəun] *n* voz *f* (*or* tono) monocorde
monotonous [mə'nɔtənəs] *adj* monótono
monsoon [mɔn'su:n] *n* monzón *m*
monster ['mɔnstə*] *n* monstruo
monstrous ['mɔnstrəs] *adj* (*huge*) enorme; (*atrocious, ugly*) monstruoso
month [mʌnθ] *n* mes *m*; **~ly** *adj* mensual ♦ *adv* mensualmente
monument ['mɔnjumənt] *n* monumento
moo [mu:] *vi* mugir
mood [mu:d] *n* humor *m*; (*of crowd, group*) clima *m*; **to be in a good/bad ~** estar de buen/mal humor; **~y** *adj* (*changeable*) de humor variable; (*sullen*) malhumorado
moon [mu:n] *n* luna; **~light** *n* luz *f* de la luna; **~lighting** *n* pluriempleo; **~lit** *adj*: **a ~lit night** una noche de luna
Moor [muə*] *n* moro/a

moor [muə*] n páramo ♦ vt (ship) amarrar ♦ vi echar las amarras

Moorish ['muərɪʃ] adj moro; (architecture) árabe, morisco

moorland ['muələnd] n páramo, brezal m

moose [mu:s] n inv alce m

mop [mɔp] n fregona; (of hair) greña, melena ♦ vt fregar; ~ up vt limpiar

mope [məup] vi estar or andar deprimido

moped ['məupɛd] n ciclomotor m

moral ['mɔrl] adj moral ♦ n moraleja; ~s npl moralidad f, moral f

morale [mɔ'rɑ:l] n moral f

morality [mə'rælɪtɪ] n moralidad f

morass [mə'ræs] n pantano

KEYWORD

more [mɔ:*] adj 1 (greater in number etc) más; ~ people/work than before más gente/trabajo que antes
2 (additional) más; do you want (some) ~ tea? ¿quieres más té?; is there any ~ wine? ¿queda vino?; it'll take a few ~ weeks tardará unas semanas más; it's 2 kms ~ to the house faltan 2 kms para la casa; ~ time/letters than we expected más tiempo del que/más cartas de las que esperábamos
♦ pron (greater amount, additional amount) más; ~ than 10 más de 10; it cost ~ than the other one/than we expected costó más que el otro/más de lo que esperábamos; is there any ~? ¿hay más?; many/much ~ muchos(as)/mucho(a) más
♦ adv más; ~ dangerous/easily (than) más peligroso/fácilmente (que); ~ and ~ expensive cada vez más caro; ~ or less más o menos; ~ than ever más que nunca

---

moreover [mɔ:'rəuvə*] adv además, por otra parte

morning ['mɔ:nɪŋ] n mañana; (early ~) madrugada ♦ cpd matutino, de la mañana; in the ~ por la mañana; 7 o'clock in the ~ las 7 de la mañana; ~

sickness n náuseas fpl matutinas

Morocco [mə'rɔkəu] n Marruecos m

moron ['mɔ:rɔn] (inf) n imbécil m/f

morphine ['mɔ:fi:n] n morfina

Morse [mɔ:s] n (also: ~ code) (código) Morse

morsel ['mɔ:sl] n (of food) bocado

mortar ['mɔ:tə*] n argamasa

mortgage ['mɔ:gɪdʒ] n hipoteca ♦ vt hipotecar; ~ company (US) n ≈ banco hipotecario

mortuary ['mɔ:tjuərɪ] n depósito de cadáveres

Moscow ['mɔskəu] n Moscú

Moslem ['mɔzləm] adj, n = **Muslim**

mosque [mɔsk] n mezquita

mosquito [mɔs'ki:təu] (pl ~es) n mosquito (SP), zancudo (AM)

moss [mɔs] n musgo

most [məust] adj la mayor parte de, la mayoría de ♦ pron la mayor parte, la mayoría ♦ adv el más; (very) muy; the ~ (also: +adj) el más; ~ of them la mayor parte de ellos; I saw the ~ yo vi el que más; at the (very) ~ a lo sumo, todo lo más; to make the ~ of aprovechar (al máximo); a ~ interesting book un libro interesantísimo; ~ly adv en su mayor parte, principalmente

MOT (BRIT) n abbr (= Ministry of Transport): the ~ (test) inspección (anual) obligatoria de coches y camiones

motel [məu'tɛl] n motel m

moth [mɔθ] n mariposa nocturna; (clothes ~) polilla

mother ['mʌðə*] n madre f ♦ adj materno ♦ vt (care for) cuidar (como una madre); ~hood n maternidad f; ~-in-law n suegra; ~ly adj maternal; ~-of-pearl n nácar m; ~-to-be n futura madre f; ~ tongue n lengua materna

motion ['məuʃən] n movimiento; (gesture) ademán m, señal f; (at meeting) moción f ♦ vt, vi: to ~ (to) sb to do sth hacer señas a uno para que haga algo; ~less adj inmóvil; ~ picture n película

motivated ['məutɪveɪtɪd] adj motivado

motive ['məʊtɪv] n motivo
motley ['mɒtlɪ] adj variado
motor ['məʊtə*] n motor m; (BRIT: inf: vehicle) coche m (SP), carro (AM), automóvil m ♦ adj motor (f: motora or motriz); ~**bike** n moto f; ~**boat** n lancha motora; ~**car** (BRIT) n coche m, carro, automóvil m; ~**cycle** n motocicleta; ~**cycle racing** n motociclismo; ~**cyclist** n motociclista m/f; ~**ing** (BRIT) n automovilismo; ~**ist** n conductor(a) m/f, automovilista m/f; ~ **racing** (BRIT) n carreras fpl de coches, automovilismo; ~ **vehicle** n automóvil m; ~**way** (BRIT) n autopista
mottled ['mɒtld] adj abigarrado
motto ['mɒtəʊ] (pl ~**es**) n lema m; (watchword) consigna
mould [məʊld] (US **mold**) n molde m; (mildew) moho ♦ vt moldear; (fig) formar; ~**y** adj enmohecido
moult [məʊlt] (US **molt**) vi mudar la piel (or las plumas)
mound [maʊnd] n montón m, montículo
mount [maʊnt] n monte m ♦ vt montar, subir a; (jewel) engarzar; (picture) enmarcar; (exhibition etc) organizar ♦ vi (increase) aumentar; ~ **up** vi aumentar
mountain ['maʊntɪn] n montaña ♦ cpd de montaña; ~ **bike** n bicicleta de montaña; ~**eer** [-'nɪə*] n montañero/a (SP), andinista m/f (AM); ~**eering** [-'nɪərɪŋ] n montañismo, andinismo; ~**ous** adj montañoso; ~ **rescue team** n equipo de rescate de montaña; ~**side** n ladera de la montaña
mourn [mɔːn] vt llorar, lamentar ♦ vi: **to ~ for** llorar la muerte de; ~**er** n doliente m/f; dolorido/a; ~**ing** n luto; **in ~ing** de luto
mouse [maʊs] (pl **mice**) n (ZOOL, COMPUT) ratón m; ~ **mat** n (COMPUT) alfombrilla; ~**trap** n ratonera
mousse [muːs] n (CULIN) crema batida; (for hair) espuma (moldeadora)
moustache [məs'tɑːʃ] (US **mustache**) n bigote m
mousy ['maʊsɪ] adj (hair) pardusco
mouth [maʊθ, pl maʊðz] n boca; (of river) desembocadura; ~**ful** n bocado; ~ **organ** n armónica; ~**piece** n (of musical instrument) boquilla; (spokesman) portavoz m/f; ~**wash** n enjuague m; ~**watering** adj apetitoso
movable ['muːvəbl] adj movible
move [muːv] n (movement) movimiento; (in game) jugada; (: turn to play) turno; (change: of house) mudanza; (: of job) cambio de trabajo ♦ vt mover; (emotionally) conmover; (POL: resolution etc) proponer ♦ vi moverse; (traffic) circular; (also: ~ **house**) trasladarse, mudarse; **to ~ sb to do sth** mover a uno a hacer algo; **to get a ~ on** darse prisa; ~ **about** or **around** vi moverse; (travel) viajar; ~ **along** vi avanzar, adelantarse; ~ **away** vi alejarse; ~ **back** vi retroceder; ~ **forward** vi avanzar; ~ **in** vi (to a house) instalarse; (police, soldiers) intervenir; ~ **on** vi ponerse en camino; ~ **out** vi (of house) mudarse; ~ **over** vi apartarse, hacer sitio; ~ **up** vi (employee) ser ascendido
moveable ['muːvəbl] adj = **movable**
movement ['muːvmənt] n movimiento
movie ['muːvɪ] n película; **to go to the ~s** ir al cine
moving ['muːvɪŋ] adj (emotional) conmovedor(a); (that moves) móvil
mow [məʊ] (pt **mowed**, pp **mowed** or **mown**) vt (grass, corn) cortar, segar; ~ **down** vt (shoot) acribillar; ~**er** n (also: **lawn~er**) cortacéspedes m inv, segadora
MP n abbr = **Member of Parliament**
MP3 n MP3 m; ~ **player** n reproductor m MP3
m.p.h. abbr = **miles per hour** (60 m.p.h. = 96 k.p.h.)
Mr ['mɪstə*] (US **Mr.**) n: ~ **Smith** (el) Sr. Smith
Mrs ['mɪsɪz] (US **Mrs.**) n: ~ **Smith** (la) Sra. Smith
Ms [mɪz] (US **Ms.**) n (= Miss or Mrs): ~ **Smith** (la) Sr(t)a. Smith
M.Sc. abbr = **Master of Science**
MSP n abbr = **Member of the Scottish Parliament**
much [mʌtʃ] adj mucho ♦ adv mucho;

(before pp) muy ♦ n or pron mucho; **how ~ is it?** ¿cuánto es?, ¿cuánto cuesta?; **too ~** demasiado; **it's not ~** no es mucho; **as ~ as** tanto como; **however ~ he tries** por mucho que se esfuerce

muck [mʌk] n suciedad f; **~ about** or **around** (inf) vi perder el tiempo; (enjoy o.s.) entretenerse; **~ up** (inf) vt arruinar, estropear

mud [mʌd] n barro, lodo

muddle ['mʌdl] n desorden m, confusión f; (mix-up) embrollo, lío ♦ vt (also: **~ up**) embrollar, confundir; **~ through** vi salir del paso

muddy ['mʌdɪ] adj fangoso, cubierto de lodo

mudguard ['mʌdgɑːd] n guardabarros m inv

muffin ['mʌfɪn] n panecillo dulce

muffle ['mʌfl] vt (sound) amortiguar; (against cold) embozar; **~d** adj (noise etc) amortiguado, apagado; **~r** (US) n (AUT) silenciador m

mug [mʌg] n taza grande (sin platillo); (for beer) jarra; (inf: face) jeta; (: fool) bobo ♦ vt (assault) asaltar; **~ging** n asalto

muggy ['mʌgɪ] adj bochornoso

mule [mjuːl] n mula

multi... [mʌltɪ] prefix multi...

multi-level [mʌltɪ'levl] (US) adj = **multistorey**

multiple ['mʌltɪpl] adj múltiple ♦ n múltiplo; **~ sclerosis** n esclerosis f múltiple

multiplex cinema ['mʌltɪpleks-] n multicines mpl

multiplication [mʌltɪplɪ'keɪʃən] n multiplicación f

multiply ['mʌltɪplaɪ] vt multiplicar ♦ vi multiplicarse

multistorey [mʌltɪ'stɔːrɪ] (BRIT) adj de muchos pisos

multitude ['mʌltɪtjuːd] n multitud f

mum [mʌm] (BRIT: inf) n mamá ♦ adj: **to keep ~** mantener la boca cerrada

mumble ['mʌmbl] vt, vi hablar entre dientes, refunfuñar

mummy ['mʌmɪ] n (BRIT: mother) mamá; (embalmed) momia

mumps [mʌmps] n paperas fpl

munch [mʌntʃ] vt, vi mascar

mundane [mʌn'deɪn] adj trivial

municipal [mjuː'nɪsɪpl] adj municipal

murder ['mɜːdə] n asesinato; (in law) homicidio ♦ vt asesinar, matar; **~er/ess** n asesino/a; **~ous** adj homicida

murky ['mɜːkɪ] adj (water) turbio; (street, night) lóbrego

murmur ['mɜːmə] n murmullo ♦ vt, vi murmurar

muscle ['mʌsl] n músculo; (fig: strength) garra, fuerza; **~ in** vi entrometerse; **muscular** ['mʌskjulə] adj muscular; (person) musculoso

muse [mjuːz] vi meditar ♦ n musa

museum [mjuː'zɪəm] n museo

mushroom ['mʌʃrum] n seta, hongo; (CULIN) champiñón m ♦ vi crecer de la noche a la mañana

music ['mjuːzɪk] n música; **~al** adj musical; (sound) melodioso; (person) con talento musical ♦ n (show) comedia musical; **~al instrument** n instrumento musical; **~ hall** n teatro de variedades; **~ian** [-'zɪʃən] n músico/a

Muslim ['mʌzlɪm] adj, n musulmán/ana m/f

muslin ['mʌzlɪn] n muselina

mussel ['mʌsl] n mejillón m

must [mʌst] aux vb (obligation): **I ~ do it** debo hacerlo, tengo que hacerlo; (probability): **he ~ be there by now** ya debe (de) estar allí ♦ n: **it's a ~** es imprescindible

mustache ['mʌstæʃ] (US) n = **moustache**

mustard ['mʌstəd] n mostaza

muster ['mʌstə] vt juntar, reunir

mustn't ['mʌsnt] = **must not**

mute [mjuːt] adj, n mudo/a m/f

muted ['mjuːtɪd] adj callado; (colour) apagado

mutiny ['mjuːtɪnɪ] n motín m ♦ vi amotinarse

mutter ['mʌtə] vt, vi murmurar

mutton ['mʌtn] n carne f de cordero
mutual ['mjuːtʃuəl] adj mutuo; (*interest*) común; ~**ly** adv mutuamente
muzzle ['mʌzl] n hocico; (*for dog*) bozal m; (*of gun*) boca ♦ vt (*dog*) poner un bozal a
my [maɪ] adj mi(s); ~ **house/brother/ sisters** mi casa/mi hermano/mis hermanas; **I've washed ~ hair/cut ~ finger** me he lavado el pelo/cortado un dedo; **is this ~ pen or yours?** ¿es este bolígrafo mío o tuyo?
myself [maɪ'self] pron (*reflexive*) me; (*emphatic*) yo mismo; (*after prep*) mí (mismo); see also **oneself**
mysterious [mɪs'tɪərɪəs] adj misterioso
mystery ['mɪstərɪ] n misterio
mystify ['mɪstɪfaɪ] vt (*perplex*) dejar perplejo
myth [mɪθ] n mito

N, n

n/a abbr (= *not applicable*) no interesa
nag [næg] vt (*scold*) regañar; ~**ging** adj (*doubt*) persistente; (*pain*) continuo
nail [neɪl] n (*human*) uña; (*metal*) clavo ♦ vt clavar; **to ~ sth to sth** clavar algo en algo; **to ~ sb down to doing sth** comprometer a uno a que haga algo; ~**brush** n cepillo para las uñas; ~**file** n lima para las uñas; ~ **polish** n esmalte m or laca para las uñas; ~ **polish remover** n quitaesmalte m; ~ **scissors** npl tijeras fpl para las uñas; ~ **varnish** (*BRIT*) n = ~ **polish**
naïve [naɪ'iːv] adj ingenuo
naked ['neɪkɪd] adj (*nude*) desnudo; (*flame*) expuesto al aire
name [neɪm] n nombre m; (*surname*) apellido; (*reputation*) fama, renombre m ♦ vt (*child*) poner nombre a; (*criminal*) identificar; (*price, date etc*) fijar; **what's your ~?** ¿cómo se llama?; **by ~** de nombre; **in the ~ of** en nombre de; **to give one's ~ and address** dar sus señas;

~**ly** adv a saber; ~**sake** n tocayo/a
nanny ['nænɪ] n niñera
nap [næp] n (*sleep*) sueñecito, siesta
nape [neɪp] n: ~ **of the neck** nuca, cogote m
napkin ['næpkɪn] n (*also*: **table ~**) servilleta
nappy ['næpɪ] (*BRIT*) n pañal m; ~ **rash** n prurito
narcotic [naː'kɒtɪk] adj, n narcótico
narrow ['nærəʊ] adj estrecho, angosto; (*fig: majority etc*) corto; (: *ideas etc*) estrecho ♦ vi (*road*) estrecharse; (*diminish*) reducirse; **to have a ~ escape** escaparse por los pelos; **to ~ sth down** reducir algo; ~**ly** adv (*miss*) por poco; ~-**minded** adj de miras estrechas
nasty ['naːstɪ] adj (*remark*) feo; (*person*) antipático; (*revolting: taste, smell*) asqueroso; (*wound, disease etc*) peligroso, grave
nation ['neɪʃən] n nación f
national ['næʃənl] adj, n nacional m/f; ~ **dress** n vestido nacional; **N~ Health Service** (*BRIT*) n servicio nacional de salud pública; ≈ Insalud m (*SP*); **N~ Insurance** (*BRIT*) n seguro social nacional; ~**ism** n nacionalismo; ~**ist** adj, n nacionalista m/f; ~**ity** [-'nælɪtɪ] n nacionalidad f; ~**ize** vt nacionalizar; ~**ly** adv (*nationwide*) en escala nacional; (*as a nation*) nacionalmente, como nación; ~ **park** (*BRIT*) n parque m nacional
nationwide ['neɪʃənwaɪd] adj en escala or a nivel nacional
native ['neɪtɪv] n (*local inhabitant*) natural m/f, nacional m/f ♦ adj (*indigenous*) indígena; (*country*) natal; (*innate*) natural, innato; **a ~ of Russia** un(a) natural m/f de Rusia; **a ~ speaker of French** un hablante nativo de francés; **N~ American** adj, n americano/a indígena, amerindio/a; ~ **language** n lengua materna
Nativity [nə'tɪvɪtɪ] n: **the ~** Navidad f
NATO ['neɪtəʊ] n abbr (= *North Atlantic Treaty Organization*) OTAN f
natural ['nætʃrəl] adj natural; ~**ly** adv

(*speak etc*) naturalmente; (*of course*) desde luego, por supuesto

nature ['neɪtʃə*] *n* (*also:* **N~**) naturaleza; (*group, sort*) género, clase *f*; (*character*) carácter *m*, genio; **by ~** por *or* de naturaleza

naught [nɔ:t] = **nought**

naughty ['nɔ:tɪ] *adj* (*child*) travieso

nausea ['nɔ:sɪə] *n* náuseas *fpl*

nautical ['nɔ:tɪkl] *adj* náutico, marítimo; (*mile*) marino

naval ['neɪvl] *adj* naval, de marina; **~ officer** *n* oficial *m/f* de marina

nave [neɪv] *n* nave *f*

navel ['neɪvl] *n* ombligo

navigate ['nævɪgeɪt] *vt* gobernar ♦ *vi* navegar; (*AUT*) ir de copiloto; **navigation** [-'geɪʃən] *n* (*action*) navegación *f*; (*science*) náutica; **navigator** *n* navegador(a) *m/f*, navegante *m/f*; (*AUT*) copiloto *m/f*

navvy ['nævɪ] (*BRIT*) *n* peón *m* caminero

navy ['neɪvɪ] *n* marina de guerra; (*ships*) armada, flota; **~-(blue)** *adj* azul marino

Nazi ['nɑ:tsɪ] *n* nazi *m/f*

NB *abbr* (= *nota bene*) nótese

near [nɪə*] *adj* (*place, relation*) cercano; (*time*) próximo ♦ *adv* cerca ♦ *prep* (*also:* **~ to**: *space*) cerca a, junto a; (: *time*) cerca de ♦ *vt* acercarse a, aproximarse a; **~by** [nɪə'baɪ] *adj* cercano, próximo ♦ *adv* cerca; **~ly** *adv* casi, por poco; **I ~ly fell** por poco me caigo; **~ miss** *n* tiro cercano; **~side** *n* (*AUT: in Britain*) lado izquierdo; (: *in US, Europe etc*) lado derecho; **~-sighted** *adj* miope, corto de vista

neat [ni:t] *adj* (*place*) ordenado, bien cuidado; (*person*) pulcro; (*plan*) ingenioso; (*spirits*) solo; **~ly** *adv* (*tidily*) con esmero; (*skilfully*) ingeniosamente

necessarily ['nesɪsrɪlɪ] *adv* necesariamente

necessary ['nesɪsrɪ] *adj* necesario, preciso

necessitate [nɪ'sesɪteɪt] *vt* hacer necesario

necessity [nɪ'sesɪtɪ] *n* necesidad *f*; **necessities** *npl* artículos *mpl* de primera necesidad

neck [nek] *n* (*of person, garment, bottle*) cuello; (*of animal*) pescuezo ♦ *vi* (*inf*) besuquearse; **~ and ~** parejos; **~lace** ['neklɪs] *n* collar *m*; **~line** *n* escote *m*; **~tie** ['nektaɪ] *n* corbata

née [neɪ] *adj:* **~ Scott** de soltera Scott

need [ni:d] *n* (*lack*) escasez *f*, falta; (*necessity*) necesidad *f* ♦ *vt* (*require*) necesitar; **I ~ to do it** tengo que *or* debo hacerlo; **you don't ~ to go** no hace falta que (te) vayas

needle ['ni:dl] *n* aguja ♦ *vt* (*fig: inf*) picar, fastidiar

needless ['ni:dlɪs] *adj* innecesario; **~ to say** huelga decir que

needlework ['ni:dlwɜ:k] *n* (*activity*) costura, labor *f* de aguja

needn't ['ni:dnt] = **need not**

needy ['ni:dɪ] *adj* necesitado

negative ['negətɪv] *n* (*PHOT*) negativo; (*LING*) negación *f* ♦ *adj* negativo; **~ equity** *n* situación que se da cuando el valor de la vivienda es menor que el de la hipoteca que pesa sobre ella

neglect [nɪ'glekt] *vt* (*one's duty*) faltar a, no cumplir con; (*child*) descuidar, desatender ♦ *n* (*of house, garden etc*) abandono; (*of child*) desatención *f*; (*of duty*) incumplimiento

negligee ['neglɪʒeɪ] *n* (*nightgown*) salto de cama

negotiate [nɪ'gəʊʃɪeɪt] *vt* (*treaty, loan*) negociar; (*obstacle*) franquear; (*bend in road*) tomar ♦ *vi:* **to ~ (with)** negociar (con); **negotiation** [-'eɪʃən] *n* negociación *f*, gestión *f*

neigh [neɪ] *vi* relinchar

neighbour ['neɪbə*] (*US* **neighbor**) *n* vecino/a; **~hood** *n* (*place*) vecindad *f*, barrio; (*people*) vecindario; **~ing** *adj* vecino; **~ly** *adj* (*person*) amable; (*attitude*) de buen vecino

neither ['naɪðə*] *adj* ni ♦ *conj:* **I didn't move and ~ did John** no me he movido, ni Juan tampoco ♦ *pron* ninguno ♦ *adv:* **~ good nor bad** ni bueno ni malo; **~ is true** ninguno/a de los/las dos es cierto/a neon ['ni:ɔn] *n* neón *m*; ~ **light** *n* lámpara de neón

nephew ['nevju:] *n* sobrino

nerve [nə:v] *n* (ANAT) nervio; (courage) valor *m*; (impudence) descaro, frescura; **a fit of ~s** un ataque de nervios; ~-racking *adj* desquiciante

nervous ['nə:vəs] *adj* (anxious, ANAT) nervioso; (timid) tímido, miedoso; ~ **breakdown** *n* crisis *f* nerviosa

nest [nɛst] *n* (of bird) nido; (wasps' ~) avispero ♦ *vi* anidar; ~ **egg** *n* (fig) ahorros *mpl*

nestle ['nɛsl] *vi*: **to ~ down** acurrucarse

net [nɛt] *n* (gen) red *f*; (fabric) tul *m* ♦ *adj* (COMM) neto, líquido ♦ *vt* coger (SP) or agarrar (AM) con red; (SPORT) marcar; **the Net** (Internet) la Red; ~**ball** *n* básquet *m*

Netherlands ['nɛðələndz] *npl*: **the ~** los Países Bajos

nett [nɛt] *adj* = **net**

netting ['nɛtɪŋ] *n* red *f*, redes *fpl*

nettle ['nɛtl] *n* ortiga

network ['nɛtwə:k] *n* red *f*

neurotic [njuə'rɔtɪk] *adj*, neurótico/a

neuter ['nju:tə*] *adj* (LING) neutro ♦ *vt* castrar, capar

neutral ['nju:trəl] *adj* (person) neutral; (colour etc, ELEC) neutro ♦ *n* (AUT) punto muerto; ~**ize** *vt* neutralizar

never ['nɛvə*] *adv* nunca, jamás; **I ~ went** no fui nunca; ~ **in my life** jamás en la vida; see also **mind**; ~-**ending** *adj* interminable, sin fin; ~**theless** [nɛvəðə'lɛs] *adv* sin embargo, no obstante

new [nju:] *adj* nuevo; (brand new) a estrenar; (recent) reciente; **N~ Age** *n* Nueva Era; ~**born** *adj* recién nacido; ~**comer** ['nju:kʌmə*] *n* recién venido/a or llegado/a; ~-**fangled** (pej) *adj* modernísimo; ~-**found** *adj* (friend) nuevo; (enthusiasm) recién adquirido; ~**ly** *adv* nuevamente, recién; ~**ly-weds** *npl* recién casados *mpl*

news [nju:z] *n* noticias *fpl*; **a piece of ~** una noticia; **the ~** (RADIO, TV) las noticias

fpl; ~ **agency** *n* agencia de noticias; ~**agent** (BRIT) *n* vendedor(a) *m/f* de periódicos; ~**caster** *n* presentador(a) *m/f*, locutor(a) *m/f*; ~ **flash** *n* noticia de última hora; ~**letter** *n* hoja informativa, boletín *m*; ~**paper** *n* periódico, diario; ~**print** *n* papel *m* de periódico; ~**reader** *n* = ~**caster**; ~**reel** *n* noticiario; ~ **stand** *n* quiosco or puesto de periódicos

newt [nju:t] *n* tritón *m*

New Year *n* Año Nuevo; ~'s Day *n* Día *m* de Año Nuevo; ~'s Eve *n* Nochevieja

New York ['nju:'jɔ:k] *n* Nueva York

New Zealand [nju:'zi:lənd] *n* Nueva Zelanda; ~er *n* neozelandés/esa *m/f*

next [nɛkst] *adj* (house, room) vecino; (bus stop, meeting) próximo; (following: page etc) siguiente ♦ *adv* después; **the ~ day** el día siguiente; ~ **time** la próxima vez; ~ **year** el año próximo or que viene; ~ **to** junto a, al lado de; ~ **to nothing** casi nada; ~ **please!** ¡el siguiente!; ~ **door** *adv* en la casa de al lado ♦ *adj* vecino, de al lado; ~-**of-kin** *n* pariente *m* más cercano

NHS *n* abbr = **National Health Service**

nib [nɪb] *n* plumilla

nibble ['nɪbl] *vt* mordisquear, mordiscar

Nicaragua [nɪkə'ræɡjuə] *n* Nicaragua; ~n *adj*, *n* nicaragüense *m/f*

nice [naɪs] *adj* (likeable) simpático; (kind) amable; (pleasant) agradable; (attractive) bonito, mono, lindo (AM); ~**ly** *adv* amablemente, bien

nick [nɪk] *n* (wound) rasguño; (cut, indentation) mella, muesca ♦ *vt* (inf) birlar, robar; **in the ~ of time** justo a tiempo

nickel ['nɪkl] *n* níquel *m*; (US) moneda de 5 centavos

nickname ['nɪkneɪm] *n* apodo, mote *m* ♦ *vt* apodar

nicotine ['nɪkəti:n] *n* nicotina

niece [ni:s] *n* sobrina

Nigeria [naɪ'dʒɪərɪə] *n* Nigeria; ~n *adj*, *n* nigeriano/a *m/f*

niggling ['nɪɡlɪŋ] *adj* (trifling) nimio,

insignificante; (*annoying*) molesto

night [naɪt] *n* noche *f*; (*evening*) tarde *f*; **the ~ before last** anteanoche; **at ~, by ~** de noche, por la noche; **~cap** *n* (*drink*) *bebida que se toma antes de acostarse*; ~ **club** *n* cabaret *m*; **~dress** (*BRIT*) *n* camisón *m*; **~fall** *n* anochecer *m*; **~gown** *n* = **~dress**

nightingale ['naɪtɪŋgeɪl] *n* ruiseñor *m*

night: ~**life** *n* vida nocturna; **~ly** *adj* de todas las noches ♦ *adv* todas las noches, cada noche; **~mare** *n* pesadilla; ~ **porter** *n* portero de noche; **~ school** *n* clase(s) *f(pl)* nocturna(s); ~ **shift** *n* turno nocturno *or* de noche; **~time** *n* noche *f*; ~ **watchman** *n* vigilante *m* nocturno

nil [nɪl] (*BRIT*) *n* (*SPORT*) cero, nada

Nile [naɪl] *n*: **the ~** el Nilo

nimble ['nɪmbl] *adj* (*agile*) ágil, ligero; (*skilful*) diestro

nine [naɪn] *num* nueve; **~teen** *num* diecinueve, diez y nueve; **~ty** *num* noventa

ninth [naɪnθ] *adj* noveno

nip [nɪp] *vt* (*pinch*) pellizcar; (*bite*) morder

nipple ['nɪpl] *n* (*ANAT*) pezón *m*

nitrogen ['naɪtrədʒən] *n* nitrógeno

KEYWORD

no [nəu] (*pl* **~es**) *adv* (*opposite of "yes"*) no; **are you coming? — ~ (I'm not)** ¿vienes? — no; **would you like some more? — ~ thank you** ¿quieres más? — no gracias

♦ *adj* (*not any*): **I have ~ money/time/ books** no tengo dinero/tiempo/libros; ~ **other man would have done it** ningún otro lo hubiera hecho; **"~ entry"** "prohibido el paso"; **"~ smoking"** "prohibido fumar"

♦ *n* no *m*

---

nobility [nəu'bɪlɪtɪ] *n* nobleza

noble ['nəubl] *adj* noble

nobody ['nəubədɪ] *pron* nadie

nod [nɔd] *vi* saludar con la cabeza; (*in*

agreement) decir que sí con la cabeza; (*doze*) dar cabezadas ♦ *vt*: **to ~ one's head** inclinar la cabeza ♦ *n* inclinación *f* de cabeza; ~ **off** *vi* dar cabezadas

noise [nɔɪz] *n* ruido; (*din*) escándalo, estrépito; **noisy** *adj* ruidoso; (*child*) escandaloso

nominate ['nɔmɪneɪt] *vt* (*propose*) proponer; (*appoint*) nombrar; **nominee** [-'niː] *n* candidato/a

non... [nɔn] *prefix* no, des..., in...; **~alcoholic** *adj* no alcohólico; **~chalant** *adj* indiferente; **~committal** *adj* evasivo; **~descript** *adj* soso

none [nʌn] *pron* ninguno/a ♦ *adv* de ninguna manera; ~ **of you** ninguno de vosotros; **I've ~ left** no me queda ninguno/a; **he's ~ the worse for it** no le ha hecho ningún mal

nonentity [nɔ'nentɪtɪ] *n* cero a la izquierda, nulidad *f*

nonetheless [nʌnðə'les] *adv* sin embargo, no obstante

non-existent *adj* inexistente

non-fiction *n* literatura no novelesca

nonplussed [nɔn'plʌst] *adj* perplejo

nonsense ['nɔnsəns] *n* tonterías *fpl*, disparates *fpl*; **~!** ¡qué tonterías!

non: **~-smoker** *n* no fumador(a) *m/f*; **~smoking** *adj* (de) no fumador; **~-stick** *adj* (*pan, surface*) antiadherente; **~-stop** *adj* continuo; (*RAIL*) directo ♦ *adv* sin parar

noodles ['nuːdlz] *npl* tallarines *mpl*

nook [nuk] *n*: **~s and crannies** escondrijos *mpl*

noon [nuːn] *n* mediodía *m*

no-one *pron* = **nobody**

noose [nuːs] *n* (*hangman's*) dogal *m*

nor [nɔː*] *conj* = **neither** ♦ *adv see* **neither**

norm [nɔːm] *n* norma

normal ['nɔːml] *adj* normal; **~ly** *adv* normalmente

north [nɔːθ] *n* norte *m* ♦ *adj* del norte, norteño ♦ *adv* al *or* hacia el norte; **N~ Africa** *n* África del Norte; **N~ America** *n* América del Norte; **~-east** *n* nor(d)este

m; ~**erly** ['nɔːðəlɪ] adj (point, direction)
norteño; ~**ern** ['nɔːðən] adj norteño, del
norte; **N~ern Ireland** n Irlanda del
Norte; **N~ Pole** n Polo Norte; **N~ Sea**
n Mar m del Norte; ~**ward(s)**
['nɔːθwəd(z)] adv hacia el norte; ~-**west** n
nor(d)oeste m

Norway ['nɔːweɪ] n Noruega; **Norwegian**
[-'wiːdʒən] adj noruego/a ♦ n noruego/a;
(LING) noruego

nose [nəuz] n (ANAT) nariz f; (ZOOL)
hocico; (sense of smell) olfato ♦ vi: **to ~**
about curiosear; ~**bleed** n hemorragia
nasal; ~-**dive** n (of plane: deliberate)
picado vertical; (: involuntary) caída en
picado; ~**y** (inf) adj curioso, fisgón/ona

nostalgia [nɔs'tældʒɪə] n nostalgia

nostril ['nɔstrɪl] n ventana de la nariz

nosy ['nəuzɪ] (inf) adj = **nosey**

not [nɔt] adv no; ~ **that ...** no es que ...;
it's too late, isn't it? es demasiado
tarde, ¿verdad or no?; ~ **yet/now**
todavía/ahora no; **why ~?** ¿por qué no?;
see also **all**; **only**

notably ['nəutəblɪ] adv especialmente

notary ['nəutərɪ] n notario/a

notch [nɔtʃ] n muesca, corte m

note [nəut] n (MUS, record, letter) nota;
(banknote) billete m; (tone) tono ♦ vt
(observe) notar, observar; (write down)
apuntar, anotar; ~**book** n libreta,
cuaderno; ~**d** ['nəutɪd] adj célebre,
conocido; ~**pad** n bloc m; ~**paper** n
papel m para cartas

nothing ['nʌθɪŋ] n nada; (zero) cero; **he**
does ~ no hace nada; ~ **new** nada
nuevo; ~ **much** no mucho; **for ~** (free)
gratis, sin pago; (in vain) en balde

notice ['nəutɪs] n (announcement) anuncio;
(warning) aviso; (dismissal) despido;
(resignation) dimisión f; (period of time)
plazo ♦ vt (observe) notar, observar; **to**
bring sth to sb's ~ (attention) llamar la
atención de uno sobre algo; **to take ~ of**
tomar nota de, prestar atención a; **at**
short ~ con poca anticipación; **until**
further ~ hasta nuevo aviso; **to hand in**

one's ~ dimitir; ~**able** adj evidente,
obvio; ~ **board** (BRIT) n tablón m de
anuncios

notify ['nəutɪfaɪ] vt: **to ~ sb (of sth)**
comunicar (algo) a uno

notion ['nəuʃən] n idea; (opinion) opinión f

notorious [nəu'tɔːrɪəs] adj notorio

nougat ['nuːgɑː] n turrón m

nought [nɔːt] n cero

noun [naun] n nombre m, sustantivo

nourish ['nʌrɪʃ] vt nutrir; (fig) alimentar;
~**ing** adj nutritivo; ~**ment** n alimento,
sustento

novel ['nɔvl] n novela ♦ adj (new) nuevo,
original; (unexpected) insólito; ~**ist** n
novelista m/f; ~**ty** n novedad f

November [nəu'vembə*] n noviembre m

novice ['nɔvɪs] n (REL) novicio/a

now [nau] adv (at the present time) ahora;
(these days) actualmente, hoy día ♦ conj:
~ **(that)** ya que, ahora que; **right ~** ahora
mismo; **by ~** ya; **just ~** ahora mismo; ~
and then, ~ **and again** de vez en
cuando; **from ~ on** de ahora en adelante;
~**adays** ['nauədeɪz] adv hoy (en) día,
actualmente

nowhere ['nəuwɛə*] adv (direction) a
ninguna parte; (location) en ninguna
parte

nozzle ['nɔzl] n boquilla

nuance ['njuːɑːns] n matiz m

nuclear ['njuːklɪə*] adj nuclear

nucleus ['njuːklɪəs] (pl **nuclei**) n núcleo

nude [njuːd] adj, n desnudo/a m/f; **in the**
~ desnudo

nudge [nʌdʒ] vt dar un codazo a

nudist ['njuːdɪst] n nudista m/f

nuisance ['njuːsns] n molestia, fastidio;
(person) pesado, latoso; **what a ~!** ¡qué
lata!

null [nʌl] adj: ~ **and void** nulo y sin efecto

numb [nʌm] adj: ~ **with cold/fear**
entumecido por el frío/paralizado de
miedo

number ['nʌmbə*] n número; (quantity)
cantidad f ♦ vt (pages etc) numerar,
poner número a; (amount to) sumar,

ascender a; **to be ~ed among** figurar entre; **a ~ of** varios, algunos; **they were ten in ~** eran diez; **~ plate** (BRIT) *n* matrícula, placa

numeral ['nju:mərəl] *n* número, cifra

numerate ['nju:mərɪt] *adj* competente en la aritmética

numerous ['nju:mərəs] *adj* numeroso

nun [nʌn] *n* monja, religiosa

nurse [nəːs] *n* enfermero/a; (*also:* **~maid**) niñera ♦ *vt* (*patient*) cuidar, atender

nursery ['nəːsərɪ] *n* (*institution*) guardería infantil; (*room*) cuarto de los niños; (*for plants*) criadero, semillero; **~ rhyme** *n* canción *f* infantil; **~ school** *n* parvulario, escuela de párvulos; **~ slope** (BRIT) *n* (SKI) cuesta para principiantes

nursing ['nəːsɪŋ] *n* (*profession*) profesión *f* de enfermera; (*care*) asistencia, cuidado; **~ home** *n* clínica de reposo

nut [nʌt] *n* (TECH) tuerca; (BOT) nuez *f*; **~crackers** *npl* cascanueces *m inv*

nutmeg ['nʌtmeg] *n* nuez *f* moscada

nutritious [nju:'trɪʃəs] *adj* nutritivo, alimenticio

nuts [nʌts] (*inf*) *adj* loco

nutshell ['nʌtʃel] *n*: **in a ~** en resumidas cuentas

nylon ['naɪlɔn] *n* nilón *m* ♦ *adj* de nilón

O, o

oak [əuk] *n* roble *m* ♦ *adj* de roble

O.A.P. (BRIT) *n abbr* = **old-age pensioner**

oar [ɔː*] *n* remo

oasis [əu'eɪsɪs] (*pl* **oases**) *n* oasis *m inv*

oath [əuθ] *n* juramento; (*swear word*) palabrota; **on** (BRIT) *or* **under ~** bajo juramento

oatmeal ['əutmiːl] *n* harina de avena

oats [əuts] *n* avena

obedience [ə'biːdɪəns] *n* obediencia

obedient [ə'biːdɪənt] *adj* obediente

obey [ə'beɪ] *vt* obedecer; (*instructions, regulations*) cumplir

obituary [ə'bɪtjuərɪ] *n* necrología

object [*n* 'ɔbdʒɪkt, *vb* əb'dʒekt] *n* objeto; (*purpose*) objeto, propósito; (LING) complemento ♦ *vi*: **to ~ to** estar en contra de; (*proposal*) oponerse a; **to ~ that** objetar que; **expense is no ~** no importa cuánto cuesta; **I ~!** ¡yo protesto!; **~ion** [əb'dʒekʃən] *n* protesta; **I have no ~ion to ...** no tengo inconveniente en que ...; **~ionable** [əb'dʒekʃənəbl] *adj* desagradable; (*conduct*) censurable; **~ive** *adj, n* objetivo

obligation [ɔblɪ'geɪʃən] *n* obligación *f*; (*debt*) deber *m*; **without ~** sin compromiso

oblige [ə'blaɪdʒ] *vt* (*do a favour for*) complacer, hacer un favor a; **to ~ sb to do sth** forzar *or* obligar a uno a hacer algo; **to be ~d to sb for sth** estarle agradecido a uno por algo; **obliging** *adj* servicial, atento

oblique [ə'bliːk] *adj* oblicuo; (*allusion*) indirecto

obliterate [ə'blɪtəreɪt] *vt* borrar

oblivion [ə'blɪvɪən] *n* olvido; **oblivious** [-ɪəs] *adj*: **oblivious of** inconsciente de

oblong ['ɔblɔŋ] *adj* rectangular ♦ *n* rectángulo

obnoxious [əb'nɔkʃəs] *adj* odioso, detestable; (*smell*) nauseabundo

oboe ['əubəu] *n* oboe *m*

obscene [əb'siːn] *adj* obsceno

obscure [əb'skjuə*] *adj* oscuro ♦ *vt* oscurecer; (*hide: sun*) esconder

observant [əb'zəːvnt] *adj* observador(a)

observation [ɔbzə'veɪʃən] *n* observación *f*; (MED) examen *m*

observe [əb'zəːv] *vt* observar; (*rule*) cumplir; **~r** *n* observador(a) *m/f*

obsess [əb'ses] *vt* obsesionar; **~ive** *adj* obsesivo; obsesionante

obsolete ['ɔbsəliːt] *adj*: **to be ~** estar en desuso

obstacle ['ɔbstəkl] *n* obstáculo; (*nuisance*) estorbo; **~ race** *n* carrera de obstáculos

obstinate ['ɔbstɪnɪt] *adj* terco, porfiado; (*determined*) obstinado

obstruct [əb'strʌkt] *vt* obstruir; (*hinder*) estorbar, obstaculizar; **~ion** [əb'strʌkʃən] *n* (*action*) obstrucción *f*; (*object*) estorbo, obstáculo

obtain [əb'teɪn] *vt* obtener; (*achieve*) conseguir

obvious ['ɒbvɪəs] *adj* obvio, evidente; **~ly** *adv* evidentemente, naturalmente; **~ly not** por supuesto que no

occasion [ə'keɪʒən] *n* oportunidad *f*, ocasión *f*; (*event*) acontecimiento; **~al** *adj* poco frecuente, ocasional; **~ally** *adv* de vez en cuando

occupant ['ɒkjupənt] *n* (*of house*) inquilino/a; (*of car*) ocupante *m/f*

occupation [ɒkju'peɪʃən] *n* ocupación *f*; (*job*) trabajo; (*pastime*) ocupaciones *fpl*; **~al hazard** *n* riesgo profesional

occupier ['ɒkjupaɪə*] *n* inquilino/a

occupy ['ɒkjupaɪ] *vt* (*seat, post, time*) ocupar; (*house*) habitar; **to ~ o.s. in doing** pasar el tiempo haciendo

occur [ə'kə:*] *vi* pasar, suceder; **to ~ to sb** ocurrírsele a uno; **~rence** [ə'kʌrəns] *n* acontecimiento; (*existence*) existencia

ocean ['əuʃən] *n* océano

o'clock [ə'klɔk] *adv*: **it is 5 ~** son las 5

OCR *n abbr* = **optical character recognition/reader**

October [ɒk'təubə*] *n* octubre *m*

octopus ['ɒktəpəs] *n* pulpo

odd [ɒd] *adj* extraño, raro; (*number*) impar; (*sock, shoe etc*) suelto; **60-~** 60 y pico; **at ~ times** de vez en cuando; **to be the ~ one out** estar de más; **~ity** *n* rareza *f*, (*person*) excéntrico; **~-job man** *n* chico para todo; **~ jobs** *npl* bricolaje *m*; **~ly** *adv* curiosamente, extrañamente; *see also* **enough**; **~ments** *npl* (*COMM*) retales *mpl*; **~s** *npl* (*in betting*) puntos *mpl* de ventaja; **it makes no ~s** da lo mismo; **at ~s** reñidos/as; **~s and ends** minucias *fpl*

odometer [ɒ'dɒmɪtə*] (*US*) *n* cuentakilómetros *m inv*

odour ['əudə*] (*US* **odor**) *n* olor *m*; (*unpleasant*) hedor *m*

KEYWORD

of [ɒv, əv] *prep* **1** (*gen*) de; **a friend ~ ours** un amigo nuestro; **a boy ~ 10** un chico de 10 años; **that was kind ~ you** eso fue muy amable por *or* de tu parte

2 (*expressing quantity, amount, dates etc*) de; **a kilo ~ flour** un kilo de harina; **there were 3 ~ them** había tres; **3 ~ us went** tres de nosotros fuimos; **the 5th ~ July** el 5 de julio

3 (*from, out of*) de; **made ~ wood** (hecho) de madera

off [ɒf] *adj, adv* (*engine*) desconectado; (*light*) apagado; (*tap*) cerrado; (*BRIT: food: bad*) pasado, malo; (: *milk*) cortado; (*cancelled*) cancelado ♦ *prep* de; **to be ~** (*to leave*) irse, marcharse; **to be ~ sick** estar enfermo *or* de baja; **a day ~** un día libre *or* sin trabajar; **to have an ~ day** tener un día malo; **he had his coat ~** se había quitado el abrigo; **10% ~** (*COMM*) (con el) 10% de descuento; **5 km ~ (the road)** a 5 km (de la carretera); **~ the coast** frente a la costa; **I'm ~ meat** (*no longer eat/like it*) paso de la carne; **on the ~ chance** por si acaso; **~ and on** de vez en cuando

offal ['ɒfl] (*BRIT*) *n* (*CULIN*) menudencias *fpl*

off-colour [ɒf'kʌlə*] (*BRIT*) *adj* (*ill*) indispuesto

offence [ə'fɛns] (*US* **offense**) *n* (*crime*) delito; **to take ~ at** ofenderse por

offend [ə'fɛnd] *vt* (*person*) ofender; **~er** *n* delincuente *m/f*

offensive [ə'fɛnsɪv] *adj* ofensivo; (*smell etc*) repugnante ♦ *n* (*MIL*) ofensiva

offer ['ɒfə*] *n* oferta, ofrecimiento; (*proposal*) propuesta ♦ *vt* ofrecer; (*opportunity*) facilitar; **"on ~"** (*COMM*) "en oferta"; **~ing** *n* ofrenda

offhand [ɒf'hænd] *adj* informal ♦ *adv* de improviso

office ['ɒfɪs] *n* (*place*) oficina; (*room*) despacho; (*position*) carga, oficio; **doctor's ~** (*US*) consultorio; **to take ~**

entrar en funciones; **~ automation** *n* ofimática, buromática; **~ block** (*US* **~ building**) *n* bloque *m* de oficinas; **~ hours** *npl* horas *fpl* de oficina; (*US: MED*) horas *fpl* de consulta
officer ['ɔfɪsə⁎] *n* (*MIL etc*) oficial *m/f*; (*also*: **police ~**) agente *m/f* de policía; (*of organization*) director(a) *m/f*
office worker *n* oficinista *m/f*
official [ə'fɪʃl] *adj* oficial, autorizado ♦ *n* funcionario, oficial *m*
offing ['ɔfɪŋ] *n*: **in the ~** (*fig*) en perspectiva
off: **~-licence** (*BRIT*) *n* (*shop*) bodega, *tienda de vinos y bebidas alcohólicas*; **~-line** *adj, adv* (*COMPUT*) fuera de línea; **~-peak** *adj* (*electricity*) de banda económica; (*ticket*) *billete de precio reducido por viajar fuera de las horas punta*; **~-putting** (*BRIT*) *adj* (*person*) asqueroso; (*remark*) desalentador(a); **~-season** *adj, adv* fuera de temporada

─────────────
│ **off-licence** │
─────────────

ⓘ *En el Reino Unido la venta de bebidas alcohólicas está estrictamente regulada y se necesita una licencia especial, con la que cuentan los bares, restaurantes y los establecimientos de* **off-licence***, los únicos lugares en donde se pueden adquirir bebidas alcohólicas para su consumo fuera del local, de donde viene su nombre. También venden bebidas no alcohólicas, tabaco, chocolatinas, patatas fritas etc y a menudo forman parte de una cadena nacional.*

offset ['ɔfset] (*irreg*) *vt* contrarrestar, compensar
offshoot ['ɔfʃuːt] *n* (*fig*) ramificación *f*
offshore [ɔfʃɔː⁎] *adj* (*breeze, island*) costera; (*fishing*) de bajura
offside ['ɔf'saɪd] *adj* (*SPORT*) fuera de juego; (*AUT*: *in UK*) del lado derecho; (*: in US, Europe etc*) del lado izquierdo
offspring ['ɔfsprɪŋ] *n inv* descendencia *f*
off: **~stage** *adv* entre bastidores; **~-the-**

peg (*US* **~-the-rack**) *adv* confeccionado; **~-white** *adj* color crudo
often ['ɔfn] *adv* a menudo, con frecuencia; **how ~ do you go?** ¿cada cuánto vas?
oh [əu] *excl* ¡ah!
oil [ɔɪl] *n* aceite *m*; (*petroleum*) petróleo; (*for heating*) aceite *m* combustible ♦ *vt* engrasar; **~can** *n* lata de aceite; **~field** *n* campo petrolífero; **~ filter** *n* (*AUT*) filtro de aceite; **~ painting** *n* pintura al óleo; **~ rig** *n* torre *f* de perforación; **~ tanker** *n* petrolero; (*truck*) camión *m* cisterna; **~ well** *n* pozo (de petróleo); **~y** *adj* aceitoso; (*food*) grasiento
ointment ['ɔɪntmənt] *n* ungüento
O.K., okay ['əu'keɪ] *excl* O.K., ¡está bien!, ¡vale! (*SP*) ♦ *adj* bien ♦ *vt* dar el visto bueno a
old [əuld] *adj* viejo; (*former*) antiguo; **how ~ are you?** ¿cuántos años tienes?, ¿qué edad tienes?; **he's 10 years ~** tiene 10 años; **~er brother** hermano mayor; **~ age** *n* vejez *f*; **~-age pensioner** (*BRIT*) *n* jubilado/a; **~-fashioned** *adj* anticuado, pasado de moda
olive ['ɔlɪv] *n* (*fruit*) aceituna; (*tree*) olivo ♦ *adj* (*also*: **~-green**) verde oliva; **~ oil** *n* aceite *m* de oliva
Olympic [əu'lɪmpɪk] *adj* olímpico; **the ~ Games, the ~s** las Olimpíadas
omelet(te) ['ɔmlɪt] *n* tortilla (*SP*), tortilla de huevo (*AM*)
omen ['əumen] *n* presagio
ominous ['ɔmɪnəs] *adj* de mal agüero, amenazador(a)
omit [əu'mɪt] *vt* omitir

────────────
│ *KEYWORD* │
────────────

on [ɔn] *prep* **1** (*indicating position*) en; sobre; **~ the wall** en la pared; **it's ~ the table** está sobre *or* en la mesa; **~ the left** a la izquierda
2 (*indicating means, method, condition etc*): **~ foot** a pie; **~ the train/plane** (*go*) en tren/avión; (*be*) en el tren/el avión; **~ the radio/television/telephone** por *or* en la radio/televisión/al teléfono; **to be ~**

drugs drogarse; (*MED*) estar a tratamiento; **to be ~ holiday/business** estar de vacaciones/en viaje de negocios 3 (*referring to time*): **~ Friday** el viernes; **~ Fridays** los viernes; **~ June 20th** el 20 de junio; **a week ~ Friday** del viernes en una semana; **~ arrival** al llegar; **~ seeing this** al ver esto 4 (*about, concerning*) sobre, acerca de; **a book ~ physics** un libro de *or* sobre física ♦ *adv* 1 (*referring to dress*): **to have one's coat ~** tener *or* llevar el abrigo puesto; **she put her gloves ~** se puso los guantes 2 (*referring to covering*): "**screw the lid ~ tightly**" "cerrar bien la tapa" 3 (*further, continuously*): **to walk** *etc* **~** seguir caminando *etc*
♦ *adj* 1 (*functioning, in operation*: *machine, radio, TV, light*) encendido/a (*SP*), prendido/a (*AM*); (: *tap*) abierto/a; (: *brakes*) echado/a, puesto/a; **is the meeting still ~?** (*in progress*) ¿todavía continúa la reunión?; (*not cancelled*) ¿va a haber reunión al fin?; **there's a good film ~ at the cinema** ponen una buena película en el cine 2: **that's not ~!** (*inf*: *not possible*) ¡eso ni hablar!; (: *not acceptable*) ¡eso no se hace!

once [wʌns] *adv* una vez; (*formerly*) antiguamente ♦ *conj* una vez que; **~ he had left/it was done** una vez que se había marchado/se hizo; **at ~** en seguida, inmediatamente; (*simultaneously*) a la vez; **~ a week** una vez por semana; **~ more** otra vez; **~ and for all** de una vez por todas; **~ upon a time** érase una vez

oncoming [ˈɒnkʌmɪŋ] *adj* (*traffic*) que viene de frente

KEYWORD

one [wʌn] *num* un(o)/una; **~ hundred and fifty** ciento cincuenta; **~ by ~** uno a uno ♦ *adj* 1 (*sole*) único; **the ~ book which** el único libro que; **the ~ man who** el único que

2 (*same*) mismo/a; **they came in the ~ car** vinieron en un solo coche
♦ *pron* 1: **this ~** éste/ésta; **that ~** ése/ésa; (*more remote*) aquél/aquella; **I've already got (a red) ~** ya tengo uno/a (rojo/a); **~ by ~** uno/a por uno/a
2: **~ another** os (*SP*), se (+*el uno al otro, unos a otros etc*); **do you two ever see ~ another?** ¿vosotros dos os veis alguna vez? (*SP*), ¿se ven ustedes alguna vez?; **the boys didn't dare look at ~ another** los chicos no se atrevieron a mirarse (el uno al otro); **they all kissed ~ another** se besaron unos a otros
3 (*impers*): **~ never knows** nunca se sabe; **to cut ~'s finger** cortarse el dedo; **~ needs to eat** hay que comer

one: **~-day excursion** (*US*) *n* billete *m* de ida y vuelta en un día; **~-man** *adj* (*business*) individual; **~-man band** *n* hombre-orquesta *m*; **~-off** (*BRIT*: *inf*) *n* (*event*) acontecimiento único

oneself [wʌnˈself] *pron* (*reflexive*) se; (*after prep*) sí; (*emphatic*) uno/a mismo/a; **to hurt ~** hacerse daño; **to keep sth for ~** guardarse algo; **to talk to ~** hablar solo

one: **~-sided** *adj* (*argument*) parcial; **~-to-~** *adj* (*relationship*) de dos; **~-way** *adj* (*street*) de sentido único

ongoing [ˈɒngəʊɪŋ] *adj* continuo

onion [ˈʌnjən] *n* cebolla

on-line *adj, adv* (*COMPUT*) en línea

onlooker [ˈɒnlʊkə*] *n* espectador(a) *m/f*

only [ˈəʊnlɪ] *adv* solamente, sólo ♦ *adj* único, solo ♦ *conj* solamente una, pero; **an ~ child** un hijo único; **not ~ ... but also ...** no sólo ... sino también ...

onset [ˈɒnset] *n* comienzo

onshore [ˈɒnfɔː*] *adj* (*wind*) que sopla del mar hacia la tierra

onslaught [ˈɒnslɔːt] *n* ataque *m*, embestida

onto [ˈɒntʊ] *prep* = **on to**

onward(s) [ˈɒnwəd(z)] *adv* (*move*) (hacia) adelante; **from that time ~** desde entonces en adelante

onyx ['ɔnɪks] n ónice m

ooze [uːz] vi rezumar

opaque [əu'peɪk] adj opaco

OPEC ['əupek] n abbr (= Organization of Petroleum-Exporting Countries) OPEP f

open ['əupn] adj abierto; (car) descubierto; (road, view) despejado; (meeting) público; (admiration) manifiesto ♦ vt abrir ♦ vi abrirse; (book etc: commence) comenzar; **in the ~ (air)** al aire libre; **~ on to** vt fus (subj: room, door) dar a; **~ up** vt abrir; (blocked road) despejar ♦ vi abrirse, empezar; **~ing** n abertura; (start) comienzo; (opportunity) oportunidad f; **~ing hours** npl horario de apertura; **~ learning** n enseñanza flexible a tiempo parcial; **~ly** adv abiertamente; **~-minded** adj imparcial; **~-necked** adj (shirt) desabrochado; sin corbata; **~-plan** adj: **~-plan office** gran oficina sin particiones

---

Open University

i *La* **Open University,** *fundada en 1969, está especializada en impartir cursos a distancia que no exigen una dedicación exclusiva. Cuenta con sus propios materiales de apoyo, entre ellos programas de radio y televisión emitidos por la* **BBC** *y para conseguir los créditos de la licenciatura es necesaria la presentación de unos trabajos y la asistencia a los cursos de verano.*

---

opera ['ɔpərə] n ópera; **~ house** n teatro de la ópera

operate ['ɔpəreɪt] vt (machine) hacer funcionar; (company) dirigir ♦ vi funcionar; **to ~ on sb** (MED) operar a uno

operatic [ɔpə'rætɪk] adj de ópera

operating table ['ɔpəreɪtɪŋ-] n mesa de operaciones

operating theatre n sala de operaciones

operation [ɔpə'reɪʃən] n operación f; (of machine) funcionamiento; **to be in ~** estar funcionando or en funcionamiento; **to have an ~** (MED) ser operado; **~al** adj operacional, en buen estado

operative ['ɔpərətɪv] adj en vigor

operator ['ɔpəreɪtə*] n (of machine) maquinista m/f, operario/a; (TEL) operador(a) m/f, telefonista m/f

opinion [ə'pɪnɪən] n opinión f; **in my ~** en mi opinión, a mi juicio; **~ated** adj testarudo; **~ poll** n encuesta, sondeo

opponent [ə'pəunənt] n adversario/a, contrincante m/f

opportunity [ɔpə'tjuːnɪtɪ] n oportunidad f; **to take the ~ of doing** aprovechar la ocasión para hacer

oppose [ə'pəuz] vt oponerse a; **to be ~d to sth** oponerse a algo; **as ~d to** a diferencia de; **opposing** adj opuesto, contrario

opposite ['ɔpəzɪt] adj opuesto, contrario a; (house etc) de enfrente ♦ adv en frente ♦ prep en frente de, frente a ♦ n lo contrario

opposition [ɔpə'zɪʃən] n oposición f

oppressive [ə'presɪv] adj opresivo; (weather) agobiante

opt [ɔpt] vi: **to ~ for** optar por; **to ~ to do** optar por hacer; **~ out** vi: **to ~ out of** optar por no hacer

optical ['ɔptɪkl] adj óptico

optician [ɔp'tɪʃən] n óptico m/f

optimist ['ɔptɪmɪst] n optimista m/f; **~ic** [-'mɪstɪk] adj optimista

option ['ɔpʃən] n opción f; **~al** adj facultativo, discrecional

or [ɔː*] conj o; (before o, ho) u; (with negative): **he hasn't seen ~ heard anything** no ha visto ni oído nada; **~ else** si no

oral ['ɔːrəl] adj oral ♦ n examen m oral

orange ['ɔrɪndʒ] n (fruit) naranja ♦ adj color naranja

orbit ['ɔːbɪt] n órbita ♦ vt, vi orbitar

orchard ['ɔːtʃəd] n huerto

orchestra ['ɔːkɪstrə] n orquesta; (US: seating) platea

orchid ['ɔːkɪd] n orquídea

ordain [ɔː'deɪn] vt (REL) ordenar, decretar

ordeal [ɔːˈdiːl] *n* experiencia horrorosa
order [ˈɔːdə*] *n* orden *m*; (*command*)
orden *f*; (*good ~*) buen estado; (COMM)
pedido ♦ *vt* (*also*: **put in ~**) arreglar,
poner en orden; (COMM) pedir;
(*command*) mandar, ordenar; **in ~** en
orden; (*of document*) en regla; **in
(working) ~** en funcionamiento; **in ~ to
do/that** para hacer/que; **on ~** (COMM)
pedido; **to be out of ~** estar
desordenado; (*not working*) no funcionar;
to ~ sb to do sth mandar a uno hacer
algo; **~ form** *n* hoja de pedido; **~ly** *n*
(MIL) ordenanza *m*; (MED) enfermero/a
(auxiliar) ♦ *adj* ordenado
ordinary [ˈɔːdnrɪ] *adj* corriente, normal;
(*pej*) común y corriente; **out of the ~**
fuera de lo común
Ordnance Survey [ˈɔːdnəns-] (BRIT) *n*
servicio oficial de topografía
ore [ɔː*] *n* mineral *m*
organ [ˈɔːgən] *n* órgano *m*; **~ic** [ɔːˈgænɪk] *adj*
orgánico; **~ism** *n* organismo
organization [ˌɔːgənaɪˈzeɪʃən] *n*
organización *f*
organize [ˈɔːgənaɪz] *vt* organizar; **~r** *n*
organizador(a) *m/f*
orgasm [ˈɔːgæzəm] *n* orgasmo
orgy [ˈɔːdʒɪ] *n* orgía
Orient [ˈɔːrɪənt] *n* Oriente *m*; **oriental**
[-ˈɛntl] *adj* oriental
orientate [ˈɔːrɪənteɪt] *vt*: **to ~ o.s.**
orientarse
origin [ˈɒrɪdʒɪn] *n* origen *m*
original [əˈrɪdʒɪnl] *adj* original; (*first*)
primero; (*earlier*) primitivo ♦ *n* original *m*;
~ly *adv* al principio
originate [əˈrɪdʒɪneɪt] *vi*: **to ~ from, to ~
in** surgir de, tener su origen en
Orkney [ˈɔːknɪ] *n* (*also*: **the Orkney
Islands**) las Orcadas
ornament [ˈɔːnəmənt] *n* adorno; (*trinket*)
chuchería; **~al** [-ˈmɛntl] *adj* decorativo, de
adorno
ornate [ɔːˈneɪt] *adj* muy ornado, vistoso
orphan [ˈɔːfn] *n* huérfano/a
orthopaedic [ɔːθəˈpiːdɪk] (US **orthopedic**)

adj ortopédico
ostensibly [ɒsˈtɛnsɪblɪ] *adv* aparentemente
ostentatious [ɒstɛnˈteɪʃəs] *adj* ostentoso
osteopath [ˈɒstɪəpæθ] *n* osteópata *m/f*
ostracize [ˈɒstrəsaɪz] *vt* hacer el vacío a
ostrich [ˈɒstrɪtʃ] *n* avestruz *m*
other [ˈʌðə*] *adj* otro ♦ *pron*: **the ~ (one)**
el/la otro/a ♦ *adv*: **~ than** aparte de; **~s**
(*~ people*) otros; **the ~ day** el otro día;
~wise *adv* de otra manera ♦ *conj* (*if not*)
si no
otter [ˈɒtə*] *n* nutria
ouch [autʃ] *excl* ¡ay!
ought [ɔːt] (*pt* **ought**) *aux vb*: **I ~ to do it**
debería hacerlo; **this ~ to have been
corrected** esto debiera haberse corregido;
he ~ to win (*probability*) debe *or* debiera
ganar
ounce [auns] *n* onza (28.35g)
our [ˈauə*] *adj* nuestro; *see also* **my**; **~s**
pron (el) nuestro/(la) nuestra *etc*; *see also*
mine[1]; **~selves** *pron pl* (*reflexive, after
prep*) nosotros; (*emphatic*) nosotros
mismos; *see also* **oneself**
oust [aust] *vt* desalojar
out [aut] *adv* fuera, afuera; (*not at home*)
fuera (de casa); (*light, fire*) apagado; **~
there** allí (fuera); **he's ~** (*absent*) no está,
ha salido; **to be ~ in one's calculations**
equivocarse (en sus cálculos); **to run ~**
salir corriendo; **~ loud** en alta voz; **~ of**
(*outside*) fuera de; (*because of: anger etc*)
por; **~ of petrol** sin gasolina; **"~ of order"**
"no funciona"; **~-and-~** *adj* (*liar, thief
etc*) redomado, empedernido; **~back** *n*
interior *m*; **~board** *adj*: **~board motor**
(motor *m*) fuera borda *m*; **~break** *n* (*of
war*) comienzo; (*of disease*) epidemia; (*of
violence etc*) ola; **~burst** *n* explosión *f*,
arranque *m*; **~cast** *n* paria *m/f*; **~come**
n resultado; **~crop** *n* (*of rock*)
afloramiento; **~cry** *n* protestas *fpl*;
~dated *adj* anticuado, fuera de moda;
~do (*irreg*) *vt* superar; **~door** *adj*
exterior, de aire libre; (*clothes*) de calle;
~doors *adv* al aire libre
outer [ˈautə*] *adj* exterior, externo; **~**

space n espacio exterior
outfit ['autfɪt] n (clothes) conjunto
out: ~going adj (character) extrovertido;
(retiring: president etc) saliente; **~goings**
(BRIT) npl gastos mpl; **~grow** (irreg) vt:
he has ~grown his clothes su ropa le
queda pequeña ya; **~house** n
dependencia; **~ing** ['autɪŋ] n excursión f,
paseo
out: ~law n proscrito ♦ vt proscribir; **~lay**
n inversión f; **~let** n salida; (of pipe)
desagüe m; (US: ELEC) toma de corriente;
(also: retail **~let**) punto de venta; **~line**
n (shape) contorno, perfil m; (sketch,
plan) esbozo ♦ vt (plan etc) esbozar; **in
~line** (fig) a grandes rasgos; **~live** vt
sobrevivir a; **~look** n (fig: prospects)
perspectivas fpl; (: for weather)
pronóstico; **~lying** adj remoto, aislado;
~moded adj anticuado, pasado de
moda; **~number** vt superar en número;
~-of-date adj (passport) caducado;
(clothes) pasado de moda; **~-of-the-way**
adj apartado; **~patient** n paciente m/f
externo/a; **~post** n puesto avanzado;
~put n (volumen m de) producción f,
rendimiento; (COMPUT) salida
outrage ['autreɪdʒ] n escándalo; (atrocity)
atrocidad f ♦ vt ultrajar; **~ous** [-'reɪdʒəs]
adj monstruoso
outright [adv aut'raɪt, adj 'autraɪt] adv (ask,
deny) francamente; (refuse)
rotundamente; (win) de manera absoluta;
(be killed) en el acto ♦ adj franco,
rotundo
outset ['autset] n principio
outside [aut'saɪd] n exterior m ♦ adj
exterior, externo ♦ adv fuera ♦ prep fuera
de; (beyond) más allá de; **at the ~** (fig) a
lo sumo; **~ lane** n (AUT: in Britain) carril
m de la derecha; (: in US, Europe etc)
carril m de la izquierda; **~ line** n (TEL)
línea (exterior); **~r** n (stranger) extraño,
forastero
out: ~size adj (clothes) de talla grande;
~skirts npl alrededores mpl, afueras fpl;
~spoken adj muy franco; **~standing**

adj excepcional, destacado; (remaining)
pendiente; **~stay** vt: **to ~stay one's
welcome** quedarse más de la cuenta;
~stretched adj (hand) extendido;
~strip vt (competitors, demand) dejar
atrás, aventajar; **~-tray** n bandeja de
salida
outward ['autwəd] adj externo; (journey)
de ida
outweigh [aut'weɪ] vt pesar más que
outwit [aut'wɪt] vt ser más listo que
oval ['əuvl] adj ovalado ♦ n óvalo
ovary ['əuvəri] n ovario
oven ['ʌvn] n horno; **~proof** adj
resistente al horno
over ['əuvə*] adv encima, por encima
♦ adj (or adv) (finished) terminado;
(surplus) de sobra ♦ prep (por) encima de;
(above) sobre; (on the other side of) al
otro lado de; (more than) más de;
(during) durante; **~ here** (por) aquí; **~
there** (por) allí or allá; **all ~** (everywhere)
por todas partes; **~ and ~ (again)** una y
otra vez; **~ and above** además de; **to ask
sb ~** invitar a uno a una casa; **to bend ~**
inclinarse
overall [adj, n 'əuvərɔːl, adv əuvər'ɔːl] adj
(length etc) total; (study) de conjunto
♦ adv en conjunto ♦ n (BRIT)
guardapolvo; **~s** npl mono (SP), overol m
(AM)
over: ~awe vt: **to be ~awed (by)** quedar
impresionado (con); **~balance** vi perder
el equilibrio; **~board** adv (NAUT) por la
borda; **~book** [əuvə'buk] vt sobrereservar
overcast ['əuvəkɑːst] adj encapotado
overcharge [əuvə'tʃɑːdʒ] vt: **to ~ sb**
cobrar un precio excesivo a uno
overcoat ['əuvəkəut] n abrigo, sobretodo
overcome [əuvə'kʌm] (irreg) vt vencer;
(difficulty) superar
over: ~crowded adj atestado de gente;
(city, country) superpoblado; **~do** (irreg)
vt exagerar; (overcook) cocer demasiado;
to ~do it (work etc) pasarse; **~dose** n
sobredosis f inv; **~draft** n saldo deudor;
~drawn adj (account) en descubierto;

~**due** adj retrasado; ~**estimate** [əuvər'estɪmeɪt] vt sobreestimar

overflow [vb əuvə'fləu, n 'əuvəfləu] vi desbordarse ♦ n (also: ~ **pipe**) (cañería de) desagüe m

overgrown [əuvə'grəun] adj (garden) invadido por la vegetación

overhaul [vb əuvə'hɔːl, n 'əuvəhɔːl] vt revisar, repasar ♦ n revisión f

overhead [adv əuvə'hed, adj, n 'əuvəhed] adv por arriba or encima ♦ adj (cable) aéreo ♦ n (US) = ~**s**; ~**s** npl (expenses) gastos mpl generales

over: ~**hear** (irreg) vt oír por casualidad; ~**heat** vi (engine) recalentarse; ~**joyed** adj encantado, lleno de alegría

overland ['əuvəlænd] adj, adv por tierra

overlap [əuvə'læp] vi traslaparse

over: ~**leaf** adv al dorso; ~**load** vt sobrecargar; ~**look** vt (have view of) dar a, tener vistas a; (miss: by mistake) pasar por alto; (excuse) perdonar

overnight [əuvə'naɪt] adv durante la noche; (fig) de la noche a la mañana ♦ adj de noche; **to stay** ~ pasar la noche

overpass ['əuvəpɑːs] (US) n paso superior

overpower [əuvə'pauə*] vt dominar; (fig) embargar; ~**ing** adj (heat) agobiante; (smell) penetrante

over: ~**rate** vt sobreestimar; ~**ride** (irreg) vt no hacer caso de; ~**riding** adj predominante; ~**rule** vt (decision) anular; (claim) denegar; ~**run** (irreg) vt (country) invadir; (time limit) rebasar, exceder

overseas [əuvə'siːz] adv (abroad: live) en el extranjero; (: travel) al extranjero ♦ adj (trade) exterior; (visitor) extranjero

overshadow [əuvə'ʃædəu] vt: **to be** ~**ed by** estar a la sombra de

overshoot [əuvə'ʃuːt] (irreg) vt excederse

oversight ['əuvəsaɪt] n descuido

oversleep [əuvə'sliːp] (irreg) vi quedarse dormido

overstep [əuvə'step] vt: **to** ~ **the mark** pasarse de la raya

overt [əu'vɜːt] adj abierto

overtake [əuvə'teɪk] (irreg) vt sobrepasar;

(BRIT: AUT) adelantar

over: ~**throw** (irreg) vt (government) derrocar; ~**time** n horas fpl extraordinarias; ~**tone** n (fig) tono

overture ['əuvətʃuə*] n (MUS) obertura; (fig) preludio

over: ~**turn** vt volcar; (fig: plan) desbaratar; (: government) derrocar ♦ vi volcar; ~**weight** adj demasiado gordo or pesado; ~**whelm** vt aplastar; (subj: emotion) sobrecoger; ~**whelming** adj (victory, defeat) arrollador(a); (feeling) irresistible; ~**work** vi trabajar demasiado; ~**wrought** [əuvə'rɔːt] adj sobreexcitado

owe [əu] vt: **to** ~ **sb sth, to** ~ **sth to sb** deber algo a uno; **owing to** prep debido a, por causa de

owl [aul] n búho, lechuza

own [əun] vt tener, poseer ♦ adj propio; **a room of my** ~ una habitación propia; **to get one's** ~ **back** tomar revancha; **on one's** ~ solo, a solas; ~ **up** vi confesar; ~**er** n dueño/a; ~**ership** n posesión f

ox [ɔks] (pl ~**en**) n buey m; ~**tail** n: ~**tail soup** sopa de rabo de buey

oxygen ['ɔksɪdʒən] n oxígeno

oyster ['ɔɪstə*] n ostra

oz. abbr = **ounce(s)**

ozone ['əuzəun]: ~ **friendly** adj que no daña la capa de ozono; ~ **hole** n agujero m de/en la capa de ozono; ~ **layer** n capa f de ozono

P, p

p [piː] abbr = **penny; pence**

P.A. n abbr = **personal assistant; public address system**

p.a. abbr = **per annum**

pa [pɑː] (inf) n papá m

pace [peɪs] n paso ♦ vi: **to** ~ **up and down** pasearse de un lado a otro; **to keep** ~ **with** llevar el mismo paso que; ~**maker** n (MED) regulador m cardíaco, marcapasos m inv; (SPORT: also: ~**setter**) liebre f

Pacific [pə'sɪfɪk] n: **the ~ (Ocean)** el (Océano) Pacífico
pack [pæk] n (*packet*) paquete m; (*of hounds*) jauría; (*of people*) manada, bando; (*of cards*) baraja; (*bundle*) fardo; (*US: of cigarettes*) paquete m; (*back ~*) mochila ♦ vt (*fill*) llenar; (*in suitcase etc*) meter, poner; (*cram*) llenar, atestar; **to ~ (one's bags)** hacerse la maleta; **to ~ sb off** despachar a uno; **~ it in!** (*inf*) ¡déjalo!
package ['pækɪdʒ] n paquete m; (*bulky*) bulto; (*also*: **~ deal**) acuerdo global; **~ holiday** n vacaciones fpl organizadas; **~ tour** n viaje m organizado
packed lunch n almuerzo frío
packet ['pækɪt] n paquete m
packing ['pækɪŋ] n embalaje m; **~ case** n cajón m de embalaje
pact [pækt] n pacto
pad [pæd] n (*of paper*) bloc m; (*cushion*) cojinete m; (*inf: home*) casa ♦ vt rellenar; **~ding** n (*material*) relleno
paddle ['pædl] n (*oar*) canalete m; (*US: for table tennis*) paleta ♦ vt impulsar con canalete ♦ vi (*with feet*) chapotear; **paddling pool** (*BRIT*) n estanque m de juegos
paddock ['pædək] n corral m
padlock ['pædlɔk] n candado
paediatrics [piːdɪ'ætrɪks] (*US* **pediatrics**) n pediatría
pagan ['peɪgən] adj, n pagano/a m/f
page [peɪdʒ] n (*of book*) página; (*of newspaper*) plana; (*also*: **~ boy**) paje m ♦ vt (*in hotel etc*) llamar por altavoz a
pageant ['pædʒənt] n (*procession*) desfile m; (*show*) espectáculo; **~ry** n pompa
pager ['peɪdʒə*] n (*TEL*) busca m
paging device ['peɪdʒɪŋ-] n = **pager**
paid [peɪd] pt, pp of **pay** ♦ adj (*work*) remunerado; (*holiday*) pagado; (*official etc*) a sueldo; **to put ~ to** (*BRIT*) acabar con
pail [peɪl] n cubo, balde m
pain [peɪn] n dolor m; **to be in ~** sufrir; **to take ~s to do sth** tomarse grandes molestias en hacer algo; **~ed** adj

(*expression*) afligido; **~ful** adj doloroso; (*difficult*) penoso; (*disagreeable*) desagradable; **~fully** adv (fig: *very*) terriblemente; **~killer** n analgésico; **~less** adj que no causa dolor; **~staking** ['peɪnzteɪkɪŋ] adj (*person*) concienzudo, esmerado
paint [peɪnt] n pintura ♦ vt pintar; **to ~ the door blue** pintar la puerta de azul; **~brush** n (*artist's*) pincel m; (*decorator's*) brocha; **~er** n pintor(a) m/f; **~ing** n pintura; **~work** n pintura
pair [peə*] n (*of shoes, gloves etc*) par m; (*of people*) pareja; **a ~ of scissors** unas tijeras; **a ~ of trousers** unos pantalones, un pantalón
pajamas [pə'dʒɑːməz] (*US*) npl pijama m
Pakistan [pɑːkɪ'stɑːn] n Paquistán m; **~i** adj, n paquistaní m/f
pal [pæl] (*inf*) n compinche m/f, compañero/a
palace ['pæləs] n palacio
palatable ['pælɪtəbl] adj sabroso
palate ['pælɪt] n paladar m
pale [peɪl] adj (*gen*) pálido; (*colour*) claro ♦ n: **to be beyond the ~** pasarse de la raya
Palestine ['pælɪstaɪn] n Palestina; **Palestinian** [-'tɪnɪən] adj, n palestino/a m/f
palette ['pælɪt] n paleta
pall [pɔːl] vi perder el sabor
pallet ['pælɪt] n (*for goods*) pallet m
pallid ['pælɪd] adj pálido
palm [pɑːm] n (*ANAT*) palma; (*also*: **~ tree**) palmera, palma ♦ vt: **to ~ sth off on sb** (*inf*) encajar algo a uno; **P~ Sunday** n Domingo de Ramos
paltry ['pɔːltrɪ] adj irrisorio
pamper ['pæmpə*] vt mimar
pamphlet ['pæmflət] n folleto
pan [pæn] n (*also*: **sauce~**) cacerola, cazuela, olla; (*also*: **frying ~**) sartén f
Panama ['pænəmɑː] n Panamá m; **the ~ Canal** el Canal de Panamá
pancake ['pænkeɪk] n crepe f
panda ['pændə] n panda m; **~ car** (*BRIT*) n

coche *m* Z (*SP*)

pandemonium [pændɪˈməʊnɪəm] *n* jaleo

pander [ˈpændə*] *vi*: **to ~ to** complacer a

pane [peɪn] *n* cristal *m*

panel [ˈpænl] *n* (*of wood etc*) panel *m*; (*RADIO, TV*) panel *m* de invitados; **~ling** (*US* **~ing**) *n* paneles *mpl*

pang [pæŋ] *n*: **a ~ of regret** (una punzada de) remordimiento; **hunger ~s** dolores *mpl* del hambre

panic [ˈpænɪk] *n* (terror *m*) pánico ♦ *vi* dejarse llevar por el pánico; **~ky** *adj* (*person*) asustadizo; **~-stricken** *adj* preso de pánico

pansy [ˈpænzɪ] *n* (*BOT*) pensamiento; (*inf*: *pej*) maricón *m*

pant [pænt] *vi* jadear

panther [ˈpænθə*] *n* pantera

panties [ˈpæntɪz] *npl* bragas *fpl*, pantis *mpl*

pantihose [ˈpæntɪhəʊz] (*US*) *n* pantimedias *fpl*

pantomime [ˈpæntəmaɪm] (*BRIT*) *n* revista musical representada en Navidad, basada en cuentos de hadas

---
pantomime

🛈 *En época navideña se ponen en escena en los teatros británicos las llamadas* **pantomimes,** *que son versiones libres de cuentos tradicionales como Aladino o El gato con botas. En ella nunca faltan personajes como la dama ("dame"), papel que siempre interpreta un actor, el protagonista joven ("principal boy"), normalmente interpretado por una actriz, y el malvado ("villain"). Es un espectáculo familiar en el que se anima al público a participar y aunque va dirigido principalmente a los niños, cuenta con grandes dosis de humor para adultos.*

---

pantry [ˈpæntrɪ] *n* despensa

pants [pænts] *n* (*BRIT: underwear: woman's*) bragas *fpl*; (: *man's*) calzoncillos *mpl*; (*US: trousers*) pantalones *mpl*

paper [ˈpeɪpə*] *n* papel *m*; (*also*: **news~**)

periódico, diario; (*academic essay*) ensayo; (*exam*) examen *m* ♦ *adj* de papel ♦ *vt* empapelar (*SP*), tapizar (*AM*); **~s** *npl* (*also*: **identity ~s**) papeles *mpl*, documentos *mpl*; **~back** *n* libro en rústica; **~ bag** *n* bolsa de papel; **~ clip** *n* clip *m*; **~ hankie** *n* pañuelo de papel; **~weight** *n* pisapapeles *m inv*; **~work** *n* trabajo administrativo

paprika [ˈpæprɪkə] *n* pimentón *m*

par [pɑː*] *n* par *f*; (*GOLF*) par *m*; **to be on a ~ with** estar a la par con

parachute [ˈpærəʃuːt] *n* paracaídas *m inv*

parade [pəˈreɪd] *n* desfile *m* ♦ *vt* (*show off*) hacer alarde de ♦ *vi* desfilar; (*MIL*) pasar revista

paradise [ˈpærədaɪs] *n* paraíso

paradox [ˈpærədɔks] *n* paradoja; **~ically** [-ˈdɔksɪklɪ] *adv* paradójicamente

paraffin [ˈpærəfɪn] (*BRIT*) *n* (*also*: **~ oil**) parafina

paragon [ˈpærəgən] *n* modelo

paragraph [ˈpærəgrɑːf] *n* párrafo

parallel [ˈpærəlel] *adj* en paralelo; (*fig*) semejante ♦ *n* (*line*) paralela; (*fig, GEO*) paralelo

paralyse [ˈpærəlaɪz] *vt* paralizar

paralysis [pəˈrælɪsɪs] *n* parálisis *f inv*

paralyze [ˈpærəlaɪz] (*US*) *vt* = **paralyse**

paramount [ˈpærəmaunt] *adj*: **of ~ importance** de suma importancia

paranoid [ˈpærənɔɪd] *adj* (*person, feeling*) paranoico

paraphernalia [pærəfəˈneɪlɪə] *n* (*gear*) avíos *mpl*

parasite [ˈpærəsaɪt] *n* parásito/a

parasol [ˈpærəsɔl] *n* sombrilla, quitasol *m*

paratrooper [ˈpærətruːpə*] *n* paracaidista *m/f*

parcel [ˈpɑːsl] *n* paquete *m* ♦ *vt* (*also*: **~ up**) empaquetar, embalar

parched [pɑːtʃt] *adj* (*person*) muerto de sed

parchment [ˈpɑːtʃmənt] *n* pergamino

pardon [ˈpɑːdn] *n* (*LAW*) indulto ♦ *vt* perdonar; **~ me!, I beg your ~!** (*I'm sorry!*) ¡perdone usted!; (*I beg your*) **~?, ~**

me? (*US*) (*what did you say?*) ¿cómo?
parent ['pɛərənt] *n* (*mother*) madre *f*;
(*father*) padre *m*; **~s** *npl* padres *mpl*; **~al**
[pə'rɛntl] *adj* paternal/maternal
parenthesis [pə'rɛnθɪsɪs] (*pl*
parentheses) *n* paréntesis *m inv*
Paris ['pærɪs] *n* París
parish ['pærɪʃ] *n* parroquia
Parisian [pə'rɪzɪən] *adj, n* parisiense *m/f*
park [paːk] *n* parque *m* ♦ *vt* aparcar,
estacionar ♦ *vi* aparcar, estacionarse
parking ['paːkɪŋ] *n* aparcamiento,
estacionamiento; **"no ~"** "prohibido
estacionarse"; **~ lot** (*US*) *n* parking *m*; **~
meter** *n* parquímetro; **~ ticket** *n* multa
de aparcamiento
parliament ['paːləmənt] *n* parlamento;
(*Spanish*) Cortes *fpl*; **~ary** [-'mɛntərɪ] *adj*
parlamentario

Parliament

❶ *El Parlamento británico (**Parliament**)
tiene como sede el palacio de
Westminster, también llamado "Houses of
Parliament" y consta de dos cámaras. La
Cámara de los Comunes ("House of
Commons"), compuesta por 650 diputados
(**Members of Parliament**) elegidos por
sufragio universal en su respectiva
circunscripción electoral (**constituency**),
se reúne 175 días al año y sus sesiones
son moderadas por el Presidente de la
Cámara (**Speaker**). La cámara alta es la
Cámara de los Lores ("House of Lords") y
está formada por miembros que han sido
nombrados por el monarca o que han
heredado su escaño. Su poder es limitado,
aunque actúa como tribunal supremo de
apelación, excepto en Escocia.*

---

parlour ['paːlə*] (*US* **parlor**) *n* sala de
recibo, salón *m*, living *m* (*AM*)
parochial [pə'rəʊkɪəl] (*pej*) *adj* de miras
estrechas
parole [pə'rəʊl] *n*: **on ~** libre bajo palabra
parquet ['paːkeɪ] *n*: **~ floor(ing)** parquet
m

parrot ['pærət] *n* loro, papagayo
parry ['pærɪ] *vt* parar
parsley ['paːslɪ] *n* perejil *m*
parsnip ['paːsnɪp] *n* chirivía
parson ['paːsn] *n* cura *m*
part [paːt] *n* (*gen, MUS*) parte *f*; (*bit*) trozo;
(*of machine*) pieza; (*THEATRE etc*) papel *m*;
(*of serial*) entrega; (*US: in hair*) raya ♦ *adv*
= partly ♦ *vt* separar ♦ *vi* (*people*)
separarse; (*crowd*) apartarse; **to take ~ in**
tomar parte *or* participar en; **to take sth
in good ~** tomar algo en buena parte; **to
take sb's ~** defender a uno; **for my ~** por
mi parte; **for the most ~** en su mayor
parte; **to ~ one's hair** hacerse la raya; **~
with** *vt fus* ceder, entregar; (*money*)
pagar; **~ exchange** (*BRIT*) *n*: **in ~
exchange** como parte del pago
partial ['paːʃl] *adj* parcial; **to be ~ to** ser
aficionado a
participant [paː'tɪsɪpənt] *n* (*in competition*)
concursante *m/f*; (*in campaign etc*)
participante *m/f*
participate [paː'tɪsɪpeɪt] *vi*: **to ~ in**
participar en; **participation** [-'peɪʃən] *n*
participación *f*
participle ['paːtɪsɪpl] *n* participio
particle ['paːtɪkl] *n* partícula; (*of dust*)
grano
particular [pə'tɪkjʊlə*] *adj* (*special*)
particular; (*concrete*) concreto; (*given*)
determinado; (*fussy*) quisquilloso;
(*demanding*) exigente; **~s** *npl*
(*information*) datos *mpl*; (*details*)
pormenores *mpl*; **in ~** en particular; **~ly**
adv (*in particular*) sobre todo; (*difficult,
good etc*) especialmente
parting ['paːtɪŋ] *n* (*act of*) separación *f*;
(*farewell*) despedida; (*BRIT: in hair*) raya
♦ *adj* de despedida
partisan [paːtɪ'zæn] *adj* partidista ♦ *n*
partidario/a
partition [paː'tɪʃən] *n* (*POL*) división *f*;
(*wall*) tabique *m*
partly ['paːtlɪ] *adv* en parte
partner ['paːtnə*] *n* (*COMM*) socio/a;
(*SPORT, at dance*) pareja; (*spouse*) cónyuge

m/f; (*lover*) compañero/a; ~ship *n* asociación *f*; (COMM) sociedad *f*

partridge ['pɑ:trɪdʒ] *n* perdiz *f*

part-time *adj, adv* a tiempo parcial

party ['pɑ:tɪ] *n* (POL) partido; (*celebration*) fiesta; (*group*) grupo; (LAW) parte *f* interesada ♦ *cpd* (POL) de partido; ~ **dress** *n* vestido de fiesta

pass [pɑ:s] *vt* (*time, object*) pasar; (*place*) pasar por; (*overtake*) rebasar; (*exam*) aprobar; (*approve*) aprobar ♦ *vi* pasar; (SCOL) aprobar, ser aprobado ♦ *n* (*permit*) permiso; (*membership card*) carnet *m*; (*in mountains*) puerto, desfiladero; (SPORT) pase *m*; (SCOL: *also*: ~ **mark**): **to get a** ~ **in** aprobar en; **to** ~ **sth through sth** pasar algo por algo; **to make a** ~ **at sb** (*inf*) hacer proposiciones a uno; ~ **away** *vi* fallecer; ~ **by** *vi* pasar ♦ *vt* (*ignore*) pasar por alto; ~ **for** *vt fus* hacer pasar por; ~ **on** *vt* transmitir; ~ **out** *vi* desmayarse; ~ **up** *vt* (*opportunity*) renunciar a; ~able *adj* (*road*) transitable; (*tolerable*) pasable

passage ['pæsɪdʒ] *n* (*also*: ~**way**) pasillo; (*act of passing*) tránsito; (*fare, in book*) pasaje *m*; (*by boat*) travesía; (ANAT) tubo

passbook ['pɑ:sbʊk] *n* libreta de banco

passenger ['pæsɪndʒə*] *n* pasajero/a, viajero/a

passer-by [pɑ:sə'baɪ] *n* transeúnte *m/f*

passing ['pɑ:sɪŋ] *adj* pasajero; **in** ~ de paso; ~ **place** *n* (AUT) apartadero

passion ['pæʃən] *n* pasión *f*; ~ate *adj* apasionado

passive ['pæsɪv] *adj* (*gen, also* LING) pasivo; ~ **smoking** *n* efectos del tabaco en fumadores pasivos

Passover ['pɑ:səʊvə*] *n* Pascua (de los judíos)

passport ['pɑ:spɔ:t] *n* pasaporte *m*; ~ **control** *n* control *m* de pasaporte; ~ **office** *n* oficina de pasaportes

password ['pɑ:swɜ:d] *n* contraseña

past [pɑ:st] *prep* (*in front of*) por delante de; (*further than*) más allá de; (*later than*) después de ♦ *adj* pasado; (*president etc*) antiguo ♦ *n* (*time*) pasado; (*of person*)

antecedentes *mpl*; **he's** ~ **forty** tiene más de cuarenta años; **ten / quarter** ~ **eight** las ocho y diez/cuarto; **for the** ~ **few/3 days** durante los últimos días/últimos 3 días; **to run** ~ **sb** pasar a uno corriendo

pasta ['pæstə] *n* pasta

paste [peɪst] *n* pasta; (*glue*) engrudo ♦ *vt* pegar

pasteurized ['pæstəraɪzd] *adj* pasteurizado

pastille ['pæstɪl] *n* pastilla

pastime ['pɑ:staɪm] *n* pasatiempo

pastry ['peɪstrɪ] *n* (*dough*) pasta; (*cake*) pastel *m*

pasture ['pɑ:stʃə*] *n* pasto

pasty¹ ['pæstɪ] *n* empanada

pasty² ['peɪstɪ] *adj* (*complexion*) pálido

pat [pæt] *vt* dar una palmadita a; (*dog etc*) acariciar

patch [pætʃ] *n* (*of material, eye* ~) parche *m*; (*mended part*) remiendo; (*of land*) terreno ♦ *vt* remendar; **(to go through) a bad** ~ (pasar por) una mala racha; ~ **up** *vt* reparar; (*quarrel*) hacer las paces en; ~**work** *n* labor *m* de retazos; ~**y** *adj* desigual

pâté ['pæteɪ] *n* paté *m*

patent ['peɪtnt] *n* patente *f* ♦ *vt* patentar ♦ *adj* patente, evidente; ~ **leather** *n* charol *m*

paternal [pə'tɜ:nl] *adj* paternal; (*relation*) paterno

path [pɑ:θ] *n* camino, sendero; (*trail, track*) pista; (*of missile*) trayectoria

pathetic [pə'θetɪk] *adj* patético, lastimoso; (*very bad*) malísimo

pathological [pæθə'lɒdʒɪkəl] *adj* patológico

pathway ['pɑ:θweɪ] *n* sendero, vereda

patience ['peɪʃns] *n* paciencia; (BRIT: CARDS) solitario

patient ['peɪʃnt] *n* paciente *m/f* ♦ *adj* paciente, sufrido

patio ['pætɪəʊ] *n* patio

patriot ['peɪtrɪət] *n* patriota *m/f*; ~**ic** [pætrɪ'ɒtɪk] *adj* patriótico

patrol [pə'trəʊl] *n* patrulla ♦ *vt* patrullar por; ~ **car** *n* coche *m* patrulla; ~**man**

(US irreg) n policía *m*

patron ['peɪtrən] *n (in shop)* cliente *m/f; (of charity)* patrocinador(a) *m/f;* ~ **of the arts** mecenas *m;* ~**ize** ['pætrənaɪz] *vt (shop)* ser cliente de; *(artist etc)* proteger; *(look down on)* condescender con; ~ **saint** *n* santo/a patrón/ona *m/f*

patter ['pætə*] *n* golpeteo; *(sales talk)* labia ♦ *vi (rain)* tamborilear

pattern ['pætən] *n (SEWING)* patrón *m; (design)* dibujo

pauper ['pɔːpə*] *n* pobre *m/f*

pause [pɔːz] *n* pausa ♦ *vi* hacer una pausa

pave [peɪv] *vt* pavimentar; **to ~ the way for** preparar el terreno para

pavement ['peɪvmənt] *(BRIT) n* acera *(SP)*, vereda *(AM)*

pavilion [pə'vɪlɪən] *n (SPORT)* caseta

paving ['peɪvɪŋ] *n* pavimento, enlosado; ~ **stone** *n* losa

paw [pɔː] *n* pata

pawn [pɔːn] *n (CHESS)* peón *m; (fig)* instrumento ♦ *vt* empeñar; ~ **broker** *n* prestamista *m/f;* ~**shop** *n* monte *m* de piedad

pay [peɪ] *(pt, pp* **paid**) *n (wage etc)* sueldo, salario ♦ *vt* pagar ♦ *vi (be profitable)* rendir; **to ~ attention (to)** prestar atención (a); **to ~ sb a visit** hacer una visita a uno; **to ~ one's respects to sb** presentar sus respetos a uno; ~ **back** *vt (money)* reembolsar; *(person)* pagar; ~ **for** *vt fus* pagar; ~ **in** *vt* ingresar; ~ **off** *vt* saldar ♦ *vi (scheme, decision)* dar resultado; ~ **up** *vt* pagar (de mala gana); ~**able** *adj:* ~**able to** pagadero a; ~ **day** *n* día *m* de paga; ~**ee** *n* portador(a) *m/f;* ~ **envelope** *(US) n* = ~ **packet;** ~**ment** *n* pago; **monthly ~ment** mensualidad *f;* ~ **packet** *(BRIT) n* sobre *m* (de paga); ~ **phone** *n* teléfono público; ~**roll** *n* nómina; ~ **slip** *n* recibo de sueldo; ~ **television** *n* televisión *f* de pago

PC *n abbr* = **personal computer;** *(BRIT)* = **police constable** ♦ *adj abbr* = **politically correct**

p.c. *abbr* = **per cent**

pea [piː] *n* guisante *m (SP)*, chícharo *(AM)*, arveja *(AM)*

peace [piːs] *n* paz *f; (calm)* paz *f,* tranquilidad *f;* ~**ful** *adj (gentle)* pacífico; *(calm)* tranquilo, sosegado

peach [piːtʃ] *n* melocotón *m (SP)*, durazno *(AM)*

peacock ['piːkɔk] *n* pavo real

peak [piːk] *n (of mountain)* cumbre *f,* cima; *(of cap)* visera; *(fig)* cumbre *f;* ~ **hours** *npl,* ~ **period** *n* horas *fpl* punta

peal [piːl] *n (of bells)* repique *m;* ~ **of laughter** carcajada

peanut ['piːnʌt] *n* cacahuete *m (SP)*, maní *m (AM);* ~ **butter** manteca de cacahuete *or* maní

pear [pɛə*] *n* pera

pearl [pɜːl] *n* perla

peasant ['pɛznt] *n* campesino/a

peat [piːt] *n* turba

pebble ['pɛbl] *n* guijarro

peck [pɛk] *vt (also:* ~ **at)** picotear ♦ *n* picotazo; *(kiss)* besito; ~**ing order** *n* orden *m* de jerarquía; ~**ish** *(BRIT: inf) adj:* **I feel ~ish** tengo ganas de picar algo

peculiar [pɪ'kjuːlɪə*] *adj (odd)* extraño, raro; *(typical)* propio, característico; ~ **to** propio de

pedal ['pɛdl] *n* pedal *m* ♦ *vi* pedalear

pedantic [pɪ'dæntɪk] *adj* pedante

peddler ['pɛdlə*] *n:* **drug ~** traficante *m/f;* camello

pedestrian [pɪ'dɛstrɪən] *n* peatón/ona *m/f* ♦ *adj* pedestre; ~ **crossing** *(BRIT) n* paso de peatones; ~ **precinct** *(BRIT),* ~ **zone** *(US) n* zona peatonal

pediatrics [piːdɪ'ætrɪks] *(US) n* = **paediatrics**

pedigree ['pɛdɪgriː] *n* genealogía; *(of animal)* raza, pedigrí *m* ♦ *cpd (animal)* de raza, de casta

pee [piː] *(inf) vi* mear

peek [piːk] *vi* mirar a hurtadillas

peel [piːl] *n* piel *f; (of orange, lemon)* cáscara; *(: removed)* peladuras *fpl* ♦ *vt* pelar ♦ *vi (paint etc)* desconcharse; *(wallpaper)* despegarse, desprenderse;

(skin) pelar

peep [pi:p] *n* (*BRIT: look*) mirada furtiva; *(sound)* pío ♦ *vi* (*BRIT: look*) mirar furtivamente; ~ **out** *vi* salir (un poco); ~**hole** *n* mirilla

peer [pɪə*] *vi*: **to ~ at** esudriñar ♦ *n* *(noble)* par *m*; *(equal)* igual *m*; *(contemporary)* contemporáneo/a; ~**age** *n* nobleza

peeved [pi:vd] *adj* enojado

peg [peg] *n* (*for coat etc*) gancho, colgadero; (*BRIT: also:* **clothes ~**) pinza

Pekingese [pi:kɪ'ni:z] *n* (*dog*) pequinés/ esa *m/f*

pelican ['pelɪkən] *n* pelícano; ~ **crossing** (*BRIT*) *n* (*AUT*) paso de peatones señalizado

pellet ['pelɪt] *n* bolita; *(bullet)* perdigón *m*

pelt [pelt] *vt*: **to ~ sb with sth** arrojarle algo a uno ♦ *vi* *(rain)* llover a cántaros: *(inf: run)* correr ♦ *n* pellejo

pen [pen] *n* (*fountain ~*) pluma; (*ballpoint ~*) bolígrafo; (*for sheep*) redil *m*

penal ['pi:nl] *adj* penal; ~**ize** *vt* castigar

penalty ['penltɪ] *n* (*gen*) pena; (*fine*) multa; (*kick*) (*FOOTBALL*) penalty *m*; (*RUGBY*) golpe *m* de castigo

penance ['penəns] *n* penitencia

pence [pens] *npl of* **penny**

pencil ['pensl] *n* lápiz *m*, lapicero (*AM*); ~ **case** *n* estuche *m*; ~ **sharpener** *n* sacapuntas *m inv*

pendant ['pendnt] *n* pendiente *m*

pending ['pendɪŋ] *prep* antes de ♦ *adj* pendiente

pendulum ['pendjuləm] *n* péndulo

penetrate ['penɪtreɪt] *vt* penetrar

penfriend ['penfrend] (*BRIT*) *n* amigo/a por carta

penguin ['peŋgwɪn] *n* pingüino

penicillin [penɪ'sɪlɪn] *n* penicilina

peninsula [pə'nɪnsjulə] *n* península

penis ['pi:nɪs] *n* pene *m*

penitentiary [penɪ'tenʃərɪ] (*US*) *n* cárcel *f*, presidio

penknife ['pennaɪf] *n* navaja

pen name *n* seudónimo

penniless ['penɪlɪs] *adj* sin dinero

penny ['penɪ] (*pl* **pennies** *or* (*BRIT*) **pence**) *n* penique *m*; (*US*) centavo

penpal ['penpæl] *n* amigo/a por carta

pension ['penʃən] *n* (*state benefit*) jubilación *f*; ~**er** (*BRIT*) *n* jubilado/a; ~ **fund** *n* caja *or* fondo de pensiones

pentagon ['pentəgən] *n*: **the P~** (*US: POL*) el Pentágono

---
Pentagon

i Se conoce como **Pentagon** al edificio de planta pentagonal que acoge las dependencias del Ministerio de Defensa estadounidense ("*Department of Defense*") en Arlington, Virginia. En lenguaje periodístico se aplica también a la dirección militar del país.

Pentecost ['pentɪkɔst] *n* Pentecostés *m*

penthouse ['penthaus] *n* ático de lujo

pent-up ['pentʌp] *adj* reprimido

people ['pi:pl] *npl* gente *f*; (*citizens*) pueblo, ciudadanos *mpl*; (*POL*): **the ~** el pueblo ♦ *n* (*nation, race*) pueblo, nación *f*; **several ~ came** vinieron varias personas; ~ **say that ...** dice la gente que ...

pep [pep] (*inf*): ~ **up** *vt* animar

pepper ['pepə*] *n* (*spice*) pimienta; (*vegetable*) pimiento ♦ *vt*: **to ~ with** (*fig*) salpicar de; ~**mint** *n* (*sweet*) pastilla de menta

peptalk ['peptɔ:k] *n*: **to give sb a ~** darle a uno una inyección de ánimo

per [pə:*] *prep* por; ~ **day/person** por día/persona; ~ **annum** al año; ~ **capita** *adj, adv* per cápita

perceive [pə'si:v] *vt* percibir; (*realize*) darse cuenta de

per cent *n* por ciento

percentage [pə'sentɪdʒ] *n* porcentaje *m*

perception [pə'sepʃən] *n* percepción *f*; (*insight*) perspicacia; (*opinion etc*) opinión *f*; **perceptive** [-'septɪv] *adj* perspicaz

perch [pə:tʃ] *n* (*fish*) perca; (*for bird*) percha ♦ *vi*: **to ~ (on)** (*bird*) posarse (en); (*person*) encaramarse (en)

percolator [ˈpəːkəleɪtə*] n (also: **coffee ~**) cafetera de filtro

perennial [pəˈrenɪəl] adj perenne

perfect [adj, n ˈpəːfɪkt, vb pəˈfekt] adj perfecto ♦ n (also: **~ tense**) perfecto ♦ vt perfeccionar; **~ly** [ˈpəːfɪktlɪ] adv perfectamente

perforate [ˈpəːfəreɪt] vt perforar

perform [pəˈfɔːm] vt (carry out) realizar, llevar a cabo; (THEATRE) representar; (piece of music) interpretar ♦ vi (well, badly) funcionar; **~ance** n (of a play) representación f; (of actor, athlete etc) actuación f; (of car, engine, company) rendimiento; (of economy) resultados mpl; **~er** n (actor) actor m, actriz f

perfume [ˈpəːfjuːm] n perfume m

perhaps [pəˈhæps] adv quizá(s), tal vez

peril [ˈperɪl] n peligro, riesgo

perimeter [pəˈrɪmɪtə*] n perímetro

period [ˈpɪərɪəd] n período; (SCOL) clase f; (full stop) punto; (MED) regla ♦ adj (costume, furniture) de época; **~ic(al)** [-ˈɔdɪk(l)] adj periódico; **~ical** [-ˈɔdɪkl] n periódico; **~ically** [-ˈɔdɪklɪ] adv de vez en cuando, cada cierto tiempo

peripheral [pəˈrɪfərəl] adj periférico ♦ n (COMPUT) periférico, unidad f periférica

perish [ˈperɪʃ] vi perecer; (decay) echarse a perder; **~able** adj perecedero

perjury [ˈpəːdʒərɪ] n (LAW) perjurio

perk [pəːk] n extra m; **~ up** vi (cheer up) animarse

perm [pəːm] n permanente f

permanent [ˈpəːmənənt] adj permanente

permeate [ˈpəːmɪeɪt] vi penetrar, trascender ♦ vt penetrar, trascender a

permissible [pəˈmɪsɪbl] adj permisible, lícito

permission [pəˈmɪʃən] n permiso

permissive [pəˈmɪsɪv] adj permisivo

permit [n ˈpəːmɪt, vt pəˈmɪt] n permiso, licencia ♦ vt permitir

perplex [pəˈpleks] vt dejar perplejo

persecute [ˈpəːsɪkjuːt] vt perseguir

persevere [pəːsɪˈvɪə*] vi persistir

Persian [ˈpəːʃən] adj, n persa m/f; **the ~ Gulf** el Golfo Pérsico

persist [pəˈsɪst] vi: **to ~ (in doing sth)** persistir (en hacer algo); **~ence** n empeño; **~ent** adj persistente; (determined) porfiado

person [ˈpəːsn] n persona; **in ~** en persona; **~al** adj personal; individual; (visit) en persona; **~al assistant** n ayudante m/f personal; **~al column** n anuncios mpl personales; **~al computer** n ordenador m personal; **~ality** [-ˈnælɪtɪ] n personalidad f; **~ally** adv personalmente; (in person) en persona; **to take sth ~ally** tomarse algo a mal; **~al organizer** n agenda; **~al stereo** n Walkman ® m; **~ify** [-ˈsɔnɪfaɪ] vt encarnar

personnel [pəːsəˈnel] n personal m

perspective [pəˈspektɪv] n perspectiva

Perspex ® [ˈpəːspeks] n plexiglás ® m

perspiration [pəːspɪˈreɪʃən] n transpiración f

persuade [pəˈsweɪd] vt: **to ~ sb to do sth** persuadir a uno para que haga algo

Peru [pəˈruː] n el Perú; **Peruvian** adj, n peruano/a m/f

perverse [pəˈvəːs] adj perverso; (wayward) travieso

pervert [n ˈpəːvəːt, vb pəˈvəːt] n pervertido/a ♦ vt pervertir; (truth, sb's words) tergiversar

pessimist [ˈpesɪmɪst] n pesimista m/f; **~ic** [-ˈmɪstɪk] adj pesimista

pest [pest] n (insect) insecto nocivo; (fig) lata, molestia

pester [ˈpestə*] vt molestar, acosar

pesticide [ˈpestɪsaɪd] n pesticida m

pet [pet] n animal m doméstico ♦ cpd favorito ♦ vt acariciar; **teacher's ~** favorito/a (del profesor); **~ hate** manía

petal [ˈpetl] n pétalo

peter [ˈpiːtə*]: **to ~ out** vi agotarse, acabarse

petite [pəˈtiːt] adj chiquita

petition [pəˈtɪʃən] n petición f

petrified [ˈpetrɪfaɪd] adj horrorizado

petrol [ˈpetrəl] (BRIT) n gasolina; **two/four-star ~** gasolina normal/súper; **~ can**

n bidón *m* de gasolina

petroleum [pə'trəʊlɪəm] *n* petróleo

petrol: ~ **pump** (*BRIT*) *n* (*in garage*) surtidor *m* de gasolina; ~ **station** (*BRIT*) *n* gasolinera; ~ **tank** (*BRIT*) *n* depósito (de gasolina)

petticoat ['petɪkəʊt] *n* enaguas *fpl*

petty ['petɪ] *adj* (*mean*) mezquino; (*unimportant*) insignificante; ~ **cash** *n* dinero para gastos menores; ~ **officer** *n* contramaestre *m*

petulant ['petjʊlənt] *adj* malhumorado

pew [pju:] *n* banco

pewter ['pju:tə*] *n* peltre *m*

phantom ['fæntəm] *n* fantasma *m*

pharmacist ['fɑ:məsɪst] *n* farmacéutico/a

pharmacy ['fɑ:məsɪ] *n* farmacia

phase [feɪz] *n* fase *f* ♦ *vt*: to ~ sth in/out introducir/retirar algo por etapas

Ph.D. *abbr* = **Doctor of Philosophy**

pheasant ['feznt] *n* faisán *m*

phenomenon [fə'nɒmɪnən] (*pl* **phenomena**) *n* fenómeno

philanthropist [fɪ'lænθrəpɪst] *n* filántropo/a

Philippines ['fɪlɪpi:nz] *npl*: the ~ las Filipinas

philosopher [fɪ'lɒsəfə*] *n* filósofo/a

philosophy [fɪ'lɒsəfɪ] *n* filosofía

phobia ['fəʊbjə] *n* fobia

phone [fəʊn] *n* teléfono ♦ *vt* telefonear, llamar por teléfono; **to be on the ~** tener teléfono; (*be calling*) estar hablando por teléfono; ~ **back** *vt*, *vi* volver a llamar; ~ **up** *vt*, *vi* llamar por teléfono; ~ **book** *n* guía telefónica; ~ **booth** *n* cabina telefónica; ~ **box** (*BRIT*) *n* = ~ **booth**; ~ **call** *n* llamada (telefónica); ~**card** *n* teletarjeta; ~**in** (*BRIT*) *n* (*RADIO, TV*) programa *m* de participación (telefónica)

phonetics [fə'netɪks] *n* fonética

phoney ['fəʊnɪ] *adj* falso

photo ['fəʊtəʊ] *n* foto *f*; ~**copier** *n* fotocopiadora; ~**copy** *n* fotocopia ♦ *vt* fotocopiar

photograph ['fəʊtəgrɑ:f] *n* fotografía ♦ *vt* fotografiar; ~**er** [fə'tɒgrəfə*] *n* fotógrafo;

~**y** [fə'tɒgrəfɪ] *n* fotografía

phrase [freɪz] *n* frase *f* ♦ *vt* expresar; ~ **book** *n* libro de frases

physical ['fɪzɪkl] *adj* físico; ~ **education** *n* educación *f* física; ~**ly** *adv* físicamente

physician [fɪ'zɪʃən] *n* médico/a

physicist ['fɪzɪsɪst] *n* físico/a

physics ['fɪzɪks] *n* física

physiotherapy [fɪzɪəʊ'θerəpɪ] *n* fisioterapia

physique [fɪ'zi:k] *n* físico

pianist ['pi:ənɪst] *n* pianista *m/f*

piano [pɪ'ænəʊ] *n* piano

pick [pɪk] *n* (*tool: also:* ~-**axe**) pico, piqueta ♦ *vt* (*select*) elegir, escoger; (*gather*) coger (*SP*), recoger; (*remove, take out*) sacar, quitar; (*lock*) abrir con ganzúa; **take your ~** escoja lo que quiera; **the ~ of** lo mejor de; **to ~ one's nose/teeth** hurgarse las narices/limpiarse los dientes; **to ~ a quarrel with sb** meterse con alguien; ~ **at** *vt fus*: **to ~ at one's food** comer con poco apetito; ~ **on** *vt fus* (*person*) meterse con; ~ **out** *vt* escoger; (*distinguish*) identificar; ~ **up** *vi* (*improve: sales*) ir mejor; (*: patient*) reponerse; (*: FINANCE*) recobrarse ♦ *vt* recoger; (*learn*) aprender; (*POLICE: arrest*) detener; (*person: for sex*) ligar; (*RADIO*) captar; **to ~ up speed** acelerarse; **to ~ o.s. up** levantarse

picket ['pɪkɪt] *n* piquete *m* ♦ *vt* piquetear

pickle ['pɪkl] *n* (*also:* ~**s**: *as condiment*) escabeche *m*; (*fig: mess*) apuro ♦ *vt* encurtir

pickpocket ['pɪkpɒkɪt] *n* carterista *m/f*

pickup ['pɪkʌp] *n* (*small truck*) furgoneta

picnic ['pɪknɪk] *n* merienda ♦ *vi* ir de merienda; ~ **area** *n* zona de picnic; (*AUT*) área de descanso

picture ['pɪktʃə*] *n* cuadro; (*painting*) pintura; (*photograph*) fotografía; (*TV*) imagen *f*; (*film*) película; (*fig: description*) descripción *f*; (*: situation*) situación *f* ♦ *vt* (*imagine*) imaginar; ~**s** *npl*: the ~**s** (*BRIT*) el cine; ~ **book** *n* libro de dibujos

picturesque [pɪktʃə'resk] *adj* pintoresco

pie [paɪ] n pastel m; (open) tarta; (small: of meat) empanada

piece [piːs] n pedazo, trozo; (of cake) trozo; (item): **a ~ of clothing/furniture/advice** una prenda (de vestir)/un mueble/un consejo ♦ vt: **to ~ together** juntar; (TECH) armar; **to take to ~s** desmontar; **~meal** adv poco a poco; **~work** n trabajo a destajo

pie chart n gráfico de sectores or tarta

pier [pɪə*] n muelle m, embarcadero

pierce [pɪəs] vt perforar

piercing [ˈpɪəsɪn] adj penetrante

pig [pɪg] n cerdo (SP), puerco (SP), chancho (AM); (pej: unkind person) asqueroso; (: greedy person) glotón/ona m/f

pigeon [ˈpɪdʒən] n paloma; (as food) pichón m; **~hole** n casilla

piggy bank [ˈpɪgɪ-] n hucha (en forma de cerdito)

pig: ~headed [ˈpɪgˈhedɪd] adj terco, testarudo; **~let** [ˈpɪglɪt] n cochinillo; **~skin** n piel f de cerdo; **~sty** [ˈpɪgstaɪ] n pocilga; **~tail** n (girl's) trenza; (Chinese, TAUR) coleta

pike [paɪk] n (fish) lucio

pilchard [ˈpɪltʃəd] n sardina

pile [paɪl] n montón m; (of carpet, cloth) pelo ♦ vt (also: **~ up**) amontonar; (fig) acumular ♦ vi (also: **~ up**) amontonarse; acumularse; **~ into** vt fus (car) meterse en; **~s** [paɪlz] npl (MED) almorranas fpl, hemorroides mpl; **~-up** n (AUT) accidente m múltiple

pilfering [ˈpɪlfərɪn] n ratería

pilgrim [ˈpɪlgrɪm] n peregrino/a; **~age** n peregrinación f, romería

pill [pɪl] n píldora; **the ~** la píldora

pillage [ˈpɪlɪdʒ] vt pillar, saquear

pillar [ˈpɪlə*] n pilar m; **~ box** (BRIT) n buzón m

pillion [ˈpɪljən] n (of motorcycle) asiento trasero

pillow [ˈpɪləu] n almohada; **~case** n funda

pilot [ˈpaɪlət] n piloto ♦ cpd (scheme etc) piloto ♦ vt pilotar; **~ light** n piloto

pimp [pɪmp] n chulo (SP), cafiche m (AM)

pimple [ˈpɪmpl] n grano

PIN n abbr (= personal identification number) número personal

pin [pɪn] n alfiler m ♦ vt prender (con alfiler); **~s and needles** hormigueo; **to ~ sb down** (fig) hacer que uno concrete; **to ~ sth on sb** (fig) colgarle a uno el sambenito de algo

pinafore [ˈpɪnəfɔː*] n delantal m; **~ dress** (BRIT) n mandil m

pinball [ˈpɪnbɔːl] n mesa americana

pincers [ˈpɪnsəz] npl pinzas fpl, tenazas fpl

pinch [pɪntʃ] n (of salt etc) pizca ♦ vt pellizcar; (inf: steal) birlar; **at a ~** en caso de apuro

pincushion [ˈpɪnkuʃən] n acerico

pine [paɪn] n (also: **~ tree, wood**) pino ♦ vi: **to ~ for** suspirar por; **~ away** vi morirse de pena

pineapple [ˈpaɪnæpl] n piña, ananás m

ping [pɪn] n (noise) sonido agudo; **~-pong** ® n pingpong ® m

pink [pɪnk] adj rosado, (color de) rosa ♦ n (colour) rosa; (BOT) clavel m, clavellina

pinpoint [ˈpɪnpɔɪnt] vt precisar

pint [paɪnt] n pinta (BRIT = 568cc; US = 473cc); (BRIT: inf: of beer) pinta de cerveza, ≈ jarra (SP)

pin-up n fotografía erótica

pioneer [paɪəˈnɪə*] n pionero/a

pious [ˈpaɪəs] adj piadoso, devoto

pip [pɪp] n (seed) pepita; **the ~s** (BRIT) la señal

pipe [paɪp] n tubo, caño; (for smoking) pipa ♦ vt conducir en cañerías; **~s** npl (gen) cañería; (also: **bag~s**) gaita; **~ cleaner** n limpiapipas m inv; **~ dream** n sueño imposible; **~line** n (for oil) oleoducto; (for gas) gasoducto; **~r** n gaitero/a

piping [ˈpaɪpɪn] adv: **to be ~ hot** estar que quema

piquant [ˈpiːkənt] adj picante; (fig) agudo

pique [piːk] n pique m, resentimiento

pirate [ˈpaɪərət] n pirata m/f ♦ vt (cassette,

book) piratear; **~ radio** (*BRIT*) *n* emisora pirata

Pisces ['paɪsiːz] *n* Piscis *m*

piss [pɪs] (*infl*) *vi* mear; **~ed** (*infl*) *adj* (*drunk*) borracho

pistol ['pɪstl] *n* pistola

piston ['pɪstən] *n* pistón *m*, émbolo

pit [pɪt] *n* hoyo; (*also:* **coal ~**) mina; (*in garage*) foso de inspección; (*also:* **orchestra ~**) platea ♦ *vt:* **to ~ one's wits against sb** medir fuerzas con uno; **~s** *npl* (*AUT*) box *m*

pitch [pɪtʃ] *n* (*MUS*) tono; (*BRIT: SPORT*) campo, terreno; (*fig*) punto; (*tar*) brea ♦ *vt* (*throw*) arrojar, lanzar ♦ *vi* (*fall*) caer(se); **to ~ a tent** montar una tienda (de campaña); **~-black** *adj* negro como boca de lobo; **~ed battle** *n* batalla campal

pitfall ['pɪtfɔːl] *n* riesgo

pith [pɪθ] *n* (*of orange*) médula

pithy ['pɪθɪ] *adj* (*fig*) jugoso

pitiful ['pɪtɪful] *adj* (*touching*) lastimoso, conmovedor(a)

pitiless ['pɪtɪlɪs] *adj* despiadado

pittance ['pɪtns] *n* miseria

pity ['pɪtɪ] *n* compasión *f*, piedad *f* ♦ *vt* compadecer(se de); **what a ~!** ¡qué pena!

pizza ['piːtsə] *n* pizza

placard ['plækɑːd] *n* letrero; (*in march etc*) pancarta

placate [plə'keɪt] *vt* apaciguar

place [pleɪs] *n* lugar *m*, sitio; (*seat*) plaza, asiento; (*post*) puesto; (*home*): **at/to his ~** en/a su casa; (*role: in society etc*) papel *m* ♦ *vt* (*object*) poner, colocar; (*identify*) reconocer; **to take ~** tener lugar; **to be ~d** (*in race, exam*) colocarse; **out of ~** (*not suitable*) fuera de lugar; **in the first ~** en primer lugar; **to change ~s with sb** cambiarse de sitio con uno; **~ of birth** lugar *m* de nacimiento

placid ['plæsɪd] *adj* apacible

plague [pleɪg] *n* plaga; (*MED*) peste *f* ♦ *vt* (*fig*) acosar, atormentar

plaice [pleɪs] *n inv* platija

plaid [plæd] *n* (*material*) tartán *m*

plain [pleɪn] *adj* (*unpatterned*) liso; (*clear*) claro, evidente; (*simple*) sencillo; (*not handsome*) poco atractivo ♦ *adv* claramente ♦ *n* llano, llanura; **~ chocolate** *n* chocolate *m* amargo; **~-clothes** *adj* (*police*) vestido de paisano; **~ly** *adv* claramente

plaintiff ['pleɪntɪf] *n* demandante *m/f*

plait [plæt] *n* trenza

plan [plæn] *n* (*drawing*) plano; (*scheme*) plan *m*, proyecto ♦ *vt* proyectar, planificar ♦ *vi* hacer proyectos; **to ~ to do** pensar hacer

plane [pleɪn] *n* (*AVIAT*) avión *m*; (*MATH, fig*) plano; (*also:* **~ tree**) plátano; (*tool*) cepillo

planet ['plænɪt] *n* planeta *m*

plank [plæŋk] *n* tabla

planner ['plænə*] *n* planificador(a) *m/f*

planning ['plænɪŋ] *n* planificación *f*; **family ~** planificación familiar; **~ permission** *n* permiso para realizar obras

plant [plɑːnt] *n* planta; (*machinery*) maquinaria; (*factory*) fábrica ♦ *vt* plantar; (*field*) sembrar; (*bomb*) colocar

plaster ['plɑːstə*] *n* (*for walls*) yeso; (*also:* **~ of Paris**) yeso mate; (*BRIT: also:* **sticking ~**) tirita (*SP*), esparadrapo, curita (*AM*) ♦ *vt* enyesar; (*cover*): **to ~ with** llenar *or* cubrir de; **~ed** (*inf*) *adj* borracho; **~er** *n* yesero

plastic ['plæstɪk] *n* plástico ♦ *adj* de plástico; **~ bag** *n* bolsa de plástico

Plasticine ® ['plæstɪsiːn] (*BRIT*) *n* plastilina ®

plastic surgery *n* cirugía plástica

plate [pleɪt] *n* (*dish*) plato; (*metal, in book*) lámina; (*dental ~*) placa de dentadura postiza

plateau ['plætəu] (*pl* **~s** *or* **~x**) *n* meseta, altiplanicie *f*

plateaux ['plætəuz] *npl of* **plateau**

plate glass *n* vidrio cilindrado

platform ['plætfɔːm] *n* (*RAIL*) andén *m*; (*stage, BRIT: on bus*) plataforma; (*at meeting*) tribuna; (*POL*) programa *m* (*electoral*)

platinum ['plætɪnəm] *adj, n* platino

platoon [pləˈtuːn] *n* pelotón *m*

platter [ˈplætə*] *n* fuente *f*

plausible [ˈplɔːzɪbl] *adj* verosímil; (*person*) convincente

play [pleɪ] *n* (*THEATRE*) obra, comedia ♦ *vt* (*game*) jugar; (*compete against*) jugar contra; (*instrument*) tocar; (*part: in play etc*) hacer el papel de; (*tape, record*) poner ♦ *vi* jugar; (*band*) tocar; (*tape, record*) sonar; **to ~ safe** ir a lo seguro; **~ down** *vt* quitar importancia a; **~ up** *vi* (*cause trouble to*) dar guerra; **~boy** *n* playboy *m*; **~er** *n* jugador(a) *m/f*; (*THEATRE*) actor/actriz *m/f*; (*MUS*) músico/a; **~ful** *adj* juguetón/ona; **~ground** *n* (*in school*) patio de recreo; (*in park*) parque *m* infantil; **~group** *n* jardín *m* de niños; **~ing card** *n* naipe *m*, carta; **~ing field** *n* campo de deportes; **~mate** *n* compañero/a de juego; **~-off** *n* (*SPORT*) (partido de) desempate *m*; **~pen** *n* corral *m*; **~thing** *n* juguete *m*; **~time** *n* (*SCOL*) recreo; **~wright** *n* dramaturgo/a

plc *abbr* (= *public limited company*) ≈ S.A.

plea [pliː] *n* súplica, petición *f*; (*LAW*) alegato, defensa; **~ bargaining** *n* (*LAW*) acuerdo entre fiscal y defensor para agilizar los trámites judiciales

plead [pliːd] *vt* (*LAW*): **to ~ sb's case** defender a uno; (*give as excuse*) poner como pretexto ♦ *vi* (*LAW*) declararse; (*beg*): **to ~ with sb** suplicar *or* rogar a uno

pleasant [ˈplɛznt] *adj* agradable; **~ries** *npl* cortesías *fpl*

please [pliːz] *excl* ¡por favor! ♦ *vt* (*give pleasure to*) dar gusto a, agradar ♦ *vi* (*think fit*): **do as you ~** haz lo que quieras; **~ yourself!** (*inf*) ¡haz lo que quieras!, ¡como quieras!; **~d** *adj* (*happy*) alegre, contento; **~d (with)** satisfecho (de); **~d to meet you** ¡encantado!, ¡tanto gusto!; **pleasing** *adj* agradable, grato

pleasure [ˈplɛʒə*] *n* placer *m*, gusto; **"it's a ~"** "el gusto es mío"

pleat [pliːt] *n* pliegue *m*

pledge [plɛdʒ] *n* (*promise*) promesa, voto

♦ *vt* prometer

plentiful [ˈplɛntɪful] *adj* copioso, abundante

plenty [ˈplɛntɪ] *n*: **~ of** mucho(s)/a(s)

pliable [ˈplaɪəbl] *adj* flexible

pliers [ˈplaɪəz] *npl* alicates *mpl*, tenazas *fpl*

plight [plaɪt] *n* situación *f* difícil

plimsolls [ˈplɪmsəlz] (*BRIT*) *npl* zapatos *mpl* de tenis

plinth [plɪnθ] *n* plinto

plod [plɒd] *vi* caminar con paso pesado; (*fig*) trabajar laboriosamente

plonk [plɒŋk] (*inf*) *n* (*BRIT: wine*) vino peleón ♦ *vt*: **to ~ sth down** dejar caer algo

plot [plɒt] *n* (*scheme*) complot *m*, conjura; (*of story, play*) argumento; (*of land*) terreno, lote *m* (*AM*) ♦ *vt* (*mark out*) trazar; (*conspire*) tramar, urdir ♦ *vi* conspirar

plough [plaʊ] (*US* **plow**) *n* arado ♦ *vt* (*earth*) arar; **to ~ money into** invertir dinero en; **~ through** *vt fus* (*crowd*) abrirse paso por la fuerza por; **~man's lunch** (*BRIT*) *n* almuerzo de pub a base de pan, queso y encurtidos

pluck [plʌk] *vt* (*fruit*) coger (*SP*), recoger (*AM*); (*musical instrument*) puntear; (*bird*) desplumar; (*eyebrows*) depilar; **to ~ up courage** hacer de tripas corazón

plug [plʌg] *n* tapón *m*; (*ELEC*) enchufe *m*, clavija; (*AUT: also:* **spark(ing) ~**) bujía ♦ *vt* (*hole*) tapar; (*inf: advertise*) dar publicidad a; **~ in** *vt* (*ELEC*) enchufar

plum [plʌm] *n* (*fruit*) ciruela

plumb [plʌm] *vt*: **to ~ the depths of** alcanzar los mayores extremos de

plumber [ˈplʌmə*] *n* fontanero/a (*SP*), plomero/a (*AM*)

plumbing [ˈplʌmɪŋ] *n* (*trade*) fontanería, plomería; (*piping*) cañería

plummet [ˈplʌmɪt] *vi*: **to ~ (down)** caer a plomo

plump [plʌmp] *adj* rechoncho, rollizo ♦ *vi*: **to ~ for** (*inf: choose*) optar por; **~ up** *vt* mullir

plunder [ˈplʌndə*] *vt* pillar, saquear

plunge [plʌndʒ] n zambullida ♦ vt sumergir, hundir ♦ vi (fall) caer; (dive) saltar; (person) arrojarse; **to take the ~** lanzarse; **plunging** adj: **plunging neckline** escote m pronunciado

pluperfect [pluːˈpəːfɪkt] n pluscuamperfecto

plural [ˈpluərl] adj plural ♦ n plural m

plus [plʌs] n (also: **~ sign**) signo más ♦ prep más, y, además de; **ten/twenty ~** más de diez/veinte

plush [plʌʃ] adj lujoso

plutonium [pluːˈtəʊnɪəm] n plutonio

ply [plaɪ] vt (a trade) ejercer ♦ vi (ship) ir y venir ♦ n (of wool, rope) cabo; **to ~ sb with drink** insistir en ofrecer a uno muchas copas; **~wood** n madera contrachapada

P.M. n abbr = **Prime Minister**

p.m. adv abbr (= post meridiem) de la tarde or noche

pneumatic [njuːˈmætɪk] adj neumático; **~ drill** n martillo neumático

pneumonia [njuːˈməʊnɪə] n pulmonía

poach [pəʊtʃ] vt (cook) escalfar; (steal) cazar (or pescar) en vedado ♦ vi cazar (or pescar) en vedado; **~ed** adj escalfado; **~er** n cazador(a) m/f furtivo/a

P.O. Box n abbr = **Post Office Box**

pocket [ˈpɔkɪt] n bolsillo; (fig: small area) bolsa ♦ vt meter en el bolsillo; (steal) embolsar; **to be out of ~** (BRIT) salir perdiendo; **~book** n (US) cartera; **~ calculator** n calculadora de bolsillo; **~ knife** n navaja; **~ money** n asignación f

pod [pɔd] n vaina

podgy [ˈpɔdʒɪ] adj gordinflón/ona

podiatrist [pɔˈdiːətrɪst] (US) n pedicuro/a

poem [ˈpəʊɪm] n poema m

poet [ˈpəʊɪt] n poeta m/f; **~ic** [-ˈɛtɪk] adj poético; **~ry** n poesía

poignant [ˈpɔɪnjənt] adj conmovedor(a)

point [pɔɪnt] n punto; (tip) punta; (purpose) fin m, propósito; (use) utilidad f; (significant part) lo significativo; (moment) momento; (ELEC) toma (de corriente); (also: **decimal ~**): **2 ~ 3 (2.3)** dos coma tres (2,3) ♦ vt señalar; (gun etc): **to ~ sth at sb** apuntar algo a uno ♦ vi: **to ~ at** señalar; **~s** npl (AUT) contactos mpl; (RAIL) agujas fpl; **to be on the ~ of doing sth** estar a punto de hacer algo; **to make a ~ of** poner empeño en; **to get/miss the ~** comprender/no comprender; **to come to the ~** ir al meollo; **there's no ~ (in doing)** no tiene sentido (hacer); **~ out** vt señalar; **~ to** vt fus (fig) indicar, señalar; **~-blank** adv (say, refuse) sin más hablar; (also: **at ~-blank range**) a quemarropa; **~ed** adj (shape) puntiagudo, afilado; (remark) intencionado; **~edly** adv intencionadamente; **~er** n (needle) aguja, indicador m; **~less** adj sin sentido; **~ of view** n punto de vista

poise [pɔɪz] n aplomo, elegancia

poison [ˈpɔɪzn] n veneno ♦ vt envenenar; **~ing** n envenenamiento; **~ous** adj venenoso; (fumes etc) tóxico

poke [pəʊk] vt (jab with finger, stick etc) empujar; (put): **to ~ sth in(to)** introducir algo en; **~ about** vi fisgonear

poker [ˈpəʊkə*] n atizador m; (CARDS) póker m

poky [ˈpəʊkɪ] adj estrecho

Poland [ˈpəʊlənd] n Polonia

polar [ˈpəʊlə*] adj polar; **~ bear** n oso polar

Pole [pəʊl] n polaco/a

pole [pəʊl] n palo; (fixed) poste m; (GEO) polo; **~ bean** (US) n ≈ judía verde; **~ vault** n salto con pértiga

police [pəˈliːs] n policía ♦ vt vigilar; **~ car** n coche-patrulla m; **~man** (irreg) n policía m, guardia m; **~ state** n estado policial; **~ station** n comisaría; **~woman** (irreg) n mujer f policía

policy [ˈpɔlɪsɪ] n política; (also: **insurance ~**) póliza

polio [ˈpəʊlɪəʊ] n polio f

Polish [ˈpəʊlɪʃ] adj polaco ♦ n (LING) polaco

polish [ˈpɔlɪʃ] n (for shoes) betún m; (for floor) cera (de lustrar); (shine) brillo, lustre m; (fig: refinement) educación f ♦ vt (shoes) limpiar; (make shiny) pulir, sacar brillo a; ~ off vt (food) despachar; ~ed adj (fig: person) elegante

polite [pə'laɪt] adj cortés, atento; ~ness n cortesía

political [pə'lɪtɪkl] adj político; ~ly adv políticamente; ~ly correct políticamente correcto

politician [pɔlɪ'tɪʃən] n político/a

politics ['pɔlɪtɪks] n política

poll [pəul] n (election) votación f; (also: **opinion ~**) sondeo, encuesta ♦ vt encuestar; (votes) obtener

pollen ['pɔlən] n polen m

polling day ['pəulɪŋ-] n día m de elecciones

polling station n centro electoral

pollute [pə'lu:t] vt contaminar

pollution [pə'lu:ʃən] n polución f, contaminación f del medio ambiente

polo ['pəuləu] n (sport) polo; ~-necked adj de cuello vuelto; ~ shirt n polo, niqui m

polyester [pɔlɪ'estə*] n poliéster m

polystyrene [pɔlɪ'staɪri:n] n poliestireno

polythene ['pɔlɪθi:n] (BRIT) n politeno

pomegranate ['pɔmɪgrænɪt] n granada

pomp [pɔmp] n pompa

pompous ['pɔmpəs] adj pomposo

pond [pɔnd] n (natural) charca; (artificial) estanque m

ponder ['pɔndə*] vt meditar

ponderous ['pɔndərəs] adj pesado

pong [pɔŋ] (BRIT: inf) n hedor m

pony ['pəunɪ] n poney m, jaca, potro (AM); ~tail n cola de caballo; ~ trekking (BRIT) n excursión f a caballo

poodle ['pu:dl] n caniche m

pool [pu:l] n (natural) charca; (also: **swimming ~**) piscina (SP), alberca (AM); (fig: of light etc) charco; (SPORT) chapolín m ♦ vt juntar; ~s npl (football ~s) quinielas fpl; **typing ~** servicio de mecanografía

poor [puə*] adj pobre; (bad) de mala calidad ♦ npl: **the ~** los pobres; ~ly adj mal, enfermo ♦ adv mal

pop [pɔp] n (sound) ruido seco; (MUS) (música) pop m; (inf: father) papá m; (drink) gaseosa ♦ vt (put quickly) meter (de prisa) ♦ vi reventar; (cork) saltar; ~ in/out vi entrar/salir un momento; ~ up vi aparecer inesperadamente; ~corn n palomitas fpl

pope [pəup] n papa m

poplar ['pɔplə*] n álamo

popper ['pɔpə*] (BRIT) n automático

poppy ['pɔpɪ] n amapola

Popsicle ® ['pɔpsɪkl] (US) n polo

pop star n estrella del pop

populace ['pɔpjuləs] n pueblo, plebe f

popular ['pɔpjulə*] adj popular

population [pɔpju'leɪʃən] n población f

porcelain ['pɔ:slɪn] n porcelana

porch [pɔ:tʃ] n pórtico, entrada; (US) veranda

porcupine ['pɔ:kjupaɪn] n puerco m espín

pore [pɔ:*] n poro ♦ vi: **to ~ over** engolfarse en

pork [pɔ:k] n carne f de cerdo (SP) or chancho (AM)

pornography [pɔ:'nɔgrəfɪ] n pornografía

porpoise ['pɔ:pəs] n marsopa

porridge ['pɔrɪdʒ] n gachas fpl de avena

port [pɔ:t] n puerto; (NAUT: left side) babor m; (wine) vino de Oporto; ~ of call puerto de escala

portable ['pɔ:təbl] adj portátil

porter ['pɔ:tə*] n (for luggage) maletero; (doorkeeper) portero/a, conserje m/f

portfolio [pɔ:t'fəuliəu] n cartera

porthole ['pɔ:thəul] n portilla

portion ['pɔ:ʃən] n porción f; (of food) ración f

portrait ['pɔ:treɪt] n retrato

portray [pɔ:'treɪ] vt retratar; (subj: actor) representar

Portugal ['pɔ:tjugl] n Portugal m

Portuguese [pɔ:tju'gi:z] adj portugués/esa ♦ n inv portugués/esa m/f; (LING) portugués m

pose [pəuz] n postura, actitud f ♦ vi (pretend): **to ~ as** hacerse pasar por ♦ vt (question) plantear; **to ~ for** posar para

posh [pɒʃ] (*inf*) *adj* elegante, de lujo

position [pə'zɪʃən] *n* posición *f*; (*job*) puesto; (*situation*) situación *f* ♦ *vt* colocar

positive ['pɒzɪtɪv] *adj* positivo; (*certain*) seguro; (*definite*) definitivo

possess [pə'zɛs] *vt* poseer; **~ion** [pə'zɛʃən] *n* posesión *f*; **~ions** *npl* (*belongings*) pertenencias *fpl*

possibility [pɒsɪ'bɪlɪtɪ] *n* posibilidad *f*

possible ['pɒsɪbl] *adj* posible; **as big as ~** lo más grande posible; **possibly** *adv* posiblemente; **I cannot possibly come** me es imposible venir

post [pəust] *n* (*BRIT: system*) correos *mpl*; (*BRIT: letters, delivery*) correo; (*job, situation*) puesto; (*pole*) poste *m* ♦ *vt* (*BRIT: send by post*) echar al correo; (*BRIT: appoint*) **to ~ to** enviar a; **~age** *n* porte *m*, franqueo; **~age stamp** *n* sello de correos; **~al** *adj* postal, de correos; **~al order** *n* giro postal; **~box** (*BRIT*) *n* buzón *m*; **~card** *n* tarjeta postal; **~code** (*BRIT*) *n* código postal

postdate [pəust'deɪt] *vt* (*cheque*) poner fecha adelantada a

poster ['pəustə*] *n* cartel *m*

poste restante [pəust'rɛstɔ̃nt] (*BRIT*) *n* lista de correos

postgraduate ['pəust'grædjuət] *n* posgraduado/a

posthumous ['pɒstjuməs] *adj* póstumo

postman ['pəustmən] (*irreg*) *n* cartero

postmark ['pəustmɑːk] *n* matasellos *m inv*

post-mortem [-'mɔːtəm] *n* autopsia

post office *n* (*building*) (oficina de) correos *m*; (*organization*): **the Post Office** Administración *f* General de Correos; **Post Office Box** *n* apartado postal (*SP*), casilla de correos (*AM*)

postpone [pəs'pəun] *vt* aplazar

postscript ['pəustskrɪpt] *n* posdata

posture ['pɒstʃə*] *n* postura, actitud *f*

postwar [pəust'wɔː*] *adj* de la posguerra

posy ['pəuzɪ] *n* ramillete *m* (de flores)

pot [pɒt] *n* (*for cooking*) olla; (*tea~*) tetera; (*coffee~*) cafetera; (*for flowers*) maceta; (*for jam*) tarro, pote *m*; (*inf: marijuana*)

chocolate *m* ♦ *vt* (*plant*) poner en tiesto; **to go to ~** (*inf*) irse al traste

potato [pə'teɪtəu] (*pl* **~es**) *n* patata (*SP*), papa (*AM*); **~ peeler** *n* pelapatatas *m inv*

potent ['pəutnt] *adj* potente, poderoso; (*drink*) fuerte

potential [pə'tɛnʃl] *adj* potencial, posible ♦ *n* potencial *m*; **~ly** *adv* en potencia

pothole ['pɒthəul] *n* (*in road*) bache *m*; (*BRIT: underground*) gruta; **potholing** (*BRIT*) *n*: **to go potholing** dedicarse a la espeleología

potluck [pɒt'lʌk] *n*: **to take ~** tomar lo que haya

potted ['pɒtɪd] *adj* (*food*) en conserva; (*plant*) en tiesto *or* maceta; (*shortened*) resumido

potter ['pɒtə*] *n* alfarero/a ♦ *vi*: **to ~ around, ~ about** (*BRIT*) hacer trabajitos; **~y** *n* cerámica; (*factory*) alfarería

potty ['pɒtɪ] *n* orinal *m* de niño

pouch [pautʃ] *n* (*ZOOL*) bolsa; (*for tobacco*) petaca

poultry ['pəultrɪ] *n* aves *fpl* de corral; (*meat*) pollo

pounce [pauns] *vi*: **to ~ on** precipitarse sobre

pound [paund] *n* libra (*weight = 453g or 16oz; money = 100 pence*) ♦ *vt* (*beat*) golpear; (*crush*) machacar ♦ *vi* (*heart*) latir; **~ sterling** *n* libra esterlina

pour [pɔː*] *vt* echar; (*tea etc*) servir ♦ *vi* correr, fluir; **to ~ sb a drink** servirle a uno una copa; **~ away or off** *vt* vaciar, verter; **~ in** *vi* (*people*) entrar en tropel; **~ out** *vi* salir en tropel ♦ *vt* (*drink*) echar, servir; (*fig*): **to ~ out one's feelings** desahogarse; **~ing** *adj*: **~ing rain** lluvia torrencial

pout [paut] *vi* hacer pucheros

poverty ['pɒvətɪ] *n* pobreza, miseria; **~-stricken** *adj* necesitado

powder ['paudə*] *n* polvo; (*face ~*) polvos *mpl* ♦ *vt* polvorear; **to ~ one's face** empolvarse la cara; **~ compact** *n* polvera; **~ed milk** *n* leche *f* en polvo; **~ room** *n* aseos *mpl*

power ['pauə*] n poder m; (strength) fuerza; (nation, TECH) potencia; (drive) empuje m; (ELEC) fuerza, energía ♦ vt impulsar; **to be in** ~ (POL) estar en el poder; ~ **cut** (BRIT) n apagón m; ~**ed** adj: ~**ed by** impulsado por; ~ **failure** n = ~ **cut**; ~**ful** adj poderoso; (engine) potente; (speech etc) convincente; ~**less** adj: ~**less (to do)** incapaz (de hacer); ~ **point** (BRIT) n enchufe m; ~ **station** n central f eléctrica

p.p. abbr (= per procurationem): ~ **J. Smith** p.p. (por poder de) J. Smith; (= pages) págs

PR n abbr = **public relations**

practical ['præktɪkl] adj práctico; ~**ity** [-'kælɪtɪ] n factibilidad f; ~ **joke** n broma pesada; ~**ly** adv (almost) casi

practice ['præktɪs] n (habit) costumbre f; (exercise) práctica, ejercicio; (training) adiestramiento; (MED: of profession) práctica, ejercicio; (MED, LAW: business) consulta ♦ vt, vi (US) = **practise**; **in** ~ (in reality) en la práctica; **out of** ~ desentrenado

practise ['præktɪs] (US **practice**) vt (carry out) practicar; (profession) ejercer; (train at) practicar ♦ vi ejercer; (train) practicar; **practising** adj (Christian etc) practicante; (lawyer) en ejercicio

practitioner [præk'tɪʃənə*] n (MED) médico/a

prairie ['prɛərɪ] n pampa

praise [preɪz] n alabanza(s) f(pl), elogio(s) m(pl) ♦ vt alabar, elogiar; ~**worthy** adj loable

pram [præm] (BRIT) n cochecito de niño

prank [præŋk] n travesura

prawn [prɔːn] n gamba; ~ **cocktail** n cóctel m de gambas

pray [preɪ] vi rezar

prayer [prɛə*] n oración f, rezo; (entreaty) ruego, súplica

preach [priːtʃ] vi (also fig) predicar; ~**er** n predicador(a) m/f

precaution [prɪ'kɔːʃən] n precaución f

precede [prɪ'siːd] vt, vi preceder

precedent ['presɪdənt] n precedente m

preceding [prɪ'siːdɪŋ] adj anterior

precinct ['priːsɪŋkt] n recinto; ~**s** npl contornos mpl; **pedestrian** ~ (BRIT) zona peatonal; **shopping** ~ (BRIT) centro comercial

precious ['preʃəs] adj precioso

precipitate [prɪ'sɪpɪtett] vt precipitar

precise [prɪ'saɪs] adj preciso, exacto; ~**ly** adv precisamente, exactamente

precocious [prɪ'kəuʃəs] adj precoz

precondition [priːkən'dɪʃən] n condición f previa

predecessor ['priːdɪsesə*] n antecesor(a) m/f

predicament [prɪ'dɪkəmənt] n apuro

predict [prɪ'dɪkt] vt pronosticar; ~**able** adj previsible; ~**ion** [-'dɪkʃən] n predicción f

predominantly [prɪ'dɒmɪnəntlɪ] adv en su mayoría

pre-empt [priː'emt] vt adelantarse a

preen [priːn] vt: **to** ~ **itself** (bird) limpiarse (las plumas); **to** ~ **o.s.** pavonearse

preface ['prefəs] n prefacio

prefect ['priːfekt] (BRIT) n (in school) monitor(a) m/f

prefer [prɪ'fəː*] vt preferir; **to** ~ **doing** or **to do** preferir hacer; ~**able** ['prefrəbl] adj preferible; ~**ably** ['prefrəblɪ] adv de preferencia; ~**ence** ['prefrəns] n preferencia; (priority) prioridad f; ~**ential** [prefə'renʃəl] adj preferente

prefix ['priːfɪks] n prefijo

pregnancy ['pregnənsɪ] n (of woman) embarazo; (of animal) preñez f

pregnant ['pregnənt] adj (woman) embarazada; (animal) preñada

prehistoric ['priːhɪs'tɔrɪk] adj prehistórico

prejudice ['predʒudɪs] n prejuicio; ~**d** adj (person) predispuesto

premarital ['priː'mærɪtl] adj prematrimonial

premature ['premətʃuə*] adj prematuro

premier ['premɪə*] adj primero, principal ♦ n (POL) primer(a) ministro/a

première ['premɪeə*] n estreno

premise ['premɪs] n premisa; ~**s** npl (of business etc) local m; **on the** ~**s** en el lugar mismo

premium ['pri:mɪəm] n premio; (*insurance*) prima; **to be at a ~** ser muy solicitado; **~ bond** (*BRIT*) n bono del estado que participa en una lotería nacional

premonition [premə'nɪʃən] n presentimiento

preoccupied [pri:'ɔkjupaɪd] adj ensimismado

prep [prep] n (*SCOL: study*) deberes mpl

prepaid [pri:'peɪd] adj porte pagado

preparation [prepə'reɪʃən] n preparación f; **~s** npl preparativos mpl

preparatory [prɪ'pærətərɪ] adj preparatorio, preliminar; **~ school** n escuela preparatoria

prepare [prɪ'pɛə*] vt preparar, disponer; (*CULIN*) preparar ♦ vi: **to ~ for** (*action*) prepararse or disponerse para; (*event*) hacer preparativos para; **~d to** dispuesto a; **~d for** listo para

preposition [prepə'zɪʃən] n preposición f

preposterous [prɪ'pɔstərəs] adj absurdo, ridículo

prep school n = **preparatory school**

prerequisite [pri:'rekwɪzɪt] n requisito

Presbyterian [prezbɪ'tɪərɪən] adj, n presbiteriano/a m/f

preschool ['pri:'sku:l] adj preescolar

prescribe [prɪ'skraɪb] vt (*MED*) recetar

prescription [prɪ'skrɪpʃən] n (*MED*) receta

presence ['prezns] n presencia; **in sb's ~** en presencia de uno; **~ of mind** aplomo

present [adj, n 'preznt, vb prɪ'zent] adj (*in attendance*) presente; (*current*) actual ♦ n (*gift*) regalo; (*actuality*): **the ~** la actualidad, el presente ♦ vt (*introduce, describe*) presentar; (*expound*) exponer; (*give*) presentar, dar, ofrecer; (*THEATRE*) representar; **to give sb a ~** regalar algo a uno; **at ~** actualmente; **to make o.s. ~able** [prɪ'zentəbl] adj: arreglarse; **~ation** [-'teɪʃən] n presentación f; (*of report etc*) exposición f; (*formal ceremony*) entrega de un regalo; **~-day** adj actual; **~er** [prɪ'zentə*] n (*RADIO, TV*) locutor(a) m/f; **~ly** adv (*soon*) dentro de poco;

(*now*) ahora

preservative [prɪ'zə:vətɪv] n conservante m

preserve [prɪ'zə:v] vt (*keep safe*) preservar, proteger; (*maintain*) mantener; (*food*) conservar ♦ n (*for game*) coto, vedado; (*often pl: jam*) conserva, confitura

president ['prezɪdənt] n presidente m/f; **~ial** [-'denʃl] adj presidencial

press [pres] n (*newspapers*): **the P~** la prensa; (*printer's*) imprenta; (*of button*) pulsación f ♦ vt empujar; (*button etc*) apretar; (*clothes: iron*) planchar; (*put pressure on: person*) presionar; (*insist*): **to ~ sth on sb** insistir en que uno acepte algo ♦ vi (*squeeze*) apretar; (*pressurize*): **to ~ for** presionar por; **we are ~ed for time/money** estamos apurados de tiempo/dinero; **~ on** vi avanzar; (*hurry*) apretar el paso; **~ agency** n agencia de prensa; **~ conference** n rueda de prensa; **~ing** adj apremiante; **~ stud** (*BRIT*) n botón m de presión; **~-up** (*BRIT*) n plancha

pressure ['preʃə*] n presión f; **to put ~ on sb** presionar a uno; **~ cooker** n olla a presión; **~ gauge** n manómetro; **~ group** n grupo de presión; **pressurized** adj (*container*) a presión

prestige [pres'ti:ʒ] n prestigio

presumably [prɪ'zju:məblɪ] adv es de suponer que, cabe presumir que

presume [prɪ'zju:m] vt: **to ~ (that)** presumir (que), suponer (que)

pretence [prɪ'tens] (*US* **pretense**) n fingimiento; **under false ~s** con engaños

pretend [prɪ'tend] vt, vi (*feign*) fingir

pretentious [prɪ'tenʃəs] adj presumido; (*ostentatious*) ostentoso, aparatoso

pretext ['pri:tekst] n pretexto

pretty ['prɪtɪ] adj bonito, (*SP*), lindo (*AM*) ♦ adv bastante

prevail [prɪ'veɪl] vi (*gain mastery*) prevalecer; (*be current*) predominar; **~ing** adj (*dominant*) predominante

prevalent ['prevələnt] adj (*widespread*) extendido

prevent [prɪ'vent] *vt*: **to ~ sb from doing sth** impedir a uno hacer algo; **to ~ sth from happening** evitar que ocurra algo; **~ative** *adj* = **preventive**; **~ive** *adj* preventivo

preview ['priːvjuː] *n* (*of film*) preestreno

previous ['priːvɪəs] *adj* previo, anterior; **~ly** *adv* antes

prewar [priː'wɔː*] *adj* de antes de la guerra

prey [preɪ] *n* presa ♦ *vi*: **to ~ on** (*feed on*) alimentarse de; **it was ~ing on his mind** le preocupaba, le obsesionaba

price [praɪs] *n* precio ♦ *vt* (*goods*) fijar el precio de; **~less** *adj* que no tiene precio; **~ list** *n* tarifa

prick [prɪk] *n* (*sting*) picadura ♦ *vt* pinchar; (*hurt*) picar; **to ~ up one's ears** aguzar el oído

prickle ['prɪkl] *n* (*sensation*) picor *m*; (*BOT*) espina; **prickly** *adj* espinoso; (*fig: person*) enojadizo; **prickly heat** *n* sarpullido causado por exceso de calor

pride [praɪd] *n* orgullo; (*pej*) soberbia ♦ *vt*: **to ~ o.s. on** enorgullecerse de

priest [priːst] *n* sacerdote *m*; **~hood** *n* sacerdocio

prim [prɪm] *adj* (*demure*) remilgado; (*prudish*) gazmoño

primarily ['praɪmərɪlɪ] *adv* ante todo

primary ['praɪmərɪ] *adj* (*first in importance*) principal ♦ *n* (*US: POL*) (elección *f*) primaria; **~ school** (*BRIT*) *n* escuela primaria

prime [praɪm] *adj* primero, principal; (*excellent*) selecto, de primera clase ♦ *n*: **in the ~ of life** en la flor de la vida ♦ *vt* (*wood, fig*) preparar; **~ example** ejemplo típico; **P~ Minister** *n* primer(a) ministro/a

primeval [praɪ'miːvəl] *adj* primitivo

primitive ['prɪmɪtɪv] *adj* primitivo; (*crude*) rudimentario

primrose ['prɪmrəuz] *n* primavera, prímula

Primus (stove) ® ['praɪməs-] (*BRIT*) *n* hornillo de camping

prince [prɪns] *n* príncipe *m*

princess [prɪn'ses] *n* princesa

principal ['prɪnsɪpl] *adj* principal, mayor ♦ *n* director(a) *m/f*; **~ity** [-'pælɪtɪ] *n* principado

principle ['prɪnsɪpl] *n* principio; **in ~** en principio; **on ~** por principio

print [prɪnt] *n* (*foot~*) huella; (*finger~*) huella dactilar; (*letters*) letra de molde; (*fabric*) estampado; (*ART*) grabado; (*PHOT*) impresión *f* ♦ *vt* imprimir; (*cloth*) estampar; (*write in capitals*) escribir en letras de molde; **out of ~** agotado; **~ed matter** *n* impresos *mpl*; **~er** *n* (*person*) impresor(a) *m/f*; (*machine*) impresora; **~ing** *n* (*art*) imprenta; (*act*) impresión *f*; **~out** *n* (*COMPUT*) impresión *f*

prior ['praɪə*] *adj* anterior, previo; (*more important*) más importante; **~ to** antes de

priority [praɪ'ɔrɪtɪ] *n* prioridad *f*; **to have ~ (over)** tener prioridad (sobre)

prison ['prɪzn] *n* cárcel *f*, prisión *f* ♦ *cpd* carcelario; **~er** *n* (*in prison*) preso/a; (*captured person*) prisionero/a; **~er-of-war** *n* prisionero de guerra

privacy ['prɪvəsɪ] *n* intimidad *f*

private ['praɪvɪt] *adj* (*personal*) particular; (*property, industry, discussion etc*) privado; (*person*) reservado; (*place*) tranquilo ♦ *n* soldado raso; **"~"** (*on envelope*) "confidencial"; (*on door*) "prohibido el paso"; **in ~** en privado; **~ enterprise** *n* empresa privada; **~ eye** *n* detective *m/f* privado/a; **~ property** *n* propiedad *f* privada; **~ school** *n* colegio particular

privet ['prɪvɪt] *n* alheña

privilege ['prɪvɪlɪdʒ] *n* privilegio; (*prerogative*) prerrogativa

privy ['prɪvɪ] *adj*: **to be ~ to** estar enterado de

prize [praɪz] *n* premio ♦ *adj* de primera clase ♦ *vt* apreciar, estimar; **~-giving** *n* distribución *f* de premios; **~winner** *n* premiado/a

pro [prəu] *n* (*SPORT*) profesional *m/f* ♦ *prep* a favor de; **the ~s and cons** los pros y los contras

probability [prɔbə'bɪlɪtɪ] *n* probabilidad *f*;

in all ~ con toda probabilidad
probable ['prɒbəbl] *adj* probable
probably ['prɒbəblɪ] *adv* probablemente
probation [prə'beɪʃən] *n*: **on ~** (*employee*) a prueba; (*LAW*) en libertad condicional
probe [prəub] *n* (*MED, SPACE*) sonda; (*enquiry*) encuesta, investigación *f* ♦ *vt* sondar; (*investigate*) investigar
problem ['prɒbləm] *n* problema *m*
procedure [prə'siːdʒə*] *n* procedimiento; (*bureaucratic*) trámites *mpl*
proceed [prə'siːd] *vi* (*do afterwards*): **to ~ to do sth** proceder a hacer algo; (*continue*): **to ~ (with)** continuar *or* seguir (con); **~ings** *npl* acto(s) (*pl*); (*LAW*) proceso; **~s** ['prəusiːdz] *npl* (*money*) ganancias *fpl*, ingresos *mpl*
process ['prəuses] *n* proceso ♦ *vt* tratar, elaborar; **~ing** *n* tratamiento, elaboración *f*; (*PHOT*) revelado
procession [prə'seʃən] *n* desfile *m*; **funeral ~** cortejo fúnebre
pro-choice [prəu'tʃɔɪs] *adj* en favor del derecho a elegir de la madre
proclaim [prə'kleɪm] *vt* anunciar
procrastinate [prəu'kræstɪneɪt] *vi* demorarse
procure [prə'kjuə*] *vt* conseguir
prod [prɒd] *vt* empujar ♦ *n* empujón *m*
prodigy ['prɒdɪdʒɪ] *n* prodigio
produce [*n* 'prɒdjuːs, *vt* prə'djuːs] *n* (*AGR*) productos *mpl* agrícolas ♦ *vt* producir; (*play, film, programme*) presentar; **~r** *n* productor(a) *m/f*; (*of film, programme*) director(a) *m/f*; (*of record*) productor(a) *m/f*
product ['prɒdʌkt] *n* producto
production [prə'dʌkʃən] *n* producción *f*; (*THEATRE*) presentación *f*; **~ line** *n* línea de producción
productivity [prɒdʌk'tɪvɪtɪ] *n* productividad *f*
profession [prə'feʃən] *n* profesión *f*; **~al** *adj* profesional ♦ *n* profesional *m/f*; (*skilled person*) perito
professor [prə'fesə*] *n* (*BRIT*) catedrático/a; (*US, Canada*) profesor(a) *m/f*

proficient [prə'fɪʃənt] *adj* experto, hábil
profile ['prəufaɪl] *n* perfil *m*
profit ['prɒfɪt] *n* (*COMM*) ganancia ♦ *vi*: **to ~ by** *or* **from** aprovechar *or* sacar provecho de; **~ability** [-ə'bɪlɪtɪ] *n* rentabilidad *f*; **~able** *adj* (*ECON*) rentable
profound [prə'faund] *adj* profundo
profusely [prə'fjuːslɪ] *adv* profusamente
programme (*US* **program**) ['prəugræm] *n* programa *m* ♦ *vt* programar; **~r** (*US* **programer**) *n* programador(a) *m/f*; **programming** (*US* **programing**) *n* programación *f*
progress [*n* 'prəugres, *vi* prə'gres] *n* progreso; (*development*) desarrollo ♦ *vi* progresar, avanzar; **in ~** en curso; **~ive** [-'gresɪv] *adj* progresivo; (*person*) progresista
prohibit [prə'hɪbɪt] *vt* prohibir; **to ~ sb from doing sth** prohibir a uno hacer algo; **~ion** [-'bɪʃn] *n* prohibición *f*; (*US*): **P~ion** Ley *f* Seca
project [*n* 'prɒdʒekt, *vb* prə'dʒekt] *n* proyecto ♦ *vt* proyectar ♦ *vi* (*stick out*) salir, sobresalir; **~ion** [prə'dʒekʃən] *n* proyección *f*; (*overhang*) saliente *m*; **~or** [prə'dʒektə*] *n* proyector *m*
pro-life [prəu'laɪf] *adj* pro-vida
prolong [prə'lɒŋ] *vt* prolongar, extender
prom [prɒm] *n abbr* = **promenade**; (*US*: *ball*) baile *m* de gala

Prom

i *El ciclo de conciertos de música clásica más conocido de Londres es el llamado* **the Proms** *(promenade concerts), que se celebra anualmente en el Royal Albert Hall. Su nombre se debe a que originalmente el público paseaba durante las actuaciones, costumbre que en la actualidad se mantiene de forma simbólica, permitiendo que parte de los asistentes permanezcan de pie. En Estados Unidos se llama* **prom** *a un baile de gala en un centro de educación secundaria o universitaria.*

promenade [promə'nɑːd] n (by sea) paseo marítimo; ~ **concert** (BRIT) n concierto (en que parte del público permanece de pie)

prominence ['prɒmɪnəns] n importancia

prominent ['prɒmɪnənt] adj (standing out) saliente; (important) eminente, importante

promiscuous [prə'mɪskjuəs] adj (sexually) promiscuo

promise ['prɒmɪs] n promesa ♦ vt, vi prometer; **promising** adj prometedor(a)

promote [prə'məut] vt (employee) ascender; (product, pop star) hacer propaganda por; (ideas) fomentar; ~**r** n (of event) promotor(a) m/f; (of cause etc) impulsor(a) m/f; **promotion** [-'məuʃən] n (advertising campaign) campaña de promoción f; (in rank) ascenso

prompt [prɒmpt] adj rápido ♦ adv: **at 6 o'clock** ~ a las seis en punto ♦ n (COMPUT) aviso ♦ vt (urge) mover, incitar; (when talking) instar; (THEATRE) apuntar; **to** ~ **sb to do sth** instar a uno a hacer algo; ~**ly** adv rápidamente; (exactly) puntualmente

prone [prəun] adj (lying) postrado; ~ **to** propenso a

prong [prɒŋ] n diente m, punta

pronoun ['prəunaun] n pronombre m

pronounce [prə'nauns] vt pronunciar; ~**d** adj (marked) marcado

pronunciation [prənʌnsɪ'eɪʃən] n pronunciación f

proof [pruːf] n prueba ♦ adj: ~ **against** a prueba de

prop [prɒp] n apoyo; (fig) sostén m ♦ vt (also: ~ **up**) apoyar; (lean): **to** ~ **sth against** apoyar algo contra

propaganda [prɒpə'gændə] n propaganda

propel [prə'pɛl] vt impulsar, propulsar; ~**ler** n hélice f

propensity [prə'pɛnsɪtɪ] n propensión f

proper ['prɒpə*] adj (suited, right) propio; (exact) justo; (seemly) correcto, decente; (authentic) verdadero; (referring to place): **the village** ~ el pueblo mismo; ~**ly** adv

(adequately) correctamente; (decently) decentemente; ~ **noun** n nombre m propio

property ['prɒpətɪ] n propiedad f; (personal) bienes mpl muebles; ~ **owner** n dueño/a de propiedades

prophecy ['prɒfɪsɪ] n profecía

prophesy ['prɒfɪsaɪ] vt (fig) predecir

prophet ['prɒfɪt] n profeta m

proportion [prə'pɔːʃən] n proporción f; (share) parte f; ~**al** adj: ~**al (to)** en proporción (con); ~**al representation** n representación f proporcional; ~**ate** adj: ~**ate (to)** en proporción (con)

proposal [prə'pəuzl] n (offer of marriage) oferta de matrimonio; (plan) proyecto

propose [prə'pəuz] vt proponer ♦ vi declararse; **to** ~ **to do** tener intención de hacer

proposition [prɒpə'zɪʃən] n propuesta

proprietor [prə'praɪətə*] n propietario/a, dueño/a

propriety [prə'praɪətɪ] n decoro

pro rata [-'rɑːtə] adv a prorrateo

prose [prəuz] n prosa

prosecute ['prɒsɪkjuːt] vt (LAW) procesar; **prosecution** [-'kjuːʃən] n proceso, causa; (accusing side) acusación f; **prosecutor** n acusador(a) m/f; (also: **public prosecutor**) fiscal m

prospect [n 'prɒspɛkt, vb prə'spɛkt] n (possibility) posibilidad f; (outlook) perspectiva ♦ vi: **to** ~ **for** buscar; ~**s** npl (for work etc) perspectivas fpl; ~**ing** n prospección f; ~**ive** [prə'spɛktɪv] adj futuro

prospectus [prə'spɛktəs] n prospecto

prosper ['prɒspə*] vi prosperar; ~**ity** [-'spɛrɪtɪ] n prosperidad f; ~**ous** adj próspero

prostitute ['prɒstɪtjuːt] n prostituta; (male) hombre que se dedica a la prostitución

protect [prə'tɛkt] vt proteger; ~**ion** [-'tɛkʃən] n protección f; ~**ive** adj protector(a)

protein ['prəutiːn] n proteína

protest [n 'prəutɛst, vb prə'tɛst] n protesta

♦ *vi*: **to ~ about** or **at/against** protestar de/contra ♦ *vt (insist)*: **to ~ (that)** insistir en (que)

Protestant ['prɒtɪstənt] *adj, n* protestante *m/f*

protester [prə'tɛstə*] *n* manifestante *m/f*

protracted [prə'træktɪd] *adj* prolongado

protrude [prə'truːd] *vi* salir, sobresalir

proud [praud] *adj* orgulloso; *(pej)* soberbio, altanero

prove [pruːv] *vt* probar; *(show)* demostrar
♦ *vi*: **to ~ (to be) correct** resultar correcto; **to ~ o.s.** probar su valía

proverb ['prɒvɜːb] *n* refrán *m*

provide [prə'vaɪd] *vt* proporcionar, dar; **to ~ sb with sth** proveer a uno de algo; **~d (that)** *conj* con tal de que, a condición de que; **~ for** *vt fus (person)* mantener a; *(problem etc)* tener en cuenta; **providing** [prə'vaɪdɪŋ] *conj*: **providing (that)** a condición de que, con tal de que

province ['prɒvɪns] *n* provincia *f*; *(fig)* esfera; **provincial** [prə'vɪnʃəl] *adj* provincial; *(pej)* provinciano

provision [prə'vɪʒən] *n (supplying)* suministro, abastecimiento; *(of contract etc)* disposición *f*; **~s** *npl (food)* comestibles *mpl*; **~al** *adj* provisional

proviso [prə'vaɪzəu] *n* condición *f*, estipulación *f*

provocative [prə'vɒkətɪv] *adj* provocativo

provoke [prə'vəuk] *vt (cause)* provocar, incitar; *(anger)* enojar

prowess ['praus] *n* destreza

prowl [praul] *vi (also: ~ about, ~ around)* merodear ♦ *n*: **on the ~** de merodeo; **~er** *n* merodeador(a) *m/f*

proxy ['prɒksɪ] *n*: **by ~** por poderes

prudent ['pruːdənt] *adj* prudente

prune [pruːn] *n* ciruela pasa ♦ *vt* podar

pry [praɪ] *vi*: **to ~ (into)** entrometerse (en)

PS *n abbr (= postscript)* P.D.

psalm [sɑːm] *n* salmo

pseudonym ['sjuːdəunɪm] *n* seudónimo

psyche ['saɪkɪ] *n* psique *f*

psychiatric [saɪkɪ'ætrɪk] *adj* psiquiátrico

psychiatrist [saɪ'kaɪətrɪst] *n* psiquiatra *m/f*

psychic ['saɪkɪk] *adj (also: ~al)* psíquico

psychoanalyse [saɪkəu'ænəlaɪz] *vt* psicoanalizar; **psychoanalysis** [-ə'nælɪsɪs] *n* psicoanálisis *m inv*

psychological [saɪkə'lɒdʒɪkl] *adj* psicológico

psychologist [saɪ'kɒlədʒɪst] *n* psicólogo/a

psychology [saɪ'kɒlədʒɪ] *n* psicología

PTO *abbr (= please turn over)* sigue

pub [pʌb] *n abbr (= public house)* pub *m*, bar *m*

pub

Un **pub** *es un local público donde se pueden consumir bebidas alcohólicas. La estricta regulación sobre la venta de alcohol prohíbe que se sirva a menores de 18 años y controla las horas de apertura, aunque éstas son más flexibles desde hace unos años. El* **pub** *es, además, un lugar de encuentro donde se sirven comidas ligeras o se juega a los dardos o al billar, entre otras actividades.*

puberty ['pjuːbətɪ] *n* pubertad *f*

public ['pʌblɪk] *adj* público ♦ *n*: **the ~** el público; **in ~** en público; **to make ~** hacer público; **~ address system** *n* megafonía

publican ['pʌblɪkən] *n* tabernero/a

publication [pʌblɪ'keɪʃən] *n* publicación *f*

public: **~ company** *n* sociedad *f* anónima; **~ convenience** *(BRIT)* *n* aseos *mpl* públicos *(SP)*, sanitarios *mpl* *(AM)*; **~ holiday** *n* día de fiesta *(SP)*, (día) feriado *(AM)*; **~ house** *(BRIT)* *n* bar *m*, pub *m*

publicity [pʌb'lɪsɪtɪ] *n* publicidad *f*

publicize ['pʌblɪsaɪz] *vt* publicitar

publicly ['pʌblɪklɪ] *adv* públicamente, en público

public: **~ opinion** *n* opinión *f* pública; **~ relations** *n* relaciones *fpl* públicas; **~ school** *n (BRIT)* escuela privada; *(US)* instituto; **~-spirited** *adj* que tiene sentido del deber ciudadano; **~ transport** *n* transporte *m* público

publish ['pʌblɪʃ] *vt* publicar; **~er** *n*

(*person*) editor(a) *m/f*; (*firm*) editorial *f*; ~ing *n* (*industry*) industria del libro

pub lunch *n* almuerzo que se sirve en un *pub*; **to go for a ~** almorzar *o* comer en un pub

pucker ['pʌkə*] *vt* (*pleat*) arrugar; (*brow etc*) fruncir

pudding ['pudɪŋ] *n* pudín *m*; (*BRIT: dessert*) postre *m*; **black ~** morcilla

puddle ['pʌdl] *n* charco

puff [pʌf] *n* soplo; (*of smoke, air*) bocanada; (*of breathing*) resoplido ♦ *vt*: **to ~ one's pipe** chupar la pipa ♦ *vi* (*pant*) jadear; **~ out** *vt* hinchar; **~ pastry** *n* hojaldre *m*; **~y** *adj* hinchado

pull [pul] *n* (*tug*): **to give sth a ~** dar un tirón a algo ♦ *vt* tirar de; (*press: trigger*) apretar; (*haul*) tirar, arrastrar; (*close: curtain*) echar ♦ *vi* tirar; **to ~ to pieces** hacer pedazos; **to not ~ one's punches** no andarse con bromas; **to ~ one's weight** hacer su parte; **to ~ o.s. together** sobreponerse; **to ~ sb's leg** tomar el pelo a uno; **~ apart** *vt* (*break*) romper; **~ down** *vt* (*building*) derribar; **~ in** *vi* (*car etc*) parar (junto a la acera); (*train*) llegar a la estación; **~ off** *vt* (*deal etc*) cerrar; **~ out** *vi* (*car, train etc*) salir ♦ *vt* sacar, arrancar; **~ over** *vi* (*AUT*) hacerse a un lado; **~ through** *vi* (*MED*) reponerse; **~ up** *vi* (*stop*) parar ♦ *vt* (*raise*) levantar; (*uproot*) arrancar, desarraigar

pulley ['pulɪ] *n* polea

pullover ['pulauvə*] *n* jersey *m*, suéter *m*

pulp [pʌlp] *n* (*of fruit*) pulpa

pulpit ['pulpɪt] *n* púlpito

pulsate [pʌl'seɪt] *vi* pulsar, latir

pulse [pʌls] *n* (*ANAT*) pulso; (*rhythm*) pulsación *f*; (*BOT*) legumbre *f*

pump [pʌmp] *n* bomba; (*shoe*) zapatilla ♦ *vt* sacar con una bomba; **~ up** *vt* inflar

pumpkin ['pʌmpkɪn] *n* calabaza

pun [pʌn] *n* juego de palabras

punch [pʌntʃ] *n* (*blow*) golpe *m*, puñetazo; (*tool*) punzón *m*; (*drink*) ponche *m* ♦ *vt* (*hit*): **to ~ sb/sth** dar un puñetazo *or* golpear a uno/algo; **~line** *n* palabras que

rematan un chiste; **~-up** (*BRIT: inf*) *n* riña

punctual ['pʌŋktjuəl] *adj* puntual

punctuation [pʌŋktju'eɪʃən] *n* puntuación *f*

puncture ['pʌŋktʃə*] (*BRIT*) *n* pinchazo ♦ *vt* pinchar

pungent ['pʌndʒənt] *adj* acre

punish ['pʌnɪʃ] *vt* castigar; **~ment** *n* castigo

punk [pʌŋk] *n* (*also*: **~ rocker**) punki *m/f*; (*also*: **~ rock**) música punk; (*US: inf: hoodlum*) rufián *m*

punt [pʌnt] *n* (*boat*) batea

punter ['pʌntə*] (*BRIT*) *n* (*gambler*) jugador(a) *m/f*; (*inf*) cliente *m/f*

puny ['pjuːnɪ] *adj* débil

pup [pʌp] *n* cachorro

pupil ['pjuːpl] *n* alumno/a; (*of eye*) pupila

puppet ['pʌpɪt] *n* títere *m*

puppy ['pʌpɪ] *n* cachorro, perrito

purchase ['pɜːtʃɪs] *n* compra ♦ *vt* comprar; **~r** *n* comprador(a) *m/f*

pure [pjuə*] *adj* puro

purée ['pjuəreɪ] *n* puré *m*

purely ['pjuəlɪ] *adv* puramente

purge [pɜːdʒ] *n* (*MED, POL*) purga ♦ *vt* purgar

purify ['pjuərɪfaɪ] *vt* purificar, depurar

purple ['pɜːpl] *adj* purpúreo; morado

purpose ['pɜːpəs] *n* propósito; **on ~** a propósito, adrede; **~ful** *adj* resuelto, determinado

purr [pɜː*] *vi* ronronear

purse [pɜːs] *n* monedero; (*US*) bolsa (*SP*), cartera (*AM*) ♦ *vt* fruncir

pursue [pə'sjuː] *vt* seguir; **~r** *n* perseguidor(a) *m/f*

pursuit [pə'sjuːt] *n* (*chase*) caza; (*occupation*) actividad *f*

push [puʃ] *n* empuje *m*, empujón *m*; (*of button*) presión *f*; (*drive*) empuje *m* ♦ *vt* empujar; (*button*) apretar; (*promote*) promover ♦ *vi* empujar; (*demand*): **to ~ for** luchar por; **~ aside** *vt* apartar con la mano; **~ off** (*inf*) *vi* largarse; **~ on** *vi* seguir adelante; **~ through** *vi* (*crowd*) abrirse paso a empujones ♦ *vt* (*measure*) despachar; ~ **up** vt (total, prices) hacer subir; ~**chair** (BRIT) n sillita de ruedas; ~**er** n (drug ~er) traficante m/f de drogas; ~**over** (inf) n: **it's a ~over** está tirado; ~-**up** (US) n plancha; ~**y** (pej) adj agresivo

puss [pus] (inf) n minino

pussy(-cat) ['pusɪ-] (inf) n = **puss**

put [put] (pt, pp **put**) vt (place) poner, colocar; (~ into) meter; (say) expresar; (a question) hacer; (estimate) estimar; ~ **about** or **around** vt (rumour) diseminar; ~ **across** vt (ideas etc) comunicar; ~ **away** vt (store) guardar; ~ **back** vt (replace) devolver a su lugar; (postpone) aplazar; ~ **by** vt (money) guardar; ~ **down** vt (on ground) poner en el suelo; (animal) sacrificar; (in writing) apuntar; (revolt etc) sofocar; (attribute): **to ~ sth down to** atribuir algo a a; ~ **forward** vt (ideas) presentar, proponer; ~ **in** vt (complaint) presentar; (time) dedicar; ~ **off** vt (postpone) aplazar; (discourage) desanimar; ~ **on** vt ponerse; (light etc) encender; (play etc) presentar; (gain): **to ~ on weight** engordar; (brake) echar; (record, kettle etc) poner; (assume) adoptar; ~ **out** vt (fire, light) apagar; (rubbish etc) sacar; (cat etc) echar; (one's hand) alargar; (inf: person): **to be ~ out** alterarse; ~ **through** vt (TEL) poner; (plan etc) hacer aprobar; ~ **up** vt (raise) levantar, alzar; (hang) colgar; (build) construir; (increase) aumentar; (accommodate) alojar; ~ **up with** vt fus aguantar

putt [pʌt] n putt m, golpe m corto; ~**ing green** n green m; minigolf m

putty ['pʌtɪ] n masilla

put-up ['putʌp] adj: ~ **job** (BRIT) amaño

puzzle ['pʌzl] n rompecabezas m inv; (also: **crossword** ~) crucigrama m; (mystery) misterio ♦ vt dejar perplejo, confundir ♦ vi: **to ~ over sth** devanarse los sesos con algo; **puzzling** adj misterioso, extraño

pyjamas [pɪ'dʒɑːməz] (BRIT) npl pijama m

pylon ['paɪlən] n torre f de conducción eléctrica

pyramid ['pɪrəmɪd] n pirámide f

Pyrenees [pɪrə'niːz] npl: **the ~** los Pirineos

python ['paɪθən] n pitón m

Q, q

quack [kwæk] n graznido; (pej: doctor) curandero/a

quad [kwɒd] n abbr = **quadrangle**; **quadruplet**

quadrangle ['kwɒdrængl] n patio

quadruple [kwɒ'drupl] vt, vi cuadruplicar

quadruplets [kwɔː'druːplɪts] npl cuatrillizos/as

quail [kweɪl] n codorniz f ♦ vi: **to ~ at** or **before** amedrentarse ante

quaint [kweɪnt] adj extraño; (picturesque) pintoresco

quake [kweɪk] vi temblar ♦ n abbr = **earthquake**

Quaker ['kweɪkə*] n cuáquero/a

qualification [kwɒlɪfɪ'keɪʃən] n (ability) capacidad f; (often pl: diploma etc) título; (reservation) salvedad f

qualified ['kwɒlɪfaɪd] adj capacitado; (professionally) titulado; (limited) limitado

qualify ['kwɒlɪfaɪ] vt (make competent) capacitar; (modify) modificar ♦ vi (in competition): **to ~ (for)** calificarse (para); (pass examination(s)): **to ~ (as)** calificarse (de), graduarse (en); (be eligible): **to ~ (for)** reunir los requisitos (para)

quality ['kwɒlɪtɪ] n calidad f; (of person) cualidad f; ~ **time** n tiempo dedicado a la familia y a los amigos

---
quality press
---

i *La expresión* **quality press** *se refiere a los periódicos que dan un tratamiento serio de las noticias, ofreciendo información detallada sobre un amplio espectro de temas y un análisis en profundidad de la actualidad. Por su tamaño, considerablemente mayor que el* *de los periódicos sensacionalistas, se les conoce también como "broadsheets".*

qualm [kwɑːm] *n* escrúpulo
quandary ['kwɒndrɪ] *n*: **to be in a ~** tener dudas
quantity ['kwɒntɪtɪ] *n* cantidad *f*; **in ~** en grandes cantidades; **~ surveyor** *n* aparejador(a) *m/f*
quarantine ['kwɒrntiːn] *n* cuarentena
quarrel ['kwɒrl] *n* riña, pelea ♦ *vi* reñir, pelearse
quarry ['kwɒrɪ] *n* cantera
quart [kwɔːt] *n* ≈ litro
quarter ['kwɔːtə*] *n* cuarto, cuarta parte *f*; (US: *coin*) moneda de 25 centavos; (*of year*) trimestre *m*; (*district*) barrio ♦ *vt* dividir en cuartos; (MIL: *lodge*) alojar; **~s** *npl* (*barracks*) cuartel *m*; (*living ~s*) alojamiento; **a ~ of an hour** un cuarto de hora; **~ final** *n* cuarto de final; **~ly** *adj* trimestral ♦ *adv* cada 3 meses, trimestralmente
quartet(te) [kwɔː'tet] *n* cuarteto
quartz [kwɔːts] *n* cuarzo
quash [kwɒʃ] *vt* (*verdict*) anular
quaver ['kweɪvə*] (BRIT) *n* (MUS) corchea ♦ *vi* temblar
quay [kiː] *n* (*also*: **~side**) muelle *m*
queasy ['kwiːzɪ] *adj*: **to feel ~** tener náuseas
queen [kwiːn] *n* reina; (CARDS etc) dama; **~ mother** *n* reina madre
queer [kwɪə*] *adj* raro, extraño ♦ *n* (*inf: highly offensive*) maricón *m*
quell [kwɛl] *vt* (*feeling*) calmar; (*rebellion etc*) sofocar
quench [kwɛntʃ] *vt*: **to ~ one's thirst** apagar la sed
query ['kwɪərɪ] *n* (*question*) pregunta ♦ *vt* dudar de
quest [kwɛst] *n* busca, búsqueda
question ['kwɛstʃən] *n* pregunta; (*doubt*) duda; (*matter*) asunto, cuestión *f* ♦ *vt* (*doubt*) dudar de; (*interrogate*) interrogar, hacer preguntas a; **beyond ~** fuera de toda duda; **out of the ~** imposible; ni

hablar; **~able** *adj* dudoso; **~ mark** *n* punto de interrogación; **~naire** [-'nɛə*] *n* cuestionario
queue [kjuː] (BRIT) *n* cola ♦ *vi* (*also*: **~ up**) hacer cola
quibble ['kwɪbl] *vi* sutilizar
quick [kwɪk] *adj* rápido; (*agile*) ágil; (*mind*) listo ♦ *n*: **cut to the ~** (*fig*) herido en lo vivo; **be ~!** ¡date prisa!; **~en** *vt* apresurar ♦ *vi* apresurarse, darse prisa; **~ly** *adv* rápidamente, de prisa; **~sand** *n* arenas *fpl* movedizas; **~-witted** *adj* perspicaz
quid [kwɪd] (BRIT: inf) *n inv* libra
quiet ['kwaɪət] *adj* (*voice, music etc*) bajo; (*person, place*) tranquilo; (*ceremony*) íntimo ♦ *n* silencio; (*calm*) tranquilidad *f* ♦ *vt, vi* (US) = **~en**; **~en** (*also*: **~en down**) *vi* calmarse; (*grow silent*) callarse ♦ *vt* calmar; hacer callar; **~ly** *adv* tranquilamente; (*silently*) silenciosamente; **~ness** *n* silencio; tranquilidad *f*
quilt [kwɪlt] *n* edredón *m*
quin [kwɪn] *n abbr* = **quintuplet**
quintet(te) [kwɪn'tet] *n* quinteto
quintuplets [kwɪn'tjuːplɪts] *npl* quintillizos/as
quip [kwɪp] *n* pulla
quirk [kwɜːk] *n* peculiaridad *f*; (*accident*) capricho
quit [kwɪt] (pt, pp **quit** or **quitted**) *vt* dejar, abandonar; (*premises*) desocupar ♦ *vi* (*give up*) renunciar; (*resign*) dimitir
quite [kwaɪt] *adv* (*rather*) bastante; (*entirely*) completamente; **that's not ~ big enough** no acaba de ser lo bastante grande; **~ a few of them** un buen número de ellos; **~ (so)!** ¡así es!, ¡exactamente!
quits [kwɪts] *adj*: **~ (with)** en paz (con); **let's call it ~** dejémoslo en tablas
quiver ['kwɪvə*] *vi* estremecerse
quiz [kwɪz] *n* concurso ♦ *vt* interrogar; **~zical** *adj* burlón(ona)
quota ['kwəʊtə] *n* cuota
quotation [kwəʊ'teɪʃən] *n* cita; (*estimate*) presupuesto; **~ marks** *npl* comillas *fpl*
quote [kwəʊt] *n* cita; (*estimate*)

presupuesto ♦ vt citar; (price) cotizar ♦ vi:
to ~ from citar de; **~s** npl (inverted
commas) comillas fpl

R, r

rabbi ['ræbaɪ] n rabino
rabbit ['ræbɪt] n conejo; **~ hutch** n
conejera
rabble ['ræbl] (pej) n chusma, populacho
rabies ['reɪbiːz] n rabia
RAC (BRIT) n abbr = **Royal Automobile
Club**
rac(c)oon [rə'kuːn] n mapache m
race [reɪs] n carrera; (species) raza ♦ vt
(horse) hacer correr; (engine) acelerar ♦ vi
(compete) competir; (run) correr; (pulse)
latir a ritmo acelerado; **~ car** (US) n
= **racing car**; **~ car driver** (US) n
= **racing driver**; **~course** n hipódromo;
~horse n caballo de carreras; **~track** n
pista; (for cars) autódromo
racial ['reɪʃl] adj racial
racing ['reɪsɪŋ] n carreras fpl; **~ car** (BRIT)
n coche m de carreras; **~ driver** (BRIT) n
corredor(a) m/f de coches
racism ['reɪsɪzəm] n racismo; **racist** [-sɪst]
adj, n racista m/f
rack [ræk] n (also: **luggage ~**) rejilla; (shelf)
estante m; (also: **roof ~**) baca,
portaequipajes m inv; (dish ~)
escurreplatos m inv; (clothes ~) percha
♦ vt atormentar; **to ~ one's brains**
devanarse los sesos
racket ['rækɪt] n (for tennis) raqueta;
(noise) ruido, estrépito; (swindle) estafa,
timo
racquet ['rækɪt] n raqueta
racy ['reɪsɪ] adj picante, salado
radar ['reɪdɑː*] n radar m
radiant ['reɪdɪənt] adj radiante (de
felicidad)
radiate ['reɪdɪeɪt] vt (heat) radiar; (emotion)
irradiar ♦ vi (lines) extenderse
radiation [reɪdɪ'eɪʃən] n radiación f
radiator ['reɪdɪeɪtə*] n radiador m

radical ['rædɪkl] adj radical
radii ['reɪdɪaɪ] npl of **radius**
radio ['reɪdɪəu] n radio f; **on the ~** por
radio
radio... [reɪdɪəu] prefix: **~active** adj
radioactivo; **~graphy** [reɪdɪ'ɔgrəfɪ] n
radiografía; **~logy** [reɪdɪ'ɔlədʒɪ] n
radiología
radio station n emisora
radiotherapy [-'θerəpɪ] n radioterapia
radish ['rædɪʃ] n rábano
radius ['reɪdɪəs] (pl **radii**) n radio
RAF n abbr = **Royal Air Force**
raffle ['ræfl] n rifa, sorteo
raft [rɑːft] n balsa; (also: **life ~**) balsa
salvavidas
rafter ['rɑːftə*] n viga
rag [ræg] n (piece of cloth) trapo; (torn
cloth) harapo; (pej: newspaper)
periodicucho; (for charity) actividades
estudiantiles benéficas; **~s** npl (torn
clothes) harapos mpl; **~ doll** n muñeca
de trapo
rage [reɪdʒ] n rabia, furor m ♦ vi (person)
rabiar, estar furioso; (storm) bramar; **it's
all the ~** (very fashionable) está muy de
moda
ragged ['rægɪd] adj (edge) desigual,
mellado; (appearance) andrajoso,
harapiento
raid [reɪd] n (MIL) incursión f; (criminal)
asalto; (by police) redada ♦ vt invadir,
atacar; asaltar
rail [reɪl] n (on stair) barandilla, pasamanos
m inv; (on bridge, balcony) pretil m; (of
ship) barandilla; (also: **towel ~**) toallero;
~s npl (RAIL) vía; **by ~** por ferrocarril;
~ing(s) n(pl) vallado; **~road** (US) n
= **~way**; **~way** (BRIT) n ferrocarril m, vía
férrea; **~way line** (BRIT) n línea (de
ferrocarril); **~wayman** (BRIT irreg) n
ferroviario; **~way station** (BRIT) n
estación f de ferrocarril
rain [reɪn] n lluvia ♦ vi llover; **in the ~** bajo
la lluvia; **it's ~ing** llueve, está lloviendo;
~bow n arco iris; **~coat** n impermeable
m; **~drop** n gota de lluvia; **~fall** n lluvia;

~forest n selvas fpl tropicales; **~y** adj lluvioso

raise [reɪz] n aumento ♦ vt levantar; (increase) aumentar; (improve: morale) subir; (: standards) mejorar; (doubts) suscitar; (a question) plantear; (cattle, family) criar; (crop) cultivar; (army) reclutar; (loan) obtener; **to ~ one's voice** alzar la voz

raisin ['reɪzn] n pasa de Corinto

rake [reɪk] n (tool) rastrillo; (person) libertino ♦ vt (garden) rastrillar

rally ['rælɪ] n (POL etc) reunión f, mitin m; (AUT) rallye m; (TENNIS) peloteo ♦ vt reunir ♦ vi recuperarse; **~ round** vt fus (fig) dar apoyo a

RAM [ræm] n abbr (= random access memory) RAM f

ram [ræm] n carnero; (also: **battering ~**) ariete m ♦ vt (crash into) dar contra, chocar con; (push: fist etc) empujar con fuerza

ramble ['ræmbl] n caminata, excursión f en el campo ♦ vi (pej: also: **~ on**) divagar; **~r** n excursionista m/f; (BOT) trepadora; **rambling** adj (speech) inconexo; (house) laberíntico; (BOT) trepador/a

ramp [ræmp] n rampa; **on/off ~** (US: AUT) vía de acceso/salida

rampage [ræm'peɪdʒ] n: **to be on the ~** desmandarse ♦ vi: **they went rampaging through the town** recorrieron la ciudad armando alboroto

rampant ['ræmpənt] adj (disease etc): **to be ~** estar extendiéndose mucho

ram raid vt atracar (rompiendo el escaparate con un coche)

ramshackle ['ræmʃækl] adj destartalado

ran [ræn] pt of **run**

ranch [rɑ:ntʃ] n hacienda, estancia; **~er** n ganadero

rancid ['rænsɪd] adj rancio

rancour ['ræŋkə*] (US **rancor**) n rencor m

random ['rændəm] adj fortuito, sin orden; (COMPUT, MATH) aleatorio ♦ n: **at ~** al azar

randy ['rændɪ] (BRIT: inf) adj cachondo

rang [ræŋ] pt of **ring**

range [reɪndʒ] n (of mountains) cadena de montañas, cordillera; (of missile) alcance m; (of voice) registro; (series) serie f; (of products) surtido; (MIL: also: **shooting ~**) campo de tiro; (also: **kitchen ~**) fogón m ♦ vt (place) colocar; (arrange) arreglar ♦ vi: **to ~ over** (extend) extenderse por; **to ~ from ... to ...** oscilar entre ... y ...

ranger [reɪndʒə*] n guardabosques m inv

rank [ræŋk] n (row) fila; (MIL) rango; (status) categoría; (BRIT: also: **taxi ~**) parada de taxis ♦ vi: **to ~ among** figurar entre ♦ adj fétido, rancio; **the ~ and file** (fig) la base

ransack ['rænsæk] vt (search) registrar; (plunder) saquear

ransom ['rænsəm] n rescate m; **to hold to ~** (fig) hacer chantaje a

rant [rænt] vi divagar, desvariar

rap [ræp] vt golpear, dar un golpecito en ♦ n (music) rap m

rape [reɪp] n violación f; (BOT) colza ♦ vt violar; **~ (seed) oil** n aceite m de colza

rapid ['ræpɪd] adj rápido; **~ity** [rə'pɪdɪtɪ] n rapidez f; **~s** npl (GEO) rápidos mpl

rapist ['reɪpɪst] n violador m

rapport [ræ'pɔ:*] n simpatía

rapturous ['ræptʃərəs] adj extático

rare [reə*] adj raro, poco común; (CULIN: steak) poco hecho

rarely ['reəlɪ] adv pocas veces

raring ['reərɪŋ] adj: **to be ~ to go** (inf) tener muchas ganas de empezar

rascal ['rɑ:skl] n pillo, pícaro

rash [ræʃ] adj imprudente, precipitado ♦ n (MED) sarpullido, erupción f (cutánea); (of events) serie f

rasher ['ræʃə*] n lonja

raspberry ['rɑ:zbərɪ] n frambuesa

rasping ['rɑ:spɪŋ] adj: **a ~ noise** un ruido áspero

rat [ræt] n rata

rate [reɪt] n (ratio) razón f; (price) precio; (: of hotel etc) tarifa; (of interest) tipo; (speed) velocidad f ♦ vt (value) tasar; (estimate) estimar; **~s** npl (BRIT: property tax) impuesto municipal; (fees) tarifa; **to ~**

sth/sb as considerar algo/a uno como;
~able value (BRIT) n valor m impuesto;
~payer (BRIT) n contribuyente m/f
rather ['rɑːðə*] adv: **it's ~ expensive** es
algo caro; (too much) es demasiado caro;
(to some extent) más bien; **there's ~ a lot**
hay bastante; **I would** or **I'd ~ go**
preferiría ir; **or ~** mejor dicho
rating ['reɪtɪŋ] n tasación f; (score) índice
m; (of ship) clase f; **~s** npl (RADIO, TV)
niveles mpl de audiencia
ratio ['reɪʃiəu] n razón f; **in the ~ of 100 to
1** a razón de 100 a 1
ration ['ræʃən] n ración f ♦ vt racionar; **~s**
npl víveres mpl
rational ['ræʃənl] adj (solution, reasoning)
lógico, razonable; (person) cuerdo,
sensato; **~e** [-'nɑːl] n razón f
fundamental; **~ize** vt justificar
rat race n lucha incesante por la
supervivencia
rattle ['rætl] n golpeteo; (of train etc)
traqueteo; (for baby) sonaja, sonajero ♦ vi
castañetear; (car, bus): **to ~ along**
traquetear ♦ vt hacer sonar agitando;
~snake n serpiente f de cascabel
raucous ['rɔːkəs] adj estridente, ronco
ravage ['rævɪdʒ] vt hacer estragos en,
destrozar; **~s** npl estragos mpl
rave [reɪv] vi (in anger) encolerizarse; (with
enthusiasm) entusiasmarse; (MED) delirar,
desvariar ♦ n (inf: party) rave m
raven ['reɪvən] n cuervo
ravenous ['rævənəs] adj hambriento
ravine [rə'viːn] n barranco
raving ['reɪvɪŋ] adj: **~ lunatic** loco/a de
atar
ravishing ['rævɪʃɪŋ] adj encantador(a)
raw [rɔː] adj crudo; (not processed) bruto;
(sore) vivo; (inexperienced) novato,
inexperto; **~ deal** (inf) n injusticia; **~
material** n materia prima
ray [reɪ] n rayo; **~ of hope** (rayo de)
esperanza
raze [reɪz] vt arrasar
razor ['reɪzə*] n (open) navaja; (safety ~)
máquina de afeitar; (electric ~) máquina

(eléctrica) de afeitar; **~ blade** n hoja de
afeitar
Rd abbr = **road**
re [riː] prep con referencia a
reach [riːtʃ] n alcance m; (of river etc)
extensión f entre dos recodos ♦ vt
alcanzar, llegar a; (achieve) lograr ♦ vi
extenderse; **within ~** al alcance (de la
mano); **out of ~** fuera del alcance; **~ out**
vt (hand) tender ♦ vi: **to ~ out for sth**
alargar or tender la mano para tomar
algo
react [riː'ækt] vi reaccionar; **~ion** [-'ækʃən]
n reacción f
reactor [riː'æktə*] n (also: **nuclear ~**)
reactor m (nuclear)
read [riːd, pt, pp red] (pt, pp **read**) vi leer
♦ vt leer; (understand) entender; (study)
estudiar; **~ out** vt leer en alta voz; **~able**
adj (writing) legible; (book) leíble; **~er** n
lector(a) m/f; (BRIT: at university)
profesor(a) m/f adjunto/a; **~ership** n (of
paper etc) (número de) lectores mpl
readily ['redɪlɪ] adv (willingly) de buena
gana; (easily) fácilmente; (quickly) en
seguida
readiness ['redɪnɪs] n buena voluntad f;
(preparedness) preparación f; **in ~**
(prepared) listo, preparado
reading ['riːdɪŋ] n lectura; (on instrument)
indicación f
ready ['redɪ] adj listo, preparado; (willing)
dispuesto; (available) disponible ♦ adv:
~-cooked listo para comer ♦ n: **at the ~**
(MIL) listo para tirar; **to get ~** vi
prepararse ♦ vt preparar; **~-made** adj
confeccionado; **~-to-wear** adj
confeccionado
real [rɪəl] adj verdadero, auténtico; **in ~
terms** en términos reales; **~ estate** n
bienes mpl raíces; **~istic** [-'lɪstɪk] adj
realista
reality [riː'ælɪtɪ] n realidad f
realization [rɪəlaɪ'zeɪʃən] n comprensión f;
(fulfilment, COMM) realización f
realize ['rɪəlaɪz] vt (understand) darse
cuenta de

really ['rɪəlɪ] *adv* realmente; (*for emphasis*) verdaderamente; (*actually*): **what ~ happened** lo que pasó en realidad; **~?** ¿de veras?; **~!** (*annoyance*) ¡vamos!, ¡por favor!

realm [rɛlm] *n* reino; (*fig*) esfera

realtor ® ['rɪəltɔ:*] (*US*) *n* corredor(a) *m/f* de bienes raíces

reap [ri:p] *vt* segar; (*fig*) cosechar, recoger

reappear [ri:ə'pɪə*] *vi* reaparecer

rear [rɪə*] *adj* trasero ♦ *n* parte *f* trasera ♦ *vt* (*cattle, family*) criar ♦ *vi* (*also*: **~ up**) (*animal*) encabritarse; **~guard** *n* retaguardia

rearmament [ri:'ɑ:məmənt] *n* rearme *m*

rearrange [ri:ə'reɪndʒ] *vt* ordenar *or* arreglar de nuevo

rear-view mirror *n* (*AUT*) (espejo) retrovisor *m*

reason ['ri:zn] *n* razón *f* ♦ *vi*: **to ~ with sb** tratar de que uno entre en razón; **it stands to ~ that** es lógico que; **~able** *adj* razonable; (*sensible*) sensato; **~ably** *adv* razonablemente; **~ing** *n* razonamiento, argumentos *mpl*

reassurance [ri:ə'ʃuərəns] *n* consuelo

reassure [ri:ə'ʃuə*] *vt* tranquilizar, alentar; **to ~ sb that** tranquilizar a uno asegurando que

rebate ['ri:beɪt] *n* (*on tax etc*) desgravación *f*

rebel [*n* 'rɛbl, *vi* rɪ'bɛl] *n* rebelde *m/f* ♦ *vi* rebelarse, sublevarse; **~lious** [rɪ'bɛljəs] *adj* rebelde; (*child*) revoltoso

rebirth ['ri:bə:θ] *n* renacimiento

rebound [*vi* rɪ'baund, *n* 'ri:baund] *vi* (*ball*) rebotar ♦ *n* rebote *m*; **on the ~** (*also fig*) de rebote

rebuff [rɪ'bʌf] *n* desaire *m*, rechazo

rebuild [ri:'bɪld] (*irreg*) *vt* reconstruir

rebuke [rɪ'bju:k] *n* reprimenda ♦ *vt* reprender

rebut [rɪ'bʌt] *vt* rebatir

recall [*vb* rɪ'kɔ:l, *n* 'ri:kɔl] *vt* (*remember*) recordar; (*ambassador etc*) retirar ♦ *n* recuerdo; retirada

recap ['ri:kæp], **recapitulate**

recapitulate [ri:kə'pɪtjuleɪt] *vt, vi* recapitular

rec'd *abbr* (= *received*) rbdo

recede [rɪ'si:d] *vi* (*memory*) ir borrándose; (*hair*) retroceder; **receding** *adj* (*forehead, chin*) huidizo; **to have a receding hairline** tener entradas

receipt [rɪ'si:t] *n* (*document*) recibo; (*for parcel etc*) acuse *m* de recibo; (*act of receiving*) recepción *f*; **~s** *npl* (*COMM*) ingresos *mpl*

receive [rɪ'si:v] *vt* recibir; (*guest*) acoger; (*wound*) sufrir; **~r** *n* (*TEL*) auricular *m*; (*RADIO*) receptor *m*; (*of stolen goods*) perista *m/f*; (*COMM*) administrador *m* jurídico

recent ['ri:snt] *adj* reciente; **~ly** *adv* recientemente; **~ly arrived** recién llegado

receptacle [rɪ'sɛptɪkl] *n* receptáculo

reception [rɪ'sɛpʃən] *n* recepción *f*; (*welcome*) acogida; **~ desk** *n* recepción *f*; **~ist** *n* recepcionista *m/f*

recess [rɪ'sɛs] *n* (*in room*) hueco; (*for bed*) nicho; (*secret place*) escondrijo; (*POL etc*: *holiday*) clausura

recession [rɪ'sɛʃən] *n* recesión *f*

recipe ['rɛsɪpɪ] *n* receta; (*for disaster, success*) fórmula

recipient [rɪ'sɪpɪənt] *n* recibidor(a) *m/f*; (*of letter*) destinatario/a

recital [rɪ'saɪtl] *n* recital *m*

recite [rɪ'saɪt] *vt* (*poem*) recitar

reckless ['rɛkləs] *adj* temerario, imprudente; (*driving, driver*) peligroso; **~ly** *adv* imprudentemente; de modo peligroso

reckon ['rɛkən] *vt* calcular; (*consider*) considerar; (*think*): **I ~ that ...** me parece que ...; **~ on** *vt fus* contar con; **~ing** *n* cálculo

reclaim [rɪ'kleɪm] *vt* (*land, waste*) recuperar; (*land: from sea*) rescatar; (*demand back*) reclamar

reclamation [rɛklə'meɪʃən] *n* (*of land*) acondicionamiento de tierras

recline [rɪ'klaɪn] *vi* reclinarse; **reclining** *adj* (*seat*) reclinable

recluse [rɪ'klu:s] *n* recluso/a

recognition [rekəg'nɪʃən] n reconocimiento; **transformed beyond ~** irreconocible

recognizable ['rekəgnaɪzəbl] adj: **~ (by)** reconocible (por)

recognize ['rekəgnaɪz] vt: **to ~ (by/as)** reconocer (por/como)

recoil [vi rɪ'kɔɪl, n 'riːkɔɪl] vi (person): **to ~ from doing sth** retraerse de hacer algo ♦ n (of gun) retroceso

recollect [rekə'lekt] vt recordar, acordarse de; **~ion** [-'lekʃən] n recuerdo

recommend [rekə'mend] vt recomendar

reconcile ['rekənsaɪl] vt (two people) reconciliar; (two facts) compaginar; **to ~ o.s. to sth** conformarse a algo

recondition [riːkən'dɪʃən] vt (machine) reacondicionar

reconnoitre [rekə'nɔɪtə*] (US **reconnoiter**) vt, vi (MIL) reconocer

reconsider [riːkən'sɪdə*] vt repensar

reconstruct [riːkən'strʌkt] vt reconstruir

record [n 'rekɔːd, vt rɪ'kɔːd] n (MUS) disco; (of meeting etc) acta; (register) registro, partida; (file) archivo; (also: **criminal ~**) antecedentes mpl; (written) expediente m; (SPORT, COMPUT) récord m ♦ vt registrar; (MUS: song etc) grabar; **in ~ time** en un tiempo récord; **off the ~** adj no oficial ♦ adv confidencialmente; **~ card** n (in file) ficha; **~ed delivery** (BRIT) n (POST) entrega con acuse de recibo; **~er** n (MUS) flauta de pico; **~ holder** n (SPORT) actual poseedor(a) m/f del récord; **~ing** n (MUS) grabación f; **~ player** n tocadiscos m inv

recount [rɪ'kaunt] vt contar

re-count ['riːkaunt] n (POL: of votes) segundo escrutinio

recoup [rɪ'kuːp] vt: **to ~ one's losses** recuperar las pérdidas

recourse [rɪ'kɔːs] n: **to have ~ to** recurrir a

recover [rɪ'kʌvə*] vt recuperar ♦ vi (from illness, shock) recuperarse; **~y** n recuperación f

recreation [rekrɪ'eɪʃən] n recreo; **~al** adj de recreo; **~al drug** droga recreativa

recruit [rɪ'kruːt] n recluta m/f ♦ vt reclutar; (staff) contratar

rectangle ['rektæŋgl] n rectángulo; **rectangular** [-'tæŋgjulə*] adj rectangular

rectify ['rektɪfaɪ] vt rectificar

rector ['rektə*] n (REL) párroco; **~y** n casa del párroco

recuperate [rɪ'kuːpəreɪt] vi reponerse, restablecerse

recur [rɪ'kəː*] vi repetirse; (pain, illness) producirse de nuevo; **~rence** [rɪ'kʌrəns] n repetición f; **~rent** [rɪ'kʌrənt] adj repetido

recycle [riː'saɪkl] vt reciclar

red [red] n rojo ♦ adj rojo; (hair) pelirrojo; (wine) tinto; **to be in the ~** (account) estar en números rojos; (business) tener un saldo negativo; **to give sb the ~ carpet treatment** recibir a uno con todos los honores; **R~ Cross** n Cruz f Roja; **~currant** n grosella roja; **~den** vt enrojecer ♦ vi enrojecerse

redeem [rɪ'diːm] vt redimir; (promises) cumplir; (sth in pawn) desempeñar; (fig, also REL) rescatar; **~ing** adj: **~ing feature** rasgo bueno or favorable

redeploy [riːdɪ'plɔɪ] vt (resources) reorganizar

red: **~-haired** adj pelirrojo; **~-handed** adj: **to be caught ~-handed** cogerse (SP) or pillarse (AM) con las manos en la masa; **~head** n pelirrojo/a; **~ herring** n (fig) pista falsa; **~-hot** adj candente

redirect [riːdaɪ'rekt] vt (mail) reexpedir

red light n: **to go through a ~** (AUT) pasar la luz roja; **red-light district** n barrio chino

redo [riː'duː] (irreg) vt rehacer

redress [rɪ'dres] vt reparar

Red Sea n: **the ~** el mar Rojo

redskin ['redskɪn] n piel roja m/f

red tape n (fig) trámites mpl

reduce [rɪ'djuːs] vt reducir; **to ~ sb to tears** hacer llorar a uno; **to be ~d to begging** no quedarle a uno otro remedio que pedir limosna; **"~ speed now"** (AUT) "reduzca la velocidad"; **at a ~d price** (of

goods) (a precio) rebajado; **reduction**
[rɪ'dʌkʃən] *n* reducción *f*; (*of price*) rebaja;
(*discount*) descuento; (*smaller-scale copy*)
copia reducida
redundancy [rɪ'dʌndənsɪ] *n* (*dismissal*)
despido; (*unemployment*) desempleo
redundant [rɪ'dʌndnt] *adj* (BRIT: *worker*)
parado, sin trabajo; (*detail, object*)
superfluo; **to be made ~** quedar(se) sin
trabajo
reed [riːd] *n* (BOT) junco, caña; (MUS)
lengüeta
reef [riːf] *n* (*at sea*) arrecife *m*
reek [riːk] *vi*: **to ~ (of)** apestar (a)
reel [riːl] *n* carrete *m*, bobina; (*of film*)
rollo; (*dance*) baile *m* escocés ♦ *vt* (*also*: ~
up) devanar; (*also*: ~ **in**) sacar ♦ *vi* (*sway*)
tambalear(se)
ref [rɛf] (*inf*) *n abbr* = **referee**
refectory [rɪ'fɛktərɪ] *n* comedor *m*
refer [rɪ'fəː] *vt* (*send: patient*) referir;
(: *matter*) remitir ♦ *vi*: **to ~** (*allude to*)
referirse a, aludir a; (*apply to*) relacionarse
con; (*consult*) consultar
referee [rɛfə'riː] *n* árbitro; (BRIT: *for job
application*): **to be a ~ for sb**
proporcionar referencias a uno ♦ *vt*
(*match*) arbitrar en
reference ['rɛfrəns] *n* referencia; (*for job
application: letter*) carta de
recomendación; **with ~ to** (COMM: *in
letter*) me remito a; **~ book** *n* libro de
consulta; **~ number** *n* número de
referencia
refill [*vt* riː'fɪl, *n* 'riːfɪl] *vt* rellenar ♦ *n*
repuesto, recambio
refine [rɪ'faɪn] *vt* refinar; **~d** *adj* (*person*)
fino; **~ment** *n* cultura, educación *f*; (*of
system*) refinamiento
reflect [rɪ'flɛkt] *vt* reflejar ♦ *vi* (*think*)
reflexionar, pensar; **it ~s badly/well on
him** le perjudica/le hace honor; **~ion**
[-'flɛkʃən] *n* (*act*) reflexión *f*; (*image*)
reflejo; (*criticism*) crítica; **on ~ion**
pensándolo bien; **~or** *n* (AUT) captafaros
m inv; (*of light, heat*) reflector *m*
reflex ['riːflɛks] *adj, n* reflejo; **~ive**

[rɪ'flɛksɪv] *adj* (LING) reflexivo
reform [rɪ'fɔːm] *n* reforma ♦ *vt* reformar;
~atory (US) *n* reformatorio
refrain [rɪ'freɪn] *vi*: **to ~ from doing**
abstenerse de hacer ♦ *n* estribillo
refresh [rɪ'frɛʃ] *vt* refrescar; **~er course**
(BRIT) *n* curso de repaso; **~ing** *adj*
refrescante; **~ments** *npl* refrescos *mpl*
refrigerator [rɪ'frɪdʒəreɪtə*] *n* nevera (SP),
refrigeradora (AM)
refuel [riː'fjuəl] *vi* repostar (combustible)
refuge ['rɛfjuːdʒ] *n* refugio, asilo; **to take ~
in** refugiarse en
refugee [rɛfju'dʒiː] *n* refugiado/a
refund [*n* 'riːfʌnd, *vb* rɪ'fʌnd] *n* reembolso
♦ *vt* devolver, reembolsar
refurbish [riː'fəːbɪʃ] *vt* restaurar, renovar
refusal [rɪ'fjuːzəl] *n* negativa; **to have first
~** tener la primera opción a
refuse[1] ['rɛfjuːs] *n* basura; **~ collection**
n recolección *f* de basuras
refuse[2] [rɪ'fjuːz] *vt* rechazar; (*invitation*)
declinar; (*permission*) denegar ♦ *vi*: **to ~
to do sth** negarse a hacer algo; (*horse*)
rehusar
regain [rɪ'geɪn] *vt* recobrar, recuperar
regal ['riːgl] *adj* regio, real
regard [rɪ'gɑːd] *n* mirada; (*esteem*)
respeto; (*attention*) consideración *f* ♦ *vt*
(*consider*) considerar; **to give one's ~s to**
saludar de su parte a; **"with kindest ~s"**
"con muchos recuerdos"; **~ing, as ~s,
with ~ to** con respecto a, en cuanto a;
~less *adv* a pesar de todo; **~less of** sin
reparar en
régime [reɪ'ʒiːm] *n* régimen *m*
regiment ['rɛdʒɪmənt] *n* regimiento; **~al**
[-'mɛntl] *adj* militar
region ['riːdʒən] *n* región *f*; **in the ~ of**
(*fig*) alrededor de; **~al** *adj* regional
register ['rɛdʒɪstə*] *n* registro ♦ *vt*
registrar; (*birth*) declarar; (*car*) matricular;
(*letter*) certificar; (*subj: instrument*)
marcar, indicar ♦ *vi* (*at hotel*) registrarse;
(*as student*) matricularse; (*make
impression*) producir impresión; **~ed** *adj*
(*letter, parcel*) certificado; **~ed**

trademark *n* marca registrada

registrar ['redʒɪstraː*] *n* secretario/a (del registro civil)

registration [redʒɪs'treɪʃən] *n* (*act*) declaración *f*; (*AUT: also:* ~ **number**) matrícula

registry ['redʒɪstrɪ] *n* registro; ~ **office** (*BRIT*) *n* registro civil; **to get married in a ~ office** casarse por lo civil

regret [rɪ'gret] *n* sentimiento, pesar *m* ♦ *vt* sentir, lamentar; ~**fully** *adv* con pesar; ~**table** *adj* lamentable

regular ['regjulə*] *adj* regular; (*soldier*) profesional; (*usual*) habitual; (: *doctor*) de cabecera ♦ *n* (*client etc*) cliente/a *m/f*; ~**ly** *adv* con regularidad; (*often*) repetidas veces

regulate ['regjuleɪt] *vt* controlar; **regulation** [-'leɪʃən] *n* (*rule*) regla, reglamento

rehearsal [rɪ'həːsəl] *n* ensayo

rehearse [rɪ'həːs] *vt* ensayar

reign [reɪn] *n* reinado; (*fig*) predominio ♦ *vi* reinar; (*fig*) imperar

reimburse [riːɪm'bəːs] *vt* reembolsar

rein [reɪn] *n* (*for horse*) rienda

reindeer ['reɪndɪə*] *n inv* reno

reinforce [riːɪn'fɔːs] *vt* reforzar; ~**d concrete** *n* hormigón *m* armado; ~**ments** *npl* (*MIL*) refuerzos *mpl*

reinstate [riːɪn'steɪt] *vt* reintegrar; (*tax, law*) reinstaurar

reiterate [riː'ɪtəreɪt] *vt* reiterar, repetir

reject [n 'riːdʒekt, vb rɪ'dʒekt] *n* (*thing*) desecho ♦ *vt* rechazar; (*suggestion*) descartar; (*coin*) expulsar; ~**ion** [rɪ'dʒekʃən] *n* rechazo

rejoice [rɪ'dʒɔɪs] *vi*: **to ~ at** *or* **over** regocijarse *or* alegrarse de

rejuvenate [rɪ'dʒuːvəneɪt] *vt* rejuvenecer

relapse [rɪ'læps] *n* recaída

relate [rɪ'leɪt] *vt* (*tell*) contar, relatar; (*connect*) relacionar ♦ *vi* relacionarse; ~**d** *adj* afín; (*person*) emparentado; ~**d to** (*subject*) relacionado con; **relating to** *prep* referente a

relation [rɪ'leɪʃən] *n* (*person*) familiar *m/f*,

pariente/a *m/f*; (*link*) relación *f*; ~**s** *npl* (*relatives*) familiares *mpl*; ~**ship** *n* relación *f*; (*personal*) relaciones *fpl*; (*also:* **family ~ship**) parentesco

relative ['relətɪv] *n* pariente/a *m/f*, familiar *m/f* ♦ *adj* relativo; ~**ly** *adv* (*comparatively*) relativamente

relax [rɪ'læks] *vi* descansar; (*unwind*) relajarse ♦ *vt* (*one's grip*) soltar, aflojar; (*control*) relajar; (*mind, person*) descansar; ~**ation** [riːlæk'seɪʃən] *n* descanso; (*of rule, control*) relajamiento; (*entertainment*) diversión *f*; ~**ed** *adj* relajado; (*tranquil*) tranquilo; ~**ing** *adj* relajante

relay ['riːleɪ] *n* (*race*) carrera de relevos ♦ *vt* (*RADIO, TV*) retransmitir

release [rɪ'liːs] *n* (*liberation*) liberación *f*; (*from prison*) puesta en libertad; (*of gas etc*) escape *m*; (*of film etc*) estreno; (*of record*) lanzamiento ♦ *vt* (*prisoner*) poner en libertad; (*gas*) despedir, arrojar; (*from wreckage*) soltar; (*catch, spring etc*) desenganchar; (*film*) estrenar; (*book*) publicar; (*news*) difundir

relegate ['relɪgeɪt] *vt* relegar; (*BRIT: SPORT*): **to be ~d to** bajar a

relent [rɪ'lent] *vi* ablandarse; ~**less** *adj* implacable

relevant ['reləvənt] *adj* (*fact*) pertinente; ~ **to** relacionado con

reliable [rɪ'laɪəbl] *adj* (*person, firm*) de confianza, de fiar; (*method, machine*) seguro; (*source*) fidedigno; **reliably** *adv*: **to be reliably informed that ...** saber de fuente fidedigna que ...

reliance [rɪ'laɪəns] *n*: ~ **(on)** dependencia (de)

relic ['relɪk] *n* (*REL*) reliquia; (*of the past*) vestigio

relief [rɪ'liːf] *n* (*from pain, anxiety*) alivio; (*help, supplies*) socorro, ayuda; (*ART, GEO*) relieve *m*

relieve [rɪ'liːv] *vt* (*pain*) aliviar; (*bring help to*) ayudar, socorrer; (*take over from*) sustituir; (: *guard*) relevar; **to ~ sb of sth** quitar algo a uno; **to ~ o.s.** hacer sus necesidades

religion [rɪˈlɪdʒən] n religión f; **religious** adj religioso

relinquish [rɪˈlɪŋkwɪʃ] vt abandonar; (plan, habit) renunciar a

relish [ˈrɛlɪʃ] n (CULIN) salsa; (enjoyment) entusiasmo ♦ vt (food etc) saborear; (enjoy): **to ~ sth** hacerle mucha ilusión a uno algo

relocate [riːləʊˈkeɪt] vt cambiar de lugar, mudar ♦ vi mudarse

reluctance [rɪˈlʌktəns] n renuencia

reluctant [rɪˈlʌktənt] adj renuente; **~ly** adv de mala gana

rely on [rɪˈlaɪ-] vt fus depender de; (trust) contar con

remain [rɪˈmeɪn] vi (survive) quedar; (be left) sobrar; (continue) quedar(se), permanecer; **~der** n resto; **~ing** adj que queda(n); (surviving) restante(s); **~s** npl restos mpl

remand [rɪˈmɑːnd] n: **on ~** detenido (bajo custodia) ♦ vt: **to be ~ed in custody** quedar detenido bajo custodia; **~ home** (BRIT) n reformatorio

remark [rɪˈmɑːk] n comentario ♦ vt comentar; **~able** adj (outstanding) extraordinario

remarry [riːˈmærɪ] vi volver a casarse

remedial [rɪˈmiːdɪəl] adj de recuperación

remedy [ˈrɛmədɪ] n remedio ♦ vt remediar, curar

remember [rɪˈmɛmbə*] vt recordar, acordarse de; (bear in mind) tener presente; (send greetings to): **~ me to him** dale recuerdos de mi parte; **remembrance** n recuerdo; **R~ Day** n ≈ día en el que se recuerda a los caídos en las dos guerras mundiales

---
Remembrance Day

ⓘ En el Reino Unido el domingo más próximo al 11 de noviembre se conoce como **Remembrance Sunday** o **Remembrance Day**, aniversario de la firma del armisticio de 1918 que puso fin a la Primera Guerra Mundial. Ese día, a las once de la mañana (hora en que se firmó el armisticio), se recuerda a los que murieron en las dos guerras mundiales con dos minutos de silencio ante los monumentos a los caídos. Allí se colocan coronas de amapolas, flor que también se suele llevar prendida en el pecho tras pagar un donativo destinado a los inválidos de guerra.

---

remind [rɪˈmaɪnd] vt: **to ~ sb to do sth** recordar a uno que haga algo; **to ~ sb of sth** (of fact) recordar algo a uno; **she ~s me of her mother** me recuerda a su madre; **~er** n notificación f; (memento) recuerdo

reminisce [rɛmɪˈnɪs] vi recordar (viejas historias); **reminiscent** adj: **to be reminiscent of sth** recordar algo

remiss [rɪˈmɪs] adj descuidado; **it was ~ of him** fue un descuido de su parte

remission [rɪˈmɪʃən] n remisión f; (of prison sentence) disminución f de pena; (REL) perdón m

remit [rɪˈmɪt] vt (send: money) remitir, enviar; **~tance** n remesa, envío

remnant [ˈrɛmnənt] n resto; (of cloth) retal m; **~s** npl (COMM) restos mpl de serie

remorse [rɪˈmɔːs] n remordimientos mpl; **~ful** adj arrepentido; **~less** adj (fig) implacable, inexorable

remote [rɪˈməʊt] adj (distant) lejano; (person) distante; **~ control** n telecontrol m; **~ly** adv remotamente; (slightly) levemente

remould [ˈriːməʊld] (BRIT) n (tyre) neumático or llanta (AM) recauchutado/a

removable [rɪˈmuːvəbl] adj (detachable) separable

removal [rɪˈmuːvəl] n (taking away) el quitar; (BRIT: from house) mudanza; (from office: dismissal) destitución f; (MED) extirpación f; **~ van** (BRIT) n camión m de mudanzas

remove [rɪˈmuːv] vt quitar; (employee) destituir; (name: from list) tachar, borrar; (doubt) disipar; (abuse) suprimir, acabar con; (MED) extirpar

Renaissance [rɪ'neɪsãns] *n*: **the ~** el Renacimiento

render ['rendə*] *vt* (*thanks*) dar; (*aid*) proporcionar, prestar; (*make*): **to ~ sth useless** hacer algo inútil; **~ing** *n* (*MUS etc*) interpretación *f*

rendezvous ['rɒndɪvuː] *n* cita

renew [rɪ'njuː] *vt* renovar; (*resume*) reanudar; (*loan etc*) prorrogar; **~able** *adj* renovable; **~al** *n* reanudación *f*; prórroga

renounce [rɪ'nauns] *vt* renunciar a; (*right, inheritance*) renunciar

renovate ['renəveɪt] *vt* renovar

renown [rɪ'naun] *n* renombre *m*; **~ed** *adj* renombrado

rent [rent] *n* (*for house*) arriendo, renta ♦ *vt* alquilar; **~al** *n* (*for television, car*) alquiler *m*

rep [rep] *n abbr* = **representative; repertory**

repair [rɪ'peə*] *n* reparación *f*, compostura ♦ *vt* reparar, componer; (*shoes*) remendar; **in good/bad ~** en buen/mal estado; **~ kit** *n* caja de herramientas

repatriate [riː'pætrɪeɪt] *vt* repatriar

repay [riː'peɪ] (*irreg*) *vt* (*money*) devolver, reembolsar; (*person*) pagar; (*debt*) liquidar; (*sb's efforts*) devolver, corresponder a; **~ment** *n* reembolso, devolución *f*; (*sum of money*) recompensa

repeal [rɪ'piːl] *n* revocación *f* ♦ *vt* revocar

repeat [rɪ'piːt] *n* (*RADIO, TV*) reposición *f* ♦ *vt* repetir ♦ *vi* repetirse; **~edly** *adv* repetidas veces

repel [rɪ'pel] *vt* (*drive away*) rechazar; (*disgust*) repugnar; **~lent** *adj* repugnante ♦ *n*: **insect ~lent** crema (*or* loción *f*) anti-insectos

repent [rɪ'pent] *vi*: **to ~ (of)** arrepentirse (de); **~ance** *n* arrepentimiento

repercussions [riːpə'kʌʃənz] *npl* consecuencias *fpl*

repertory ['repətərɪ] *n* (*also*: **~ theatre**) teatro de repertorio

repetition [repɪ'tɪʃən] *n* repetición *f*

repetitive [rɪ'petɪtɪv] *adj* repetitivo

replace [rɪ'pleɪs] *vt* (*put back*) devolver a su sitio; (*take the place of*) reemplazar, sustituir; **~ment** *n* (*act*) reposición *f*; (*thing*) recambio; (*person*) suplente *m/f*

replay ['riːpleɪ] *n* (*SPORT*) desempate *m*; (*of tape, film*) repetición *f*

replenish [rɪ'plenɪʃ] *vt* rellenar; (*stock etc*) reponer

replica ['replɪkə] *n* copia, reproducción *f* (exacta)

reply [rɪ'plaɪ] *n* respuesta, contestación *f* ♦ *vi* contestar, responder

report [rɪ'pɔːt] *n* informe *m*; (*PRESS etc*) reportaje *m*; (*BRIT: also*: **school ~**) boletín *m* escolar; (*of gun*) estallido ♦ *vt* informar de; (*PRESS etc*) hacer un reportaje sobre; (*notify: accident, culprit*) denunciar ♦ *vi* (*make a report*) presentar un informe; (*present o.s.*): **to ~ (to sb)** presentarse (ante uno); **~ card** *n* (*US, Scottish*) cartilla escolar; **~edly** *adv* según se dice; **~er** *n* periodista *m/f*

repose [rɪ'pəuz] *n*: **in ~** (*face, mouth*) en reposo

reprehensible [reprɪ'hensɪbl] *adj* reprensible, censurable

represent [reprɪ'zent] *vt* representar; (*COMM*) ser agente de; (*describe*): **to ~ sth as** describir algo como; **~ation** [-'teɪʃən] *n* representación *f*; **~ations** *npl* (*protest*) quejas *fpl*; **~ative** *n* representante *m/f*; (*US: POL*) diputado/a *m/f* ♦ *adj* representativo

repress [rɪ'pres] *vt* reprimir; **~ion** [-'preʃən] *n* represión *f*

reprieve [rɪ'priːv] *n* (*LAW*) indulto; (*fig*) alivio

reprisals [rɪ'praɪzlz] *npl* represalias *fpl*

reproach [rɪ'prəutʃ] *n* reproche *m* ♦ *vt*: **to ~ sb for sth** reprochar algo a uno; **~ful** *adj* de reproche, de acusación

reproduce [riːprə'djuːs] *vt* reproducir ♦ *vi* reproducirse; **reproduction** [-'dʌkʃən] *n* reproducción *f*

reprove [rɪ'pruːv] *vt*: **to ~ sb for sth** reprochar algo a uno

reptile ['reptaɪl] *n* reptil *m*

republic [rɪ'pʌblɪk] *n* república; **~an** *adj*,

n republicano/a *m/f*

repudiate [rɪ'pjuːdɪeɪt] *vt* rechazar; (*violence etc*) repudiar

repulsive [rɪ'pʌlsɪv] *adj* repulsivo

reputable ['repjutəbl] *adj* (*make etc*) de renombre

reputation [repju'teɪʃən] *n* reputación *f*

reputed [rɪ'pjuːtɪd] *adj* supuesto; ~ly *adv* según dicen *or* se dice

request [rɪ'kwest] *n* petición *f*; (*formal*) solicitud *f* ♦ *vt*: **to ~ sth of** *or* **from sb** solicitar algo a uno; ~ **stop** (*BRIT*) *n* parada discrecional

require [rɪ'kwaɪə*] *vt* (*need: subj: person*) necesitar, tener necesidad de; (: *thing, situation*) (*want*) pedir; **to ~ sb to do sth** pedir a uno que haga algo; ~ment *n* requisito; (*need*) necesidad *f*

requisition [rekwɪ'zɪʃən] *n*: ~ **(for)** solicitud *f* (de) ♦ *vt* (*MIL*) requisar

rescue ['reskjuː] *n* rescate *m* ♦ *vt* rescatar; ~ **party** *n* expedición *f* de salvamento; ~r *n* salvador(a) *m/f*

research [rɪ'sɜːtʃ] *n* investigaciones *fpl* ♦ *vt* investigar; ~er *n* investigador(a) *m/f*

resemblance [rɪ'zembləns] *n* parecido

resemble [rɪ'zembl] *vt* parecerse a

resent [rɪ'zent] *vt* tomar a mal; ~ful *adj* resentido; ~ment *n* resentimiento

reservation [rezə'veɪʃən] *n* reserva

reserve [rɪ'zɜːv] *n* reserva; (*SPORT*) suplente *m/f* ♦ *vt* (*seats etc*) reservar; ~s *npl* (*MIL*) reserva; **in** ~ de reserva; ~d *adj* reservado

reshuffle [riː'ʃʌfl] *n*: **Cabinet** ~ (*POL*) remodelación *f* del gabinete

residence ['rezɪdəns] *n* (*formal: home*) domicilio; (*length of stay*) permanencia; ~ **permit** (*BRIT*) *n* permiso de permanencia

resident ['rezɪdənt] *n* (*of area*) vecino/a; (*in hotel*) huésped(a) *m/f* ♦ *adj* (*population*) permanente; (*doctor*) residente; ~ial [-'denʃəl] *adj* residencial

residue ['rezɪdjuː] *n* resto

resign [rɪ'zaɪn] *vt* renunciar a ♦ *vi* dimitir; **to ~ o.s. to** (*situation*) resignarse a; ~ation [rezɪg'neɪʃən] *n* dimisión *f*; (*state of*

mind) resignación *f*; ~ed *adj* resignado

resilient [rɪ'zɪlɪənt] *adj* (*material*) elástico; (*person*) resistente

resist [rɪ'zɪst] *vt* resistir, oponerse a; ~ance *n* resistencia

resolute ['rezəluːt] *adj* resuelto; (*refusal*) tajante

resolution [rezə'luːʃən] *n* (*gen*) resolución *f*

resolve [rɪ'zɒlv] *n* resolución *f* ♦ *vt* resolver ♦ *vi*: **to ~ to do** resolver hacer; ~d *adj* resuelto

resort [rɪ'zɔːt] *n* (*town*) centro turístico; (*recourse*) recurso ♦ *vi*: **to ~ to** recurrir a; **in the last** ~ como último recurso

resounding [rɪ'zaundɪŋ] *adj* sonoro; (*fig*) clamoroso

resource [rɪ'sɔːs] *n* recurso; ~s *npl* recursos *mpl*; ~ful *adj* despabilado, ingenioso

respect [rɪs'pekt] *n* respeto ♦ *vt* respetar; ~s *npl* recuerdos *mpl*, saludos *mpl*; **with ~ to** con respecto a; **in this** ~ en cuanto a eso; ~able *adj* respetable; (*large: amount*) apreciable; (*passable*) tolerable; ~ful *adj* respetuoso

respective [rɪs'pektɪv] *adj* respectivo; ~ly *adv* respectivamente

respite ['respaɪt] *n* respiro

respond [rɪs'pɒnd] *vi* responder; (*react*) reaccionar; **response** [-'pɒns] *n* respuesta; reacción *f*

responsibility [rɪspɒnsɪ'bɪlɪtɪ] *n* responsabilidad *f*

responsible [rɪs'pɒnsɪbl] *adj* (*character*) serio, formal; (*job*) de confianza; (*liable*): ~ **(for)** responsable (de)

responsive [rɪs'pɒnsɪv] *adj* sensible

rest [rest] *n* descanso, reposo; (*MUS, pause*) pausa, silencio; (*support*) apoyo; (*remainder*) resto ♦ *vi* descansar; (*be supported*): **to ~ on** descansar sobre ♦ *vt* (*lean*): **to ~ sth on/against** apoyar algo en *or* sobre/contra; **the ~ of them** (*people, objects*) los demás; **it ~s with him to ...** depende de él el que ...

restaurant ['restərən] *n* restaurante *m*; ~

car (BRIT) n (RAIL) coche-comedor m
restful ['restful] *adj* descansado, tranquilo
rest home n residencia para jubilados
restive ['restɪv] *adj* inquieto; (*horse*) rebelón(ona)
restless ['restlɪs] *adj* inquieto
restoration [restə'reɪʃən] n restauración f; devolución f
restore [rɪ'stɔ:*] *vt* (*building*) restaurar; (*sth stolen*) devolver; (*health*) restablecer; (*to power*) volver a poner a
restrain [rɪs'treɪn] *vt* (*feeling*) contener, refrenar; (*person*): **to ~ (from doing)** disuadir (de hacer); **~ed** *adj* reservado; **~t** n (*restriction*) restricción f; (*moderation*) moderación f; (*of manner*) reserva
restrict [rɪs'trɪkt] *vt* restringir, limitar; **~ion** [-kʃən] n restricción f, limitación f; **~ive** *adj* restrictivo
rest room n (US) n aseos mpl
result [rɪ'zʌlt] n resultado ♦ *vi*: **to ~ in** terminar, tener por resultado; **as a ~ of** a consecuencia de
resume [rɪ'zju:m] *vt* reanudar ♦ *vi* comenzar de nuevo
résumé ['reɪzju:meɪ] n resumen m; (US) currículum m
resumption [rɪ'zʌmpʃən] n reanudación f
resurgence [rɪ'sə:dʒəns] n resurgimiento m
resurrection [rezə'rekʃən] n resurrección f
resuscitate [rɪ'sʌsɪteɪt] *vt* (MED) resucitar
retail [rɪ'teɪl] *adj, adv* al por menor; **~er** n detallista m/f; **~ price** n precio de venta al público
retain [rɪ'teɪn] *vt* (*keep*) retener, conservar; **~er** n (*fee*) anticipo
retaliate [rɪ'tælɪeɪt] *vi*: **to ~ (against)** tomar represalias (contra); **retaliation** [-'eɪʃən] n represalias fpl
retarded [rɪ'tɑ:dɪd] *adj* retrasado
retch [retʃ] *vi* dársele a uno arcadas
retentive [rɪ'tentɪv] *adj* (*memory*) retentivo
retire [rɪ'taɪə*] *vi* (*give up work*) jubilarse; (*withdraw*) retirarse; (*go to bed*) acostarse; **~d** *adj* (*person*) jubilado; **~ment** n (*giving up work: state*) retiro; (: *act*) jubilación f; **retiring** *adj* (*leaving*)

saliente; (*shy*) retraído
retort [rɪ'tɔ:t] *vi* contestar
retrace [ri:'treɪs] *vt*: **to ~ one's steps** volver sobre sus pasos, desandar lo andado
retract [rɪ'trækt] *vt* (*statement*) retirar; (*claws*) retraer; (*undercarriage, aerial*) replegar
retrain [ri:'treɪn] *vt* reciclar; **~ing** n readaptación f profesional
retread ['ri:tred] n neumático (SP) or llanta (AM) recauchutado/a
retreat [rɪ'tri:t] n (*place*) retiro; (MIL) retirada ♦ *vi* retirarse
retribution [retrɪ'bju:ʃən] n desquite m
retrieval [rɪ'tri:vəl] n recuperación f
retrieve [rɪ'tri:v] *vt* recobrar; (*situation, honour*) salvar; (COMPUT) recuperar; (*error*) reparar; **~r** n perro cobrador
retrospect ['retrəspekt] n: **in ~** retrospectivamente; **~ive** [-'spektɪv] *adj* retrospectivo; (*law*) retroactivo
return [rɪ'tə:n] n (*going or coming back*) vuelta, regreso; (*of sth stolen etc*) devolución f; (FINANCE: *from land, shares*) ganancia, ingresos mpl ♦ *cpd* (*journey*) de regreso; (BRIT: *ticket*) de ida y vuelta; (*match*) de vuelta ♦ *vi* (*person etc: come or go back*) volver, regresar; (*symptoms etc*) reaparecer; (*regain*): **to ~ to** recuperar ♦ *vt* devolver; (*favour, love etc*) corresponder a; (*verdict*) pronunciar; (POL: *candidate*) elegir; **~s** npl (COMM) ingresos mpl; **in ~ (for)** a cambio (de); **by ~ of post** a vuelta de correo; **many happy ~s (of the day)!** ¡feliz cumpleaños!
reunion [ri:'ju:nɪən] n (*of family*) reunión f; (*of two people, school*) reencuentro
reunite [ri:ju:'naɪt] *vt* reunir; (*reconcile*) reconciliar
rev [rev] (AUT) n abbr (= revolution) revolución f ♦ *vt* (*also*: **~ up**) acelerar
reveal [rɪ'vi:l] *vt* revelar; **~ing** *adj* revelador(a)
revel ['revl] *vi*: **to ~ in sth/in doing sth** gozar de algo/con hacer algo
revenge [rɪ'vendʒ] n venganza; **to take ~**

on vengarse de

revenue ['revənjuː] *n* ingresos *mpl*, rentas *fpl*

reverberate [rɪ'vɜːbəreɪt] *vi* (*sound*) resonar, retumbar; (*fig: shock*) repercutir

reverence ['revərəns] *n* reverencia

Reverend ['revərənd] *adj* (*in titles*): **the ~ John Smith** (*Anglican*) el Reverendo John Smith; (*Catholic*) el Padre John Smith; (*Protestant*) el Pastor John Smith

reversal [rɪ'vɜːsl] *n* (*of order*) inversión *f*; (*of direction, policy*) cambio; (*of decision*) revocación *f*

reverse [rɪ'vɜːs] *n* (*opposite*) contrario; (*back: of cloth*) revés *m*; (: *of coin*) reverso; (: *of paper*) dorso; (*AUT: also:* **~ gear**) marcha atrás; (*setback*) revés *m* ♦ *adj* (*order*) inverso; (*direction*) contrario; (*process*) opuesto ♦ *vt* (*decision, AUT*) dar marcha atrás a; (*position, function*) invertir ♦ *vi* (*BRIT: AUT*) dar marcha atrás; **~-charge call** (*BRIT*) *n* llamada a cobro revertido; **reversing lights** (*BRIT*) *npl* (*AUT*) luces *fpl* de retroceso

revert [rɪ'vɜːt] *vi*: **to ~ to** volver a

review [rɪ'vjuː] *n* (*magazine, MIL*) revista; (*of book, film*) reseña; (*US: examination*) repaso, examen *m* ♦ *vt* repasar, examinar; (*MIL*) pasar revista a; (*book, film*) reseñar; **~er** *n* crítico/a

revise [rɪ'vaɪz] *vt* (*manuscript*) corregir; (*opinion*) modificar; (*price, procedure*) revisar ♦ *vi* (*study*) repasar; **revision** [rɪ'vɪʒən] *n* corrección *f*; modificación *f*; (*for exam*) repaso

revival [rɪ'vaɪvl] *n* (*recovery*) reanimación *f*; (*of interest*) renacimiento; (*THEATRE*) reestreno; (*of faith*) despertar *m*

revive [rɪ'vaɪv] *vt* resucitar; (*custom*) restablecer; (*hope*) despertar; (*play*) reestrenar ♦ *vi* (*person*) volver en sí; (*business*) reactivar

revolt [rɪ'vəult] *n* rebelión *f* ♦ *vi* rebelarse, sublevarse ♦ *vt* dar asco a, repugnar; **~ing** *adj* asqueroso, repugnante

revolution [revə'luːʃən] *n* revolución *f*; **~ary** *adj, n* revolucionario/a *m/f*; **~ize** *vt*

revolucionar

revolve [rɪ'vɔlv] *vi* dar vueltas, girar; (*life, discussion*): **to ~ (a)round** girar en torno a

revolver [rɪ'vɔlvə*] *n* revólver *m*

revolving [rɪ'vɔlvɪŋ] *adj* (*chair, door etc*) giratorio

revue [rɪ'vjuː] *n* (*THEATRE*) revista

revulsion [rɪ'vʌlʃən] *n* asco, repugnancia

reward [rɪ'wɔːd] *n* premio, recompensa ♦ *vt*: **to ~ (for)** recompensar *or* premiar (por); **~ing** *adj* (*fig*) valioso

rewind [riː'waɪnd] (*irreg*) *vt* rebobinar

rewire [riː'waɪə*] *vt* (*house*) renovar la instalación eléctrica de

rheumatism ['ruːmətɪzəm] *n* reumatismo, reúma *m*

Rhine [raɪn] *n*: **the ~** el (río) Rin

rhinoceros [raɪ'nɔsərəs] *n* rinoceronte *m*

rhododendron [rəudə'dɛndrn] *n* rododendro

Rhone [rəun] *n*: **the ~** el (río) Ródano

rhubarb ['ruːbɑːb] *n* ruibarbo

rhyme [raɪm] *n* rima; (*verse*) poesía

rhythm ['rɪðm] *n* ritmo

rib [rɪb] *n* (*ANAT*) costilla ♦ *vt* (*mock*) tomar el pelo a

ribbon ['rɪbən] *n* cinta; **in ~s** (*torn*) hecho trizas

rice [raɪs] *n* arroz *m*; **~ pudding** *n* arroz *m* con leche

rich [rɪtʃ] *adj* rico; (*soil*) fértil; (*food*) pesado; (: *sweet*) empalagoso; (*abundant*): **~ in** (*minerals etc*) rico en; **the ~** *npl* los ricos; **~es** *npl* riqueza; **~ly** *adv* ricamente; (*deserved, earned*) bien

rickets ['rɪkɪts] *n* raquitismo

rid [rɪd] (*pt, pp* **rid**) *vt*: **to ~ sb of sth** librar a uno de algo; **to get ~ of** deshacerse *or* desembarazarse de

ridden ['rɪdn] *pp of* **ride**

riddle ['rɪdl] *n* (*puzzle*) acertijo; (*mystery*) enigma *m*, misterio ♦ *vt*: **to be ~d with** ser lleno *or* plagado de

ride [raɪd] (*pt* **rode**, *pp* **ridden**) *n* paseo; (*distance covered*) viaje *m*, recorrido ♦ *vi* (*as sport*) montar; (*go somewhere: on horse, bicycle*) dar un paseo, pasearse;

(*travel: on bicycle, motorcycle, bus*) viajar ♦ *vt* (*a horse*) montar a; (*a bicycle, motorcycle*) andar en; (*distance*) recorrer; **to take sb for a ~** (*fig*) engañar a uno; **~r** *n* (*on horse*) jinete/a *m/f*; (*on bicycle*) ciclista *m/f*; (*on motorcycle*) motociclista *m/f*

ridge [rɪdʒ] *n* (*of hill*) cresta; (*of roof*) caballete *m*; (*wrinkle*) arruga

ridicule ['rɪdɪkjuːl] *n* irrisión *f*, burla ♦ *vt* poner en ridículo, burlarse de; **ridiculous** [-'dɪkjuləs] *adj* ridículo

riding ['raɪdɪŋ] *n* equitación *f*; **I like ~** me gusta montar a caballo; **~ school** *n* escuela de equitación

rife [raɪf] *adj*: **to be ~** ser muy común; **to be ~ with** abundar en

riffraff ['rɪfræf] *n* gentuza

rifle ['raɪfl] *n* rifle *m*, fusil *m* ♦ *vt* saquear; **~ through** (*papers*) registrar; **~ range** *n* campo de tiro; (*at fair*) tiro al blanco

rift [rɪft] *n* (*in clouds*) claro; (*fig: disagreement*) desavenencia

rig [rɪg] *n* (*also*: **oil ~**: *at sea*) plataforma petrolera ♦ *vt* (*election etc*) amañar; **~ out** (*BRIT*) *vt* disfrazar; **~ up** *vt* improvisar; **~ging** *n* (*NAUT*) aparejo

right [raɪt] *adj* (*correct*) correcto, exacto; (*suitable*) indicado, debido; (*proper*) apropiado; (*just*) justo; (*morally good*) bueno; (*not left*) derecho ♦ *n* bueno; (*title, claim*) derecho; (*not left*) derecha ♦ *adv* bien, correctamente; (*not left*) a la derecha; (*exactly*): **~ now** ahora mismo ♦ *vt* enderezar; (*correct*) corregir ♦ *excl* ¡bueno!, ¡está bien!; **to be ~** (*person*) tener razón; (*answer*) ser correcto; **is that the ~ time?** (*of clock*) ¿es esa la hora buena?; **by ~s** en justicia; **on the ~** a la derecha; **to be in the ~** tener razón; **~ away** en seguida; **in the middle** exactamente en el centro; **~ angle** *n* ángulo recto; **~eous** ['raɪtʃəs] *adj* justado, honrado; (*anger*) justificado; **~ful** *adj* legítimo; **~-handed** *adj* diestro; **~-hand man** *n* brazo derecho; **~-hand side** *n*

derecha; **~ly** *adv* correctamente, debidamente; (*with reason*) con razón; **~ of way** *n* (*on path etc*) derecho de paso; (*AUT*) prioridad *f*; **~-wing** *adj* (*POL*) derechista

rigid ['rɪdʒɪd] *adj* rígido; (*person, ideas*) inflexible

rigmarole ['rɪgmərəul] *n* galimatías *m inv*

rigorous ['rɪgərəs] *adj* riguroso

rile [raɪl] *vt* irritar

rim [rɪm] *n* borde *m*; (*of spectacles*) aro; (*of wheel*) llanta

rind [raɪnd] *n* (*of bacon*) corteza; (*of lemon etc*) cáscara; (*of cheese*) costra

ring [rɪŋ] (*pt* **rang**, *pp* **rung**) *n* (*of metal*) aro; (*on finger*) anillo; (*of people*) corro; (*of objects*) círculo; (*gang*) banda; (*for boxing*) cuadrilátero; (*of circus*) pista; (*bull ~*) ruedo, plaza; (*sound of bell*) toque *m* ♦ *vi* (*on telephone*) llamar por teléfono; (*bell*) repicar; (*doorbell, phone*) sonar; (*also*: **~ out**) sonar; (*ears*) zumbar ♦ *vt* (*BRIT*: *TEL*) llamar, telefonear; (*bell etc*) hacer sonar; (*doorbell*) tocar; **to give sb a ~** (*BRIT*: *TEL*) llamar *or* telefonear a alguien; **~ back** (*BRIT*) *vt, vi* (*TEL*) devolver la llamada; **~ off** (*BRIT*) *vi* (*TEL*) colgar, cortar la comunicación; **~ up** (*BRIT*) *vt* (*TEL*) llamar, telefonear; **~ing** *n* (*of bell*) repique *m*; (*of phone*) el sonar; (*in ears*) zumbido; **~ing tone** *n* (*TEL*) tono de llamada; **~leader** *n* (*of gang*) cabecilla *m*; **~lets** ['rɪŋlɪts] *npl* rizos *mpl*, bucles *mpl*; **~ road** (*BRIT*) *n* carretera periférica *or* de circunvalación

rink [rɪŋk] *n* (*also*: **ice ~**) pista de hielo

rinse [rɪns] *n* aclarado; (*dye*) tinte *m* ♦ *vt* aclarar; (*mouth*) enjuagar

riot ['raɪət] *n* motín *m*, disturbio ♦ *vi* amotinarse; **to run ~** desmandarse; **~ous** *adj* alborotado; (*party*) bullicioso

rip [rɪp] *n* rasgón *m*, rasgadura ♦ *vt* rasgar, desgarrar ♦ *vi* rasgarse, desgarrarse; **~cord** *n* cabo de desgarre

ripe [raɪp] *adj* maduro; **~n** *vt* madurar; (*cheese*) curar ♦ *vi* madurar

ripple ['rɪpl] *n* onda, rizo; (*sound*)

murmullo ♦ *vi* rizarse

rise [raɪz] (*pt* **rose**, *pp* **risen**) *n* (*slope*) cuesta, pendiente *f*; (*hill*) altura; (*BRIT: in wages*) aumento; (*in prices, temperature*) subida; (*fig: to power etc*) ascenso ♦ *vi* subir; (*waters*) crecer; (*sun, moon*) salir; (*person: from bed etc*) levantarse; (*also:* ~ **up**: *rebel*) sublevarse; (*in rank*) ascender; **to give** ~ **to** dar lugar or origen a; **to** ~ **to the occasion** ponerse a la altura de las circunstancias; **risen** ['rɪzn] *pp of* **rise**; **rising** *adj* (*increasing: number*) creciente; (*: prices*) en aumento or alza; (*tide*) creciente; (*sun, moon*) naciente

risk [rɪsk] *n* riesgo, peligro ♦ *vt* arriesgar; (*run the* ~ *of*) exponerse a; **to take** or **run the** ~ **of doing** correr el riesgo de hacer; **at** ~ en peligro; **at one's own** ~ bajo su propia responsabilidad; ~**y** *adj* arriesgado, peligroso

rissole ['rɪsəʊl] *n* croqueta

rite [raɪt] *n* rito; **last** ~**s** exequias *fpl*

ritual ['rɪtjʊəl] *adj* ritual ♦ *n* ritual *m*, rito

rival ['raɪvl] *n* rival *m/f*; (*in business*) competidor(a) *m/f* ♦ *adj* rival, opuesto ♦ *vt* competir con; ~**ry** *n* competencia

river ['rɪvə*] *n* río ♦ *cpd* (*port*) de río; (*traffic*) fluvial; **up/down** ~ río arriba/abajo; ~**bank** *n* orilla (del río); ~**bed** *n* lecho, cauce *m*

rivet ['rɪvɪt] *n* roblón *m*, remache *m* ♦ *vt* (*fig*) captar

Riviera [rɪvɪ'eərə] *n*: **the (French)** ~ la Costa Azul (francesa)

road [rəʊd] *n* camino; (*motorway etc*) carretera; (*in town*) calle *f* ♦ *cpd* (*accident*) de tráfico; **major/minor** ~ carretera principal/secundaria; ~ **accident** *n* accidente de tráfico; ~**block** *n* barricada; ~**hog** *n* loco/a del volante; **map** *n* mapa *m* de carreteras; ~ **rage** *n* agresividad en la carretera; ~ **safety** *n* seguridad *f* vial; ~**side** *n* borde *m* (del camino); ~**sign** *n* señal *f* de tráfico; ~ **user** *n* usuario/a de la vía pública; ~**way** *n* calzada; ~**works** *npl* obras *fpl*; ~**worthy** *adj* (*car*) en buen estado para

circular

roam [rəʊm] *vi* vagar

roar [rɔ:*] *n* rugido; (*of vehicle, storm*) estruendo; (*of laughter*) carcajada ♦ *vi* rugir; hacer estruendo; **to** ~ **with laughter** reírse a carcajadas; **to do a** ~**ing trade** hacer buen negocio

roast [rəʊst] *n* carne *f* asada, asado ♦ *vt* asar; (*coffee*) tostar; ~ **beef** *n* rosbif *m*

rob [rɒb] *vt* robar; **to** ~ **sb of sth** robar algo a uno; (*fig: deprive*) quitar algo a uno; ~**ber** *n* ladrón/ona *m/f*; ~**bery** *n* robo

robe [rəʊb] *n* (*for ceremony etc*) toga; (*also:* **bath~**, *US*) albornoz *m*

robin ['rɒbɪn] *n* petirrojo

robot ['rəʊbɒt] *n* robot *m*

robust [rəʊ'bʌst] *adj* robusto, fuerte

rock [rɒk] *n* roca; (*boulder*) peña, peñasco; (*US: small stone*) piedrecita; (*BRIT: sweet*) ≈ pirulí ♦ *vt* (*swing gently: cradle*) balancear, mecer; (*: child*) arrullar; (*shake*) sacudir ♦ *vi* mecerse, balancearse; sacudirse; **on the** ~**s** (*drink*) con hielo; (*marriage etc*) en ruinas; ~ **and roll** *n* rocanrol *m*; ~~**bottom** *n* (*fig*) punto más bajo; ~**ery** *n* cuadro alpino

rocket ['rɒkɪt] *n* cohete *m*

rocking ['rɒkɪŋ]: ~ **chair** *n* mecedora; ~ **horse** *n* caballo de balancín

rocky ['rɒkɪ] *adj* rocoso

rod [rɒd] *n* vara, varilla; (*also: fishing* ~) caña

rode [rəʊd] *pt of* **ride**

rodent ['rəʊdnt] *n* roedor *m*

roe [rəʊ] *n* (*species: also:* ~ **deer**) corzo; (*of fish*): **hard/soft** ~ hueva/lecha

rogue [rəʊg] *n* pícaro, pillo

role [rəʊl] *n* papel *m*

roll [rəʊl] *n* rollo; (*of bank notes*) fajo; (*also:* **bread** ~) panecillo; (*register, list*) lista, nómina; (*sound: of drums etc*) redoble *m* ♦ *vt* hacer rodar; (*also:* ~ **up**: *string*) enrollar; (*: sleeves*) arremangar; (*cigarette*) liar; (*also:* ~ **out**: *pastry*) aplanar; (*flatten: road, lawn*) apisonar ♦ *vi* rodar; (*drum*) redoblar; (*ship*) balancearse; ~ **about** or

around vi (*person*) revolcarse; (*object*)
rodar (por); **~ by** vi (*time*) pasar; **~ over**
vi dar una vuelta; **~ up** vi (*inf: arrive*)
aparecer ♦ vt (*carpet*) arrollar; **~ call** n:
to take a ~ call pasar lista; **~er** n rodillo;
(*wheel*) rueda; (*for road*) apisonadora; (*for
hair*) rulo; **~erblade** n patín m (en
línea); **~er coaster** n montaña rusa;
~er skates npl patines mpl de rueda

rolling ['rəʊlɪŋ] adj (*landscape*) ondulado;
~ pin n rodillo (de cocina); **~ stock** n
(*RAIL*) material m rodante

ROM [rɔm] n abbr (*COMPUT: = read only
memory*) ROM f

Roman ['rəʊmən] adj romano/a; **~
Catholic** adj, n católico/a m/f (romano/
a)

romance [rə'mæns] n (*love affair*) amor m;
(*charm*) lo romántico; (*novel*) novela de
amor

Romania [ruː'meɪnɪə] n = **Rumania**

Roman numeral n número romano

romantic [rə'mæntɪk] adj romántico

Rome [rəʊm] n Roma

romp [rɔmp] n retozo, juego ♦ vi (*also: ~
about*) jugar, brincar

rompers ['rɔmpəz] npl pelele m

roof [ruːf] (*pl ~s*) n (*gen*) techo; (*of house*)
techo, tejado ♦ vt techar, poner techo a;
the ~ of the mouth el paladar; **~ing** n
techumbre f; **~ rack** n (*AUT*) baca,
portaequipajes m inv

rook [rʊk] n (*bird*) graja; (*CHESS*) torre f

room [ruːm] n cuarto, habitación f, pieza
(*esp AM*); (*also:* **bed~**) dormitorio; (*in
school etc*) sala; (*space, scope*) sitio,
cabida; **~s** npl (*lodging*) alojamiento; **"~s
to let", "~s for rent"** (*US*) "se alquilan
cuartos"; **single/double ~** habitación
individual/doble or para dos personas;
~ing house (*US*) n pensión f; **~mate** n
compañero/a de cuarto; **~ service** n
servicio de habitaciones; **~y** adj
espacioso; (*garment*) amplio

roost [ruːst] vi pasar la noche

rooster ['ruːstə*] n gallo

root [ruːt] n raíz f ♦ vi arraigarse; **~ about**

vi (*fig*) buscar y rebuscar; **~ for** vt fus
(*support*) apoyar a; **~ out** vt desarraigar

rope [rəʊp] n cuerda; (*NAUT*) cable m ♦ vt
(*tie*) atar or amarrar con (una) cuerda;
(*climbers: also:* **~ together**) encordarse;
(*an area: also:* **~ off**) acordonar; **to know
the ~s** (*fig*) conocer los trucos (del oficio);
~ in vt (*fig*): **to ~ sb in** persuadir a uno a
tomar parte

rosary ['rəʊzərɪ] n rosario

rose [rəʊz] pt of **rise** ♦ n rosa; (*shrub*)
rosal m; (*on watering can*) roseta

rosé ['rəʊzeɪ] n vino rosado

rosebud ['rəʊzbʌd] n capullo de rosa

rosebush ['rəʊzbʊʃ] n rosal m

rosemary ['rəʊzmərɪ] n romero

roster ['rɔstə*] n: **duty ~** lista de deberes

rostrum ['rɔstrəm] n tribuna

rosy ['rəʊzɪ] adj rosado, sonrosado; **a ~
future** un futuro prometedor

rot [rɔt] n podredumbre f; (*fig: pej*)
tonterías fpl ♦ vt pudrir ♦ vi pudrirse

rota ['rəʊtə] n (*sistema* m de) turnos mpl

rotary ['rəʊtərɪ] adj rotativo

rotate [rəʊ'teɪt] vt (*revolve*) hacer girar, dar
vueltas a; (*jobs*) alternar ♦ vi girar, dar
vueltas; **rotating** adj rotativo; **rotation**
[-'teɪʃən] n rotación f

rotten ['rɔtn] adj podrido; (*dishonest*)
corrompido; (*inf: bad*) pocho; **to feel ~**
(*ill*) sentirse fatal

rotund [rəʊ'tʌnd] adj regordete

rouble ['ruːbl] (*US* **ruble**) n rublo

rough [rʌf] adj (*skin, surface*) áspero;
(*terrain*) quebrado; (*road*) desigual; (*voice*)
bronco; (*person, manner*) tosco, grosero;
(*weather*) borrascoso; (*treatment*) brutal;
(*sea*) picado; (*town, area*) peligroso;
(*cloth*) basto; (*plan*) preliminar; (*guess*)
aproximado ♦ n (*GOLF*): **in the ~** en las
hierbas altas; **to ~ it** vivir sin
comodidades; **to sleep ~** (*BRIT*) pasar la
noche al raso; **~age** n fibra(s) f(pl); **~-
and-ready** adj improvisado; **~ copy** n
borrador m; **~ draft** n = **~ copy**; **~ly**
adv (*handle*) torpemente; (*make*)
toscamente; (*speak*) groseramente;

(*approximately*) aproximadamente; **~ness** *n* (*of surface*) aspereza; (*of person*) rudeza
roulette [ru:'let] *n* ruleta
Roumania [ru:'meɪnɪə] *n* = **Rumania**
round [raund] *adj* redondo ♦ *n* círculo; (*BRIT: of toast*) rebanada; (*of policeman*) ronda; (*of milkman*) recorrido; (*of doctor*) visitas *fpl*; (*game: of cards, in competition*) partida; (*of ammunition*) cartucho; (*BOXING*) asalto; (*of talks*) ronda ♦ *vt* (*corner*) doblar ♦ *prep* alrededor de; (*surrounding*): **~ his neck/the table** en su cuello/alrededor de la mesa; (*in a circular movement*): **to move ~ the room/sail ~ the world** dar una vuelta a la habitación/circunnavegar el mundo; (*in various directions*): **to move ~ a room/house** moverse por toda la habitación/casa; (*approximately*) alrededor de ♦ *adv*: **all ~** por todos lados; **the long way ~** por el camino menos directo; **all the year ~** durante todo el año; **it's just ~ the corner** (*fig*) está a la vuelta de la esquina; **~ the clock** *adv* las 24 horas; **to go ~ to sb's (house)** ir a casa de uno; **to go ~ the back** pasar por atrás; **enough to go ~** bastante (para todos); **a ~ of applause** una salva de aplausos; **a ~ of drinks/sandwiches** una ronda de bebidas/bocadillos; **~ off** *vt* (*speech etc*) acabar, poner término a; **~ up** *vt* (*cattle*) acorralar; (*people*) reunir; (*price*) redondear; **~about** (*BRIT*) *n* (*AUT*) isleta; (*at fair*) tiovivo ♦ *adj* (*route, means*) indirecto; **~ers** *n* (*game*) juego similar al béisbol; **~ly** *adv* (*fig*) rotundamente; **~trip** *n* viaje *m* de ida y vuelta; **~up** *n* rodeo; (*of criminals*) redada; (*of news*) resumen *m*
rouse [rauz] *vt* (*wake up*) despertar; (*stir up*) suscitar; **rousing** *adj* (*cheer, welcome*) caluroso
route [ru:t] *n* ruta, camino; (*of bus*) recorrido; (*of shipping*) derrota
routine [ru:'ti:n] *adj* rutinario ♦ *n* rutina; (*THEATRE*) número
rove [rəuv] *vt* vagar *or* errar por

row[1] [rəu] *n* (*line*) fila, hilera; (*KNITTING*) pasada ♦ *vi* (*in boat*) remar ♦ *vt* conducir remando; **4 days in a ~** 4 días seguidos
row[2] [rau] *n* (*racket*) escándalo; (*dispute*) bronca, pelea; (*scolding*) regaño ♦ *vi* pelear(se)
rowboat ['rəubəut] (*US*) *n* bote *m* de remos
rowdy ['raudɪ] *adj* (*person: noisy*) ruidoso; (*occasion*) alborotado
rowing ['rəuɪŋ] *n* remo; **~ boat** (*BRIT*) *n* bote *m* de remos
royal ['rɔɪəl] *adj* real; **R~ Air Force** *n* Fuerzas *fpl* Aéreas Británicas; **~ty** *n* (*~ persons*) familia real; (*payment to author*) derechos *mpl* de autor
rpm *abbr* (= *revs per minute*) r.p.m.
R.S.V.P. *abbr* (= *répondez s'il vous plaît*) SRC
Rt. Hon. *abbr* (*BRIT*: = *Right Honourable*) título honorífico de diputado
rub [rʌb] *vt* frotar; (*scrub*) restregar ♦ *n*: **to give sth a ~** frotar algo; **to ~ sb up** *or* **~ sb** (*US*) **the wrong way** entrarle uno por mal ojo; **~ off** *vi* borrarse; **~ off on** *vt fus* influir en; **~ out** *vt* borrar
rubber ['rʌbə*] *n* caucho, goma; (*BRIT: eraser*) goma de borrar; **~ band** *n* goma, gomita; **~ plant** *n* ficus *m*
rubbish ['rʌbɪʃ] *n* basura; (*waste*) desperdicios *mpl*; (*fig: pej*) tonterías *fpl*; (*junk*) pacotilla; **~ bin** (*BRIT*) *n* cubo (*SP*) *or* bote *m* (*AM*) de la basura; **~ dump** *n* vertedero, basurero
rubble ['rʌbl] *n* escombros *mpl*
ruble ['ru:bl] (*US*) *n* = **rouble**
ruby ['ru:bɪ] *n* rubí *m*
rucksack ['rʌksæk] *n* mochila
rudder ['rʌdə*] *n* timón *m*
ruddy ['rʌdɪ] *adj* (*face*) rubicundo; (*inf: damned*) condenado
rude [ru:d] *adj* (*impolite: person*) mal educado; (*: word, manners*) grosero; (*crude*) crudo; (*indecent*) indecente; **~ness** *n* descortesía
ruffle ['rʌfl] *vt* (*hair*) despeinar; (*clothes*) arrugar; **to get ~d** (*fig: person*) alterarse

rug [rʌg] *n* alfombra; (*BRIT*: blanket) manta
rugby ['rʌgbɪ] *n* (*also*: ~ **football**) rugby *m*
rugged ['rʌgɪd] *adj* (*landscape*)
accidentado; (*features*) robusto
ruin ['ruːɪn] *n* ruina ♦ *vt* arruinar; (*spoil*)
estropear; ~**s** *npl* ruinas *fpl*, restos *mpl*
rule [ruːl] *n* (*norm*) norma, costumbre *f*;
(*regulation, ruler*) regla; (*government*)
dominio ♦ *vt* (*country, person*) gobernar
♦ *vi* gobernar; (*LAW*) fallar; **as a** ~ por
regla general; ~ **out** *vt* excluir; ~**d** *adj*
(*paper*) rayado; ~**r** *n* (*sovereign*) soberano;
(*for measuring*) regla; **ruling** *adj* (*party*)
gobernante; (*class*) dirigente ♦ *n* (*LAW*)
fallo, decisión *f*
rum [rʌm] *n* ron *m*
Rumania [ruːˈmeɪnɪə] *n* Rumanía; ~**n** *adj*
rumano/a ♦ *n* rumano/a *m/f*; (*LING*)
rumano
rumble ['rʌmbl] *n* (*noise*) ruido sordo ♦ *vi*
retumbar, hacer un ruido sordo;
(*stomach, pipe*) sonar
rummage ['rʌmɪdʒ] *vi* (*search*) hurgar
rumour ['ruːmə*] (*US* **rumor**) *n* rumor *m*
♦ *vt*: **it is ~ed that ...** se rumorea que ...
rump [rʌmp] *n* (*of animal*) ancas *fpl*,
grupa; ~ **steak** *n* filete *m* de lomo
rumpus ['rʌmpəs] *n* lío, jaleo
run [rʌn] (*pt* **ran**, *pp* **run**) *n* (*fast pace*): **at**
a ~ corriendo; (*SPORT, in tights*) carrera;
(*outing*) paseo, excursión *f*; (*distance
travelled*) trayecto; (*series*) serie *f*;
(*THEATRE*) temporada; (*SKI*) pista ♦ *vt*
correr; (*operate: business*) dirigir;
(: *competition, course*) organizar; (: *hotel,
house*) administrar, llevar; (*COMPUT*)
ejecutar; (*pass: hand*) pasar; (*PRESS:
feature*) publicar ♦ *vi* correr; (*work:
machine*) funcionar, marchar; (*bus, train:
operate*) circular, ir; (: *travel*) ir; (*continue:
play*) seguir; (: *contract*) ser válido; (*flow:
river*) fluir; (*colours, washing*) desteñirse;
(*in election*) ser candidato; **there was a ~
on** (*meat, tickets*) hubo mucha demanda
de; **in the long** ~ a la larga; **on the** ~ en
fuga; **I'll ~ you to the station** te llevaré a
la estación (en coche); **to ~ a risk** correr

un riesgo; **to ~ a bath** llenar la bañera; ~
about *or* **around** *vi* (*children*) correr por
todos lados; ~ **across** *vt fus* (*find*) dar
or topar con; ~ **away** *vi* huir; ~ **down**
vt (*production*) ir reduciendo; (*factory*) ir
restringiendo la producción en; (*subj: car*)
atropellar; (*criticize*) criticar; **to be ~ down**
(*person: tired*) estar debilitado; ~ **in** (*BRIT*)
vt (*car*) rodar; ~ **into** *vt fus* (*meet:
person, trouble*) tropezar con; (*collide with*)
chocar con; ~ **off** *vt* (*water*) dejar correr;
(*copies*) sacar ♦ *vi* huir corriendo; ~ **out**
vi (*person*) salir corriendo; (*liquid*) irse;
(*lease*) caducar, vencer; (*money etc*)
acabarse; ~ **out of** *vt fus* quedar sin; ~
over *vt* (*AUT*) atropellar ♦ *vt fus* (*revise*)
repasar; ~ **through** *vt fus* (*instructions*)
repasar; ~ **up** *vt* (*debt*) contraer; **to ~ up
against** (*difficulties*) tropezar con; ~**away**
adj (*horse*) desbocado; (*truck*) sin frenos;
(*child*) escapado de casa
rung [rʌŋ] *pp of* **ring** ♦ *n* (*of ladder*)
escalón *m*, peldaño
runner ['rʌnə*] *n* (*in race: person*)
corredor(a) *m/f*; (: *horse*) caballo; (*on
sledge*) patín *m*; ~ **bean** (*BRIT*) *n* ≈ judía
verde; ~**-up** *n* subcampeón/ona *m/f*
running ['rʌnɪŋ] *n* (*sport*) atletismo;
(*business*) administración *f* ♦ *adj* (*water,
costs*) corriente; (*commentary*) continuo;
to be in/out of the ~ for sth tener/no
tener posibilidades de ganar algo; **6 days**
~ 6 días seguidos; ~ **commentary** *n*
(*TV, RADIO*) comentario en directo; (*on
guided tour etc*) comentario detallado; ~
costs *npl* gastos *mpl* corrientes
runny ['rʌnɪ] *adj* fluido; (*nose, eyes*)
gastante
run-of-the-mill *adj* común y corriente
runt [rʌnt] *n* (*also pej*) redrojo, enano
run-up *n*: ~ **to** (*election etc*) período
previo a
runway ['rʌnweɪ] *n* (*AVIAT*) pista de
aterrizaje
rural ['ruərl] *adj* rural
rush [rʌʃ] *n* ímpetu *m*; (*hurry*) prisa;
(*COMM*) demanda repentina; (*current*)

corriente f fuerte; (of feeling) torrente;
(BOT) junco ♦ vt apresurar; (work) hacer
de prisa ♦ vi correr, precipitarse; ~ hour
n horas fpl punta
rusk [rʌsk] n bizcocho tostado
Russia ['rʌʃə] n Rusia; ~n adj ruso/a ♦ n
ruso/a m/f; (LING) ruso
rust [rʌst] n herrumbre f, moho ♦ vi
oxidarse
rustic ['rʌstɪk] adj rústico
rustle ['rʌsl] vi susurrar ♦ vt (paper) hacer
crujir
rustproof ['rʌstpruːf] adj inoxidable
rusty ['rʌstɪ] adj oxidado
rut [rʌt] n surco; (ZOOL) celo; to be in a ~
ser esclavo de la rutina
ruthless ['ruːθlɪs] adj despiadado
rye [raɪ] n centeno

S, s

Sabbath ['sæbəθ] n domingo; (Jewish)
sábado
sabotage ['sæbətɑːʒ] n sabotaje m ♦ vt
sabotear
saccharin(e) ['sækərɪn] n sacarina
sachet ['sæʃeɪ] n sobrecito
sack [sæk] n (bag) saco, costal m ♦ vt
(dismiss) despedir; (plunder) saquear; to
get the ~ ser despedido; ~ing n despido;
(material) arpillera
sacred ['seɪkrɪd] adj sagrado, santo
sacrifice ['sækrɪfaɪs] n sacrificio ♦ vt
sacrificar
sad [sæd] adj (unhappy) triste; (deplorable)
lamentable
saddle ['sædl] n silla (de montar); (of
cycle) sillín m ♦ vt (horse) ensillar; to be
~d with sth (inf) quedar cargado con
algo; ~bag n alforja
sadistic [sə'dɪstɪk] adj sádico
sadly ['sædlɪ] adv lamentablemente; to be
~ lacking in estar por desgracia carente
de
sadness ['sædnɪs] n tristeza
s.a.e. abbr (= stamped addressed

envelope) sobre con las propias señas de
uno y con sello
safari [sə'fɑːrɪ] n safari m
safe [seɪf] adj (out of danger) fuera de
peligro; (not dangerous, sure) seguro;
(unharmed) ileso ♦ n caja de caudales,
caja fuerte; ~ and sound sano y salvo;
(just) to be on the ~ side para mayor
seguridad; ~-conduct n salvoconducto;
~-deposit n (vault) cámara acorazada;
(box) caja de seguridad; ~guard n
protección f, garantía ♦ vt proteger,
defender; ~keeping n custodia; ~ly adv
seguramente, con seguridad; to arrive
~ly llegar bien; ~ sex n sexo seguro or
sin riesgo
safety ['seɪftɪ] n seguridad f; ~ belt n
cinturón m (de seguridad); ~ pin n
imperdible m (SP), seguro (AM); ~ valve
n válvula de seguridad
saffron ['sæfrən] n azafrán m
sag [sæg] vi aflojarse
sage [seɪdʒ] n (herb) salvia; (man) sabio
Sagittarius [sædʒɪ'tɛərɪəs] n Sagitario
Sahara [sə'hɑːrə] n: the ~ (Desert) el
(desierto del) Sáhara
said [sed] pt, pp of **say**
sail [seɪl] n (on boat) vela; (trip): to go for
a ~ dar un paseo en barco ♦ vt (boat)
gobernar ♦ vi (travel: ship) navegar;
(SPORT) hacer vela; (begin voyage) salir;
they ~ed into Copenhagen arribaron a
Copenhague; ~ through vt fus (exam)
aprobar sin ningún problema; ~boat (US)
n velero, barco de vela; ~ing n (SPORT)
vela; to go ~ing hacer vela; ~ing boat n
barco de vela; ~ing ship n velero; ~or
n marinero, marino
saint [seɪnt] n santo; ~ly adj santo
sake [seɪk] n: for the ~ of por
salad ['sæləd] n ensalada; ~ bowl n
ensaladera; ~ cream n (BRIT) (especie f
de) mayonesa; ~ dressing n aliño
salary ['sælərɪ] n sueldo
sale [seɪl] n venta; (at reduced prices)
liquidación f, saldo; (auction) subasta; ~s
npl (total amount sold) ventas fpl,

facturación f; **"for ~"** "se vende"; **on ~** en venta; **on ~ or return** (*goods*) venta por reposición; **~room** n sala de subastas; **~s assistant** (*US* **~s clerk**) n dependiente/a m/f; **salesman/woman** (*irreg*) n (*in shop*) dependiente/a m/f; (*representative*) viajante m/f

salmon ['sæmən] n *inv* salmón m

salon ['sælɒn] n (*hairdressing* ~) peluquería; (*beauty* ~) salón m de belleza

saloon [sə'luːn] n (*US*) bar m, taberna; (*BRIT: AUT*) (coche m de) turismo; (*ship's lounge*) cámara, salón m

salt [sɔlt] n sal f ♦ vt salar; (*put ~ on*) poner sal en; ~ **cellar** n salero; **~water** adj de agua salada; **~y** adj salado

salute [sə'luːt] n saludo; (*of guns*) salva ♦ vt saludar

salvage ['sælvɪdʒ] n (*saving*) salvamento, recuperación f; (*things saved*) objetos mpl salvados ♦ vt salvar

salvation [sæl'veɪʃən] n salvación f; **S~ Army** n Ejército de Salvación

same [seɪm] adj mismo ♦ pron: **the ~** el/la mismo/a, los/las mismos/as; **the ~ book as** el mismo libro que; **at the ~ time** (*at the ~ moment*) al mismo tiempo; (*yet*) sin embargo; **all** or **just the ~** sin embargo, aun así; **to do the ~ (as sb)** hacer lo mismo (que uno); **the ~ to you!** ¡igualmente!

sample ['sɑːmpl] n muestra ♦ vt (*food*) probar; (*wine*) catar

sanction ['sæŋkʃən] n aprobación f ♦ vt sancionar; aprobar; **~s** npl (*POL*) sanciones fpl

sanctity ['sæŋktɪtɪ] n santidad f; (*inviolability*) inviolabilidad f

sanctuary ['sæŋktjuərɪ] n santuario; (*refuge*) asilo, refugio; (*for wildlife*) reserva

sand [sænd] n arena; (*beach*) playa ♦ vt (*also:* ~ **down**) lijar

sandal ['sændl] n sandalia

sand: **~box** (*US*) n = **~pit**; **~castle** n castillo de arena; ~ **dune** n duna; **~paper** n papel m de lija; **~pit** n (*for children*) cajón m de arena; **~stone** n

piedra arenisca

sandwich ['sændwɪtʃ] n bocadillo (*SP*), sandwich m, emparedado (*AM*) ♦ vt intercalar; **~ed between** apretujado entre; **cheese/ham ~** sandwich de queso/jamón; ~ **course** (*BRIT*) n curso de medio tiempo

sandy ['sændɪ] adj arenoso; (*colour*) rojizo

sane [seɪn] adj cuerdo; (*sensible*) sensato

sang [sæŋ] pt of **sing**

sanitary ['sænɪtərɪ] adj sanitario; (*clean*) higiénico; ~ **towel** (*US* ~ **napkin**) n paño higiénico, compresa

sanitation [sænɪ'teɪʃən] n (*in house*) servicios mpl higiénicos; (*in town*) servicio de desinfección; ~ **department** (*US*) n departamento de limpieza y recogida de basuras

sanity ['sænɪtɪ] n cordura; (*of judgment*) sensatez f

sank [sæŋk] pt of **sink**

Santa Claus [sæntə'klɔːz] n San Nicolás, Papá Noel

sap [sæp] n (*of plants*) savia ♦ vt (*strength*) minar, agotar

sapling ['sæplɪŋ] n árbol nuevo or joven

sapphire ['sæfaɪə*] n zafiro

sarcasm ['sɑːkæzm] n sarcasmo

sardine [sɑː'diːn] n sardina

Sardinia [sɑː'dɪnɪə] n Cerdeña

sash [sæʃ] n faja

sat [sæt] pt, pp of **sit**

Satan ['seɪtn] n Satanás m

satchel ['sætʃl] n (*child's*) cartera (*SP*), mochila (*AM*)

satellite ['sætəlaɪt] n satélite m; ~ **dish** n antena de televisión por satélite; ~ **television** n televisión f vía satélite

satin ['sætɪn] n raso ♦ adj de raso

satire ['sætaɪə*] n sátira

satisfaction [sætɪs'fækʃən] n satisfacción f

satisfactory [sætɪs'fæktərɪ] adj satisfactorio

satisfy ['sætɪsfaɪ] vt satisfacer; (*convince*) convencer; **~ing** adj satisfactorio

Saturday ['sætədɪ] n sábado

sauce [sɔːs] n salsa; (*sweet*) crema; jarabe m; **~pan** n cacerola, olla

saucer ['sɔːsə*] n platillo
Saudi ['saudɪ]: ~ **Arabia** n Arabia Saudí or Saudita; ~ **(Arabian)** adj, n saudí m/f, saudita m/f
sauna ['sɔːnə] n sauna
saunter ['sɔːntə*] vi: **to ~ in/out** entrar/salir sin prisa
sausage ['sɔsɪdʒ] n salchicha; ~ **roll** n empanadita de salchicha
sauté ['səuteɪ] adj salteado
savage ['sævɪdʒ] adj (cruel, fierce) feroz, furioso; (primitive) salvaje ♦ n salvaje m/f ♦ vt (attack) embestir
save [seɪv] vt (rescue) salvar, rescatar; (money, time) ahorrar; (put by, keep: seat) guardar; (COMPUT) salvar (y guardar); (avoid: trouble) evitar; (SPORT) parar ♦ vi (also: ~ up) ahorrar ♦ n (SPORT) parada ♦ prep salvo, excepto
saving ['seɪvɪŋ] n (on price etc) economía ♦ adj: **the ~ grace of** el único mérito de; ~**s** npl ahorros mpl; ~**s account** n cuenta de ahorros; ~**s bank** n caja de ahorros
saviour ['seɪvjə*] (US **savior**) n salvador(a) m/f
savour ['seɪvə*] (US **savor**) vt saborear; ~**y** adj sabroso; (dish: not sweet) salado
saw [sɔː] (pt **sawed**, pp **sawed** or **sawn**) pt of **see** ♦ n (tool) sierra ♦ vt serrar; ~**dust** n (a)serrín m; ~**mill** n aserradero; ~**-off shotgun** n escopeta de cañones recortados
saxophone ['sæksəfəun] n saxófono
say [seɪ] (pt, pp **said**) n: **to have one's ~** expresar su opinión ♦ vt decir; **to have a** or **some ~ in sth** tener voz or tener que ver en algo; **to ~ yes/no** decir que sí/no; **could you ~ that again?** ¿podría repetir eso?; **that is to ~** es decir; **that goes without ~ing** ni que decir tiene; ~**ing** n dicho, refrán m
scab [skæb] n costra; (pej) esquirol m
scaffold ['skæfəuld] n cadalso; ~**ing** n andamio, andamiaje m
scald [skɔːld] n escaldadura ♦ vt escaldar
scale [skeɪl] n (gen, MUS) escala; (of fish)

escama; (of salaries, fees etc) escalafón m ♦ vt (mountain) escalar; (tree) trepar; ~**s** npl (for weighing: small) balanza; (: large) báscula; **on a large ~** en gran escala; ~ **of charges** tarifa, lista de precios; ~ **down** vt reducir a escala
scallop ['skɔləp] n (ZOOL) venera; (SEWING) festón m
scalp [skælp] n cabellera ♦ vt escalpar
scampi ['skæmpɪ] npl gambas fpl
scan [skæn] vt (examine) escudriñar; (glance at quickly) dar un vistazo a; (TV, RADAR) explorar, registrar ♦ n (MED): **to have a ~** pasar por el escáner
scandal ['skændl] n escándalo; (gossip) chismes mpl
Scandinavia [skændɪ'neɪvɪə] n Escandinavia; ~**n** adj, n escandinavo/a m/f
scant [skænt] adj escaso; ~**y** adj (meal) insuficiente; (clothes) ligero
scapegoat ['skeɪpgəut] n cabeza de turco, chivo expiatorio
scar [skɑː] n cicatriz f; (fig) señal f ♦ vt dejar señales en
scarce [skɛəs] adj escaso; **to make o.s. ~** (inf) esfumarse; ~**ly** adv apenas; **scarcity** n escasez f
scare [skɛə*] n susto, sobresalto; (panic) pánico ♦ vt asustar, espantar; **to ~ sb stiff** dar a uno un susto de muerte; **bomb ~** amenaza de bomba; ~ **off** or **away** vt ahuyentar; ~**crow** n espantapájaros m inv; ~**d** adj: **to be ~d** estar asustado
scarf [skɑːf] (pl ~**s** or **scarves**) n (long) bufanda; (square) pañuelo
scarlet ['skɑːlɪt] adj escarlata; ~ **fever** n escarlatina
scarves [skɑːvz] npl of **scarf**
scary ['skɛərɪ] (inf) adj espeluznante
scathing ['skeɪðɪŋ] adj mordaz
scatter ['skætə*] vt (spread) esparcir, desparramar; (put to flight) dispersar ♦ vi desparramarse; dispersarse; ~**brained** adj ligero de cascos
scavenger ['skævəndʒə*] n (person) basurero/a

scenario [sɪˈnɑːrɪəu] n (THEATRE) argumento; (CINEMA) guión m; (fig) escenario

scene [siːn] n (THEATRE, fig etc) escena; (of crime etc) escenario; (view) panorama m; (fuss) escándalo; **~ry** n (THEATRE) decorado; (landscape) paisaje m; **scenic** adj pintoresco

scent [sɛnt] n perfume m, olor m; (fig: track) rastro, pista

sceptic [ˈskɛptɪk] (US **skeptic**) n escéptico/a; **~al** adj escéptico

sceptre [ˈsɛptə*] (US **scepter**) n cetro

schedule [ˈʃɛdjuːl, (US) ˈskɛdjuːl] n (timetable) horario; (of events) programa m; (list) lista ♦ vt (visit) fijar la hora de; **to arrive on ~** llegar a la hora debida; **to be ahead of/behind ~** estar adelantado/en retraso; **~d flight** n vuelo regular

scheme [skiːm] n (plan) plan m, proyecto; (plot) intriga; (arrangement) disposición f; (pension ~ etc) sistema m ♦ vi (intrigue) intrigar; **scheming** adj intrigante ♦ n intrigas fpl

schizophrenic [skɪtzəˈfrɛnɪk] adj esquizofrénico

scholar [ˈskɔlə*] n (pupil) alumno/a; (learned person) sabio/a, erudito/a; **~ship** n erudición f; (grant) beca

school [skuːl] n escuela, colegio; (in university) facultad f ♦ cpd escolar; **~ age** n edad f escolar; **~book** n libro de texto; **~boy** n alumno; **~ children** npl alumnos mpl; **~girl** n alumna; **~ing** n enseñanza; **~master/mistress** n (primary) maestro/a; (secondary) profesor(a) m/f; **~teacher** n (primary) maestro/a; (secondary) profesor(a) m/f

schooner [ˈskuːnə*] n (ship) goleta

sciatica [saɪˈætɪkə] n ciática

science [ˈsaɪəns] n ciencia; **~ fiction** n ciencia-ficción f; **scientific** [-ˈtɪfɪk] adj científico; **scientist** n científico/a

scissors [ˈsɪzəz] npl tijeras fpl; **a pair of ~** unas tijeras

scoff [skɔf] vt (BRIT: inf: eat) engullir ♦ vi: **to ~ (at)** (mock) mofarse (de)

scold [skəuld] vt regañar

scone [skɔn] n pastel de pan

scoop [skuːp] n (for flour etc) pala; (PRESS) exclusiva; **~ out** vt excavar; **~ up** vt recoger

scooter [ˈskuːtə*] n moto f; (toy) patinete m

scope [skəup] n (of plan) ámbito; (of person) competencia; (opportunity) libertad f (de acción)

scorch [skɔːtʃ] vt (clothes) chamuscar; (earth, grass) quemar, secar

score [skɔː*] n (points etc) puntuación f; (MUS) partitura; (twenty) veintena ♦ vt (goal, point) ganar; (mark) rayar; ♦ vi marcar un tanto; (FOOTBALL) marcar (un) gol; (keep score) llevar el tanteo; **~s** de (very many) decenas de; **on that ~** en lo que se refiere a eso; **to ~ 6 out of 10** obtener una puntuación de 6 sobre 10; **~ out** vt tachar; **~ over** vt fus obtener una victoria sobre; **~board** n marcador m

scorn [skɔːn] n desprecio; **~ful** adj desdeñoso, despreciativo

Scorpio [ˈskɔːpɪəu] n Escorpión m

scorpion [ˈskɔːpɪən] n alacrán m

Scot [skɔt] n escocés/esa m/f

Scotch [skɔtʃ] n whisky m escocés

Scotland [ˈskɔtlənd] n Escocia

Scots [skɔts] adj escocés/esa; **~man/ woman** (irreg) n escocés/esa m/f; **Scottish** [ˈskɔtɪʃ] adj escocés/esa; **Scottish Parliament** n Parlamento escocés

scoundrel [ˈskaundrl] n canalla m/f, sinvergüenza m/f

scout [skaut] n (MIL, also: **boy ~**) explorador m; **girl ~** (US) niña exploradora; **~ around** vi reconocer el terreno

scowl [skaul] vi fruncir el ceño; **to ~ at sb** mirar con ceño a uno

scrabble [ˈskræbl] vi (claw): **to ~ (at)** arañar; (also: **~ around**: search) revolver todo buscando ♦ n: **S~** ® Scrabble ® m

scraggy [ˈskrægɪ] adj descarnado

scram [skræm] (inf) vi largarse

scramble [ˈskræmbl] n (climb) subida

(difícil); (*struggle*) pelea ♦ *vi*: **to ~ through/out** abrirse paso/salir con dificultad; **to ~ for** pelear por; ~**d eggs** *npl* huevos *mpl* revueltos

scrap [skræp] *n* (*bit*) pedacito; (*fig*) pizca; (*fight*) riña, bronca; (*also*: **~ iron**) chatarra, hierro viejo ♦ *vt* (*discard*) desechar, descartar ♦ *vi* reñir, armar (una) bronca; **~s** *npl* (*waste*) sobras *fpl*, desperdicios *mpl*; ~**book** *n* álbum *m* de recortes; **~ dealer** *n* chatarrero/a

scrape [skreɪp] *n*: **to get into a ~** meterse en un lío ♦ *vt* raspar; (*skin etc*) rasguñar; (~ *against*) rozar ♦ *vi*: **to ~ through** (*exam*) aprobar por los pelos; **~ together** *vt* (*money*) arañar, juntar

scrap: **~ heap** *n* (*fig*): **to be on the ~ heap** estar acabado; **~ merchant** (*BRIT*) *n* chatarrero/a; **~ paper** *n* pedazos *mpl* de papel

scratch [skrætʃ] *n* rasguño; (*from claw*) arañazo ♦ *cpd*: **~ team** equipo improvisado ♦ *vt* (*paint, car*) rayar; (*with claw, nail*) rasguñar, arañar; (*rub: nose etc*) rascarse ♦ *vi* rascarse; **to start from ~** partir de cero; **to be up to ~** cumplir con los requisitos

scrawl [skrɔːl] *n* garabatos *mpl* ♦ *vi* hacer garabatos

scrawny ['skrɔːnɪ] *adj* flaco

scream [skriːm] *n* chillido ♦ *vi* chillar

screech [skriːtʃ] *vi* chirriar

screen [skriːn] *n* (*CINEMA, TV*) pantalla; (*movable barrier*) biombo ♦ *vt* (*conceal*) tapar; (*from the wind etc*) proteger; (*film*) proyectar; (*candidates etc*) investigar a; ~**ing** *n* (*MED*) investigación *f* médica; ~**play** *n* guión *m*; **~ saver** *n* (*COMPUT*) protector *m* de pantalla

screw [skruː] *n* tornillo ♦ *vt* (*also*: **~ in**) atornillar; **~ up** *vt* (*paper etc*) arrugar; **to ~ up one's eyes** arrugar el entrecejo; ~**driver** *n* destornillador *m*

scribble ['skrɪbl] *n* garabatos *mpl* ♦ *vt, vi* garabatear

script [skrɪpt] *n* (*CINEMA etc*) guión *m*; (*writing*) escritura, letra

Scripture(s) ['skrɪptʃə*(z)] *n(pl)* Sagrada Escritura

scroll [skrəul] *n* rollo

scrounge [skraundʒ] (*inf*) *vt*: **to ~ sth off** *or* **from sb** obtener algo de uno de gorra ♦ *n*: **on the ~** de gorra; ~**r** *n* gorrón/ona *m/f*

scrub [skrʌb] *n* (*land*) maleza ♦ *vt* fregar, restregar; (*inf: reject*) cancelar, anular

scruff [skrʌf] *n*: **by the ~ of the neck** por el pescuezo

scruffy ['skrʌfɪ] *adj* desaliñado, piojoso

scrum(mage) ['skrʌm(mɪdʒ)] *n* (*RUGBY*) melée *f*

scruple ['skruːpl] *n* (*gen pl*) escrúpulo

scrutinize ['skruːtɪnaɪz] *vt* escudriñar; (*votes*) escrutar; **scrutiny** ['skruːtɪnɪ] *n* escrutinio, examen *m*

scuff [skʌf] *vt* (*shoes, floor*) rayar

scuffle ['skʌfl] *n* refriega

sculptor ['skʌlptə*] *n* escultor(a) *m/f*

sculpture ['skʌlptʃə*] *n* escultura

scum [skʌm] *n* (*on liquid*) espuma; (*pej: people*) escoria

scurry ['skʌrɪ] *vi* correr; **to ~ off** escabullirse

scuttle ['skʌtl] *n* (*also*: **coal ~**) cubo, carbonera ♦ *vt* (*ship*) barrenar ♦ *vi* (*scamper*): **to ~ away, ~ off** escabullirse

scythe [saɪð] *n* guadaña

SDP (*BRIT*) *n abbr* = **Social Democratic Party**

sea [siː] *n* mar *m* ♦ *cpd* de mar, marítimo; **by ~** (*travel*) en barco; **on the ~** (*boat*) en el mar; (*town*) junto al mar; **to be all at ~** (*fig*) estar despistado; **out to ~, at ~** en alta mar; ~**board** *n* litoral *m*; ~**food** *n* mariscos *mpl*; **~ front** *n* paseo marítimo; ~**going** *adj* de altura; ~**gull** *n* gaviota

seal [siːl] *n* (*animal*) foca; (*stamp*) sello ♦ *vt* (*close*) cerrar; **~ off** *vt* (*area*) acordonar

sea level *n* nivel *m* del mar

sea lion *n* león *m* marino

seam [siːm] *n* costura; (*of metal*) juntura; (*of coal*) veta, filón *m*

seaman ['siːmən] (*irreg*) *n* marinero

seance ['seɪɒns] *n* sesión *f* de espiritismo

seaplane ['si:pleɪn] *n* hidroavión *m*
seaport ['si:pɔ:t] *n* puerto de mar
search [sɜ:tʃ] *n* (*for person, thing*) busca, búsqueda; (*COMPUT*) búsqueda; (*inspection: of sb's home*) registro ♦ *vt* (*look in*) buscar en; (*examine*) examinar; (*person, place*) registrar ♦ *vi*: **to ~ for** buscar; **in ~ of** en busca de; **~ through** *vt fus* registrar; **~ engine** *n* (*COMPUT*) buscador *m*; **~ing** *adj* penetrante; **~light** *n* reflector *m*; **~ party** *n* pelotón *m* de salvamento; **~ warrant** *n* mandamiento (judicial)
sea: **~shore** *n* playa, orilla del mar; **~sick** *adj* mareado; **~side** *n* playa, orilla del mar; **~side resort** *n* centro turístico costero
season ['si:zn] *n* (*of year*) estación *f*; (*sporting etc*) temporada; (*of films etc*) ciclo ♦ *vt* (*food*) sazonar; **in/out of ~** en sazón/fuera de temporada; **~al** *adj* estacional; **~ed** *adj* (*fig*) experimentado; **~ing** *n* condimento, aderezo; **~ ticket** *n* abono
seat [si:t] *n* (*in bus, train*) asiento; (*chair*) silla; (*PARLIAMENT*) escaño; (*buttocks*) culo, trasero; (*of trousers*) culera ♦ *vt* sentar; (*have room for*) tener cabida para; **to be ~ed** sentarse; **~ belt** *n* cinturón *m* de seguridad
sea: **~ water** *n* agua del mar; **~weed** *n* alga marina; **~worthy** *adj* en condiciones de navegar
sec. *abbr* = **second(s)**
secluded [sɪ'klu:dɪd] *adj* retirado
seclusion [sɪ'klu:ʒən] *n* reclusión *f*
second ['sekənd] *adj* segundo ♦ *adv* en segundo lugar ♦ *n* segundo; (*AUT: also:* **~ gear**) segunda; (*COMM*) artículo con algún desperfecto; (*BRIT: SCOL: degree*) *título de licenciado con calificación de notable* ♦ *vt* (*motion*) apoyar; **~ary** *adj* secundario; **~ary school** *n* escuela secundaria; **~-class** *adj* de segunda clase ♦ *adv* (*RAIL*) en segunda; **~hand** *adj* usado; **~ hand** *n* (*on clock*) segundero; **~ly** *adv* en segundo lugar; **~ment**

[sɪ'kɒndmənt] (*BRIT*) *n* traslado temporal; **~-rate** *adj* de segunda categoría; **~ thoughts** *npl*: **to have ~ thoughts** cambiar de opinión; **on ~ thoughts** *or* **thought** (*US*) pensándolo bien
secrecy ['si:krəsɪ] *n* secreto
secret ['si:krɪt] *adj*, *n* secreto; **in ~** en secreto
secretarial [sekrɪ'teərɪəl] *adj* de secretario; (*course, staff*) de secretariado
secretary ['sekrətərɪ] *n* secretario/a; **S~ of State (for)** (*BRIT: POL*) Ministro (de)
secretive ['si:krətɪv] *adj* reservado, sigiloso
secretly ['si:krɪtlɪ] *adv* en secreto
sect [sekt] *n* secta; **~arian** [-'teərɪən] *adj* sectario
section ['sekʃən] *n* sección *f*; (*part*) parte *f*; (*of document*) artículo; (*of opinion*) sector *m*; (*cross-~*) corte *m* transversal
sector ['sektə*] *n* sector *m*
secular ['sekjʊlə*] *adj* secular, seglar
secure [sɪ'kjʊə*] *adj* seguro; (*firmly fixed*) firme, fijo ♦ *vt* (*fix*) asegurar, afianzar; (*get*) conseguir
security [sɪ'kjʊərɪtɪ] *n* seguridad *f*; (*for loan*) fianza; (: *object*) prenda
sedate [sɪ'deɪt] *adj* tranquilo ♦ *vt* tratar con sedantes
sedation [sɪ'deɪʃən] *n* (*MED*) sedación *f*
sedative ['sedɪtɪv] *n* sedante *m*, sedativo
seduce [sɪ'dju:s] *vt* seducir; **seduction** [-'dʌkʃən] *n* seducción *f*; **seductive** [-'dʌktɪv] *adj* seductor(a)
see [si:] (*pt* **saw**, *pp* **seen**) *vt* ver; (*accompany*): **to ~ sb to the door** acompañar a uno a la puerta; (*understand*) ver, comprender ♦ *vi* ver ♦ *n* (*arz*)obispado; **to ~ that** (*ensure*) asegurar que; **~ you soon!** ¡hasta pronto!; **~ about** *vt fus* atender a, encargarse de; **~ off** *vt* despedir; **~ through** *vt fus* (*fig*) calar ♦ *vt* (*plan*) llevar a cabo; **~ to** *vt fus* atender a, encargarse de
seed [si:d] *n* semilla; (*in fruit*) pepita; (*fig: gen pl*) germen *m*; (*TENNIS etc*) preseleccionado/a; **to go to ~** (*plant*) granar; (*fig*) descuidarse; **~ling** *n* planta

de semillero; **~y** *adj* (*shabby*) desaseado, raído

seeing ['si:ɪŋ] *conj*: **~ (that)** visto que, en vista de que

seek [si:k] (*pt, pp* **sought**) *vt* buscar; (*post*) solicitar

seem [si:m] *vi* parecer; **there ~s to be ...** parece que hay ...; **~ingly** *adv* aparentemente, según parece

seen [si:n] *pp of* **see**

seep [si:p] *vi* filtrarse

seesaw ['si:sɔ:] *n* subibaja

seethe [si:ð] *vi* hervir; **to ~ with anger** estar furioso

see-through *adj* transparente

segment ['segmənt] *n* (*part*) sección *f*; (*of orange*) gajo

segregate ['segrɪgeɪt] *vt* segregar

seize [si:z] *vt* (*grasp*) agarrar, asir; (*take possession of*) secuestrar; (: *territory*) apoderarse de; (*opportunity*) aprovecharse de; **~ (up)on** *vt fus* aprovechar; **~ up** *vi* (*TECH*) agarrotarse

seizure ['si:ʒə*] *n* (*MED*) ataque *m*; (*LAW, of power*) incautación *f*

seldom ['seldəm] *adv* rara vez

select [sɪ'lekt] *adj* selecto, escogido ♦ *vt* escoger, elegir; (*SPORT*) seleccionar; **~ion** [-'lekʃən] *n* selección *f*, elección *f*; (*COMM*) surtido

self [self] (*pl* **selves**) *n* uno mismo; **the ~** el yo ♦ *prefix* auto...; **~-assured** *adj* seguro de sí mismo; **~-catering** (*BRIT*) *adj* (*flat etc*) con cocina; **~-centred** (*US* **~-centered**) *adj* egocéntrico; **~-confidence** *n* confianza en sí mismo; **~-conscious** *adj* cohibido; **~-contained** (*BRIT*) *adj* (*flat*) con entrada particular; **~-control** *n* autodominio; **~-defence** (*US* **~-defense**) *n* defensa propia; **~-discipline** *n* autodisciplina; **~-employed** *adj* que trabaja por cuenta propia; **~-evident** *adj* patente; **~-governing** *adj* autónomo; **~-indulgent** *adj* autocomplaciente; **~-interest** *n* egoísmo; **~-ish** *adj* egoísta; **~-ishness** *n* egoísmo; **~-less** *adj* desinteresado; **~-**

made *adj*: **~-made man** hombre *m* que se ha hecho a sí mismo; **~-pity** *n* lástima de sí mismo; **~-portrait** *n* autorretrato; **~-possessed** *adj* sereno, dueño de sí mismo; **~-preservation** *n* propia conservación *f*; **~-respect** *n* amor *m* propio; **~-righteous** *adj* santurrón/ona; **~-sacrifice** *n* abnegación *f*; **~-satisfied** *adj* satisfecho de sí mismo; **~-service** *adj* de autoservicio; **~-sufficient** *adj* autosuficiente; **~-taught** *adj* autodidacta

sell [sel] (*pt, pp* **sold**) *vt* vender ♦ *vi* venderse; **to ~ at** *or* **for £10** venderse a 10 libras; **~ off** *vt* liquidar; **~ out** *vi*: **to ~ out of tickets/milk** vender todas las entradas/toda la leche; **~-by date** *n* fecha de caducidad; **~er** *n* vendedor(a) *m/f*; **~ing price** *n* precio de venta

Sellotape ® ['seləuteɪp] (*BRIT*) *n* cinta adhesiva, celo (*SP*), scotch *m* (*AM*)

selves [selvz] *npl of* **self**

semblance ['sembləns] *n* apariencia

semen ['si:mən] *n* semen *m*

semester [sɪ'mestə*] (*US*) *n* semestre *m*

semi... [semɪ] *prefix* semi..., medio...; **~circle** *n* semicírculo; **~colon** *n* punto y coma; **~conductor** *n* semiconductor *m*; **~detached (house)** *n* (*casa*) semiseparada; **~final** *n* semi-final *m*

seminar ['semɪnɑ:*] *n* seminario

seminary ['semɪnərɪ] *n* (*REL*) seminario

semiskilled ['semɪskɪld] *adj* (*work, worker*) semi-cualificado

semi-skimmed (milk) *n* leche semidesnatada

senate ['senɪt] *n* senado; **senator** *n* senador(a) *m/f*

send [send] (*pt, pp* **sent**) *vt* mandar, enviar; (*signal*) transmitir; **~ away** *vt* despachar; **~ away for** *vt fus* pedir; **~ back** *vt* devolver; **~ for** *vt fus* mandar traer; **~ off** *vt* (*goods*) despachar; (*BRIT: SPORT: player*) expulsar; **~ out** *vt* (*invitation*) mandar; (*signal*) emitir; **~ up** *vt* (*person, price*) hacer subir; (*BRIT: parody*) parodiar; **~er** *n* remitente *m/f*;

~-off n: **a good ~-off** una buena despedida

senior ['si:nɪə*] adj (older) mayor, más viejo; (: on staff) de más antigüedad; (of higher rank) superior; **~ citizen** n persona de la tercera edad; **~ity** [-'ɔrɪtɪ] n antigüedad f

sensation [sen'seɪʃən] n sensación f; **~al** adj sensacional

sense [sens] n (faculty, meaning) sentido; (feeling) sensación f; (good ~) sentido común, juicio ♦ vt sentir, percibir; **it makes ~** tiene sentido; **~less** adj estúpido, insensato; (unconscious) sin conocimiento; **~ of humour** n sentido del humor

sensible ['sensɪbl] adj sensato; (reasonable) razonable, lógico

sensitive ['sensɪtɪv] adj sensible; (touchy) susceptible

sensual ['sensjuəl] adj sensual

sensuous ['sensjuəs] adj sensual

sent [sent] pt, pp of **send**

sentence ['sentns] n (LING) oración f; (LAW) sentencia, fallo ♦ vt: **to ~ sb to death/to 5 years (in prison)** condenar a uno a muerte/a 5 años de cárcel

sentiment ['sentɪmənt] n sentimiento; (opinion) opinión f; **~al** [-'mentl] adj sentimental

sentry ['sentrɪ] n centinela m

separate [adj 'seprɪt, vb 'sepəreɪt] adj separado; (distinct) distinto ♦ vt separar; (part) dividir ♦ vi separarse; **~s** npl (clothes) coordinados mpl; **~ly** adv por separado; **separation** [-'reɪʃən] n separación f

September [sep'tembə*] n se(p)tiembre m

septic ['septɪk] adj séptico; **~ tank** n fosa séptica

sequel ['si:kwl] n consecuencia, resultado; (of story) continuación f

sequence ['si:kwəns] n sucesión f, serie f; (CINEMA) secuencia

sequin ['si:kwɪn] n lentejuela

serene [sɪ'ri:n] adj sereno, tranquilo

sergeant ['sa:dʒənt] n sargento

serial ['sɪərɪəl] n (TV) telenovela, serie f televisiva; (BOOK) serie f; **~ize** vt emitir como serial; **~ killer** n asesino/a múltiple; **~ number** n número de serie

series ['sɪərɪ:s] n inv serie f

serious ['sɪərɪəs] adj serio; (grave) grave; **~ly** adv en serio; (ill, wounded etc) gravemente

sermon ['sə:mən] n sermón m

serrated [sɪ'reɪtɪd] adj serrado, dentellado

serum ['sɪərəm] n suero

servant ['sə:vənt] n servidor(a) m/f; (house ~) criado/a

serve [sə:v] vt servir; (customer) atender; (subj: train) pasar por; (apprenticeship) hacer; (prison term) cumplir ♦ vi (at table) servir; (TENNIS) sacar; **to ~ as/for/to do** servir de/para/para hacer ♦ n (TENNIS) saque m; **it ~s him right** se lo tiene merecido; **~ out** vt (food) servir; **~ up** vt = **~ out**

service ['sə:vɪs] n servicio; (REL) misa; (AUT) mantenimiento; (dishes etc) juego ♦ vt (car etc) revisar; (: repair) reparar; **the S~s** npl las fuerzas armadas; **to be of ~ to sb** ser útil a uno; **~ included/not included** servicio incluido/no incluido; **~able** adj servible, utilizable; **~ area** n (on motorway) área de servicio; **~ charge** (BRIT) n servicio; **~man** n militar m; **~ station** n estación f de servicio

serviette [sə:vɪ'et] (BRIT) n servilleta

session ['seʃən] n sesión f; **to be in ~** estar en sesión

set [set] (pt, pp set) n juego; (RADIO) aparato; (TV) televisor m; (of utensils) batería; (of cutlery) cubierto; (of books) colección f; (TENNIS) set m; (group of people) grupo; (CINEMA) plató m; (THEATRE) decorado; (HAIRDRESSING) marcado ♦ adj (fixed) fijo; (ready) listo ♦ vt (place) poner, colocar; (fix) fijar; (adjust) ajustar, arreglar; (decide: rules etc) establecer, decidir ♦ vi (sun) ponerse; (jam, jelly) cuajarse; (concrete) fraguar; (bone) componerse; **to be ~ on doing sth** estar empeñado en hacer algo; **to ~ to**

music poner música a; **to ~ on fire** incendiar, poner fuego a; **to ~ free** poner en libertad; **to ~ sth going** poner algo en marcha; **to ~ sail** zarpar, hacerse a la vela; **~ about** *vt fus* ponerse a; **~ aside** *vt* poner aparte, dejar de lado; (*money, time*) reservar; **~ back** *vt* (*cost*): **to ~ sb back £5** costar a uno cinco libras; (: *in time*): **to ~ back (by)** retrasar (por); **~ off** *vi* partir ♦ *vt* (*bomb*) hacer estallar; (*events*) poner en marcha; (*show up well*) hacer resaltar; **~ out** *vi* partir ♦ *vt* (*arrange*) disponer; (*state*) exponer; **to ~ out to do sth** proponerse hacer algo; **~ up** *vt* establecer; **~back** *n* revés *m*, contratiempo; **~ menu** *n* menú *m*

settee [se'ti:] *n* sofá *m*

setting ['setɪŋ] *n* (*scenery*) marco; (*position*) disposición *f*; (*of sun*) puesta; (*of jewel*) engaste *m*, montadura

settle ['setl] *vt* (*argument*) resolver; (*accounts*) ajustar, liquidar; (MED: *calm*) calmar, sosegar ♦ *vi* (*dust etc*) depositarse; (*weather*) serenarse; (*also:* **~ down**) instalarse; tranquilizarse; **to ~ for sth** convenir en aceptar algo; **to ~ on sth** decidirse por algo; **~ in** *vi* instalarse; **~ up** *vi*: **to ~ up with sb** ajustar cuentas con uno; **~ment** *n* (*payment*) liquidación *f*; (*agreement*) acuerdo, convenio; (*village etc*) pueblo; **~r** *n* colono/a, colonizador(a) *m/f*

setup ['setʌp] *n* sistema *m*; (*situation*) situación *f*

seven ['sevn] *num* siete; **~teen** *num* diez y siete, diecisiete; **~th** *num* séptimo; **~ty** *num* setenta

sever ['sevə*] *vt* cortar; (*relations*) romper

several ['sevərl] *adj, pron* varios/as *m/fpl*, algunos/as *m/fpl*; **~ of us** varios de nosotros

severance ['sevərəns] *n* (*of relations*) ruptura; **~ pay** *n* indemnización *f* por despido

severe [sɪ'vɪə*] *adj* severo; (*serious*) grave; (*hard*) duro; (*pain*) intenso; **severity** [sɪ'verɪtɪ] *n* severidad *f*; gravedad *f*;

intensidad *f*

sew [səu] (*pt* **sewed**, *pp* **sewn**) *vt, vi* coser; **~ up** *vt* coser, zurcir

sewage ['su:ɪdʒ] *n* aguas *fpl* residuales

sewer ['su:ə*] *n* alcantarilla, cloaca

sewing ['səuɪŋ] *n* costura; **~ machine** *n* máquina de coser

sewn [səun] *pp of* **sew**

sex [seks] *n* sexo; (*lovemaking*): **to have ~** hacer el amor; **~ist** *adj, n* sexista *m/f*; **~ual** ['seksjuəl] *adj* sexual; **~y** *adj* sexy

shabby ['ʃæbɪ] *adj* (*person*) desharrapado; (*clothes*) raído, gastado; (*behaviour*) ruin *inv*

shack [ʃæk] *n* choza, chabola

shackles ['ʃæklz] *npl* grillos *mpl*, grilletes *mpl*

shade [ʃeɪd] *n* sombra; (*for lamp*) pantalla; (*for eyes*) visera; (*of colour*) matiz *m*, tonalidad *f*; (*small quantity*): **a ~ (too big/more)** un poquitín (grande/más) ♦ *vt* dar sombra a; (*eyes*) proteger del sol; **in the ~** en la sombra

shadow ['ʃædəu] *n* sombra ♦ *vt* (*follow*) seguir y vigilar; **~ cabinet** (BRIT) *n* (POL) *gabinete paralelo formado por el partido de oposición*; **~y** *adj* oscuro; (*dim*) indistinto

shady ['ʃeɪdɪ] *adj* sombreado; (*fig: dishonest*) sospechoso; (: *deal*) turbio

shaft [ʃɑːft] *n* (*of arrow, spear*) astil *m*; (AUT, TECH) eje *m*, árbol *m*; (*of mine*) pozo; (*of lift*) hueco, caja; (*of light*) rayo

shaggy ['ʃægɪ] *adj* peludo

shake [ʃeɪk] (*pt* **shook**, *pp* **shaken**) *vt* sacudir; (*building*) hacer temblar; (*bottle, cocktail*) agitar ♦ *vi* (*tremble*) temblar; **to ~ one's head** (*in refusal*) negar con la cabeza; (*in dismay*) mover o menear la cabeza, incrédulo; **to ~ hands with sb** estrechar la mano a uno; **~ off** *vt* sacudirse; (*fig*) deshacerse de; **~ up** *vt* agitar; (*fig*) reorganizar; **shaky** *adj* (*hand, voice*) trémulo; (*building*) inestable

shall [ʃæl] *aux vb*: **~ I help you?** ¿quieres que te ayude?; **I'll buy three, ~ I?** compro tres, ¿no te parece?

shallow ['ʃæləʊ] *adj* poco profundo; (*fig*) superficial

sham [ʃæm] *n* fraude *m*, engaño ♦ *vt* fingir, simular

shambles ['ʃæmblz] *n* confusión *f*

shame [ʃeɪm] *n* vergüenza ♦ *vt* avergonzar; **it is a ~ that/to do** es una lástima que/hacer; **what a ~!** ¡qué lástima!; **~ful** *adj* vergonzoso; **~less** *adj* desvergonzado

shampoo [ʃæm'puː] *n* champú *m* ♦ *vt* lavar con champú; **~ and set** *n* lavado y marcado

shamrock ['ʃæmrɔk] *n* trébol *m* (*emblema nacional irlandés*)

shandy ['ʃændɪ] *n* mezcla de cerveza con gaseosa

shan't [ʃɑːnt] = **shall not**

shantytown ['ʃæntɪtaʊn] *n* barrio de chabolas

shape [ʃeɪp] *n* forma ♦ *vt* formar, dar forma a; (*sb's ideas*) formar; (*sb's life*) determinar; **to take ~** tomar forma; **~ up** *vi* (*events*) desarrollarse; (*person*) formarse; **-~d** *suffix*: **heart~d** en forma de corazón; **~less** *adj* informe, sin forma definida; **~ly** *adj* (*body etc*) esbelto

share [ʃeə*] *n* (*part*) parte *f*, porción *f*; (*contribution*) cuota; (*COMM*) acción *f* ♦ *vt* dividir; (*have in common*) compartir; **to ~ out (among or between)** repartir (entre); **~holder** (*BRIT*) *n* accionista *m/f*

shark [ʃɑːk] *n* tiburón *m*

sharp [ʃɑːp] *adj* (*blade, nose*) afilado; (*point*) puntiagudo; (*outline*) definido; (*pain*) intenso; (*MUS*) desafinado; (*contrast*) marcado; (*voice*) agudo; (*person: quick-witted*) astuto; (*: dishonest*) poco escrupuloso ♦ *n* (*MUS*) sostenido ♦ *adv*: **at 2 o'clock ~** a las 2 en punto; **~en** *vt* afilar; (*pencil*) sacar punta a; (*fig*) agudizar; **~ener** *n* (*also*: **pencil ~ener**) sacapuntas *m inv*; **~-eyed** *adj* de vista aguda; **~ly** *adv* (*turn, stop*) bruscamente; (*stand out, contrast*) claramente; (*criticize, retort*) severamente

shatter ['ʃætə*] *vt* hacer añicos *or* pedazos;

(*fig: ruin*) destruir, acabar con ♦ *vi* hacerse añicos

shave [ʃeɪv] *vt* afeitar, rasurar ♦ *vi* afeitarse, rasurarse ♦ *n*: **to have a ~** afeitarse; **~r** *n* (*also*: **electric ~r**) máquina de afeitar (eléctrica)

shaving ['ʃeɪvɪŋ] *n* (*action*) el afeitarse, rasurado; **~s** *npl* (*of wood etc*) virutas *fpl*; **~ brush** *n* brocha (de afeitar); **~ cream** *n* crema de afeitar; **~ foam** *n* espuma de afeitar

shawl [ʃɔːl] *n* chal *m*

she [ʃiː] *pron* ella; **~-cat** *n* gata

sheaf [ʃiːf] (*pl* **sheaves**) *n* (*of corn*) gavilla *f*; (*of papers*) fajo

shear [ʃɪə*] (*pt* **sheared**, *pp* **sheared** *or* **shorn**) *vt* esquilar, trasquilar; **~s** *npl* (*for hedge*) tijeras *fpl* de jardín

sheath [ʃiːθ] *n* vaina; (*contraceptive*) preservativo

sheaves [ʃiːvz] *npl of* **sheaf**

shed [ʃed] (*pt, pp* **shed**) *n* cobertizo ♦ *vt* (*skin*) mudar; (*tears, blood*) derramar; (*load*) derramar; (*workers*) despedir

she'd [ʃiːd] = **she had; she would**

sheen [ʃiːn] *n* brillo, lustre *m*

sheep [ʃiːp] *n inv* oveja; **~dog** *n* perro pastor; **~skin** *n* piel *f* de carnero

sheer [ʃɪə*] *adj* (*utter*) puro, completo; (*steep*) escarpado; (*material*) diáfano ♦ *adv* verticalmente

sheet [ʃiːt] *n* (*on bed*) sábana; (*of paper*) hoja; (*of glass, metal*) lámina; (*of ice*) capa

sheik(h) [ʃeɪk] *n* jeque *m*

shelf [ʃelf] (*pl* **shelves**) *n* estante *m*

shell [ʃel] *n* (*on beach*) concha; (*of egg, nut etc*) cáscara; (*explosive*) proyectil *m*, obús *m*; (*of building*) armazón *f* ♦ *vt* (*peas*) desenvainar; (*MIL*) bombardear

she'll [ʃiːl] = **she will; she shall**

shellfish ['ʃelfɪʃ] *n inv* crustáceo; (*as food*) mariscos *mpl*

shell suit *n* chándal *m* de calle

shelter ['ʃeltə*] *n* abrigo, refugio ♦ *vt* (*aid*) amparar, proteger; (*give lodging to*) abrigar ♦ *vi* abrigarse, refugiarse; **~ed** *adj* (*life*) protegido; (*spot*) abrigado; **~ed**

housing *n* viviendas vigiladas para ancianos y minusválidos

shelve [ʃelv] *vt* (*fig*) aplazar; ~s *npl of* shelf

shepherd ['ʃepəd] *n* pastor *m* ♦ *vt* (*guide*) guiar, conducir; ~'s pie (*BRIT*) *n* pastel de carne y patatas

sherry ['ʃeri] *n* jerez *m*

she's [ʃiːz] = she is; she has

Shetland ['ʃetlənd] *n* (*also:* the ~ Isles) las Islas de Zetlandia

shield [ʃiːld] *n* escudo; (*protection*) blindaje *m* ♦ *vt*: to ~ (from) proteger (de)

shift [ʃift] *n* (*change*) cambio; (*at work*) turno ♦ *vt* trasladar; (*remove*) quitar ♦ *vi* moverse; ~ work *n* trabajo a turnos; ~y *adj* tramposo; (*eyes*) furtivo

shimmer ['ʃimə*] *n* reflejo trémulo

shin [ʃin] *n* espinilla

shine [ʃain] (*pt, pp* shone) *n* brillo, lustre *m* ♦ *vi* brillar, relucir ♦ *vt* (*shoes*) lustrar, sacar brillo a; to ~ a torch on sth dirigir una linterna hacia algo

shingle ['ʃiŋgl] *n* (*on beach*) guijarros *mpl*; ~s *n* (*MED*) herpes *mpl or fpl*

shiny ['ʃaini] *adj* brillante, lustroso

ship [ʃip] *n* buque *m*, barco ♦ *vt* (*goods*) embarcar; (*send*) transportar *or* enviar por vía marítima; ~building *n* construcción *f* de buques; ~ment *n* (*goods*) envío; ~ping *n* (*act*) embarque *m*; (*traffic*) buques *mpl*; ~wreck *n* naufragio ♦ *vt*: to be ~wrecked naufragar; ~yard *n* astillero

shire ['ʃaiə*] (*BRIT*) *n* condado

shirt [ʃəːt] *n* camisa; in (one's) ~ sleeves en mangas de camisa

shit [ʃit] (*inf!*) *excl* ¡mierda! (!)

shiver ['ʃivə*] *n* escalofrío ♦ *vi* temblar, estremecerse; (*with cold*) tiritar

shoal [ʃəul] *n* (*of fish*) banco *m*; (*fig: also:* ~s) tropel *m*

shock [ʃɔk] *n* (*impact*) choque *m*; (*ELEC*) descarga (eléctrica); (*emotional*) conmoción *f*; (*start*) sobresalto, susto; (*MED*) postración *f* nerviosa ♦ *vt* dar un susto a; (*offend*) escandalizar; ~

absorber *n* amortiguador *m*; ~ing *adj* (*awful*) espantoso; (*outrageous*) escandaloso

shoddy ['ʃɔdi] *adj* de pacotilla

shoe [ʃuː] (*pt, pp* shod) *n* zapato; (*for horse*) herradura ♦ *vt* (*horse*) herrar; ~brush *n* cepillo para zapatos; ~lace *n* cordón *m*; ~ polish *n* betún *m*; ~shop *n* zapatería; ~string *n* (*fig*): on a ~string con muy poco dinero

shone [ʃɔn] *pt, pp of* shine

shook [ʃuk] *pt of* shake

shoot [ʃuːt] (*pt, pp* shot) *n* (*on branch, seedling*) retoño, vástago ♦ *vt* disparar; (*kill*) matar a tiros; (*wound*) pegar un tiro; (*execute*) fusilar; (*film*) rodar, filmar ♦ *vi* (*FOOTBALL*) chutar; ~ down *vt* (*plane*) derribar; ~ in/out *vi* entrar corriendo/ salir disparado; ~ up *vi* (*prices*) dispararse; ~ing *n* (*shots*) tiros *mpl*; (*HUNTING*) caza con escopeta; ~ing star *n* estrella fugaz

shop [ʃɔp] *n* tienda; (*workshop*) taller *m* ♦ *vi* (*also:* go ~ping) ir de compras; ~ assistant (*BRIT*) *n* dependiente/a *m/f*; ~ floor (*BRIT*) *n* (*fig*) taller *m*, fábrica; ~keeper *n* tendero/a; ~lifting *n* mechería; ~per *n* comprador(a) *m/f*; ~ping *n* (*goods*) compras *fpl*; ~ping bag *n* bolsa de (compras); ~ping centre (*US* ~ping center) *n* centro comercial; ~-soiled *adj* deteriorado; ~ steward (*BRIT*) *n* (*INDUSTRY*) enlace *m* sindical; ~ window *n* escaparate *m* (*SP*), vidriera (*AM*)

shore [ʃɔː*] *n* orilla ♦ *vt*: to ~ (up) reforzar; on ~ en tierra

shorn [ʃɔːn] *pp of* shear

short [ʃɔːt] *adj* corto; (*in time*) breve, de corta duración; (*person*) bajo; (*curt*) brusco, seco; (*insufficient*) insuficiente; (a pair of) ~s (unos) pantalones *mpl* cortos; to be ~ of sth estar falto de algo; in ~ en pocas palabras; ~ of doing ... fuera de hacer ...; it is ~ for es la forma abreviada de; to cut ~ (*speech, visit*) interrumpir, terminar inesperadamente; everything ~

of ... todo menos ...; **to fall ~ of** no alcanzar; **to run ~ of** quedarle a uno poco; **to stop ~** parar en seco; **to stop ~ of** detenerse antes de; **~age** *n*: **a ~age of** una falta de; **~bread** *n especie de mantecada*; **~change** *vt* no dar el cambio completo a; **~circuit** *n* cortocircuito; **~coming** *n* defecto, deficiencia; **~(crust) pastry** (*BRIT*) *n* pasta quebradiza; **~cut** *n* atajo; **~en** *vt* acortar; (*visit*) interrumpir; **~fall** *n* déficit *m*; **~hand** (*BRIT*) *n* taquigrafía; **~hand typist** (*BRIT*) *n* taquimecanógrafo/a; **~ list** (*BRIT*) *n* (*for job*) lista de candidatos escogidos; **~-lived** *adj* efímero; **~ly** *adv* en breve, dentro de poco; **~-sighted** (*BRIT*) *adj* miope; (*fig*) imprudente; **~-staffed** *adj*: **to be ~-staffed** estar falto de personal; **~ story** *n* cuento; **~-tempered** *adj* enojadizo; **~-term** *adj* (*effect*) a corto plazo; **~wave** *n* (*RADIO*) onda corta

shot [ʃɒt] *pt, pp of* **shoot** *n* (*sound*) tiro, disparo; (*try*) tentativa; (*injection*) inyección *f*; (*PHOT*) toma, fotografía; **to be a good/poor ~** (*person*) tener buena/mala puntería; **like a ~** (*without any delay*) como un rayo; **~gun** *n* escopeta

should [ʃʊd] *aux vb*: **I ~ go now** debo irme ahora; **he ~ be there now** debe de haber llegado (ya); **I ~ go if I were you** yo en tu lugar me iría; **I ~ like to** me gustaría

shoulder [ˈʃəʊldə*] *n* hombro *vt* (*fig*) cargar con; **~ bag** *n* cartera de bandolera; **~ blade** *n* omóplato

shouldn't [ˈʃʊdnt] = **should not**

shout [ʃaʊt] *n* grito *vt* gritar *vi* gritar, dar voces; **~ down** *vt* acallar a gritos; **~ing** *n* griterío

shove [ʃʌv] *n* empujón *m* *vt* empujar; (*inf: put*): **to ~ sth in** meter algo a empellones; **~ off** (*inf*) *vi* largarse

shovel [ˈʃʌvl] *n* pala; (*mechanical*) excavadora *vt* mover con pala

show [ʃəʊ] (*pt* **showed**, *pp* **shown**) *n* (*of emotion*) demostración *f*; (*semblance*) apariencia; (*exhibition*) exposición *f*; (*THEATRE*) función *f*, espectáculo; (*TV*) show *m* *vt* mostrar, enseñar; (*courage etc*) mostrar, manifestar; (*exhibit*) exponer; (*film*) proyectar *vi* mostrarse; (*appear*) aparecer; **for ~** para impresionar; **on ~** (*exhibits etc*) expuesto; **~ in** *vt* (*person*) hacer pasar; **~ off** (*pej*) *vi* presumir *vt* (*display*) lucir; **~ out** *vt*: **to ~ sb out** acompañar a uno a la puerta; **~ up** *vi* (*stand out*) destacar; (*inf: turn up*) aparecer *vt* (*unmask*) desenmascarar; **~ business** *n* mundo del espectáculo; **~down** *n* enfrentamiento (final)

shower [ˈʃaʊə*] *n* (*rain*) chaparrón *m*, chubasco; (*of stones etc*) lluvia; (*for bathing*) ducha (*SP*), regadera (*AM*) *vi* llover *vt* (*fig*): **to ~ sb with sth** colmar a uno de algo; **to have a ~** ducharse; **~proof** *adj* impermeable

showing [ˈʃəʊɪŋ] *n* (*of film*) proyección *f*

show jumping *n* hípica

shown [ʃəʊn] *pp of* **show**

show: **~-off** (*inf*) *n* (*person*) presumido/a; **~piece** *n* (*of exhibition etc*) objeto cumbre; **~room** *n* sala de muestras

shrank [ʃræŋk] *pt of* **shrink**

shrapnel [ˈʃræpnl] *n* metralla

shred [ʃred] *n* (*gen pl*) triza, jirón *m* *vt* hacer trizas; (*CULIN*) desmenuzar; **~der** *n* (*vegetable ~der*) picadora; (*document ~der*) trituradora (de papel)

shrewd [ʃruːd] *adj* astuto

shriek [ʃriːk] *n* chillido *vi* chillar

shrill [ʃrɪl] *adj* agudo, estridente

shrimp [ʃrɪmp] *n* camarón *m*

shrine [ʃraɪn] *n* santuario, sepulcro

shrink [ʃrɪŋk] (*pt* **shrank**, *pp* **shrunk**) *vi* encogerse; (*be reduced*) reducirse; (*also: ~ away*) retroceder *vt* encoger *n* (*inf: pej*) loquero/a; **to ~ from (doing) sth** no atreverse a hacer algo; **~wrap** *vt* embalar con película de plástico

shrivel [ˈʃrɪvl] (*also: ~ up*) *vt* (*dry*) secar *vi* secarse

shroud [ʃraʊd] *n* sudario *vt*: **~ed in mystery** envuelto en el misterio

Shrove Tuesday ['ʃrəuv-] n martes m de carnaval

shrub [ʃrʌb] n arbusto; **~bery** n arbustos mpl

shrug [ʃrʌg] n encogimiento de hombros ♦ vt, vi: **to ~ (one's shoulders)** encogerse de hombros; **~ off** vt negar importancia a

shrunk [ʃrʌŋk] pp of **shrink**

shudder ['ʃʌdə*] n estremecimiento, escalofrío ♦ vi estremecerse

shuffle ['ʃʌfl] vt (cards) barajar ♦ vi: **to ~ (one's feet)** arrastrar los pies

shun [ʃʌn] vt rehuir, esquivar

shunt [ʃʌnt] vt (train) maniobrar; (object) empujar

shut [ʃʌt] (pt, pp **shut**) vt cerrar ♦ vi cerrarse; **~ down** vt, vi cerrar; **~ off** vt (supply etc) cortar; **~ up** vi (inf: keep quiet) callarse ♦ vt (close) cerrar; (silence) hacer callar; **~ter** n contraventana; (PHOT) obturador m

shuttle ['ʃʌtl] n lanzadera; (also: **~ service**) servicio rápido y continuo entre dos puntos; (: AVIAT) puente m aéreo; **~cock** n volante m; **~ diplomacy** n viajes mpl diplomáticos

shy [ʃaɪ] adj tímido; **~ness** n timidez f

Sicily ['sɪsɪlɪ] n Sicilia

sick [sɪk] adj (ill) enfermo; (nauseated) mareado; (humour) negro; (vomiting): **to be ~** (BRIT) vomitar; **to feel ~** tener náuseas; **to be ~ of** (fig) estar harto de; **~ bay** n enfermería; **~en** vt dar asco a; **~ening** adj (fig) asqueroso

sickle ['sɪkl] n hoz f

sick: **~ leave** n baja por enfermedad; **~ly** adj enfermizo; (smell) nauseabundo; **~ness** n enfermedad f, mal m; (vomiting) náuseas fpl; **~ pay** n subsidio de enfermedad

side [saɪd] n (gen) lado m; (of body) costado; (of lake) orilla; (of hill) ladera; (team) equipo; ♦ adj (door, entrance) lateral ♦ vi: **to ~ with sb** tomar el partido de uno; **by the ~ of** al lado de; **~ by ~** juntos/as; **from ~ to ~** de un lado para otro; **from**

all ~s de todos lados; **to take ~s (with)** tomar partido (con); **~board** n aparador m; **~boards** (BRIT) npl = **~burns**; **~burns** npl patillas fpl; **~ drum** n tambor m; **~ effect** n efecto secundario; **~light** n (AUT) luz f lateral; **~line** n (SPORT) línea de banda; (fig) empleo suplementario; **~long** adj de soslayo; **~ order** n plato de acompañamiento; **~ show** n (stall) caseta; **~step** vt (fig) esquivar; **~ street** n calle f lateral; **~track** vt (fig) desviar (de su propósito); **~walk** (US) n acera; **~ways** adv de lado

siding ['saɪdɪŋ] n (RAIL) apartadero, vía muerta

siege [siːdʒ] n cerco, sitio

sieve [sɪv] n colador m ♦ vt cribar

sift [sɪft] vt cribar; (fig: information) escudriñar

sigh [saɪ] n suspiro ♦ vi suspirar

sight [saɪt] n (faculty) vista; (spectacle) espectáculo; (on gun) mira, alza ♦ vt divisar; **in ~** a la vista; **out of ~** fuera de (la) vista; **on ~** (shoot) sin previo aviso; **~seeing** n excursionismo, turismo; **to go ~seeing** hacer turismo

sign [saɪn] n (with hand) señal f, seña; (trace) huella, rastro; (notice) letrero; (written) signo ♦ vt firmar; (SPORT) fichar; **to ~ sth over to sb** firmar el traspaso de algo a uno; **~ on** vi (BRIT: as unemployed) registrarse como desempleado; (for course) inscribirse ♦ vt (MIL) alistar; (employee) contratar; **~ up** vi (MIL) alistarse; (for course) inscribirse ♦ vt (player) fichar

signal ['sɪgnl] n señal f ♦ vi señalizar ♦ vt (person) hacer señas a; (message) comunicar por señales; **~man** (irreg) n (RAIL) guardavía m

signature ['sɪgnətʃə*] n firma; **~ tune** n sintonía de apertura de un programa

signet ring ['sɪgnət-] n anillo de sello

significance [sɪg'nɪfɪkəns] n (importance) trascendencia

significant [sɪg'nɪfɪkənt] adj significativo; (important) trascendente

signify ['sɪgnɪfaɪ] *vt* significar

sign language *n* lenguaje *m* para sordomudos

signpost ['saɪnpəʊst] *n* indicador *m*

silence ['saɪlns] *n* silencio ♦ *vt* acallar; (*guns*) reducir al silencio; ~**r** *n* (*on gun*, BRIT: AUT) silenciador *m*

silent ['saɪlnt] *adj* silencioso; (*not speaking*) callado; (*film*) mudo; **to remain** ~ guardar silencio; ~ **partner** *n* (COMM) socio/a comanditario/a

silhouette [sɪluː'et] *n* silueta

silicon chip ['sɪlɪkən-] *n* plaqueta de silicio

silk [sɪlk] *n* seda ♦ *adj* de seda; ~**y** *adj* sedoso

silly ['sɪlɪ] *adj* (*person*) tonto; (*idea*) absurdo

silt [sɪlt] *n* sedimento

silver ['sɪlvə*] *n* plata; (*money*) moneda suelta ♦ *adj* de plata; (*colour*) plateado; ~ **paper** (BRIT) *n* papel *m* de plata; ~-**plated** *adj* plateado; ~**smith** *n* platero/a; ~**ware** *n* plata; ~**y** *adj* argentino

similar ['sɪmɪlə*] *adj*: ~ **(to)** parecido *or* semejante (a); ~**ity** [-'lærɪtɪ] *n* semejanza; ~**ly** *adv* del mismo modo

simmer ['sɪmə*] *vi* hervir a fuego lento

simple ['sɪmpl] *adj* (*easy*) sencillo; (*foolish*, COMM: *interest*) simple; **simplicity** [-'plɪsɪtɪ] *n* sencillez *f*; **simplify** ['sɪmplɪfaɪ] *vt* simplificar

simply ['sɪmplɪ] *adv* (*live*, *talk*) sencillamente; (*just*, *merely*) sólo

simulate ['sɪmjuːleɪt] *vt* fingir, simular; ~**d** *adj* simulado; (*fur*) de imitación

simultaneous [sɪməl'teɪnɪəs] *adj* simultáneo; ~**ly** *adv* simultáneamente

sin [sɪn] *n* pecado ♦ *vi* pecar

since [sɪns] *adv* desde entonces, después ♦ *prep* desde ♦ *conj* (*time*) desde que; (*because*) ya que, puesto que; ~ **then**, **ever** ~ desde entonces

sincere [sɪn'sɪə*] *adj* sincero; ~**ly** *adv*: **yours** ~**ly** (*in letters*) le saluda atentamente; **sincerity** [-'serɪtɪ] *n* sinceridad *f*

sinew ['sɪnjuː] *n* tendón *m*

sing [sɪŋ] (*pt* **sang**, *pp* **sung**) *vt*, *vi* cantar

Singapore [sɪŋə'pɔː*] *n* Singapur *m*

singe [sɪndʒ] *vt* chamuscar

singer ['sɪŋə*] *n* cantante *m/f*

singing ['sɪŋɪŋ] *n* canto

single ['sɪŋgl] *adj* único, solo; (*unmarried*) soltero; (*not double*) simple, sencillo ♦ *n* (BRIT: *also*: ~ **ticket**) billete *m* sencillo; (*record*) sencillo, single *m*; ~**s** *npl* (TENNIS) individual *m*; ~ **out** *vt* (*choose*) escoger; ~ **bed** cama individual; ~-**breasted** *adj* recto; ~ **file** *n*: **in** ~ **file** en fila de uno; ~-**handed** *adv* sin ayuda; ~-**minded** *adj* resuelto, firme; ~ **parent** *n* padre *m* soltero, madre *f* soltera (*o divorciado etc*); ~ **parent family** familia monoparental; ~ **room** *n* cuarto individual

singly ['sɪŋglɪ] *adv* uno por uno

singular ['sɪŋgjulə*] *adj* (*odd*) raro, extraño; (*outstanding*) excepcional ♦ *n* (LING) singular *m*

sinister ['sɪnɪstə*] *adj* siniestro

sink [sɪŋk] (*pt* **sank**, *pp* **sunk**) *n* fregadero ♦ *vt* (*ship*) hundir, echar a pique; (*foundations*) excavar ♦ *vi* (*gen*) hundirse; **to** ~ **sth into** hundir algo en; ~ **in** *vi* (*fig*) penetrar, calar

sinner ['sɪnə*] *n* pecador(a) *m/f*

sinus ['saɪnəs] *n* (ANAT) seno

sip [sɪp] *n* sorbo ♦ *vt* sorber, beber a sorbitos

siphon ['saɪfən] *n* sifón *m*; ~ **off** *vt* desviar

sir [sə*] *n* señor *m*; **S~ John Smith** Sir John Smith; **yes** ~ sí, señor

siren ['saɪərn] *n* sirena

sirloin ['səːlɔɪn] *n* (*also*: ~ **steak**) solomillo

sister ['sɪstə*] *n* hermana; (BRIT: *nurse*) enfermera jefe; ~-**in-law** *n* cuñada

sit [sɪt] (*pt*, *pp* **sat**) *vi* sentarse; (*be sitting*) estar sentado; (*assembly*) reunirse; (*for painter*) posar ♦ *vt* (*exam*) presentarse a; ~ **down** *vi* sentarse; ~ **in on** *vt fus* asistir a; ~ **up** *vi* incorporarse; (*not go to bed*) velar

sitcom ['sɪtkɔm] *n abbr* (= *situation comedy*) comedia de situación

site [saɪt] *n* sitio; (*also:* **building ~**) solar *m* ♦ *vt* situar

sit-in *n* (*demonstration*) sentada

sitting ['sɪtɪŋ] *n* (*of assembly etc*) sesión *f*; (*in canteen*) turno; **~ room** *n* sala de estar

situated ['sɪtjueɪtɪd] *adj* situado

situation [sɪtjuˈeɪʃən] *n* situación *f*; "**~s vacant**" (*BRIT*) "ofrecen trabajo"

six [sɪks] *num* seis; **~teen** *num* diez y seis, dieciséis; **~th** *num* sexto; **~ty** *num* sesenta

size [saɪz] *n* tamaño; (*extent*) extensión *f*; (*of clothing*) talla; (*of shoes*) número; **~ up** *vt* formarse una idea de; **~able** *adj* importante, considerable

sizzle ['sɪzl] *vi* crepitar

skate [skeɪt] *n* patín *m*; (*fish: pl inv*) raya ♦ *vi* patinar; **~board** *n* monopatín *m*; **~boarding** *n* monopatín *m*; **~r** *n* patinador(a) *m/f*; **skating** *n* patinaje *m*; **skating rink** *n* pista de patinaje

skeleton ['skelɪtn] *n* esqueleto; (*TECH*) armazón *f*; (*outline*) esquema *m*; **~ staff** *n* personal *m* reducido

skeptic *etc* ['skeptɪk] (*US*) = **sceptic**

sketch [sketʃ] *n* (*drawing*) dibujo; (*outline*) esbozo, bosquejo; (*THEATRE*) sketch *m* ♦ *vt* dibujar; (*plan etc: also:* **~ out**) esbozar; **~ book** *n* libro de dibujos; **~y** *adj* incompleto

skewer ['skjuːə*] *n* broqueta

ski [skiː] *n* esquí *m* ♦ *vi* esquiar; **~ boot** *n* bota de esquí

skid [skɪd] *n* patinazo ♦ *vi* patinar

ski: **~er** *n* esquiador(a) *m/f*; **~ing** *n* esquí *m*; **~ jump** *n* salto con esquís

skilful ['skɪlful] (*BRIT*) *adj* diestro, experto

ski lift *n* telesilla *m*, telesquí *m*

skill [skɪl] *n* destreza, pericia; técnica; **~ed** *adj* hábil, diestro; (*worker*) cualificado; **~full** (*US*) *adj* = **skilful**

skim [skɪm] *vt* (*milk*) desnatar; (*glide over*) rozar, rasar ♦ *vi*: **to ~ through** (*book*) hojear; **~med milk** *n* leche *f* desnatada

skimp [skɪmp] *vt* (*also:* **~ on:** *work*) chapucear; (*cloth etc*) escatimar; **~y** *adj*

escaso; (*skirt*) muy corto

skin [skɪn] *n* piel *f*; (*complexion*) cutis *m* ♦ *vt* (*fruit etc*) pelar; (*animal*) despellejar; **~ cancer** *n* cáncar *m* de piel; **~-deep** *adj* superficial; **~ diving** *n* buceo; **~ny** *adj* flaco; **~tight** *adj* (*dress etc*) muy ajustado

skip [skɪp] *n* brinco, salto; (*BRIT: container*) contenedor *m* ♦ *vi* brincar; (*with rope*) saltar a la comba ♦ *vt* saltarse

ski: **~ pass** *n* forfait *m* (de esquí); **~ pole** *n* bastón *m* de esquiar

skipper ['skɪpə*] *n* (*NAUT, SPORT*) capitán *m*

skipping rope ['skɪpɪŋ-] (*BRIT*) *n* comba

skirmish ['skəːmɪʃ] *n* escaramuza

skirt [skəːt] *n* falda (*SP*), pollera (*AM*) ♦ *vt* (*go round*) ladear; **~ing board** (*BRIT*) *n* rodapié *m*

ski slope *n* pista de esquí

ski suit *n* traje *m* de esquí

ski tow *n* remonte *m*

skittle ['skɪtl] *n* bolo; **~s** *n* (*game*) boliche *m*

skive [skaɪv] (*BRIT: inf*) *vi* gandulear

skull [skʌl] *n* calavera; (*ANAT*) cráneo

skunk [skʌŋk] *n* mofeta

sky [skaɪ] *n* cielo; **~light** *n* tragaluz *m*, claraboya; **~scraper** *n* rascacielos *m inv*

slab [slæb] *n* (*stone*) bloque *m*; (*flat*) losa; (*of cake*) trozo

slack [slæk] *adj* (*loose*) flojo; (*slow*) de poca actividad; (*careless*) descuidado; **~s** *npl* pantalones *mpl*; **~en** (*also:* **~en off**) *vi* aflojarse ♦ *vt* aflojar; (*speed*) disminuir

slag heap ['slæg-] *n* escorial *m*, escombrera

slag off (*BRIT: inf*) *vt* poner como un trapo

slam [slæm] *vt* (*throw*) arrojar (violentamente); (*criticize*) criticar duramente ♦ *vi* (*door*) cerrarse de golpe; **to ~ the door** dar un portazo

slander ['slɑːndə*] *n* calumnia, difamación *f*

slang [slæŋ] *n* argot *m*; (*jargon*) jerga

slant [slɑːnt] *n* sesgo, inclinación *f*; (*fig*)

interpretación f; **~ed** adj (fig) parcial;
~ing adj inclinado; (eyes) rasgado
slap [slæp] n palmada; (in face) bofetada
♦ vt dar una palmada or bofetada a;
(paint etc): **to ~ sth on sth** embadurnar
algo con algo ♦ adv (directly)
exactamente, directamente; **~dash** adj
descuidado; **~stick** n comedia de golpe
y porrazo; **~-up** adj: **a ~-up meal** (BRIT)
un banquetazo, una comilona
slash [slæʃ] vt acuchillar; (fig: prices)
fulminar
slat [slæt] n tablilla, listón m
slate [sleɪt] n pizarra ♦ vt (fig: criticize)
criticar duramente
slaughter ['slɔ:tə*] n (of animals) matanza;
(of people) carnicería ♦ vt matar; **~house**
n matadero
Slav [slɑ:v] adj eslavo
slave [sleɪv] n esclavo/a ♦ vi (also: **~
away**) sudar tinta; **~ry** n esclavitud f
slay [sleɪ] (pt slew, pp slain) vt matar
sleazy ['sli:zɪ] adj de mala fama
sledge [sledʒ] n trineo; **~hammer** n
mazo
sleek [sli:k] adj (shiny) lustroso; (car etc)
elegante
sleep [sli:p] (pt, pp slept) n sueño ♦ vi
dormir; **to go to ~** quedarse dormido; **~
around** vi acostarse con cualquiera; **~
in** vi (oversleep) quedarse dormido; **~er** n
(person) durmiente m/f; (BRIT: RAIL: on
track) traviesa; (: train) coche-cama m;
~ing bag n saco de dormir; **~ing car** n
coche-cama m; **~ing partner** (BRIT) n
(COMM) socio comanditario; **~ing pill** n
somnífero; **~less** adj: a **~less night** una
noche en blanco; **~walker** n
sonámbulo/a; **~y** adj soñoliento; (place)
soporífero
sleet [sli:t] n aguanieve f
sleeve [sli:v] n manga; (TECH) manguito;
(of record) portada; **~less** adj sin mangas
sleigh [sleɪ] n trineo
sleight [slaɪt] n: **~ of hand** escamoteo
slender ['slendə*] adj delgado; (means)
escaso

slept [slept] pt, pp of **sleep**
slew [slu:] pt of **slay** ♦ vi (BRIT: veer)
torcerse
slice [slaɪs] n (of meat) tajada; (of bread)
rebanada; (of lemon) rodaja; (utensil) pala
♦ vt cortar (en tajos); rebanar
slick [slɪk] adj (skilful) hábil, diestro; (clever)
astuto ♦ n (also: **oil ~**) marea negra
slide [slaɪd] (pt, pp slid) n (movement)
descenso, desprendimiento; (in
playground) tobogán m; (PHOT)
diapositiva; (BRIT: also: **hair ~**) pasador m
♦ vt correr, deslizar ♦ vi (slip) resbalarse;
(glide) deslizarse; **sliding** adj (door)
corredizo; **sliding scale** n escala móvil
slight [slaɪt] adj (slim) delgado; (frail)
delicado; (pain etc) leve; (trivial)
insignificante; (small) pequeño ♦ n desaire
m ♦ vt (insult) ofender, desairar; **not in
the ~est** en absoluto; **~ly** adv
ligeramente, un poco
slim [slɪm] adj delgado, esbelto; (fig:
chance) remoto ♦ vi adelgazar
slime [slaɪm] n limo, cieno
slimming ['slɪmɪŋ] n adelgazamiento
slimy ['slaɪmɪ] adj cenagoso
sling [slɪŋ] (pt, pp slung) n (MED)
cabestrillo; (weapon) honda ♦ vt tirar,
arrojar
slip [slɪp] n (slide) resbalón m; (mistake)
descuido; (underskirt) combinación f; (of
paper) papelito ♦ vt (slide) deslizar ♦ vi
deslizarse; (stumble) resbalar(se); (decline)
decaer; (move smoothly): **to ~ into/out of**
(room etc) introducirse en/salirse de; **to
give sb the ~** eludir a uno; **a ~ of the
tongue** un lapsus; **to ~ sth on/off**
ponerse/quitarse algo; **~ away** vi
escabullirse; **~ in** vt meter ♦ vi meterse;
~ out vi (go out) salir (un momento); **~
up** vi (make mistake) equivocarse; meter
la pata; **~ped disc** n vértebra dislocada
slipper ['slɪpə*] n zapatilla, pantufla
slippery ['slɪpərɪ] adj resbaladizo
slip: ~ road (BRIT) n carretera de acceso;
~-up n (error) desliz m; **~way** n grada,
gradas fpl

slit [slɪt] (*pt, pp* **slit**) *n* raja; (*cut*) corte *m* ♦ *vt* rajar; cortar

slither ['slɪðə*] *vi* deslizarse

sliver ['slɪvə*] *n* (*of glass, wood*) astilla; (*of cheese etc*) raja

slob [slɔb] (*inf*) *n* abandonado/a

slog [slɔg] (*BRIT*) *vi* sudar tinta; **it was a ~** costó trabajo (hacerlo)

slogan ['sləugən] *n* eslogan *m*, lema *m*

slope [sləup] *n* (*up*) cuesta, pendiente *f*; (*down*) declive *m*; (*side of mountain*) falda, vertiente *m* ♦ *vi*: **to ~ down** estar en declive; **to ~ up** inclinarse; **sloping** *adj* en pendiente; en declive; (*writing*) inclinado

sloppy ['slɔpɪ] *adj* (*work*) descuidado; (*appearance*) desaliñado

slot [slɔt] *n* ranura ♦ *vt*: **to ~ into** encajar en

slot machine *n* (*BRIT: vending machine*) distribuidor *m* automático; (*for gambling*) tragaperras *m inv*

slouch [slautʃ] *vi* andar *etc* con los hombros caídos

Slovenia [sləu'vi:nɪə] *n* Eslovenia

slovenly ['slʌvənlɪ] *adj* desaliñado, desaseado; (*careless*) descuidado

slow [sləu] *adj* lento; (*not clever*) lerdo; (*watch*): **to be ~** atrasar ♦ *adv* lentamente, despacio ♦ *vt, vi* (*also: ~ down, ~ up*) retardar; "**~**" (*road sign*) "disminuir velocidad"; **~down** (*US*) *n* huelga de manos caídas; **~ly** *adv* lentamente, despacio; **~ motion** *n*: **in ~ motion** a cámara lenta

sludge [slʌdʒ] *n* lodo, fango

slug [slʌg] *n* babosa; (*bullet*) posta; **~gish** *adj* lento; (*person*) perezoso

sluice [slu:s] *n* (*gate*) esclusa; (*channel*) canal *m*

slum [slʌm] *n* casucha

slump [slʌmp] *n* (*economic*) depresión *f* ♦ *vi* hundirse; (*prices*) caer en picado

slung [slʌŋ] *pt, pp of* **sling**

slur [slə:*] *n*: **to cast a ~ on** insultar ♦ *vt* (*speech*) pronunciar mal

slush [slʌʃ] *n* nieve *f* a medio derretir

slut [slʌt] *n* putona

sly [slaɪ] *adj* astuto; (*smile*) taimado

smack [smæk] *n* bofetada ♦ *vt* dar con la mano a; (*child, on face*) abofetear ♦ *vi*: **to ~ of** saber a, oler a

small [smɔ:l] *adj* pequeño; **~ ads** (*BRIT*) *npl* anuncios *mpl* por palabras; **~ change** *n* suelto, cambio; **~holder** (*BRIT*) *n* granjero/a, parcelero/a; **~ hours** *npl*: **in the ~ hours** a las altas horas (de la noche); **~pox** *n* viruela; **~ talk** *n* cháchara

smart [smɑ:t] *adj* elegante; (*clever*) listo, inteligente; (*quick*) rápido, vivo ♦ *vi* escocer, picar; **~en up** *vi* arreglarse ♦ *vt* arreglar

smash [smæʃ] *n* (*also:* **~-up**) choque *m*; (*MUS*) exitazo ♦ *vt* (*break*) hacer pedazos; (*car etc*) estrellar; (*SPORT: record*) batir ♦ *vi* hacerse pedazos; (*against wall etc*) estrellarse; **~ing** (*inf*) *adj* estupendo

smattering ['smætərɪŋ] *n*: **a ~ of** algo de

smear [smɪə*] *n* mancha; (*MED*) frotis *m inv* ♦ *vt* untar; **~ campaign** *n* campaña de desprestigio

smell [smɛl] (*pt, pp* **smelt** *or* **smelled**) *n* olor *m*; (*sense*) olfato ♦ *vt, vi* oler; **~y** *adj* maloliente

smile [smaɪl] *n* sonrisa ♦ *vi* sonreír

smirk [smə:k] *n* sonrisa falsa *or* afectada

smith [smɪθ] *n* herrero; **~y** ['smɪðɪ] *n* herrería

smog [smɔg] *n* esmog *m*

smoke [sməuk] *n* humo ♦ *vi* fumar; (*chimney*) echar humo ♦ *vt* (*cigarettes*) fumar; **~d** *adj* (*bacon, glass*) ahumado; **~r** *n* (*person*) fumador(a) *m/f*; (*RAIL*) coche *m* fumador; **~ screen** *n* cortina de humo; **~ shop** (*US*) *n* estanco (*SP*), tabaquería (*AM*); **smoking** *n*: "**no smoking**" "prohibido fumar"; **smoky** *adj* (*room*) lleno de humo; (*taste*) ahumado

smolder ['sməuldə*] (*US*) *vi* = **smoulder**

smooth [smu:ð] *adj* liso; (*sea*) tranquilo; (*flavour, movement*) suave; (*sauce*) fino; (*person: pej*) meloso ♦ *vt* (*also:* **~ out**) alisar; (*creases, difficulties*) allanar

smother ['smʌðə*] *vt* sofocar; (*repress*) contener

smoulder ['sməuldə*] (*US* **smolder**) *vi* arder sin llama

smudge [smʌdʒ] *n* mancha ♦ *vt* manchar

smug [smʌg] *adj* presumido; orondo

smuggle ['smʌgl] *vt* pasar de contrabando; **~r** *n* contrabandista *m/f*; **smuggling** *n* contrabando

smutty ['smʌti] *adj* (*fig*) verde, obsceno

snack [snæk] *n* bocado; **~ bar** *n* cafetería

snag [snæg] *n* problema *m*

snail [sneil] *n* caracol *m*

snake [sneik] *n* serpiente *f*

snap [snæp] *n* (*sound*) chasquido; (*photograph*) foto *f* ♦ *adj* (*decision*) instantáneo ♦ *vt* (*break*) quebrar; (*fingers*) castañetear ♦ *vi* quebrarse; (*fig: speak sharply*) contestar bruscamente; **to ~ shut** cerrarse de golpe; **~ at** *vt fus* (*subj: dog*) intentar morder; **~ off** *vi* partirse; **~ up** *vt* agarrar; **~ fastener** (*US*) *n* botón *m* de presión; **~py** (*inf*) *adj* (*answer*) instantáneo; (*slogan*) conciso; **make it ~py!** (*hurry up*) ¡date prisa!; **~shot** *n* foto *f* (instantánea)

snare [snɛə*] *n* trampa

snarl [snɑːl] *vi* gruñir

snatch [snætʃ] *n* (*small piece*) fragmento ♦ *vt* (**~ away**) arrebatar; (*fig*) agarrar; **to ~ some sleep** encontrar tiempo para dormir

sneak [sniːk] (*pt* (*US*) **snuck**) *vi*: **to ~ in/out** entrar/salir a hurtadillas ♦ *n* (*inf*) soplón/ona *m/f*; **to ~ up on sb** aparecérsele de improviso a uno; **~ers** *npl* zapatos *mpl* de lona; **~y** *adj* furtivo

sneer [snɪə*] *vi* reír con sarcasmo; (*mock*): **to ~ at** burlarse de

sneeze [sniːz] *vi* estornudar

sniff [snɪf] *vi* sollozar ♦ *vt* husmear, oler; (*drugs*) esnifar

snigger ['snɪgə*] *vi* reírse con disimulo

snip [snɪp] *n* tijeretazo; (*BRIT: inf: bargain*) ganga ♦ *vt* tijeretear

sniper ['snaɪpə*] *n* francotirador(a) *m/f*

snippet ['snɪpɪt] *n* retazo

snob [snɔb] *n* (e)snob *m/f*; **~bery** *n* (e)snobismo; **~bish** *adj* (e)snob

snooker ['snuːkə*] *n* especie de billar

snoop [snuːp] *vi*: **to ~ about** fisgonear

snooze [snuːz] *n* siesta ♦ *vi* echar una siesta

snore [snɔː*] *n* ronquido ♦ *vi* roncar

snorkel ['snɔːkl] *n* (tubo) respirador *m*

snort [snɔːt] *n* bufido ♦ *vi* bufar

snout [snaut] *n* hocico, morro

snow [snəu] *n* nieve *f* ♦ *vi* nevar; **~ball** *n* bola de nieve ♦ *vi* (*fig*) agrandarse, ampliarse; **~bound** *adj* bloqueado por la nieve; **~drift** *n* ventisquero; **~drop** *n* campanilla; **~fall** *n* nevada; **~flake** *n* copo de nieve; **~man** (*irreg*) *n* figura de nieve; **~plough** (*US* **~plow**) *n* quitanieves *m inv*; **~shoe** *n* raqueta (de nieve); **~storm** *n* nevada, nevasca

snub [snʌb] *vt* (*person*) desairar ♦ *n* desaire *m*, repulsa; **~-nosed** *adj* chato

snuff [snʌf] *n* rapé *m*

snug [snʌg] *adj* (*cosy*) cómodo; (*fitted*) ajustado

snuggle ['snʌgl] *vi*: **to ~ up to sb** arrimarse a uno

KEYWORD

so [səu] *adv* **1** (*thus, likewise*) así, de este modo; **if ~** de ser así; **I like swimming — ~ do I** a mí me gusta nadar — a mí también; **I've got work to do — ~ has Paul** tengo trabajo que hacer — Paul también; **it's 5 o'clock — ~ it is!** son las cinco — ¡pues es verdad!; **I hope/think ~** espero/creo que sí; **~ far** hasta ahora; (*in past*) hasta este momento

2 (*in comparisons etc: to such a degree*) tan; **~ quickly (that)** tan rápido (que); **~ big (that)** tan grande (que); **she's not ~ clever as her brother** no es tan lista como su hermano; **we were ~ worried** estábamos preocupadísimos

3: **~ much** *adj, adv* tanto; **~ many** tantos/as

4 (*phrases*): **10 or ~** unos 10, 10 o así; **~ long!** (*inf: goodbye*) ¡hasta luego!

♦ conj 1 (expressing purpose): ~ as to do para hacer; ~ (that) para que +sub 2 (expressing result) así que; ~ you see, I could have gone así que ya ves, (yo) podría haber ido

soak [sauk] vt (drench) empapar; (steep in water) remojar ♦ vi remojarse, estar a remojo; ~ **in** vi penetrar; ~ **up** vt absorber

soap [saup] n jabón m; ~**flakes** npl escamas fpl de jabón; ~ **opera** n telenovela; ~ **powder** n jabón m en polvo; ~**y** adj jabonoso

soar [sɔ:*] vi (on wings) remontarse; (rocket, prices) dispararse; (building etc) elevarse

sob [sɔb] n sollozo ♦ vi sollozar

sober ['saubə*] adj (serious) serio; (not drunk) sobrio; (colour, style) discreto; ~ **up** vt quitar la borrachera

so-called adj así llamado

soccer ['sɔkə*] n fútbol m

social ['sauʃl] adj social ♦ n velada, fiesta; ~ **club** n club m; ~**ism** n socialismo; ~**ist** adj, n socialista m/f; ~**ize** vi: to ~**ize (with)** alternar (con); ~**ly** adv socialmente; ~ **security** n seguridad f social; ~ **work** n asistencia social; ~ **worker** n asistente/a m/f social

society [sə'saɪətɪ] n sociedad f; (club) asociación f; (also: **high ~**) alta sociedad

sociology [sausɪ'ɔlədʒɪ] n sociología f

sock [sɔk] n calcetín m (SP), media (AM)

socket ['sɔkɪt] n cavidad f; (BRIT: ELEC) enchufe m

sod [sɔd] n (of earth) césped m; (BRIT: inf!) cabrón/ona m/f (!)

soda ['saudə] n (CHEM) sosa; (also: ~ **water**) soda; (US: also: ~ **pop**) gaseosa

sofa ['saufə] n sofá m

soft [sɔft] adj (lenient, not hard) blando; (gentle, not bright) suave; ~ **drink** n bebida no alcohólica; ~**en** ['sɔfn] vt ablandar; suavizar; (effect) amortiguar ♦ vi ablandarse; suavizarse; ~**ly** adv suavemente; (gently) delicadamente, con

delicadeza; ~**ness** n blandura; suavidad f; ~**ware** n (COMPUT) software m

soggy ['sɔgɪ] adj empapado

soil [sɔɪl] n (earth) tierra, suelo ♦ vt ensuciar; ~**ed** adj sucio

solar ['saulə*] adj: ~ **energy** n energía solar; ~ **panel** n panel m solar

sold [sauld] pt, pp of **sell**; ~ **out** adj (COMM) agotado

solder ['saulda*] vt soldar ♦ n soldadura

soldier ['sauldʒə*] n soldado; (army man) militar m

sole [saul] n (of foot) planta; (of shoe) suela; (fish: pl inv) lenguado ♦ adj único

solemn ['sɔləm] adj solemne

sole trader n (COMM) comerciante m exclusivo

solicit [sə'lɪsɪt] vt (request) solicitar ♦ vi (prostitute) importunar

solicitor [sə'lɪsɪtə*] (BRIT) n (for wills etc) ≈ notario/a; (in court) ≈ abogado/a

solid ['sɔlɪd] adj sólido; (gold etc) macizo ♦ n sólido; ~**s** npl (food) alimentos mpl sólidos

solidarity [sɔlɪ'dærɪtɪ] n solidaridad f

solitary ['sɔlɪtərɪ] adj solitario, solo; ~ **confinement** n incomunicación f

solo ['saulau] n solo ♦ adv (fly) en solitario; ~**ist** n solista m/f

soluble ['sɔljubl] adj soluble

solution [sə'lu:ʃən] n solución f

solve [sɔlv] vt resolver, solucionar

solvent ['sɔlvənt] adj (COMM) solvente ♦ n (CHEM) solvente m

KEYWORD

some [sʌm] adj 1 (a certain amount or number of): ~ **tea / water / biscuits** té/ agua/(unas) galletas; **there's ~ milk in the fridge** hay leche en el frigo; **there were ~ people outside** había algunas personas fuera; **I've got ~ money, but not much** tengo algo de dinero, pero no mucho
2 (certain: in contrasts) algunos/as; ~ **people say that ...** hay quien dice que ...; ~ **films were excellent, but most**

were mediocre hubo películas
excelentes, pero la mayoría fueron
mediocres
3 (*unspecified*): ~ **woman was asking for
you** una mujer estuvo preguntando por
ti; **he was asking for ~ book (or other)**
pedía un libro; ~ **day** algún día; ~ **day
next week** un día de la semana que
viene
♦ *pron* **1** (*a certain number*): **I've got ~**
(*books etc*) tengo algunos/as
2 (*a certain amount*) algo; **I've got ~**
(*money, milk*) tengo algo; **could I have ~
of that cheese?** ¿me puede dar un poco
de ese queso?; **I've read ~ of the book**
he leído parte del libro
♦ *adv*: ~ **10 people** unas 10 personas,
una decena de personas

some: ~body ['sʌmbədɪ] *pron* =
someone; ~how *adv* de alguna manera;
(*for some reason*) por una u otra razón;
~one *pron* alguien; **~place** (*US*) *adv*
= **somewhere**
somersault ['sʌməsɔːlt] *n* (*deliberate*) salto
mortal; (*accidental*) vuelco ♦ *vi* dar un
salto mortal; dar vuelcos
some: ~thing *pron* algo; **would you like
~thing to eat/drink?** ¿te gustaría cenar/
tomar algo?; **~time** *adv* (*in future*) algún
día, en algún momento; (*in past*): **~time
last month** durante el mes pasado;
~times *adv* a veces; **~what** *adv* algo;
~where *adv* (*be*) en alguna parte, (*go*)
a alguna parte; **~where else** (*be*) en otra
parte; (*go*) a otra parte
son [sʌn] *n* hijo
song [sɒŋ] *n* canción *f*
son-in-law *n* yerno
soon [suːn] *adv* pronto, dentro de poco; ~
afterwards poco después; *see also* **as**;
~er *adv* (*time*) antes, más temprano;
(*preference*): **I would ~er do that** preferiría
hacer eso; **~er or later** tarde o temprano
soot [sut] *n* hollín *m*
soothe [suːð] *vt* tranquilizar; (*pain*) aliviar
sophisticated [sə'fɪstɪkeɪtɪd] *adj*

sofisticado
sophomore ['sɒfəmɔː*] (*US*) *n* estudiante
m/f de segundo año
sopping ['sɒpɪŋ] *adj*: ~ **(wet)** empapado
soppy ['sɒpɪ] (*pej*) *adj* tonto
soprano [sə'prɑːnəu] *n* soprano *f*
sorcerer ['sɔːsərə*] *n* hechicero
sore [sɔː*] *adj* (*painful*) doloroso, que duele
♦ *n* llaga; **~ly** *adv*: **I am ~ly tempted to**
estoy muy tentado a
sorrow ['sɒrəu] *n* pena, dolor *m*; **~s** *npl*
pesares *mpl*; **~ful** *adj* triste
sorry ['sɒrɪ] *adj* (*regretful*) arrepentido;
(*condition, excuse*) lastimoso; **~!** ¡perdón!,
¡perdone!; **~?** ¿cómo?; **to feel ~ for sb**
tener lástima a uno; **I feel ~ for him** me
da lástima
sort [sɔːt] *n* clase *f*, género, tipo ♦ *vt* (*also:
~ out: papers*) clasificar; (*: problems*)
arreglar, solucionar; **~ing office** *n* sala
de batalla
SOS *n* SOS *m*
so-so *adv* regular, así así
soufflé ['suːfleɪ] *n* suflé *m*
sought [sɔːt] *pt, pp of* **seek**
soul [səul] *n* alma; **~ful** *adj* lleno de
sentimiento
sound [saund] *n* (*noise*) sonido, ruido;
(*volume: on TV etc*) volumen *m*; (*GEO*)
estrecho ♦ *adj* (*healthy*) sano; (*safe, not
damaged*) en buen estado; (*reliable:
person*) digno de confianza; (*sensible*)
sensato, razonable; (*secure: investment*)
seguro ♦ *adv*: **~ asleep** profundamente
dormido ♦ *vt* (*alarm*) sonar ♦ *vi* sonar,
resonar; (*fig: seem*) parecer; **to ~ like**
sonar a; ~ **out** *vt* sondear; ~ **barrier** *n*
barrera del sonido; **~bite** *n* cita jugosa; ~
effects *npl* efectos *mpl* sonoros; **~ly** *adv*
(*sleep*) profundamente; (*defeated*)
completamente; **~proof** *adj*
insonorizado; **~track** *n* (*of film*) banda
sonora
soup [suːp] *n* (*thick*) sopa; (*thin*) caldo; ~
plate *n* plato sopero; **~spoon** *n*
cuchara sopera
sour ['sauə*] *adj* agrio; (*milk*) cortado; **it's**

~ **grapes** (fig) están verdes
source [sɔːs] n fuente f
south [sauθ] n sur m ♦ adj del sur, sureño
♦ adv al sur, hacia el sur; **S~ Africa** n
África del Sur; **S~ African** adj, n
sudafricano/a m/f; **S~ America** n
América del Sur, Sudamérica; **S~
American** adj, n sudamericano/a m/f;
~-east n sudeste m; **~erly** ['sʌðəlɪ] adj
sur; (from the ~) del sur; **~ern** ['sʌðən] adj
del sur, meridional; **S~ Pole** n Polo Sur;
~ward(s) adv hacia el sur; **~-west** n
suroeste m
souvenir [suːvə'nɪə*] n recuerdo
sovereign ['sɔvrɪn] adj, n soberano/a m/f;
~ty n soberanía
soviet ['səuvɪət] adj soviético; **the S~
Union** la Unión Soviética
sow[1] [səu] (pt **sowed**, pp **sown**) vt
sembrar
sow[2] [sau] n cerda (SP), puerca (SP),
chancha (AM)
soy [sɔɪ] (US) n = **soya**
soya ['sɔɪə] (BRIT) n soja; ~ **bean** n haba
de soja; ~ **sauce** n salsa de soja
spa [spɑː] n balneario
space [speɪs] n espacio; (room) sitio ♦ cpd
espacial ♦ vt (also: ~ **out**) espaciar; **~craft**
n nave f espacial; **~man/woman** (irreg)
n astronauta m/f, cosmonauta m/f;
~ship n = **~craft**; **spacing** n espaciado
spacious ['speɪʃəs] adj amplio
spade [speɪd] n (tool) pala, laya; **~s** npl
(CARDS: British); (: Spanish)
espadas fpl
spaghetti [spə'gɛtɪ] n espaguetis mpl,
fideos mpl
Spain [speɪn] n España
span [spæn] n (of bird, plane) envergadura;
(of arch) luz f; (in time) lapso ♦ vt
extenderse sobre, cruzar; (fig) abarcar
Spaniard ['spænjəd] n español(a) m/f
spaniel ['spænjəl] n perro de aguas
Spanish ['spænɪʃ] adj español(a) ♦ n
(LING) español m, castellano; **the ~** npl los
españoles
spank [spæŋk] vt zurrar

spanner ['spænə*] (BRIT) n llave f (inglesa)
spare [spɛə*] adj de reserva; (surplus)
sobrante, de más ♦ n = ~ **part** ♦ vt (do
without) pasarse sin; (refrain from hurting)
perdonar; **to ~** (surplus) sobrante, de
sobra; ~ **part** n pieza de repuesto; ~
time n tiempo libre; ~ **wheel** n (AUT)
rueda de recambio
sparingly ['spɛərɪŋlɪ] adv con moderación
spark [spɑːk] n chispa; (fig) chispazo;
~(ing) plug n bujía
sparkle ['spɑːkl] n centelleo, destello ♦ vi
(shine) relucir, brillar; **sparkling** adj
(eyes, conversation) brillante; (wine)
espumoso; (mineral water) con gas
sparrow ['spærəu] n gorrión m
sparse [spɑːs] adj esparcido, escaso
spartan ['spɑːtən] adj (fig) espartano
spasm ['spæzəm] n (MED) espasmo
spastic ['spæstɪk] n espástico/a
spat [spæt] pt, pp of **spit**
spate [speɪt] n (fig): a ~ **of** un torrente de
spawn [spɔːn] vi desovar, frezar ♦ n
huevas fpl
speak [spiːk] (pt **spoke**, pp **spoken**) vt
(language) hablar; (truth) decir ♦ vi
hablar; (make a speech) intervenir; **to ~
sb/of** or **about sth** hablar con uno/de or
sobre algo; ~ **up!** ¡habla fuerte!; **~er** n (in
public) orador(a) m/f; (also: **loud~er**)
altavoz m; (for stereo etc) bafle m; (POL):
the S~er (BRIT) el Presidente de la
Cámara de los Comunes; (US) el
Presidente del Congreso
spear [spɪə*] n lanza ♦ vt alancear; **~head**
vt (attack etc) encabezar
spec [spɛk] (inf) n: **on ~** como
especulación
special ['spɛʃl] adj especial; (edition etc)
extraordinario; (delivery) urgente; **~ist** n
especialista m/f; **~ity** [spɛʃɪ'ælɪtɪ] (BRIT) n
especialidad f; **~ize** vi: **to ~ize (in)**
especializarse (en); **~ly** adv sobre todo,
en particular; **~ty** n (US) = **~ity**
species ['spiːʃiːz] n inv especie f
specific [spə'sɪfɪk] adj específico; **~ally**
adv específicamente

specify ['spɛsɪfaɪ] *vt, vi* especificar, precisar
specimen ['spɛsɪmən] *n* ejemplar *m*;
(*MED: of urine*) espécimen *m* (: *of blood*)
muestra
speck [spɛk] *n* grano, mota
speckled ['spɛkld] *adj* moteado
specs [spɛks] (*inf*) *npl* gafas *fpl* (*SP*),
anteojos *mpl*
spectacle ['spɛktəkl] *n* espectáculo; **~s**
npl (*BRIT: glasses*) gafas *fpl* (*SP*), anteojos
mpl; **spectacular** [-'tækjulə*] *adj*
espectacular; (*success*) impresionante
spectator [spɛk'teɪtə*] *n* espectador(a) *m/f*
spectrum ['spɛktrəm] (*pl* **spectra**) *n*
espectro
speculate ['spɛkjuleɪt] *vi*: **to ~ (on)**
especular (en); **speculation**
[spɛkju'leɪʃən] *n* especulación *f*
speech [spi:tʃ] *n* (*faculty*) habla; (*formal
talk*) discurso; (*spoken language*) lenguaje
m; **~less** *adj* mudo, estupefacto; **~
therapist** *n* especialista que corrige
defectos de pronunciación en los niños
speed [spi:d] *n* velocidad *f*; (*haste*) prisa;
(*promptness*) rapidez *f*; **at full** *or* **top ~** a
máxima velocidad; **~ up** *vi* acelerarse
♦ *vt* acelerar; **~boat** *n* lancha motora;
~ily *adv* rápido, rápidamente; **~ing** *n*
(*AUT*) exceso de velocidad; **~ limit** *n*
límite *m* de velocidad, velocidad *f*
máxima; **~ometer** [spɪ'dɒmɪtə*] *n*
velocímetro; **~way** *n* (*sport*) pista de
carrera; **~y** *adj* (*fast*) veloz, rápido;
(*prompt*) pronto
spell [spɛl] (*pt, pp* **spelt** (*BRIT*) *or* **spelled**)
n (*also*: **magic ~**) encanto, hechizo;
(*period of time*) rato, período ♦ *vt*
deletrear; (*fig*) anunciar, presagiar; **to cast
a ~ on sb** hechizar a uno; **he can't ~**
pone faltas de ortografía; **~bound** *adj*
embelesado, hechizado; **~ing** *n*
ortografía
spend [spɛnd] (*pt, pp* **spent**) *vt* (*money*)
gastar; (*time*) pasar; (*life*) dedicar; **~thrift**
n derrochador(a) *m/f*, pródigo/a
sperm [spə:m] *n* esperma
sphere [sfɪə*] *n* esfera

sphinx [sfɪŋks] *n* esfinge *f*
spice [spaɪs] *n* especia ♦ *vt* condimentar
spicy ['spaɪsɪ] *adj* picante
spider ['spaɪdə*] *n* araña
spike [spaɪk] *n* (*point*) punta; (*BOT*) espiga
spill [spɪl] (*pt, pp* **spilt** *or* **spilled**) *vt*
derramar, verter ♦ *vi* derramarse; **to ~
over** desbordarse
spin [spɪn] (*pt, pp* **spun**) *n* (*AVIAT*) barrena;
(*trip in car*) paseo (en coche); (*on ball*)
efecto ♦ *vt* (*wool etc*) hilar; (*ball etc*) hacer
girar ♦ *vi* girar, dar vueltas
spinach ['spɪnɪtʃ] *n* espinaca; (*as food*)
espinacas *fpl*
spinal ['spaɪnl] *adj* espinal; **~ cord** *n*
columna vertebral
spin doctor *n* informador(a) parcial al
servicio de un partido político etc
spin-dryer (*BRIT*) *n* secador *m* centrífugo
spine [spaɪn] *n* espinazo, columna
vertebral; (*thorn*) espina; **~less** *adj* (*fig*)
débil, pusilánime
spinning ['spɪnɪŋ] *n* hilandería; **~ top** *n*
peonza
spin-off *n* derivado, producto secundario
spinster ['spɪnstə*] *n* soltera
spiral ['spaɪərl] *n* espiral *f* ♦ *vi* (*fig: prices*)
subir desorbitadamente; **~ staircase** *n*
escalera de caracol
spire ['spaɪə*] *n* aguja, chapitel *m*
spirit ['spɪrɪt] *n* (*soul*) alma *f*; (*ghost*)
fantasma *m*; (*attitude, sense*) espíritu *m*;
(*courage*) valor *m*, ánimo; **~s** *npl* (*drink*)
licor(es) *m(pl)*; **in good ~s** alegre, de
buen ánimo; **~ed** *adj* enérgico, vigoroso
spiritual ['spɪrɪtjuəl] *adj* espiritual ♦ *n*
espiritual *m*
spit [spɪt] (*pt, pp* **spat**) *n* (*for roasting*)
asador *m*, espetón *m*; (*saliva*) saliva ♦ *vi*
escupir; (*sound*) chisporrotear; (*rain*)
lloviznar
spite [spaɪt] *n* rencor *m*, ojeriza ♦ *vt* causar
pena a, mortificar; **in ~ of** a pesar de,
pese a; **~ful** *adj* rencoroso, malévolo
spittle ['spɪtl] *n* saliva, baba
splash [splæʃ] *n* (*sound*) chapoteo; (*of
colour*) mancha ♦ *vt* salpicar ♦ *vi* (*also*: **~**

about) chapotear

spleen [spli:n] *n* (*ANAT*) bazo

splendid ['splendid] *adj* espléndido

splint [splint] *n* tablilla

splinter ['splɪntə*] *n* (*of wood etc*) astilla; (*in finger*) espigón *m* ♦ *vi* astillarse, hacer astillas

split [split] (*pt, pp* **split**) *n* hendedura, raja; (*fig*) división *f*; (*POL*) escisión *f* ♦ *vt* partir, rajar; (*party*) dividir; (*share*) repartir ♦ *vi* dividirse, escindirse; ~ **up** *vi* (*couple*) separarse; (*meeting*) acabarse

spoil [spɔɪl] (*pt, pp* **spoilt** *or* **spoiled**) *vt* (*damage*) dañar; (*mar*) estropear; (*child*) mimar, consentir; ~**s** *npl* despojo, botín *m*; ~**sport** *n* aguafiestas *m inv*

spoke [spəuk] *pt of* **speak** ♦ *n* rayo, radio

spoken ['spəukn] *pp of* **speak**

spokesman ['spəuksmən] (*irreg*) *n* portavoz *m*; **spokeswoman** ['spəukswumən] (*irreg*) *n* portavoz *f*

sponge [spʌndʒ] *n* esponja; (*also*: ~ **cake**) bizcocho ♦ *vt* (*wash*) lavar con esponja ♦ *vi*: **to** ~ **off** *or* **on sb** vivir a costa de uno; ~ **bag** *n* (*BRIT*) esponjera

sponsor ['spɒnsə*] *n* patrocinador(a) *m/f* ♦ *vt* (*applicant, proposal etc*) proponer; ~**ship** *n* patrocinio

spontaneous [spɒn'teɪnɪəs] *adj* espontáneo

spooky ['spu:kɪ] (*inf*) *adj* espeluznante, horripilante

spool [spu:l] *n* carrete *m*

spoon [spu:n] *n* cuchara; ~**-feed** *vt* dar de comer con cuchara a; (*fig*) tratar como un niño a; ~**ful** *n* cucharada

sport [spɔ:t] *n* deporte *m*; (*person*): **to be a good** ~ ser muy majo ♦ *vt* (*wear*) lucir, ostentar; ~**ing** *adj* deportivo; (*generous*) caballeroso; **to give sb a** ~**ing chance** darle a uno una (buena) oportunidad; ~ **jacket** (*US*) *n* = ~**s jacket**; ~**s car** *n* coche *m* deportivo; ~**s jacket** (*BRIT*) *n* chaqueta deportiva; ~**sman** (*irreg*) *n* deportista *m*; ~**smanship** *n* deportividad *f*; ~**swear** *n* trajes *mpl* de deporte *or* sport; ~**swoman** (*irreg*) *n*

deportista; ~**y** *adj* deportista

spot [spɔt] *n* sitio, lugar *m*; (*dot: on pattern*) punto, mancha; (*pimple*) grano; (*RADIO*) cuña publicitaria; (*TV*) espacio publicitario; (*small amount*): **a** ~ **of** un poquito de ♦ *vt* (*notice*) notar, observar; **on the** ~ allí mismo; ~ **check** *n* reconocimiento rápido; ~**less** *adj* perfectamente limpio; ~**light** *n* foco, reflector *m*; (*AUT*) faro auxiliar; ~**ted** *adj* (*pattern*) de puntos; ~**ty** *adj* (*face*) con granos

spouse [spauz] *n* cónyuge *m/f*

spout [spaut] *n* (*of jug*) pico; (*of pipe*) caño ♦ *vi* salir en chorro

sprain [spreɪn] *n* torcedura ♦ *vt*: **to** ~ **one's ankle/wrist** torcerse el tobillo/la muñeca

sprang [spræŋ] *pt of* **spring**

sprawl [sprɔ:l] *vi* tumbarse

spray [spreɪ] *n* rociada; (*of sea*) espuma; (*container*) atomizador *m*; (*for paint etc*) pistola rociadora; (*of flowers*) ramita ♦ *vt* rociar; (*crops*) regar

spread [spred] (*pt, pp* **spread**) *n* extensión *f*; (*for bread etc*) pasta para untar; (*inf: food*) comilona ♦ *vt* extender; (*butter*) untar; (*wings, sails*) desplegar; (*work, wealth*) repartir; (*scatter*) esparcir ♦ *vi* (*also*: ~ **out**: *stain*) extenderse; (*news*) diseminarse; ~ **out** *vi* (*move apart*) separarse; ~**-eagled** *adj* a pata tendida; ~**sheet** *n* hoja electrónica *or* de cálculo

spree [spri:] *n*: **to go on a** ~ ir de juerga

sprightly ['spraɪtlɪ] *adj* vivo, enérgico

spring [sprɪŋ] (*pt* **sprang**, *pp* **sprung**) *n* (*season*) primavera; (*leap*) salto, brinco; (*coiled metal*) resorte *m*; (*of water*) fuente *f*, manantial *m* ♦ *vi* saltar, brincar; ~ **up** *vi* (*thing: appear*) aparecer; (*problem*) surgir; ~**board** *n* trampolín *m*; ~**clean(ing)** *n* limpieza general; ~**time** *n* primavera

sprinkle ['sprɪŋkl] *vt* (*pour: liquid*) rociar; (: *salt, sugar*) espolvorear; **to** ~ **water** *etc* **on,** ~ **with water** *etc* rociar *or* salpicar de agua *etc*; ~**r** *n* (*for lawn*) rociadera; (*to*

put out fire) aparato de rociadura automática
sprint [sprɪnt] *n* esprint *m* ♦ *vi* esprintar
sprout [spraut] *vi* brotar, retoñar; **(Brussels) ~s** *npl* coles *fpl* de Bruselas
spruce [spru:s] *n inv* (*BOT*) pícea ♦ *adj* aseado, pulcro
sprung [sprʌŋ] *pp of* **spring**
spun [spʌn] *pt, pp of* **spin**
spur [spə:*] *n* espuela; (*fig*) estímulo, aguijón *m* ♦ *vt* (*also*: **~ on**) estimular, incitar; **on the ~ of the moment** de improviso
spurious ['spjuərɪəs] *adj* falso
spurn [spə:n] *vt* desdeñar, rechazar
spurt [spə:t] *n* chorro; (*of energy*) arrebato ♦ *vi* chorrear
spy [spaɪ] *n* espía *m/f* ♦ *vi*: **to ~ on** espiar a ♦ *vt* (*see*) divisar, lograr ver; **~ing** *n* espionaje *m*
sq. *abbr* = **square**
squabble ['skwɔbl] *vi* reñir, pelear
squad [skwɔd] *n* (*MIL*) pelotón *m*; (*POLICE*) brigada; (*SPORT*) equipo
squadron ['skwɔdrn] *n* (*MIL*) escuadrón *m*; (*AVIAT, NAUT*) escuadra
squalid ['skwɔlɪd] *adj* vil; (*fig: sordid*) sórdido
squall [skwɔ:l] *n* (*storm*) chubasco; (*wind*) ráfaga
squalor ['skwɔlə*] *n* miseria
squander ['skwɔndə*] *vt* (*money*) derrochar, despilfarrar; (*chances*) desperdiciar
square [skwɛə*] *n* cuadro; (*in town*) plaza; (*inf: person*) carca *m/f* ♦ *adj* cuadrado; (*inf: ideas, tastes*) trasnochado ♦ *vt* (*arrange*) arreglar; (*MATH*) cuadrar; (*reconcile*) compaginar; **all ~** igual(es); **to have a ~ meal** comer caliente; **2 metres ~** 2 metros en cuadro; **2 ~ metres** 2 metros cuadrados; **~ly** *adv* de lleno
squash [skwɔʃ] *n* (*BRIT: drink*): **lemon/orange ~** zumo (*SP*) or jugo (*AM*) de limón/naranja; (*US: BOT*) calabacín *m*; (*SPORT*) squash *m*, frontenis *m* ♦ *vt* aplastar

squat [skwɔt] *adj* achaparrado ♦ *vi* (*also*: **~ down**) agacharse, sentarse en cuclillas; **~ter** *n persona que ocupa ilegalmente una casa*
squeak [skwi:k] *vi* (*hinge*) chirriar, rechinar; (*mouse*) chillar
squeal [skwi:l] *vi* chillar, dar gritos agudos
squeamish ['skwi:mɪʃ] *adj* delicado, remilgado
squeeze [skwi:z] *n* presión *f*; (*of hand*) apretón *m*; (*COMM*) restricción *f* ♦ *vt* (*hand, arm*) apretar; **~ out** *vt* exprimir
squelch [skwɛltʃ] *vi* chapotear
squid [skwɪd] *n inv* calamar *m*; (*CULIN*) calamares *mpl*
squiggle ['skwɪgl] *n* garabato
squint [skwɪnt] *vi* bizquear, ser bizco ♦ *n* (*MED*) estrabismo
squirm [skwə:m] *vi* retorcerse, revolverse
squirrel ['skwɪrəl] *n* ardilla
squirt [skwə:t] *vi* salir a chorros ♦ *vt* chiscar
Sr *abbr* = **senior**
St *abbr* = **saint; street**
stab [stæb] *n* (*with knife*) puñalada; (*of pain*) pinchazo; (*inf: try*): **to have a ~ at (doing) sth** intentar (hacer) algo ♦ *vt* apuñalar
stable ['steɪbl] *adj* estable ♦ *n* cuadra, caballeriza
stack [stæk] *n* montón *m*, pila ♦ *vt* amontonar, apilar
stadium ['steɪdɪəm] *n* estadio
staff [stɑ:f] *n* (*work force*) personal *m*, plantilla; (*BRIT: SCOL*) cuerpo docente ♦ *vt* proveer de personal
stag [stæg] *n* ciervo, venado
stage [steɪdʒ] *n* escena; (*point*) etapa; (*platform*) plataforma; (*profession*): **the ~** el teatro ♦ *vt* (*play*) poner en escena, representar; (*organize*) montar, organizar; **in ~s** por etapas; **~coach** *n* diligencia; **~ manager** *n* director(a) *m/f* de escena
stagger ['stægə*] *vi* tambalearse ♦ *vt* (*amaze*) asombrar; (*hours, holidays*) escalonar; **~ing** *adj* asombroso
stagnant ['stægnənt] *adj* estancado

stag party n despedida de soltero
staid [steɪd] adj serio, formal
stain [steɪn] n mancha; (*colouring*) tintura
♦ vt manchar; (*wood*) teñir; **~ed glass**
window n vidriera de colores; **~less**
steel n acero inoxidable; **~ remover** n
quitamanchas m inv
stair [steə*] n (*step*) peldaño, escalón m;
~s npl escaleras fpl; **~case** n = **~way**;
~way n escalera
stake [steɪk] n estaca, poste m; (*COMM*)
interés m; (*BETTING*) apuesta ♦ vt (*money*)
apostar; (*life*) arriesgar; (*reputation*) poner
en juego; (*claim*) presentar una
reclamación; **to be at ~** estar en juego
stale [steɪl] adj (*bread*) duro; (*food*)
pasado; (*smell*) rancio; (*beer*) agrio
stalemate ['steɪlmeɪt] n tablas fpl (por
ahogado); (*fig*) estancamiento
stalk [stɔːk] n tallo, caña ♦ vt acechar,
cazar al acecho; **~ off** vi irse airado
stall [stɔːl] n (*in market*) puesto; (*in stable*)
casilla (de establo) ♦ vt (*AUT*) calar; (*fig*)
dar largas a ♦ vi (*AUT*) calarse; (*fig*)
andarse con rodeos; **~s** npl (*BRIT: in
cinema, theatre*) butacas fpl
stallion ['stælɪən] n semental m
stamina ['stæmɪnə] n resistencia
stammer ['stæmə*] n tartamudeo ♦ vi
tartamudear
stamp [stæmp] n sello (*SP*), estampilla
(*AM*); (*mark, also fig*) marca, huella; (*on
document*) timbre m ♦ vi (*also: ~ one's
foot*) patear ♦ vt (*mark*) marcar; (*letter*)
poner sellos or estampillas en; (*with
rubber ~*) sellar; **~ album** n álbum m
para sellos or estampillas; **~ collecting** n
filatelia
stampede [stæm'piːd] n estampida
stance [stæns] n postura
stand [stænd] n (*pt, pp stood*) n (*position*)
posición f, postura; (*for taxis*) parada; (*hall ~*) perchero; (*music ~*) atril m;
(*SPORT*) tribuna; (*at exhibition*) stand m
♦ vi (*be*) estar, encontrarse; (*be on foot*)
estar de pie; (*rise*) levantarse; (*remain*)
quedar en pie; (*in election*) presentar

candidatura ♦ vt (*place*) poner, colocar;
(*withstand*) aguantar, soportar; (*invite to*)
invitar; **to make a ~** (*fig*) mantener una
postura firme; **to ~ for parliament** (*BRIT*)
presentarse (como candidato) a las
elecciones; **~ by** vi (*be ready*) estar listo
♦ vt fus (*opinion*) aferrarse a; (*person*)
apoyar; **~ down** vi (*withdraw*) ceder el
puesto; **~ for** vt fus (*signify*) significar;
(*tolerate*) aguantar, permitir; **~ in for** vt
fus suplir a; **~ out** vi destacarse; **~ up** vi
levantarse, ponerse de pie; **~ up for** vt
fus defender; **~ up to** vt fus hacer frente
a
standard ['stændəd] n patrón m, norma;
(*level*) nivel m; (*flag*) estandarte m ♦ adj
(*size etc*) normal, corriente; (*text*) básico;
~s npl (*morals*) valores mpl morales; **~**
lamp (*BRIT*) n lámpara de pie; **~ of**
living n nivel m de vida
stand-by ['stændbaɪ] n (*reserve*) recurso
seguro; **to be on ~** estar sobre aviso; **~**
ticket n (*AVIAT*) (billete m) standby m
stand-in ['stændɪn] n suplente m/f
standing ['stændɪŋ] adj (*on foot*) de pie,
en pie; (*permanent*) permanente ♦ n
reputación f; **of many years' ~** que lleva
muchos años; **~ joke** n broma
permanente; **~ order** (*BRIT*) n (*at bank*)
orden f de pago permanente; **~ room** n
sitio para estar de pie
stand: **~point** n punto de vista; **~still** n:
at a ~still (*industry, traffic*) paralizado;
(*car*) parado; **to come to a ~still** quedar
paralizado; pararse
stank [stæŋk] pt of **stink**
staple ['steɪpl] n (*for papers*) grapa ♦ adj
(*food etc*) básico ♦ vt grapar; **~r** n
grapadora
star [stɑː*] n estrella; (*celebrity*) estrella,
astro ♦ vt (*THEATRE, CINEMA*) ser el/la
protagonista de; **the ~s** npl (*ASTROLOGY*)
el horóscopo
starboard ['stɑːbəd] n estribor m
starch [stɑːtʃ] n almidón m
stardom ['stɑːdəm] n estrellato
stare [steə*] n mirada fija ♦ vi: **to ~ at**

mirar fijo
starfish ['stɑːfɪʃ] *n* estrella de mar
stark [stɑːk] *adj* (*bleak*) severo, escueto
♦ *adv*: **~ naked** en cueros
starling ['stɑːlɪŋ] *n* estornino
starry ['stɑːrɪ] *adj* estrellado; **~-eyed** *adj*
(*innocent*) inocentón/ona, ingenuo
start [stɑːt] *n* principio, comienzo;
(*departure*) salida; (*sudden movement*)
salto, sobresalto; (*advantage*) ventaja ♦ *vt*
empezar, comenzar; (*cause*) causar;
(*found*) fundar; (*engine*) poner en marcha
♦ *vi* comenzar, empezar; (*with fright*)
asustarse, sobresaltarse; (*train etc*) salir; **to
~ doing** *or* **to do sth** empezar a hacer
algo; **~ off** *vi* empezar, comenzar; (*leave*)
salir, ponerse en camino; **~ up** *vi*
comenzar; (*car*) ponerse en marcha ♦ *vt*
comenzar; poner en marcha; **~er** *n* (*AUT*)
botón *m* de arranque; (*SPORT: official*) juez
m/f de salida; (*BRIT: CULIN*) entrada; **~ing
point** *n* punto de partida
startle ['stɑːtl] *vt* asustar, sobrecoger;
startling *adj* alarmante
starvation [stɑːˈveɪʃən] *n* hambre *f*
starve [stɑːv] *vi* tener mucha hambre; (*to
death*) morir de hambre ♦ *vt* hacer pasar
hambre
state [steɪt] *n* estado ♦ *vt* (*say, declare*)
afirmar; **the S~s** los Estados Unidos; **to
be in a ~** estar agitado; **~ly** *adj*
majestuoso, imponente; **~ly home** *n*
casa señorial, casa solariega; **~ment** *n*
afirmación *f*; **~sman** (*irreg*) *n* estadista *m*
static ['stætɪk] *n* (*RADIO*) parásitos *mpl*
♦ *adj* estático; **~ electricity** *n* estática
station ['steɪʃən] *n* (*gen*) estación *f*; (*RADIO*)
emisora; (*rank*) posición *f* social ♦ *vt*
colocar, situar; (*MIL*) apostar
stationary ['steɪʃnərɪ] *adj* estacionario, fijo
stationer ['steɪʃnə*] *n* papelero/a; **~'s
(shop)** (*BRIT*) *n* papelería; **~y** [-nərɪ] *n*
papel *m* de escribir, artículos *mpl* de
escritorio
station master *n* (*RAIL*) jefe *m* de
estación
station wagon (*US*) *n* ranchera

statistic [stəˈtɪstɪk] *n* estadística; **~s** *n*
(*science*) estadística
statue ['stætjuː] *n* estatua
status ['steɪtəs] *n* estado; (*reputation*)
estatus *m*; **~ symbol** *n* símbolo de
prestigio
statute ['stætjuːt] *n* estatuto, ley *f*;
statutory *adj* estatutario
staunch [stɔːntʃ] *adj* leal, incondicional
stay [steɪ] *n* estancia ♦ *vi* quedar(se); (*as
guest*) hospedarse; **to ~ put** seguir en el
mismo sitio; **to ~ the night/5 days** pasar
la noche/estar 5 días; **~ behind** *vi*
quedar atrás; **~ in** *vi* quedarse en casa; **~
on** *vi* quedarse; **~ out** *vi* (*of house*) no
volver a casa; (*on strike*) permanecer en
huelga; **~ up** *vi* (*at night*) velar, no
acostarse; **~ing power** *n* aguante *m*
stead [sted] *n*: **in sb's ~** en lugar de uno;
to stand sb in good ~ ser muy útil a uno
steadfast ['stedfɑːst] *adj* firme, resuelto
steadily ['stedɪlɪ] *adv* constantemente;
(*firmly*) firmemente; (*work, walk*) sin parar;
(*gaze*) fijamente
steady ['stedɪ] *adj* (*firm*) firme; (*regular*)
regular; (*person, character*) sensato,
juicioso; (*boyfriend*) formal; (*look, voice*)
tranquilo ♦ *vt* (*stabilize*) estabilizar;
(*nerves*) calmar
steak [steɪk] *n* (*gen*) filete *m*; (*beef*) bistec
m
steal [stiːl] (*pt* **stole**, *pp* **stolen**) *vt* robar
♦ *vi* robar; (*move secretly*) andar a
hurtadillas
stealth [stelθ] *n*: **by ~** a escondidas,
sigilosamente; **~y** *adj* cauteloso, sigiloso
steam [stiːm] *n* vapor *m*; (*mist*) vaho,
humo *m* (*CULIN*) cocer al vapor ♦ *vi*
echar vapor; **~ engine** *n* máquina de
vapor; **~er** *n* (*buque m de*) vapor *m*;
~roller *n* apisonadora; **~ship** *n* = **~er**;
~y *adj* (*room*) lleno de vapor; (*window*)
empañado; (*heat, atmosphere*)
bochornoso
steel [stiːl] *n* acero ♦ *adj* de acero;
~works *n* acería
steep [stiːp] *adj* escarpado, abrupto; (*stair*)

empinado; (price) exorbitante, excesivo
♦ vt empapar, remojar
steeple ['sti:pl] n aguja; **~chase** n
carrera de obstáculos
steer [stɪə*] vt (car) conducir (SP), manejar
(AM); (person) dirigir ♦ vi conducir,
manejar; **~ing** n (AUT) dirección f; **~ing
wheel** n volante m
stem [stem] n (of plant) tallo; (of glass) pie
m ♦ vt detener; (blood) restañar; **~ from**
vt fus ser consecuencia de
stench [stentʃ] n hedor m
stencil ['stensl] n (pattern) plantilla ♦ vt
hacer un cliché de
stenographer [ste'nɔgrəfə*] (US) n
taquígrafo/a
step [step] n paso; (on stair) peldaño,
escalón m ♦ vi: **to ~ forward/back** dar
un paso adelante/hacia atrás; **~s** npl
(BRIT) = **~ladder**; **in/out of ~ (with)**
acorde/en disonancia (con); **~ down** vi
(fig) retirarse; **~ on** vt fus pisar; **~ up** vt
(increase) aumentar; **~brother** n
hermanastro; **~daughter** n hijastra;
~father n padrastro; **~ladder** n escalera
doble or de tijera; **~mother** n madrastra;
~ping stone n pasadera; **~sister** n
hermanastra; **~son** n hijastro
stereo ['stɪərɪəu] n estéreo ♦ adj (also:
~phonic) estéreo, estereofónico
sterile ['sterail] adj estéril; **sterilize**
['sterilaiz] vt esterilizar
sterling ['stɜ:lɪŋ] adj (silver) de ley ♦ n
(ECON) (libras fpl) esterlinas fpl; **one
pound ~** una libra esterlina
stern [stɜ:n] adj severo, austero ♦ n (NAUT)
popa
stew [stju:] n cocido (SP), estofado (SP),
guisado (AM) ♦ vt estofar, guisar; (fruit)
cocer
steward ['stju:əd] n camarero; **~ess** n
(esp on plane) azafata
stick [stik] (pt, pp **stuck**) n palo; (of
dynamite) barreno; (as weapon) porra;
(walking ~) bastón m ♦ vt (glue) pegar;
(inf: put) meter; (: tolerate) aguantar,
soportar; (thrust): **to ~ sth into** clavar or

hincar algo en ♦ vi pegarse; (be
unmoveable) quedarse parado; (in mind)
quedarse grabado; **~ out** vi sobresalir; **~
up** vi sobresalir; **~ up for** vt fus
defender; **~er** n (label) etiqueta
engomada; (with slogan) pegatina; **~ing
plaster** n esparadrapo
stick-up ['stikʌp] (inf) n asalto, atraco
sticky ['stiki] adj pegajoso; (label)
engomado; (fig) difícil
stiff [stif] adj rígido, tieso; (hard) duro;
(manner) estirado; (difficult) difícil;
(person) inflexible; (price) exorbitante
♦ adv: **scared/bored ~** muerto de
miedo/aburrimiento; **~en** vi (muscles etc)
agarrotarse; **~ neck** n tortícolis m inv;
~ness n rigidez f, tiesura
stifle ['staifl] vt ahogar, sofocar; **stifling**
adj (heat) sofocante, bochornoso
stigma ['stigmə] n (fig) estigma m
stile [stail] n portillo, portilla
stiletto [sti'letəu] (BRIT) n (also: **~ heel**)
tacón m de aguja
still [stil] adj inmóvil, quieto ♦ adv todavía;
(even) aun; (nonetheless) sin embargo,
aun así; **~born** adj nacido muerto; **~ life**
n naturaleza muerta
stilt [stilt] n zanco; (pile) pilar m, soporte
m
stilted ['stiltid] adj afectado
stimulate ['stimjuleit] vt estimular
stimulus ['stimjuləs] (pl **stimuli**) n
estímulo, incentivo
sting [stiŋ] (pt, pp **stung**) n picadura;
(pain) escozor m, picazón f; (organ)
aguijón m ♦ vt, vi picar
stingy ['stindʒi] adj tacaño
stink [stiŋk] (pt **stank**, pp **stunk**) n hedor
m, tufo ♦ vi heder, apestar; **~ing** adj
hediondo, fétido; (fig: inf) horrible
stint [stint] n tarea, trabajo ♦ vi: **to ~ on**
escatimar
stir [stɜ:*] n (fig: agitation) conmoción f
♦ vt (tea etc) remover; (fig: emotions)
provocar ♦ vi moverse; **~ up** vt (trouble)
fomentar
stirrup ['stirəp] n estribo

stitch [stɪtʃ] *n* (*SEWING*) puntada; (*KNITTING*) punto; (*MED*) punto (de sutura); (*pain*) punzada ♦ *vt* coser; (*MED*) suturar

stoat [stəut] *n* armiño

stock [stɔk] *n* (*COMM: reserves*) existencias *fpl*, stock *m*; (*: selection*) surtido; (*AGR*) ganado, ganadería; (*CULIN*) caldo; (*descent*) raza, estirpe *f*; (*FINANCE*) capital *m* ♦ *adj* (*fig: reply etc*) clásico ♦ *vt* (*have in* ∼) tener existencias de; **∼s and shares** acciones y valores; **in** ∼ en existencia *or* almacén; **out of** ∼ agotado; **to take** ∼ **of** (*fig*) asesorar, examinar; ∼ **up with** *vt fus* abastecerse de; **∼broker** [ˈstɔkbrəukə*] *n* agente *m/f or* corredor(a) *m/f* de bolsa; ∼ **cube** (*BRIT*) *n* pastilla de caldo; ∼ **exchange** *n* bolsa

stocking [ˈstɔkɪŋ] *n* media

stock: ∼ **market** *n* bolsa (de valores); **∼pile** *n* reserva ♦ *vt* acumular, almacenar; **∼taking** (*BRIT*) *n* (*COMM*) inventario

stocky [ˈstɔkɪ] *adj* (*strong*) robusto; (*short*) achaparrado

stodgy [ˈstɔdʒɪ] *adj* indigesto, pesado

stoke [stəuk] *vt* atizar

stole [stəul] *pt of* **steal** ♦ *n* estola

stolen [ˈstəuln] *pp of* **steal**

stomach [ˈstʌmək] *n* (*ANAT*) estómago; (*belly*) vientre *m* ♦ *vt* tragar, aguantar; **∼ache** *n* dolor *m* de estómago

stone [stəun] *n* piedra; (*in fruit*) hueso; *= 6.348 kg; 14 libras* ♦ *adj* de piedra ♦ *vt* apedrear; (*fruit*) deshuesar; **∼-cold** *adj* helado; **∼-deaf** *adj* sordo como una tapia; **∼work** *n* (*art*) cantería; **stony** *adj* pedregoso; (*fig*) frío

stood [stud] *pt, pp of* **stand**

stool [stu:l] *n* taburete *m*

stoop [stu:p] *vi* (*also:* ∼ **down**) doblarse, agacharse; (*also:* **have a** ∼) ser cargado de espaldas

stop [stɔp] *n* parada; (*in punctuation*) punto ♦ *vt* parar, detener; (*break off*) suspender; (*block: pay*) suspender; (*: cheque*) invalidar; (*also:* **put a** ∼ **to**) poner término a ♦ *vi* pararse, detenerse; (*end*) acabarse; **to** ∼ **doing sth** dejar de hacer algo; ∼ **dead** *vi* pararse en seco; ∼ **off** *vi* interrumpir el viaje; ∼ **up** *vt* (*hole*) tapar; **∼gap** *n* (*person*) interino/a; (*thing*) recurso provisional; **∼over** *n* parada; (*AVIAT*) escala

stoppage [ˈstɔpɪdʒ] *n* (*strike*) paro; (*blockage*) obstrucción *f*

stopper [ˈstɔpə*] *n* tapón *m*

stop press *n* noticias *fpl* de última hora

stopwatch [ˈstɔpwɔtʃ] *n* cronómetro

storage [ˈstɔ:rɪdʒ] *n* almacenaje *m*; ∼ **heater** *n* acumulador *m*

store [stɔ:*] *n* (*stock*) provisión *f*; (*depot: BRIT: large shop*) almacén *m*; (*US*) tienda; (*reserve*) reserva, repuesto ♦ *vt* almacenar; **∼s** *npl* víveres *mpl*; **in** ∼ (*fig*): **to be in** ∼ **for sb** esperarle a uno; ∼ **up** *vt* acumular; **∼room** *n* despensa

storey [ˈstɔ:rɪ] (*US* **story**) *n* piso

stork [stɔ:k] *n* cigüeña

storm [stɔ:m] *n* tormenta; (*fig: of applause*) salva; (*: of criticism*) nube *f* ♦ *vi* (*fig*) rabiar ♦ *vt* tomar por asalto; **∼y** *adj* tempestuoso

story [ˈstɔ:rɪ] *n* historia; (*lie*) mentira; (*US*) = **storey**; **∼book** *n* libro de cuentos

stout [staut] *adj* (*strong*) sólido; (*fat*) gordo, corpulento; (*resolute*) resuelto ♦ *n* cerveza negra

stove [stəuv] *n* (*for cooking*) cocina; (*for heating*) estufa

stow [stəu] *vt* (*also:* ∼ **away**) meter, poner; (*NAUT*) estibar; **∼away** *n* polizón/ona *m/f*

straggle [ˈstrægl] *vi* (*houses etc*) extenderse; (*lag behind*) rezagarse

straight [streɪt] *adj* recto, derecho; (*frank*) franco, directo; (*simple*) sencillo ♦ *adv* derecho, directamente; (*drink*) sin mezcla; **to put** *or* **get sth** ∼ dejar algo en claro; ∼ **away**, ∼ **off** en seguida; **∼en** *vt* (*also:* **∼en out**) enderezar, poner derecho; **∼-faced** *adj* serio; **∼forward** *adj* (*simple*) sencillo; (*honest*) honrado, franco

strain [streɪn] *n* tensión *f*; (*TECH*) presión *f*; (*MED*) torcedura; (*breed*) tipo, variedad *f*

♦ *vt* (*back etc*) torcerse; (*resources*) agotar; (*stretch*) estirar; (*food, tea*) colar; **~s** *npl* (MUS) son *m*; **~ed** *adj* (*muscle*) torcido; (*laugh*) forzado; (*relations*) tenso; **~er** *n* colador *m*

strait [streɪt] *n* (GEO) estrecho; **to be in dire ~** pasar grandes apuros; **~-jacket** *n* camisa de fuerza; **~-laced** *adj* mojigato, gazmoño

strand [strænd] *n* (*of thread*) hebra; (*of hair*) trenza; (*of rope*) ramal *m*

stranded ['strændɪd] *adj* (*person: without money*) desamparado; (: *without transport*) colgado

strange [streɪndʒ] *adj* (*not known*) desconocido; (*odd*) extraño, raro; **~ly** *adv* de un modo raro; *see also* **enough**; **~r** *n* desconocido/a; (*from another area*) forastero/a

strangle ['stræŋgl] *vt* estrangular; **~hold** *n* (*fig*) dominio completo

strap [stræp] *n* correa; (*of slip, dress*) tirante *m*

strategic [strə'ti:dʒɪk] *adj* estratégico

strategy ['strætɪdʒɪ] *n* estrategia

straw [strɔː] *n* paja; (*drinking ~*) caña, pajita; **that's the last ~!** ¡eso es el colmo!

strawberry ['strɔːbərɪ] *n* fresa (SP), frutilla (AM)

stray [streɪ] *adj* (*animal*) extraviado; (*bullet*) perdido; (*scattered*) disperso ♦ *vi* extraviarse, perderse

streak [stri:k] *n* raya; (*in hair*) raya ♦ *vt* rayar ♦ *vi*: **to ~ past** pasar como un rayo

stream [stri:m] *n* riachuelo, arroyo; (*of people, vehicles*) riada, caravana; (*of smoke, insults etc*) chorro ♦ *vt* (SCOL) dividir en grupos por habilidad ♦ *vi* correr, fluir; **to ~ in/out** (*people*) entrar/ salir en tropel

streamer ['stri:mə*] *n* serpentina

streamlined ['stri:mlaɪnd] *adj* aerodinámico

street [stri:t] *n* calle *f*; **~car** (US) *n* tranvía *m*; **~ lamp** *n* farol *m*; **~ plan** *n* plano; **~wise** (*inf*) *adj* que tiene mucha calle

strength [streŋθ] *n* fuerza; (*of girder, knot etc*) resistencia; (*fig: power*) poder *m*; **~en** *vt* fortalecer, reforzar

strenuous ['strenjuəs] *adj* (*energetic, determined*) enérgico

stress [stres] *n* presión *f*; (*mental strain*) estrés *m*; (*accent*) acento ♦ *vt* subrayar, recalcar; (*syllable*) acentuar

stretch [stretʃ] *n* (*of sand etc*) trecho ♦ *vi* estirarse; (*extend*): **to ~ to** *or* **as far as** extenderse hasta ♦ *vt* extender, estirar; (*make demands of*) exigir el máximo esfuerzo a; **~ out** *vi* tenderse ♦ *vt* (*arm etc*) extender; (*spread*) estirar

stretcher ['stretʃə*] *n* camilla

strewn [stru:n] *adj*: **~ with** cubierto *or* sembrado de

stricken ['strɪkən] *adj* (*person*) herido; (*city, industry etc*) condenado; **~ with** (*disease*) afectado por

strict [strɪkt] *adj* severo; (*exact*) estricto; **~ly** *adv* severamente; estrictamente

stride [straɪd] (*pt* **strode**, *pp* **stridden**) *n* zancada, tranco ♦ *vi* dar zancadas, andar a trancos

strife [straɪf] *n* lucha

strike [straɪk] (*pt, pp* **struck**) *n* huelga; (*of oil etc*) descubrimiento; (*attack*) ataque *m* ♦ *vt* golpear, pegar; (*oil etc*) descubrir; (*bargain, deal*) cerrar ♦ *vi* declarar la huelga; (*attack*) atacar; (*clock*) dar la hora; **on ~** (*workers*) en huelga; **to ~ a match** encender un fósforo; **~ down** *vt* derribar; **~ up** *vt* (MUS) empezar a tocar; (*conversation*) entablar; (*friendship*) trabar; **~r** *n* huelguista *m/f*; (SPORT) delantero; **striking** *adj* llamativo

string [strɪŋ] (*pt, pp* **strung**) *n* (*gen*) cuerda; (*row*) hilera ♦ *vt*: **to ~ together** ensartar; **to ~ out** extenderse; **the ~s** *npl* (MUS) los instrumentos de cuerda; **to pull ~s** (*fig*) mover palancas; **~ bean** *n* judía verde, habichuela; **~(ed) instrument** *n* (MUS) instrumento de cuerda

stringent ['strɪndʒənt] *adj* riguroso, severo

strip [strɪp] *n* tira; (*of land*) franja; (*of metal*) cinta, lámina ♦ *vt* desnudar; (*paint*) quitar; (*also*: **~ down**: *machine*) desmontar ♦ vi desnudarse; ~ **cartoon** n tira cómica (SP), historieta (AM)

stripe [straɪp] n raya; (MIL) galón m; ~**d** adj a rayas, rayado

strip lighting n alumbrado fluorescente

stripper ['strɪpə*] n artista m/f de striptease

strive [straɪv] (pt **strove**, pp **striven**) vi: to ~ **for sth/to do sth** luchar por conseguir/hacer algo

strode [strəud] pt of **stride**

stroke [strəuk] n (blow) golpe m; (SWIMMING) brazada; (MED) apoplejía; (of paintbrush) toque m ♦ vt acariciar; **at a** ~ de un solo golpe

stroll [strəul] n paseo, vuelta ♦ vi dar un paseo or una vuelta; ~**er** (US) n (for child) sillita de ruedas

strong [strɒŋ] adj fuerte; **they are 50** ~ son 50; ~**hold** n fortaleza; (fig) baluarte m; ~**ly** adv fuertemente, con fuerza; (believe) firmemente; ~**room** n cámara acorazada

strove [strəuv] pt of **strive**

struck [strʌk] pt, pp of **strike**

structure ['strʌktʃə*] n estructura; (building) construcción f

struggle ['strʌgl] n lucha ♦ vi luchar

strum [strʌm] vt (guitar) rasguear

strung [strʌŋ] pt, pp of **string**

strut [strʌt] n puntal m ♦ vi pavonearse

stub [stʌb] n (of ticket etc) talón m; (of cigarette) colilla; **to ~ one's toe on sth** dar con el dedo (del pie) contra algo; ~ **out** vt apagar

stubble ['stʌbl] n rastrojo; (on chin) barba (incipiente)

stubborn ['stʌbən] adj terco, testarudo

stuck [stʌk] pt, pp of **stick** ♦ adj (jammed) atascado; ~-**up** adj engreído, presumido

stud [stʌd] n (shirt ~) corchete m; (of boot) taco; (earring) pendiente m (de bolita); (also: ~ **farm**) caballeriza; (also: ~ **horse**) caballo semental ♦ vt (fig): ~**ded with** salpicado de

student ['stju:dənt] n estudiante m/f ♦ adj estudiantil; ~ **driver** (US) n aprendiz(a)

m/f

studio ['stju:dɪəu] n estudio; (artist's) taller m; ~ **flat** (US ~ **apartment**) n estudio

studious ['stju:dɪəs] adj estudioso; (studied) calculado; ~**ly** adv (carefully) con esmero

study ['stʌdɪ] n estudio ♦ vt estudiar; (examine) examinar, investigar ♦ vi estudiar

stuff [stʌf] n materia; (substance) material m, sustancia; (things) cosas fpl ♦ vt llenar; (CULIN) rellenar; (animals) disecar; (inf: push) meter; ~**ing** n relleno; ~**y** adj (room) mal ventilado; (person) de miras estrechas

stumble ['stʌmbl] vi tropezar, dar un traspié; **to ~ across, ~ on** (fig) tropezar con; **stumbling block** n tropiezo, obstáculo

stump [stʌmp] n (of tree) tocón m; (of limb) muñón m ♦ vt: **to be ~ed for an answer** no saber qué contestar

stun [stʌn] vt dejar sin sentido

stung [stʌŋ] pt, pp of **sting**

stunk [stʌŋk] pp of **stink**

stunning ['stʌnɪŋ] adj (fig: news) pasmoso; (: outfit etc) sensacional

stunt [stʌnt] n (in film) escena peligrosa; (publicity ~) truco publicitario; ~**man** (irreg) n doble m

stupid ['stju:pɪd] adj estúpido, tonto; ~**ity** [-'pɪdɪtɪ] n estupidez f

sturdy ['stɜ:dɪ] adj robusto, fuerte

stutter ['stʌtə*] n tartamudeo ♦ vi tartamudear

sty [staɪ] n (for pigs) pocilga

stye [staɪ] n (MED) orzuelo

style [staɪl] n estilo; **stylish** adj elegante, a la moda

stylus ['staɪləs] n aguja

suave [swɑ:v] adj cortés

sub... [sʌb] prefix sub...; ~**conscious** adj subconsciente; ~**contract** vt subcontratar; ~**divide** vt subdividir

subdue [səb'dju:] vt sojuzgar; (passions) dominar; ~**d** adj (light) tenue; (person) sumiso, manso

subject [n 'sʌbdʒɪkt, vb səb'dʒɛkt] n súbdito; (SCOL) asignatura; (matter) tema m; (GRAMMAR) sujeto ♦ vt: **to ~ sb to sth** someter a uno a algo; **to be ~ to** (law) estar sujeto a; (subj: person) ser propenso a; **~ive** [-'dʒɛktɪv] adj subjetivo; **~ matter** n (content) contenido

sublet [sʌb'lɛt] vt subarrendar

submarine [sʌbmə'riːn] n submarino

submerge [səb'məːdʒ] vt sumergir ♦ vi sumergirse

submissive [səb'mɪsɪv] adj sumiso

submit [səb'mɪt] vt someter ♦ vi: **to ~ to sth** someterse a algo

subnormal [sʌb'nɔːməl] adj anormal

subordinate [sə'bɔːdɪnət] adj, n subordinado/a m/f

subpoena [səb'piːnə] n (LAW) citación f

subscribe [səb'skraɪb] vi suscribir; **to ~ to** (opinion, fund) suscribir, aprobar; (newspaper) suscribirse a; **~r** n (to periodical) suscriptor(a) m/f; (to telephone) abonado/a

subscription [səb'skrɪpʃən] n abono; (to magazine) suscripción f

subsequent [sʌbsɪkwənt] adj subsiguiente, posterior; **~ly** adv posteriormente, más tarde

subside [səb'saɪd] vi hundirse; (flood) bajar; (wind) amainar; **subsidence** [-'saɪdns] n hundimiento; (in road) socavón m

subsidiary [səb'sɪdɪərɪ] adj secundario ♦ n sucursal f, filial f

subsidize ['sʌbsɪdaɪz] vt subvencionar

subsidy ['sʌbsɪdɪ] n subvención f

subsistence [səb'sɪstəns] n subsistencia; **~ allowance** n salario mínimo

substance ['sʌbstəns] n sustancia

substantial [səb'stænʃl] adj sustancial, sustancioso; (fig) importante

substantiate [səb'stænʃɪeɪt] vt comprobar

substitute ['sʌbstɪtjuːt] n (person) suplente m/f; (thing) sustituto ♦ vt: **to ~ A for B** sustituir A por B, reemplazar B por A

subtitle ['sʌbtaɪtl] n subtítulo

subtle ['sʌtl] adj sutil; **~ty** n sutileza

subtotal [sʌb'təutl] n total m parcial

subtract [səb'trækt] vt restar, sustraer; **~ion** [-'trækʃən] n resta, sustracción f

suburb ['sʌbəːb] n barrio residencial; **the ~s** las afueras (de la ciudad); **~an** [sə'bəːbən] adj suburbano; (train etc) de cercanías; **~ia** [sə'bəːbɪə] n barrios mpl residenciales

subway ['sʌbweɪ] n (BRIT) paso subterráneo or inferior; (US) metro

succeed [sək'siːd] vi (person) tener éxito; (plan) salir bien ♦ vt suceder a; **to ~ in doing** lograr hacer; **~ing** adj (following) sucesivo

success [sək'sɛs] n éxito; **~ful** adj exitoso; (business) próspero; **to be ~ful (in doing)** lograr (hacer); **~fully** adv con éxito

succession [sək'sɛʃən] n sucesión f, serie f

successive [sək'sɛsɪv] adj sucesivo, consecutivo

succinct [sək'sɪŋkt] adj sucinto

such [sʌtʃ] adj tal, semejante; (of that kind): **~ a book** tal libro; (so much): **~ courage** tanto valor ♦ adv tan; **~ a long trip** un viaje tan largo; **~ a lot of** tanto(s)/a(s); **~ as** (like) tal como; **as ~** como tal; **~-and-~** adj tal o cual

suck [sʌk] vt chupar; (bottle) sorber; (breast) mamar; **~er** n (ZOOL) ventosa; (inf) bobo, primo

suction ['sʌkʃən] n succión f

Sudan [su'dæn] n Sudán m

sudden ['sʌdn] adj (rapid) repentino, súbito; (unexpected) imprevisto; **all of a ~** de repente; **~ly** adv de repente

suds [sʌdz] npl espuma de jabón

sue [suː] vt demandar

suede [sweɪd] n ante m (SP), gamuza (AM)

suet ['suɪt] n sebo

Suez ['suːɪz] n: **the ~ Canal** el Canal de Suez

suffer ['sʌfə*] vt sufrir, padecer; (tolerate) aguantar, soportar ♦ vi sufrir; **to ~ from** (illness etc) padecer; **~er** n víctima; (MED) enfermo/a; **~ing** n sufrimiento

sufficient [sə'fɪʃənt] *adj* suficiente, bastante; **~ly** *ad* suficientemente, bastante

suffocate ['sʌfəkeɪt] *vi* ahogarse, asfixiarse; **suffocation** [-'keɪʃən] *n* asfixia

sugar ['ʃʊgə*] *n* azúcar *m* ♦ *vt* echar azúcar a, azucarar; **~ beet** *n* remolacha; **~ cane** *n* caña de azúcar

suggest [sə'dʒɛst] *vt* sugerir; **~ion** [-'dʒɛstʃən] *n* sugerencia; **~ive** (*pej*) *adj* indecente

suicide ['sʊɪsaɪd] *n* suicidio; (*person*) suicida *m/f*; *see also* **commit**

suit [suːt] *n* (*man's*) traje *m*; (*woman's*) conjunto; (*LAW*) pleito; (*CARDS*) palo ♦ *vt* convenir; (*clothes*) sentar a, ir bien a; (*adapt*): **to ~ sth to** adaptar *or* ajustar algo a; **well ~ed** (*well matched*: *couple*) hecho el uno para el otro; **~able** *adj* conveniente; (*apt*) indicado; **~ably** *adv* convenientemente; (*impressed*) apropiadamente

suitcase ['suːtkeɪs] *n* maleta (*SP*), valija (*AM*)

suite [swiːt] *n* (*of rooms, MUS*) suite *f*; (*furniture*): **bedroom/dining room ~** (juego de) dormitorio/comedor

suitor ['suːtə*] *n* pretendiente *m*

sulfur ['sʌlfə*] (*US*) *n* = **sulphur**

sulk [sʌlk] *vi* estar de mal humor; **~y** *adj* malhumorado

sullen ['sʌlən] *adj* hosco, malhumorado

sulphur ['sʌlfə*] (*US* **sulfur**) *n* azufre *m*

sultana [sʌl'tɑːnə] *n* (*fruit*) pasa de Esmirna

sultry ['sʌltrɪ] *adj* (*weather*) bochornoso

sum [sʌm] *n* suma; (*total*) total *m*; **~ up** *vt* resumir ♦ *vi* hacer un resumen

summarize ['sʌmərɑɪz] *vt* resumir

summary ['sʌmərɪ] *n* resumen *m* ♦ *adj* (*justice*) sumario

summer ['sʌmə*] *n* verano ♦ *cpd* de verano; **in ~** en verano; **~ holidays** *npl* vacaciones *fpl* de verano; **~house** *n* (*in garden*) cenador *m*, glorieta; **~time** *n* (*season*) verano; **~ time** *n* (*by clock*) hora de verano

summit ['sʌmɪt] *n* cima, cumbre *f*; (*also*: **~ conference, ~ meeting**) (conferencia) cumbre *f*

summon ['sʌmən] *vt* (*person*) llamar; (*meeting*) convocar; (*LAW*) citar; **~ up** *vt* (*courage*) armarse de; **~s** *n* llamamiento, llamada ♦ *vt* (*LAW*) citar

sump [sʌmp] (*BRIT*) *n* (*AUT*) cárter *m*

sumptuous ['sʌmptjʊəs] *adj* suntuoso

sun [sʌn] *n* sol *m*; **~bathe** *vi* tomar el sol; **~block** *n* filtro solar; **~burn** *n* (*painful*) quemadura; (*tan*) bronceado; **~burnt** *adj* quemado por el sol

Sunday ['sʌndɪ] *n* domingo; **~ school** *n* catequesis *f* dominical

sundial ['sʌndaɪəl] *n* reloj *m* de sol

sundown ['sʌndaʊn] *n* anochecer *m*

sundry ['sʌndrɪ] *adj* varios/as, diversos/as; **all and ~** todos sin excepción; **sundries** *npl* géneros *mpl* diversos

sunflower ['sʌnflaʊə*] *n* girasol *m*

sung [sʌŋ] *pp of* **sing**

sunglasses ['sʌnglɑːsɪz] *npl* gafas *fpl* (*SP*) *or* anteojos *mpl* de sol

sunk [sʌŋk] *pp of* **sink**

sun: ~light *n* luz *f* del sol; **~lit** *adj* iluminado por el sol; **~ny** *adj* soleado; (*day*) de sol; (*fig*) alegre; **~rise** *n* salida del sol; **~ roof** *n* (*AUT*) techo corredizo; **~screen** *n* protector *m* solar; **~set** *n* puesta del sol; **~shade** *n* (*over table*) sombrilla; **~shine** *n* sol *m*; **~stroke** *n* insolación *f*; **~tan** *n* bronceado; **~tan oil** *n* aceite *m* bronceador

super ['suːpə*] (*inf*) *adj* genial

superannuation [suːpərænju'eɪʃən] *n* cuota de jubilación

superb [suː'pəːb] *adj* magnífico, espléndido

supercilious [suːpə'sɪlɪəs] *adj* altanero

superfluous [suː'pəːflʊəs] *adj* superfluo, de sobra

superhuman [suːpə'hjuːmən] *adj* sobrehumano

superimpose ['suːpərɪm'pəʊz] *vt* sobreponer

superintendent [suːrɪn'tɛndənt] *n*

director(a) *m/f*; (*POLICE*) subjefe/a *m/f*
superior [su'pɪərɪə*] *adj* superior; (*smug*) desdeñoso ♦ *n* superior *m*; **~ity** [-'ɔrɪtɪ] *n* superioridad *f*
superlative [su'pə:lətɪv] *n* superlativo
superman ['su:pəmæn] (*irreg*) *n* superhombre *m*
supermarket ['su:pəmɑ:kɪt] *n* supermercado
supernatural [su:pə'nætʃərəl] *adj* sobrenatural ♦ *n*: **the ~** lo sobrenatural
superpower ['su:pəpauə*] *n* (*POL*) superpotencia
supersede [su:pə'si:d] *vt* suplantar
superstar ['su:pəstɑ:*] *n* gran estrella
superstitious [su:pə'stɪʃəs] *adj* supersticioso
supertanker ['su:pətæŋkə*] *n* superpetrolero
supervise ['su:pəvaɪz] *vt* supervisar; **supervision** [-'vɪʒən] *n* supervisión *f*; **supervisor** *n* supervisor(a) *m/f*
supper ['sʌpə*] *n* cena
supple ['sʌpl] *adj* flexible
supplement [*n* 'sʌplɪmənt, *vb* sʌplɪ'mənt] *n* suplemento ♦ *vt* suplir; **~ary** [-'mentərɪ] *adj* suplementario; **~ary benefit** (*BRIT*) *n* subsidio suplementario de la seguridad social
supplier [sə'plaɪə*] *n* (*COMM*) distribuidor(a) *m/f*
supply [sə'plaɪ] *vt* (*provide*) suministrar; (*equip*): **to ~ (with)** proveer (de) ♦ *n* provisión *f*; (*gas, water etc*) suministro; **supplies** *npl* (*food*) víveres *mpl*; (*MIL*) pertrechos *mpl*; **~ teacher** *n* profesor(a) *m/f* suplente
support [sə'pɔ:t] *n* apoyo; (*TECH*) soporte *m* ♦ *vt* apoyar; (*financially*) mantener; (*uphold, TECH*) sostener; **~er** *n* (*POL etc*) partidario/a; (*SPORT*) aficionado/a
suppose [sə'pəuz] *vt* suponer; (*imagine*) imaginarse; (*duty*): **to be ~d to do sth** deber hacer algo; **~dly** [sə'pəuzɪdlɪ] *adv* según cabe suponer; **supposing** *conj* en caso de que
suppress [sə'pres] *vt* suprimir; (*yawn*)

ahogar
supreme [su'pri:m] *adj* supremo
surcharge ['sə:tʃɑ:dʒ] *n* sobretasa, recargo
sure [ʃuə*] *adj* seguro; (*definite, convinced*) cierto; **to make ~ of sth/that** asegurarse de algo/asegurar que; **~!** (*of course*) ¡claro!, ¡por supuesto!; **~ enough** efectivamente; **~ly** *adv* (*certainly*) seguramente
surf [sə:f] *n* olas *fpl*
surface ['sə:fɪs] *n* superficie *f* ♦ *vt* (*road*) revestir ♦ *vi* (*also fig*) salir a la superficie; **by ~ mail** por vía terrestre
surfboard ['sə:fbɔ:d] *n* tabla (de surf)
surfeit ['sə:fɪt] *n*: **a ~ of** un exceso de
surfing ['sə:fɪŋ] *n* surf *m*
surge [sə:dʒ] *n* oleada, oleaje *m* ♦ *vi* (*wave*) romper; (*people*) avanzar en tropel
surgeon ['sə:dʒən] *n* cirujano/a
surgery ['sə:dʒərɪ] *n* cirugía; (*BRIT: room*) consultorio; **~ hours** (*BRIT*) *npl* horas *fpl* de consulta
surgical ['sə:dʒɪkl] *adj* quirúrgico; **~ spirit** (*BRIT*) *n* alcohol *m* de 90°
surname ['sə:neɪm] *n* apellido
surpass [sə:'pɑ:s] *vt* superar, exceder
surplus ['sə:pləs] *n* excedente *m*; (*COMM*) superávit *m* ♦ *adj* excedente, sobrante
surprise [sə'praɪz] *n* sorpresa ♦ *vt* sorprender; **surprising** *adj* sorprendente; **surprisingly** *adv*: **it was surprisingly easy** me *etc* sorprendió lo fácil que fue
surrender [sə'rendə*] *n* rendición *f*, entrega ♦ *vi* rendirse, entregarse
surreptitious [sʌrəp'tɪʃəs] *adj* subrepticio
surrogate ['sʌrəgɪt] *n* sucedáneo; **~ mother** *n* madre *f* portadora
surround [sə'raund] *vt* rodear, circundar; (*MIL etc*) cercar; **~ing** *adj* circundante; **~ings** *npl* alrededores *mpl*, cercanías *fpl*
surveillance [sə:'veɪləns] *n* vigilancia
survey [*n* 'sə:veɪ, *vb* sə'veɪ] *n* inspección *f*, reconocimiento; (*inquiry*) encuesta ♦ *vt* examinar, inspeccionar; (*look at*) mirar, contemplar; **~or** *n* agrimensor(a) *m/f*
survival [sə'vaɪvl] *n* supervivencia

survive [sə'vaɪv] *vi* sobrevivir; (*custom etc*) perdurar ♦ *vt* sobrevivir a; **survivor** *n* superviviente *m/f*

susceptible [sə'sɛptəbl] *adj*: **~ (to)** (*disease*) susceptible (a); (*flattery*) sensible (a)

suspect [*adj, n* 'sʌspɛkt, *vb* səs'pɛkt] *adj, n* sospechoso/a *m/f* ♦ *vt* (*person*) sospechar de; (*think*) sospechar

suspend [səs'pɛnd] *vt* suspender; **~ed sentence** *n* (*LAW*) libertad *f* condicional; **~er belt** *n* portaligas *m inv*; **~ers** *npl* (*BRIT*) ligas *fpl*; (*US*) tirantes *mpl*

suspense [səs'pɛns] *n* incertidumbre *f*, duda; (*in film etc*) suspense *m*; **to keep sb in ~** mantener a uno en suspense

suspension [səs'pɛnʃən] *n* (*gen, AUT*) suspensión *f*; (*of driving licence*) privación *f*; **~ bridge** *n* puente *m* colgante

suspicion [səs'pɪʃən] *n* sospecha; (*distrust*) recelo; **suspicious** [-ʃəs] *adj* receloso; (*causing suspicion*) sospechoso

sustain [səs'teɪn] *vt* sostener, apoyar; (*suffer*) sufrir, padecer; **~able** *adj* sostenible; **~ed** *adj* (*effort*) sostenido

sustenance ['sʌstɪnəns] *n* sustento

swab [swɔb] *n* (*MED*) algodón *m*

swagger ['swægə*] *vi* pavonearse

swallow ['swɔləʊ] *n* (*bird*) golondrina ♦ *vt* tragar; (*fig, pride*) tragarse; **~ up** *vt* (*savings etc*) consumir

swam [swæm] *pt of* **swim**

swamp [swɔmp] *n* pantano, ciénaga ♦ *vt* (*with water etc*) inundar; (*fig*) abrumar, agobiar; **~y** *adj* pantanoso

swan [swɔn] *n* cisne *m*

swap [swɔp] *n* canje *m*, intercambio ♦ *vt*: **to ~ (for)** cambiar (por)

swarm [swɔːm] *n* (*of bees*) enjambre *m*; (*fig*) multitud *f* ♦ *vi* (*bees*) formar un enjambre; (*people*) pulular; **to be ~ing with** ser un hervidero de

swastika ['swɔstɪkə] *n* esvástika

swat [swɔt] *vt* aplastar

sway [sweɪ] *vi* mecerse, balancearse ♦ *vt* (*influence*) mover, influir en

swear [swɛə*] (*pt* **swore**, *pp* **sworn**) *vi*

(*curse*) maldecir; (*promise*) jurar ♦ *vt* jurar; **~word** *n* taco, palabrota

sweat [swɛt] *n* sudor *m* ♦ *vi* sudar

sweater ['swɛtə*] *n* suéter *m*

sweatshirt ['swɛtʃəːt] *n* suéter *m*

sweaty ['swɛtɪ] *adj* sudoroso

Swede [swiːd] *n* sueco/a

swede [swiːd] (*BRIT*) *n* nabo

Sweden ['swiːdn] *n* Suecia; **Swedish** ['swiːdɪʃ] *adj* sueco ♦ *n* (*LING*) sueco

sweep [swiːp] (*pt, pp* **swept**) *n* (*act*) barrido; (*also*: **chimney~**) deshollinador(a) *m/f* ♦ *vt* barrer; (*with arm*) empujar; (*subj*: *current*) arrastrar ♦ *vi* barrer; (*arm etc*) moverse rápidamente; (*wind*) soplar con violencia; **~ away** *vt* barrer; **~ past** *vi* pasar majestuosamente; **~ up** *vi* barrer; **~ing** *adj* (*gesture*) dramático; (*generalized*): *statement*) generalizado

sweet [swiːt] *n* (*candy*) dulce *m*, caramelo; (*BRIT*: *pudding*) postre *m* ♦ *adj* dulce; (*fig*: *kind*) dulce, amable; (: *attractive*) mono; **~corn** *n* maíz *m*; **~en** *vt* (*add sugar to*) poner azúcar a; (*person*) endulzar; **~heart** *n* novio/a; **~ness** *n* dulzura; **~ pea** *n* guisante *m* de olor

swell [swɛl] (*pt* **swelled**, *pp* **swollen** or **swelled**) *n* (*of sea*) marejada, oleaje *m* ♦ *adj* (*US*: *inf*: *excellent*) estupendo, fenomenal ♦ *vt* hinchar, inflar ♦ *vi* (*also*: **~ up**) hincharse; (*numbers*) aumentar; (*sound, feeling*) ir aumentando; **~ing** *n* (*MED*) hinchazón *f*

sweltering ['swɛltərɪŋ] *adj* sofocante, de mucho calor

swept [swɛpt] *pt, pp of* **sweep**

swerve [swəːv] *vi* desviarse bruscamente

swift [swɪft] *n* (*bird*) vencejo ♦ *adj* rápido, veloz; **~ly** *adv* rápidamente

swig [swɪg] (*inf*) *n* (*drink*) trago

swill [swɪl] *vt* (*also*: **~ out, ~ down**) lavar, limpiar con agua

swim [swɪm] (*pt* **swam**, *pp* **swum**) *n*: **to go for a ~** ir a nadar *or* a bañarse ♦ *vi* nadar; (*head, room*) dar vueltas ♦ *vt* nadar; (*the Channel etc*) cruzar a nado; **~mer** *n* nadador(a) *m/f*; **~ming** *n*

natación f; **~ming cap** n gorro de baño;
~ming costume (*BRIT*) n bañador m,
traje m de baño; **~ming pool** n piscina
(*SP*), alberca (*AM*); **~ming trunks** n
bañador m (de hombre); **~suit** n
= **~ming costume**
swindle ['swɪndl] n estafa ♦ vt estafar
swine [swaɪn] (*inf!*) canalla (!)
swing [swɪŋ] (*pt, pp* **swung**) n (*in
playground*) columpio; (*movement*)
balanceo, vaivén m; (*change of direction*)
viraje m; (*rhythm*) ritmo ♦ vt balancear;
(*also*: **~ round**) voltear, girar ♦ vi
balancearse, columpiarse; (*also*: **~ round**)
dar media vuelta; **to be in full ~** estar en
plena marcha; **~ bridge** n puente m
giratorio; **~ door** (*US* **~ing door**) n
puerta giratoria
swingeing ['swɪndʒɪŋ] (*BRIT*) adj (*cuts*)
atroz
swipe [swaɪp] vt (*hit*) golpear fuerte; (*inf*:
steal) guindar; **~ card** n tarjeta
magnética deslizante, tarjeta swipe
swirl [swəːl] vi arremolinarse
Swiss [swɪs] adj, n inv suizo/a m/f
switch [swɪtʃ] n (*for light etc*) interruptor
m; (*change*) cambio ♦ vt (*change*)
cambiar de; **~ off** vt apagar; (*engine*)
parar; **~ on** vt encender (*SP*), prender
(*AM*); (*engine, machine*) arrancar; **~board**
n (*TEL*) centralita (de teléfonos) (*SP*),
conmutador m (*AM*)
Switzerland ['swɪtsələnd] n Suiza
swivel ['swɪvl] vi (*also*: **~ round**) girar
swollen ['swəulən] pp of **swell**
swoon [swuːn] vi desmayarse
swoop [swuːp] n (*by police etc*) redada
♦ vi (*also*: **~ down**) calarse
swop [swɔp] = **swap**
sword [sɔːd] n espada; **~fish** n pez m
espada
swore [swɔːʳ] pt of **swear**
sworn [swɔːn] pp of **swear** ♦ adj
(*statement*) bajo juramento; (*enemy*)
implacable
swot [swɔt] (*BRIT*) vt, vi empollar
swum [swʌm] pp of **swim**

swung [swʌŋ] pt, pp of **swing**
sycamore ['sɪkəmɔː] n sicomoro
syllable ['sɪləbl] n sílaba
syllabus ['sɪləbəs] n programa m de
estudios
symbol ['sɪmbl] n símbolo
symmetry ['sɪmɪtrɪ] n simetría
sympathetic [sɪmpə'θɛtɪk] adj
(*understanding*) comprensivo; (*likeable*)
simpático; (*showing support*): **~ to(wards)**
bien dispuesto hacia
sympathize ['sɪmpəθaɪz] vi: **to ~ with**
(*person*) compadecerse de; (*feelings*)
comprender; (*cause*) apoyar; **~r** n (*POL*)
simpatizante m/f
sympathy ['sɪmpəθɪ] n (*pity*) compasión f;
sympathies npl (*tendencies*) tendencias
fpl; **with our deepest ~** nuestro más
sentido pésame; **in ~** en solidaridad
symphony ['sɪmfənɪ] n sinfonía
symptom ['sɪmptəm] n síntoma m, indicio
synagogue ['sɪnəgɔg] n sinagoga
syndicate ['sɪndɪkɪt] n (*gen*) sindicato; (*of
newspapers*) agencia (de noticias)
syndrome ['sɪndrəum] n síndrome m
synopsis [sɪ'nɔpsɪs] (*pl* **synopses**) n
sinopsis f inv
synthesis ['sɪnθəsɪs] (*pl* **syntheses**) n
síntesis f inv
synthetic [sɪn'θɛtɪk] adj sintético
syphilis ['sɪfɪlɪs] n sífilis f
syphon ['saɪfən] = **siphon**
Syria ['sɪrɪə] n Siria; **~n** adj, n sirio/a
syringe [sɪ'rɪndʒ] n jeringa
syrup ['sɪrəp] n jarabe m; (*also*: **golden ~**)
almíbar m
system ['sɪstəm] n sistema m; (*ANAT*)
organismo; **~atic** [-'mætɪk] adj
sistemático, metódico; **~ disk** n
(*COMPUT*) disco del sistema; **~s analyst**
n analista m/f de sistemas

T, t

ta [tɑː] (*BRIT: inf*) *excl* ¡gracias!
tab [tæb] *n* lengüeta; (*label*) etiqueta; **to keep ~s on** (*fig*) vigilar
tabby ['tæbɪ] *n* (*also:* **~ cat**) gato atigrado
table ['teɪbl] *n* mesa; (*of statistics etc*) cuadro, tabla ♦ *vt* (*BRIT: motion etc*) presentar; **to lay** *or* **set the ~** poner la mesa; **~cloth** *n* mantel *m*; **~ of contents** *n* índice *m* de materias; **~ d'hôte** [tɑːblˈdəʊt] *adj* del menú; **~ lamp** *n* lámpara de mesa; **~mat** *n* (*for plate*) posaplatos *m inv*; (*for hot dish*) salvamantel *m*; **~spoon** *n* cuchara de servir; (*also:* **~spoonful:** *as measurement*) cucharada
tablet ['tæblɪt] *n* (*MED*) pastilla, comprimido; (*of stone*) lápida
table tennis *n* ping-pong *m*, tenis *m* de mesa
table wine *n* vino de mesa
tabloid ['tæblɔɪd] *n* periódico popular sensacionalista

┌─ **tabloid press** ─────────────

i El término **tabloid press** *o* **tabloids** se usa para referirse a la prensa popular británica, por el tamaño más pequeño de los periódicos. A diferencia de los de la llamada *quality press*, estas publicaciones se caracterizan por un lenguaje sencillo, una presentación llamativa y un contenido sensacionalista, centrado a veces en los escándalos financieros y sexuales de los famosos, por lo que también reciben el nombre peyorativo de *"gutter press"*.

└──────────────────────────

tack [tæk] *n* (*nail*) tachuela; (*fig*) rumbo ♦ *vt* (*nail*) clavar con tachuelas; (*stitch*) hilvanar ♦ *vi* virar
tackle ['tækl] *n* (*fishing ~*) aparejo (de pescar); (*for lifting*) aparejo ♦ *vt* (*difficulty*) enfrentarse con; (*challenge: person*) hacer frente a; (*grapple with*) agarrar; (*FOOTBALL*) cargar; (*RUGBY*) placar
tacky ['tækɪ] *adj* pegajoso; (*pej*) cutre
tact [tækt] *n* tacto, discreción *f*; **~ful** *adj* discreto, diplomático
tactics ['tæktɪks] *n, npl* táctica
tactless ['tæktlɪs] *adj* indiscreto
tadpole ['tædpəʊl] *n* renacuajo
tag [tæg] *n* (*label*) etiqueta; **~ along** *vi* ir (*or* venir) también
tail [teɪl] *n* cola; (*of shirt, coat*) faldón *m* ♦ *vt* (*follow*) vigilar a; **~s** *npl* (*formal suit*) levita; **~ away** *vi* (*in size, quality etc*) ir disminuyendo; **~ off** *vi* = **~ away**; **~back** (*BRIT*) *n* (*AUT*) cola; **~ end** *n* cola, parte *f* final; **~gate** *n* (*AUT*) puerta trasera
tailor ['teɪlə*] *n* sastre *m*; **~ing** *n* (*cut*) corte *m*; (*craft*) sastrería; **~-made** *adj* (*also fig*) hecho a la medida
tailwind ['teɪlwɪnd] *n* viento de cola
tainted ['teɪntɪd] *adj* (*food*) pasado; (*water, air*) contaminado; (*fig*) manchado
take [teɪk] (*pt* **took**, *pp* **taken**) *vt* tomar; (*grab*) coger (*SP*), agarrar (*AM*); (*gain: prize*) ganar; (*require: effort, courage*) exigir; (*tolerate: pain etc*) aguantar; (*hold: passengers etc*) tener cabida para; (*accompany, bring, carry*) llevar; (*exam*) presentarse a; **to ~ sth from** (*drawer etc*) sacar algo de; (*person*) quitar algo a; **I ~ it that ...** supongo que ...; **~ after** *vt fus* parecerse a; **~ apart** *vt* desmontar; **~ away** *vt* (*remove*) quitar; (*carry off*) llevar; (*MATH*) restar; **~ back** *vt* (*return*) devolver; (*one's words*) retractarse de; **~ down** *vt* (*building*) derribar; (*letter etc*) apuntar; **~ in** *vt* (*deceive*) engañar; (*understand*) entender; (*include*) abarcar; (*lodger*) acoger, recibir; **~ off** *vi* (*AVIAT*) despegar ♦ *vt* (*remove*) quitar; **~ on** *vt* (*work*) aceptar; (*employee*) contratar; (*opponent*) desafiar a uno; **~ out** *vt* sacar; **~ over** *vt* (*business*) tomar posesión de; (*country*) tomar el poder ♦ *vi*: **to ~ over from sb** reemplazar a uno; **~ to** *vt fus* (*person*) coger cariño a, encariñarse con; (*activity*) aficionarse a; **~ up** *vt* (*a dress*)

acortar; (*occupy: time, space*) ocupar;
(*engage in: hobby etc*) dedicarse a;
(*accept*): **to ~ sb up on** aceptar; **~away**
(*BRIT*) *adj* (*food*) para llevar ♦ *n* tienda (*or*
restaurante *m*) de comida para llevar;
~off *n* (*AVIAT*) despegue *m*; **~out** (*US*) *n*
= **~away**; **~over** *n* (*COMM*) absorción *f*

takings ['teɪkɪŋz] *npl* (*COMM*) ingresos *mpl*

talc [tælk] *n* (*also:* **~um powder**) (polvos
de) talco

tale [teɪl] *n* (*story*) cuento; (*account*)
relación *f*; **to tell ~s** (*fig*) chivarse

talent ['tælnt] *n* talento; **~ed** *adj* de
talento

talk [tɔːk] *n* charla; (*conversation*)
conversación *f*; (*gossip*) habladurías *fpl*,
chismes *mpl* ♦ *vi* hablar; **~s** *npl* (*POL etc*)
conversaciones *fpl*; **to ~ about** hablar de;
to ~ sb into doing sth convencer a uno
para que haga algo; **to ~ sb out of doing
sth** disuadir a uno de que haga algo; **to ~
shop** hablar del trabajo; **~ over** *vt*
discutir; **~ative** *adj* hablador(a); **~ show**
n programa *m* de entrevistas

tall [tɔːl] *adj* alto; (*object*) grande; **to be 6
feet ~** (*person*) ≈ medir 1 metro 80

tally ['tælɪ] *n* cuenta ♦ *vi*: **to ~ (with)**
corresponder (con)

talon ['tælən] *n* garra

tambourine [tæmbə'riːn] *n* pandereta

tame [teɪm] *adj* domesticado; (*fig*)
mediocre

tamper ['tæmpə*] *vi*: **to ~ with** tocar,
andar con

tampon ['tæmpən] *n* tampón *m*

tan [tæn] *n* (*also:* **sun~**) bronceado ♦ *vi*
ponerse moreno ♦ *adj* (*colour*) marrón

tang [tæŋ] *n* sabor *m* fuerte

tangent ['tændʒənt] *n* (*MATH*) tangente *f*;
to go off at a ~ (*fig*) salirse por la
tangente

tangerine [tændʒə'riːn] *n* mandarina

tangle ['tæŋgl] *n* enredo; **to get in(to) a ~**
enredarse

tank [tæŋk] *n* (*water* ~) depósito, tanque
m; (*for fish*) acuario; (*MIL*) tanque *m*

tanker ['tæŋkə*] *n* (*ship*) buque *m* cisterna;

(*truck*) camión *m* cisterna

tanned [tænd] *adj* (*skin*) moreno

tantalizing ['tæntəlaɪzɪŋ] *adj* tentador(a)

tantamount ['tæntəmaunt] *adj*: **~ to**
equivalente a

tantrum ['tæntrəm] *n* rabieta

tap [tæp] *n* (*BRIT: on sink etc*) grifo (*SP*),
canilla (*AM*); (*gas ~*) llave *f*; (*gentle blow*)
golpecito ♦ *vt* (*hit gently*) dar golpecitos
en; (*resources*) utilizar, explotar;
(*telephone*) intervenir; **on ~** (*fig: resources*)
a mano; **~ dancing** *n* claqué *m*

tape [teɪp] *n* (*also:* **magnetic ~**) cinta
magnética; (*cassette*) cassette *f*, cinta;
(*sticky ~*) cinta adhesiva; (*for tying*) cinta
♦ *vt* (*record*) grabar (en cinta); (*stick with
~*) pegar con cinta adhesiva; **~ deck** *n*
grabadora; **~ measure** *n* cinta métrica,
metro

taper ['teɪpə*] *n* cirio ♦ *vi* afilarse

tape recorder *n* grabadora

tapestry ['tæpɪstrɪ] *n* (*object*) tapiz *m*; (*art*)
tapicería

tar [tɑː] *n* alquitrán *m*, brea

target ['tɑːgɪt] *n* (*gen*) blanco

tariff ['tærɪf] *n* (*on goods*) arancel *m*; (*BRIT:
in hotels etc*) tarifa

tarmac ['tɑːmæk] *n* (*BRIT: on road*)
asfaltado; (*AVIAT*) pista de aterrizaje)

tarnish ['tɑːnɪʃ] *vt* deslustrar

tarpaulin [tɑː'pɔːlɪn] *n* lona
impermeabilizada

tarragon ['tærəgən] *n* estragón *m*

tart [tɑːt] *n* (*CULIN*) tarta; (*BRIT: inf:
prostitute*) puta ♦ *adj* agrio, ácido; **~ up**
(*BRIT: inf*) *vt* (*building*) remozar; **to ~ o.s.
up** acicalarse

tartan ['tɑːtn] *n* tejido escocés *m*

tartar ['tɑːtə*] *n* (*on teeth*) sarro; **~(e)
sauce** *n* salsa tártara

task [tɑːsk] *n* tarea; **to take to ~** reprender;
~ force *n* (*MIL, POLICE*) grupo de
operaciones

taste [teɪst] *n* (*sense*) gusto; (*flavour*) sabor
m; (*also: after~*) sabor *m*, dejo; (*sample*):
have a ~! ¡prueba un poquito!; (*fig*)
muestra, idea ♦ *vt* (*also fig*) probar ♦ *vi*:

to ~ of *or* **like** (*fish, garlic etc*) saber a;
you can ~ the garlic (in it) se nota el
sabor a ajo; **in good/bad ~** de buen/mal
gusto; **~ful** *adj* de buen gusto; **~less**
adj (*food*) soso; (*remark etc*) de mal gusto;
tasty *adj* sabroso, rico

tatters ['tætəz] *npl*: **in ~** hecho jirones

tattoo [tə'tu:] *n* tatuaje *m*; (*spectacle*)
espectáculo militar ♦ *vt* tatuar

tatty ['tætɪ] (*BRIT: inf*) *adj* cochambroso

taught [tɔ:t] *pt, pp of* **teach**

taunt [tɔ:nt] *n* burla ♦ *vt* burlarse de

Taurus ['tɔ:rəs] *n* Tauro

taut [tɔ:t] *adj* tirante, tenso

tax [tæks] *n* impuesto ♦ *vt* gravar (con un
impuesto); (*fig: memory*) poner a prueba
(*: patience*) agotar; **~able** *adj* (*income*)
gravable; **~ation** [-'seɪʃən] *n* impuestos
mpl; **~ avoidance** *n* evasión *f* de
impuestos; **~ disc** (*BRIT*) *n* (*AUT*) pegatina
del impuesto de circulación; **~ evasion**
n evasión *f* fiscal; **~-free** *adj* libre de
impuestos

taxi ['tæksɪ] *n* taxi *m* ♦ *vi* (*AVIAT*) rodar por
la pista; **~ driver** *n* taxista *m/f*; **~ rank**
(*BRIT*), **~ stand** *n* parada de taxis

tax: **~ payer** *n* contribuyente *m/f*; **~
relief** *n* desgravación *f* fiscal; **~ return** *n*
declaración *f* de ingresos

TB *n abbr* = **tuberculosis**

tea [ti:] *n* té *m*; (*BRIT: meal*) ≈ merienda
(*SP*); cena; **high ~** (*BRIT*) merienda-cena
(*SP*); **~ bag** *n* bolsita de té; **~ break**
(*BRIT*) *n* descanso para el té

teach [ti:tʃ] (*pt, pp* **taught**) *vt*: **to ~ sb
sth, ~ sth to sb** enseñar algo a uno ♦ *vi*
(*be a teacher*) ser profesor(a), enseñar;
~er *n* (*in secondary school*) profesor(a)
m/f; (*in primary school*) maestro/a,
profesor/a de EGB; **~ing** *n* enseñanza

tea cosy *n* cubretetera *m*

teacup ['ti:kʌp] *n* taza para el té

teak [ti:k] *n* (madera de) teca

team [ti:m] *n* equipo; (*of horses*) tiro;
~work *n* trabajo en equipo

teapot ['ti:pɔt] *n* tetera

tear¹ [tɪə*] *n* lágrima; **in ~s** llorando

tear² [tɛə*] (*pt* **tore**, *pp* **torn**) *n* rasgón *m*,
desgarrón *m* ♦ *vt* romper, rasgar ♦ *vi*
rasgarse; **~ along** *vi* (*rush*) precipitarse;
~ up *vt* (*sheet of paper etc*) romper

tearful ['tɪəfəl] *adj* lloroso

tear gas ['tɪə-] *n* gas *m* lacrimógeno

tearoom ['ti:ru:m] *n* salón *m* de té

tease [ti:z] *vt* tomar el pelo a

tea set *n* servicio de té

teaspoon *n* cucharita; (*also*: **~ful**: *as
measurement*) cucharadita

teat [ti:t] *n* (*of bottle*) tetina

teatime ['ti:taɪm] *n* hora del té

tea towel (*BRIT*) *n* paño de cocina

technical ['teknɪkl] *adj* técnico; **~
college** (*BRIT*) *n* ≈ escuela de artes y
oficios (*SP*); **~ity** [-'kælɪtɪ] *n* (*point of law*)
formalismo; (*detail*) detalle *m* técnico; **~ly**
adv en teoría; (*regarding technique*)
técnicamente

technician [tek'nɪʃn] *n* técnico/a

technique [tek'ni:k] *n* técnica

technological [teknə'lɔdʒɪkl] *adj*
tecnológico

technology [tek'nɔlədʒɪ] *n* tecnología

teddy (bear) ['tedɪ-] *n* osito de felpa

tedious ['ti:dɪəs] *adj* pesado, aburrido

teem [ti:m] *vi*: **to ~ with** rebosar de; **it is
~ing (with rain)** llueve a cántaros

teenage ['ti:neɪdʒ] *adj* (*fashions etc*)
juvenil; (*children*) quinceañero; **~r** *n*
quinceañero/a

teens [ti:nz] *npl*: **to be in one's ~** ser
adolescente

tee-shirt ['ti:ʃə:t] *n* = **T-shirt**

teeter ['ti:tə*] *vi* balancearse; (*fig*): **to ~ on
the edge of ...** estar al borde de ...

teeth [ti:θ] *npl of* **tooth**

teethe [ti:ð] *vi* echar los dientes

teething ['ti:ðɪŋ]: **~ ring** *n* mordedor *m*;
~ troubles *npl* (*fig*) dificultades *fpl*
iniciales

teetotal ['ti:'təutl] *adj* abstemio

telegram ['telɪgræm] *n* telegrama *m*

telegraph ['telɪgrɑ:f] *n* telégrafo; **~ pole**
n poste *m* telegráfico

telepathy [tə'lepəθɪ] *n* telepatía

telephone ['tɛlɪfəʊn] *n* teléfono ♦ *vt* llamar por teléfono, telefonear; (*message*) dar por teléfono; **to be on the ~** (*talking*) hablar por teléfono; (*possessing ~*) tener teléfono; **~ booth** *n* cabina telefónica; **~ box** (*BRIT*) *n* = **~ booth**; **~ call** *n* llamada (telefónica); **~ directory** *n* guía (telefónica); **~ number** *n* número de teléfono; **telephonist** [təˈlɛfənɪst] (*BRIT*) *n* telefonista *m/f*

telesales ['tɛlɪseɪlz] *npl* televenta(s) *f(pl)*

telescope ['tɛlɪskəʊp] *n* telescopio

television ['tɛlɪvɪʒən] *n* televisión *f*; **on ~** en la televisión; **~ set** *n* televisor *m*

teleworking ['tɛlɪˌwɜːkɪŋ] *n* teletrabajo

tell [tɛl] (*pt, pp* **told**) *vt* decir; (*relate: story*) contar; (*distinguish*): **to ~ sth from** distinguir algo de ♦ *vi* (*talk*): **to ~ (of)** contar; (*have effect*) tener efecto; **to ~ sb to do sth** mandar a uno hacer algo; **~ off** *vt*: **to ~ sb off** regañar a uno; **~er** *n* (*in bank*) cajero/a; **~ing** *adj* (*remark*) revelador(a); **~tale** *adj* (*sign*) indicador(a)

telly ['tɛlɪ] (*BRIT: inf*) *n abbr* (= *television*) tele *f*

temp [tɛmp] *n abbr* (*BRIT*: = *temporary*) temporero/a

temper ['tɛmpə*] *n* (*nature*) carácter *m*; (*mood*) humor *m*; (*bad ~*) (mal) genio; (*fit of anger*) acceso de ira ♦ *vt* (*moderate*) moderar; **to be in a ~** estar furioso; **to lose one's ~** enfadarse, enojarse

temperament ['tɛmprəmənt] *n* (*nature*) temperamento

temperate ['tɛmprət] *adj* (*climate etc*) templado

temperature ['tɛmprətʃə*] *n* temperatura; **to have** *or* **run a ~** tener fiebre

temple ['tɛmpl] *n* (*building*) templo; (*ANAT*) sien *f*

tempo ['tɛmpəʊ] *n* (*pl* **tempos** *or* **tempi**) (*MUS*) tempo, tiempo; (*fig*) ritmo

temporarily ['tɛmpərərɪlɪ] *adv* temporalmente

temporary ['tɛmpərərɪ] *adj* provisional; (*passing*) transitorio; (*worker*) temporero; (*job*) temporal

tempt [tɛmpt] *vt* tentar; **to ~ sb into doing sth** tentar *or* inducir a uno a hacer algo; **~ation** [-'teɪʃən] *n* tentación *f*; **~ing** *adj* tentador(a); (*food*) apetitoso/a

ten [tɛn] *num* diez

tenacity [təˈnæsɪtɪ] *n* tenacidad *f*

tenancy ['tɛnənsɪ] *n* arrendamiento, alquiler *m*

tenant ['tɛnənt] *n* inquilino/a

tend [tɛnd] *vt* cuidar ♦ *vi*: **to ~ to do sth** tener tendencia a hacer algo

tendency ['tɛndənsɪ] *n* tendencia

tender ['tɛndə*] *adj* (*person, care*) tierno, cariñoso; (*meat*) tierno; (*sore*) sensible ♦ *n* (*COMM: offer*) oferta; (*money*): **legal ~** moneda de curso legal ♦ *vt* ofrecer; **~ness** *n* ternura; (*of meat*) blandura

tenement ['tɛnəmənt] *n* casa de pisos (*SP*)

tennis ['tɛnɪs] *n* tenis *m*; **~ ball** *n* pelota de tenis; **~ court** *n* cancha de tenis; **~ player** *n* tenista *m/f*; **~ racket** *n* raqueta de tenis

tenor ['tɛnə*] *n* (*MUS*) tenor *m*

tenpin bowling ['tɛnpɪn-] *n* (juego de los) bolos

tense [tɛns] *adj* (*person*) nervioso; (*moment, atmosphere*) tenso; (*muscle*) tenso, en tensión ♦ *n* (*LING*) tiempo

tension ['tɛnʃən] *n* tensión *f*

tent [tɛnt] *n* tienda (de campaña) (*SP*), carpa (*AM*)

tentative ['tɛntətɪv] *adj* (*person, smile*) indeciso; (*conclusion, plans*) provisional

tenterhooks ['tɛntəhʊks] *npl*: **on ~** sobre ascuas

tenth [tɛnθ] *num* décimo

tent peg *n* clavija, estaca

tent pole *n* mástil *m*

tenuous ['tɛnjʊəs] *adj* tenue

tenure ['tɛnjʊə*] *n* (*of land etc*) tenencia; (*of office*) ejercicio

tepid ['tɛpɪd] *adj* tibio

term [tɜːm] *n* (*word*) término; (*period*) período; (*SCOL*) trimestre *m* ♦ *vt* llamar; **~s** *npl* (*conditions, COMM*) condiciones *fpl*; **in the short/long ~** a corto/largo plazo; **to be on good ~s with sb** llevarse bien

con uno; **to come to ~s with** (*problem*)
aceptar
terminal ['tə:mınl] *adj* (*disease*) mortal;
(*patient*) terminal ♦ *n* (COMPUT) terminal
m; (*also*: **air ~**) terminal *f*; (BRIT: *also*:
coach ~) (estación *f*) terminal *f*
terminate ['tə:mıneıt] *vt* terminar
terminus ['tə:mınəs] (*pl* **termini**) *n*
término, (estación *f*) terminal *f*
terrace ['terəs] *n* terraza; (BRIT: *row of
houses*) hilera de casas adosadas; **the ~s**
(BRIT: SPORT) las gradas *fpl*; **~d** *adj*
(*garden*) en terrazas; (*house*) adosado
terrain [te'reın] *n* terreno
terrible ['terıbl] *adj* terrible, horrible; (*inf*)
atroz; **terribly** *adv* terriblemente; (*very
badly*) malísimamente
terrific [tə'rıfık] *adj* (*very great*) tremendo;
(*wonderful*) fantástico, fenomenal
terrify ['terıfaı] *vt* aterrorizar
territory ['terıtərı] *n* (*also fig*) territorio
terror ['terə*] *n* terror *m*; **~ism** *n*
terrorismo; **~ist** *n* terrorista *m/f*
test [test] *n* (*gen*, CHEM) prueba; (MED)
examen *m*; (SCOL) examen *m*, test *m*;
(*also*: **driving ~**) examen *m* de conducir
♦ *vt* probar, poner a prueba; (MED, SCOL)
examinar
testament ['testəmənt] *n* testamento; **the
Old/New T~** el Antiguo/Nuevo
Testamento
testicle ['testıkl] *n* testículo
testify ['testıfaı] *vi* (LAW) prestar
declaración; **to ~ to sth** atestiguar algo
testimony ['testımənı] *n* (LAW) testimonio
test: **~ match** *n* (CRICKET, RUGBY) partido
internacional; **~ tube** *n* probeta
tetanus ['tetənəs] *n* tétano
tether ['teðə*] *vt* atar ♦ *n*: **to be at the
end of one's ~** no aguantar más
text [tekst] *n* texto; **~book** *n* libro de
texto; **~ message** *n* mensaje *m* (de
texto); **~ messaging** *n* envío de
mensajes (de texto)
textiles ['tekstaılz] *npl* textiles *mpl*; (*textile
industry*) industria textil
texting ['tekstıŋ] *n* (COMPUT) envío de

mensajes (de texto)
texture ['tekstʃə*] *n* textura
Thailand ['taılænd] *n* Tailandia
Thames [temz] *n*: **the ~** el (río) Támesis
than [ðaen] *conj* (*in comparisons*): **more ~
10/once** más de 10/una vez; **I have
more/less ~ you/Paul** tengo más/
menos que tú/Paul; **she is older ~ you
think** es mayor de lo que piensas
thank [θaeŋk] *vt* dar las gracias a,
agradecer; **~ you (very much)** muchas
gracias; **~ God!** ¡gracias a Dios!; **~s** *npl*
gracias *fpl* ♦ *excl* (*also*: **many ~s, ~s a
lot**) ¡gracias!; **~s to** *prep* gracias a; **~ful**
adj: **~ful (for)** agradecido (por); **~less**
adj ingrato; **T~sgiving (Day)** *see box*

KEYWORD

that [ðaet] (*pl* **those**) *adj* (*demonstrative*)
ese/a, *pl* esos/as; (*more remote*) aquel/
aquella, *pl* aquellos/as; **leave those
books on the table** deja esos libros sobre
la mesa; **~ one** ése/ésa; (*more remote*)
aquél/aquélla; **~ one over there** ése/ésa
de ahí; aquél/aquélla de allí
♦ *pron* **1** (*demonstrative*) ése/a, *pl* ésos/as;
(*neuter*) eso; (*more remote*) aquél/aquélla,
pl aquéllos/as; (*neuter*) aquello; **what's ~?**
¿qué es eso (*or* aquello)?; **who's ~?**
¿quién es ése (*or* aquél/aquélla)?; **is ~
you?** ¿eres tú?; **will you eat all ~?** ¿vas a
comer todo eso?; **~'s my house** ésa es
mi casa; **~'s what he said** eso es lo que

dijo; **~ is (to say)** es decir
2 (*relative: subject, object*) que; (*with preposition*) (el/la) que *etc*, el/la cual *etc*; **the book (~) I read** el libro que leí; **the books ~ are in the library** los libros que están en la biblioteca; **all (~) I have** todo lo que tengo; **the box (~) I put it in** la caja en la que *or* donde lo puse; **the people (~) I spoke to** la gente con la que hablé
3 (*relative: of time*) que; **the day (~) he came** el día (en) que vino
♦ *conj* que; **he thought ~ I was ill** creyó que yo estaba enfermo
♦ *adv* (*demonstrative*): **I can't work ~ much** no puedo trabajar tanto; **I didn't realise it was ~ bad** no creí que fuera tan malo; **~ high** así de alto

thatched [θætʃt] *adj* (*roof*) de paja; (*cottage*) con tejado de paja
thaw [θɔ:] *n* deshielo ♦ *vi* (*ice*) derretirse; (*food*) descongelarse ♦ *vt* (*food*) descongelar

KEYWORD

the [ði:, ðə] *def art* **1** (*gen*) el, *f* la, *pl* los, *fpl* las (*NB* = el *immediately before f n beginning with stressed (h)a*; a+el = al; de+el = del); **~ boy/girl** el chico/la chica; **~ books/flowers** los libros/las flores; **to ~ postman/from ~ drawer** al cartero/del cajón; **I haven't ~ time/money** no tengo tiempo/dinero
2 (*+adj to form n*) los; lo; **~ rich and ~ poor** los ricos y los pobres; **to attempt ~ impossible** intentar lo imposible
3 (*in titles*): **Elizabeth ~ First** Isabel primera; **Peter ~ Great** Pedro el Grande
4 (*in comparisons*): **~ more he works ~ more he earns** cuanto más trabaja más gana

theatre ['θɪətə*] (*US* **theater**) *n* teatro; (*also:* **lecture ~**) aula; (*MED: also:* **operating ~**) quirófano; **~-goer** *n* aficionado/a al teatro

theatrical [θɪ'ætrɪkl] *adj* teatral
theft [θeft] *n* robo
their [ðɛə*] *adj* su; **~s** *pron* (el) suyo/(la) suya *etc*; *see also* **my; mine¹**
them [ðem, ðəm] *pron* (*direct*) los/las; (*indirect*) les; (*stressed, after prep*) ellos/ellas; *see also* **me**
theme [θi:m] *n* tema *m*; **~ park** *n* parque de atracciones (*en torno a un tema central*); **~ song** *n* tema *m* (*musical*)
themselves [ðəm'selvz] *pl pron* (*subject*) ellos mismos/ellas mismas; (*complement*) se; (*after prep*) sí (mismos/as); *see also* **oneself**
then [ðen] *adv* (*at that time*) entonces; (*next*) después; (*later*) luego, después; (*and also*) además ♦ *conj* (*therefore*) en ese caso, entonces ♦ *adj*: **the ~ president** el entonces presidente; **by ~** para entonces; **from ~ on** desde entonces
theology [θɪ'ɔlədʒɪ] *n* teología
theory ['θɪərɪ] *n* teoría
therapist ['θerəpɪst] *n* terapeuta *m/f*
therapy ['θerəpɪ] *n* terapia

KEYWORD

there ['ðɛə*] *adv* **1**: **~ is, ~ are** hay; **~ is no-one here/no bread left** no hay nadie aquí/no queda pan; **~ has been an accident** ha habido un accidente
2 (*referring to place*) ahí; (*distant*) allí; **it's ~** está ahí; **put it in/on/up/down ~** ponlo ahí dentro/encima/arriba/abajo; **I want that book ~** quiero ese libro de ahí; **~ he is!** ¡ahí está!
3: **~, ~** (*esp to child*) ea, ea

there: ~abouts *adv* por ahí; **~after** *adv* después; **~by** *adv* así, de ese modo; **~fore** *adv* por lo tanto; **~'s** = **there is**; **there has**
thermal ['θə:ml] *adj* termal; (*paper*) térmico
thermometer [θə'mɔmɪtə*] *n* termómetro
Thermos ® ['θə:məs] *n* (*also:* **~ flask**) termo
thermostat ['θə:məustæt] *n* termostato

thesaurus [θɪ'sɔːrəs] *n* tesoro

these [ðiːz] *pl adj* estos/as ♦ *pl pron* éstos/as

thesis ['θiːsɪs] (*pl* **theses**) *n* tesis *f inv*

they [ðeɪ] *pl pron* ellos/ellas; (*stressed*) ellos (mismos)/ellas (mismas); **~ say that ...** (*it is said that*) se dice que ...; **~'d = they had; they would; ~'ll = they shall; they will; ~'re = they are; ~'ve = they have**

thick [θɪk] *adj* (*in consistency*) espeso; (*in size*) grueso; (*stupid*) torpe ♦ *n*: **in the ~ of the battle** en lo más reñido de la batalla; **it's 20 cm ~** tiene 20 cm de espesor; **~en** *vi* espesarse ♦ *vt* (*sauce etc*) espesar; **~ness** *n* espesor *m*; grueso; **~set** *adj* fornido

thief [θiːf] (*pl* **thieves**) *n* ladrón/ona *m/f*

thigh [θaɪ] *n* muslo

thimble ['θɪmbl] *n* dedal *m*

thin [θɪn] *adj* (*person, animal*) flaco; (*in size*) delgado; (*in consistency*) poco espeso; (*hair, crowd*) escaso ♦ *vt*: **to ~ (down)** diluir

thing [θɪŋ] *n* cosa; (*object*) objeto, artículo; (*matter*) asunto; (*mania*) : **to have a ~ about sth/sb** estar obsesionado con uno/algo; **~s** *npl* (*belongings*) efectos *mpl* (personales); **the best ~ would be to ...** lo mejor sería ...; **how are ~s?** ¿qué tal?

think [θɪŋk] (*pt, pp* **thought**) *vi* pensar ♦ *vt* pensar, creer; **what did you ~ of them?** ¿qué te parecieron?; **to ~ about sth/sb** pensar en algo/uno; **I'll ~ about it** lo pensaré; **to ~ of doing sth** pensar en hacer algo; **I ~ so/not** creo que sí/no; **to ~ well of sb** tener buen concepto de uno; **~ over** *vt* reflexionar sobre, meditar; **~ up** *vt* (*plan etc*) idear; **~ tank** *n* gabinete *m* de estrategia

thinly ['θɪnlɪ] *adv* (*cut*) fino; (*spread*) ligeramente

third [θɜːd] *adj* (*before n*) tercer(a); (*following n*) tercero/a ♦ *n* tercero/a; (*fraction*) tercio; (*BRIT: SCOL: degree*) título de licenciado con calificación de aprobado; **~ly** *adv* en tercer lugar; **~ party insurance** (*BRIT*) *n* seguro contra

terceros; **~-rate** *adj* (*de calidad*) mediocre; **T~ World** *n* Tercer Mundo

thirst [θɜːst] *n* sed *f*; **~y** *adj* (*person, animal*) sediento; (*work*) que da sed; **to be ~y** tener sed

thirteen ['θɜː'tiːn] *num* trece

thirty ['θɜːtɪ] *num* treinta

KEYWORD
---

this [ðɪs] (*pl* **these**) *adj* (*demonstrative*) este/a; *pl* estos/as; (*neuter*) esto; **~ man/woman** este hombre/esta mujer; **these children/flowers** estos chicos/estas flores; **~ one (here)** éste/a, esto (de aquí) ♦ *pron* (*demonstrative*) éste/a; *pl* éstos/as; (*neuter*) esto; **who is ~?** ¿quién es éste/ésta?; **what is ~?** ¿qué es esto?; **~ is where I live** aquí vivo; **~ is what he said** esto es lo que dijo; **~ is Mr Brown** (*in introductions*) le presento al Sr. Brown; (*photo*) éste es el Sr. Brown; (*on telephone*) habla el Sr. Brown ♦ *adv* (*demonstrative*): **~ high/long** *etc* así de alto/largo *etc*; **~ far** hasta aquí

---

thistle ['θɪsl] *n* cardo

thorn [θɔːn] *n* espina

thorough ['θʌrə] *adj* (*search*) minucioso; (*wash*) a fondo; (*knowledge, research*) profundo; (*person*) meticuloso; **~bred** *adj* (*horse*) de pura sangre; **~fare** *n* calle *f*; **"no ~fare"** "prohibido el paso"; **~ly** *adv* (*search*) minuciosamente; (*study*) profundamente; (*wash*) a fondo; (*utterly: bad, wet etc*) completamente, totalmente

those [ðəʊz] *pl adj* esos/esas; (*more remote*) aquellos/as

though [ðəʊ] *conj* aunque ♦ *adv* sin embargo

thought [θɔːt] *pt, pp of* **think** ♦ *n* pensamiento; (*opinion*) opinión *f*; **~ful** *adj* pensativo; (*serious*) serio; (*considerate*) atento; **~less** *adj* desconsiderado

thousand ['θaʊzənd] *num* mil; **two ~** dos mil; **~s of** miles de; **~th** *num* milésimo

thrash [θræʃ] *vt* azotar; (*defeat*) derrotar; **~ about** *or* **around** *vi* debatirse; **~ out** *vt* discutir a fondo

thread [θrɛd] *n* hilo; (*of screw*) rosca ♦ *vt* (*needle*) enhebrar; **~bare** *adj* raído

threat [θrɛt] *n* amenaza; **~en** *vi* amenazar ♦ *vt*: **to ~en sb with/to do** amenazar a uno con/con hacer

three [θriː] *num* tres; **~-dimensional** *adj* tridimensional; **~-piece suit** *n* traje *m* de tres piezas; **~-piece suite** *n* tresillo; **~-ply** *adj* (*wool*) de tres cabos

threshold ['θrɛʃhəuld] *n* umbral *m*

threw [θruː] *pt of* **throw**

thrifty ['θrɪftɪ] *adj* económico

thrill [θrɪl] *n* (*excitement*) emoción *f*; (*shudder*) estremecimiento ♦ *vt* emocionar; **to be ~ed** (*with gift etc*) estar encantado; **~er** *n* novela (*or obra or película*) de suspense; **~ing** *adj* emocionante

thrive [θraɪv] (*pt, pp* **thrived**) *vi* (*grow*) crecer; (*do well*): **to ~ on sth** sentarle muy bien a uno algo; **thriving** *adj* próspero

throat [θrəut] *n* garganta; **to have a sore ~** tener dolor de garganta

throb [θrɒb] *vi* latir; dar punzadas; vibrar

throes [θrəuz] *npl*: **in the ~ of** en medio de

throne [θrəun] *n* trono

throng [θrɒŋ] *n* multitud *f*, muchedumbre *f* ♦ *vt* agolparse en

throttle ['θrɒtl] *n* (*AUT*) acelerador *m* ♦ *vt* estrangular

through [θruː] *prep* por, a través de; (*time*) durante; (*by means of*) por medio de, mediante; (*owing to*) gracias a ♦ *adj* (*ticket, train*) directo ♦ *adv* completamente, de parte a parte; de principio a fin; **to put sb ~ to sb** (*TEL*) poner *or* pasar a uno con uno; **to be ~** (*TEL*) tener comunicación; (*have finished*) haber terminado; **"no ~ road"** (*BRIT*) "calle sin salida"; **~out** *prep* (*place*) por todas partes de, por todo; (*time*) durante todo ♦ *adv* por *or* en todas partes

throw [θrəu] (*pt* **threw**, *pp* **thrown**) *n* tiro; (*SPORT*) lanzamiento ♦ *vt* tirar, echar; (*SPORT*) lanzar; (*rider*) derribar; (*fig*)

desconcertar; **to ~ a party** dar una fiesta; **~ away** *vt* tirar; (*money*) derrochar; **~ off** *vt* deshacerse de; **~ out** *vt* tirar; (*person*) echar; expulsar; **~ up** *vi* vomitar; **~away** *adj* para tirar, desechable; (*remark*) hecho de paso; **~-in** *n* (*SPORT*) saque *m*

thru [θruː] (*US*) = **through**

thrush [θrʌʃ] *n* zorzal *m*, tordo

thrust [θrʌst] (*pt, pp* **thrust**) *vt* empujar (con fuerza)

thud [θʌd] *n* golpe *m* sordo

thug [θʌg] *n* gamberro/a

thumb [θʌm] *n* (*ANAT*) pulgar *m*; **to ~ a lift** hacer autostop; **~ through** *vt fus* (*book*) hojear; **~tack** (*US*) *n* chincheta (*SP*)

thump [θʌmp] *n* golpe *m*; (*sound*) ruido seco *or* sordo ♦ *vt* golpear ♦ *vi* (*heart etc*) palpitar

thunder ['θʌndə*] *n* trueno ♦ *vi* tronar; (*train etc*): **to ~ past** pasar como un trueno; **~bolt** *n* rayo; **~clap** *n* trueno; **~storm** *n* tormenta; **~y** *adj* tormentoso

Thursday ['θɜːzdɪ] *n* jueves *m inv*

thus [ðʌs] *adv* así, de este modo

thyme [taɪm] *n* tomillo

thyroid ['θaɪrɔɪd] *n* (*also*: **~ gland**) tiroides *m inv*

tic [tɪk] *n* tic *m*

tick [tɪk] *n* (*sound: of clock*) tictac *m*; (*mark*) palomita; (*ZOOL*) garrapata; (*BRIT*: *inf*): **in a ~** en un instante ♦ *vi* hacer tictac ♦ *vt* marcar; **~ off** *vt* marcar; (*person*) reñir; **~ over** *vi* (*engine*) girar en marcha lenta; (*fig*) ir tirando

ticket ['tɪkɪt] *n* billete *m* (*SP*), tíquet *m*, boleto (*AM*); (*for cinema etc*) entrada (*SP*), boleto (*AM*); (*in shop: on goods*) etiqueta; (*for raffle*) papeleta; (*for library*) tarjeta; (*parking ~*) multa por estacionamiento ilegal; **~ collector** *n* revisor(a) *m/f*; **~ office** *n* (*THEATRE*) taquilla (*SP*), boletería (*AM*), (*RAIL*) despacho de billetes (*SP*) *or* boletos (*AM*)

tickle ['tɪkl] *vt* hacer cosquillas a ♦ *vi* hacer cosquillas; **ticklish** *adj* (*person*)

cosquilloso; (*problem*) delicado
tidal ['taɪdl] *adj* de marea; **~ wave** *n*
maremoto
tidbit ['tɪdbɪt] (*US*) *n* = **titbit**
tiddlywinks ['tɪdlɪwɪŋks] *n juego infantil
con fichas de plástico*
tide [taɪd] *n* marea; (*fig: of events etc*)
curso, marcha; **~ over** *vt* (*help out*)
ayudar a salir del apuro
tidy ['taɪdɪ] *adj* (*room etc*) ordenado; (*dress,
work*) limpio; (*person*) (bien) arreglado
♦ *vt* (*also:* **~ up**) poner en orden
tie [taɪ] *n* (*string etc*) atadura; (*BRIT: also:*
neck~) corbata; (*fig: link*) vínculo, lazo;
(*SPORT etc: draw*) empate *m* ♦ *vt* atar ♦ *vi*
(*SPORT etc*) empatar; **to ~ in a bow** atar
con un lazo; **to ~ a knot in sth** hacer un
nudo en algo; **~ down** *vt* (*fig: person:
restrict*) atar; (*: to price, date etc*) obligar
a; **~ up** *vt* (*parcel*) envolver; (*dog, person*)
atar; (*arrangements*) concluir; **to be ~d up**
(*busy*) estar ocupado
tier [tɪə*] *n* grada; (*of cake*) piso
tiger ['taɪgə*] *n* tigre *m*
tight [taɪt] *adj* (*rope*) tirante; (*money*)
escaso; (*clothes*) ajustado; (*bend*) cerrado;
(*shoes, schedule*) apretado; (*budget*)
ajustado; (*security*) estricto; (*inf: drunk*)
borracho ♦ *adv* (*squeeze*) muy fuerte;
(*shut*) bien; **~en** *vt* (*rope*) estirar; (*screw,
grip*) apretar; (*security*) reforzar ♦ *vi*
estirarse; apretarse; **~-fisted** *adj* tacaño;
~ly *adv* (*grasp*) muy fuerte; **~rope** *n*
cuerda floja; **~s** (*BRIT*) *npl* panti *mpl*
tile [taɪl] *n* (*on roof*) teja; (*on floor*) baldosa;
(*on wall*) azulejo; **~d** *adj* de tejas;
embaldosado; (*wall*) alicatado
till [tɪl] *n* caja (registradora) ♦ *vt* (*land*)
cultivar ♦ *prep, conj* = **until**
tilt [tɪlt] *vt* inclinar ♦ *vi* inclinarse
timber ['tɪmbə*] *n* (*material*) madera
time [taɪm] *n* tiempo; (*epoch: often pl*)
época; (*by clock*) hora; (*moment*)
momento; (*occasion*) vez *f*; (*MUS*) compás
m ♦ *vt* calcular *or* medir el tiempo de;
(*race*) cronometrar; (*remark, visit etc*)
elegir el momento para; **a long ~** mucho

tiempo; **4 at a ~** de 4 en 4; **4 a la vez**;
for the ~ being de momento, por ahora;
from ~ to ~ de vez en cuando; **at ~s** a
veces; **in ~** (*soon enough*) a tiempo; (*after
some time*) con el tiempo; (*MUS*) al
compás; **in a week's ~** dentro de una
semana; **in no ~** en un abrir y cerrar de
ojos; **any ~** cuando sea; **on ~** a la hora; **5
~s 5** 5 por 5; **what ~ is it?** ¿qué hora
es?; **to have a good ~** pasarlo bien,
divertirse; **~ bomb** *n* bomba de efecto
retardado; **~less** *adj* eterno; **~ limit** *n*
plazo; **~ly** *adj* oportuno; **~ off** *n* tiempo
libre; **~r** *n* (*in kitchen etc*) programador *m*
horario; **~ scale** (*BRIT*) *n* escala de
tiempo; **~-share** *n* apartamento (*or*
casa) a tiempo compartido; **~ switch**
(*BRIT*) *n* interruptor *m* (horario); **~table** *n*
horario; **~ zone** *n* huso horario
timid ['tɪmɪd] *adj* tímido
timing ['taɪmɪŋ] *n* (*SPORT*) cronometraje *m*;
the ~ of his resignation el momento que
eligió para dimitir
tin [tɪn] *n* estaño; (*also:* **~ plate**) hojalata;
(*BRIT: can*) lata; **~foil** *n* papel *m* de
estaño
tinge [tɪndʒ] *n* matiz *m* ♦ *vt*: **~d with**
teñido de
tingle ['tɪŋgl] *vi* (*person*): **to ~ (with)**
estremecerse (de); (*hands etc*) hormiguear
tinker ['tɪŋkə*]: **~ with** *vt fus* jugar con,
tocar
tinned [tɪnd] (*BRIT*) *adj* (*food*) en lata, en
conserva
tin opener [-əupnə*] (*BRIT*) *n* abrelatas *m
inv*
tinsel ['tɪnsl] *n* (guirnalda de) espumillón
m
tint [tɪnt] *n* matiz *m*; (*for hair*) tinte *m*;
~ed *adj* (*hair*) teñido; (*glass, spectacles*)
ahumado
tiny ['taɪnɪ] *adj* minúsculo, pequeñito
tip [tɪp] *n* (*end*) punta; (*gratuity*) propina;
(*BRIT: for rubbish*) vertedero; (*advice*)
consejo ♦ *vt* (*waiter*) dar una propina a;
(*tilt*) inclinar; (*empty: also:* **~ out**) vaciar,
echar; (*overturn: also:* **~ over**) volcar; **~-**

off *n* (*hint*) advertencia; **~ped** (*BRIT*) *adj* (*cigarette*) con filtro

Tipp-Ex ® ['tɪpɛks] *n* Tipp-Ex ® *m*

tipsy ['tɪpsɪ] (*inf*) *adj* alegre, mareado

tiptoe ['tɪptəʊ] *n*: **on ~** de puntillas

tire ['taɪə*] *n* (*US*) = **tyre** ♦ *vt* cansar ♦ *vi* (*gen*) cansarse; (*become bored*) aburrirse; **~d** *adj* cansado; **to be ~d of sth** estar harto de algo; **~less** *adj* incansable; **~some** *adj* aburrido; **tiring** *adj* cansado

tissue ['tɪʃu:] *n* tejido; (*paper handkerchief*) pañuelo de papel, kleenex ® *m*; **~ paper** *n* papel *m* de seda

tit [tɪt] *n* (*bird*) herrerillo común; **to give ~ for tat** dar ojo por ojo

titbit ['tɪtbɪt] (*US* **tidbit**) *n* (*food*) golosina; (*news*) noticia sabrosa

title ['taɪtl] *n* título; **~ deed** *n* (*LAW*) título de propiedad; **~ role** *n* papel *m* principal

TM *abbr* = **trademark**

KEYWORD

---

to [tu:, tə] *prep* **1** (*direction*) a; **to go ~ France/London/school/the station** ir a Francia/Londres/al colegio/a la estación; **to go ~ Claude's/the doctor's** ir a casa de Claude/al médico; **the road ~ Edinburgh** la carretera de Edimburgo

2 (*as far as*) hasta, a; **from here ~ London** de aquí a *or* hasta Londres; **to count ~ 10** contar hasta 10; **from 40 ~ 50 people** entre 40 y 50 personas

3 (*with expressions of time*): **a quarter/twenty ~ 5** las 5 menos cuarto/veinte

4 (*for, of*): **the key ~ the front door** la llave de la puerta principal; **she is secretary ~ the director** es la secretaria del director; **a letter ~ his wife** una carta a *or* para su mujer

5 (*expressing indirect object*) a; **to give sth ~ sb** darle algo a alguien; **to talk ~ sb** hablar con alguien; **to be a danger ~ sb** ser un peligro para alguien; **to carry out repairs ~ sth** hacer reparaciones en algo

6 (*in relation to*): **3 goals ~ 2** 3 goles a 2; **30 miles ~ the gallon** ≈ 9,4 litros a los cien (kms)

7 (*purpose, result*): **to come ~ sb's aid** venir en auxilio *or* ayuda de alguien; **to sentence sb ~ death** condenar a uno a muerte; **~ my great surprise** con gran sorpresa mía

♦ **with vb 1** (*simple infin*): **~ go/eat** ir/comer

2 (*following another vb*): **to want/try/start ~ do** querer/intentar/empezar a hacer; *see also relevant vb*

3 (*with vb omitted*): **I don't want ~** no quiero

4 (*purpose, result*) para; **I did it ~ help you** lo hice para ayudarte; **he came ~ see you** vino a verte

5 (*equivalent to relative clause*): **I have things ~ do** tengo cosas que hacer; **the main thing is ~ try** lo principal es intentarlo

6 (*after adj etc*): **ready ~ go** listo para irse; **too old ~ ...** demasiado viejo (como) para ...

♦ *adv*: **pull/push the door ~** tirar de/empujar la puerta

---

toad [təʊd] *n* sapo; **~stool** *n* hongo venenoso

toast [təʊst] *n* (*CULIN*) tostada; (*drink, speech*) brindis *m* ♦ *vt* (*CULIN*) tostar; (*drink to*) brindar por; **~er** *n* tostador *m*

tobacco [tə'bækəʊ] *n* tabaco; **~nist** *n* estanquero/a (*SP*), tabaquero/a (*AM*); **~nist's (shop)** (*BRIT*) *n* estanco (*SP*), tabaquería (*AM*)

toboggan [tə'bɒgən] *n* tobogán *m*

today [tə'deɪ] *adv, n* (*also fig*) hoy *m*

toddler ['tɒdlə*] *n* niño/a (que empieza a andar)

toe [təʊ] *n* dedo (del pie); (*of shoe*) punta; **to ~ the line** (*fig*) conformarse; **~nail** *n* uña del pie

toffee ['tɒfɪ] *n* toffee *m*; **~ apple** (*BRIT*) *n* manzana acaramelada

together [tə'gɛðə*] *adv* juntos; (*at same time*) al mismo tiempo, a la vez; **~ with** junto con

toil [tɔɪl] *n* trabajo duro, labor *f* ♦ *vi*

trabajar duramente

toilet ['tɔɪlət] n retrete m; (BRIT: room)
servicios mpl (SP), wáter m (SP), sanitario
(AM) ♦ cpd (soap etc) de aseo; ~ **paper**
n papel m higiénico; **~ries** npl artículos
mpl de tocador; ~ **roll** n rollo de papel
higiénico

token ['təʊkən] n (sign) señal f, muestra;
(souvenir) recuerdo; (disc) ficha ♦ adj
(strike, payment etc) simbólico; **book/
record ~** (BRIT) vale m para comprar
libros/discos; **gift ~** (BRIT) vale-regalo

Tokyo ['təʊkjəʊ] n Tokio, Tokío

told [təʊld] pt, pp of **tell**

tolerable ['tɔlərəbl] adj (bearable)
soportable; (fairly good) pasable

tolerant ['tɔlərnt] adj: ~ **of** tolerante con

tolerate ['tɔləreɪt] vt tolerar

toll [təʊl] n (of casualties) número de
víctimas; (tax, charge) peaje m ♦ vi (bell)
doblar

tomato [tə'mɑːtəʊ] (pl ~**es**) n tomate m

tomb [tuːm] n tumba

tomboy ['tɔmbɔɪ] n marimacho

tombstone ['tuːmstəʊn] n lápida

tomcat ['tɔmkæt] n gato (macho)

tomorrow [tə'mɔrəʊ] adv, n (also: fig)
mañana; **the day after ~** pasado mañana;
~ **morning** mañana por la mañana

ton [tʌn] n tonelada (BRIT = 1016 kg; US
= 907 kg); (metric ~) tonelada métrica;
~s of (inf) montones de

tone [təʊn] ♦ vi (also: ~ **in**)
armonizar; ~ **down** vt (criticism) suavizar;
(colour) atenuar; ~ **up** vt (muscles)
tonificar; **~-deaf** adj con mal oído

tongs [tɔŋz] npl (for coal) tenazas fpl;
(curling ~) tenacillas fpl

tongue [tʌŋ] n lengua; ~ **in cheek**
irónicamente; **~-tied** adj (fig) mudo; **~-
twister** n trabalenguas m inv

tonic ['tɔnɪk] n (MED, also fig) tónico; (also:
~ **water**) (agua) tónica

tonight [tə'naɪt] adv, n esta noche; esta
tarde

tonsil ['tɔnsl] n amígdala; **~litis** [-'laɪtɪs] n
amigdalitis f

too [tuː] adv (excessively) demasiado; (also)
también; ~ **much** demasiado; ~ **many**
demasiados/as

took [tʊk] pt of **take**

tool [tuːl] n herramienta; ~ **box** n caja de
herramientas

toot [tuːt] n pitido ♦ vi tocar el pito

tooth [tuːθ] (pl **teeth**) n (ANAT, TECH)
diente m; (molar) muela; **~ache** n dolor
m de muelas; **~brush** n cepillo de
dientes; **~paste** n pasta de dientes;
~pick n palillo

top [tɔp] n (of mountain) cumbre f, cima;
(of tree) copa; (of head) coronilla; (of
ladder, page) lo alto; (of table) superficie f;
(of cupboard) parte f de arriba; (lid: of
box) tapa; (: of bottle, jar) tapón m; (of
list etc) cabeza; (toy) peonza; (garment)
blusa; camiseta ♦ adj de arriba; (in rank)
principal, primero; (best) mejor ♦ vt
(exceed) exceder; (be first in) encabezar;
on ~ of (above) sobre, encima de; (in
addition to) además de; **from ~ to bottom**
de pies a cabeza; ~ **off** (US) vt = ~ **up**; ~
up vt llenar; ~ **floor** n último piso; ~
hat n sombrero de copa; **~-heavy** adj
(object) mal equilibrado

topic ['tɔpɪk] n tema m; **~al** adj actual

top-: ~less adj (bather, bikini) topless inv;
~-level adj (talks) al más alto nivel;
~most adj más alto

topple ['tɔpl] vt derribar ♦ vi caerse

top-secret adj de alto secreto

topsy-turvy ['tɔpsɪ'tɜːvɪ] adj al revés
♦ adv patas arriba

torch [tɔːtʃ] n antorcha; (BRIT: electric)
linterna

tore [tɔː*] pt of **tear²**

torment [n 'tɔːment, vt tɔː'ment] n
tormento ♦ vt atormentar; (fig: annoy)
fastidiar

torn [tɔːn] pp of **tear²**

torrent ['tɔrnt] n torrente m

tortoise ['tɔːtəs] n tortuga; **~shell**
['tɔːtəʃel] adj de carey

torture ['tɔːtʃə*] n tortura ♦ vt torturar;
(fig) atormentar

Tory ['tɔːrɪ] (BRIT) adj, n (POL) conservador(a) m/f

toss [tɔs] vt tirar, echar; (one's head) sacudir; **to ~ a coin** echar a cara o cruz; **to ~ up for sth** jugar a cara o cruz algo; **to ~ and turn** (in bed) dar vueltas

tot [tɔt] n (BRIT: drink) copita; (child) nene/a m/f

total ['təutl] adj total, entero; (emphatic: failure etc) completo, total ♦ n total m, suma ♦ vt (add up) sumar; (amount to) ascender a; **~ly** adv totalmente

touch [tʌtʃ] n tacto; (contact) contacto ♦ vt tocar; (emotionally) conmover; **a ~ of** (fig) un poquito de; **to get in ~ with sb** ponerse en contacto con uno; **to lose ~** (friends) perder contacto; **~ on** vt fus (topic) aludir (brevemente) a; **~ up** vt (paint) retocar; **~-and-go** adj arriesgado; **~down** n aterrizaje m; (on sea) amerizaje m; (US: FOOTBALL) ensayo; **~ed** adj (moved) conmovido; **~ing** adj (moving) conmovedor(a); **~line** n (SPORT) línea de banda; **~y** adj (person) quisquilloso

tough [tʌf] adj (material) resistente; (meat) duro; (problem etc) difícil; (policy, stance) inflexible; (person) fuerte; **~en** vt endurecer

toupée ['tuːpeɪ] n peluca

tour ['tuə*] n viaje m, vuelta; (also: **package ~**) viaje m todo comprendido; (of town, museum) visita; (by band etc) gira ♦ vt recorrer, visitar; **~ guide** n guía m turístico, guía f turística

tourism ['tuərɪzm] n turismo

tourist ['tuərɪst] n turista m/f ♦ cpd turístico; **~ office** n oficina de turismo

tousled ['tauzld] adj (hair) despeinado

tout [taut] vi: **to ~ for business** solicitar clientes ♦ n (also: **ticket ~**) revendedor(a) m/f

tow [təu] vt remolcar; **"on or in (US) ~"** (AUT) "a remolque"

toward(s) [tə'wɔːd(z)] prep hacia; (attitude) respecto a, con; (purpose) para

towel ['tauəl] n toalla; **~ling** n (fabric) felpa; **~ rail** (US **~ rack**) n toallero

tower ['tauə*] n torre f; **~ block** (BRIT) n torre f (de pisos); **~ing** adj muy alto, imponente

town [taun] n ciudad f; **to go to ~** ir a la ciudad; (fig) echar la casa por la ventana; **~ centre** n centro de la ciudad; **~ council** n ayuntamiento, consejo municipal; **~ hall** n ayuntamiento; **~ plan** n plano de la ciudad; **~ planning** n urbanismo

towrope ['təurəup] n cable m de remolque

tow truck (US) n camión m grúa

toy [tɔɪ] n juguete m; **~ with** vt fus jugar con; (idea) acariciar; **~shop** n juguetería

trace [treɪs] n rastro ♦ vt (draw) trazar, delinear; (locate) encontrar; (follow) seguir la pista de; **tracing paper** n papel m de calco

track [træk] n (mark) huella, pista; (path: gen) camino, senda; (: of bullet etc) trayectoria; (: of suspect, animal) pista, rastro; (RAIL) vía; (SPORT) pista; (on tape, record) canción f ♦ vt seguir la pista de; **to keep ~ of** mantenerse al tanto de, seguir; **~ down** vt (prey) seguir el rastro de; (sth lost) encontrar; **~suit** n chandal m

tract [trækt] n (GEO) región f

traction ['trækʃən] n (power) tracción f; **in ~** (MED) en tracción

tractor ['træktə*] n tractor m

trade [treɪd] n comercio; (skill, job) oficio ♦ vi negociar, comerciar ♦ vt (exchange): **to ~ sth (for sth)** cambiar algo (por algo); **~ in** vt (old car etc) ofrecer como parte del pago; **~ fair** n feria comercial; **~mark** n marca de fábrica; **~ name** n marca registrada; **~r** n comerciante m/f; **~sman** (irreg) n (shopkeeper) tendero; **~ union** n sindicato; **~ unionist** n sindicalista m/f

tradition [trə'dɪʃən] n tradición f; **~al** adj tradicional

traffic ['træfɪk] n (gen, AUT) tráfico, circulación f, tránsito (AM) ♦ vi: **to ~ in** (pej: liquor, drugs) traficar en; **~ circle**

(*US*) *n* isleta; ~ **jam** *n* embotellamiento;
~ **lights** *npl* semáforo; ~ **warden** *n*
guardia *m/f* de tráfico
tragedy ['trædʒədɪ] *n* tragedia
tragic ['trædʒɪk] *adj* trágico
trail [treɪl] *n* (*tracks*) rastro, pista; (*path*)
camino, sendero; (*dust, smoke*) estela ♦ *vt*
(*drag*) arrastrar; (*follow*) seguir la pista de
♦ *vi* arrastrar; (*in contest etc*) ir perdiendo;
~ **behind** *vi* quedar a la zaga; ~**er** *n*
(*AUT*) remolque *m*; (*caravan*) caravana;
(*CINEMA*) trailer *m*, avance *m*; ~**er truck**
(*US*) *n* trailer *m*
train [treɪn] *n* tren *m*; (*of dress*) cola;
(*series*) serie *f* ♦ *vt* (*educate, teach skills to*)
formar; (*sportsman*) entrenar; (*dog*)
adiestrar; (*point: gun etc*): **to ~ on** apuntar
a ♦ *vi* (*SPORT*) entrenarse; (*learn a skill*): **to**
~ **as a teacher** *etc* estudiar para profesor
etc; **one's ~ of thought** el razonamiento
de uno; ~**ed** *adj* (*worker*) cualificado;
(*animal*) amaestrado; ~**ee** [treɪ'niː] *n*
aprendiz(a) *m/f*; ~**er** *n* (*SPORT: coach*)
entrenador(a) *m/f*; (: *shoe*): ~**ers**
zapatillas *fpl* (de deporte); (*of animals*)
domador(a) *m/f*; ~**ing** *n* formación *f*;
entrenamiento; **to be in ~ing** (*SPORT*)
estar entrenando; ~**ing college** *n* (*gen*)
colegio de formación profesional; (*for
teachers*) escuela de formación del
profesorado; ~**ing shoes** *npl* zapatillas
fpl (de deporte)
trait [treɪt] *n* rasgo
traitor ['treɪtə*] *n* traidor(a) *m/f*
tram [træm] (*BRIT*) *n* (*also:* ~**car**) tranvía *m*
tramp [træmp] *n* (*person*) vagabundo/a;
(*inf. pej: woman*) puta
trample ['træmpl] *vt*: **to ~ (underfoot)**
pisotear
trampoline ['træmpəliːn] *n* trampolín *m*
tranquil ['træŋkwɪl] *adj* tranquilo; ~**lizer** *n*
(*MED*) tranquilizante *m*
transact [træn'zækt] *vt* (*business*)
despachar; ~**ion** [-'zækʃən] *n* transacción
f, operación *f*
transfer [*n* 'trænsfəː*, *vb* træns'fəː*] *n* (*of
employees*) traslado; (*of money, power*)

transferencia; (*SPORT*) traspaso; (*picture,
design*) calcomanía ♦ *vt* trasladar;
transferir; **to ~ the charges** (*BRIT: TEL*)
llamar a cobro revertido
transform [træns'fɔːm] *vt* transformar
transfusion [træns'fjuːʒən] *n* transfusión *f*
transient ['trænzɪənt] *adj* transitorio
transistor [træn'zɪstə*] *n* (*ELEC*) transistor
m; ~ **radio** *n* transistor *m*
transit ['trænzɪt] *n*: **in ~** en tránsito
transitive ['trænzɪtɪv] *adj* (*LING*) transitivo
transit lounge *n* sala de tránsito
translate [trænz'leɪt] *vt* traducir;
translation [-'leɪʃən] *n* traducción *f*;
translator *n* traductor(a) *m/f*
transmit [trænz'mɪt] *vt* transmitir; ~**ter** *n*
transmisor *m*
transparency [træns'pɛərnsɪ] *n*
transparencia; (*BRIT: PHOT*) diapositiva
transparent [træns'pærnt] *adj*
transparente
transpire [træns'paɪə*] *vi* (*turn out*)
resultar; (*happen*) ocurrir, suceder; **it ~d
that ...** se supo que ...
transplant ['trænsplɑːnt] *n* (*MED*)
transplante *m*
transport [*n* 'trænspɔːt, *vt* træns'pɔːt] *n*
transporte *m*; (*car*) coche *m* (*SP*), carro
(*AM*), automóvil *m* ♦ *vt* transportar;
~**ation** [-'teɪʃən] *n* transporte *m*; ~ **café**
(*BRIT*) *n* bar-restaurant *m* de carretera
transvestite [trænz'vɛstaɪt] *n* travestí *m/f*
trap [træp] *n* (*snare, trick*) trampa;
(*carriage*) cabriolé *m* ♦ *vt* coger (*SP*) or
agarrar (*AM*) en una trampa; (*trick*)
engañar; (*confine*) atrapar; ~ **door** *n*
escotilla
trapeze [trə'piːz] *n* trapecio
trappings ['træpɪŋz] *npl* adornos *mpl*
trash [træʃ] *n* (*rubbish*) basura; (*pej*): **the
book/film is** ~ el libro/la película no vale
nada; (*nonsense*) tonterías *fpl*; ~ **can** (*US*)
n cubo (*SP*) or balde *m* (*AM*) de la basura
travel ['trævl] *n* viaje *m* ♦ *vi* viajar ♦ *vt*
(*distance*) recorrer; ~**s** *npl* (*journeys*) viajes
mpl; ~ **agent** *n* agente *m/f* de viajes;
~**ler** (*US* ~**er**) *n* viajero/a; ~**ler's**

cheque (*US* ~**er's check**) *n* cheque *m* de viajero; ~**ling** (*US* ~**ing**) *n* los viajes, el viajar; ~ **sickness** *n* mareo

trawler ['trɔ:lə*] *n* pesquero de arrastre

tray [treɪ] *n* bandeja; (*on desk*) cajón *m*

treacherous ['tretʃərəs] *adj* traidor, traicionero; (*dangerous*) peligroso

treacle ['tri:kl] (*BRIT*) *n* melaza

tread [tred] (*pt* **trod**, *pp* **trodden**) *n* (*step*) paso, pisada; (*sound*) ruido de pasos; (*of stair*) escalón *m*; (*of tyre*) banda de rodadura ♦ *vi* pisar; ~ **on** *vt fus* pisar

treason ['tri:zn] *n* traición *f*

treasure ['treʒə*] *n* (*also fig*) tesoro ♦ *vt* (*value: object, friendship*) apreciar; (: *memory*) guardar

treasurer ['treʒərə*] *n* tesorero/a

treasury ['treʒərɪ] *n*: **the T~** el Ministerio de Hacienda

treat [tri:t] *n* (*present*) regalo ♦ *vt* tratar; **to ~ sb to sth** invitar a uno a algo

treatment ['tri:tmənt] *n* tratamiento *m*

treaty ['tri:tɪ] *n* tratado *m*

treble ['trebl] *adj* triple ♦ *vi* triplicar ♦ *vi* triplicarse; ~ **clef** *n* (*MUS*) clave *f* de sol

tree [tri:] *n* árbol *m*; ~ **trunk** tronco (de árbol)

trek [trek] *n* (*long journey*) viaje *m* largo y difícil; (*tiring walk*) caminata

trellis ['trelɪs] *n* enrejado

tremble ['trembl] *vi* temblar

tremendous [trɪ'mendəs] *adj* tremendo, enorme; (*excellent*) estupendo

tremor ['tremə*] *n* temblor *m*; (*also:* **earth ~**) temblor *m* de tierra

trench [trentʃ] *n* zanja

trend [trend] *n* (*tendency*) tendencia; (*of events*) curso; (*fashion*) moda; ~**y** *adj* de moda

trespass ['trespəs] *vi*: **to ~ on** entrar sin permiso en; **"no ~ing"** "prohibido el paso"

trestle ['tresl] *n* caballete *m*

trial ['traɪəl] *n* (*LAW*) juicio, proceso; (*test: of machine etc*) prueba; ~**s** *npl* (*hardships*) dificultades *fpl*; **by ~ and error** a fuerza de probar

triangle ['traɪæŋgl] *n* (*MATH, MUS*) triángulo

tribe [traɪb] *n* tribu *f*

tribunal [traɪ'bju:nl] *n* tribunal *m*

tributary ['trɪbjutərɪ] *n* (*river*) afluente *m*

tribute ['trɪbju:t] *n* homenaje *m*, tributo; **to pay ~ to** rendir homenaje a

trick [trɪk] *n* (*skill, knack*) tino, truco; (*conjuring ~*) truco; (*joke*) broma; (*CARDS*) baza ♦ *vt* engañar; **to play a ~ on sb** gastar una broma a uno; **that should do the ~** a ver si funciona así; ~**ery** *n* engaño

trickle ['trɪkl] *n* (*of water etc*) goteo ♦ *vi* gotear

tricky ['trɪkɪ] *adj* difícil; delicado

tricycle ['traɪsɪkl] *n* triciclo

trifle ['traɪfl] *n* bagatela; (*CULIN*) dulce de bizcocho borracho, gelatina, fruta y natillas ♦ *adv*: **a ~ long** un poquito largo; **trifling** *adj* insignificante

trigger ['trɪgə*] *n* (*of gun*) gatillo; ~ **off** *vt* desencadenar

trim [trɪm] *adj* (*house, garden*) en buen estado; (*person, figure*) esbelto ♦ *n* (*haircut etc*) recorte *m*; (*on car*) guarnición *f* ♦ *vt* (*neaten*) arreglar; (*cut*) recortar; (*decorate*) adornar; (*NAUT: a sail*) orientar; ~**mings** *npl* (*CULIN*) guarnición *f*

trip [trɪp] *n* viaje *m*; (*excursion*) excursión *f*; (*stumble*) traspié *m* ♦ *vi* (*stumble*) tropezar; (*go lightly*) andar a paso ligero; **on a ~** de viaje; ~ **up** *vi* tropezar, caerse ♦ *vt* hacer tropezar *or* caer

tripe [traɪp] *n* (*CULIN*) callos *mpl*

triple ['trɪpl] *adj* triple; **triplets** ['trɪplɪts] *npl* trillizos/as *mpl/fpl*; **triplicate** ['trɪplɪkət] *n*: **in triplicate** por triplicado

trite [traɪt] *adj* trillado

triumph ['traɪʌmf] *n* triunfo ♦ *vi*: **to ~ (over)** vencer; ~**ant** [traɪ'ʌmfənt] *adj* (*team etc*) vencedor(a); (*wave, return*) triunfal

trivia ['trɪvɪə] *npl* trivialidades *fpl*

trivial ['trɪvɪəl] *adj* insignificante; (*commonplace*) banal

trod [trɔd] *pt of* **tread**

trodden ['trɔdn] *pp of* **tread**

trolley ['trɔlɪ] *n* carrito; (*also*: ~ **bus**) trolebús *m*

trombone [trɔm'bəun] *n* trombón *m*

troop [tru:p] *n* grupo, banda; **~s** *npl* (*MIL*) tropas *fpl*; ~ **in/out** *vi* entrar/salir en tropel; **~ing the colour** *n* (*ceremony*) presentación *f* de la bandera

trophy ['trəufɪ] *n* trofeo

tropical ['trɔpɪkl] *adj* tropical

trot [trɔt] *n* trote *m* ♦ *vi* trotar; **on the ~** (*BRIT*: *fig*) seguidos/as

trouble ['trʌbl] *n* problema *m*, dificultad *f*; (*worry*) preocupación *f*; (*bother, effort*) molestia, esfuerzo; (*unrest*) inquietud *f*; (*MED*): **stomach** *etc* ~ problemas *mpl* gástricos *etc* ♦ *vt* (*disturb*) molestar; (*worry*) preocupar, inquietar ♦ *vi*: **to ~ to do sth** molestarse en hacer algo; **~s** *npl* (*POL etc*) conflictos *mpl*; (*personal*) problemas *mpl*; **to be in ~** estar en un apuro; **it's no ~!** ¡no es molestia (ninguna)!; **what's the ~?** (*with broken TV etc*) ¿cuál es el problema?; (*doctor to patient*) ¿qué pasa?; **~d** *adj* (*person*) preocupado; (*country, epoch, life*) agitado; **~maker** *n* agitador(a) *m/f*; (*child*) alborotador *m*; **~shooter** *n* (*in conflict*) conciliador(a) *m/f*; **~some** *adj* molesto

trough [trɔf] *n* (*also*: **drinking ~**) abrevadero; (*also*: **feeding ~**) comedero; (*depression*) depresión *f*

troupe [tru:p] *n* grupo

trousers ['trauzəz] *npl* pantalones *mpl*; **short ~** pantalones *mpl* cortos

trousseau ['tru:səu] (*pl* **~x** *or* **~s**) *n* ajuar *m*

trout [traut] *n inv* trucha

trowel ['trauəl] *n* (*of gardener*) palita; (*of builder*) paleta

truant ['truənt] *n*: **to play ~** (*BRIT*) hacer novillos

truce [tru:s] *n* tregua

truck [trʌk] *n* (*lorry*) camión *m*; (*RAIL*) vagón *m*; ~ **driver** *n* camionero; ~ **farm** (*US*) *n* huerto

true [tru:] *adj* verdadero; (*accurate*) exacto;

(*genuine*) auténtico; (*faithful*) fiel; **to come ~** realizarse

truffle ['trʌfl] *n* trufa

truly ['tru:lɪ] *adv* (*really*) realmente; (*truthfully*) verdaderamente; (*faithfully*): **yours ~** (*in letter*) le saluda atentamente

trump [trʌmp] *n* triunfo

trumpet ['trʌmpɪt] *n* trompeta

truncheon ['trʌntʃən] *n* porra

trundle ['trʌndl] *vi*: **to ~ along** ir sin prisas

trunk [trʌŋk] *n* (*of tree, person*) tronco; (*of elephant*) trompa; (*case*) baúl *m*; (*US*: *AUT*) maletero; **~s** *npl* (*also*: **swimming ~s**) bañador *m* (de hombre)

truss [trʌs] *vt*: ~ (**up**) atar

trust [trʌst] *n* confianza; (*responsibility*) responsabilidad *f*; (*LAW*) fideicomiso *f* ♦ *vt* (*rely on*) tener confianza en; (*hope*) esperar; (*entrust*): **to ~ sth to sb** confiar algo a uno; **to take sth on ~** aceptar algo a ojos cerrados; **~ed** *adj* de confianza; **~ee** [trʌs'ti:] *n* (*LAW*) fideicomisario; (*of school*) administrador *m*; **~ful** *adj* confiado; **~ing** *adj* confiado; **~worthy** *adj* digno de confianza

truth [tru:θ, *pl* tru:ðz] *n* verdad *f*; **~ful** *adj* veraz

try [traɪ] *n* tentativa, intento; (*RUGBY*) ensayo ♦ *vt* (*attempt*) intentar; (*test*: *also*: ~ **out**) probar, someter a prueba; (*LAW*) juzgar, procesar; (*strain*: *patience*) hacer perder ♦ *vi* probar; **to have a ~** probar suerte; **to ~ to do sth** intentar hacer algo; ~ **again!** ¡vuelve a probar!; ~ **harder!** ¡esfuérzate más!; **well, I tried** al menos lo intenté; ~ **on** *vt* (*clothes*) probarse; **~ing** *adj* (*experience*) cansado; (*person*) pesado

T-shirt ['ti:ʃə:t] *n* camiseta

T-square *n* regla en T

tub [tʌb] *n* cubo (*SP*), balde *m* (*AM*); (*bath*) tina, bañera

tube [tju:b] *n* tubo; (*BRIT*: *underground*) metro; (*for tyre*) cámara de aire

tuberculosis [tjubə:kju'ləusɪs] *n* tuberculosis *f inv*

tube station (*BRIT*) *n* estación *f* de metro

tubular ['tju:bjulə*] *adj* tubular

TUC (*BRIT*) *n abbr* (= *Trades Union Congress*) *federación nacional de sindicatos*

tuck [tʌk] *vt* (*put*) poner; ~ **away** *vt* (*money*) guardar; (*building*): **to be ~ed away** esconderse, ocultarse; ~ **in** *vt* meter dentro; (*child*) arropar ♦ *vi* (*eat*) comer con apetito; ~ **up** *vt* (*child*) arropar; ~ **shop** *n* (*SCOL*) tienda; ≈ bar *m* (del colegio) (*SP*)

Tuesday ['tju:zdɪ] *n* martes *m inv*

tuft [tʌft] *n* mechón *m*; (*of grass etc*) manojo

tug [tʌg] *n* (*ship*) remolcador *m* ♦ *vt* tirar de; **~-of-war** *n* lucha de tiro de cuerda; (*fig*) tira y afloja *m*

tuition [tju:'ɪʃən] *n* (*BRIT*) enseñanza; (: *private* ~) clases *fpl* particulares; (*US: school fees*) matrícula

tulip ['tju:lɪp] *n* tulipán *m*

tumble ['tʌmbl] *n* (*fall*) caída ♦ *vi* caer; **to ~ to sth** (*inf*) caer en la cuenta de algo; **~down** *adj* destartalado; ~ **dryer** (*BRIT*) *n* secadora

tumbler ['tʌmblə*] *n* (*glass*) vaso

tummy ['tʌmɪ] (*inf*) *n* barriga, tripa

tumour ['tju:mə*] (*US* **tumor**) *n* tumor *m*

tuna ['tju:nə] *n inv* (*also*: ~ **fish**) atún *m*

tune [tju:n] *n* melodía ♦ *vt* (*MUS*) afinar; (*RADIO, TV, AUT*) sintonizar; **to be in/out of** ~ (*instrument*) estar afinado/desafinado; (*singer*) cantar afinadamente/desafinar; **to be in/out of** ~ **with** (*fig*) estar de acuerdo/en desacuerdo con; ~ **in** *vi*: **to ~ in (to)** (*RADIO, TV*) sintonizar (con); ~ **up** *vi* (*musician*) afinar (su instrumento); **~ful** *adj* melodioso; **~r** *n*: **piano ~r** afinador(a) *m/f* de pianos

tunic ['tju:nɪk] *n* túnica

Tunisia [tju:'nɪzɪə] *n* Túnez *m*

tunnel ['tʌnl] *n* túnel *m*; (*in mine*) galería ♦ *vi* construir un túnel/una galería

turban ['tə:bən] *n* turbante *m*

turbulent ['tə:bjulənt] *adj* turbulento

tureen [tə'ri:n] *n* sopera

turf [tə:f] *n* césped *m*; (*clod*) tepe *m* ♦ *vt* cubrir con césped; ~ **out** (*inf*) *vt* echar a la calle

Turk [tə:k] *n* turco/a

Turkey ['tə:kɪ] *n* Turquía

turkey ['tə:kɪ] *n* pavo

Turkish ['tə:kɪʃ] *adj, n* turco

turmoil ['tə:mɔɪl] *n*: **in** ~ revuelto

turn [tə:n] *n* turno; (*in road*) curva; (*of mind, events*) rumbo; (*THEATRE*) número; (*MED*) ataque *m* ♦ *vt* girar, volver; (*collar, steak*) dar la vuelta a; (*page*) pasar; (*change*): **to ~ sth into** convertir algo en ♦ *vi* volver; (*person: look back*) volverse; (*reverse direction*) dar la vuelta; (*milk*) cortarse; (*become*): **to ~ nasty/forty** ponerse feo/cumplir los cuarenta; **a good** ~ un favor; **it gave me quite a** ~ me dio un susto; "**no left ~**" (*AUT*) "prohibido girar a la izquierda"; **it's your** ~ te toca a ti; **in** ~ por turnos; **to take ~s (at)** turnarse (en); ~ **away** *vi* apartar la vista ♦ *vi* rechazar; ~ **back** *vi* volverse atrás ♦ *vi* hacer retroceder; (*clock*) retrasar; ~ **down** *vt* (*refuse*) rechazar; (*reduce*) bajar; (*fold*) doblar; ~ **in** *vi* (*inf: go to bed*) acostarse ♦ *vt* (*fold*) doblar hacia dentro; ~ **off** *vi* (*from road*) desviarse ♦ *vt* (*light, radio etc*) apagar; (*tap*) cerrar; (*engine*) parar; ~ **on** *vt* (*light, radio etc*) encender (*SP*), prender (*AM*); (*tap*) abrir; (*engine*) poner en marcha; ~ **out** *vt* (*light, gas*) apagar; (*produce*) producir ♦ *vi* (*voters*) concurrir; **to ~ out to be ...** resultar ser ...; ~ **over** *vi* (*person*) volverse ♦ *vt* (*object*) dar la vuelta a; (*page*) volver; ~ **round** *vi* volverse; (*rotate*) girar; ~ **up** *vi* (*person*) llegar, presentarse; (*lost object*) aparecer ♦ *vt* (*gen*) subir; **~ing** *n* (*in road*) vuelta; **~ing point** *n* (*fig*) momento decisivo

turnip ['tə:nɪp] *n* nabo

turn: **~out** *n* concurrencia; **~over** *n* (*COMM: amount of money*) volumen *m* de ventas; (: *of goods*) movimiento; **~pike** (*US*) *n* autopista de peaje; **~stile** *n* torniquete *m*; **~table** *n* plato; **~-up** (*BRIT*) *n* (*on trousers*) vuelta

turpentine ['tə:pəntaɪn] *n* (*also*: **turps**)

trementina
turquoise ['tɜːkwɔɪz] *n* (*stone*) turquesa
♦ *adj* color turquesa
turret ['tʌrɪt] *n* torreón *m*
turtle ['tɜːtl] *n* galápago *m*; **~neck**
(sweater) *n* jersey *m* de cuello vuelto
tusk [tʌsk] *n* colmillo
tutor ['tjuːtə*] *n* profesor(a) *m/f*; **~ial**
[-'tɔːrɪəl] (*SCOL*) *n* seminario
tuxedo [tʌk'siːdəu] (*US*) *n* smóking *m*,
esmoquin *m*
TV [tiː'viː] *n abbr* (= *television*) tele *f*
twang [twæŋ] *n* (*of instrument*) punteado;
(*of voice*) timbre *m* nasal
tweezers ['twiːzəz] *npl* pinzas *fpl* (de
depilar)
twelfth [twɛlfθ] *num* duodécimo
twelve [twɛlv] *num* doce; **at ~ o'clock**
(*midday*) a mediodía; (*midnight*) a
medianoche
twentieth ['twɛntɪɪθ] *adj* vigésimo
twenty ['twɛntɪ] *num* veinte
twice [twaɪs] *adv* dos veces; **~ as much**
dos veces más
twiddle ['twɪdl] *vi*: **to ~ (with) sth** dar
vueltas a algo; **to ~ one's thumbs** (*fig*)
estar mano sobre mano
twig [twɪg] *n* ramita
twilight ['twaɪlaɪt] *n* crepúsculo
twin [twɪn] *adj*, *n* gemelo/a *m/f* ♦ *vt*
hermanar; **~-bedded room** *n*
habitación *f* doble
twine [twaɪn] *n* bramante *m* ♦ *vi* (*plant*)
enroscarse
twinge [twɪndʒ] *n* (*of pain*) punzada; (*of
conscience*) remordimiento
twinkle ['twɪŋkl] *vi* centellear; (*eyes*) brillar
twirl [twɜːl] *vt* dar vueltas a ♦ *vi* dar
vueltas
twist [twɪst] *n* (*action*) torsión *f*; (*in road,
coil*) vuelta; (*in wire, flex*) doblez *f*; (*in
story*) giro ♦ *vt* torcer; (*weave*) trenzar;
(*roll around*) enrollar; (*fig*) deformar ♦ *vi*
serpentear
twit [twɪt] (*inf*) *n* tonto
twitch [twɪtʃ] *n* (*pull*) tirón *m*; (*nervous*) tic
m ♦ *vi* crisparse

two [tuː] *num* dos; **to put ~ and ~
together** (*fig*) atar cabos; **~-door** *adj*
(*AUT*) de dos puertas; **~-faced** *adj* (*pej*:
person) falso; **~-fold** *adv*: **to increase
~fold** doblarse; **~-piece (suit)** *n* traje *m*
de dos piezas; **~-piece (swimsuit)** *n*
dos piezas *m inv*, bikini *m*; **~some** *n*
(*people*) pareja; **~-way** *adj*: **~-way traffic**
circulación *f* de dos sentidos
tycoon [taɪ'kuːn] *n*: **(business) ~ magnate**
m
type [taɪp] *n* (*category*) tipo, género;
(*model*) tipo; (*TYP*) tipo, letra ♦ *vt* (*letter
etc*) escribir a máquina; **~cast** *adj*
(*actor*) encasillado; **~face** *n* letra;
~script *n* texto mecanografiado;
~writer *n* máquina de escribir; **~written**
adj mecanografiado
typhoid ['taɪfɔɪd] *n* tifoidea
typical ['tɪpɪkl] *adj* típico
typing ['taɪpɪŋ] *n* mecanografía
typist ['taɪpɪst] *n* mecanógrafo/a
tyrant ['taɪərnt] *n* tirano/a
tyre ['taɪə*] (*US* **tire**) *n* neumático (*SP*),
llanta (*AM*); **~ pressure** *n* presión *f* de
los neumáticos

U, u

U-bend ['juː'bɛnd] *n* (*AUT, in pipe*) recodo
udder ['ʌdə*] *n* ubre *f*
UFO ['juːfəu] *n abbr* = (*unidentified flying
object*) OVNI *m*
ugh [əːh] *excl* ¡uf!
ugly ['ʌglɪ] *adj* feo; (*dangerous*) peligroso
UHT *abbr*: **~ milk** leche *f* UHT, leche *f*
uperizada
UK *n abbr* = **United Kingdom**
ulcer ['ʌlsə*] *n* úlcera; (*mouth ~*) llaga
Ulster ['ʌlstə*] *n* Ulster *m*
ulterior [ʌl'tɪərɪə*] *adj*: **~ motive** segundas
intenciones *fpl*
ultimate ['ʌltɪmət] *adj* último, final;
(*greatest*) máximo; **~ly** *adv* (*in the end*)
por último, al final; (*fundamentally*) a *or*
en fin de cuentas

umbilical cord [ʌm'bɪlɪkl-] n cordón m umbilical

umbrella [ʌm'brelə] n paraguas m inv; (for sun) sombrilla

umpire ['ʌmpaɪə*] n árbitro

umpteen [ʌmp'tiːn] adj enésimos/as; ~**th** adj: **for the ~th time** por enésima vez

UN n abbr (= United Nations) NN. UU.

unable [ʌn'eɪbl] adj: **to be ~ to do sth** no poder hacer algo

unaccompanied [ʌnə'kʌmpənɪd] adj no acompañado; (song) sin acompañamiento

unaccustomed [ʌnə'kʌstəmd] adj: **to be ~ to** no estar acostumbrado a

unanimous [juː'nænɪməs] adj unánime

unarmed [ʌn'ɑːmd] adj (defenceless) inerme; (without weapon) desarmado

unattached [ʌnə'tætʃt] adj (person) soltero y sin compromiso; (part etc) suelto

unattended [ʌnə'tendɪd] adj desatendido

unattractive [ʌnə'træktɪv] adj poco atractivo

unauthorized [ʌn'ɔːθəraɪzd] adj no autorizado

unavoidable [ʌnə'vɔɪdəbl] adj inevitable

unaware [ʌnə'weə*] adj: **to be ~ of** ignorar; ~**s** adv de improviso

unbalanced [ʌn'bælənst] adj (report) poco objetivo; (mentally) trastornado

unbearable [ʌn'beərəbl] adj insoportable

unbeatable [ʌn'biːtəbl] adj (team) invencible; (price) inmejorable; (quality) insuperable

unbelievable [ʌnbɪ'liːvəbl] adj increíble

unbend [ʌn'bend] (irreg) vi (relax) relajarse ♦ vt (wire) enderezar

unbiased [ʌn'baɪəst] adj imparcial

unborn [ʌn'bɔːn] adj que va a nacer

unbroken [ʌn'brəukən] adj (seal) intacto; (series) continuo; (record) no batido; (spirit) indómito

unbutton [ʌn'bʌtn] vt desabrochar

uncalled-for [ʌn'kɔːldfɔː*] adj gratuito, inmerecido

uncanny [ʌn'kænɪ] adj extraño

unceremonious ['ʌnserɪ'məunɪəs] adj (abrupt, rude) brusco, hosco

uncertain [ʌn'səːtn] adj incierto; (indecisive) indeciso

unchanged [ʌn'tʃeɪndʒd] adj igual, sin cambios

uncivilized [ʌn'sɪvɪlaɪzd] adj inculto; (fig: behaviour etc) bárbaro; (hour) inoportuno

uncle ['ʌŋkl] n tío

uncomfortable [ʌn'kʌmfətəbl] adj incómodo; (uneasy) inquieto

uncommon [ʌn'kɔmən] adj poco común, raro

uncompromising [ʌn'kɔmprəmaɪzɪŋ] adj intransigente

unconcerned [ʌnkən'səːnd] adj indiferente, despreocupado

unconditional [ʌnkən'dɪʃənl] adj incondicional

unconscious [ʌn'kɔnʃəs] adj sin sentido; (unaware): **to be ~ of** no darse cuenta de ♦ n: **the ~** el inconsciente

uncontrollable [ʌnkən'trəuləbl] adj (child etc) incontrolable; (temper) indomable; (laughter) incontenible

unconventional [ʌnkən'venʃənl] adj poco convencional

uncouth [ʌn'kuːθ] adj grosero, inculto

uncover [ʌn'kʌvə*] vt descubrir; (take lid off) destapar

undecided [ʌndɪ'saɪdɪd] adj (character) indeciso; (question) no resuelto

under ['ʌndə*] prep debajo de; (less than) menos de; (according to) según, de acuerdo con; (sb's leadership) bajo ♦ adv debajo, abajo; ~ **there** allí abajo; ~ **repair** en reparación

under... ['ʌndə*] prefix sub-; ~**age** adj menor de edad; (drinking etc) de los menores de edad; ~**carriage** (BRIT) n (AVIAT) tren m de aterrizaje; ~**charge** vt cobrar menos de la cuenta; ~**clothes** npl ropa interior (SP) or íntima (AM); ~**coat** n (paint) primera mano; ~**cover** adj clandestino; ~**current** n (fig) corriente f oculta; ~**cut** irreg vt vender más barato que; ~**developed** adj subdesarrollado; ~**dog** n desvalido/a; ~**done** adj (CULIN) poco hecho;

~estimate vt subestimar; **~exposed** adj (PHOT) subexpuesto; **~fed** adj subalimentado; **~foot** adv con los pies; **~go** vt irreg sufrir; (treatment) recibir; **~graduate** n estudiante m/f; **~ground** n (BRIT: railway) metro; (POL) movimiento clandestino ♦ adj (car park) subterráneo ♦ adv (work) en la clandestinidad; **~growth** n maleza; **~hand(ed)** adj (fig) socarrón; **~lie** vt irreg (fig) ser la razón fundamental de; **~line** vt subrayar; **~mine** vt socavar, minar; **~neath** [ʌndə'ni:θ] adv debajo ♦ prep debajo de, bajo; **~paid** adj mal pagado; **~pants** npl calzoncillos mpl; **~pass** (BRIT) n paso subterráneo; **~privileged** adj desposeído; **~rate** vt menospreciar, subestimar; **~shirt** (US) n camiseta; **~shorts** (US) npl calzoncillos mpl; **~side** n parte f inferior; **~skirt** (BRIT) n enaguas fpl

understand [ʌndə'stænd] (irreg) vt, vi entender, comprender; (assume) tener entendido; **~able** adj comprensible; **~ing** adj comprensivo ♦ n comprensión f, entendimiento; (agreement) acuerdo

understatement ['ʌndəsteɪtmənt] n modestia (excesiva); **that's an ~!** ¡eso es decir poco!

understood [ʌndə'stud] pt, pp of **understand** ♦ adj (agreed) acordado; (implied): **it is ~ that** se sobreentiende que

understudy ['ʌndəstʌdɪ] n suplente m/f

undertake [ʌndə'teɪk] (irreg) vt emprender; **to ~ to do sth** comprometerse a hacer algo

undertaker ['ʌndəteɪkə*] n director(a) m/f de pompas fúnebres

undertaking ['ʌndəteɪkɪŋ] n empresa; (promise) promesa

under: **~tone** n: **in an ~tone** en voz baja; **~water** adv bajo el agua ♦ adj submarino; **~wear** n ropa interior (SP) or íntima (AM); **~world** n (of crime) hampa, inframundo; **~writer** n (INSURANCE) asegurador(a) m/f

undesirable [ʌndɪ'zaɪrəbl] adj (person) indeseable; (thing) poco aconsejable

undo [ʌn'du:] (irreg) vt (laces) desatar; (button etc) desabrochar; (spoil) deshacer; **~ing** n ruina, perdición f

undoubted [ʌn'dautɪd] adj indudable

undress [ʌn'dres] vi desnudarse

undulating ['ʌndjuleɪtɪŋ] adj ondulante

unduly [ʌn'dju:lɪ] adv excesivamente, demasiado

unearth [ʌn'ə:θ] vt desenterrar

unearthly [ʌn'ə:θlɪ] adj (hour) inverosímil

uneasy [ʌn'i:zɪ] adj intranquilo, preocupado; (feeling) desagradable; (peace) inseguro

uneducated [ʌn'edjukeɪtɪd] adj ignorante, inculto

unemployed [ʌnɪm'plɔɪd] adj parado, sin trabajo ♦ npl: **the ~** los parados

unemployment [ʌnɪm'plɔɪmənt] n paro, desempleo

unending [ʌn'endɪŋ] adj interminable

unerring [ʌn'ə:rɪŋ] adj infalible

uneven [ʌn'i:vn] adj desigual; (road etc) lleno de baches

unexpected [ʌnɪk'spektɪd] adj inesperado; **~ly** adv inesperadamente

unfailing [ʌn'feɪlɪŋ] adj (support) indefectible; (energy) inagotable

unfair [ʌn'fɛə*] adj: **~ (to sb)** injusto (con uno)

unfaithful [ʌn'feɪθful] adj infiel

unfamiliar [ʌnfə'mɪlɪə*] adj extraño, desconocido; **to be ~ with** desconocer

unfashionable [ʌn'fæʃnəbl] adj pasado or fuera de moda

unfasten [ʌn'fa:sn] vt (knot) desatar; (dress) desabrochar; (open) abrir

unfavourable [ʌn'feɪvərəbl] (US **unfavorable**) adj desfavorable

unfeeling [ʌn'fi:lɪŋ] adj insensible

unfinished [ʌn'fɪnɪʃt] adj inacabado, sin terminar

unfit [ʌn'fɪt] adj bajo de forma; (incompetent): **~ (for)** incapaz (de); **~ for work** no apto para trabajar

unfold [ʌn'fəuld] vt desdoblar ♦ vi abrirse

unforeseen [ˈʌnfɔːˈsiːn] *adj* imprevisto
unforgettable [ʌnfəˈgetəbl] *adj*
inolvidable
unfortunate [ʌnˈfɔːtʃnət] *adj* desgraciado;
(*event, remark*) inoportuno; **~ly** *adv*
desgraciadamente
unfounded [ʌnˈfaundɪd] *adj* infundado
unfriendly [ʌnˈfrendlɪ] *adj* antipático;
(*behaviour, remark*) hostil, poco amigable
ungainly [ʌnˈgeɪnlɪ] *adj* desgarbado
ungodly [ʌnˈgɒdlɪ] *adj*: **at an ~ hour** a una
hora inverosímil
ungrateful [ʌnˈgreɪtful] *adj* ingrato
unhappiness [ʌnˈhæpɪnɪs] *n* tristeza,
desdicha
unhappy [ʌnˈhæpɪ] *adj* (*sad*) triste;
(*unfortunate*) desgraciado; (*childhood*)
infeliz; **~ about/with** (*arrangements etc*)
poco contento con, descontento de
unharmed [ʌnˈhɑːmd] *adj* ileso
unhealthy [ʌnˈhelθɪ] *adj* (*place*) malsano;
(*person*) enfermizo; (*fig: interest*) morboso
unheard-of *adj* inaudito, sin precedente
unhurt [ʌnˈhɜːt] *adj* ileso
unidentified [ʌnaɪˈdentɪfaɪd] *adj* no
identificado, sin identificar; *see also* **UFO**
uniform [ˈjuːnɪfɔːm] *n* uniforme *m* ♦ *adj*
uniforme
unify [ˈjuːnɪfaɪ] *vt* unificar, unir
uninhabited [ʌnɪnˈhæbɪtɪd] *adj* desierto
unintentional [ʌnɪnˈtenʃənəl] *adj*
involuntario
union [ˈjuːnjən] *n* unión *f*; (*also*: **trade ~**)
sindicato ♦ *cpd* sindical; **U~ Jack** *n*
bandera del Reino Unido
unique [juːˈniːk] *adj* único
unison [ˈjuːnɪsn] *n*: **in ~** (*speak, reply, sing*)
al unísono
unit [ˈjuːnɪt] *n* unidad *f*; (*section: of
furniture etc*) elemento; (*team*) grupo;
kitchen ~ módulo de cocina
unite [juːˈnaɪt] *vt* unir ♦ *vi* unirse; **~d** *adj*
unido; (*effort*) conjunto; **U~d Kingdom**
n Reino Unido; **U~d Nations
(Organization)** *n* Naciones *fpl* Unidas;
U~d States (of America) *n* Estados
mpl Unidos

unit trust (*BRIT*) *n* bono fiduciario
unity [ˈjuːnɪtɪ] *n* unidad *f*
universe [ˈjuːnɪvɜːs] *n* universo
university [juːnɪˈvɜːsɪtɪ] *n* universidad *f*
unjust [ʌnˈdʒʌst] *adj* injusto
unkempt [ʌnˈkempt] *adj* (*appearance*)
descuidado; (*hair*) despeinado
unkind [ʌnˈkaɪnd] *adj* poco amable;
(*behaviour, comment*) cruel
unknown [ʌnˈnəun] *adj* desconocido
unlawful [ʌnˈlɔːful] *adj* ilegal, ilícito
unleaded [ʌnˈledɪd] *adj* (*petrol, fuel*) sin
plombo
unless [ʌnˈles] *conj* a menos que; **~ he
comes** a menos que venga; **~ otherwise
stated** salvo indicación contraria
unlike [ʌnˈlaɪk] *adj* (*not alike*) distinto de
or a; (*not like*) poco propio de ♦ *prep* a
diferencia de
unlikely [ʌnˈlaɪklɪ] *adj* improbable;
(*unexpected*) inverosímil
unlimited [ʌnˈlɪmɪtɪd] *adj* ilimitado
unlisted [ʌnˈlɪstɪd] (*US*) *adj* (*TEL*) que no
consta en la guía
unload [ʌnˈləud] *vt* descargar
unlock [ʌnˈlɒk] *vt* abrir (con llave)
unlucky [ʌnˈlʌkɪ] *adj* desgraciado; (*object,
number*) que da mala suerte; **to be ~**
tener mala suerte
unmarried [ʌnˈmærɪd] *adj* soltero
unmistak(e)able [ʌnmɪsˈteɪkəbl] *adj*
inconfundible
unnatural [ʌnˈnætʃrəl] *adj* (*gen*)
antinatural; (*manner*) afectado; (*habit*)
perverso
unnecessary [ʌnˈnesəsərɪ] *adj*
innecesario, inútil
unnoticed [ʌnˈnəutɪst] *adj*: **to go** *or* **pass
~** pasar desapercibido
UNO [ˈjuːnəu] *n abbr* (= *United Nations
Organization*) ONU *f*
unobtainable [ʌnəbˈteɪnəbl] *adj*
inconseguible; (*TEL*) inexistente
unobtrusive [ʌnəbˈtruːsɪv] *adj* discreto
unofficial [ʌnəˈfɪʃl] *adj* no oficial; (*news*)
sin confirmar
unorthodox [ʌnˈɔːθədɒks] *adj* poco

ortodoxo; (REL) heterodoxo
unpack [ʌnˈpæk] vi deshacer las maletas
♦ vt deshacer
unpalatable [ʌnˈpælətəbl] adj incomible;
(truth) desagradable
unparalleled [ʌnˈpærəleld] adj
(unequalled) incomparable
unpleasant [ʌnˈplɛznt] adj (disagreeable)
desagradable; (person, manner) antipático
unplug [ʌnˈplʌg] vt desenchufar,
desconectar
unpopular [ʌnˈpɔpjulə*] adj impopular,
poco popular
unprecedented [ʌnˈprɛsɪdəntɪd] adj sin
precedentes
unpredictable [ʌnprɪˈdɪktəbl] adj
imprevisible
unprofessional [ʌnprəˈfɛʃənl] adj
(attitude, conduct) poco ético
unqualified [ʌnˈkwɔlɪfaɪd] adj sin título,
no cualificado; (success) total
unquestionably [ʌnˈkwɛstʃənəblɪ] adv
indiscutiblemente
unreal [ʌnˈrɪəl] adj irreal; (extraordinary)
increíble
unrealistic [ʌnrɪəˈlɪstɪk] adj poco realista
unreasonable [ʌnˈriːznəbl] adj
irrazonable; (demand) excesivo
unrelated [ʌnrɪˈleɪtɪd] adj sin relación;
(family) no emparentado
unreliable [ʌnrɪˈlaɪəbl] adj (person)
informal; (machine) poco fiable
unremitting [ʌnrɪˈmɪtɪŋ] adj constante
unreservedly [ʌnrɪˈzɜːvɪdlɪ] adv sin
reserva
unrest [ʌnˈrɛst] n inquietud f, malestar m;
(POL) disturbios mpl
unroll [ʌnˈrəul] vt desenrollar
unruly [ʌnˈruːlɪ] adj indisciplinado
unsafe [ʌnˈseɪf] adj peligroso
unsaid [ʌnˈsɛd] adj: **to leave sth ~** dejar
algo sin decir
unsatisfactory [ˈʌnsætɪsˈfæktərɪ] adj poco
satisfactorio
unsavoury [ʌnˈseɪvərɪ] (US **unsavory**) adj
(fig) repugnante
unscrew [ʌnˈskruː] vt destornillar

unscrupulous [ʌnˈskruːpjuləs] adj sin
escrúpulos
unsettled [ʌnˈsɛtld] adj inquieto,
intranquilo; (weather) variable
unshaven [ʌnˈʃeɪvn] adj sin afeitar
unsightly [ʌnˈsaɪtlɪ] adj feo
unskilled [ʌnˈskɪld] adj (work) no
especializado; (worker) no cualificado
unspeakable [ʌnˈspiːkəbl] adj indecible;
(awful) incalificable
unstable [ʌnˈsteɪbl] adj inestable
unsteady [ʌnˈstɛdɪ] adj inestable
unstuck [ʌnˈstʌk] adj: **to come ~**
despegarse; (fig) fracasar
unsuccessful [ʌnsəkˈsɛsful] adj (attempt)
infructuoso; (writer, proposal) sin éxito; **to
be ~** (in attempting sth) no tener éxito,
fracasar; **~ly** adv en vano, sin éxito
unsuitable [ʌnˈsuːtəbl] adj inapropiado;
(time) inoportuno
unsure [ʌnˈʃuə*] adj inseguro, poco
seguro
unsuspecting [ˈʌnsəsˈpɛktɪŋ] adj
desprevenido
unsympathetic [ʌnsɪmpəˈθɛtɪk] adj poco
comprensivo; (unlikeable) antipático
unthinkable [ʌnˈθɪŋkəbl] adj
inconcebible, impensable
untidy [ʌnˈtaɪdɪ] adj (room) desordenado;
(appearance) desaliñado
untie [ʌnˈtaɪ] vt desatar
until [ənˈtɪl] prep hasta ♦ conj hasta que; **~
he comes** hasta que venga; **~ now** hasta
ahora; **~ then** hasta entonces
untimely [ʌnˈtaɪmlɪ] adj inoportuno;
(death) prematuro
untold [ʌnˈtəuld] adj (story) nunca
contado; (suffering) indecible; (wealth)
incalculable
untoward [ʌntəˈwɔːd] adj adverso
unused [ʌnˈjuːzd] adj sin usar
unusual [ʌnˈjuːʒuəl] adj insólito, poco
común; (exceptional) inusitado
unveil [ʌnˈveɪl] vt (statue) descubrir
unwanted [ʌnˈwɔntɪd] adj (clothing) viejo;
(pregnancy) no deseado
unwelcome [ʌnˈwɛlkəm] adj inoportuno;

(*news*) desagradable

unwell [ʌnˈwɛl] *adj*: **to be/feel ~** estar indispuesto/sentirse mal

unwieldy [ʌnˈwiːldɪ] *adj* difícil de manejar

unwilling [ʌnˈwɪlɪŋ] *adj*: **to be ~ to do sth** estar poco dispuesto a hacer algo; **~ly** *adv* de mala gana

unwind [ʌnˈwaɪnd] (*irreg: like* wind²) *vt* desenvolver ♦ *vi* (*relax*) relajarse

unwise [ʌnˈwaɪz] *adj* imprudente

unwitting [ʌnˈwɪtɪŋ] *adj* inconsciente

unworthy [ʌnˈwəːðɪ] *adj* indigno

unwrap [ʌnˈræp] *vt* desenvolver

unwritten [ʌnˈrɪtn] *adj* (*agreement*) tácito; (*rules, law*) no escrito

---
KEYWORD
---

up [ʌp] *prep*: **to go/be ~ sth** subir/estar subido en algo; **he went ~ the stairs/the hill** subió las escaleras/la colina; **we walked/climbed ~ the hill** subimos la colina; **they live further ~ the street** viven más arriba en la calle; **go ~ that road and turn left** sigue por esa calle y gira a la izquierda

♦ *adv* **1** (*upwards, higher*) más arriba; **~ in the mountains** en lo alto (de la montaña); **put it a bit higher ~** ponlo un poco más arriba *or* alto; **~ there** ahí *or* allí arriba; **~ above** en lo alto, por encima, arriba

2: **to be ~** (*out of bed*) estar levantado; (*prices, level*) haber subido

3: **~ to** (*as far as*) hasta; **~ to now** hasta ahora *or* la fecha

4: **to be ~ to** (*depending on*): **it's ~ to you** depende de ti; **he's not ~ to it** (*job, task etc*) no es capaz de hacerlo; **his work is not ~ to the required standard** su trabajo no da la talla; (*inf: be doing*): **what is he ~ to?** ¿que estará tramando?

♦ *n*: **~s and downs** altibajos *mpl*

---

upbringing [ˈʌpbrɪŋɪŋ] *n* educación *f*

update [ʌpˈdeɪt] *vt* poner al día

upgrade [ʌpˈgreɪd] *vt* (*house*) modernizar; (*employee*) ascender

upheaval [ʌpˈhiːvl] *n* trastornos *mpl*; (*POL*) agitación *f*

uphill [ʌpˈhɪl] *adj* cuesta arriba; (*fig: task*) penoso, difícil ♦ *adv*: **to go ~** ir cuesta arriba

uphold [ʌpˈhəuld] (*irreg*) *vt* defender

upholstery [ʌpˈhəulstərɪ] *n* tapicería

upkeep [ˈʌpkiːp] *n* mantenimiento

upon [əˈpɔn] *prep* sobre

upper [ˈʌpə*] *adj* superior, de arriba ♦ *n* (*of shoe: also*: **~s**) empeine *m*; **~-class** *adj* de clase alta; **~ hand** *n*: **to have the ~ hand** tener la sartén por el mango; **~most** *adj* el más alto; **what was ~most in my mind** lo que me preocupaba más

upright [ˈʌpraɪt] *adj* derecho; (*vertical*) vertical; (*fig*) honrado

uprising [ˈʌpraɪzɪŋ] *n* sublevación *f*

uproar [ˈʌprɔː*] *n* escándalo

uproot [ʌpˈruːt] *vt* (*also fig*) desarraigar

upset [*n* ˈʌpset, *vb, adj* ʌpˈset] *n* (*to plan etc*) revés *m*, contratiempo; (*MED*) trastorno ♦ (*irreg*) *vt* (*glass etc*) volcar; (*plan*) alterar; (*person*) molestar, disgustar ♦ *adj* molesto, disgustado; (*stomach*) revuelto

upshot [ˈʌpʃɔt] *n* resultado

upside-down *adv* al revés; **to turn a place ~** (*fig*) revolverlo todo

upstairs [ʌpˈstɛəz] *adv* arriba ♦ *adj* (*room*) de arriba ♦ *n* el piso superior

upstart [ˈʌpstɑːt] *n* advenedizo/a

upstream [ʌpˈstriːm] *adv* río arriba

uptake [ˈʌpteɪk] *n*: **to be quick/slow on the ~** ser muy listo/torpe

uptight [ʌpˈtaɪt] *adj* tenso, nervioso

up-to-date *adj* al día

upturn [ˈʌptəːn] *n* (*in luck*) mejora; (*COMM: in market*) resurgimiento económico

upward [ˈʌpwəd] *adj* ascendente; **~(s)** *adv* hacia arriba; (*more than*): **~(s) of** más de

urban [ˈəːbən] *adj* urbano

urchin [ˈəːtʃɪn] *n* pilluelo, golfillo

urge [əːdʒ] *n* (*desire*) deseo ♦ *vt*: **to ~ sb to do sth** animar a uno a hacer algo

urgent [ˈəːdʒənt] *adj* urgente; (*voice*)

perentorio
urinate ['juərɪneɪt] *vi* orinar
urine ['juərɪn] *n* orina, orines *mpl*
urn [ə:n] *n* urna; (*also*: **tea ~**) cacharro
metálico grande para hacer té
Uruguay ['juerəgwaɪ] *n* (el) Uruguay; **~an**
[-'gwaɪən] *adj*, *n* uruguayo/a *m/f*
US *n abbr* (= *United States*) EE. UU.
us [ʌs] *pron* nos; (*after prep*) nosotros/as;
see also **me**
USA *n abbr* (= *United States* (*of America*))
EE. UU.
usage ['ju:zɪdʒ] *n* (LING) uso
use [*n* ju:s, *vb* ju:z] *n* uso, empleo;
(*usefulness*) utilidad *f* ♦ *vt* usar, emplear;
she ~d to do it (ella) solía *or*
acostumbraba hacerlo; **in ~** en uso; **out**
of ~ en desuso; **to be of ~** servir; **it's no**
~ (*pointless*) es inútil; (*not useful*) no sirve;
to be ~d to estar acostumbrado a,
acostumbrar; **~ up** *vt* (*food*) consumir;
(*money*) gastar; **~d** *adj* (*car*) usado; **~ful**
adj útil; **~fulness** *n* utilidad *f*; **~less** *adj*
(*unusable*) inservible; (*pointless*) inútil;
(*person*) inepto; **~r** *n* usuario/a; **~r-**
friendly *adj* (*computer*) amistoso
usher ['ʌʃə*] *n* (*at wedding*) ujier *m*; **~ette**
[-'rɛt] *n* (*in cinema*) acomodadora
USSR *n* (HIST): **the ~** la URSS
usual ['ju:ʒuəl] *adj* normal, corriente; **as ~**
como de costumbre; **~ly** *adv*
normalmente
utensil [ju:'tɛnsl] *n* utensilio; **kitchen ~s**
batería de cocina
uterus ['ju:tərəs] *n* útero
utility [ju:'tɪlɪtɪ] *n* utilidad *f*; (*public ~*)
(empresa de) servicio público; **~ room** *n*
ofis *m*
utilize ['ju:tɪlaɪz] *vt* utilizar
utmost ['ʌtməust] *adj* mayor ♦ *n*: **to do**
one's ~ = hacer todo lo posible
utter ['ʌtə*] *adj* total, completo ♦ *vt*
pronunciar, proferir; **~ly** *adv*
completamente, totalmente
U-turn ['ju:'tə:n] *n* viraje *m* en redondo

V, v

v. *abbr* = **verse; versus;** (= *volt*) v;
(= *vide*) véase
vacancy ['veɪkənsɪ] *n* (BRIT: *job*) vacante *f*;
(*room*) habitación *f* libre; **"no**
vacancies" "completo"
vacant ['veɪkənt] *adj* desocupado, libre;
(*expression*) distraído
vacate [və'keɪt] *vt* (*house, room*)
desocupar; (*job*) dejar (vacante)
vacation [və'keɪʃən] *n* vacaciones *fpl*
vaccinate ['væksɪneɪt] *vt* vacunar
vaccine ['væksi:n] *n* vacuna
vacuum ['vækjum] *n* vacío; **~ cleaner** *n*
aspiradora; **~-flask** (BRIT) *n* termo; **~-**
packed *adj* empaquetado al vacío
vagina [və'dʒaɪnə] *n* vagina
vagrant ['veɪgrnt] *n* vagabundo/a
vague [veɪg] *adj* vago; (*memory*) borroso;
(*ambiguous*) impreciso; (*person: absent-
minded*) distraído; (: *evasive*): **to be ~** no
decir las cosas claramente; **~ly** *adv*
vagamente; distraídamente; con evasivas
vain [veɪn] *adj* (*conceited*) presumido;
(*useless*) vano, inútil; **in ~** en vano
valentine ['væləntaɪn] *n* (*also*: **~ card**)
tarjeta del Día de los Enamorados
valet ['væleɪ] *n* ayuda *m* de cámara
valid ['vælɪd] *adj* válido; (*ticket*) valedero;
(*law*) vigente
valley ['vælɪ] *n* valle *m*
valuable ['væljuəbl] *adj* (*jewel*) de valor;
(*time*) valioso; **~s** *npl* objetos *mpl* de
valor
valuation [vælju'eɪʃən] *n* tasación *f*,
valuación *f*; (*judgement of quality*)
valoración *f*
value ['vælju:] *n* valor *m*; (*importance*)
importancia ♦ *vt* (*fix price of*) tasar,
valorar; (*esteem*) apreciar; **~s** *npl*
(*principles*) principios *mpl*; **~ added tax**
(BRIT) *n* impuesto sobre el valor añadido;
~d *adj* (*appreciated*) apreciado
valve [vælv] *n* válvula

van [væn] n (AUT) furgoneta (SP), camioneta (AM)
vandal ['vændl] n vándalo/a; **~ism** n vandalismo; **~ize** vt dañar, destruir
vanilla [və'nɪlə] n vainilla
vanish ['vænɪʃ] vi desaparecer
vanity ['vænɪtɪ] n vanidad f
vantage point ['vɑːntɪdʒ-] n (for views) punto panorámico
vapour ['veɪpə*] (US **vapor**) n vapor m; (on breath, window) vaho
variable ['vɛərɪəbl] adj variable
variation [vɛərɪ'eɪʃən] n variación f
varicose ['værɪkəus] adj: **~ veins** varices fpl
varied ['vɛərɪd] adj variado
variety [və'raɪətɪ] n (diversity) diversidad f; (type) variedad f; **~ show** n espectáculo de variedades
various ['vɛərɪəs] adj (several: people) varios/as; (reasons) diversos/as
varnish ['vɑːnɪʃ] n barniz m; (nail ~) esmalte m ♦ vt barnizar; (nails) pintar (con esmalte)
vary ['vɛərɪ] vt variar; (change) cambiar ♦ vi variar
vase [vɑːz] n florero
Vaseline ® ['væsɪliːn] n vaselina ®
vast [vɑːst] adj enorme
VAT [væt] (BRIT) n abbr (= value added tax) IVA m
vat [væt] n tina, tinaja
Vatican ['vætɪkən] n: **the ~** el Vaticano
vault [vɔːlt] n (of roof) bóveda; (tomb) panteón m; (in bank) cámara acorazada ♦ vt (also: **~ over**) saltar (por encima de)
vaunted ['vɔːntɪd] adj: **much ~** cacareado, alardeado
VCR n abbr = **video cassette recorder**
VD n abbr = **venereal disease**
VDU n abbr (= visual display unit) UPV f
veal [viːl] n ternera
veer [vɪə*] vi (vehicle) virar; (wind) girar
vegan ['viːgən] n vegetariano/a estricto/a, vegetaliano/a
vegeburger ['vɛdʒɪbɜːgə*] n hamburguesa vegetal

vegetable ['vɛdʒtəbl] n (BOT) vegetal m; (edible plant) legumbre f, hortaliza ♦ adj vegetal; **~s** npl (cooked) verduras fpl
vegetarian [vɛdʒɪ'tɛərɪən] adj, n vegetariano/a m/f
vehement ['viːɪmənt] adj vehemente, apasionado
vehicle ['viːɪkl] n vehículo; (fig) medio
veil [veɪl] n velo ♦ vt velar; **~ed** adj (fig) velado
vein [veɪn] n vena; (of ore etc) veta
velocity [vɪ'lɒsɪtɪ] n velocidad f
velvet ['vɛlvɪt] n terciopelo
vending machine ['vɛndɪŋ-] n distribuidor m automático
veneer [və'nɪə*] n chapa, enchapado; (fig) barniz m
venereal disease [vɪ'nɪərɪəl-] n enfermedad f venérea
Venetian blind [vɪ'niːʃən-] n persiana
Venezuela [vɛnɪ'zweɪlə] n Venezuela; **~n** adj, n venezolano/a m/f
vengeance ['vɛndʒəns] n venganza; **with a ~** (fig) con creces
venison ['vɛnɪsn] n carne f de venado
venom ['vɛnəm] n veneno; (bitterness) odio; **~ous** adj venenoso; lleno de odio
vent [vɛnt] n (in jacket) respiradero; (in wall) rejilla (de ventilación) ♦ vt (fig: feelings) desahogar
ventilator ['vɛntɪleɪtə*] n ventilador m
venture ['vɛntʃə*] n empresa ♦ vt (opinion) ofrecer ♦ vi arriesgarse, lanzarse; **business ~** empresa comercial
venue ['vɛnjuː] n lugar m
veranda(h) [və'rændə] n terraza
verb [vɜːb] n verbo; **~al** adj verbal
verbatim [vɜː'beɪtɪm] adj, adv palabra por palabra
verdict ['vɜːdɪkt] n veredicto, fallo; (fig) opinión f, juicio
verge [vɜːdʒ] (BRIT) n borde m; **"soft ~s"** (AUT) "arcén m no asfaltado"; **to be on the ~ of doing sth** estar a punto de hacer algo; **~ on** vt fus rayar en
verify ['vɛrɪfaɪ] vt comprobar, verificar
vermin ['vɜːmɪn] npl (animals) alimañas

fpl; (*insects, fig*) parásitos *mpl*
vermouth [ˈvəːməθ] *n* vermut *m*
versatile [ˈvəːsətaɪl] *adj* (*person*) polifacético; (*machine, tool etc*) versátil
verse [vəːs] *n* poesía; (*stanza*) estrofa; (*in bible*) versículo
version [ˈvəːʃən] *n* versión *f*
versus [ˈvəːsəs] *prep* contra
vertebra [ˈvəːtɪbrə] (*pl ~e*) *n* vértebra
vertical [ˈvəːtɪkl] *adj* vertical
verve [vəːv] *n* brío
very [ˈverɪ] *adv* muy ♦ *adj*: **the ~ book which** el mismo libro que; **the ~ last** el último de todos; **at the ~ least** al menos; **~ much** muchísimo
vessel [ˈvesl] *n* (*ship*) barco; (*container*) vasija; *see* **blood**
vest [vest] *n* (*BRIT*) camiseta; (*US: waistcoat*) chaleco; **~ed interests** *npl* (*COMM*) intereses *mpl* creados
vet [vet] *vt* (*candidate*) investigar ♦ *n abbr* (*BRIT*) = **veterinary surgeon**
veteran [ˈvetərn] *n* veterano
veterinary surgeon [ˈvetrɪnərɪ] (*US* **veterinarian**) *n* veterinario/a *m/f*
veto [ˈviːtəu] (*pl ~es*) *n* veto ♦ *vt* prohibir, poner el veto a
vex [veks] *vt* fastidiar; **~ed** *adj* (*question*) controvertido
VHF *abbr* (= *very high frequency*) muy alta frecuencia
via [ˈvaɪə] *prep* por, por medio de
vibrant [ˈvaɪbrənt] *adj* (*lively*) animado; (*bright*) vivo; (*voice*) vibrante
vibrate [vaɪˈbreɪt] *vi* vibrar
vicar [ˈvɪkə*] *n* párroco (de la Iglesia Anglicana); **~age** *n* parroquia
vice [vaɪs] *n* (*evil*) vicio; (*TECH*) torno de banco
vice- [vaɪs] *prefix* vice-; **~-chairman** *n* vicepresidente *m*
vice squad *n* brigada antivicio
vice versa [ˈvaɪsɪˈvəːsə] *adv* viceversa
vicinity [vɪˈsɪnɪtɪ] *n*: **in the ~ (of)** cercano (a)
vicious [ˈvɪʃəs] *adj* (*attack*) violento; (*words*) cruel; (*horse, dog*) resabido; **~**

circle *n* círculo vicioso
victim [ˈvɪktɪm] *n* víctima
victor [ˈvɪktə*] *n* vencedor(a) *m/f*
victory [ˈvɪktərɪ] *n* victoria
video [ˈvɪdɪəu] *cpd* video ♦ *n* (*~ film*) videofilm *m*; (*also: ~ cassette*) videocassette *f*; (*also: ~ cassette recorder*) magnetoscopio; **~ game** *n* videojuego; **~ tape** *n* cinta de vídeo
vie [vaɪ] *vi*: **to ~ (with sb for sth)** competir (con uno por algo)
Vienna [vɪˈenə] *n* Viena
Vietnam [vjetˈnæm] *n* Vietnam *m*; **~ese** [-nəˈmiːz] *n inv, adj* vietnamita *m/f*
view [vjuː] *n* vista; (*outlook*) perspectiva; (*opinion*) opinión *f*, criterio ♦ *vt* (*look at*) mirar; (*fig*) considerar; **on ~** (*in museum etc*) expuesto; **in full ~ (of)** en plena vista (de); **in ~ of the weather/the fact that** en vista del tiempo/del hecho de que; **in my ~** en mi opinión; **~er** *n* espectador(a) *m/f*; (*TV*) telespectador(a) *m/f*; **~finder** *n* visor *m* de imagen; **~point** *n* (*attitude*) punto de vista; (*place*) mirador *m*
vigour [ˈvɪɡə*] (*US* **vigor**) *n* energía, vigor *m*
vile [vaɪl] *adj* vil, infame; (*smell*) asqueroso; (*temper*) endemoniado
villa [ˈvɪlə] *n* (*country house*) casa de campo; (*suburban house*) chalet *m*
village [ˈvɪlɪdʒ] *n* aldea; **~r** *n* aldeano/a
villain [ˈvɪlən] *n* (*scoundrel*) malvado/a; (*in novel*) malo; (*BRIT: criminal*) maleante *m/f*
vindicate [ˈvɪndɪkeɪt] *vt* vindicar, justificar
vindictive [vɪnˈdɪktɪv] *adj* vengativo
vine [vaɪn] *n* vid *f*
vinegar [ˈvɪnɪɡə*] *n* vinagre *m*
vineyard [ˈvɪnjɑːd] *n* viña, viñedo
vintage [ˈvɪntɪdʒ] *n* (*year*) vendimia, cosecha ♦ *cpd* de época; **~ wine** *n* vino añejo
vinyl [ˈvaɪnl] *n* vinilo
viola [vɪˈəulə] *n* (*MUS*) viola
violate [ˈvaɪəleɪt] *vt* violar
violence [ˈvaɪələns] *n* violencia
violent [ˈvaɪələnt] *adj* violento; (*intense*) intenso

violet ['vaɪələt] *adj* violado, violeta ♦ *n* (*plant*) violeta

violin [vaɪə'lɪn] *n* violín *m*; **~ist** *n* violinista *m/f*

VIP *n abbr* (= *very important person*) VIP *m*

virgin ['vɜːdʒɪn] *n* virgen *f*

Virgo ['vɜːgəʊ] *n* Virgo

virtually ['vɜːtjʊəlɪ] *adv* prácticamente

virtual reality ['vɜːtjʊəl-] *n* (*COMPUT*) mundo *or* realidad *f* virtual

virtue ['vɜːtjuː] *n* virtud *f*; (*advantage*) ventaja; **by ~ of** en virtud de

virtuous ['vɜːtjʊəs] *adj* virtuoso

virus ['vaɪərəs] *n* (*also*: *COMPUT*) virus *m*

visa ['viːzə] *n* visado (*SP*), visa (*AM*)

visible ['vɪzəbl] *adj* visible

vision ['vɪʒən] *n* (*sight*) vista; (*foresight, in dream*) visión *f*

visit ['vɪzɪt] *n* visita ♦ *vt* (*person: US: also: ~ with*) visitar, hacer una visita a; (*place*) ir a, (ir a) conocer; **~ing hours** *npl* (*in hospital etc*) horas *fpl* de visita; **~or** *n* (*in museum*) visitante *m/f*; (*invited to house*) visita; (*tourist*) turista *m/f*

visor ['vaɪzə*] *n* visera

visual ['vɪzjʊəl] *adj* visual; **~ aid** *n* medio visual; **~ display unit** *n* unidad *f* de presentación visual; **~ize** *vt* imaginarse

vital ['vaɪtl] *adj* (*essential*) esencial, imprescindible; (*dynamic*) dinámico; (*organ*) vital; **~ly** *adv*: **~ly important** de primera importancia; **~ statistics** *npl* (*fig*) medidas *fpl* vitales

vitamin ['vɪtəmɪn] *n* vitamina

vivacious [vɪ'veɪʃəs] *adj* vivaz, alegre

vivid ['vɪvɪd] *adj* (*account*) gráfico; (*light*) intenso; (*imagination, memory*) vivo; **~ly** *adv* gráficamente; (*remember*) como si fuera hoy

V-neck ['viːnɛk] *n* cuello de pico

vocabulary [vəʊ'kæbjʊlərɪ] *n* vocabulario

vocal ['vəʊkl] *adj* vocal; (*articulate*) elocuente; **~ cords** *npl* cuerdas *fpl* vocales

vocation [vəʊ'keɪʃən] *n* vocación *f*; **~al** *adj* profesional

vodka ['vɒdkə] *n* vodka *m*

vogue [vəʊg] *n*: **in ~** en boga, de moda

voice [vɔɪs] *n* voz *f* ♦ *vt* expresar; **~ mail** *n* fonobuzón *m*

void [vɔɪd] *n* vacío; (*hole*) hueco ♦ *adj* (*invalid*) nulo, inválido; (*empty*): **~ of** carente *or* desprovisto de

volatile ['vɒlətaɪl] *adj* (*situation*) inestable; (*person*) voluble; (*liquid*) volátil

volcano [vɒl'keɪnəʊ] (*pl* **~es**) *n* volcán *m*

volition [və'lɪʃən] *n*: **of one's own ~** de su propia voluntad

volley ['vɒlɪ] *n* (*of gunfire*) descarga; (*of stones etc*) lluvia; (*fig*) torrente *m*; (*TENNIS etc*) volea; **~ball** *n* vol(e)ibol *m*

volt [vəʊlt] *n* voltio; **~age** *n* voltaje *m*

volume ['vɒljuːm] *n* (*gen*) volumen *m*; (*book*) tomo

voluntary ['vɒləntərɪ] *adj* voluntario

volunteer [vɒlən'tɪə*] *n* voluntario/a ♦ *vt* (*information*) ofrecer ♦ *vi* ofrecerse (de voluntario); **to ~ to do** ofrecerse a hacer

vomit ['vɒmɪt] *n* vómito ♦ *vt*, *vi* vomitar

vote [vəʊt] *n* voto; (*votes cast*) votación *f*; (*right to ~*) derecho de votar; (*franchise*) sufragio ♦ *vt* (*chairman*) elegir; (*propose*): **to ~ that** proponer que ♦ *vi* votar, ir a votar; **~ of thanks** voto de gracias; **~r** *n* votante *m/f*; **voting** *n* votación *f*

vouch [vaʊtʃ]: **to ~ for** *vt fus* garantizar, responder de

voucher ['vaʊtʃə*] *n* (*for meal, petrol*) vale *m*

vow [vaʊ] *n* voto ♦ *vt*: **to ~ to do/that** jurar hacer/que

vowel ['vaʊəl] *n* vocal *f*

voyage ['vɔɪdʒ] *n* viaje *m*

vulgar ['vʌlgə*] *adj* (*rude*) ordinario, grosero; (*in bad taste*) de mal gusto; **~ity** [-'gærɪtɪ] *n* grosería; mal gusto

vulnerable ['vʌlnərəbl] *adj* vulnerable

vulture ['vʌltʃə*] *n* buitre *m*

W, w

wad [wɔd] n bolita; (of banknotes etc) fajo

waddle ['wɔdl] vi anadear

wade [weɪd] vi: to ~ through (water) vadear; (fig: book) leer con dificultad; **wading pool** (US) n piscina para niños

wafer ['weɪfə*] n galleta, barquillo

waffle ['wɔfl] n (CULIN) gofre ♦ vi dar el rollo

waft [wɔft] vt llevar por el aire ♦ vi flotar

wag [wæg] vt menear, agitar ♦ vi moverse, menearse

wage [weɪdʒ] n (also: ~s) sueldo, salario ♦ vt: to ~ war hacer la guerra; ~ **earner** n asalariado/a; ~ **packet** n sobre m de paga

wager ['weɪdʒə*] n apuesta

wag(g)on ['wægən] n (horse-drawn) carro; (BRIT: RAIL) vagón m

wail [weɪl] n gemido ♦ vi gemir

waist [weɪst] n cintura, talle m; ~**coat** (BRIT) n chaleco; ~**line** n talle m

wait [weɪt] n (interval) pausa ♦ vi esperar; **to lie in ~ for** acechar a; **I can't ~ to** (fig) estoy deseando; **to ~ for** esperar (a); ~ **behind** vi quedarse; ~ **on** vt fus servir a; ~**er** n camarero; ~**ing** n: "**no ~ing**" (BRIT: AUT) "prohibido estacionarse"; ~**ing list** n lista de espera; ~**ing room** n sala de espera; ~**ress** n camarera

waive [weɪv] vt suspender

wake [weɪk] (pt **woke** or **waked**, pp **woken** or **waked**) vt (also: ~ **up**) despertar ♦ vi (also: ~ **up**) despertarse ♦ n (for dead person) vela, velatorio; (NAUT) estela; **waken** vt, vi = **wake**

Wales [weɪlz] n País m de Gales; **the Prince of ~** el príncipe de Gales

walk [wɔːk] n (stroll) paseo; (hike) excursión f a pie, caminata; (gait) paso, andar m; (in park etc) paseo, alameda ♦ vi andar, caminar; (for pleasure, exercise) pasear ♦ vt (distance) recorrer a pie, andar; (dog) pasear; **10 minutes' ~**

from here a 10 minutos de aquí andando; **people from all ~s of life** gente de todas las esferas; ~ **out** vi (workers) declararse en huelga; ~ **out on** (inf) vt fus abandonar; ~**er** n (person) paseante m/f, caminante m/f; ~**ie-talkie** ['wɔːkɪ'tɔːkɪ] n walkie-talkie m; ~**ing** n el andar; ~**ing shoes** npl zapatos mpl para andar; ~**ing stick** n bastón m; **W~man** ® ['wɔːkmən] n Walkman ® m; ~**out** n huelga; ~**over** (inf) n: **it was a ~over** fue pan comido; ~**way** n paseo

wall [wɔːl] n pared f; (exterior) muro; (city ~ etc) muralla; (garden) con tapia; ~**ed** adj amurallado

wallet ['wɔlɪt] n cartera (SP), billetera (AM)

wallflower ['wɔːlflauə*] n alhelí m; **to be a ~** (fig) comer pavo

wallow ['wɔləu] vi revolcarse

wallpaper ['wɔːlpeɪpə*] n papel m pintado ♦ vt empapelar

walnut ['wɔːlnʌt] n nuez f; (tree) nogal m

walrus ['wɔːlrəs] (pl ~ or ~**es**) n morsa

waltz [wɔːlts] n vals m ♦ vi bailar el vals

wand [wɔnd] n (also: **magic ~**) varita (mágica)

wander ['wɔndə*] vi (person) vagar; deambular; (thoughts) divagar ♦ vt recorrer, vagar por

wane [weɪn] vi menguar

wangle ['wæŋgl] (BRIT: inf) vt agenciarse

want [wɔnt] vt querer, desear; (need) necesitar ♦ n: **for ~ of** por falta de; ~**s** npl (needs) necesidades fpl; **to ~ to do** querer hacer; **to ~ sb to do sth** querer que uno haga algo; ~**ed** adj (criminal) buscado; "~**ed**" (in advertisements) "se busca"; ~**ing** adj: **to be found ~ing** no estar a la altura de las circunstancias

WAP [wæp] n abbr (COMPUT: = wireless application protocol) WAP f

war [wɔː*] n guerra; **to make ~ (on)** (also fig) declarar la guerra (a)

ward [wɔːd] n (in hospital) sala; (POL) distrito electoral; (LAW: child: also: ~ **of court**) pupilo/a; ~ **off** vt (blow) desviar, parar; (attack) rechazar

warden ['wɔːdn] n (BRIT: of institution)
director(a) m/f; (of park, game reserve)
guardián/ana m/f; (BRIT: also: **traffic ~**)
guardia m/f
warder ['wɔːdə*] n (BRIT) guardián/ana m/
f, carcelero/a
wardrobe ['wɔːdrəub] n armario,
guardarropa, ropero (esp AM)
warehouse ['wɛəhaus] n almacén m,
depósito
wares [wɛəz] npl mercancías fpl
warfare ['wɔːfɛə*] n guerra
warhead ['wɔːhed] n cabeza armada
warily ['wɛərɪlɪ] adv con cautela,
cautelosamente
warm [wɔːm] adj caliente; (thanks) efusivo;
(clothes etc) abrigado; (welcome, day)
caluroso; **it's ~** hace calor; **I'm ~** tengo
calor; **~ up** vi (room) calentarse; (person)
entrar en calor; (athlete) hacer ejercicios
de calentamiento ♦ vt calentar; **~-
hearted** adj afectuoso; **~ly** adv
afectuosamente; **~th** n calor m
warn [wɔːn] vt avisar, advertir; **~ing** n
aviso, advertencia; **~ing light** n luz f de
advertencia; **~ing triangle** n (AUT)
triángulo señalizador
warp [wɔːp] vi (wood) combarse ♦ vt
combar; (mind) pervertir
warrant ['wɔrnt] n autorización f; (LAW: to
arrest) orden f de detención; (: to search)
mandamiento de registro
warranty ['wɔrəntɪ] n garantía
warren ['wɔrən] n (of rabbits) madriguera;
(fig) laberinto
warrior ['wɔrɪə*] n guerrero/a
Warsaw ['wɔːsɔː] n Varsovia
warship ['wɔːʃɪp] n buque m o barco de
guerra
wart [wɔːt] n verruga
wartime ['wɔːtaɪm] n: **in ~** en tiempos de
guerra, en la guerra
wary ['wɛərɪ] adj cauteloso
was [wɔz] pt of **be**
wash [wɔʃ] vt lavar ♦ vi lavarse; (sea etc):
to ~ against/over sth llegar hasta/cubrir
algo ♦ n (clothes etc) lavado; (of ship)

estela; **to have a ~** lavarse; **~ away** vt
(stain) quitar lavando; (subj: river etc)
llevarse; **~ off** vi quitarse (al lavar); **~ up**
vi (BRIT) fregar los platos; (US) lavarse;
~able adj lavable; **~basin** (US **~bowl**) n
lavabo; **~ cloth** (US) n manopla; **~er**
(TECH) arandela; **~ing** n (dirty) ropa sucia;
(clean) colada; **~ing machine** n
lavadora; **~ing powder** (BRIT) n
detergente m (en polvo)
Washington ['wɔʃɪŋtən] n Washington m
wash: ~ing-up (BRIT) n fregado, platos
mpl (para fregar); **~ing-up liquid** (BRIT)
n líquido lavavajillas; **~-out** (inf) n
fracaso; **~room** (US) n servicios mpl
wasn't ['wɔznt] = **was not**
wasp [wɔsp] n avispa
wastage ['weɪstɪdʒ] n desgaste m; (loss)
pérdida
waste [weɪst] n derroche m, despilfarro;
(of time) pérdida; (food) sobras fpl;
(rubbish) basura, desperdicios mpl ♦ adj
(material) de desecho; (left over) sobrante;
(land) baldío, descampado ♦ vt
malgastar, derrochar; (time) perder;
(opportunity) desperdiciar; **~s** npl (area of
land) tierras fpl baldías; **~ away** vi
consumirse; **~ disposal unit** (BRIT) n
triturador m de basura; **~ful** adj
derrochador(a); (process) antieconómico;
~ ground (BRIT) n terreno baldío;
~paper basket n papelera; **~ pipe** n
tubo de desagüe
watch [wɔtʃ] n (also: **wrist ~**) reloj m; (MIL:
group of guards) centinela m; (act)
vigilancia; (NAUT: spell of duty) guardia
♦ vt (look at) mirar, observar; (: match,
programme) ver; (spy on, guard) vigilar;
(be careful of) cuidarse de, tener cuidado
de ♦ vi ver, mirar; (keep guard) montar
guardia; **~ out** vi cuidarse, tener cuidado;
~dog n perro guardián; (fig) persona u
organismo encargado de asegurarse de que
las empresas actúan dentro de la legalidad;
~ful adj vigilante, sobre aviso; **~maker**
n relojero/a; **~man** (irreg) n see **night**; **~
strap** n pulsera (de reloj)

water ['wɔːtə*] *n* agua ♦ *vt* (*plant*) regar
♦ *vi* (*eyes*) llorar; (*mouth*) hacerse la boca
agua; **~ down** *vt* (*milk etc*) aguar; (*fig:
story*) dulcificar, diluir; **~ closet** *n* wáter
m; **~colour** *n* acuarela; **~cress** *n* berro;
~fall *n* cascada, salto de agua; **~ heater**
n calentador *m* de agua; **~ing can** *n*
regadera; **~ lily** *n* nenúfar *m*; **~line** *n*
(*NAUT*) línea de flotación; **~logged** *adj*
(*ground*) inundado; **~ main** *n* cañería del
agua; **~melon** *n* sandía; **~proof** *adj*
impermeable; **~shed** *n* (*GEO*) cuenca;
(*fig*) momento crítico; **~-skiing** *n* esquí
m acuático; **~tight** *adj* hermético; **~way**
n vía fluvial o navegable; **~works** *n*
central *f* depuradora; **~y** *adj* (*coffee etc*)
aguado; (*eyes*) lloroso

watt [wɔt] *n* vatio

wave [weɪv] *n* (*of hand*) señal *f* con la
mano; (*on water*) ola; (*RADIO, in hair*)
onda; (*fig*) oleada ♦ *vi* agitar la mano;
(*flag etc*) ondear ♦ *vt* (*handkerchief, gun*)
agitar; **~length** *n* longitud *f* de onda

waver ['weɪvə*] *vi* (*voice, love etc*) flaquear;
(*person*) vacilar

wavy ['weɪvɪ] *adj* ondulado

wax [wæks] *n* cera ♦ *vt* encerar ♦ *vi*
(*moon*) crecer; **~ paper** *n* (*US*) papel *m*
apergaminado; **~works** *n* museo de cera
♦ *npl* figuras *fpl* de cera

way [weɪ] *n* camino; (*distance*) trayecto,
recorrido; (*direction*) dirección *f*, sentido;
(*manner*) modo, manera; (*habit*)
costumbre *f*; **which ~? – this ~** ¿por
dónde?, ¿en qué dirección? — por aquí;
on the ~ (*en route*) en (el) camino; **to be
on one's ~** estar en camino; **to be in the
~** bloquear el camino; (*fig*) estorbar; **to
go out of one's ~ to do sth** desvivirse
por hacer algo; **under ~** en marcha; **to
lose one's ~** extraviarse; **in a ~** en cierto
modo *or* sentido; **no ~!** (*inf*) ¡de eso
nada!; **by the ~** ... a propósito ...; **"~ in"**
(*BRIT*) "entrada"; **"~ out"** (*BRIT*) "salida";
the ~ back el camino de vuelta; **"give
~"** (*BRIT: AUT*) "ceda el paso"

waylay [weɪ'leɪ] (*irreg*) *vt* salir al paso a

wayward ['weɪwəd] *adj* díscolo

W.C. *n* (*BRIT*) wáter *m*

we [wiː] *pl pron* nosotros/as

weak [wiːk] *adj* débil, flojo; (*tea etc*) claro;
~en *vi* debilitarse; (*give way*) ceder ♦ *vt*
debilitar; **~ling** *n* debilucho/a; (*morally*)
persona de poco carácter; **~ness** *n*
debilidad *f*; (*fault*) punto débil; **to have a
~ness for** tener debilidad por

wealth [welθ] *n* riqueza; (*of details*)
abundancia; **~y** *adj* rico

wean [wiːn] *vt* destetar

weapon ['wepən] *n* arma

wear [weə*] (*pt* **wore**, *pp* **worn**) *n* (*use*)
uso; (*deterioration through use*) desgaste
m; (*clothing*): **sports/baby~** ropa de
deportes/de niños ♦ *vt* (*clothes*) llevar;
(*shoes*) calzar; (*damage: through use*)
gastar, usar ♦ *vi* (*last*) durar; (*rub through
etc*) desgastarse; **evening ~** ropa de
etiqueta; **~ away** *vt* gastar ♦ *vi* desgastarse;
~ down *vt* gastar; (*strength*) agotar; **~ off**
vi (*pain etc*) pasar, desaparecer; **~ out** *vt*
desgastar; (*person, strength*) agotar; **~
and tear** *n* desgaste *m*

weary ['wɪərɪ] *adj* cansado; (*dispirited*)
abatido ♦ *vi*: **to ~ of** cansarse de

weasel ['wiːzl] *n* (*ZOOL*) comadreja

weather ['weðə*] *n* tiempo ♦ *vt* (*storm, crisis*)
hacer frente a; **under the ~** (*fig: ill*)
indispuesto, pachucho; **~-beaten** *adj* (*skin*)
curtido; (*building*) deteriorado por la
intemperie; **~cock** *n* veleta; **~forecast** *n*
boletín *m* meteorológico; **~man** (*irreg: inf*)
n hombre *m* del tiempo; **~ vane** *n* = **~cock**

weave [wiːv] (*pt* **wove**, *pp* **woven**) *vt*
(*cloth*) tejer; (*fig*) entretejer; **~r** *n*
tejedor(a) *m/f*; **weaving** *n* tejeduría

web [web] *n* (*of spider*) telaraña; (*on duck's
foot*) membrana; (*network*) red *f*; **the
(World Wide) W~** el *or* la Web

webcam ['webkæm] *n* webcam *f*

webcast ['webkɑːst] *n* (*COMPUT*)
transmisión por Internet

website ['websaɪt] *n* sitio Web

wed [wed] (*pt, pp* **wedded**) *vt* casar ♦ *vi*
casarse

we'd [wi:d] = **we had; we would**
wedding ['wedɪŋ] n boda, casamiento; **silver ~ (anniversary)** bodas fpl de plata; **~ day** n día m de la boda; **~ dress** n traje m de novia; **~ present** n regalo de boda; **~ ring** n alianza
wedge [wedʒ] n (of wood etc) cuña; (of cake) trozo ♦ vt acuñar; (push) apretar
Wednesday ['wednzdɪ] n miércoles m inv
wee [wi:] (Scottish) adj pequeñito
weed [wi:d] n mala hierba, maleza ♦ vt escardar, desherbar; **~killer** n herbicida m; **~y** adj (person) mequetréfico
week [wi:k] n semana; **a ~ today/on Friday** de hoy/del viernes en ocho días; **~day** n día m laborable; **~end** n fin m de semana; **~ly** adv semanalmente, cada semana ♦ adj semanal ♦ n semanario
weep [wi:p] (pt, pp **wept**) vi, vt llorar; **~ing willow** n sauce m llorón
weigh [weɪ] vt, vi pesar; **to ~ anchor** levar anclas; **~ down** vt sobrecargar; (fig: with worry) agobiar; **~ up** vt sopesar
weight [weɪt] n peso; (metal ~) pesa; **to lose/put on ~** adelgazar/engordar; **~ing** n (allowance): (London) **~ing** dietas (por residir en Londres); **~lifter** n levantador m de pesas; **~y** adj pesado; (matters) de relevancia or peso
weir [wɪə*] n presa
weird [wɪəd] adj raro, extraño
welcome ['welkəm] adj bienvenido ♦ n bienvenida ♦ vt dar la bienvenida a; (be glad of) alegrarse de; **thank you – you're ~** gracias — de nada
weld [weld] n soldadura ♦ vt soldar
welfare ['welfeə*] n bienestar m; (social aid) asistencia social; **~ state** n estado del bienestar
well [wel] n fuente f, pozo ♦ adv bien ♦ adj: **to be ~** estar bien (de salud) ♦ excl ¡vaya!, ¡bueno!; **as ~** también; **as ~ as** además de; **~ done!** ¡bien hecho!; **get ~ soon!** ¡que te mejores pronto!; **to do ~** (business) ir bien; (person) tener éxito; **~ up** vi (tears) saltar
we'll [wi:l] = **we will; we shall**

well: ~-behaved adj bueno; **~-being** n bienestar m; **~-built** adj (person) fornido; **~-deserved** adj merecido; **~-dressed** adj bien vestido; **~-groomed** adj de buena presencia; **~-heeled** (inf) adj (wealthy) rico
wellingtons ['welɪŋtənz] npl (also: **wellington boots**) botas fpl de goma
well: ~-known adj (person) conocido; **~-mannered** adj educado; **~-meaning** adj bienintencionado; **~-off** adj acomodado; **~-read** adj leído; **~-to-do** adj acomodado; **~-wisher** n admirador(a) m/f
Welsh [welʃ] adj galés/esa ♦ n (LING) galés m; **the ~** npl los galeses; **the ~ Assembly** el Parlamento galés; **~man** (irreg) n galés m; **~ rarebit** n pan m con queso tostado; **~woman** (irreg) n galesa
went [went] pt of **go**
wept [wept] pt, pp of **weep**
were [wə:*] pt of **be**
we're [wɪə*] = **we are**
weren't [wə:nt] = **were not**
west [west] n oeste m ♦ adj occidental, del oeste ♦ adv al or hacia el oeste; **the W~** el Oeste, el Occidente; **W~ Country** (BRIT) n: **the W~ Country** el suroeste de Inglaterra; **~erly** adj occidental; (wind) del oeste; **~ern** adj occidental ♦ n (CINEMA) película del oeste; **W~ Germany** n Alemania Occidental; **W~ Indian** adj, n antillano/a m/f; **W~ Indies** npl Antillas fpl; **~ward(s)** adv hacia el oeste
wet [wet] adj (damp) húmedo; (~ through) mojado; (rainy) lluvioso ♦ (BRIT) n (POL) conservador(a) m/f moderado/a; **to get ~** mojarse; **"~ paint"** "recién pintado"; **~suit** n traje m térmico
we've [wi:v] = **we have**
whack [wæk] vt dar un buen golpe a
whale [weɪl] n (ZOOL) ballena
wharf [wɔ:f] (pl **wharves**) n muelle m

KEYWORD
---

what [wɔt] adj **1** (in direct/indirect questions) qué; **~ size is he?** ¿qué talla usa?; **~ colour/shape is it?** ¿de qué color/forma es?

2 (*in exclamations*): **~ a mess!** ¡qué desastre!; **~ a fool I am!** ¡qué tonto soy! ♦ *pron* **1** (*interrogative*) qué; **~ are you doing?** ¿qué haces *or* estás haciendo?; **~ is happening?** ¿qué pasa *or* está pasando?; **~ is it called?** ¿cómo se llama?; **~ about me?** ¿y tú qué?; **~ about doing ...?** ¿qué tal si hacemos ...?

2 (*relative*) lo que; **I saw ~ you did / was on the table** vi lo que hiciste/había en la mesa ♦ *excl* (*disbelieving*) ¡cómo!; **~, no coffee!** ¡que no hay café!

whatever [wɔtˈɛvə*] *adj*: **~ book you choose** cualquier libro que elijas ♦ *pron*: **do ~ is necessary** haga lo que sea necesario; **~ happens** pase lo que pase; **no reason** ~ ninguna razón sea la que sea; **nothing ~** nada en absoluto

whatsoever [wɔtsəuˈɛvə*] *adj* = **whatever**

wheat [wiːt] *n* trigo

wheedle [ˈwiːdl] *vt*: **to ~ sb into doing sth** engatusar a uno para que haga algo; **to ~ sth out of sb** sonsacar algo a uno

wheel [wiːl] *n* rueda; (*AUT: also:* **steering ~**) volante *m*; (*NAUT*) timón *m* ♦ *vt* (*pram etc*) empujar ♦ *vi* (*also:* **~ round**) dar la vuelta, girar; **~barrow** *n* carretilla; **~chair** *n* silla de ruedas; **~ clamp** *n* (*AUT*) cepo

wheeze [wiːz] *vi* resollar

KEYWORD

when [wɛn] *adv* cuando; **~ did it happen?** ¿cuándo ocurrió?; **I know ~ it happened** sé cuándo ocurrió

♦ *conj* **1** (*at, during, after the time that*) cuando; **be careful ~ you cross the road** ten cuidado al cruzar la calle; **that was ~ I needed you** fue entonces que te necesité

2 (*on, at which*): **on the day ~ I met him** el día en qué le conocí

3 (*whereas*) cuando

whenever [wɛnˈɛvə*] *conj* cuando; (*every time that*) cada vez que ♦ *adv* cuando sea

where [wɛə*] *adv* dónde ♦ *conj* donde; **this is ~** aquí es donde; **~abouts** *adv* dónde ♦ *n*: **nobody knows his ~abouts** nadie conoce su paradero; **~as** *conj* visto que, mientras; **~by** *pron* por lo cual; **wherever** [-ˈɛvə*] *conj* dondequiera que; (*interrogative*) dónde; **~withal** *n* recursos *mpl*

whether [ˈwɛðə*] *conj* si; **I don't know ~ to accept or not** no sé si aceptar o no; **~ you go or not** vayas o no vayas

KEYWORD

which [wɪtʃ] *adj* **1** (*interrogative: direct, indirect*) qué; **~ picture(s) do you want?** ¿qué cuadro(s) quieres?; **~ one?** ¿cuál?

2: **in ~ case** en cuyo caso; **we got there at 8 pm, by ~ time the cinema was full** llegamos allí a las 8, cuando el cine estaba lleno

♦ *pron* **1** (*interrogative*) cuál; **I don't mind ~** el/la que sea

2 (*relative: replacing noun*) que; (: *replacing clause*) lo que; (: *after preposition*) (el/la) que *etc*, el/la cual *etc*; **the apple ~ you ate / ~ is on the table** la manzana que comiste/que está en la mesa; **the chair on ~ you are sitting** la silla en la que estás sentado; **he said he knew, ~ is true / I feared** dijo que lo sabía, lo cual *or* lo que es cierto/me temía

whichever [wɪtʃˈɛvə*] *adj*: **take ~ book you prefer** coja (*SP*) el libro que prefiera; **~ book you take** cualquier libro que coja

while [waɪl] *n* rato, momento ♦ *conj* mientras; (*although*) aunque; **for a ~** durante algún tiempo; **~ away** *vt* pasar

whim [wɪm] *n* capricho

whimper [ˈwɪmpə*] *n* sollozo ♦ *vi* lloriquear

whimsical [ˈwɪmzɪkl] *adj* (*person*) caprichoso; (*look*) juguetón/ona

whine [waɪn] *n* (*of pain*) gemido; (*of*

engine) zumbido; (of siren) aullido ♦ vi gemir; zumbar; (fig: complain) gimotear

whip [wɪp] n látigo; (POL: person) *encargado de la disciplina partidaria en el parlamento* ♦ vt azotar; (CULIN) batir; (move quickly): **to ~ sth out/off** sacar/quitar algo de un tirón; **~ped cream** n nata or crema montada; **~-round** (BRIT) n colecta

whirl [wəːl] vt hacer girar, dar vueltas a ♦ vi girar, dar vueltas; (leaves etc) arremolinarse; **~pool** n remolino; **~wind** n torbellino

whirr [wəː*] vi zumbar

whisk [wɪsk] n (CULIN) batidor m ♦ vt (CULIN) batir; **to ~ sb away** or **off** llevar volando a uno

whiskers ['wɪskəz] npl (of animal) bigotes mpl; (of man) patillas fpl

whiskey ['wɪskɪ] (US, Ireland) n = whisky

whisky ['wɪskɪ] n whisky m

whisper ['wɪspə*] n susurro ♦ vi, vt susurrar

whistle ['wɪsl] n (sound) silbido; (object) silbato ♦ vi silbar

white [waɪt] adj blanco; (pale) pálido ♦ n blanco; (of egg) clara; **~ coffee** (BRIT) n café m con leche; **~-collar worker** n oficinista m/f; **~ elephant** n (fig) maula; **~ lie** n mentirilla; **~ paper** n (POL) libro rojo; **~wash** n (paint) jalbegue m, cal f ♦ vt (also fig) blanquear

whiting ['waɪtɪŋ] n inv (fish) pescadilla

Whitsun ['wɪtsn] n pentecostés m

whizz [wɪz] vi: **to ~ past** or **by** pasar a toda velocidad; **~ kid** (inf) n prodigio

who [huː] pron 1 (interrogative) quién; **~ is it?, ~'s there?** ¿quién es?; **~ are you looking for?** ¿a quién buscas?; **I told her ~ I was** le dije quién era yo
2 (relative) que; **the man/woman ~ spoke to me** el hombre/la mujer que habló conmigo; **those ~ can swim** los que saben or sepan nadar

whodun(n)it [huːˈdʌnɪt] (inf) n novela policíaca

whoever [huːˈɛvə*] pron: **~ finds it** cualquiera or quienquiera que lo encuentre; **ask ~ you like** pregunta a quien quieras; **~ he marries** no importa con quién se case

whole [həʊl] adj (entire) todo, entero; (not broken) intacto ♦ n todo; (all): **the ~ of the town** toda la ciudad, la ciudad entera ♦ n (total) total m; (sum) conjunto; **on the ~, as a ~** en general; **~food(s)** n(pl) alimento(s) m(pl) integral(es); **~hearted** adj sincero, cordial; **~meal** adj integral; **~sale** n venta al por mayor ♦ adj al por mayor; (fig: destruction) sistemático; **~saler** n mayorista m/f; **~some** adj sano; **~wheat** adj = **~meal**; **wholly** adv totalmente, enteramente

whom [huːm] pron 1 (interrogative): **~ did you see?** ¿a quién viste?; **to ~ did you give it?** ¿a quién se lo diste?; **tell me from ~ you received it** dígame de quién lo recibió
2 (relative) que; **to ~** a quien(es); **of ~** de quien(es), del/de la que etc; **the man ~ I saw/to ~ I wrote** el hombre que vi/a quien escribí; **the lady about/with ~ I was talking** la señora de (la) que/con quien or (la) que hablaba

whooping cough ['huːpɪŋ-] n tos f ferina

whore [hɔː*] (inf: pej) n puta

whose [huːz] adj 1 (possessive: interrogative): **~ book is this?, ~ is this book?** ¿de quién es este libro?; **~ pencil have you taken?** ¿de quién es el lápiz que has cogido?; **~ daughter are you?** ¿de quién eres hija?
2 (possessive: relative) cuyo/a, pl cuyos/as; **the man ~ son you rescued** el hombre cuyo hijo rescataste; **those ~ passports I**

have aquellas personas cuyos pasaportes
tengo; **the woman ~ car was stolen** la
mujer a quien le robaron el coche
♦ *pron* de quién; **~ is this?** ¿de quién es
esto?; **I know ~ it is** sé de quién es

KEYWORD

why [waɪ] *adv* por qué; **~ not?** ¿por qué
no?; **~ not do it now?** ¿por qué no lo
haces (*or* hacemos *etc*) ahora?
♦ *conj*: **I wonder ~ he said that** me
pregunto por qué dijo eso; **that's not ~
I'm here** no es por eso (por lo) que estoy
aquí; **the reason ~** la razón por la que
♦ *excl* (*expressing surprise, shock,
annoyance*) ¡hombre!, ¡vaya! (*explaining*):
~, it's you! ¡hombre, eres tú!; **~, that's
impossible!** ¡pero sí eso es imposible!

wicked ['wɪkɪd] *adj* malvado, cruel
wicket ['wɪkɪt] *n* (CRICKET: *stumps*) palos
mpl (: *grass area*) terreno de juego
wide [waɪd] *adj* ancho; (*area, knowledge*)
vasto, grande; (*choice*) amplio ♦ *adv*: **to
open ~** abrir de par en par; **to shoot ~**
errar el tiro; **~-angle lens** *n* objetivo de
gran angular; **~-awake** *adj* bien
despierto; **~ly** *adv* (*travelled*) mucho;
(*spaced*) muy; **it is ~ly believed/known
that ...** mucha gente piensa/sabe que ...;
~n *vt* ensanchar; (*experience*) ampliar ♦ *vi*
ensancharse; **~ open** *adj* abierto de par
en par; **~spread** *adj* extendido,
general
widow ['wɪdəʊ] *n* viuda; **~ed** *adj* viudo;
~er *n* viudo
width [wɪdθ] *n* anchura; (*of cloth*) ancho
wield [wiːld] *vt* (*sword*) blandir; (*power*)
ejercer
wife [waɪf] (*pl* **wives**) *n* mujer *f*, esposa
wig [wɪg] *n* peluca
wiggle ['wɪgl] *vt* menear
wild [waɪld] *adj* (*animal*) salvaje; (*plant*)
silvestre; (*person*) furioso, violento; (*idea*)
descabellado; (*rough: sea*) bravo; (: *land*)
agreste; (: *weather*) muy revuelto; **~s** *npl*

regiones *fpl* salvajes, tierras *fpl* vírgenes;
~erness ['wɪldənɪs] *n* desierto; **~life** *n*
fauna; **~ly** *adv* (*behave*) locamente; (*lash
out*) a diestro y siniestro; (*guess*) a lo loco;
(*happy*) a más no poder
wilful ['wɪlful] (*US* **willful**) *adj* (*action*)
deliberado; (*obstinate*) testarudo

KEYWORD

will [wɪl] *aux vb* **1** (*forming future tense*): **I
~ finish it tomorrow** lo terminaré *or* voy
a terminar mañana; **I ~ have finished it
by tomorrow** lo habré terminado para
mañana; **~ you do it? – yes I ~/no I
won't** ¿lo harás? — sí/no
2 (*in conjectures, predictions*): **he ~** *or*
he'll be there by now ya habrá *or* debe
(de) haber llegado; **that ~ be the
postman** será *or* debe ser el cartero
3 (*in commands, requests, offers*): **~ you
be quiet!** ¿quieres callarte?; **~ you help
me?** ¿quieres ayudarme?; **~ you have a
cup of tea?** ¿te apetece un té?; **I won't
put up with it!** ¡no lo soporto!
♦ *vt* (*pt, pp* **willed**): **to ~ sb to do sth**
desear que alguien haga algo; **he ~ed
himself to go on** con gran fuerza de
voluntad, continuó
♦ *n* voluntad *f*; (*testament*) testamento

willing ['wɪlɪŋ] *adj* (*with goodwill*) de
buena voluntad; (*enthusiastic*) entusiasta;
he's ~ to do it está dispuesto a hacerlo;
~ly *adv* con mucho gusto; **~ness** *n*
buena voluntad
willow ['wɪləʊ] *n* sauce *m*
willpower ['wɪlpaʊə*] *n* fuerza de
voluntad
willy-nilly [wɪlɪ'nɪlɪ] *adv* quiérase o no
wilt [wɪlt] *vi* marchitarse
win [wɪn] (*pt, pp* **won**) *n* victoria, triunfo
♦ *vt* ganar; (*obtain*) conseguir, lograr ♦ *vi*
ganar; **~ over** *vt* convencer a; **~ round**
(*BRIT*) *vt* = **~ over**
wince [wɪns] *vi* encogerse
winch [wɪntʃ] *n* torno
wind¹ [wɪnd] *n* viento; (*MED*) gases *mpl*

♦ *vt* (*take breath away from*) dejar sin aliento a

wind² [waɪnd] (*pt, pp* **wound**) *vt* enrollar; (*wrap*) envolver; (*clock, toy*) dar cuerda a ♦ *vi* (*road, river*) serpentear; ~ **up** *vt* (*clock*) dar cuerda a; (*debate, meeting*) concluir, terminar

windfall ['wɪndfɔ:l] *n* golpe *m* de suerte

winding ['waɪndɪŋ] *adj* (*road*) tortuoso; (*staircase*) de caracol

wind instrument [wɪnd-] *n* (*MUS*) instrumento de viento

windmill ['wɪndmɪl] *n* molino de viento

window ['wɪndəu] *n* ventana; (*in car, train*) ventanilla; (*in shop etc*) escaparate *m* (*SP*), vitrina (*AM*); ~ **box** *n* jardinera de ventana; ~ **cleaner** *n* (*person*) limpiador *m* de cristales; ~ **ledge** *n* alféizar *m*, repisa; ~ **pane** *n* cristal *m*; ~ **seat** *n* asiento junto a la ventana; ~-**shopping** *n*: **to go** ~-**shopping** ir de escaparates; ~**sill** *n* alféizar *m*, repisa

windpipe ['wɪndpaɪp] *n* tráquea

wind power *n* energía eólica

windscreen ['wɪndskri:n] (*US* **windshield**) *n* parabrisas *m inv*; ~ **washer** *n* lavaparabrisas *m inv*; ~ **wiper** *n* limpiaparabrisas *m inv*

windswept ['wɪndswept] *adj* azotado por el viento

windy ['wɪndɪ] *adj* de mucho viento; **it's** ~ hace viento

wine [waɪn] *n* vino; ~ **bar** *n* enoteca; ~ **cellar** *n* bodega; ~ **glass** *n* copa (para vino); ~ **list** *n* lista de vinos; ~ **waiter** *n* escanciador *m*

wing [wɪŋ] *n* ala; (*AUT*) aleta; ~**s** *npl* (*THEATRE*) bastidores *mpl*; ~**er** *n* (*SPORT*) extremo *m*

wink [wɪŋk] *n* guiño, pestañeo ♦ *vi* guiñar, pestañear

winner ['wɪnə*] *n* ganador(a) *m/f*

winning ['wɪnɪŋ] *adj* (*team*) ganador(a); (*goal*) decisivo; (*smile*) encantador(a); ~**s** *npl* ganancias *fpl*

winter ['wɪntə*] *n* invierno ♦ *vi* invernar; **wintry** ['wɪntrɪ] *adj* invernal

wipe [waɪp] *n*: **to give sth a** ~ pasar un trapo sobre algo ♦ *vt* limpiar; (*tape*) borrar; ~ **off** *vt* limpiar con un trapo; (*remove*) quitar; ~ **out** *vt* (*debt*) liquidar; (*memory*) borrar; (*destroy*) destruir; ~ **up** *vt* limpiar

wire ['waɪə*] *n* alambre *m*; (*ELEC*) cable *m* (eléctrico); (*TEL*) telegrama *m* ♦ *vt* (*house*) poner la instalación eléctrica en; (*also*: ~ **up**) conectar; (*person: telegram*) telegrafiar

wireless ['waɪəlɪs] (*BRIT*) *n* radio *f*

wiring ['waɪərɪŋ] *n* instalación *f* eléctrica

wiry ['waɪərɪ] *adj* (*person*) enjuto y fuerte; (*hair*) crespo

wisdom ['wɪzdəm] *n* sabiduría, saber *m*; (*good sense*) cordura; ~ **tooth** *n* muela del juicio

wise [waɪz] *adj* sabio; (*sensible*) juicioso

...wise [waɪz] *suffix*: **time**~ en cuanto a or respecto al tiempo

wish [wɪʃ] *n* deseo ♦ *vt* querer; **best** ~**es** (*on birthday etc*) felicidades *fpl*; **with best** ~**es** (*in letter*) saludos *mpl*, recuerdos *mpl*; **to** ~ **sb goodbye** despedirse de uno; **he** ~**ed me well** me deseó mucha suerte; **to** ~ **to do/sb to do sth** querer hacer/ que alguien haga algo; **to** ~ **for** desear; ~**ful** *adj*: **it's** ~**ful thinking** eso sería soñar

wisp [wɪsp] *n* mechón *m*; (*of smoke*) voluta

wistful ['wɪstful] *adj* pensativo

wit [wɪt] *n* ingenio, gracia; (*also*: ~**s**) inteligencia; (*person*) chistoso/a

witch [wɪtʃ] *n* bruja; ~**craft** *n* brujería; ~-**hunt** *n* (*fig*) caza de brujas

KEYWORD

with [wɪð, wɪθ] *prep* **1** (*accompanying*) con (con+mí, ti, sí = conmigo, contigo, consigo); **I was** ~ **him** estaba con él; **we stayed** ~ **friends** nos quedamos en casa de unos amigos; **I'm (not)** ~ **you** (*understand*) (no) te entiendo; **to be** ~ **it** (*inf: person: up-to-date*) estar al tanto; (: *alert*) ser despabilado

2 (*descriptive, indicating manner etc*) con; de; **a room** ~ **a view** una habitación con vistas; **the man** ~ **the grey hat/blue eyes** el hombre del sombrero gris/de los ojos azules; **red ~ anger** rojo de ira; **to shake ~ fear** temblar de miedo; **to fill sth ~ water** llenar algo de agua

withdraw [wɪθ'drɔː] (*irreg*) *vt* retirar, sacar ♦ *vi* retirarse; **to ~ money (from the bank)** retirar fondos (del banco); **~al** *n* retirada; (*of money*) reintegro; **~al symptoms** *npl* (*MED*) síndrome *m* de abstinencia; **~n** *adj* (*person*) reservado, introvertido

wither ['wɪðə*] *vi* marchitarse

withhold [wɪθ'həuld] (*irreg*) *vt* (*money*) retener; (*decision*) aplazar; (*permission*) negar; (*information*) ocultar

within [wɪð'ɪn] *prep* dentro de ♦ *adv* dentro; **~ reach (of)** al alcance (de); **~ sight (of)** a la vista (de); **~ the week** antes de acabar la semana; **~ a mile (of)** a menos de una milla (de)

without [wɪð'aut] *prep* sin; **to go ~ sth** pasar sin algo

withstand [wɪθ'stænd] (*irreg*) *vt* resistir a

witness ['wɪtnɪs] *n* testigo *m/f* ♦ *vt* (*event*) presenciar; (*document*) atestiguar la veracidad de; (*fig*) ser testimonio de; **~ box** *n* tribuna de los testigos; **~ stand** (*US*) *n* = **~ box**

witty ['wɪtɪ] *adj* ingenioso

wives [waɪvz] *npl of* **wife**

wk *abbr* = **week**

wobble ['wɒbl] *vi* temblar; (*chair*) cojear

woe [wəu] *n* desgracia

woke [wəuk] *pt of* **wake**

woken ['wəukən] *pp of* **wake**

wolf [wulf] *n* lobo; **wolves** [wulvz] *npl of* **wolf**

woman ['wumən] (*pl* **women**) *n* mujer *f*; **~ doctor** *n* médica; **women's lib** (*inf: pej*) *n* liberación *f* de la mujer; **~ly** *adj* femenino

womb [wuːm] *n* matriz *f*, útero

women ['wɪmɪn] *npl of* **woman**

won [wʌn] *pt, pp of* **win**

wonder ['wʌndə*] *n* maravilla, prodigio; (*feeling*) asombro ♦ *vi*: **to ~ whether/why** preguntarse si/por qué; **to ~ at**

asombrarse de; **to ~ about** pensar sobre *or* en; **it's no ~ (that)** no es de extrañarse (que +*subjun*); **~ful** *adj* maravilloso

won't [wəunt] = **will not**

wood [wud] *n* (*timber*) madera; (*forest*) bosque *m*; **~ carving** *n* (*act*) tallado en madera; (*object*) talla en madera; **~ed** *adj* arbolado; **~en** *adj* de madera; (*fig*) inexpresivo; **~pecker** *n* pájaro carpintero; **~wind** *n* (*MUS*) instrumentos *mpl* de viento de madera; **~work** *n* carpintería; **~worm** *n* carcoma

wool [wul] *n* lana; **to pull the ~ over sb's eyes** (*fig*) engatusar a uno; **~en** (*US*) *adj* = **~len**; **~len** *adj* de lana; **~lens** *npl* géneros *mpl* de lana; **~ly** *adj* lanudo, de lana; (*fig: ideas*) confuso; **~y** (*US*) *adj* = **~ly**

word [wəːd] *n* palabra; (*news*) noticia; (*promise*) palabra (de honor) ♦ *vt* redactar; **in other ~s** en otras palabras; **to break/keep one's ~** faltar a la palabra/ cumplir la promesa; **to have ~s with sb** reñir con uno; **~ing** *n* redacción *f*; **~ processing** *n* proceso de textos; **~ processor** *n* procesador *m* de textos

wore [wɔː*] *pt of* **wear**

work [wəːk] *n* trabajo; (*job*) empleo, trabajo; (*ART, LITERATURE*) obra ♦ *vi* trabajar; (*mechanism*) funcionar, marchar; (*medicine*) ser eficaz, surtir efecto ♦ *vt* (*shape*) trabajar; (*stone etc*) tallar; (*mine etc*) explotar; (*machine*) manejar, hacer funcionar; **~s** *n* (*BRIT: factory*) fábrica ♦ *npl* (*of clock, machine*) mecanismo; **to be out of ~** estar parado, no tener trabajo; **to ~ loose** (*part*) desprenderse; (*knot*) aflojarse; **~ on** *vt fus* trabajar en, dedicarse a; (*principle*) basarse en; **~ out** *vi* (*plans etc*) salir bien, funcionar ♦ *vt* (*problem*) resolver; (*plan*) elaborar; **it ~s out at £100** suma 100 libras; **~ up** *vt*: **to get ~ed up** excitarse; **~able** *adj* (*solution*) práctico, factible; **~aholic** [wəːkə'hɒlɪk] *n* trabajador(a) obsesivo/a *m/f*; **~er** *n* trabajador(a) *m/f*, obrero/a; **~force** *n* mano *f* de obra; **~ing class** *n*

clase f obrera; **~ing-class** adj obrero;
~ing order n: **in ~ing order** en
funcionamiento; **~man** (irreg) n obrero;
~manship n habilidad f, trabajo;
~sheet n hoja de trabajo; **~shop** n
taller m; **~ station** n puesto or estación f
de trabajo; **~-to-rule** (BRIT) n huelga de
celo
world [wɜːld] n mundo ♦ cpd (champion)
del mundo; (power, war) mundial; **to
think the ~ of sb** (fig) tener un concepto
muy alto de uno; **~ly** adj mundano; **~-
wide** adj mundial, universal; **W~-Wide
Web** n: **the W~-Wide Web** el World
Wide Web
worm [wɜːm] n (also: **earth~**) lombriz f
worn [wɔːn] pp of **wear** ♦ adj usado; **~-
out** adj (object) gastado; (person)
rendido, agotado
worried ['wʌrɪd] adj preocupado
worry ['wʌrɪ] n preocupación f ♦ vt
preocupar, inquietar ♦ vi preocuparse;
~ing adj inquietante
worse [wɜːs] adj, adv peor ♦ n lo peor; **a
change for the ~** un empeoramiento; **~n**
vt, vi empeorar; **~ off** adj (financially): **to
be ~ off** tener menos dinero; (fig): **you'll
be ~ off this way** de esta forma estarás
peor que nunca
worship ['wɜːʃɪp] n adoración f ♦ vt
adorar; **Your W~** (BRIT: to mayor) señor
alcalde; (: to judge) señor juez
worst [wɜːst] adj, adv peor ♦ n lo peor; **at
~** en lo peor de los casos
worth [wɜːθ] n valor m ♦ adj: **to be ~**
valer; **it's ~ it** vale or merece la pena; **to
be ~ one's while (to do)** merecer la pena
(hacer); **~less** adj sin valor; (useless)
inútil; **~while** adj (activity) que merece la
pena; (cause) loable
worthy ['wɜːðɪ] adj respetable; (motive)
honesto; **~ of** digno de

┌─────────────┐
│ KEYWORD   │
└─────────────┘

would [wʊd] aux vb **1** (conditional tense):
if you asked him he ~ do it si se lo
pidieras, lo haría; **if you had asked him**

he ~ have done it si se lo hubieras
pedido, lo habría or hubiera hecho
2 (in offers, invitations, requests): **~ you
like a biscuit?** ¿quieres una galleta?;
(formal) ¿querría una galleta?; **~ you ask
him to come in?** ¿quiere hacerle pasar?;
~ you open the window please? ¿quiere
or podría abrir la ventana, por favor?
3 (in indirect speech): **I said I ~ do it** dije
que lo haría
4 (emphatic): **it WOULD have to snow
today!** ¡tenía que nevar precisamente
hoy!
5 (insistence): **she ~n't behave** no quiso
comportarse bien
6 (conjecture): **it ~ have been midnight**
sería medianoche; **it ~ seem so** parece
ser que sí
7 (indicating habit): **he ~ go there on
Mondays** iba allí los lunes

would-be (pej) adj presunto
wouldn't ['wʊdnt] = **would not**
wound[1] [wuːnd] n herida ♦ vt herir
wound[2] [waʊnd] pt, pp of **wind**
wove [wəʊv] pt of **weave**
woven ['wəʊvən] pp of **weave**
wrap [ræp] vt (also: **~ up**) envolver; **~per**
n (on chocolate) papel m; (BRIT: of book)
sobrecubierta; **~ping paper** n papel m
de envolver; (fancy) papel m de regalo
wreak [riːk] vt: **to ~ havoc (on)** hacer
estragos (en); **to ~ vengeance (on)**
vengarse de
wreath [riːθ, pl riːðz] n (funeral ~) corona
wreck [rek] n (ship: destruction) naufragio;
(: remains) restos mpl del barco; (pej:
person) ruina ♦ vt (car etc) destrozar;
(chances) arruinar; **~age** n restos mpl; (of
building) escombros mpl
wren [ren] n (ZOOL) reyezuelo
wrench [rentʃ] n (TECH) llave f inglesa;
(tug) tirón m; (fig) dolor m ♦ vt arrancar;
to ~ sth from sb arrebatar algo
violentamente a uno
wrestle ['resl] vi: **to ~ (with sb)** luchar
(con or contra uno); **~r** n luchador(a) m/f

(de lucha libre); **wrestling** *n* lucha libre

wretched ['retʃɪd] *adj* miserable

wriggle ['rɪgl] *vi* (*also*: ~ **about**) menearse, retorcerse

wring [rɪŋ] (*pt, pp* **wrung**) *vt* retorcer; (*wet clothes*) escurrir; (*fig*): **to ~ sth out of sb** sacar algo por la fuerza a uno

wrinkle ['rɪŋkl] *n* arruga ♦ *vt* arrugar ♦ *vi* arrugarse

wrist [rɪst] *n* muñeca; **~watch** *n* reloj *m* de pulsera

writ [rɪt] *n* mandato judicial

write [raɪt] (*pt* **wrote**, *pp* **written**) *vt* escribir; (*cheque*) extender ♦ *vi* escribir; ~ **down** *vt* escribir; (*note*) apuntar; ~ **off** *vt* (*debt*) borrar (como incobrable); (*fig*) desechar por inútil; ~ **out** *vt* escribir; ~ **up** *vt* redactar; **~-off** *n* siniestro total; **~r** *n* escritor(a) *m/f*

writhe [raɪð] *vi* retorcerse

writing ['raɪtɪŋ] *n* escritura; (*hand-*) letra; (*of author*) obras *fpl*; **in** ~ por escrito; ~ **paper** *n* papel *m* de escribir

written ['rɪtn] *pp of* **write**

wrong [rɔŋ] *adj* (*wicked*) malo; (*unfair*) injusto; (*incorrect*) equivocado, incorrecto; (*not suitable*) inoportuno, inconveniente; (*reverse*) del revés ♦ *adv* equivocadamente ♦ *n* injusticia ♦ *vt* ser injusto con; **you are ~ to do it** haces mal en hacerlo; **you are ~ about that, you've got it ~** en eso estás equivocado; **to be in the ~** no tener razón, tener la culpa; **what's ~?** ¿qué pasa?; **to go ~** (*person*) equivocarse; (*plan*) salir mal; (*machine*) estropearse; **~ful** *adj* injusto; **~ly** *adv* mal, incorrectamente; (*by mistake*) por error; ~ **number** *n* (*TEL*): **you've got the ~ number** se ha equivocado de número

wrote [rəut] *pt of* **write**

wrought iron [rɔːt-] *n* hierro forjado

wrung [rʌŋ] *pt, pp of* **wring**

wt. *abbr* = **weight**

WWW *n abbr* (= *World Wide Web*) WWW *m*

X, x

Xmas ['eksməs] *n abbr* = **Christmas**

X-ray ['eksreɪ] *n* radiografía ♦ *vt* radiografiar, sacar radiografías de

xylophone ['zaɪləfəun] *n* xilófono

Y, y

yacht [jɔt] *n* yate *m*; **~ing** *n* (*sport*) balandrismo; **~sman/woman** (*irreg*) *n* balandrista *m/f*

Yank [jæŋk] (*pej*) *n* yanqui *m/f*

Yankee ['jæŋki] (*pej*) *n* = **Yank**

yap [jæp] *vi* (*dog*) aullar

yard [jɑːd] *n* patio; (*measure*) yarda; **~stick** *n* (*fig*) criterio, norma

yarn [jɑːn] *n* hilo; (*tale*) cuento, historia

yawn [jɔːn] *n* bostezo ♦ *vi* bostezar; **~ing** *adj* (*gap*) muy abierto

yd(s). *abbr* = **yard(s)**

yeah [jeə] (*inf*) *adv* sí

year [jɪə*] *n* año; **to be 8 ~s old** tener 8 años; **an eight-~-old child** un niño de ocho años (de edad); **~ly** *adj* anual ♦ *adv* anualmente, cada año

yearn [jəːn] *vi*: **to ~ for sth** añorar algo, suspirar por algo

yeast [jiːst] *n* levadura

yell [jel] *n* grito, alarido ♦ *vi* gritar

yellow ['jeləu] *adj* amarillo

yelp [jelp] *n* aullido ♦ *vi* aullar

yes [jes] *adv* sí ♦ *n* sí *m*; **to say/answer ~** decir/contestar que sí

yesterday ['jestədɪ] *adv* ayer ♦ *n* ayer *m*; ~ **morning/evening** ayer por la mañana/tarde; **all day** ~ todo el día de ayer

yet [jet] *adv* ya; (*negative*) todavía ♦ *conj* sin embargo, a pesar de todo; **it is not finished ~** todavía no está acabado; **the best ~** el/la mejor hasta ahora; **as ~** hasta ahora, todavía

yew [juː] *n* tejo

yield [jiːld] *n* (*AGR*) cosecha; (*COMM*)

rendimiento ♦ *vt* ceder; (*results*) producir, dar; (*profit*) rendir ♦ *vi* rendirse, ceder; (*US: AUT*) ceder el paso

YMCA *n abbr* (= *Young Men's Christian Association*) Asociación *f* de Jóvenes Cristianos

yog(h)ourt ['jəugət] *n* yogur *m*

yog(h)urt ['jəugət] *n* = **yog(h)ourt**

yoke [jəuk] *n* yugo

yolk [jəuk] *n* yema (de huevo)

KEYWORD
---

you [ju:] *pron* **1** (*subject: familiar*) tú, *pl* vosotros/as (*SP*), ustedes (*AM*); (*polite*) usted, *pl* ustedes; **~ are very kind** eres/es *etc* muy amable; **~ Spanish enjoy your food** a vosotros (*or* ustedes) los españoles os (*or* les) gusta la comida; **~ and I will go** iremos tú y yo

2 (*object: direct: familiar*) te, *pl* os (*SP*), les (*AM*); (*polite*) le, *pl* les, *f* la, *pl* las; **I know ~** te/le *etc* conozco

3 (*object: indirect: familiar*) te, *pl* os (*SP*), les (*AM*); (*polite*) le, *pl* les; **I gave the letter to ~ yesterday** te/os *etc* di la carta ayer

4 (*stressed*): **I told YOU to do it** te dije a ti que lo hicieras, es a ti a quien dije que lo hicieras; *see also* **3, 5**

5 (*after prep: NB*: con+ti = contigo: *familiar*) ti, *pl* vosotros/as (*SP*), ustedes (*AM*); (*: polite*) usted, *pl* ustedes; **it's for ~** es para ti/vosotros *etc*

6 (*comparisons: familiar*) tú, *pl* vosotros/as (*SP*), ustedes (*AM*); (*: polite*) usted, *pl* ustedes; **she's younger than ~** es más joven que tú/vosotros *etc*

7 (*impersonal: one*): **fresh air does ~ good** el aire puro (te) hace bien; **~ never know** nunca se sabe; **~ can't do that!** ¡eso no se hace!

you'd [ju:d] = **you had; you would**

you'll [ju:l] = **you will; you shall**

young [jʌŋ] *adj* joven ♦ *npl* (*of animal*) cría; (*people*): **the ~** los jóvenes, la juventud; **~er** *adj* (*brother etc*) menor;

~ster *n* joven *m/f*

your [jɔː*] *adj* tu; (*pl*) vuestro; (*formal*) su; *see also* **my**

you're [juə*] = **you are**

yours [jɔːz] *pron* tuyo; (*pl*) vuestro; (*formal*) suyo; *see also* **faithfully; mine¹; sincerely**

yourself [jɔː'self] *pron* tú mismo; (*complement*) te; (*after prep*) tí (mismo); (*formal*) usted mismo; (*: complement*) se; (*: after prep*) sí (mismo); **yourselves** *pl pron* vosotros mismos; (*after prep*) vosotros (mismos); (*formal*) ustedes (mismos); (*: complement*) se; (*: after prep*) sí mismos; *see also* **oneself**

youth [ju:θ, *pl* ju:ðz] *n* juventud *f*; (*young man*) joven *m*; **~ club** *n* club *m* juvenil; **~ful** *adj* juvenil; **~ hostel** *n* albergue *m* de juventud

you've [ju:v] = **you have**

Yugoslav ['ju:gəuslɑ:v] *adj, n* yugo(e)slavo/a *m/f*

Yugoslavia [ju:gəu'slɑ:vɪə] *n* Yugoslavia

yuppie ['jʌpɪ] (*inf*) *adj, n* yupi *m/f*, yupy *m/f*

YWCA *n abbr* (= *Young Women's Christian Association*) Asociación *f* de Jóvenes Cristianas

Z, z

zany ['zeɪnɪ] *adj* estrafalario

zap [zæp] *vt* (*COMPUT*) borrar

zeal [zi:l] *n* celo, entusiasmo; **~ous** ['zɛləs] *adj* celoso, entusiasta

zebra ['zi:brə] *n* cebra; **~ crossing** (*BRIT*) *n* paso de peatones

zero ['zɪərəu] *n* cero

zest [zest] *n* ánimo, vivacidad *f*; (*of orange*) piel *f*

zigzag ['zɪgzæg] *n* zigzag *m* ♦ *vi* zigzaguear, hacer eses

zinc [zɪŋk] *n* cinc *m*, zinc *m*

zip [zɪp] *n* (*also*: **~ fastener,** (*US*) **~per**) cremallera (*SP*), cierre *m* (*AM*) ♦ *vt* (*also*: **~ up**) cerrar la cremallera de; **~ code** (*US*)

n código postal
zodiac ['zəudɪæk] *n* zodíaco
zone [zəun] *n* zona
zoo [zu:] *n* (jardín *m*) zoo *m*
zoology [zu'ɔlədʒɪ] *n* zoología

zoom [zu:m] *vi*: **to ~ past** pasar
zumbando; **~ lens** *n* zoom *m*
zucchini [zu:'ki:nɪ] (*US*) *n(pl)*
calabacín(ines) *m(pl)*